HARRAP'S
French
Business

English-French/French-English

HARRAP'S
French
Business

English-French/French-English

Edited by
Françoise Laurendeau-Collin
Jane Pratt
Peter Collin
Revised and Edited by
Helen Knox

London   Paris

First published in this edition in Great Britain 1991
by HARRAP BOOKS Ltd 1991
Chelsea House, 26 Market Square, Bromley, Kent BR1 1NA

© HARRAP BOOKS Ltd 1991

ISBN 0 245-60407-3

Typeset by B.P. Integraphics, Bath
Printed and bound in Denmark
by Nørhaven Rotation

PREFACE

The new *French and English Business* Dictionary includes terms and expressions used in a wide range of commercial contexts: Banking, Stock Exchange, Accountancy, Insurance, Commerce, Law. Also included are specific terms relating to EEC commercial practices. The work has been based on terms commonly found in commercial correspondence, business newspapers and magazines put out by commercial companies, banks, etc.

The aim of the dictionary is to provide a basic translating tool for everyday business language. As in all Harrap dictionaries, the emphasis has been laid on providing practical examples to show terms and phrases used in context—rendering the dictionary of great value to the translator, the businessman, the secretary, the sales manager, the business-school student.

In addition to the main text, the dictionary provides useful supplementary material concerning international currencies, international organizations and their abbreviations, comparison between balance sheets in English and French to mention but a few.

It should be noted that in contrast to other business dictionaries, the *Harrap's French and English Business Dictionary* gives only the strictly commercial meanings of words, leaving non-commercial meanings for a general dictionary. Superfluous non-business matter has been kept to the absolute minimum.

We want to thank all those who worked on this dictionary, in particular Marie-Noëlle Gérard of Bristol Polytechnic, the late C. B. Johnson and Janet Kernachan.

F.L.-C.
J.P.
P.H.C.

PREFACE 2nd edition

The new edition of the *Harrap's French and English Business Dictionary* is a completely revised and substantially increased edition which was updated bearing in mind that American business terms often differ from those used in the British day-to-day business language. For this reason, a new supplement with explanations and translations, was compiled listing a great many of these up to date americanisms.

Also completely new, a legal and contractual supplement which lists a series of verbs, adverbs and expressions and their translations, used frequently in contracts and other legal documents.

The balance-sheet in both French and English has been updated to a more recent one and the existing supplements on international currencies and acronyms of international organizations were also completely revised.

We want to thank Jill Harry and Norman Howell who helped revise the dictionary, Nicholas Berry for his important contribution, particularly in the field of americanisms, and Michael Mould and Anne Paquette who compiled the supplement on legal and contractual terms.

F.L.-C.

PREFACE 3rd edition

This completely revised edition of the *Harrap's French and English Business Dictionary* has been considerably expanded and updated. Since 1986 many changes have taken place in the world of finance, especially on the international stock exchanges. The vocabulary has therefore increased and many new terms have been included in this revision. The list of American Business terms has also been revised and updated, and many common American terms will also be found in the main section of the dictionary.

The lists of abbreviations and acronyms have also been considerably expanded and the existing supplement on international currencies has been completely revised and updated.

The layout of the dictionary has not been altered, but a considerable number of glosses in italics have been included for ease of consultation.

I am indebted to and would like to thank my French consultant Constantin Kinsky for his invaluable advice and help during the revision of this dictionary.

I.K.

PRÉFACE

Ce nouveau dictionnaire, le *Harrap's French and English Business Dictionary*, contient des termes et expressions employés dans la langue des affaires, c'est-à-dire des termes de banque, d'assurance, de comptabilité, de Bourse, de commerce, de publicité et de nombreux termes juridiques et autres expressions propres aux affaires de la CEE.

Comme tous les autres dictionnaires Harrap, le *Business Dictionary* a pour politique de donner autant d'exemples que possible. Ces exemples proviennent de lettres d'affaires, de journaux et revues économiques aussi bien que de matériel publicitaire émis par des entreprises commerciales, des banques et autres organisations. Notre dictionnaire devient ainsi un outil précieux pour le traducteur, l'homme d'affaires, la secrétaire, le directeur commercial ou l'étudiant de l'école de commerce.

Le *Harrap's French and English Business Dictionary* contient un supplément dans lequel on trouve une foule de renseignements utiles tels que les listes des devises internationales, d'organisations nationales et internationales et leur sigle sans oublier plusieurs pages, en français et en anglais, tirées du rapport annuel bilingue d'une société.

Le *Harrap's French and English Business Dictionary* étant un dictionnaire pour spécialistes, les éditeurs ont pris soin de ne donner que la traduction du sens commercial des mots à moins qu'une traduction plus générale n'ait été considérée utile même dans le domaine des affaires.

Nous tenons à remercier les personnes qui ont travaillé à ce dictionnaire, dont en particulier Marie-Noëlle Gérard de Bristol Polytechnic, C. B. Johnson† et Janet Kernachan.

F.L.-C.
M.P.
P.H.C.

PREFACE 2ème édition

Cette nouvelle édition revue et corrigée du *Harrap's French and English Business Dictionary* offre à l'utilisateur un dictionnaire entièrement mis à jour, ayant été augmenté d'un grand nombre de mots et expressions tirés du domaine des affaires, en tenant surtout compte du fait que la langue américaine contient des expressions qui lui sont propres. Ces différences font l'objet d'un supplément spécial tout à fait nouveau sur les américanismes.

En plus une liste inédite d'adverbes, verbes et expressions particulières aux contrats et autres documents légaux vient s'ajouter aux suppléments déjà existants.

Le bilan, dans les deux langues, est tiré d'un rapport annuel plus récent tandis que la liste des devises internationales et celle des sigles des organismes internationaux ont été corrigées et augmentées.

Nous tenons à remercier Jill Harry et Norman Howell qui ont contribué à la révision du dictionnaire, Nicholas Berry pour son apport particulièrement important dans le domaine des américanismes, ainsi que Michael Mould et Anne Paquette qui ont préparé le supplément contenant les termes légaux et contractuels.

F.L.-C.

PRÉFACE 3ème édition

Cette nouvelle édition entièrement revue et corrigée du *Harrap's French and English Business Dictionary* a été considérablement agrandie et mise à jour. Depuis 1986, il y a eu beaucoup de changements dans le monde des affaires, en particulier sur les bourses internationales. Par conséquent le vocabulaire a augmenté et de nombreux termes nouveaux ont été ajoutés à cette révision. La liste des termes des affaires américains a également été revue et mise à jour, et on trouvera aussi de nombreux termes américains dans la section principale du dictionnaire.

La liste des abréviations et sigles a également été considérablement augmentée et la liste des devises internationales a été entièrement revue et mise à jour.

La présentation du dictionnaire n'a pas été modifiée, mais un nombre considérable de gloses en italique a été ajouté pour faciliter la consultation du dictionnaire.

Je tiens à remercier M. Constantin Kinsky pour sa collaboration et ses conseils pendant la révision de ce dictionnaire.

H.K.

ABBREVIATIONS USED IN THE DICTIONARY—
ABRÉVIATIONS UTILISÉES DANS LE DICTIONNAIRE

a.	adjective	adjectif
abbr.	abbreviation	abréviation
Adm:	administration	administration
adv.	adverb	adverbe
adv.phr.	adverbial phrase	locution adverbiale
Aut:	motoring; motor industry	automobilisme; industrie automobile
Av:	aviation; aircraft	aviation; avions
Bank:	banking	opérations de banque
Book-k:	book-keeping	comptabilité
Br:	British	britannique
Cmptr:	computers; data processing	ordinateurs; informatique
coll.	collective	collectif
Const:	construction industry	industrie du bâtiment
Corr:	correspondence	correspondance
Cust:	customs	douane
Econ:	economics	économie
EEC:	Common Market term	terme du Marché commun
e.g.	for example	par exemple
esp.	especially	surtout
etc.	et cetera	et caetera
Euph:	euphemism	euphémisme
f.	feminine	féminin
F:	colloquialism	familier; style de la conversation
Fin:	finance	terme de finance
FrC:	French Canadian	mot utilisé au Canada français
Hist:	history	histoire
Ind:	industry	industrie
Ins:	insurance	assurance
inv.	invariable	invariable
Journ:	journalism	journalisme
Jur:	legal term	terme de droit
Lt.phr.	latin phrase	locution latine
m.	masculine	masculin
Meas:	weights and measures	poids et mesures
MIns:	marine insurance	assurance maritime
Mkt:	advertising and marketing	publicité et marketing
n.	noun	nom
NAm:	United States and Canada	États-Unis et Canada
Nau:	nautical term	terme de marine
num.	numeral	numéral
occ.	occasionally	parfois
Pej:	pejorative	péjoratif
pers.	person	personne
Pharm:	pharmacy	pharmacie
pl.	plural	pluriel
PN:	public notice	avis au public
PolEc:	political economy	économie politique
Post:	postal services	postes
pref.	prefix	préfixe
prep.phr.	prepositional phrase	locution prépositive
Publ:	publishing	édition
qch.	something	quelque chose
qn	someone	quelqu'un
Rail:	railways/railroads	chemins de fer
Rtm:	registered trademark	marque déposée

ABBREVIATIONS USED IN THE DICTIONARY
ABRÉVIATIONS UTILISÉES DANS LE DICTIONNAIRE

Scot:	Scotland; Scottish	mot utilisé en Écosse
sg.const.	singular construction	avec verbe au singulier
s.o.	someone	quelqu'un
Stat:	statistics	statistiques
StExch:	Stock Exchange	terme de Bourse
sth.	something	quelque chose
SwFr:	Swiss French	mot utilisé en Suisse
Tchn:	technical	terme technique
Tel:	telephone	téléphone
Th:	theatre	théâtre
Trans:	transport	transports
TV:	television	télévision
Typ:	typography	typographie
US:	United States	États-Unis
usu.	usually	d'ordinaire
v.	verb	verbe
Veh:	vehicles	véhicules
v.i.	intransitive verb	verbe intransitif
v.pr.	pronominal verb	verbe pronominal
v.tr.	transitive verb	verbe transitif
WTel:	telegraph	télégraphe

/	synonym or alternative	synonyme ou alternative
=	nearest equivalent (of an institution an office, etc., when systems vary in the different countries)	équivalent le plus proche (d'un terme désignant une institution, une charge, etc., dans les cas où les systèmes varient dans les différents pays)

ENGLISH-FRENCH

A

A1, *a. MIns:* le meilleur; **ship registered A1,** navire enregistré en parfaite condition.

abandonment, *n. MIns:* délaissement *m* (d'un navire); **notice of abandonment,** avis *m* de délaissement; **abandonment of an option,** abandon *m* d'une prime; **abandonment of a right,** désistement *m* d'un droit/ renonciation *f* à un droit.

abatement, *n.* diminution *f*/rabais *m*/ réduction *f*/remise *f* (sur le prix); **abatement of taxes/tax abatement,** dégrèvement *m* d'impôt.

abeyance, *n.* **work in abeyance,** travail *m* en souffrance; **the matter is still in abeyance,** la question est toujours pendante/en suspens.

abode, *n.* **place of abode,** résidence *f.*

above-the-line, 1. *a. Book-k: (expenditure, etc.),* au-dessus de la ligne; **above-the-line accounts,** comptes *mpl* de résultats courants *2. n. Mkt:* coût *m* média.

absenteeism, *n.* absentéisme *m.*

absorb, *v.tr. (a)* **to absorb a surplus,** résorber un excédent/un surplus *(b)* **the business has been absorbed by a competitor,** l'entreprise a été absorbée par un concurrent.

absorption, *n.* absorption *f* (d'une entreprise par une autre, etc.).

abstract, *n.* résumé *m*/abrégé *m*/sommaire *m*/précis *m*/extrait *m*; **abstract of an article,** sommaire/précis d'un article.

acceleration, *n.* accélération *f.*

accelerator, *n.* **accelerator principle,** principe *m* d'accélération.

accept, *v.tr.* **to accept a bill,** accepter un effet; **to accept (delivery of/shipment of) goods,** prendre livraison de marchandises.

acceptance, *n. (a) (agreement)* acceptation *f; (document)* effet accepté/effet à payer; **to present a bill for acceptance,** présenter une traite à l'acceptation; *NAm:* **acceptance bank/acceptance house,** banque d'acceptation; **bank/banker's acceptance,** acceptation de banque/ bancaire; **non-acceptance,** refus *m* d'acceptation; **qualified acceptance,** acceptation sous réserve; **general/clean/ unconditional acceptance,** acceptation sans réserve *(b)* réception *f* (d'un article commandé) *(c) Mkt:* **brand acceptance,** acceptabilité *f* de la marque; **consumer acceptance,** réceptivité *f* des consommateurs.

accepted, *a. (written on accepted bill)* accepté/bon pour acceptation; **accepted bill,** effet accepté.

accepting, *a. Br:* **accepting house,** banque *f* d'acceptation.

acceptor, *n.* accepteur, -euse (d'une lettre de change).

access, *n.* **to have/to demand access to the books of a company,** avoir/demander communication des livres d'une société; *Cmptr:* **random access,** accès *m* aléatoire; **access time,** temps *m* d'accès.

accident, *n.* **industrial accident,** accident *m* du travail; **accident insurance,** assurance *f* (contre les) accidents; **accident policy,** police *f* d'assurance accidents.

accommodation, *n.* prêt *m* (à court terme); **accommodation bill,** billet *m* effet

1

m /traite *f*/papier *m* de complaisance; effet/
papier/traite de cavalerie.

accord, *n.* (*a*) **accord and satisfaction**,
libération *f* (d'une obligation) à titre onéreux (*b*) *US:* (*agreement*) convention *f*/
accord *m*.

accordance, *n.* **in accordance with your instructions**, en conformité avec/conformé-
ment à vos ordres; selon vos ordres.

according, *prep. phr.* **according to instructions**, selon/suivant les ordres; conformément aux ordres.

account, *n.* (*a*) compte *m*/note *f*; **let me
have your account**, envoyez-moi votre
note/votre compte; **detailed/itemized
account**, compte détaillé; **accounts payable**, dettes passives; **accounts receivable**,
dettes actives; **to have an account with s.o.**,
avoir un compte chez qn/être en compte
avec qn; **charge it to my account**, in-
scrivez-le/mettez-le à mon compte;
account card, carte *f* de crédit (d'un magasin); **cash or account?** vous payez/réglez
comptant ou est-ce que vous avez un
compte chez nous? **to pay a sum on
account**, donner une somme en acompte/à
compte/à valoir; verser un acompte/un
à-valoir/une provision/des arrhes *fpl*; **to
pay £10 on account**, donner un acompte
de £10; **to account rendered/as per account
rendered**, suivant compte remis/suivant
relevé remis; **to settle an account**, régler
une note/un compte/une facture (*b*)
accounts, (*of firm, etc.*) comptabilité *f*;
accounts department, (service *m* de) la
comptabilité; **annual accounts**, comptes
de clôture/de fin d'exercice; rapport
annuel; **final accounts**, compte définitif;
management accounts, compte de gestion;
profit and loss account, compte de résultat; **income and expenditure account**,
compte de dépenses et recettes; **cash
account**, compte de caisse; **trading
account**/*NAm:* **operating account**, compte
d'exploitation; **purchase account**, compte
d'achats; **capital account**, compte de capital; **sales account**, compte des ventes;
contra account, compte contre-partie;
impersonal accounts, comptes qui ne mon-
trent pas les créditeurs et débiteurs; **per-**

sonal account, *StExch:* compte de
tiers; *Book-k:* compte propre/personnel;
account book, livre *m* de comptes; registre
m de comptabilité; **to keep the accounts**,
tenir les livres/les écritures *f*/la comptabilité; **to keep separate accounts**, faire
bourse à part; **to keep (a) strict account of
expenses**, tenir un compte rigoureux des
dépenses (*c*) *Bank:* **agio account**, compte
d'agio; **bank**/*NAm:* **banking account**,
compte en banque/compte bancaire;
current account, compte courant; **dead
account**, compte inactif; **escrow account**,
compte bloqué; **deposit account**, compte
de dépôt/compte rémunéré; (*when notice
has to be given before withdrawal*) compte
à terme; **foreign account**, compte étranger
(National) Girobank account = compte
chèque postal (CCP); **loan account**,
compte de prêt; crédit *m*; compte d'avances; **numbered account**, (*esp in Switzerland*)
compte numéroté; **cheque-book/cheque**
NAm: **checking account**, compte (de
chèques (CC); **joint account**, compte joint/
conjoint; **office/business account**, compte
professionnel/commercial; **saving
account**, compte d'épargne/de caiss
d'épargne; compte sur livret; *NAm:* **zero
balance account**, compte débiteur e
chambre de compensation; **credit account**
compte créditeur; **debit account**, compt
débiteur; **to open an account**, (se faire
ouvrir un compte; **to close an account**
fermer un compte; **account holder**
titulaire *mf* d'un compte; **account number**
numéro *m* de compte; **to pay money int
one's account**, verser de l'argent à so
compte/faire créditer son compte d'un
somme/alimenter son compte; **to pay
s.o.'s salary directly into his/her account**
verser le salaire de qn par virement direc
sur son compte; **to apply for an account**
faire une demande d'ouverture d
compte; **to overdraw an account**, mettre u
compte à découvert; **statement of account**
relevé *m*/état *m*/bordereau *m* de compte
exchange equalization account, fonds *m* d
stabilisation des changes (*d*) *StExch*
(trading) account, période boursièr
(*généralement quinze jours*); **account day**
jour de liquidation (boursière) (*e*) *Mk*

(advertising) account, budget *m* (publicitaire)/client *m* (*f*) exposé *m*/état *m*/mémoire *m*/note *f*; **account of one's transactions,** état/exposé de ses opérations (*g*) **to set up in business on one's own account,** s'installer à son compte/prendre à son compte/se mettre à son compte.

accountable, *a.* **accountable receipt,** reçu certifié/pièce *f* comptable.

accountancy, *n.* comptabilité *f*; expertise *f* comptable.

accountant, *n.* (*a*) agent *m* comptable; comptable *mf*; **chief accountant,** chef *m* de la comptabilité/chef comptable; **cost accountant,** comptable de prix de revient (*b*) **chartered accountant (CA)**/*NAm:* **certified public accountant (CPA),** (*i*) expert *m* comptable/*FrC:* comptable agréé (CA) (*ii*) conseiller fiscal; **financial accountant,** trésorier *m* d'entreprise.

account for, *v.tr. Book-k:* **to account for (sth.),** comptabiliser (une dépense, etc.); justifier (une dépense).

accounting, *n.* comptabilité *f*; expertise *f* comptable; **cost accounting,** comptabilité de prix de revient/comptabilité analytique; **current cost accounting,** comptabilité en coûts réels/déflatés/de remplacement; **standard cost accounting,** méthode des coûts standards; **direct cost accounting,** comptabilité analytique des coûts variables/proportionnels; **accounting period,** exercice *m*; **accounting policies/procedures,** méthodes *f*/pratiques *f* comptables; **accounting system,** plan *m* comptable; **automatic accounting,** comptabilité *f* mécanographique.

accredited, *a.* accrédité/autorisé/attitré.

accrual, *n.* accumulation *f*; **accrual basis method,** méthode *f* du coupon couru; **accrual of dividend,** échéance *f* de dividende.

accrue, *v.i.* (*of interest*) courir/s'accumuler; **interest accrues (as) from ...,** les intérêts *mpl* courent à partir de ...; **accruing interest,** intérêts à échoir.

accrued, *a.* (*interest*) couru/accumulé; **accrued charges/expenses,** effets *mpl* à payer/frais (ac)cumulés; **accrued income,** intérêts courus non échus; **accrued benefits,** (*under pension scheme*) points *mpl* de retraite.

accumulate, *v.i.* **to allow one's dividends to accumulate,** laisser accumuler ses dividendes; **accumulated dividends,** dividendes accumulés.

accumulation, *n.* **accumulation of capital/capital accumulation,** accumulation *f* du capital.

acknowledge, *v.tr.* **to acknowledge (receipt of) a letter,** accuser réception d'une lettre; **I acknowledge receipt of your letter,** j'accuse réception de votre lettre/j'ai bien reçu votre lettre.

acknowledg(e)ment, *n.* (*a*) reçu *m*/récépissé *m*/quittance *f* (d'un paiement) (*b*) **acknowledg(e)ment (of receipt),** accusé *m* de réception (d'une lettre, etc.); **acknowledg(e)ment of debt,** reconnaissance *f* de dette.

acquire, *v.tr.* acquérir (un bien, un droit); faire l'acquisition de (une propriété, etc.).

acquired, *a.* acquis; **acquired surplus,** surplus acquis.

acquisition, *n.* acquisition *f*.

acquisitive, *a.* (*company*) en (phase de) croissance externe; (*society*) d'acquisition.

acquittance, *n.* acquittement *m* (d'une dette); décharge *f*/quittance *f*.

across-the-board, *a.* **an across-the-board increase,** une augmentation générale.

act[1], *n.* **1. Companies Act,** loi *f*/législation *f* sur les sociétés; **Factory Act/Health and Safety at Work Act,** loi sur les accidents du travail/législation industrielle; **Finance Act,** loi de Finances **2. act of God,** (cas *m* de) force majeure/cas fortuit; fléau *m*/désastre naturel.

act[2], *v.i.* (*a*) **to act as (secretary, etc.),** exercer les fonctions de (secrétaire, etc.) (*b*) **to**

act on a letter, donner suite à une lettre (c) **to act for/on behalf of s.o.,** agir au nom de qn/représenter qn.

acting, a. suppléant; intérimaire; **acting manager,** directeur intérimaire.

action, n. **1.** (to take) **industrial action,** (i) (voter/organiser un) mouvement revendicatif (ii) se mettre en grève; **day of action,** journée d'action **2.** Jur: **action at law,** action f en justice/procès (civil ou criminel); **legal action,** action juridique/ procès; **action for libel,** action/procès/ plainte f en diffamation; **action for damages,** action en dommages intérêts/ dommages et intérêts; **action for payment,** action en paiement; **action for an account,** action en reddition de compte; **to bring an action against s.o.,** intenter une action contre qn/intenter un procès à ou contre qn/exercer des poursuites f contre qn/ déposer une plainte contre qn/(faire) appeler qn en justice **3.** (equity stake) capitaux mpl propres/fonds mpl propres.

activation, n. activation f.

active, a. **active balance,** balance f excédentaire; **active market,** marché animé/ actif; **active money,** monnaie circulante; **active partner,** associé-gérant m/ commandité, -ée; **active population,** population active; StExch: **active stock,** valeurs actives; **there is an active demand for oils,** les valeurs pétrolières sont très recherchées/il y a une forte demande de valeurs pétrolières.

actual, **1.** a. (a) **to give the actual figures,** donner les chiffres réels; **actual employment,** emploi effectif; **the figures represent the actual value,** les chiffres représentent la valeur réelle (b) **actual cost,** prix m (i) d'achat (ii) de revient **2.** n.pl. (a) **the actuals,** les chiffres réels (b) **actuals,** (on commodities market) livraisons fpl physiques/marchandises livrées au comptant.

actuarial, a. (calculation, etc.) actuariel.

actuary, n. actuaire mf.

acumen, n. **business acumen,** sens m des affaires.

ad, n. F: pub f; (private, in newspaper) annonce f; **to put an ad in the paper,** mettre/insérer une annonce dans le journal; **classified/small ads,** annonces classées/petites annonces; **ad agency,** agence publicitaire/de publicité.

add, v.tr. & i. (a) **to add the interest to the capital,** ajouter l'intérêt au capital (b) **to add up a column of figures,** additionner/ totaliser une colonne de chiffres (c) **the assets add up to two million(s),** l'actif m s'élève à deux millions; **the figures don't add up,** les chiffres sont faux; **the accounts won't add up,** je n'arrive pas à faire accorder/balancer les comptes (d) **this adds to our expenses,** cela augmente (le montant de) nos dépenses.

adder, n. Cmptr: additionneur m.

adding, n. addition f; **adding machine,** machine f à calculer/à additionner.

addition, n. (a) addition f; **additions to the staff,** adjonction f de personnel (b) **addition to the stock,** augmentation f du capital (par incorporation de réserves).

additional, a. **additional charges,** supplément(s) m/frais mpl supplémentaires; **additional investment,** investissement m supplémentaire; **additional payment,** supplément; **additional clause,** avenant m.

address¹, n. adresse f; **accommodation address,** siège social-boîte aux lettres; **business address,** (of company) (adresse du) siège social; (of person) adresse du bureau; **home address,** adresse du domicile.

address², v.tr. (a) **to address a letter,** mettre/écrire l'adresse sur une enveloppe; **please address all enquiries to ...,** faire parvenir toute demande de renseignements à ... (b) **he is to address the meeting,** il doit prendre la parole à la réunion.

addressed, a. (enveloppe, etc.) qui porte l'adresse (du destinataire); **this parcel is addressed to me,** ce colis m'est adressé; **please send a stamped addressed envelope.** NAm: **self-addressed stamped envelope**

(sae, *NAm:* **sase),** pour la réponse joindre une enveloppe timbrée à votre adresse.

addressee, *n.* destinataire *mf.*

addressing, *n.* **addressing machine,** machine *f* à adresser.

Addressograph, *n.* (*Rtm: of machines manufactured by Addressograph Multigraph Corporation*) Adressographe *m;* machine *f* à imprimer les adresses.

adjourn, **1.** *v.tr.* **to adjourn a meeting,** ajourner une réunion **2.** *v.i.* **the meeting adjourned at 3 o'clock,** on a levé la séance à 3 heures.

adjournment, *n.* ajournement *m/*renvoi *m,* remise *f* (d'une séance).

adjudicate, *v.tr.* juger; *Adm:* adjuger; **to adjudicate a claim,** (ad)juger une réclamation; **to adjudicate s.o. (to be) bankrupt,** déclarer qn en faillite.

adjudication, *n.* jugement *m/*décision *f; Adm:* adjudication *f;* **adjudication order/ adjudication of bankruptcy,** jugement déclaratif de faillite; **adjudication of a bankrupt's debts,** répartition *f* des dettes d'un failli.

adjudicative, *a. Jur:* (acte) déclaratif/ déclaratoire.

adjudicator, *n.* arbitre *m/*juge *m.*

adjust, *v.tr.* r(é)ajuster (les salaires); **income adjusted for inflation,** revenu réel compte tenu de l'inflation.

adjustable, *a.* **adjustable rate,** (à) taux variable.

adjuster, *NAm:* **adjustor** *n. Ins:* **average adjuster/loss adjuster,** expert, -erte en assurances; répartiteur *m* d'avaries; **claims/insurance adjuster,** expert en assurances.

adjustment, *n. Ins:* **average adjustment,** répartition *f* d'avaries; **seasonal adjustment,** rectification saisonnière; **tax adjustment,**

redressement fiscal; **wage adjustment,** r(é)ajustement *m* des salaires.

adjustor, *n.* = **adjuster.**

adman, *n. F:* publicitaire *m.*

admin, *n. F:* = **administration.**

administered, *a. NAm:* **administered price,** prix imposé.

administration, *n.* (*a*) administration *f/* gestion *f* (des affaires); **administration expenses,** frais *mpl* d'administration/de gestion; *NAm:* **the Administration,** le gouvernement (fédéral) (*b*) liquidation *f* (d'une société).

administrative, *a.* administratif; **administrative details,** détails *m* d'ordre administratif.

administrator, *n.* administrateur, -trice; gérant, -ante (d'une entreprise); gestionnaire *mf.*

admission, *n.* **admission (fee),** (prix *m* d')entrée *f;* **admission free,** entrée libre/ gratuite; **admission £2** = entrée 20 Fr; **admission requirements,** conditions *f* d'admission.

admittance, *n.* entrée *f;* **no admittance,** entrée interdite.

adopt, *v.tr.* approuver (les minutes d'un conseil d'administration); **to adopt a resolution (at a meeting),** adopter une motion (à une réunion).

ad referendum, *Lt. phr.* au référendum/au vote direct (des citoyens ou des membres d'un groupement); **ad referendum contract,** contrat dûment signé qui contient certaines dispositions à discuter davantage.

ad valorem, *Lt. phr.* **ad valorem duty/tax,** droit *m/*taxe *f* sur la valeur; droit/taxe ad valorem; droit proportionnel; **to pay a duty ad valorem,** payer un droit sur/d'après la valeur des marchandises; **ad valorem revenue stamp,** timbre fiscal selon la valeur.

advance[1], *n.* **1.** (*a*) **to pay in advance,** payer d'avance; **to pay a sum in advance,** verser un acompte/une provision; avancer de l'argent; **payable in advance,** payable à l'avance; **fixed in advance,** fixé à l'avance; (prix) forfaitaire; *Corr:* **thanking you in advance,** en vous remerciant d'avance; avec mes remerciements anticipés (*b*) **advance payment,** provision; arrhes *fpl*; paiement anticipé; **advance booking,** location *f*/réservation *f* de places (à l'avance) **2.** (*a*) avance *f* (de fonds); à-bon-compte *m inv*; à-valoir *m inv*; **bank advance,** avance bancaire; **cash advance,** avance en numéraire; **advance on current account,** avance en compte courant; **to make an advance of £10 to s.o.,** faire à qn une avance de £10/avancer £10 à qn; **advance account,** compte *m* d'avances; **advance on a contract,** acompte *m* sur contrat; arrhes; **advance against security,** avance/prêt *m* sur nantissement; **advances on securities/ against collateral,** prêts sur titres; **standing advance,** avance permanente; **secured advances,** avances sur nantissement/garanties; **unsecured advances,** avances à découvert/sur notoriété (*b*) augmentation *f*/hausse *f* (de prix); renchérissement *m*; **the general advance in prices,** la hausse/ l'augmentation générale des prix; **there is an advance on wheat,** les blés sont à la hausse/ont subi une hausse; (*at auction*) **any advance?** qui dit mieux?

advance[2], **1.** *v.tr.* (*a*) **to advance s.o. money,** avancer/prêter de l'argent à qn; **I will advance him £1000 on your note of hand,** je lui avancerai/je lui ferai une avance de £1000 sur un billet de vous; **sum advanced,** avance *f*/provision *f*; arrhes *fpl*; mise *f* hors (*b*) augmenter/hausser (les prix) **2.** *v.i.* (*of shares, etc.*) augmenter de prix/monter; **prices are advancing,** les prix *m* augmentent/montent.

advancement, *n.* **1. economic advancement,** essor *m* économique **2.** avancement *m*/promotion *f*.

advantage, *n.* **absolute advantage,** avantage absolu.

adverse, *a.* **adverse budget,** budget *m* déficitaire; **adverse balance of trade,** balance *f* commerciale déficitaire.

advert, *n.* *F:* réclame *f*/annonce *f* (publicitaire).

advertise, *v.tr. & i.* (*a*) **to advertise in a paper,** (faire) insérer/mettre une annonce dans un journal; **to advertise for a translator,** faire paraître une annonce pour recruter les services d'un traducteur (*b*) faire de la réclame/de la publicité (pour un produit); **to advertise widely to launch sth. on the market,** faire appel à la grande publicité pour lancer un article; **(goods) as advertised (on television),** (marchandises *f*) conformes à la spécification publicitaire (télévisée).

advertisement, *n.* (*a*) publicité *f*/réclame *f*/annonce *f* publicitaire (*b*) (*in newspaper*) annonce; **classified advertisements,** annonces classées/petites annonces; **advertisement manager,** annoncier, -ière.

advertiser, *n.* annonceur *m*.

advertising, *n.* publicité *f*/réclame *f*; annonces *fpl*; **advertising account,** budget *m* publicitaire; **advertising agency,** agence *f* publicitaire/de publicité; **advertising agent,** agent *m* de publicité; **advertising campaign,** campagne *f* de publicité; **advertising expenses,** dépenses *fpl* publicitaires/frais *mpl* de publicité; **advertising man/woman,** publicitaire *mf*; **advertising manager,** chef *m* de publicité; **advertising medium,** organe *m* de publicité; **advertising media,** supports *m* publicitaires; **advertising schedule,** programme *m* des annonces; **advertising sheet,** feuille *f* d'annonces; **advertising space,** espace *m*/ emplacement *m* réservé à la publicité; **cheapness can be a bad advertising point,** le bon marché peut être une contre-publicité; **above-the-line advertising,** coût *m* média; **below-the-line advertising,** coût promotion; **competitive advertising,** publicité concurrentielle; **informative/ persuasive advertising,** publicité instructive/persuasive; **poster advertising,** publicité par affichage/par affiches.

dvice, *n.* (*a*) **advice note/letter of advice,** lettre *f*/note *f* d'avis; **as per advice,** suivant avis (*b*) **until further advice,** jusqu'à nouvel avis; **to take legal advice,** consulter un avocat; **we have received advices from Hong Kong,** nous avons reçu des avis/des informations *f* de Hong Kong.

dvise, *v.tr.* **to advise a draft,** aviser d'une traite/donner avis d'une traite.

dviser, advisor, *n.* conseiller, -ère; **economic adviser,** conseiller économique.

dvisory, *a.* **advisory board,** comité consultatif; *Bank:* **advisory committee,** comité de restructuration.

ffidavit, *n.* déclaration faite sous serment/affidavit *m.*

ffiliate, *n.* *NAm:* société affiliée/filiale *f.*

ffiliated, *a.* **affiliated company,** société affiliée/filiale *f.*

freightment, *n.* transport *m* de marchandises par navire.

loat, *a.* **to keep (s.o., a business) afloat,** renflouer (qn, une entreprise); **to keep bills afloat,** faire circuler des effets.

oresaid, *a. & adv. Jur:* susmentionné/susdit/mentionné ci-dessus/mentionné plus haut.

ter, *prep.* (*of a bill of exchange*) **after date,** délai *m* de date; **after sight,** délai de vue.

termarket, *n.* état du marché pour une action après son entrée en Bourse.

ainst, *prep.* **the franc is weak against the other currencies, especially against the DMark,** le franc est faible contre les autres devises, notamment vis-à-vis du DMark; *MIns:* **against all risks,** contre tous risques.

e, *n.* **age group,** groupe *m* d'âge; **age limit,** limite *f* d'âge.

ency, *n.* (*a*) agence *f*/bureau *m*; **sole agency for a firm,** représentation exclusive d'une maison; **credit agency,** agence le rating; bureau de cotation/d'évalua-

tion; **news/press agency,** agence de presse; **employment agency,** bureau/agence de placement; agence pour l'emploi; **estate agency,** agence immobilière; **land agency,** agence foncière; **customs agency,** agence en douane; **shipping agency/forwarding agency,** agence maritime; **travel agency,** agence de voyage(s)/de tourisme; **literary agency,** agence littéraire; **agency account,** compte *m* agence; **agency agreement,** contrat *m* de mandat/traité *m* d'agence/accord *m* du mandataire; **agency contract,** contrat d'agence; **agency fee,** commission *f* de gestion (*b*) *Bank:* (*i*) succursale *f*/agence (de banque) (*ii*) direction *f* (d'une succursale)/agence (de banque) (*c*) comptoir *m* (à l'étranger).

agenda, *n.* ordre *m* du jour/programme *m* (d'une réunion); **to draw up an agenda,** dresser l'ordre du jour; **to place a question on the agenda,** inscrire une question à l'ordre du jour.

agent, *n.* agent *m*/représentant *m*; **agent for the firm of ...,** représentant de la maison ...; **appointed/authorized agent,** mandataire *mf*; (agent) agréé (*m*); fondé *m* de pouvoir; **to be sole agent for ...,** avoir la représentation exclusive de ...; **sole agent for a brand,** seul dépositaire/concessionnaire d'une marque; agent (commercial) exclusif; **commission agent,** commissionnaire *m*; **fiscal agent,** représentant fiscal; **forwarding agent/transport agent,** transitaire *m*; **insurance agent,** agent d'assurances; **managing agent,** agent-gérant *m*; **manufacturer's agent,** concessionnaire *m*; représentant (de commerce); **mercantile agent,** affactureur *m*; agent/société *f* d'affacturage; **local agent,** agent sur le terrain; **(real-)estate agent,** agent immobilier; **general agent,** agent d'affaires; **literary agent,** agent littéraire; **universal agent,** mandataire général.

aggregate, 1. *a.* total/global; **aggregate economic activity,** ensemble *m* des activités économiques; **aggregate output,** production globale; **aggregate demand/supply,** demande/offre globale;

aggregate net increment, accroissement global net **2.** *n.* somme totale/montant global.

agio, *n.* agio *m*; prix *m* du change; **agio account,** compte *m* d'agio.

agiotage, *n.* agiotage *m*.

agree, *v.tr.* **to agree the accounts/the books,** faire accorder les écritures/les livres; **the figures were agreed between the accountants,** les chiffres ont été acceptés (d'un commun accord) par les experts-comptables; **to agree on a price,** convenir d'un prix.

agreed, *a.* convenu; forfaitaire; **agreed price,** prix convenu; **contract at an agreed price,** contrat *m* à forfait/contrat forfaitaire; **agreed consideration,** (*i*) prix convenu (*ii*) contrepartie convenue.

agreement, *n.* **1.** convention *f*/acte *m*/ contrat *m*/traité *m*/arrangement *m*; **written agreement,** convention écrite; **gentleman's agreement,** convention verbale reposant sur l'honneur; **agreement for sale,** contrat/acte de vente; **blanket agreement,** accord-cadre *m*; **collective agreement,** contrat collectif; **collective wage agreement,** convention collective des salaires; **to work by agreement,** entreprendre un travail à prix convenu/à forfait; **to break an agreement,** rompre un marché; **to enter into an agreement with s.o.,** passer un traité/un contrat avec qn; **an agreement has been concluded between the two parties,** un accord est intervenu entre les deux parties; **to sign an agreement,** signer un contrat/une convention; **to sign a legal agreement,** s'engager (par) devant notaire (**to do sth.,** à faire qch.); **to abide by the agreement,** s'en tenir à la convention/s'en tenir à ce qui a été convenu **2.** accord *m*/entente *f*; **as per agreement,** comme (il a été) convenu; **by mutual agreement,** de gré à gré/à l'amiable/d'un commun accord; **marketing agreement,** accord de commercialisation; **General Agreement on Tariffs and Trade (GATT),** Accord général sur les tarifs douaniers et le commerce.

agribusiness, *n.* agrinégoce *m*.

agricultural, *a.* (produit, etc.) agrico**; agricultural engineer,** ingénieur ag**; nome; agricultural processing indust**; agro-industrie *f*; **agricultural show,** exp; sition *f* agricole/comice *m* agrico; **common agricultural policy (CAP),** pc; tique agricole commune.

agriculture, *n.* agriculture *f*.

agri-financial, *a.* agro-financier.

agri-foodstuffs, *a. & npl.* (secteur) ag; alimentaire.

agri-monetary, *a.* (mesure) ag; monétaire.

aid, *n.* aide *f*/assistance *f*; **economic a**; aide économique; **in aid of,** au profit;

aided, *a.* **state-aided/government-aid**; subventionné par l'État.

air, *n.* **by air,** (*letter, freight*) par avion/**; voie aérienne; **air cargo,** transport *m*; avion; fret aérien; **air transport,** tra; ports aériens; **air company,** compagni; de navigation aérienne; **air carrier,** transporteur aérien (*ii*) compag; aérienne; **air travel,** voyages *mpl*; avion; **air letter,** aérogramme *m*.

aircraft, *n. inv.* avion *m*/appareil; **charter aircraft,** (*i*) avion affrété/avion; lisé/charter *m* (*ii*) avion-taxi *m*; **aircr**; **charter agreement,** contrat *m* d'af; tement aérien; **commercial aircraft,** av; commercial; **the aircraft industry,** l; dustrie *f* aéronautique; **aircraft manu**; **turer/aircraft constructor,** constructeu; d'avions/avionneur *m*.

airfreight[1], *v.tr.* acheminer/transpo; par avion.

airfreight[2], *n.* transport *m* par av**; (*price*) fret *m*/frais *mpl* (de transport; avion); (*cargo*) fret aérien.

airline, *n.* ligne aérienne/compag; aérienne/service *m* de transports aéri**;

airmail[1], *n.* (*a*) poste aérienne; ser; postal aérien; **by airmail,** par avion courrier *m* par avion; **airmail letter,** lettre (envoyée) par avion; **airmail paper,** papier *m* avion/papier pelure; **airmail sticker,** autocollant *m* 'par avion'.

airmail², *v.tr.* envoyer/expédier (une lettre, etc.) par avion.

airport, *n.* aéroport *m.*

all-in, *a.* **all-in price,** prix *m* tout compris/prix forfaitaire; *Ins:* **all-in policy,** police *f* tous risques.

allocate, *v.tr.* allouer/assigner (qch. à qn, à qch.); **to allocate a sum to sth.,** affecter/assigner une somme à qch.

allocation, *n.* **1.** (*a*) allocation *f*/affectation *f* (d'une somme); **allocation of capital,** affectation des investissements; **allocation to reserve funds,** dotation *f* au fonds de réserve/au compte de provisions (*b*) répartition *f* (de dépenses, etc.); attribution *f* (de fonctions) (*c*) **allocation of contract,** adjudication *f;* **allocation to the lowest tender,** adjudication au mieux-disant; **allocation to the highest bidder,** adjudication à la surenchère **2.** part assignée/somme assignée.

allocatur, *n.* certificat *m* de l'état de frais (*pour le calcul de l'impôt*).

allonge, *n.* allonge *f* (d'une lettre de change).

allot, *v.tr.* répartir/distribuer (des actions); **all the shares have been allotted,** toutes les actions ont été réparties.

allotment, *n.* (*a*) affectation *f* (d'une somme à un but) (*b*) **allotment of shares,** attribution *f* d'actions; **letter of allotment,** (lettre *f* d')avis *m* de répartition/lettre d'allocation; bulletin *m* de souscription; **payment in full on allotment,** libération *f* à la répartition; **to pay so much on allotment,** payer tant lors de la répartition (*c*) (*method of warehousing*) allotissement *m* (de marchandises).

all-out, *a.* (*strike, etc.*) tous azimuts.

allow, *v.tr.* (*a*) **to allow s.o. a discount,** consentir/accorder/faire une remise à qn; **to**

allow 5%, déduire 5%/faire une remise de 5%; **to allow 5% interest on deposits,** allouer/attribuer 5% d'intérêt sur les dépôts (*b*) **to allow a claim,** admettre un recours (*c*) **to allow for sums paid in advance,** faire déduction des sommes payées d'avance; **packing is not allowed for,** (le prix de) l'emballage n'est pas compris/inclus; **after allowing for ...,** déduction faite de ...; **to allow for the tare,** défalquer la tare; **to allow so much for carriage,** (*i*) ajouter (*ii*) déduire tant pour le port (*d*) **to allow s.o. £500 a year,** allouer à qn la somme annuelle de £500.

allowable, *a.* admissible/admis/permis/légitime; **allowable claim,** réclamation *f* recevable; **allowable expenses,** dépense *f* déductible/dépense remboursable.

allowance, *n.* **1.** **cost-of-living allowance,** indemnité *f* de vie chère/de cherté de vie; **accommodation/housing allowance,** indemnité de logement; **allocation-logement;** **allowance against tax,** dégrèvement *m*/abattement fiscal; **income tax allowance,** déduction *f* avant impôt/déduction fiscale; **personal allowance,** abattement *m* à la base; **earned income allowance,** déduction au titre des revenus salariaux ou professionnels; **office/entertainment allowance,** frais *mpl* de bureau/de représentation; **relocation/removal allowance,** prime *f*/indemnité de déplacement; **travel allowance,** indemnité de déplacement; **foreign currency allowance,** allocation en devises **2.** (*a*) remise *f*/rabais *m*/déduction/concession *f;* (*for bad quality, etc.*) réfaction *f;* **to make an allowance on an article,** faire/accorder un rabais sur un article (*b*) provisions *fpl;* **allowance to cashier for errors,** passe *f* de caisse; **allowance for exchange fluctuations,** provisions pour fluctuations du change; **allowance for loss,** provisions pour pertes; **depreciation allowance/wear-and-tear allowance,** provisions pour amortissement.

alphanumeric, *a.* **alphanumeric filing,** classement *m* (par ordre) alphanumérique.

alphanumerics, *n. Cmptr:* caractères alphanumériques.

amalgamate, 1. *v.tr.* amalgamer/fusionner (des sociétés, etc.); unifier (des industries); **to amalgamate shares,** fusionner des actions **2.** *v.i.* (*of companies*) fusionner/opérer une fusion.

amalgamation, *n.* fusion *f*/fusionnement *m* (de deux sociétés, *Fin:* d'actions); **amalgamation of industries,** fusion industrielle.

amazing, *a.* **amazing offer!** offre exceptionnelle!

amend, *v.tr.* (*a*) **to amend a resolution,** amender une proposition (*b*) rectifier (un compte); modifier.

amendment, *n.* (*a*) amendement *m* (d'une proposition) (*b*) rectification *f* (d'un compte); modification *f*.

amortizable, *a.* amortissable.

amortization, *n.* amortissement *m* (d'une dette, etc.); **amortization quota,** cote *f*/taux *m* d'amortissement; **authorized quota amortization,** contingent *m* d'amortissement autorisé.

amortize, *v.tr.* amortir (une dette).

amount[1], *n.* somme *f*/montant *m*/total *m* (d'une facture, etc.); valeur *f*; quantité *f* (d'une marchandise); **amount of expenses,** chiffre *m* de la dépense; **amount paid,** somme versée; **amount paid on account,** acompte versé; **what is the amount of their turnover?** quel est leur chiffre d'affaires? **gross amount,** montant brut; **net amount,** montant net; **total amount,** somme totale; **amount invested (in a company),** mise *f* de fonds; **amounts of stock negotiable,** quotités *f* de titres négociables; **amounts to be made good,** masse créancière; **amount insured/amount of the risk,** montant assuré; **amount written off,** amortissement *m*; *NAm:* **face amount,** valeur nominale/nominal *m*; *Book-k:* **amount brought in,** report *m* des exercices antérieurs; **amount carried forward,** report à nouveau/somme

à reporter; **amount entered twice,** double empioi *m*.

amount[2], *v.i.* (*of money, etc.*) s'élever/se monter (**to, à**); **the stocks amount to 2 500,** les stocks *m* s'élèvent à 2 500/atteignen 2 500.

analyse, *v.tr.* **to analyse an account,** dépouiller/décomposer un compte.

analysis, *n.* analyse *f*; **analysis of account,** dépouillement *m*/décomposition *f*/analyse d'un compte; **economic analysis,** analyse/étude *f* économique; **fundamental analysis,** analyse fondamentale; **statistical analysis,** analyse statistique; **cost benefit analysis,** analyse des coûts e rendements/analyse coût-profit; **cost effectiveness analysis,** étude *f* de coût e d'efficacité; **job analysis,** analyse de tâches; **operating costs analysis,** comptabilité *f* analytique d'exploitation; **project analysis,** étude de projet; **sales/marke analysis,** analyse des ventes/du marché; **supply and demand analysis,** analyse d l'offre et de la demande; **systems analysis,** analyse des systèmes; **technical analysis,** analyse sur graphiques.

analyst, *n.* analyste *mf*; **financial analyst,** analyste financier; **systems analyst,** analyste-programmeur *m*; **fundamental market analyst,** analyste *mf* fondamental(e); **chart analyst,** *NAm:* **technical market analyst,** prévisionniste *mf*/chartiste *mf*/analyste sur graphiques.

analytical, *a.* **analytical training,** formation *f* par étapes.

annual, *a.* annuel; **annual leave,** congé annuel; **annual report,** rapport annuel d gestion; **annual abstract of statistic** annuaire *m* de statistiques; **he has a annual salary of £30,000,** il gagne trent mille livres par an.

annualized, *a.* **the annualized figures,** montant total pour un an; **annualized percentage rate (A.P.R.),** taux annualisé.

annually, *adv.* annuellement; tous les ans.

annuitant, *n.* rentier, -ière (en viager).

annuity, *n.* 1. **annuity in redemption of debt**, annuité *f* 2. rente *f* (annuelle); **government annuity**, rente sur l'État; **perpetual annuity**, rente perpétuelle; **terminable annuity**, rente à terme; annuité résiliable; **life annuity**, rente viagère; **annuity in reversion/reversionary annuity**, rente réversible; **survivorship annuity**, rente viagère avec réversion; **deferred annuity**, annuité différée; **contingent annuity**, annuité contingente; **to invest money in an annuity/to buy an annuity**, placer son argent en viager/à fonds perdu.

annul, *v.tr.* annuler/résilier/résoudre (un contrat).

annullable, *a.* (contrat) annulable/résiliable/résoluble.

annulling[1], *a.* qui annule; **annulling clause**, clause *f* abrogative/abrogatoire.

annulling[2], **annulment**, *n.* annulation *f*/résiliation *f*/abrogation *f*/résolution *f* (d'un contrat, etc.).

answer[1], *n.* réponse *f*; **in answer to your letter**, en réponse à votre lettre.

answer[2], *v.tr.* **I answered this letter**, j'ai répondu à cette lettre; **to answer the telephone**, répondre au téléphone; prendre une communication.

answering, *a.* **answering machine**, répondeur *m* (téléphonique); répondeur-enregistreur *m*.

antedate[1], *n.* antidate *f*.

antedate[2], *v.tr.* antidater (un document, etc.).

anticipate, *v.tr.* prévoir; **to anticipate demand**, prévoir la demande; **anticipated sales**, (taux de) ventes prévues.

anticipation, *n.* **in anticipation of a price rise**, en prévision d'une augmentation de prix.

anti-inflationary, *a.* **anti-inflationary measures**, mesures anti-inflationnistes.

antitrust, *a.* antitrust *inv*; *esp. NAm:* **antitrust laws**, législation *f* antitrust.

appeal, *n.* **sales appeal**, attraction commerciale.

appear, *v.i.* apparaître/figurer/être inscrit; **item which appears in the books**, article *m* qui figure dans les livres.

appliance, *n.* appareil *m*; **electrical (household) appliance**, appareil électroménager.

applicant, *n.* **applicant for a job**, candidat, -ate à un emploi/postulant, -ante; **applicant for a patent**, demandeur *m* d'un brevet; **applicant for shares**, souscripteur *m* à des actions; **applicant for a trademark**, déposant *m* d'une marque.

application, *n.* (*a*) **application (for a job, for a patent)**, demande *f* (d'emploi, de brevet); **application form**, formulaire *m* de demande (d'emploi, etc.); bulletin *m* d'abonnement (à un journal); **closing date for application**, date limite de dépôt de candidatures; **to send in/to submit an application**, faire une demande (par écrit); **samples are sent on application**, on envoie des échantillons sur demande (*b*) *Fin:* **application for shares**, souscription *f* d'actions; demande de titres en souscription; **payable on application**, payable à la souscription; **application form**, (*for shares*) bulletin de souscription; **application money**, versement *m* de souscription; **application receipt**, reçu *m* de souscription; **application and allotment**, souscription *f* et allocation *f* (d'actions) (*c*) **commercial application**, application commerciale (d'une invention, etc.).

apply, 1. *v.tr.* **to apply a payment to a particular debt**, imputer/affecter un paiement à une dette spécifiée 2. *v.i.* (*a*) **to apply for a job**, poser sa candidature à un poste; solliciter/postuler un emploi; **apply within**, s'adresser ici; **to apply in writing**, écrire; **to apply in person**, se présenter (*b*) **to apply for shares**, souscrire (à) des actions.

appoint, *v.tr.* **to appoint s.o. to a post**, nommer qn à un emploi/désigner qn à un poste; **Mr X has been appointed general manager,** M. X s'est vu confié le poste de/est devenu/a été nommé directeur général.

appointee, *n.* candidat(e) retenu(e)/choisi(e); nouveau/nouvelle titulaire d'un poste.

appointed, *a.* **appointed agent,** agent attitré; **our newly appointed sales manager,** notre nouveau chef de vente/le chef de vente que nous venons de nommer.

appointment, *n.* **1.** (*for business*) entrevue *f*; **to make/fix an appointment with s.o.,** fixer un rendez-vous/donner rendez-vous (à qn); **to make an appointment with s.o. for three o'clock,** prendre un rendez-vous pour trois heures; **to break an appointment,** manquer au rendez-vous; **to cancel an appointment,** annuler un rendez-vous; **to meet s.o. by appointment,** avoir (un) rendez-vous avec qn; **have you an appointment?** avez-vous un rendez-vous? **by appointment only,** sur rendez-vous **2.** (*a*) nomination *f*/désignation *f* (de qn à un emploi) (*b*) (*of shop, etc.*) **by appointment to Her Majesty,** fournisseur breveté/attitré/officiel de sa Majesté (*c*) poste *m*/emploi *m*; **to hold an appointment,** être préposé à un emploi; (*in newspaper*) **appointments vacant,** offres *f* d'emploi; **appointments wanted,** demandes *f* d'emploi.

apportion, *v.tr.* répartir/ventiler (les frais).

apportionment, *n.* partage *m*/répartition *f*/imputation *f*/affectation *f* (d'impôts, de dépenses, etc.); ventilation *f* (de frais, etc.).

appraisal, *n.* estimation *f*/évaluation *f*; expertise *f*; **market appraisal,** évaluation *f* du marché; **investment appraisal,** appréciation *f* des investissements.

appraiser, *n.* commissaire-priseur *m*.

appreciate, *v.i.* (*of goods, etc.*) augmenter de valeur/augmenter de prix/accuser une plus-value; **appreciated surplus,** plus-value; **the franc has appreciated in terms of**

other currencies, le franc s'est apprécié vis-à-vis des autres monnaies.

appreciation, *n.* **1.** appréciation *f* (du prix/de la valeur de qch.); estimation *f* (de la valeur de qch.); évaluation *f* **2.** augmentation *f*/hausse *f* de valeur amélioration *f*/valorisation *f*/plus-value *f*; **these shares show an appreciation,** ces actions *f* ont enregistré une plus-value **appreciation of assets,** plus-value d'actif **appreciation of the exchange,** plus-value du change; **appreciation in prices,** amélioration des cours/des prix.

apprentice[1], *n.* apprenti, -ie.

apprentice[2], *v.tr.* **to apprentice s.o. to s.o.** placer/mettre qn en apprentissage chez qn.

apprenticeship, *n.* apprentissage *m*; **to serve one's apprenticeship with s.o.,** faire son apprentissage chez qn.

appro, *n.* *F:* **on appro,** à l'essai/à condition **to buy (sth.) on appro,** acheter (qch.) à condition/à l'essai.

appropriate, *v.tr.* destiner/affecter consacrer (**a sum to/for a purpose,** une somme à un projet); **funds appropriated for the new library,** fonds affectés à la nouvelle bibliothèque; **appropriated profits,** bénéfices distribués.

appropriation, *n.* affectation *f* de fonds attribution *f*/distraction *f* (d'une somme) **appropriation account,** compte *m* de perte et profits; **appropriation of payment to a debt,** imputation *f* d'un paiement une dette; **appropriation to the reserve,** dotation *f* au compte de provisions; **prior appropriation,** prélèvement *m* prioritaire

approval, *n.* **1.** approbation *f*/agrément *m* **subject to approval/for approval,** soumis l'approbation; **to submit for approval (to s.o.),** soumettre à l'approbation (de qn) **2** ratification *f*/homologation *f* (d'un document) **3.** (*a*) **on approval,** à condition l'essai; **to buy sth. on approval,** acheter qch. à l'essai/à condition; **tools sent on approval,** outils envoyés à titre d'essai **book sent on approval,** livre envoyé l'examen/en communication (*b*) *NAm:* **approvals,** marchandises envoyées à l'essai.

approve, *v.tr.* approuver/sanctionner (une action); ratifier/homologuer (un document); approuver (les comptes); **read and approved,** lu et approuvé; **the proposal was approved (of),** la proposition a été approuvée/agréée.

approximation, *n.* approximation *f*/ évaluation approximative.

arb, *n. NAm: abbr of* **arbitrage.**

arbitrage, *n.* (*a*) *Fin:* arbitrage *m;* **stock arbitrage,** arbitrage sur des valeurs; *US:* **index arbitrage,** gestion indicielle; couverture *f* sur indice; *US:* **risk arbitrage,** arbitrage risque (*b*) *PolEc:* **arbitrage syndicate,** syndicat *m* arbitragiste.

arbitrage(u)r, *n.* arbitragiste *mf.*

arbitrate, **1.** *v.tr.* arbitrer/juger/trancher (un différend) **2.** *v.i.* décider en qualité d'arbitre; arbitrer.

arbitration, *n.* **1.** arbitrage *m;* **arbitration board,** commission *f* paritaire d'arbitrage; **procedure by arbitration,** procédure arbitrale; **settlement by arbitration,** règlement *m* par arbitrage; solution arbitrale; **to refer a question to arbitration,** soumettre une question à l'arbitrage; **to submit an affair for arbitration,** soumettre un différend à l'arbitrage; **difference submissible to arbitration,** litige *m* arbitral; **to go to arbitration,** soumettre un différend à l'arbitrage/recourir à l'arbitrage; **arbitration tribunal,** tribunal arbitral; **arbitration court/court of arbitration,** tribunal arbitral; **arbitration clause,** clause *f* d'arbitrage; clause compromissoire; **arbitration analysis,** analyse arbitrale **2. arbitration of exchange,** arbitrage du change.

arbitrator, *n.* arbitre *m;* médiateur *m;* amiable compositeur *m.*

arcade, *n.* **shopping arcade,** galerie marchande.

area, *n.* (*a*) **residential area,** quartier résidentiel; **shopping area,** quartier commerçant (*b*) **free trade area,** zone *f* de libre-échange; **currency area,** zone monétaire; **the sterling/dollar/franc area,** la zone sterling/dollar/franc (*c*) **growth area,** secteur *m* de croissance; **problem area,** zone critique (*d*) superficie *f*.

Ariel, *n.* système *m* informatique qui rend possible les opérations boursières entre souscripteurs sans passer par la Bourse de Londres.

arrangement, *n.* **to make an arrangement/ to come to an arrangement with s.o.,** faire un arrangement avec qn; **private arrangement,** accord à l'amiable; **price by arrangement,** prix *m* à débattre/à discuter/ à négocier; (*after bankruptcy*) concordat *m.*

arrears, *n.pl.* arriéré *m*/arrérages *mpl*; **in arrears,** à terme échu; **rent arrears,** arriéré/arrérages de loyer; **tax arrears,** arriéré/arrérages d'impôt; **arrears of wages,** arrérages de salaires/rappel *m* de salaires; **arrears of interest,** intérêts non payés; arrérages; **to get into arrears,** s'arrérager; arrérager; **to let one's rent fall into arrears,** être en retard pour payer son loyer; laisser son loyer s'arrérager; **interest on arrears,** intérêts moratoires; **salary with arrears effective as from March 1st,** traitement *m* avec effet rétroactif au 1er mars.

arrival, *n.* arrivage *m* (de marchandises); arrivée *f* (d'un avion, etc.), (*on letters*) **to await arrival,** prière d'attendre l'arrivée.

arrive, *v.i.* **to arrive at a price,** calculer/ fixer un prix; convenir d'un prix.

article[1], *n.* **1.** article *m*/clause *f* (d'une convention, d'un traité); **articles of apprenticeship,** contrat *m* d'apprentissage; **he is under articles,** il fait son apprentissage/il est en apprentissage; **articles of a partnership,** contrat de société/acte *m* d'association; **the articles of a contract,** les stipulations *f* d'un contrat; **articles of association,** statuts *m* (*d'une société à responsabilité limitée*); **appointed/provided by the articles,** statutaire; **under the articles/in accordance with the articles,** statutairement; (*of sale, contract*) **articles and conditions,** cahier *m* des charges **2.** article *m*; produit *m*; marchandise *f*; **to put an article on the market,** lancer un produit sur le marché.

article[2], *v.tr.* **to article s.o. to an architect,** placer qn (comme élève) chez un architecte; **articled clerk,** clerc d'avoué/de notaire (*lié par un contrat d'apprentissage*).

assembly, *n.* (*a*) assemblée *f* (*b*) **assembly line,** chaîne *f* de montage; **assembly workshop,** atelier *m* de montage.

assess, *v.tr.* **to assess the damage,** évaluer les dommages/les dégâts; **to assess the damages at £100,** fixer les dommages-intérêts à £100; **to assess a property (for taxation),** évaluer une propriété.

assessable, *a.* **assessable income,** revenu *m* imposable.

assessment, *n.* évaluation *f*; **assessment of damages,** évaluation des dommages-intérêts/dommages et intérêts; **tax assessment,** détermination *f* de l'assiette de l'impôt/de l'assiette fiscale; **additional tax assessment,** redressement fiscal; **year of assessment,** année d'imposition.

asset, *n.pl.* **assets,** actif *m*/avoir(s) *m*(*pl*); masse active (d'une liquidation après faillite); **assets and liabilities,** actif et passif; **asset-based loan,** prêt fondé sur des actifs réels; **available assets,** actif disponible/liquide; **capital assets,** actif immobilisé/valeurs immobilisées; **circulating assets,** capitaux circulants; **current/floating/working asset,** actif circulant/valeurs *f* disponibles/valeurs réalisables; **fixed assets,** immobilisations (corporelles)/ actif immobilisé/valeurs immobilisées/actif stable; **foreign currency assets,** avoirs en devises étrangères; **frozen assets,** fonds bloqués/non liquides; **intangible/invisible asset,** actif incorporel/ immobilisations (incorporelles); **liquid assets/quick assets,** actif liquide/disponible/négociable/réalisable; **tangible assets,** valeurs matérielles; **net tangible asset value,** valeur comptable nette; **nonperforming assets,** actifs hors exploita-

tion; **realizable assets,** actif réalisable; **personal assets,** biens *m* meubles; **real assets,** biens immobiliers; **total assets,** total de l'actif; **excess of assets over liabilities,** excédent *m* de l'actif sur le passif; **assets brought in,** apport *m*; **asset play,** valeur *f* d'actif; **asset stripping,** démantèlement *m* d'entreprise; raid financier; **asset turnover,** rotation *f* des capitaux; **asset value,** valeurs *fpl* des actifs; **asset valuation,** réserve *f*/provision *f* pour évaluation d'actif.

assign, *v.tr.* assigner (**to,** à); **to assign a right to s.o.,** attribuer un droit à qn/faire cession d'un droit à qn; **to assign shares to s.o.,** transmettre/céder des actions à qn.

assignation, *n.* cession *f*/transfert *m* (de dettes, etc.); **assignation of shares/of patent,** transmission *f* d'actions/de brevet; **deed of assignation,** acte *m* de transfert; acte attributif.

assignee, *n.* cessionnaire *mf* (d'une créance, etc.); ayant cause *m*.

assignment, *n.* (*a*) cession *f*/transfert *m* (de biens, de dettes, etc.); **deed of assignment,** acte attributif/acte de transfert (*b*) **job assignment,** affectation *f* des tâches.

assignor, *n.* cédant, -ante.

assistance, *n.* **financial assistance,** appui financier.

assistant[1], *a.* auxiliaire; adjoint; **assistant manager,** sous-directeur *m*; **assistant general manager/general manager's assistant,** directeur général adjoint.

assistant[2], *n.* assistant, -ante; aide *mf*; adjoint, -ointe/ auxiliaire *mf*; collaborateur, -trice; **shop assistant,** vendeur, -euse; **personal assistant (PA),** assistant, -ante/ secrétaire particulier, -ière.

associate[1], *a.* **associate company,** société affiliée; **associate director,** directeur adjoint.

associate[2], *n.* associé, -ée; adjoint, -ointe; **business associate,** associé, -ée.

association, *n.* association *f*; société *f*; **trade association,** association professionnelle; **employers' association,** syndicat patronal; **producers' association,** syndicat de producteurs; *NAm:* **Savings and Loan Association** = crédit foncier; **to form an association,** constituer une société.

assume, *v.tr.* **to assume all risks,** assumer tous les risques.

assurance, *n.* assurance *f*; **life assurance,** assurance sur la vie/assurance-vie *f*; **term assurance,** assurance-décès *f*; **assurance company,** compagnie *f* d'assurances; **assurance policy,** police *f* d'assurance.

assure, *v.tr.* **to assure s.o.'s life,** assurer la vie de qn; **to assure one's life,** s'assurer (sur la vie); **to have one's life assured,** se faire assurer sur la vie.

assured, *n.* assuré, -ée.

assurer, assuror, *n.* assureur *m*.

at best, *prep. phr.* au mieux/au meilleur prix; **order at best,** ordre *m* au mieux.

at call, *prep. phr.* à vue/à présentation/sur demande.

at par, *prep. phr.* au pair; **repayable at par,** remboursable au pair.

at limit, *prep. phr. StExch:* (ordre) à cours limite.

at sight, *prep. phr.* à vue/à présentation/sur demande.

attachment, *n. Jur:* saisie *f*; saisie-arrêt *f*; **attachment of property,** saisie immobilière.

attention, *n.* **your orders shall have our best attention,** vos commandes seront exécutées avec le plus grand soin; **(for the) attention (of) Mr X,** à l'attention de M. X.

attested, *a.* **attested copy,** copie certifiée conforme.

attorney, *n.* (*a*) agréé(e) (au tribunal de commerce) (*b*) procureur *m*/fondé *m* de pouvoir; **attorney in fact,** mandataire *m*; **power of attorney,** procuration *f*/mandat *m*/pouvoirs *mpl* (*c*) *NAm:* avocat *m* (*ins-*

crit au Barreau); avoué *m*; *NAm:* **district attorney** = procureur de la République.

attractive, *a.* **attractive prices,** prix intéressants.

attributable, *a.* **attributable profits,** bénéfices *m* distribuables.

auction[1]**,** *n.* (*a*) **(sale by) auction/auction sale,** vente *f* à l'enchère/aux enchères/à l'encan; (*of certain goods, e.g. fish*) (vente à la) criée *f*; **by auction,** par voie d'adjudication; **to sell goods by auction/***NAm:* **at auction,** vendre des marchandises aux enchères; **to put sth. up to/for auction,** mettre qch. à l'enchère; **auction room,** salle *f* des ventes; **Dutch auction,** vente à la baisse/au rabais (*b*) (*of treasury bonds*) adjudication *f*.

auction[2]**,** *v.tr.* vendre (qch.) à l'enchère/aux enchères/à l'encan; mettre (qch.) aux enchères; (*certain goods, e.g. fish*) vendre à la criée; **to auction sth. off,** vendre qch. aux enchères (*pour s'en débarrasser*).

auctioneer, *n.* (*a*) **auctioneer and valuer,** commissaire-priseur *m* (*b*) (*at a sale*) directeur *m* de la vente.

audiotyping, *n.* dactylographie *f* au magnétophone.

audiotypist, *n.* dactylo *f* au magnétophone/audiotypiste *mf*.

audit[1]**,** *n.* vérification *f*/apurement *m* (des comptes); vérification(s) comptable(s); audit *m*/contrôle *m*; **audit manager,** directeur *m*/chef *m* du service d'audit; **external audit,** audit/contrôle externe; **internal audit,** audit/contrôle interne.

audit[2]**,** *v.tr.* vérifier/apurer/examiner (les comptes); **to audit the accounts of a company,** vérifier et certifier la comptabilité d'une société.

auditing, *n.* vérification *f* et certification *f* des écritures; vérification des comptes; apurement *m*; **balance sheet auditing,** contrôle *m* du bilan.

auditor, *n.* vérificateur *m* comptable/audit(eur) *m*/réviseur *m*/commissaire *m* aux comptes (d'une société); **auditor's final discharge,** quitus *m*; **external auditor,** audit(eur) externe; **internal auditor,** audit(eur)/vérificateur interne.

auditorship, *n.* commissariat *m* des comptes.

austerity, *n.* **austerity measures,** mesures *f* d'austérité.

autarchy, autarky, *n.* autarcie *f*.

authenticate, *v.tr.* authentifier.

authority, *n.* autorité *f*; administration *f*; **the (Public) Authorities,** les pouvoirs publics.

authorize, *v.tr.* autoriser.

authorized, *a.* **authorized agent,** mandataire *mf*; **authorized capital,** capital social/nominal; **authorized dealer,** concessionnaire *mf*/distributeur agréé.

automated, *a.* automatisé.

automatic, *a.* automatique; **automatic data processing (ADP),** traitement *m* automatique des données.

automation, *n.* automatisation *f*/automation *f*.

autonomy, *n.* autonomie (financière).

availability, *n.* disponibilité *f* (de matériaux, etc.); (durée et rayon de) validité *f* (d'un billet); **subject to availability,** selon disponibilité.

available, *a.* (*a*) disponible; (*pers.*) libre; **available at all branches,** en vente dans toutes nos/les succursales; **no longer available,** qu'on ne peut plus se procurer; introuvable; **it's no longer available,** ça ne se fait plus; **items available in stock,** disponibilités *f* du stock; **available assets,** actif *m* disponible/liquide; **available funds,** fonds *m* liquides/fonds disponibles/disponibilités *fpl*; **capital that can be made available,** capitaux *m* mobilisables; **sum available for dividend,** affectation *f* aux actions (*b*) valable; **(ticket) available on day of issue only,** (billet) valable le jour d'émission seulement.

average[1], *n.* (*a*) moyenne *f*; **moving average,** moyenne mobile; **rough average** moyenne approximative; **sales average** moyenne des ventes; **weighted average** moyenne pondérée; **to take an average** faire la moyenne (*b*) *MIns:* avarie(s) *f*(*pl* **particular average,** avarie particulière **general average,** avaries communes; **free from average,** franc d'avaries; **average adjustment/average statement,** répartition *f* d'avaries; **average adjuster/***NAm* **adjustor,** répartiteur *m* d'avaries; **average bond,** compromis *m* d'avarie (*c*) indice *n NAm:* **Stock average,** indice des titres **Dow Jones average,** indice Dow Jones.

average[2], *a.* moyen; **average cost per uni** coût unitaire moyen; **average price,** pri moyen; **average specimen,** échantillo normal; **average due date,** échéanc moyenne; *NAm:* **average tax rate,** tau d'imposition effectif/moyen; **averag yield,** rendement *m* moyen; **taking as basis the average figures for the last fiv years,** en adoptant comme base l moyenne des cinq dernières années.

average out, *v.i.* faire la moyenne de; **averages out at ...,** cela donne e moyenne ....

averager, *n.* *MIns:* répartiteur d'avaries.

averaging, *n.* *StExch:* moyennes *fp* communes *fpl*.

avoidance, *n.* **avoidance of an agreemen** (*owing to breach, etc.*), résolution annulation *f*/résiliation *f* d'un contrat; (*a contract*) **condition of avoidance,** co dition *f* résolutoire; **action for avoidan of contract,** action *f* en nullité; **avoidan of contract owing to mistake or misrepr sentation,** rescision *f*; **tax avoidance,** év sion fiscale.

avoirdupois, *n.* poids *m* du commerc **ounce avoirdupois,** once *f* avoirdupo once du commerce.

award[1], *n.* arbitrage *m*; sentence arbitra décision *f* (arbitrale)/adjudication *f*; **make an award,** rendre un jugement (arb tral); prononcer/rendre un arrêt; **to enforce an award,** rendre obligatoire une sentence; **to set aside an award,** annuler une sentence.

award[2], *v.tr.* adjuger/décerner **(sth. to s.o.,** qch. à qn); adjuger (un marché); **to award a wage increase,** accorder une augmentation de salaire; **to award damages,** accorder des dommages-intérêts.

awarding, *n.* adjudication *f* (d'un marché).

axe[1], *n. Fig:* **the axe,** coupe *f* sombre; coupe *f* (dans les prévisions budgétaires); réductions *fpl* (sur les traitements); diminutions *fpl* (de personnel); **to give s.o. the axe,** se débarrasser de qn/sa(c)quer qn.

axe[2], *v.tr. F:* **to axe public expenditure,** porter la hache dans les dépenses publiques; **to axe officials,** renvoyer des fonctionnaires (*pour des raisons d'économie*).

B

B, 'B' School (= **Business School**), école supérieure de commerce.

back[1], *n.* dos *m*/verso *m* (d'un chèque); **bills as per back,** effets *m* comme au verso; **back-to-back credit,** crédit adossé; **back to back loan/operation,** opération *f* de face à face; contrat *m* de prêt direct.

back[2], *a.* **back orders,** commandes *f* en souffrance/en retard; **back interest,** arrérages *mpl*; **back pay/payment,** rappel *m* de traitement; **back rent,** arriéré *m* de loyer; *Fin:* **back door,** réescompte *m*.

back[3], *v.tr.* **to back s.o.,** financer/soutenir qn; **to back a bill,** avaliser/endosser un effet/donner son aval *m* à un effet; **to back a project,** donner son appui à un projet; **Government-backed,** garanti par le gouvernement.

backdate, *v.tr.* antidater; **the contract is backdated,** le contrat est antidaté; **increase backdated to May 1st,** augmentation *f* avec effet rétroactif au 1er mai.

backer, *n.* (*a*) **backer of a bill,** avaliseur, -euse/avaliste *mf* (*b*) **financial backer,** bailleur, -euse, de fonds/commanditaire *m*; **the enterprise has an American backer,** le bailleur de fonds est américain.

backhander, *n.* pot-de-vin *m*/dessous-de-table *m*.

backing, *n.* (*a*) **backing of the currency,** couverture *f*/garantie *f* de la monnaie (*b*) **financial backing,** fonds *mpl*; aide financière/soutien financier.

backlog, *n.* arriéré *m*; **backlog of orders,** commandes non exécutées/en souffrance; arriéré *m* de commandes.

back-up, **1.** *a.* **back-up service/sales back-up,** service *m* après-vente **2.** aide (financière)/support (financier).

backwardation, *n.* déport *m*.

bad, **1.** *a.* **bad debt,** mauvaise créance/créance irrécouvrable/créance douteuse; **bad name,** mauvaise réputation **2.** *n.* **he is 5000 francs to the bad,** il est en perte de 5000 francs.

bail, *n.* **to go/to stand bail for s.o.,** se porter garant de qn/caution pour qn.

bailee, *n.* dépositaire *mf* (de biens sous contrat).

bailer, *n.* = **bailor.**

bailiff, *n.* huissier *m*.

bailment, *n.* (acte *m* de) dépôt *m*; contrat *m* de gage/de dépôt.

bailor, *n.* déposant, -ante (de biens sous contrat).

bail out, *see* **bale**[2].

bailout, *n.* *US:* plan *m* de sauvetage (pour une entreprise en difficulté).

balance[1], *n.* (*a*) solde *m*; reliquat *m* d'un compte; **balance of account,** solde de compte; **bank balance,** solde en banque/bancaire; **credit balance,** solde créditeur; **debit balance,** solde débiteur; **balance in hand,** solde en caisse; **balance carried forward,** report *m*/solde à reporter; **balance brought forward,** report/solde reporté; **balance due,** reste dû/solde (de compte); **payment of balance,** paiement *m* pour solde de compte; **to pay the balance,** régler le solde; **balance book,** livre *m* d'inventaire; **balance sheet,** bilan *m*/balance *f* d'inventaire; **off the balance**

18

sheet, hors de bilan; **trial balance,** balance générale/de vérification (*b*) **trade balance/ balance of trade/visible balance,** balance commerciale; **balance of payments,** balance des paiements.

balance², **1.** *v.tr.* balancer (un compte); compenser (une dette); **to balance the books,** clôturer les comptes; dresser/ établir le bilan; **to balance the budget,** équilibrer le budget; **to balance an adverse budget,** rétablir un budget déficitaire **2.** *v.i.* (*of accounts*) balancer/s'équilibrer.

balancing, *n.* **balancing of accounts,** règlement *m*/arrêté *m* de comptes.

bale¹, *n.* balle *f*/ballot *m* (de marchandises, etc.); **bale of cotton,** balle de coton (pesant de 160 à 500 livres); **bale of paper,** ballot (de dix rames) de papier.

bale², *v.tr.* **1.** emballer/emballotter/empaqueter (des marchandises) **2.** **bale out/bail out,** renflouer (qn); renflouer/injecter du capital dans (une entreprise en difficulté); **bale/bail out clause,** échappatoire *f*; *Jur:* clause *f* commissoire.

baling, *n.* mise *f* en balles.

ballasting *n.* lestage *m*.

ballot, *n.* (*a*) scrutin *m* (*b*) *StExch:* (*when shares are oversubscribed*) allocation *f* d'actions par tirage au sort.

band, *n.* plage *f*; **rate band,** plage de taux.

bang, *v.tr.* *StExch:* **to bang the market,** faire baisser les prix/écraser le marché/casser les cours.

bank¹, *n.* (*a*) banque *f*; **central bank,** banque centrale; **commercial bank,** banque de dépôt; **correspondent bank,** banque correspondante; **the High Street banks,** les grandes banques centrales; **agricultural bank/land bank,** banque territoriale/ banque hypothécaire; crédit foncier; **investment bank,** banque d'investissement/de placement/d'affaires; **merchant bank,** banque d'affaires/ commerciale; **private bank,** banque privée; **savings bank,** caisse *f*/banque d'épargne; **National Savings Bank,** Caisse

nationale d'épargne; **the Bank of England,** la Banque d'Angleterre; **the World Bank,** la Banque Mondiale; **bank account,** compte *m* en banque/compte bancaire; **bank acceptance,** acceptation *f* de banque; **bank annuities,** rente perpétuelle/fonds consolidés; **bank bill,** effet (tiré par une banque sur une autre); **bank book,** livret *m*/carnet *m* de banque; **bank charges,** frais *mpl* bancaires; **bank credit,** crédit bancaire; **bank clerk,** employé, -ée, de banque; **bank draft,** chèque *m* de banque; **bank loan,** prêt *m* de banque/prêt bancaire; **bank manager,** directeur *m* de banque; **bank messenger,** garçon *m* de recettes; **bank holiday,** jour férié; **bank rate,** taux (officiel) d'escompte; **bank roll,** ressources *f* monétaires (*b*) (bureau de) banque; **bank transfer,** virement *m* bancaire.

bank², *v.tr.* & *i.* mettre/déposer (de l'argent) à la banque; **he banked his salary,** il a déposé son salaire à la banque; **to bank with ...,** avoir un compte (bancaire) chez ...; **where do you bank?** qui est votre banquier?/à quelle banque avez-vous votre compte?/avec quelle banque faites-vous affaire?

bankable, *a.* (effet *m*) bancable/ banquable/négociable (en banque).

banker, *n.* banquier *m*; **banker's card,** carte *f* bancaire; carte de crédit/de garantie (d'une banque); **banker's draft,** traite *f*; **banker's order,** ordre de virement *m* bancaire.

banking, *n.* (*a*) opération(s) de banque/ bancaire(s); **consumer/retail banking,** banque *f* de particuliers; **electronic/high-tech banking,** banque électronique; **investment banking,** banque d'affaires; **banking house,** maison *f* de banque/ établissement *m* bancaire; **big banking houses,** les grandes sociétés bancaires; *NAm:* **banking account,** compte *m* en banque/compte bancaire; **banking hours,** heures *f* d'ouverture de la banque; **banking business,** trafic *m* bancaire (*b*) profession *f* de banquier; la banque.

banknote, *n.* billet *m* de banque.

bankroll¹, *n.* *NAm:* fortune personnelle.

bankroll², *v.tr.* *F:* financer (une opération)/ fournir les capitaux (à qn, pour un projet).

bankrupt¹, *a. & n.* (commerçant) failli (*m*); **fraudulent/negligent bankrupt**, banqueroutier, -ière; **to go bankrupt**, (*i*) faire faillite (*ii*) (*fraudulently*) faire banqueroute; **to be bankrupt**, être en faillite; **to adjudge/to adjudicate s.o. bankrupt**, déclarer qn en faillite; **bankrupt's certificate**, concordat *m*; **undischarged bankrupt**, failli non réhabilité.

bankrupt², *v.tr.* mettre (qn) en faillite.

bankruptcy, *n.* (*a*) faillite *f*; *Jur:* **act of bankruptcy**, acte *m* manifeste d'insolvabilité (entraînant la faillite); **bankruptcy petition/petition in bankruptcy**, dépôt *m* de bilan; **to present/to file one's petition in bankruptcy**, déposer son bilan; **the Bankruptcy Act**, le code de procédure régissant les faillites (*b*) **fraudulent bankruptcy**, banqueroute *f*/faillite frauduleuse.

bar, *n.* (*a*) lingot *m* (d'or) (*b*) *Mkt:* **bar code**, code-barre *m*/code *m* à barres; **bar coded label**, étiquette *f* portant un code à barres; **bar chart**, graphique *m* à bâtons.

bargain¹, *n.* (*a*) marché *m*/affaire *f*; **a good bargain**, une bonne affaire/un bon marché/un marché avantageux; **a bad bargain**, une mauvaise affaire; **to strike a bargain with s.o.**, conclure/faire un marché avec qn; *StExch:* **bargains done**, cours faits; **early bargain**, opération effectuée après la clôture officielle de la Bourse; **matched bargain**, opération d'application; **time bargain**, marché à terme/à livrer; vente *f* à livrer; *Jur:* **bargain and sale**, contrat *m* de vente impliquant le transfert de la propriété à titre onéreux (*b*) **bargain counter**, rayon *m* des soldes; **bargain basement**, sous-sol *m* d'économie; **bargain hunter**, chercheur, -euse, d'occasions/acheteur, -euse, à la recherche de soldes; **bargain offer**, offre exceptionnelle; **bargain sale**, marchan-dises *fpl* en solde *m*; vente-réclame *f*; **bargain price(s)**, prix *m* de solde/prix exceptionnel(s); (*of article*) **a real bargain**, une véritable occasion/une occasion unique/une aubaine; **to snap up a bargain**, sauter sur une occasion.

bargain², *v.i.* (*a*) entrer en négociations; négocier/traiter (**with s.o.**, avec qn); faire un marché (avec qn) (*b*) (*haggle*) **to bargain with s.o.**, marchander avec qn; **to bargain over a second-hand book**, marchander un livre d'occasion.

bargaining, *n.* négociations *fpl*; (*haggling*) marchandage *m*; **bargaining unit**, groupement négociateur; **bargaining position**, situation *f* permettant de négocier; **bargaining power**, pouvoir *m* de négocia-tion; pouvoir de contestation; **bargaining table**, table *f* des négociations; **(free) collective bargaining**, négociations collec-tives; **collective bargaining agreement**, convention collective.

barker card, *n.* *Mkt:* affichette *f* de rayonnage.

barometer, *n.* baromètre *m* (du marché).

barratry, *n.* *Jur: Nau:* baraterie *f*.

barrel, *n.* fût *m*/tonneau *m* (de vin, de bière); caque *f* (de harengs); baril *m* (de pétrole).

barrier, *n.* barrière *f*/obstacle *m*/entrave *f*; **customs/tariff barrier**, barrière douanière; **trade barrier**, barrière commerciale; **barrier to entry**, barrières *fpl* à l'entrée.

barrister, *n.* **barrister (at law)**, avocat *m*.

barter¹, *n.* (accord *m* de) troc *m*; échange *m*.

barter², *v.* (*a*) *v.tr.* **to barter sth. for sth.**, échanger qch. contre qch./troquer une chose contre une autre (*b*) *v.i.* faire le commerce d'échanges/faire le troc.

bartering, *n.* *US:* contre-achat *m*/barter-ing *m*/échange *m* marchandise (*mélange de troc basique et de techniques plus sophis-tiquées*).

base, *n.* **base date/year**, date *f*/année *f* de base; *Bank:* **base rate**, taux *m* de base (bancaire) (*b*) **base stock (method)**, comptabilisation *f* en premier entré dernier sorti/en dernier entré premier sorti (*c*) *Mkt:* **base line**, signature *f.*

basic, *a.* **basic pay**, salaire *m* de base/de départ; **basic commodity**, denrée *f* témoin; **basic statistics**, statistiques fondamentales.

basis, *n.* base *f*/fondement *m*/assiette *f*/ régime *m.*

basket, *n. PolEc:* **the shopping basket**, le panier de la ménagère; **basket of currencies**, panier de monnaies.

batch, *n.* lot *m* (de marchandises, etc.).

batched, *a.* **batched consignment/dispatch**, envoi groupé.

bay, *n.* **loading bay**, quai *m* de chargement.

bear[1], *n. StExch:* (*a*) baissier *m*/spéculateur *m* à la baisse; **bear closing**, arbitrage *m* à la baisse; **bear market**, marché *m* à la baisse; **bear position**, position à la baisse; **bear sale**, vente *f* à découvert; **bear slide**, retournement *m* du marché à la baisse; **bear speculation**, spéculation *f* à la baisse; **to sell a bear**, vendre à découvert (*b*) **bear hug**, communiqué *m* d'information annonçant une OPA immédiate.

bear[2], *StExch:* (*a*) *v.tr.* **to bear the market**, chercher à faire baisser les cours (*b*) *v.i.* jouer à la baisse; spéculer sur la baisse.

bear[3] *v.tr.* **to bear interest**, porter intérêt; **to bear the costs**, prendre les frais à sa charge.

bearer, *n.* **bearer (of a letter/of a cheque)** porteur, -euse (d'une lettre/d'un chèque); **bearer bond**, obligation *f* au porteur; **cheque made payable to bearer**, chèque (payable) au porteur.

bearing, *a.* **interest-bearing capital**, capital productif d'intérêts/capital qui rapporte.

bearish, *a. StExch:* **bearish market**, marché baissier; **bearish tendency**, tendance *f* à la baisse.

bed, *n.* **bed and breakfast**, chambre *f* avec petit déjeuner; *StExch:* **bed and breakfast deal**, aller et retour *m.*

behalf, *n.* **payment on behalf of s.o.**, (*i*) versement *m* au compte/à l'acquit *m* de qn (*ii*) de la part de qn/au nom de qn.

belly up, *v.i. NAm: F:* faire faillite.

below-the-line, **1.** *a. Book-k:* (*expenditure*) au-dessous de la ligne; **below-the-line accounts**, comptes *mpl* de résultats exceptionnels **2.** *n. Mkt:* coût *m* promotion.

benchmark, *n.* point *m* de repère.

beneficial, *a.* **beneficial owner/beneficial occupant**, usufruitier, -ière.

beneficiary, *n.* **the beneficiaries**, les bénéficiaires/les ayants droit.

benefit[1], *n.* **1. fringe benefits**, avantages sociaux **2.** prestation *f*/indemnité *f*/allocation *f*; **industrial injuries benefit**, indemnité pour accidents du travail; **National Insurance benefits**, prestations sociales; **unemployment benefit**, indemnité de chômage; **sickness benefit/medical benefit**, indemnité de maladie/prestation de l'assurance-maladie; **to pay out benefits**, verser des prestations.

benefit[2], **1.** *v.tr.* faire du bien/être avantageux/profiter à (qn/qch.); **a steady exchange rate benefits trade**, un taux d'échange stable est avantageux au commerce/favorise le commerce **2.** *v.i.* **to benefit by/from sth.**, profiter de qch./ bénéficier de qch./tirer avantage de qch.; **to benefit from a rise in prices**, profiter/ tirer profit d'une hausse de prix.

bequeath, *v.tr. Jur:* léguer/faire un legs.

bequest, *n.* legs *m.*

best-seller, *n.* (*author*) auteur à succès; (*book*) succès *m* de librairie/best-seller *m*; livre *m* à gros tirage.

best-selling, *a.* à grand succès/de grosse vente; **best-selling author**, auteur à succès/ auteur d'un best-seller.

bet[1], *n.* pari *m*; **to make a bet,** faire un pari/parier.

bet[2], *v.tr.* parier/faire un pari.

beta, *n.* *StExch:* **beta (factor/coefficient),** coefficient *m* B/beta.

better, *adv.* **to go better,** (*of shares*) monter; être en hausse.

betterment, *n.* plus-value *f*; appréciation *f*; **betterment levy/tax,** impôt *m* sur les plus-values; **additions and betterments,** extensions *f* et embellissements *m*.

biannual, *a.* qui se produit deux fois par an; semestriel.

bid[1], *n.* (*a*) enchère *f*/offre *f*/mise *f*; **to make a bid of £250 000 for a property,** faire une offre de £250 000 pour un immeuble; mettre une enchère de £250 000 sur un immeuble; **to make the first bid/opening bid,** faire la première mise/première enchère; **to make a higher/further/better bid,** surenchérir/faire une offre plus élevée; **cash bid,** offre au comptant; **higher/further/better bid,** offre supérieure/surenchère *f*/suroffre *f*; **closing/last bid,** dernière mise/dernière enchère; **takeover bid,** offre publique d'achat (OPA); **hostile (takeover) bid,** OPA hostile/inamicale; **friendly (takeover) bid,** OPA amicale (*b*) *StExch: NAm:* **bid and asked,** l'offre et la demande/prix d'achat et de vente (*c*) tentative *f*; **in a bid to reopen negotiations,** dans une tentative de relancer les négociations.

bid[2], *v.tr. & i.* **1.** (*at auction sale*) **to bid for sth.,** faire une offre pour qch./mettre une enchère sur qch.; **to bid a high price,** offrir une grosse somme; **to bid £10,** faire une offre de dix livres/miser dix livres; **to bid another pound,** faire une surenchère d'une livre; **to bid over s.o./more than s.o.,** enchérir sur qn/surenchérir; **to bid in (a lot),** racheter un lot (pour le compte du vendeur); **the buyers were bidding (up) well,** les enchères montaient vite **2. to bid for/on a contract,** soumissionner à une adjudication; **to bid for/on the new hospital,** faire une soumission pour le nouvel hôpital/soumissionner la construction du nouvel hôpital.

bidder, *n.* **1.** (*at sale*) enchérisseur, -euse; **there were no bidders,** il n'y a pas eu de prenants; **the lowest bidder,** le moins disant; **the highest bidder,** le plus offrant/le dernier enchérisseur; l'adjudicataire *m*; **allocation to the highest bidder,** adjudication *f* à la surenchère/au plus offrant; **hostile bidder,** enchérisseur hostile/inamical **2.** soumissionnaire *mf*.

bidding, *n.* **1.** enchères *fpl*/mises *fpl*; **the bidding was very brisk,** les enchères étaient vives; la vente a été bonne/a bien marché; **to start the bidding for a picture at £5 000,** mettre un tableau à prix £5 000; **bidding ring,** groupe *m* (de marchands, d'investisseurs) agissant de concert (*pratique illégale*) **2. the cheapest or best bidding,** la soumission la plus basse/favorable.

biennial, *a.* bisannuel/biennal.

big, *a.* **to earn big money,** gagner gros; **there's big money in it,** cela rapporte/rapportera gros; **big drop in prices,** forte baisse de prix; **to do a big trade,** faire de grosses affaires.

Big Bang (the), *n.* *StExch: F:* le big bang/le grand chambardement (*du 27 octobre 1986*).

bilateralism, *n.* *PolEc:* bilatéralisme *m*.

bill[1], *n.* **1.** note *f*/facture *f*/mémoire *m*; **to make out a bill,** dresser/faire/établir/rédiger une facture; **the bill was made out to me/in my name,** la facture a été émise/faite à mon nom; **to pay a bill,** payer/régler une facture; **you have not paid your bill,** vous n'avez pas réglé (la facture/la note/l'addition); vous n'avez pas payé votre facture; **shall I charge it on the bill?** faut-il le facturer/le porter sur la note? **to foot the bill,** payer la note/les dépenses; **wage(s) bill,** masse globale des salaires; *Jur:* **bill of costs,** état *m* de frais **2.** (*a*) effet *m*/papier *m* (de commerce); **accommodation bill,** billet *m* de complaisance; **bill of exchange,** lettre *f* de change/traite *f*; **blank bill,** traite en blanc; **bill of debt,** reconnaissance *f* de dette; **long bill,** effet à long terme/à longue échéance; **short bill,**

effet à court terme/à courte échéance; **sight bill/bill payable at sight,** effet payable à vue/à présentation; **period/term bill,** effet à terme; **usance bill,** effet à usance; **bills payable,** effets à payer; **bills receivable,** effets à recevoir; **bills in hand,** effets en portefeuille/portefeuille *m* effets; **bills in a set,** effet en plusieurs exemplaires; **bill broker/discounter,** courtier *m* de change/ agent *m* de change (*b*) *NAm:* billet de banque; **five-dollar bill,** billet de cinq dollars (*c*) **exchequer bill,** bon *m* du Trésor (britannique); **Treasury bill,** bon du Trésor (à court terme) **3.** affiche *f*/écriteau *m*; **stick no bills!** défense d'afficher! **4. bill of lading,** *Nau:* connaissement *m*; *Rail: NAm:* feuille *f* d'expédition; *Cust:* **bill of entry,** déclaration *f* (d'entrée) en douane; **bill of sight,** déclaration (en douane) provisoire; **transit bill,** passavant *m*; **victualling bill,** autorisation *f* d'embarquer des provisions soumises aux droits **5. bill of sale,** acte *m* de vente/ contrat *m* de vente/facture.

bill², *v.tr.* facturer (des marchandises); **they billed me twice for the spare parts,** les pièces de rechange m'ont été facturées deux fois.

biller, *n. NAm:* **1.** (*pers.*) facturier, -ière **2.** (*machine*) facturière *f*/machine *f* à facturer.

billing, *n.* facturation *f* (de marchandises); **billing machine,** machine *f* à facturer/ facturière *f*; **billing price,** prix *m* de facture.

billion, *n.* milliard *m*; **10 billion dollars,** 10 milliards de dollars.

bimonthly, *a.* (*i*) deux fois par mois/ bimensuel (*ii*) tous les deux mois.

binary, *a.* **binary number,** nombre binaire.

bind, *v.tr.* obliger (par contrat); lier (les parties).

binder, *n.* **1.** convention *f* liant le vendeur **2. loose-leaf/ring binder,** reliure *f*/classeur *m* à anneaux.

binding, *a.* obligatoire; **legally binding,** qui oblige en droit; **binding agreement,** con-

vention *f*/obligation *f* irrévocable; **decision binding on all parties,** décision *f* obligatoire pour tous; **obligation binding on all parties,** obligation solidaire.

biodegradable, *a.* biodégradable.

birth, *n.* naissance *f*; **birth rate,** natalité *f*/ taux *m* des naissances.

birthplace, *n.* lieu *m* de naissance.

biweekly, *a.* (*a*) deux fois par semaine; (*adj. only*) bihebdomadaire (*b*) tous les quinze jours.

black¹, 1. *a.* **black market,** marché parallèle/marché noir; **black economy,** économie *f* souterraine/parallèle **2.** *n. F:* **in the black,** solvable/sans dettes; **to move into the black,** avoir un compte bénéficiaire.

black², *v.tr.* boycotter (des marchandises, etc.).

blackleg, *n.* briseur *m* de grève.

black list¹, *n.* liste noire.

blacklist², *v.tr.* inscrire/mettre (qn, une entreprise, etc.) sur la liste noire.

Black Monday, *n.* jour *m* du krach (boursier) (*le lundi 19 octobre 1987*).

blank¹, *a.* **blank credit,** crédit *m* en blanc/ dont le montant n'est pas spécifié; **blank cheque,** chèque *m* en blanc; *NAm:* **blank check,** (formule de) chèque.

blank², *n.* (*in document, etc.*) blanc *m*/case *f*; **to fill in the blanks (of a form),** remplir (une formule); **cheque signed in blank,** chèque signé en blanc; **endorsement in blank/blank endorsement,** endossement *m* en blanc/titre *m* au porteur.

blanket, *a.* général/applicable à tous les cas; **blanket agreement,** accord-cadre *m*; **blanket order,** commande globale/d'une portée générale; **blanket mortgage,** hypothèque générale; **blanket policy,** police globale (tous risques); *Rail: etc:* **blanket rate,** tarif *m* de groupe/tarif global.

blister, *n.* **blister pack,** habillage transparent; *FrC:* emballage-coque *m.*

blockade, *n.* blocus *m* économique.

block¹, *n.* (*a*) **block of shares,** bloc *m*/paquet *m* d'actions; **block booking,** location *f* (de places de théâtre, de films, etc.) en bloc; **block purchase,** achat *m* en bloc; **block trading,** négociations *fpl* de bloc (*b*) **to write in block letters,** écrire en caractères d'imprimerie/en majuscules/en capitales.

block², *v.tr.* **to block (prices, imports),** bloquer (les prix, les importations); **blocked account,** compte bloqué; **blocked currency,** monnaie bloquée/non convertible.

blue, *a.* **blue chip (stock),** valeur sûre/valeur de père de famille/valeur vedette/titre *m* de premier ordre/blue chip.

blue-collar, *a.* **blue-collar worker,** travailleur, -euse, manuel(le).

blue-ribbon, *a.* **blue-ribbon committee,** commission spéciale/extraordinaire.

blue-sky, *a.* **blue-sky security,** titre *m* hautement spéculatif/à haut risque.

blurb, *n.* (*a*) baratin *m* publicitaire (*b*) (*on book jacket, etc.*) texte *m* publicitaire.

board, *n.* (*a*) conseil *m*/comité *m*; **price control board,** commission *f* de contrôle des prix; **advisory board,** comité consultatif; **marketing board,** office *m* de régularisation de vente; fonds *m* de stabilisation du marché; **board of directors, the board,** direction générale (d'une société); directoire *m*; **executive board,** conseil d'administration; **the bank is represented on the board,** la banque fait partie du conseil; **board meeting,** réunion *f* du conseil d'administration; **board of inquiry,** commission d'enquête; **Tourist Board,** office *m* de tourisme; **Board of Trade,** Ministère du Commerce et de l'Industrie (*b*) *Nau:* **free on board (fob),** franco bord (*c*) **board and lodging/room and board,** chambre et pension; **half board,** demi-pension *f;* **full board,** pension complète; **with board and** lodging, nourri et logé (*d*) *NAm:* **the Big Board,** la Bourse de New York.

boardroom, *n.* salle *f* (de réunion) du conseil (d'administration).

body, *n.* **professional bodies,** organisations professionnelles.

bogus, *a.* **bogus company,** (*i*) société *f* qui n'existe pas/société fantôme (*ii*) société véreuse; **bogus identity card,** fausse carte *f* d'identité.

boiler-room, *n.* *NAm:* organisation *f* qui vend au public des produits financiers très spéculatifs ou sans valeur.

bomb, *v.i.* s'effondrer/faire un plongeon, chuter.

bona fide, *a.* de bonne foi; sérieux; **bona fide offer,** offre sérieuse/ferme.

bonanza, 1. *n.* **the new store proved (to be) a bonanza,** le nouveau magasin est devenu une vraie mine d'or **2.** *a.* prospère, favorable; **bonanza year,** année *f* de prospérité/d'abondance.

bona vacantia, *npl.* biens non réclamés.

bond¹, *n.* **1.** (*a*) engagement *m*/contrat *m* (*b Jur:* obligation *f*/engagement; **to enter into a bond (with s.o.),** contracter une obligation/un engagement (envers qn); **mortgage bond,** titre *m*/obligation hypothécaire; **contract bond/performance bond,** garantie *f* d'exécution (d'un contrat) (*c*) *Fin:* bon *m*; obligation; **bond issue,** émission *f* obligataire/d'obligations; **bearer bond/coupon bond,** obligation au porteur; **bulldog bond,** obligation bulldog; **convertible bond,** obligation convertible; **straight bond,** obligation classiques; **corporate bond,** obligation de sociétés; **income bond,** valeur *f* de rendement; **bond market,** marché obligataire; **registered bond,** bon nominatif; **government bond/treasury bond,** (*i*) rente *f* sur l'État (*ii*) titre de rente; bon du trésor à long terme; **long/medium/short bond,** obligation longue/moyenne/courte; **yankee bond,** obligation yankee; **yearling bond,** yearling *m*; = certificat *m* de dépôt

2. *Cust:* dépôt *m*/entrepôt *m*; *(of goods)* **to be in bond,** être à l'entrepôt de la douane; **tobacco in bond,** tabac *m* en garenne; **goods in bond,** marchandises *fpl* à l'entrepôt de la douane/marchandises entreposées; **goods out of bond,** marchandises sorties de l'entrepôt/dédouanées; **to take goods out of bond,** dédouaner des marchandises/faire sortir des marchandises de l'entrepôt de la douane; **taking out of bond,** dédouanage *m*; **bond note,** acquit-à-caution *m*.

bond[2], *v.tr. Cust:* entreposer/mettre en dépôt/mettre à l'entrepôt (des marchandises).

bonded, *a.* **1.** *Cust: (of goods)* entreposé/en dépôt/à l'entrepôt/en douane; **bonded warehouse,** entrepôt *m* de douane **2.** *Fin:* (dette) garantie par obligations.

bonder, *n.* *(pers.)* entrepositaire *m.*

bondholder, *n.* *Fin:* obligataire *m*/porteur *m* d'obligation.

bonding, *n.* *Cust:* entreposage *m* (de marchandises).

bonus, *n.* gratification *f*/sursalaire *m*/boni *m*/bonification *f*/prime *f*; **work on a bonus system,** travail *m* à la prime; **cost-of-living bonus,** indemnité *f* de vie chère/de cherté de vie; **bonus share,** action gratuite/action d'attribution/action donnée en prime; **bonus on shares,** dividende *m* supplémentaire/bonification sur les actions; *Ins:* **bonus to policy holder,** bénéfice additionnel alloué aux assurés; **no-claims bonus,** bonus *m*; **no-claims bonus system,** système du bonus-malus; **reversionary bonus,** prime de participation; **terminal bonus,** prime libératoire de fin de contrat; **Christmas bonus** = gratification du jour de l'an/de fin d'année; 13ᵉ mois; **group bonus,** prime collective/d'équipe; **incentive bonus/productivity bonus,** *NAm:* **merit bonus,** prime de rendement.

boodle, *n.* *F.* pot-de-vin *m.*

book[1], *n.* **1.** livre *m*; **the book trade,** l'industrie *f* du livre; **book publishing,** l'édition *f*; **book club,** club *m* du livre; **book token,** chèque-livre *m* **2.** registre *m*;

account book, livre de comptes/registre de comptabilité/livre *m* journal; **to keep the books (of a firm),** tenir les livres/les écritures/la comptabilité (d'une maison); **bill book,** échéancier *m*; **black book,** plan *m* de défense contre une OPA hostile/plan de défense anti-OPA; **Blue Book,** *(National Income and Expenditure)* rapport annuel des comptes de la nation; **purchase book/bought book,** journal *m* des achats; **sales book,** journal des ventes; **waste book,** main courante; **book of original/prime entry,** journal; **book credit,** crédit *m* compte; **book debts,** comptes fournisseurs; **book entry,** écriture *f* (comptable); **book value,** valeur *f* comptable; **bank book,** livret *m*/carnet *m* de banque; **cash book,** livre de caisse; **cheque book,** carnet de chèques/chéquier *m*; **order book,** carnet de commandes.

book[2], *v.tr. (a)* inscrire/enregistrer (une commande)/prendre note (d'une commande); **we are heavily booked,** nous avons beaucoup de commandes à exécuter/notre carnet de commandes est bien rempli *(b)* retenir (une chambre à l'hôtel); retenir/réserver/louer (une place au théâtre); réserver (une place dans un avion, etc.); **to book s.o. into a hotel,** retenir une chambre d'hôtel pour qn; **to book a ticket through to Paris,** prendre un billet direct pour Paris; **we are booked up/fully booked,** c'est complet/il n'y a plus de places/il n'y a plus de chambres disponibles.

booking, *n.* location *f*/réservation *f*; **booking office,** guichet *m*/bureau de réservation/de location; **booking clerk,** préposé(e) à la location/au guichet/à la vente des billets; **double booking,** surréservation *f.*

bookkeeper, *n.* aide-comptable *mf*; commis *m*/employé, -ée aux écritures.

bookkeeping, *n.* tenue *f* de livres/comptabilité *f*; **single-entry book-keeping,** comptabilité à/en partie simple; tenue de livres en partie simple; **double-entry book-keeping,** comptabilité à/en partie double; tenue de livres en partie double; digraphie *f.*

booklet, *n.* livret *m*/brochure *f*; **descriptive booklet**, notice descriptive (d'une machine, etc.).

bookseller, *n.* libraire *m*; **secondhand bookseller**, bouquiniste *m*; **new and secondhand bookseller**, librairie *f* de neuf et d'occasion; **bookseller and publisher**, libraire-éditeur *m.*

bookselling, *n.* (commerce de) librairie *f*; commerce/vente *f* des livres.

bookwork, *n.* tenue *f* de livres/des écritures.

boom[1], *n.* boom *m*/essor *m* économique/ vague *f* de prospérité/(période de) haute conjoncture; **baby boom**, baby-boom *m*/boom des naissances.

boom[2], *v.i.* être en hausse; **trade/business is booming**, les affaires *f* marchent bien/sont en plein essor.

booming, *a.* **we have a booming economy**, nous traversons une période d'essor économique.

boost[1], *n.* **to give a boost to an industry**, relancer une industrie.

boost[2], *v.tr.* augmenter; **to boost production**, relancer/augmenter la production; **to boost the economy**, relancer l'économie.

boosting, *n.* réclame *f*/battage *m.*

booth, *n.* *NAm:* stand *m* (d'exposition).

border, *n.* frontière *f.*

borrow, *v.tr. & i.* emprunter (**from**, à); **to borrow (money) from s.o.**, faire un emprunt à qn/emprunter (de l'argent) à qn; **to borrow on mortgage**, emprunter sur hypothèque; **to borrow on/at interest**, emprunter à intérêt; **to borrow long**, emprunter à long terme/à longue échéance; **to borrow short**, emprunter à court terme/à courte échéance; *StExch:* **to borrow stock**, (faire) reporter des titres.

borrowed, *a.* emprunté/d'emprunt; **borrowed capital**, capitaux empruntés/ d'emprunt.

borrower, *n.* emprunteur, -euse; **borrower's credit**, crédit *m* de l'emprunteur.

borrowing, *n.* emprunts *mpl*; **financed by borrowing**, financé par des emprunts; **borrowing power**, capacité *f* de crédit; **borrowing requirement**, besoin *m* de crédit.

boss, *n.* patron *m*; contremaître *m.*

bottom, 1. *n.* **the bottom has fallen out of the market**, le marché s'est effondré 2. *a.* **bottom price**, le prix le plus bas 3. **bottom line** = résultat net (de l'exercice); **black bottom line**, solde créditeur; **red bottom line**, solde débiteur; *Fig:* **the bottom line is profit**, ce qui compte c'est de faire des bénéfices.

bottom out, *vi.* **the dollar has bottomed out**, le dollar s'est effondré; **bottoming out**, retournement *m* à la baisse.

bottomry, *n. Nau:* **bottomry bond**, obligation *f* hypothécaire (*pour fournir les fonds nécessaires pour terminer un voyage*); **bottomry interest**, profit *m* maritime.

bought, *see* **buy**[1].

bounce, *v.i. F:* **I hope this cheque won't bounce**, j'espère que ce n'est pas un chèque sans provision/*F:* en bois.

bouncer, *n. F:* chèque *m* sans provision/*F:* en bois.

bouncing, *a. F:* **bouncing cheque**, chèque *m* sans provision/*F:* en bois.

bounty, *n.* (*reward, premium*) prime *f* d'encouragement; prime (à l'exportation, etc.); (*government subsidy*) subvention *f*; **system of bounties**, système *m* de primes.

Bourse, *n.* Bourse *f* (de valeurs).

boutique, *n.* (*a*) (petit) magasin de modes; (*in department store*) boutique *f*; **teenage boutique**, le coin/la boutique des jeunes (*b*) magasin *m*/supermarché *m* financier/ de services financiers.

box 27 **break-up**

box[1], *n.* (*a*) boîte *f*; (**cardboard**) **box,** (caisse *f* en) carton *m* (*b*) **cash box,** caisse *f* (*c*) **PO Box 301,** boîte *f* postale 301/BP 301; (*in advertisements*) **Box number 301,** Référence 301/Ref. 301 (*d*) case *f* (d'un formulaire) (*e*) *Trans: Av:* **black box,** boîte noire.

box[2], *v.tr.* encaisser/encartonner (qch.)/mettre (qch.) dans une boîte; coffrer; **to box an article for sale,** conditionner un article pour la vente.

boxed, *a.* dans une boîte/dans un étui/sous étui.

boycott[1], *n.* grève *f* des achats; boycott *m*/boycottage *m* (d'un produit).

boycott[2], *v.tr.* boycotter (un produit).

bracket, *n.* **income bracket,** tranche *f* des revenus; **wage bracket,** fourchette *f* des salaires; **the middle income bracket,** la tranche des revenus moyens; **tax bracket,** tranche *f* d'imposition.

brain-drain, *n.* fuite *f* des cerveaux.

brainstorming, *n. Mkt:* remue-méninges *m*/brainstorming *m*.

branch[1], *n.* (*a*) **the different branches of industry,** les différentes branches de l'industrie (*b*) succursale *f*/filiale *f* (d'une société, d'une maison de commerce); succursale/comptoir *m* (d'une banque); **branch banking,** banque *f* à réseau; **branch manager,** directeur de (la) succursale (d'une banque); (*of a business*) **main branch,** établissement principal/maison mère; siège (social); **branch office,** (*i*) agence *f* (*ii*) bureau *m* de quartier; **this shop has a branch in Lyon,** ce magasin a une succursale à Lyon.

branch[2], *v.i.* (*of an organization, etc.*) **to branch out into …,** étendre ses activités *f*/son commerce à …

brand[1], *n.* (*trademark*) marque *f* (de fabrique/de commerce); **brand image,** image *f* de marque; **brand leader,** marque de tête; **brand loyalty,** fidélité *f* à la marque; **brand name,** marque (de fabrique); *Mkt:* **brand name recall,** mémomarque *f*; **brand piracy,**

contrefaçon *f*; **a good brand of cigars,** une bonne marque de cigares; **brand benefit acceptance,** bénéfice *m* publicitaire; **brand manager,** chef *m* de produit.

brand[2], *v.tr.* donner une marque (de fabrique) à (un produit).

branded, *a.* **branded goods,** produits *m* de marque.

breach, *n.* **breach of contract,** rupture *f* de contrat; **breach of trust,** abus *m* de confiance; **breach of warranty,** violation *f* de garantie.

break,[1] *n.* (*a*) effondrement *m* (du marché) (*b*) rupture (de négociations) (*c*) pause-café *f*.

break[2], **1.** *v.tr.* (*a*) **to break a contract,** résilier/rompre un contrat (*b*) **to break the 10% ceiling,** crever le plafond de 10% (*c*) **the market broke on the downside,** le marché s'est effondré **2.** *v.i.* **to break into Western markets,** percer sur/entrer sur les marchés de l'ouest.

breakage, *n.* (*i*) casse *f*/avarie *f* (*ii*) colis endommagé/avarié: **to pay for breakages,** payer la casse.

break down, *v.tr.* ventiler (les dépenses); **to break down an account,** faire un décompte/faire le détail d'un compte.

breakdown, *n.* analyse *f*/décomposition *f*/détail *m*; **statistical breakdown,** analyse statistique; **breakdown of expenses,** ventilation *f* des dépenses/décompte *m*.

break even, *v.i.* équilibrer son budget; ne faire ni pertes ni profits; rentrer dans ses frais/dans son argent.

break-even, *a.* **break-even deal,** affaire blanche; **break-even point,** seuil *m* de rentabilité; point mort.

breakout, *n. StExch:* cassure *f*.

break up, *v.i.* (*of meeting*) se séparer; **when the meeting broke up,** à l'issue de la réunion.

break-up, *n.* (*a*) vente *f* par appartement (*b*) démandèlement *m* (d'entreprise).

bribe¹, *n.* pot-de-vin *m.*

bribe², *v.tr.* offrir un pot-de-vin à (qn).

bribery, *n.* corruption *f.*

bridge, *n.* **bridge financing**, crédit-relais *m.*

bridging, *a.* **bridging loan**, prêt-relais *m*; **bridging value**, valeur *f* de récupération.

brief¹, *n. Jur:* dossier *m*; cause *f.*

brief², *v.tr.* donner des instructions (préalables) à quelqu'un; faire un résumé de ce qui va suivre.

briefing, *n.* réunion *f* préparatoire/ briefing *m*; *FrC:* bref *m*/breffage *m.*

bring down, *v.tr.* (*a*) *Book-k:* **balance brought down**, solde *m* à nouveau (*b*) abaisser/faire baisser (les prix); réduire (le taux de l'inflation); avilir (la monnaie, les prix); **to bring down the price of an article to £5,** baisser le prix d'un article jusqu'à £5.

bring forward, *v.tr.* **to bring forward an amount,** reporter une somme; **brought forward,** à reporter; report *m.*

bring in, *v.tr.* (*of capital investment*) **to bring in interest,** rapporter/porter intérêt; **investment that brings in 6%,** placement *m* qui porte intérêt à 6%/qui rapporte un intérêt de 6%.

bring out, *v.tr.* introduire (des valeurs sur le marché); **to bring out a new book,** publier/lancer un nouveau livre; **to bring out a new model,** sortir un nouveau modèle.

brisk, *a.* actif/animé; **brisk competition,** concurrence dynamique; **brisk trade,** commerce actif; **brisk market,** marché actif/animé; **business is brisk,** les affaires *f* marchent.

British, *a.* britannique/de la Grande-Bretagne; **British goods,** produits *mpl*/ marchandises *fpl* britanniques.

broadside, *n. NAm:* dépliant *m.*

brochure, *n.* brochure *f*/dépliant *m*; prospectus *m* publicitaire.

broker, *n.* courtier *m* (de commerce); **bill broker,** courtier de change; **cotton broker,** courtier en coton; **insurance broker,** courtier/agent *m* d'assurances/assureur *m*; **loading broker,** courtier affréteur; **ship broker,** courtier maritime; **broker's commission,** (frais *mpl* de) courtage *m*; commission *f*; **broker's contract,** courtage *m*; **foreign exchange broker,** cambiste *m*/ agent *m* de change; *StExch:* **(stock)broker,** agent de change/courtier en valeurs mobilières; **floor broker,** courtier membre du parquet; **government broker,** = Spécialiste *mf* en Valeurs du Trésor (SUT); **intermediate broker,** intermédiaire *m*/remisier *m* (en Bourse); **money broker,** prêteur, -euse sur titre/en réméré; **outside broker,** courtier libre/ courtier marron/courtier non autorisé; **running broker,** remisier *m.*

brokerage, *n.* **1.** (*profession of broker*) courtage *m*; **brokerage houses,** maisons de courtage (auprès de la Bourse); **outside brokerage,** affaires *fpl* de banque **2.** (frais *mpl* de) courtage *m*; commission *f.*

broking, *n.* courtage *m.*

bubble, *n.* **bubble pack,** habillage transparent; *FrC:* emballage-coque *m.*

buck, *n. F:* dollar *m* (américain).

bucket shop, *n.* (*a*) *F:* bureau *m* de courtier marron (*b*) agence *f* de voyages à prix réduits.

budget¹, *n.* (*a*) budget *m*; prévisions *f* budgétaires; crédits *m* budgétaires; **balanced budget,** budget équilibré; **budget constraint,** contrainte *f* budgétaire; **budget deficit,** déficit *m* budgétaire; **cash budget,** budget de trésorerie; **flexible budget,** budget flexible/adaptable; **to fix the budget,** établir le budget; **to balance the budget,** équilibrer le budget; **family/ household budget,** budget familial; **master budget,** budget global; **publicity budget,** budget de publicité/publicitaire; **sales and marketing budget,** budget commercial/des ventes; **operating budget,** budget d'exploitation; *Parl:* **budget statement for the year, the Budget,** situation *f* budgétaire de l'année; **to open/to introduce the budget,** présenter le budget (*b*) **budget account,** compte *m* crédit (*avec mensualités payées d'avance*)/compte d'abonnement/compte permanent; **budget department,** rayon *m* des prix modiques/sous-sol *m* d'économie; **budget prices,** prix avantageux/raisonnables/modiques (*c*) *Bank:* **budget account** = compte crédit.

budget[2], *v.i. Fin: Parl:* **to budget for (a certain expenditure),** budgétiser (certaines dépenses); **I have to budget for the whole year,** il me faut établir mon budget pour toute l'année.

budgetary, *a.* budgétaire; **budgetary policy,** politique *f* budgétaire; **budgetary control,** contrôle *m* budgétaire/gestion prévisionnelle.

budgeting, *n.* (*i*) budgétisation *f* (*ii*) établissement *m* du budget.

buffer, *n.* **buffer stock,** (*of shares*) matelas *m*; (*of raw materials*) stock *m* de sécurité/de précaution; stock tampon.

build, *v.tr. esp. NAm:* **to build (sth.) into a product,** incorporer (qch.) dans un produit.

building, *n.* (*a*) bâtiment *m*/édifice *m*/immeuble *m*; **office building,** immeuble à usage de bureaux; **public buildings,** édifices publics; **residential building,** immeuble à usage d'habitation (*b*) construction *f*; **building contractor,** entrepreneur *m* de bâtiments; **building land,** terrain(s) *m* à bâtir; **building plot,** lotissement *m*; **building estate,** lotissement; **building materials,** matériaux *m* de construction; **building society/**NAm **building and loan association,** caisse *f* d'épargne-logement; = société (commune) de crédit immobilier (hypothécaire); **building trade/industry,** l'industrie *f* du bâtiment; = bâtiments, travaux publics (BTP).

build up, *v.tr.* (*a*) **to build up one's business,** développer son affaire *f*/son commerce (*b*) faire de la publicité pour (un produit).

build-up, *n.* 1. publicité tapageuse 2. accumulation *f* (de stock).

bulk, *n.* (*a*) **bulk orders,** commandes par quantité; **in bulk,** en grande quantité; en bloc; **to buy in bulk,** acheter en bloc/en grosse quantité; **bulk buying is cheaper,** c'est moins cher d'acheter en bloc (*b*) en vrac; **to ship (sth.) in bulk,** transporter (qch.) en vrac; **bulk carrier,** vraquier *m*.

bulky, *a.* volumineux/encombrant; **bulky cargo,** chargement volumineux.

bull[1], *n. StExch:* haussier, -ière/spéculateur, -trice, à la hausse; **stale bull,** haussier qui ne peut pas faire de bénéfices sur une vente; **bull market,** marché à la hausse; **bull transaction,** opération *f* à la hausse; **to buy a bull,** spéculer à la hausse.

bull[2], *StExch:* (*a*) *v.tr.* **to bull the market,** chercher à faire hausser les cours/pousser les actions à la hausse (*b*) *v.i.* spéculer à la hausse (*c*) *v.i.* (*of stocks, etc.*) être en hausse.

bullet, *n.* remboursement *m* in fine.

bullion, *n.* or *m* en barres; or/argent *m* en lingot(s); valeurs *fpl* en espèces; *Fin:* métal *m*; **gold bullion standard,** étalon *m* lingot-or; **bullion reserve,** réserve *f* métallique.

bullish, *a. StExch:* **bullish market,** marché haussier/à la hausse; **bullish tendency,** tendance *f* à la hausse.

bumpf, *n.* paperasse *f.*

bumper, *a.* **bumper crop,** récolte exceptionnelle.

buoyant, *a.* **buoyant market,** marché animé/porteur.

burden[1], *n. NAm:* frais généraux; **tax burden,** le poids de la fiscalité.

burden[2], *v.tr.* grever (d'impôt, d'hypothèque); **burdened with tax,** lourd d'impôts.

bureau, *n.* bureau *m*/agence *f*; **bureau de change,** bureau *m* de change; **employment bureau,** bureau/agence de placement; **visitors' bureau,** centre *m* d'accueil.

bureaucracy, *n.* bureaucratie *f.*

bureaucratic, *a.* bureaucratique.

bureaucratize, *vtr.* bureaucratiser.

bushel, *n.* boisseau *m (8 gallons, approx. 36 litres).*

business, *n.* (*a*) les affaires *f*; **business is business**, les affaires sont les affaires; **what's his line of business?** qu'est-ce qu'il fait (comme métier)? **to do business with s.o.**, faire affaire avec qn; **to lose business**, perdre de la clientèle; **shop that does a thriving business**, commerce *m* qui fait de bonnes affaires; **to be in business**, être dans les affaires; **to give up business**, se retirer des affaires; **to go out of business**, (*i*) faire faillite (*ii*) fermer boutique; **I'm going to London on business**, je vais à Londres pour affaires; **to be away on business**, être en déplacement (pour affaires); **how's business?** comment vont les affaires? **business is slow**, les affaires ne marchent pas; **volume of business**, volume *m* de la production; **to talk business**, parler affaires; **big business**, les grosses entreprises commerciales; les consortiums *m*; les trusts *m*; **the tourist trade is big business today**, le tourisme est une affaire de grande importance aujourd'hui (*b*) entreprise *f*/maison *f*/firme *f*/établissement *m*; fonds *m* de commerce; **a profitable business**, une entreprise lucrative/rentable; **to run a business**, diriger un commerce; **to set up in business**, ouvrir un magasin/un commerce; **he is the owner of a small business**, il est propriétaire (*i*) d'une petite entreprise (*ii*) d'un petit commerce/d'un petit magasin; **the small business sector**, la petite entreprise; **his business is near the station**, son établissement/son atelier *m*/son usine *f* est près de la gare (*c*) **business agent**, agent *m* d'affaires; **business bank**, banque *f* d'affaires; **business card**, carte *f* (de visite) d'affaires; **business call**, visite *f* d'affaires; **business career**, carrière *f* dans les affaires; **business centre**, centre *m* des affaires; **business college/school**, école de commerce et de gestion; **business concern**, entreprise commerciale; **business corre-**

spondence, correspondance commerciale; **business cycle**, cycle *m* économique; **business game**, jeu *m* d'entreprise; **business hours**, (*office*) heures *f* de travail/de bureau; (*shop*) heures d'ouverture; **business intelligence system**, réactique *f*; **business letter**, lettre commerciale; **business lunch**, déjeuner *m* d'affaires; **business management**, gestion *f* d'entreprise; **business manager**, gérant, -ante, d'entreprise; **business name**, raison sociale; nom commercial; **business quarter**, quartier commerçant; **business trip**, voyage *m* d'affaires; **business world**, le monde des affaires; **business year**, exercice *m* (financier).

businesslike, *a.* sérieux/pratique.

businessman, *n.* (*i*) homme *m* d'affaires (*ii*) commerçant *m*; **to be a good businessman**, s'entendre aux affaires.

businesswoman, *n.* (*i*) femme *f* d'affaires (*ii*) commerçante *f.*

bust, *a.* F: **to go bust**, faire faillite.

buy[1], *v.tr. & i.* acheter (**sth. from s.o.**, qch. à qn); **to buy for cash**, acheter au comptant; **to buy on credit**, acheter à crédit/à terme; **bought of**, doit à; **to buy earnings**, investir en valeurs de croissance; chercher la plus-value.

buy[2], *n.* achat *m*; affaire *f*; **to give a buy order**, donner un ordre d'achat; **it's a good buy**, c'est un bon placement/c'est une occasion/une affaire; **to make a bad buy**, faire un mauvais achat/une mauvaise affaire/un mauvais placement.

buy back, *v.tr.* racheter.

buyer, *n.* 1. acheteur, -euse; acquéreur *m*; preneur, -euse; **potential/prospective buyer**, acheteur potentiel/éventuel; **buyer's market**, marché *m* à la baisse; **buyer's option**, prime *f* acheteur; *StExch:* **buyers over**, excès *m* d'acheteurs; **(home) loans for first time buyers**, prêt pour la première accession 2. (*for firm*) acheteur;

commissionnaire *m* d'achat; **head buyer/ chief buyer,** acheteur, -euse, principal(e).

uy in, *v.tr.* (*a*) (*at auction sale*) racheter (pour le compte du vendeur); **the diamonds were bought in at £65 000,** les diamants ont été retirés de la vente à £65 000 (*b*) *StExch:* **to buy in against a client,** exécuter un client.

uying, *n.* achat(s) *m(pl)*; **speculative buying,** achats spéculatifs; (*in shop*) **impulse buying,** achat d'impulsion/achat stimulé; **shop buying,** achats professionnels (à la Bourse); **buying back,** rachat *m*; **buying in,** rachat; *StExch:* exécution *f* (d'un client); **buying order,** ordre *m* d'achat; **buying out,** désintéressement *m* (d'un associé); (*of shares, etc.*) **buying rate/ quote/quotation,** cours *m* d'achat (des valeurs).

buy into, *v.i.* **to buy into a company,** acheter des actions d'une société.

buy out, *v.tr.* désintéresser (un associé, etc.); **we bought him out for £90 000,** nous lui avons acheté sa part/son intérêt *m* dans l'affaire pour £90 000; nous avons payé son commerce £90 000.

buyout, *n.* **leveraged buyout (LBO),** acquisition *f* d'une société par effet de levier; **(leveraged) management buyout ((L)MBO),** rachat *m* d'entreprise par les salariés/reprise *f* d'entreprise par les salariés/RES.

buy up, *v.tr.* acheter (qch.) en masse.

by(e)-laws, *n.* statuts *mpl*/règlements *mpl* (d'une société).

by-product, *n.* sous-produit *m*/(produit) dérivé *m*.

C

cabinet, *n.* **filing cabinet**, fichier *m*/classeur *m*.

cable[1], *n.* (*international telegram*) câble *m*; **cable address**, adresse *f* télégraphique; **cable transfer**, virement *m* télégraphique.

cable[2], (*a*) *v.tr.* câbler (un message) (*b*) *v.tr. & i.* **to cable (to) s.o.**, câbler à qn/ aviser qn par câble/envoyer un câble à qn.

cablegram, *n.* câble *m*.

calculate, *v.tr. & i.* (*a*) calculer/évaluer; chiffrer; supputer; estimer (*b*) faire un calcul/compter.

calculating, *adj.* **calculating machine**, machine *f* à calculer; calculatrice *f*.

calculation, *n.* calcul *m*; estimation *f*; **to make a calculation**, faire un calcul/calculer; **to be out in one's calculations**, être loin de son compte; **rough calculation**, calcul approximatif.

calculator, *n.* (*on desk*) machine *f* à calculer; calculatrice *f*; **pocket calculator**, calculatrice de poche/calculette *f*; **electronic calculator**, calculatrice électronique; **print-out calculator/calculator with a listing**, calculatrice imprimante.

calendar, *n.* calendrier *m*; **calendar month**, mois civil/commun; **calendar year**, année civile.

call[1], *n.* **1.** (*claim*) demande *f* (d'argent); *Fin:* **call (up)**, appel *m* de fonds/de versement; **call letter**, avis *m* d'appel de fonds; **payable at call**, payable sur demande/à présentation/à vue; **call money/ money at call**, argent au jour le jour; dépôt à court terme; **call loan**, prêt à vue/ prêt remboursable sur demande; **with-**drawal at call, retrait *m* à vue **2.** *StExch:* c... option, option *f* d'achat; **call over**, marc... *m* à la criée; **call premium**, prime *f* ... remboursement; **call price**, cours *m* ... dont; **call on a hundred shares**, option ... cent actions; **call of more**, option *f* ... double; **call of twice more**, option ... double à prime **3. there's no call for th...** article, cet article n'est pas très deman... **4.** appel *m* téléphonique/communicati... *f*; **call box**, cabine *f* (téléphonique); loc... call, communication urbaine; **person-t...** person call, appel avec préavis; **tra...** ferred charge call/*NAm:* collect call, app... en PCV; **trunk call/long distance ca...** communication interurbaine; **to take...** receive a (phone) call, prendre/recevoir ... appel **5.** (*of reps, etc.*) visite *f*; **to do...** round of calls, faire une tournée; **cold ca...** approche directe; **cold call sales**, ventes... par approche directe/marketing dire... marketing téléphonique/vente par té... phone/vente directe.

call[2], *v.tr. & i.* **1.** *StExch:* appeler remboursement **2. to call s.o. on the te...** phone, téléphoner à qn/appeler qn téléphone **3. to call on s.o.**, rendre visit... qn/aller voir qn (chez lui, au bureau) **to call a strike**, ordonner une grève/lan... un ordre de grève; **to call a meeting**, co... voquer une réunion.

callable, *a.* **callable bonds**, obligation... remboursables avant échéance/ob... gations avec amortissement anticipé.

called-up, *a.* **called-up capital**, capi... appelé.

call for, *v.i.* **to call for a wage increa...** demander/réclamer une augmentation salaire; **to call for additional cover**, fa... un appel de marge.

call in, *v.tr.* (*a*) retirer (une monnaie) de la circulation (*b*) **to call in one's money,** faire rentrer ses fonds.

calling in, *n.* retrait *m* (de monnaies).

call off, *v.tr.* **to call off a deal,** rompre/annuler un marché; **the strike was called off,** on a annulé la grève/mis fin à la grève.

cambist, *n.* cambiste *m*; agent *m* de change.

campaign, *n.* **sales campaign,** campagne *f* de vente; **advertising campaign,** campagne publicitaire/de publicité; **press campaign,** campagne de presse.

can[1], *n.* **1.** bidon *m* (de lait, d'huile) **2.** boîte *f* (de conserve, de bière).

can[2], *v.tr.* mettre en conserve (de la viande, etc.).

cancel, *v.tr.* **1.** annuler (un chèque, une commande, une réunion); annuler/faire remise de (une dette); *Jur:* annuler/résilier/résoudre/révoquer/rescinder (un marché, un contrat); décommander (un rendez-vous, des marchandises, qn); **to consider an agreement as cancelled,** considérer un contrat comme nul et non avenu; **to cancel a stamp,** oblitérer un timbre **2.** *Book-k:* contrepasser; (*of two entries*) **to cancel each other,** s'annuler.

cancellation, *n.* annulation *f*/révocation *f*/résiliation *f*/résolution *f* (d'un contrat, d'une vente); annulation (d'une commande).

cancelled, *a.* annulé/décommandé/révoqué/supprimé; (contrat) nul et non avenu/rescindé.

canned, *a.* en boîte/en conserve; **canned food,** conserves *fpl.*

cannery, *n.* conserverie *f.*

canning, *n.* mise *f* en conserve; **canning industry,** conserverie *f*/industrie *f* des conserves alimentaires; **canning factory,** conserverie.

canvass[1], *n.* sollicitation *f* (de commandes); prospection *f* (de la clientèle).

canvass[2], *v.tr. & i.* solliciter (des commandes); sonder (des opinions); **to canvass s.o.,** solliciter la clientèle de qn/solliciter des commandes de qn; *Pol:* solliciter des voix de qn; **to canvass an area,** faire du démarchage dans une région/démarcher une région; **to canvass for customers,** prospecter la clientèle; **to canvass from door to door,** faire du porte(-)à(-)porte.

canvasser, *n.* démarcheur, -euse; placier *m* (de marchandises); *Pol:* agent électoral.

canvassing, *n.* démarchage *m*/prospection *f*; *Pol:* démarchage (électoral).

cap, *n.* couverture *f* à la hausse/taux plafonné/cap *m.*

capacity, *n.* **1.** (*a*) rendement *m*; débit *m*; **manufacturing capacity/production capacity,** capacité *f* de production; **yield capacity,** productivité *f*; **to work at full capacity,** travailler à plein rendement; **capacity output,** production *f* maximum; **idle capacity,** potentiel non utilisé; **capacity utilization rate,** taux *mpl* d'utilisation de la capacité; **excess capacity,** surcapacité *f*; **plant capacity,** capacité de l'usine; **profit-earning capacity,** rentabilité *f* (*b*) **capacity (content),** capacité (d'un tonneau, etc.); **storage capacity,** capacité de stockage **2.** (*talent, ability*) capacité (**for,** pour, de); aptitude *f* (à faire qch.); **business capacity,** capacité pour les affaires **3. to have the capacity to do sth.,** être qualifié pour faire qch.; savoir/pouvoir faire qch.; **in the capacity of …,** en qualité de …; **to act in one's official capacity,** agir dans l'exercice de ses fonctions.

capital, *n.* capital *m*/capitaux *mpl*/fonds *mpl*; **authorized/registered/nominal/capital,** capital autorisé/capital déclaré/capital social; **capital account,** compte *m* de capital; **capital accumulation,** accumulation *f* de capital; **capital allowances,** déductions (fiscales) sur frais d'établissement; **capital assets,** actif *m* immobilisé/valeurs immobilisées; **capital**

bonus, actions gratuites; **capital budget,** budget *m* d'investissement; **capital expenditure/outlay,** dépenses *fpl* en capital/mise *f* de fonds/frais *mpl* d'établissement; **capital gains/profits,** plus-value *f*; **capital gains tax,** impôt *m* sur les plus-values; **capital goods,** biens *mpl* d'équipement; **capital loss,** moins-value *f*; **capital market,** marché *m* des capitaux/marché financier; **capital movements,** mouvements *mpl* des capitaux; *NAm:* **capital stock,** capital social/capital-actions; **capital structure,** plan financier; **circulating capital,** capital circulant/roulant; **fixed capital,** capital fixe; **human capital,** capital humain; **issued capital,** capital émis; **medium-term capital,** dettes *fpl* à moyen terme; **paid-up capital,** capital versé; **primary capital,** capitaux de départ/capitaux propres initiaux; **share capital,** capital social/capital-actions; **short-term capital,** dettes à court terme; **subscribed capital,** capital souscrit; **uncalled capital,** capital non appelé/actions non libérées; **venture capital,** capital risque; **working capital,** capital d'exploitation/capital de roulement/fonds de roulement/actifs circulants; **company with a capital of ...,** société au capital social de ....

capital-intensive, *a.* (*industry*) lourd/à forte intensité capitalistique.

capitalised, *a. NAm:* **to be well capitalised,** posséder une grande fortune/des capitaux élevés.

capitalism, *n.* capitalisme *m*; **popular capitalism,** capitalisme populaire.

capitalist, 1. *a.* capitaliste **2.** *n.* (*a*) capitaliste *mf*; **the great capitalists,** les grands financiers; la haute finance (*b*) bailleur *m* de fonds.

capitalization, *n.* capitalisation *f* (des intérêts, etc.); **(market) capitalization,** capitalisation boursière; **capitalization issue,** attributions *fpl* d'actions gratuites; **capitalization of reserves,** incorporation *f* de réserves au capital.

capitalize, *v.tr.* capitaliser (une rente, etc.); **your income, if capitalized, would run**

to ..., votre revenu, en termes de capital, se monterait à ...; **company capitalized at £100 000,** société *f* au capital de £100 000 **capitalized value,** valeur capitalisée.

captive, *a.* **captive market,** marché captif

capture, *v.tr.* **to capture the market,** accaparer la vente/conquérir le marché.

car[1], *n.* **(motor) car,** automobile *f*/voiture *f* **the car industry,** l'industrie *f* de l'automobile; **car manufacturer,** constructeur *n* (d')automobile(s); **car insurance,** assurance *f* automobile; **car licence** = carte grise; **car (tele)phone,** téléphone *m* de voiture; **company car,** voiture de fonction/de société.

car[2], *n. StExch:* (*futures contract*) contrat *n* d'opérations à terme.

carat, *n.* **18-carat gold,** or à 18 carats.

card, *n.* (*a*) **business card,** carte *f* (de visite professionnelle; *Com* carte d'affaires **(bank) cheque card/cheque guarantee card banker's card,** carte chèque/cart (d'identité) bancaire/carte de garanti (d'une banque); **cash card,** carte bancaire **charge card,** carte de paiement; *NAm* **courtesy card,** carte de recommandation **credit card,** carte accréditive/carte d crédit; **store card,** carte privative/de crédi maison; **smart card,** carte à mémoire/ puce; **phone card,** carte de publiphone (*b* **bin card,** (*in warehousing*) bon-magasi *m*/bordereau *m* d'inventaire/bordereau d magasin; **show card,** (*i*) étiquette *f* (de v trine, etc.) (*ii*) carte d'échantillons (*c* **(index) card,** fiche *f*; **card index,** fichier *n* **tabulating card,** carte mécanographique perforée; **punch(ed) card,** carte perforée **card punch,** perforatrice *f* de cartes (*a* **letter card,** carte-lettre *f*; **reply card,** cart réponse *f* (*e*) carte (de sécurité sociale); *I* **to get one's cards,** être renvoyé; **to give s.** **his cards,** renvoyer qn (*f*) **clock car** carte de pointage.

cardboard, *n.* carton *m*/cartonnage *m*; **fin cardboard,** bristol *m*; **corrugated cardboar**

carton d'emballage/carton ondulé; **cardboard box,** boîte *f* en carton/carton *m*.

card-index, *v.tr.* mettre (des informations) sur fiches.

card-indexing, *n.* mise *f* sur fiches.

cardphone, *n.* publiphone *m* à carte.

care, *n.* care of (^c/_o) **Mr Martin,** aux (bons) soins de M. Martin/chez M. Martin.

cargo, *n.* (*a*) cargaison *f*/chargement *m*/ marchandises *fpl*; **to take on/to take in/to embark cargo,** charger des marchandises/ prendre du fret/prendre un chargement; **full cargo,** plein chargement; **air cargo,** fret aérien; **deck cargo,** pontée *f*; **general/ mixed cargo,** cargaison mixte/marchandises diverses; **cargo outward,** chargement/fret *m* d'aller; **cargo homeward,** chargement/fret de retour (*b*) **cargo boat/cargo ship,** cargo *m*; **cargo plane,** avion-cargo *m*; avion *m* de fret.

carriage, *n.* fret *m*/port *m*/transport *m*; **carriage free,** franc de port/franco de port; **carriage paid,** (en) port payé; **carriage forward,** (en) port dû; **carriage (expenses),** frais *mpl* de port/de transport; **to pay the carriage,** payer le factage/le camionnage/le transport.

carrier, *n.* entrepreneur *m* de transports; transporteur *m*; camionneur *m*; **industrial carrier,** transporteur pour compte propre.

carry[1], *n.* *StExch:* prêt *m*/emprunt *m* (*pour financer les opérations à terme*).

carry[2], *v.tr.* **1.** transporter (des marchandises, etc.) **2.** (*i*) adopter (une proposition) (*ii*) faire adopter/faire passer (une proposition); (*of a bill, etc.*) **to be carried,** passer/être adopté/être voté **3.** (*a*) **to carry interest,** porter intérêt; **to carry an interest of 4%,** rapporter un intérêt de 4% (*b*) (*of shop*) avoir (des marchandises) en magasin/en stock; **we don't carry this brand of cigar,** nous ne vendons pas cette marque de cigares **4.** *StExch:* (*of broker*) accorder un crédit à (un client).

carry back, *v.tr. Book-k:* **to carry an item back,** faire un report rétrospectif/faire un report sur les exercises précédents.

carry forward, *v.tr. Book-k:* **balance carried forward,** report à nouveau; **to carry an item forward,** faire un report prospectif/faire un report sur les exercises suivants; **to be carried forward,** à reporter.

carrying, *n.* **1.** *NAm:* (*a*) **carrying charges,** frais *mpl* de possession/de jouissance; **carrying cost,** coût *m* de conservation en portefeuille (*b*) **carrying cost/value,** valeur *f* comptable **2.** *StExch:* pratique *f* d'emprunts/de prêts (*par financer les operations à terme*).

carry on, *v.tr.* **to carry on a trade/a business,** exercer/diriger un commerce; diriger une entreprise.

carry over, *v.tr.* **1.** *Book-k:* faire un report/ reporter (une somme d'une page à une autre); **to carry over a balance,** reporter un solde **2.** *StExch:* **to carry over stock,** reporter des titres; prendre des titres en report; **stock carried over,** titres *mpl* en report.

carry-over, *n.* report *m*; **carry-over rate,** taux *m* de report.

cart, *n.* **cart note,** (*a*) bordereau *m* d'expédition (*b*) permis de sortie/d'enlèvement de marchandises (*de l'entrepôt de douane après dédouanement*).

cartage, *n.* (*a*) transport *m* par voiture/par camion; camionnage *m* (*b*) frais *mpl* de transport; **cartage note,** bordereau *m* d'expédition.

cartel, *n.* cartel *m*.

carter, *n.* camionneur *m*.

carton, *n.* (*box*) carton *m*/boîte *f* en carton; **carton of milk/milk carton,** brique *f* de lait/lait *m* en brique; **a carton of 200 cigarettes,** une cartouche de 200 cigarettes.

cartridge, *n.* **film cartridge,** chargeur *m*; **ink cartridge,** cartouche *f* d'encre.

case[1], *n.* **(packing) case,** caisse *f*/boîte *f* (d'emballage); **case of goods,** caisse de marchandises; **glass case/show case,** vitrine *f.*

case[2], *n.* (*a*) law case, affaire contentieuse; **case law,** jurisprudence *f*; **case study,** étude *f* de cas (*b*) **case of need,** endossement *m* d'une lettre de change.

case[3], *v.tr.* to case goods, emballer des marchandises/mettre des marchandises en caisse(s).

cash[1], *n.* (*no pl*) espèces *fpl*; numéraire *m*; argent comptant; valeurs *fpl* en espèces; **hard cash,** argent liquide/liquide *m*; **cash balance,** solde actif/solde de caisse; **cash budget,** budget *m* de trésorerie; **cash discount,** escompte *m* (de caisse)/remise *f*/escompte sur paiement (au) comptant; **cash float,** caisse *f*; **cash management,** gestion *f* de trésorerie; **cash price,** prix *m* (au) comptant; **to buy for cash,** acheter (au) comptant; **cash purchase,** achat *m* (au) comptant; **to pay cash (down),** payer comptant/cash; **to pay in cash,** payer en espèces/en liquide; **cash payment/settlement in cash/cash settlement/cash down,** paiement *m* (au) comptant/versement *m*/règlement *m* en espèces; **cash reserve,** (*i*) encaisse *f* liquide (*ii*) réserve en espèce (d'une banque); **to sell for cash,** vendre (au) comptant; **cash transaction/cash sale,** transaction *f*/vente *f* au comptant; **cash with order,** payable à la commande; **terms cash/cash terms,** payable au comptant; **cash less discount,** comptant avec escompte; **cash before delivery,** paiement avant la livraison; **cash on delivery (COD),** paiement à la livraison; livraison contre remboursement; **cash account,** compte *m* de caisse; **cash and carry,** payer-prendre *m inv*; **cash store,** magasin *m* qui ne fait pas de crédit; *Jur:* **cash offer,** offre réelle; **cash position,** situation de (la) caisse; **cash requirements,** besoins *m* de trésorerie; *Fin:* **cash shares,** actions *f* de numéraire/en numéraire; **shares issued for cash,** actions émises contre espèces; **securities dealt for in cash,** valeurs au comptant; **cash at maturity,** valeur aux échéances; *Book-k:* **cash in hand,** fonds *mpl*/espèces en caisse/caisse *f*/encaisse *f* dis-

ponible; **petty cash,** petite caisse; **menu monnaie; ready cash,** argent *m* en main liquide; **to have cash in hand,** avoir d l'argent en caisse; **to keep the cash,** teni la caisse; **to balance the cash,** faire l caisse; **cash shorts and overs,** déficits *m* e excédents *m* de caisse; **cash box,** caisse cassette *f*; **cash desk,** caisse; **would yo please go to the cash desk,** veuillez passe à la caisse; **cash card,** carte *f* bancaire **cash dispenser,** guichet *m* automatique d banque (GAB)/distributeur (automa tique) de billets (DAB)/billetterie *f*; **cas register,** caisse enregistreuse: caiss comptable.

cash[2], *v.tr.* toucher/encaisser (un chèque/u mandat-poste); encaisser (un effet, u coupon); escompter (un effet); **to cash cheque for s.o.,** (*of bank*) payer un chèqu à qn.

cashable, *a.* encaissable/payable (à vue)

cash-book,cash book, *n.* livre *m* d caisse; **counter cash-book,** chiffrier *n* main courante de caisse; **paid cash-boo** main courante de sorties de caisse.

cash cow, *n. F:* vache *f* à lait.

cashed up, *a.* **the company was well cashe up,** les liquidités de la société étaient pl que suffisantes.

cash flow, *n.* cash flow *m*; marge *f* bru d'autofinancement (MBA); **discount cash flow (DCF),** cash flow actualis méthode *f* DCF; **they have cash flow pro lems,** ils ont des problèmes de trésoreri

cashier, *n.* caissier, -ière/préposé(e) à caisse; **cashier's desk/office,** caisse comptoir-caisse *m*; **she's the cashier, e** tient la caisse.

cash in, 1. *v.i.* (*a*) (*of salesman, etc.*) vers sa recette à la caisse; régler ses compt (*b*) (*after attendance at board meetin etc.*) toucher ses jetons **2.** *v.tr.* **to cash in cheque,** toucher un chèque.

cashpoint, *n.* point *m* retrait/guichet automatique de banque (GAB)/distr buteur *m* automatique de billets/billetterie *f.*

cash up, *v.i.* faire la caisse.

cask, *n.* barrique *f*/baril *m*/fût *m*/futaille *f*/tonneau *m*; **to put wine into casks,** mettre le vin en fût(s)/en tonneau(x)/en barrique; **wine in the cask,** vin en fût/en cercles; vin en pièce; vin logé.

casting, *a.* **casting vote,** voix prépondérante (*accordée au président d'un conseil, etc., quand les avis sont également partagés*); **the chairman has the casting vote,** la voix du président est prépondérante; **to give the casting vote,** départager les voix/ les votes.

casual, *a.* **casual labour,** main-d'œuvre occasionnelle/temporaire; **casual worker,** travailleur, -euse/employé(e) occasionnel(le)/temporaire.

cataloging, *n. NAm:* = **cataloguing.**

catalogue[1], *NAm:* **catalog,** *n.* catalogue *m*/liste *f*/répertoire *m*/nomenclature *f*; **mail order catalogue,** catalogue (d'achat par correspondance); **trade catalogue,** catalogue général (complet)/tarif *m*; **to buy by catalogue,** acheter sur catalogue.

catalogue[2], *NAm:* **catalog,** *v.tr.* cataloguer/inscrire (qch.) dans un catalogue.

cataloguing, *NAm:* **cataloging** *n.* catalogage *m*.

cater, *v.i.* **to cater for (schools, etc.),** préparer les repas pour (les écoles, etc.)

caterer, *n.* traiteur *m*.

catering, *n.* (*a*) **catering department,** rayon *m* d'alimentation (d'un grand magasin) (*b*) **catering/the catering industry,** la restauration; **the catering was done by Messrs Long,** la maison Long a fourni/ préparé le repas.

cattle, *n. coll. inv.* bétail *m*/bestiaux *mpl*; **cattle market,** marché *m* aux bestiaux.

caution, *n.* **caution money,** cautionnement *m*/caution *f*.

caveat, *n. Jur:* (*a*) opposition *f* (**to,** à); **to**

enter/put in a caveat, former/mettre opposition (**against,** à); **caveat against unfair practices,** avertissement *m* contre la concurrence déloyale (*b*) avis *m* d'opposition (au renouvellement d'un brevet d'invention, etc.); **caveat emptor,** aux risques de l'acheteur; **caveat subscriptor,** aux risques du signataire.

ceiling, *n.* plafond *m*; **credit ceiling,** plafond de crédit; **price ceiling,** plafond des prix; **output has reached its ceiling,** la production plafonne; **prices have reached the ceiling of ...,** les prix plafonnent à ...; **ceiling price,** prix plafond; **monetary ceilings,** plafonds monétaires; **to fix a ceiling to a budget,** fixer un plafond à un budget.

census, *n.* recensement *m*/dénombrement *m* (de la population).

cent, *n.* (*coin*) cent *m*; **a five cent coin,** une pièce de cinq cents; **it costs ten cents,** ça coûte dix cents.

central, *a.* **central purchasing office,** centrale *f* d'achats; **the central bank,** la banque centrale.

centralization, *n.* centralisation *f*.

centre, *NAm:* **center,** *n.* (*a*) **business centre,** centre *m* des affaires; **commercial centre,** centre commercial; **industrial centre,** centre industriel; **shopping centre,** centre commercial; *FrC:* centre d'achat(s); **tourist centre,** centre de tourisme (*b*) **budget centre,** centre *m* budgétaire; **cost centre,** centre de coût(s).

cereal, *a. & n.* céréale *f*; **cereal crops,** céréales.

certificate, *n.* (*a*) certificat *m*; **bearer certificate,** titre *m* au porteur; **loan certificate,** titre de prêt; **negotiable exchange certificate,** certificat d'échange négociable; **savings certificate,** bon *m* d'emprunt/bon d'épargne; **scrip certificate,** certificat provisoire; **share/ stock certificate,** certificat d'action(s); **registered share certificate,** certificat nominatif d'action(s); *Bank:* **certificate of deposit,** bon de caisse; **certificate of insurance,** attestation *f* d'assurance; **certificate**

of compliance, certificat de conformité; **certificate of approval,** certificat d'homologation; **certificate of origin,** certificat d'origine; *Ins:* **certificate of damage,** certificat d'avarie; *Nau:* **certificate of receipt,** certificat de chargement; **certificate of registration,** certificat d'inscription maritime; **tonnage certificate,** certificat de jauge; *Av:* **certificate of airworthiness,** certificat de navigabilité; *Aut:* **test certificate** = certificat d'aptitude à rouler; **international certificate for motor vehicles,** certificat international pour automobiles (b) *Jur:* **(bankrupt's) certificate** = (acte *m* de) concordat *m* (*entre un failli et ses créanciers*).

certificated, *a.* **1.** diplômé/titré **2.** *Jur:* **certificated bankrupt,** failli *m*/concordataire *mf.*

certification, *n.* **certification of transfer,** certificat *m* de transfert.

certify, *v.tr.* (a) certifier/déclarer/attester; **to certify (this) a true copy,** certifier copie conforme; **certified as a true copy,** copie certifiée conforme; *Fin:* **certified transfers,** transferts déclarés (b) authentiquer/homologuer/légaliser (un document); **certified cheque,** chèque certifié/*FrC:* chèque visé (pour provision); *NAm:* **certified letter** = lettre recommandée.

cesser, *n. Jur:* **cesser clause,** clause *f* de cessation.

cession, *n.* **1.** cession *f*; abandon *m* (de marchandises/de droits) **2.** *Jur:* cession de biens (aux créanciers).

cessionary *a.* cessionnaire **2.** *n. Jur:* ayant cause *m.*

chain, *n.* **chain of distribution,** circuit *m*/réseau *m* de distribution.

chain-store, *n.* (a) magasin *m* à succursales (multiples) (b) succursale *f* (de grand magasin).

chair¹, *n.* fauteuil *m* (de président); **to be in the chair,** occuper le fauteuil présidentiel/présider/diriger les débats; **to be voted into the chair,** être élu président; **Mr James**

was in the chair, M. James présidait la réunion/la réunion était sous la présidence de M. James; **to speak from the chair,** parler en tant que président; **to leave/vacate the chair,** lever la séance; **to support the chair,** se ranger à l'avis du président; **to address/appeal to the chair,** s'adresser/en appeler au président; **chair! (chair!),** à l'ordre!

chair², *v.tr.* **to chair a meeting,** présider une réunion.

chairman, *n.* président, -ente; **to act as chairman,** présider (une séance); **a committee with Mr Finch as chairman,** un comité sous la présidence de M. Finch; **Mr Chairman/Madam Chairman,** Monsieur le Président/Madame la Présidente; **chairman's report,** rapport (annuel) du président; **Chairman of the Board,** Président(e) du Conseil d'Administration; **he was chairman of the firm for ten years,** il a été président/président-directeur général de la maison pendant dix ans.

chairmanship, *n.* présidence *f*; **under the chairmanship of Mrs Brown,** sous la présidence de Mme Brown.

chairperson, *n.* président, -ente.

chairwoman, *n.* présidente *f* (d'une séance, etc.).

chamber, *n.* **Chamber of Commerce,** Chambre *f* de commerce; **Chamber of Trade,** Chambre de métiers.

chandler, *n.* **ship chandler,** fournisseur *m* maritime.

change¹, *n.* **1.** **(small) change,** (petite) monnaie; **to give change for £2,** donner/rendre la monnaie de £2; **keep the change,** gardez la monnaie; **change machine,** distributeur *m* de monnaie **2.** changement *m*; variation *f* (de prix); remaniement *m*; renouvellement *m.*

change², *v.tr.* **to change a £5 note into francs,** changer un billet de £5 en francs; **could you change me a note?** pouvez-vous me faire de la monnaie?

channel, *n.* **to go through the official channel**

nels, suivre la filière/la voie hiérarchique; **to open up new channels for trade,** créer de nouveaux débouchés pour le commerce; **channels of distribution,** canaux *m* de distribution.

hapter, *n.* (*a*) chapitre *m* (d'un livre) (*b*) *US:* **chapter 11,** clause *f* de liquidation; **they were in chapter 11,** ils étaient en état de suspension de paiements.

harge[1], *n.* frais *mpl*/prix *m*; **admittance/ entry charge,** (prix d')entrée *f*; **there is no charge (for admittance),** l'entrée est gratuite; **advertising charges,** frais de publicité; **annual charges,** (*net income*) revenu net; **list of charges,** tarif *m*; **scale of charges,** barème *m* des prix; **handling charges,** frais de manutention; **inclusive charge,** tarif tout compris; **extra charge,** supplément *m*; **customs charges,** frais de douane; **bank charges,** frais bancaires; **capital charge,** intérêt *m*/service *m* des capitaux (investis); **fixed charge,** (*asset*) bien hypothéqué; (*fixed costs*) coûts fixes; **interest charges,** frais financiers/intérêt *m* (à payer); *Bank:* (*on overdrawn account*) agios *mpl*; **social charges** (*levied on employers*), charges sociales; *NAm:* **charge account,** compte *m* crédit d'achats; *NAm:* **charge plate,** carte *f* de crédit; **to make a charge for sth.,** compter qch.; **no charge is made for packing,** on ne compte pas l'emballage/ l'emballage n'est pas facturé/l'emballage est gratuit; **free of charge,** (*i*) exempt de frais/sans frais (*ii*) gratis/franco (*iii*) à titre gratuit/à titre gracieux; **at a charge of . . .,** moyennant . . .; **at a small charge,** moyennant une faible rétribution; **charges forward,** frais à percevoir à la livraison; (en) port dû; **service charge,** prestation *f* (de service).

arge[2], *v.tr.* (*a*) charger/imputer; **to charge an account with all the expenses,** charger un compte de tous les frais; **to charge the postage to the customer,** débiter les frais de poste au client; **commission charged by the bank,** commission prélevée par la banque; **to charge an expense on/to an account,** imputer/passer/mettre une dépense à un compte; **to charge a sum to the**

debit of an account, inscrire/passer une somme au débit d'un compte; débiter un compte d'une somme; **charge it on the bill,** portez-le sur la note/facturez-le (*b*) **property charged as security for a debt,** immeuble affecté à la garantie d'une créance (*c*) **to charge s.o. £5 for sth.,** prendre/compter/demander £5 à qn pour qch.; **we are charging you the old prices,** nous vous faisons encore les anciens prix; **to charge ten francs a metre,** demander dix francs du mètre; **how much will you charge for the lot?** combien demandez-vous pour le tout?/quel est votre prix pour le tout?

chargeable, *a.* (*a*) à la charge (**to,** de); **repairs chargeable to/against the owner,** réparations *f* à la charge du propriétaire (*b*) *Fin:* **sum chargeable to a reserve,** somme *f* imputable sur une réserve (*c*) **chargeable asset,** actif imposable sur les plus-values; **chargeable gain,** bénéfice *m* imposable.

chargee, *n. Jur:* créancier privilégié.

chargehand, *n. Ind:* chef *m* d'équipe.

charge off, *vtr. NAm:* réduire/amortir (le capital).

chart, *n.* graphique *m*; **activity chart,** graphique des activités; **bar chart,** graphique à bâtons; **organization chart,** organigramme *m*; **pie chart,** diagramme *m*/ graphique à secteurs; **flow chart,** graphique *m* d'évolution; *Cmptr:* organigramme; **below the important chart point of 10%,** en dessous du seuil psychologique de 10%/de la barre des 10%.

charter[1], *n.* **1.** charte *f*/statuts *mpl*/acte *m* de constitution (d'une société); privilège *m*; **bank charter,** privilège de la banque **2.** *Nau: Av:* affrètement *m*/nolisement *m*; **charter plane,** charter *m*/avion nolisé *m*; **charter flight,** (vol *m*) charter; **on charter,** (*i*) affrété/nolisé/loué (*ii*) sous contrat **3.** *Nau:* **bareboat charter,** affrètement coque nue; **charter party,** charte partie *f*/contrat *m* d'affrètement.

charter[2], *v.tr.* **1.** instituer (une compagnie) par charte/accorder une charte à (une compagnie, etc.) **2.** affréter/fréter/noliser (un navire, un avion); prendre (un navire) à fret; **to charter a coach,** affréter un car.

chartered, *a.* **1. chartered company,** compagnie privilégiée/à charte; **chartered bank,** banque privilégiée; **chartered accountant (CA)** = expert *m* comptable/ *FrC:* comptable agréé **2. chartered ship,** navire affrété; **chartered aircraft/plane,** avion affrété/nolisé; charter *m.*

charterer, *n. Nau:* affréteur *m.*

chartering, *n.* affrètement *m*/nolisement *m* (d'un navire, etc.); **chartering agent,** agent *m* d'affrètement.

chartism, *n.* analyse *f* sur graphiques/ prévision *f* économique par graphiques.

chartist, *n. Econ:* chartiste *mf*/prévisionniste *mf*/opérateur *m* sur graphiques.

chattel, *n. Jur:* bien *m* meuble; bien mobilier; **goods and chattels,** biens et effets *m* (personnels); **pledged chattels,** biens nantis.

cheap, *a. & adv.* (*a*) (à) bon marché/(à) bon compte/pas cher; **exceptionally cheap article,** article *m* très bon marché; **cheap rate,** tarif réduit; **to buy sth. cheap,** acheter qch. (à) bon marché/à bon compte/pour pas cher; **cheaper,** (à) meilleur marché/à meilleur compte; moins coûteux/moins cher; **it comes (out)/works out cheaper to buy 10 kilos,** on a avantage à acheter 10 kilos à la fois/cela revient moins cher d'acheter 10 kilos à la fois; **to obtain cheaper credit,** obtenir du crédit à meilleur compte; **cheaper and cheaper,** de moins en moins cher; **cheapest,** le meilleur marché/le moins cher; **dead/dirt cheap,** à vil prix/pour rien/à un prix défiant toute concurrence; **it's dirt cheap,** c'est donné/c'est d'un bon marché ridicule; *F:* (*of shopkeeper*) **he's very cheap,** il n'est pas cher/il ne prend pas cher; **to buy sth. on the cheap,** acheter qch. au rabais/à bas prix; **cheap jack,** vendeur *m* au rabais; vendeur sur saisies (*b*) *Fin:* **cheap money,** facilités *fpl* d'escompte/argent *m* à bon marché.

cheapie, *n. F:* (tout ce) qui n'est pas ch▮ article bon marché.

cheaply, *adv.* (à) bon marché/à bas prix▮ peu de frais; **they can manufacture mo▮ cheaply than we do,** ils sont à même ▮ fabriquer à meilleur marché que nous.

cheapness, *n.* bon marché/bas prix.

check[1], *n.* **1.** (*restraint*) frein *m*; **to put▮ check on production,** freiner la producti▮ **2.** contrôle *m*/vérification *f* (d'un comp▮ etc.); **check sample,** échantillon *m* témo▮ **3. luggage/baggage check,** bulletin *m* bagages **4.** *NAm:* (*in restaurant*) additi▮ *f* **5.** *NAm:* = **cheque.**

check[2], *v.tr.* **1.** arrêter/enrayer (la hau▮ des prix); freiner (la production) **2.** ▮ rifier/apurer (un compte); examiner (▮ documents); **all the sales are check▮** toutes les ventes sont contrôlées; **to che▮ (off/over) goods,** vérifier des march▮ dises; **to check and sign for goods on ▮ livery,** réceptionner des marchandises▮ *NAm:* mettre (les bagages) à la consig▮

check in, (*a*) *v.i.* (*at hotel*) s'inscrire▮ l'arrivée/se faire enregistrer; (*at airp▮* se présenter à l'enregistrement (*b*) ▮ (*at airport*) **to check one's luggage in,** (faire) enregistrer ses bagages (*ii*) me▮ ses bagages à la consigne.

check-in, *n.* (*at airport*) enregistremen▮ (des bagages); **check-in time is 30 min▮ prior to departure,** (*à l'aéroport*) les vo▮ geurs sont priés de se présenter à l'e▮ gistrement 30 minutes avant l'heure ▮ départ; **check-in counter,** guichet ▮ d'enregistrement.

checking, *n.* **1.** contrôle *m*/vérificatio▮ apurement *m*; pointage *m*; (*on Lon▮ Stock Exchange*) ajustement *m* (*sur ▮ dinateur*) **2.** *NAm:* **checking acco▮** compte *m* en banque/compte de chèq▮ compte courant.

checkless, *a. NAm:* = **chequeless.**

check out, *v.i.* (*at hotel*) régler (sa note▮ départ; quitter l'hôtel.

checkout, *n.* (*a*) (*in supermarket*) chec▮

(point), caisse f (de sortie) (b) **checkout time is at 12 noon,** les clients doivent quitter la chambre avant midi (le jour du départ).

heckroom, n. *NAm:* (*left-luggage office*) consigne f.

heque, n. chèque m; **bank cheque,** chèque bancaire; **banker's cheque,** chèque de banque; **cheque for ten pounds,** chèque de dix livres (sterling); **cheque to order,** chèque à ordre; **cheque to bearer,** chèque au porteur; **crossed cheque,** chèque barré; **open/uncrossed cheque,** chèque ouvert/ non barré; **blank cheque,** chèque en blanc; **certified cheque,** chèque certifié/*FrC:* visé; **pay cheque,** (chèque de) traitement m/ salaire m; **stale cheque,** chèque périmé; **traveller's cheque,** chèque de voyage; **cheque without cover/rubber cheque**/*F:* **dud cheque,** chèque sans provision/*F* chèque en bois; **cheque book,** carnet m de chèques/chéquier m; **cheque paper,** papier m de sûreté; **cheque counterfoil/stub,** talon m de chèque/souche f; **to cash a cheque,** toucher un chèque; **to endorse a cheque,** endosser un cheque; **to make out a cheque to . . . ,** établir/faire un chèque à l'ordre de ...; **to pay by cheque,** régler par chèque; **to pay a cheque into the bank/into one's account,** déposer un chèque à la banque/ verser de l'argent à son compte; **to refer a cheque to drawer,** refuser d'honorer un chèque; **to stop a cheque,** suspendre le paiement d'un chèque; **to write (out)/to draw a cheque,** faire/émettre un chèque.

hequeless, *NAm:* **checkless,** a. cheque-less society, société f sans chèques.

hief, a. **chief accountant**/*NAm:* **Chief Financial Officer (CFO),** chef comptable; directeur financier; **chief executive**/*NAm:* **Chief Executive Officer (CEO),** directeur général.

hinese wall, n. *StExch:* murailles fpl de Chine; frontière f séparant les analystes des opérateurs financiers (*empêchant les délits d'initiés*).

hip, n. **1. blue chip (investment),** investissement sûr/de père de famille/titre m de premier ordre/blue chip **2.** *Cmptr:* **(micro/ silicon) chip,** puce f/microplaquette f.

chit, n. note f/facture f (de consommation) (*dans un club*).

choice, a. **choice article,** article m de choix/ article surfin; **choice quality,** qualité f de choix; **choice raisins,** raisins m surchoix; **choice wine,** vin m de première qualité; vin de marque.

churning, n. *F: StExch:* rotation f d'actifs/ de portefeuille.

circular, 1. a. **circular letter,** circulaire f; **circular letter of credit,** lettre de crédit circulaire **2.** n. (a) circulaire f (b) (*advertisement*) prospectus m.

circularize, v.tr. envoyer/expédier (des circulaires/des prospectus).

circulate, 1. v.i. (*of money*) **to circulate freely,** circuler librement; rouler **2.** v.tr. (a) mettre en circulation/émettre (des billets de banque) (b) = **circularize.**

circulating[1], a. circulant; *Fin:* **circulating capital,** capitaux circulants/fonds roulants.

circulating[2], n. circulation f; *Fin:* **circulating medium,** agent m monétaire/monnaie f d'échange/moyen m d'échange.

circulation, n. (a) **circulation of capital,** roulement m de fonds/circulation f des capitaux; **to withdraw capital from its natural channels of circulation,** enlever des capitaux à leur circuit naturel (b) (*of money*) **to be in circulation,** circuler; **notes in circulation,** billets m en circulation; **credit circulation,** circulation f fiduciaire (c) **circulation (of a newspaper),** tirage m (d'un journal); **newspaper with a wide circulation,** journal à grand/gros tirage.

City (the), n. la Cité de Londres (*centre des affaires*); **City man,** homme d'affaires (*de la Cité de Londres*); financier m; **he's in the City,** il est dans la finance (*dans la Cité de Londres*); *Journ:* **City article,** bulletin financier/compte rendu de la Bourse et du commerce; **The City,** Bourse/finance/

commerce; **City editor,** rédacteur *m* de la rubrique financière.

civil, *a.* civil service, administration *f*/fonction publique; **civil servant,** fonctionnaire *mf.*

claim[1], *n.* **1.** revendication *f*/réclamation *f*; **wage claims,** revendications de salaire/salariales **2.** droit *m*/titre *m*/prétention *f* (**to sth.,** à qch.); **legal claim to sth.,** titre juridique à qch.; **to put in a claim,** faire valoir ses droits **3.** *Jur:* (*debt*) créance *f*; **claims and liabilities,** créances et engagements *m*; **contractual claim,** créance contractuelle; **preferential claim,** créance privilégiée; privilège *m* du créancier **4.** *Ins:* demande *f* d'indemnité; **claim form,** formulaire *m* de demande d'indemnité; **claims manager,** chef *m* du service des réclamations; **to lay claim to sth.,** prétendre à qch; **to set up a claim,** faire une réclamation; **to make/put in a claim for damages,** demander une indemnité/réclamer des dommages-intérêts; **disputed claims office,** le contentieux; **the claims being disputed,** les contentieux en cours; **small claims court,** tribunal *m* des petites créances.

claim[2], *v.tr.* réclamer/revendiquer (un droit, etc.); *Ins:* **to claim damages,** réclamer des dommages-intérêts.

claimant, *n.* prétendant, -ante; revendicateur, -trice; *Jur:* réclamant, -ante; demandeur, -eresse; partie requérante; **rightful claimant,** ayant droit *m*; **claimant for a patent,** demandeur d'un brevet.

claim back, *v.tr.* to claim back VAT, récupérer la TVA.

claimer, *n.* = **claimant.**

claiming, *n.* réclamation *f*/revendication *f*; *Jur:* **claiming back,** action *f* en restitution.

clamp-down, *n.* clamp-down on credit, resserrement *m* du crédit.

class, *n. Av:* **economy class,** classe *f* économique; **first class,** première classe; *Rail:* **second class coach,** wagon *m* de seconde/de 2e classe; **to travel first/secon class,** voyager en première/en second *Post:* **first class rate** = tarif norma **second class rate** = tarif réduit.

classification, *n.* **job classification** classification *f* des fonctions.

classified, *a.* (*information*) (classé) secre

clause, *n.* clause *f*/article *m* (d'un traité **clauses of a law,** dispositions *f* d'une lo **additional clause,** clause additionnell **capital clause,** (*in memorandum of assoc ation*) constitution *f* du capital socia *Ins:* avenant *m* (d'une police); **claus governing a sale,** conditions *f* d'une vent **customary clause,** clause d'usage; **form clause,** clause de style; **penalty claus** clause pénale; **arbitration clause,** claus compromissoire; **saving clause,** clause c sauvegarde/clause restrictive; réservatic *f*; **restrictive clauses,** modalités *f*.

claw back, *n.* (*a*) récupération *f* (d'un d grèvement d'impôt) (*b*) *NAm:* retour *m* ε arrière.

clean, *a. Fin:* **clean bill,** effet *m* libre; **clea receipt,** reçu *m* sans réserve.

clear[1], *a.* **1.** (*a*) **clear profit,** bénéfice clair net; **clear loss,** perte sèche (*b*) *Jur:* **thr clear days,** trois jours francs **2.** **cle accounts,** comptes *m* en règle.

clear[2], *v.tr.* **1.** liquider/acquitter (u dette); **to clear goods,** solder/liquider d marchandises; **to clear,** (en) solde; **mu be cleared,** vente *f* à tout prix **2.** **to clear ship,** expédier un navire; faire la décl ration à la sortie; **to clear goods throu; customs,** passer des marchandises douane/dédouaner des marchandise retirer des marchandises de la douane **to clear 10%,** réaliser 10% tous fr; payés/faire un bénéfice net de 10%; **not clear one's expenses,** ne pas faire ses fra **I cleared a hundred pounds,** cela *m* rapporté cent livres net **4.** *Bank:* compe ser (un chèque); **to clear a bill,** régler ■ effet.

clearance, *n.* **1. clearance (sale),** vente *f*

soldes; liquidation *f* **2.** *Cust: Nau:* acquit *m*/acquittement *m* (de marchandises); déclaration *f* en douane à la sortie/ dédouanement *m*; congé *m*; **clearance inward(s),** (*i*) déclaration d'entrée (*ii*) permis *m* d'entrée; acquit; **clearance outward(s),** (*i*) déclaration de sortie (*ii*) permis de sortie; congé des douanes; **clearance certificate,** lettre *f* de mer; **to effect customs clearance,** procéder aux formalités de la douane **3.** *Bank:* compensation *f* (d'un chèque).

clearing, *n.* **1. clearing (off) of goods/ merchandise,** liquidation *f*/solde *m* **2.** (*a*) acquittement *m* des droits (sur des marchandises)/dédouanement *m* (*b*) **clearing (off) of a debt,** liquidation *f*/ acquittement (d'une dette) (*c*) liquidation (d'un compte) (*d*) *Fin:* compensation *f*/clearing *m* (de chèques); **general clearing,** compensation de chèques en dehors de Londres; **town clearing,** compensation de chèques à Londres; **under the clearing procedure,** par voie de compensation; **clearing agreement,** accord *m* de compensation/de clearing; **clearing bank,** banque *f* de clearing; **clearing account,** compte *m* de compensation; *Bank:* **clearing house,** chambre *f* de compensation; **to pass a cheque through the clearing house,** compenser un chèque.

clear off, *v.tr.* **to clear off a debt,** rembourser une dette.

clerical, *a.* (*a*) **clerical error,** faute *f* de copiste; *Book-k:* erreur *f* d'écriture (*b*) **clerical job,** poste *m* d'employé; **clerical work,** travail *m* de bureau; **clerical worker,** employé, -ée de bureau; **clerical staff,** personnel *m* de bureau; employés de bureau.

clerk[1], *n.* **1.** employé, -ée de bureau; commis *m*; **bank clerk,** employé/commis de banque; **chief clerk/senior clerk/head clerk,** chef *m* de bureau; commis principal/premier commis; **junior clerk,** petit employé; **shipping clerk,** (commis) expéditionnaire *m*/employé à l'expédition; **filing clerk/**NAm: **file clerk,** préposé, -ée/ employé aux dossiers; **records clerk,** employé aux archives; **booking clerk,** pré-

posé au guichet/à la location/à la vente des billets **2.** *NAm:* (*a*) **sales clerk,** vendeur, -euse/commis (de magasin) (*b*) préposé à la réception (d'un hôtel).

clerk[2], *v.i.* *NAm:* travailler comme employé, -ée de bureau/de banque/ comme vendeur, -euse dans un magasin.

clerkess, *n.* employée *f* de bureau.

client, *n.* client, -ente; **our clients,** nos clients/notre clientèle *f*.

clientele, clientèle, *n.* clientèle *f* (d'un magasin/d'un restaurant, etc.).

clinch, *v.tr.* **to clinch a deal,** faire/conclure une affaire.

clip, *n.* **money clip,** pince *f* à billets.

clock, *v.i.* **to clock in,** pointer (à l'arrivée); **to clock out,** pointer (au départ/à la sortie).

clocking, *n.* **clocking in/out,** pointage *m* (à l'arrivée/à la sortie/au départ).

close[1], *n.* *StExch:* (*on financial futures market*) clôture *f*; (*closing price*) cours *m* de clôture.

close[2], **1.** *v.tr.* (*a*) *Book-k:* **to close the books,** balancer les comptes (*b*) clôturer/ arrêter (un compte); conclure/clore (un marché/une négociation); conclure (une affaire); *StExch:* liquider (une opération); *Jur:* clôturer (une faillite); **to close the yearly accounts,** arrêter les comptes de l'exercice; *StExch:* **to close a position,** couvrir une position **2.** *v.i.* (*a*) *StExch:* **the shares closed at £10,** les actions *f* ont clôturé/terminé à £10 (*b*) (*of shop*) **closed,** (magasin) fermé; **closed on Saturdays,** fermé le samedi **3. closed shop,** monopole syndical de l'embauche; entreprise *f*/atelier *m* qui n'embauche que du personnel syndiqué.

closed, *a.* fermé; **closed card,** (société d'investissement) à capital fixe.

closed-end, *a.* **closed-end (investment) fund/trust,** société *f* d'investissement à capital fixe (SICAF); **closed-end mortgage,** prêt hypothécaire à montant fixe.

close down, 1. *v.tr.* fermer (définitivement); **2000 factories closed down in 1982,** 2000 usines ont fermé leur(s) porte(s) en 1982 **2.** *v.i. (of factory)* fermer; arrêter/cesser la production; chômer; *(of shop)* fermer boutique.

close-down *n.* fermeture (définitive).

close out, *NAm:* **1.** *v.tr. (a)* solder (des marchandises)/écouler (des marchandises) à bas prix *(b)* fermer/arrêter/clôturer (un compte) **2.** *v.i.* fermer boutique; *StExch:* liquider sa position (en Bourse).

closing[1], *a.* dernier/final; **the closing bid,** la dernière enchère; **closing date (for application),** date *f* limite; **closing price,** dernier cours/prix *m* de clôture; **the closing quotations,** les cotes *f* en clôture; **closing stock,** stock *m* à l'inventaire.

closing[2], *n.* **1.** fermeture *f* (d'un magasin); fermeture/chômage *m* (d'une usine); **Sunday closing,** chômage du dimanche; repos *m* hebdomadaire; **closing time,** heure *f* de fermeture (d'un pub, etc.); **early closing day,** jour *m* où les magasins sont fermés l'après-midi **2.** *(i)* clôture *f* (d'un compte) *(ii)* règlement *m* (d'un compte); clôture/conclusion *f* (d'un marché/d'une affaire); levée *f*/clôture (d'une séance); **closing costs,** frais de clôture/de conclusion (d'une transaction, d'une opération); **closing meeting,** scéance de clôture (d'une transaction).

closing down, *n.* **1.** cessation *f* de commerce **2.** fermeture *f*/chômage *m* (d'une usine); fermeture/liquidation *f* (d'un magasin); **closing down sale,** solde *m* de fermeture.

closing out, *n. NAm:* fermeture *f*/liquidation *f* (d'un magasin, d'une position en Bourse); **closing out sale,** solde *m* de fermeture.

closure, *n.* fermeture *f*; *NAm:* **closure at 6 pm,** fermeture à 18 heures; **store/factory closure,** fermeture (des portes) d'un ma**gasin/d'une usine *(causée par la faillite)*

clothing, *n.* habillement *m*; *(clothes* vêtements *mpl*; **article of clothing,** vête ment *m*; **the clothing trade,** l'industrie *f* d vêtement/de l'habillement; *NAm:* **cloth ing store,** magasin *m* de drapier/de confec tions.

co-creditor, *n. Jur:* cocréancier, -ière.

code, *n.* **post(al) code,** *NAm:* **zip code,** cod postal; *Tel:* **area code,** indicatif départ mental/*FrC:* régional; **country code,** i dicatif du pays; **international code,** préfix *m* d'accès à l'automatique internationa *Com:* **ABC code/commercial code,** cod commercial; *StExch:* **model code,** code c déontologie boursière.

co-director, *n.* codirecteur, -trice; c administrateur *m*.

coin, *n.* **1.** pièce *f* de monnaie; **gold coin** pièces d'or **2.** *coll. (no pl)* monnaie(s) *(pl)*/pièces/numéraire *m*/espèces *fpl*; **co and bullion,** métal monnayé et métal barres; **in coin,** en espèces/en numéraire **coin machine/coin-operated machine/coi in-the-slot machine,** distributeur *m* aut matique.

coinage, *n. (a)* système *m* monétaire (d' pays) *(b)* monnaie(s) *f(pl)*; numéraire

co-insurance, *n.* coassurance *f*.

collapse[1], *n. (a)* débâcle *f*/écroulement (d'un établissement) *(b) Fin:* **the collap of the market,** l'effondrement *m* marché/des cours de la Bourse; **t collapse of the franc,** la dégringolade franc.

collapse[2], *v.i. (of prices)* s'effondrer.

collar, *n.* **blue collar worker,** ouvrier *m*/c bleu/employé manuel; **gold coll worker,** col doré; **white collar work** employé *m* de bureau/col blanc.

collateral, *a. & n.* **collateral (security)/c lateral evidence,** garantie additionnel accessoire/complémentaire; nantisseme *m*; **loan on collateral,** prêt sur nantis:

ment/prêt garanti; **to lodge as collateral,** fournir/déposer en nantissement; **the bank prefers not to lend without collateral,** de préférence, la banque ne prête pas sans nantissement.

collateralize, *v.tr.* garantir par nantissement.

collect[1], *v.tr.* percevoir/lever/recouvrer (des impôts); toucher (une traite); **to collect a debt,** recouvrer/récupérer/faire rentrer une créance; **to collect moneys due,** faire la recette (des traites).

collect[2], **1.** *a. NAm:* **collect call,** appel *m* (téléphonique) en PCV; **to make a collect call,** faire un appel/téléphoner en PCV; *FrC:* (faire) renverser les frais (d'appel) **2.** *adv. NAm:* **to call collect,** faire un appel/téléphoner en PCV; **to send a parcel collect,** envoyer un colis en port dû/payable à destination.

collectable, 1. *n.pl.* **collectables,** *NAm:* **collectibles,** pièces *fpl* pour collectionneurs/pour amateurs d'art **2.** *a. (of money)* recouvrable/récupérable; *(of tax)* percevable; *(of coupon)* encaissable.

collectible, *see* **collectable.**

collecting, *a.* **collecting clerk,** garçon *m* de recettes; **collecting banker,** banquier encaisseur; **collecting agency,** banque *f* de recouvrement; **collecting department,** service *m* de recouvrement.

collection, *n. (a)* perception *f*/recouvrement *m*/levée *f*/rentrée *f* (des impôts); **debt collection,** recouvrement de créances *(b)* encaissement *m*; **bill for collection,** effet *m* à l'encaissement; **list of bills for collection,** bordereau *m* d'encaissement; **collection bank,** banque *f* d'encaissement; **collection charges,** frais *m* d'encaissement/de recouvrement; **statement of collections,** décompte *m* des encaissements; **collection rates,** tarifs *m* d'encaissement; **to hand in for collection,** donner à l'encaissement; **to send for collection,** envoyer à l'encaissement.

collective, *a.* collectif; **(free) collective bargaining,** négociation *f* de convention collective; **collective contract,** contrat collectif; **collective ownership,** propriété collective; **collective liability,** responsabilité collective.

collectivism, *n. Econ:* collectivisme *m*.

collector, *n. (a)* encaisseur *m* (d'un chèque, etc.) *(b) Adm:* percepteur *m* (des contributions directes); receveur *m* (des contributions indirectes); **debt collector,** agent *m* de recouvrement.

column, *n.* colonne *f* (créditrice, débitrice).

combine, *n.* combinaison financière; entente industrielle; cartel *m*; trust *m*; **horizontal combine,** cartel horizontal/consortium *m*.

combined, *a.* **combined totals,** les données globales.

commerce, *n.* commerce *m*; **Chamber of Commerce,** Chambre *f* de commerce.

commercial[1], *a.* commercial; **commercial artist,** dessinateur, -trice de publicité; **commercial attaché,** attaché commercial; **commercial bank,** banque commerciale/de commerce; banque de dépôt; **commercial college,** école supérieure de commerce; **commercial court,** tribunal *m* de commerce; **commercial designer,** dessinateur, -trice de publicité; **commercial efficiency (of a machine),** rendement *m* économique/effet *m* utile (d'une machine); **commercial law,** droit commercial/le Code de commerce; **commercial paper,** effet commercial; billet *m* de trésorerie; **commercial port,** port *m* de commerce; **commercial district,** quartier commerçant; **commercial traveller,** représentant *m*/voyageur *m* de commerce; courtier *m*; **commercial television,** télévision commerciale; **commercial value,** valeur marchande; **sample of no commercial value,** échantillon *m* sans valeur marchande; **commercial vehicle,** véhicule *m* utilitaire.

commercial[2], *n. WTel: TV:* publicité *f*; **the commercials,** la publicité.

commercialism, n. esprit commercial; *Pej:* mercantilisme m.

commercialization, n. commercialisation f.

commercialize, v.tr. commercialiser.

commercially, adv. commercialement.

commission, n. **1.** commission f/pourcentage m; **commission on sale,** commission sur vente; **work done on commission,** travail fait sur commande; **sale on commission,** vente f à (la) commission; **to get three per cent commission,** toucher trois pour cent de commission; **to charge/to receive 5% commission,** prendre/toucher une commission de 5%; **to appoint s.o. as buyer on commission,** commissionner qn; **illicit commission,** remise f illicite/*F:* pot m de vin; **commission agent,** représentant m à la commission; commissionnaire m agréé; *Nau:* **address commission,** frêt-à-bord m; **over-riding commission,** (*paid to broker*) commission d'arrangement **2. commission of inquiry,** commission d'enquête; **control commission,** commission de contrôle; **Economic Commission for Europe (ECE),** Commission économique pour l'Europe **3.** *NAm:* **commission broker,** courtier m à la commission.

Commissioner, n. **Commissioner of Audit** = auditeur m à la Cour des comptes.

commitment, n. **commitment fee,** commission f d'engagement.

committee, n. comité m/commission f/ conseil m; **to be on/to sit on a committee,** être membre/faire partie d'un comité; **management committee,** comité de direction/conseil d'administration; **joint production committee,** comité d'entreprise; **works committee,** comité d'entreprise; **the Stock Exchange Committee** = la Chambre syndicale des agents de change.

commodity, n. marchandise f/denrée f/ produit m; *StExch:* matière première; **commodities such as tea, coffee and sugar,** denrées telles que le thé, le café et le sucre; **primary commodity/basic com-**

modity, produit de base; **standard commodity,** bien m étalon; article m de référence; **rice is the staple commodity of China,** le riz est la ressource principale de la Chine; **commodity market,** Bourse de commerce/marché m des denrées et matières premières; **commodity broker,** commissionnaire agréé (auprès de la Bourse de commerce de Paris); **commodity exchange,** bourse f de(s) marchandises; **commodity credits,** crédits commerciaux; **commodity futures,** opérations à terme su^r marchandises/sur matières premières; **(Paris) commodity futures market,** marché à terme de marchandises (de la Bourse de Commerce de Paris); **to trade commodities,** spéculer sur les marchés à terme des matières premières; **commodity money/commodity currency,** monnaie marchandise; **international commodity agreements,** accords internationaux su^r les produits de base.

common, a. **1.** ordinaire; *NAm:* **common stock/common equity,** actions f ordinaire **2. the Common Market,** le marché commun; **common customs tariff,** tari^f douanier commun; **common external tariff,** tarif externe commun.

communism, n. *PolEcon:* communisme m

community, n. (a) **the (European Economic) Community (EEC),** la communaut^é (économique) européenne (CEE) (b) **business community,** monde m de^s affaires; milieu m/gens mpl d'affaires; **financial community,** monde de la haute finance; **community charge,** = taxe locale

commutation, n. **commutation ticket,** carte f (d'abonnement).

commute, v.i. faire la navette (**to work,** pour se rendre à son travail).

commuter, n. banlieusard, -arde; **commuter belt,** banlieue f; **commuter train,** train de banlieue.

commuting, n. trajets journaliers.

company, n. (a) société f/compagnie f, entreprise f; **joint stock company,** société anonyme par actions; *NAm:* société eⁿ

commandite; **limited (liability) company/ company limited by shares,** (*i*) société à responsabilité limitée (SARL) (*ii*) société anonyme (SA); **private (limited) company** = société à responsabilité limitée; **public limited company** = société anonyme (SA); **affiliated/subsidiary company,** filiale *f*/compagnie affiliée; **dependant/ daughter company,** compagnie/société captive; **assurance company/insurance company,** compagnie d'assurances; **bogus company,** société fantôme; **close/***NAm:* **closed/***NAm:* **closely-held company,** société contrôlée par un maximum de cinq personnes et qui n'est pas cotée en Bourse; **family company,** société de famille; **independent company,** compagnie/société indépendante; **joint venture company,** société d'exploitation en commun; **listed company,** société cotée; **management company,** société de gérance; compagnie d'exploitation; **parent company,** compagnie mère; **real estate company,** société immobilière; **shell company,** société qui n'existe que de nom; **shipping company,** compagnie de navigation; société de transports maritimes; **statutory company,** entreprise *f*/établissement *m* de service public; *US:* **threshold company,** entreprise en développement; **unlimited company,** société à responsabilité infinie; **Companies Act,** loi *f* sur les sociétés; **Company law,** droit des sociétés; **name of a company,** raison sociale; **and Co.,** et Cie; **to form/to incorporate a company,** constituer une société; **to liquidate/to wind up a company,** liquider une société; **a (good) company man,** un homme qui se dévoue aux intérêts de l'entreprise; **company doctor,** redresseur *m*/repreneur *m* d'entreprises; **company funds,** fonds social; **one company town,** agglomération construite pour les employés d'une entreprise (*b*) corporation *f* de marchands; **the City Companies,** les corporations de la Cité de Londres.

comparability, *n.* **pay comparability,** alignement *m* des salaires (*sur ceux d'autres industries*).

comparative, *a.* **comparative advantage,** avantage comparatif.

compensate, *v.tr.* (*a*) **to compensate s.o. for sth.,** dédommager/indemniser qn de qch.; **to compensate a workman for injuries,** dédommager un ouvrier pour blessures (*b*) rémunérer (qn).

compensation, *n.* (*a*) compensation *f*; (*for loss/injury*) dédommagement *m*; (*for damage*) indemnité compensatrice/ indemnisation *f*; *Jur:* réparation civile/ composition *f*; *EEC:* **monetary compensation amount,** montant *m* compensatoire monétaire; **to pay s.o. compensation in cash,** indemniser qn en argent (*b*) **executive compensation,** rémunération *f* des cadres; *NAm:* **hourly compensation,** gain *m* horaire.

compete, *v.i.* **to compete with s.o.,** faire concurrence à qn/concurrencer qn; **we cannot compete successfully with . . .,** nous ne pouvons pas soutenir la concurrence de . . ./nous ne pouvons pas lutter contre . . .; **to compete with one another,** se faire concurrence.

competence, competency *n.* attributions *fpl* (d'un fonctionnaire); *Jur:* compétence *f*; **this lies within his competence,** cela rentre dans ses attributions; **to be within the competence of a court,** être de la compétence/du ressort d'un tribunal; **to fall beyond the competence of . . .,** ne pas relever/ne pas être de la compétence de . . .

competent, *a.* 1. capable; **I am looking for a competent manager,** je cherche un gérant qualifié/compétent 2. compétent (**in a matter,** en une matière); **competent to do sth.,** capable de faire qch.; compétent/ qualifié pour faire qch. 3. *Jur:* (*court*) compétent.

competing, *a.* **competing firms,** entreprises concurrentielles; **competing products,** produits concurrents.

competition, *n.* concurrence *f*; **free competition,** libre concurrence; **monopolistic/ imperfect competition,** concurrence monopolistique; **perfect/pure competition,** concurrence *f* pure et parfaite; **unfair competition,** concurrence déloyale.

competitive, *a.* concurrentiel/concurrent/ compétitif; **in competitive conditions,** en conditions de concurrence; **competitive price,** prix concurrentiel/compétitif; prix défiant toute concurrence; **competitive products,** produits concurrents/compétitifs; **full competitive costs,** coûts concurrentiels intégraux; **competitive supply and demand,** l'offre et la demande concurrentielles; **competitive bidding,** appel *m* d'offres.

competitiveness, *n.* compétitivité *f* (des prix, des produits).

competitor, *n.* concurrent, -ente; rival, -ale; **my competitors in trade,** mes concurrents.

complaint, *n.* (*a*) plainte *f*; **the complaints by the employers of the scarcity of skilled labour,** les plaintes formulées par les patrons sur la rareté de la main-d'œuvre spécialisée (*b*) plainte/réclamation *f*; **to lodge/make a complaint against s.o.,** porter plainte contre qn/déposer une plainte contre qn; **to lodge a complaint with s.o.,** réclamer auprès de qn; **complaints office,** service *m* des réclamations.

completion, *n.* **completion of a contract,** signature *f* d'un contrat.

complex, *n.* centre *m*/complexe *m* (industriel).

complimentary, *a.* **complimentary copy (of a book),** exemplaire (d'un livre) envoyé à titre gracieux; **complimentary ticket,** billet *m* de faveur.

composition, *n.* arrangement *m*/accommodement *m* (*avec ses créanciers*); concordat préventif (*à la faillite*); **to make a composition,** composer; **composition of fifty pence in the pound,** décharge *f* de cinquante pour cent.

compound[1]**,** *a.* *Book-k:* **compound entry,** article composé/collectif/récapitulatif; *Fin:* **compound interest,** intérêts composés.

compound[2]**,** *v.i.* composer/transiger/ concorder/arriver à un concordat/

s'accommoder/s'arranger (avec ses créanciers).

comprehensive, *a.* (*study, view*) d'ensemble; (*programme*) complet; (*insurance*) multirisque.

comptroller, *n.* = **controller.**

compulsory, *a.* obligatoire; **compulsory purchase order,** (ordre d')expropriation *f* (pour cause d'utilité publique).

computable, *a.* calculable.

computation, *n.* (*a*) compte *m*/calcul *m*, estimation *f*; **to make a computation of sth.,** faire le calcul de qch/calculer, estimer qch; **at the lowest computation it will cost …,** en mettant les choses au plus bas, cela va coûter … (*b*) **electronic computation,** calcul électronique.

computational, *a.* de calcul; **computational error,** erreur *f* de calcul.

compute, *v.tr.* calculer.

computer, *n.* ordinateur *m*/calculateur *m*; **analog computer,** ordinateur analogique; **business computer,** ordinateur de gestion; **digital computer,** calculateur numérique; **home computer,** ordinateur familial; **micro computer,** micro-ordinateur *m*; **personal computer (PC),** ordinateur individuel; **computer department,** service *n* informatique; **computer accounting,** comptabilité *f* par ordinateur; **computer analyst,** analyste *mf*; **computer engineer,** ingénieur-informaticien *m*; **computer expert,** informaticien, -ienne; **computer map,** carte *f* infographique; **computer programmer,** programmeur, -euse; **the computer industry,** industrie *f* informatique; **computer science,** informatique *f*.

computerize, *v.tr.* (*a*) informatiser/équiper (une organisation) d'ordinateurs (*b*) **to computerize wages,** informatiser de salaires.

computerized, *a.* informatisé; **computerized data,** données *fpl* informatiques/ automatisées.

computing, *n.* informatique *f*; **commercia**

computing, informatique de gestion; **home computing,** informatique familiale; **computing speed/computing time,** vitesse *f*/durée *f* de calcul.

con, *a.* **con man,** escroc *m*; **con game/trick,** escroquerie *f*/duperie *f.*

concealment, *n. Jur:* dissimulation *f* de certains faits/de défauts (de la marchandise); *Fin:* **concealment of assets,** dissimulation d'actif.

concern[1], *n.* entreprise *f*/affaire *f*/exploitation *f*/maison *f* (de commerce, etc.); fonds *m* de commerce; **business concern,** entreprise commerciale; **manufacturing concern,** entreprise industrielle; **the whole concern is for sale,** toute l'entreprise est mise en vente/est à vendre; **going concern,** affaire qui marche; (*of shop, etc.*) **to be sold as a going concern,** à vendre avec fonds.

concern[2], *v.tr.* intéresser (qn); **to whom it may concern,** à qui de droit; **those/the persons concerned,** les intéressés.

concert, *n.* concert *m*; *F:* **concert party,** groupe qui agit de concert pour contrôler des actions en Bourse.

concession, *n.* (*a*) concession *f*; **mining concession,** concession minière (*b*) **(price) concession,** réduction *f*; **tax concession,** avoir fiscal.

concessionaire, *n.* concessionnaire *mf.*

concessionary, **1.** *a.* (*a*) (*company, etc.*) concessionnaire (*b*) (*subsidy, etc.*) concédé (*c*) **concessionary fare,** tarif réduit **2.** *n.* concessionnaire *mf.*

conciliation, *n. Ind:* **conciliation service,** service *m* de médiation *f.*

conciliator, *n. Ind:* médiateur, -trice.

condition, *n.* **1.** condition *f*; **conditions of sale,** conditions de vente; **conditions laid down in an agreement,** stipulations *f* d'un contrat; **conditions of the contract,** cahier *m* des charges; **conditions of employment,** conditions d'emploi: *Fin:* **terms and conditions of an issue/of repayment,** modalités *f* d'une émission/d'un rem-

boursement; **express condition,** condition expresse; **implied condition,** condition tacite; **on condition,** sous réserve **2.** état *m*/situation *f*; état d'entretien (du matériel, etc.); **living conditions,** conditions de vie; **working conditions (in a factory),** conditions de travail (dans une usine); **in good (working) condition,** en bonne condition/en bon état (de marche); **in bad condition,** en mauvais état; (*of goods*) **in fair condition,** acceptable; **economic conditions,** conditions économiques; conjoncture *f*; **the condition of the market,** l'état du marché; **minimum cost condition,** hypothèse *f* du coût minimum.

conditional, *a.* **conditional offer,** offre conditionnelle.

condominium, condo, *n. NAm:* (*building*) (immeuble *m* en) copropriété *f*; (*apartment*) appartement *m* dans une copropriété.

conference, *n.* **1.** conférence *f*/entretien *m*/consultation *f*; **to be in conference with one's colleagues,** être en conférence/en consultation avec ses collègues; *Tel:* **conference call,** appel *m* par Réunion-Téléphone (*Rtm*); **conference line,** Réunion-Téléphone *f* (*Rtm*) **2.** congrès *m*; conférence; colloque *m*; **publishers' conference,** congrès d'éditeurs.

confidence, *n.* confiance *f*; **confidence trick,** escroquerie *f*/duperie *f*; **confidence trickster,** escroc *m.*

confirm, *v.tr.* **to confirm a booking,** confirmer une réservation.

confirmation, *n.* confirmation *f*; **confirmation note,** avis *m* de confirmation (de crédit, etc.).

conglomerate, *n.* conglomérat *m.*

congress, *n.* congrès *m*; réunion *f.*

consensus, *n.* consensus *m*; unanimité *f.*

consent, *v.tr.* **to consent a reduction in price,** consentir une réduction/faire un rabais.

consideration, *n.* **1.** **for a consideration,**

moyennant paiement; **contract without consideration,** contrat *m* sans contrepartie; **agreed consideration,** prix convenu; **for good consideration,** (*i*) à titre amical (*ii*) à titre onéreux **2.** cause *f*/provision *f* **(for,** de); **to give consideration for a bill,** provisionner une lettre de change; **consideration given for a bill of exchange,** cause *f* d'un billet.

consign, *v.tr.* consigner/envoyer/expédier (des marchandises) (**to s.o.,** à qn/à l'adresse de qn); envoyer (des marchandises) en consignation (à qn).

consignation, *n.* consignation *f*; **to ship goods to the consignation of s.o.,** consigner des marchandises à qn; envoyer des marchandises en consignation à qn.

consignee, *n.* consignataire *mf*; destinataire *mf*.

consignment, *n.* **1.** (*a*) envoi *m*/expédition *f* (de marchandises); **goods for consignment to the provinces and abroad,** articles *m* à destination de la province et de l'étranger; **consignment note,** lettre *f* de voiture; bon *m*/bordereau *m* d'expédition; *Rail:* récépissé *m* (*b*) **on consignment,** en consignation/en dépôt (permanent) **2.** (*goods sent*) envoi/arrivage *m* (de marchandises); **your consignment of books has arrived,** votre envoi de livres nous est bien parvenu; **I am expecting a large consignment of . . .,** j'attends un fort arrivage de . . . .

consignor, *n.* consignateur, -trice/expéditeur, -trice.

consolidate, *v.tr.* (*a*) regrouper/fusionner/unir/réunir (deux entreprises, etc.) (*b*) *Fin:* consolider/unifier (une dette).

consolidated, *a.* (*a*) consolidé/intégré; *Fin:* **consolidated accounts,** comptes consolidés/intégrés; **consolidated annuities/stock,** fonds consolidés/les consolidés; **consolidated balance-sheet,** bilan consolidé; **consolidated statement of income,** résultats consolidés; **net consolidated profit**/*NAm:* **income,** bénéfices nets consolidés; **consolidated cash transactions,** ré-

capitulation *f*/regroupement *m* des opérations de caisse (*b*) réuni; **consolidated shipping,** compagnie des armateurs réunis.

consolidation, *n.* **1.** *Fin:* regroupement *m* (d'actions) **2.** consolidation *f*/unification *f* (d'une dette).

CONSOL, *n. abbr. Consolidated Stock/Consolidated Loan*) *Fin:* fonds consolidés/les consolidés *m*; **CONSOL certificate,** titre consolidé.

consortium, *n.* consortium *m*.

constant, *a.* **constant francs/dollars,** francs/dollars constants.

consultancy, *n.* **consultancy firm,** cabinet *m* d'ingénieur(s)-conseil(s)/etc.; **consultancy service,** service *m*/assistance *f* technique; **management consultancy practice,** cabinet de conseil en gestion.

consultant *n.* conseil *m*/consultant, -ante **engineering consultant,** ingénieur-conseil *m*; **finance consultant,** conseil financier **management consultant,** conseiller *m* de gestion/de direction; **tax consultant,** conseil fiscal/fiscaliste *mf*; **consultant service** assistance *f*/service *m* technique.

consulting, *a.* **consulting engineer,** ingénieur-conseil *m*.

consumable, *a.* (*a*) (aliment *m*) consommable; *PolEc:* consomptible; **consumable goods,** produits *m* de consommation (*b*) *n.pl.* **consumables,** aliments/comestible *m*/denrées *f*.

consumer, *n.* consommateur, -trice; **gas consumers,** les abonnés *m* du gaz; *PolEc:* **producers and consumers,** producteurs *n* et consommateurs; **consumer council** comité (consultatif) des consommateurs **Consumers' Association** = Institut national de la consommation; **(mass) consumer goods/products,** biens *m* d (grande) consommation; **consumer durables,** biens de consommation durables **consumer credit,** crédit *m* à la consommation; **consumer industry,** industrie de con sommation; **consumer price,** prix à l consommation; **consumer research,** recherche *f* des besoins des consommateurs; consommatique *f*; **consumer society,** société *f* de consommation; **consumer spending/consumer expenditure,** dépenses *fpl* de consommation; **consumer price index,** indice *m* des prix à la consommation.

consumerism, *n.* consommatisme *m*/consommaction *f*/consommérisme *m*.

consumption, *n.* consommation *f*; **energy consumption,** consommation d'énergie; **home consumption,** consommation intérieure; **world consumption,** consommation mondiale; (*of car*) **petrol consumption,** consommation d'essence; **for current consumption,** destiné à la consommation courante; **unfit for human consumption,** non comestible.

contact, *n.* **business contact,** relation *f* d'affaires; **contact man,** agent *m* de liaison.

container, *n.* (*a*) récipient *m*; réservoir *m*; bac *m* (pour aliments); boîte *f*/caisse *f* (*b*) *Trans:* conteneur *m*/container *m*; **container ship,** (navire) porte-conteneurs *m*; **container shipping,** transports *m* maritimes par conteneurs; **container berth,** poste *m* à quai pour porte-conteneurs; **to put into containers,** conteneuriser.

containerization, *n.* *Trans:* conteneurisation *f*; transport *m* par conteneurs; **the dock strike was against containerization,** la grève des dockers avait pour origine l'opposition à l'adoption des conteneurs.

containerize, *v.tr.* conteneuriser.

contango[1], *n.* *StExch:* (*i*) report *m* (*ii*) taux *m* de report; **contango day,** jour *m* des reports; **money on contango,** capitaux *mpl* en report; **contangoes are low,** les reports sont bon marché; **payer of contango,** reporté *m*.

contango[2], *v.tr. & i. StExch:* reporter (une position).

contangoable, *a. StExch:* reportable.

content, *n.* **the content (of a letter),** le con-

tenu (d'une lettre); **the contents (of a bottle, box, parcel),** le contenu (d'une bouteille/d'une boîte/d'un colis); **gold content,** teneur *f* en or; **work contents,** contenu du travail.

contingency, *n.* **contingency analysis,** analyse *f* de contingence; **contingency fund,** fonds *m* de prévoyance; **contingency reserve,** réserve *f* de prévoyance; *pl.* **contingencies,** faux frais/frais divers; **to provide for/to allow for contingencies,** parer à l'imprévu/tenir compte de l'imprévu.

contingent, *a.* éventuel/fortuit/accidentel/aléatoire; **contingent expenses,** dépenses imprévues; **contingent profit,** profit *m* aléatoire; **contingent liability,** (élément de) passif éventuel.

continuation, *n. StExch:* **continuation operation,** opération *f* de report; **continuation rate,** prix du report.

contra[1], *n. Book-k:* **per contra,** par contre; **as per contra,** en contrepartie/porté ci-contre; **settlement per contra,** compensation *f*; **to settle a debt per contra,** compenser une dette avec une autre; **contra entry,** article *m* inverse/écriture *f* inverse; **contra account,** compte *m* d'autre part; compte contrepartie.

contra[2], *v.tr. Book-k:* contrepasser (des écritures, etc.).

contraband, *n.* contrebande *f*; **contraband goods,** marchandises *f* de contrebande.

contract[1], *n.* **1.** (*a*) contrat *m*/convention *f*; **contract of employment**/*NAm:* **labor contract,** contrat de travail; **contract of insurance,** contrat d'assurance; **group contract,** contrat collectif; **parole contract,** contrat verbal; **simple contract,** contrat ordinaire; **social contract,** convention sociale; **to bind oneself by contract,** s'engager par contrat/contractuellement; **to acquire sth. under a contract,** acquérir/obtenir qch. par contrat; **to draw up a contract,** dresser/rédiger un contrat; **to sign a contract,** signer un contrat; **to annul/terminate/cancel a contract,** résilier/annuler un contrat; **bound by contract/under contract,** lié par contrat (*b*) acte *m* de vente; contrat translatif de propriété; **law of contract,** droit *m* des obligations; **contract note,** note *f*/bordereau *m* de contrat; *StExch:* avis *m* d'exécution; **private contract,** contrat sous seing privé; **by private contract,** à l'amiable/de gré à gré **2.** entreprise *f*; soumission *f*; adjudication *f*; convention forfaitaire; marché *m*; **building contract,** contrat d'entreprise; **to make a contract for supplying wood,** faire/passer un marché pour une fourniture de bois; **contract for a bridge,** entreprise d'un pont; **contract work,** travail en sous-traitance; **contract price,** prix *m* forfaitaire/contractuel; *Adm:* prix de série; **to enter into a contract,** (*of pers.*) passer un contrat (**with,** avec); (*of thg*) faire partie d'un contrat; **contract labour,** main-d'œuvre contractuelle; **worker on contract,** contractuel, -elle; **to put work up for contract,** mettre un travail en adjudication; **to put work out to contract,** mettre un travail à l'entreprise; **to place/to give/to award a contract,** concéder/adjuger l'exécution (d'un travail); passer un contrat (à qn) pour l'exécution (d'un travail); **to tender for a contract,** soumissionner à une adjudication; **to get/to secure a contract for sth.,** être déclaré adjudicataire d'un contrat; **conditions of contract,** cahier *m* des charges; **conditions as per contract,** conditions contractuelles; **contract date,** date contractuelle; **breach of contract,** rupture *f* de contrat; *Jur:* **action for breach of contract,** action *f* en rescision/pour inexécution d'un contrat; action contractuelle; **action for specific performance of contract,** action en exécution de contrat; **penalty for non-fulfilment of contract,** peine contractuelle; **to claim under a contract,** intenter une action en exécution de contrat.

contract², *v.* **1.** *v.tr.* (*a*) **to contract to do sth.,** entreprendre de faire qch./s'engager par traité à faire qch. (*b*) **to contract a loan,** faire/contracter un emprunt **2.** *v.i.* **to contract for a supply of sth.,** entreprendre une fourniture de qch.; **to contract for work,** prendre qch. à l'entreprise; **to con-**

tract with s.o., traiter avec qn; faire/passer un marché avec qn; **the work was contracted out to s.o.,** on a donné le travail à un sous-traitant; **to contract out (of an agreement),** se dégager d'un contrat; **to contract in,** s'engager par contrat préalable.

contracting, *a.* **contracting partner,** cocontractant, -ante; **contracting party,** contractant *m*/parties contractantes; *esp.* adjudicataire *mf.*

contractor, *n.* entrepreneur *m*; **employment contractor,** entreprise *f* de travail temporaire; **haulage contractor,** entrepreneur de transports.

contractual, *a.* contractuel/forfaitaire; **contractual claims,** créances contractuelles.

contribution, *n.* contribution *f*/apport *m*/cotisation *f*; **contribution pro rata,** contribution proportionnelle/quote-part *f*; **employer's and employee's contributions,** cotisations patronales et ouvrières; **health insurance contributions,** cotisations maladies; **National Insurance contributions** = (*paid by employee*) cotisation à la Sécurité sociale; (*paid by employer*) charges sociales; **to pay one's (National Insurance) contributions,** cotiser à la Sécurité sociale; **additional voluntary contribution,** supplément *m* de cotisation (*payé volontairement*); *Fin:* **contribution of capital,** apport de capitaux; **contribution to the capital of a company,** contribution au capital d'une compagnie/apport d'actif.

contributor, *n. Fin:* **contributor of capital,** apporteur *m*/société apporteuse/personne apporteuse de capitaux.

contributory, 1. *n.* actionnaire *mf* responsable proportionnellement à son apport **2.** *a.* **contributory pension plan,** régime de retraite financé par les cotisations patronales et ouvrières.

control¹, *n.* **1.** autorité *f*; **to have control of a business,** être à la tête d'une entreprise **2.** contrôle *m*; **accounting control,** contrôle de la comptabilité; **budgetary control,** contrôle *m* budgétaire; **credit control,**

encadrement *m* des crédits; **(foreign) exchange control,** contrôle des changes; **management control,** contrôle de gestion; **money/monetary control,** contrôle monétaire; **price control,** réglementation *f/* contrôle (des prix); **production control,** gestion *f* de (la) production; **rent control,** contrôle/réglementation des loyers; **quality control,** contrôle de (la) qualité; **stock control,** contrôle/gestion *f* des stocks.

control², *v.tr.* **1.** diriger/réglementer (des affaires); **to control a business,** diriger une entreprise/être à la tête d'une entreprise **2. to control inflation,** contenir l'inflation; **to control the rise in the cost of living,** enrayer la hausse du coût de la vie; **controlled currency,** monnaie dirigée; **controlled economy,** économie dirigée; **controlled market,** marché réglementé; **controlled prices,** prix réglementés/taxés.

controller, *n.* (*i*) vérificateur *m* des comptes (*ii*) directeur des services comptables/ des finances (*iii*) contrôleur *m* de gestion.

controlling, *a.* **controlling interest (in a firm),** majorité *f/*participation *f* majoritaire/participation qui donne le contrôle (dans une société); **controlling shareholding,** bloc *m* de contrôle.

convene, 1. *v.tr.* convoquer/réunir (une assemblée); réunir/assembler (une conférence, etc.); **to convene a meeting of shareholders,** convoquer une assemblée d'actionnaires **2.** *v.i.* s'assembler/se réunir/se rencontrer.

convener, convenor, *n.* convocateur *m.*

convenience, *n.* **convenience food,** prêt-à-manger *m*; **convenience store,** bazarette *f.*

convention, *n.* contrat *m/*accord *m/* convention *f.*

conversion, *n.* (*a*) détournement *m* de fonds (*b*) *StExch:* conversion *f* (d'un titre); **conversion issue,** émission *f* de conversion; **conversion loan,** emprunt *m* de conversion; **conversion price,** prix *m* de conversion.

convert¹, *n.* *NAm: Fin:* obligation *f* convertible (en actions).

convert², *v.tr.* (*a*) convertir (*b*) **to convert funds to another purpose,** affecter des fonds à un autre usage/à d'autres fins; *Jur:* **to convert funds to one's own use,** détourner des fonds.

convertibility, *n.* convertibilité *f* (d'une monnaie, d'une obligation).

convertible, *a.* *Fin:* **convertible bond/ convertible loan stock/***n.* **convertible,** obligation *f* convertible (en actions); **convertible currency,** monnaie *f* convertible.

convey, *v.tr.* **to convey goods,** transporter des marchandises.

conveyance, *n.* *Jur:* (*a*) cession *f/*transfert *m* de biens (*b*) **deed of conveyance,** acte de cession/acte translatif de propriété.

conveyancing, *n.* *Jur:* rédaction *f* d'actes de cession/d'actes translatifs de propriété.

cook, *v.tr.* *F:* **to cook the books,** falsifier/ truquer/tripoter les comptes.

cooking, *n.* *F:* **cooking of accounts,** falsification *f/*trucage *m* des comptes; tripatouillage *m* d'une comptabilité; irrégularités *fpl* d'écriture.

cooling off, *a.* **cooling off period,** période *f* de réflexion; temps d'arrêt; pause *f.*

co-op = **co-operative,** *n.* la coopé.

co-operative, 1. *a.* **co-operative society,** société coopérative/coopérative *f* **2.** *n.* coopérative *f*; **agricultural co-operative,** coopérative agricole; **consumers' co-operative,** coopérative de consommation; **wine co-operative,** coopérative vinicole.

co-owner, *n.* copropriétaire *mf.*

co-ownership, *n.* copropriété *f.*

copartner, *n.* coassocié(e)/coparticipant(e).

copartnership, *n.* coassociation *f/*coparticipation *f*; société *f* en nom collectif;

industrial copartnership, actionnariat ouvrier.

coproperty, *n.* copropriété *f.*

coproprietor, *n.* copropriétaire *mf.*

copy, *n.* (*a*) copie *f*/transcription *f* (d'une lettre, etc.); **advertising copy,** texte *m* publicitaire; *Typ:* **carbon copy,** double *m*/ copie conforme/duplicata *m*; **hard copy,** copie sur (support) papier/copie en clair/ tirage *m*/facsim *m*; **top copy,** original *m*; **rough copy,** brouillon *m*; **fair/final copy,** copie au net/au propre (*b*) *Jur:* expédition *f* (d'un acte/d'un titre); **certified copy,** copie authentique; **certified true copy,** pour copie conforme/copie certifiée (conforme); copie authentique; **true copy,** copie conforme; **file copy,** exemplaire *m* des archives (*c*) (*of a book*) exemplaire *m*; **presentation copy,** spécimen gratuit; (*of magazine, etc.*) numéro *m*.

copying, *n.* **copying machine,** duplicateur *m.*

copyright[1], *n.* droit *m* de reproduction/ d'auteur; copyright *m*; **copyright act,** loi *f* sur le droit de reproduction; **out of copyright,** (tombé) dans le domaine public; **infringement of copyright,** violation *f* du droit de reproduction; **copyright reserved,** tous droits réservés/droit de reproduction réservé; **copyright notice,** mention *f* de réserve; *Journ:* mention d'interdiction.

copyright[2], *v.tr.* déposer (un livre à la Bibliothèque Nationale).

copyright[3], *a.* (livre) qui est protégé par le droit de reproduction/d'auteur; (livre) qui n'est pas dans le domaine public; (article) dont le droit de reproduction est réservé; **copyright (in all countries),** tous droits de reproduction et de traduction réservés (pour tous pays).

copyrighted, *a.* (*book*) déposé.

copyrighting, *n.* dépôt légal (d'une publication).

copywriter, *n.* (concepteur-)rédacteur *m.*

corn, *n. coll.* grains *mpl*/blé(s) *m*(*pl*)/ céréales *fpl*; *NAm:* maïs *m*; **Corn Exchange,** bourse *f* des céréales; halle *f* aux blés; **corn chandler/dealer/merchant,** marchand *m* de blé/de grains; grainetier *m*; **corn trade,** commerce *m* des grains/des céréales.

corner[1], *n.* monopole *m*; trust *m* d'accapareurs; corner *m*; **to make a corner in wheat,** accaparer le blé.

corner[2], *v.tr.* accaparer (une denrée); manipuler/accaparer (le marché).

cornering, *n.* accaparement *m* (d'une denrée); manipulation *f* (du marché).

corporate, *a.* corporatif/de société/d'entreprise; **corporate body/body corporate,** personne morale; société *f*/compagnie *f*; **corporate culture,** culture *f* d'entreprise; **corporate finance,** finance *f* d'entreprise; **corporate finance manager,** financier *m* d'entreprise; **corporate hospitality (CH),** invitations *fpl* de complaisance; **corporate income,** revenu de société; **corporate name,** raison sociale; **corporate image/ identity,** image *f* de marque (d'une société); *US:* **corporate licensing,** marchandisage *m*; **corporate profit,** profit *m* des sociétés; **corporate income tax,** impôt sur les bénéfices des sociétés.

corporation, *n.* **1.** société commerciale; compagnie *f* **2.** *Fin:* (*a*) **corporation stocks,** emprunts *mpl* de ville (*b*) **corporation tax,** impôt *m* sur les sociétés; **advance corporation tax,** impôt anticipé sur les sociétés; = avoir fiscal.

correction, *n.* correction *f* (des variations saisonnières); **technical market correction,** correction technique du marché.

correlation, *n.* corrélation *f*; **correlation ratio,** rapport *m* de corrélation.

correspond, *v.i.* **1. to correspond to sample,** être conforme à l'échantillon **2. to correspond with s.o.,** correspondre avec qn/ écrire à qn/échanger des lettres avec qn.

correspondence, *n.* (*a*) correspondance *f*/échange *m* de lettres; **to be in correspon-**

dence with s.o., être en correspondance avec qn (*b*) correspondance/courrier *m*; **correspondence clerk,** correspondancier *m*.

correspondent, *n.* correspondant, -ante.

corresponding, *a. Book-k:* **corresponding entry,** écriture *f* conforme/de conformité.

co-signatory, *n. Jur:* co-signataire *mf.*

cost¹, *n.* **1.** coût *m*/frais *mpl*; **cost of living,** coût de la vie; **increased cost of living,** augmentation *f* du coût de la vie; **cost-of-living allowance/bonus,** indemnité *f* de cherté de vie/de vie chère; **cost of borrowed capital,** coût de l'endettement; **the cost of an undertaking,** les frais d'une entreprise; **costs to be borne by ...,** frais à la charge de ...; **economic cost,** coût économique; **first cost/prime cost,** coût premier; prix initial; **actual cost/net cost,** prix de revient/prix d'achat; **cost price,** prix coûtant/valeur *f* en fabrique; **cost unit,** unité *f* de coût; **committed costs,** frais engagés; **gross cost,** prix de revient brut; **total cost,** coût total; **to sell at cost (price),** vendre au prix coûtant; **to sell under cost price,** vendre à perte; **cost analysis,** analyse *f* des charges/du prix de revient/des coûts; **direct costs,** charges directes; **fixed costs,** coût constant/fixe; charge *f* fixe; frais *mpl* fixes; **incidental costs,** faux frais; **indirect costs,** charges indirectes; **labour costs,** (coût de la) main-d'œuvre *f*; **operating costs,** frais d'exploitation; **sunk costs,** frais non amortissables; argent investi à fonds perdu; **cost, insurance and freight (CIF),** coût, assurance, fret (CAF); **cost keeping,** comptabilité de prix coûtants; **cost account,** compte *m* des charges; **cost accountant,** comptable *mf* de prix de revient; **cost accounting,** comptabilité *f* de prix de revient/comptabilité analytique; **current cost accounting,** comptabilité en coûts réels/déflatés/de remplacement; **full cost accounting,** méthode de capitalisation du coût entier; **cost book,** livre *m* de(s) charges; *StExch:* **cost of a share,** valeur *f* d'achat d'une action; **cost of acquisition and disposal (of securities),** frais d'acquisition et de cession (de titres) **2.** *pl. Jur:* frais d'instance; dépens *mpl*; **to pay**

costs, payer les condamnations/les frais et dépens; **order to pay costs,** exécutoire *m* de dépens.

cost², **1.** *v.i. & tr.* coûter; **how much does it cost?** combien cela coûte-t-il?/ça coûte combien? **it costs five pounds,** ça coûte cinq livres **2.** *v.tr.* **to cost an article,** établir le prix de revient d'un article; **to cost a job,** évaluer le coût d'une entreprise/d'un travail.

cost-benefit, *n.* **cost-benefit analysis,** analyse *f* coût-profit/analyse des coûts et rendements.

cost-effective, *a.* rentable.

cost-effectiveness, *n.* **cost-effectiveness analysis,** analyse *f* coût-efficacité.

costing, *n.* évaluation *f* du prix de revient; **direct costing,** méthode *f* de coût variable/proportionnel; **full costing,** méthode de capitalisation du coût entier; **production costing,** comptabilité analytique/industrielle.

cost-plus, *n.* taux *m* de marque.

coterminous, *a. Jur:* (*leases*) à échéance simultanée.

co-trustee, *n. Jur:* co-administrateur, -trice.

cottage, *n.* **cottage industry,** industrie artisanale.

cotton, *n.* coton *m*; **cotton industry,** industrie cotonnière/du coton; **cotton trade,** commerce *m* des cotons; **cotton broker,** courtier *m* en coton; **cotton goods/stuffs,** tissus *m* de coton; cotonnades *f.*

council, *n.* conseil *m*; assemblée *f*; **Council for Mutual Economic Aid (COMECON),** Conseil de l'aide économique mutuelle (COMECON); **Council of Europe,** Counseil de l'Europe; **Council flat/house** = habitation *f* à loyer modéré/HLM.

counsel, *n.* avocat-conseil *m.*

counseling, *n.* (*advice*) conseils professionnels; (*career guidance*) orientation professionnelle.

counter, *n.* (*a*) (*in bank, etc.*) guichets *mpl*/caisse *f*; **payable over the counter,** payable au guichet (*b*) (*in shop*) comptoir *m*; **sold over the counter,** vendu (au) comptant; **drugs sold over the counter,** médicaments vendus sans ordonnance; **to sell under the counter,** vendre en cachette; **goods from under the counter,** des marchandises *f* de l'arrière-boutique; **counter hand,** vendeur, -euse.

counterbid, *n.* suroffre *f*; surenchère *f*.

counterfeit, *n.* contrefaçon *f*; faux billets.

counterfoil, *n.* souche *f*/talon *m* (de chèque, de quittance); **counterfoil book,** cahier *m*/carnet *m*/registre *m*/livre *m* à souche.

countermand, *v.tr.* **to countermand the order for sth.,** décommander qch.; **unless countermanded,** sauf contrordre/sauf contravis.

countermarketing, *n.* campagne *f* de dénigrement.

countermove, *n.* contremarché *m*/contre-offensive *f*/contre-attaque *f*.

counter-offer, *n.* contre-offre *f*.

counterpart, *n.* duplicata *m*/double *m* (d'un document); contrepartie *f*; **tally counterpart,** souche *f* (d'un reçu).

counterproductive, *a.* qui nuit à/gêne (la productivité).

countersign, *v.tr.* contresigner.

countersignature, *n.* contreseing.

countervailing, *a.* *Fin:* compensateur; compensatoire.

coupon, *n.* coupon *m*; **(free) gift coupon,** bon-prime *m*; **coupon redeemable for cash,** timbre *m*/chèque *m* ristourne; **reply coupon,** coupon-réponse *m*; *Fin:* **interest coupon,** coupon (d'intérêts); **cum coupon,** coupon attaché; **ex coupon,** coupon détaché; **due date of coupon,** échéance *f* de coupon; **outstanding coupons,** coupons en souffrance.

court, *n.* *Jur:* cour *f*/tribunal *m*.

covenant[1]**,** *n.* **1.** convention *f*; **deed of co-**venant, pacte *m*/engagement *m* **2.** *NAm:* **the lessee is a good covenant,** le locataire a une bonne capacité de remboursement/ une solvabilité assurée.

covenant[2]**,** *v.tr.* s'engager (par contrat) à verser (un montant fixe, régulièrement, pendant un temps déterminé).

cover[1]**,** *n.* (*a*) couverture *f*/provision *f*/ garantie *f*; *Ins:* couverture *f*; *Fin:* marge *f* de sécurité; **to operate with/without cover,** opérer avec couverture/à découvert; **call for additional cover,** appel *m* de marge; *Ins:* **full cover,** garantie totale; *Ins:* **disability cover,** assurance invalidité; **open cover,** traité facultatif obligatoire/facob *m*; **cover note,** lettre *f* de couverture; *Jur:* **to lodge stock as cover,** déposer des titres en nantissement (*b*) (*in restaurant*) **cover charge,** couvert *m* (*c*) **to send sth. under separate cover,** faire parvenir qch. sous pli séparé.

cover[2]**,** *v.tr.* (*a*) couvrir (un risque/son banquier); (*of creditor*) **to be covered,** être à couvert; **to cover a bill,** faire la provision d'une lettre de change; *StExch:* **to cover short sales/shorts,** racheter des titres; **to cover a short account/position,** couvrir un découvert; **to cover by buying back,** se couvrir en rachetant; **the application is covered,** la souscription est couverte; *Ins:* **he is covered against fire,** son assurance *f* couvre le risque d'incendie/il est assuré contre les incendies (*b*) **to cover one's expenses,** faire ses frais/couvrir ses dépenses/rentrer dans ses frais; **to cover a deficit,** combler un déficit.

coverage, *n.* *Ins:* couverture *f*/provision *f*, garantie *f*.

covering, *a.* **1. covering letter,** lettre explicative; lettre d'introduction/lettre annexe; lettre de confirmation; **covering note,** garantie *f* **2.** *StExch:* **covering purchases,** rachats *m*; **bear/short covering** rachat des vendeurs à découvert.

crab, *n.* *Publ:* **crabs,** invendus *mp* (retournés à l'éditeur).

crack, *vtr.* **to crack the market,** percer su un marché.

crash[1], *n.* **financial crash/business crash,** débâcle financière/krach *m.*

crash[2], *v.i.* (*of business*) faire faillite; (*of prices*) s'effondrer.

crate, *n.* cageot *m* (à légumes)/caisse *f* à claire-voie.

cream, *v.tr.* **to cream the market,** écrémer le marché; **to cream off the profits,** se beurrer.

creation, *n.* **the job creation programme** = le pacte pour l'emploi.

credibility, *n.* crédibilité *f.*

credit[1], *n.* (*a*) crédit *m*; **to give s.o. credit,** faire crédit à qn; **to sell on credit,** vendre à crédit/à terme; **long/short credit,** crédit à long/court terme; **blank credit/open credit,** crédit en blanc/à découvert; **revolving credit,** crédit renouvelable/permanent/revolving; **trade credit,** crédit commercial; **credit bank/credit establishment,** banque *f*/établissement *m* de crédit; **credit facilities,** facilités *f* de paiement; **credit freeze/squeeze,** blocage *m*/restriction *f*/encadrement *m* du crédit; **credit union,** société *f* de crédit; *Bank:* **letter of credit,** accréditif *m*/lettre de créance/de crédit/lettre accréditive; **documentary letter of credit,** crédit documentaire; **extended credit,** accréditif prolongé; **permanent credit,** accréditif permanent; **credit account,** (*i*) compte créditeur (*ii*) compte crédit d'achats; **to open a credit account with s.o.,** ouvrir un crédit chez qn; **to open a credit,** loger un accréditif; **to give s.o. credit facilities,** accréditer qn (auprès d'une banque); **to open credit facilities with a bank,** loger un accréditif sur une banque; **to give s.o. a bank credit,** ouvrir un crédit en banque à qn/accréditer qn; **credit card,** carte *f* de crédit/carte accréditive; **credit circulation,** circulation *f* fiduciaire; **credit instrument,** instrument *m* de crédit; **credit insurance,** assurance *f* contre les mauvaises créances;**credit limit,** limite *f*/plafond *m* de crédit; réserve *f* d'achat; **credit agency/***NAm:* **bureau,** agence *f* de rating; bureau *m* de cotation/d'évaluation; **credit rating,** degré *m* de solvabilité; **credit worthy,** qui a une réputation de solvabilité/digne de confiance; **credit worthiness,** degré *m*/réputation *f* de solvabilité; crédit sur le marché; **to live on credit,** vivre à crédit; **no credit (allowed),** on ne fait pas (de) crédit (*b*) *Book-k:* **debit and credit,** doit *m* et avoir *m*; **credit (entry),** article porté au crédit d'un compte; **credit side,** avoir; **credit balance,** solde créditeur; **account in credit/account showing a credit balance,** compte bénéficiaire; *Bank:* **credit note,** note *f* d'avoir/note de crédit/bordereau *m* de crédit; *Bank:* **credit slip,** bulletin *m* de versement; **to enter/put a sum to s.o.'s credit,** porter une somme au crédit/à l'actif de qn; alimenter le compte de qn; **to pay in a sum to s.o.'s credit,** payer une somme à la décharge de qn; **bank credit,** crédit bancaire; **investment credits,** crédit d'impôt/avoir fiscal; **tax credit,** déductions fiscales; *StExch:* avoir *m* fiscal/crédit d'impôt; **frozen credits,** créances gelées.

credit[2], *v.tr.* **to credit an account with a sum/to credit a sum to an account,** créditer un compte d'une somme/créditer une somme à un compte/porter une somme au crédit d'un compte/passer (un montant) en profit.

creditor, *n.* **1.** créancier, -ière; **to be s.o.'s creditor for 1000 francs,** devoir 1000 francs à qn; **simple-contract creditor,** créancier chirographaire/créancier en vertu d'un contrat sous seing privé; **joint creditor,** cocréancier, -ière; **trade creditor,** créancier d'exploitation; **unsecured creditor,** créancier chirographaire; (*in bankruptcy*) **creditor of a creditor,** créancier en sous-ordre **2.** créditeur, -trice; *Book-k:* (*of balance*) **creditor side,** crédit *m*/avoir *m* **3.** *pl.* **creditors,** dette passive.

creditworthy, *a.* qui a une réputation de solvabilité.

critical, *a.* **critical path analysis/method,** analyse *f*/méthode *f* du chemin critique.

cross, *v.tr.* barrer (un chèque); **crossed cheque,** chèque barré.

crowd, *n. StExch:* groupe *m*.

cum, *Lt. phr.* avec; **cum all**, tout compris/ tous bénéfices inclus; **cum dividend/cum div.**, coupon/dividende attaché.

cumulative, *a.* **cumulative dividend**, dividende cumulatif; **cumulative share**, action à dividende cumulatif; **cumulative preference shares**, actions privilégiées.

curb, *v.tr.* **to curb inflation**, contenir l'inflation; **to curb imports**, freiner les importations.

currency, *n.* unité *f* monétaire (d'un pays)/monnaie *f*; devise(s) *f(pl)*; **payable in currency**, payable en espèces; **currency area**, zone monétaire; **currency dealer**, cambiste *m*; **foreign currency**, devises étrangères; **bill in foreign currency**, effet *m* en devises étrangères; **decimal currency**, système monétaire décimal; **firm currency**, devise soutenue; **foreign currency allowance**, allocation *f* en devises; **hard/scarce currency**, devise forte; **soft currency**, devise faible; **legal (tender) currency**, monnaie légale/courante/libératoire; **paper currency**, papier-monnaie *m*/monnaie fiduciaire; **silver currency**, monnaie/numéraire *m* d'argent; **currency note**, coupure *f*/billet *m* (de banque); **questions of currency**, questions *f* monétaires.

current, *a.* **current account**, compte courant; *StExch:* liquidation courante; **money on current account**, dépôt *m* à vue; **current earnings**, bénéfices de l'exercice; **current liabilities**, passif *m* exigible/exigibilités *fpl*; dette *f* à court terme; **current assets**, actif *m* réalisable et disponible/ actifs de roulement; **current price**, prix courant/prix du marché; **the current rate of exchange in Paris**, le taux de change en cours à Paris; **current quotations**, cours *mpl* actuels; **money that is no longer current**, monnaie qui n'est plus courante/ qui n'a plus cours; **current loan**, prêt en cours/non remboursé/consenti; **current (fiscal) year**, l'exercice *m* en cours.

curve, *n.* courbe *f*/ligne *f*; **growth curve**, courbe de croissance.

custom, *n.* **1.** (*a*) (*of business*) clientèle *f* (*b*) patronage *m*/pratique *f* (du client); **to lose s.o.'s custom**, perdre un client/perdre la clientèle de qn; **custom(-)built/ custom(-)made/custom-tailored**, (fait) sur commande/sur mesure; adapté aux goûts/ aux besoins du client **2.** *pl* **customs**, douane *f*; **customs broker**, agent *m* en douane; **customs declaration**, déclaration *f* de/en douane; **customs duties**, droits *m* de douane; **customs house**, (bureau *m* de) douane; **customs officer**, douanier *m*; **customs regime/tariff**, régime/tarif douanier; **customs union**, union douanière; **customs value**, valeur de douane; **to get/to go through customs**, passer la douane/en douane/par la douane; **to get/to take sth. through the customs**, faire passer qch. à la douane; **customs examination/ formalities**, formalités *f* de douane; **customs clearance**, dédouanement *m*; **to effect customs clearance**, procéder aux formalités de la douane/dédouaner.

customer, *n.* (*of shop, etc.*) client, -ente; (*of public house, etc.*) consommateur *m*; (*of bank, etc.*) déposant, -ante; **current account customer**, titulaire *mf* d'un compte courant; (*of restaurant, etc.*) **regular customer**, habitué(e).

customize, *v.tr.* faire sur commande; personnaliser; faire sur mesure(s).

cut[1], *n.* réduction *f* (de prix, de dépenses); **(drastic) cut**, coupe *f* (sombre) (dans le personnel, etc.); **budget cuts**, coupe budgétaires; **salary cuts/cuts in salary**, réductions de salaires/sur les traitements; **spending cuts**, diminutions *f*/réduction des dépenses; **tax cuts**, réduction d'impôts.

cut[2], (*a*) *v.tr.* **to cut costs**, réduire les frais; **to cut (back) prices**, baisser les prix; **to cut (back) production**, diminuer la production (*b*) *p.p.* **cut price**, prix *m* de rabais; **to sell at cut price**, vendre au rabais/au dessous des cours.

cutback, *n.* réduction *f*/diminution *f* (de la production/d'un budget).

cut-price, *a.* à prix réduit.

cut-rate, *a.* **(to sell at) cut-rate prices,** (vendre au) rabais.

cut-throat, *a.* **cut-throat competition,** concurrence acharnée.

cutting, *n.* **cutting (down) of prices,** réduction *f* des prix/rabais *m.*

cycle, *n.* cycle *m*; **economic cycle/trade cycle,** cycle économique.

cyclical, **1.** *a.* **cyclical variations,** variations *f* cycliques **2.** *npl* **cyclicals,** valeurs *fpl* cycliques.

D

dabble, *v.i.* **to dabble on the Stock Exchange,** boursicoter.

dabbler, *n.* **dabbler on the Stock Exchange,** boursicoteur, -euse.

dabbling, *n. StExch:* boursicotage *m.*

daily, *a.* journalier/quotidien/de tous les jours; **daily consumption,** consommation journalière; **daily paper,** (journal) quotidien *m;* **daily returns,** recettes journalières/relevés journaliers; *Fin:* **daily loans,** prêts *m* au jour le jour; *StExch:* **daily closing prices,** cours *m* de clôture quotidiens.

dairy, *n.* **1.** laiterie *f;* **co-operative dairy,** coopérative laitière; **dairy farming,** industrie laitière; **dairy produce,** produits laitiers **2.** (*shop*) laiterie/crémerie *f.*

dairying, *n.* l'industrie laitière.

daisy wheel, *n. Typ:* marguerite *f;* **daisy wheel printer,** imprimante *f* à marguerite.

damage[1]**,** *n.* **1.** dommage(s) *m(pl)/* dégât(s) *m(pl);* (*to ship, cargo*) avarie(s) *f(pl);* **damage in transit,** avaries de route; **to suffer damage,** subir un dommage; **damage to property,** dommages matériels; **the insurance will pay for the damage,** les assurances *f* vont payer les dommages; *Ins:* **damage survey,** expertise *f* des dégâts/ des avaries **2.** *pl. Jur:* dommages-intérêts *mpl*/dommages et intérêts/indemnité *f;* réparation *f* de dommages; **exemplary damages,** réparation *f* d'un préjudice moral; **nominal damages,** dommages-intérêts symboliques; **substantial damages,** réparation d'un préjudice réel; **to bring an action for damages against s.o./to sue s.o. for damages,** poursuivre qn en dommages-intérêts; **to be liable for damages,** être tenu

des dommages-intérêts; (*in respect of act committed by third party*) être civilement responsable; **to claim £1 000 damages,** réclamer des dommages-intérêts/une indemnité de £1 000; **to pay the damages,** payer/acquitter les condamnations.

damage[2]**,** *v.tr.* endommager/abîmer; avarier (une marchandise).

damaged, *a.* avarié/endommagé/abîmé/ qui a subi un dommage; **damaged goods,** marchandises avariées.

damp down, *v.tr.* **to damp down the market,** freiner le marché; **to damp down consumption,** réduire la consommation.

data, *n.* données *f*/information *f;* **data acquisition,** collecte *f*/saisie *f* de données; **data processing,** informatique *f* traitement *m* de l'information/des données; **data processing department,** service *m* informatique; **data handling,** maniement *m* de données; **data bank,** banque *f* de données; **data base,** base *f* de données; **data input,** introduction *f*/entrée *f* de données; **data processing card,** carte perforée/mécanographique.

date[1]**,** *n.* (*a*) date *f;* **date stamp,** (*object*) (tampon *m*) dateur *m;* (*mark*) cachet *m;* **date of delivery,** date/jour *m* de livraison; **dispatch date,** date d'envoi (*b*) **up to date,** à jour; (*well-informed*) au courant (**on,** de); **I am up to date with my work,** mon travail est à jour; **to bring/to keep sth. up to date,** mettre/tenir qch. à jour (*c*) **to date,** à ce jour/jusqu'ici; **interest to date,** intérêts *m* à ce jour (*d*) **out of date,** (passeport/chèque, etc.) périmé; (vêtement) démodé (*e*) *Fin:* **date of a bill,** terme *m*/ échéance *f* d'un billet; **three months after date/at three months' date,** à trois mois de date/d'échéance; **due date,** (date d')échéance; **final/latest date,** terme *m* de rigueur; **to buy at long/short date,** acheter à long/à court terme; **to pay at fixed dates,** payer à échéances fixes.

date[2], *v.tr.* (*a*) dater (une lettre, etc.); **the cheque is dated March 24th,** le chèque a été émis le 24 mars/est daté du 24 mars; **to date back,** antidater; **to date forward,** postdater (*b*) composter (un billet); **dating and numbering machine,** composteur *m.*

datebook, *n. NAm:* agenda *m.*

dated, *a.* daté; **thank you for your letter dated June 15th,** je vous remercie de votre lettre datée/en date du 15 juin; (*in compounds*) *Fin:* **long-dated,** à longue échéance/à long terme; **short-dated,** à courte échéance/à court terme.

day, *n.* 1. (*a*) jour *m*; journée *f*; **day off,** jour de congé; **eight-hour day,** journée de huit heures; **pay day,** jour de paie; **working day,** jour ouvrable; *StExch:* **making up day/settlement day,** jour de liquidation/du règlement; **trading day,** jour de Bourse; **last trading day,** dernier jour de négociation (*b*) **day labour,** travail *m* à la journée; **day labourer,** journalier *m*/ouvrier *m* à la journée; *StExch:* **day order,** ordre *m* valable pour la journée; **day trader,** spéculateur *m* à la journée; *Ind:* **day shift,** équipe *f* de jour; (*of workman*) **to be on day shift,** être de jour; *Rail: etc:* **day return,** aller et retour *m* (*pour une journée*); *Fin:* **day bill,** effet *m* à date fixe; **day-to-day loan,** prêt *m* au jour le jour; **one-day option,** prime *f* au lendemain; **last-day money,** emprunt *m* remboursable fin courant 2. (= *24 hours*) **clear day,** jour franc/plein; **ten clear days' notice,** préavis *m* de dix jours francs.

daybook, *n.* livre journal *m*/livre *m* de commerce/main courante/brouillard *m.*

dead, *a.* 1. (*inactive*) **dead season,** morte-saison *f*; **dead period,** période *f* d'inactivité; *Fin:* **dead account,** compte inactif; **dead money,** argent mort/qui dort; **dead loan,** emprunt *m* irrécouvrable; **dead market,** marché mort; **dead freight,** faux fret; dédit *m* pour défaut de chargement 2. **dead loss,** perte sèche.

deadline, *n.* date *f* limite; **to meet a deadline,** faire qch. dans un délai prescrit.

deadweight, *n. Nau:* portée *f* en poids/chargement *m* en lourd/port *m* en lourd; **deadweight cargo,** marchandises lourdes; **deadweight cargo capacity,** port en marchandises; **ton deadweight,** tonneau *m* de portée en lourd/d'affrètement.

deal[1], *n.* affaire *f*/marché *m*; **it's a deal,** d'accord; marché conclu! **to make a deal/to strike a deal/***NAm:* **to cut a deal with s.o.,** conclure une affaire/un accord avec qn; **to negotiate a deal,** négocier une affaire; **to call off a deal,** annuler un marché; **fair deal,** traitement *m*/arrangement *m* équitable; **financial deal,** opération financière/transaction *f*; **firm deal,** marché ferme; *esp. US:* **bought deal,** mobilisation *f* d'actifs; **cash deal,** transaction *f* au comptant; **deal on joint account,** opération *f* en participation; **option deal,** opération à prime; **package deal,** contrat global/panier *m*; **paper deal,** transaction sur papier; **even deal,** opération blanche; **swap credit deal,** facilités *f* de crédit réciproques; **upstairs deal,** affaire conclue à huis clos; **a big deal,** une grosse affaire; **deal on the Stock Exchange,** coup *m* de Bourse.

deal[2], *v.i.* 1. **to deal with a piece of business,** se charger d'une affaire; **to deal with an order,** donner suite à une commande 2. **to deal with s.o.,** traiter/négocier avec qn; **to deal in leather/in wool,** faire le commerce des cuirs/des laines; **I don't deal in that line,** je ne fais pas cet article; *Fin:* **to deal in options,** faire le commerce des primes.

dealer, *n.* (*a*) négociant *m* (**in,** en); distributeur *m* (**in,** de); stockiste *m* (*b*) marchand(e)/fournisseur *m* (**in,** de); **retail dealer,** détaillant(e); **wholesale dealer,** grossiste *mf*; **secondhand dealer,** revendeur, -euse; brocanteur, -euse; **exchange dealer,** courtier *m* de change/cambiste *m*;

authorized dealer, concessionnaire *mf*/distributeur agréé; **art dealer,** marchand(e) de tableaux; **you can obtain this article from your usual dealer,** vous trouverez cet article chez votre fournisseur habituel (*c*) *StExch:* courtier, -ière/cambiste-commis opérateur.

dealing, *n.* **1. dealing in wool/in wines,** commerce *m* des laines/des vins; *StExch:* **dealings for the account/for the settlement,** négociations *f* à terme; **dealing room,** salle *f* des changes; **cash dealings,** opérations *f* au comptant; **exchange dealings,** opérations boursières; **after hours dealing,** transactions *fpl* hors bourse/marché hors bourse; **forward dealings,** négociations/opérations *f* de change à terme; **margin dealing,** (*method of dealing commodities or financial futures*) cotation *f* par appel de marge; (*high-gear dealing*) arbitrage *m* à la marge/marginal; (*transactions on margin of loan*) arbitrage sur dépôt de titres de garantie; **option dealing,** opérations à prime/à option; **telephone dealing,** cotation *f* par téléphone **2. to have dealings with s.o.,** être en relations d'affaires/faire affaire/traiter avec qn **3. fair/square dealing,** loyauté *f*/honnêteté *f* (en affaires).

dear, *a.* **1.** cher/coûteux/onéreux; (*of food, etc.*) **to get dear/dearer,** augmenter/renchérir; **apples are much dearer this year,** le prix des pommes a beaucoup augmenté cette année; **dear money,** argent cher **2. Dear Madam,** Madame/Mademoiselle; **Dear Mr Martin,** Cher Monsieur (Martin); **Dear Sir,** Monsieur; **Dear Sirs,** Messieurs.

dearth, *n.* pénurie *f* (de marchandise).

death, *n.* décès *m*/mort *f*; **death duties/** *NAm:* **tax,** droits *m* de succession; **death rate,** taux *m* de mortalité; *StExch:* **death valley days,** jours creux.

debenture, *n. Fin:* obligation *f*;**first/second/third debenture,** obligation de premier/de deuxième/de troisième rang; **bearer debenture,** obligation au porteur; **convertible debenture,** obligation conver-

tible (en action); **mortgage debenture,** obligation hypothécaire; **unsecured/naked/simple debenture,** obligation non garantie; **issue of debentures/debenture issue,** émission *f* d'obligations; **unissued debentures,** obligations à la souche; **debenture bond,** titre *m*/certificat d'obligation; **debenture capital,** capital-obligations *m*; **debenture holder,** porteur *m* d'obligations/obligataire *mf*; **debenture loan,** emprunt *m* obligataire; **debenture register,** registre *m* des obligataires; **debenture stock,** obligations.

debit[1], *n. Book-k:* débit *m*/doit *m*; **debit and credit,** doit et avoir *m*/débit et crédit *m*; **debit (entry),** article porté au débit d'un compte; **debit side,** débit d'un compte; **to enter sth. on the debit (side) of an account,** porter/inscrire qch. au débit d'un compte; **debit note,** note *f*/ bordereau *m* de débit; **debit account,** compte débiteur; **debit balance,** solde débiteur; **account showing a debit balance,** compte déficitaire/qui présente un déficit; **debit card,** carte *f* de débit; **debit column,** colonne *f* des débits; **(by) direct debit,** (par) prélèvement *m* bancaire (automatique).

debit[2], *v.tr. Book-k:* **1.** débiter (un article/un compte); **to whom shall I debit the amount?** au débit de qui dois-je porter le montant? **2. to debit s.o. with a sum,** porter une somme au débit de qn/débiter (le compte de) qn d'une somme.

debitable, *a.* **charge debitable to the profit and loss account,** charge *f* à porter au débit du compte de résultat.

debt, *n.* dette *f*; créance *f*; **National/***US:* **Federal Debt,** la dette publique/de l'État; **bad debt,** mauvaise créance/créance irrécouvrable; **doubtful debt,** créance douteuse; **good debt,** bonne créance/dette; **unpaid/undischarged debt,** dette non acquittée; **debt due,** créance exigible; **debt limit,** limite *f* d'endettement; **privileged debt,** dette privilégiée; **secured/unsecured debt,** créance garantie/sans garantie; **debt owed by us/by the firm,** dette passive; **debt owed to us,** dette active; **to be in debt,** être endetté/avoir des dettes; **to be out of debt,**

avoir payé ses dettes; **to get out of debt,** rembourser/payer ses dettes; s'acquitter de ses dettes; **to pay off a debt,** rembourser/payer une dette; **to run into debt,** s'endetter; **external debt,** dette extérieure; **floating debt,** dette publique flottante/dette non consolidée/dette courante; **funded debt/consolidated debt,** fonds consolidés; dette consolidée; dette publique en rentes sur l'État; **senior debt,** dette de premier rang/dette senior; **debt-for-equity,** ratio *m* d'endettement sur fonds propres; **debt collector,** agent *m* de recouvrements; **to collect a debt,** recouvrer une dette; **debt security,** titre *m* de créance.

ebtnocrat, *n.* employé(e) de banque spécialisé(e) dans les prêts de haut niveau (*souvent aux pays du Tiers Monde*).

ebtor, *n.* 1. débiteur *m*; **joint debtor,** codébiteur 2. *Book-k:* **debtor side,** débit *m*/doit *m*; **debtor account,** compte débiteur; **debtor and creditor account,** compte par doit et avoir; **debtor nation,** nation débitrice; *pl.* **debtors,** dette active.

ebug, *v.tr. Cmptr:* déboguer/éliminer les bogues de/(un système, un programme).

ebut, *n.* (cours *m* d')introduction *f*.

ecentralization, *n.* décentralisation *f*.

ecentralize, *v.tr.* décentraliser.

ecile, *n. Stat:* décile *m*.

ecimal, 1. *a.* **decimal point** = virgule *f* (**3.5** = 3,5)/*FrC:* point *m* (décimal); **decimal system,** système décimal 2. *n.* décimale *f*.

ecimalization, *n.* décimalisation *f*.

ecimalize, *v.tr.* appliquer le système décimal.

ecimate, *v.tr.* **we have to decimate our workforce,** il nous faut réduire notre main-d'œuvre.

ecision, *n.* **to make a decision,** prendre

une décision; **decision making,** prise *f* de décision(s).

declaration, *n.* (*a*) **statutory declaration,** attestation *f*; **declaration of bankruptcy,** jugement déclaratif de faillite; **declaration of income,** déclaration *f* de revenu; **VAT declaration,** déclaration de TVA; **customs declaration,** déclaration de/en douane (*b*) *StExch:* **declaration of options,** réponse *f* des primes.

declare, *v.tr. Cust:* **have you anything to declare?** avez-vous quelque chose à déclarer? **nothing to declare,** rien à déclarer (*b*) *StExch:* **to declare an option,** répondre/donner la réponse à une prime (*c*) **to declare s.o. bankrupt,** constater l'état de faillite de qn; *Fin:* **to declare a dividend of 10%,** déclarer un dividende de 10%.

declared, *a.* **declared dividend,** dividende déclaré; **declared value,** valeur déclarée.

declining, *a.* (marché, prix) en baisse; (valeur) décroissante.

decontrol, *v.tr.* libérer (le commerce, etc.) des contraintes du gouvernement; **to decontrol the price of meat,** détaxer la viande; **to decontrol prices/to decontrol wages,** débloquer les prix/débloquer les salaires.

decrease[1]**,** *n.* diminution *f*/baisse *f*/décroissance *f*/amoindrissement *m*; **decrease in price,** baisse de prix; **decrease in value,** diminution de valeur/moins-value *f*; **the decrease in wheat,** la raréfaction du blé; **our imports are on the decrease,** nos importations *f* sont en baisse.

decrease[2]**,** *v.i.* diminuer/décroître/ s'amoindrir/aller en diminuant/aller en décroissant; **our imports are decreasing,** nos importations *f* diminuent/baissent.

deduct, *v.tr.* déduire/défalquer/retrancher (**from,** de); **to deduct sth. from the price,** décompter/déduire qch. du prix/rabattre qch. sur le prix; **to deduct a sum (of money),** décompter une somme; **to deduct 5% from the salaries,** faire une retenue de/ prélever 5% sur les salaires; **after deduct-**

ing ..., après déduction de .../déduction faite de ...; **to be deducted,** à déduire.

deductible, *a.* déductible; **tax deductible,** déductible de l'impôt.

deduction, *n.* décompte *m*/déduction *f*/ défalcation *f*/imputation *f* **(from a quantity,** sur une quantité); (*of pay*) retenue *f*; **after deduction of taxes,** après déduction des impôts; **fixed deduction,** déduction *f* forfaitaire; **tax deduction,** déduction fiscale; **deduction from salary/deduction at source,** retenue sur le salaire/prélèvement *m*.

deed, *n. Jur:* acte notarié sur papier timbré et signé par les parties contractantes; **deed privately executed by the parties/private deed,** acte sous seing privé; **deed of assignment,** acte attributif; acte de transfert; **to draw up a deed,** rédiger un acte; **mortgage deed,** acte hypothécaire; **title deed/deed of title,** titre (constitutif) de propriété; acte; **deed of covenant,** pacte *m*/engagement *m*; **deed of partnership,** acte constitutif/acte de société; **deed of transfer,** feuille *f* de transfert.

de facto, *Lt. phr:* de facto; de fait.

defalcation, *n. NAm:* détournement *m* de fonds.

default[1], *n.* (*a*) *Jur:* défaut *m* de comparaître (*b*) **default in paying,** défaut de paiement/non-paiement *m*; **default interest,** intérêts *mpl* pour défaut de paiement/ intérêts moratoires; **in default of payment,** à défaut de paiement.

default[2], *v.i.* ne pas faire face à ses engagements/manquer à ses engagements.

defaulter, *n.* partie défaillante/débiteur défaillant.

defeasible, *a. Jur:* révocable.

defect, *n.* défaut *m*/imperfection *f*/malfaçon *f*/défectuosité *f*/vice *m* (de construction)/tare *f*; **latent defects,** défauts/vices cachés; **manufacturing defect,** défaut de fabrication; **patent defects,** défauts/vices apparents.

defendant, *n. Jur:* défendeur, -eresse.

defensive, *a.* **defensive tactics,** techniqu *fpl*/tactiques *fpl* de défense contre-OPA

defer, *v.tr.* différer (un paiement, u échéance).

deferment, *n.* **deferment of payment,** dé *m* de paiement.

deferred, *a.* (*of share, etc.*) différé; **deferr stock,** actions différées; **deferred calls** shares, appels différés sur actions; **d ferred charges,** frais reportés/différés; **d ferred liabilities,** passif reporté; **deferr payment,** paiement différé; (*by stalments*) paiement par versements éch lonnés; **deferred results,** résultats *m* longue échéance.

deficiency, *n.* (*a*) découvert *m*; **to make a deficiency,** combler un déficit (*b*) défi budgétaire/découvert; **deficiency bil deficiency advances,** avances *f* provisoir crédits *m* budgétaires/crédits intérimair collectifs *m* budgétaires (*c*) **deficien payment,** subvention compensatrice (a agriculteurs, etc.).

deficit, *n.* déficit *m*/excédent *m* de c penses/découvert *m*; **trade deficit,** défi commercial; **budget that shows a defic budget** *m* déficitaire; **to make good/ma up the deficit,** combler le déficit.

definite, *a.* **definite order,** comman ferme.

deflate, *v.tr.* **to deflate (the currenc** amener la déflation de la monnaie; minuer la circulation fiduciaire.

deflation, *n. Fin:* déflation *f*/baisse *f* c prix.

deflationary, *a.* (politique) de désinf tion; (mesures) désinflationnistes.

defray, *v.tr. NAm:* défrayer (qn)/couv les frais (de qn).

defunct, *a.* **defunct company,** société d soute.

degearing, *n.* diminution *f*/réduction *f* ratio d'endettement; désendettement *n*

del credere, *a. & n.* **del credere (comm**

sion), (commission) ducroire *m*; del credere agent, agent *m* ducroire.

degree, *n.* degré *m* (de liquidité, etc.).

delegate[1], *n.* délégué(e).

delegate[2], *v.tr.* (*a*) déléguer qn (*b*) déléguer (des pouvoirs).

delegation, *n.* (*a*) délégation *f* (de qn) (*b*) délégation (de pouvoirs) (*c*) **to send a delegation,** envoyer une délégation; **trade delegation,** délégation commerciale.

delete, *v.tr.* **delete where inapplicable,** rayer la/les mention(s) inutile(s).

deliver, *v.tr.* livrer/délivrer (des marchandises); **delivered free,** livraison gratuite/ expédié franc de port/livraison franco; **deliver free as far as the French border,** livraison franco frontière française; **delivered on board,** rendu à bord; **goods delivered at/to any address,** livraison *f* à domicile.

delivery, *n.* (*a*) **delivery of goods,** livraison *f*/transport *m*/envoi *m*/factage *m* de marchandises; **parcels awaiting delivery,** colis *m* en souffrance; **delivery area,** réception *f* des marchandises; **delivery charges,** frais *mpl* d'expédition; **delivery office,** bureau *m* de distribution; **delivery order form,** bulletin *m* de livraison; **delivery note,** bon *m* de réception; **delivery price,** prix rendu; **delivery van,** voiture *f*/ camion *m* de livraison; **express/special delivery,** envoi *m* par exprès *m*; **recorded delivery,** envoi recommandé; **for immediate delivery,** à livrer de suite; **free delivery,** envoi livraison franco; **next day delivery,** livraison lendemain; **delivery within a month,** délai de livraison, moins d'un mois; **delivery man/boy/girl/woman,** livreur, -euse; **to pay on delivery,** payer à la livraison/livrer contre remboursement; **cash on delivery (COD),** livraison contre remboursement/payable à la livraison; **delivery date,** date *f* de livraison; **purchase for future delivery,** achat *m* à terme; **to accept/to take delivery of sth.,** prendre livraison de qch./réceptionner (des marchandises) (*b*) *Fin:* **delivery of stocks,**

cession *f*/remise *f* de titres; **to take delivery of stocks,** prendre livraison de titres; (*of stocks*) **for delivery,** au comptant; **to sell for delivery,** vendre à couvert; **sale for delivery,** vente *f* à livrer (*c*) *Jur:* tradition *f*/transfert *m* (d'un bien, d'une marchandise).

demand, *n.* 1. (*a*) demande *f*/réclamation *f*/revendication *f*/requête *f*; *Jur:* sommation *f*; **the Trade Union demands,** les revendications syndicales; **payable on demand,** payable sur demande/à vue/à bureau ouvert/à présentation; **promissory note payable on demand,** billet *m* payable à volonté/sur demande; **demand bill,** traite *f* à vue; *Fin:* **demand deposit,** dépôt *m* à vue (*b*) (*for taxes, rates*) avertissement *m*; (*for bills*) **final demand,** dernier rappel 2. demande; **supply and demand,** l'offre *f* et la demande; **the demand is slack/seasonal/keen/steady,** la demande est faible/saisonnière/forte/ stable; **to be in (great) demand,** être (très) demandé/ recherché; **to be in little demand,** être peu demandé/peu recherché.

demographic, *a.* (étude) démographique.

demography, *n.* démographie *f.*

demonetization, *n.* démonétisation *f.*

demonetize, *v.tr.* démonétiser.

demonstration, *n.* (*of apparatus*) démonstration *f* (d'un appareil); **demonstration model,** appareil *m* ayant servi aux démonstrations/appareil de démonstrations.

demonstrator, *n.* démonstrateur, -trice.

demurrage, *n.* 1. *Nau:* (*a*) surestarie(s) *f(pl)* (*b*) indemnité *f* de/pour surestaries 2. *Rail:* (*a*) magasinage *m* (*b*) droits *mpl* de magasinage 3. *Fin:* retenue *f* pour frais de fabrication (perçue sur l'or en barres versé à la Banque d'Angleterre).

denationalization, *n.* dénationalization *f.*

denationalize, *v.tr.* dénationaliser.

denomination, *n.* **coins of all denomi-**

nations, pièces *f* de toutes valeurs; **(notes of) small denominations,** petites coupures.

department, *n.* (*a*) département *m*/service *m*/branche *f*; **accounts department,** (service de) la comptabilité/services comptables; **after-sales department/ customer service department,** service après-vente; **(capital-)issue department,** service des émissions; **complaints department,** service des réclamations; **design department,** service technique/de stylique; **dispatch department,** service des expéditions; **equipment/supply department,** service du matériel/service fournisseur; **export department,** service des exportations; **head of department,** chef *m* de service; **legal department,** service du contentieux; **personnel department,** service du personnel; **sales department,** service *m* des ventes; **to solve a problem between the departments concerned,** résoudre un problème interdépartemental (*b*) (*in shop*) rayon *m*; comptoir *m*; **dress department,** rayon des robes; **department store,** grand magasin/magasin à rayons.

departmental, *a.* (*a*) départemental/qui se rapporte à un service; **departmental manager,** chef *m* de service/de rayon (*b*) **departmental store,** grand magasin/ magasin à rayons.

depauperization, *n.* développement *m.*

dependent, *n.* personne *f* à charge.

depletion, *n.* épuisement *m* (des stocks).

deposit[1], *n.* **1.** *Bank:* dépôt *m*; **bank deposit,** dépôt bancaire/en banque; **deposit bank,** banque *f* de dépôt; **deposit money,** monnaie scripturale; **minimum deposit,** acompte *m* minimum; **on deposit,** en dépôt; **deposit account,** compte *m* d'épargne; **fixed deposit/deposit for a fixed period/***NAm:* **time deposit,** dépôt à échéance fixe; argent *m* en dépôt à terme; **deposit at seven days' notice,** dépôt à sept jours de préavis; **deposit slip,** bordereau *m*/bulletin *m* de versement; **safe deposit,** dépôt en coffre-fort **2.** (*a*) *Bank:* consignation *f* (d'une somme) (*b*) (*against damages*) caution *f*/cautionnement *m*; (*for*

contract) arrhes *fpl*; (*for apartment* caution; (*for bottle*) consigne *f*; (*part pay ment*) acompte *m*; (*on bottles*) **no dep osit** = (bouteilles) non consignées; t leave/to make/to pay a deposit on sth.,** ver ser une somme/un acompte en garanti de qch.; donner des arrhes/verser un provision; **to leave £10 as (a) deposit** verser un acompte de £10 (*c*) *Fin: StExch* dépôt *m* de garantie/deposit *m.* **3.** *Pub legal deposit,** dépôt légal.

deposit[2], *v.tr.* (*a*) déposer (de l'argent à l banque); **to deposit documents with bank,** mettre des documents en dépôt dans une banque; *Publ:* **to deposit dut copies of a publication (for copyright),** dé poser des exemplaires d'un livre (= dépôt légal) (*b*) **to deposit £100,** verse £100 d'arrhes/verser £100 à titre de pro vision; *Cust:* **to deposit the duty (repay able),** cautionner les droits.

depositary, *n.* dépositaire *mf*/consigna taire *mf.*

depositor, *n.* *Bank:* déposant, -ante/épar gnant, -ante; **depositor's book,** livret n minatif.

depository, *n.* **1.** dépôt *m*/magasin *n* entrepôt *m*; **furniture depository,** garde meubles *m inv* **2.** = **depositary** *NAm:* **depository institution,** banque *f* d dépôt.

depot, *n.* dépôt *m*/entrepôt *m*; **goods depot** dépôt de marchandises/hangar *m* marchandises; **petrol storage depot,** dépô d'essence.

depreciable, *a.* *NAm:* **depreciable bas** assiette *f* de l'amortissement.

depreciate, **1.** *v.tr.* (*a*) déprécier/rabaiss (la valeur de qch.); avilir (les marcha dises); **to depreciate the franc,** déprécie dévaloriser le franc (*b*) amortir (mobilier, l'outillage, etc.) **2.** *v.i.* se dépr cier/diminuer de valeur; (*of prices, share etc.*) baisser.

depreciation, *n.* (*a*) dépréciation *f*/dév lorisation *f* (de la monnaie); dépréciatic (du matériel); moins-value *f*/décote *f* (d actions); avilissement *m* (des marchandises); **depreciation of money,** érosion *f* monétaire; **shares that show a depreciation,** actions *f* qui ont enregistré une moins-value/une baisse (de prix) (*b*) *Ind: Book-k:* **annual depreciation,** dépréciation annuelle/amortissement annuel; **depreciation allowance,** provision *f* pour amortissement; **depreciation base,** assiette *f* de l'amortissement; **depreciation rate,** taux *m* d'amortissement; **accelerated depreciation,** amortissement accéléré; **straight line depreciation,** méthode *f* de l'amortissement constant/méthode linéaire.

depress, *v.tr.* faire languir/faire végéter (le commerce); faire baisser (le prix de qch.).

depressed, *a.* (marché) languissant/déprimé/dans le marasme.

depression, *n.* crise *f*/affaissement *m*/marasme *m*/stagnation *f* (des affaires); **economic depression,** dépression *f* économique/récession *f*.

deputy, *n.* fondé *m* de pouvoir; représentant *m* (de qn); délégué *m* (d'un fonctionnaire); **to act as deputy for s.o.,** suppléer qn; **deputy chairman,** vice-président *m*; **deputy manager/manageress,** directeur adjoint/directrice adjointe; sous-directeur, -trice; **deputy managing director,** directeur général adjoint/adjoint(e) au directeur général.

deregulate, *vtr.* déréguler.

deregulation, *n.* dérégulation *f*.

description, *n.* désignation *f* (de marchandises); **Trade Descriptions Act,** loi *f* qui empêche la publicité mensongère (*b*) **job description,** description *f* d'un poste/définition *f* d'une fonction.

design, *n.* dessin *m*/type *m*/modèle *m*/motif *m*/stylique *f*/design *m*/conception *f* (d'une machine/d'un produit); **computer aided design,** conception assistée par ordinateur; **industrial design,** dessin industriel/design industriel; **product design,** conception d'un produit; **our latest design,** notre dernier modèle; **car of the**

latest design, voiture *f* dernier modèle; **The Design Centre,** Centre *m* d'exposition de modèles.

designate, *v.tr.* désigner; (*past participle*) **the president designate,** le président désigné.

designation, *n.* désignation *f* (d'une marchandise).

designer, *n.* stylicien, -ienne; *Mkt:* créatif, -ive; dessinateur, -trice; **project designer,** concepteur(-projeteur) *m*/designer *m*.

desk, *n.* **1. (office) desk,** bureau *m*; **desk pad,** sous-main *m inv*; (*note-pad*) bloc-notes *m*; **desk work,** travail *m* de bureau **2.** (*in shop*) caisse *f*; *Mkt: Publ:* rédaction *f*; *Journ:* service *m*; **pay at the desk,** payez à la caisse; (*in hotel*) **(reception) desk,** réception; *Mkt:* **desk research,** recherche *f* documentaire.

desktop, *n.* *Cmptr:* desktop publishing, publication assistée par ordinateur.

despatch, *n. & v.* = **dispatch** [1, 2].

destabilize, *vtr.* déstabiliser (le gouvernement, etc.).

destock, *v.tr. & i.* déstocker.

destocking, *n.* déstockage *m*.

detail, *n.* **for further/fuller details,** pour tous renseignements supplémentaires/pour de plus amples renseignements.

determination, *n.* **1.** détermination *f*/fixation *f* (d'une date/des prix) **2.** *Jur:* expiration *f* (d'un contrat, etc.); (*annulment*) résiliation *f* (d'un contrat).

determine, *v.tr.* **1.** déterminer/fixer (une date/des prix); **conditions to be determined,** conditions *f* à définir **2.** *Jur:* **to determine a contract/a lease,** résilier un contrat/un bail.

devaluation, *n.* dévaluation *f*.

devalue, *v.tr.* dévaluer; **the franc has been devalued,** le franc a été dévalué; **the franc**

has devalued by 3%, le franc s'est dévalué de 3%.

developing, *a.* **developing country,** pays en voie de développement.

development, *n.* (*a*) exploitation *f*/mise *f* en valeur (d'une région); aménagement *m* (d'un terrain); **development area,** zone *f* de développement/zone d'aménagement (*b*) **research and development,** recherche *f* et développement; **development expenditure,** frais *mpl* de développement.

deviation, *n.* (*a*) *MIns:* déroutement *m* (d'un navire) (*entraînant l'annulation des polices d'assurance et de la chartepartie*) (*b*) *Stat:* écart *m*; **standard deviation,** écart type.

device, *n.* dispositif *m*/système *m*/ mécanisme *m*.

diagram, *n.* schéma *m*; diagramme *m*; **flow diagram,** organigramme *m*/ordinogramme *m*; **block diagram,** schéma fonctionnel/synoptique.

diagrammatic, *a.* graphique; schématique.

dial, *v.tr. & i.* faire/composer (un numéro de téléphone); **to dial direct,** appeler/ obtenir une communication par l'automatique.

dialling, *n.* **dialling code,** indicatif *m*; **dialling tone,** tonalité *f*; **international direct dialling,** automatique *m* international; **push-button dialling**/*NAm:* **touch dialling telephone,** téléphone *m* à touches/à clavier.

diary, *n.* agenda *m*/calendrier *m*/semainier *m*; **bill diary,** carnet *m* d'échéances/ échéancier *m*; **desk diary,** bloc *m* calendrier; agenda de bureau.

Dictaphone, *n. R.t.m.* Dictaphone *m*/ appareil *m* à dicter.

dictate, *v.tr.* dicter (une lettre).

dictating, *n.* dictée *f* (d'une lettre); **dictating machine,** appareil *m* à dicter.

dictation, *n.* dictée *f.*

difference, *n.* différence *f*/écart *m* (**between,** entre); **differences in price,** écarts de prix; *StExch:* **difference between cash and settlement prices,** report *m*; **speculation in difference and contangoes,** spéculation *f* sur les différences et les reports.

differential, 1. *a.* **differential duties,** droits différentiels; **differential tariff,** tarif différentiel **2.** *n.* écart *m* (de prix, de salaires); **wage differential,** hiérarchie salariale.

diluted, *a.* **fully diluted earnings per share,** bénéfice net dilué par action.

dilution, *n.* **dilution of equity/equity dilution,** dilution *f* du bénéfice par action; **dilution of shareholding,** dilution des actions.

dilutive, *a.* **dilutive effect,** effet *m* de dilution.

dime, *n. NAm:* (pièce *f* de) dix cents *mpl*.

diminishing, *a.* décroissant; **diminishing balance,** méthode *f* de calcul de la moins value par la déduction d'une proportion fixe de la valeur totale d'un actif chaque année; amortissement proportionnel; **diminishing returns/diminishing marginal product,** rendements décroissants.

dinks, *npl.* (*abbr. of double income no kids.* F: couple *m* à deux revenus sans enfants.

dip, *v.i.* (*of shares, etc.*) baisser.

direct[1], *v.tr.* diriger/mener/gérer/régir/ administrer (une entreprise).

direct[2], *a.* **direct action,** (tentative *f* de) prise *f* de contrôle/raid *m*; **direct costing,** méthode *f* de coût *m* variable/proportionnel; **direct cost accounting,** (méthode de) comptabilité *f* des coûts variables; *Bank:* **direct debit,** prélèvement *m* (bancaire) automatique; **direct expenses/charges,** charges directes/coûts directs; **direct labour,** main-d'œuvre directe; **direct mail(ing),** publicité directe; **direct selling,** vente directe; **direct tax,** impôt direct; **direct taxation,** contribution directe.

direction, *n.* (*a*) direction *f*/administration

f (d'une société); conduite *f* (des affaires) (*b*) **directions for use,** mode *m* d'emploi.

director, *n.* directeur *m*/administrateur *m* (d'une société); **managing director,** directeur général; **chairman and managing director,** président-directeur général (P-DG); **board of directors,** conseil *m* d'administration/direction générale.

directorate, *n.* (conseil *m* d')administration *f*.

directorship, *n.* direction *f*; poste *m*/fonctions *fpl* de directeur; **during his directorship,** pendant sa direction.

directory, *n.* **commercial directory,** annuaire *m* du commerce; **street directory,** guide *m* des rues; **telephone directory,** annuaire (des téléphones);**electronic directory,** annuaire électronique.

directress, *n. NAm:* directrice *f*.

dirty, *a.* **dirty money,** argent *m* mal acquis/ de source douteuse.

disburse, *v.tr.* débourser (de l'argent).

disbursement, *n.* **1.** déboursement *m*/ versement *m*/paiement *m* **2.** *pl.* **disbursements,** déboursé *m*/frais *mpl*/débours *mpl*.

disc, *n.* **(road) tax disc,** vignette *f* (automobile).

discharge[1], *n.* **1.** (*of ship*) déchargement *m*; (*of cargo*) déchargement/débarquement *m*/débardage *m* **2.** *Jur:* **discharge in bankruptcy/order of discharge,** réhabilitation *f* (d'un failli) **3.** (*a*) paiement *m* (d'une dette) (*b*) quittance *f*/décharge *f*/libération *f*/acquit *m*; **in full discharge,** pour acquit; **final discharge,** quitus *m*.

discharge[2], *v.tr.* **1.** (*ship*) décharger; (*cargo*) décharger/débarquer **2.** *Jur:* réhabiliter/décharger (un failli); **discharged bankrupt,** failli réhabilité **3.** acquitter/ liquider/solder/payer (une dette); payer/ apurer/faire l'apurement de (un compte); **payment in full discharge of debt,** paiement *m*/versement *m* libératoire; **to discharge one's liabilities,** payer/régler ses dettes

4. to discharge an employee, renvoyer/ congédier/licencier un employé.

dischargeable, *a.* **1.** (*bankrupt*) réhabilitable **2.** (*debt*) acquittable/payable.

disclosure, *n.* (devoir *m* d')information financière; (*i*) publication *f* des comptes/ dépôts des comptes et statuts au greffe du tribunal de Commerce (*ii*) obligation *f* d'information.

discontinue, *v.tr.* arrêter/cesser (la production, etc.).

discontinued, *a.* **discontinued line,** modèle discontinué.

discount[1], *n.* **1.** remise *f*/rabais *m*/escompte *m*/ristourne *f*; **to give a discount,** faire une remise; **to sell sth. at a discount,** vendre qch. au rabais; **discount for quantities,** réduction *f* sur la quantité; **discount for cash/cash discount,** escompte (sur paiement) au comptant/escompte de caisse; **settlement discount,** ristourne/escompte; **trade discount,** remise/escompte d'usage; **additional discount,** surremise *f*; **to allow a discount of 10%/a 10% discount,** consentir un rabais de dix pour cent; **discount player,** vendeur, -euse au rabais; **discount price,** prix *m* faible **2.** *Fin:* escompte; **bank discount,** escompte en dehors; **discount market,** marché de l'escompte; **true discount,** escompte en dedans; **discount bank/ house,** banque spécialisée dans l'escompte des effets de commerce/banque d'escompte; *NAm:* **discount house,** (magasin) minimarge (*m*); **discount rate,** taux *m* d'escompte; **discount store,** magasin de discount; (*of shares*) **to be/to stand at a discount,** être en perte/accuser une perte.

discount[2], *v.tr. Fin:* escompter (un effet)/prendre (un effet) à l'escompte/ faire l'escompte de (un effet); **to discount a rise in shares,** escompter sur une hausse des valeurs; **discounted value,** valeur actualisée.

discountable, *a. Fin:* escomptable.

discounter, *n.* **1.** (*pers.*) escompteur *m* **2.** *NAm:* (= **discount store**) magasin *m* de demi-gros/magasin minimarge/centre distributeur.

discounting, n. escompte m; actualisation f; **discounting bank,** banque f/maison f d'escompte; **invoice discounting,** escompte de traites/de créances; affacturage m; **discounting banker,** banquier m escompteur.

discrepancy, n. écart m/différence f; **statistical discrepancy,** écart statistique; **there is a discrepancy in the accounts,** les comptes m ne sont pas justes.

discretionary, a. StExch: **discretionary account,** compte m avec procuration; **discretionary fund,** compte sous mandat de gestion; **discretionary order,** ordre m à appréciation.

dishonour, v.tr. **to dishonour a bill,** ne pas honorer/ne pas accepter un effet/refuser de payer un effet; **dishonoured cheque,** chèque impayé/non honoré.

disinflation, n. désinflation f.

disinflationary, a. désinflationniste.

disintermediation, n. désintermédiation f.

disinvestment, n. désinvestissement m.

disk, n. Cmptr: **hard disk,** disque dur/rigide; **floppy disk,** disquette f/disque m souple; **magnetic disk,** disque magnétique; **disk drive,** unité f de disques.

diskette, n. Cmptr: disquette f/disque m souple.

dismiss, v.tr. **to dismiss an employee,** congédier/licencier un employé; **to be dismissed,** recevoir son congé/être congédié/se faire mettre à la porte.

dismissal, n. renvoi m/congédiement m/licenciement m; **unfair dismissal/wrongful dismissal,** licenciement abusif.

dispatch[1]**,** n. expédition f/envoi m; **dispatch service/dispatch department,** service m des expéditions; **dispatch manager,** chef m du service des expéditions; **dispatch note,** bulletin m/bordereau m d'expédition;

dispatch rider, coursier, -ière (à motocyclette).

dispatch[2]**,** v.tr. **1.** expédier/envoyer/acheminer (une lettre/des marchandises); **to dispatch goods to Paris,** acheminer des marchandises sur/vers Paris **2.** expédier (une affaire).

dispatcher, n. expéditeur, -trice.

dispatching, n. expédition f/envoi m/acheminement m/répartition f/ventilation f (des marchandises/du courrier).

dispenser, n. appareil m/étui m/distributeur m; **automatic dispenser,** distributeur automatique; **cash dispenser,** distributeur (automatique) de billets (DAB)/guichet m automatique de banque (GAB)/billetterie f.

displaced, a. StExch: **displaced shares,** actions déclassées.

displacement, n. StExch: déclassement m (d'actions); déplacement m de fonds.

display[1]**,** n. étalage m/exposition f (de marchandises); **display pack,** emballage m de présentation/emballage présentoir m; **display window/display cabinet/display case,** vitrine f; **display unit/stand,** présentoir m; Cmptr: **visual display unit terminal (VDU/VDT),** visuel m.

display[2]**,** v.tr. étaler/exposer (des marchandises).

disposable, 1. a. (a) disponible; **disposable income,** surplus m/revenu m disponible; **disposable funds,** disponibilités f/valeurs disponibles (b) à jeter après usage/jetable **2.** npl. **disposables,** biens mpl de consommation non durables.

disposal, n. **1.** disposition f/cession f (onéreuse)/vente f (de biens); **for disposal,** vendre/à céder; **disposal of securities,** cession de titres **2. to have a car at one's disposal,** disposer d'une voiture.

dispose, v.i. **to dispose of goods/of an article,** écouler (des marchandises/

vendre/placer (un produit); **to dispose of one's business,** céder son fonds.

ispute, *n.* litige *m*; différend *m*; **commercial dispute,** litige commercial; **industrial dispute,** conflit *m* du travail.

issolution, *n.* dissolution *f* (d'une société, etc.).

istraint, *n. Jur:* saisie *f*.

istress, *n.* détresse *f*; misère *f*; **to be in financial distress,** être dans l'embarras financier; **distress merchandise,** vente *f* sur saisie; marchandises vendues sur saisie/en liquidation de stocks.

istressed, *a.* **distressed areas,** régions affligées par la crise économique.

istributable, *a.* **distributable profits,** bénéfices distribuables.

istribute, *v.tr.* être concessionnaire d'un produit; vendre/distribuer (un produit).

istribution, *n.* (mise *f* en) distribution *f*; répartition *f*; **distribution channels/network,** canaux *mpl*/réseau *m* de distribution; **distribution costs,** frais *mpl* de distribution/coût *m* de la distribution; **distribution manager,** chef *m* de la distribution; **distribution slip,** bordereau *m* de circulation/liste *f* de(s) destinataires; **wholesale and retail distribution,** commerce *m* de gros et de détail; *Fin:* (*in bankruptcy*) **distribution of debts,** répartition *f* des dettes.

istributor, *n.* distributeur, -trice (d'automobiles, etc.).

istrict, *n.* **district bank,** banque régionale; **district manager,** directeur régional.

isturbed, *a. StExch:* **disturbed market,** marché agité.

iversification, *n.* **product diversification,** diversification *f* des produits.

iversify, *v.tr.* **to diversify production,** diversifier la production.

ividend, *n.* dividende *m*; (*from cooperative society*) ristourne *f*; **the company has declared a dividend of 10%,** la société a

déclaré un dividende de 10%; **dividend cover,** taux *m* de couverture du dividende; **dividend on shares,** dividende d'actions; **accrued dividend,** dividende proportionnel; **final dividend,** solde *m* de dividende; **interim dividend,** dividende intérimaire; **cum dividend/***NAm:* **dividend on,** avec le dividende/coupon attaché; **ex dividend/***NAm:* **dividend off,** ex-dividende/sans intérêt; **dividend mandate,** ordonnance *f* de paiement; **dividend warrant,** chèque-dividende *m*/coupon d'arrérages; **dividend yield,** taux de rendement (en dividendes).

dock, *n.* bassin *m* (d'un port); (*wharf*) **loading dock,** embarcadère *m*; **unloading dock,** débarcadère *m*; **the docks,** les docks *m*.

docker, *n.* docker *m*/débardeur *m*.

docket, *n.* (*a*) étiquette *f*/fiche *f* (*b*) bordereau *m* (de livraison, etc.) (*c*) récépissé *m* (de douane).

dockyard, *n.* chantier *m* maritime/naval.

document, *n.* document *m*/pièce *f*/titre *m*/ papier *m*; **legal document,** acte *m* authentique; acte notarié; **commercial documents,** papiers d'affaires; **working document,** document de travail.

documentary, *a.* documentaire; **documentary bill,** traite *f* documentaire; traite accompagnée de documents; **documentary credit,** crédit *m* documentaire.

dogsbody, *n. Pej:* factotum *m*.

dole, *n.* **dole (money),** allocation *f*/ indemnité *f* de chômage; **to be/to go on the dole,** être/s'inscrire au chômage.

dollar, *n.* dollar (américain/canadien/ australien/malais/etc.); **a five dollar note/** *NAm:* **bill,** un billet de cinq dollars; **dollar area,** zone *f* dollar; **dollar balances,** balances *f* dollar; **dollar crisis,** crise *f* du dollar; **dollar premium,** prime *f* sur le dollar.

domestic, *a.* (commerce) intérieur; **domestic credit expansion (DCE),** croissance *f* de la masse monétaire; **domestic produc-**

tion, production nationale; **domestic products,** denrées *f* du pays.

domicile[1], *n.* domicile *m.*

domicile[2], *v.tr.* domicilier (un effet); **bills domiciled in France,** traites *f* payables/compensables en France.

domiciliation, *n.* domiciliation *f* (d'un effet).

donation, *n. Jur:* donation *f.*

donee, *n. Jur:* donataire *mf.*

donor, *n. Jur:* donateur, -trice.

door-to-door, *a.* **door-to-door transport/canvassing/selling,** porte-à-porte *m;* **to be a door-to-door salesman,** être placier *m*/être démarcheur *m*/faire du porte-à-porte.

double, *a.* **double bottom,** cours *m* qui touche/qui retrouve son plus bas; **double top,** cours qui touche/qui retrouve son plus haut.

down, *a.* **down payment,** acompte *m;* versement *m* à la commande/versement initial.

downgrade, *vtr.* attribuer une classification inférieure à (une valeur, etc.).

downside, *n.* mise *f* (en jeu); perte maximale; engagement *m.*

downstream, *adv. & a. (of company)* en aval.

downturn, *n.* repli *m*/régression *f;* désescalade *f.*

downward, *a.* **downward trend (of prices),** tendance *f* à la baisse.

draft[1], *n.* (*a*) tirage *m* (d'un effet) (*b*) traite *f*/lettre *f* de change/mandat *m*/disposition *f*/effet *m;* bon *m* (sur une banque); **bank draft,** chèque *m* de banque; **banker's draft,** traite *f;* **time draft,** traite/effet à terme; **to make a draft on s.o.,** faire traite/tirer sur qn (*c*) **draft of a contract/draft contract,** projet *m* de contrat; **draft agreement,** projet de convention.

draft[2], *v.tr.* rédiger (un acte/un projet); **to**

draft a letter, faire le brouillon d'une lettr **to draft a contract,** préparer/faire le proj d'un contrat.

drafter, *n.* rédacteur, -trice (d'un act etc.).

drafting, *n.* rédaction *f* (d'un acte, etc.)

drain, *n.* **drain of money,** drainage *m* capitaux; **drain on the resources,** cause d'épuisement des ressources; **the bra drain,** la fuite des cerveaux.

draughtsman, -woman, *n.* dessinateu -trice industriel, -elle.

draw, *v.tr.* (*a*) **to draw a commission,** p lever/demander une commission (*b*) **draw money from the bank/from account,** retirer de l'argent de la banqu d'un compte; **to draw one's salary,** touch son salaire (*c*) **to draw (a cheque) on bank,** tirer un chèque sur une banq fournir sur une banque; **to draw thr months' bill on London,** fournir à 3 m sur Londres (*d*) **money drawing intere** argent *m* qui produit des intérêts.

drawback, *n. Cust:* drawback *m*/rembo sement *m* à l'exportation des dro d'entrée.

drawee, *n.* tiré *m* (d'une lettre de chang

drawer, *n.* tireur *m* (d'une lettre change); **to refer a cheque to drawer,** re ser d'honorer un chèque.

drawing, *n.* (*a*) *NAm:* prélèvement retrait *m* (d'une somme d'argent de banque) (*b*) traite *f* (de chèques, d'effe **drawing on s.o.,** disposition *f* sur **drawing account,** compte courant/com de dépôt à vue; *NAm:* **Special Draw Rights (SDR),** droits de tirage spéciau

draw up, *v.tr.* établir/dresser/rédiger (bilan).

dress up, *v.tr. NAm:* **the accounts w dressed up,** les comptes avaient été fa fiés.

drift, *n.* tendance *f* à la hausse (des p des salaires).

drive, *n.* campagne *f;* **economy drive, p**

gramme m/effort m de réduction des coûts/ des charges; **sales drive,** campagne de vente.

drop[1], *n.* **1.** chute *f*/baisse *f*/abaissement *m*; **drop in prices,** chute/baisse de prix; **heavy drop in cottons,** débâcle *f* des cotons; **sales show a drop of 10%,** les ventes *f* accusent une régression/enregistrent une baisse de 10%; *Fin:* **drop in value/in takings,** moins-value *f* **2.** *F:* livraison *f*; **I have four drops to make,** j'ai quatre livraisons à faire.

drop[2], *v.i.* (*of prices*) baisser; *Fin:* **receipts have dropped,** les recettes *f* ont baissé/ accusent une moins-value; *StExch:* **shares dropped a point,** les actions *f* ont reculé d'un point; **the pound dropped 10% against the dollar,** la livre a baissé de 10% contre le dollar.

drop dead fee,*n.* commission *f* de désinté-ressement.

drop dead rate,*n.* taux *m*/cours *m* de dé-sintéressement.

drug, *n.* (*a*) drogue *f* (*b*) produit phar-maceutique (*c*) **drug on the market,** article *m* invendable/marchandise *f* invendable.

drugstore, *n. NAm:* pharmacie *f*/ drug-store *m*.

dry, *a.* (*a*) **dry money,** argent sec (*b*) **dry goods,** marchandises sèches; *NAm:* articles *m* de nouveauté; étoffes *f*/tissus *m*; mercerie *f*; *NAm:* **dry goods store,** ma-gasin *m* de nouveautés; *Nau:* **dry cargo,** cargaison sèche (*c*) **dry hole,** puits *m* de pé-trole stérile; *Fin:* opération *f* à rendement insuffisant.

dud, *F:* **1.** *a.* (*a*) **dud stock,** marchandises *f* invendables; rossignols *mpl* (*b*) **dud cheque,** chèque *m* sans provision/*F:* chèque en bois; **dud note,** faux billet de banque **2.** *n.* **the note was a dud,** le billet était faux.

due, *a.* **1.** (*of debt*) exigible; **not due,** inexi-gible; **bill due on 1st May,** effet *m* payable le premier mai; **contributions still due,** cotisations *f* à percevoir; **balance due (to us),** solde créditeur; **balance due (by us),** solde débiteur; **debts due to us/to the firm,** dettes actives/créances *f*; **debts due by us/by the firm,** dettes passives; **amounts due within one year,** échéances *f* à moins d'un an; **sums due from banks,** créances sur les banques; **bond due for repayment,** obligation amortie; *NAm:* **due bill,** reconnaissance *f* de dette; **to fall/become due,** échoir/arriver à échéance/venir à échéance; **past due,** en souffrance; **when due,** à l'échéance; **due date,** (date d')éché-ance/(date d')exigibilité *f*; **average due date,** échéance moyenne; **redemption before due date,** remboursement/amortissement anticipé **2. in due form,** dans les formes voulues/en bonne forme/en règle/dans les règles; **contract drawn up in due form,** contrat rédigé en bonne et due forme; **re-ceipt in due form,** quittance régulière **3.** *n.* commande notée.

due-date, *v.tr.* coter (un effet).

dues, *n.pl.* droits *m*/frais *mpl*; **taxes and dues,** impôts *m* et taxes *f*; **market dues,** hallage *m*; **port dues,** droits de port.

dull, *a.* (marché) calme/inactif/lourd/plat/ inanimé/languissant; **the dull season,** la morte-saison; **business is dull,** les affaires *f* languissent/le marché est calme.

dul(l)ness,*n.* stagnation *f*/marasme *m* (des affaires); inactivité *f*/inaction *f*/peu d'ac-tivité (du marché).

duly, *adv.* **1.** dûment; **duly authorized rep-resentative,** représentant dûment accré-dité; **I duly received your letter of ...,** j'ai bien reçu votre lettre du ... **2.** en temps voulu/en temps utile; **I duly sent it back,** je l'ai renvoyé en temps voulu.

dummy, *a. & n.* (*of pers.*) mannequin *m*; (*of book, etc.*) maquette *f*; **dummy (pack),** em-ballage *m* factice; **dummy box,** boîte *f* factice; **dummy company,** société *f* prête-nom.

dump, *v.tr.* **to dump goods on a foreign market,** écouler à perte des marchandises à l'étranger/faire du dumping.

dump bin, *n. Mkt:* panier *m* (présentoir).

dumper, *n.* **1.** commerçant *m* (*esp.* exportateur *m*) qui fait du dumping **2. dumper truck,** camion *m* à benne.

dumping, *n.* dumping *m*/délestage *m*; vente *f* à perte; prix *m* de bataille; **panic dumping,** délestage de panique.

duopoly, *n.* duopole *m.*

duopsony, *n.* marché *m* duopsone.

duplicate[1], *a.* double/en double; **duplicate receipt,** duplicata *m* d'un reçu.

duplicate[2], *n.* duplicata *m*/double *m*/ contrepartie *f* (d'un écrit); **in duplicate,** (en) double/en duplicata/en double exemplaire; **to draw a bill of exchange in duplicate,** tirer une lettre de change en duplicata.

duplicate[3], **1.** *v.i. Book-k:* (*of entry*) **to duplicate with another,** faire double emploi avec un autre **2.** *v.tr.* **to duplicate a circular letter,** reproduire/tirer une lettre circulaire à plusieurs exemplaires (au duplicateur)/polycopier une lettre circulaire.

duplicating, *n.* **1.** répétition *f*; **duplicating book,** manifold *m* **2.** reproduction *f*/ tirage *m* à plusieurs exemplaires (au duplicateur); **duplicating machine,** duplicateur *m*/machine *f* à polycopier; **duplicating paper,** papier *m* pour duplicateurs.

duplication, *n.* répétition *f*/reproductio *f*; *Book-k:* double emploi *m* (d'une écr ture).

duplicator, *n.* duplicateur *m*/machine *f* polycopier.

durable, **1.** *a.* durable; **durable good** biens permanents/biens durables; bien produits *m* d'usage **2.** *n.* **(consumer) du ables,** biens de consommation durables.

duration, *n.* **duration of a lease,** durée d'un bail.

dutiable, *a.* soumis à des droits; passib de droits/imposable/taxable; *Cus* soumis aux droits de douane/*F:* décla rable.

duty, *n.* droit *m*; **customs duty,** droit c douane; **import duty,** droit d'entré estate/death duties, droits de succession **liable to duty,** passible de droits; soum aux droits; **duty on silk,** droits d'entrée s les soieries; **duty-paid goods,** marcha dises acquittées/dédouanées; **to take tl duty off goods,** exonérer des marchan dises; **stamp duty,** droit de timbre.

duty-free, *a.* exempt de droit/franc de to droit; (importé) en franchise de douan **duty-free shop,** boutique franche/magas *m* hors taxe; **duty-free goods,** marchan dises *f* hors taxe.

E

arly, *a.* **1. early closing day,** jour *m* de fermeture des magasins l'après-midi **2. at an early date,** prochainement/à une date prochaine; **at your earliest convenience,** le plus tôt (qu'il vous sera) possible/dès que possible/dans les meilleurs délais.

armark, *v.tr.* **to earmark funds for a purpose,** assigner/affecter une somme à un projet.

arn, *v.tr.* gagner (de l'argent); **to earn interest,** rapporter des intérêts; **to earn one's living by writing,** gagner sa vie en écrivant.

arned, *a.* **earned income,** revenus salariaux; revenus professionnels; *NAm:* **earned surplus,** profits *mpl* excédentaires.

arner, *n.* **the biggest profit earner,** la plus grande source de profit(s).

arnest, *a. NAm:* **earnest money,** (*deposit*) arrhes *fpl*; dépôt *m* de garantie; (*margin on futures market*) marge *f* de garantie.

arning, *a.* profitable/qui rapporte/lucratif; **earning capacity,** capacité *f* bénéficiaire; profitabilité *f*/rentabilité *f*; **earning power,** productivité financière; **earning potential,** capacité bénéficiaire.

arnings, *n.pl.* **1.** salaire *m*; rémunération *f*; appointements *mpl*; **loss of earnings,** perte *f* de salaire **2.** profits *m*/bénéfices *m*/gains *m*/revenus *mpl* (d'une entreprise); bénéfices financiers; **earnings per share (EPS),** bénéfice/gain par action; **earnings growth,** accroissement *m*/augmentation *f* des bénéfices; **earnings performance,** rentabilité *f*; **gross earnings,** bénéfices bruts/recettes brutes; **invisible earnings,** revenus *m* invisibles; **price earnings ratio (PER),** rapport *m* cours-bénéfices; taux *m* de capitalisation des bénéfices/price

earnings ratio; **retained earnings,** bénéfices non distribués.

earn-out, *n.* plan *m* de participation des salariés aux fruits de l'expansion.

easement, *n. Jur:* servitude *f*; **affirmative/negative easement,** servitude active/passive.

easy, *a.* **1. by easy payments/on easy terms,** avec facilités *f* de paiement **2. easy market,** marché *m* tranquille/calme; **share prices are easier today,** le prix des actions fléchit **3. easy money,** argent *m* à bon marché; facilités *fpl* d'escompte.

echelon, *n.* **the higher echelons of industry,** les niveaux/les échelons supérieurs de l'industrie.

econometrics, *n.* économétrie *f*.

economic, *a.* (*a*) qui se rapporte à l'économie politique; (problème, situation) économique; **economic climate,** climat *m* économique; **economic crisis,** crise *f* économique; **economic development,** croissance *f* par habitant/per capita; **economic growth,** croissance *f* économique; **economic lot size (ELS),** quantité *f* économique à commander/quantité économique de réapprovisionnement; **economic policy,** politique *f*/système *m* économique; **economic prospects,** prévisions conjoncturelles/économiques; **economic sanctions,** sanctions *f* économiques; **economic situation,** conjoncture *f* économique; **economic strategy,** stratégie conjoncturelle; **economic trend(s),** évolution *f*/conjoncture économique; tendances conjoncturelles; **European Economic Community (EEC),** Communauté économique européenne (CEE) (*b*) **economic**

proposition, affaire *f* rentable; **economic rent,** loyer *m* bon marché.

economical, *a.* économique; **economical car,** voiture *f* économique.

economics, *n.pl.* (*usu. with sg. const.*). **1.** science *f* économique/économie *f* politique; **welfare economics,** l'économie du bien-être **2.** rentabilité *f* (d'un projet); **the economics of town planning,** les aspects financiers de l'urbanisme.

economist, *n.* **(political) economist,** économiste *m*; **agricultural economist,** agronome *m*.

economize, **1.** *v.i.* **to economize on food,** économiser/faire des économies sur la nourriture **2.** *v.tr.* **to economize £500 on rent,** économiser £500 sur le prix du loyer.

economy, *n.* **1.** économie *f* (d'argent, de temps, etc.); **to practise economy/ economies,** économiser; **economy of scale,** économie d'échelle/de dimension; *Aut:* **economy run,** concours *m* de consommation; *Av:* **economy class,** classe *f* touriste **2.** (*a*) **capitalist economy,** économie capitaliste/libérale; **controlled economy,** économie dirigée; **domestic economy,** économie interne; **free market economy,** économie de marché; **mixed economy,** économie mixte; **natural economy,** économie de troc/non monétaire; **open/closed economy,** économie ouverte/fermée; **planned economy,** économie planifiée; **political economy,** économie politique; **service economy,** (rendement total du) secteur *m* tertiaire/secteur des services; économie à dominante de services; **share economy,** capitalisation boursière du pays; économie d'actionnariat populaire/ économie de participation; **sleeping economy,** économie à ressources sous-exploitées/à fort potentiel de croissance inexploité; **socialist commodity economy,** économie socialiste à propriété collective des moyens de production; **underground economy,** marché *m* parallèle; **wage economy,** revenu national/économie salariale (*b*) **to disturb the economy of the country,** déranger l'économie/le régime économique du pays.

econospeak, *n.* jargon *m* économique.

edge, *n.* **competitive edge,** avance concurrentielle/sur les concurrents.

effect¹, *n.* **1.** (*a*) effet *m*/action *f*/influence résultat *m*/conséquence *f* (d'un fait) (*of regulation, etc.*) **to take effect/to com into effect,** entrer en vigueur; **to take effe on/with effect from January 1st,** applicable à compter du/qui entre en vigueu le 1er janvier; **to remain in effect,** demeur en vigueur/être toujours en vigueur (sens *m*/teneur *f* (d'un document); **with proviso to the effect that ...,** avec u clause conditionnelle portant q ...,/dont la teneur est que ...; **we ha made provisions to this effect,** nous avo pris des dispositions dans ce sens **2.** *p* (**personal) effects,** effets/biens personnel *Jur:* **movable effects,** biens meubles/effe mobiliers; *Bank:* **no effects,** pas de pr vision/défaut *m* de provision.

effect², *v.tr.* effectuer/accomplir/opére réaliser/exécuter (qch.); **to effect a pa ment,** effectuer un paiement; **to effe customs clearance,** procéder aux forma tés douanières; **to effect a settleme between two parties,** arriver à un acco entre deux parties/réussir à mettre l deux parties d'accord; *Book-k:* **to effect corresponding entry,** passer une écritu conforme.

effective, *a.* (*a*) (*output, productio* effectif; *PolEc:* **effective demand,** d mande effective; **effective managemen** direction *f*/gestion *f* efficace; **effecti rate,** taux effectif; **effective yield,** rend ment effectif; *Fin:* **effective money,** mo naie effective/réelle (*b*) *Adm:* **effecti date,** date *f* d'entrée en vigueur; **effecti on/as from October 10th,** applicable partir du 10 octobre/qui entre en vigue le 10 octobre.

effectiveness, *n.* efficacité *f*; **cost effe tiveness,** coût-efficacité *m*.

effectual, *a.* (*contract*) valide; (*regulatic rule*) en vigueur.

efficiency, *n.* **1.** (*a*) efficacité *f* (du travail, etc.); performances *fpl* (d'une administration); **with a high degree of efficiency,** exceptionnellement performant; **absolute efficiency,** efficience absolue/efficacité parfaite; **economic efficiency,** efficience *f*/efficacité économique; **relative efficiency,** efficience/efficacité relative; **technical efficiency,** efficacité technique (*b*) productivité *f*/haut rendement *m* (d'une machine); (*in chain production*) **motion efficiency,** rendement du geste; **efficiency expert,** expert *m* en organisation/en rendement **2.** (*of pers.*) compétence *f*/capacité *f*; valeur professionnelle (de la main-d'œuvre); *Ind:* **efficiency wages,** salaire proportionné à la production/basé sur le rendement.

efficient, *a.* (*a*) (*method, work*) efficace; (*organization*) efficace/performant; **efficient working (of apparatus),** bon fonctionnement (d'un appareil); **efficient machine,** machine *f* à haut rendement/performante (*c*) (*pers.*) capable/compétent/efficace.

efficiently, *adv.* **1.** efficacement **2.** avec compétence.

efflux, *n. PolEc:* **efflux of capital,** exode *m* de capitaux; **efflux of gold,** sortie *f* d'or.

elastic, *a. PolEc:* (offre, demande) élastique.

elasticity, *n. PolEc:* **the elasticity of supply and demand,** l'élasticité *f* de l'offre et de la demande.

electronic, *a.* électronique; **electronic banking,** paiement *m* électronique; **electronic computer,** calculateur *m* électronique; **electronic data processing (EDP),** traitement *m* électronique de l'information (TEI); **the EDP industry,** l'industrie *f* de l'informatique; **electronic funds transfer (EFT),** transfert *m* électronique de fonds; **electronic point of sale (EPS),** point *m* de vente électronique/terminal *m* de paiement/caisse *f* électronique; **electronic funds transfer at point of sale (EFTPOS),** transfert électronique de fonds au point de vente.

electronics, *n.pl.* (*usu. with sg. const.*) électronique *f*; **electronics industry,** industrie *f* électronique; **electronics engineer,** electronicien, -ienne.

elephant, *n. F:* (*large corporate entity*) dinausore *m*.

email, *n.* (*abbr.* **electronic mail**) messagerie *f* (électronique).

embargo[1], *n.* embargo *m*; séquestre *m*; *Nau:* saisie *f*; **to lay an embargo on a ship,** mettre l'embargo sur un navire/saisir un navire; (*of ship, goods*) **to be under an embargo,** être séquestré; **to put/to impose an embargo on the import of horses,** mettre un embargo sur/défendre l'importation des chevaux; **to lift/to remove an embargo,** lever un embargo.

embargo[2], *v.tr.* mettre l'embargo sur/séquestrer (un navire, des marchandises).

embark, *v.tr.* (*of ship*) prendre à bord (des marchandises, etc.).

embarkation, *n.* embarquement *m*; **port of embarkation,** port *m* d'embarquement.

embezzle, **1.** *v.tr.* détourner/distraire/s'approprier (des fonds) **2.** *v.i.* commettre des détournements (de fonds).

embezzlement, *n.* malversation *f*; détournement *m* de fonds.

embezzler, *n.* auteur *m* d'un détournement de fonds/d'une malversation.

emergency, *n.* situation *f* critique/nécessité urgente/cas urgent/crise *f*; imprévu *m*; **emergency fund,** fonds *m* de secours.

emerging, *a.* **emerging market,** marché émergent.

emoluments, *n.pl.* appointements *mpl*/traitement *m*/rémunération *f*/émoluments *mpl*.

employ, *v.tr.* (*a*) employer (qn) à son service; **to employ twenty workmen,** employer vingt ouvriers (*b*) (*only of new staff*) embaucher.

employed, **1.** *a.* employé; **to be fully em-**

ployed, travailler à plein temps; **gainfully employed,** rémunéré; **the gainfully employed population,** la population active; **capital employed,** capital investi **2.** *n.* **employers and employed,** le patronat et le salariat/les patrons et les ouvriers.

employee, *n.* employé(e); **the employees of a firm,** le personnel d'une maison; **relations between management and employees,** relations *f* entre la direction et le personnel; **to take on employees,** engager/recruter du personnel; embaucher de la main-d'œuvre.

employer, *n.* employeur, -euse/patron, -onne/chef *m* d'entreprise; **the big employers of labour,** les grands employeurs de main-d'œuvre; **(body of) employers,** patronat *m*; **organization of employers/employers' association,** organisation patronale/syndicat patronal; **chamber of employers,** chambre patronale; **employers' liability insurance,** assurance *f* des patrons contre les accidents du travail; assurance réparation; **employer's contribution,** cotisation patronale.

employment, *n.* **1.** (*use*) emploi *m* (de l'argent, etc.) **2.** (*occupation*) emploi/travail *m*/place *f*/situation *f*/occupation *f*; *PolEc:* **full employment,** plein emploi/plein-emploi *m*; **full-time employment,** travail à plein temps; **part-time employment,** travail à mi-temps/travail à temps partiel; **temporary employment,** travail temporaire; **to be without employment,** être sans emploi/sans travail/au chômage; **to find alternative employment for an employee,** transférer un(e) employé(e)/placer un(e) employé(e) ailleurs; **to give s.o. employment,** donner un emploi à qn; **to seek employment,** chercher un emploi/de l'emploi; **employment bureau/employment agency/employment office,** bureau *m*/agence *f* de placement; (*for workmen*) service *m* d'embauche/de la main-d'œuvre; **employment exchange/** *NAm:* **employment bureau** = agence nationale pour l'emploi (ANPE); **employment tax,** taxe *f* sur l'emploi; **conditions of employment,** conditions *f* d'em-

bauche; **security of employment/guaranteed employment,** sécurité *f* d l'emploi.

emporium, *n.* **1.** entrepôt *m*; centre *m* c commerce; marché *m* **2.** grand magasin

empties, *n.pl.* emballages *mpl* vides; caisses *f*/bouteilles *f* vides; **returne empties,** emballages retournés vide **empties are not returnable,** on ne repren pas les bouteilles vides.

emption, *n. Jur:* achat *m*; **right of emptio** droit *m* d'emption/droit d'achat.

emptor, *n.* acheteur, -euse.

encash, *v.tr.* encaisser/toucher (u chèque); **when encashed,** après encaiss ment.

encashable, *a.* encaissable.

encashment, *n.* **1.** encaissement *m* **2.** r cette *f*/rentrée *f*.

enclose, *v.tr.* **to enclose sth. in a letter,** joi dre qch. à une lettre; **letter enclosing cheque,** lettre *f* contenant un chèqu **enclosed herewith,** sous ce pli; **please fin enclosed ...,** veuillez trouver ci-joir sous ce pli ....

enclosure, *n.* pièce jointe; document c joint/annexe; **enclosures,** pièces joint (PJ).

encumbrance, *n.* servitude *f*; **free from a encumbrance,** sans servitudes ni hypoth ques.

end¹, *n.* bout *m*/fin *f* (du mois, etc.); fi (d'une réunion); terme *m* (d'un procè etc.); **to come to an end,** prendre fin; arr ver à son terme; **at the end of the month/** **the year,** à la fin du mois/de l'année; **the end of the six months allowed,** au bo des six mois; *NAm:* **end price,** prix c détail; **end product,** produit/article fin **end user,** consommateur, -trice.

end², **1.** *v.tr.* finir/terminer/achever; co clure (un discours); clore/clôturer (un séance) **2.** *v.i.* finir/se terminer (at/i dans/en); **your subscription ends on M**

31st, votre abonnement *m* expire le 31 mai.

endorse, *v.tr.* endosser (un chèque); **to endorse a bill,** avaliser/endosser/donner son aval *m* à un effet; **to endorse a project,** approuver/sanctionner/appuyer un projet; **to endorse a bill of exchange,** endosser une lettre de change; **to endorse over a bill to s.o.,** transmettre par voie d'endossement une lettre de change à qn; **to endorse back a bill to drawer,** contrepasser un effet au tireur; **endorsed driving licence,** permis *m* de conduire portant la mention d'une infraction.

endorsee, *n. Fin:* endossataire *mf*/bénéficiaire *mf* (d'un billet par endos); tiers porteur d'un chèque.

endorsement, *n.* (*a*) *Fin: etc:* endossement *m*/endos *m* (d'un chèque, d'une lettre de change); aval *m* (d'un effet); **blank endorsement,** cheque *m* en blanc endossé; **facultative endorsement,** = levée *f* (*b*) *Ins:* avenant *m*.

endorser, *n. Fin:* endosseur, -euse/cessionnaire *m* (d'un chèque, etc.); avaliste *m*/avaliseur *m* (d'un effet); **second endorser (of bill),** tiers porteur *m*.

endowment, *n. Ins:* **(pure) endowment assurance/endowment policy,** assurance *f* en cas de vie; assurance à capital différé/à terme fixe/à dotation; **combined endowment and whole-life insurance,** assurance en cas de vie et de décès; **(ordinary) endowment assurance,** assurance à capital différé; **endowment mortgage,** prêt-logement lié à une assurance en cas de vie.

energetics, *n.* énergétique *f*.

energy, *n.* énergie *f*; **energy consumption bill,** facture *f* énergétique.

engage, *v.tr. & i.* (*a*) **I am engaged, I can't come,** je ne peux pas venir, je suis pris(e) (*b*) *Tel:* **the number is engaged,** la ligne est occupée.

engagement, *n.* **1.** engagement *m* **2.** rendez-vous; **I have an engagement,** je suis pris(e).

engineer, *n.* (*a*) ingénieur *m*; **civil engineer,** ingénieur des travaux publics; (*government employee*) = ingénieur des ponts et chaussées (*b*) **consulting engineer,** ingénieur conseil; **knowledge engineer,** cognoticien, -ienne; **management/ industrial engineer,** ingénieur en organisation/d'exploitation/des méthodes; **project/design engineer,** ingénieur d'études; **planning/work-study engineer,** ingénieur de planification/en organisation; **programming engineer,** ingénieur programmeur/de programmation; **product engineer,** (*profession*) ingénieur de produit; (*job title, in firm*) ingénieur du produit; **production engineer,** ingénieur (chargé) de la production; **process development engineer,** (ingénieur-/technicien-)gammiste *m*; **sales engineer,** ingénieur commercial/chef *m* du service des ventes; **technical sales engineer,** ingénieur technico-commercial.

engineering, *n.* ingénierie *f*; **(civil) engineering,** génie civil; les travaux publics; **financial engineering,** ingénierie financière; **food engineering,** génie alimentaire; **human engineering,** ergonomie *f*; **industrial engineering,** organisation industrielle; **management engineering,** organisation de la gestion des entreprises; **product engineering,** ingénierie du produit; **production engineering,** technique *f* de la production; **methods engineering/process engineering,** étude *f* des méthodes (industrielles); **engineering company/firm,** compagnie *f* d'ingénieurs-conseils; **engineering department,** service *m* technique; **engineering and design department,** bureau *m* d'études; **engineering consultant,** ingénieur-conseil *m*.

enquiry, *n. see* **inquiry.**

enter, 1. *v.tr.* (*a*) *Cust:* **to enter goods,** déclarer des marchandises en douane; **to enter a ship (inwards, outwards),** faire la déclaration (d'entrée, de sortie) (*b*) comptabiliser (une dépense, etc.); **to enter (sth. in the accounts),** comptabiliser (un montant); **to enter (up) an item in the ledger,** inscrire/porter un article au grand(-)livre; passer une écriture; **to enter**

(up) an amount in the profits, employer une somme en recette **2.** *v.i.* (*a*) **to enter into relations with s.o.,** entrer en relations avec qn/entamer des relations avec qn; **to enter into negotiations with s.o.,** engager des négociations avec qn; **to enter into partnership with s.o.,** s'associer à/avec qn; **to enter into a bargain/an agreement/a contract,** conclure un marché/un accord; passer un contrat (**with,** avec) (*b*) *Jur:* **to enter into the rights of a creditor,** demeurer subrogé aux droits d'un créancier.

entering, *n.* **entering (up),** inscription *f*/ enregistrement *m*/comptabilisation *f*; **entering clerk,** commis *m* aux écritures.

enterprise, *n.* entreprise *f*; **free enterprise,** la libre entreprise; **private enterprise,** l'entreprise privée/le secteur privé; **state enterprise,** le secteur public; **small-scale enterprise,** entreprise artisanale; **Enterprise Allowance Scheme (EAS),** Fonds d'aide à la création d'entreprise; **enterprise zone,** zone *f*/pole *m* de développement d'entreprises; (zone de) pépinière *f* d'entreprise; zone franche.

enterpriser, *n.* entrepreneur *m*.

entertainment, *n.* **entertainment allowance,** indemnité *f* de fonction; **entertainment expenses,** frais *mpl* de représentation.

entitled, *a.* **to be entitled to (sth.),** avoir droit à qch; **those entitled (to a benefit),** les ayants droit (à une prestation); **entitled to represent the firm,** habilité à représenter la société.

entitlement, *n.* (*on forms*) montant auquel on a droit; ce qui revient de droit; **holiday entitlement,** congé annuel.

entity, *n.* entité *f*; **legal entity,** personne morale.

entrepôt, *n.* entrepôt *m*; **entrepôt port,** port franc.

entrepreneur, *n.* entrepreneur *m*; *NAm:* créateur *m* d'entreprise.

entrepreneurial, *a.* (activités, décision) d'entrepreneur; **entrepreneurial veteran,** entrepreneur chevronné; **entrepreneuria virgin,** entrepreneur débutant.

entry, *n.* **1.** (*appearance of a company on market*) entrée *f*/pénétration *f* d'un marché; **entry and exit,** taux *m* de renou vellement **2.** *Book-k:* (*a*) passation d'écriture/inscription *f* (dans un livre de commerce); **single-entry bookkeeping** comptabilité *f* à/en partie simple; **double entry bookkeeping,** comptabilité à/en partie double (*b*) article *m*/écriture *f*; to contra an entry,** contre-passer une écri ture; **to make an entry,** passer une écri ture; **to make an entry of a transaction** passer une transaction en écriture; to make an entry against s.o.,** débiter qn **compound entry,** article composé collectif/récapitulatif; **contra entry,** con trepassation *f*/contre-passement *m*; **pos entry,** écriture postérieure/subséquente **wrong entry,** faux emploi **3.** *Cust:* **custom house entry/customs entry,** passage *m* e douane; **to pass a customs entry of manu factured goods,** faire une déclaration e douane de produits manufacturés; t make an entry of goods,** déclarer de marchandises à la douane; **(bill of) entr entry inwards,** déclaration *f* d'entrée (e douane); **entry under bond,** acquit-à caution *m*; **post entry,** déclaration add tionnelle **4. entry form,** feuille d'inscription.

envelope, *n.* enveloppe *f*; **apertur envelope,** enveloppe à panneau découpé fenêtre découpée; **adhesive envelope,** env loppe gommée; **airmail envelope,** env lope avion; **buff/brown envelop** enveloppe bulle; **manil(l)a envelop** enveloppe kraft; **envelope with met fastener,** pochette *f*; **window envelop panel envelope,** enveloppe à fenêtre; **to p a letter in an envelope,** mettre une lett sous enveloppe; **in a sealed envelope,** so pli cacheté; **envelope file,** chemise *f* (c carton); **stamped addressed envelo (s.a.e),** enveloppe timbrée à votre adress

environment, *n.* environnement *m* (éc nomique).

environmental, *a.* **environmental econ mics,** économie *f* de l'environnement.

equal, *a.* égal; paritaire; **equal pay for equal work,** à travail égal, salaire égal; **equal opportunity organization,** organisation où les emplois sont ouverts à tous sans distinction ni discrimination.

equalization, *n.* **1.** *Fin:* régularisation *f* (de dividendes); *Adm:* péréquation *f* (de contributions, de traitements) **2.** *Fin:* **exchange equalization account,** fonds *m* de stabilisation des changes.

equalize, *v.tr.* **to equalize wages,** faire la péréquation des salaires; **to equalize dividends,** régulariser les dividendes.

equalizing, *n.* péréquation *f* (des prix, des salaires).

equation, *n.* **equation of payments,** échéance commune (de billets de change).

equilibrium, *n.* équilibre *m*; **equilibrium price,** prix *m* d'équilibre.

equip, *v.tr.* outiller/équiper (une usine); **to equip a workman with tools,** outiller un ouvrier; **to equip a works with new plant,** équiper une usine d'un matériel neuf.

equipment, *n.* matériel *m*/équipement *m*; machines *fpl*; outillage *m* (d'une usine); **heavy equipment,** matériel lourd; **equipment leasing,** crédit–bail mobilier; **capital equipment,** biens *m* d'équipement/biens durables; capitaux *m* fixes; **machinery and equipment,** matériel et outillage; **technical equipment,** capital *m* technique.

equity, *n.* **1.** *Jur:* droit *m* (équitable); **equity of redemption,** droit de rachat, après forclusion, d'un bien hypothéqué **2.** **equity (capital),** capital-actions *m*; **shareholders'/stockholders' equity,** capitaux *mpl*/fonds *m* propres; avoir *m* des actionnaires; **equity derivative/quasi-equity,** quasi fonds propres; **equity-linked policy,** assurance-vie libellée/investie en actions/en parts; **equity market,** marché des actions; **equity play,** stratégie *f* d'actions/d'investissement en valeurs mobilières; *pl.* **equities**/*NAm:* **common equities,** actions *f* ordinaires; **equities trader,** courtier *m* sur actions; **equity trading,** négociation *f* d'actions/courtage *m* sur actions.

equivalence, *n.* *Fin:* **equivalences of exchange,** parités *f* de change.

equivalent, **1.** *a.* équivalent; **to be equivalent to sth.,** être équivalent à qch./équivaloir à qch. **2.** *n.* *PolEc:* **man equivalent,** unité-travailleur *f.*

ergonomics, *n.pl.* (*usu. with sg. const.*) ergonomie *f.*

ergonomist, *n.* ergonomiste *mf.*

error, *n.* erreur *f*/faute *f*; **error of calculation,** erreur de calcul/faux calcul; **margin of error,** marge *f* d'erreur; **error in printing/printing error,** coquille *f*; **typing error,** faute de frappe; **errors and omissions excepted (E & OE),** sauf erreur ou omission; **sent by error,** envoyé par erreur.

escalate, *v.i.* (*of prices*) monter en flèche.

escalation, *n.* hausse *f*/augmentation *f* (rapide)/flambée *f* (des prix); **escalation clause,** clause d'indexation.

escalator, *n.* **escalator clause,** clause *f* d'indexation.

escape, *n.* **escape clause,** clause *f* échappatoire.

escrow, *n.* **funds held in escrow,** argent placé en dépôt légal/en séquestre/déposé en main tierce/*FrC:* entiercé; *NAm:* **escrow account,** compte bloqué; compte à échéance/à terme; **escrow agent,** dépositaire légal.

establish, *v.tr.* fonder (une maison de commerce); édifier (un système); créer (une agence); **to establish a tax on tobacco,** taxer le tabac; **to establish oneself (in business),** s'établir dans les affaires; **to establish oneself in a job,** se faire une (bonne) réputation.

establishment, *n.* **1.** établissement *m* (d'une industrie, etc.); création *f* (d'un système, d'un bureau); fondation *f* (d'une maison de commerce) **2.** établissement/maison *f*; **business establishment,** maison de commerce; **establishment charges,** frais généraux/dépenses *f* de la maison **3. to be on the establishment/to form part of the establishment,** faire partie du personnel **4. the Establishment,** les classes dirigeantes.

estate, *n.* **1.** (*a*) bien *m*; domaine *m*; immeuble *m*; **landed estate,** propriété foncière; **real estate,** biens immobiliers (*b*) succession *f* (d'un défunt); **estate duty/** *NAm:* **estate tax,** droits *mpl* de succession (*c*) actif *m* (d'un failli) **2.** (*a*) terre *f*/ propriété *f*; **country estate for sale,** domaine à vendre (*b*) **housing estate,** (*i*) lotissement *m* (*ii*) cité ouvrière; groupe *m* de H.L.M.; **industrial/trading estate,** zone industrielle (*c*) **(real) estate agent,** agent immobilier; **(real) estate agency,** agence immobilière; agence de location; **real estate investments,** placements immobiliers.

estimate[1], *n.* **1.** aperçu *m*/évaluation *f*/ calcul *m*; **rough estimate,** chiffre approximatif; **these figures are only a rough estimate,** ces chiffres sont très approximatifs; **conservative estimate,** évaluation prudente **2.** devis (estimatif)/état estimatif/état appréciatif; **budget estimates,** prévisions *f* budgétaires; **building estimate,** devis de construction; **estimate of expenditure,** chiffre prévu pour les dépenses; **printing estimate,** devis d'imprimerie; **preliminary estimate/rough estimate,** devis de prévision/devis approximatif; **estimate on demand,** devis sur demande; **to give/to put in an estimate,** établir un devis; soumissionner; **to ask for an estimate,** (*i*) faire évaluer/faire estimer qch (*ii*) demander un devis (pour un travail).

estimate[2], *v.tr.* estimer/évaluer/apprécier (les frais); évaluer (la production d'un puits de pétrole, etc.).

estimated, *a.* **estimated cost,** coût estimatif/estimation *f*; **estimated value,** valeur estimée; **it is only an estimated figure,** ce n'est qu'une estimation.

estimation, *n.* estimation *f*/appréciation *f*/évaluation *f*/calcul *m* (des frais, etc.).

estoppel, *n. Jur:* le fait d'être dans l'im-

possibilité de poursuivre sa voie en raison d'une action commise au préalable par soi-même.

eurobond, *n.* euro-obligation *f*.

eurocheque, *n.* eurochèque *m*.

eurocrat, *n.* eurocrate *m*.

eurocredit, *n.* eurocrédit *m*.

eurocurrency, *n.* eurodevise *f*/euro-monnaie; **the eurocurrency market,** le marché des eurodevises *f*.

eurodollars, *n.* eurodollars *m*.

euromarket, *n.* euromarché *m*.

euroyen, *n.* euroyen *m*.

evaluation, *n.* étude *f*/analyse *f*; **job evaluation,** évaluation *f* des tâches; *NAm:* (*of staff*) **performance evaluation,** notation *f* du personnel; *Stat:* **formative evaluation,** évaluation réflexe.

evasion, *n.* **tax evasion,** fraude fiscale/ fraude à l'impôt.

evidence, *n.* preuve *f*; **documentary evidence,** preuve écrite/authentique; **to give evidence,** témoigner.

ex, *prep.* **1. ex wharf/ex quay** = à quai; **price ex works/ex factory,** prix *m* départ usine/prix sortie (d')usine; **ex ship,** à bord; **ex warehouse,** à (prendre à) l'entrepôt/en entrepôt **2.** (*without*) *Fin:* **ex allotment** ex-répartition; **stock ex rights/ex new,** titre *m* ex-droit; **shares quoted ex dividend** actions citées ex-dividende/sans intérêts; coupon détaché/ex-coupon; **this stock goes ex coupon on August 1st,** le coupon de cette action se détache le premier août

exceed, *v.tr.* excéder; **demand exceeds supply,** la demande excède/dépasse l'offre.

excess, *n.* excédent *m* (de poids, de dépenses, etc.); **excess of expenditure over revenue,** excédent des dépenses sur les recettes; **excess charges/excess fare,** supplément *m*; **excess luggage,** excédent de bagages; **excess supply,** surproduction *f*; **excess weight,** poids *m* excédentaire surcharge *f*; **in excess,** en surplus; *Ins:* **excess clause,** franchise *f*; **excess profits,** surplus *m* des bénéfices; (*unexpected*) bénéfices exceptionnels/extraordinaires; *Fin:* **excess profits tax,** impôt *m* sur les bénéfices exceptionnels.

exchange[1], *n.* **1.** échange *m* (de marchandises); **exchange and barter,** troc *m*; **(car, etc. taken in) part exchange,** reprise *f* **2.** *Fin:* (*a*) change *m*; devises *fpl*; **dollar exchange,** change du dollar/en dollar(s); **(foreign) exchange broker/dealer,** agent *m* de change/cambiste *m*; **exchange control/ restrictions,** contrôle *m* des changes; **exchange list,** la cote des changes; **exchange market,** marché *m* des changes; **(foreign) exchange office,** bureau *m* de change; **exchange premium/premium on exchange,** agio *m*/prix *m* du change; **foreign exchange reserves,** réserves en devises (étrangères); **exchange value,** valeur *f* d'échange; **fixed/direct exchange,** le certain; **floating/fluctuating exchange,** l'incertain; **foreign exchange (FOREX),** devises (étrangères); change; **foreign exchange transaction,** opération *f* de change; **rate of exchange/exchange rate,** cours *m*/taux *m* de change; taux de conversion (de l'argent); **fixed/floating exchange rate,** taux de change fixe/flottant; **at the current rate of exchange,** au cours du jour; au taux de change courant/en vigueur; **official exchange rate,** taux de change officiel; (*at the top of foreign bill*) **exchange for £ ...,** bon pour ... (*b*) **bill of exchange,** effet *m*/traite *f*/lettre *f* de change; **short exchange,** papier court; **first of exchange,** première *f* de change; primata *m* de change; **second of exchange,** seconde *f* de change; copie *f* de change **3.** bourse *f* (des valeurs); **commodity/produce exchange/**(*in London*) **the Royal Exchange,** bourse de(s) marchandises; Bourse de commerce; **the Stock Exchange,** la Bourse; **Corn Exchange,** Bourse des céréales; halle *f* aux blés; **employment exchange,** l'agence nationale pour l'emploi (ANPE) **4. (telephone) exchange,** central *m* (téléphonique).

exchange[2], *v.tr.* (*a*) échanger (des

marchandises); **to exchange a dress for one of a bigger size,** échanger une robe contre une de la taille au-dessus (*b*) **to exchange contracts,** signer les contrats de vente et d'achat d'une propriété (*c*) **to exchange francs for pounds,** changer des francs en livres (*d*) troquer/faire un troc.

exchangeable, *a.* **1.** échangeable **(for,** contre); **exchangeable value,** valeur *f* d'échange.

exchanger, *n.* échangeur, -euse; *Jur:* échangiste *m*.

exchanging, *n.* échange *m* (de marchandises); troc *m* (de denrées).

exchequer, *n.* (*in the UK*) **the Exchequer,** (*i*) la Trésorerie; le fisc (*ii*) le Trésor public (*iii*) = le Ministère des Finances; **the Chancellor of the Exchequer** = le Ministre des Finances; **exchequer bill,** bon *m* du Trésor.

excisable, *a.* imposable; (*of goods*) soumis aux droits de régie.

excise[1], *n.* **1.** droit *m*; taxe *f*; contributions indirectes **2.** service *m* des contributions indirectes; la régie; **Customs and Excise,** la Régie; **Excise officer,** (*i*) receveur, euse des contributions indirectes (*ii*) employé, -ée de la régie; **excise duties,** droits de régie; **excise duty,** impôt indirect; *Cust:* **excise bond,** acquit-à-caution *m*.

excise[2], *v.tr.* imposer (une denrée etc.)/frapper (qch.) d'un droit de régie; soumettre (qn) à un droit de régie.

exciseman, *n.* employé *m* de la régie.

exclusive, 1. *a.* exclusif; **exclusive rights,** droits exclusifs (de vendre)/exclusivité *f* **2.** *prep.* **exclusive of wrappings,** emballage non compris; **exclusive of tax,** hors taxe (HT); **turnover exclusive of tax,** chiffre d'affaires HT.

exclusivity, *n.* exclusivité *f*.

ex-directory, *a.* (*telephone number*) sur la liste rouge; **to be ex-directory,** être sur la liste rouge.

execution, *n.* (*of law*) **to enforce execution,**

appliquer (les dispositions d')une loi; **(of contract) to demand execution,** exiger l'exécution d'un contrat.

executive, 1. *a.* (*power*) exécutif; (*ability*) d'exécution; (*job*) de cadre; (*car, plane*) de direction; **executive director,** cadre supérieur/dirigeant; **executive member,** membre du comité de direction; **executive officer,** cadre supérieur; **executive secretary,** secrétaire *mf* de direction; *NAm:* **Chief Executive Officer (CEO),** = président-directeur général (PDG) **2.** *n.* directeur, -trice; cadre *m*; chef *m* de service; (*board, committee*) bureau *m*; **chief executive,** directeur général; **account executive,** chargé *m* de comptes/d'affaires; *Mkt:* cadre commercial; (*in public relations*) relationniste-conseil *m*; *NAm: Fin:* agent *m* de change; **business executive,** directeur commercial; **sales executive,** directeur/cadre commercial; **junior executive,** jeune cadre; **(senior) executive,** cadre supérieur/dirigeant.

executor, *n.* exécuteur, -trice (d'un ordre); exécuteur, -trice testamentaire.

exempt[1], *a.* exempt/dispensé/exempté **(from,** de); **exempt from taxes/tax exempt,** exonéré/exempt/franc d'impôt.

exempt[2], *v.tr.* **to exempt s.o. (from sth.),** exempter/exonérer/dégrever qn (d'un impôt, etc.).

exemption, *n.* exemption *f*/exonération *f*/dégrèvement *m* (d'impôt); **exemption clause,** clause *f* d'exonération; **tax exemption,** exonération/exemption d'impôt.

exercise[1], *n.* (*a*) exercice *m* (de ses fonctions, etc.) (*b*) *StExch:* **exercise of an option,** levée *f* d'une prime; **exercise notice,** assignation *f*; **exercise price,** cours *m* de base.

exercise[2], *v.tr.* (*a*) exercer (ses fonctions, etc.) (*b*) *Fin:* **to exercise an option,** lever une prime/une option/l'option.

ex gratia, *a.* **ex gratia payment,** paiement *m* à titre de faveur.

ex-growth, *n. Euph:* (*decline*) baisse *f*.

exhibit[1], *n.* objet *m*/marchandise *f* exposé(e).

exhibit[2], *v.tr.* **1. to exhibit large profits,** faire ressortir de gros bénéfices **2. to exhibit goods in shop windows,** mettre/exposer des marchandises à l'étalage/en vitrine.

exhibition, *n.* **1.** exposition *f* (de tableaux); étalage *m* (de marchandises) **2.** (*a*) exposition; **Ideal Home Exhibition,** = Salon *m* des Arts ménagers (*b*) **exhibition room/hall,** salon d'exposition; **exhibition stand,** stand *m* (d'exposition).

exhibitor, *n.* (*at exhibition*) exposant, -ante.

exit, *v.i.* liquider un portefeuille; fermer une usine; cesser la production.

ex officio, 1. *adv.* (agir) d'office **2.** *a.* nommé d'office.

expand, *v.tr. & i.* (*of industry*) (s')agrandir/(se) développer.

expanding, *a.* en expansion.

expansion, *n.* **1. currency expansion,** expansion *f* monétaire **2.** (*a*) expansion (d'un commerce, etc.) (*b*) *PolEc:* relance *f* (économique).

expansionist, *a. PolEc:* expansionniste.

ex parte, *a. Jur:* unilatéral.

expectation, *n.* prévision(s) *f* (à long, à court terme); **sales expectation,** prévisions des ventes.

expenditure, *n.* **1.** (*spending*) dépense *f* (d'argent, etc.) **2.** (*amount spent*) dépense(s)/frais *mpl*; **it entails heavy expenditure,** cela entraîne une forte dépense/de fortes dépenses; **capital expenditure,** dépenses en capital/en immobilisations *fpl*; **current expenditure,** dépenses courantes; frais d'exploitation.

expense, *n.* **1.** dépense *f*/frais *mpl*; **book published at author's expense,** livre publié à compte d'auteur; **at great expense,** à grands frais; **regardless of expense,** sans regarder à la dépense; **it is not worth the**

expense, c'est trop cher pour ce que c'est **2.** (*a*) **expense account,** note de/indemnité pour frais professionnels (*b*) frais *mpl*; **administration expenses,** frais de gestion; **overhead/general/standing/business expenses,** frais généraux; **fixed expenses,** coûts *mpl* fixes; **incidental expenses,** faux frais; **legal expenses,** frais d'avocat/de notaire; **preliminary expenses (of a company),** frais d'établissement (d'une société); **petty expenses,** menues dépenses; **running expenses,** (*of car*) frais d'entretien; (*of business*) frais d'exploitation; **sundry expenses,** frais *m* divers; **travelling expenses,** frais de représentation/de déplacement; **to cut down on expenses,** réduire les frais/les dépenses; **all expenses paid,** tous frais payés/remboursés; **no expenses,** exempt de frais; (*on bill*) (retour) sans frais/sans protêt.

e x p e n s i v e , *a.* coûteux/cher/onéreux; **to be expensive,** coûter cher; **this shop is expensive,** ce magasin vend cher.

e x p e r t , *n.* expert *m*/spécialiste *mf*; **the experts,** les gens *m* du métier/les spécialistes; **he is an expert in this field,** il est expert en la matière/il s'y connaît; **expert's report,** expertise *f.*

e x p e r t i s e , *n.* évaluation *f*/expertise *f.*

e x p i r a t i o n , *n.* échéance *f* (d'un marché à prime); fin *f* (d'un terme); **expiration of a lease,** expiration *f* d'un bail; *Ins:* **expiration of a policy,** expiration/échéance *f* d'une police; **to repay before the expiration of a period,** rembourser par anticipation.

e x p i r e , *v.i.* (*of term, etc.*) expirer/échoir/ prendre fin/venir à échéance/à expiration; **expired bill,** effet périmé; *Ins:* **expired policy,** police échue; **his passport has expired,** son passeport est expiré/périmé.

e x p i r y , *n.* expiration *f*/fin *f*/échéance *f*/ terminaison *f* (d'un terme); terme *m* (d'une période); **expiry date,** date d'échéance.

e x p o r t¹, *n.* **1.** marchandise exportée; *pl.* **exports,** (*i*) articles *m* d'exportation (*ii*) exportations *f* (d'un pays); **invisible exports,** exportations invisibles; **visible exports,** exportations visibles; **to increase exports to Britain,** augmenter les exportations vers la Grande-Bretagne **2.** exportation/sortie *f*; **export agent,** commissionnaire exportateur; **export credit,** crédit *m* à l'exportation/crédit export; **export credit rate,** taux *m* de crédit export; **export price,** prix *m* à l'export/prix export; **export trade,** commerce *m* d'exportation; **export duty,** droit(s) *m*(*pl*) de sortie; **export quotas,** contingents *mpl* d'exportation; *EEC:* **export restitution/ refund,** restitution *f* à l'exportation; **prohibition of exports,** prohibitions *fpl* de sortie.

e x p o r t², *v.tr.* exporter (des marchandises) **(from,** de).

e x p o r t a t i o n , *n.* exportation *f*/sortie *f* (de marchandises).

e x p o r t e r , *n.* exportateur, -trice.

e x p o r t i n g , *a.* (marchand, pays, etc.) exportateur.

e x p o s u r e , *n.* sensibilité *f*/exposition *f* à un risque; **currency exposure,** risque *m* de change.

e x p r e s s , *a.* exprès (*inv*); **express letter/ delivery,** lettre *f*/livraison *f* exprès.

e x t e n d , *v.tr.* **1. to extend credit to s.o.,** accorder des facilités de crédit à qn **2.** prolonger (un délai); proroger (l'échéance d'un billet); *Bank:* **to extend the validity of a credit until March,** proroger jusqu'en mars l'échéance d'un accréditif.

e x t e n s i o n , *n.* **1.** *Book-k:* transport *m*/ report *m* (d'une balance) **2.** (*growing*) extension *f*/accroissement *m* (des affaires, etc.) **3.** prolongation *f* (d'échéance, etc.); **to get an extension of time,** obtenir un délai/une prorogation de délai; **arrangement for an extension of time,** atermoiement *m*; *Bank:* **extension of credit,** prolongation d'un accréditif **4.** *Tel:* **extension 136,** poste *m* 136.

e x t e r n a l , *a.* (*of trade, etc.*) étranger/

extérieur; **external account** = compte *m* d'étranger/*FrC:* compte de non-résident; **external debt,** dette extérieure; **external trade,** commerce extérieur.

extortionate, *a.* **extortionate price,** prix exorbitant.

extra, 1. *a.* en sus/en plus; supplémentaire; **extra charge,** prix *m* en sus; supplément *m*; **extra cost,** surcoût *m*; **to charge extra,** percevoir un supplément; facturer en sus; *Ins:* **extra premium,** surprime *f* **2.** *adv.* **service extra,** service non compris **3.** *n.pl.* **extras,** frais *m*/dépenses *f* supplémentaires.

extracurricular, *a.* paraprofessionnel.

extraordinary, *a.* **to call an extraordinary general meeting (EGM) of the shareholders,** convoquer d'urgence les sociétaires/convoquer une assemblée générale extraordinaire; *Book-k:* **extraordinary items,** pertes et profits exceptionnels/éléments exceptionnels.

F

face, *n.* **1. face value**/*NAm:* **amount**, valeur nominale/nominal *m*; valeur faciale (d'un timbre) **2.** recto *m* (d'un document, etc.).

facility, *n.* **1.** facilité *f*; **facilities for payment**, facilités de paiement; **overdraft facilities**, facilités de caisse **2.** *usu. pl.* installations *fpl*; **storage facilities**, entrepôt *m*/magasin *m*; **transport facilities**, moyens *m* de transport; *Nau:* **harbour facilities**, installations portuaires; *Trans:* **loading and unloading facilities**, installations/ quais *m* de chargement et de déchargement; **we have no facilities for it**, nous ne sommes pas équipés/outillés pour cela.

facsimile, *n.* (*exact copy*) fac-similé *m*/ copie *f*/reproduction exacte; (*telegraphic system and copy*) télécopie *f*/fac-similé *m*; **facsimile machine**, télécopieur *m*.

factor, *n.* **1.** (*a*) (*pers.*) agent *m* (dépositaire); courtier *m* de marchandises (*b*) factor *m*/société *f* d'affacturage **2.** indice *m*/coefficient *m*; **the sales increased by a factor of ten**, les ventes sont dix fois plus élevées/l'indice des vente est dix fois plus haut **3.** élément *m*/facteur *m*; **seasonal factors**, facteurs saisonniers; **factors of production**, les facteurs de la production; **human factor**, facteur humain; **cost factor**, facteur coût/prix.

factorage, *n.* (*a*) courtage *m*/commission *f* (*b*) commission d'affacturage.

factoring, *n.* affacturage *m*/factoring *m*; **factoring charges**, commission *f* d'affacturage.

factory, *n.* usine *f*/fabrique *f*; **biscuit factory**, biscuiterie *f*; **car factory**, usine d'automobiles; **shoe factory**, fabrique de chaussures; **arms factory**, manufacture *f* d'armes; **factory unit**, unité *f* de fabrication; **factory-installed component**, pièce *f* d'origine; **factory hand/factory worker**, ouvrier, -ière d'usine; **factory inspector**, inspecteur *m* du travail; **factory inspection**, inspection *f* du travail; **factory overheads**, frais généraux de fabrication; **factory price**, prix *m* (sortie) usine.

facture in, *v.tr. NAm:* comptabiliser (une somme).

failed, *a.* **failed firm**, maison *f* en faillite.

failing[1], *n.* faillite *f*.

failing[2], *prep.* à défaut de; **failing payment within thirty days**, à défaut de paiement dans les trente jours; **failing your advice to the contrary**, sauf avis contraire de votre part.

failure, *n.* **1. failure to pay a bill**, défaut *m* de paiement d'un effet **2.** (*a*) insuccès *m*/ non-réussite *f*; avortement *m* (d'un projet, etc.); échec *m* (dans une entreprise) (*b*) (*bankruptcy*) faillite *f*.

fair[1], *n.* foire *f*/exposition *f*/salon *m*; **book fair**, salon/foire du livre; **world fair**, exposition universelle.

fair[2], *a.* **to have a reputation for fair (and square) dealing**, avoir une réputation de loyauté en affaires; **fair deal**, traitement *m*/arrangement *m* équitable; **to charge a fair price**, vendre à un prix modéré/ raisonnable; **fair price provisions**/*NAm:* **fair-price amendments**, clause *f* de maintien de cours; **to make fair profits**, réaliser des bénéfices raisonnables; **fair trade**, libre échange basé sur des conditions de réciprocité; **fair wages**, salaire *m* équitable; **fair wear and tear**, usure normale.

faith, *n.* **good faith,** bonne foi; **purchaser in good faith,** acquéreur *m* de bonne foi.

faithfully, *adv. Corr:* **(we remain) yours faithfully,** veuillez agréer nos meilleures salutations/nos salutations distinguées/ nos respectueuses salutations; recevez l'expression de nos sentiments distingués/ de nos sentiments les meilleurs.

fake[1], *n.* faux *m*; contrefaçon *f*; falsification *f*/imitation *f*.

fake[2], *v.tr.* falsifier/maquiller (un document, etc.); contrefaire/truquer/falsifier (des calculs); **faked balance-sheet,** bilan truqué.

fall[1], *n.* baisse *f* (des prix, des actions); **heavy fall,** forte baisse/débâcle *f*; **fall of the currency,** dépréciation *f* de la monnaie; chute *f* des cours; **fall in the minimum lending rate,** baisse/fléchissement *m* du taux officiel d'escompte; *StExch:* **dealing for a fall,** opération *f* à la baisse; **to buy on a fall,** acheter à la baisse.

fall[2], *v.i.* (*a*) (*of price*) baisser/subir une baisse; (*of money*) se déprécier; (*of value*) baisser/diminuer/fléchir (*b*) **to fall due,** venir à échéance.

fall back, *v.i.* (*a*) *StExch: Fin:* se replier; **shares fell back a point,** les actions se sont repliées d'un point (*b*) **to fall back on one's capital,** avoir recours à/recourir à son capital.

falling[1], *a.* **falling market,** marché baissier/ marché orienté à la baisse/en baisse; **to sell on a rising market and buy on a falling market,** vendre en hausse et acheter en baisse; **the falling pound,** la livre qui se dévalorise/qui se déprécie.

falling[2], *n.* (*a*) abaissement *m*/baisse *f* (de prix); fléchissement *m*/baisse (de la valeur de qch.) (*b*) *StExch: Fin:* **falling back,** repli *m* (*c*) **falling off,** diminution *f*/ décroissement *m* (de chiffres, de taux, etc.); dépérissement *m* (d'une industrie); ralentissement *m* (de commandes, des affaires).

fall off, *v.i.* (*of profits*) diminuer; **the**

takings are falling off, les recettes *f* diminuent.

false, *a.* **1.** (*incorrect*) faux/erroné; **false weight,** faux poids **2. false balance-sheet,** faux bilan **3.** (*document, etc.*) forgé; (*coin, etc.*) faux/contrefait.

falsification, *n.* falsification *f* (des comptes, etc.).

falsify, *v.tr.* falsifier (un document); fausser (un bilan).

fancy, *a.* (*a*) **fancy goods,** nouveautés *f*/ objets *m* de fantaisie; *NAm:* **fancy chocolates,** chocolats *m* de choix/surchoix (*b*) **fancy price,** prix trop élevé/fantaisiste.

fare, *n.* prix *m* du billet/du voyage/de la place; (*in taxi*) prix de la course; (*ticket*) billet *m*; **cheap fares,** tarif réduit; **full fare/ adult fare,** (billet) plein tarif/place entière; *Av:* **full fare,** (classe) plein service; **half fare (ticket),** demi-tarif *m*/ demi-place *f*; **single fare,** (prix du) billet simple/(prix d'un) aller (simple); **return fare**/*NAm:* **round-trip fare,** aller et retour *m*.

farm, *n.* ferme *f*/exploitation *f* agricole; **dairy farm,** ferme laitière; **fish farm,** établissement *m* piscicole; **poultry farm,** exploitation avicole/élevage de volailles; **sheep farm,** élevage *m* de moutons; **farm cooperative,** coopérative *f* agricole; **farm labourer,** ouvrier *m* agricole.

farmer, *n.* agriculteur *m*/cultivateur -trice/exploitant, -ante agricole.

farming, *n.* exploitation *f* agricole; culture *f*/agriculture *f*; **mixed farming,** polyculture *f*; **single-crop farming,** monoculture *f*; **fish farming,** pisciculture *f*/élevage *m* de poissons; **poultry farming,** aviculture *f*/élevage *m* de volailles; **sheep farming,** élevage de moutons; **stock farming,** élevage de bestiaux; **farming lease,** bail *m* à ferme.

farm out, *v.tr.* **to farm out work,** donner un travail à un sous-contractant/donner un travail en sous-traitance.

fast-food, *n.* prêt-à-manger *m*/fast-food *m*/restauration *f* rapide.

fatigue, *n.* usure *f*; **fatigue allowance**, provision *f* pour usure.

faulty, *a.* défectueux.

favourable, *a.* (*of terms, etc.*) bon/avantageux; **on favourable terms**, à bon compte.

Fax, *n. Rtm:* **Fax (machine)**, télécopieur *m*; **to send a Fax**, transmettre/envoyer une télécopie/un fac-similé.

feasibility, *n.* **feasibility report**, rapport *m* de faisabilité; **feasibility study**, étude *f* préalable/étude de faisabilité.

featherbedding, *n.* (*i*) utilisation excessive de la main-d'œuvre (par rapport aux besoins réels) (*ii*) subvention *f* à une industrie (par rapport aux besoins réels).

Fed, *n. US:* = **the Federal Reserve**, la Réserve Fédérale/le Fed.

federal, *a.* fédéral; *US:* **Federal Reserve (system)**, (système de) Réserve fédérale; *US:* **Federal Reserve Bank**, banque *f* membre de la Réserve fédérale; *US:* **federal fund**, fonds fédéraux/réserves *fpl* obligataires.

federation, *n.* fédération *f*; **employers' federation**, syndicat patronal.

fee, *n.* (*a*) honoraires *mpl* (d'un médecin consultant, d'un avocat, etc.); jeton *m* de présence (d'un administrateur); prestation *f* (de services); redevance *f*; **consultancy fee**, frais *mpl* d'expertise; **finders' fee**, commission *f*; prestation de démarcheur; **flat fee**, commission immédiate; **management fee**, commission de chef de file; **to draw one's fees**, toucher ses honoraires, etc. (*b*) droits *mpl*; **admission fee**, (droit d')entrée *f*; **patent fee**, taxe *f* de droits de brevet; **registration fee**, droits d'inscription; droits d'enregistrement; **subscription fee**, prix *m* de l'abonnement (à un journal, etc.); cotisation *f* (à une organisation); **for a small fee**, moyennant une légère redevance/contre une somme modique; **to charge a fee**, demander une prestation de service/des honoraires, etc.

(*c*) *Jur:* **fee simple**, propriété inconditionnelle.

feedback, *n.* effet *m* de retour/rétroaction *f*/feed-back *m*.

fetch, *v.tr.* (*i*) rapporter (*ii*) atteindre (un certain prix); **it fetched a high price**, cela s'est vendu cher; **it won't fetch much**, cela ne rapportera pas beaucoup; **the table will fetch about £200**, la table rapportera dans les £200.

fiat, *n. Fin: NAm:* **fiat money**, monnaie fiduciaire/fictive; papier-monnaie *m* inconvertible.

fictitious, *a.* fictif; **fictitious assets**, actif fictif; *Fin:* **fictitious bill**, traite *f* en l'air.

fiduciary, *a. Jur: Fin:* (prêt, monnaie, etc.) fiduciaire.

field, *n.* (*a*) marché *m* (pour un produit) (*b*) **field study/survey**, recherche *f* sur le terrain/sur les lieux; **field work**, démarchage *m* auprès de la clientèle (*c*) **field of activity**, sphère *f*/secteur *m* d'activité (*d*) **coal field**, bassin *m* houiller; **oil field**, gisement *m* pétrolifère.

fifty-fifty **1.** *a.* **a fifty-fifty venture**, un accord d'entreprise en coparticipation à 50% **2.** *adv.* **to share the costs fifty-fifty**, partager les frais moitié-moitié.

figure, *n.* (*a*) chiffre *m*; **in round figures**, en chiffres ronds; **to work out the figures**, faire les calculs; **to find a mistake in the figures**, trouver une erreur de calcul; **sales figures**, chiffre d'affaires/chiffres de vente; **his income runs into five figures** = il a un revenu de plus de dix mille francs; **we cannot allow you credit beyond this figure**, nous ne pouvons pas vous accorder un crédit plus important/un crédit au-delà de ce montant (*b*) *pl.* **figures**, données *f* numériques/détails chiffrés (d'un projet, etc.); statistiques *f*; **the figures for next year look good**, les statistiques pour l'année prochaine semblent favorables.

figuring, *n.* chiffrage *m* (des dépenses, etc.).

file[1], *n.* **1.** classeur *m*; **card-index file**, fichier *m*; **suspension file,** dossier suspendu **2.** *pl.* **files,** archives *f*; dossier *m*; **we have placed your report in/on the file,** nous avons ajouté votre rapport au dossier; **to keep s.o.'s name on file,** prendre note des coordonnées de qqn; *esp. NAm:* **file clerk,** documentaliste *mf*; **file copy,** exemplaire *m*/pièce *f* d'archives.

file[2], *v.tr.* **1. to file (away),** classer (des fiches, des documents, etc.) **2. to file one's petition (in bankruptcy),** enregistrer/déposer une requête de mise en faillite/déposer son bilan; **to file an application for a patent,** déposer une demande de brevet; *NAm:* **to file one's tax return,** remplir sa déclaration de revenus/d'impôts.

filing, *n.* (*a*) classement *m* (de documents, de fiches, etc.); **filing cabinet,** classeur *m*; **filing tray/filing basket,** corbeille *f* pour correspondance/pour documents à classer; **filing drawer,** tiroir *m* classeur; **filing clerk,** documentaliste *mf*; **filing system,** (méthode *f* de) classement (*b*) dépôt *m* d'une demande/d'une requête; envoi *m* d'une déclaration de revenus.

fill, *v.tr.* **1. to fill a post/a vacancy,** suppléer/ pourvoir à une vacance; nommer qn à un poste **2. to fill an order,** exécuter une commande.

fill in, *v.tr.* remplir (un formulaire, une formule, un bordereau); **to fill in the date,** insérer la date.

fill out, *v.tr. NAm:* remplir (un formulaire, une formule, un bordereau).

fill up, *v.tr.* remplir (un formulaire, une formule, un bordereau).

final, *a.* final/dernier; **final date (for payment),** délai *m* de rigueur; **final demand (for payment),** dernier rappel; **final instalment,** dernier versement/versement libératoire; **final product,** produit fini.

finalize, *v.tr.* compléter.

finance[1], *n.* finance *f*; **public finance,** finances publiques; **high finance,** la haute finance; **the world of finance,** le monde de la finance; **questions of finance,** la fi- nance/les questions financières; **Finance Act,** loi *f* de finances; **finance company/ finance house,** société *f* financière/de crédits/de prêts; **finance development corporation,** fonds *m* de développement économique.

finance[2], *v.tr.* financer/commanditer (qn, une entreprise, etc.); supporter tous les frais de (une entreprise); **we have someone to finance the business,** nous avons un bailleur de fonds; **to finance the cost of the undertaking,** fournir les fonds nécessaires à l'entreprise; **operation 100% debt financed,** opération entièrement financée par emprunt.

financial, *a.* financier; **financial adviser,** conseiller, -ère financier, -ière; **financial analyst,** analyste financier; **financial assistance,** appui financier; **financial backer,** bailleur, -euse de fonds; **financial director,** directeur financier; **financial institution,** établissement *m* de crédit; société financière; **financial market,** marché financier; **financial news,** informations financières; **financial position,** situation financière; **financial pressure,** embarras financier; **financial resources,** ressources *fpl*/finances *fpl*; **financial statement,** situation *f* de trésorerie/état financier; bilan *m*; **the financial world,** le monde de la finance; **financial year,** exercice *m* (comptable); année *f* budgétaire.

financially, *adv.* financièrement; **financially sound,** solvable/solide du point de vue financier.

financier, *n.* **1.** (grand) financier *m* **2.** bailleur, -euse de fonds.

financing, *n.* financement *m* (d'une entreprise, etc.); **compensatory official financing,** financement compensatoire officiel; **debt financing,** consolidation *f* de la dette/ financement par emprunt.

find, *v.tr.* (*a*) **to find the money for an undertaking,** procurer les capitaux/fournir l'argent pour une entreprise (*b*) **£100 all found,** £100 logé et nourri; **I pay her £150 all found,** je lui donne £150 tout compris

(c) *Jur:* **to find for the accused,** se prononcer en faveur de l'accusé.

finder, *n.* démarcheur *m*; **finder's fee,** commission *f*; prestation *f* de démarcheur.

findings, *n.* **clear report of findings,** certificat *m* de conformité; **the findings of a commission of inquiry,** les conclusions *f*/le verdict d'une commission d'enquête.

fine[1], *n.* amende *f*; **to have to pay a fine of £300,** avoir une amende de £300 à payer.

fine[2], *v.tr.* **to fine s.o.,** condamner qn à une amende.

fine[3], *a.* **fine bill,** beau papier; **fine trade bill,** papier de haut commerce/de première catégorie.

fine[4], *adv.* **prices are cut very fine,** les prix *m* sont au plus bas; **profits cut very fine,** profits réduits à presque rien.

finish, *n.* *StExch:* **price at the finish,** prix de clôture; **trading at the finish,** opération(s) *f(pl)* de clôture.

fire, *v.tr.* **to fire s.o.,** mettre qn à la porte/licencier qn/renvoyer qn.

firm[1], *n.* maison *f* de commerce/société (commerciale); société en nom collectif; entreprise *f*/firme *f*; **name/style of a firm,** raison sociale; **a large firm,** une grosse entreprise; **firm of solicitors,** = étude *f* de notaire.

firm[2], *a.* (*of market, offer, sale*) ferme; (*of contango rates*) tendu; **firm stock,** valeur ferme/soutenue; **these shares remain firm at …,** ces actions se maintiennent à …; **article in firm demand,** article constamment demandé.

firm[3], *v.i.* **the market firmed during the day's trading,** le marché s'est stabilisé au cours de la journée.

firmness, *n.* **the firmness of the pound,** la stabilité de la livre.

first, *n.* (*a*) **first of exchange,** première *f* de change (*b*) **first-class paper,** effet *m* de première catégorie; **first-rate products,** produits de première qualité/de premier

ordre; *pl.* **firsts,** articles *m* de première qualité/produits *m* surchoix (*c*) **first-line manager,** agent *m* de maîtrise (*d*) **first in first out/ FIFO** = premier entré premier sorti/PEPS; **last in first out/LIFO** dernier entré premier sorti/DEPS (*e*) *Trans:* première (classe); *Post:* **first class rate** = tarif normal.

fiscal, *a.* fiscal; **fiscal period/fiscal year,** exercice *m* (financier); année *f* budgétaire; **fiscal policy,** politique *f* budgétaire.

fiver, *n.* *F:* billet de cinq livres (sterling).

fix, *v.tr.* fixer/établir (une indemnité, un prix, le taux de l'intérêt, etc.); **to fix the budget,** déterminer le budget; **to fix a meeting for three o'clock,** fixer une séance pour trois heures; **the date is not yet fixed,** la date n'est pas encore fixée/déterminée/arrêtée; **on the date fixed,** à la date prescrite.

fixed, *a.* **1.** **fixed charges,** frais *m* fixes; **fixed cost,** coût *m* fixe/constant; **fixed price,** prix *m* fixe/forfaitaire; prix fait/coté; **fixed in advance,** forfaitaire/à forfait; **fixed deposit,** dépôt *m* à terme (fixe)/à échéance fixe; **fixed income,** revenu *m* fixe; **fixed salary,** appointements *m* fixes/salaire *m* fixe/un fixe; **fixed-interest security,** valeur *f* à intérêt fixe **2.** **fixed capital/assets,** capital fixe/capital immobilisé/immobilisations *fpl*/valeurs immobilisées.

fixing, *n.* (*a*) fixage *m*/établissement *m*/détermination *f* (des prix, des droits, etc.); **gold fixing,** fixage du cours de l'or (*b*) **price fixing,** contrôle illégal des prix (par un cartel, etc.).

fixture, *n.* meuble *m* fixe/installation *fpl*; **fixtures and fittings (f&f),** reprise *f*.

flagging, *a.* languissant; chancelant; faible; **flagging economy,** économie languissante/chancelante.

flat[1], *n.* appartement *m*; **block of flats,** immeuble *m* (d'appartements).

flat[2], *a.* (*a*) **flat market,** marché calme/languissant (*b*) **flat rate,** taux *m* fixe/tarif *m* fixe/forfait *m*/tarif forfaitaire; **flat rate of pay,** taux uniforme de salaires; **flat-rate subscription,** abonnement *m* à forfait; *NAm:* **flat quotation,** cotation *f* sans intérêts.

fledgeling, *n.* **fledgeling business,** affaire *f* qui démarre.

fleet, *n.* parc *m*; **fleet of cars,** parc automobile.

flexibility, *n.* **price flexibility,** flexibilité *f* des prix.

flexible, *a.* **flexible budget,** budget *m* adaptable/flexible; **flexible prices,** prix *m* flexibles; **flexible (working) hours,** horaire *m* flexible/souple/variable.

flexitime, *n.,* **flextime,** *n.* horaire *m* souple/flexible/variable.

flight, *n.* (*a*) (*of aircraft*) vol *m* (*b*) **capital flight,** fuite *f* des capitaux (vers l'étranger); **flight capital,** capitaux en fuite.

float¹, *n.* **1. (cash) float,** caisse *f*/monnaie *f* **2.** *StExch:* flottant *m*; **clean float,** taux *m* de changes libres/flottants; **dirty float,** taux de change concertés.

float², *v.tr.* **1.** créer/fonder/lancer (une compagnie, etc.); **to float a loan,** émettre/lancer un emprunt **2. to float the pound,** laisser flotter la livre (sterling).

floatation, *n.* = **flotation.**

floater, *n.* **1.** (*pers.*) lanceur *m* (d'une compagnie, etc.) **2.** (*a*) *StExch: F:* titre *m* de premier rang (*b*) *Ins:* police flottante (*c*) (*loan*) prêt *m*; (*money borrowed*) argent emprunté.

floating¹, *n.* **the floating of the pound,** le flottement de la livre (sterling).

floating², *a.* **1. floating cargo,** cargaison *f* sur mer **2. floating capital/assets,** capital circulant/flottant/mobile/disponible; fonds *mpl* de roulement/capitaux roulants; **floating debt,** dette flottante/non consolidée; **floating exchange rate,** taux de change flottant; **floating pound,** livre *f* (sterling) qui flotte/flottante; *Ins:*

floating policy, police d'abonnement/flottante.

floor, *n.* **1.** (*in factory*) **shop floor,** l'atelier *m* **2.** *NAm:* (*in shop*) **floor manager,** chef *m* de rayon **3. floor figure,** valeur *f* de base; **floor price,** prix *m* plancher; **floor trader,** boursier professionnel qui travaille à la corbeille pour son propre compte; **floor trading,** cotation *f* à la corbeille.

floorwalker, *n.* (*in a store*) inspecteur, -trice; surveillant, -ante; chef *m* de rayon; (*in a bank*) surveillant,-ante.

flotation, *n.* lancement *m* (d'un emprunt, etc.); émission *f* d'actions.

flotsam, *n.* épave(s) flottante(s); **flotsam and jetsam,** choses *fpl* de flot et de mer.

flourish, *v.i.* (*of business, etc.*) être florissant/prospérer; **trade will flourish,** le commerce prendra de l'extension/deviendra florissant.

flourishing, *a.* **flourishing trade,** commerce *m* prospère.

flow¹, *n.* (*a*) **flow of capital,** mouvement *m* de capital; **flow of money,** flux *m* monétaire/financier; **work flow,** déroulement *m* des opérations (*b*) **cash flow,** marge brute d'autofinancement/cashflow *m*; **discounted cash flow (DCF),** cashflow actualisé (méthode DCF); **they have cash flow problems,** ils ont des problèmes de trésorerie (*c*) **flow chart,** graphique *m* d'évolution; organigramme *m*.

flow², *v.i.* (*of money*) circuler.

flow in, *v.i.* (*of money*) affluer.

flow-through, *a. NAm:* (*of tax*) **flow-through method of accounting,** méthode *f* de l'impôt exigible.

fluctuate, *v.i.* (*of markets, values*) fluctuer/osciller; **prices fluctuate between £2000 and £2500,** les prix flottent/varient entre £2000 et £2500.

fluctuating, *a.* (*prices, etc.*) oscillant/fluctuant/variable.

fluctuation, *n.* **fluctuation of the franc,**

fluctuation *f*/variation *f* du (cours du) franc; **market fluctuations,** fluctuations du marché; **maximum fluctuation,** variation maximale autorisée; **minimum fluctuation,** variation de cours minimale; **seasonal fluctuations,** variations saisonnières.

flush, *a.* **flush with money,** qui a beaucoup d'argent.

fly-by-night, *n.* **fly-by-night operation/firm,** opération *f*/société *f* véreuse.

fold(up), *v.i. F: (of business, etc.)* cesser ses activités/fermer ses portes/fermer boutique.

folder, *n.* **1.** dépliant *m*/prospectus *m* **2.** *(for papers, etc.)* chemise *f*/dossier *m*.

folio¹, *n. Book-k:* **posting folio,** rencontre *f*.

folio², *v.tr. Book-k:* paginer (un registre, etc.) à livre ouvert.

following, *a. StExch:* **following settlement/following account,** liquidation suivante.

follow up, *v.tr.* faire suivre (une lettre) d'une seconde lettre.

follow-up, *n.* **follow-up (system),** relance *f* (du client, de la publicité, etc.); **follow-up work,** travail *m* complémentaire; **follow-up letter,** (lettre de) rappel *m*; *Mkt:* **follow-up (of order),** suivi *m* (d'une commande).

food, *n.* *(a)* aliments *mpl*; **food counter/**(*in large store*) **food hall/food store/food department,** rayon *m* d'alimentation; **food packaging,** emballage *m* des produits alimentaires; **food products,** produits *m* alimentaires/comestibles *m*/denrées *f*; **food and drink trade,** restauration *f*; **the food industry,** l'industrie *f* alimentaire; **food manufacturer,** fabricant *m* de produits comestibles; **food value,** valeur nutritive *(b)* aliment; **canned/tinned foods,** conserves *f* (alimentaires)/aliments en conserve/aliments en boîtes; **health foods,** produits (d'alimentation) naturels.

foodstuffs, *n.pl.* produits *m* alimentaires/produits d'alimentation/denrées *f* (alimentaires)/comestibles *m*; **essential foodstuffs,** denrées de première nécessité.

foolscap, *n.* papier *m* ministre; (papier) tellière (*m*).

foot¹, *n. Meas:* pied (anglais) *m* (= 0,3048 m).

foot², *v.tr.* **1.** **to foot the bill,** payer la note/les dépenses **2.** *NAm:* **to foot (up) an account,** additionner un compte.

footsie, FOOTSIE, *n. (FTSE 100) F:* indice *m* du *Financial Times*.

force, *n.* *(a)* **to be in force,** être en vigueur; **to come into force,** entrer en vigueur; **rates in force,** tarifs *m* en vigueur *(b)* **sales force,** équipe *f* de vente.

forced, *a.* **forced sale,** vente forcée; *Fin:* **forced currency,** cours forcé.

force down, *v.tr.* **to force down prices,** faire baisser les prix.

force up, *v.tr.* **to force up prices,** faire hausser/faire monter les prix.

forecast¹, *n. & a.* **sales forecast,** prévision *f* des ventes; **earnings forecast,** résultats prévisionnels; **forecast operating budget,** budget *m* d'exploitation prévisionnel; **forecast plan,** plan prévisionnel.

forecast², *v.tr.* prévoir/faire des prévisions; **he forecasts sales of £1m,** il prévoit un chiffre de vente de £1 m.

foreclose, *v.tr. Jur:* **to foreclose the mortgagor (from the equity of redemption)/to foreclose the mortgage,** saisir/poursuivre la vente de l'immeuble hypothéqué.

foreclosure, *n. Jur:* forclusion *f*; saisie *f* (d'une hypothèque).

foreign, *a.* étranger; **foreign bill,** effet *m*/lettre *f* de change sur l'extérieur; **foreign currency,** devises *f* étrangères; **foreign debt,** dette extérieure/endettement extérieur; **foreign exchange,** devises (étrangères)/change (étranger); **foreign exchange transfer,** transfert *m* de devises; **foreign exchange broker/dealer,** cambiste *m*/courtier *m* en devises; **foreign goods,** marchandises *fpl* qui viennent de l'étranger; **foreign in-vestments,** investissements *mpl* à l'étranger; **foreign money order,** mandat international; **Foreign Office,** Ministère *m* des Affaires étrangères/*FrC:* Ministère des Affaires extérieures; **foreign trade,** commerce extérieur.

foreman, *n.* contremaître *m.*

forfeit[1], **1.** *n.* (*a*) (*for non-performance of contract*) dédit *m*; **forfeit clause (of a contract),** clause *f* de dédit (*b*) *StExch:* **to relinquish the forfeit,** abandonner la prime **2. the goods were declared forfeit,** les marchandises ont été confisquées.

forfeit[2], *v.tr.* perdre (qch.) par confiscation; **to forfeit a deposit,** perdre les arrhes; *Jur:* **to forfeit a patent,** déchoir d'un brevet.

forfeiting, *n.* affacturage *m* à forfait.

forfeiture, *n.* **1.** *Jur: Fin:* déchéance *f*/ forfaiture *f* (d'un droit, etc.); **action for forfeiture of patent,** action *f* en déchéance de brevet **2.** bien(s) confisqué(s).

forge, *v.tr.* contrefaire (une signature, des billets de banque).

forged, *a.* (document, billet de banque, etc.) faux/contrefait/falsifié; **forged document,** faux *m.*

forgery, *n.* **1.** contrefaçon *f* (d'une signature, de billets de banque); falsification *f* (de documents) **2.** faux *m*; **the signature was a forgery,** la signature était contrefaite.

form[1], *n.* **1. receipt in due form,** quittance régulière/en bonne forme **2. (printed) form,** formule *f*/formulaire *m*/bulletin *m*; **printed form of receipt,** formule de quittance; **form for bill of exchange,** formule d'effet de commerce; **form 20,** formulaire numéro 20; **form of tender,** modèle *m* de soumission; **inquiry form,** bulletin de demande de renseignements; **application form,** formulaire de demande; (*for shares*) bulletin de souscription; **blank form,** formulaire en blanc; **order form,** bon *m*/bulletin de commande;

Bank: **cheque form,** (*i*) formule (*ii*) volant *m* (de chèque) (*iii*) chèque *m*; **listing forms,** bordereaux *m* en blanc; **form of return,** feuille *f* de déclaration (de revenu, etc.) **3.** *Nau:* **long/short form,** connaissement complet/abrégé.

form[2], *v.tr.* former/organiser/constituer (une société, etc.).

formal, *a.* (*a*) officiel; **formal demand,** demande officielle (*b*) **formal notice,** mise *f* en demeure.

formality, *n.* formalité *f*; **customs formalities,** formalités de douanes.

formation, forming, *n.* constitution *f* (d'une société, etc.); **capital formation,** formation *f* de capital.

forward[1], *a. Fin:* **forward book,** échéancier *m* des devises livrables à terme; *StExch:* **forward deals/sales/ trading,** opérations *f*/ventes *f* à terme; **forward delivery,** livraison *f* à terme; **forward contract,** contrat *m* à terme de gré à gré; **forward exchange contract,** opération *f* de change à terme; **forward market,** marché *m* à terme; (*on Paris Stock Exchange*) (marché du) règlement mensuel (RM); *Bank:* **forward rates,** taux *m* pour les opérations à terme.

forward[2], *adv.* **1.** (*a*) **to date forward a cheque,** postdater un chèque; **a forward dated cheque,** un chèque postdaté; **carriage forward,** (en) port dû; **charges forward,** frais *m* à percevoir à la livraison (*b*) **to buy forward,** acheter à terme; **to sell forward,** vendre à terme **2.** *Book-k:* **to carry the balance forward,** reporter le solde à nouveau; **(carried) forward,** à reporter; report *m.*

forward[3], *v.tr.* (*a*) expédier/envoyer/transiter (des marchandises, etc.); **to forward sth. to s.o.,** faire parvenir qch à qn; **to forward goods to Paris,** diriger des marchandises sur Paris; acheminer des marchandises sur/vers Paris (*b*) transmettre/faire suivre/réexpédier (une lettre); **to be forwarded/please forward,** (prière de) faire suivre/faire suivre s.v.p.

forwarder, *n.* (*a*) expéditeur, -trice (d'un

colis, etc.)/envoyeur, -euse (d'un paquet, etc.) (*b*) = **forwarding agent.**

orwarding, *n.* (*a*) expédition *f*/envoi *m*; acheminement *m* (d'un colis); **forwarding agent,** entrepreneur *m* de transports/(agent) expéditeur (*m*)/transporteur *m*; transitaire *m*; **forwarding agency,** entreprise *f* de transports; société *f*/compagnie *f*/maison *f* d'expédition; maison de transit; **forwarding charges,** frais *mpl* de transport/d'expédition; **forwarding time,** durée *f* d'acheminement; **international forwarding,** transport international; **forwarding instructions,** indications *f* concernant l'expédition (*b*) réexpédition *f* (d'une lettre); **forwarding address,** adresse *f* de réexpédition/ nouvelle adresse.

oul, *a.* **foul bill of lading,** connaissement *m* avec réserves.

ounder, *n.* fondateur *m* (d'une maison de commerce/d'une société); **founder member,** membre fondateur; **founder's shares,** parts *f* bénéficiaires/de fondateur.

our, *a.* quatre; **the Big Four** = les quatre grandes banques (*Lloyds, National Westminster, Barclays, Midland*).

action, *n.* (*a*) fraction *f*/nombre *m* fractionnaire; **fractions of a franc are charged as a franc,** l'addition est arrondie au franc supérieur (*b*) *Fin:* fraction/ rompu *m* (d'action, d'obligation).

actional, *a.* fractionnaire; **fractional part,** fraction *f*; **fractional coins,** monnaie *f* divisionnaire/d'appoint; *NAm:* **fractional note,** (billet *m* de banque de) petite coupure.

agile, *a.* fragile.

anc, *n.* franc *m* (français, suisse, belge, etc.); **franc account,** compte (tenu) en francs; **new franc,** franc lourd.

anchise, *n.* **1.** concession *f*/contrat *m* de franchisage/franchise *f*; **franchise outlet,** boutique franchisée **2.** *MIns:* minimum *m* d'avaries au-dessous duquel l'assureur

est libéré de toute responsabilité/ franchise *f*.

franchisee, *n.* franchisé, -ée.

franchiser, *n.* **1.** franchisé, -ée **2.** franchiseur *m*.

franchising, *n.* franchisage *m*/franchising *m*; **franchising operation,** franchisage.

franchisor, *n.* franchiseur *m*.

franco, *adv.* franco; **franco price,** prix franco.

frank, *v.tr.* **to frank a letter,** affranchir une lettre.

franking, *a.* **franking machine,** machine *f* à affranchir les lettres.

fraud, *n.* fraude *f*; **to obtain sth. by fraud,** obtenir qch. par fraude/frauduleusement; **frauds relating to goods,** tromperie *f* sur la marchandise.

fraudster, *n.* *F:* escroc *m*/fraudeur *m*.

fraudulent, *a.* frauduleux; **fraudulent balance-sheet,** faux bilan; **fraudulent transaction,** transaction frauduleuse/ entachée de fraude; **fraudulent clause (in a contract),** clause dolosive; **fraudulent bankrupt,** banqueroutier frauduleux.

fraudulently, *adv.* frauduleusement/par fraude; **goods imported fraudulently,** marchandises passées en fraude.

free[1], *a.* **1.** *Fin:* **to set money free,** mobiliser de l'argent/débloquer des fonds; **setting free,** mobilisation *f* (de l'argent) **2.** franc (**of,** de); **interest free of tax,** intérêts nets d'impôts/exempts d'impôt/en franchise d'impôt; **interest-free,** en franchise d'intérêt; **(interest) free credit,** crédit gratuit; **post free,** en franchise postale; *Cust:* **free of duty/duty free,** exempt de droits d'entrée; en franchise douanière; **to import sth. free of duty/duty free,** faire entrer qch. en franchise; **free list,** liste *f* d'exemptions **3.** gratuit; gratis; **free** sample, échantillon gratuit; **free of charge,** gratuit; gratis; **free ticket,** billet gratuit/de faveur; **free trial,** essai gratuit; **we are sending you the machine for free**

trial, nous vous envoyons l'appareil gratuitement à l'essai/à titre d'essai; **free demonstration in the home,** démonstration ƒ à domicile à titre gracieux; **delivery free,** franc de port; sans frais de transport; **delivered free as far as the French frontier,** livraison franco frontière française; **free on rail,** franco de rail/franco wagon; **free on truck (FOT),** franco camion; **free alongside ship (FAS)/free at quay/on wharf,** franco long du bord; franco de quai; vente FAS; **free over side,** franco allège; **free on board (FOB),** franco à bord; vente FOB; **free in and out,** bord à bord **4. free enterprise,** libre entreprise ƒ; **free port,** port franc; **free trade,** libre-échange *m*; **free trade area/zone,** zone ƒ de libre-échange; **free trade policy,** politique ƒ antiprotectionniste/politique libre-échangiste/politique de libre-échange; **free trader,** libre-échangiste *mf*/antiprotectionniste *mf*; *NAm:* commerçant indépendant des consortiums.

free[2], *adv.* franc de port/en port payé/franco; **free of charge,** gratuitement; **catalogue sent free on request** = demandez notre catalogue gratuit.

free[3], *v.tr.* (*a*) mettre (des denrées réglementées) en vente libre (*b*) détaxer (des denrées taxées).

freebie, *n. F:* journal gratuit/visite gratuite; ce qui est offert gratuitement.

free-flowing, *a.* **free-flowing capital,** libre circulation ƒ des capitaux; capitaux flotants.

Freefone, *n. Rtm: Tel:* numéro vert.

freehold, *n.* **freehold property,** propriété ƒ sans réserve; pleine propriété.

freepost, *n.* libre-réponse ƒ.

freeze[1], *n.* **prices and wages freeze,** blocage *m*/gel *m* des prix et des salaires.

freeze[2], *v.tr.* **to freeze credits,** geler/bloquer les crédits; **to freeze wages,** geler/bloquer les salaires.

freeze out, *v.tr.* étrangler (une maison de commerce qui vous fait concurrence).

freeze-out, *n.* étranglement *m* (d'une maison de commerce qui vous fait concurrence).

freezing, *n.* blocage *m* (des salaires, de crédits, d'une dette, etc.).

freight[1], *n.* **1.** fret *m*; transport maritime e aérien; *NAm:* transport par camion/pa chemin de fer; **air freight,** fret aérien; **sen by air freight,** envoyé par avion/expédi par voie aérienne **2.** (*a*) (*cargo, load*) fre cargaison ƒ/chargement *m* (d'un navire) **to take in freight,** prendre du fret; **dea freight,** (*i*) faux fret (*ii*) dédit *m* pou défaut de chargement; **homeward freigh onward freight,** fret de retour; **outwar freight,** fret d'aller (*b*) (*goods*) marchan dises (transportées); *NAm:* **freight trair train** *m* de marchandises; *NAm:* **freigh car,** wagon *m* à/de marchandises; **A freight plane,** avion *m* de fret; **freigh depot,** gare ƒ de marchandises; **freigh elevator,** monte-charge *m inv*; **freight rat tarif** *m* marchandise; **freight shippin messageries** ƒ maritimes **3.** (*cost*) fre (frais de) port *m*/transport; **freight b weight,** fret au poids; **to pay the freigh payer** le fret; **freight charges paid,** po payé.

freight[2], *v.tr.* **1.** affréter (un navire) **2. freight (out) a ship,** donner un navire à fr **3.** charger (un navire) **4.** transporter d marchandises; faire transporter/envoye des marchandises (par bateau, par avio *also NAm:* par camion, par train).

freightage, *n.* **1.** affrètement *m* **2.** fret *n* cargaison ƒ **3.** *NAm:* frais *mpl* de tran port/fret.

freighter, *n.* **1.** affréteur *m* (d'un navire) consignataire *m* (de marchandises à tran porter) **3.** entrepreneur *m* de transport exportateur *m* **4.** (*a*) cargo *m*; navire *m* charge (*b*) *Av:* avion *m* de fret.

freightliner, *n.* train *m* de marchandis en conteneurs.

fringe, *n.* **fringe benefits/***NAm: F:* **fringe avantages** *m* accessoires; suppléments de salaire (en nature); avantages sociau **fringe market,** marché marginal.

front, *n.* **1. front company,** société-écran

front man, (*i*) prête-nom *m* (*ii*) représentant, -ante (d'une société); porteparole *m* (d'une organisation); **front money,** capital initial/de départ **2. he demanded the money up front,** il a demandé d'être payé en avance.

front-end, *n.* (*a*) **front-end loading,** (méthode de) prélèvement des frais (d'achat) sur les premiers versements (*b*) *NAm:* section *f* de commercialisation *f* (d'une société).

fronting, *n. Ins:* façade *f*.

front-runner, *n.* candidat favori/principal concurrent.

frozen, *a. Fin:* (*account*) gelé/bloqué; **frozen assets,** fonds *m* non liquides/fonds gelés/fonds bloqués; **frozen credits,** créances gelées/crédits bloqués.

frustrated, *a.* **frustrated exports,** produits destinés à l'exportation en souffrance.

fulfil, *v.tr.* exécuter (un contrat); remplir (une obligation).

fulfilment, *n.* exécution *f* (d'un contrat).

full[1], *a.* **full fare,** (billet) plein tarif/place entière; *Av:* (classe) plein service; **full measure,** mesure *f* juste/mesure comble; **full price,** prix fort; **full payment,** remboursement intégral; **full weight,** poids *m* juste; *Ins:* **full cover,** garantie totale; *Fin:* **full discharge,** quitus *m*.

full[2], *n.* **money refunded in full,** remboursement complet; **vous serez intégralement remboursé de la somme versée; capital paid in full,** capital entièrement versé; **in full of all demands,** pour fin de compte/pour solde de tout compte; **acceptance in full of the conditions,** acceptation intégrale des conditions.

full-time, 1. *adv.* **to work full-time,** travailler à plein temps **2.** *a.* **full-time employment/job,** emploi *m* à temps complet/à plein temps; **full-time employee,** employé, -ée qui travaille à plein temps.

fully, *adv.* pleinement/entièrement/complètement; **fully paid,** payé intégralement; **until fully paid,** jusqu'à règlement complet/parfait paiement; **capital fully paid (up),** capital entièrement versé; **fully paid-up shares,** actions entièrement libérées.

functional, *a.* fonctionnel; **functional approach,** démarche *f* pragmatique; **functional organization,** organisation fonctionnelle/horizontale.

fund[1], *n.* (*a*) fonds *m*; caisse *f*; **International Monetary Fund (IMF),** Fonds Monétaire International (FMI); **pension fund/ retirement fund,** caisse de retraites; **fund of funds/fund management company,** Organisme *m* de Placements Collectifs en Valeurs Mobilières (OPCVM); **captive fund,** fonds dédié/fonds de capital-risque maison; **consolidated fund,** compte *m* du Trésor Public; **index fund,** fonds à gestion indicielle/fonds indiciel; **low-load fund,** fonds à faible frais d'entrée; **managed fund,** fonds géré; **money market fund,** fonds monétaires (*b*) *pl.* **funds,** fonds; masse *f*; ressources *f* pécuniaires; **funds of a company,** fonds social/masse sociale; (*of company*) **to make a call for funds,** faire un appel de capital; **funds on which an annuity is secured,** assiette *f* d'une rente; *Bank:* **no funds,** défaut *m* de provision/ manque *m* de fonds; pas d'encaisse; **not sufficient funds,** (chèque) sans provision; **sinking fund,** fonds d'amortissement; **fund raiser,** tapeur, -euse de fonds (*c*) *pl.* **public funds,** la dette publique; **The Funds,** les bons du Trésor; **fund holder,** rentier, -ière.

fund[2], *v.tr. Fin:* **1.** consolider (une dette publique) **2. to fund money,** placer de l'argent dans les fonds publics; acheter des bons du Trésor **3.** pourvoir (une société, etc.) de fonds/verser des fonds (dans une société); **to fund a project,** financer un projet/une entreprise.

fundamentalist, *n. NAm:* analyste *mf* fondamental(e).

funded, *a.* **funded capital,** capitaux investis; **long-term funded capital,** capitaux consolidés à long terme; **funded debt,** dette consolidée; **funded property,** biens *mpl* en rentes.

funding, *n.* consolidation *f* (d'une dette); assiette *f* (d'une rente); **funding loan,** emprunt *m* de consolidation; **BP will put up half of the funding,** BP financera le projet à 50%.

fungible, *a.* **fungible securities,** titres *mpl* en suspens.

funnel, *v.tr.* **he funnelled profits into another company,** il a acheminé/dirigé/canalisé les profits vers une autre société; il a fait profiter une autre société des profits réalisés.

further, *a.* **further orders,** commandes ultérieures/nouvelles commandes; **further to your letter of the 15th,** (comme) suite à/en réponse à votre lettre du 15 courant; **further to your telephone call,** (comme) suite à notre conversation téléphonique; **further to our letter,** nous référant à notre lettre; **a further £50 on account,** un nouvel acompte de cinquante livres; **to ask for a further credit,** demander un crédit supplémentaire; **for further information/details/particulars,** pour (obtenir de) plus amples renseignements/pour renseignements supplémentaires.

future, *a.* **your future orders,** vos nouvelles commandes; **future delivery,** livraison *f* à terme; **goods for future delivery,** marchandises *f* livrables ultérieurement/à terme; *Fin:* **exchange for future delivery,** opérations *f* de change à terme; **to sell for future delivery,** vendre livrable à terme.

futures, *n.pl. Fin:* contrats/opérations *f* transactions *f* à terme; **(quotations for) futures,** cotations *f*/livraisons *f* à terme; **financial futures,** contrat *m* à terme d'instruments financiers (CATIF); **gold futures,** le marché à terme de l'or; **(financial) futures market,** marché *m* à terme d'instruments financiers (MATIF); marché de contrats à terme; **selling of futures/sale for futures,** vente *f* à forfait/à découvert; **futures option,** option *f* sur contrats à terme.

G

G5 (countries), *n.* le G5/le groupe des 5.

G7 (countries), *n.* le G7/le groupe des 7.

gain[1], *n.* **1.** (*profit*) gain *m*/profit *m*/bénéfice *m*; **capital gains tax,** impôt *m* sur les plus-values **2.** (*increase*) accroissement *m*/augmentation *f.*

gain[2], *v.tr. & i.* gagner; bénéficier (de); faire un profit.

gainer, *n. Fin:* valeur *f* en hausse.

gainsharing, *n.* participation *f* aux bénéfices; participation des salariés.

gallon, *n. Meas:* gallon *m* (**Imperial gallon** = 4,546 litres; **US gallon** = 3,785 litres); (*of car*) **to do 28 miles to the gallon** = consommer 10 litres aux 100 (kilomètres).

gamble[1], *n.* coup risqué; **pure gamble,** pure spéculation/affaire de chance.

gamble[2], *v.i.* **to gamble on the Stock Exchange,** boursicoter/jouer à la Bourse/spéculer.

gambler, *n.* **gambler on the Stock Exchange,** joueur, -euse/spéculateur, -trice/boursicoteur, -euse.

gambling, *n.* **gambling on the Stock Exchange,** spéculation *f.*

gap, *n.* écart *m*; **gap study,** étude *f* des écarts; **gap in the market,** créneau *m*; **trade gap,** déficit commercial; découvert *m* de la balance commerciale; **the dollar gap,** la pénurie de dollars.

garnishee, *n.* tiers saisi; **garnishee order,** ordonnance *f* de saisie-arrêt.

gazette, *n.* **London Gazette/Edinburgh Gazette** = Le Journal officiel/l'Officiel.

gazetted, *a.* (*information*) publié dans l'Officiel.

gazump, *v.tr.* (*a*) (*vendor*) revenir sur une promesse de vente pour accepter une suroffre; (*purchaser*) faire une suroffre (dans l'immobilier); **I have been gazumped,** quelqu'un a fait une suroffre qui a été acceptée et l'affaire est tombée à l'eau (*b*) augmenter le prix de vente (d'une propriété) avant l'échange des contrats.

gazumping, *n.* suroffre *f*; surenchère *f* des prix (dans l'immobilier).

gear, *v.tr.* (*a*) **wages geared to the cost of living,** salaires indexés au coût de la vie; **a company geared up for expansion,** une société tournée/orientée vers l'expansion (*b*) **highly geared company,** société avec ratio *m* d'endettement élevé.

gearing, *n. Fin:* (*leverage*) effet *m* de levier; (*expressed as percentage*) ratio *m* d'endettement.

general, *a.* (*a*) **general meeting,** assemblée générale; (*on agenda of meeting*) **general business,** questions diverses; **general expenses,** frais généraux; **general and administrative expenses (G & A),** frais généraux et frais de gestion; *MIns:* **general average,** avaries communes; **general acceptance,** acceptation *f* sans réserve; **general balance-sheet,** bilan *m* d'ensemble; **general bill of lading,** connaissement collectif; **General Agreement on Tariffs and Trade (GATT),** Accord général sur les tarifs douaniers et le commerce/agétac *m*; **general ledger,** grand(-)livre *m*; **general partnership,** société (commerciale) en nom collectif; **general trend,** tendance/orientation générale (*b*) **general store(s),** alimentation générale (*c*) **secretary general,** secrétaire général.

generate, *v.tr.* créer/produire (un revenu).

generic, 1. *a* générique **2.** *n. NAm: Pharm:* produit générique; **branded generic,** produit générique de fantaisie; **commodity generic,** produit générique vrai.

genuine, *a.* (*a*) authentique/véritable; **genuine article,** article garanti d'origine (*b*) **genuine purchaser,** acheteur sérieux.

genuineness, *n.* authenticité *f* (d'une marque de fabrique, etc.).

get, *v.tr.* **1.** (*a*) (*obtain*) se procurer/obtenir; (*buy*) acheter; **I got this car cheap,** j'ai eu/j'ai acheté cette voiture (*à*) bon marché (*b*) recevoir/gagner; **to get £35000 a year,** gagner £35000 par an; **to get 10% interest,** recevoir un intérêt de 10%; **I get only a small profit,** il ne me revient/je n'en retire qu'un léger bénéfice **2.** recevoir (une lettre, etc.); **I got his answer this morning,** j'ai eu/j'ai reçu sa réponse ce matin **3.** he **got himself appointed chairman,** il s'est fait nommer président **4.** he **got (himself) into debt,** il s'est endetté **5. I can't get hold of him,** je n'arrive pas à le joindre **6.** he **gets on well with his colleagues,** il s'entend bien avec ses collègues **7.** we **must get down to work,** il nous faut nous mettre au travail.

get through, *v.tr.* **to get sth. through the customs,** (faire) passer qch. à la douane.

get up, *v.tr.* apprêter/présenter (un article pour la vente); habiller (des bouteilles).

getup, get-up, *n.* façon *f*/présentation *f* (de marchandises); habillage *m* (de bouteilles); présentation (d'un livre).

giant, *a.* **giant packet,** carton géant.

gift, *n.* (*a*) don *m*; donation *f*; *Jur:* **as a gift,** à titre d'avantage; **deed of gift,** (acte *m* de) donation entre vifs (*b*) cadeau *m*; **gift shop,** magasin *m* de nouveautés; **gift cheque/token,** chèque-cadeau *m*; **gift coupon/gift voucher,** bon-cadeau *m* (*c*) (*on presentation of coupons*) prime *f*.

gilt, *n.* = **gilt-edged stock.**

gilt-edged, *a. StExch:* (*a*) **gilt-edged stock(s)/securities,** fonds *m* d'État; valeurs *f* de haute qualité/de premier choix; valeurs refuge/*F:* valeurs de père de famille; **gilt switches,** arbitrage *m* sur valeurs du Trésor (*b*) *US:* **gilt-edged bond,** valeur *f* du Trésor américain.

giro, *n. Bank:* (*a*) **giro system/bank giro,** giro bancaire; **giro cheque,** chèque *m* de virement; **bank giro transfer,** virement *m* bancaire (*b*) *F:* allocation *f* de Sécurité Sociale (*payée par chèque tous les quinze jours*).

Girobank, *n. Post:* = service *m* de chèques postaux; **Girobank account** = compte courant postal/compte chèque postal (CCP).

give, *v.tr.* **1.** (*a*) donner; **to give a good price for sth.,** donner/payer un bon prix pour qch.; **what did you give for it?** combien l'avez-vous payé? **I'll give you £10 for it,** je vous en donnerai £10; **what will you give me for it?** combien m'en offrez-vous? **to give a week's notice,** donner ses huit jours (de préavis); **to give s.o. a rise,** augmenter (le salaire de) qqn; **to give credit,** faire crédit (*b*) *StExch:* **to give for the call,** acheter la prime à livrer; **to give for the put,** acheter la prime à recevoir **2.** (*a shop*) **I gave him an order for ten new cars,** je lui ai passé une commande de dix voitures neuves **3. investment that gives 10%,** placement *m* qui rapporte 10% **4.** *Jur:* **to give evidence,** témoigner.

giveaway, *n. F:* **giveaway (price),** prix *n.* dérisoire; **it's a giveaway!** c'est donné!

given, *a.* donné; **at a given price,** à un cour donné/déterminé.

give on, *v.tr. StExch:* faire reporter (de titres).

glass, *n.* **1.** (*a*) **the glass industry,** l'industri *f* du verre/la verrerie (*b*) (*on parce.* **glass** = (*sur un colis*) fragile.

global, *a.* **global finance,** financement *n* aux entreprises; **global equities marke**

marché mondial des actions/cotation mondiale des actions; **global village,** le village planétaire.

glut[1], *n.* surabondance *f*/pléthore *f* (d'une denrée, etc.); *Fin:* **glut of money,** pléthore de capitaux.

glut[2], *v.tr.* encombrer/inonder/écraser/ surcharger (le marché); créer une pléthore sur (le marché).

glutting, *n.* **glutting of the markets,** encombrement *m*/engorgement *m* des marchés.

gnome, *n.* requin *m* de la finance.

go-between, *n.* intermédiaire *mf*/médiateur (dans un conflit).

godown, *n.* entrepôt *m* (*dans les pays orientaux*).

go down, *v.i.* (*of prices, value*) baisser.

gofer, *n.* factotum *m.*

going, *a.* **1.** qui marche; **going concern,** affaire *f* qui marche/prospère **2. the going price,** le prix courant/actuel.

gold, *n.* (*a*) or *m*; **gold content,** teneur *f* en or; **pure gold,** or pur (*b*) *Fin:* **gold currency/gold money,** monnaie *f* d'or; pièces *fpl* d'or/en or; **gold specie,** or monnayé; **gold bullion,** or en lingots; **gold coin and bullion,** encaisse *f* or; **gold franc,** franc *m* or; **France's gold reserves,** le stock/la réserve d'or de la France; **gold standard,** étalon-or *m*; **gold bullion standard,** étalon-or lingot; **gold exchange standard,** étalon *m* de change-or; **gold ratio,** rapport *m* de l'encaisse en or à la monnaie en circulation; **export/outgoing gold point,** point *m* de sortie de l'or/gold-point *m* de sortie; **import/incoming gold point,** point d'entrée de l'or/gold-point d'entrée; *StExch:* **gold bond,** obligation *f* or; **gold shares/F: s.pl. golds,** valeurs *f* aurifères (*c*) *US:* **gold bug,** investisseur-or *m*/investisseur patrimonial en or.

golden, *a.* (*a*) doré; *NAm:* **Golden Boys,** jeunes spéculateurs *mpl* sur le marché à options; **golden handcuffs,** contrat alléchant (*qui encourage les employés à rester avec le même employeur*); **golden handshake,** indemnité *f* de départ; **golden hello,** indemnité de transfert (*offerte par un nouvel employeur*); (faire) un pont d'or (à qn); **golden parachute,** indemnité contractuelle de départ/de licenciement; parapluie doré (*b*) *StExch:* **golden fixing,** cotation *f* de l'or; cours officiel.

good, *a.* (*a*) bon, valable; **ticket good for one month,** billet *m* valable pour un mois (*b*) **in good faith,** de bonne foi; **in good time,** en temps utile; **at a good price,** à un prix intéressant.

goods, *n.pl.* (*a*) *Jur:* biens *m*/effets *m*/biens meubles (*b*) marchandises *f*/denrées *f*/ objets *m*/articles *m*; **capital goods,** biens d'équipement; **consumer goods,** biens de consommation; **durable goods,** biens permanents/durables; **luxury goods,** articles de luxe; **manufactured goods,** produits fabriqués/manufacturés; **perishable goods,** denrées périssables; *NAm:* **soft goods,** articles de nouveauté; *NAm:* **hard goods,** biens de consommation durables; **wet goods,** liquides *m*; **white/brown goods,** produits blancs/bruns (*c*) *Rail:* **goods train,** train *m* de marchandises; **goods station/goods depot,** gare *f*/dépôt *m* de marchandises.

good-till-cancelled (GTC), *n.* ordre *m* (valable jusqu'à) révocation.

goodwill, *n.* survaloir *m*/survaleur *f*/goodwill *m*/éléments incorporels/fonds *m* de commerce; surcote *f* d'intégration.

go-slow, *a.* & *n.* **go-slow (strike),** grève perlée; **go-slow policy,** politique *f* d'attente.

go up, *v.i.* (*of prices, etc.*) monter/ augmenter; **the cost of living is going up,** le coût de la vie augmente; **the bidding went up to £2000,** les enchères *f* ont monté jusqu'à £2000.

Government, *n.* gouvernement *m*; État *m*; **government bonds,** obligations *f* d'État; **government papers/securities/ stock,** effets publics/rentes sur l'État/fonds d'État; **government loan,** emprunt public.

g r a c e, *n.* **days of grace,** délai (*accordé pour le paiement d'un effet*); *Ins:* délai (*accordé pour le paiement des primes d'assurance sur la vie*); **to give a creditor seven days' grace,** accorder à un créancier sept jours de grâce/de faveur.

g r a d e[1], *n.* (*of employee*) échelon *m*; (*of products*) **high-grade/top-grade/choice-grade,** de qualité supérieure/de (tout) premier choix; surchoix; *F:* (de qualité) extra; **low-grade/below-grade,** de qualité inférieure; *Aut:* **high-grade/premium-grade petrol** = supercarburant *m*/super *m*; **low-grade petrol** = ordinaire *m*.

g r a d e[2], *v.tr.* **1.** classer/trier (des marchandises, etc.) selon leur qualité/calibrer **2. graded tax,** (*i*) impôt progressif (*ii*) impôt dégressif; **graded advertising rates,** tarif *m* d'annonces dégressif **3. graded hotels,** hôtels classés.

g r a d i n g, *n.* (*of employee*) échelon *m*.

g r a d u a t e[1], *n.* diplômé, -ée; licencié, -ée; **graduate entry,** échelon *m* d'entrée pour les diplômés; **graduate training scheme,** programme *m* de formation professionnelle pour les diplômés.

g r a d u a t e[2], *v.tr.* **to graduate a tax according to the taxpayer's income,** établir un impôt proportionnellement au revenu du contribuable; **graduated pension scheme** = régime *m* de retraites complémentaires (obligatoires); **graduated income tax,** impôt progressif; impôt proportionnel au revenu du contribuable; **graduated taxation,** taxes imposées par paliers.

g r a i n, *n.* céréales *fpl*; **grain market,** marché *m* des grains.

g r a m, *n. Meas:* gramme *m* (*abbr:* g) (= 0.0353 oz); **250 gram(s)/250g,** 250 grammes/250g.

g r a n d, *a.* **grand total,** total global/général.

g r a n t[1], *n.* aide *f* pécuniaire; subvention *f*/ allocation *f*/prime *f*; **grant-aided,** subven-

tionné par l'État; **investment grant,** subvention pour investissement.

g r a n t[2], *v.tr.* accorder/allouer (une subvention à qn); **to grant a loan,** consentir un prêt; **to grant an overdraft,** consentir un découvert (**to,** à); *Jur:* **to grant bail,** accorder une liberté (provisoire) à qn sous caution.

g r a p h, *n.* courbe *f*; graphe *m*; graphique *m*; diagramme *m*; **graph paper,** papier quadrillé; **to plot a graph,** tracer un graphique.

g r a t u i t y, *n.* pourboire *m*/gratification *f*.

g r e e n, *a.* **green franc,** franc vert; **green pound,** livre verte; **green rate,** taux vert; **green baize door,** frontière *f* séparant les analystes des opérateurs financiers (*empêchant les délits d'initiés*); *F:* **green book,** (*Unlisted Securities Market*) marché *m* hors cote.

g r e e n b a c k, *n.* dollar *m* (américain); le billet vert.

g r e y, *a.* **grey market,** marché gris; **grey zone,** zone grise.

g r i d, *n.* **grid structure,** structure *f* en grille; **managerial grid,** grille *f* de gestion.

g r o s s[1], *n.* douze douzaines *f*/grosse *f*; **six gross of pencils,** six grosses de crayons; **great gross,** douze grosses.

g r o s s[2], *a.* (*a*) brut; **gross amount,** montant brut (d'une facture, etc.); **gross cost,** prix de revient brut; **gross margin,** marge brute/profit brut; **gross mark-up,** marge (bénéficiaire) brute; **gross proceeds,** produit brut (d'une opération commerciale ou financière); **gross profit,** bénéfice brut; **gross loss,** perte brute; **gross national income,** revenu national brut; **gross domestic product (GDP),** produit intérieur brut (PIB); **gross national product (GNP),** produit national brut (PNB) (*b*) **gross weight,** poids brut; **gross (register) ton,** tonneau *m* de jauge brute; **gross (register) tonnage,** (tonnage *m* de) jauge brute/ tonnage brut (*c*) *MIns:* **gross average,** grosse(s) avarie(s) commune(s).

g r o s s[3], *v.tr.* produire un montant brut/

donner des recettes brutes; **they grossed £10 million,** cela leur a rapporté brut £10 millions.

rossing up, *n.* majoration *f.*

round, *n.* (*a*) terrain *m*; **building ground,** terrain à bâtir (*b*) **the dollar lost ground,** le dollar a perdu du terrain (*c*) **ground rent,** rente foncière.

roup, *n.* (*a*) *Ind: etc:* groupe *m*/groupement *m*/société *f*/groupe d'entreprises/ groupe industriel; **the Shell Group,** le Groupe Shell; *Ins:* **group insurance,** contrat *m* de groupe; **group ticket,** billet collectif; **group decision,** décision collective; **Group of Ten,** le groupe des dix (*b*) **group accounts,** comptes consolidés/intégrés.

rowth, *n.* accroissement *m*/augmentation *f* (en quantité)/développement *m* (des affaires); expansion *f* (des affaires, d'une maison de commerce); **economic growth,** développement/croissance *f* économique; **growth index,** indice *m* de croissance; **growth industry,** industrie *f* en croissance rapide; **growth sector,** secteur *m* de croissance; **growth share/stock,** valeur *f* de croissance; **growth of productivity,** accroissement *m* de la productivité; **sales growth,** accroissement/augmentation des ventes; **growth rate/ rate of growth,** taux *m* d'expansion/de croissance/d'accroissement; **annual compound growth rate,** taux de croissance annualisé/composé annuellement; **ex growth,** (titre) dont la possibilité de croissance est réduite.

uarantee[1], *n.* **1.** (*pers.*) garant, -ante; caution *f*; **to go guarantee for s.o.,** se porter garant de qn/se porter caution pour qn/cautionner qn **2.** garantie *f*; **certificate of guarantee,** bulletin *m* de garantie; **under guarantee,** sous garantie; **I bought it secondhand, without guarantee,** je l'ai acheté d'occasion et sans garantie;

guarantee of a bill of exchange, aval *m* d'une lettre de change; **guarantee fund,** fonds *m* de garantie; **guarantee company/ guarantee society,** société *f* de sécurité; **guarantee commission,** ducroire *m* **3.** (*security*) garantie/cautionnement *m*; **bank guarantee,** caution bancaire; **to leave £5 as a guarantee,** verser un cautionnement de £5; **to secure all guarantees,** s'assurer toutes les garanties nécessaires.

guarantee[2], *v.tr.* **1.** (*a*) garantir/cautionner (qn, qch.)/se porter garant de/se porter caution pour (qn, qch.); **to guarantee a debt,** garantir une dette (*b*) **to guarantee an endorsement,** avaliser la signature (sur une traite); **to guarantee a bill of exchange,** avaliser une lettre de change **2.** garantir (une montre, un appareil)/vendre sous garantie; **watch guaranteed for two years,** montre garantie pour deux ans.

guaranteed, *a.* (*a*) garanti; **guaranteed bonds/stocks,** obligations/valeurs garanties (*b*) (*of bill*) signé pour aval/avalisé.

guarantor, *n.* garant, -ante/caution *f*/ répondant, -ante; avaliste *m*/donneur *m* d'aval (d'une lettre de change); **to stand as guarantor for s.o.,** appuyer qn de sa garantie/cautionner qn/se porter garant de qn.

guaranty, *n.* = **guarantee**[1] **2.** and **3.**

guardian, *n.* *Jur:* **(legal) guardian,** tuteur, -trice.

guesstimate, *n.* *F:* estimation approximative.

guild, *n.* *Hist:* corporation *f*; **merchant guild,** g(u)ilde *f* de commerçants; **trade guild,** corps *m* de métier.

guinea, *n.* guinée *f* (= £1.05).

gyration, *n.* fluctuations *fpl* (du marché).

H

habilitate, *v.tr. NAm:* avancer les fonds pour l'exploitation (d'une usine).

habilitator, *n. NAm:* bailleur *m* de fonds.

hacker, *n. Cmptr:* pirate *m* informatique.

hacking, *n. Cmptr:* piratage *m* informatique.

haggle, *v.i.* marchander.

half, 1. *n.* moitié *f*; **the first half (of the year),** le premier semestre; **reduced by half,** réduit de moitié 2. *a.* demi; **half day,** demi-journée *f*; **to work half days,** faire des demi-journées; *NAm:* **half a dollar,** (valeur de) cinquante cents; **a half dozen/half a dozen,** une demi-douzaine; **a rebate of half percent,** une ristourne d'un demi pour cent; **half fare/half-price ticket,** (*in train, bus*) demi-place *f*; (*in cinema*) demi-tarif *m*; **at half price,** à moitié prix; **on half profits,** de compte à demi; *StExch:* **half commission,** remise *f*; **half-commission man,** remisier *m*.

half-dollar, *n. NAm:* (pièce de) cinquante cents.

half(-)year, *n.* semestre *m*; **first half(-)year,** semestre de janvier/d'hiver; **second half(-)year,** semestre de juillet/d'été.

half-yearly, 1. *a.* semestriel; **half-yearly meeting,** assemblée semestrielle; **to draw up the half-yearly accounts,** dresser le bilan semestriel; **half-yearly dividend/payment/rent,** semestre *m* 2. *adv.* par semestre/tous les six mois.

hallmark[1], *n.* poinçon *m* (de contrôle, de maître) (*sur les objets d'orfèvrerie*).

hallmark[2], *v.tr.* poinçonner (l'orfèvrerie).

hammer[1], *n.* marteau *m* (de commissaire-

priseur); **to come under the hammer,** êt mis/vendu aux enchères.

hammer[2], *v.tr.* (*a*) *StExch:* (*of stockbroke* hammered, déclaré insolvable/exécu (*b*) *F:* **to hammer prices,** faire baisser l prix (*c*) **to hammer out a contract,** sign un contrat (après de longues négoci tions).

hammering, *n. StExch:* déclaration d'i solvabilité (d'un courtier, etc.).

hand, *n.* 1. (*a*) (*of business, etc.*) **to chan hands,** changer de propriétaire (*b*) **to ha so much money in hand,** avoir ta d'argent disponible; **cash in har** encaisse *f*; montant *m* en caisse; **stock hand,** marchandises *fpl* en magasin; **wo in hand,** travail *m* en cours/en chantier **work on hand,** travail en cours; travail faire; **goods left on hand,** marchandis non vendues/laissées pour compte **your order is not to hand at prese** l'article que vous avez commandé n' pas disponible en ce moment 2. (*per* ouvrier, -ière; manœuvre *m*; **to take hands,** embaucher de la main-d'œuvre signature *f*; *Jur:* **to set one's hand to a de** apposer sa signature à un acte; **note hand,** billet *m* à ordre.

handbook, *n.* manuel *m* (de références)

handicraft, *n.* artisanat *m*/travail arti nal.

hand in, *v.tr.* remettre/déposer qch.; **hand in one's resignation,** démissionn donner sa démission.

handle, *v.tr.* (*a*) **to handle a lot of mon** manier de grosses sommes d'argent; **don't handle these goods,** nous ne ten pas ces articles; **we can handle orders**

overseas, nous prenons des commandes pour l'étranger; **we are in a position to handle any sort of business,** nous sommes à même d'exécuter n'importe quelle opération (*b*) (*on parcels*) **handle with care** = fragile.

handler, *n.* manutentionnaire *mf.*

handling, *n.* (*a*) manutention *f* (de marchandises, etc.); **handling charges,** frais *mpl* de manutention; **industrial handling,** manutention industrielle; **handling capacity,** capacité *f* de traitement (*b*) distribution *f.*

hand(-)made, *a.* fait (à la) main/fabriqué à la main.

hand over, *v.tr.* remettre (qch. à qn); **the letter was handed over to him personally,** on lui a remis la lettre en main(s) propre(s).

handout, *n.* (*a*) prospectus *m*/circulaire *f* publicitaire (*b*) cadeau *m* publicitaire.

handshake, *n.* *F:* **golden handshake,** indemnité *f* de départ/cadeau *m* d'adieu; **to give s.o. a golden handshake,** remercier qn de ses services en le dédommageant grassement.

handwork, *n.* travail *m* à la main; travail manuel.

handwriting, *n.* **send your application in your own handwriting,** envoyez une demande manuscrite.

harbour, *n.* port *m*; **commercial harbour,** port commercial; **fishing harbour,** port de pêche; **harbour dues,** droits *m* de port/de mouillage; **harbour installations/harbour facilities/harbour works,** installations *f* portuaires.

hard, *a.* **1.** *Fin:* (*of stock, rates, etc.*) soutenu/ferme **2. article that is hard to sell,** article difficile à vendre/qui ne se vend pas bien/d'écoulement difficile **3. hard currency,** devise *f* forte.

harden, *v.i.* *Fin:* (*of shares, etc.*) **to harden (up),** se raffermir; **prices are hardening,** les prix *m* sont en hausse/se raffermissent.

hardening, *n.* (*of prices*) raffermissement *m.*

hardness, *n.* *Fin:* tension *f* (du marché, des actions).

hard sell, *n.* publicité poussée à fond/publicité agressive/battage *m* (publicitaire); **to give s.o. the hard sell,** imposer une vente à qn.

hardware, *n.* *Cmptr:* matériel *m* (de traitement de l'information)/équipement *m*/hardware *m.*

haul[1], *n.* transport *m*; **length of haul,** distance *f* de transport; **short haul,** transport à/sur courte distance; **medium haul,** transport à/sur moyenne distance; **long haul,** transport sur longue distance/à grande distance.

haul[2], *v.tr.* transporter (des marchandises) par camion/camionner.

haulage, *n.* **1.** roulage *m*/camionnage *m*; **haulage contractor,** entrepreneur *m* de transports/de roulage; **road haulage,** transports routiers; **road haulage depot,** gare routière (de marchandises) **2.** (*costs*) frais *mpl* de roulage/de transport.

haulier, *n.* (*a*) entrepreneur *m* de transports (*b*) entreprise *f* de roulage.

hawk, *v.tr.* colporter (des marchandises); crier des marchandises.

hawker, *n.* (*a*) colporteur *m*/marchand ambulant/camelot *m* (*b*) (*of fruit, vegetables*) marchand des quatre saisons.

hawking, *n.* colportage *m*; **share hawking,** colportage de titres.

head, *n.* **1.** (*headings*) **he signed heads of agreement,** il a signé le protocole d'accord **2.** (*pers.*) (*a*) chef *m*; directeur, -trice; **head of department,** chef de service; (*in store*) chef de rayon (*b*) **head agent,** agent principal; **head clerk,** premier commis/commis principal; chef de bureau; **head foreman,** chef d'atelier; **head office,** siège social/bureau principal **3. to**

pay so much per head/so much a head, payer tant par tête/par personne.

headed, *a.* **headed notepaper**, papier *m* à en-tête.

headhunter, *n.* chasseur *m* de têtes.

heading, *n.* (*a*) en-tête *m* (d'une page, d'une lettre, d'une facture) (*b*) poste *m*/rubrique *f*; **see under the heading 'sales'**, voir sous la rubrique "vente".

headquarters, *n.pl.* siège social/bureau principal; **to have its headquarters at …**, avoir son siège à ….

health, *n.* santé *f*; **health insurance**, assurance *f* maladie.

hearing, *n. Jur:* audience *f*/audition *f*.

heavy, *a.* **1. the market is heavy**, le marché est lourd **2. heavy expenditure**, dépenses *f* considérables/grosses dépenses; **heavy industry**, industrie lourde; **heavy losses**, lourdes/fortes pertes; **heavy percentage**, pourcentage élevé; **heavy sales**, ventes massives; **contangoes are heavy**, les reports sont chers **3.** (*oppressive*) **heavy tax**, impôt lourd; **heavy charge on the budget**, charge onéreuse pour le budget **4. heavy hitters**, hommes de poids (dans le domaine de la vente).

hedge[1], *n. StExch:* **hedge (operation)**, (*i*) arbitrage *m* (*ii*) (opération de) couverture *f*; **hedge against inflation**, sauvegarde *f*/couverture *f* contre l'inflation; **hedge clause**, clause de sauvegarde (*insérée dans un contrat*).

hedge[2], *v.i. & tr. StExch:* (*i*) faire une opération d'arbitrage/arbitrer (des valeurs) (*ii*) se couvrir; **to hedge by a sale for the account**, se couvrir par une vente à terme.

hedger, *n. StExch:* arbitragiste *m* en couverture de risque.

hedging, *n.* (*a*) *StExch:* arbitrage *m* (à terme)/opération *f* de couverture/endiguement *m*/hedging *m* (*b*) *NAm:* contrepartie *f*.

hereafter, *adv.* ci-après/ci-dessous.

hereby, *adv.* **we hereby declare that …** nous déclarons, par la présente, que ….

hereditable, *a.* **hereditable bond**, effet *m* transmissible par (voie de) succession.

hereditament, *n. Jur:* (*a*) bien transmissible par (voie de) succession (*b*) *pl* **hereditaments**, biens composant une succession/legs *m*.

herewith, *adv.* **I am sending you herewith** je vous envoie ci-joint/ci-inclus/sous cpli.

heritage, *n.* patrimoine *m*.

hidden, *a. Fin:* **hidden cost**, coût caché **hidden reserves**, réserves secrètes occultes.

high[1], **higher**, **highest**, *a.* (*a*) **high/higher executives**, cadres supérieurs; **to be in** **high position**, être haut placé (*b*) **high prices**, prix élevés; **to fetch a high price**, s vendre cher; **highest price**, chiffre *m* maximum; **the highest and lowest prices** cours *m* extrêmes; **to make a higher bid** faire une offre supérieure; **high rate of interest**, taux d'intérêt élevé (*c*) **the highes efficiency**, (*i*) la plus grande compétence (*ii*) le rendement maximum.

high[2], *adv.* (*of price*) **to run high**, être élevé **expenditure is running high**, les dépenses sont élevées.

high[3], *n.* **prices have reached a new high**, le prix *m* ont atteint un nouveau maximum **to reach an all-time high**, atteindre u nouveau record/plafond; *StExch:* **high and lows**, les (cours) extrêmes/les (cour les plus) hauts et les (cours les plus) ba

high-end, *a.* (*goods*) haut de gamme.

high-grade, *a.* (marchandise, etc.) de pre mière qualité/de (premier) choix; **high grade petrol**, supercarburant *m*/ super *n*

high-level, *a.* **high-level staff**, les cadre supérieurs; **high-level decision**, décisio prise à un niveau supérieur.

highly, *adv.* **1. highly placed official**, hau fonctionnaire **2. his services are high**

paid, ses services sont largement rétribués/on paie très cher ses services.

high-pressure, *a.* **high-pressure salesman,** vendeur importun/agressif/qui force la main; **high-pressure salesmanship,** l'art *m* de vendre coûte que coûte (en forçant la main).

high-quality, *a.* de première qualité/de premier ordre/de (premier) choix.

high-tech, *a.* (*design*) résolument moderne; (*look*) ultra-sophistiqué; (*conception*) issu de la recherche de pointe/de haute technologie.

hire[1], *n.* **1.** (*a*) *NAm:* embauchage *m* (de main-d'œuvre) (*b*) location *f* (de voiture, etc.); **cars for hire,** voitures à louer; **car hire service,** location *f* de voitures; **hire car,** voiture *f* de location (*c*) **hire purchase,** (*i*) achat *m* à crédit/à tempérament (*ii*) location-vente *f;* **hire purchase agreement,** contrat *m* de location-vente; **to buy sth. on hire purchase,** acheter qch. à crédit/à tempérament **2.** *NAm:* (*i*) salaire *m* (*ii*) prix *m* de la location.

hire[2], **1.** *v.tr.* (*a*) *esp. NAm:* engager (un ouvrier, un employé); **the personnel manager has the power to hire and fire,** le chef du personnel a tous droits d'embauche et de renvoi (*b*) louer (une voiture, etc.)/prendre (qch.) en location **2.** *v.i. NAm:* **he hired (himself) out as a waiter,** il a accepté un emploi comme garçon de restaurant.

hired, *a.* **hired car,** voiture *f* de location.

hire out, *v.tr.* donner en location.

hiring, *n.* (*a*) embauchage *m* (d'un ouvrier) (*b*) location *f* (d'une voiture, etc.).

histogram, *n.* histogramme *m.*

historical, *a.* **historical cost,** coût *m* historique/à l'origine.

hive off, *v.tr.* (*a*) *F:* mettre de côté/mettre à l'écart (*b*) **the subsidiary company will be hived off,** la filiale deviendra indépendante.

hoarding, *n.* **1.** thésaurisation *f* (de capitaux) **2.** panneau *m* d'affichage.

hold, *v.tr.* **1. to hold stocks as security,** détenir des titres en garantie; **to hold stocks for a rise,** conserver des valeurs en vue d'une hausse **2. this product is still holding its own after all these years,** ce produit, lancé depuis des années, se vend toujours bien **3.** tenir (une séance); **the Motor Show is held in October,** le Salon de l'Automobile a lieu/se tient au mois d'octobre; **to hold an auction,** faire/procéder à une vente aux enchères; **the meeting will be held at 8 p.m.,** la réunion aura lieu à huit heures du soir/à 20 heures **4.** *Tel:* **hold the line please,** ne quittez pas, s'il vous plaît; **the line's engaged, will you hold?,** voulez-vous attendre que le poste soit libre?

hold back, *v.i.* **buyers are holding back,** les acheteurs *m* s'abstiennent.

holder, *n.* (*a*) (*pers.*) détenteur, -trice (de titres, d'une lettre de change); porteur, -euse (de titres, d'un effet); titulaire *mf* (d'un droit, d'un poste, d'un permis, d'un compte en banque, d'une carte de crédit); concessionnaire *mf* (d'un brevet, d'une marque, d'un produit); propriétaire *mf* (d'une terre); **holder of insurance policy,** assuré, -ée; *Jur:* **holder (on trust) of s.o.'s securities,** dépositaire *mf* des valeurs de qn; **holders of debt claims,** créanciers *m;* **holder in due course,** porteur régulier/de bonne foi (*b*) **message holder,** classe-notes *m*/spirale *f* de classement.

holding, *n. Fin:* avoir *m* (en actions); effets *mpl* en portefeuille; dossier *m;* holding *m;* **he has holdings in several companies,** il est actionnaire de plusieurs sociétés; **core holding,** investissement *m* de base (*dans le portefeuille des investisseurs institutionnels*); **cross holdings,** participations croisées; **majority holding,** participation *f* majoritaire; **holding company,** tenante *f*/(société) holding *m*/société de portefeuille/société de contrôle.

hold over, *v.tr.* arriérer/différer (un paiement); **bills held over,** effets *m* en souffrance/en suspens.

hold up, 1. *v.tr.* **goods held up at the customs,** marchandises *f* en consigne/en souffrance/immobilisées à la douane; **payment is held up,** (*i*) on refuse de régler tout de suite (*ii*) les paiements sont suspendus **2.** *v.i.* **the shares held up well,** les actions se sont bien défendues; **the market is holding up well,** le marché tient toujours.

holiday, *n.* (*a*) (jour de) fête *f*/jour férié; **statutory / legal / official / national / public/ bank holiday,** fête légale (*b*) (jour de) congé *m* (*c*) **a month's holiday,** un mois de vacances; **paid holidays,** congé payé; **the summer holidays,** les grandes vacances; **to stagger holidays,** étaler les vacances.

home, *n.* **1. the Ideal Home Exhibition** = le Salon des Arts Ménagers **2.** (*a*) *NAm: Ind:* **home office,** siège social (d'une compagnie) (*b*) (*referring to the nation*) **the Home Office,** le Ministère de l'Intérieur; **home trade,** (*i*) commerce intérieur (*ii*) cabotage national; **home market,** marché intérieur; **home products/ home produce,** produits nationaux/du pays (*c*) **to work at home,** travailler/faire du travail à domicile **3. home loan,** prêt *m* hypothécaire.

homeward, *a.* **homeward freight,** fret *m* de retour; **homeward journey,** voyage *m* de retour.

homewards, *adv. Nau:* **loading homewards,** chargement *m* pour le retour; chargement de retour; **cargo homewards,** cargaison *f* de retour.

honorary, *a.* (*a*) (emploi, service) honoraire/non rétribué/bénévole; **honorary duties,** fonctions *f* sans rétribution/travail à titre gratuit/travail bénévole (*b*) **honorary president,** président *m* d'honneur/honoraire.

honour¹, *n.* **acceptance (of protested bill) for honour,** acceptation *f* par intervention; **the acceptor for honour,** l'avaliseur, -euse/l'avaliste *mf*; le donneur d'aval; **act of honour,** acte *m* d'intervention; **for the honour of ...,** pour l'honneur de ....

honour², *v.tr.* **to honour a bill,** faire honneur à/honorer/payer une lettre de change; **honoured bill,** traite payée/acquittée; **to honour one's signature,** honorer/faire honneur à sa signature.

horizontal, *a.* (*a*) *NAm:* **horizontal increase in salaries of 10%,** augmentation *f* uniforme de 10% sur toutes les rétributions (*b*) **horizontal integration,** intégration *f* horizontale.

horse-trading, *n.* maquignonnage *m.*

hostess, *n. Av:* **air hostess,** hôtesse *f* de l'air; **ground hostess,** hôtesse au sol.

hostile, *a.* (*takeover bid*) hostile/inamical sauvage.

hotel, *n.* hôtel *m;* **hotel accommodation,** chambre *f* d'hôtel; **hotel bill/expenses,** frais de séjour à l'hôtel; **hotel manager,** le directeur de l'hôtel; **private/residential hotel** = pension *f* de famille; **the hotel trade,** l'industrie hôtelière/l'hôtellerie *f.*

hour, *n.* heure *f;* **to pay s.o. by the hour,** payer qn à l'heure; **to be paid £5 an hour,** être payé £5 (de) l'heure; **output per hour,** puissance *f* horaire/rendement *m* à l'heure; **eight-hour day,** journée *f* (de travail) de huit heures; **37-hour week,** semaine de 37 heures; **business hours,** heures d'affaires/de bureau; heures d'ouverture et de clôture; **office hours,** heures de bureau; **I do this work out of hours,** je fais ce travail en dehors de mes heures (de bureau, d'atelier, etc.); **rush/ peak hours,** heures de pointe/d'affluence.

hourly, 1. *a* (débit, rendement, salaire) par heure/à l'heure/horaire; **hourly paid workers,** ouvriers payés à l'heure; **hourly rate,** tarif *m* horaire; **workmen's hourly rate pay,** salaire horaire ouvrier **2.** *adv* toutes les heures; d'heure en heure.

house, *n.* **1.** maison *f;* **house property,** immeubles *mpl;* **to invest in house property,** placer son argent en immeubles; **house agent,** agent immobilier; **house agency,** agence immobilière **2.** (*a*) **finance house,** maison de finance; **publishing house,** maison d'édition (*b*) **house magazine/ organ,** journal *m* interne d'entreprise

house telephone, téléphone intérieur; *Fin:* **house bill,** lettre de change creuse (*c*) *StExch:* **the House,** la Bourse (de Londres); **members of the House,** agents *m* de change.

household, *n. PolEc:* ménage *m*/famille *f*; **household expenses,** budget *m* du ménage.

householder, *n.* propriétaire *mf*/occupant, -ante (d'une maison); **householders' association,** syndicat de(s) propriétaires.

house-to-house, *a.* (vente, etc.) à domicile; **house-to-house canvassing,** porte(-)à(-)porte *m*/démarchage *m*.

hovercraft, *n.* aéroglisseur *m*; *F:* hovercraft *m*.

hoverport, *n.* hoverport *m*.

huckster, *n. NAm:* agent *m* de publicité agressif.

huckstering, *n. NAm:* vente agressive/exagérée/excessive.

hull, *n. MIns:* corps *m*; **hull insurance,** assurance *f* sur corps; **hull underwriter,** assureur *m* sur corps.

hundredweight, *n.* (*abbr.* **c.w.t.**), poids *m* de 112 livres/quintal *m* (= 50 kg).

hush-money, *n.* pot-de-vin *m*.

hydrofoil, *n.* hydroglisseur *m*.

hype, *v.tr.* exagérer le prix/la valeur (d'un produit, de titres, etc.).

hyped up, *a.* (produits, titres) dont la valeur a été exagérée.

hyperinflation, *n.* hyperinflation *f*.

hypermarket, *n.* hypermarché *m*.

hypothecate *v.tr. Jur:* hypothéquer (une terre); déposer (des titres) en nantissement.

hypothecation, *n.* fait *m* d'hypothéquer; inscription *f* hypothécaire/nantissement *m*; **letter of hypothecation,** lettre *f* hypothécaire/de nantissement.

I

idle, *a.* (*a*) (*of employees*) qui chôme/en chômage; (*of machine*) au repos/arrêté (*b*) (*of money*) **to lie idle,** dormir; **capital lying idle,** capital oisif; fonds dormants/ inemployés/improductifs/morts; **to let one's money lie idle,** laisser dormir son argent (*c*) **idle time,** temps mort.

illegal, *a.* illégal.

illegality, *n.* illégalité *f.*

illegally, *adv.* illégalement.

illicit, *a.* illicite; **illicit profits,** profits *m* illicites.

illiquidity, *n.* non-liquidité *f.*

image, *n.* **brand image,** image *f* de marque; **corporate image,** image de marque (de l'entreprise).

imbalance, *n.* déséquilibre *m*; **trade imbalance,** déficit commercial.

immobilization, *n.* immobilisation *f* (de capitaux).

immovable, *Jur:* **1.** *a.* **immovable property,** biens immobiliers/biens immeubles; **seizure of immovable property,** saisie immobilière **2.** *n. pl.* **immovables,** biens immobiliers/biens immeubles.

immunity, *n.* exemption *f* (**from,** de); **to claim immunity from certain taxes,** demander à être exempté/exonéré/dispensé de certains impôts.

impact, *n.* répercussion(s) *f(pl)*/impact *m*; **the impact of high wages on production costs,** l'incidence *f* des hauts salaires sur les prix de revient; **the impact of a publicity campaign,** l'impact d'une campagne publicitaire.

imperfect, *a.* imparfait; **imperfect competition,** concurrence imparfaite.

impersonal, *a.* **impersonal account,** compte fictif/compte anonyme.

implement, *v.tr.* exécuter/mettre à exécution (un projet); appliquer (une loi).

implementation, *n.* application *f*/exécution *f*/mise à exécution/mise à effet (d'un règlement, d'un programme).

implicit, *a.* (coût, intérêt) implicite.

implied, *a.* implicite/tacite; **implied terms,** termes implicites (d'un contrat).

import[1], *n.* (*a*) *usu. pl.* **imports,** (*i*) (*coll.*) importations *f* (*ii*) articles *m* d'importation; **the imports and exports of a country,** les importations et les exportations *f* d'un pays; **visible and invisible imports,** importations visibles et invisibles (*b*) **import agent,** commissionnaire importateur **import ban,** prohibition *f*/interdiction d'importation; prohibition d'entrée **import duty,** droit *m* d'entrée/de douane **import firm,** maison *f* d'importation **import licence/permit,** licence *f*/permis *m* d'importation; **import list,** (*i*) liste *f* des importations (*ii*) tarif *m* d'entrée; **import quotas,** contingent *m* d'importation; con tingentement *m* des importations; **import specie point,** point *m* d'entrée de l'or **import trade,** commerce *m* d'importation commerce passif; **import (and) export company,** entreprise *f* d'import-export.

import[2], *v.tr.* importer (des marchandises) **imported goods,** articles *m* d'importation importations *f*; **goods imported from France,** produits de provenance française importations françaises.

importable, *a.* importable.

importation, *n.* 1. importation *f* (de marchandises); **for temporary importation**, en franchise *f* temporaire 2. *NAm:* (article *m* d')importation.

importer, *n.* importateur, -trice; maison *f* d'importation; **importers' entry of goods**, règlements *mpl* à l'importation.

importing[1], *a.* importateur; **the importing countries**, les pays importateurs; **importing house**, maison *f* d'importation.

importing[2], *n.* importation *f* (de marchandises).

impose, *v.tr.* **to impose a tax on sugar**, imposer le sucre/taxer le sucre/frapper le sucre d'une taxe; **to impose a tax on small business**, imposer les petits commerces.

imposition, *n.* imposition *f*/impôt *m*/taxe *f*; *pl.* contributions *fpl.*

impound, *v.tr. Jur:* (*a*) confisquer/saisir (des marchandises) (*b*) faire déposer (des documents) au greffe.

impounding, *n. Jur:* (*a*) arrêt *m*/saisie *f* (de marchandises) (*b*) prise *f* de possession (de documents).

imprest, *n. Adm:* avance *f* de fonds (à un fournisseur de l'État); **imprest account**, compte *m* d'avances (à montant fixe); **imprest system**, comptabilité *f* de prévision.

imprint, *n.* **publisher's imprint**, nom *m*/firme *f*/rubrique *f* de l'éditeur; **published under the Harrap imprint**, publié par la maison Harrap.

imprinter, *n.* **(credit card) imprinter**, presse imprimante (de cartes de crédit).

improve, 1. *v.ind.tr.* **to improve on s.o.'s offer**, enchérir sur l'offre de qn 2. *v.i.* (*a*) s'améliorer; **his business is improving**, son commerce est en voie de relèvement; **business is improving/things are improving**, il y a une amélioration dans les affaires/les affaires reprennent (*b*) (*of prices, markets*) monter; être en hausse.

improved, *a.* (*a*) (*of invention, method*) per-

fectionné (*b*) **improved offer**, offre supérieure.

improvement, *n.* amélioration *f*; **job improvement**, amélioration des tâches; **house improvement**, travaux *mpl* de modernisation (d'une maison); **improvement of the dollar against the florin**, appréciation *f* du dollar vis-à-vis du florin.

impulse, *n.* **impulse buying**, achat spontané/achat d'impulsion.

imputation, *n.* imputation *f*; **imputation system**, système *m* de l'avoir fiscal.

imputed, *a.* **imputed payments**, paiements imputés; **imputed value**, valeur imputée/implicite.

in, *a.* **in tray**, entrées *fpl*; *Fin:* **in book**, livre *m* du dedans/registre *m* des chèques à rembourser.

inactive, *a.* inactif.

incentive, *n.* **incentive bonus/pay**, prime *f* de rendement; **incentive scheme**, programme *m* de stimulants salariaux/de salaires au rendement; **incentive (tour/travel)**, voyage *m* de stimulation; **group incentive**, prime (de rendement) d'équipe/prime collective; **production incentives**, stimulants de la production/primes de rendement/encouragements à la production; **tax incentives**, incitations fiscales.

inch, *n. Meas:* pouce *m* (=2.54 cm).

incidence, *n.* incidence *f*.

incidental, 1. *a.* **incidental expenses/n.pl. incidentals**, faux frais/frais accessoires; dépenses imprévues.

in-clearing, *a. Fin:* **in-clearing book**, livre *m* du dedans/registre *m* des chèques à rembourser.

include, *v.tr.* comprendre/renfermer/embrasser; **including carriage**, y compris le port/port compris; **up to and including December 31st**, jusqu'au 31 décembre inclusivement.

inclusive, *a.* **inclusive sum**, somme globale/totale; **all inclusive/inclusive price/ inclusive terms,** (prix) tout compris/(*in hotel, etc.*) prix net; **inclusive of all taxes,** toutes taxes comprises (TTC); **from 4th to 12th February inclusive,** du 4 au 12 février inclusivement.

income, *n.* **1.** revenu *m*/revenus *mpl*; **annual income,** revenu annuel; **disposable income,** revenu disponible; **fixed income,** revenu fixe; **source of income,** source(s) *f(pl)* de revenu; **earned income,** revenu(s) du travail; revenus salariaux; revenus professionnels; **independent income,** fortune personnelle; **notional income,** gain *m* d'opportunité; **regular income,** revenu régulier; **taxable/non-taxable income,** revenu imposable/non imposable; **unearned income/private income,** rente(s) *f(pl)*; revenus non professionnels; **to have a private/an unearned income of £3000 a year,** avoir trois mille livres de rente; **land that brings in a good income,** terre *f* de bon rapport; **income group/income bracket,** tranche *f* de salaire/de revenu; **higher-income / lower-income / middle-income groups,** groupes *m* (de contribuables) à revenus élevés/faibles/moyens; **incomes policy,** politique *f* des revenus; *PolEc:* **gross national income,** revenu national brut; **income tax,** impôt *m* (cédulaire) sur le revenu; **income-tax return,** déclaration fiscale/déclaration *f* de revenu/déclaration d'impôt sur le revenu **2.** recettes *fpl*/revenus/rentrées *fpl*/bénéfice *m*; **income statement/statement of income,** compte *m* de résultat; **net income,** bénéfice net; **income debenture,** obligation *f* à revenus variables.

incomings, *n.pl.* recettes *f*/revenus *m*/ rentrées *f*; **his incomings and outgoings,** ses recettes et ses dépenses *f*.

incontestability, *n. Ins:* **incontestability clause,** clause *f* d'incontestabilité.

inconvertible, *a.* (*paper money, etc.*) inconvertible/non convertible (**into,** en).

incorporate, 1. *v.tr.* constituer (une association) en société commerciale; constituer une société **2.** *v.i.* se constituer en société commerciale.

incorporated, *a. NAm:* **incorporated company (Inc.),** association constituée en société commerciale/société enregistrée; société à responsabilité limitée.

incorporation, *n.* constitution *f* d'une société; **instrument/articles of incorporation,** statuts *mpl* (d'une société); acte *m* de constitution (d'une société).

incoterms, (*abbr. of international commercial terms*) incoterms *mpl*/termes *mpl* de commerce international.

increase¹, *n.* (*a*) augmentation *f*/accroissement *m*/progression *f*; **natural increase,** accroissement naturel; **increase of capital,** augmentation de capital; **increase in demand,** accroissement de la demande; **increase in price,** augmentation de prix/ hausse *f* de prix; **increase in the cost of living/cost-of-living increase;** hausse du coût de la vie; **increase in value (of property, etc.),** plus-value *f* (d'une propriété, etc.); **increase in wages/pay increase(s),** augmentation/relèvement *m*/hausse *f* de salaire(s); **I've had an increase in salary,** j'ai reçu une augmentation (de salaire)/*F:* j'ai été augmenté; **an increase of 30% on last week('s),** une augmentation/une plus-value de 30% sur la semaine dernière (*b*) **to be on the increase,** augmenter/aller en augmentant.

increase², **1.** *v.i.* augmenter/progresser; grandir; croître; s'accroître; **to increase in size,** augmenter de volume; **to increase in value,** augmenter de valeur; **to increase in price,** devenir plus cher; augmenter de prix; **to go on increasing,** aller en augmentant **2.** *v.tr.* augmenter (la production); relever/augmenter (les salaires); augmenter/majorer (les prix, les impôts); **to increase the expenditure,** augmenter la dépense.

increased, *a.* accru; **increased demand,** demande accrue.

increasing, *a.* croissant; **increasing cost,** coût croissant.

increment, *n.* **1.** augmentation *f*/accroissement *m*; **a salary of £36000 plus annual**

increments of ..., un salaire de £36000 avec augmentation annuelle de ... **2.** profit *m*; (*of land, shares*) **unearned increment,** plus-value *f.*

incremental, *a.* **incremental cost,** coût marginal; **incremental increase,** hausse graduelle/pas à pas.

incumbrance, *n. Jur:* charge *f*; servitude *f.*

incur, *v.tr.* courir (un risque); éprouver/ subir (une perte); contracter (des dettes); entraîner (des frais); **expenses incurred,** frais encourus.

indebted, *a.* endetté; **to be heavily indebted to s.o.,** devoir une forte somme à qn.

indebtedness, *n.* endettement *m*; dette(s) *f(pl)*; **indebtedness day/date,** = date *f* de clôture de l'exercice.

indemnification, *n.* **1.** indemnisation *f/* dédommagement *m* (**of s.o.,** de qn) **2.** indemnité *f/*dédommagement/compensation *f*; **to pay a sum of money by way of indemnification,** payer une somme à titre d'indemnité.

indemnify, *v.tr.* indemniser/dédommager (qn) (**for a loss,** d'une perte).

indemnity, *n.* **1.** garantie *f/*assurance *f* (contre une perte, etc.); **indemnity bond,** obligation indemnitaire; **(letter of) indemnity,** cautionnement *m/*(lettre *f* de) garantie *f* **2.** indemnité *f/*dédommagement *m/*compensation *f*; **to pay full indemnity to s.o.,** indemniser qn totalement/de tous ses frais; **receiver of an indemnity,** indemnitaire *mf;* **professional indemnity,** indemnité professionnelle.

indent¹, *n.* commande *f* de marchandises/ ordre *m* d'achat; *esp.* commande reçue de l'étranger; **closed indent,** commande spécifiant le fournisseur; **open indent,** commande ne spécifiant pas le fournisseur.

indent², *v.i.* **to indent on s.o. for sth.,** passer une commande (de qch) à qn.

indenter, *n.* client *m* qui passe une commande de marchandises venant de l'étranger.

indenture¹, *n. Jur:* (*a*) acte *m*; contrat *m* synallagmatique; contrat bilatéral/réciproque (*b*) *usu.pl.* **indentures,** contrat d'apprentissage.

indenture², *v.tr.* (*a*) lier (qn) par contrat; **indentured labour,** main-d'œuvre engagée à long terme (*b*) mettre (qn) en apprentissage (**to s.o.,** chez qn) (sous contrat).

index, *n.* **1.** (*pl.* **indexes**) (*a*) index *m/* table *f* alphabétique (*b*) répertoire *m/*catalogue *m*; **card index,** fichier *m* **2.** (*pl.* **indices**) **index number** (nombre) indice *m*; **growth index,** indice de croissance; **bond index,** indice des obligations; **consumer price index,** indice des prix à la consommation; **cost of living index,** indice du coût de la vie; **Financial Times/FT index,** indice du Financial Times; **Dow Jones index,** indice Dow Jones; **stock/share index,** indice de la Bourse; **retail price index,** indice des prix de détail; **wholesale price index,** indice des prix de gros; **overall index,** indice général/global.

indexation, *n.* indexation *f.*

index-linked, *a.* indexé; (*salary*) indexé sur l'indice du coût de la vie.

index-linking, *n.* indexation *f.*

indicator, *n.* **retail-price indicator,** indice *m* des prix de détail; **all-items indicator,** indice général des cours; *PolEc:* **economic indicators,** indicateurs *m* d'activité économique/indicateurs d'alerte/*F:* clignotants *m*; **leading business indicators,** principaux indicateurs économiques; *NAm:* **leading price indicator,** indice *m* composite des principaux indicateurs; **market indicator,** indicateur de marché.

indirect, *a.* indirect; **indirect charges/ indirect expenses,** frais généraux/charges indirectes; **indirect labour,** main-d'œuvre indirecte; **indirect selling,** vente indirecte; **indirect taxes,** impôts indirects.

indorse, *v.tr.* = **endorse.**

induction, *n.* **induction course**, stage *m* de mise au courant/d'accueil.

indulge, *v.tr.* accorder un délai à (une lettre de change, au payeur d'une lettre de change).

indulgence, *n.* délai *m* de paiement (accordé au payeur d'une lettre de change).

industrial, *a.* (*a*) industriel; **industrial centre**, centre industriel; **industrial complex/industrial estate**, complexe industriel/zone industrielle; **industrial exhibition**, salon *m* de l'industrie; **industrial product**, produit industriel; **industrial training**, formation *f* à l'usine/dans l'entreprise (*b*) **industrial action**, action revendicative; **to take industrial action**, se mettre en grève; **industrial dispute**, conflit ouvrier/du travail; **industrial unrest**, agitation ouvrière; **conflits sociaux**; **industrial relations**, relations industrielles/professionnelles; **industrial disease**, maladie professionnelle; **industrial espionage**, espionage industriel; **industrial injuries**, accidents *m* du travail; **industrial insurance**, assurance *f* contre les accidents du travail; **industrial sabotage**, concurrence déloyale (*c*) *PolEc:* **industrial unit**, atelier *m* (*d*) *Fin:* **industrial bank**, banque industrielle; **industrial shares/n.pl. industrials**, valeurs industrielles.

industrialism, *n.* industrialisme *m.*

industrialist, *n.* industriel *m.*

industrialization, *n.* industrialisation *f.*

industrialize, 1. *v.tr.* industrialiser; **newly industrialized countries**, pays nouvellement industrialisés **2.** *v.i.* s'industrialiser.

industry, *n.* (*a*) industrie *f;* **basic industry**, industrie de base; **processing industry**, industrie de transformation (*b*) **infant industry**, industrie naissante; **growing/growth industry**, industrie en plein essor; **consumer goods industry**, industrie de consommation (*c*) **cottage industry**, industrie artisanale/artisanat *m;* **heavy industry**, l'industrie lourde; **light industry**, l'industrie légère; **primary in-**dustry, industrie primaire/secteur *m* primaire; **sector of industry**, secteur industriel; branche *f* d'industrie (*d*) **agricultural industries**, industries agricoles; **aircraft industry**, industrie aéronautique; **building industry**, industrie du bâtiment/le bâtiment; **chemical industry**, industrie chimique; **computer industry**, industrie (de l')informatique; **engineering industry**, industrie mécanique; **electronics industry**, industrie électronique; **hotel industry**, industrie hôtelière; **mining industry**, industrie minière/industrie extractive; **metal industry**, industrie métallurgique; **motor industry/car industry**, industrie automobile; **oil industry/petroleum industry**, industrie pétrolière/industrie du pétrole; **plastics industry**, industrie pétrochimique; **precision industry**, industrie de précision; **service industry**, (*sector*) secteur tertiaire; (*business*) société de services; **shipping industry**, (*i*) industrie des transports maritimes (*ii*) industrie de constructions navales; **textile industry**, les industries textiles.

inefficiency, *n.* (*a*) inefficacité *f* (des mesures prises, etc.) (*b*) incapacité (professionnelle); incompétence *f*/manque *m* de compétence.

inefficient, *a.* (*a*) (*of measure, etc.*) inefficace/ineffectif (*b*) (*of pers.*) incapable, incompétent.

inelastic, *a.* (demande, etc.) fixe/qui ne change pas.

inertia, *n.* **inertia selling**, vente *f* par obtention abusive/frauduleuse de commande, vente forcée.

inexecution, *n.* inexécution *f* (d'un contrat, etc.)

inexpensive, *a.* peu coûteux/bon marché (qui ne coûte) pas cher.

inexpensively, *adv.* (à) bon marché/à bas prix/à peu de frais/à bon compte; **to live inexpensively**, vivre économiquement/à peu de frais.

inferior, *a.* inférieur; **inferior goods**

marchandises inférieures; **inferior quality,** qualité inférieure/mauvaise qualité.

inflate, *v.tr.* (*a*) grossir/charger (un compte); gonfler (une facture) (*b*) hausser/faire monter (les prix) (*c*) *PolEc:* **to inflate the currency,** accroître artificiellement la circulation fiduciaire; recourir à l'inflation.

inflated, *a.* (*a*) (prix) exagéré/gonflé (*b*) *PolEc:* **inflated currency,** circulation fiduciaire artificiellement accrue/inflation monétaire.

inflation, *n.* *PolEc:* **rate of inflation,** taux *m* d'inflation; **the danger of inflation,** le danger inflationniste; **to fight inflation,** lutter contre l'inflation; **creeping/ crawling inflation,** inflation rampante; **galloping inflation,** inflation galopante; **measures to combat inflation,** mesures déflationnistes; **monetary inflation,** inflation monétaire; **repressed/suppressed inflation,** inflation continue; **inflation of the currency,** inflation fiduciaire; **price inflation,** inflation des prix; **cost-push inflation,** inflation par les coûts; **demand-pull inflation,** inflation par la demande; **double-digit/double-figure inflation,** taux d'inflation de plus de 10%.

inflationary, *a.* (politique, etc.) inflationniste/d'inflation; **inflationary spiral,** spirale *f* inflationniste; **inflationary tendency,** tendance *f* inflationniste/à l'inflation.

inflationism, *n.* *PolEc:* inflationnisme *m.*

inflationist, *n.* inflationniste *mf.*

inflow, *n.* afflux *m* (de marchandises, etc.); **capital inflow,** entrée *f* de capitaux.

influx, *n.* entrée *f*/afflux *m*; **influx of gold,** afflux d'or.

info, *n.* informations *fpl*/renseignements *mpl*; **a piece/a bit of info,** un renseignement; **info quote,** cotation fournie (seulement) à titre de renseignement.

inform, *v.tr.* *Corr:* **we are writing to inform you of the dispatch of ...,** nous vous avisons de l'envoi de ...; **I am pleased to**

inform you that ..., j'ai le plaisir/l'honneur de vous annoncer/de vous informer que ...; **I regret to have to inform you that ...,** j'ai le regret de vous annoncer/de vous faire savoir que ...; **we are informed that ...,** on nous apprend/on nous fait savoir/on nous informe que ....

information, *n.* renseignement(s) *m(pl)*/ information(s) *f(pl)*; **all the necessary/ relevant information,** tous (les) renseignements utiles; **I am sending you for your information/by way of information ...,** je vous envoie à titre d'information/de renseignement ...; *Adm:* **information copy,** copie *f* pour information; **(strictly) confidential information,** renseignement (strictement) confidentiel; **information retrieval,** recherche *f* documentaire (de données); **information technology (IT),** informatique *f*; **piece of information,** renseignement; indication *f*; **request for information,** demande *f* de renseignement(s); **for further information apply to ...,** pour de plus amples renseignements s'adresser à/écrire à ...; **processing of information,** traitement *m* de l'information; *Adm:* **information bureau,** bureau *m* de renseignements/centre *m* d'information; **tourist information bureau,** = Syndicat *m* d'Initiative; **information services,** marché *m* de l'information.

infraction, *n.* infraction *f* (à la loi).

infrastructure, *n.* *PolEc: Adm:* infrastructure *f.*

infringe, *v.tr.* **to infringe a patent,** (*i*) contrefaire un objet breveté (*ii*) empiéter sur un brevet; **to infringe a copyright,** violer les droits d'auteur; commettre un délit de contrefaçon.

infringement, *n.* **infringement of a patent,** contrefaçon *f* (d'un brevet); **infringement of (literary) copyright,** contrefaçon (littéraire); violation *f* des droits d'auteur; **patent infringement suit,** procès en contrefaçon/pour délit de contrefaçon.

ingot, *n.* lingot *m* (d'or, d'argent); **ingot gold,** or *m* en lingot.

inheritance, n. héritage m; succession f; *NAm:* **inheritance tax,** droits mpl de succession.

in-house, a. interne; établi par la maison; sur place; **in-house training,** formation f interne.

initial[1]**,** a. **initial capital,** capital initial/ d'apport; **initial (capital) expenditure/ expenses/investment/outlay,** frais mpl de premier établissement; **initial cost,** coût initial; (*of manufactured product*) prix m de revient; **initial value,** valeur f de départ; **initial public offering (IPO),** introduction f en bourse; **initial public offering window/ IPO window,** délai m d'introduction en bourse.

initial[2]**,** v.tr. parafer/parapher/viser (une lettre, un document).

inject, v.tr. **to inject capital into a business,** injecter du capital dans une entreprise.

injection, n. **injection of capital into a business,** injection f/apport m de capital dans une entreprise.

injunction, n. *Jur:* arrêt m de suspension/ de sursis.

injured, a. **injured party,** partie lésée.

inland, a. **inland trade,** commerce intérieur; **inland postage rates,** (tarif m d')affranchissement m en régime intérieur; **inland bill,** traite f sur le pays; effet m/ lettre f de change sur l'intérieur; **the Inland Revenue (Department),** le fisc; **inland revenue stamp,** timbre fiscal.

input, n. input m; entrée f; facteur m (de production); *Cmptr:* **input-output,** entrée-sortie.

inquiry, n. (demande f de) renseignement m; **inquiry office,** bureau m de renseignements; **board/commission of inqury,** commission f d'enquête; *Corr:* **with reference to your inquiry of May 5th ...,** en réponse à votre demande du 5 mai ....

inscribed, a. *Fin:* **inscribed stock,** actions inscrites (au grand-livre).

insider, n. *StExch:* **the insiders,** les initiés; **insider dealing/trading,** délit m d'initié(s).

insolvency, n. insolvabilité f; **to be in a state of insolvency,** être insolvable/en état de cessation de paiements.

insolvent, 1. a. (débiteur, société) insolvable; **to become insolvent,** être en état de cessation de paiements; **to declare oneself insolvent,** déposer son bilan 2. n. failli m.

inspect, v.tr. inspecter/visiter (une fabrique, etc.); contrôler/vérifier/examiner (les livres d'un négociant); vérifier/ inspecter (une machine, etc.).

inspecting[1]**,** a. **inspecting officer,** inspecteur, -trice.

inspecting[2]**,** n. inspection f; **inspecting order,** ordre m d'inspection.

inspection, n. (*a*) examen m/vérification f (de documents, etc.); **to buy goods on inspection,** acheter des marchandises sur examen; *Publ:* **inspection copy,** spécimen m (*b*) inspection f/visite f (d'un établissement, etc.); contrôle m (du personnel, du matériel, etc.); **inspection committee,** comité m de surveillance; **periodical inspection of factories,** visite périodique des fabriques; **tour of inspection,** inspection; **sanitary inspection,** visite/contrôle sanitaire; **to make an inspection,** faire une inspection; *Cust:* **inspection order,** bon m de visite; *Adm:* **inspection stamp,** cachet m de vérification; (*punch*) poinçon m de contrôle.

inspector, n. inspecteur, -trice; **tax inspector/inspector of taxes,** inspecteur/ contrôleur m des contributions directes; **inspector of weights and measures,** vérificateur m des poids et mesures.

instability, n. instabilité f (financière).

instal(l)ment, n. fraction f (de paiement); acompte m; paiement m à compte; versement m; (*monthly*) mensualité f; **annual instalment,** annuité f; **debt payable by annual instalments,** dette f annuitaire; **final instalment,** paiement pour solde/

versement libératoire; **to pay an instalment,** verser un acompte; faire un versement; **to pay in/by instalments,** payer par versements; échelonner/fractionner les paiements; **payable in two instalments,** payable en deux versements; **payable in monthly instalments,** payable par mensualités *f*; **repayable by instalments,** remboursable par paiements à terme/par versements échelonnés/en plusieurs versements; *NAm:* **to buy on the instalment plan,** acheter à tempérament/à crédit; *NAm:* **instalment credit,** crédit *m* à tempérament; **to vote credits in instalments,** voter des crédits par tranches.

instant, *a. (abbr.* **inst.***) Corr:* courant; **my letter of the 5th inst.,** ma lettre du 5 courant/du 5 ct.

institute, *v.tr.* **to institute proceedings against s.o.,** intenter un procès contre qn.

institution, *n. Fin:* **credit institution,** établissement *m* de crédit; **investment institution,** société *f* de placement.

institutional, *a. (a)* **institutional advertising,** publicité *f* de prestige *(b)* **institutional investors,** investisseurs *mpl* institutionnels/grands investisseurs.

instruction, *n. Corr:* **we await your instructions,** nous attendons vos instructions/vos ordres; **instructions for use,** mode *m* d'emploi.

instrument, *n. Jur:* instrument *m*/acte *m*/document *m*; **investment instrument,** instrument de placement; **negotiable instrument,** effet *m* de commerce; titre *m* au porteur.

insurable, *a.* assurable; **insurable interest,** intérêt *m* pécuniaire.

insurance, *n. (a)* assurance *f*; **to take out an insurance on sth./against a risk,** contracter une assurance/prendre une assurance/s'assurer/se faire assurer contre un risque; **his furniture was covered by an insurance,** il avait assuré son mobilier; **to pay the insurance on a car,** payer l'assurance/les primes d'assurance d'une voiture; **accident insurance,** assurance contre les accidents/assurance-accidents *f*; **buildings insurance,** assurance habitation; **burglary insurance/theft insurance,** assurance contre le vol; **cancellation insurance,** assurance annulation; **car/motor insurance,** assurance-automobile *f*; **contents insurance,** assurance mobilier/habitation; **credit insurance/loan repayment insurance,** assurance-crédit *f*; **endowment insurance,** *(i)* assurance en cas de vie *(ii)* assurance à terme fixe; **fire insurance,** assurance contre l'incendie/assurance-incendie *f*; **freight insurance,** assurance sur fret; **(private) medical insurance,** assurance maladie; **life insurance,** assurance sur la vie/assurance-vie *f*; **marine insurance,** assurance maritime; *NAm:* **no fault insurance,** assurance non-responsabilité/sans égard à la responsabilité; **permanent health insurance (PHI),** assurance longue maladie; **public liability insurance,** assurance responsabilité civile; **third-party (liability) insurance,** assurance au tiers; **workmen's compensation insurance/employers' liability insurance,** assurance (des employeurs) contre les accidents du travail; **whole-life insurance,** assurance-décès *f*; **all-risk insurance/all-in insurance/comprehensive insurance,** assurance tous risques; assurance multirisque; *SwFr:* assurance casco; **collective insurance/group insurance,** assurance collective; **double insurance,** assurance cumulative; **index(-linked) insurance,** assurance indexée; **term insurance,** assurance temporaire *(b)* **insurance agent,** agent *m* d'assurance(s); **insurance broker,** courtier *m* d'assurance(s); assureur *m*; **insurance charges,** frais *m* d'assurance; **insurance claim,** demande *f* d'indemnité; **insurance company,** compagnie/société d'assurances; **insurance cover,** couverture *f*; **insurance money,** indemnité *f* d'assurance; **insurance policy/contract,** police *f*/contrat *m* d'assurance; **insurance premium,** prime *f* d'assurance; **insurance value,** valeur *f* d'assurance; **he's in insurance,** il est/il travaille dans les assurances *(c) Adm:* **National Insurance,** assurance sociale/= sécurité sociale; **unemployment insurance,** assurance chômage.

insure, 1. *v.tr.* (*i*) assurer (*ii*) faire assurer (des marchandises, un mobilier, etc.); **to insure one's life,** s'assurer sur la vie/se faire assurer sur la vie/contracter une assurance-vie **2.** *v.i.* **to insure against theft,** s'assurer/se faire assurer contre le vol.

insured, *a. & n.* assuré, -ée; **the house was insured,** la maison était assurée; **insured value,** valeur assurée; *Post:* **parcel insured for £25,** colis chargé avec valeur déclarée £25.

insurer, *n.* assureur *m.*

intangible, *a.* **intangible assets/n.pl. intangibles,** valeurs immatérielles; actif incorporel/immobilisations incorporelles.

intascale, *n.* (= **inter-tanker nominal freight scale**) barème mondial des taux de fret nominaux.

integration, *n.* intégration *f*/concentration *f*; **backward integration,** intégration ascendante; **forward integration,** intégration descendante; **horizontal integration,** concentration horizontale; **vestical integration,** intégration/concentration verticale.

intellectual, *a.* **intellectual property,** propriété intellectuelle.

intent, *n.* **letter of intent,** lettre *f* d'intention.

inter, *pref.* **inter(-)company items,** opérations intersociétés.

interbank, *a.* (opération, etc.) interbancaire/entre banques; **interbank loans,** prêts *m* de banque à banque/entre banques; **interbank offered rate (IBOR),** taux *m* interbancaire offert.

interbranch, *a.* (opérations) entre succursales (d'une même entreprise).

interdepartmental, *a.* interdépartemental; *Adm: etc:* **interdepartmental problems,** problèmes communs à plusieurs services.

interest, *n.* (*a*) *Fin:* intérêt *m*; **back interest,** arrérage(s) d'intérêts; **compound interest,** intérêt composé; **simple interest,** intérêt simple; **accrued interest,** intérêt couru/produits financiers à recevoir; **beneficial interest,** usufruit *m*; **fixed interest,** intérêt fixe; **fixed interest market,** marché *m* des obligations; **high interest,** intérêt élevé/gros rendement; **interest charges,** intérêts (à payer); frais financiers; (*on overdraft*) agios *mpl*; **interest coupon/warrant,** coupon *m* (d'intérêt); **interests due/payable,** intérêts échus/à recevoir; **interest income,** revenu *m* d'intérêt/produits financiers/bénéfices financiers; **interest on capital,** intérêt du capital; **interest on a loan,** intérêt sur prêt; **interest on £100,** intérêt sur £100; **interest rate/rate of interest,** taux *m* d'intérêt/de l'intérêt; **long-term interest rate,** taux d'intérêt à long terme; **short interest,** taux (d'intérêt) à court terme; **the interest rate is 4%,** le taux d'intérêt est de 4%; **to bear/to yield/to carry interest,** porter intérêt/rapporter; **shares that yield a 5% interest,** actions *f* portant intérêt au taux de 5%; **interest-bearing loan,** prêt *m* à intérêt; **interest-bearing securities,** titres *m* qui produisent des intérêts; **interest cover,** couverture *f* de l'intérêt; **interest-free,** sans intérêt; **interest-free credit,** crédit gratuit; **life interest,** usufruit *m*; **to pay interest,** payer des intérêts; **money earning no interest,** argent improductif/dormant; **to allow interest to accumulate,** laisser courir des intérêts (*b*) intérêt/participation *f*; **controlling interest,** majorité *f*/participation majoritaire/participation qui donne le contrôle; **majority interest,** participation majoritaire; **minority interest,** participation minoritaire; **to have an interest in the profits,** participer aux bénéfices; **I have no vested interests in the business,** je n'ai pas de capitaux/je n'ai pas d'intérêts/je ne suis pas intéressé dans cette entreprise; **his interest in the company is £10 000,** il a une commandite de £10 000 (*c*) *StExch:* **open/short interest,** position ouverte/vendeur.

interested, *a.* **the interested parties,** les parties intéressées; *Jur:* **interested party,** ayant droit *m.*

interface, *n. Cmptr:* interface *f.*

interim, *a.* **interim accounts,** comptes semestriels/trimestriels; **interim dividend,** dividende *m* intérimaire/accompte *m* sur dividende; **interim report,** rapport *m* intérimaire.

intermediary, *n.* intermédiaire *mf;* **financial intermediary,** intermédiaire financier.

intermediate, *a. Fin:* **intermediate credit,** crédit *m* à moyen terme; **intermediate goods/products,** biens *mpl* intermédiaires.

internal, *a.* **internal check,** audit *m* interne/ contrôle *m*/vérification *f;* **internal control,** contrôle interne; **internal revenue,** recettes fiscales; *NAm:* **internal rate of return,** taux *m* de rentabilité interne; **Internal Revenue Service (IRS),** le fisc; **internal trade,** commerce intérieur.

international, *a.* international; **international law,** droit international.

intertrade, *n.* commerce *m* réciproque.

intervention, *n. EEC:* **intervention price,** prix *m* d'intervention.

interview[1]**,** *n.* entretien *m*/entrevue *f*/ interview *f;* **to give an interview,** accorder une interview.

interview[2]**,** *v.tr.* interviewer (qn)/soumettre (qn) à une interview.

interviewer, *n.* interviewer *m*/intervieweur, -euse.

intestacy, *n.* fait *m* de meurir intestat.

intestate, *a.* intestat.

intrapreneur, *n.* entrepreneur *m* qui travaille au sein d'une compagnie.

intrinsic, *a.* **intrinsic value,** valeur *f* intrinsèque.

introduce, *v.tr.* lancer (une marchandise); *StExch:* introduire (des actions).

introduction, *n. St Exch:* introduction *f* au marché hors cote.

introductory, *a.* **introductory price/offer,** (*i*) prix *m* de lancement/de vente publicitaire/prix-réclame *m* (*ii*) vente-réclame *f* (*iii*) promotion *f.*

invalid, *a.* périmé/qui n'est pas valable/ qui n'est plus valable.

invalidate, *v.tr.* invalider/rendre invalide (un contrat).

invalidation, *n.* invalidation *f* (d'un document, d'un contrat).

invalidity, *n.* invalidité *f* (d'un contract, etc.).

inventory[1]**,** *n.* **1.** inventaire *m;* **to take/to draw up an inventory,** faire/dresser un inventaire; **inventory of fixtures,** état *m* des lieux; **inventory book,** livre *m* d'inventaires; *Book-k:* **book inventory,** inventaire comptable; **ingoing inventory,** inventaire d'entrée (dans un immeuble); **outgoing inventory,** inventaire de sortie (d'un immeuble); **inventory with valuation,** inventaire avec prisée **2.** (*a*) stock(s) *m(pl);* **inventory management/control,** gestion *f* des stocks/du stock; **inventory turnover,** rotation *f* des stocks; **beginning/ ending inventory,** stock d'ouverture/de fermeture; **excess inventory,** surplus de stock (*b*) (établissement, levée *f,* d')inventaire; **perpetual inventory,** inventaire permanent.

inventory[2]**,** *v.tr.* inventorier (les biens de qn); dresser l'inventaire (des biens de qn); **furniture that inventories at £10 000,** meubles *mpl* dont l'inventaire se monte à £10,000.

invest, *v.tr. Fin:* placer/investir (son argent, des fonds); **to invest money,** faire des placements; **to invest money in a business,** mettre de l'argent/placer des fonds dans un commerce; **to invest one's money to good account,** faire valoir son argent; **money invested in an annuity,** argent constitué en viager; **capital invested,** mise *f* de fonds; capital engagé/investi; *Ind:* capital d'établissement; **to invest in real estate,** faire des placements immobiliers.

investibles, *n.pl. NAm:* pièces *fpl* pour collectionneurs/pour amateurs d'art.

investment, *n. Fin:* placement *m*/investissement *m* (de capitaux); mise *f* de fonds; (titre de) participation *f*; **bond investment,** placement obligataire; **equity investment,** placement en actions; *NAm:* **failure investment,** investissement en valeurs de redressement/de retournement; **fixed investment,** (montant des) immobilisations *f*; **good investment,** placement avantageux; **safe/blue-chip investment,** placement sûr/valeur *f* de tout repos; valeur refuge; **long-term investment,** placement à long terme; **short-term investment,** placement à court terme; **unquoted investments,** valeurs non cotées; **investment in industry,** investissement industriel; **investment in real estate,** placements/investissements immobiliers; **investments in securities,** placements en valeurs; **employee investment in the capital of a business,** actionnariat ouvrier; **to make investments,** investir des capitaux/faire des investissements/faire des placements; **(list of) investments,** portefeuille *m* titres; valeurs en portefeuille; dossier *m*; **investment adviser,** conseiller en placements; **investment analyst,** analyste *mf* en placements; **investment banking,** banque *f* d'affaires; **investment company,** société *f* de portefeuille/d'investissement(s)/de placement(s); **investment credit,** crédit *m* d'investissement; **investment fund,** fonds *m* commun de placement; **investment market,** marché *m* des capitaux; **investment securities/investment stock,** valeurs en portefeuille/valeurs de placement; valeurs classées; **investment trusts,** sociétés de placement(s); fonds *m* de placement(s).

investor, *n.* actionnaire *mf*; investisseur *m*; **small/private investors,** petits actionnaires/petits épargnants; l'épargne privée/la petite épargne.

invisible, *PolEc:* **1.** *a.* **invisible exports,** exportations *f* invisibles; **invisible imports,** importations *f* invisibles **2.** *n.pl.* **invisibles,** invisibles *mpl.*

invitation, *n. Fin:* **invitation to the public (to subscribe to a loan),** appel *m* au public (pour la souscription d'un emprunt); **invitation for tenders,** appel d'offres.

invite, *v.tr. Fin:* **to invite shareholders to subscribe (a new issue),** faire un appel de fonds; **to invite bids/tenders,** faire un appel d'offres.

invoice[1], *n.* facture *f* (de débit); note *f* (de frais); **shipping invoice,** facture d'expédition; **invoice of origin/original invoice,** facture originale; **the amount was included in my invoice,** le montant m'a été facturé; **to make out an invoice,** établir/faire une facture; **to settle an invoice,** régler une facture; **as per invoice,** suivant la facture; **invoice book,** facturier *m*; copie *f* des factures; livre *m* des achats; **invoice clerk,** facturier, -ière; **invoice price,** prix *m* de facture; **invoice work,** travaux *mpl* de facturation.

invoice[2], *v.tr.* facturer (des marchandises)/porter (une marchandise) sur une facture.

invoicing, *n.* facturation *f* (de marchandises, de frais d'emballage, etc.); **invoicing machine,** machine *f* à facturer; facturière *f*; **VAT invoicing,** facturation de la TVA.

inward, *a.* **inward charges,** frais *m* à l'entrée (d'un navire dans un port); **inward bill of lading,** connaissement *m* d'entrée; **inward investment,** investissements *mpl* à l'étranger; **inward manifest,** manifeste *m* d'entrée; **inward mission,** visite *f* d'un groupe d'hommes d'affaires venant de l'étranger; *Book-k:* **inward payment,** paiement reçu; encaissement *m*.

inwards, *adv.* pour l'importation; **clearance inwards,** (*i*) déclaration *f* d'entrée (*ii*) permis *m* d'entrée.

IOU, *n.* (= **I owe you**) reconnaissance *f* (de dette)/billet *m* à ordre.

irrecoverable, *a.* (créance *f*) irrécouvrable.

irredeemable, *a. Fin:* (fonds *m*) irréalisable/irremboursable; (papier *m*) non convertible; **irredeemable bonds/**n.pl. **ir-**

redeemables, obligations *f* non amortissables.

irregulars, *n.pl. NAm:* articles *m* de deuxième qualité/de qualité moyenne.

issuance, *n.* émission *f.*

issue[1], *n.* (*a*) *Adm: Fin:* émission *f* (d'un emprunt, de billets de banque, d'actions, de timbres, etc.); **block issues,** émission par série; **capitalisation issue/scrip issue/bonus issue/free issue,** attribution *f* d'actions gratuites/action attribuée gratuitement/action gratuite; **equity issue,** augmentation *f* du capital par émission d'actions; **home currency issues,** billets émis à l'intérieur du pays; **share issue,** émission d'actions; **issue premium,** prime *f* d'émission; **issue price,** taux *m*/prix *m*/valeur *f* d'émission; *Bank:* **issue department,** service *m* des émissions; **rights issue,** droits préférentiels de souscription (*b*) *Adm:* **issue card,** carte *f* (de) sortie de stock (*c*) **the latest issue of a magazine,** le dernier numéro d'une revue.

issue[2], *v.tr.* émettre (des billets de banque, des timbres, etc.); **to issue a letter of credit,** fournir une lettre de crédit; **to issue a draft on s.o.,** fournir une traite sur qn.

issued, *a* **issued capital,** capital émis/souscrit; **number of shares issued,** nombre d'actions émises.

issuing[1], *a. Fin:* **issuing company,** société émettrice; **issuing bank/house,** banque *f* de placement.

issuing[2], *n.* émission *f.*

item, **1.** *adv. Book-k.* item **2.** *n.* (*a*) article *m*; **please send us the following items,** prière de nous envoyer les articles suivants (*b*) *Book-k:* écriture *f*/article; poste *m*/détail *m*; **cash item,** article de caisse; **item of expenditure/expense item,** article/chef *m* de dépense; **credit item,** poste créditeur; **balance-sheet items,** détails du bilan; **exceptional/extraordinary items,** éléments exceptionnels; résultat *m*/compte *m* exceptionnel; **to give the items on an invoice,** donner les détails d'une facture/détailler une facture; **this item does not appear in our books,** cette écriture ne figure pas dans nos livres (*c*) **the second item of the contract,** l'article deux du contrat; **the items on the agenda,** les questions *f* à l'ordre du jour.

itemize, *v.tr.* détailler (une facture, etc.); **itemized account,** compte spécifié/détaillé.

J

jacket, *n.* **book jacket,** jaquette *f.*

jet, *n.* **jet (aeroplane)/jet-propelled aircraft,** avion *m* à réaction/jet *m;* **jumbo jet,** (avion) gros porteur/jumbo-jet *m.*

jetliner, *n.* avion commercial à réaction/ avion de ligne à réaction.

jetsam, *n.* marchandise jetée à la mer (*pour alléger le navire*).

jingle, *n.* (advertising) **jingle,** sonal *m.*

job, *n.* **1.** tâche *f/*ouvrage *m/*travail (particulier); **to do a job,** exécuter/faire un travail; **job ticket,** bon *m* de travail; **job wage,** salaire *m* à forfait; **precision job,** travail *m* de précision **2.** emploi *m/*place *f/*poste *m/*fonctions *fpl/*situation *f/F:* job *m/*boulot *m;* **off-the-job training,** formation extérieure/institutionnelle; **on-the-job training,** apprentissage *m/*formation sur le tas; **to look for a job,** chercher un emploi/du travail; **to lose one's job,** perdre son emploi/sa place; **to resign/ throw up one's job,** donner sa démission; **to be out of a job,** être au chômage/sans travail; *Adm:* **job analysis,** analyse *f* de la tâche/de la fonction; **job assignment,** assignation *f* des tâches; **Job Centre =** Agence nationale pour l'emploi (ANPE); **job classification,** classification *f* des emplois; **job creation,** création *f* d'entreprise/d'emplois; **job description,** description *f* d'un poste/d'une fonction; **job evaluation,** évaluation *f* des tâches; **600 job reductions/600 jobs lost,** 600 suppressions *f* d'emploi; **job offers,** offres d'emploi; **job satisfaction,** satisfaction *f* dans le travail; **job security,** sécurité *f* d'emploi; **job specification,** spécification *f* de la fonction **3.** **job lot,** soldes *mpl;* articles *mpl/*marchandises *fpl* d'occasion;

articles dépareillés; lot *m* de marchandises; **to buy a job lot of books,** acheter des livres en vrac; **to buy sth. as a job lot,** acheter qch. à forfait; **job-lot quantities,** petites séries (de fabrication).

jobber, *n.* **1.** ouvrier, -ière à la tâche **2.** revendeur *m;* (*in contract work*) sous-entrepreneur *m* **3.** *StExch:* (*obsolete*) **(stock) jobber,** intermédiaire *m/*jobber *m;* marchand *m* de titres; **jobber's turn,** marge *f* d'un intermédiaire **4.** *NAm:* cambiste–commis opérateur.

jobbing[1]**,** *a.* **1.** qui travaille à la tâche/à la pièce; **jobbing workman,** (ouvrier) façonnier (*m*); ouvrier à la tâche; ouvrier à façon; **jobbing gardener,** jardinier *m* à la journée **2.** *Typ:* **jobbing hand,** homme *m* en conscience.

jobbing[2]**,** *n.* **1.** (*i*) ouvrage *m* à la tâche; (*ii*) travail *m* à façon **2.** commerce *m* d'intermédiaire; vente *f* en demi-gros **3.** *StExch:* (*a*) négoce *m* d'actions; spéculation *f; Pej:* agiotage *m* (*b*) **jobbing in contangoes,** arbitrage *m* de reports.

jobless, **1.** *a* sans travail/au chômage **2.** *n.* **the jobless,** les sans-travail *inv/*les chômeurs.

job out, *v.tr. NAm:* donner en sous-traitance; sous-traiter (une affaire).

job-share, *n.* emploi *m* à temps partagé.

join, *v.tr.* **1.** **the documents joined to the report,** les documents annexés au procès-verbal **2.** (*a*) **to join a company,** (commencer à) travailler chez ... (*b*) **to join an association,** adhérer à une organisation/devenir membre d'une société.

joint, *a.* **1.** (*of work, etc.*) commun/en commun/conjoint; **joint commission,** com-

122

mission *f* mixte; **joint committee,** comité *m* mixte/paritaire; **joint orders/ordering,** groupage *m* de commandes; **joint report,** rapport collectif; **joint undertaking/venture,** entreprise conjointe; coparticipation *f*; cofinancement *m*; *Bank:* **joint account,** compte joint/compte (en) commun; **deal on joint account,** opération *f* en participation; *Fin:* **joint shares,** actions indivises; **joint stock,** capital social; **joint stock bank,** banque *f*/société *f* de dépôt; **joint stock company,** société anonyme par actions; *NAm:* société en commandite; *Publ:* **edition published at the joint expense of publisher and author,** édition (faite) en participation **2.** co-/associé; **joint author,** coauteur *m*; **joint beneficiaries,** bénéficiaires conjoints/indivis; **joint creditor,** co-créancier, -ière; **joint debt,** dette *f* conjointe; **joint debtor,** codébiteur *m*; **joint director/directress,** codirecteur, -trice; **joint enterprise,** entreprise en participation; **joint guaranty,** cautionnement solidaire; **joint holder,** codétenteur *m*; **joint management,** cogérance *f*/cogestion *f*/codirection *f*; **joint manager/manageress,** cogérant(e)/codirecteur, -trice; **joint obligation,** coobligation *f*; **joint owner,** copropriétaire *mf*; **joint ownership,** copropriété *f*; **joint partner,** coassocié(e); **joint partnership,** coassociation *f*; **joint production,** coproduction *f*; **joint purchase,** coacquisition *f*; **joint purchaser,** co-acquéreur *m*; **joint seller,** covendeur, -euse; **joint signature,** signature collective; signature en commun; **joint surety (contract),** cautionnement *m* solidaire; **joint tenant,** colocataire *mf*.

jointly, *adv.* ensemble/conjointement; **we manage the firm jointly,** nous sommes cogérants de la maison; **to start a company jointly with ...,** créer une société en commun avec ...; **to possess sth. jointly,** posséder qch. conjointement/indivisément/par indivis; *Jur:* **jointly liable/jointly responsible,** solidaire; **to act jointly,** agir solidairement; **jointly and severally liable,** responsables conjointement et solidairement.

journal, *n.* (*a*) *Book-k:* (livre *m*) journal *m*; **journal entry,** écriture *f* comptable; **sales journal,** livre *m* des ventes (*b*) revue *f*; **do you subscribe to our (professional) journal?** êtes-vous abonné à notre revue professionnelle? **house journal,** journal *m* d'entreprise.

journalism, *n.* journalisme *m*.

journalist, *n.* journaliste *mf*.

journalize, *v.tr. Book-k:* porter (une écriture comptable) au journal/journaliser.

judge, *n.* juge *m*.

judgement, *n.* **to give judgement,** prononcer un jugement/un arrêt.

judicial, *a.* judiciaire; **judicial enquiry,** enquête *f* judiciaire.

jump¹, *n.* **jump in prices,** brusque hausse *f*/flambée *f* des prix; **rents have gone up with a jump,** les loyers ont fait un bond.

jump², *v.i.* **prices have jumped 10%,** les prix *m* ont monté/progressé de 10%.

jumpy, *a.* **the market is jumpy,** le marché est instable.

junior, *a. & n.* (*a*) (*in rank*) junior; subalterne (*m*); **junior clerk,** petit commis; **junior executive,** jeune cadre; **office junior,** employé, -ée subalterne; **junior partner,** associé, -ée en second; adjoint, -ointe (*b*) *Fin:* **junior bonds,** obligations *fpl* de deuxième rang; **junior stocks,** actions *f* de dividende.

junk, *n.* **junk bonds,** obligations *fpl* à haut rendement mais à haut risque; **junk mail,** imprimé(s) publicitaire(s) souvent non personnalisés (envoyés par la poste).

jurisdiction, *n.* juridiction *f*; compétence *f*; **general jurisdiction of a court,** compétence générale d'une cour; **this matter does not come within our jurisdiction,** cette matière n'est pas de notre compétence.

jury, *n.* jury *m*; **member of the jury,** juré *m*.

justice, *n.* justice *f*; **natural justice,** principe *m* d'impartialité et de loyauté.

K

K, *n.* mille *m inv.*

kaffir, *n. F:* valeur or sud-africaine.

kangaroo, *n. F:* valeur australienne.

keen, *a.* **keen competition,** concurrence acharnée/âpre; **there is a keen demand for these stocks,** ces fonds sont activement recherchés; **keen prices,** prix compétitifs.

keep, *v.tr.* **1. keep dry,** craint l'humidité; **keep upright,** ne pas renverser **2. to keep an appointment,** aller à un rendez-vous **3. to keep the books,** tenir les livres/les écritures/la comptabilité **4.** tenir/avoir en magasin (des marchandises) **5. to keep prices down,** empêcher les prix de monter/d'augmenter; **to keep prices up,** maintenir les prix fermes **6. to keep £10 back from s.o.'s salary,** retenir (une somme de) £10 sur le salaire de qn.

kerb, *n. StExch:* **kerb market,** marché *m* hors cote; **to buy/sell on the kerb,** acheter/vendre après la clôture officielle de la Bourse.

key, *n.* (*a*) **key money,** pas *m* de porte (*b*) d'une importance capitale/vitale; **key factor,** facteur *m* clé; **key post,** poste *m* clé; **key industry,** industrie *f* clé; **key man,** cheville *f* (ouvrière)/pilier *m*/pivot *m* (d'un établissement, d'une organisation); **he is a key man,** il occupe une position clé; **key personnel/workers/staff,** personnel *m* de base.

keyboard[1], *n.* clavier *m* (d'un ordinateur, d'une machine à écrire).

keyboard[2], *v.tr. & i.* introduire (des données) par clavier/pianoter (des données).

Keynesianism, *n.* keynésianisme *m*.

Keynesian, *n.* keynésien, -ienne.

kick, *v.tr.* **to kick s.o. upstairs,** donner une promotion à qn dont on se veut se débarrasser.

kickback, *n.* ristourne *f*; dessous-de-table *m*.

kicker, *n.* commission *f*; ristourne *f*; pourcentage *m* (des recettes).

killing, *n. F:* **to make a killing,** faire une affaire d'or.

kilo/kilogram(me), *n. Meas:* kilogramme *m*/kilo *m* (*abbr.* **kg**) (= 2.2046 lb).

kilometre, *n. Meas:* kilomètre *m* (*abbr.* **km**) (= 0.6214 mile); **cost per kilometre,** coût kilométrique; **distance in kilometres,** distance *f* kilométrique.

kind, *n.* **to pay in kind,** payer en nature.

king-size(d), *n.* (format) géant; **king-sized cigarettes,** cigarettes extra longues.

kite, *n. Fin: F:* cerf-volant *m*; traite *f* en l'air; billet *m* de complaisance; **kite flyer,** tireur *m* en l'air/à découvert; **kite flying,** tirage *m* en l'air/en blanc/à découvert; **to fly/to send up a kite,** tirer en l'air/tirer en blanc/tirer à découvert.

kiting, *n.* **1.** tirage *m* (d'un chèque) en l'air/à découvert **2.** fraude *f* par tirage en l'air/à découvert **3.** falsification *f* (du montant) d'un chèque.

knight, *n.* **white/black knight,** chevalier blanc/noir.

kitty, *n.* cagnotte *f*/caisse commune (d'un groupe).

knock, *n. Aut: Ins:* **knock-for-knock agreement,** convention entre compagnies d'assurance par laquelle chacune s'engage à dédommager son client, sans chercher à départager les responsabilités.

knockdown, *a.* **knockdown prices,** prix *m* cassés/prix (de) réclame/prix-choc.

knock down[2], *v.tr.* **to knock down prices,** abaisser/réduire les prix considérablement.

knock-on, *n.* **they said that the knock-on effect of increases would be large,** ils ont dit que la répercussion des augmentations de salaires serait considérable.

know-how, *n.* savoir-faire *m*; expertise *f*; connaissances *f* techniques.

Krugerrand, *n.* krugerrand *m.*

L

label[1], *n.* (*a*) étiquette *f*; **address label,** étiquette-adresse; **gummed label,** étiquette gommée; **(self-)adhesive/stick-on label,** étiquette (auto)adhésive/autocollante; autocollant *m*; **tie-on label,** étiquette à œillet; **price label,** étiquette (portant le prix) (*b*) label *m*/étiquette; **own label goods,** marque *f* d'un magasin particulier; **quality label,** label/étiquette de qualité; **guarantee label,** label/étiquette de garantie.

label[2], *v.tr.*(*a*) étiqueter; apposer/attacher une étiquette à/coller une étiquette sur (un paquet, etc.) (*b*) attribuer un label (de garantie, de qualité, etc.) à (un produit).

labelling, *n.* (*a*) étiquetage *m*; **price labelling,** étiquetage du prix (*b*) attribution *f* d'un label (de garantie, de qualité).

labor, *n. NAm:* = **labour.**

labour, *n.* 1. travail *m*; **manual labour,** travail manuel; travail de manœuvre; **material and labour,** main-d'œuvre *f* et matériel *m*; **division of labour,** division *f* du travail 2. (*a*) main-d'œuvre/travailleurs *mpl*; **cheap labour,** main-d'œuvre à bon marché; **direct labour,** main-d'œuvre directe; **labour force,** (*i*) effectif *m*; main-d'œuvre (*ii*) *PolEc:* population active; **local labour,** main-d'œuvre locale; **skilled labour,** main-d'œuvre qualifiée/spécialisée; **cost of labour,** prix *m* de la main-d'œuvre; **shortage of labour,** pénurie *f*/crise *f*/rareté *f* de la main-d'œuvre; **labour intensive industry,** industrie qui dépend d'une main-d'œuvre considérable (*b*) **capital and labour,** le capital et la main-d'œuvre; **labour disputes/conflicts/troubles,** conflits *m* du travail; **labour unrest,** agitation ouvrière/malaise ou-

vrier; **labour market,** marché *m* du travail; **labour relations,** relations syndicales/relations du travail; **Minister of Labour,** Ministre *m* du travail; **International Labour Organization,** Organisation Internationale du Travail.

labourer, *n.* ouvrier *m*; travailleur manuel; **agricultural labourer,** ouvrier agricole.

labour-saving, *a.* qui rend le travail plus facile; **labour-saving device** = appareil électroménager.

laches, *n. Jur:* négligence *f* (coupable); inaction *f*.

lack[1], *n.* manque *m*/absence *f*/pénurie *f* (de capitaux, de main-d'œuvre, etc.); **lack of funds,** pénurie de fonds; **for lack of sufficient data,** à défaut de données suffisantes.

lack[2], *v.tr.* manquer de (disponibilités, etc.); faire défaut; **he lacks experience,** il manque d'expérience; **they lack capital,** les capitaux *m* leur font défaut.

lacklustre, *a.* (*stuck market rating*) inattractif; (*day on the stock exchange*) creux.

laden, *a. Nau:* chargé; **fully laden ship,** navire *m* en pleine charge; **laden in bulk,** chargé en vrac; **laden draught,** tirant *m* d'eau en charge.

lading, *n.* (*a*) chargement *m* (d'un navire) (*b*) embarquement *m*/mise *f* à bord (de marchandises); **bill of lading,** connaissement *m*; **through bill of lading,** connaissement direct/à forfait.

lag[1], *n.* retard *m*/décalage *m*; **time lag,** décalage; **input lag,** retard dans l'adaptation des facteurs de production.

land[1], *n. Jur:* terre(s) *f(pl)*; fonds *m* de terre/biens-fonds *m*/propriété foncière; **land and buildings,** terrains *m* et bâtiments *m*; **land reform/law,** réforme *f*/loi *f* agraire; **land tax,** contributions foncières (sur les propriétés non bâties); impôt foncier; **land agent,** (*i*) intendant *m*/régisseur *m* d'un domaine; administrateur foncier (*ii*) agent immobilier; **land agency,** (*i*) agence immobilière (*ii*) gérance *f* d'immeubles/de propriétés; **land register,** cadastre *m*; **land registration,** inscription *f* (d'un bien-fonds) au cadastre; **land registry (office),** bureau *m*/service *m* du cadastre.

land[2], *v.tr.* **1.** débarquer (des marchandises) **2.** *v.i. Av:* atterrir.

landed, *a.* **landed cost,** prix *m* à quai.

landing, *n.* (*i*) *Nau: etc.* débarquement *m*/mise *f* à quai (*ii*) *Av:* atterrissage *m*; **landing certificate,** certificat *m* de déchargement; **landing charges,** frais *mpl* de déchargement; *Av:* frais d'atterrissage; **landing permit/order,** permis *m* de débarquement/ *Av:* d'atterrissage.

landlady, *n.* propriétaire *f*; logeuse *f*; hôtelière *f*.

landlord, *n.* propriétaire *m*; hôtelier *m*.

landowner, *n.* propriétaire *m* foncier.

language, *n.* **business language,** langue *f* des affaires/langage *m* de gestion; **computer language/machine language,** langage machine.

lapse[1], *n.* **1.** déchéance *f* (d'un droit) **2.** laps *m* de temps; **after a lapse of three months,** après un délai de trois mois/au bout de trois mois.

lapse[2], *v.i. Jur: (of right, patent, etc.)* se périmer/tomber en désuétude; *Ins: (of policy, etc.)* cesser d'être en vigueur; *(of subscription)* prendre fin; **to have lapsed,** être périmé.

lapsed, *a.* (billet, etc.) périmé; *Jur:* (droit) périmé; (contrat) caduc.

large, *a.* **a large sum,** une grosse/forte somme; une somme considérable; **to incur** large losses, éprouver/subir des pertes sensibles; **to trade on a large scale,** traiter des affaires sur une grande échelle.

last, *a.* **last in first out (LIFO),** dernier entré, premier sorti (DEPS).

late[1], *a.* **1.** **late delivery,** livraison retardée **2.** **at a later date,** à une date ultérieure; **latest date,** terme *m* de rigueur/délai *m* de rigueur **3.** **latest models,** derniers modèles; **the very latest improvements,** les tout derniers perfectionnements.

late[2], *adv.* en retard.

launch, *v.tr.* **to launch a product,** lancer un produit/mettre un produit sur le marché; **to launch a £3m cash bid,** lancer une offre au comptant de £3 million.

launching, *n.* lancement *m* (de nouveaux produits).

launder, *v.tr.* blanchir (de l'argent, des capitaux).

laundering, *n.* blanchissement *m* (de l'argent).

law, *n.* **1.** (*a*) **labour laws,** législation *f* du travail (*b*) loi *f*; *PolEc:* **law of supply and demand,** loi de l'offre et de la demande; **law of diminishing returns,** loi des rendements décroissants **2.** droit *m*; **civil law,** droit civil; **common law,** droit coutumier; **commercial law/mercantile law/law merchant,** droit commercial; code *m* de commerce; **Company law/corporation law,** droit des sociétés; **international law,** droit international; **maritime law,** droit maritime; **law of contract** = droit des obligations **3.** (*justice*) **case law,** jurisprudence *f*; **court of law,** cour *f* de justice; tribunal *m*; **law courts,** palais *m* de justice; **to go to law,** avoir recours à la justice/recourir à la justice/aller en justice; **action at law,** action *f* en justice; **law costs,** frais *mpl* de procédure; **law department,** bureau *m*/service *m* du contentieux; le contentieux.

lawful, *a.* **1.** légal **2.** permis/licite; **lawful trade,** commerce *m* licite **3.** (droit etc.) légitime; (contrat) valide; **lawful currency,** cours légal.

lawfully, *adv.* légalement; légitimement.

lawfulness, *n.* légalité *f*; légitimité *f*.

lawsuit, *n.* procès *m*; poursuites *f* judiciaires; litige *m*; *F:* affaire *f*; **to bring a lawsuit against s.o.,** intenter un procès à qn.

lawyer, *n.* (*i*) avocat *m* (*ii*) avoué *m*.

lay, *n. Nau:* **lay day,** jour *m* de starie/d'estarie/de planche.

lay-away, *n.* **lay-away plan,** vente réservée/vente à terme.

laying-off, *n.* licenciement *m*/débauchage *m* (de la main-d'œuvre).

lay-off, *n. Ind:* (période *f* de) licenciement *m* (temporaire); chômage *m* technique; **the lay-offs,** les employés en chômage technique.

lay off, *v.tr.* (*a*) licencier/débaucher/renvoyer temporairement (des ouvriers); mettre des employés en chômage technique (*b*) *Ins:* **to lay off a risk,** effectuer une réassurance.

layout, *n.* **1. layout of a factory,** implantation *f* **2. layout of an article,** mise *f* en page d'un article **3. layout of a plan,** étude *f*/tracé *m* d'un projet; *Mkt:* **simple/rough layout,** crayonné *m*/esquisse *f*.

lay out, *v.tr.* **1.** faire une étude/un tracé (de projet) **2. to lay out money,** dépenser/débourser de l'argent.

lead, *n.* **lead time,** délai *m* (d'approvisionnement); **delivery lead time,** délai de livraison; **lead manager,** chef-de-file *m*.

leader, *n. St Exch:* **(equity) leader,** valeur *f* vedette; **strike leader,** meneur, -euse de grève; **the leader of the French glass industry,** le leader/le numéro 1 français du verre; **market leaders,** chef *m* de file du marché.

leading, *a.* (*a*) principal; **leading shares,** valeurs dirigeantes/vedettes; **a leading shareholder,** un des principaux actionnaires/un gros actionnaire (*b*) **available from all leading jewellers,** en vente chez tous les grands bijoutiers; **one of the leading firms in the country,** une des plus importantes entreprises du pays (*c*) **leading article,** article *m* (de) réclame.

leaf, *n.* volant *m* (d'un chèque).

lease[1], *n.* (*a*) *Jur:* bail *m*; **long lease,** bail à long terme/à longue échéance; bail emphytéotique; **operating lease,** contrat *m* de location-exploitation; **term of a lease,** durée *f* d'un bail; **to take (sth.) on lease,** louer/prendre (qch.) à bail; affermer (une terre); **to take out a lease on a house,** louer une maison/prendre une maison à bail; **to renew a lease,** renouveler un bail; **to sign a lease,** signer un bail; **expiration of a lease,** expiration *f* d'un bail; **my lease runs out in May,** mon bail expire en mai (*b*) **oil and gas leases,** concessions pétrolières et gazéifères (*c*) **lease financing,** leasing *m*; location *f* avec option d'achat.

lease[2], *v.tr.* **1. to lease (out),** louer/céder (une maison) à bail; affermer (une terre) **2.** prendre (une maison) à bail/louer (une maison); affermer (une terre).

lease-back, *n.* cession-bail *f*/location après-vente.

leasehold, 1. *n.* (*a*) tenure *f* à bail, *esp* tenure en vertu d'un bail emphytéotique (*b*) immeuble *m* loué à bail **2.** *a.* tenu à bail.

leaseholder, *n.* locataire *mf*.

leasing, *n.* **(financial) leasing,** (*i*) crédit bail *m*/leasing *m* (*ii*) location-vente *f*; **leasing company,** entreprise *f*/société *f* de leasing; **equipment leasing,** crédit-bail mobilier/bail avec option d'achat.

leave, *n.* **leave (of absence),** congé *m*; autorisation *f*/permission *f* de s'absenter; **sick leave,** congé de maladie; **annual leave,** congé annuel; **leave pay,** salaire *m* de congé; **on leave,** en congé.

ledger, *n. Book-k:* grand(-)livre *m*/livre *r* de comptabilité générale; **bought ledger,** grand(-)livre des achats; **sales ledger,** grand(-)livre des ventes; **ledger clerk,** employé, -ée aux écritures; **loose-lea**

ledger, grand(-)livre à feuillets mobiles; **payroll ledger,** grand(-)livre de paie; **share ledger,** registre *m* des actionnaires.

legacy, *n. Jur:* legs *m*; donation *f* testamentaire; **residuary legacy/***NAm:* **universal legacy,** legs universel.

legal, *a.* 1. légal; licite; **legal commerce,** commerce *m* licite 2. (*a*) légal; judiciaire; juridique; selon les lois; **legal charges,** (*in an action*) frais *m* judiciaires; (*in a transaction*) frais juridiques; **legal document,** acte *m* authentique/document *m* juridique; **legal entity,** personne civile/morale (*b*) (*of bank, etc.*) **legal department,** service *m*/bureau *m* du contentieux; le contentieux; **legal expert,** jurisconsulte *m*; avocat *m* conseil; **legal adviser,** conseiller *m* juridique; **to take legal advice,** consulter un avocat/un notaire; **to take legal action,** engager des poursuites judiciaires.

legality, *n.* légalité *f.*

legalization, *n.* légalisation *f.*

legalize, *v.tr.* légaliser/certifier/authentiquer (un document).

legally, *adv.* légalement; (*i*) licitement (*ii*) judiciairement (*iii*) juridiquement; **legally responsible,** responsable en droit.

legatee, *n. Jur:* légataire *mf*/héritier, -ière/ bénéficiaire *mf* d'un legs.

leisure, *n.* **leisure industry,** industrie *f* du temps libre/des loisirs.

lend, *v.tr.* **to lend sth. to s.o./to lend s.o. sth.,** prêter qch. à qn; **to lend money at interest,** prêter de l'argent à intérêt; **to lend against security,** prêter sur nantissement; **to lend stock on contango,** placer des titres en report.

lender, *n.* prêteur, -euse; **money lender,** bailleur *m* de fonds; **lender of the last resort,** Institut *m* monétaire.

lending, *n.* prêt *m* (d'un objet, d'argent); *Fin:* prestation *f* (de capitaux); *StExch:* placement *m* (de titres en report); **lending bank,** banque *f* de crédit; **lending limit,** plafond *m* de crédit; **lending officer,** agent

prêteur (d'un établissement de crédit); *Bank:* **minimum lending rate,** taux (officiel) d'escompte.

less, 1. *a.* **of less value,** d'une valeur moindre/de moindre valeur; **quantities/ sums less than ...,** quantités *f*/sommes *f* au-dessous de ... 2. *prep.* **purchase price less 10%,** prix *m* d'achat moins 10%; **interest less tax amounts to £50,** les intérêts nets s'élèvent à £50 3. *n.* **to sell sth. at less than cost price,** vendre qch. à moins du prix de revient/à un prix inférieur au prix de revient.

lessee, *n.* 1. locataire *mf* (à bail) (d'un immeuble, etc.); preneur, -euse 2. concessionnaire *mf.*

lessor, *n.* bailleur, -eresse; propriétaire *mf.*

let, *v.tr.* louer (une maison); **house to (be) let,** maison *f* à louer.

let-out, *n. F:* **let-out (clause),** clause *f* échappatoire.

letter, *n.* (*a*) lettre *f*; **business letter,** lettre d'affaires/lettre commerciale; **covering letter,** note/lettre explicative; lettre d'introduction/lettre d'envoi; **follow-up letter,** lettre de relance (à un client); **letter file,** classeur *m* de lettres/classe-lettres *m inv*; **letter of acknowledgement,** accusé *m* de réception; **letter of application,** lettre de demande (d'emploi, etc.); **letter of appointment,** lettre de nomination/d'affectation; **letter of complaint,** (lettre de) réclamation *f*; **letter of reference,** lettre de recommandation; **setform letter,** lettre type/ lettre passe-partout/lettre modèle; **side letter,** papillon *m* (*b*) *Post:* **air(mail) letter,** (*i*) lettre par avion (*ii*) aérogramme *m*; **express letter,** lettre exprès; **letter rate,** tarif *m* (d'affranchissement des) lettres; **registered letter,** lettre recommandée; **to send a letter first class** = envoyer une lettre à tarif normal; **to send a letter second class** = envoyer une lettre à tarif réduit (*c*) **letters patent,** brevet *m* d'invention (*d*) **letter of advice,** lettre d'avis; **letter of credit,** lettre de crédit; **letter of exchange,** lettre de change; **letter of guar-**

anty, lettre d'aval; **letter of intent,** lettre d'intention; *StExch:* **letter of allotment,** avis *m* d'attribution/de répartition.

letter-card, *n.* carte-lettre *f.*

letterheading, *n.* **write your name on a company letterheading,** envoyez votre nom sur une feuille de papier à en-tête de votre société.

letting, *a.* location *f*; **letting agency,** agence *f* de location.

level[1], *n.* niveau *m* (des prix, des salaires, etc.); **to maintain prices at a high level,** maintenir les prix à un niveau élevé.

level[2], *v.tr.* niveler (des cours, des taux, etc.).

levelling, *n.* nivellement *m* (des revenus, etc.).

level off, *v.i. (of prices, etc.)* se stabiliser.

level out, *v.i. (of prices)* s'équilibrer.

leverage, *n. (gearing)* effet *m* de levier; *(expressed as percentage)* ratio *m* d'endettement.

leveraged, *a.* bénéficiant de l'effet de levier; **the company is highly leveraged,** la société est fortement endettée; **leveraged buyout (LBO),** rachat *m* d'une société par effet de levier/LBO *f*; **leveraged management buyout,** = rachat/reprise *f* d'entreprise par les salariés (RES).

levy[1], *n.* **1.** perception *f* (d'une taxe, d'un impôt) **2.** impôt *m*/contribution *f*; **capital levy,** prélèvement *m* sur le capital; *EEC:* **(variable import) levy,** prélèvement *m* (à l'importation).

levy[2], *v.tr. (a)* percevoir (une taxe, un impôt); **to levy a duty on goods,** imposer des marchandises; frapper des marchandises d'un droit; **to levy a tax on sth,** taxer qch; frapper qch d'une taxe; percevoir une taxe sur qch *(b)* **£50 a year is levied on members' salaries for the pension fund,** les traitements des membres sont sujets à un prélèvement annuel de £50 comme contribution à la caisse de retraite.

levying, *n.* perception *f* (d'impôts).

liability, *n.* **1.** *(a) Jur:* responsabilité *f* **joint liability,** responsabilité conjointe collective; **several liability,** responsabilité séparée; **joint and several liability,** responsabilité (conjointe et) solidaire solidarité *f (b)* **third party liability** responsabilité au tiers; **public liability insurance,** assurance *f* responsabilité civile *(c)* **limited liability,** responsabilité limitée **limited liability company,** *(i)* société *f* à responsabilité limitée (SARL) *(ii)* société anonyme (SA) *(d)* **employer's liability,** responsabilité patronale/de l'employeur (pour les accidents du travail) *(e)* **absolute liability,** responsabilité totale/obligation inconditionnelle; **contractual liability,** responsabilité contractuelle; obligation contractée souscrite **2.** *Fin: (a)* **contingent liability,** *(i)* engagements éventuels; passif éventuel/exigible *(ii)* tierce caution *Bank:* **contingent liability in respect of acceptances,** débiteurs *mpl* par aval *(b) p* **liabilities,** ensemble *m* des dettes; obligations/valeurs passives/dettes passives; passif; *(in bankruptcy)* masse passive (d'une liquidation après faillite); **assets and liabilities,** actif *m* et passif; **current liabilities,** dettes à court terme/passif exigible/exigibilités *f*; **deferred liability,** passif reporté; **long-term liability,** dette passif à long terme; **to meet one's liabilities,** faire face à ses engagements/à ses échéances *(c) (on bills of exchange)* encours *m*; **liability as drawer,** encours tiré; **liability as maker/as transferor** encours cédant.

liable, *a.* **1.** *Jur:* responsable/passible **(for,** de); **liable at law,** responsable civilement **to hold oneself liable (for),** se porter garant (de) **2.** sujet/assujetti/tenu/astreint **(to,** à); redevable/passible **(to,** de); **liable to stamp duty,** assujetti au timbre; **liable to tax,** assujetti à un impôt; redevable/passible d'un impôt; **dividends liable to income tax,** dividendes soumis à l'impôt sur le revenu; **to make sth. liable to a tax,** assujettir qch. à un impôt **3.** sujet/exposé **(to,** à); **goods liable to go bad,** marchandises *f* susceptibles de s'avarier.

libel, *n.* diffamation *f*; **to sue for libel**, intenter un procès en diffamation.

liberal, *a.* (offre) généreuse; ample (provision de qch).

liberate, *v.tr. Fin:* **to liberate capital**, mobiliser des capitaux.

liberation, *n. Fin:* **liberation of capital**, mobilisation *f* de capitaux.

licence[1], *n.* permis *m*/autorisation *f*/licence *f*/privilège *m*; **licence to sell beer, wines and spirits**, permis/licence de débit de boissons; **trading licence**, carte *f* de commerce; **manufacturing licence**, brevet *m*/licence de fabrication; **exclusive licence**, licence exclusive; **made/manufactured under licence**, fabriqué sous licence; **import licence**, licence d'importation; **export licence**, licence d'exportation; **licence holder**, titulaire *mf* d'un permis; **car/vehicle licence** = carte grise; **driving licence**, permis de conduire; **heavy goods (vehicle) licence**, permis poids lourds; **road fund licence** = vignette *f* automobile.

licence[2], *v.tr. NAm:* = **license**[1].

license[1], *v.tr.* accorder un permis/une autorisation/une licence/un privilège à (qn); **licensed to sell beer, wines and spirits**, autorisé à vendre des boissons alcoolisées/*FrC:* licencié; **to be licensed to sell sth.**, avoir un permis de vente/avoir l'autorisation de vendre qch.

license[2], *n. NAm:* = **licence**[1].

licensed, *a.* autorisé(e); **licensed premises** = débit *m* de boissons (*avec licence de plein exercice*).

licensee, *n.* titulaire *mf*/détenteur, -trice d'un permis (*pour vendre de l'alcool*).

licensing, *n.* autorisation *f* (à faire qch.); octroi *m* d'un permis/d'une autorisation (à qn); **cross licensing**, concession *f* réciproque de licences; **licensing requirements**, conditions *f* d'autorisation; **licensing acts/laws**, lois relatives aux débits de boissons (alcoolisées).

lien, *n. Jur:* privilège *m* (sur un bien meuble, etc.); droit *m* de rétention; **equitable lien**, privilège indépendant de la possession; **general lien**, privilège général; **particular lien**, nantissement *m*/gage *m*; **vendor's lien**, privilège du vendeur; **(possessory) lien on goods**, droit de rétention de marchandises; **lien on shares**, actions gagées/nantissement d'actions.

life, *n.* (*a*) **working life**, période *f*/années *f pl* d'activité (*b*) **life annuity/life pension**, pension/rente viagère; pension à vie; **life interest**, usufruit *m* (d'un bien); viager *m*; rente viagère; **life tenant**, usufruitier, -ière (*c*) *Ins:* **life assurance/life insurance**, assurance *f* sur la vie/assurance-vie *f* (*d*) *Fin:* **life of a loan**, durée *f* d'un emprunt; **(product) life expectancy**, durée *f* (utile) (d'un produit)/courbe *f* de vie (d'un produit).

limit, *n.* **age limit**, limite *f* d'âge; **time limit**, délai *m* (de paiement, etc.); **size limit/weight limit**, limite de dimension/de poids; **limit of free delivery area**, rayon *m*/périmètre *m* de livraison gratuite; *Fin: etc:* **credit limit**, limite/plafond *m* de crédit; réserve *f* d'achat; **they set voluntary limits to their exports**, ils autolimitent leurs exportations/ils appliquent une limitation volontaire de leurs exportations; *StExch:* fluctuation *f* de prix maximum (*pour la durée d'une séance*); **limit (order)**, ordre *m* limite; **limit up/down**, limite de la hausse/de la baisse; limite supérieure/inférieure.

limitation, *n.* **1.** limitation *f*/restriction *f*; **limitation of liability**, limitation de responsabilité **2.** *Jur:* prescription (extinctive); **term of limitation**, délai *m* de prescription; (*in a suit*) **time limitation**, péremption *f*.

limited, *a.* limité/borné/restreint; **limited edition**, (édition à) tirage limité; **limited market**, marché étroit/restreint; **the expenditure, however limited ...**, les dépenses, si réduites soient-elles...; **limited (liability) company (Ltd)**, (*i*) société *f* à responsabilité limitée (SARL) (*ii*) société anonyme (SA); **limited partner**, commanditaire *m*; **limited partnership**, société en commandite; *StExch:* **limited prices,** cours limités.

limiting, *a.* limitatif; *Jur:* **limiting clause,** clause/condition restrictive (d'un contrat, etc.).

line, *n.* **1. air line,** compagnie *f* aérienne; **shipping line,** compagnie de navigation; messageries *f* maritimes **2.** série *f* (d'articles); gamme *f* (de produits); **leading lines,** articles *m*/spécialités *f* de réclame **3. assembly line,** chaîne *f* de montage **4.** *Bank:* **credit line,** ligne *f* de crédit/autorisation *f* de crédit **5. line organization/management,** organisation hiérarchique/verticale; **line and staff organization/management,** structure *f* mixte **6. to bring salaries/prices into line with those of other companies,** aligner les salaires/les prix sur ceux des autres sociétés.

liner, *n.* (*i*) paquebot *m* de grande ligne/ liner *m* (*ii*) (avion) gros porteur *m*; **cargo liner,** navire de charge régulier; **liner freighting,** affrètement *m* à la cueillette; **liner rate,** fret *m* à (la) cueillette.

liquid, *a.* *Fin:* (argent) liquide/disponible; **liquid assets,** valeurs *f* disponibles/actif *m* liquide/disponibilités *fpl*; **liquid debt,** dette *f* liquide/claire.

liquidate, *v.tr.* liquider (une société, une dette); amortir (une dette).

liquidation, *n.* liquidation *f* (d'une société, d'une dette); amortissement *m* (d'une dette); mobilisation *f* (de capitaux); (*of company*) **to go into liquidation,** déposer son bilan; **compulsory liquidation,** liquidation forcée; **voluntary liquidation,** liquidation volontaire; **liquidation subject to supervision of court,** liquidation judiciaire.

liquidator, *n.* liquidateur, -trice (d'une société en liquidation).

liquidity, *n.* *Fin:* liquidité *f* (d'une dette); **cash liquidity,** liquidités; **liquidity ratio,** coefficient *m*/taux *m* de liquidité.

list[1], *n.* (*a*) liste *f*; bordereau *m*; inventaire *m* (d'actif, de passif, de portefeuille); *Fin:* **list of applicants/of applications,** liste des souscripteurs (à un emprunt, etc.); *StExch:* **list of quotations,** bulletin *m* des cours; **official list,** cote officielle; *Cust:* **free list,** liste des marchandises importées en franchise; *Bank: etc:* **list of investments,** (bordereau de) portefeuille *m*; **list of bills for collection/for discount,** bordereau d'effets à l'encaissement/à l'escompte; bordereau d'encaissement/d'escompte; **mailing list,** liste d'envoi; liste des abonnés; **waiting list,** liste d'attente (*b*) **list price,** prix *m* (de) catalogue; prix public; **(current) price list,** tarif *m*; **market price list,** mercuriale *f*.

list[2], *v.tr.* inscrire/mettre/porter (des noms, etc.) sur une liste; enregistrer (qch.); inventorier (des marchandises, etc.); *Cmptr:* lister; *Fin:* **listed securities/stock,** valeurs cotées; valeurs admises/inscrites à la cote (officielle); **these articles are listed in the catalogue,** ces articles figurent au catalogue.

listing, *n.* *Cmptr:* liste *f*/listage *m*; sortie *f* d'imprimante; *StExch:* cotation *f*; admission *f* à la cote officielle; valeur cotée en Bourse; **to have a listing,** être coté en Bourse; **listing agreement,** (dossier *m* de) demande *f* d'introduction en Bourse.

liter, *n.* *NAm:* = **litre.**

literature, *n.* prospectus *m*/brochures *fpl*.

litre, *n.* *Meas:* litre *m* (*abbr.* l) (= 0.220 gallon).

live, *a.* *Fin:* **live claims,** créances *f* valables qui subsistent (*à l'égard d'un établissement de crédit*).

livelihood, *n.* moyens *mpl* de subsistance; gagne-pain *m*.

lively, *a.* *Fin:* (*of market*) animé.

living, *n.* **1. cost of living,** coût *m* de la vie; **standard of living,** niveau *m* de vie; **to earn one's living,** gagner sa vie **2. living allowance,** indemnité *f* de séjour; **living wage,** minimum vital/salaire minimal.

load[1], *n.* **1.** (*a*) charge *f*/chargement *m* (d'u...

camion, d'un navire, d'un avion, etc.); **average load,** charge moyenne; **axle load,** charge par essieu; **commercial load/pay load,** charge utile; **constant/dead load,** charge constante/poids à vide/poids mort; **load carrying capacity,** charge utile/charge maximale/charge limite; **load limit,** charge limite; **maximum load,** charge maximale; **permitted pay load/ regulation carrying capacity,** charge utile réglementaire; **test load,** charge d'essai; **lorry load**/*NAm:* **truck load,** charge complète (*b*) (*contents of vehicle*) camion *m* (de gravier, etc.); chargement *m*; cargaison *f* (d'un navire) **2.** commission *f*; frais *mpl* d'acquisition (d'unités de fonds mutuels).

load², 1. *v.tr.* (*a*) charger (un camion, un navire, etc.); embarquer (des marchandises) (*b*) *Ins:* majorer (une prime); imposer une surprime **2.** *v.i.* (*of ship, etc.*) **to be loaded,** prendre charge; faire la cargaison; **loading for Bombay,** en charge pour Bombay; **ship loading,** navire *m* en chargement/en charge.

loaded, *a.* **1.** (camion, navire, etc.) chargé **2.** *Ins:* **loaded premium,** prime majorée/ surprime *f*.

loading, *n.* **1.** chargement *m* (d'un camion, d'un wagon, d'un navire, d'un avion); embarquement *m* (de marchandises, passagers); **bulk loading,** chargement en vrac; **loading point,** point *m* de chargement; **loading ramp/rack,** rampe *f* de chargement; **loading chute,** couloir *m* de chargement; **loading board,** pont volant; **loading bay,** quai *m* de chargement; **loading dock,** embarcadère *m* **2.** *Ins:* surprime *f*/majoration *f* (d'une prime).

loan¹, *n.* **1.** (*money lent*) prêt *m*/avance *f*; (*money borrowed*) emprunt *m*/avance *f*; **loan capital/loan stock,** capital-obligations *m*; **loan at interest,** prêt à intérêt; **loan at call/loan repayable on demand,** prêt/emprunt remboursable sur demande; **loan at notice,** prêt/emprunt à terme; **loan back,** cession-bail *f*; **dead loan,** emprunt irrécouvrable; **long-term loan,** prêt/emprunt à long terme; **margin loan,** prêt de second rang/prêt subordonné; **short(-term) loan,** prêt/emprunt à court terme; **soft loan,** prêt bonifié/à taux bonifié; **term loan,** prêt/emprunt à terme fixe; **loan by the week,** prêt/emprunt à la petite semaine; **loan on collateral,** prêt sur gage/sur nantissement; prêt garanti/nanti; **loan on mortgage/mortgage loan,** emprunt hypothécaire/sur hypothèque; **loan on securities/on stock,** emprunt sur titres; **loan on trust,** prêt d'honneur; **secured loan,** prêt/emprunt garanti; **unsecured loan/loan without security/loan on overdraft,** prêt/emprunt à découvert; **tied loan,** prêt conditionnel/emprunt à emploi spécifié; prêt lié; *MIns:* **loan on respondentia,** prêt/emprunt à la grosse sur facultés; **loan office,** (*i*) caisse *f* d'emprunts (*ii*) maison *f* de prêts; **loan bank,** caisse de prêt; **loan society/company,** société *f* de crédit; **loan charges,** frais financiers; **loan department,** service *m* des crédits; **loan certificate,** titre *m* de prêt; **to apply for a loan,** demander/solliciter un prêt; **application for a loan,** demande *f* de prêt; **to allow/to grant a loan,** accorder/ consentir un prêt; **to contract/to raise/to take up a loan,** contracter/faire un emprunt; **to collect a loan,** toucher un emprunt; **to repay a loan,** amortir/rembourser un emprunt; **loan guarantee scheme (LGS),** prêts bonifiés d'aide à l'investissement/au développement des entreprises **2.** *Fin:* emprunt; **bank loan,** emprunt bancaire/de la banque; **day-to-day/day loan**/*NAm:* **call loan,** prêt/crédit au jour le jour; **government loan,** emprunt d'État; **public loan,** emprunt public; **perpetual loan,** emprunt perpétuel; **personal loan,** emprunt personnel; **refunding loan,** emprunt de remboursement; **consolidation loan/ funding loan,** emprunt de consolidation; **consolidated loan,** emprunt consolidé; **conversion loan,** emprunt de conversion; **debenture loan,** emprunt obligataire; **indexed loan,** emprunt indexé; **to issue a loan,** émettre/lancer un emprunt; **issue of a loan,** émission *f* d'un emprunt; **to float a loan,** lancer un emprunt; **to service a loan,**

assurer le service d'un emprunt; **to sub-cribe to a loan,** souscrire à un emprunt.

loan[2], *v.tr.* prêter (**sth. to s.o.,** qch. à qn).

locking up, *n.* **locking up of capital,** immobilisation *f* de capitaux.

lock out, *v.tr. Ind:* lock(-)outer (le personnel); fermer (les ateliers).

lockout, *n. Ind:* fermeture *f* (des portes)/lock-out *m inv.*

lock up, *v.tr. Fin:* **to lock up capital,** immobiliser/bloquer/engager/des capitaux.

loco, *adv.* loco; **loco price,** prix *m* loco/sur place.

lodge, *v.tr.* déposer/remettre; **to lodge money with s.o.,** consigner/déposer de l'argent chez qn; confier/remettre de l'argent à qn; **to lodge securities with a bank,** déposer des titres dans une banque; **securities lodged as collateral,** titres déposés/remis en nantissement.

lodging, lodg(e)ment, *n.* dépôt *m*/consignation *f*/remise *f* (d'argent, de valeurs) **(with,** chez).

logo, *n.* logo(type) *m.*

lollipop, *n. F:* récompense *f*/prime *f* (*offerte par une société*).

lombard rate, *n.* taux *n* lombard.

long, *a. & n.* **longs,** titres longs/obligations longues; **long end of the market,** taux longs/taux à long terme; **to take a long position/to go long,** acheter à la hausse/prendre une position longue; **long ton,** tonne forte.

long-dated, *a. Fin:* à longue échéance; **long-dated bills,** billets *m*/papiers *m* à longue échéance; **long-dated securities,** titres longs/obligations longues.

long-distance, *a.* **long-distance (telephone) call,** communication interurbaine; **long-distance lorry driver,** routier *m.*

long-range, *a.* (prévisions) à long terme.

longstanding, *a.* ancien; de longue date; de vieille date; **longstanding accounts,** notes dues depuis longtemps/vieux comptes.

long-term, *a.* à long terme; **long-term credit,** crédit *m*/emprunt *m* à long terme; **long-term debt,** dette *f* à long terme; **long-term policy,** politique *f* à long terme/à longue échéance.

loop, *n.* (chaîne *f* d')autocontrôle *m.*

loophole, *n.* échappatoire *f*/porte *f* de sortie.

loose, *a.* **loose cash/change,** menue monnaie; **loose goods,** marchandises *f* en vrac

lorry, *n.* camion *m*; **five-ton lorry,** camion de cinq tonnes; **heavy lorry,** camion lourd/de fort tonnage; poids lourd; **articulated lorry,** semi-remorque *fm*; **lorry driver,** conducteur *m*/chauffeur *m* de camion de poids lourd; *F:* routier *m.*

lose, *v.tr.* (*a*) perdre (qch.) (*b*) **to lose in value,** perdre de sa valeur (*c*) **to lose a customer,** perdre un client.

loser, *n. Fin:* valeur *f* en baisse.

loss, *n.* **1.** perte *f*; **loss of custom,** perte de clientèle; **loss of market,** perte de marché; **loss of profit/earnings,** manque *m* à gagner **2.** (*a*) déficit *m*; **to sustain/suffer heavy losses,** subir de grosses/fortes pertes; **to make up one's losses,** compenser ses pertes; **dead loss,** perte sèche; **net loss,** perte nette; **tax loss,** déficit fiscal reportable; **trading loss,** perte *f* d'arbitrage/de trading/de gestion; *F:* une paume; **loss leader,** produit *m* d'appel; **to sell at a loss,** vendre à perte; **sale of goods at a loss,** vente *f* de marchandises; **to minimize one's losses,** atténuer ses pertes; **to cut one's losses,** faire la part du feu; **loss carry back,** report *m* en arrière de déficit; **loss carry forward,** report en avance de déficit (*I. Ins:* sinistre *m*; **to estimate the loss,** évaluer le sinistre; **loss assessment,** fixation des dommages; **(actual) total loss,** perte totale; *MIns:* **constructive total loss,** perte censée totale; *MIns:* **partial loss,** perte partielle/sinistre partiel **3.** *Ind/Trans:* freinte *f*/frainte *f*/diminution *f* (du poids d'un produit en cours de fabrica) tion ou de transport); **loss in transit,** freinte/déchet *m* de route.

loss-making, *a.* déficitaire.

lot, *n.* **1.** *Fin:* **the debentures are redeemed by lot,** les obligations sont rachetées par voie de tirage **2.** (*a*) (*at auction*) lot *m* (*b*) lot; paquet *m*; **lot of goods,** lot de marchandises; **to buy in one lot,** acheter en bloc; *Fin:* **lots of shares,** paquet de titres/d'actions; **to sell shares in small lots,** vendre des actions par petits paquets.

lottery, *n.* loterie *f*; **lottery ticket,** billet *m* de loterie; *Fin:* **lottery loan,** emprunt *m* à lots.

low[1], *a.* bas; **low-grade,** de qualité inférieure; **low price,** bas prix; prix faible; **low wages,** salaires peu élevés; **at a low figure/at a low price,** à bas prix/à bon compte/à bon marché; **to keep prices low,** maintenir les prix bas; **the lowest price,** le dernier prix; **prices are at their lowest,** les prix sont au plus bas; **the rate of exchange is low,** le taux du change est bas; **highs and lows,** (cours les plus) hauts et les (cours les plus) bas.

low[2], *n.* **the share index has reached an all-time low,** l'indice des actions est descendu à son plus bas niveau; **to reach a new low,** descendre à un niveau encore jamais atteint.

lower, *v.tr.* rabaisser (un prix); **to lower rents,** diminuer/baisser les loyers; **to lower the minimum lending rate,** abaisser le taux d'escompte.

lowering, *n.* **lowering of prices,** rabais *m*/réduction *f* (de prix).

lucrative, *a.* lucratif, -ive.

luggage, *n.* bagages *mpl*; **hand luggage/cabin luggage,** bagages à main; **free luggage allowance,** franchise *f* de bagages; **luggage registration office,** (bureau d') enregistrement *m* (des bagages); **registered luggage,** bagages enregistrés; **(un)checked luggage,** bagages (non) enregistrés.

lump, *n.* **1. to sell sth. in the lump,** vendre qch. en bloc/en gros/globalement; **lump sum,** (*i*) montant global/somme globale; prix global (*ii*) prix forfaitaire; paiement *m* forfaitaire; **lump sum contract,** forfait *m*; **lump system,** système *m* de paiement forfaitaire.

luxury, *n.* **luxury goods,** articles *m*/produits *m*/objets *m* de luxe; **luxury tax,** taxe *f* de luxe.

M

M, *n.* **M0, M1, M2, M3, etc,** M0, M1, M2, M3, etc.

machine, *n.* (*a*) (*for office use, etc.*) **adding machine,** machine à additionner/à calculer; **copying machine,** machine à (poly)copier; duplicateur *m*; **dictating machine,** machine à dicter (*b*) **machine production,** production *f* en série/production à la machine/production mécanisée; **machine work,** travail *m* à la machine; usinage *m*; **machine-made,** fait à la machine/en série; **vending machine,** distributeur *m* automatique (*c*) **the industrial machine,** les rouages *m*/l'organisation *f* de l'industrie.

machinery, *n.* **administrative machinery,** l'appareil administratif/la machine administrative; *Fin:* **compensation machinery,** mécanisme de compensation.

machining, *n.* usinage *m*.

macroeconomic, *a.* macroéconomique.

macroeconomics, *n.pl.* macroéconomie *f*.

made, *a.* fait/fabriqué/confectionné; **made in France,** fabriqué en France; **French made cars,** voitures de fabrication française; *see also* **make**².

made-up, *a.* **made-up box,** caisse assemblée.

mag, *n.* = **magazine.**

magazine, *n.* revue *f*/publication *f*; périodique *m*; **fashion magazine,** journal *m*/revue de mode; **illustrated magazine,** revue illustrée/magazine *m*; *Publ:* **magazine rights,** droits *m* de reproduction dans les périodiques.

magistrate, *n.* magistrat *m*; **magistrates' court,** tribunal *m* d'instance.

magnate, *n.* magnat *m*.

mail¹, *n.* **1.** courrier *m*; lettres *fpl*; **incomin‖ mail,** courrier (à l')arrivée; **outgoing mai‖** courrier (au) départ; courrier à expédie‖ **inward mail,** courrier en provenance (*i*) d‖ l'étranger (*ii*) de la province; **outwa‖ mail,** courrier (en partance) (*i*) pou‖ l'étranger (*ii*) pour la province; **to ope‖ one's mail/to deal with one's mail,** d‖ pouiller/lire son courrier; **we put it in th‖ mail yesterday,** nous l'avons mis à ‖ poste hier **2. mail order,** commande *f* p‖ correspondance; **mail order busines‖** (achat et) vente *f* par correspandanc‖ (VPC)/sur catalogue; **mail order firr‖ house,** maison *f* de vente par co‖ respondance; **mail order catalogu‖** catalogue *m* de vente par correspondanc‖ **3. direct mail advertising,** publicité direc‖ (par correspondance) **4.** *Cmptr:* **electr‖ nic mail,** messagerie *f* (électronique).

mail², *v.tr.* envoyer par la poste/expédi‖ (une lettre, un paquet) par la post‖ mettre (une lettre) à la poste.

mailable, *a.* qu'on peut envoyer par poste.

mailing, *n.* publipostage *m*; **direct mailin‖** publicité directe (par correspondanc‖ **mailing list,** liste *f* de diffusion; lis‖ d'adresses; **mailing piece/mailing sho‖** prospectus *m*/dépliant *m*/envoi *m* (‖ publicité directe); **please add our name‖ your mailing list,** veuillez nous faire pa‖ venir régulièrement votre docume‖ tation/vos catalogues/vos tarifs.

main, *a.* principal; premier; essentiel; **ma‖ office,** direction (générale); siège soci‖ **factory contained in three main buildin‖** usine *f* en trois corps de bâtiment; *Cmp‖*

main frame (computer), unité centrale de traitement.

maintain, *v.tr.* (*a*) entretenir (des relations, une correspondance) (*b*) **to maintain the exchange above the gold-point,** maintenir le change au-dessus du gold point; **the dividend maintains at 5%,** le dividende se maintient à 5%.

maintenance, *n.* **1. resale price maintenance,** prix imposés **2.** (*a*) entretien *m*/conservation *f* (du matériel, des bâtiments, etc.); maintenance *f*; **planned maintenance,** maintenance programmée/entretien systématique; **preventive maintenance,** entretien préventif; **routine maintenance/scheduled maintenance,** entretien courant/périodique/de routine; **maintenance allowance,** allocation *f* d'entretien; **maintenance charges/maintenance expenses,** frais *mpl* d'entretien; **maintenance equipment,** matériel *m* d'entretien; **maintenance personnel/maintenance staff,** personnel *m* d'entretien/équipe(s) *f(pl)* d'entretien; **maintenance engineer,** ingénieur *m*/technicien *m* d'entretien (*b*) **maintenance programme/maintenance project,** programme *m* de maintenance; **maintenance requirements,** moyens *m* de maintenance exigés/indispensables; *StExch:* marge *f*/couverture *f* exigée pour maintenir une position en Bourse; **maintenance resources,** moyens *mpl* de maintenance (dont on dispose); **maintenance service,** location *f* entretien **3.** *Jur:* aide pécuniaire (apportée à une des parties); pension *f* alimentaire.

major, *n. NAm:* société *f* de premier ordre/d'importance majeure.

majority, *n.* majorité *f* (des voix, etc.); **absolute majority,** majorité absolue; **majority decision,** décision prise à la majorité (des voix); **majority holding/interest/stake,** participation *f* majoritaire; **majority shareholder,** actionnaire *mf* (à participation) majoritaire.

make¹, *n.* (*a*) façon *f*/forme *f*/fabrication *f*/construction *f* (*b*) marque *f* (d'un pro-duit); **of French make,** de fabrication française; **our own make,** notre propre marque; **cars of all makes,** voitures de toutes marques; **a good make (of car, etc.),** (voiture, etc.) de marque connue/d'excellente fabrication; **standard make,** marque courante.

make², *v.tr.* **1.** (*a*) fabriquer/faire/construire (une machine, une boîte, etc.) (*b*) *Fin:* **to make a promissory note,** souscrire un billet à ordre; **to make a bill of exchange,** libeller une lettre de change (*c*) **to make a payment,** effectuer/faire un versement; **to make a market,** créer un marché (*d*) **to make a speech,** faire un discours (*e*) **to make an appointment,** prendre rendez-vous (*f*) **to make good,** réparer **2.** (*acquire*) faire (de l'argent); **to make £100 a week,** gagner/se faire £100 par semaine; **to make profits,** réaliser des bénéfices; **to make a deal,** conclure un marché/faire une affaire (avec qn); **to make a good deal by ...,** tirer beaucoup de profit de ...; (*of goods*) **to make a price,** faire un prix; accorder un rabais; **the prices made yesterday,** les cours pratiqués hier **3.** faire la fortune de ...; **the cotton trade made Manchester,** l'industrie cotonnière a fait la prospérité de Manchester.

make out, *v.tr.* faire/établir/dresser (une liste, etc.); dresser/rédiger (un mémoire); établir/dresser/relever (un compte); **to make out a cheque to ...,** faire/libeller/établir un chèque à l'ordre de ...; **to make out a document in duplicate,** établir un document en double (exemplaire).

make over, *v.tr.* céder/transférer/transmettre (**sth. to s.o.,** qch. à qn).

maker, *n.* (*a*) fabricant *m* (de drap, etc.); constructeur *m* (de machines); **biscuit maker,** fabricant de biscuits; **maker's price,** prix *m* de fabrique/prix départ usine (*b*) **maker (of a promissory note),** signataire *mf* (d'une lettre de change) (*c*) *StExch:* **market maker,** teneur *m* de marché.

make up, 1. *v.tr.* (*a*) compléter/parfaire (une somme); exécuter (une commande); combler/suppléer à (un déficit); **to make**

up the difference, combler la différence; **to make up the even money,** faire l'appoint (*b*) **to make up back payments,** régler/ solder l'arriéré; **the lost day will be made up,** la journée chômée sera récupérée (*c*) faire (un paquet); **to make up goods into a parcel,** faire un paquet des marchandises (*d*) faire/confectionner/ façonner (des vêtements); dresser (une liste); établir/ arrêter (un compte); clôturer (les comptes); dresser (un bilan); **customer's own material made up** = on travaille à façon/tailleur *m* à façon; **to make up one's accounts,** arrêter ses comptes (*e*) rassembler/réunir (une compagnie); rassembler (une somme d'argent) (*f*) **the payments make up a considerable total,** ces versements atteignent une somme considérable **2.** *v.i.* (*a*) **to make up for one's losses,** compenser ses pertes; **that will make up for your losses,** cela vous dédommagera de vos pertes (*b*) **to make up on a competitor,** gagner sur un concurrent.

making, *n.* **1.** fabrication *f* (de la toile, du papier); confection *f*/façon *f* (de vêtements); construction *f* (d'une machine); création *f* (d'un poste); **decision making,** prise *f* de décision; **the making of a profit,** la réalisation d'un bénéfice **2. making up,** (*i*) compensation *f* (**for losses,** de pertes) (*ii*) arrêté *m* (de comptes); clôture *f* (d'un bilan); *StExch:* **making a price,** action *f* de coter une valeur; **making up day,** jour *m* de liquidation/du règlement; **making up price,** cours *m* de compensation.

maladjustment, *n. PolEc:* **maladjustment in the balance of trade,** déséquilibre *m* dans la balance commerciale.

maladministration, *n.* mauvaise administration/mauvaise gestion.

mala fide, *a. & adv. Jur:* de mauvaise foi.

malpractice, *n.* négligence professionnelle.

mammoth, *a.* géant/énorme/gigantesque/ colossal; **mammoth reduction,** énorme réduction; **on a mammoth scale,** sur une

échelle colossale; **mammoth size, paque** *m* géant.

man[1], *n.* **1.** homme *m*; **a married man, un** homme marié; **a single man,** un homm non marié/célibataire/un célibataire; **mar in the street,** homme moyen; **a salarie man,** un salarié **2.** (*a*) **men's department** rayon *m* (de vêtements pour) hommes (*b* **the men on a site,** les ouvriers *mpl* d'u chantier.

man[2], *v.tr.* fournir du personnel à (un organisation, etc.); assurer le service d (une machine)/la manœuvre de (u appareil); **to man a night-shift, compose** une équipe de nuit; **to man a stanc** affecter du personnel à un stand/assure la surveillance d'un stand; garder u stand/surveiller un stand.

manage, *v.tr.* conduire (une entrepris etc.); administrer/diriger/gérer (une a faire, une société, une banque, etc.); régi gérer (une propriété, une exploitatio agricole, etc.); mener (une affaire); **t manage s.o.'s affairs,** gérer les affaires d qn.

manageable, *a.* (*undertaking*) praticabl faisable; **business grown too big to b manageable,** entreprise devenue si gross qu'on ne peut plus la diriger.

management, *n.* **1.** gestion *f*/administra tion *f*/direction *f*/management *m* (d'un entreprise, d'une société etc.); **asset ma agement,** gestion de capital; **business ma agement,** administration; gestion d affaires; **divisional management,** gestio cellulaire/par département; **office ma agement,** organisation *f* des bureaux; **pe sonnel/staff management,** directio *f*/administration *f* du personnel; **pr duction management,** gestion/organisa tion de la production; **sales managemen** direction commerciale/administratio des ventes; **management accountin** comptabilité *f* de gestion; **manageme auditor,** contrôleur *m* de gestion; **manag ment chart,** organigramme *m*; **manag ment committee,** comité *m* de directio **management consultant,** ingénieur-conse *m*; conseil *m* en gestion; conseiller *m* de direction; **management fee,** commission *f* de chef de file; **management by objectives (MBO),** direction par objectifs (DPO); **passive management,** gestion passive/ gestion indicielle répliquée; **total quality management (TQM),** gestion zéro-défaut/ gestion de qualité totale; **management operating system,** système intégré de gestion; **management science,** science *f* de la gestion; **management team,** équipe *f* de direction; **management techniques,** techniques *f* de gestion; **management theory,** théorie *f* de la gestion de l'entreprise; **bad management,** mauvaise organisation; **owing to bad management,** faute d'organisation; **under new management,** changement *m* de propriétaire/de direction; nouvelle direction **2.** *coll.* les administrateurs *m*/les directeurs *m*/les dirigeants *m* (d'une société); l'administration/la direction; **general management,** direction générale; **joint management,** codirection *f*; **line management,** organisation *f* hiérarchique/verticale; **line and staff management,** structure *f* mixte; **management training,** formation *f* des cadres; **middle management,** cadres moyens; **supervisory management,** agents *mpl* de maîtrise *f*; **top/senior management,** cadres supérieurs/dirigeants; haute direction; **the management regrets any inconvenience caused by the rebuilding,** la direction s'excuse auprès de ses clients de tout inconvénient causé par les travaux (de construction).

manager, *n.* **1.** (*i*) directeur *m*/gérant *m* (d'une société, etc.); chef *m*/dirigeant *m* d'une entreprise; manageur, -euse/ manager *m*; administrateur *m* (*ii*) régisseur *m* (d'une propriété); **account manager,** chargé *m*/responsable *m* de budget; **advertising/publicity manager,** chef *m* de publicité/directeur de la publicité/responsable du service (de) publicité; **art manager,** directeur artistique; **assistant manager,** sous-directeur *m*/sous-chef *m*; **branch manager,** directeur de succursale; **business manager,** (*i*) gérant d'affaires (*ii*)

directeur commercial (*iii*) *Journ:* administrateur (*iv*) *Th:* impresario *m* (d'une chanteuse, etc.); **company manager,** chef d'entreprise; directeur d'une entreprise; (*in store*) **department manager,** chef de rayon (*dans un grand magasin*); **departmental manager,** chef *m* de service; (*in shop*) chef de rayon; **deputy manager,** directeur adjoint; **distribution manager,** chef de distribution; **district manager,** directeur régional; **engineering manager,** directeur technique; **general manager,** directeur général; **hotel manager,** directeur d'hôtel; **joint manager,** directeur adjoint/cogérant; **marketing manager,** directeur commercial/du marketing; **middle manager,** cadre moyen; **office manager,** chef de bureau; **personnel/staff manager,** chef/directeur du personnel; **plant manager,** directeur d'usine; **production manager,** directeur de la production; *Publ:* chef *m* de fabrication; **purchasing manager,** chef des achats; **sales manager,** directeur commercial; **senior manager,** cadre supérieur; **works manager,** chef du service (des) ateliers **2.** *Jur:* **receiver and manager,** administrateur (d'une faillite, etc.); syndic *m* de faillite.

manageress, *n.* directrice *f*/gérante *f*; **joint manageress,** directrice adjointe/cogérante.

managerial, *a.* directorial; **managerial control,** contrôle *m* de direction; **managerial position,** poste *m* d'encadrement; poste de cadre; **the managerial staff,** les cadres *m*; le personnel d'encadrement; **managerial structure,** hiérarchie *f*.

managership, *n.* direction *f*/gérance *f* (d'une entreprise, etc.).

managing, *a.* **managing board,** comité *m* de direction; **managing director,** directeur général; **chairman and managing director,** président-directeur général (P-DG).

mandate, *n.* mandat *m*/procuration *f*; *Bank:* **mandate form,** lettre *f* de signatures autorisées.

mandatory, *a.* obligatoire.

man-hour, n. heure f de travail (d'un homme)/heure d'ouvrier.

manifest[1], n. (a) Nau: (**inward, outward**) **manifest,** manifeste m (d'entrée, de sortie) (b) Av: état m de chargement.

manifest[2], v.tr. Nau: (a) déclarer (une cargaison) en douane (b) faire figurer (une marchandise) sur un manifeste.

manipulate, v.tr. manœuvrer; manipuler; Pej: **to manipulate accounts,** tripoter/ cuisiner/arranger des comptes; StExch: **to manipulate the market,** agir sur le marché/ travailler le marché; provoquer des mouvements de Bourse.

manipulation, n. Pej: tripotage m; **manipulation of the market,** tripotages en Bourse; agiotage m.

manipulator, n. Pej: tripoteur m; StExch: agioteur m.

man-made, a. artificiel/synthétique; **man-made fibres,** fibres f synthétiques.

manned, a. (a) (administrative, technical agency) = service assuré; **the service is manned 24 hours a day,** il y a une permanence (b) (machine, apparatus, stand) = surveillance assurée.

manning, n. affectation f de personnel (à une organisation, au fonctionnement d'une machine, etc.).

manpower, n. coll. Ind: main-d'œuvre f; effectifs mpl; **manpower forecasting,** prévision f de l'emploi; **manpower management,** gestion f d'effectifs/gestion de l'emploi; **manpower planning,** planification f de l'emploi; **shortage of manpower,** crise f de main-d'œuvre/d'effectifs.

manual[1], n. manuel m (d'utilisation).

manual[2], a. manuel; **manual labour,** la main-d'œuvre; **manual work,** travail manuel; travail de manœuvre; **manual worker,** un(e) manuel(le)/travailleur manuel/travailleuse manuelle; **manual operation,** fonctionnement m à la main.

manually, adv. manuellement/à la main.

manufacture[1], n. 1. usinage m; production f; fabrication f (d'un produit industriel); confection f (de vêtements, etc.); **articles of foreign manufacture,** articles fabriqués à l'étranger/de fabrication étrangère 2 usu. pl. produits fabriqués/manufacturés

manufacture[2], v.tr. fabriquer/manufacturer (un produit industriel); confectionne (des vêtements, etc.); **manufactured goods** produits manufacturés.

manufacturer, n. (i) fabricant, -ante; producteur, -trice (ii) industriel m; **cloth manufacturer,** fabricant de textiles; **boiler manufacturer,** constructeur m de chaudières; **manufacturer's price,** prix m (de fabrique.

manufacturing[1], a. industriel; **manufacturing industry/firm/concern,** entreprise industrielle/industrie de fabrication; **manufacturing rights,** droits m(pl) de fabrication; **manufacturing town,** ville industrielle.

manufacturing[2], n. fabrication f; confection f (de vêtements); **economic manufacturing quantity,** quantité f économique de production; **manufacturing capacity** capacité f de production; **manufacturing control,** contrôle m de fabrication; **manufacturing costs/manufacturing overheads** frais mpl/coût m de fabrication; **manufacturing industry,** industrie f de fabrication **manufacturing process,** procédé m de fabrication.

margin[1], n. (a) marge f/écart m; **the margin between the rates of interest,** l'écart entre les taux d'intérêt; **profit margin,** marge bénéficiaire; **gross margin,** marge brute **net margin,** marge nette; **operating margin,** marge nette d'exploitation **margin of error,** marge d'erreur; **to allow margin for error,** prévoir une marge d'erreur; **margin of £100 for unforeseen expenses,** disponibilité f d'imprévus de £100; **the margin of permitted fluctuation** la marge de fluctuation; **safety margin** marge de sécurité (b) Fin: marge de garantie/couverture f/provision f (versée à u courtier); **initial margin,** marge initiale dépôt *m* de marge/deposit *m*; **speculative margin,** couverture sur opération spéculative; **call for margin/margin call,** appel de couverture/de marge; **margin requirements,** couverture obligatoire/deposit *m* obligatoire (*pour initier une position en Bourse*); **to buy on margin,** acheter à crédit (*en déposant seulement un pourcentage de la somme globale de son investissement*).

margin², *v.i. esp. NAm: StExch:* **to margin (up),** verser les couvertures requises.

marginal, *a.* marginal; **marginal cost,** coût marginal; **marginal costing/cost pricing,** comptabilité marginale/méthode *f* des coûts marginaux; **marginal return on capital,** rendement marginal du capital; **marginal profit,** bénéfice marginal; **firm with only a marginal profit,** entreprise marginale; **marginal productivity,** productivité marginale; **marginal revenue,** revenu marginal; **marginal utility,** utilité marginale.

marine, 1. *a.* **marine insurance,** assurance *f* maritime **2.** *n.* **merchant/mercantile marine,** marine marchande/de commerce.

maritime, *a.* maritime; **maritime law,** droit *m*/législation *f* maritime; **maritime loan,** (*i*) prêt *m* (*ii*) emprunt *m* à la grosse; *Ins:* **maritime peril,** péril *m*/fortune *f* de mer; **maritime risk,** risque *m* maritime/risque de mer; **maritime trade,** commerce *m* maritime.

mark¹, *n.* (*a*) **certification mark,** marque *f* de garantie; (*on gold and silver*) **(assay) mark,** poinçon *m* de garantie (*b*) **below the 3% mark,** en-dessous de la barre des 3%; **below the psychologically important 3% mark,** en-dessous du seuil psychologique de 3%.

mark², *v.tr.* **1.** marquer/chiffrer/estampiller (*des marchandises*); **marked 'breakable',** revêtu de la mention 'fragile' **2. to mark (the price of) an article,** fixer le prix d'un article; *StExch:* **to mark stock,** coter des valeurs.

mark³, mark *m*/Deutschmark *m*.

mark down, *v.tr.* **to mark down (the price**

of) goods, baisser le prix de marchandises/démarquer des marchandises; *StExch:* **prices have been marked down,** les cours se sont inscrits en baisse.

mark-down, *n.* rabais *m*/remise *f.*

market¹, *n.* **1.** marché *m*; **covered market,** halle(s) *f(pl)*/marché couvert; **open-air market,** marché en plein air; **cattle market,** marché aux bestiaux; **fish market,** marché aux poissons; **market day,** jour *m* de marché; **market place,** la place du marché; **to go to the market,** aller au marché **2.** (*a*) **the Common Market,** le Marché commun; *EEC:* **market outside the Community,** marché tiers; **foreign market/overseas market,** marché extérieur/marché d'outre-mer; **free/open market,** marché libre; *StExch:* **to buy shares on the open market,** acheter des actions en bourse; **home market,** marché intérieur; **the teenage market,** le marché des adolescents/des jeunes (*b*) *StExch:* **bear/bearish market,** marché (orienté) à la baisse/marché baissier; **bull market,** marché (orienté) à la hausse/marché haussier; **bond market,** marché obligataire/des obligations; **cash/spot/non-contract market,** marché au comptant/du disponible/du physique; **capital market,** marché financier; **commodity market,** marché de matières premières; **cotton market,** marché du coton; **foreign exchange market,** marché des changes; **forward exchange market,** marché des changes à terme; **forward market,** marché à terme; (*on French Stock Exchange*) règlement mensuel (RM); **futures market,** marché à terme d'instruments financiers (MATIF); **gold market,** marché de l'or; **international money market,** marché monétaire international; **loan market,** marché des prêts; **metal market,** marché des métaux; **world market,** marché mondial; **settlement market,** marché à terme (des valeurs); **the property market,** le marché immobilier; **stock market/the market,** marché des valeurs/la Bourse (des valeurs) (*c*) **black market,** marché noir/marché parallèle; **to buy on the black market,** acheter au noir; **buyer's market,**

marché acheteur/marché à la baisse; **fringe market,** marché marginal; **grey/ semi-black market,** marché gris; **dull/inactive market,** marché inactif; **jumpy market,** marché instable; **limited market,** marché étroit; **official market,** marché officiel; **primary market/new issues market,** marché primaire; **seller's market,** marché vendeur/marché à la hausse; **steady market,** marché ferme/soutenu; **unofficial market/ over-the-counter market (OTC),** marché hors bourse; **third market,** marché hors cote; **unlisted securities market (USM),** second marché (d) **market analysis,** analyse f de marchés; **market appraisal,** évaluation f du marché; **market forces,** tendances fpl du marché; **market forecast,** prévisions du marché; **market intelligence,** information commerciale; *StExch:* **market opening/close,** ouverture f/clôture f du marché; **market opportunity/opening/gap in the market,** créneau m; **market maker,** teneur m de marché; **market price,** prix du marché/ cours (de la bourse); **market rate of discount,** taux m d'escompte hors banque; **market research,** étude de marché; **test market,** marché-test m; **market tending,** manipulation f du cours sur l'indice; **market trends,** tendances f du marché; **market value,** valeur marchande/prix m du marché; **down market,** bas de gamme; **up market,** haut de gamme; **up market store,** magasin haut de gamme/magasin chic/magasin de luxe; **to be in the market for sth.,** être acheteur/chercher à acheter quelque chose; **to be on the market/to come into the market/onto the market,** être en vente; *StExch:* **to buy, sell at (the) market,** acheter, vendre au mieux/au prix/au cours du marché; **to buy at the top of the market,** acheter au prix/au cours le plus élevé; **to corner a market,** accaparer un marché; **his house is on the market,** sa maison est à vendre; **he put his house on the market,** il a mis sa maison en vente; **to find a market for sth.,** trouver un débouché pour qch.; **to find a ready market,** trouver à vendre facilement; **to make a market/to rig a market,** se porter contrepartiste mf (occulte); **market rigger,** contrepartiste occulte; **market making rigging,** contrepartie f dissimulé occulte; **to play the market,** spéculer; **price oneself out of the market,** perdre s clientèle en demandant trop cher; **th bottom has fallen out of the market,** marché s'est effondré.

market[2], *v.tr.* vendre; trouver des d bouchés m pour (ses marchandises lancer (un produit).

marketability, *n.* valeur marchand commerciale (d'un produit).

marketable, *a.* (a) (*of goods*) vendabl d'un débit facile (b) **marketable secur ties,** titres négociables (en Bourse **marketable value,** valeur marchand vénale.

marketing, *n.* commercialisation marketing m/mercatique f (d'un produit techniques commerciales; **creati marketing,** créativité commercia **marketing agreement,** accord m commercialisation; **marketing costs,** fra mpl de commercialisation; **marketing d partment,** service m du marketin **marketing executive,** animateur m d ventes; **marketing manager,** directeur commercial/chef m du marketing/dire teur du marketing; **marketing mi** marchéage m; **marketing policy,** politiq f de commercialisation; **marketi specialist,** mercaticien, -ienne.

marketmaker, *n.* agent m de change (*q intervient sur le marché comme principal comme agent*).

marking, *n. StExch:* cotation f (des v leurs).

mark off, *v.i.* **to mark off (a sum again sth.),** déduire/défalquer/soustraire (d' montant).

mark up, *v.tr.* augmenter le prix de (qch majorer un prix/une facture; *StExc* **prices have been marked up,** les cours so en hausse.

mark-up, *n.* marge f (bénéficiair augmentation f/majoration f (d'un pri

mark-up pricing, fixation f du prix au coût moyen majoré; **we operate a 2.5 times mark-up,** nous appliquons une marge de 2,5/notre marge est de 2,5.

mart, $n.$ **1.** centre m de commerce; marché m; **money mart,** marché monétaire **2. (auction) mart,** salle f de vente; **car mart,** marché (des) autos; **trade mart,** expomarché $m.$

marzipan layer, $n.$ $F:$ cadres moyens.

mass, $n.$ (*large quantity*) **mass dismissal,** licenciement collectif; **mass production,** fabrication f/production f en série; **massproduction car,** voiture f de série; **mass unemployment,** chômage massif.

mass-produce, $v.tr.$ fabriquer en série; **mass-produced cars,** voitures de série.

matched, $a.$ $StExch:$ **matched bargains/ sales,** mariages mpl; $NAm:$ **matched orders,** ordres couplés d'achat et de vente (*pour stimuler le marché*).

matching, $n.$ $StExch:$ $NAm:$ application $f.$

material, $n.$ **1.** matière f; matériau m; **raw material(s),** matière(s) première(s); **unprocessed/unrefined material,** matière brute/non traitée (industriellement); **synthetic material,** matière/produit synthétique; **building materials,** matériaux de construction **2.** $Tex:$ tissu m; étoffe f; **dress materials,** tissus (de confection) **3.** matériel m; **artists' materials,** matériel d'artiste; **camping material,** matériel de camping.

materiality, $n.$ (*in accounts*) importance f (relative) (d'une erreur, d'un élément); pertinence f (d'un procédé, etc.).

matter, $n.$ **1.** (*a*) **matter of dispute,** sujet m de controverse (*b*) **postal matter,** lettres fpl et paquets postaux; **printed matter,** imprimé m **2.** affaire f/chose f/cas m; **we'll deal with this matter tomorrow,** nous nous occuperons de ce problème demain; **business matters,** affaires; **money matters,** affaires d'argent; $Jur:$ **in the matter of the Companies Act,** vu la loi sur les Sociétés;

a matter of business, une question d'affaires; **matter of form,** pure formalité.

mature[1], $a.$ (*a*) **mature economy,** économie f en pleine maturité (*b*) $Fin:$ (papier) échu.

mature[2], $v.i.$ $Fin:$ (*of bill*) échoir; arriver à échéance; **bills to mature,** papier m à échéance.

matured, $a.$ $Fin:$ échu; arrivé à échéance; **matured capital,** capitaux mpl dont la date de paiement est échue; **matured bonds,** obligations échues/arrivées à échéance.

maturing, $a.$ **maturing bills,** papiers qui arrivent à échéance.

maturity, $n.$ (*a*) $Fin:$ **(date of) maturity/ maturity date,** échéance f (d'une traite, d'un billet); **payable at maturity,** payable à l'échéance (*b*) $NAm:$ **current maturities,** versements mpl (sur une dette à long terme) exigibles à moins d'un an/exigibles à court terme.

maximization, $n.$ maximation f/maximisation f; **profit maximization,** maximisation du profit/des profits; **the maximization of total utility,** la maximisation de l'utilité totale.

maximize, $v.tr.$ maximaliser/maximiser; porter (qch.) au maximum.

maximizing = maximization.

maximum, 1. $n.$ maximum m; **to the maximum,** au maximum; **up to a maximum of …,** jusqu'à concurrence de …; **to raise production to a maximum,** porter la production au maximum **2.** $a.$ maximum; $occ.$ maximal; **maximum efficiency,** maximum de rendement; **maximum load,** charge f maximale/limite; **maximum price,** prix m maximum; **maximum output,** rendement m maximum.

mean[1], $n.$ moyenne $f.$

mean[2], $a.$ moyen; **mean price,** prix moyen; **mean due date,** échéance moyenne/ commune; **mean tare,** tare commune.

means, $n.pl.$ moyens mpl (de vivre); ressources *fpl*; **private means,** ressources personnelles/fortune personnelle; **this car is beyond my means,** cette voiture est hors de ma portée/n'est pas dans mes prix; **means of payment,** moyens de paiement; *Adm:* **means test** = enquête *f* sur la situation (de fortune).

measure[1], *n.* **1.** (*a*) mesure *f*; **linear measure,** mesure linéaire; **square measure,** mesure de superficie/de surface; **cubic measure,** mesure de volume; **liquid measure,** mesure de capacité pour les liquides; **dry measure,** mesure de capacité; **weights and measures,** poids *m* et mesures (*b*) **made to measure,** fait sur mesure; **to have a suit made to measure,** se faire faire un costume sur mesure (*c*) *Nau:* cubage *m*; jaugeage *m*; **measure goods,** marchandises *f* de cubage/d'encombrement **2.** (*instrument for measuring*) (*a*) mesure (à grains, à lait, etc.) (*b*) **tape measure,** centimètre *m* (de couturière)/mètre *m* (à ruban) **3.** mesure/démarche *f*/manœuvre *f*; **security/safety measures,** mesures de sécurité; **measures of conciliation,** voies *f* d'accommodement; **as a measure of economy/as an economy measure,** par mesure d'économie; **austerity measures,** mesures d'austérité; **deflationary measures,** mesures déflationnistes; **retaliatory measures,** mesures de rétorsion.

measure[2], *v.tr.* (*a*) mesurer (une distance, etc.) (*b*) **to measure the tonnage of a ship,** jauger un navire (*c*) mesurer (qn)/prendre les mesures/prendre les mensurations (de qn).

measurement, *n.* **1.** mesure *f*; mesurage *m*; **performance measurement,** mesure de la performance; **productivity measurement,** mesure de la productivité **2.** *Nau:* (*a*) jaugeage *m* (d'un navire) (*b*) cubage *m*/encombrement *m* (du fret); **measurement converted into weight,** cubage converti en poids; **to pay for cargo by measurement,** payer le fret au cubage/au volume; **measurement freight,** fret selon encombrement/selon volume; **measurement goods,** marchandises *f* de cubage/d'encombrement; **measurement ton,** tonneau *m* d'encombrement/de mer **3. to take a customer's measurements,** mesurer un client/prendre les mesures/prendre les mensurations d'un client.

mechanism, *n.* mécanisme *m*; **banking mechanism,** mécanisme bancaire; **discount mechanism,** mécanisme de l'escompte; **market mechanism,** mécanisme du marché; **price mechanism,** mécanisme des prix.

mechanization, *n.* mécanisation *f.*

mechanize, *v.tr.* mécaniser (une industrie).

media, *n.* média *m* (*pl* **médias**); **TV is a media,** la télévision est un média; **advertising media,** média publicitaire; **the new mass media,** les nouveaux mass(-)média; **media mix,** mixte média; **media planning,** médialisation *f*/plan *m* média; **media planner,** médiaplaneur *m*/médialiste *mf*; **media research,** médialogie *f.*

median, *n.* médiane *f.*

mediate, *v.i.* (*of pers.*) agir en médiateur/servir de médiateur/servir d'intermédiaire (**between ... and ...,** entre ... et ...).

mediation, *n.* médiation *f*/intervention (amicale); **offer of mediation,** offre *f* d'intervention; **through the mediation of ...,** par l'entremise *f* de ....

mediator, *n.* médiateur, -trice/intermédiaire *mf*/arbitre *m.*

medical, *a.* **medical certificate,** certificat médical; *Ind:* **medical officer,** médecin *m* du travail; **medical profession,** corps médical.

medicine, *n.* médecine *f*; **industrial medicine,** médecine *f* du travail.

medium, *n.* (*a*) intermédiaire *m*/entremise *f*; **through the medium of the press,** par l'intermédiaire de la presse/par voie de presse (*b*) moyen *m* (de communication, etc.); agent *m*/organe *m*; **advertising medium,** organe de publicité/support *m* publicitaire/support de publicité.

medium-dated, *a.* à échéance moyenne.

medium-size(d), *a.* de taille/grandeur moyenne; **small and medium-size firms,** petites et moyennes entreprises (PME).

medium-term, *a.* **medium-term finance,** financement *m* à moyen terme.

meet, 1. *v.tr.* (*a*) rejoindre/retrouver (qn); **to arrange to meet s.o.,** donner rendez-vous à qn; fixer un rendez-vous avec qn; **I arranged to meet him at three o'clock,** j'ai pris rendez-vous avec lui pour trois heures (*b*) faire la connaissance de (qn); **it was a great pleasure to meet you/meeting you,** je suis enchanté d'avoir fait votre connaissance; **I hope to meet you soon,** j'espère avoir sous peu le plaisir de faire votre connaissance (*c*) faire des concessions *f* à (qn); **I'll do my best to meet your price,** on peut s'arranger quant au prix (*d*) satisfaire à (un besoin, une demande); **to meet the demand,** satisfaire à la demande; **to meet s.o.'s requirements,** donner satisfaction à qn; **he met my request by saying that . . .,** en réponse à ma demande il a dit que . . . (*e*) faire honneur à/faire bon accueil à/accueillir (un effet, une lettre de change); honorer (un chèque); **to meet one's commitments,** faire honneur à ses engagements; remplir ses engagements (*f*) **to meet expenses,** faire face aux dépenses/à ses dépenses; subvenir aux frais; **he met all expenses,** il a subvenu à tout **2.** *v.i.* (*a*) (*of pers.*) se rencontrer/se voir (*b*) (*of society, assembly*) se réunir (en session); s'assembler (*c*) **to meet with a loss,** éprouver/subir une perte; **to meet with a refusal,** essuyer un refus.

meeting, *n.* assemblée *f*/réunion *f*/séance *f*; **annual general meeting (AGM),** assemblée générale annuelle; **board meeting,** réunion du conseil d'administration; **meeting place/meeting point,** lieu *m* de réunion; rendez-vous *m*; **to hold a meeting,** tenir une réunion; **the association holds its meetings at . . .,** l'association *f* se réunit à . . .; **the meeting will be held tomorrow at 3 o'clock,** la réunion est prévue pour demain/aura lieu demain à 15 heures; **notice of meeting,** convocation *f*; **to call a meeting of shareholders,** convoquer les actionnaires; *Jur:* **meeting of creditors,** assemblée de créanciers; **at the meeting in London,** lors de la séance tenue à Londres; **to open the meeting,** déclarer la séance ouverte; **to close the meeting,** lever la séance; **to address the meeting,** prendre la parole; **to put a resolution to the meeting,** mettre une résolution aux voix.

mega-, *pref.* méga-/grand; **mega deal,** une très grosse affaire/une affaire très importante.

megamerger, *n.* méga-fusion *f.*

member, *n.* membre *m* (d'une société, etc.); **ordinary members/paying members of an association,** cotisants *m*; **member countries of the EEC,** les pays membres de la CEE.

membership, *n.* **1.** qualité *f* de membre; adhésion *f*; **qualifications for membership,** conditions *f*/titres *m* d'éligibilité; **conditions of membership,** conditions *f* d'adhésion/d'admission; **membership card,** carte *f* de membre/de sociétaire; **to apply for membership,** faire une demande d'adhésion; **to pay one's membership (fee),** payer sa cotisation/son abonnement *m*; **to renew one's membership,** renouveler sa carte (de membre) **2.** nombre *m* de membres/effectif *m* (d'une société, etc.); **club with a membership of a thousand,** club *m* de mille membres; **the opinion of the majority of our membership,** l'avis *m* de la majorité de nos membres.

memo, *n.* *F:* note *f*; **memo pad,** bloc-notes *m.*

memorandum, *n.* **1.** note *f*; *Pol Com* mémorandum *m*; **to make a memorandum of sth.,** prendre note de qch.; noter qch. **2.** (*a*) mémoire *m* (d'un contrat, d'une vente, etc.); sommaire *m* des articles (d'un contrat) (*b*) *Jur:* **memorandum of association,** charte constitutive d'une société à responsabilité limitée; acte *m* de constitution d'une société; **memorandum and articles of association,** statuts *mpl*; **memorandum of satisfaction,** document *m* certifiant le paiement d'une hypothèque; **memorandum of understanding,** protocole *m* d'accord **3.** bordereau *m*; **memorandum book,** carnet *m*/calepin *m*/agenda *m.*

mercantile, *a.* marchand/commercial/commerçant/de commerce; **mercantile operations**, opérations *f* mercantiles; **mercantile nation**, nation commerçante; **mercantile broker**, agent *m* de change; **mercantile agency**, agence commerciale; **mercantile agent**, agent commercial; **mercantile marine**, marine marchande; **mercantile law**, droit commercial/code *m* de commerce.

mercantilism, *n.* mercantilisme *m.*

merchandise[1], *n.* marchandise(s) *f(pl)*.

merchandise[2], *v.tr.* marchandiser; commercialiser.

merchandiser, *n.* (*object*) présentoir *m*; (*person*) marchandiseur *m.*

merchandising, *n.* marchandisage *m/* merchandising *m*; promotion *f* des ventes; commercialisation *f.*

merchandizable, *a.* en état d'être livré au commerce; vendable.

merchant[1], *n.* (*a*) négociant, -ante; commerçant, -ante; marchand, -ande en gros; **wine merchant**, négociant en vins (*b*) *Scot: & NAm:* marchand, -ande/boutiquier, -ière **2.** *a.* (*a*) marchand/du commerce; **merchant bank**, banque *f* d'affaires; **merchant marine/merchant navy/merchant service/merchant shipping**, marine marchande; **merchant ship/merchant vessel**, navire marchand/navire de commerce.

merchantable, *a.* **1.** en état d'être livré au commerce; vendable **2.** de débit facile/de bonne vente.

merchantman, *n.* navire marchand/navire de commerce.

merge, **1.** *v.tr.* fusionner (deux systèmes, etc.); amalgamer (**sth. in/into sth.**, qch. avec qch.) **2.** *v.i.* (*of banks, companies*) s'amalgammer/fusionner.

merger, *n. Fin:* fusion *f* (de plusieurs sociétés en une seule); absorption *f* (d'une société par une autre); **industrial merger**, fusion/concentration *f* industrielle; **merger company**, sociétés réunies.

merging, *n.* fusion *f*; fusionnement *m.*

merit, *n.* **1.** mérite *m*; **to discuss the merits of sth.**, discuter le pour et le contre de qch. **2.** valeur *f*/mérite; *Ind: etc:* **merit bonus**, prime *f* de rendement; **merit rating**, (*i*) appréciation *f* du mérite (*ii*) notation *f* du personnel.

message, *n.* message *m*; communication *f* (téléphonique, etc.); **advertising message**, message publicitaire; **to leave a message for s.o.**, laisser un message/un mot pour qn; **I'll give him the message**, je lui transmettrai le message; **message handling**, messagerie *f* (électronique).

messenger, *n.* (*a*) messager, -ère; coursier, -ière (*b*) commissionnaire *m*; **by messenger**, par porteur; **messenger boy**, garçon *m* de courses; **auctioneer's messenger**, garçon de salle; **office messenger**, garçon de bureau.

Messrs, *n.m.pl.* Messieurs, *abbr.* MM; **Messrs J. Martin & Co.**, Monsieur J. Martin & Cie.

meter, *n.* **1.** *NAm:* = **metre 2.** compteur *m* (à gaz, à eau, d'électricité).

method, *n.* (*a*) (*research, science*) méthode *f* (*b*) méthode/manière *f* (**of doing sth.**, de faire qch.); procédé *m* (pour faire qch.); modalités *fpl*; **method of payment**, modalités de paiement; *Ind:* **production method**, procédé(s) de fabrication; **method of operation**, méthode d'exploitation; **method of working**, méthode de travail; **sampling method**, échantillonnage *m/* sondage *m* (*c*) *Ind:* **methods engineer**, ingénieur *m* des méthodes; **methods engineering/methods study**, étude *f* des méthodes; **methods office**, bureau *m* des méthodes; **time and methods study**, étude des temps et des méthodes.

methodical, *a.* méthodique.

metre, *n. Meas:* mètre *m* (*abbr.* **m**) (= 1.0936 yards); **square metre**, mètre carré;

cubic metre, mètre cube; **stacked cubic metre,** stère *m* (de bois).

metric, *a.* *Meas:* métrique; **metric unit,** unité *f* métrique; **the metric system,** le système métrique; **metric ton,** tonne *f* (métrique); (*of country*) **to go metric,** adopter le système métrique.

metricate, *v.tr. & i.* introduire/adopter le système métrique.

metrication, *n.* adoption *f*/introduction *f*/utilisation *f* du système métrique.

mezzanine, *n.* **mezzanine debt,** dette *f* subordonnée/dette mezzanine; **mezzanine finance,** méthode de financement d'une partie du capital nécessaire pour acheter une entreprise (*utilisée principalement par ses employés*).

microcomputer, *n.* micro-ordinateur *m.*

micro-computing, *n.* micro-informatique *f.*

microeconomic, *a.* microéconomique.

microeconomics, *n.pl.* microéconomie *f.*

microfiche, *n.* microfiche *f.*

microfilm, *n.* microfilm *m.*

microprocessing, *n.* micro-informatique *f.*

microprocessor, *n.* microprocesseur *m.*

mid, *a.* mi-/du milieu; **from mid June to mid August,** de la mi-juin à la mi-août; *StExch:* **mid month account/settlement,** le 15 du mois/la liquidation de quinzaine.

middle, *n.* **middle management,** cadres moyens; **middle (market) price,** prix/cours moyen.

middleman, *n.* intermédiaire *mf.*

migrant, *a. & n.* **migrant (worker),** (travailleur) migrant.

mile, *n.* *Meas:* mille *m*; **five miles,** cinq milles (= huit kilomètres); **speed limit of 50 miles an hour,** vitesse limitée à 50 milles à l'heure/= à 80 kilomètres à l'heure; **my car does 25 miles to the gallon/25 miles per gallon (m.p.g.)** = ma voiture consomme (environ) onze litres aux 100 kilomètres (11L/100 km).

mileage, *n.* distance *f* en milles/= kilométrage *m*; **daily mileage** = parcours kilométrique journalier; (*for taxi, etc.*) **mileage rate** = tarif *m* au kilomètre; **mileage allowance,** indemnité *f* de déplacement.

milk, *v.tr.* **to milk a business,** saigner une société à blanc.

mill, *n.* usine *f*; **cotton mill,** filature *f* de coton.

milligram, *Meas:* milligramme *m* (*abbr.* **mg**) (0.0154 gram).

millilitre, *n.* *Meas:* millilitre *m* (*abbr.* **ml**).

millimetre, *n.* *Meas:* millimètre *m* (*abbr.* **mm**) (= 0.0394 in); **millimetre scale,** échelle *f* millimétrique.

million, *n.* million *m*; **one thousand million,** un milliard; **two million men,** deux millions d'hommes; (*of pers.*) **worth millions/worth ten million,** riche à millions/dix fois millionnaire; **a two-million pound machine,** une machine coûtant deux millions de livres.

mineral, *a.* **mineral rights,** droits miniers.

minicomputer, *n.* mini-ordinateur *m.*

minimal, *a.* minimal/minimum; **minimal amount,** (*i*) quantité *f* minimum (*ii*) montant *m* minimum; **minimal value,** valeur minimale/minimum; **minimal weight,** poids *m* minimum.

minimarket, *n.* supérette *f.*

minimization, *n.* minimisation *f*/réduction *f* au minimum; **cost minimization,** réduction *f* des coûts.

minimize, *v.tr.* minimiser/réduire au minimum; **to minimize a loss,** atténuer une perte.

minimizing, *n.* = **minimization.**

minimum, *pl.* 1. *n.* minimum *m*; **to reduce expenses to a minimum,** réduire les frais au minimum 2. *a.* **minimum quantity,** quantité *f* minimum; **minimum prices,** prix *m* minimums/minima; **the minimum**

number of shares, le nombre minimum d'actions; **(index-linked) minimum wage,** = salaire minimum interprofessionnel de croissance (SMIC).

mining, *a.* **mining shares,** valeurs minières.

minor, 1. *a.* petit/menu/peu important/ mineur(e); **minor expenses,** menus frais. 2. *n. Jur:* mineur, -eure.

minority, *n.* minorité *f*; **minority holding/ interest/stake,** participation *f*/intérêt *m* minoritaire; **minority shareholders,** petits actionnaires/actionnaires minoritaires/les minoritaires.

mint[1], *n.* **the Mint** = l'Hôtel *m* de la Monnaie/l'Hôtel des Monnaies/la Monnaie; **in mint condition,** à l'état neuf; *Fin:* **mint par,** pair *m* intrinsèque/pair théorique.

mint[2], *v.tr.* **to mint money,** frapper de la monnaie/battre monnaie.

mintage, *n.* 1. monnayage *m*; frappe *f* de la monnaie 2. espèces monnayées (de telle date, de telle Monnaie) 3. droit *m* de monnayage; droit de frappe.

minute, *n.* (*a*) **minutes of a meeting,** procès-verbal *m*/compte-rendu *m* d'une réunion; **to confirm the minutes of the last meeting,** approuver le procès-verbal de la dernière réunion; **to read the minutes (of a meeting),** lire le procès-verbal (d'une réunion); **to take the minutes of a meeting,** rédiger le procès-verbal d'une réunion; **minute book,** registre *m* des procès-verbaux/des délibérations; *Adm:* journal *m* de correspondance et d'actes (*b*) **Treasury minute,** approbation *f* de la Trésorerie; communiqué *m* de la Trésorerie.

misapplication, *n.* emploi injustifié (d'une somme d'argent); détournement *m* (de fonds).

misapply, *v.tr.* faire un emploi injustifié (d'une somme d'argent); détourner (des fonds).

misappropriate, *v.tr.* détourner (des fonds).

misappropriation, *n.* détournement *m* (de fonds); malversation *f.*

miscalculate, *v.tr.* mal calculer (une somme, etc.).

miscalculation, *n.* faux calcul/calcul erroné; mécompte *m*; erreur *f* de calcul/ erreur de compte.

miscellaneous, *a.* varié; divers; **miscellaneous shares,** valeurs diverses; **miscellaneous expenses,** (frais) divers *mpl.*

miscount[1], *n.* (*a*) erreur *f* de calcul; faux calcul (*b*) erreur d'addition.

miscount[2], (*a*) *v.tr.* mal compter (*b*) *v.i.* faire une erreur de calcul.

misdate, *v.tr.* mal dater (une lettre, un chèque, etc.).

misdirect, *v.tr.* mal adresser/mal acheminer (une lettre).

misenter, *v.tr. Book-k:* contre-poser.

misentry, *n. Book-k:* contre-position *f.*

mismanage, *v.tr.* mal diriger/mal administrer/mal gérer (une affaire, une entreprise).

mismanagement, *n.* mauvaise administration/mauvaise gestion.

misprint, *n.* coquille *f*; faute *f* d'impression.

misrepresent, *v.tr.* dénaturer des faits; présenter (des faits) sous un faux jour; faire un faux rapport/une fausse déclaration.

misrepresentation, *n.* faux rapport/faux exposé/fausse déclaration.

misroute, *v.tr.* mal acheminer (un paquet, etc.).

misrouting, *n.* erreur *f* d'acheminement (d'un paquet, etc.); fausse direction.

Miss, *n.* mademoiselle *f*; **Miss Thomas,** Mademoiselle (Mlle) Thomas.

mission, *n.* **trade mission,** mission *f* commerciale.

mistake, *n.* erreur *f*/faute *f*; méprise *f*; **mis-**

take in labelling, erreur d'étiquetage; **mistake in the date,** erreur de date; **to make a mistake,** faire une faute; commettre une faute/une erreur; se méprendre/se tromper.

misuse, *n.* abus *m*/mauvais usage/emploi abusif/mauvais emploi (de qch.); **misuse of authority,** abus d'autorité; abus de pouvoir; *Jur:* **fraudulent misuse of funds,** détournement *m* de fonds.

mixed, *a.* mixte; **mixed costs,** frais *m*/coûts *m* semi-variables; **mixed economy,** économie *f* mixte; *Ins:* **mixed policy,** police *f* au temps et au voyage; **mixed sea and land risks,** risques *m* mixtes maritimes et terrestres; *Nau:* **mixed cargo,** cargaison *f* mixte.

mixture, *n.* assortiment *m*.

mobility, *n.* mobilité *f* (des capitaux, de la main-d'œuvre, du personnel).

mobilizable, *a.* mobilisable.

mobilization, *n.* mobilisation *f* (de capitaux, etc.).

mobilize, *v.tr.* mobiliser (des capitaux, etc.).

mock-up, *n.* maquette *f*.

mode, *n.* mode *m*; méthode *f*.

model, *n.* (*a*) modèle *m*/maquette *f*/modèle réduit (*b*) **new model (of a car),** nouveau modèle (d'une voiture) (*c*) **econometric models,** modèles prévisionnels.

modem, *n. Cmptr:* (= **modulator-demodulator),** modem *m* (= modulateur-démodulateur).

moderate, *a.* modéré/moyen/raisonnable; **moderate price,** prix modéré/modique/moyen; **moderate income,** revenu *m* modique.

modernization, *n.* modernisation *f*.

modernize, *v.tr.* moderniser; rénover.

modular, *a. Const: etc:* modulaire; fait d'éléments normalisés (préfabriqués); **modular construction/modular design,** construction au moyen d'éléments normalisés.

mom, *n. NAm:* **mom and pop operation,** petite affaire/entreprise.

monetarism, *n.* monétarisme *m*.

monetary, *a.* monétaire; **monetary area,** zone *f* monétaire; **monetary convention,** convention *f* monétaire; **monetary policy/ monetary management,** politique *f* monétaire; **monetary reform,** réforme *f*/assainissement *m* monétaire; **monetary standard,** étalon *m* monétaire; **monetary unit,** unité *f* monétaire; **European Monetary System (EMS),** système *m* monétaire européen (SME); **International Monetary Fund (IMF),** Fonds *m* monétaire international (FMI).

money, *n.* **1.** monnaie *f*; argent *m*; espèces *fpl*; numéraire *m*; (*coins*) **gold/silver money,** monnaie d'or/d'argent; **to coin/to mint money,** frapper de la monnaie; *Bank:* **bank money/deposit money,** monnaie de banque/monnaie scripturale; **broad money,** M3; **narrow money,** M0/ monnaie *f* Banque Centrale; **commodity money,** monnaie marchandise; **current money,** monnaie qui a cours; **divisional/ fractional money,** monnaie divisionnaire/ monnaie d'appoint; **electronic money,** Monétique (*Rtm:*); **fiduciary money,** billets *mpl* sans couverture; **money of account,** monnaie de compte; **paper money,** monnaie de papier; billets *mpl* (de banque); papier-monnaie *m*; **plastic money,** monnaie électronique; **token money,** monnaie fiduciaire; *Fin:* **cheap/ easy money,** argent à bon marché; **call money/money at call,** argent au jour le jour; argent/dépôt *m* à vue; **danger money,** prime *f* de risque(s); **free money,** argent gratuit; **hot money,** capitaux *mpl* flottants/spéculatifs/fébriles; **new money,** crédit *m* de restructuration; **seed/front money,** capital de départ; **money rate,** taux *m* de l'argent; **money market,** marché monétaire/marché des changes; marché financier; **money supply,** masse *f* monétaire; ressources *fpl* monétaires;

price of money, loyer *m* de l'argent; **ready money**, argent comptant/argent liquide; **to pay in ready money**, payer (au) comptant; *Post:* **money order**, mandat (postal)/mandat-poste *m*; **international/foreign money order**, mandat international; **to be worth a lot of money**, (*i*) (*of thg*), valoir cher/avoir de la valeur (*ii*) (*of pers.*) être riche/avoir de la fortune; **to be short of money**, être à court d'argent; **to get one's money back**, (*i*) se faire rembourser (*ii*) rentrer dans ses fonds; **to raise money**, se procurer de l'argent/des capitaux **2.** *Jur: pl:* **moneys/monies** argent/fonds *mpl*; sommes *fpl* (d'argent); **monies paid out**, versements (opérés); **monies paid in**, recettes (effectuées); **public monies**, deniers publics; le trésor public; **sundry monies owing to him**, diverses sommes à lui dues; **monies owing to us**, nos créances *f*.

moneychanger, *n.* (*a*) courtier *m* de change (*b*) *NAm:* (*machine*) distributeur *m* de monnaie.

moneylender, *n.* prêteur *m* (d'argent); bailleur *m* de fonds; maison *f* de prêt.

moneymaker, *n.* (*a*) personne qui sait gagner de l'argent (*b*) article *m* à succès (*c*) (*trade, etc*) qui rapporte.

money-spinner, *n.* (produit, etc.) qui rapporte; *F:* mine d'or.

monitor, *n.* *Cmptr:* (*a*) (programme *m*) moniteur *m* (*b*) appareil de surveillance/de contrôle.

monitoring, *n.* *Mkt:* contrôle continu/surveillance *f*.

monometallism, *n.* *Fin:* monométallisme *m*.

monopolist, *a.* & *n.* monopoliste (*mf*)/monopoleur, -euse.

monopolistic, *a.* monopolistique.

monopolization, *n.* monopolisation *f*.

monopolize, *v.tr.* monopoliser/accaparer (un marché).

monopolizing, *n.* monopolisation *f*.

monopoly, *n.* monopole *m*; **to have a**

monopoly of sth./*NAm:* **on sth.**, avoir le monopole de qch.; avoir l'exclusivité *f* de qch.; **State monopoly**, monopole d'État; **monopoly control**, contrôle *m* monopolistique; **monopoly service**, service monopoleur; **oil company with a monopoly**, société pétrolière monopoliste; **price monopoly**, monopole des prix; **Monopolies and Mergers Commission**, = Commission *f* de la Concurrence et des Prix.

monopsony, *n.* monopsone *m*.

month, *n.* mois *m*; **calendar month**, mois du calendrier/mois civil; **in the month of August**, au mois d'août; **at the end of the (current) month**, fin courant; **once a month**, une fois par mois; mensuellement; **a month's credit**, un mois de crédit; *Fin:* **bill at three months**, papier *m* à trois mois (d'échéance); **to pay an employee by the month**, mensualiser un employé.

monthly[1], *a.* (*a*) mensuel; **monthly payment/monthly instalment**, mensualité *f*; **monthly statement (of account)**, relevé *m*/situation *f* de fin de mois (*b*) *Rail: etc:* **monthly season ticket**, carte *f* (d'abonnement) valable pour un mois; (*on underground and buses*) = carte orange.

monthly[2], *adv.* mensuellement/une fois par mois/chaque mois/tous les mois.

moonlight, *v.i.* *F:* faire du travail noir/travailler au noir.

moonlighter, *n.* *F:* travailleur, -euse au noir/personne qui travaille au noir.

moonlighting, *n.* *F:* travail (au) noir.

mop up, *v.tr.* **losses that mop up all the profits**, pertes *f* qui engloutissent tous les bénéfices.

moratorium, *n.* *Fin:* moratorium *m*/moratoire *m*; **to announce a moratorium**, décréter un moratoire; **debt for which a moratorium has been granted**, dette *f* moratoire.

moratory, *a.* moratoire.

mortgage[1], *n.* hypothèque *f*/prêt-logement

m; **blanket mortgage/general mortgage,** hypothèque générale; **chattel mortgage,** hypothèque mobilière/hypothèque sur biens meubles; **discharge of a mortgage,** mainlevée *f* d'une hypothèque; **first/prior mortgage,** hypothèque de premier rang/première hypothèque; **puisne mortgage,** hypothèque (*non appuyée par la production du titre de propriété*); **second mortgage,** seconde hypothèque; **top-up mortgage,** = hypothèque de second rang; **burdened/encumbered with mortgage,** grevé d'hypothèque; **free from mortgage,** libre d'hypothèque; **by/on mortgage,** sur hypothèque/hypothécairement; **to borrow on mortgage,** emprunter sur hypothèque; **to create a mortgage,** constituer une hypothèque; **to foreclose a mortgage,** saisir un bien hypothéqué; **to take out/to raise a mortgage,** contracter une hypothèque/obtenir un prêt-logement; **to buy a house on mortgage,** prendre une hypothèque pour acheter une maison/acheter une maison sur hypothèque; **to secure a debt by mortgage,** hypothéquer une créance; **to register a mortgage on a property,** inscrire une hypothèque sur un bien; **to pay off/redeem a mortgage,** purger une hypothèque; **mortgage bond/mortgage debenture,** obligation *f* hypothécaire; **first mortgage bonds,** obligations de première hypothèque; **mortgage charge,** affectation *f* hypothécaire; **mortgage creditor,** créancier *m* hypothécaire; **mortgage claim,** créance *f* hypothécaire; **mortgage debtor,** débiteur *m* hypothécaire; **mortgage deed,** contrat *m*/acte *m* hypothécaire; **mortgage registrar,** conservateur *m* des hypothèques; **mortgage registration,** inscription *f* hypothécaire; **mortgage registry,** conservation *f* des hypothèques.

mortgage², *v.tr.* hypothéquer (une terre, un immeuble, des titres); engager/mettre en gage (des marchandises, des titres); déposer (des titres) en nantissement; **mortgaged estate,** domaine hypothéqué.

mortgageable, *a.* hypothécable.

mortgagee, *n.* créancier *m* hypothécaire.

mortgager, mortgagor, *n.* débiteur *m* hypothécaire.

mothball, *v.tr.* (*plan*) mettre en réserve.

motion, *n.* **1.** mouvement *m*; *Ind: etc:* **motion analysis,** analyse *f* des mouvements; **motion efficiency,** rendement *m* du geste; **time and motion consultant,** organisateur-conseil *m*; **time and motion study,** étude *f* des temps et des mouvements **2.** (*a*) motion *f*/proposition *f*; **to carry a motion,** faire adopter une motion; **to put forward the motion,** mettre la proposition aux voix; **to speak for the motion/to support the motion,** soutenir la motion; **to speak against the motion,** soutenir la contrepartie (*b*) *Jur:* demande *f*/ requête *f*.

motivated, *a.* **the staff must be motivated,** le personnel doit être motivé.

motivation, *n.* motifs *mpl*/motivation *f*.

motivational, *a.* **motivational studies/research,** études *f*/recherche *f* de motivation.

motivator, *n.* mobile *m*/motivation *f*.

motive, *n.* **profit motive,** motivation *f* par le profit.

mount up, *v.i.* croître/monter/augmenter.

movable = **moveable.**

moveable, 1. *a.* *Jur:* mobilier/meuble; **moveable effects/property,** effets mobiliers/biens *m* meubles; **moveable assets,** valeurs mobilières **2.** *n.pl.* **moveables,** (*a*) mobilier *m* (*b*) *Jur:* biens mobiliers/biens meubles; meubles *mpl*.

movement, *n.* *PolEc: etc:* circulation *f* (des capitaux, etc.); mouvement *m* (de baisse, de hausse) (des prix, des valeurs, en bourse); activité *f* (du marché); **free movement of labour/of workers,** libre circulation des travailleurs/de la main-d'œuvre; **cyclical movements,** mouvements cycliques/conjoncturels.

move up, *v.i.* *StExch:* (*of shares*) se relever/reprendre (de la valeur).

moving, *a.* mobile; **moving averages,** moyennes *f* mobiles.

Mr, (*form of address*) **Mr Thomas,** Monsieur/M. Thomas.

Mrs, (*form of address*) **Mrs Thomas,** Madame/Mme Thomas.

Ms, M/s, (*form of address*) **Ms, M/s Thomas,** (*i*) Mademoiselle/Mlle Thomas (*ii*) Madame/Mme Thomas.

multilateral, *a.* multilatéral.

multilateralism, *n.* *PolEc:* multilatéralisme *m.*

multimillionaire, *a. & n.* multimillionnaire (*mf*)/milliardaire (*mf*).

multinational, *a. & n.* **multinational company/corporation,** (société) multinationale *f.*

multiple, *a. & n.* multiple; **multiple management,** direction *f* multiple; **multiple stores/multiples,** magasins *m* à succur-

sales (multiples); **multiple ownership,** multipropriété *f* (d'un immeuble, etc.); *PolEc:* **multiple-use principle,** principe *m* de polyvalence.

multiplication, *n.* multiplication *f.*

multiplier, *n.* multiplicateur *m.*

multiply, 1. *v.tr.* multiplier; **to multiply two numbers together,** multiplier deux nombres **2.** *v.i.* se multiplier.

mutual, *a.* mutuel/réciproque; **to arrange a transaction on mutual principles/on mutual terms,** conclure un marché stipulant un échange de services/avec stipulation de réciprocité; **mutual benefit society,** société *f* de secours mutuels; **member of a mutual benefit society,** mutualiste *mf*; **mutual assurance,** coassurance *f*; **mutual assurance company,** société *f* d'assurances mutuelles; mutuelle *f*; *NAm:* **mutual fund(s)/**n.pl.* **mutuals** = société *f* d'investissement à capital variable (SICAV).

N

naked, *a.* sans garantie; **naked debenture,** obligation *f* chirographaire/sans garantie.

name, *n.* **1.** nom *m*; **full name,** nom et prénoms *mpl*; *StExch:* **name day,** deuxième jour *m* de liquidation; **name of a firm/of a company/corporate name,** raison sociale (d'une maison de commerce, d'une société); **the company trades under the name of ...,** la société a pour dénomination ...; **name of an account,** intitulé *m* d'un compte; **name of the payee,** nom du bénéficiaire; **brand name,** marque *f* de fabrique; **registered trade name,** nom déposé; **to set/put one's name to a document,** signer un document/apposer sa signature à un document; **list of names,** liste nominative; **the shares are in my name,** les actions *f* sont à mon nom **2.** réputation *f*/renommée *f*; **trademark with a good name,** marque réputée; **a big name in the business world,** un nom bien connu dans le monde des affaires.

named, *a.* nommé; **on the named day/on the day named,** à jour nommé; *Ins:* **party named/person named,** accrédité, -ée; **named policy/policy to a named person,** police nominative.

narration, *n.* = **narrative.**

narrative, *n.* *Book-k:* note explicative justifiant une écriture (*dans un livre de commerce*).

narrow, *a.* **narrow market,** marché étroit.

nation, *n.* nation *f*; **United Nations,** Nations Unies; **debtor nation,** nation débitrice.

national, *a.* national; de l'État; **National debt,** la dette publique/la dette de l'État; **(gross, net) national income,** revenu national (brut, net); **(gross, net) national product,** produit national (brut, net); **national expenditure,** dépenses *fpl* de l'État; **National Health Service (NHS),** service *m* de santé publique.

nationality, *n.* nationalité *f*.

nationalization, *n.* nationalisation *f*/étatisation *f* (d'une industrie, etc.).

nationalize, *v.tr.* nationaliser/étatiser (une industrie, etc.); **nationalized industries,** entreprises/industries nationalisées; les nationalisées *fpl*.

natural, *a.* naturel; **natural resources,** ressources *f* naturelles; **natural resources company,** exploitation *f* de diverses ressources naturelles; *Jur:* **natural or legal persons,** personnes physiques et morales.

nature, *n.* **nature of contents,** nature *f*/désignation *f* du contenu; **nature and extent of risk,** nature et étendue *f* d'un risque.

navigation, *n.* navigation *f*; **navigation company,** compagnie *f* de navigation/de transports maritimes; **navigation dues,** droits *m* de navigation.

negative, *a.* négatif; **negative income tax,** impôt négatif sur le revenu.

neglected, *a.* *StExch:* **neglected stocks,** fonds négligés/délaissés.

negligence, *n.* négligence; **through negligence,** par négligence; *Jur:* **criminal negligence,** négligence coupable/criminelle; **gross negligence,** négligence grave; *Ins:* **negligence clause,** clause dite négligence.

negotiability, *n.* négociabilité *f* (d'un effet de commerce).

negotiable, *a. Fin etc:* (effet, titre, etc.) négociable; **stocks negotiable on the Stock Exchange,** titres négociables en Bourse; **not negotiable,** non négociable; (*on cheque*) non à ordre.

negotiate, 1. *v.tr.* négocier/traiter (une affaire) (*b*) **to negotiate a bill,** négocier une lettre de change 2. *v.i.* **to be negotiating with s.o. for ...,** être en pourparlers avec qn au sujet de ...; négocier une affaire avec qn; **they refuse to negotiate,** ils refusent de négocier.

negotiation, *n.* négociation *f* (d'un emprunt, d'une lettre de change); **under negotiation,** en (cours de) négociation; **by negotiation,** par (voie de) négociations; de gré à gré; **the price is a matter for negotiation,** le prix est à débattre; **to be in negotiation with s.o.,** être en pourparlers avec qn; **to enter into negotiations with s.o./to start negotiations with s.o.,** engager/entamer des négociations avec qn; entrer en pourparlers/entamer des pourparlers avec qn; **to break off negotiations,** rompre les négociations; **to resume negotiations,** reprendre les négociations; **joint negotiations,** négociations paritaires.

negotiator, *n.* négociateur, -trice.

nervous, *a.* (*market*) agité/instable.

net[1], 1. *a.* (*weight, price, etc.*) net; **net amount,** montant net; **net assets,** actif net; **net asset value,** valeur *f* d'actif net/actif net; **net income,** revenu net; **net margin,** marge nette; (*on pay slip*) **net pay,** net à payer; **net present value,** valeur actuelle nette; **net proceeds of a sale,** produit net d'une vente; **net profit,** bénéfice net; **net receipts,** recettes nettes; **net weight,** poids net; **net worth,** valeur nette/situation nette; **terms strictly net,** sans déduction; payable au comptant; **turnover net of tax,** chiffre *m* d'affaires hors taxe 2. *n.* le (poids/prix/montant) net.

net[2], *v.tr.* 1. (*of pers.*) toucher net/gagner net (tant de bénéfices, etc.); **I netted (a full profit of) £2000,** cela m'a rapporté un bénéfice net de £2000; il me reste £2000

net 2. (*of enterprise, etc.*) rapporter net/produire net (une certaine somme).

nett, *a.* = **net**[1].

network, *n.* réseau *m*; **broadcasting networks,** réseaux de transmission; **distribution network,** réseau de distribution.

networking, *n. NAm:* fait *m* d'établir des contacts d'affaire.

never-never, *n. F:* **to buy sth. on the never-never,** acheter qch. à crédit/à tempérament.

new, *a.* 1. nouveau; **new capital,** capitaux frais; **new departure,** nouvelle orientation; **new issue (of shares),** nouvelle émission (d'actions); **under new management,** changement *m* de direction; **new money,** crédit *m* de restructuration; **new shares,** actions nouvelles; **two new shares for each five shares held,** deux actions nouvelles pour cinq anciennes; **to open up new channels for trade,** créer de nouveaux débouchés au commerce 2. neuf; **as new,** à l'état (de) neuf.

news, *n.pl.* (*usu. with sg. const.*) 1. nouvelle(s) *f*(*pl*)/actualités *fpl*/informations *fpl*; **news agency,** agence *f* de presse; **financial news,** chronique financière/informations financières.

newsagent, *n.* marchand, -ande/dépositaire *mf* de journaux.

newsletter, *n.* bulletin *m* (d'informations); circulaire *f*.

newspaper, *n.* journal *m*.

niche, *n. Mkt:* secteur spécialisé; (**market**) **niche,** position *f* d'une société dans un marché; niche *f*.

nickel, *n.* (*a*) nickel *m* (*b*) (pièce de) 5 cents (au Canada et aux USA).

night, *n.* nuit *f*; **night rate,** tarif *m* de nuit; **night work,** travail *m* de nuit; **to do night work/to be on night duty/F: to work nights/to be on nights,** travailler la nuit/*F:* être de nuit; **night shift,** équipe *f* de nuit; **he's on (the) night shift,** il est de nuit; *Bank:* **night safe,** coffre(-fort) *m* de nuit.

nil, *n.* (*on report sheet, etc.*) néant *m*/zéro *m*; **the balance is nil,** le solde est nul; **nil growth,** croissance *f* zéro; (*rights issues*) **nil paid,** capital non appelé/capital appelé non versé.

nomenclature, *n.* nomenclature *f.*

nominal, *a.* **1.** (*a*) nominal/de peu d'importance; **nominal rent,** loyer insignifiant/loyer symbolique (*b*) *Book-k:* **nominal account,** compte *m* d'exploitation générale; **nominal ledger,** grand(-)livre général; *Fin:* **nominal capital,** capital nominal/social; **nominal price,** prix théorique/nominal/fictif; **nominal value,** valeur nominale; **nominal wages,** salaire nominal; **nominal yield/rate,** taux nominal **2.** nominatif; **nominal list (of shareholders),** liste nominative (des actionnaires).

nominate, *v.tr.* (*a*) nommer/choisir/désigner (qn); **to nominate s.o. to a post,** nommer qn à un emploi (*b*) proposer/présenter (un candidat).

nomination, *n.* nomination *f.*

nominee, *n.* **1.** (*for an annuity, etc.*) personne dénommée/désignée **2.** (*for a post*) personne nommée/choisie; candidat(e) désigné(e)/choisi(e) **3.** prête-nom *m*; *Jur:* personne interposée.

non-acceptance, *n.* non-acceptation *f*; refus *m* d'acceptation (d'un effet, d'une traite).

non-assessable, *a. Adm:* (revenu, etc.) non imposable.

non-assessment, *n. Adm:* non-imposition *f* (d'un revenu, etc.).

non-cancellable, *a.* non résiliable.

non-capitalized, *a.* non capitalisé.

non-contributory, *a.* **non-contributory pension scheme,** caisse *f* de retraite sans versements de la part des bénéficiaires.

non-cumulative, *a. Fin:* **non-cumulative shares,** actions non cumulatives.

non-current, *a.* **non-current liabilities,** passif *m* non exigible/passif à long terme.

non-delivery, *n.* non-livraison *f*; défaut *m* de livraison; non-réception *f* (de marchandises, etc.); non-remise *f* (d'une lettre).

non-domiciled, *a.* non-domicilié/non-résident.

none, *pron. Adm:* (*in schedules, forms, etc.*) néant.

non-execution, *n.* non-exécution *f* (d'un contrat, etc.).

non-executive, *a.* **non-executive director,** administrateur *m.*

non-forfeiture, *n. Jur:* non-déchéance *f*/non-résiliation *f*/prolongation *f*/reconduction *f*; *Ins:* **non-forfeiture clause,** clause *f* de reconduction automatique.

non-fulfilment, *n.* non-exécution *f* (d'un contrat, etc.).

non-liability, *n. Jur:* non-responsabilité *f*; **non-liability clause,** clause *f* de non-responsabilité.

non-member, *n.* **open to non-members,** ouvert au public.

non-negotiable, *a.* (billet, etc.) non négociable.

non-participating, *a. Ins:* (police) sans participation aux bénéfices.

non-payment, *n.* non-paiement *m*; défaut *m* de paiement; **in case of non-payment,** en cas de non-paiement; à défaut de paiement; faute *f* de paiement.

non-profit, *a.* **non-profit organization,** société *f* sans but lucratif.

non-profit-making, *a.* (*a*) déficitaire (*b*) **non-profit-making organization,** société *f* sans but lucratif.

non-qualifying, *a.* **non-qualifying policy,** régime *m* de retraite non défiscalisé.

non-recurring, *a.* **non-recurring expenditure,** frais *m*/dépenses *f* extraordinaires.

non-resident, *n.* non-résident, -ente; **bar**

open to non-residents, bar ouvert au public.

non-returnable, *a.* perdu; **non-returnable container/packaging,** emballage perdu/non repris; bouteille non consignée.

non-taxable, *a.* *Adm:* (revenu) non imposable.

non-tariff, *a.* **non-tariff barriers,** barrières *f* non tarifaires.

non-union, *a.* (ouvrier) non syndiqué.

non-unionist, *n.* non-syndiqué, -ée.

non-warranty, *n.* non-garantie *f*; **non-warranty clause,** clause *f* de non-garantie.

notarial, *a.* *Jur:* (*a*) (*functions, etc.*) notarial (*b*) (*deed, etc.*) notarié.

notary, *n.* *Jur:* **notary (public),** notaire *m*; **contract drawn up before a notary,** contrat fait devant notaire.

note[1], *n.* 1. note *f*/mémorandum *m* 2. (*a*) billet *m*/bordereau *m*; **commission note,** bon *m* de commission; *Ins:* **cover note,** certificat *m* provisoire d'assurance; **discount note,** bordereau d'escompte; **credit note,** note/facture *f* d'avoir; bordereau de crédit; **debit note,** note/bordereau de débit; **note of hand,** reconnaissance *f* (de dette); billet (simple); **promissory note,** billet à ordre (simple) (*b*) **advice note,** bon de livraison; **delivery note,** bon de réception; **dispatch note,** bulletin *m*/bordereau/feuille *f* d'expédition; **customhouse note,** bordereau de douane/facture douanière (*c*) *StExch:* **contract note,** bordereau d'achat/de vente; **delivery note,** avis *m* de livraison; (*sent by broker to client*) **sold (contract) note,** avis d'exécution d'un ordre 3. billet (de banque); **hundred franc note,** coupure *f*/billet de cent francs.

note[2], *v.tr.* **we duly note that ...,** nous prenons bonne note (de ce) que ...; **you will note that there is an error in the account,** nous vous faisons remarquer qu'il s'est glissé une erreur dans le compte; **we have noted your order,** nous avons pris bonne note de votre commande.

notice, *n.* (*a*) avis *m*/notification *f*; **notice of delivery,** accusé *m* de réception (*b*) préavis *m*; avertissement *m*; **until further notice,** jusqu'à nouvel ordre/jusqu'à nouvel avis/jusqu'à avis contraire (*c*) (*at work*) préavis *m* (de congé); **to give one's notice,** donner sa démission; **advance notice,** préavis; **period/term of notice,** délai-congé *m*/délai *m* de congé/délai de préavis; préavis de licenciement; **to give six months' notice,** donner un préavis de six mois; **to require three months' notice,** exiger un préavis de trois mois (*d*) délai *m*; **at short notice,** à bref délai; **can be delivered at three days' notice,** livrable dans un délai de trois jours; *Fin:* **realizable at short notice,** réalisable à court terme; *Bank:* **deposit at seven days' notice,** dépôt *m* à sept jours de préavis; **notice of withdrawal,** mandat *m*; avis de retrait de fonds (*e*) **notice (to quit),** (avis de) congé *m*; *Jur:* intimation *f* de vider les lieux; **formal notice,** mise *f* en demeure; **to be under notice to quit,** avoir reçu son congé; **what notice do you require?** quel est le terme du congé? **to give notice,** (*of landlord*) donner congé/signifier son congé à un locataire (*of tenant*) donner congé au propriétaire; **you have to give a month's notice,** il faut donner congé un mois d'avance.

notification, *n.* avis *m*/notification *f*/annonce *f* (d'un fait, etc.); **notification to the contrary,** contre-ordre *m*; **letter of notification,** lettre notificative.

notify, *v.tr.* **to notify s.o. of sth.,** avertir/aviser qn de qch.; notifier qch. à qn; **to be notified of sth.,** recevoir notification de qch.; être avisé/averti de qch.

notional, *a.* fictif; **notional rent,** loyer insignifiant/symbolique.

notwithstanding, *prep.* malgré/en dépit de/nonobstant; **notwithstanding any provision to the contrary,** nonobstant toute clause contraire.

novation, *n.* *Jur:* novation *f* (de contrat, etc.).

novelty, *n.* (article de) nouveauté *f*.

null, *a.* *Jur: etc:* (*of decree, etc.*) nul; **null**

and void, nul et de nul effet/nul et sans effet/nul et non avenu; **to declare a contract null and void,** déclarer un contrat nul et non avenu; **to render null,** annuler/infirmer (un décret, etc.).

nullification, *n.* annulation *f*/infirmation *f.*

nullify, *v.tr.* annuler/infirmer (un acte).

number[1], *n.* **1.** nombre *m*; **total number of shares,** nombre total d'actions; **number of hours worked,** nombre d'heures de travail; *PolEc:* **index number,** indice *m*/nombre index; **the number of computers in service,** le parc d'ordinateurs **2.** numéro *m*; **reference number,** numéro de référence/d'abonnement, etc.; **order number,** numéro de commande; **lot number,** numéro de lot; (*in hotel*) **room number,** numéro de chambre; *Ind:* **serial number,** numéro de série/de fabrication; **National Insurance number** = matricule *m* de Sécurité Sociale; **telephone number,** numéro de téléphone; *Bank:* **cheque number,** numéro de chèque.

number[2], *v.tr.* (*consecutively*) numéroter.

numerical, *a.* (valeur, etc.) numérique; **numerical analysis,** analyse *f* numérique; **numerical data,** données *f* numériques.

O

oath, *n.* serment *m*; **under oath,** sous serment.

objective, *n.* but *m*/objectif *m*; **long-term objective,** objectif lointain; **short-term objective,** objectif à court terme; **management by objectives (MBO),** direction *f* par objectifs (DPO).

obligate, *v.tr.* **1.** *Jur:* **to obligate s.o. to do sth.,** imposer à qn l'obligation de faire qch.; **to be obligated to do sth.,** avoir l'obligation de faire qch. **2.** *NAm: Fin:* (*a*) obliger (un bien) (*b*) affecter (des fonds, des crédits).

obligation, *n.* (*a*) obligation *f*; **to be under an obligation (to do sth),** être dans l'obligation de/être forcé de/être tenu de (faire qch.); **you are under no obligation,** sans engagement *m* de votre part; **without obligation,** sans engagement; (*in shop*) **no obligation to buy** = entrée *f* libre (*b*) *Jur:* **joint and several obligation,** obligation solidaire; **moral obligation,** obligation morale.

observer, *n.* observateur *m*.

obsolescence, *n.* (*a*) obsolescence *f*/vieillissement *m*/désuétude *f*: *Ind:* obsolescence (d'un outillage); **built-in obsolescence,** obsolescence prévue systématiquement; **planned obsolescence,** obsolescence prévue/désuétude calculée (*b*) *Ins:* **obsolescence clause,** clause *f* de vétusté.

obsolescent, *a.* obsolescent; qui tombe en désuétude.

obsolete, *a.* obsolescent; vieilli.

obtainable, *a.* procurable; **where is that book obtainable?** où peut-on se procurer ce livre?

occupancy, *n.* **1.** *Jur:* possession *f* à titre de premier occupant **2.** (*a*) occupation *f*/habitation *f* (d'un immeuble); *NAm:* **(for) residential occupancy,** (à) usage *m* d'habitation; **(for) commercial occupancy,** (à) usage commercial; **industrial occupancy,** location *f* par une entreprise industrielle; (*of house, etc.*) **immediate occupancy,** possession immédiate (*b*) *NAm:* immeuble occupé; appartement occupé.

occupant, *n.* (*a*) (*i*) occupant, -ante (d'un lieu) (*ii*) locataire *mf* (d'une maison) (*b*) *Jur:* premier occupant.

occupation, *n.* **1.** *Jur:* prise *f* de possession (*d'un bien à titre de premier occupant*) **2.** métier *m*/emploi *m*/profession *f*; **what is his occupation?** quel est son métier? quel est son emploi?

occupational, *a.* **occupational accident,** accident du travail; **occupational disease,** maladie professionnelle; **occupational hazards,** risques professionnels/risques du métier.

occupier, *n.* occupant, -ante.

occupy, *v.tr.* **1.** occuper/habiter (une maison, etc.) **2.** occuper/remplir (une fonction, un emploi); **to occupy an important post,** occuper un poste important.

ocean-going, *a.* **ocean-going ship,** navire *m* au long cours/long-courrier *m*.

odd, *a.* **1.** (*a*) (nombre) impair (*b*) **a hundred-odd packing cases,** cent et quelques caisses; une centaine de caisses; **a few odd grammes over,** quelques grammes de plus; **to make up the odd money,** faire l'appoint **2.** (*a*) disparate; (*of one of a set, of a pair*) dépareillé; **odd one (of pair),** demi-paire *f* (*b*) **odd lot,** (*i*) solde *m* (*ii*) lot *m* d'appoint (iii) *StExch: NAm:* unité *f* de moins de 100 actions **3.** non usuel; **odd size,** dimension spéciale/non courante; **odd sizes,** tailles non suivies.

odd-even, *a.* **odd-even system,** système *m* des numéros pairs et impairs (des plaques minéralogiques) correspondants aux jours pairs et impairs (*pour la vente de l'essence*).

odd-lot, *a.* *StExch: NAm:* **odd-lot-trading,** achats *mpl* et ventes *fpl* de lots de moins de 100 actions; **odd-lot order,** ordre *m* de moins de 100 actions.

oddment, *n.* article dépareillé; article en solde; coupon *m* d'étoffe; *pl.* **oddments,** fins *fpl* de série.

off, 1. *adv.* (*a*) **the deal is off,** le marché est rompu/l'affaire est manquée; **the strike is off,** la grève n'aura pas lieu/la grève est annulée (*b*) **to allow 5% off for cash payment,** faire une réduction/une remise de 5% pour paiement (au) comptant; **5p off,** remise/réduction de 5p **2.** *prep.* (*a*) **to take sth. off the price,** faire une remise; **a third off everything,** rabais général d'un tiers; **to borrow money off s.o.,** emprunter de l'argent à qn (*b*) **to have/to take time off (work),** avoir du temps (de) libre; **an afternoon off,** un après-midi de congé; **day off,** jour *m* de congé; **to give the staff a day off,** donner congé à son personnel pour la journée; **to arrange to take two days off,** se libérer pour deux jours.

off-board, *a.* *NAm:* **off-board market,** marché *m* hors-cote.

off-book, *a.* *NAm:* **off-book fund,** caisse noire.

offence, *n.* délit *m*.

offer¹, *n.* (*a*) offre *f*/proposition *f*; **firm offer,** offre ferme; **general offer,** offre publique; **godfather offer,** offre irrésistible; **(this house is) under offer,** on a fait une offre d'achat (pour cette maison); **verbal offer,** offre verbale; **written offer,** offre écrite; **to make an offer (for sth.),** faire une offre (pour qch.); **that's the best offer I can make,** c'est le plus que je puis offrir; c'est

mon dernier mot; **we made a better offer,** nous avons fait une suroffre; **on offer,** en réclame/en vente; **special offer,** article *m* (en) réclame; offre spéciale; **job offers,** offres d'emploi (*b*) **offer for sale,** mise *f* sur le marché; **offer by prospectus,** offre publique de vente (OPV); **offer to purchase,** offre publique d'achat (OPA).

offer², *v.tr.* (*a*) offrir; **he was offered the post,** on lui a offert le poste (*b*) **to offer goods (for sale),** mettre des marchandises en vente; **house offered for sale,** maison mise en vente; **to offer one's services,** proposer ses services (*c*) *StExch:* **prices offered,** cours offerts/cours vendeurs.

offering, *n.* offre *f*; mise *f* sur le marché (de nouvelles actions); *US:* **offering circular,** note *f* d'information.

office, *n.* **1.** (*a*) fonctions *fpl*; **to perform the office of secretary,** faire office de secrétaire; **to be in office,** être au pouvoir; exercer une fonction; **public office,** administration publique (*b*) charge *f*/emploi *m*/place *f*/fonctions *fpl*; **high office/important office,** poste élevé **2.** (*a*) bureau *m*; étude *f* (d'un avocat, d'un notaire); cabinet *m*; **branch office,** succursale *f*; **business office,** bureau commercial; **head office/registered offices (of a company),** bureau principal/bureau central/siège social; administration centrale; **new office technology/office automation (OA),** bureautique *f*; **office boy,** coursier *m*/garçon *m* de courses; **office building/office block,** immeuble *m* de bureaux/bâtiment administratif; **office clerk,** employé,-ée de bureau; **office copy,** double *m*; **office equipment,** matériel *m* de bureau; **office expenses,** frais *mpl* de bureau; **office hours,** heures *f* de bureau; **office management,** organisation *f* des bureaux; **office manager,** chef *m* de bureau; **office premises/office space,** locaux *mpl* pour bureaux; **office requisites/office supplies,** articles *m*/fournitures *f* de bureau; **office staff,** personnel *m* de bureau; **for office use only,** (cadre) réservé à l'administration; **office work,** travail *m* de bureau; **office worker,** employé, -ée de bureau (*b*) **private office,** cabinet particulier; **the manager's office**, le bureau du directeur; **the secretary's office**, le secrétariat (c) **booking office**/(in theatre) **box office**, bureau de location; guichet m; **cash office**, caisse f; **inquiry office**, bureau des renseignements; **registration office**, bureau d'enregistrement; **tourist office**, bureau de tourisme; Syndicat m d'Initiative (c) **the Audit Office**, la Cour des comptes.

officer, n. **customs officer**, douanier m; NAm: **executive officer**, cadre supérieur; administrateur m; directeur m; **training officer**, directeur m de formation/cadre chargé de la formation professionnelle.

official, 1. a. (a) officiel; **official document**, document officiel; **to act in one's official capacity (as)**, agir en sa qualité de ... (b) (of statement, source, journal, etc.) officiel; Fin: **Official List**, cote officielle; **official market**, marché officiel; parquet m; **official quotations**, cours m officiel; Bank: **official rate**, taux officiel d'escompte; **official receiver**, administrateur m judiciaire/mandataire(-)liquidateur m; **official strike**, grève officielle/réglementaire (c) Post: (on Government envelopes) **official paid** = franchise postale **2.** n. fonctionnaire m; Pej: bureaucrate m; **higher officials**, hauts fonctionnaires; **minor officials**, petits fonctionnaires.

officialese, n. jargon administratif.

officially, adv. officiellement; **stock quoted officially**, valeurs admises à la cote officielle.

off-licence, n. (permit) licence f permettant exclusivement la vente des boissons alcoolisées à emporter; (shop) magasin m de vins et de spiritueux.

offload, v.tr. débarquer (un excédent de marchandises, etc.).

off-peak, a. **off-peak day**, jour creux; **off-peak hours**, heures creuses; **off-peak season**, période creuse.

off-price, a. **off-price store**, superminimarge m.

off-season, 1. n. morte-saison f **2.** adv. pendant la morte-saison **3.** a. hors saison; **off-season tariff**, tarif m hors saison.

offset[1], n. (a) compensation f/dédommagement m; **as an offset to my losses**, en compensation de mes pertes (b) Book-k: compensation (d'une écriture).

offset[2], v.tr. (a) (printing) imprimer (un livre) en offset (b) contrebalancer; compenser (des pertes, etc.) (c) StExch: prendre une position inverse sur le marché.

offsetting, a. **offsetting entry**, écriture f de compensation.

offshore, a. (a) **offshore oilfield**, gisement m pétrolifère marin/en mer/off-shore (b) **offshore funds**, fonds placés à l'étranger; **offshore investment**, investissement extraterritorial.

offtake, n. écoulement m (de marchandises, etc.).

off-the-job, a. **off-the-job training**, formation extérieure/institutionelle.

oil, n. (a) huile f; **crude oil**, pétrole brut/le brut; **diesel oil**, gas-oil m; **fuel oil**, (i) pétrole (ii) mazout m; **oil field**, gisement m pétrolifère/gisement de pétrole; **oil producing countries**, pays producteurs de pétrole/pays pétroliers; **oil refinery**, raffinerie f de pétrole; **oil rig**, appareil m de sondage; installation f de forage; (off-shore) plate-forme (pétrolière); **oil tanker**, pétrolier m; **oil company**, société pétrolière; **big oil**, grandes sociétés pétrolières (b) StExch: **oil market**, marché pétrolier; **oil prices** prix pétroliers; **oil products**, produits pétroliers; **oil shares/oils**, valeurs pétrolières/les pétroles.

oligopoly, n. PolEc: oligopole m.

ombudsman, n. ombudsman m; médiateur, -trice.

omission, n. omission f; **errors and omissions excepted**, sauf erreurs et omission

omnium, n. StExch: omnium m.

on, prep. **1.** (a) sur; **tax on tobacco**, taxe su

le tabac (*b*) **to be on the committee,** être membre du comité; **to be on the staff,** faire partie du personnel **2. on a commercial basis,** sur une base commerciale; **on an average,** en moyenne; **interest on capital,** intérêt *m* d'un capital; **to borrow money on security,** emprunter de l'argent sur nantissement; **to retire on a pension of £15000 a year,** prendre sa retraite avec une pension de £15000 par an; **to buy sth. on good terms,** acheter qch. à d'excellentes conditions **3.** (*a*) **on Monday,** lundi (prochain ou dernier); **on Mondays,** le lundi; **on April 3rd,** le trois avril; **on and after the 15th,** à partir du quinze; à dater du quinze; **on or about the 12th,** vers le douze (*b*) **on account,** à valoir; **on application/on request,** sur demande; **on condition,** sous réserve; **on examination,** après examen; **on hand,** disponible; **on stream,** (mise) en service; **on trial,** à l'essai; **payable on demand,** payable sur demande/à vue; **payable on sight,** payable à vue **4. on the cheap,** à bon marché; **on the house,** aux frais de la maison **5. on sale,** en vente; **on display,** exposé; en vitrine **6. I am here on business,** je suis ici pour affaires; **on holiday,** en congé/en vacances; **to be working on sth.,** travailler à qch. **7.** (*a*) **decision binding on s.o.,** décision *f* obligatoire pour qn/qui lie qn (*b*) **cheque on a bank/on Paris,** chèque *m* (tiré) sur une banque/sur Paris.

oncost, *n.* frais généraux.

one, 1. *num.a.* un **2.** *n.* (*a*) **number one,** numéro un (*b*) **goods that are sold in ones,** marchandises *f* qui se vendent à la pièce/à l'unité; **two for the price of one,** deux pour le prix d'un (*c*) *StExch:* unité *f*; unité de mille livres (*au prix nominal des actions*); **to issue shares in ones,** émettre des actions en unités.

one-legged, *a. F:* (contrat, etc.) inégal.

one-man, *a.* **one-man business,** entreprise individuelle.

one-off, *a.* (article) spécial/hors série; ponctuel; *Publ:* (livre) qui ne fait pas partie d'une série; **one-off deal,** affaire exclusive/qui ne se répète pas.

one-price, *a.* **one-price counter,** rayon *m* à prix unique; **one-price store,** magasin *m* à prix unique/prix *m* unique.

onerous, *a.* **1.** (devoir, impôt, etc.) onéreux **2.** *Jur: esp. Scot:* **onerous contract,** contrat *m* à titre onéreux.

one-sided, *a.* (*of contract*) unilatéral; inégal.

one-way, *a.* **one-way packing,** emballage perdu; **one-way ticket,** aller *m* (simple).

on-floor, *a.* **on-floor transactions,** opérations *fpl*/négociations *fpl* à la corbeille.

on-line, *a. Cmptr:* en ligne; **on-line data service,** serveur *m.*

onshore, *a.* **onshore oil/field,** pétrole *m*/gisement *m* on-shore.

on-the-job, *a.* **on-the-job training,** formation *f* pratique; apprentissage *m*/formation sur le tas.

open¹, *a.* **1.** (*a*) ouvert; *PolEc:* **policy of the open door/open-door policy,** politique *f* de la porte ouverte (*b*) (*box, etc.*) ouvert; (*parcel*) défait; (*envelope*) (*not sealed*) non cacheté; (*opened*) décacheté (*c*) **open all (the) year round,** ouvert toute l'année; **the offices are open from ten to five,** les bureaux sont ouverts de dix heures à cinq heures (*d*) *StExch:* **to buy on the open market,** acheter en Bourse **2. open to any reasonable offer,** disposé à considérer toute offre raisonnable **3. to keep a job open,** ne pas pourvoir à un emploi **4.** (*a*) **open contract,** contrat *m* dont toutes les stipulations ne sont pas encore arrêtées (*b*) *MIns:* **open policy,** police (d'assurance) flottante/d'abonnement; police d'assurance ouverte **5.** *Fin:* **open account,** compte ouvert; compte courant; **open cheque,** chèque ouvert/non barré; **open credit,** crédit *m* à découvert; facilité *f* de caisse; **open ticket,** billet ouvert.

open², 1. *v.tr.* (*a*) décacheter (une lettre); défaire (un paquet); (*on box*) **open here,** côté à ouvrir; **to open the mail,** dépouiller le courrier (*b*) **to open a new shop,** ouvrir un nouveau magasin; **the company is**

opening its own bank, la société va ouvrir sa propre banque (c) commencer; **to open negotiations,** entamer/engager des négociations (d) **to open a bank account,** (se faire) ouvrir un compte bancaire; **to open a line of credit,** ouvrir un crédit (e) **to open a loan,** ouvrir un emprunt **2.** v.i. (a) (of shop, etc.) ouvrir; **the bank opens at ten,** la banque ouvre (ses portes) à dix heures; **as soon as the season opens,** dès l'ouverture f de la saison (b) StExch: coter à l'ouverture; **coppers opened firm,** les valeurs f cuprifères ont ouvert fermes.

open-end, a. NAm: Fin: **open-end trust/ fund** = société f d'investissement à capital variable (SICAV); (invested in equity) SICAV actions; (invested in bonds) SICAV obligations.

open-ended, a. (of agreement, mortgage) sans date limite; non déterminé; extensible; **open-ended trust** = société f d'investissement à capital variable (SICAV).

opening[1], n. **1.** (a) ouverture f (d'un magasin, d'un bureau, d'un compte, d'un crédit); décachetage m (d'une lettre); dépouillement m (du courrier) (b) **opening of an additional workshop,** mise f en service d'un nouvel atelier (c) ouverture (de négociations) (d) **the opening (up) of new markets/of new channels of trade,** l'ouverture de nouveaux débouchés (pour une marchandise); **have you any openings for school-leavers?** avez-vous des débouchés pour les jeunes qui quittent l'école? (e) **opening hours,** heures f d'ouverture; **late opening Friday** = nocturne m le vendredi; **opening time,** heure d'ouverture (d'un pub) (f) StExch: (**opening day,** jour m d'ouverture; F: **the opening,** le cours d'ouverture.

opening[2], a. Book-k: **opening entry,** écriture f d'ouverture; StExch: **opening price,** (i) cours m d'ouverture/premier cours (d'une séance boursière) (ii) cours d'introduction (d'une nouvelle valeur en bourse).

open up, v.tr. (a) **to open up a country to trade,** ouvrir un pays au commerce (b) ouvrir (une boutique, une maison de commerce, une succursale).

operate, 1. v.i. (a) opérer; agir; **to operate without cover,** opérer à découvert (b) **the rise in wages will operate from January 1st,** l'augmentation f des salaires entrera en vigueur le premier janvier (c) StExch: **to operate for a rise,** spéculer à la hausse; **to operate for a fall,** spéculer à la baisse; **to operate against one's client,** faire de la contrepartie **2.** v.tr. (a) (i) (of pers.) **to operate a machine,** faire fonctionner un appareil (ii) (of machine) **how to operate** = fonctionnement m (b) gérer/diriger (une maison de commerce, etc.).

operating, n. NAm: **chief operating officer** = président-directeur général; **operating budget,** budget m d'exploitation **operating costs,** frais m d'exploitation **operating losses,** pertes f d'exploitation **operating profits,** bénéfices m d'exploitation.

operation, n. (a) entreprise f/affaire f (b) **firm's operations,** les activités f d'une entreprise; **operations breakdown,** décomposition f des tâches; **operations management,** gestion f des opérations; NAm: **operations research (OR),** recherche opérationnelle (RO); StExch: Bank: **bank operation,** opération f bancaire **credit operation,** opération à terme **selling**/NAm: **vending operation,** opération de vente; **stock exchange operation,** opération de Bourse.

operational, a. (a) opérationnel; **operational audit,** audit opérationnel; **operational costs,** coûts opérationnels **operational efficiency,** efficacité opérationnelle; **operational planning,** planification f des opérations; **operations research (OR),** recherche opérationnelle (RO) (b) **to become operational,** être (mis) en service/en marche.

operative, 1. a. (a) **to become operative,** entrer en vigueur/prendre effet; **the rise in wages has been operative since May 1st,** l'augmentation f des salaires est entrée e vigueur le premier mai (b) **the operative side of an industry,** les ateliers m **2.** n. (pers.) ouvrier, -ière; artisan, -ane.

operator, n. (a) opérateur, -trice; **(telephone) operator,** opérateur, -trice/téléphoniste mf; **switchboard operator,** standardiste mf; **to call the operator,** appeler la standardiste/la téléphoniste (b) opérateur (d'une machine); **operator's handbook,** manuel m de l'utilisateur (c) exploitant, -ante (d'une entreprise) (d) StExch: boursier; m **operator for a fall,** spéculateur m à la baisse; **operator for a rise,** spéculateur à la hausse (e) **tour operator,** voyagiste mf/organisateur, -trice de voyages.

operatorship, n. exploitation f.

opinion, n. (a) **opinion poll/survey,** sondage m (d'opinion); **public opinion,** opinion publique (b) Jur: **to take counsel's opinion,** consulter un avocat/un conseiller juridique.

opportunity, n. **1.** occasion f (favorable)/ opportunité f; **Equal Opportunity Commission** = commission f d'égalité des chances; **investment opportunities,** occasions/opportunités d'investissement; **job opportunities,** débouchés m; **market opportunity,** créneau m; **unique sales opportunities,** occasions exceptionnelles **2. opportunity cost,** coût d'opportunité/ d'option/de substitution; **productive opportunity,** possibilité f de production; **the industry is rising to the height of its opportunity,** l'industrie f atteint peu à peu son développement maximum.

optimal, a. optimal; optimum; **optimal resource allocation,** répartition optimale des ressources.

optim(al)ization, n. optimisation f.

optim(al)ize, v.tr. optimiser.

optimum, 1. n. optimum m **2.** a. **optimum conditions,** les conditions les meilleures; les conditions optima/optimales; **optimum employment of resources,** emploi m optimum des ressources.

option, n. **1.** option f (d'achat); faculté f (d'achat); **to rent a building with option of purchase,** prendre un immeuble (i) en crédit-bail (ii) en location-vente **2.** StExch: option; **at-the-money option,** option à l'argent/à la monnaie/au cours; **call option,** option d'achat; **compound option,** option synthétique; **double option,** double option/stellage m; **in-the-money option,** option en dedans; **out-of-the money option,** option en dehors/hors des cours; **naked option,** option d'achat vendue à découvert; **option day,** (jour de la) réponse des primes; **option dealings/ trading,** opérations à prime/à option; **options market,** marché m à options; marché à primes; **multiple options facility,** ligne f de crédit à options multiples; **option money,** (montant m de la) prime; acompte m de préférence; **option price,** prix m de l'option; **put option,** option de vente; **put and call option,** double option/ stellage; **stock option,** option de titres; **stock option plan,** plan d'options sur titres; **traded option,** option cotée (sur un marché organisé); **traditional option,** option traditionnelle; **to declare an option,** donner la réponse à/répondre à (une prime, une option); **to take up/to exercise an option,** lever une option/une prime.

optional, a. facultatif; **optional extras,** accessoires m au choix (de l'acheteur); **optional retirement at sixty,** retraite f à soixante ans sur demande.

optionee, n. bénéficiaire mf d'options.

order[1], n. **1.** (a) **in order,** en règle; **is your passport in order?** est-ce que votre passeport est en règle? (b) en bon état; **machine in good (working) order,** machine f en bon état (de fonctionnement, de marche); **out of order,** hors service; (téléphone) en dérangement **2. pay to the order of J. Martin,** payez à l'ordre de J. Martin; **pay J. Martin or order,** payez à J. Martin ou à son ordre; **bill to order/order bill,** billet m à ordre; **cheque to order/order cheque,** chèque m à ordre **3.** commande f/ordre m; **order book,** carnet m de commandes; **(tele)phone order,** commande téléphonique/par téléphone; **standing order,** commande permanente; (*in restaurant*) **have you given your order?** avez-vous commandé? **to fill an order,** exécuter une commande; **to place an order with (s.o.)/to give (s.o.) an order,** faire/passer une commande à (qn); commander qch. chez qn; **he gave us an order for five tons of fertilizer,** il a commandé/il nous a passé une commande de cinq tonnes d'engrais; **as per order,** conformément à votre commande; **cash with order,** payable à la commande; **order form,** bon *m* de commande; **to put goods on order,** commander des marchandises; **economic order quantity,** quantité *f* économique à commander; **it's on order,** c'est commandé; **by order and for account of J. Martin,** d'ordre et pour compte de J. Martin; (*of furniture, etc.*) **made to order,** fabriqué sur commande/à la demande **4.** (*goods ordered*) **to deliver an order,** livrer une commande **5.** (*a*) **order to pay/order for payment,** ordonnance *f* de paiement; **order to view,** permis *m* de visiter (une maison à vendre, etc.) (*b*) bon *m*; **delivery order,** bon de livraison; **issue order,** bon de sortie (de magasin, etc.); **purchase order,** bon d'achat/de commande (*c*) mandat *m*; **order on a bank,** mandat sur une banque; **postal order/money order,** (*i*) mandat-poste *m* (*ii*) mandat-lettre *m* (*iii*) mandat-carte *m*; Bank: **banker's order/ standing order,** ordre de virement/de paiement automatique; **to pay by banker's/standing order,** payer par virement automatique (*d*) **open/resting order,** ordre à révocation **6.** StExch: ordre *m* (de Bourse); **discretionary order,** ordre à appréciation; **market order,** ordre (à faire exécuter) au prix du marché; **order at best,** ordre à faire exécuter au mieux; **to give/ place an order,** passer un ordre; **all or none order,** ordre tout ou rien; **stop order,** ordre stop; **limit order,** ordre à cours limite.

order², *v.tr.* commander/demander/commissioner (qch.); faire/passer une commande; **to order goods from Paris,** commander des articles de Paris; **to order a taxi,** demander un taxi/faire venir un taxi.

ordering, *n.* passation *f* de commandes.

ordinary, *a.* (*a*) ordinaire; normal; courant; **ordinary scale of remuneration,** barème courant de rémunération (*b*) Fin: **ordinary share,** action *f* ordinaire.

organization, *n.* **1.** organisation *f*; Ind: **organization and methods (O and M),** méthodes *f* et organisation; **functional organization/staff organization,** organisation fonctionnelle/horizontale; **line organization,** structure hiérarchique/ verticale; **organization chart,** organigramme *m* **2.** organisation/organisme *m* (politique, international, etc.); **travel organization,** organisation de tourisme/de voyage.

organize, *v.tr.* organiser; **organized labour** = les organisations ouvrières.

organizer, *n.* organisateur, -trice.

organizing, *n.* organisation *f*; **organizing committee,** comité *m* d'organisation.

organogram, *n.* organigramme *m*.

orientation, *n.* orientation *f*; **customer orientation,** orientation du client.

oriented, *a.* orienté; **profit-oriented organization,** entreprise *f* à but lucratif; **export-oriented economy,** économie orientée vers les exportations.

origin, *n.* origine *f*; **country of origin,** pays *m* de provenance; **goods of foreign origin,** marchandises *f* de provenance étrangère; Cust: **certificate of origin,** certificat *m* d'origine.

original, 1. *a.* (*a*) original; initial/premier primitif; **original cost,** coût *m* d'acquisition/coût initial; **original value,** valeur initiale à l'origine; **original packing,** emballage *m* d'origine; Fin: **original capital,** capital d'origine/primitif (*b*) **original bill cheque/receipt,** effet/chèque/récépissé original; **original document,** (*i*) Book-k: pièce *f* comptable (*ii*) Jur: primordial *m* **original invoice,** facture originale **2.** *n.* original *m* (d'une facture, etc.); Fin: pri mata (d'une traite); **to copy sth. from the original,** copier qch. sur l'original.

ounce, *n. Meas:* once *f*; (*measure of weight*) **avoirdupois ounce** = 28,35 g; **Troy ounce** = 31,1035 g; (*measure of capacity*) **fluid ounce** = 28 cl.

out, 1. *adv.* (*a*) **the workmen are out (on strike),** les ouvriers sont en grève; **money out (on loan),** argent prêté; prêts *mpl* (*b*) dans l'erreur; **to be out in one's calculations,** être loin du compte; s'être trompé dans ses calculs; **he is five pounds out (in his accounts),** il y a une erreur de cinq livres (dans ses comptes) (*c*) **the lease is out,** le bail est expiré **2.** *prep. phr.* **my passport is out of date,** mon passeport est périmé; **(article) out of stock,** (article) épuisé; **to be out of blue pens,** ne plus avoir (en stock)/être à court de stylos bleus; **to be out of work,** être au chômage; **(to be) out of order,** (être) en dérangement; (être) hors service **3.** *a.* **out (tray),** (corbeille à courrier) sorties *fpl*; *Book-k:* **out book,** livre *m* du dehors.

outbid, *v.tr.* (*at auction*) enchérir (sur qn)/surenchérir/faire une surenchère.

outbidding, *n.* surenchère *f*.

outbound, *a.* (*a*) (navire) en partance; (avion, train) en partance (*b*) (navire, avion) effectuant un voyage d'aller (*c*) **outbound freight,** fret *m* de sortie.

out-clearing, *n. Fin: Bank:* **out-clearing book,** livre *m* du dehors.

outcome, *n.* résultat *m*.

outfit, *n.* établissement *m*/organisation *f*.

outflow, *n. Fin:* **outflow of gold,** sortie *f* d'or; **inflow and outflow of currencies,** opérations *fpl* sur devises.

outgo, *n. NAm:* dépenses *fpl*/sorties *fpl* de fonds.

outgoing, *a.* (*a*) *Ind:* **outgoing shift,** équipe sortante/relevée (*b*) **outgoing mail,** courrier *m* à expédier/au départ (*c*) *Fin:* **outgoing gold-point,** gold-point *m* de sortie.

outgoings, *n.pl.* dépenses *fpl*/frais *mpl*/

débours *mpl*; sorties *fpl* (de fonds); **the outgoings exceed the incomings,** les dépenses excèdent les recettes; il y a plus de sorties que de rentrées.

outlay, *n.* frais *mpl*/dépenses *fpl*/débours *mpl*; investissement *m*; **first/initial/capital outlay,** première mise de fonds/frais d'établissement; **to get back/recover one's outlay,** rentrer dans ses fonds; **without any great outlay/considerable outlay,** sans mise de fonds importante; à peu de frais.

outlet, *n.* débouché *m* (pour marchandises); **retail outlet,** magasin *m*; **sales outlet,** point *m*/lieu *m* de vente; **tied outlet,** magasin astreint par bail à vendre la marchandise d'un certain fabricant.

outlook, *n.* perspective *f*.

out-of-court, *a.* **out-of-court settlement,** règlement *m* à l'amiable.

out-of-date, *a.* désuet; **out-of-date cheque,** chèque périmé.

out-of-pocket, *a.* **out-of-pocket expenses,** menues dépenses; débours *mpl*; **to be left out-of-pocket,** ne pas rentrer dans ses frais/en être pour ses frais.

outplacement, *n. NAm:* **outplacement advisor,** (bureau *m* de) conseiller *m* pour cadres (*désirant trouver un emploi après licenciement*).

output, *n.* production *f*/rendement *m* (d'un travailleur, etc.); débit *m* (d'une machine); **this represents 25% of the total output,** cela représente 25% de la production totale; **daily output of a worker,** production journalière/rendement journalier d'un ouvrier; **unit price of output,** prix *m* unitaire du produit; **output per hour,** production horaire/production à l'heure; **capacity/maximum/peak output,** production maximale/maximum; rendement maximal/maximum; **output bonus,** prime *f* de rendement; **output ceiling,** plafond *m* de la production; **input-output tables,** tableaux *m* d'échanges industriels.

outright, *adv.* **to buy sth. outright,** acheter

qch. au comptant; **to buy rights outright,** acquérir des droits en bloc.

outsell, *v.tr.* **1.** (*of goods*) (*i*) se vendre en plus grande quantité que/être plus demandé que (qch.) (*ii*) se vendre plus cher que (qch.) **2.** vendre plus (qu'un autre).

outside, *a.* (*a*) **outside worker,** travailleur, -euse/employé, -ée à domicile (*b*) *StExch:* **outside broker,** courtier *m* marron/coulissier *m*; **outside market,** marché *m* hors cote; coulisse *f*; **outside price,** prix *m* maxima.

outsider, *n. StExch:* courtier *m* marron; courtier libre.

outsize, *n.* grande taille/taille exceptionnelle; (*in men's clothes*) très grand patron; **outsize dress,** robe *f* en taille exceptionnelle; **outsize shoes,** pointure *f* hors série.

outstanding, *a.* (*account*) impayé/dû; à percevoir; (*payment*) arriéré/en retard; (*interest*) échu; **outstanding balance,** solde *m* à découvert; **outstanding debts (due to us),** créances *f* (à recouvrer); **total of bills/ credits outstanding at any (given) time,** encours *m*; **outstanding coupons,** coupons *m* en souffrance; **outstanding shares,** actions en cours/en circulation; **outstanding notes,** billets *m* effectivement en circulation; **there is nothing outstanding,** tout est réglé.

out-turn, *n.* production nette/rendement net.

outvote, *v.tr.* obtenir une majorité sur (qn); **we were outvoted,** la majorité des voix a été contre nous.

outward, *a.* **outward voyage,** voyage *m* d'aller; **outward cargo,** cargaison *f*/chargement *m* d'aller; **the outward and the homeward voyages,** l'aller *m* et le retour; **outward bill of lading,** connaissement *m* de sortie; **outward freight,** fret *m* de sortie; **outward mission,** visite *f* (d'un groupe d'hommes d'affaires) à l'étranger/mission *f* à l'étranger.

outwork, *n.* travail *m* (fait) à domicile.

outworker, *n.* employé, -ée qui travaille à domicile.

over, 1. *prep.* (*a*) **over fifty pounds,** plus de cinquante livres; **not over 250 grams,** jusqu'à 250 g; **he receives tips over and above his wages,** il reçoit des pourboires en plus/en sus de son salaire (*b*) **an increase of 10% over last year,** une augmentation de 10% par rapport à l'année dernière (*c*) **over the last three years,** au cours des trois dernières années **2.** *adv.* (*a*) **difference over or under,** différence *f* en plus ou en moins; *StExch:* **buyers/sellers over,** excès *m* d'acheteurs/de vendeurs (*b*) **bills held over,** effets *m* en souffrance/en suspens **3.** *n.* **over in the cash,** excédent *n* dans l'encaisse; **shorts and overs,** déficits *m* et excédents; **we agree to supply 5% overs,** nous acceptons de vous fournir un excédent de 5% (du nombre commandé).

overage, *n. NAm:* excédent *m*/surplus *m*.

overall, *a.* (*a*) hors tout; total; **overall length,** longueur totale/hors tout; **overall consumption,** consommation totale (*b*) général; global; total; **overall demand,** demande globale; **overall efficiency,** (*i*) efficacité totale (*ii*) rendement global; **overall plan,** plan *m* d'ensemble; **overall company objectives,** objectifs globaux de l'entreprise; **overall financial budget deficit,** impasse *f* budgétaire; **overall indexation,** indexation généralisée.

overassessment, *n.* surtaux *m*; surimposition *f*.

overbid[1], *n.* (*a*) surenchère *f*; suroffre *f* (*b*) enchère exagérée/offre exagérée.

overbid[2], **1.** *v.tr.* surenchérir; enchérir sur (qn) **2.** *v.i.* (*at sale*) faire une offre exagérée.

overbook, *v.i.* **to be overbooked,** avoir accepté des réservations *f* en surnombre/en trop.

overbooking, *n.* réservations *f* en surnombre/surréservation *f*.

overbought, *a. StExch:* (marché) survalué/suracheté.

overbuy, *v.i.* acheter au delà de (*i*) ses moyens (*ii*) ce qu'on pourra écouler.

overcapacity, *n. PolEc:* surcapacité *f.*

overcapitalization, *n. Fin:* surcapitalisation *f.*

overcapitalize, *v.tr. Fin:* surcapitaliser (une société).

overcharge[1], *n.* excédent *m*; surmarquage *m*; **to pay a £5 overcharge,** payer £5 d'excédent/payer £5 en trop; **overcharge on an account,** majoration *f* d'un compte.

overcharge[2], *v.tr.* faire payer trop cher un article à (qn); surmarquer (un article); survendre (un article); **you have overcharged me £2,** vous m'avez compté £2 en trop; **to overcharge (on) an account,** majorer une facture/compter qch. en trop sur une facture.

overconsumption, *n.* surconsommation *f.*

overdevelop, *v.tr. PolEc:* surdévelopper.

overdevelopment, *n. PolEc:* surdéveloppement *m.*

overdraft, *n.* (bank) overdraft, découvert *m* (d'un compte); solde débiteur; avance *f* bancaire; **unsecured overdraft,** découvert en blanc; **to allow s.o. an overdraft of £1000,** accorder à qn un découvert de £1000; **to grant a firm overdraft facilities,** consentir des facilités de caisse à une maison.

overdraw, *v.tr. Bank:* **to overdraw (one's account),** mettre son compte à découvert; tirer à découvert; **account overdrawn,** compte (à) découvert/désapprovisionné; **to be overdrawn at the bank,** avoir un découvert à la banque.

overdue, *a.* (*of account*) arriéré/échu/en retard/en souffrance; **interest on overdue payments,** intérêts *m* moratoires; **the interest is overdue,** l'intérêt n'a pas été payé à l'échéance.

overemployment, *n.* suremploi *m.*

overestimate, *v.tr.* surévaluer (qch.)/surestimer (la valeur de qch.).

overexposure, *n.* risque accru/double risque.

overextend, *v.pr.* **to overextend oneself,** prendre des engagements *m* en excès de ses moyens (financiers).

overfreight, *n.* poids *m* en excès; surcharge *f.*

overfull, *a.* **overfull production,** production *f* excédentaire.

overfunding, *n.* déflation *f* budgétaire.

overhead, **1.** *a.* (*a*) **overhead expenses/costs,** frais généraux (*b*) **overhead projection,** rétroprojection *f*; **overhead projector (OHP),** rétroprojecteur *m* **2.** *n.pl* overheads/*NAm:* **overhead,** frais généraux (d'administration, de fabrication, etc.); **manufacturing overheads,** frais de/coût *m* de (la) fabrication.

overindustrialization, *n.* surindustrialisation *f.*

overinsurance, *n.* surassurance *f.*

overinsure, *v.tr.* surassurer.

overissue[1], *n. Fin:* surémission *f*/émission excessive (de papier-monnaie, etc.).

overissue[2], *v.tr. Fin:* faire une surémission de (papier-monnaie, etc.).

overlap, *n. Mkt:* débordement *m.*

overlapping, *n.* **overlapping of two jobs,** chevauchement *m* de deux emplois; empiétement *m* d'un emploi sur l'autre.

overload, *v.tr.* surcharger (un navire, le marché, etc.); **overloaded market,** marché alourdi/surchargé.

overman, *v.tr.* **to be overmanned,** avoir un personnel trop nombreux; avoir un surplus de main-d'œuvre.

overmanning, *n.* sureffectifs *mpl*; **the industry suffers from overmanning,** l'industrie souffre d'un excédent de personnel/de main-d'œuvre.

overnight, *n. Fin:* **overnight loans,** prêts *m* du jour au lendemain.

overpay, *v.tr.* surpayer; trop payer (qn);

overpaid workmen, ouvriers surpayés/trop payés; **it appears that I am overpaid,** il paraît que je suis payé au-dessus du taux normal; il paraît que mon salaire est trop élevé.

overpayment, *n.* (*a*) surpaye *f*/surpaie *f*/paiement *m* en trop; (*of taxes*) trop-perçu *m* (*b*) rémunération/rétribution excessive (d'un employé, etc.).

overprice, *v.tr.* demander/vendre trop cher.

overproduce, *v.tr. & i.* surproduire.

overproduction, *n.* surproduction *f.*

overrate, *v.tr.* **1.** surévaluer/surestimer/surfaire (la valeur d'une action, etc.) **2.** *Adm:* surtaxer (un contribuable à l'impôt foncier).

overriding, *a.* principal; essentiel; (redevance, etc.) prioritaire/de priorité/de premier rang; **overriding importance,** importance primordiale; *Jur:* **overriding clause,** clause *f* dérogatoire.

overrun, *n.* *NAm:* (*a*) **overrun (costs),** dépassement *m* du coût estimé (*b*) excédent *m*/surplus *m* (de production, etc.).

overseas, 1. *a.* (commerce, etc.) d'outre-mer; **overseas debt,** dette extérieure; **overseas market,** marché étranger/d'outre-mer **2.** *adv.* **from overseas,** d'outremer.

overseer, *n.* surveillant, -ante; inspecteur, -trice; *Ind:* contremaître, -tresse; chef *m* d'atelier.

oversell, *v.tr.* (*a*) vendre plus (de qch.) qu'on ne peut livrer/survendre (*b*) surfaire la valeur de qch (*c*) *StExch:* **the market is oversold/is in an oversold condition,** le marché a baissé à un niveau non justifié.

overshoot, *vtr.* casser une tendance/une moyenne à la hausse.

oversold, *a.* *StExch:* (marché) sous-évalué.

overspend[1], *v.tr.* dépenser au-delà de (ses moyens, etc.); **to overspend one's income by £1000,** dépenser £1000 de plus que le montant de son revenu; *Fin:* **amount overspent,** découvert *m.*

overspend[2], *n.* découvert *m.*

overspill, *n.* dépassement *m*; débordement *m*; surplus *m*; trop-plein *m.*

overstaffed, *a.* qui a un personnel trop nombreux/un excédent de personnel.

overstock[1], *n.* *NAm:* **overstocks** *npl* surplus *m*/excédent *m* (d'un stock)/surstock *m.*

overstock[2], *v.tr.* encombrer (le marché etc.) (**with,** de); **to overstock a shop with (sth.),** encombrer un magasin de stocks (de qch.).

oversubscribe, *v.tr.* *Fin:* sursouscrire (une émission).

oversubscription, *n.* *Fin:* **oversubscription of a loan/an issue,** sursouscription d'un emprunt/d'une émission.

overt, *a.* **market overt,** marché public.

overtax, *v.tr.* surtaxer/surimposer (qn).

over-the-counter, *a.* **over-the-counter sales,** ventes *f* au comptant; **over-the-counter market/OTC market,** marché *n* des valeurs hors cote; marché des trans actions hors séance/marché THS.

overtime, 1. *n.* *Ind:* (*a*) heures *f* supplé mentaires (de travail); **an hour of over time/an hour's overtime,** une heur supplémentaire; **overtime ban,** grève *f* de heures supplémentaires (*b*) **the salar does not include overtime,** les heure supplémentaires ne sont pas comprise comptées dans le salaire **2.** *adv.* **to wor overtime/to be on overtime,** faire de heures supplémentaires.

overtrade, *v.i.* prendre trop de position en Bourse par rapport à ses moyens o par rapport aux risques encourus.

over-trading, *n.* marché sur-acheté.

overvaluation, *n.* surestimation *f* (de valeur de qch.)/surévaluation *f* (de qch

overvalue[1], *n.* survaleur *f* (des monnaies).

overvalue[2], *v.tr.* surévaluer; estimer/ évaluer (un objet) au-dessus de sa valeur.

overweight, 1. *n.* (*a*) surpoids *m*; poids *m* en excès (*b*) excédent *m* (de bagages) **2.** *a.* au-dessus du poids réglementaire; **parcel 50 grams overweight,** colis *m* qui excède de 50 grammes le poids réglementaire/ qui a un excédent de 50 grammes.

owe, *v.tr.* devoir; **to owe s.o. sth./to owe sth. to s.o.,** devoir qch. à qn; **the sum owed (to) her,** le montant qui lui est dû; **I still owe you for the petrol,** je vous dois encore l'essence/j'ai encore à vous payer l'essence.

owing, *a.* dû; **all the money owing to me,** tout l'argent qui m'est dû; **the moneys/ monies owing to us,** nos créances *f*; **the rent owing,** l'arriéré *m* du loyer.

own[1], *a.* propre; **to have one's own business/ to work on one's own account,** travailler à son propre compte.

own[2], *v.tr.* posséder; **majority-owned subsidiaries,** filiales dans lesquelles une personne/une compagnie détient une participation majoritaire; **50% owned company,** société détenue à 50%; **State-owned company,** compagnie nationalisée/ étatisée/qui appartient à l'État.

owner, *n.* propriétaire *mf*; exploitant, -ante; possesseur *m*; patron, -onne (d'une maison de commerce); **rightful owner,** possesseur légitime; *Jur:* ayant droit *m*; **sole owner,** propriétaire unique; **bare owner,** nu propriétaire; **joint owner,** copropriétaire *mf*; **owner-occupied,** occupé par le propriétaire; **owner-occupier,** propriétaire occupant *m*; **ship owner,** armateur *m*.

ownership, *n.* (droit *m* de) propriété *f*; possession *f*; participation *f* (dans une société); *Jur:* **bare ownership,** nue propriété; **common ownership,** collectivité *f*; **home ownership,** accession *f* à la propriété; **joint ownership,** copropriété *f*; **propriété commune; private ownership,** (régime *m* de) propriété privée; **social ownership,** propriété collective; **change of ownership,** (*i*) *Jur:* mutation *f* (*ii*) *P.N:* changement *m* de propriétaire; *Jur:* **claim of ownership,** action *f* pétitoire.

P

p, *abbr.* = **penny**, *pl.* **pence**; **one p,** un penny; **a book costing 50p,** un livre qui coûte cinquante pence; **a 10p (postage) stamp,** un timbre de dix pence; **10p off,** remise *f* de 10p/10 pence.

pack[1], *n.* paquet *m*; ballot *m* (de marchandises, etc.); balle *f* (de coton, etc.); *NAm:* **pack of cigarettes,** paquet de cigarettes; **pack goods,** marchandises *f* en balle(s) (*b*) emballage *m*; **blister pack/bubble pack,** habillage transparent; *FrC:* emballage-coque *m*; **vacuum pack,** emballage sous vide.

pack[2], *v.tr.* emballer/empaqueter (des marchandises).

package[1], *n.* **1.** (*i*) empaquetage *m*/emballage *m*/habillage *m* (*ii*) conditionnement *m* **2.** (*a*) paquet *m*/colis *m*; ballot *m* (*b*) *NAm:* **package store,** débit *m* où on vend des boissons à emporter **3.** achat groupé/forfait *m*/package *m*; **package deal,** contrat global/train *m* de propositions; **package tour,** voyage *m* à forfait/à prix forfaitaire; voyage organisé; **package tour organiser,** forfaitiste *mf*; *Ins:* **package policies,** garanties *f* multirisques; *Cmptr:* **software package,** progiciel *m*; **accounting package,** progiciel de comptabilité.

package[2], *v.tr.* (*i*) empaqueter/emballer (*ii*) conditionner.

packaging, *n.* (*i*) empaquetage *m*/emballage *m*/habillage *m* (*ii*) conditionnement *m*; **packaging industries,** industries *f* de conditionnement.

packet, *n.* (*a*) paquet *m* (de thé, de biscuits, de cigarettes, etc.); **packet soup,** potage *m* en sachet (*b*) **(postal) packet,** colis (postai).

packing, *n.* **1.** emballage *m*/empaquetage

m/habillage *m*; **packing charges,** frais *mp* d'emballage; **packing extra,** emballage non compris/en sus; **packing included,** emballage compris; **packing case,** caisse *f*/boîte *f* d'emballage; **packing crate** caisse (d'emballage); **packing cloth** **canvas,** toile *f* d'emballage; **packing slip** bon *m* de livraison **2.** matériel *m* d'emballage; **non-returnable packing,** emballage perdu.

pacman defence, *n.* *US:* (*illegal practice* défense *f* du Pacman/contre-OPA *f*.

pad[1], *n.* bloc *m* (de papier à écrire, etc.) **desk pad,** sous-main *m inv*; **memo pad** **scribbling pad,** bloc-notes *m*; **inking pad** tampon encreur.

pad[2], *v.tr.* gonfler (un budget, un relevé d dépenses, etc.).

paging, *n.* **paging (service),** recherche *f* d personne.

paid, *a.* **1.** appointé/payé/rétribué rémunéré/salarié; **paid assistant,** aide ré tribué(e); **paid holidays,** congés payés **paid work,** travail rémunéré/rétribué; **pai worker,** (travailleur, -euse) salarié(e **(employee) paid by the hour,** (employé -ée) payé à l'heure **2.** (*a*) (*goods, etc.* payé; (*on bills*) pour acquit/payé/acquitté **paid bills,** rentrées *fpl*; **paid cash book** main courante de dépenses/de sorties (*b* (*member*) **(fully) paid up,** qui a payé/qu est à jour de sa cotisation; *Fin:* **paid u capital,** capital appelé/versé; **paid u shares,** actions libérées; **tax paid,** (impôt payé (*ii*) net versé.

pallet, *n.* palette *f*; plate-forme *f* de manu tention.

palletization, *n.* palettisation *f* (d marchandises).

170

palletize, *v.tr.* palettiser (des marchandises); mettre (des marchandises) sur palette(s); **palletized goods,** marchandises pallettisées/sur palette(s).

panel, *n.* **1. advertisement panel,** panneau *m* d'affichage/de publicité; panneau-réclame *m* **2. consumer panel,** groupe-témoin *m*/panel *m* de consommateurs.

panic, *n.* **panic buying,** (faire des) achats *mpl* de précaution.

paper, *n.* **1.** (*a*) papier *m*; **blotting paper,** (papier) buvard *m*; **carbon paper,** papier carbone; **brown paper/wrapping paper,** papier kraft/papier d'emballage; **graph paper,** papier quadrillé; **greaseproof paper,** papier beurre/papier jambon/ papier parcheminé; **typing paper,** papier pour machine à écrire/*F:* papier machine; **ruled/lined paper,** papier réglé (*b*) **a sheet/a piece of paper,** une feuille/un morceau de papier; **paper bag,** pochette *f*/sac *m* de papier (*c*) **the paper industry,** l'industrie du papier; **paper making,** papeterie *f*; **paper-mill,** usine *f* de papeterie; **paper maker/manufacturer,** fabricant *m* de papier (*d*) **paper profits,** profits fictifs/ théoriques **2.** (*a*) écrit *m*/document *m*/pièce *f*; **the papers of a firm,** les écritures *f* d'une entreprise; **relevant papers,** pièces justificatives; **ship's papers,** papiers/ documents de bord; **clearance papers,** papiers d'expédition (*b*) **paper clip/paper fastener,** trombone *m*/agrafe *f* (*c*) *Fin:* papier valeur; **accommodation paper,** papier de complaisance; **bankable/ unbankable paper,** papier bancable/non bancable; **commercial/mercantile/trade paper,** papier commercial/de commerce; **guaranteed paper,** papier fait; **long paper,** papier à long terme; **short paper,** papier à court terme; **negotiable paper,** papier négociable; **paper loss,** moins-value *f* sur titres; **paper securities,** papiers valeurs/ titres *m* fiduciaires (*d*) billets *mpl* (de banque); **paper money/paper currency,** papier-monnaie *m* **3.** journal *m*; **daily paper,** quotidien *m*; **weekly paper,** hebdomadaire *m*; **Sunday paper,** journal du dimanche; **trade paper,** revue *f* (de commerce) spécialisée.

paperwork, *n.* travail *m* de bureau; écritures (administratives); *F:* paperasserie (administrative); **VAT makes a lot of paperwork for shopkeepers,** la TVA complique les écritures des commerçants.

par, *n. Fin:* pair *m*; **above par,** au-dessus du pair; **below par,** au-dessous du pair; **par of exchange,** pair du change; **par value,** valeur *f* au pair/valeur nominale; **no par value,** aucune parité; sans valeur nominale; **repayable at par,** remboursable au pair; **to issue shares at par,** émettre des actions au pair.

parallel, *a.* **parallel market,** marché parallèle; marché noir; **parallel rate of exchange,** cours *m* parallèle.

parameter, *n.* paramètre *m*; **fixed parameters,** paramètres invariables.

parcel[1], *n.* (*a*) paquet *m*/colis *m*; **to make/do up a parcel,** faire un paquet; **to do up goods into parcels,** empaqueter des marchandises; **parcel(s) delivery,** livraison *f*/remise *f* de colis à domicile; factage *m*/service *m* de messageries; **parcels-delivery company,** entreprise *f* de factage; **parcel(s) office,** (bureau *m* de(s)) messageries *f*; **parcel post,** service *m* (*i*) des colis postaux (*ii*) de messageries; **to send sth. by parcel post,** envoyer/expédier qch. par colis postal; **parcel rates,** tarif *m* colis postal (*b*) **parcel of land,** terrain *m*/lot *m* (*c*) *StExch:* bloc *m* de titres.

parcel[2], *v.tr.* empaqueter; **to parcel up a consignment of books,** mettre en paquets/ emballer un envoi de livres.

parent, *n.* **parent company,** société mère/ maison mère.

pari passu, *Lt. phr.* pari passu (**with,** avec).

parity, *n.* **1.** *Fin:* **exchange at parity,** change *m* à (la) parité/au pair; **fixed parity,** parité fixe; **gold parity,** parité-or; **parity of exchange,** parité de change; **parity ratio,** rapport *m* de parité; **parity table,** table *f* des parités; **parity value,** valeur *f* au pair **2.** *n.pl.* **parities,** taux *mpl* des changes.

part, *n.* (*a*) **as part of this expansion pro-**

gramme, dans le cadre de ce programme d'expansion; **it is part of his job to ...,** il lui appartient de ... (b) **to pay in part,** payer partiellement; **to contribute in part to the expenses,** contribuer en partie/ partiellement aux frais (c) Ind: pièce f/ élément m; **spare parts,** pièces détachées/de rechange (d) **part owner,** copropriétaire mf; **part ownership,** copropriété f; indivision f (e) **to work part time,** travailler à temps partiel/à mi-temps; **part time worker/part timer,** employé, -ée qui travaille à temps partiel/à mi-temps (f) **part exchange,** reprise f; **part load,** charge incomplète; **part payment,** acompte m; Nau: **part shipment,** expédition partielle/chargement partiel.

partial, a. partiel; en partie; **partial damage to goods,** avarie f d'une partie de la marchandise; **partial loss,** perte partielle/sinistre partiel; **partial acceptance of a bill,** acceptation partielle d'une traite.

participant, n. **market participant,** intervenant, -ante sur le marché.

participation, n. participation f (**in sth.,** à qch.); **employee-worker participation,** participation des salariés/participation ouvrière/intéressement m du personnel; Bank: Ins: **participation loan,** crédit syndical.

participative, a. participatif; **participative management,** gestion participative/ paritaire.

particular, 1. a. particulier; spécial 2. n. détail m/particularité f; **to give particulars of sth.,** donner des détails de qch.; **particulars of an account,** détail d'un compte; **to give full particulars,** donner les menus détails/tous les détails; **to ask for fuller particulars about sth.,** demander des précisions f/des indications f supplémentaires sur qch.; **for further particulars apply to ...,** pour tous renseignements/pour obtenir des renseignements supplémentaires, écrire à/ s'adresser à ...; **particulars of sale,** description f de la propriété à vendre; cahier m des charges; Book-k: **the**

particulars of an entry, le libellé d'un article/d'une écriture (comptable).

partition, n. Ins: **partition of average,** répartition f d'avaries; Jur: **partition of property,** partage m des biens (entre les héritiers).

partly, adv. partiellement; en partie **partly paid (up) (share, capital),** (action) non (complètement) libérée; (capital) non entièrement versé; **partly secured creditor,** créancier partiellement nanti.

partner, n. associé, -ée; **active partner** commandité, -ée; **contracting partner** contractant, -ante; **full partner,** associé à part entière; **general partner,** associé en nom collectif; **joint partner,** coassocié -ée; **junior partner,** associé en second **limited partner,** (associé) commanditaire m; **nominal partner,** associé apporteur de la marque; **sleeping partner,** associé passif; bailleur m de fonds; **senior part ner,** associé principal; **trading partner** associé commercial.

partnership, n. 1. association f/société f **to enter/go into partnership with s.o.** s'associer à/avec qn; **to take up a part nership in a business,** s'associer à/avec qn s'intéresser dans une affaire; **to take s.o into partnership,** s'adjoindre un associé prendre qn comme associé; **to dissolve a partnership,** dissoudre une association **deed/articles of partnership,** contrat de so ciété/acte m d'association; **partnership a will,** association de fait 2. société; **genera partnership,** société commerciale en non collectif; **limited partnership,** (société en commandite f (simple); **limited part nership/partnership limited with shares** (société en) commandite par actions; **in dustrial partnership,** participation f des salariés aux bénéfices/participation ou vrière/intéressement m du personne **trading partnership,** partenariat m.

party, n. 1. Adm: etc: **working party** comité m d'étude/groupe m de travail 2 (a) Jur: **party (to a suit, to a dispute** partie f; **the contracting parties,** les partie contractantes (b) **to become a party to a agreement,** devenir partie à un contra

parties to a bill of exchange, intéressé(e)s à une lettre de change; **a third party,** un tiers/une tierce personne; **to deposit a sum in the hands of a third party,** déposer une somme en main tierce; **for the account of a third party,** pour compte d'autrui; **payment on behalf of a third party,** paiement *m* par intervention; **third party insurance,** assurance *f* au tiers; **third party risks,** risques *m* de préjudice au tiers (*c*) *Tel:* **party line,** ligne partagée.

pass[1], *n.* laissez-passer *m inv*; **pass book,** carnet *m*/livret *m* de banque.

pass[2], *v.tr.* **1. to pass a dividend,** conclure un exercice sans payer de dividende; **passed dividend,** dividende non déclaré **2.** (*a*) **to pass an invoice,** approuver une facture; (*of company*) **to pass a dividend of 5%,** approuver un dividende de 5% (*b*) **to pass a law,** voter une loi; **to pass a resolution,** passer/voter/adopter une résolution **3.** *Book-k:* **to pass an item to current account,** passer/porter un article en compte courant **4. the tax will be passed on to the consumers,** la taxe se répercutera sur les consommateurs.

passenger, *n.* (*on train*) voyageur, -euse; (*on ship, aircraft*) passager, -ère; **passenger train,** train *m* de voyageurs.

passive, *a.* passif, -ive; **passive debt,** dette passive/ne portant pas d'intérêt; balance *f* de paiement déficitaire.

passport, *n.* passeport *m.*

patent[1], **1.** *a.* (*a*) *Jur:* **letters patent,** brevet *m* d'invention/d'inventeur (*b*) **patent goods,** articles brevetés; **patent medicine,** spécialité *f* pharmaceutique **2.** *n.* (*a*) brevet d'invention; **patent relating to improvements,** brevet de perfectionnement; **to take out a patent for an invention,** prendre un brevet pour une invention/faire breveter une invention; **patent applied for/patent pending,** demande (de brevet) déposée; **infringement of a patent,** contrefaçon *f;* (*of invention*) **patent expired,** invention tombée dans le domaine public; **commissioner of patents,** directeur *m* de brevets; **patent agent,** agent

m en brevets (d'invention); **patent engineer,** ingénieur *m* conseil (*en matière de propriété industrielle*); **patent office,** bureau *m* des brevets; **patent rights,** propriété industrielle; **patent rolls,** registres *mpl* portant nomenclature des brevets d'invention; **patent trading,** échange *m* de brevets (*b*) invention/fabrication brevetée.

patent[2], *v.tr.* protéger par un brevet/faire breveter (une invention); prendre un brevet pour (une invention).

patentable, *a.* brevetable.

patented, *a.* breveté.

patentee, *n.* titulaire *mf* d'un brevet.

patronage, *n.* mécénat *m.*

pattern, *n.* **1.** échantillon *m;* **pattern book/card,** livre *m*/carte *f* d'échantillons **2.** patron *m* (de robe, etc.) **3. price pattern,** structure *f* de(s) prix; **the normal pattern of trade,** la tendance normale du marché.

pawn[1], *n.* **in pawn,** en gage; **to put sth. in pawn,** mettre qch. en gage/engager qch.; déposer qch. au crédit municipal; **to take sth. out of pawn,** dégager/désengager qch.; **pawn ticket,** reconnaissance *f* (de dépôt de gage).

pawn[2], *v.tr.* (*a*) mettre (qch.) en gage; engager (qch.) (*b*) *StExch:* **pawned stock,** titres *mpl* en pension.

pawnbroker, *n.* prêteur, -euse sur gage(s); commissionnaire *m* au crédit municipal.

pawnee, *n.* prêteur, -euse sur gage(s).

pawner, *n.* *Jur:* emprunteur, -euse sur gage(s).

pawnshop, *n.* bureau *m* de prêt sur gage(s)/ mont-de-piété *m;* crédit municipal.

pay[1], *n.* **1.** salaire *m;* appointements *mpl;* traitement *m* (d'un cadre); **back pay,** rappel *m* de traitement/arrérage *m* de salaire; **basic pay,** salaire de base; **equal pay,** égalité *f* des salaires (*entre hommes et femmes*); **holidays with pay,** congés payés; **rate of pay,** taux *m* de salaire;

severance pay, prime f de licenciement; **take-home pay,** salaire net/traitement net (moins impôt, etc. retenu à la source); **unemployment pay,** allocation f/indemnité f/secours m de chômage; **to draw one's pay,** toucher son salaire/son traitement/ son mois; **pay day,** jour m de paie; *StExch:* (jour de) liquidation f; **pay slip,** bulletin m/feuille f de paie; **pay cheque,** chèque m de règlement/de traitement/de salaire; **pay packet/pay envelope** = salaire (payé en espèces); **pay policy,** politique salariale; **pay talks,** négociations fpl salariales **2. pay desk,** caisse f; **pay office,** caisse; guichet m **3. pay phone,** téléphone payant; **pay TV,** télévision f à péage.

pay², *v.tr. & i.* (*a*) **to pay s.o.** £100, payer £100 à qn; **he paid him £100 for it,** il le/la lui a payé(e) £100; **how much do you pay for tea?** combien payez-vous le thé? **you have paid too much for it,** vous l'avez payé trop cher; **to pay cash (down)/spot cash,** payer (argent) comptant/payer (au) comptant; payer cash; **to pay in cash,** payer en espèces; **to pay in advance,** payer d'avance; **to pay in full,** payer intégralement/en totalité; *NAm:* **to pay as you go,** (*i*) payer ses factures promptement (*ii*) ne jamais dépenser plus que l'on ne gagne; **£1000 to be paid in four instalments,** £1000 payable en quatre versements; **advance to be paid back within a year,** avance f remboursable dans un an au plus tard; **to pay sth. (down) on account,** verser une (somme à titre de) provision; verser des arrhes f (*b*) **pay as you earn (PAYE)/**$NAm:$ **pay as you go** = retenue f (de l'impôt sur le revenu) à la source; **to pay at maturity/at due date,** payer à échéance; **to pay on demand/on presentation,** payer à vue/à présentation; **dividend paid out of capital,** dividende prélevé sur le capital; **pay to the order of ...,** payez à l'ordre de ...; (*on cheque*) **pay self/pay cash,** payez à (l'ordre de) moi-même; **pay to bearer,** payez au porteur; **to pay a cheque into the bank/to pay in a cheque,** remettre/déposer un chèque à la banque; faire porter un chèque au crédit de son compte/sur son compte; **to pay money into s.o.'s account,** verser de l'argent au compte de qn; **to pay the balance,** régler/verser le solde (*c*) payer (ses employés, etc.); **to be paid by th hour/by the week,** être payé à l'heure/à l. semaine; **badly paid job,** situation ma payée/mal rémunérée; **to pay (off) a deb** payer / solder / liquider / régler / acquitter rembourser (une dette); **to pay (off) creditor,** rembourser/désintéresser u créancier; **to pay off a mortgage,** purge une hypothèque; **to pay a bill/an account** payer/régler un compte; acquitter un facture; (*on receipted bill*) **paid,** pou acquit/payé; **carriage paid,** (en) port pay (par l'envoyeur); *Cust:* **to pay duty on sth** payer des droits sur qch. (*e*) **business tha doesn't pay,** affaire f qui ne rapport pas/qui n'est pas rentable.

payable, *a.* payable/acquittable; exigibl (emprunt) remboursable; **payable a sight/to order/to bearer,** payable à vue ordre/au porteur; **payable on presentatio** payable à vue/à présentation; **payable o delivery,** payable à la livraison; **bill pay able in one month,** lettre f de change à un usance/à trente jours; **payable on the 15 prox.,** valeur au 15 prochain; **to make bill, a cheque) payable to s.o.,** faire/libe ler (un billet, un chèque) à l'ordre de q **cheque payable to bearer,** chèque m a porteur; **bonds made payable in franc** bons libellés en francs; **accounts payabl** *NAm:* *n.* **payables,** comptabilité fou nisseurs/comptes fournisseurs/compte passif; **rates payable by the tenant,** impôts locatifs/charges locatives (impôts à la charge du locataire; **bi payable,** effets à payer.

payback, *n.* récupération f (du capital i vesti); **payback period,** délai m de r cupération.

paycheck, *n. NAm:* chèque m de tr tement/de salaire.

PAYE, *abbr:* = pay as you earn, retenu (de l'impôt sur le revenu) à la source.

payee, *n.* (*a*) bénéficiaire mf; **payable**

address of payee, payable à domicile; (*added to crossed cheque*) **account payee,** à l'ordre de… (*b*) porteur *m* (d'un effet).

payer, *n.* **tax payer,** contribuable *mf*; *StExch:* **payer of contango,** reporté *m*.

paying[1], *a.* **1. paying guest,** pensionnaire *mf* **2.** (*of business, etc.*) rentable/lucratif/ profitable/qui rapporte **3.** payant; **paying banker,** banquier payant; **paying third system,** système *m* du tiers payant.

paying[2], *n.* **1.** paiement *m*/versement *m* (d'argent) **2.** (*a*) **paying back,** remboursement *m*/restitution *f* (d'un emprunt) (*b*) versement (d'argent à la banque, etc.); **paying-in slip,** bordereau *m* de versement/ de paiement; **paying-in book,** carnet *m* de versements (*c*) **paying off,** (*i*) liquidation *f*/règlement *m*/amortissement *m*/ remboursement *m* (d'une dette); purge *f* (d'une hypothèque) (*ii*) congédiement *m* (des ouvriers, etc.) (*d*) **paying out/up,** déboursement *m*; débours *m*.

payload, *n.* charge payante/charge commerciale/charge utile (d'un véhicule); *Av:* poids *m* utile.

payment, *n.* (*a*) paiement *m*/versement *m* (d'argent); **cash payment,** paiement (au) comptant/en argent comptant; **payment in advance/advance payment,** paiement par anticipation/anticipé; **down payment,** acompte *m*/arrhes *fpl*/provision *f*; **monthly paiements,** mensualités *f*(*pl*); **on payment of £100,** contre paiement de £100/moyennant (le paiement de) £100; **payment by cheque,** paiement par chèque; **payment in cash,** paiement en espèces/en numéraire; **payment in full,** paiement intégral; **payment in kind,** paiement en nature; **in easy payments,** avec facilités de paiement; *StExch:* **payment in full on allotment,** libération *f* (d'actions) à la répartition; **payment on account,** paiement partiel; versement/acompte/provision/arrhes; **payment on delivery,** livraison *f* contre remboursement *m*; **subject to payment,** à titre onéreux/moyennant paiement; **without payment,** à titre gracieux/à titre bénévole (*b*) paiement/règlement *m* (d'une

dette); remboursement *m* (d'un créancier); **deferment of payment,** délai *m* de paiement; **deferred payment,** paiement différé/retardé; **non payment,** défaut *m* de paiement; **payment by instalments,** paiement par versements/paiement échelonné; **payment of balance,** paiement pour solde; **payment of interest,** paiement des intérêts; **to authorize payment,** autoriser le paiement d'un compte (*c*) **to present a cheque for payment,** présenter un chèque à l'encaissement; **to stop payment of a cheque,** faire opposition à un chèque; **payment card,** carte *f* de débit (*d*) salaire *m*; **back payment,** rappel *m*/arrérage *m* de salaire; **payment by results,** salaire *m* au rendement.

payoff, *v.tr. & i.* **1.** congédier (des ouvriers, etc.) **2. to pay off the capital,** rembourser le capital **3. it will pay off in a few years,** ce sera rentable d'ici quelques années.

payoff, *n.* *NAm:* (*a*) paiement *m*/règlement *m* (*b*) **£40 000 payoff for company head,** indemnité *f* de £40 000 offerte au président de la société (*c*) (*return*) rendement *m*.

pay out[1], *n.* *NAm:* récupération *f* (d'un investissement).

pay out[2], *v.tr. & i.* payer/débourser/verser.

payout, *n.* *Ins:* remboursement *m*.

payroll, *n.* livre *m* de paie/registre *m* des salaires; **to be on the payroll,** faire partie du personnel.

pay up, *v.tr. & i.* payer; se libérer (de ses dettes, etc.); **paid up member,** membre *m* (d'un club, etc.) qui a payé/qui est à jour de sa cotisation.

peak, *n.* **peak hours,** heures de pointe; **peak output,** (niveau) record (*m*) de production; **peak year,** année *f* record; **production was at its peak,** la production était à son maximum.

peak out, *v.i.* atteindre son (prix, niveau) maximum.

peculation, *n.* détournement *m* de fonds (*esp* par un fonctionnaire).

pecuniary, *a.* pécuniaire; **pecuniary diffi-**

culties, embarras financiers; ennuis *m* d'argent; *Jur:* **for pecuniary gain,** dans un but lucratif; **pecuniary offence,** délit puni d'une amende.

pedlar, *n.* colporteur *m.*

peg[1], *n.* **1.** **off the peg clothes,** vêtements *m* de confection; le prêt-à-porter; **to buy a dress off the peg,** acheter une robe de confection **2.** *Fin:* **crawling/sliding peg,** parité *f* à crémaillère/parité rampante/taux *m* de change rampant/flottant.

peg[2], *v.tr.* **1.** **to peg (back) prices,** bloquer les prix; **pegged prices,** prix *m* de soutien **2.** *StExch: Fin:* **to peg the market,** stabiliser le marché (en achetant et en vendant); maintenir le marché ferme; **to peg the exchanges,** maintenir le cours du change.

pegging, *n.* *StExch: Fin:* stabilisation *f* (du marché, etc.); blocage *m* (de la livre sterling, des prix, etc.); soutien *m* des prix; **pegging the exchanges,** maintien *m* du cours du change.

pen, *n.* stylo *m; Cmptr:* **light pen,** photostyle *m.*

penalty, *n.* (*a*) amende *f* (pour retard de livraison, etc.) (*b*) *Adm:* pénalité *f*/sanction (pénale); (*in contract*) **penalty clause,** clause pénale (de dommages-intérêts); **penalty for non-performance of contract,** dédit *m.*

pence, *n.pl. see* **penny.**

pending, 1. *a.* (*a*) (négociations) en cours; *Jur:* (affaire) en instance; **patent pending,** demande de brevet déposée (*b*) **pending tray,** travail en attente/en souffrance **2.** *prep.* **pending your decision,** en attendant votre décision.

penetrate, *v.tr.* pénétrer (des marchés étrangers, etc.).

penny, *n.* **1.** *pl.* **pence** (*abbr.* **p**) (*coin = 1/100th of £1*) **(new) penny,** penny *m*; **a ten pence piece/a ten p piece,** une pièce de dix pence; **a five pence stamp,** un timbre de 5 pence; (*value*) **I paid 60 pence for it,** je l'ai payé 60 pence; **penny shares,** actions d'une

valeur de moins d'une livre sterling **2.** *NAm: F:* (*coin*) *pl.* **pennies,** cent *m*; **penny stock,** actions (spéculatives) valant moins d'un dollar (américain).

pension, *n.* pension *f*; **state/Government pension,** pension de l'État; **disability pension,** pension d'invalidité; **old-age pension,** pension/retraite *f* de vieillesse (*versée aux personnes âgées de plus de 80 ans*); **retirement pension,** pension de retraite; **widow's pension,** pension de veuve; **pension plan/scheme,** régime *m* de retraite; **contributory pension plan,** régime de retraite financé par les cotisations patronales et ouvrières; **earnings-related pension (plan),** (régime de) retraite indexée sur le revenu; (*between 1961 & 1975*) **graduated pension scheme,** = régime obligatoire de retraites complémentaires; **deferred/preserved pension,** = indemnité *f* de pré-retraite; **executive pension,** retraite des cadres; **guaranteed minimum pension (GMP),** retraite minimum; **loanback pension,** retraite par capitalisation; **occupational pension scheme,** fonds *mpl* de retraite maison/d'entreprise/de groupe; **private pension,** retraite complémentaire; **self-employed pension,** = régime de retraite des artisans, commerçants et professions libérales; **pension funds,** caisses *fpl* de retraite; **to retire on a pension,** prendre sa retraite; **to commute a pension,** liquider une pension.

pensionable, *a.* **1.** (*of pers.*) qui a droit à une pension/à sa retraite **2.** (*injury, etc.*) qui donne droit à une pension; **pensionable age,** âge *m* de la mise à la retraite **3.** (emploi) donnant droit à une pension.

pensioner, *n.* bénéficiaire *mf* d'une pension; **old age pensioner (OAP),** retraité, -ée.

pensioning, *n.* **pensioning (off),** mise *f* à la retraite.

pension off, *v.tr.* **to pension s.o. off,** mettre qn à la retraite.

peppercorn, *n.* **peppercorn rent,** loyer nominal.

per, *prep.* (*a*) par; *Jur:* **per pro,** par procuration (*b*) **as per invoice,** suivant facture; selon/d'après facture; **as per sample,** conformément à l'échantillon; **per contra,** par contre; **credited as per contra,** crédité ci-contre (*c*) **ten francs per kilo,** dix francs le kilo; **100 km per hour,** 100 kilomètres à l'heure/100 kilomètres-heure/100 Km/h; **per cent,** pour cent; **seven per cent interest,** intérêt de sept pour cent (*d*) **per annum/ per year,** par an; **how much do you earn per annum?** quel est votre salaire annuel? **to receive so much per year,** recevoir tant par an; **per week,** par semaine; **per day/per diem,** par jour; *NAm:* **the per diem,** le salaire journalier; **per capita,** par tête/par habitant/par personne; **per capita income/ income per capita,** salaire individuel (*e*) **per-share earnings,** bénéfices *m* par action.

percentage, *n.* pourcentage *m*; **percentage of profit,** pourcentage de bénéfices; **directors' percentage of profits,** tantième *m*; **rates three percentage points higher than they are today,** taux supérieur/plus élevé de 3% au taux d'aujourd'hui.

percentile, *n. Stat:* centile *m*.

perfecting, *n.* **perfecting the sight,** compléter un billet à ordre.

performance, *n.* **1.** exécution *f* (d'un contrat); **not to make specific performance of a contract,** ne pas exécuter un contrat à la lettre; **performance bond,** garantie *f* de bonne fin **2.** (*i*) fonctionnement *m*/marche *f* (d'une machine) (*ii*) rendement *m*/ performance *f* (d'un appareil, etc.); **performance rating,** rendement effectif; **performance fund,** fonds *m* (à rendement) garanti; **good profit performance,** résultats performants **3.** rendement/résultat *m*; **performance against objectives,** réalisations comparées aux projets; **performance appraisal/evaluation,** évaluation *f* du rendement; **job performance,** rendement au travail; **earnings performance,** rentabilité *f*.

peril, *n. MIns:* **peril(s) of the sea,** fortune *f* de mer; risque(s) *m(pl)* de mer.

period, *n.* **1.** période *f*; durée *f*; délai *m*; **for a period of three months/for a three months' period/for a three-month period,** pendant (une période de) trois mois; **to discharge a liability within the agreed period,** liquider une créance dans les délais convenus; **base period,** période de référence; *Bank:* **deposit for a fixed period,** dépôt *m* à terme fixe **2. accounting period,** exercice *m*; **period under review,** exercice écoulé.

periodical, **1.** *a.* périodique **2.** *n.* périodique *m*/publication *f* périodique; journal *m*.

peripheral, *a. & n. Cmptr:* périphérique (*m*); **peripheral equipment/unit,** unité *f* périphérique.

perishable, **1.** *a.* périssable; sujet à s'altérer/à se détériorer; *Nau:* **perishable cargo,** denrées *f* périssables; chargement *m* périssable **2.** *n.pl.* **perishables,** denrées périssables.

perks, *n.pl.* avantages sociaux; privilèges *mpl.*

permanency, *n.* emploi permanent.

permanent, *a.* (*a*) permanent; **permanent job,** situation permanente; **to be on the permanent staff (of a firm),** avoir un emploi permanent/être titulaire d'un poste (*b*) *Fin:* **permanent assets,** actif immobilisé; capital immobilisé.

permission, *n.* permission *f*; autorisation *f*; **written permission,** autorisation écrite; *StExch:* **permission to deal,** visa *m* (*de la* COB).

permit, *n.* **1.** permis *m*; permission *f*/autorisation *f*; **building permit,** permis de construire; **work permit,** permis de travail **2.** *Cust:* acquit-à-caution *m*; passavant *m*.

perpetual, **1.** *a.* perpétuel/à vie; **perpetual loans,** emprunts perpétuels; **perpetual inventory,** inventaire permanent **2.** *npl* **subordinated perpetuals,** titres subordonnés à durée indéterminée/TSDI.

perquisites, *n.pl.* = **perks.**

person, *n.* personne *f*; individu *m*; **private**

person, (simple) particulier *m*; **legal person,** personne morale; **natural person,** personne physique; **to act through a third person,** passer par une tierce personne/par personne interposée; **the persons concerned,** les intéressés; **person named,** accrédité, ée; **policy to a named person,** police nominative; **to be delivered to the addressee in person,** à remettre en main(s) propre(s); *Tel: NAm:* **person-to-person call,** appel *m* avec préavis.

personal, *a. Cust:* **articles for personal use/personal effects,** effets usagers/effets personnels; *Bank:* **personal account,** compte (en banque) personnel/particulier; *Fin:* **personal income,** revenu personnel; **personal share,** action nominative; *Com:* **personal selling,** vente directe au consommateur; *Ins:* **personal accident insurance,** assurance *f* contre les accidents corporels/contre les accidents à personnes; *Adm: (on letter)* **personal,** personnel; **personal assistant (PA),** secrétaire particulier, -ière; assistant, -ante; *Tel:* **personal call,** appel *m* avec préavis.

personalize, *v.tr.* personnaliser; **personalized sales techniques,** publicité personnalisée; **personalized cheque,** chèque personnalisé.

personalty, *n. Jur:* biens *m* meubles/effets mobiliers; **to convert realty into personalty,** ameublir un bien; **conversion of realty into personalty,** ameublissement *m* d'un bien.

personnel, *n. Ind: etc:* personnel *m*; **personnel department,** service *m*/direction *f* du personnel; **personnel manager/officer,** directeur *m*/chef *m* du personnel; **personnel management,** direction *f*/administration *f*/gestion *f* du personnel; **personnel rating,** appréciation *f* du personnel.

pertinent, *a.* **pertinent cost,** coût approprié.

petition, *n.* **petition in bankruptcy,** (*i*) requête *f* des créanciers (*ii*) requête du négociant insolvable; **to file a petition in bankruptcy,** déposer son bilan.

petrocurrency, *n.* pétromonnaies *fpl.*

petrodollar, *n.* pétrodollar *m.*

petroleum, *n.* pétrole *m*; **crude petroleum,** pétrole brut/le brut; **refined petroleum,** pétrole raffiné; **the petroleum industry,** l'industrie pétrolière/du pétrole; **petroleum products,** produits pétroliers.

petties, *npl* (*abbr. petty cash*) menues dépenses.

petty, *a.* **petty cash,** petite caisse; menue monnaie; **petty cash book,** livre *m* de petite caisse; **petty expenses,** menues dépenses.

petty-cash, *v.t.r.* faire passer sur la caisse courante.

phase, *n.* phase *f.*

phase in, *v.tr.* adopter/introduire progressivement (de nouvelles méthodes, etc.); mettre en place progressivement (de nouvelles installations, etc.).

phase out, *v.tr.* éliminer progressivement (de vieilles méthodes, etc.); éliminer/remplacer progressivement (de vieux équipements, etc.).

phone[1], *n. F:* téléphone *m*; **to be on the phone,** (*i*) être/parler au téléphone (*ii*) être abonné au téléphone; **to answer the phone,** répondre au téléphone; **to speak to s.o. on the phone,** parler à qn au téléphone; **phone book,** annuaire *m* téléphonique/du téléphone; **phone box,** cabine *f* téléphonique; **phone call,** appel *m* (téléphonique)/coup *m* de téléphone/coup de fil.

phone[2], *v.tr. & i.* **to phone s.o.,** téléphoner à qn/appeler qn au téléphone/donner un coup de fil à qn; **I'll phone you,** je vous téléphonerai; **to phone for sth.,** demander qch./faire venir qch. par téléphone; **to phone for a taxi,** appeler un taxi; **to phone a piece of news,** téléphoner une nouvelle.

phonecard, *n.* Télécarte *f* (*Rtm:*).

photocopier, *n.* photocopieur *m*/photocopieuse *f*/copieur *m.*

photocopy[1], *n.* photocopie *f.*

photocopy[2], *v.tr.* photocopier.

photostat[1], *n.* photostat (copy), photostat *m.*

photostat[2], *v.tr. & i.* faire un photostat.

physical, *a.* physique; matériel; *NAm:* **physical inventory**, inventaire *m* (du matériel, des marchandises, etc.).

picket[1], *n. Ind: etc:* **flying pickets**, piquets *mpl* de grève volants; **strike pickets/picket line**, piquets de grève/de grévistes.

picket[2], *v.tr.* **to picket a factory**, faire le piquet de grève; se tenir en faction devant une usine (pour en interdire l'accès); **the workers are picketing the factory**, les ouvriers font le piquet de grève devant l'usine.

picketing, *n. Ind: etc:* **there is no picketing**, il n'y a pas de piquets de grève (en faction); **secondary picketing**, piquet *m* de grève devant une entreprise étrangère au conflit.

pick up, *v.i.* **business is picking up**, les affaires *f* reprennent; **prices are picking up**, les cours *m* reprennent.

piece, *n.* pièce *f* (de drap, etc.); **to sell sth. by the piece**, vendre qch. à la pièce; **piece of land**, terrain *m*; **piece of news**, nouvelle *f*; **piece of information**, renseignement *m*; **piece of the action**, participation *f* aux activités; *Tex:* **piece goods**, marchandises *f/* tissus *m* à la pièce; **piece rate**, salaire *m* à la pièce/aux pièces; **to be paid piece rates/** *esp. NAm:* **by the piece**, être payé à la pièce.

piecework, *n.* travail *m* (rémunéré) à la pièce/aux pièces; travail à la tâche.

pie-chart, *n.* graphique *m* rond à secteurs; *F:* camembert *m.*

pigeonhole, *n.* case *f/*casier *m* (pour le courrier).

pill, *n.* (*used in hostile takeover bid*) **poison pill**, pilule empoisonnée.

pilot, *n.* **pilot factory/pilot plant**, usine *f* pilote; installation *f* d'essai; **pilot project**, projet *m* pilote; **pilot series/pilot run**, présérie *f.*

PIN, *n.* **PIN (number)** (*Personal Identification Number*) code personnel.

pint, *n. Meas:* (*i*) pinte *f* = 0,568 litre; *FrC:* chopine *f* (*ii*) *NAm:* = 0,473 litre; **imperial pint**, pinte légale.

pioneer[1], *n.* pionnier *m*; **pioneer products**, innovations *f.*

pioneer[2], *v.i.* innover.

pipeline, *n.* (*a*) pipeline *f/*pipe-line *f*; (*for oil*) oléoduc *m*; (*for gas*) gazoduc *m* (*b*) *F:* **project in the pipeline**, projet *m* d'avenir.

pit, *n. StExch:* corbeille *f.*

pitch, *n.* (*a*) **sales pitch**, baratin *m* de vendeur (*b*) territoire *m* (de vente).

placard, *n.* écriteau *m*; affiche *f/*placard *m.*

place[1], *n. Fin: Bank:* **place of payment**, lieu *m* de paiement.

place[2], *v.tr.* **1.** placer/mettre; **to place an amount (of money) to s.o.'s credit**, verser une somme au crédit de qn; **to place goods**, placer/vendre des marchandises; **difficult to place**, de vente/d'écoulement difficile; **to place an order (for goods)**, placer/passer une commande; **to place a loan**, placer/négocier un emprunt; **to place £10 000 in bonds**, investir £10 000/faire un placement de £10 000 en obligations; **to place a contract**, adjuger/concéder un contrat **2.** trouver un emploi à (qn); **I could place her as a typist**, je pourrais lui trouver un travail de dactylo.

placement, *n.* (*private*) placement privé; (*public*) syndication *f.*

placing, *n.* (*a*) émission *f/*titres réservés/titres en placement privé (*b*) placement *m/*écoulement *m/*vente *f* (de marchandises); placement (d'un emprunt); passation *f* (d'ordre, de commande).

plaintiff, *n.* demandeur, -eresse; plaignant, -ante; requérant, -ante.

plan[1], *n.* plan *m/*projet *m/*programme *m*; **general plan**, plan d'ensemble; **action plan**, plan d'action; *Fin:* **investment plan**,

plan d'investissement; **savings plan,** plan (d')épargne; *PolEc:* **economic plan,** plan économique; **five-year plan,** plan quinquennal; *StExch:* **stock option plan/stock purchase plan,** plan d'options sur titres.

plan², *v.tr. PolEc:* planifier (la production, etc.).

planned, *a. PolEc:* planifié; **planned economy,** économie dirigée/planifiée; dirigisme *m* économique; **planned maintenance,** entretien *m* systématique.

planner, *n. PolEc:* planificateur, -trice; **economic planner,** conjoncturiste *mf;* **town planner,** urbaniste *mf.*

planning, *n.* **1. town planning,** urbanisme *m;* aménagement *m* des villes; **planning permission,** = permis *m* de construire **2.** *PolEc: etc:* dirigisme *m/*planification *f/* planning *m;* **economic planning,** planification économique **3.** *Ind:* **company/corporate planning,** planification dans l'entreprise; **long-term planning,** planification à long terme; **short-term planning,** planification à court terme; **planning and allocation of resources,** estimation *f* des besoins et répartition *f* des moyens; **planning, programming and budgeting system (PPBS),** rationalisation *f* des choix budgétaires (RCB); **planning department,** service *m* planning/bureau *m* de planning; **product planning,** plan de développement des produits; **sales planning,** planification/planning des ventes.

plant, *n. Ind:* (*a*) appareil(s) *m(pl)/*outillage *m;* équipement (industriel)/matériel (industriel); **plant-hire,** location *f* d'équipement; **to equip with plant,** outiller (*b*) usine *f;* **plant capacity,** capacité *f* de l'usine; **plant layout,** schéma *m* d'installation; **plant manager,** directeur *m* d'usine.

plastic, *a. & n. F:* **plastic (money),** carte(s) *f(pl)* bancaire(s).

plead, *v.tr. & i. Jur:* plaider (une cause).

pledge¹, *n.* gage *m/*nantissement *m;* **pledge holder,** détenteur, -trice, de gage(s);

unredeemed pledge, gage non retiré; **to borrow on pledge,** emprunter sur gage; **to give/put sth. in pledge,** donner/mettre qch. en gage; **to hold in pledge,** (dé)tenir en gage/en nantissement; **to realize a pledge,** réaliser un gage; **to redeem a pledge,** retirer un gage; **to set aside as a pledge,** affecter en gage.

pledge², *v.tr.* donner/mettre (qch.) en gage; déposer (qch.) en gage/en nantissement/ en garantie; engager (qch.); **to pledge one's property,** engager/gager son bien; **to pledge securities,** déposer des titres en garantie/en nantissement; **pledged securities,** valeurs nanties.

pledgee, *n. Jur:* (créancier) gagiste *m;* prêteur, -euse sur gage(s).

pledger, *n.* emprunteur, -euse sur gage(s)/ gageur, -euse.

ploughback, *n.* bénéfices *mpl* réinvestis.

plough back, *v.tr.* **to plough back the profits into the company,** autofinancer la société; réinvestir/réinjecter les bénéfices dans la société.

ploughing back, *n.* **ploughing back of profits,** autofinancement *m;* affectation *f* de profits aux investissements.

plow back, *NAm:* = **plough back.**

plug¹, *n. F:* (*a*) *Publ: NAm:* ouvrage *m* qui se vend mal (*b*) réclame (tapageuse)/ battage *m.*

plug², *v.tr. F:* faire l'article/faire de la réclame/faire du battage pour (un produit, etc.).

plummet, *v.i.* (*of prices*) dégringoler; s'effondrer.

plunge, *v.i.* (*a*) *StExch:* risquer de grosses sommes (*b*) (*of prices*) dégringoler.

plunger, *n. StExch:* (spéculateur, -trice) risque-tout (*m inv*).

plus, 1. *prep.* plus; **purchase price plus brokerage,** le prix *m* d'achat plus le courtage **2.** *a.* (*a*) (*of quantity, number, etc.*) positif (*b*) **on the plus side of the**

account, à l'actif du compte; **plus or minus difference,** différence f en plus ou en moins **3.** *n.* avantage *m*/atout *m* **4.** *adv.* **she earns £16 000 plus,** elle reçoit un salaire de plus de £16 000.

poach, *v.i.* braconner sur les terres d'autrui; **he poached their new Director,** il est allé chercher leur nouveau directeur (pour le nommer chez lui).

pocket, *n.* **to be in pocket,** faire un bénéfice/ un gain; **to be £10 in pocket,** prendre un bénéfice de £10; gagner £10; **to be out of pocket (over a transaction),** être en perte; ne pas retrouver son argent; ne pas rentrer dans ses fonds; **to be £10 out of pocket,** essuyer une perte de £10/en être de sa poche pour £10.

point, *n.* **1.** (*a*) **point of arrival/of departure,** point *m* d'arrivée/point de départ; **loading/unloading point,** point de chargement/point de déchargement (*b*) **point-of-sale,** point/lieu *m* de vente; **point-of-sale material,** matériel *m* de publicité sur le lieu de vente/matériel PLV; **point-of-sale terminals,** terminaux-points de vente (*c*) **break-even point,** point mort/seuil *m* de rentabilité (*d*) **decimal point** = virgule f (*e*) *NAm:* **he is the point man,** il occupe la position clé **2.** *StExch:* (*of price*) **to decline/to lose one point,** baisser d'un point; **to gain/to rise one point,** gagner un point/ hausser d'un point; **basis point,** point de base; **silver-point,** silver-point *m*; **silver import point,** point d'entrée de l'argent/ silver-point d'entrée; **silver export point,** point de sortie de l'argent/silver-point de sortie.

policy[1], *n.* (*a*) politique f; ligne f de conduite; tactique f; **economic policy,** politique économique; **exchange policy,** politique en matière de change; **free trade policy,** politique de libre échange; **policy of deflation,** politique de déflation/politique déflationniste; **prices and incomes policy,** politique des prix et des salaires; **to adopt a policy,** adopter une ligne de conduite (*b*) **company policy,** politique de l'entreprise; **dividend policy,** politique de distribution; **policy statement,** rapport

annuel; **product policy,** politique de lancement d'un produit (sur le marché); **sales policy,** politique de vente; **our policy is to satisfy our customers,** nous avons pour politique de satisfaire nos clients.

policy[2], *n.* **(insurance) policy,** police f (d'assurance); **(fully) comprehensive/all-risks policy,** (police) omnium (*m*)/police tous risques; **business interruption policy,** assurance f de perte d'exploitation; **buyout policy,** caisse f/fonds *mpl*/régime *m*/police de retraite ouvert(e); **franchise policy,** assurance en franchise; **life insurance policy,** police d'assurance (sur la) vie; **joint policy,** police conjointe; **master/ general policy,** police générale; **standard policy,** police type; **valued policy,** assurance forfaitaire; **whole-of-life policy,** assurance-décès f; **policy for a specific amount,** police à forfait; **policy holder,** titulaire *mf*/détenteur, -trice d'une police d'assurance; assuré, -ée; **to draw up/make out a policy,** établir une police; **to take out a policy,** prendre une police/souscrire à une police (d'assurance); **marine insurance policy,** police maritime; **cargo policy,** police sur facultés; **floating policy,** police flottante; **open policy,** police d'abonnement/police ouverte; **hull/ship policy,** police sur corps; **time policy,** police à temps.

poll, *n.* **(public) opinion poll,** sondage *m* d'opinion (publique); **Gallup poll,** sondage Gallup; **to carry out a poll,** faire un sondage.

pool[1], *n.* (*a*) groupe *m* (de travail); pool *m*; **typing pool,** service général de dactylographie; central *m* dactylographique; pool de dactylos (*b*) groupement *m* (pour opérations en commun); syndicat *m* de placement/de répartition (de marchandises, de commandes, etc.); *Fin: Bank:* tour *m* de table; (*underwriting group*) syndicat de prise ferme/de garantie; **pool banks,** pool bancaire (*c*) *PolEc: etc:* fonds commun/*F:* pool.

pool[2], *v.tr.* (*a*) mettre en commun (ses capitaux, ses bénéfices, etc.); grouper (ses moyens) (*b*) grouper (les commandes).

pooling, *n.* mise *f* en commun (de fonds, etc.); groupement *m* (des intérêts, des commandes, etc.); **pooling arrangements,** dispositions *fpl* de mise en commun (des ressources); **pooling of interests (method),** (méthode) de groupement/de fusion/de mise en commun des intérêts (de deux sociétés).

poor, *a.* pauvre; **poor quality,** qualité inférieure; mauvaise qualité; **poor quality goods,** *F:* camelote *f*; **it's of poor quality,** c'est de la camelote.

popular, *a.* populaire/à la mode/goûté du public; **popular prices,** prix *m* à la portée de tous.

popularity, *n.* popularité *f*; succès *m* (d'un produit, etc.) auprès du (grand) public.

population, *n.* population *f;* **population statistics,** statistique(s) *f(pl)* démographique(s); **floating population,** population flottante; **the working/the active population,** la population active.

port, *n.* port *m*; **the port of London,** le port de Londres; **inland port,** port intérieur; **river port,** port fluvial; **in port,** au port; **to call at a port,** faire escale à un port; relâcher dans un port; **port of call,** port d'escale; **port authority,** autorité *f* portuaire; **port capacity,** capacité *f* portuaire; **port charge/dues,** droits *mpl* de port; **fishing port,** port de pêche; **commercial port,** port de commerce/port marchand; **free port,** port franc; **home port,** port d'attache; **oil port,** port pétrolier; **open port,** port ouvert.

portable, *a.* portatif; transportable; mobile; roulant; **portable typewriter,** machine à écrire portative.

porter, *n.* porteur *m* (de bagages, etc.); chasseur *m*/garçon *m* (d'hôtel); **bank porter,** garçon de recette.

porterage, *n.* 1. transport *m*/manutention *f*/factage *m* (de marchandises, de colis); **porterage facilities,** service *m* de porteurs 2. prix *m*/frais *mpl* de transport; factage.

portfolio, *n.* (*a*) cartable *m* (pour documents, etc.) (*b*) portefeuille *m* (d'assurances, etc.) (*c*) *Fin:* **investment portfolio,** portefeuille d'investissements; **discretionary portfolio,** portefeuille avec mandat; **indexed portfolio,** gestion indicielle/portefeuille indexé; **securities in portfolio,** valeurs *f* en portefeuille; **portfolio analysis,** analyse *f* de portefeuille; **portfolio insurance,** amélioration *f* du rendement d'un portefeuille; **portfolio management,** gestion *f* de portefeuille.

position, *n.* 1. *Post: Bank:* guichet *m*; **position closed,** guichet fermé 2. état *m*/situation *f*; **financial position,** situation financière; **the cash position is not good,** la situation de la caisse laisse à désirer; **what is the position of the firm?** quelle est la situation (financière) de cette maison? 3. **key position,** position *f* clé; **position of trust,** poste *m* de confiance 4. *StExch:* **to close a position,** liquider/déboucler/couvrir une position; **bear/bull position,** position à la baisse/à la hausse; **open position,** position ouverte/nue.

possession, *n.* possession *f*/jouissance *f* (**of,** de); **to take possession of an estate,** entrer en possession/avoir la jouissance d'un bien; *Jur:* **actual possession,** possession effective; **adverse possession,** possession de fait; **vacant possession,** libre possession (d'un immeuble); **house to let with vacant possession,** maison *f* à louer avec jouissance immédiate/avec possession immédiate/clefs en main.

possessor, *n.* propriétaire *mf*; *Jur:* possesseur *m*.

post[1], *v.tr.* 1. **to post (up),** placarder; coller (des affiches, etc.); afficher (un avis, etc.); **the market rates are posted (up),** les cours sont affichés; **posted price,** prix affiché 2. *MIns:* porter (un navire) disparu 3. *NAm:* **to post an entry,** passer une écriture.

post[2], *n.* (*a*) courrier *m*; **by return of post,** par retour du courrier; **the first post,** la première distribution (*b*) la poste; **the Post Office** = les Postes et Télécommunications *f*; **to send sth. by post,** envoyer qch. par la poste (*c*) **post office,**

(bureau *m* de) poste; **Post Office (PO)** = Postes et Télécommunications (P et T); **sub post office,** bureau *m* auxiliaire (des postes); bureau de quartier; **post office clerk,** employé, -ée des postes; **post office directory,** annuaire *m* des postes; **post office box (PO Box),** boîte postale (BP)/*FrC:* case postale.

post[3], *n.* poste *m*/emploi *m*; **the post is still vacant,** vous n'avons pas encore pourvu à cet emploi.

post[4], *v.tr.* (*a*) **to post a letter,** mettre une lettre à la poste/poster une lettre; **I'll post it to you,** je vous l'enverrai par la poste (*b*) *Book-k:* **to post (up) the books,** passer les écritures *f*; **to post an entry,** passer écriture d'un article; **to post an item in the ledger/to post up an item,** porter/inscrire/passer/reporter/rapporter/transcrire un article au grand(-)livre; **to post up the ledger,** arrêter le grand(-)livre; mettre le grand(-)livre à jour.

postage, *n.* affranchissement *m*/port *m*; tarif postal (d'une lettre, etc.); **postage stamp,** timbre-poste *m*; (*on insufficiently stamped letter*) **additional postage,** surtaxe (postale); **postage included,** port compris; **postage paid,** affranchi; port payé/port perçu; **postage free,** franc de port/franco *inv.*

postal, *a.* postal; **postal authorities,** l'Administration *f* des Postes; **postal charges,** frais *mpl* d'envoi/frais de port (d'une lettre, etc.); **postal money,** monnaie postale; **postal order,** mandat-poste *m*; **postal rates,** tarifs *mpl* postaux; **postal receipt,** récépissé postal; **postal services,** les services postaux/les Postes *f* et Télécommunications *f*; les postes; **postal transfer,** virement postal; **postal transfer form,** mandat *m* de virement.

post-bang, *n.* événements *mpl* qui ont eu lieu après le big bang d'octobre 1986.

postcard, *n.* carte postale.

postcode, *n.* code postal.

postdate, *v.tr.* postdater (un chèque, un document).

poster, *n.* affiche murale; placard *m* (de publicité); poster *m*.

poste restante, *n.* poste restante.

post free, *adv.* franc de port/sans frais de poste.

posting, *n.* (*a*) envoi *m* (d'une lettre) par la poste; mise *f* à la poste (d'une lettre); **certificate of posting,** récépissé postal (*b*) *Book-k:* passation *f* (d'écritures); report *m*/entrée *f* (au grand(-)livre); transcription *f* (du journal) (*c*) affichage *m* (de prix, etc.).

post-paid, *a.* affranchi; port payé.

postpone, *v.tr.* remettre/ajourner/renvoyer à plus tard/reporter à plus tard/différer/reculer (un départ, un projet, etc.); **to postpone a payment,** différer un paiement.

postponement, *n.* remise *f* à plus tard; ajournement *m* (d'une réunion, d'une cause); renvoi *m* (d'une cause); sursis *m*.

potential, **1.** *a.* **potential buyer/customer,** acheteur/client éventuel; **potential manager** = futur cadre **2.** *n.* potentiel *m*; **industrial potential,** potentiel industriel; **growth potential,** potentiel de croissance; **market potential,** potentiel du marché; **sales potential,** potentiel de vente.

pound, *n.* **1.** (*poids*) livre *f* (= 453,6 grammes); **to sell sth. by the pound,** vendre qch. à la livre; **40 pence a pound,** quarante pence la livre **2.** (*monnaie*) **pound (sterling),** livre *f* (sterling); **pound note,** billet *m*/coupure *f* d'une livre; **five pound note (£5),** billet de cinq livres (£5).

poundage, *n.* **1.** (droit *m* de) commission *f*; remise *f* de tant par livre (sterling) **2.** taux *m* de tant par livre (de poids).

poverty, *n.* **poverty line,** seuil *m* de pauvreté.

power, *n.* **1.** pouvoir *m*; **bargaining power,** pouvoir de négociation; **earning power,** capacité *f* bénéficiaire; **purchasing power,** pouvoir d'achat; **power lunch,** déjeuner d'affaires important **2.** (*a*) pouvoir/influence *f*/autorité *f*; **executive power,**

pouvoir exécutif; **power of attorney,** procuration *f* (*b*) **to act with full powers,** agir de pleine autorité **3. power station,** centrale *f* électrique.

practice, *n.* **1.** (*a*) habitude *f*/coutume *f*/usage *m*; **trade practices,** usages commerciaux (*b*) *Ind:* technique *f*/méthodes *fpl*; **shop practice,** technique d'atelier; **management practices,** procédures *f* de gestion **2.** clientèle *f* **3.** (*a*) (*of doctor, lawyer, etc.*) **to be in practice,** exercer (*b*) étude *f* (d'un avocat); cabinet *m* (d'un médecin); **private practice,** cabinet (médical) privé.

pre-acquisition, *n.* acquisition faite au préalable.

precinct, *n.* **shopping precinct,** (*i*) centre commercial (*ii*) galerie marchande; **pedestrian precinct,** (*i*) rue piétonnière (*ii*) aire piétonnière.

predecessor, *n.* prédécesseur *m*.

pre-empt, *v.tr.* acheter/acquérir (une propriété, un monopole, etc.) par priorité.

pre-emption, *n. Jur:* (droit *m* de) préemption *f*.

pre-emptive, *a.* **pre-emptive right,** droit *m* de préemption.

pre-emptor, *n.* acquéreur, -euse (en vertu d'un droit de préemption).

preference, *n.* (*a*) préférence *f* (*b*) *PolEc:* tarif *m*/régime *m* de faveur; traitement préférentiel; préférence; **imports entitled to preference,** importations *f* ayant droit à un régime de faveur (*c*) droit *m* de priorité; *Fin:* **preference shares,** actions à dividende prioritaire/préférentiel; actions préférentielles; actions de premier rang; **liquidity preference,** préférence pour la liquidité; *Jur:* **preference clause,** pacte *m* de préférence.

preferential, *a.* **1.** (*a*) (traitement, etc.) préférentiel; **preferential price,** prix *m* de faveur (*b*) *Cust:* **preferential duty,** préférences *fpl* douanières; **preferential tariff,** tarif préférentiel/de faveur **2.** *Jur:* **prefer-**

ential claim/preferential right, droit *m* de préférence/préférentiel; privilège *m*; **creditor's preferential claim,** droit de préférence/privilège du créancier; créance privilégiée; **preferential creditor,** créancier privilégié; **preferential debt,** créance privilégiée; **preferential dividend,** dividende privilégié/dividende de priorité.

preferred, *a. Fin:* **preferred creditors,** créanciers privilégiés; **preferred (convertible) stock,** actions préférentielles (convertibles).

prefinancing, *n.* préfinancement *m*; **prefinancing of export transactions,** (crédits de) préfinancement d'exportations.

pre-funding, *n. US:* préfinancement *m*/ financement anticipé.

prejudice[1], *n.* préjudice *m*/tort *m*/ dommage *m*; **without prejudice to any claim they may otherwise have,** sans préjudice pour tous les droits et recours qu'ils pourraient avoir; **without prejudice,** sous toutes réserves; **to the prejudice of ...,** au préjudice de ....

prejudice[2], *v.tr.* porter préjudice (à qn); compromettre.

preliminary, *a.* préliminaire; **preliminary scheme,** avant-projet *m*.

premises, *n.pl.* local *m*/immeuble *m*; **business premises,** locaux commerciaux; **shop premises,** (locaux à l'usage de) magasin(s) *m(pl)*; **drinks to be consumed on the premises,** boissons à consommer sur place; **off the premises,** hors de l'établissement.

premium, *n.* **1.** prime *f*/prix *m*/récompense *f*; *Ind:* **premium bonus,** prime de rendement **2.** (*a*) **(insurance) premium,** prime (d'assurance); **additional/extra premium,** surprime *f*; **annual premium,** prime annuelle; **low-premium insurance,** assurance *f* à prime réduite; **risk premium,** prime de risque (*b*) reprise locative/ redevance *f* (à payer au début d'un bail); **flat to let, no premium,** appartement *m* à louer sans reprise **3.** *Fin:* (*a*) **(exchange) premium,** agio *m*; prix du change; **dollar**

premium, prime sur le dollar; **premium on gold,** agio sur l'or; **the (quoted) premium,** le report (*b*) *StExch:* **bond premium,** prime d'émission (d'obligations); **issue premium,** prime d'émission; **share premium,** prime d'émission; **to issue shares at a premium,** émettre des actions au-dessus du pair/de leur valeur nominale; **to sell at a premium,** vendre à prime/à bénéfice; **premium on redemption,** prime de remboursement; **premium (savings) bonds,** obligations *f* à primes (*c*) **antiques are at a premium,** les antiquités (*i*) sont très recherchées (*ii*) se vendent à prix d'or **4. premium grade petrol** = supercarburant *m/F:* super *m.*

prepack, prepackage, *v.tr.* conditionner; emballer.

prepaid, *a.* payé d'avance/prépayé; (*of letter, etc.*) affranchi; **carriage prepaid,** (*i*) port payé; payé au départ (*ii*) franc de port/franco *inv;* **prepaid answer/reply prepaid,** réponse payée/prépayée.

prepay, *v.tr.* payer/régler (qch.) d'avance; prépayer; affranchir (une lettre, etc.).

prepayment, *n.* paiement *m* d'avance; paiement par anticipation; affranchissement *m* (d'une lettre, etc.).

prerequisite, *n.* condition *f* préalable.

present[1], *a.* actuel; d'aujourd'hui; **the present year,** l'année courante; **present value,** valeur actuelle; **present capital,** capital appelé.

present[2], *v.tr.* présenter; **to present a bill for payment,** présenter un billet à l'encaissement; **to present a bill for acceptance,** présenter une traite à l'acceptation.

presentation, *n.* présentation *f;* **cheque payable on presentation,** chèque *m* payable à présentation/à vue; **payable on presentation of the coupon,** payable contre remise du coupon.

presentment, *n.* **presentment of a bill (for acceptance),** présentation *f* d'une traite à l'acceptation.

preservative, *n.* agent conservateur/de conservation; **without artificial colour or preservatives,** sans colorant ni conservateur.

preside, *v.i.* (*a*) **to preside at/over a meeting,** présider une réunion (*b*) exercer les fonctions de président.

president, *n. NAm:* président directeur général (d'une société anonyme).

press, *n.* (*a*) **to pass (a book) for press,** donner le bon à tirer (*b*) *Mkt:* **press kit/pack,** dossier *m* de presse; **press office,** service *m* de presse.

press-button, *n.* **press-button industry,** industrie entièrement automatisée.

pressure, *n.* pression *f;* **financial pressure,** embarras financiers; **pressure group,** groupe *m* de pression; **copper prices came under renewed pressure,** nouvelle baisse/faiblesse des cours du cuivre.

prestige, *n.* prestige *m;* **prestige advertising,** publicité *f* de prestige.

prestocking, *n.* préstockage *m.*

pre-tax, *a.* **pre-tax profit,** bénéfice brut/avant impôt(s).

prevailing, *a.* **prevailing economic climate,** climat *m* économique actuel.

preventive, *a.* préventif; **preventive maintenance,** entretien préventif; **preventive measures,** mesures préventives/de précaution.

previous, *a.* antérieur; préalable; **previous year,** année précédente; **without previous notice,** sans avis préalable/sans préavis.

price[1], *n.* (*a*) prix *m;* **actual price,** prix réel; **administered price,** prix imposé; **agreed price,** prix convenu; **he paid the asking price,** il a payé le prix demandé; **the asking price of this house is too high,** le prix qu'on demande pour cette maison est trop élevé; **attractive price,** prix intéressant; **average price,** prix moyen; **bargain price,** prix exceptionnel/de solde; **basic price,** prix initial; **cash price,** prix (au) comptant; **catalogue price,** prix public/prix (de) catalogue/prix fort (de vente); **ceiling price,** prix plafond; **competitive price,** prix compétitif; **cost price,** prix coûtant/prix de revient; **current price,** prix actuel/courant/pratiqué; **cut price,** prix de rabais; **direct price,** prix de gros; **discount price,** prix de rabais; **firm price/steady price,** prix ferme; **fixed price,** prix fixe/prix forfaitaire; forfait *m*; **floor price,** prix plancher; **full price,** prix fort; *Rail: Th: etc:* **half price,** demi-place *f*; demitarif *m*; **children travel at half price,** les enfants paient demi-tarif; **to sell sth. at half price,** vendre qch. à moitié prix; **high price,** prix élevé; **highest price,** prix maximum; **inclusive price,** prix tout compris/tous frais compris; **list price,** prix (de) catalogue/prix public; **low price,** bas prix; **at a low price,** à bas prix/à un prix avantageux; **lowest price/rock bottom price,** le prix le plus bas/le dernier prix; **manufacturer's price,** prix de fabrique; **manufacturer's recommended price (MRP),** prix conseillé/recommandé; **marked price,** prix marqué; **moderate price,** prix modique/modéré; **net(t) price,** prix net; **purchase price,** prix d'achat; prix coûtant; **recommended retail price (RRP),** prix recommandé/conseillé; **at a reduced price,** à prix réduit/au rabais; **retail price,** prix de détail; **retail price maintenance (RPM),** prix imposé; **sell price,** prix (du) comptant; **selling price,** prix de vente; **standard price,** prix officiel/prix taxé; **sticker price,** prix à la vente/prix affiché; *EEC:* **target price/average price,** prix d'équilibre/cours *m* pivot; *EEC:* **threshold price,** prix du seuil; **trade price,** prix de demi-gros; **wholesale price,** prix de gros; **price control,** contrôle *m* des prix; **price cutting/slashing,** forte réduction des prix; **price increase,** hausse *f* de prix; **hidden price increase,** hausse de prix déguisée; **price index,** indice des prix; **price level,** niveau *m* des prix; **(current) price list,** tarif *m*; **price mechanism/system,** régime *m* des prix; **price range,** échelle *f*/éventail *m* des prix; **price regulation,** réglementation *f* des prix; **price war,** guerre *f* des prix; **what price is that book?** combien coûte ce livre? quel est le prix de ce livre? **what price did you pay for it?** combien cela vous a-t-il coûté? combien l'avez-vous payé? **to increase in price,** augmenter de prix; **to push up prices,** faire monter les prix; **to mark up/mark down prices,** augmenter/baisser les prix; **to make a (special) price,** faire un prix (de faveur); **to quote/to name a price,** fixer un prix (*b*) *Bank: Fin:* **price of money,** loyer *m*/prix de l'argent; **price ring,** monopole *m* des prix (*c*) *StExch:* **choice price,** prix d'équilibre/prix de marché; **closing price,** cours *m* de fermeture; **exercise price/striking price,** cours de base; prix d'exercise; **fine price,** prix concurrenciel/marge étroite; **forward price,** prix à terme; **grant price,** prix d'exercice d'une stock-option; **market price,** cours du marché/de la Bourse; **market price list,** mercuriale *f*; **at current market price,** suivant le cours du marché; **opening price,** (*i*) cours d'introduction (*ii*) cours d'ouverture; **probate price,** = prix moyen; **put and call price,** cours de l'option; **bid price,** cours acheteur/cours demandé; **offer price,** cours vendeur/cours offert; **price differential,** écart *m* des prix; **price earnings ratio (PER),** taux de capitalisation des bénéfices/rapport *m* cours-bénéfice/price earning ratio/PER; **price for the account,** cours à terme; **price of option/option price,** cours de la prime; **spot price,** cours du comptant; **slump in prices,** effondrement *m* des prix/des cours.

price², *v.tr.* **1.** déterminer le prix (de qch.); fixer un prix pour (qch.); **the book is priced at £4 net,** le livre se vend (au prix de) £4 net **2.** (*a*) s'informer du prix de (qch.) (*b*) évaluer qch/estimer la valeur de qch **3. to price competitors out of the market,** fixer des prix si bas que les concurrents ne peuvent continuer à vendre; **we shall be priced out of the market/we shall price ourselves out of the market,** nos prix (trop élevés) nous feront perdre le marché **4.** *PolEc:* valoriser (une quantité).

pricey, *a. F:* cher/coûteux; **too pricey,** trop cher.

pricing, *n.* détermination *f*/établissement *m*/fixation *f* du prix (**of sth.,** de qch.);

évaluation *f*; **average cost pricing**, (comptabilisation *f* au) coût moyen pondéré; **competitive pricing**, fixation concurrentielle des prix; **delivered pricing**, prix franco; **double pricing**, prix soldés/prix démarqués; **pricing policy**, politique *f* des prix.

primage, *n. Nau:* primage *m*.

primary, *a.* **primary market**, marché *m* primaire; **primary product**, matière première/produit brut; produit de base; **primary industries**, secteur *m* primaire; *NAm:* **primary earnings per share**, bénéfices premiers par action.

prime, *a.* **1.** premier; principal; de premier ordre; **prime cost**, prix *m* coûtant; prix de revient (de production) **2.** (*a*) excellent/de qualité supérieure/de première qualité; **prime quality meat**, viande *f* de première qualité/de premier choix; viande surchoix; **prime (grade) beef**, bœuf de premier choix (*b*) *Fin:* **prime bills**, papier commercial de premier ordre; **prime bond**, obligation *f* de premier ordre; *NAm:* **prime (lending) rate** = taux *m* de base/taux d'escompte (pour les *prime bills*).

principal, *n.* (*a*) *Jur:* (*in transaction*) mandant *m*/commettant *m*; **principal and agent**, mandant et mandataire *m* (*b*) *StExch:* donneur *m* d'ordre; **undisclosed principal**, acheteur non identifié/anonyme (*c*) capital *m*/principal *m* (d'une dette); **principal and interest**, capital et intérêts *mpl*.

printed, *a.* imprimé; *Post:* **printed matter**, imprimé *m*; **printed form**, formulaire *m*.

printer, *n.* (*a*) imprimeur *m* (*b*) *Cmptr:* imprimante *f*; **daisy wheel printer**, imprimante à marguerite; **dot matrix printer**, imprimante par points.

print-out, *n. Cmptr:* sortie *f* d'imprimante; listage *m*/listing *m*; **print-out calculator**, calculatrice *f* à imprimante.

prior, *a.* préalable/précédent; antérieur; (**to sth.**, à qch.).

priority, *n.* priorité *f*; antériorité *f*; **to have priority**, avoir la priorité/être prioritaire; **top priority** = urgent; *Jur:* **priority of a creditor**, privilège *m*/priorité d'un créancier; *StExch:* **priority shares**, actions *f* de priorité.

private, *a.* **1.** privé; **private and confidential**, secret et confidentiel; **private conversation**, entretien privé; **private interview**, (*i*) entretien *m* à huis clos (*ii*) entretien privé; **to mark a letter "private"**, marquer sur une lettre "confidentiel"/"personnel"; *Jur:* **private agreement/contract/treaty**, acte *m* sous seing privé/sous-seing *m*; **to sell by private treaty/contract**, vendre de gré-à-gré **2.** **private bank**, banque privée; **private company**, société à responsabilité limitée; **private enterprise/industry/the private sector**, le secteur privé; **going private**, retrait *m* d'une société de la Bourse/radiation *f* d'une société de la Cote **3.** **private income/money/means**, rentes *fpl*; fortune personelle; **private property**, propriété privée; (*as sign*) = entrée interdite.

privately, *adv.* **privately-held**, détenu par des intérêts privés; **a privately-held company**, une société privée; **to sell sth. privately**, vendre qch. de gré-à-gré.

privatization, *n.* privatisation *f*.

privatize, *v.tr.* privatiser.

privileged, *a.* (créancier, etc.) privilégié.

pro = **procuration**.

probate,[1] *n. Jur* validation *f*/homologation *f* (d'un testament).

probate[2], *v.tr. Jur:* homologuer/entériner (un document).

probation, *n.* **period of probation**, période *f*/stage *m* probatoire; période d'essai; **to take s.o. on probation**, prendre qn à l'essai.

probationary, *a.* (*period*) d'essai.

problem, *n.* problème *m*; **problem analysis**, analyse *f* de problème(s); **problem area**, source *f* de difficultés/d'incidents (techniques); zone *f* critique.

procedure, *n.* procédure *f*/marche *f* à suivre/méthode *f*; **administrative procedure**, méthodes administratives; **order of procedure**, règles *fpl* de procédure.

proceed, *v.i.* (*a*) **negotiations are now proceeding**, des négociations *f* sont en cours (*b*) *Jur:* **to proceed against s.o.**, procéder contre qn; poursuivre qn (en justice); intenter un procès à/contre qn.

proceedings, *n.pl.* (*a*) débats *mpl* (d'une assemblée) (*b*) *Jur:* **(legal) proceedings**, procès *m;* poursuites *f* judiciaires/en justice; **to take/institute proceedings (against s.o.)**, intenter une action/un procès (à/ contre qn); engager/entamer des poursuites (judiciaires) (contre qn); introduire une instance.

proceeds, *n.pl.* produit *m*/montant *m* (d'une vente, etc.); **the net proceeds**, les recettes nettes.

process, *v.tr.* (*a*) *Adm: esp. NAm:* faire l'analyse préalable (*i*) de documents (*ii*) de candidats à un poste (*b*) *Ind:* traiter (des aliments, des produits industriellement) (*c*) *Cmptr:* élaborer (des données).

processable, *a.* (*information*) traitable.

processing, *n.* (*a*) traitement *m*; **data processing/information processing**, traitement des données (de l'information); informatique *f*; **word processing (programme)**, (programme *m* de) traitement *m* de texte (*b*) *Adm:* examen *m*/analyse *f* préalable (*i*) de documents (*ii*) de candidats à un poste (*c*) **inward processing**, transformation active; **outward processing**, transformation passive (*d*) **processing lead time**, délai *m* de lancement (*e*) **processing industry**, industrie de transformation.

processor, *n.* **data processor**, ordinateur *m*; **word processor**, machine *f* de traitement de textes; éditeur *m* de textes.

process-server, *n.* huissier *m*.

procuration, *n.* (*a*) négociation *f* (d'un emprunt); (*abbr:* **pro**) **per pro (pp)**, par procuration (*b*) **procuration (fee)**, commission payée (à un agent) pour l'obtention d'un prêt.

procurator, *n. Jur:* fondé *m* de pouvoir.

procure, *v.tr.* obtenir; se procurer.

procurement, *n.* obtention *f*; approvisionnement *m.*

produce[1], *n. coll.* produits *mpl*/denrées *fpl*; **home-grown produce**, produits du pays/ produits indigènes; **foreign produce**, produits étrangers/exotiques; **agricultural produce**, produits agricoles; **farm produce**, produits de ferme/produits fermiers; **market garden produce**, produits maraîchers; **raw produce**, matières premières.

produce[2], *v.tr.* 1. présenter/produire (des documents); **I can produce the documents**, je peux fournir les documents 2. *Ind:* fabriquer (des marchandises) 3. rapporter; **shares that produce five per cent**, actions *f* qui rapportent un intérêt de cinq pour cent.

producer, *n.* producteur, -trice; fabricant *m* (**of**, de); **producers' co-operative**, coopérative *f* de production; **producer goods**, biens *m* de production/d'équipement; **producer price index**, indice des prix à la production.

producing[1], *a.* producteur; productif; **producing capacity**, capacité *f* de production; productivité *f*; **producing centre**, centre *m* de production; **producing country**, pays producteur; **producing industry**, industrie productrice.

producing[2], *n.* = **production 1.**

product, *n.* produit *m*; *Ind:* **basic product**, produit de base; **by-product**, dérivé *m*; **end product/finished product**, produit fini; **secondary product**, produit secondaire; sous-produit *m*; **semi-manufactured product**, produit semi-fini/semi-produit; **waste products**, déchet *m*/produits de rejet; **product advertising**, publicité *f* de produit; **product analysis**, analyse *f* de produit; **product design**, conception *f* du produit; **product development,** mise au point d'un produit; **product image,** image *f* de produit; **product line/range,** gamme *f* de produits; *PolEc:* **gross national product (GNP),** produit national brut (PNB); **per capita gross national product,** produit national brut par habitant; **gross domestic product,** produit intérieur brut/ production intérieure brute; **net domestic product,** produit intérieur net.

production, *n.* **1.** production *f*/communication *f* (de documents); **on production of (your ticket, etc),** sur présentation de (votre billet, etc.) **2.** *(a)* production/ fabrication *f* (de marchandises); **batch production,** fabrication par lots; **direct production,** autarcie *f* économique; **indirect production,** économie *f* de marché; **machine production,** production mécanisée; **mass production,** production/fabrication en série; **planned production,** production planifiée/dirigée; **primary production,** production de matières premières; **secondary production,** production manufacturée; **production to order,** production sur commande; **rate of production,** taux *m* de (la) production *(b)* **production bonus,** prime *f* de rendement/ de productivité; **production capacity,** capacité de production; **production chart/ sheet,** graphique *m* d'évolution (de la production); **production cost,** coût *m*/frais *mpl* de production; **production department,** service *m* de la production; **production engineering,** productique *f*; **production line,** chaîne *f* de montage; **production line system,** production/travail *m* à la chaîne; **to work on a production line,** travailler à la chaîne; **production management,** gestion *f* de la production; **production manager,** chef *m*/directeur, -trice de la production; *Publ:* chef de fabrication; **production plant,** usine *f*; **production schedule,** programme de fabrication; **production unit,** *(i)* unité *f* *(ii)* équipe *f* de production; **to cease production,** arrêter la production; **to slow down production,** ralentir/freiner la production; **to stimulate production,** encourager la production.

productive, *a.* *(a)* (travail, etc) productif; (capital) productif d'intérêts; **the productive life (of a machine),** la vie physique (d'une machine) *(b)* profitable/utile.

productivity, *n.* productivité *f*/rendement *m*; **productivity bargaining,** négociation syndicale d'un contrat de productivité; **productivity bonus,** prime *f* de rendement; **productivity deal,** contrat *m* de productivité; **productivity drive/campaign,** campagne *f* de productivité.

profession, *n.* profession *f*; métier *m*.

professional, 1. *a.* professionnel; **professional association,** association professionnelle; **professional fees,** frais professionnels; **professional secrecy,** secret professionnel **2.** *n.* professionnel, -elle; *(executive, lawyer, etc.)* membre *m* des professions libérales.

proficiency, *n.* compétence *f* **(in a subject,** en une matière); **proficiency in English,** connaissance *f* pratique de l'anglais.

proficient, *a.* capable/compétent.

profile, *n.* profil *m*; **company profile,** profil d'entreprise; **customer profile,** profil de la clientèle; **job profile,** description *f* de fonction; **market profile,** profil du marché.

profit, *n.* profit *m*/bénéfice *m*; **capital profit,** plus-value *f*; **clear profit,** profit net; **economic profit,** résultat *m* économique; **gross profit,** profit brut; **net (operating) profit,** bénéfice net (d'exploitation); **paper profit,** profits théoriques/ fictifs non matérialisés; **profit balance,** solde *m* bénéficiaire; **profit graph,** courbe *f* de rentabilité; **profit and loss,** pertes et profits; **profit and loss account,** compte *m* de résultat; **profit margin,** marge *f* bénéficiaire; **profit optimization,** optimisation *f* des profits; **profit target,** objectif *m* de profits; **profit tax,** impôts *mpl* sur les bénéfices; **profit after tax(ation)/after-tax profit,** bénéfice net/bénéfice après impôt; **profit before tax(ation)/pre-tax profit,** bénéfice brut/bénéfice avant impôt; **loss of profit,** manque *m* à gagner; **to bring/to**

yield/to show a profit, donner un bénéfice; être bénéficiaire; **firm showing a profit,** société *f* bénéficiaire; **to derive a profit from sth.,** tirer/retirer un profit de qch.; **to make a large profit,** réaliser de gros bénéfices; (*of business*) **to move into profit,** devenir rentable; **to sell sth. at a profit,** prendre/faire un bénéfice sur une vente; **profit-earning,** rentable; **profit-earning (capacity),** rentabilité *f*; **profit-making,** réalisation *f* de bénéfices; **profit-making association,** association *f* à but lucratif; **non profit-making association,** association à but non lucratif/sans but lucratif; *Ind:* **profit-sharing (scheme),** participation *f* aux bénéfices; intéressement *m*; participation ouvrière; participation des salariés; intéressement du personnel aux fruits de l'expansion/aux bénéfices; **profit-sharing employee,** employé(e) intéressé(e); **profit-sharing bond,** obligation participante; *PolEc:* **profit system,** économie basée sur le profit; économie de libre entreprise; **profit-taking,** prise *f* de bénéfices.

profitability, *n.* rentabilité *f*; profitabilité *f*.

profitable, *a.* profitable/avantageux; (*of speculation, etc.*) lucratif; (*emploi*) rémunérateur; (*of business*) rentable.

profiteer[1], *n.* profiteur *m*/affairiste *mf*.

profiteer[2], *v.i.* faire des bénéfices excessifs.

profiteering, *n.* mercantilisme *m*; affairisme *m*.

profitless, *a.* sans profit; **profitless deal,** affaire blanche.

pro forma, *n. & adj. phr.* **pro forma (invoice),** facture *f* pro forma.

programme[1], *NAm:* **program** *n.* programme *m*; **development programme,** programme de développement; **investment programme,** programme d'investissements; **research programme,** programme de recherche(s); **training programme,** programme d'instruction/de formation/d'entraînement; **to draw up/arrange a programme,** arrêter un pro-

gramme/dresser un emploi du temps; *Cmptr:* **programme language,** langage de programmation.

programme[2], *NAm:* **program,** *v.tr.* *Cmptr:* programmer; **programmed management,** gestion programmée.

programmer, *n. Cmptr:* programmeur, -euse.

programming, *n. Cmptr:* programmation *f*; **programming department,** service *m* (de la) programmation; **programming manager,** chef *m* du service (de) programmation; **programming staff,** personnel chargé de la programmation.

progress, *n.* avancement *m* (d'un travail, etc.); **to make progress,** avancer/faire des progrès; *Ind:* **progress of the work through the different departments,** cheminement *m* des pièces à travers les différents services; **progress payments,** paiements proportionnels (à l'avancement des travaux/au prorata de l'avancement des travaux); **progress report,** compte rendu (de l'avancement) des travaux/rapport *m* périodique; **work progress,** avancement des travaux; **the work is now in progress,** le travail est en voie d'exécution/en cours; **the negotiations in progress,** les négociations *f* en cours.

progression, *n.* progression *f*; **salary progression curve,** courbe *f* d'augmentation de salaire.

progressive, *a.* progressif; **progressive tax,** impôt progressif; **progressive increase in taxation,** progressivité *f* de l'impôt; *Fin:* (*of interest*) **at a progressive rate,** à taux progressif.

prohibitive, *a.* (prix) prohibitif/inabordable; *Cust:* (droits) prohibitifs; **the price of caviare is prohibitive,** le caviar est hors de prix.

project[1], *n.* projet *m*; plan *m*; **capital project evaluation,** étude *f* de projet d'investissement; **project analysis,** étude de projet.

project[2], *v.tr.* prévoir; **he's projecting a**

40% slide in May, il prévoit une baisse de 40% au mois de mai.

projected, *a.* **projected sales,** ventes prévues.

projection, *n.* projection *f*; prévision *f*; **sales projection,** prévision des ventes.

promise, *n.* promesse *f*; **promise to pay,** promesse de payer; **promise of sale,** promesse de vente.

promissory, *a.* **promissory note,** billet *m* à ordre.

promote, *v.tr.* **1.** promouvoir (qn); donner de l'avancement à (qn); **to promote s.o. to a post,** promouvoir qn à un poste plus élevé; **to be promoted,** être promu; avancer; recevoir de l'avancement **2.** (*a*) encourager (un projet, etc.) (*b*) **to promote a company,** lancer/fonder une société (*c*) (*i*) lancer (un produit) (*ii*) stimuler la vente (d'un produit).

promoter, *n.* (*a*) **company promoter,** promoteur *m*/fondateur *m* d'une société anonyme; *Fin:* **promoters' shares,** parts *fpl* de fondateurs (*b*) **sales promoter,** promoteur des ventes.

promotion, *n.* **1.** promotion *f*/avancement *m*; **to gain promotion,** avoir/recevoir/obtenir de l'avancement; **promotion by seniority,** avancement à l'ancienneté; **prospect/chance of promotion,** possibilité *f* d'avancement; (*in ads*) poste *m* d'avenir/poste évolutif **2.** fondation *f*/lancement *m* (d'une société anonyme); promotion (immobilière); **promotion money,** frais *mpl* de fondation (d'une société anonyme); frais d'établissement; coût *m* de premier établissement **3.** lancement (d'un produit); stimulation *f* (de la vente d'un produit); **promotion budget,** budget promotionnel; **promotion team,** équipe promotionnelle; **in-store promotion,** publicité *f* au point de vente; **sales promotion,** promotion des ventes.

promotional, *a.* promotionnel; **promotional campaign/sale,** campagne/vente promotionnelle; **promotional material,**

matériel *m* de promotion/promotionnel/publicitaire.

prompt, 1. *a.* (*a*) prompt; vif/rapide; diligent; **prompt service,** service *m* rapide (*b*) immédiat; instantané; **prompt reply,** réponse *f* par retour du courrier (*c*) **prompt cotton,** coton *m* livrable sur-le-champ et comptant **2.** *n.* terme *m* (de paiement); délai *m* limite; **prompt note,** mémoire *m* de vente (*avec indication du délai de paiement*); **prompt day,** jour *m*/date *f* de paiement.

promptly, *adv.* promptement; ponctuellement.

proof, *n.* preuve *f*; **proof of ownership,** titre *m* de propriété; *Ins:* **proof of claim,** preuve de sinistre.

property, *n.* **1.** (droit de) propriété *f*; **literary property,** propriété littéraire **2.** (*a*) propriété/biens *mpl*/avoir(s) *m(pl)*; *Fin:* patrimoine *m*; **private/public property,** propriété privée/publique; *Jur:* **funded property,** biens en rentes; **personal property,** biens personnels/mobiliers; effets personnels; **real property,** biens immeubles; **damage to property,** dommages matériels (*b*) immeuble(s) *m(pl)*; propriété (foncière)/terre *f*; **commercial property,** locaux commerciaux; **property companies,** sociétés immobilières; **property developer,** promoteur immobilier/promoteur-constructeur; **property investment,** investissement(s) immobilier(s); **property loan,** prêt immobilier; **property market,** le marché (de l')immobilier/l'immobilier *m*; **property tax,** impôt foncier; **property for sale,** immeuble/maison *f*/propriété à vendre.

proportion[1]**,** *n.* proportion *f*/quota *m*/quotité *f*/pourcentage *m*.

proportion[2]**,** *v.tr.* **to proportion one's expenditures to one's profits,** mesurer ses dépenses sur ses profits.

proportional, *a.* proportionnel; en proportion (**to,** de); proportionné (**to,** à); **compensation proportional to the damage,** compensation proportionnelle au dommage subi; *Adm:* **proportional assessment,** coéquation *f*; **proportional scale,** échelle proportionnelle.

proportionment, *n.* distribution proportionnelle/au prorata.

proposal, *n.* proposition *f*/offre *f*; **to make a proposal,** faire/formuler une proposition; **proposals for ...,** propositions relatives à ...; **proposal of insurance,** proposition d'assurance.

propose, *v.tr.* proposer; **to propose a candidate,** proposer un candidat; **to propose a motion,** faire une motion.

proposition, *n.* (*a*) proposition *f*/offre *f* (*b*) *F:* affaire *f*; **it's a big proposition,** c'est une grosse affaire; **economic/paying proposition,** affaire rentable/qui rapporte.

proprietary, *a.* **proprietary insurance company,** compagnie *f* d'assurance à primes; **proprietary article,** spécialité *f*/article breveté; **proprietary medicine,** spécialité *f* pharmaceutique.

proprietor, *n.* propriétaire *mf*; **hotel proprietor,** propriétaire/patron *m* d'un hôtel; **sole proprietor,** seul propriétaire.

proprietorship, *n.* (*a*) droit *m* de propriété (*b*) propriété *f*/possession *f.*

proprietress, *n.* propriétaire *f*; patronne *f* (d'un hôtel, etc.).

pro rata, *adv. & a. phr.* au prorata/ proportionnel.

prorate, *v.tr. Fin: etc:* partager proportionnellement.

prosecute, *v.tr.* poursuivre (en justice).

prosecution, *n.* poursuites *fpl* judiciaires; **the prosecution,** l'accusation *f.*

prospect, *n.* (*a*) perspective *f*/expectative *f*; **economic prospects,** perspectives économiques; **market prospects,** perspectives commerciales; **no prospect of agreement,** aucune perspective d'accord (*b*) **future prospects of an undertaking,** perspectives d'avenir d'une entreprise (*c*) *NAm:* client éventuel/possible.

prospective, *a.* **prospective buyer,** acheteur éventuel.

prospectus, *n.* **1.** prospectus *m inv* **2.** *Fin:* appel *m* de souscription publique.

protect, *v.tr.* protéger; sauvegarder (les intérêts de qn, etc.); *StExch:* **to protect a book,** défendre une position; **to protect a bill of exchange,** garantir le bon accueil d'une lettre de change; faire provision pour une lettre de change.

protectionism, *n.* protectionnisme *m.*

protectionist, *a.* (politique) protectionniste.

protective, *a.* protecteur; *PolEc:* **protective tariff,** tarif protecteur; **protective clause,** clause de sauvegarde.

protest[1], *n.* **1.** protêt *m*; **certified protest,** protêt authentique; **protest for nonacceptance,** protêt faute d'acceptation; **protest for non-payment,** protêt faute de paiement; **to make a protest,** lever/faire protêt **2.** **ship's protest,** rapport *m* de mer; déclaration *f* d'avaries; procès-verbal *m* des avaries; **to note a protest,** faire un rapport de mer.

protest[2], *v.tr.* **to protest a bill,** (faire) protester un effet/une lettre de change; lever protêt d'une lettre de change.

prototype, *n.* prototype *m*; **exhibit prototype,** prototype de démonstration; **prototype car,** voiture *f* prototype; *Ind:* **prototype series,** présérie *f.*

prove up, *v.i. NAm:* (*a*) donner satisfaction (*b*) **to prove up on a claim,** faire valoir ses droits à une revendication; **to prove up on a concession,** accomplir toutes les formalités requises pour obtenir une concession.

provide, 1. *v.i.* pourvoir à; prévoir; **expenses provided for in the budget,** dépenses prévues au budget; **this has been provided for,** on y a pourvu; *Ins:* **this risk is not provided for in the policy,** ce risque n'est pas prévu dans la police; **to provide for a bill,** faire provision pour une lettre de change **2.** (*a*) *v.tr.* stipuler (**that,** que +

ind.); **the contract provides that ...**, dans le contrat il est stipulé que ... (*b*) fournir; **to provide s.o. with sth.**, fournir qch. à qn; pourvoir/munir/fournir/approvisionner qn de qch.; **to provide a bill with acceptance**, revêtir un effet de l'acceptation.

provident, *a.* **provident fund**, caisse *f* de prévoyance.

provision, *n.* (*a*) **we have made provisions to this effect**, nous avons pris des dispositions *fpl* dans ce sens (*b*) *Book-k:* provisions *fpl*/réserve *f*; **allocation to a provision**, dotation *f* (*c*) *pl.* **provisions**, provisions (de bouche)/comestibles *m*; *NAm:* **provision store**, alimentation *f* (*d*) clause *f*/stipulation *f*/disposition *f* (d'un contrat); **fair-price provisions**, clauses de vérité des prix; **loan-loss provisions**, provisions pour créances douteuses; **there is no provision to the contrary**, il n'y a pas de clause contraire.

provisional, *a.* provisoire; **provisional duties**, fonctions *f* intérimaires/temporaires.

provisionally, *adv.* provisoirement/par provision/par intérim; **to sign an agreement provisionally**, signer un engagement sous condition.

proviso, *n.* clause conditionnelle; condition *f* (d'un contrat); stipulation *f*; **with the proviso that ...**, à condition que ....

provisory, *a.* (*of clause, etc.*) qui énonce une stipulation; conditionnel.

proximo, *adv. Com:* (du mois) prochain.

proxy, *n.* (*a*) *Jur:* procuration *f*; **by proxy**, par procuration (*b*) (*of pers.*) mandataire *mf.*

psychographics, *n.pl.* psychologie sociale.

psychology, *n.* psychologie *f*; **economic psychology**, psychologie économique; **industrial psychology**, psychologie industrielle/psychotechnique *f.*

public, **1.** *a.* **public authorities**, pouvoirs publics; **public expenditure**, dépense(s) *f* publique(s); **public finance**, finances publiques; **public holiday**, fête légale; **public image**, image *f* de marque; **public relations (PR)**, relations publiques; **public sector**, secteur *m* publique; **public sector borrowing requirement (PSBR)**, besoins *mpl* d'emprunt du secteur public (*non couverts par les rentrées fiscales*); **public servant**, fonctionnaire *mf*; employé, -ée d'un service public; **public utilities**, services publics; **public transport**, transports *mpl* en commun; (*of firm*) **to go public**, émettre/placer des actions dans le public **2.** *n.* **the (general) public**, le (grand) public.

publication, *n.* (*a*) publication *f*/parution *f*; **publication date**, date *f* de parution (*b*) ouvrage publié/publication.

publicity, *n.* publicité *f*/réclame *f*; **advance publicity**, publicité d'amorçage; **publicity bureau/agency**, bureau *m*/ agence *f* de publicité; **publicity campaign**, campagne *f* de publicité; **publicity department**, (service *m* de) la publicité; **publicity expenses**, dépenses *f* publicitaires; **publicity man/woman**, publicitaire *mf*; publiciste *mf*; **publicity manager**, chef *m* de (la) publicité.

publicize, *v.tr.* faire de la publicité/de la réclame pour (un produit).

publish, *v.tr.* publier; **just published**, vient de paraître.

publisher, *n.* éditeur *m.*

publishing, *n. & a.* **publishing house/firm**, maison *f* d'édition; **publishing trade**, (le monde de) l'édition *f*; *Cmptr:* **desktop publishing**, publication assistée par ordinateur (PAO).

puff[1], *n.* réclame (tapageuse).

puff[2], *v.tr.* prôner/pousser/vanter (ses marchandises).

pull, *vi F:* se retirer (**from,** de); annuler un marché.

pull down, *v.tr.* **to pull down prices**, faire baisser les prix.

punter, *n.* (*a*) parieur *m* (aux courses) (*b*) boursicoteur *m.*

purchase[1], *n.* (*a*) achat *m*; **cash purchase,** achat au comptant; **closing purchase,** couverture optionnelle; **credit purchase,** achat à crédit; **forward purchase,** achat à terme; *Book-k:* **purchase book/purchase journal,** livre *m* des achats; *StExch:* **purchase contract,** bordereau *m* d'achat; **purchase money,** prix *m* d'achat; **purchase method,** méthode *f* d'achat au prix coûtant; **purchase price,** prix d'achat/prix coûtant; **purchase tax,** taxe *f* à l'achat; **to make a purchase,** faire un achat (*b*) loyer *m*; **sold at twenty years purchase,** vendu moyennant vingt ans de loyer.

purchase[2], *v.tr.* acheter/acquérir/faire l'acquisition de qch.; **to purchase for cash,** acheter (au) comptant; **to purchase sth. on credit,** acheter qch. à crédit.

purchaser, *n.* (*a*) acheteur, -euse; acquéreur *m*; (*at auction*) adjudicataire *mf*; **purchasers' association,** coopérative *f* d'achats (*b*) preneur, -euse; **to have found a purchaser for sth.,** avoir (trouvé) preneur pour qch.

purchasing[1], *a.* **purchasing party,** acquéreur; (*at auction*) partie *f* adjudicataire.

purchasing[2], *n.* achat *m*/acquisition *f*; **central purchasing,** politique *f* d'achats centralisés; *NAm:* **purchasing agent,** acheteur, -euse; **purchasing costs,** frais *mpl* de passation de commande; **purchasing department,** service *m* de l'approvisionnement; service *m* des achats; **purchasing manager,** chef *m* des achats; *PolEc:* **purchasing power,** pouvoir *m* d'achat.

pure, *a. Ins:* **pure premium,** prime nette.

purpose, *n.* but *m*/raison *f*; **for tax purposes,** pour le calcul de l'impôt.

push, *v.tr.* pousser; **to push the market higher,** faire monter les prix.

push-button, *n.* **push-button telephone,** téléphone *m* à touches/à clavier.

put[1], *n. StExch:* **put option,** option *f* de vente; **put band,** période *f* de validité d'une option de vente; **put of more,** la demande de plus; l'encore autant *m*; **put and call,** double option/stellage *m.*

put[2], *v.tr.* **1.** mettre; **to put an article on sale,** mettre un article en vente; **to put a new article on the market,** lancer une marchandise; **to put an advertisement in the paper,** (faire) insérer une annonce dans le journal; **to put one's signature to sth.,** signer qch.; *Book-k:* **to put an amount in the receipts/in the expenditure,** employer une somme en recette/en dépense; *StExch:* **to put stock at a certain price,** délivrer/fournir des actions à un certain prix; **to put money into an undertaking,** verser des fonds/placer de l'argent dans une affaire **2. to put a resolution to the meeting,** présenter une résolution à l'assemblée; **I shall put your proposal to the Board,** je porterai votre proposition à la connaissance du conseil d'administration; **to put a resolution to the vote,** mettre une résolution aux voix.

put out, *v.tr.* (*a*) **to put out work,** donner du travail en sous-traitance; donner du travail à faire à domicile (*b*) **to put out money at interest,** placer de l'argent.

put up, *v.tr.* (*a*) fournir (une somme d'argent); **to put up the money for an undertaking,** fournir les fonds d'une entreprise (*b*) **to put up prices,** monter/augmenter les prix (*c*) **to put sth. up for sale,** mettre qch en vente; **to put sth. up for auction,** mettre qch aux enchères.

pyramid, *n.* **pyramid selling,** = chaîne *f* de vente à domicile.

Q

qualification, *n.* **1.** aptitude *f*/compétence *f*/talent *m*/capacité *f*; **to have the necessary qualifications for a job,** avoir la compétence nécessaire pour remplir une fonction; posséder les qualités requises/les titres *m*/les qualifications *f* nécessaires pour un poste; **professional qualifications,** qualifications professionnelles **2.** **qualification shares,** actions *f* statutaires.

qualified, *a.* **1.** qui a les qualités requises (pour un poste, etc.); **to be qualified to do sth.,** être qualifié pour faire qch.; **qualified accountant,** comptable diplômé; **qualified persons,** personnes compétentes/personnes qualifiées **2.** restreint/mitigé/modéré; **qualified acceptance,** acceptation conditionnelle/sous condition (d'une traite, etc.); **qualified approval,** approbation *f* avec réserve; **qualified endorsement,** endos conditionnel.

qualify, *v.i.* acquérir les qualifications professionnelles/les connaissances requises/l'expérience *f* nécessaire **(for sth.,** pour qch.); **he is not qualified,** il ne possède pas les qualifications requises/les diplômes nécessaires.

qualifying, *a.* **1.** **qualifying period,** période *f* d'essai **2.** *Fin:* **qualifying shares,** actions *f* statutaires.

quality, *n.* **1.** (*a*) qualité *f*; **of good/high quality,** de bonne qualité/de qualité supérieure; **poor quality goods,** marchandises *f* de qualité inférieure; **of first rate quality/of the best quality,** de première qualité; de premier choix (*b*) **quality control,** contrôle *m* de la qualité; **quality goods,** marchandises *f* de qualité; **quality newspaper,** journal sérieux.

Quango, *n.* **(Quasi autonomous non-governmental organization)** = société nationale de service public.

quantify, *v.tr.* déterminer la quantité de (qch); quantifier; mesurer/évaluer avec précision.

quantity, *n.* **1.** (*a*) quantité *f*; **a small quantity of ...,** une petite quantité de ...; **a (large) quantity of ...,** une (grande) quantité de ...; **to buy sth. in large quantities,** acheter qch. en grande quantité/en quantité considérable; **quantity rebate/discount,** remise *f* sur la quantité; *Cust:* **the quantity permitted,** la tolérance/la quantité permise (de tabac, etc.); **economic manufacturing quantity,** quantité économique de production (*b*) *Const:* **to survey a building for quantities,** faire le métré d'un immeuble; **bill of quantities,** devis *m*; **quantity surveyor,** métreur *m* vérificateur; **quantity surveying,** métré *m* **2.** **marketable quantity of shares,** quotité *f* négociable de valeurs.

quart, *n.* *Meas:* le quart d'un gallon/*FrC:* pinte *f*; **a quart of milk,** *FrC:* une pinte de lait; **(British quart** = 1.136 litre; **American liquid quart** = 0.946 litre; **American dry quart** = 1.101 litre).

quarter, *n.* **1.** quart *m*; **three quarters,** trois quarts; **three and a quarter,** trois et un quart; **a quarter (of a pound) of coffee,** un quart (de livre) de café; **a quarter cheaper,** d'un quart meilleur marché; **I can buy it for a quarter of the price,** je peux l'avoir au quart du prix/quatre fois moins cher **2.** trimestre *m*; terme *m* (de loyer); **every quarter I receive a statement of account,** on m'envoie un relevé de compte tous les trimestres/tous les 3 mois; **a quarter's rent,** un terme/un trimestre (de loyer); **quarter day,** (jour de) terme.

quarterly, 1. *a.* trimestriel; **quarterly statement,** relevé (de compte) trimestriel **2.** *n.* publication trimestrielle **3.** *adv.* trimestriellement; par trimestre; tous les 3 mois.

quasi, *pref. & a.* quasi; **quasi contract,** quasi-contrat *m*; **quasi-money,** quasi-monnaie *f.*

quay, *n.* quai *m*; (*of goods*) **ex quay,** à prendre/livrable à quai.

quayage, *n.* droit(s) *m(pl)* de quai.

quick, *a.* rapide; **quick recovery,** reprise *f* rapide; **quick returns,** profits *m* rapides; **quick sale,** prompt débit; vente *f* facile; **quick assets,** actif *m* disponible/actif négociable/disponibilités *f.*

quid pro quo, *Lat. phr.* équivalent *m*; compensation *f*; échange *m.*

quiet, *a.* calme; **quiet market,** marché *m* calme; **business is very quiet,** les affaires *f* sont très calmes.

quorum, *n.* quorum *m*; nombre suffisant; nombre voulu; **to have/to form a quorum,** atteindre le quorum.

quota, *n.* (*a*) quote-part *f*/quotité *f*; cotisation *f*; **to contribute one's quota,** payer/apporter sa quote-part; *Adm:* **taxable quota,** quotité *f* imposable (*b*) contingent *m*/quota *m*; **sales quota,** quota de ventes (*c*) **quota sampling,** échantillonnage *m*/sondage *m* par quota (*d*) taux *m* de contingentement; **import/export quotas,** quotas d'importation/d'exportation;

quota system (of distribution), contingentement; **to fix quotas for an import,** contingenter une importation/déterminer les quotas d'une importation.

quotable, *a. StExch:* (valeur, etc.) cotable.

quotation, *n.* (*a*) *StExch:* cotation *f*/cote *f*/cours *m*/prix *m*; **actual quotations,** cours effectifs; prix effectifs cotés; **buying quotation,** cours d'achat; **closing quotation,** cours *m* de clôture; *NAm:* **flat quotation,** cotation sans intérêt; **the latest quotations,** les derniers cours; **market quotation,** cotation au cours du marché; **stock admitted to quotation,** valeurs admises à la cote officielle; **to seek a share quotation,** faire une demande d'admission à la cote (*b*) *Ind:* devis *m*; **quotation for paint,** prix pour la peinture.

quote¹, *n. F:* = **quotation.**

quote², *v.tr.* **1.** *Adm:* (*in reply*) **please quote this number,** prière de rappeler ce numéro **2.** (*a*) établir/indiquer/fixer (un prix); **to quote s.o. a price for sth.,** fixer à qn un prix pour qch. (*b*) *StExch:* coter (une valeur); **quoted company,** société à la Cote Officielle; **quoted investment,** valeurs mobilières de placement; **quoted price,** cours *m* inscrit à la cote officielle; **quoted shares/stock,** actions inscrites à la cote officielle/valeurs cotées en Bourse; **shares quoted at 90p,** valeurs qui cotent à 90p.

quote-driven, *a.* (*stock market*) gouverné par les prix.

R

rack rent, *n.* (*i*) loyer à la valeur du marché; prix courant d'un loyer (*ii*) loyer *m* exorbitant.

radiopager, *n.* récepteur *m* de poche/ récepteur (de recherche de personne)/ récepteur d'appel (de personne).

radiopaging, *n.* radiorecherche *f* de personne.

radiotelephone, *n.* radiotéléphone *m*.

raid[1], *n.* raid *m*; **bear raid,** raid /chasse *f* (en Bourse); **dawn raid,** achat *m* d'un nombre considérable d'actions d'une société-cible au début de l'ouverture souvent à un prix plus élevé que normal (*pour ensuite lancer une OPA*); **raid on the banks,** retrait massif d'argent.

raid[2], *v.tr.* **to raid the bears,** chasser le découvert.

raider, *n.* lanceur *m* d'OPA/prédateur *m*/ raider *m*.

rail, *n.* chemin *m* de fer/voie ferrée; **free on rail,** franco wagon; **price on rail,** prix *m* sur le wagon.

railroad, *n. NAm:* = **railway**.

railway, *n.* chemin *m* de fer/voie ferrée; **railway transport,** transport *m* ferroviaire/ par chemin de fer; **works with railway facilities,** usine *f* avec facilités d'accès/ avec raccordement au réseau ferroviaire.

raise[1], *n. NAm:* augmentation *f* (de salaire); **I've had a raise,** j'ai reçu une augmentation de salaire/j'ai été augmenté.

raise[2], *v.tr.* **1. to raise a question,** soulever une question **2.** *NAm:* **to raise a cheque,** (*i*) augmenter (frauduleusement) le montant d'un chèque (*ii*) faire un chèque **3.** (*a*) **to raise capital,** mobiliser des fonds/ procurer des capitaux; **to raise funds,** collecter des fonds/faire une collecte de fonds; **to raise funds by subscription,** réunir des fonds par souscription; **to raise money,** trouver/se procurer de l'argent (*b*) **to raise taxes,** lever des impôts; **to raise a loan,** (*i*) lancer (*ii*) émettre un emprunt (*c*) **to raise the price (of sth.),** augmenter le prix (de qch); **the dividend is raised by 25%,** le dividende marque une progression/a augmenté de 25%.

raising, *n.* **1.** relèvement *m*/hausse *f*/ augmentation *f*; **the raising of the minimum lending rate,** le relèvement du taux officiel d'escompte **2.** (*a*) levée *f* (d'un impôt); (*i*) lancement *m* (*ii*) émission *f* (d'un emprunt) (*b*) **fund raising,** (méthode *f* de) collecte *f* de fonds; mobilisation *f* de fonds.

rake in, *v.tr. F:* amasser (de l'argent).

rake-off, *n. F:* pourcentage *m* (*illicite ou non*); commission *f*/ristourne *f*; **to get a rake-off on each sale,** toucher une commission/un pourcentage/une guelte sur chaque vente.

rally[1], *n.* reprise *f* (des prix); reprise/redressement *m* des affaires.

rally[2], *v.i. StExch:* **shares rallied,** les actions se sont redressées/ont repris.

rallying, *n.* reprise *f*/redressement *m* (des prix, etc.).

random, 1. *n.* **at random,** au hasard **2.** *a.* aléatoire; (fait) au hasard; **random sampling,** échantillonnage *m* aléatoire/ sondage *m* probabiliste; **random check,**

contrôle *m* par sondage(s); *Stat:* **random error,** erreur *f* aléatoire.

range[1], *n.* (*a*) **price range,** échelle *f*/éventail *m* des prix; **range of products,** gamme *f* de produits; **range of sizes,** éventail/choix *m* de dimensions; **salary range,** éventail de salaires (*c*) fourchette *f*/écart *m*; *StExch:* **opening/closing range,** fourchette de cours d'ouverture/de clôture; **trading range,** fourchette de cotation; **narrow trading-range,** écarts de prix restreints (*c*) **range of activities,** rayon *m* d'action (*d*) **long/short range,** à long/à court terme.

range[2], *v.i.* **incomes ranging from £15 000 to £36 000,** revenus *m* de l'ordre de £15 000 à £36 000.

rank[1], *n.* **1. the rank and file of union members,** la masse des syndiqués **2.** *Fin:* rang *m* (d'une créance, d'une hypothèque, etc.); **to assign a rank to a debt,** assigner un rang à une créance; *Stat:* **rank order statistics,** méthodes *f* statistiques de rang.

rank[2], **1.** *v.tr. Jur:* **to rank creditors (in bankruptcy),** colloquer des créanciers **2.** *v.i.* (*a*) (*of creditor, claimant, etc.*) **to rank after s.o.,** prendre rang/passer après qn; **to rank before s.o.,** prendre rang/passer avant qn/avoir la priorité; **to rank equally with s.o.,** prendre/avoir le même rang que qn (*b*) *Jur:* (*of claim in bankruptcy*) être accepté à la vérification des créances; **to rank after sth.,** (*of mortgage*) prendre rang après qch.; (*of share*) être primé par qch.; **to rank before sth.,** (*of mortgage*) prendre rang avant qch.; (*of share*) avoir la priorité (sur qch.); **to rank equally with sth.,** prendre le même rang que qch.; **preference shares of all issues shall rank equally,** les actions de toutes les émissions prendront (le) même rang.

ranking, *n.* **1.** rang *m*; *Jur:* **ranking of a creditor,** collocation *f* de créanciers **2.** hiérarchie *f.*

ratable, *a.* = **rateable.**

rate[1], *n.* **1.** taux *m*; **birth rate,** (taux de) natalité *f*; **burn rate,** (*of company*) point mort; **to be paid at the rate of £5 an hour,**

être payé au taux de/à raison de £5 l'heure; **time rate,** rémunération *f* au temps passé/ = aux pièces **2.** (*a*) taux/prix *m*/tarif *m*; **average rate,** taux/tarif moyen; **fixed rate,** taux/tarif/prix forfaitaire; **flat rate,** taux/tarif/prix uniforme; **full rate,** plein tarif; **letter rate,** tarif lettre; **night rates,** tarifs de nuit; **postal rates,** tarifs postaux; **printed paper rate,** tarif imprimés; *Cust:* **preferential rates,** tarifs de faveur/préférentiels; **rates of insurance,** taux/tarifs d'assurance; **rates of pay,** barème *m* des salaires; **reduced rate,** tarif réduit; **standard rate,** tarif normal/uniforme; **rate fixing,** tarification *f*; **to fix a rate,** tarifer (*b*) taux/pourcentage *m*; **rate of interest/interest rate,** taux d'intérêt; **rate of return,** rentabilité/taux de rendement (*c*) *Bank:* (*obsolescent*) **bank rate,** taux d'escompte; **base rate,** taux de base (bancaire); **bill rate,** taux d'escompte; **minimum lending rate (MLR)**/*NAm* **discount rate,** taux (officiel) d'escompte; *NAm:* **prime rate,** taux d'escompte (pour les meilleurs clients)/prime rate/*FrC:* taux (d'intérêt) préférentiel (*d*) cours *m*/taux; **conversion rate,** taux de conversion; **exchange cross rate,** taux de change entre devises tierces; **rate of exchange/exchange rate,** cours/taux du change; **the rate of the dollar,** le cours du dollar; **today's rate,** le cours du jour (*e*) *StExch:* **backwardation rate,** cours/taux de déport; **carry-over/contango rate,** cours/taux de report; **forward rate,** cours/taux (pour les opérations) à terme; **market rate,** taux du marché (*f*) ratio *m*; **rate of turnover,** ratio de rotation des stocks **3.** (*a*) taux d'un impôt local (= centime le franc) (*b*) impôts locaux, (*i*) contribution foncière (*ii*) impôt mobilier; cotisation *f*; **rates and taxes,** impôts et contributions.

rate[2], *v.tr.* **1.** estimer/évaluer (qch.)/fixer la valeur de (qch.) **2.** (*a*) imposer/taxer (qn qch.); tarifer (qch.); **to rate s.o./a property at,** taxer qn/un immeuble à; **heavily rated building,** immeuble fortement taxé (*b*) *Ins:* **to rate s.o. up,** faire payer à qn une prime plus élevée.

rateable, *a.* **1.** évaluable **2.** imposable; **rateable value,** (*i*) loyer matriciel/valeur locative imposable (d'un immeuble) (*ii*) évaluation cadastrale (d'un terrain à bâtir).

ratepayer, *n.* contribuable *mf.*

ratification, *n. Jur:* ratification *f*/homologation *f*/validation *f.*

ratify, *v.tr. Jur:* ratifier/sanctionner/valider/homologuer; **to ratify a contract,** approuver un contrat.

rating, *n.* **1.** (*a*) estimation *f*/évaluation *f* (d'une pièce de monnaie/etc.) (*b*) tarification *f* (des transports, etc.); taxation *f* (d'une marchandise); répartition *f* des impôts locaux (*c*) classement *m*/classification *f* (d'une auto, etc.) **2.** évaluation (assignée à qch.); **credit rating,** réputation *f* de solvabilité; **market rating,** cours *m* en Bourse; **merit rating,** appréciation *f*/notation *f* du personnel; (*of machine*) **performance rating,** rendement effectif; **personnel rating,** appréciation/notation *f* du personnel; **workforce rating,** notation *f* de la main-d'œuvre.

ratio, *n.* **1.** raison *f*/rapport *m*/coefficient *m*/proportion *f*/ratio *m*; **in the ratio of one to three,** dans le rapport/dans la proportion de un à trois; **ten-to-one ratio,** proportion décuple; **accounting ratio,** ratio comptable; **acid-test ratio,** ratio de fonds de roulement net; **assets-to-equity ratio,** ratio de capitalisation; **capital-labour ratio,** ratio capital-travail/ratio d'intensité capitalistique; **capital-output ratio,** ratio d'intensité de capital; *Fin: Book-k:* **cash ratio,** coefficient de trésorerie; **cost-benefit ratio,** rapport coût-bénéfice; **current assets ratio/ratio of quick current assets to current liabilities,** coefficient de liquidité; **debt-to-equity ratio,** ratio d'endettement; **liquid assets ratio,** ratio de liquidité; **net profit ratio,** ratio de rentabilité nette/taux de profit net; **price-earnings ratio,** rapport cours-bénéfice; **profit-volume ratio,** rapport profit sur ventes; **quality-price ratio,** rapport qualité-prix; **ratio of working expenses/***NAm:*

operating ratio, coefficient d'exploitation **2.** taux *m*; **cover ratio,** taux de couverture; **mark-up ratio,** taux de marge.

rationale, *n.* analyse raisonnée/exposé raisonné (d'un procédé).

rationalization, *n.* rationalisation *f* (d'une industrie, etc.); organisation rationnelle (de l'industrie).

rationalize, *v.tr.* rationaliser (une industrie, etc.).

rationing, *n.* rationnement *m*; **capital rationing,** rationnement de capitaux.

rat-race, *n. F:* **the rat-race,** le panier de crabes/la foire d'empoigne/la course au bifteck.

raw, *a.* **raw material,** matière(s) première(s); matériaux bruts; *Cmptr:* **raw data,** données brutes/à traiter/non traitées.

re, *prep.* **re your letter of March 8th,** relativement à/me référant à/au sujet de votre lettre du 8 mars.

react, *v.i.* (*of prices*) réagir.

reaction, *n.* réaction *f*; **sharp reaction of sterling on the foreign market exchange,** vive réaction du sterling sur le marché des changes.

read, *v.tr.* lire (un livre, une lettre, etc.); *Adm:* **read and approved,** lu et approuvé; **to read a report (to the meeting),** donner lecture d'un rapport (à l'assemblée).

readjust, *v.tr.* **to readjust the wage structure,** r(é)ajuster les salaires.

readjustment, *n.* **the unions are demanding a readjustment of the wage structure,** les syndicats *m* réclament un r(é)ajustement des salaires.

readvertise, *v.tr.* annoncer de nouveau/faire passer une deuxième annonce.

readvertisement, *n.* deuxième annonce (pour le même poste).

ready, *a.* **1. ready money,** argent comptant/liquide; **to pay in ready money,** payer (au) comptant 2. **goods that meet with a ready sale,** marchandises *f* de vente courante/marchandises qui s'écoulent rapidement.

ready-to-wear, *a.* **ready-to-wear clothes,** (le) prêt-à-porter.

real, *a.* **1.** véritable/réel; **real accounts,** compte *m* de valeur; **real cost,** coût réel; **real income,** revenu réel/effectif; **real terms,** termes *m* réels/effectifs; **in real terms,** en monnaie constante; *Cmptr:* **real time,** temps *m* réel; *Fin:* **real value,** valeur effective; **real wages,** salaires réels **2.** *Jur:* **real estate,** propriété immobilière/biens immobiliers/immeubles *mpl*; (*landed property only*) propriété foncière/biens fonciers; bien-fonds *mpl*; *NAm:* **real estate agent,** agent immobilier; **real estate agency,** agence *f* immobilière; **real estate leasing,** crédit-bail *m* immobilier; **commercial and residential real estate,** agence de location et vente d'immeubles commerciaux et résidentiels.

realignment, *n.* **realignment of currencies,** réalignement *m* monétaire; **realignment of exchange rates,** réalignement des taux de change.

realizable, *a.* (*a*) (projet) réalisable (*b*) **realizable assets,** actif *m* réalisable.

realization, *n.* (*a*) réalisation *f* (d'un projet, etc.) (*b*) *Fin:* conversion *f* en espèces; réalisation (d'un placement, d'une propriété); mobilisation *f* (d'une indemnité); **realization account,** compte de liquidation (*c*) *Jur:* conversion (de biens meubles) en biens immeubles.

realize, *v.tr.* (*a*) réaliser (un projet, etc.) (*b*) *Fin:* convertir (des biens) en espèces; vendre/réaliser (une propriété, un placement); mobiliser (une indemnité); **these shares cannot be realized,** il n'y a pas de marché pour ces titres (*c*) réaliser (des bénéfices) (*d*) *Jur:* convertir (des biens meubles en biens immeubles) (*e*) (*of goods*) **to realize a high price,** atteindre/rapporter un bon prix.

realtor, *n. NAm:* agent immobilier.

realty, *n. Jur:* (*a*) bien immobilier (*b*) *coll.*

biens immobiliers; (biens) immeubles *mpl.*

reapply, *v.i.* faire une nouvelle demande; écrire de nouveau.

reappoint, *v.tr.* réintégrer (qn) dans ses fonctions.

reappraisal, *n.* réévaluation *f.*

reasonable, *a.* raisonnable; **reasonable prices,** prix modérés/raisonnables/abordables; **reasonable offer,** offre *f* acceptable/raisonnable.

reassess, *v.tr.* (*a*) réévaluer/réviser le taux d'imposition (d'un contribuable) (*b*) réévaluer (des dommages, un immeuble, etc.).

reassessment, *n.* (*a*) révision *f* du taux d'imposition (*b*) réévaluation *f.*

reassign, *v.tr.* **to reassign funds to their original use,** réaffecter des fonds à leur destination première.

reassignment, *n.* réaffectation *f* (de fonds).

reassurance, *n. Ins:* réassurance *f.*

reassure, *v.tr. Ins:* réassurer.

rebate, *n.* **1.** rabais *m*/remise *f*/escompte *m*; bonification *f*/ristourne *f*; remboursement *m*; (*on goods not up to sample*) réfaction *f*; **to allow a rebate on an account,** faire une remise sur un compte; *Adm:* **rent rebate,** remise de loyer; **tax rebate,** dégrèvement *m*/crédit *m* d'impôt.

rebound, *n.* **sharp rebound of the market,** reprise vigoureuse du marché; **a technical rebound,** une réaction technique.

recapitalization, *n. Fin:* changement *n* de la structure financière (d'une société)

recapitalize, *v.tr. Fin:* **to recapitalize a company,** changer la structure financière d'une société.

recede, *v.i.* décliner (en valeur); *StExch:* **oil shares receded three points,** les pétrole *m* ont reculé/baissé de trois points.

receipt[1], *n.* **1.** (*a*) recette *f*; *pl.* **receipts,** re cettes/rentrées *f*/encaissements *m*; **receipts and expenditure,** recettes et dépenses *f*; **receipts and payments,** rentrées et sorties *f* (*b*) réception *f*; **to acknowledge receipt of a letter,** accuser réception d'une lettre; **I am in receipt of your letter of June 9th,** j'ai bien reçu votre lettre du 9 juin; **on receipt of (this letter, your parcel),** au reçu de/dès réception de (cette lettre, votre envoi); **to pay on receipt,** payer à (la) réception; **within ten days of receipt,** dans les dix jours suivant réception **2.** reçu *m*/récépissé *m*/acquit *m*/quittance *f* (**for goods, money,** de marchandises, d'argent); **customs receipt,** récépissé de douane; **formal receipt,** quittance comptable; **receipt book,** carnet *m* de quittances; **receipt for a loan,** reconnaissance *f* de dette; **receipt form,** formule *f* d'acquit; **receipt for payment,** acquit/quittance/reçu; **receipt in full (discharge),** reçu pour solde de tout compte; **receipt on account,** reçu à valoir; **receipt for a registered parcel,** récépissé postal (d'un envoi recommandé); **receipt stamp,** timbre *m* de quittance/timbre-quittance *m*; **rent receipt,** quittance de loyer; **warehouse receipt,** récépissé d'entrepôt: *Fin:* **application receipt for shares,** récépissé de souscription à des actions; **to give a receipt,** donner un reçu; **send it with the receipt,** envoyez-le avec la facture acquittée.

receipt², *v.tr.* acquitter/quittancer/décharger (une facture); (*with rubber stamp*) apposer le tampon "acquitté"/"pour acquit" sur (une facture); **to receipt a bill in the margin,** émarger une facture.

receivable, *a.* **accounts receivable/n.pl. receivables,** *n.* créances *f*; comptes-clients *m*/compte d'actif/comptabilité clients; **bills receivable,** effets *m* à recevoir.

receive, *v.tr.* recevoir (une nouvelle, une lettre, etc.); **on receiving your letter,** dès réception de votre lettre; **I have received your letter,** votre lettre m'est parvenue; j'ai bien reçu votre lettre; **to receive money,** recevoir/toucher de l'argent; **to receive one's salary,** toucher son salaire; **received the sum of £100,** reçu la somme

de £100; (*on bill*) **received with thanks,** acquitté/payé/pour acquit.

receiver, *n.* **1.** (*a*) personne *f* qui reçoit (qch.); destinataire *mf* (d'une lettre, etc.); *Jur:* réceptionnaire *mf* (d'un envoi) (*b*) *NAm:* receveur *m* (des deniers publics); **receiver's office,** recette *f* (*c*) *Jur:* **receiver in bankruptcy/official receiver,** administrateur *m* judiciaire/mandataire-liquidateur *m*; **to be in the hands of the receiver,** être en règlement judiciaire (*d*) *StExch:* **receiver of contango,** reporteur *m* **2.** (**telephone) receiver,** récepteur *m*/écouteur *m*.

receivership, *n.* **to go into receivership,** se mettre en règlement judiciaire.

receiving¹, *a.* **receiving clerk,** réceptionnaire *mf*; **receiving department,** service *m* de la réception.

receiving², *n.* (*a*) réception *f*; **receiving of goods,** réception de marchandises; **receiving certificate,** certificat *m* de réception; **receiving office,** *Post:* bureau *m* de réception; *Rail:* bureau de(s) messageries (*b*) *Jur:* **receiving order,** mandat *m* d'action; ordonnance *f* de mise sous séquestre.

reception, *n.* **1.** (*at hotel*) **the reception desk/office,** la réception/le bureau de réception; *NAm:* **reception clerk,** réceptionniste *mf*/préposé, -ée à la réception; **chief reception clerk,** chef *m* de (la) réception **2.** (bureau d')accueil *m* **3.** réception (officielle, etc.).

receptionist, *n.* préposé, -ée à la réception/réceptionniste *mf* (d'un hôtel, etc.); (*in tourist centre, etc.*) hôtesse *f* d'accueil; **head receptionist,** chef *m* de (la) réception.

recession, *n. PolEc:* récession *f*; crise *f* économique; (*of business*) ralentissement *m* des affaires.

recipient, *n.* destinataire *mf* (d'une lettre, etc.); bénéficiaire *mf* (d'un chèque, d'un effet); *Jur:* donataire *mf*; **recipient of an allowance,** allocataire *mf*.

reciprocal, *a.* réciproque/mutuel; **reciprocal agreements,** accords *m* réciproques; **reciprocal concessions,** concessions *f* réciproques; *Jur:* **reciprocal contract,** contrat réciproque/bilatéral; *StExch:* **reciprocal holdings,** participations croisées.

reciprocate, *v.tr.* *Book-k:* **to reciprocate an entry,** passer écriture conforme; passer une écriture en conformité.

reciprocity, *n.* réciprocité *f* (de concessions).

reckon, **1.** *v.tr* compter/calculer/faire le compte de; supputer (une somme, etc.); **to reckon the cost of sth.,** calculer les frais de (qch.) **2.** *v.i.* compter/calculer.

recognition, *n.* **brand recognition,** identification *f* d'une marque.

recognized, *a.* **recognized agent,** agent accrédité; **recognized merchant,** commerçant attitré.

recommend, *v.tr.* recommander; **to recommend s.o. to an employer,** recommander qn à un employeur; **to recommend a candidate for a post,** recommander un candidat pour un emploi; **to recommend a (good) hotel,** recommander un (bon) hôtel; **recommended retail price,** prix *m* recommandé/conseillé.

recommendation, *n.* **1.** recommandation *f*; **I have come on the recommendation of one of your customers,** je viens sur la recommandation d'un de vos clients; *Fin:* **recommendation of a dividend,** proposition *f* de dividende **2.** **stockbroker's list of recommendations,** liste *f* de placements conseillés par un courtier; **buy recommendation,** recommandation d'acheter.

reconcile, *v.tr.* *Book-k:* **to reconcile one account with another,** faire accorder un compte avec un autre.

reconciliation, *n.* *Book-k:* ajustement *m* (des écritures); **reconciliation account,** compte collectif.

reconstruction, *n.* reconstitution *f* (d'une société, etc.); **economic and financial reconstruction,** restauration économique et financière.

record¹, *n.* **1.** (*a*) note *f*/mention *f*; **to be shown only as a record,** ne figurer que pour mémoire; **off the record,** officieux; officieusement (*b*) registre *m* **2.** *pl.* **records,** archives *f*; registres *m* **3.** carrière *f*/dossier *m*/antécédents *mpl* (de qn); **service record,** état *m* de service; **track record,** (*i*) expérience professionnelle (de qn) (*ii*) résultats obtenus (par une entreprise) **4.** record *m*; **record figure,** chiffre *m* record; **record production/output,** production *f* record/sans précédent; **record year,** année *f* record.

record², *v.tr.* enregistrer; *Adm:* recenser (des faits, etc.); **(to send a letter by) recorded delivery,** (envoyer une lettre) en recommandé.

record-breaking, *a.* **record-breaking production,** production *f* record.

recording, *n.* (prise de) note *f* (d'une commande).

recoup, *v.tr.* **1.** dédommager (qn); **to recoup (one's losses),** se rattraper (de ses pertes); récupérer son argent. **2.** *Jur:* défalquer/faire le décompte de (qch.).

recoupment, *n.* *NAm:* dédommagement *m*.

recourse, *n.* *Fin: Jur:* **to have recourse to the endorser of a bill,** avoir recours contre l'endosseur d'un effet; **endorsement without recourse,** endossement *m* à forfait; **to reserve right of recourse,** se réserver le recours/un droit de recours; **recourse against third parties,** recours contre des tiers.

recover, *v.tr. & i.* (*a*) recouvrer/regagner/ rentrer en possession de (ses biens); rentrer dans (ses dépenses); recouvrer/ récupérer/faire rentrer (une créance); **to recover one's money,** récupérer son argent/rentrer en possession de son argent/se (faire) rembourser; **to recover money advanced,** récupérer ses avances; **to recover damages from s.o.,** obtenir des dommages-intérêts de qn; se faire dédommager par qn (*b*) **the market is recovering,** le marché reprend/se ranime; **oils recovered five pence,** les valeurs pétrolières ont remonté de cinq pence; **prices are recovering,** les prix *m* se relèvent/les cours *m* reprennent.

recoverable, *a.* (*of loss, etc.*) recouvrable/récupérable.

recovery, *n.* **1.** recouvrement *m*/récupération *f*; **losses beyond/past recovery,** pertes *f* irrécupérables; **recovery of debts,** recouvrement de créances; **recovery of expenses,** recouvrement des dépenses/récupération des frais **2.** *Jur:* **recovery of payment made by mistake,** répétition *f* d'indu; **action for recovery of property,** (action en) revendication *f*; **recovery of damages,** obtention *f* de dommages-intérêts **3.** redressement *m*/relèvement *m* (économique, etc.); reprise *f* (des affaires); **trade recovery/industrial recovery,** reprise/relance *f* économique; **recovery of prices,** reprise des cours.

recredit, *v.tr. Book-k: Fin:* faire une extourne.

recruit, *v.tr.* recruter (du personnel).

recruiting, recruitment, *n.* recrutement *m* (de personnel).

rectification, *n.* rectification *f*/correction *f* (d'une erreur, etc.).

rectify, *v.tr.* rectifier/corriger (un calcul, une erreur); *Book-k:* **to rectify an entry,** modifier/rectifier une écriture.

recurrent, *a.* **recurrent expenses,** dépenses *f* qui reviennent périodiquement.

recycle, *v.tr.* recycler (des journaux, etc.).

red, *n. F:* **red tape,** paperasserie *f*/bureaucratie *f*/chinoiseries administratives; *F:* **to be in the red/to go into the red,** avoir un découvert/un compte *m* à découvert; **the company is in the red again,** la société est retombée dans le rouge; **to be out of the red,** avoir un compte créditeur.

redeem, *v.tr.* (*a*) racheter/dégager (une propriété, un nantissement, etc.) (*b*) rembourser (une obligation, une annuité, etc.); **to redeem a bill,** honorer une traite; **to redeem a debt,** amortir une dette/se

libérer d'une dette; **to redeem a mortgage,** (*of mortgagor*) éteindre une hypothèque; (*of purchaser of mortgaged property*) purger une hypothèque (*c*) obtenir le remboursement (d'obligations remboursables, etc.); encaisser (un bon de caisse, etc.).

redeemable, *a. Fin:* (*of stock, etc.*) rachetable/remboursable/amortissable.

redeeming, *n.* (*a*) rachat *m*/dégagement *m* (d'un objet mis en gage, d'une propriété hypothéquée) (*b*) remboursement *m*/amortissement *m* (d'une obligation); **redeeming of a mortgage,** (*by mortgagor*) extinction *f* d'une hypothèque; (*by purchaser of mortgaged property*) purge *f* d'une hypothèque.

redemption, *n.* (*a*) *Fin:* remboursement *m*/amortissement *m* (d'une obligation); rachat *m*/*Jur:* rédemption *f* (d'un emprunt, d'une concession); **debt redemption,** amortissement de la dette publique; **interim redemption/redemption before due date,** amortissement/remboursement anticipé; **optional redemption date,** remboursement à période d'option; **redemption date,** amortissement obligatoire; **redemption fund,** caisse *f* d'amortissement; **redemption loan,** emprunt *m* d'amortissement; **redemption fee/premium,** prime *f* de remboursement; **redemption table,** plan *m* d'amortissement (d'une dette, etc.); **redemption value/price,** valeur *f* de rachat/de remboursement; **redemption yield,** rendement *m* sur remboursement; **terms of redemption,** (*i*) condition *f* de rachat/de remboursement (*ii*) plan d'amortissement (*b*) **redemption (of a pledge, of a security),** dégagement *m*/retrait *m* (d'un gage, d'un nantissement); **redemption of a mortgage,** (*by mortgagor*) extinction *f*; (*by purchaser of mortgaged property*) purge *f* d'une hypothèque (*c*) *Jur:* **sale with power/option of redemption,** vente *f* avec faculté de rachat; vente à réméré; **covenant of redemption,** pacte *m* de rachat.

redeploy, *v.tr. Econ:* redéployer; *Adm: Ind:* réorganiser (un service); redistribuer/

reclasser/procéder à une nouvelle répartition de (la main-d'œuvre, etc.).

redeployment, *n. Econ:* redéploiement *m; Adm: Ind:* réorganisation *f* (d'un service); réorganisation/reclassement *m* (de la main-d'œuvre).

rediscount[1], *n.* 1. réescompte *m* 2. *F:* papier réescompté.

rediscount[2], *v.tr.* réescompter.

rediscountable, *a.* réescomptable.

redistribute, *v.tr.* redistribuer.

redistribution, *n.* redistribution *f;* nouvelle distribution.

reduce, *v.tr.* réduire/baisser/rabaisser/diminuer (le prix, etc.); **reduced to £5 from £10,** prix réduit de £10 à £5; **to reduce taxes,** alléger les impôts; **to reduce the rates on a house,** dégrever un immeuble; **to reduce expenses,** diminuer/réduire les dépenses; *Ind:* **to reduce the output,** ralentir la production; **to reduce the working week from 42 to 40 hours,** ramener la semaine de 42 heures à 40 heures; **to reduce the cost of living,** faire baisser le coût de la vie.

reduced, *a.* réduit; **reduced goods,** soldes *mpl;* **reduced price,** prix réduit; **bought at reduced prices,** acheté à prix réduit/à rabais/en solde; **reduced assessment on property,** dégrèvement *m.*

reduction, *n.* (*a*) réduction *f*/diminution *f*/baisse *f* (des prix, des salaires); **cost reduction,** réduction des frais; **reduction of taxes/of taxation,** allègement *m* d'dégrèvement *m* d'impôts; **reduction of expenses,** réduction *f* des dépenses; **reduction of share capital,** réduction du capital social; **staff reduction,** réduction du personnel; **600 job reductions,** 600 suppressions d'emploi (*b*) rabais *m*/remise *f;* **to make a reduction on an article,** faire un rabais/une remise sur un article.

redundancy, *n.* licenciement *m;* chômage partiel; **redundancy pay(ment),** indemnité

f/prime *f* de licenciement; **voluntary redundancy,** départ *m* volontaire.

redundant, *a.* **redundant capital,** surplus *m* (de capital)/capital en trop; *Ind:* **to be made redundant,** être (déclaré en surnombre et) licencié; être en chômage technique; **person made redundant,** licencié économique.

re-employ, *v.tr.* reprendre/réembaucher (qn); remployer/réemployer (qch.).

re-employment, *n.* réemploi *m* (de qn qch.); *Fin:* remploi *m* (de fonds).

re-engage, *v.tr.* rengager/réembaucher (des employés).

re-establish, *v.tr.* rétablir; **to re-establish a company's credit,** raffermir le crédit d'une maison.

re-establishment, *n.* rétablissement *m.*

re-export[1], *n.* réexportation *f;* **re-export trade,** commerce *m* intermédiaire réexportation *f;* **re-exports,** produits réexportés.

re-export[2], *v.tr.* réexporter.

re-exportation, *n.* réexportation *f.*

refer, 1. *v.tr.* (*of bank*) **to refer a cheque t drawer,** refuser d'honorer un chèqu (*faute de provision*); **referred to drawer** retour au tireur 2. *v.i.* **I shall have to refe (back) to the board,** il faudra que je con sulte le conseil de direction; **to refer to document,** se reporter à un documen **referring to your letter,** (comme) suite votre lettre/(nous, me) référant à votr lettre.

referee, *n.* 1. *Jur:* arbitre *m*/médiateur *m* **board of referees,** commission arbitrale 2 répondant, -ante; **to give s.o. as a refere** se recommander de qn.

reference, *n.* 1. (*a*) renvoi *m* (d'une affair devant arbitre; renvoi/référence *f* (d'ur question à une autorité, etc.) (*b*) comp tence *f*/pouvoirs *mpl* (d'un tribunal **terms of reference of a commission/order** **reference,** délimitation *f* des pouvoi d'une commission; mandat *m*/attr butions *fpl* d'une commission; **under these terms of reference,** aux termes des instructions données **2. with reference to your letter of June 9th,** nous référant à votre lettre/comme suite à votre lettre du 9 juin **3.** (*at head of letter*) **our reference,** N/Réf(érence); **your reference,** V/Réf(érence); **please quote this reference number,** numéro à rappeler; **when replying quote reference no. RL3U,** adresser sous référence RL3U **4.** (*a*) renseignements *mpl*; références *fpl* (d'employé, etc.); **to give a reference (about s.o.),** fournir des références sur qn; **to take up s.o.'s references,** prendre des renseignements sur qn; **to have good references,** avoir de bonnes références/de bonnes recommandations; **banker's/ bank reference,** référence bancaire; **to ask for references,** solliciter une recommandation; **letter of reference,** lettre de recommandation (*b*) répondant, -ante; **who are your references?** quelles sont les personnes qui peuvent fournir des références? **to give s.o. as a reference,** se recommander/se réclamer de qn; **you may use my name as (a) reference,** vous pouvez donner mon nom comme référence.

refinancing, *n.* (*a*) refinancement *m* (*b*) emprunt *m* de remboursement.

reflate, *v.tr. PolEc:* ranimer/relancer *f* (l'économie, etc.).

reflation, *n. PolEc:* relance (économique).

refloat, *v.tr. Fin:* (*a*) émettre de nouveau (un emprunt) (*b*) renflouer (une entreprise, une société).

reform, *n.* réforme *f*.

refresher, *n.* **to attend a refresher course,** se recycler/suivre un cours de recyclage/suivre un cours de perfectionnement.

refrigerate, *v.tr. Ind:* réfrigérer/garder au réfrigérateur; **refrigerated lorry,** camion frigorifique/réfrigéré; **refrigerated ship,** navire *m* frigorifique.

refrigeration, *n.* réfrigération *f*; **to keep under refrigeration,** garder au réfrigéra-

teur; **refrigeration plant,** installation *f* frigorifique.

refund[1], *n.* (*a*) remboursement *m*; **to obtain a refund,** être remboursé/se faire rembourser/obtenir un remboursement (*b*) *Jur:* restitution *f* d'indu.

refund[2], **1.** *v.tr.* (*a*) rembourser (de l'argent, un paiement) (**to s.o.,** à qn); **to refund s.o.,** rembourser qn; **to refund the cost of postage,** rembourser les frais de port; **to have one's money refunded,** obtenir un remboursement; **money refunded if not satisfied,** satisfaction garantie ou argent remis (*b*) ristourner (un paiement en trop); restituer (de l'argent) **2.** *v.i. Jur:* faire restitution d'indu.

refundable, *a.* remboursable (**over 25 years,** sur une période de 25 ans); (*when hiring*) **deposit refundable,** caution *f*/ acompte *m* remboursable; **bottle with refundable deposit,** bouteille consignée.

refunding, *n.* remboursement *m*; **refunding loan/***NAm* **refunding,** emprunt *m* de remboursement; **refunding clause,** clause *f* de remboursement.

refusal, *n.* **1.** (*a*) refus *m*; **refusal to pay,** refus de paiement (*b*) **refusal of goods,** refus de marchandises **2.** droit *m* de refuser; droit de préemption; **to have (the) first refusal,** avoir la première offre de qch; **right of first refusal,** droit de préférence.

refuse, *v.tr.* **1.** refuser (une offre, etc.) **2.** (*a*) rejeter/repousser (une requête) (*b*) **to refuse to pay,** refuser de payer.

regard, *n.* (*a*) **with regard to,** en ce qui concerne (*b*) **my kindest regards,** mon meilleur souvenir/mes sincères amitiés.

region, *n.* **it will cost in the region of £50,** cela coûtera dans les £50/environ £50.

register[1], *n.* (*a*) registre *m*; journal *m*; *Adm: etc:* sommier *m*; **Lloyd's register,** classification *f* de navires marchands; *Cust:* **register of goods in bond,** sommier d'entrepôt; *Nau:* **ship's register,** livre *m* de bord; **plant register,** plan *m* de charge d'une usine; **to enter an item in a register,**

rapporter/inscrire/noter/mettre un article sur/dans un registre; **register of debenture holders/of debentures,** registre/livre des obligataires; **shareholder's register,** registre/livre des actionnaires: **share register,** registre des actions (*b*) **commercial register,** registre de commerce (*tenu par un commerçant*); *Adm:* **companies register/register of companies/trade register** = registre du commerce; **cadastral/land register,** registre du cadastre; **charges register/register of charges,** extrait *m* du registre du cadastre.

register[2], *v.tr.* enregistrer/inscrire/immatriculer/enrôler; **to register a company,** immatriculer (une société) au registre du commerce; **to register a security,** immatriculer une valeur; **to register a trademark,** déposer une marque de fabrique.

registered, *a.* (*a*) enregistré/inscrit/immatriculé; **registered design,** modèle déposé (*b*) *Fin:* **registered bond/debenture,** obligation nominative; **registered capital,** capital déclaré; **registered stock/securities,** effets/titres nominatifs; **registered trade mark,** marque déposée; **registered value,** valeur enregistrée/constatée (*c*) *Post:* **registered letter/parcel,** (*i*) lettre recommandée/colis recommandé; (envoi en) recommandé *m* (*ii*) lettre/colis avec valeur déclarée; **by registered post,** en recommandé (*d*) **registered office(s),** siège social.

registering, *n.* (*a*) enregistrement *m*/inscription *f*/immatriculation *f* (*b*) *Post:* recommandation *f* (d'une lettre, d'un colis).

registrar, *n.* employé, -ée/préposé, -ée aux registres; *Adm:* **registrar of mortgages,** conservateur *m* des hypothèques; **companies registrar/registrar of companies,** directeur *m* du registre des sociétés.

registration, *n.* enregistrement *m*/inscription *f*; immatriculation *f* (d'une valeur, etc.); **land registration,** inscription au cadastre; **vehicle registration document,** titre *m* de propriété d'un véhicule/*F:* = carte grise; *Fin:* **registration and transfer fees,** droits *m* d'inscription et de transfert; **registration certificate,** matricule *f*; **registration fees,** *Post:* taxe *f* de recommandation; *Adm:* droit d'inscription; frais *mpl* d'enregistrement; **registration number,** *Aut:* numéro *m* d'immatriculation/numéro minéralogique; *Adm:* numéro matricule; **registration of luggage,** enregistrement des bagages; **registration of mortgages,** inscriptions hypothécaires/des hypothèques; **registration of (a) trademark,** dépôt *m* d'une marque de fabrique.

registry, *n.* (*i*) bureau *m* d'enregistrement (*ii*) greffe *m*; **land registry,** bureau du cadastre; **registry books,** livres *mp*. d'ordre/registres *mpl*; *Nau:* **certificate of registry,** lettre *f* de mer; **port of registry,** port *m* d'attache/d'immatriculation.

regression, *n.* **regression analysis,** analyse *f* de régression.

regular, *a.* 1. régulier; **regular customer,** (bon) client *m*; habitué, -ée; **regular income,** revenu régulier; **regular salary,** salaire *m* fixe; **regular staff,** employés permanents 2. *Ind:* **regular model,** modèle courant; type courant; **regular price,** prix *m* ordinaire/prix de règle.

regulate, *v.tr.* régler; réglementer; **the price is regulated by supply and demand,** le prix est déterminé par l'offre et la demande; **regulated price,** prix réglementé.

regulation, *n.* 1. règlement *m*/réglementation *f* (des affaires, etc.) 2. règlement/arrêté *m*/ordonnance *f*/prescription *f*; **regulations,** règlement(s)/réglementation/prescriptions *fpl*/dispositions *fpl*; **customs regulations,** règlements de la douane; **price regulation,** réglementation des prix; **Stock Exchange regulations,** règlement de Bourse; **safety regulations,** règles *fpl* de sécurité.

reimbursable, *a.* remboursable (**over 2 years,** sur une période de 25 ans).

reimburse, *v.tr.* 1. rembourser (de l'argent) 2. **to reimburse s.o. (for) sth,** rembourser qn de qch.; désintéresser qn

to be reimbursed, rentrer dans ses frais/se faire rembourser; obtenir un remboursement.

reimport[1], *n.* réimportation *f.*

reimport[2], *v.tr.* réimporter.

reimportation, *n.* réimportation *f.*

reinflate, *v.tr.* relancer/ranimer (l'économie).

reinstate, *v.tr.* (*a*) réintégrer (qn) (dans ses fonctions); **to reinstate s.o. in his former job,** réaffecter qn à son premier emploi (*b*) rétablir (une loi).

reinstatement, *n.* (*a*) réintégration *f* (de qn dans ses fonctions) (*b*) rétablissement *m* (d'une loi).

reinsurance, *n. Ins:* réassurance *f*; contre-assurance *f*; **reinsurance broker,** courtier *m* de réassurance; **reinsurance policy,** police *f* de réassurance.

reinsure, *v.tr. Ins:* réassurer.

reinsurer, *n. Ins:* réassureur *m.*

reinvest, *v.tr. Fin:* (*a*) replacer (des fonds); trouver un nouveau placement pour (des fonds) (*b*) réinvestir/reverser des bénéfices (dans une entreprise).

reinvestment, *n. Fin:* (*a*) nouveau placement (*b*) bénéfices réinvestis.

reissue[1], *n.* (*a*) *Fin:* nouvelle émission (de billets de banque, etc.) (*b*) nouvelle édition/réédition *f* (d'un livre).

reissue[2], *v.tr. Fin:* émettre de nouveau (des actions, etc.).

reject[1], *n.* (pièce *f* de) rebut *m*; **export reject,** article (de rebut) non destiné à l'exportation; **reject shop,** solderie *f*/magasin *m* de vente d'articles déclassés.

reject[2], *v.tr.* (*a*) rejeter/repousser (une offre, une proposition) (*b*) refuser (des marchandises, un candidat, etc.).

relate, *v.i.* se rapporter/avoir rapport/avoir trait (**to,** à); **agreement relating**

to . . ., convention *f* ayant trait à/concernant . . . .

related, *a.* (*a*) **related company,** société affiliée; **related markets,** marchés liés/connexes (*b*) **earnings(-)related pension,** pension proportionnelle au salaire.

relation, *n.* (*a*) **in/with relation to . . .,** en/pour ce qui concerne . . .; par rapport à (*b*) *pl.* relations *fpl*; **to have business relations with s.o.,** être en relations d'affaires avec qn; **industrial relations,** relations industrielles; **labour relations,** relations syndicales; relations ouvrières; relations du travail; **labour-management relations,** rapports patrons-ouvriers; **public relations (PR) officer,** chef *m* du service des relations publiques.

relative, *a.* (*of share, commodity*) **relative strength,** taux *m* de correlation/coefficient *m* beta.

release[1], *n.* 1. (*a*) décharge *f*/libération *f* (**from an obligation,** d'une obligation) (*b*) **day release,** congé de formation rémunéré; jour de permission accordé aux employés d'une maison pour se perfectionner (*c*) (*of records, etc.*) **new release,** (dernière) nouveauté/vient de paraître (*d*) *Cust:* **release of wine from bond,** congé pour le transport des vins; **release of goods against payment,** libération de marchandises; **release of mortgage,** mainlevée *f* d'une hypothèque 2. acquit *m*/quittance *f*/reçu *m.*

release[2], *v.tr.* 1. (*a*) décharger/acquitter/libérer (qn d'une obligation); libérer (un débiteur) (*b*) sortir/mettre en vente (un nouveau disque, etc.) (*c*) **to release funds,** débloquer des fonds 2. *Jur:* (*a*) **to release a debt/a tax,** remettre une dette/un impôt; faire (à qn) la remise d'une dette/d'un impôt (*b*) abandonner/renoncer à (un droit, une créance).

reliability, *n.* (*of machine*) fiabilité *f.*

reliable, *a.* (*person*) sérieux/digne de confiance/sur qui on peut compter/à qui on peut se fier; (*renseignement*) sûr; (*of machine*) fiable/sûr; **reliable firm,** maison *f* de confiance; **reliable guarantee,** garantie *f* solide; **to have sth. from a reliable source,** tenir qch. de bonne source/de source sûre.

relief, *n.* **tax relief,** réduction *f*/dégrèvement *m* d'impôt; allègement *m*/allégement *m* (fiscal); **marginal relief,** dégrèvement marginal.

relocate, *v.tr.* réimplanter (une usine); transférer; déménager.

relocation, *n.* déménagement *m*; transfert *m*; **relocation allowance,** indemnité *f* de déménagement.

remainder[1], *n.* (exemplaire(s) d'un livre) invendu *m*; livre(s) en solde.

remainder[2], *v.tr.* **to remainder (books),** solder (une édition/les invendus).

reminder, *n.* (*a*) (lettre *f* de) rappel *m*; avertissement *m*; **reminder of account due/of due date,** rappel d'échéance (*b*) *Publ:* (lettre de) relance *f.*

remission, *n.* remise *f* (d'une dette, etc.); **remission of a tax,** remise d'un impôt; détaxe *f*; **remission of taxes,** exonération *f.*

remit, *v.tr.* (*a*) remettre (une dette) (*b*) **to remit a sum of money to s.o.,** envoyer/remettre une somme à qn; faire remise d'une somme à qn; **kindly remit by cheque,** prière de régler par chèque.

remittance, *n.* règlement *m*; **send your remittance (to),** faites parvenir votre règlement (à).

remnant, *n.* coupon *m* (de tissu); **remnants,** soldes *m*; fins *f* de série.

remunerate, *v.tr.* (*a*) rémunérer (**s.o. for his services,** qn de ses services) (*b*) rémunérer/rétribuer (un service).

remuneration, *n.* rémunération *f* (**for,** de)/rétribution *f*/paiement *m*; **in remuneration for ...,** en rémunération de ....

remunerative, *a.* (travail, prix) rémunérateur.

render, *v.tr.* **to render an account to s.o.,** remettre un compte à qn; **as per account rendered/to account rendered,** suivan compte remis.

renew, *v.tr.* renouveler; **to renew a lease** renouveler un bail; **to renew one's sub scription to a newspaper,** se réabonner un journal; **to renew a bill,** prolonger un lettre de change; *Fin:* **to renew the coupon of a share certificate,** recouponner u certificat d'action.

renewal, *n.* **renewal (of subscription),** réa bonnement *m* (**to,** à); **renewal of a bil** atermoiement *m*/prolongation *f* d'un lettre de change; **renewal of a lease,** r nouvellement *m* d'un bail; *Ju* reconduction *f* (d'un contrat); *Fin:* r newal of coupons, recouponnement *m.*

rent[1], *n.* (*a*) loyer *m*; (prix de) location (d'une maison, etc.); **high rent,** gros loye loyer élevé; **low rent,** petit loyer/loye peu élevé; **nominal/peppercorn rent,** loye symbolique; **rack rent,** loyer très élev **rent back,** location-vente *f*; **rent free,** gr tuit; **to owe three months' rent,** devoir tro mois de loyer; **quarter's rent,** term *m*/loyer trimestriel; **rent roll,** registre des loyers/liste *f* des locataires (*b*) **grour rent,** redevance *f* emphytéotique/ren foncière.

rent[2], *v.tr.* (*a*) (*let*) louer (une maison) (*hire*) louer/prendre en location (un maison, etc.); **rented accomodation,** loge ment locatif; **rented car,** voiture *f* de loca tion/de louage; **to rent a house from th tenant,** sous-louer une maison (*c*) **th house rents at £200 a week,** cette maison loue £200 par semaine.

rental, *n.* (*a*) loyer *m*/location *f*; prix *m* d la location; **car rental,** location de vo tures; **rental income,** revenu locatif; **rent value,** valeur locative (d'un immeuble **yearly rental,** redevance annuelle/loye annuel (*b*) revenu locatif/revenu pr venant des loyers.

rentier, *n.* *Pol.Ec:* rentier *m.*

renting, *n.* location *f*/louage *m* (d'un maison, d'une voiture, etc.).

renunciation, *n.* cession *f* en pleine propriété/en usufruit.

reopen, 1. *v.tr.* rouvrir (un compte, etc.) **2.** *v.i.* **the shops will reopen on Monday,** la réouverture des magasin aura lieu lundi.

reopening, *n.* réouverture *f* (d'un magasin, etc.); **reopening day,** jour *m* de réouverture.

reorder[1], *n.* (*i*) commande renouvelée (*ii*) réapprovisionnement *m*; **reorder level/point,** seuil *m* de réapprovisionnement.

reorder[2], *v.tr.* renouveler une commande/faire une nouvelle commande (d'une marchandise, etc.)/commander à nouveau; faire une commande de réapprovisionnement.

reorganization, *n.* réorganisation *f.*

reorganize, 1. *v.tr.* réorganiser (les finances) **2.** *v.i.* (*of company, etc.*) se réorganiser.

rep, *n. F:* (= **representative**) représentant, -ante/délégué, -ée commercial(e).

repack, *v.tr.* rempaqueter/remballer/rencaisser (des marchandises).

repacking, *n.* rempaquetage *m*/remballage *m*/rencaissage *m* (de marchandises).

repair[1], *n.* réparation *f* (d'un bâtiment, d'une machine, etc.); **to be under repair/to be undergoing repairs,** être en réparation.

repair[2], *v.tr.* réparer (un bâtiment, une machine, etc.).

repatriation, *n.* **repatriation of funds,** rapatriement *m* de fonds.

repay, *v.tr.* rembourser (qn) **(for,** de); **to repay a debt,** rembourser/payer une dette; **to repay a debt in full,** amortir une dette; **to repay s.o.,** rembourser qn.

repayable, *a.* remboursable **(over 25 years,** sur une période de 25 ans).

repayment, *n.* remboursement *m* (d'une somme); **bond due for repayment,** obligation amortie; **repayment mortgage,** prêt-

logement *m* (*qui n'est pas lié à une assurance-vie*).

repeal[1], *n.* abrogation *f.*

repeal[2], *v.tr. Jur:* abroger.

repeat[1], *n.* **repeat (order),** commande renouvelée.

repeat[2], *v.tr.* renouveler (une commande); (*of special offer*) **cannot be repeated,** sans suite.

replace, *v.tr.* remplacer (qn, qch.).

replaceable, *a.* remplaçable.

replacement, *n.* (*a*) remplacement *m*/substitution *f*; **replacement cost,** coût *m* de remplacement; *Ins:* **replacement markets,** débouchés *m*/marchés *m* de (produits de) remplacement(s); **replacement value,** valeur *f* de remplacement (*b*) *Ind:* pièce *f* de rechange/pièce détachée (*c*) (*pers.*) remplaçant, -ante.

replevin, *n. Jur* main levée *f* de saisie.

reply[1], *n.* réponse *f*; **in reply to your letter,** en réponse à votre lettre/(comme) suite à votre lettre; *Post:* **reply card,** carte-réponse *f*; **reply-paid card,** carte-réponse affranchie; **(international) reply coupon,** coupon-réponse (international); (*of telegram, envelope*) **reply paid,** réponse payée.

reply[2], *v.i.* répondre **(to,** à).

report[1], *n.* (*a*) rapport *m* **(on,** sur); compte rendu; (*of meeting*) procès-verbal *m*; exposé *m*; récit *m* (d'une affaire); **to make/draw up a report on sth.,** faire/rédiger un rapport sur qch.; **to present a report to s.o. on sth.,** présenter/soumettre un rapport à qn sur qch.; **annual report (of a company),** rapport de gestion (d'une société); **audit(ors) report,** rapport des commissaires (aux comptes); **chairman's/manager's/president's report,** rapport du président; **progress report,** rapport périodique; rapport d'avancement (des travaux); **treasurer's report,** rapport financier; *StExch:* **stock market report,** bulletin *m* des cours de la Bourse; *Nau:* **damage report,** rapport d'avarie(s) (*b*) nouvelle *f*;

newspaper report, reportage *m*; **to confirm a report,** confirmer une nouvelle.

report[2], *v.tr.* (*a*) rapporter (un fait); rendre compte de (qch.); annoncer (les résultats de l'exercice écoulé); **to report progress to s.o.,** tenir qn au courant de la marche d'une affaire; **to report to s.o./to report on sth.,** envoyer/présenter un rapport à qn; faire un rapport sur qch./rendre compte de qch. (*b*) **please report to our branch in Paris,** veuillez vous rendre/vous présenter à notre succursale de Paris; *Cust:* **to report a vessel,** déclarer un navire; faire la déclaration d'entrée.

represent, *v.tr.* représenter (une maison de commerce, etc.)

representation, *n.* (*a*) représentation *f*; **worker representation,** représentation du personnel (*b*) **joint representation,** démarche collective.

representative, 1. *a.* typique; **representative sample,** échantillon *m* type **2.** *n.* représentant, -ante; **educational representative,** délégué, ée pédagogique; **foreign representative,** représentant, -ante à l'étranger; **sales representative,** représentant, -ante (de commerce)/délégué, -ée commercial(e); attaché commercial; **sole representatives of a firm,** seuls représentants d'une société; **trade representative,** délégué, -ée commercial(e).

reprocess, *v.tr.* recycler.

reprocessing, *n.* recyclage *m*.

repudiate, *v.tr.* nier (une dette); refuser d'honorer (un contrat).

repurchasable, *a.* rachetable.

repurchase[1], *n.* rachat *m/Jur:* réméré *m*; **sale with option of repurchase,** vente *f* à réméré/avec faculté de rachat; **repurchase agreement,** faculté *f* de rachat.

repurchase[2], *v.tr.* racheter; **sale with right to repurchase,** vente *f* à réméré.

request[1], *n.* demande *f*/prière *f*/requête *f*; **request for money/funds,** demande

d'argent/de crédits; **samples sent on request,** échantillons *m* sur demande.

request[2], *v.tr.* **to request s.o. to do sth.,** demander à qn de faire qch./prier qn de faire qch.; **as requested,** conformément à vos instructions/(comme) suite à votre demande.

requirement, *n.* condition *f*; besoin *m*; exigence *f*; **cash requirements,** besoins de trésorerie; **margin requirements,** couverture *f* obligatoire (en Bourse); **to meet your requirements,** (*i*) répondre à vos besoins (*ii*) accepter vos conditions.

requisition, *n.* demande *f*; **requisition for materials/for supplies,** demande/réquisition *f* de matériaux; commande *f* de fournitures; **requisition number,** numéro *m* de référence (d'une demande).

resale, *n.* revente *f* (d'un fonds de commerce, etc.); **resale price maintenance (RPM),** prix imposé(s) (par le fabricant); **resale value,** valeur *f* à la revente; **right on resale,** droit *m* de revente/de prise en vente.

resaleable, *a.* revendable.

rescind, *v.tr.* annuler/résoudre/résilier; rescinder (un contrat).

rescindable, *a.* annulable/résiliable/rescindable.

rescinding[1], *a.* (clause, etc.) abrogatoire

rescinding[2], **rescission,** *n.* recision *f*/annulation *f*/résolution *f*/résiliation (d'un contrat).

rescheduling, *n.* nouvelle programmation; (*of debt*) restructuration *f*.

research[1], *n.* recherche *f*; **advertising research,** études *f* publicitaires; **consumer research,** recherche des besoins des consommateurs; **economic research,** études économiques; **field research,** prospection sur le terrain; **industrial research,** recherche appliquée; **market research,** étude de marché; **marketing research,** recherche commerciale; **product research,** recherche de produits; **research and de-**

velopment **(R & D)**, recherche-développement *f*; **research and development department,** atelier *m*/service *m* d'études; **research centre/department,** centre *m*/ service de recherche; bureau *m* d'études; **research work,** recherches/travaux *mpl* de recherche; **research worker/assistant,** (*i*) chercheur *m* (scientifique) (*ii*) documentaliste *mf*; **to do research/to be engaged in research,** faire des recherches/de la recherche.

research², *v.i. & tr.* faire des recherches (scientifiques, etc.) (sur qch.).

researcher, *n.* (*a*) chercheur *m* (scientifique) (*b*) documentaliste *mf*.

reservation, *n.* réserve *f*/restriction *f*; **to enter a reservation in respect of a contract,** apporter une réserve à un contrat (*b*) réservation *f*; **to make a reservation,** retenir (une place, une chambre, etc.).

reserve¹, *n.* **1.** réserve *f* (d'argent, etc.); *Fin:* **bank reserves,** réserves bancaires; **capital reserves,** profits mis en réserve; **cash reserves,** réserve de caisse; réserve en espèces (d'une banque); **gold and dollar reserves,** avoir *m* en or et en dollars; **gold and foreign exchange reserves,** avoir en or et en devises; **contingency reserve,** réserve de prévoyance; **foreign reserves,** réserves de la Banque Centrale en devises; **general reserves,** réserves non disbribuées; **hidden/ secret reserves,** réserves secrètes/occultes; **legal reserve,** réserve légale; **reserve account,** compte *m* de réserve/de provisions; **reserve for bad debts,** réserves/ provisions *f* pour créances douteuses; **reserve capital,** capital *m* de réserve/ provision; **reserve currency,** monnaie *f* de réserve; **reserve deposit,** dépôt *m* de couverture; **reserve fund,** fonds *m* de réserve/ de prévoyance; **statutory reserve,** réserve statutaire; **to draw on the reserves,** puiser dans les réserves; **in reserve,** en réserve **2.** (*a*) *Bank:* **under reserve,** sauf bonne fin (*b*) (*at auction*) **reserve price,** mise *f* à prix/ prix *m* initial minimal **3.** *NAm:* **Federal Reserve (Fed.),** la Réserve fédérale (aux USA).

reserve², *v.tr.* réserver; **to reserve a room at**

a hotel, retenir une chambre d'hôtel; **to reserve a table (at a restaurant),** retenir/ réserver une table (au restaurant); **to reserve a seat,** retenir/réserver/louer une place; *Publ:* **all rights reserved,** tous droits (de reproduction, etc.) réservés.

reshipment, *n.* réexpédition *f* (de marchandises).

resident, *n.* résident, -ente.

residential, *a.* résidentiel; à usage d'habitation.

residue, *n.* (*a*) actif net; reste *m* (*b*) reliquat *m* d'une succession; héritage résiduel.

resign, (*a*) *v.tr.* résigner (une fonction)/se démettre (de ses fonctions)/donner sa démission (*b*) *v.i.* démissionner/donner sa démission/résigner ses fonctions/sa charge.

resignation, *n.* démission *f*; **to give (in)/to hand in/to send in/to tender one's resignation,** donner sa démission/ démissionner.

resistance, *n.* résistance *f*; **consumer resistance,** résistance des consommateurs.

resolution, *n.* résolution *f*/proposition *f*; **special resolution,** résolution extraordinaire; **to put a resolution to the meeting,** soumettre/proposer une résolution; **to pass/carry/adopt a resolution,** adopter une résolution/une proposition; **to reject a resolution,** rejeter une proposition/une résolution.

resource, *n.* (*a*) ressource *f*; **resource allocation,** allocation *f*/affectation *f* des ressources; **financial resources,** ressources financières; **limited resources,** moyens limités (*b*) *pl. NAm: Fin:* actif disponible/ liquide.

respect¹, *n.* **with respect to .../in respect of ...,** en ce qui concerne .../concernant .../quant à ....

respect², *v.tr.* **to respect a clause in a con-**

tract, respecter une clause dans un contrat.

respite, *n.* **to grant a respite for payment,** différer un paiement/accorder un sursis de paiement.

responsibility, *n.* responsabilité *f*; **allocation of responsibilities,** répartition *f* des responsabilités; **linear responsibility,** responsabilité hiérarchique; **without responsibility on our part,** sans engagement *m* ni responsabilité de notre part; **to disclaim all responsibility,** décliner toute responsabilité.

responsible, *a.* **1. responsible to s.o.,** responsable devant qn; **the commission is responsible to the government,** la commission relève du gouvernement; **to be responsible for s.o.,** répondre de qn; **to be responsible for sth.,** être responsable de qch. **2.** (*a*) capable/compétent/digne de confiance/sur qui on peut compter; **a responsible man,** un homme sérieux (*b*) **responsible job,** poste *m* qui entraîne des responsabilités; responsabilité *f*.

restitution, *n. EEC:* **export restitution,** restitution *f* (à l'exportation).

restock, *v.tr.* réapprovisionner (un magasin); **to restock with wine,** se réapprovisionner en vin.

restocking, *n.* réapprovisionnement *m* (d'un magasin).

restoration, *n.* **1.** restitution *f* d'objets trouvés **2.** restauration *f* (d'un bâtiment, d'un meuble) **3.** rétablissement *m*.

restore, *v.tr.* **1.** restituer/rendre qch à qn **2.** restaurer/rénover (un bâtiment, un meuble) **3.** rétablir; réintégrer (qn dans ses droits).

restraint, *n.* **restraint of trade/trade restraint,** atteinte *f* à la liberté du commerce; restriction *f* de concurrence (entre sociétés); **wage restraint,** restriction salariale; limitation *f* des salaires.

restrict, *v.tr.* restreindre (les dépenses, la production, etc.); **to restrict credits,** encadrer le crédit; **restricted credit,** crédit

restreint; **restricted market,** débouchés réduits.

restriction, *n.* restriction *f*/limitation *f*; **credit restrictions,** encadrement *m*/restriction du crédit; **import restrictions,** restrictions sur les importations; **restriction of expenditure,** réduction *f* des dépenses; **to impose/to lift restrictions,** imposer/abolir des restrictions.

restrictive, *a.* restrictif; **restrictive clause,** clause restrictive; **restrictive indorsement,** endossement restrictif; **restrictive practices,** (*i*) *Ind:* pratiques restrictives (*ii*) *Jur:* ententes *f*.

restructure, *v.tr.* restructurer.

restructuring, *n.* restructuration *f*.

result, *n.* résultat *m* (**of,** de); **payment by results,** salaire *m* au rendement; **trading/company results,** résultats de l'exercice/de l'exploitation; résultats financiers; **to yield results,** donner des résultats.

retail[1], *n.* détail *m*; vente *f* au détail; **to sell goods by**/*NAm:* **at retail,** vendre des marchandises au détail/détailler des marchandises; **retail dealer,** marchand-ande au détail/détaillant, -ante/marchand détaillant; **retail price,** prix *m* de détail; **retail price index,** indice *m* des prix de détail; **the retail trade,** le détail; **wholesale and retail business,** commerce *m* de gros et de détail; **retail banking,** banque *f* de détail.

retail[2], **1.** *v.tr.* détailler/vendre au détail (des marchandises) **2.** *v.i.* (*of goods*) se vendre au détail/se détailler; **these pencils retail at 8p,** ces crayons se détaillent à 8p/le prix de détail de ces crayons est de 8p.

retailer, *n.* marchand, -ande au détail/détaillant, -ante/marchand détaillant.

retain, *v.tr.* (*a*) **to retain s.o.'s services,** retenir les services de qn (*b*) **retaining fee,** honoraires versés à qn pour s'assurer son concours éventuel; provision *f*/avance *f*/acompte *m*.

retained, *a.* **retained earnings,** bénéfice

non distribués; **retained profit**, bénéfice non distribué.

retainer, *n.* provision *f*/avance *f*/acompte *m*; **to pay a retainer**, verser une avance/ une provision.

retention, *n.* **retention money**, retenue *f* de garantie; **retentions**, bénéfice(s) non distribué(s).

retest, *n. Ind: etc:* contre-essai *m.*

retire, **1.** (*a*) *v.tr.* mettre (qn) à la retraite (*b*) *Fin:* retirer/rembourser (un effet) **2.** *v.i.* se démettre (de ses fonctions); démissionner; **to retire (from business)**, se retirer des affaires; **to retire (on a pension)**, prendre sa retraite.

retired, *a.* (négociant, etc.) retiré des affaires; (fonctionnaire) retraité/à la retraite; **retired pay**, pension *f* de retraite.

retiree, *n. NAm:* retraité, -ée.

retirement, *n.* **1.** retraite *f*; **early retirement**, retraite anticipée/pré(-)retraite *f*; **optional retirement**, retraite sur demande; **compulsory/mandatory retirement**, retraite d'office; **retirement on account of age**, retraite par limite d'âge; **retirement pension**, (pension *f* de) retraite; retraite de vieillesse **2.** *Fin:* retrait *m*/remboursement *m* (d'un effet); retrait (de monnaies).

retiring, *n.* **retiring age**, âge *m* de la retraite.

retrace, *v.tr.* **the market retraced most of its gains**, le marché a reperdu une bonne partie de ses gains.

retracement, *n.* réaction *f* (technique) de Bourse.

retractable, *a.* avec option de remboursement avant l'échéance finale.

retrain, **1.** *v.tr.* recycler (qn) **2.** *v.i.* se recycler.

retraining, *n.* recyclage *m* (de qn); **job retraining**, recyclage.

retrenchment, *n.* réduction *f* (des dé-

penses); **policy of retrenchment**, politique *f* d'économies/de redressement.

retrieval, *n.* **information retrieval (system)**, (système de) recherche *f* documentaire; interrogation *f* de banque de données.

retroactive, *a.* (avec effet) rétroactif.

retrospective, *a.* (avec effet) rétroactif; (*study*) rétrospectif.

return[1], *n.* **1.** (*a*) retour *m*; *Post:* **by return (of post)**, par retour (du courrier) (*b*) *Rail: etc:* **day return**, billet d'aller et retour (*bon pour la journée seulement*); **cheap day return**, billet d'aller et retour à tarif réduit (*bon pour la journée seulement*); **return fare**, prix *m*/tarif *m* de l'aller et retour; **return journey**, (*i*) (voyage de) retour (*ii*) voyage (d')aller et retour; **to buy a return (ticket)**, prendre un (billet d')aller et retour (*c*) **empty return**, retour à vide; **loaded return**, retour en charge; **return cargo/freight**, cargaison *f*/chargement *m*/fret *m* de retour **2.** (*a*) *pl.* **returns**, recettes *f*/rentrées (*provenant des ventes*); **quick returns**, un prompt débit/ une vente rapide (*b*) revenu *m*/gain *m*/ profit *m*/rendement *m*; **to bring (in) a fair return**, rapporter un bénéfice raisonnable; **gross return**, rendement brut; **rate of return**, rentabilité *f*/taux *m* de rendement; **compound annual return**, taux *m* de rentabilité annualisé/composé annuellement; **return on capital invested**, rentabilité/taux de rendement des capitaux investis; **return on investment**, retour *m* sur investissements; *PolEc:* **law of diminishing returns**, loi *f* du rendement non proportionnel **3.** (*a*) renvoi *m*/retour; réexpédition *f* (de marchandises avariées, etc.); **return (of bill to drawer)**, contre-passation *f* (d'un effet de commerce); **on sale or return**, (marchandises) vendues avec faculté de retour/en dépôt (avec reprise des invendus)/à condition; **to deliver goods on sale or return**, livrer des marchandises en dépôt temporaire; *Post:* **return address**, adresse *f* de l'expéditeur (*b*) *pl.* **returns**, (*of books, newspapers*) invendus *m*/rendus *m*/retours *m*/bouillons *m* (*c*) ristourne *f* (d'une somme payée en trop); *Fin:* **return**

of a capital sum, remboursement *m* d'un capital; **return commission,** commission allouée en retour **4.** (*a*) rapport officiel; état *m*/exposé *m*; compte rendu/relevé *m*; statistique *f*; *Adm:* recensement *m* (de la population, etc.); **nil return,** état néant; **the official returns,** les relevés officiels; **return of expenses,** état de frais/de dépenses; **bank return,** situation *f* de la banque; **the weekly bank return,** le bilan hebdomadaire; **quarterly return,** rapport trimestriel; **annual return,** = bilan social (d'une société); **sales return,** statistique des ventes; **trade returns,** statistique de commerce (*b*) **income tax return,** déclaration *f* de revenu/déclaration d'impôts/déclaration fiscale; (*form*) formule *f*/formulaire *m* de déclaration d'impôts.

return², *v.tr.* **1.** rendre (un dépôt, etc.); rembourser (un emprunt); **to return an amount paid in excess,** ristourner/rembourser une somme payée en trop; **to return an article,** retourner une marchandise; **returned books,** invendus *mpl*; **returned empties,** bouteilles consignées/reprises *f*; **returned goods,** rendus *m*/retours *m*; *Fin:* **to return a bill to drawer,** contre-passer un effet; *Post:* **return to sender,** retour à l'envoyeur **2.** *Fin:* rapporter/donner (un bénéfice); **investment that returns good interest,** placement *m* qui produit un intérêt élevé/placement avantageux **3. to return one's income at £4 000,** faire une déclaration de £4 000 de revenu; **the liabilities are returned at £10 000,** le passif est estimé/évalué à £10 000.

returnable, *a.* qui peut être rendu/ renvoyé/retourné; restituable; **returnable bottle,** bouteille consignée; (*on goods*) **not returnable,** sans consigne/non consigné; ne peut être échangé ni rendu.

returning, *n.* renvoi *m* (de marchandises, etc.).

revalorization, *n. Fin:* revalorisation *f* (du franc, etc.).

revalorize, *v.tr. Fin:* revaloriser (le franc, etc.).

revaluation, *n.* réévaluation *f* (des actifs, etc.); réestimation *f*; *Fin:* revalorisation *f*/réévaluation *f* (du franc, etc.).

revalue, *v.tr.* réestimer; réévaluer (une propriété, etc.); *Fin:* revaloriser (le franc, etc.).

revenue, *n.* **1.** revenu *m*/rentes *fpl*; rapport *m* (**from an estate,** d'une terre); **advertising revenue,** recettes *fpl* de publicité; **average revenue,** produit moyen; **revenue account,** compte *m* des recettes et des dépenses **2.** *Adm:* **(tax) revenue,** recettes fiscales; **Inland Revenue**/*NAm:* **Internal Revenue Service (IRS),** le fisc; **the revenue authorities,** les agents *m* du fisc; **revenue office,** (bureau *m* de) perception *f*; **revenue officer,** inspecteur *m* des contributions.

reversal, *n.* (*a*) revers *m* (de fortune); **reverse takeover,** centre-OPA *f* (*b*) *Book-k:* contre-passation *f*; annulation *f* (d'une écriture).

reverse¹, *a.* à rebours/inversé; *Book-k:* **reverse entry,** écriture *f* inverse.

reverse², *v.tr. Book-k:* **to reverse an entry,** contre-passer/annuler une écriture.

reversing, *n. Book-k:* **reversing of entry,** contre-passation *f*/d'une écriture.

reversion, *n. Jur:* réversion *f*; **annuity in reversion on the death of the holder,** rente *f* réversible après la mort du titulaire.

reversionary, *a.* (droit) de réversion; **reversionary annuity,** annuité *f* réversible; rente viagère avec réversion.

review¹, *n.* **1. financial review,** examen financier **2.** *Publ:* revue *f*; périodique *m.*

review², *v.tr.* **to review salaries,** réviser les salaires.

revival, *n.* **economic revival,** relance *f* économique; **business revival,** reprise *f* des affaires.

revive, 1. *v.i.* (*of business, commerce*) reprendre/se relever; **industry is reviving,** l'industrie *f* commence à revivre/l'industrie se relève; **credit is reviving,** le crédit se rétablit **2.** *v.tr.* relancer (l'économie); **to revive trade,** ranimer le commerce.

revoke, *v.tr.* révoquer; annuler; retirer (un permis de conduire).

revolving, *a.* **revolving credit,** crédit permanent/renouvelable; crédit revolving; prêt *m* à la carte; **credit-revolving,** (avec) crédit permanent/renouvelable/à la carte; **revolving credit card,** carte revolving.

rider, *n.* ajouté *m*/annexe *f*/papillon *m* (d'un document); allonge *f* (d'un effet de commerce).

rig[1], *n.* *StExch:* (*i*) hausse *f* factice (*ii*) baisse *f* factice; coup *m* de bourse.

rig[2], *v.tr.* *Fin: StExch:* **to rig the market,** spéculer/agioter; provoquer (*i*) une hausse factice (*ii*) une baisse factice.

rigger, *n.* *StExch:* spéculateur *m*/agioteur *m*.

rigging, *n.* *StExch:* spéculation *f*; agiotage *m*.

right, *n.* (*a*) droit *m*/titre *m*; privilège *m*; *Jur:* **rights granted by contract,** droits contractuels; **right of priority,** droit d'antériorité; **(industrial) property rights,** droits de propriété (industrielle); **to exercise a right,** exercer un droit; **women's rights,** droits de la femme (*b*) *Fin:* **application rights,** droit(s)/privilège de souscription; **rights issue,** droit préférentiel de souscription; **with right of transfer,** avec faculté *f* de transfert (*c*) *Publ:* **foreign rights,** droits étrangers; **publishing rights,** droits d'édition; **all rights reserved,** tous droits réservés.

rightful, *a.* (*a*) légitime/véritable; en droit; **rightful owner,** propriétaire *mf* légitime (*b*) (*of claim*) légitime/juste/justifié.

rim, *n.* *US:* **rim country,** nouveau pays industriel (NPI).

ring, *n.* (*a*) syndicat *m*; cartel *m*; **price ring,** monopole *m* des prix (*b*) *StExch:* **the Ring,** le Parquet.

ring back, *v.tr.* *Tel:* rappeler (qn).

ring off, *v.i.* *Tel:* raccrocher.

ring up, *v.tr.* *Tel:* **to ring s.o. up,** téléphoner à qn/donner un coup de téléphone à qn/ appeler qn au téléphone (*b*) enregistrer (une somme) (sur une caisse enregistreuse).

rip-off, *n.* vol *m*/escroquerie *f*; **it's a rip-off,** c'est du vol!

rise[1], *n.* augmentation *f*/élévation *f*/hausse *f* (de prix); augmentation (de salaire); renchérissement *m* (des denrées); **the rise in the price of petrol,** la hausse du prix de l'essence; **rise in value,** augmentation de valeur; plus-value *f*; appréciation *f* (d'une monnaie); **rise in the minimum lending rate,** relèvement *m* du taux d'escompte; **the rise in the cost of living,** la hausse du coût de la vie; la montée des prix; *StExch:* **to speculate on/operate for a rise,** jouer à la hausse; **to ask (one's employer) for a rise,** demander une augmentation (de salaire).

rise[2], *v.i.* (*of prices*) monter; **prices are rising,** les prix *m* montent/sont en hausse; **prices have risen considerably,** les prix ont subi une forte hausse; **the pound sterling has risen against the dollar,** la livre sterling s'est appréciée vis-à-vis du dollar; **bread has risen by 5p,** le (prix du) pain a augmenté de 5p; **everything has risen (in price),** tout a augmenté de prix/ tout a renchéri.

risk, *n.* (*a*) risque *m*/péril *m*/aléa *m*/hasard *m*; **the risks of an undertaking,** les aléas d'une entreprise; **to run/to incur a risk,** courir un risque; **calculated risk,** risque calculé (*b*) **risk capital,** capital *m* à risques/capital-risque *m*; **risk management,** prévention-assurance *f*; **market risk,** risque de marché (*c*) *Ins:* risque; **risk subscribed,** risque assuré; **theft/fire/war risk,** risque de vol/d'incendie/de guerre; **at owner's risks,** au(x) risque(s) du propriétaire; **risks and perils at sea,** risques et périls de la mer; péril de mer; fortune *f* de mer; **comprehensive all risks policy,** police *f* tous risques; **third-party risk,** risque de recours de tiers; **tenant's third-party risk,**

risque locatif; (*pers., thg*) **a good/bad risk,** un bon/mauvais risque; **to underwrite a risk,** souscrire un risque.

rival, *a. & n.* rival, -ale; concurrent, -ente.

road, *n.* route *f*; chemin *m*; voie *f*; **road transport,** transports routiers; **to be on the road,** être représentant; (*of representative*) être en tournée/en déplacement.

robotics, *n.* robotique *f*.

rock, *n.* **rock(-)bottom price,** le prix le plus bas; **prices have reached rock bottom,** les prix sont au plus bas.

rocket, *v.i.* (*of prices*) monter en flèche.

roll[1], *n.* tableau *m*/liste *f*; rôle *m*; **tax roll,** rôle d'impôt.

roll[2], *n.* *NAm: F:* **sales went into a roll,** les ventes ont chuté/il y a eu une dégringolade des ventes.

rollback, *n. NAm:* réduction *f*/baisse *f* des prix (à son niveau précédent).

roll back, *v.tr. NAm:* baisser (un prix) à son niveau précédent.

rollercoaster, *n. NAm:* **rollercoaster market,** marché *m* volatile.

rollover, *a.* **rollover credit,** crédit *m* à taux révisable.

roster, *n.* liste *f*/rôle *m*/feuille *f*; *Adm:* **promotion roster/advancement roster,** tableau *m* d'avancement; **duty roster,** tableau de service.

rotation, *n.* rotation *f*; **job rotation,** rotation des postes; **rotation of directors,** renouvellement *m* par tiers du conseil d'administration.

rough[1], *a.* approximatif; **rough average,** moyenne approximative; **rough calculation,** calcul approximatif; **rough estimate,** évaluation *f* en gros; estimation approximative/devis approximatif; **rough layout,** crayonné *m*/esquisse *f*; **rough sketch,** ébauche *f* (de projet).

rough[2], *n. Mkt: etc:* crayonné *m*/ esquisse *f*.

roughman, *n. Mkt:* visualiseur *m*.

round[1], *n.* **there were several financing rounds,** il y a eu plusieurs séries de discussions sur les finances.

round[2], *a.* (*a*) **round dozen,** bonne douzaine; **round figure,** chiffre rond; **in round figures,** en chiffres ronds; **round sum,** compte rond (*b*) **round trip,** *NAm:* voyage *m* d'aller et retour/aller et retour; (*on futures market*) aller-retour *m*; *StExch:* **round turn,** transaction *f* à terme menée à échéance.

roundsman, *n.* livreur *m*.

round up, *v.tr.* arrondir une somme (au chiffre supérieur).

route[1], *n.* itinéraire *m*; route *f*/voie *f*/chemin *m*; **commercial/trade route,** route commerciale; **shipping route,** route de navigation.

route[2], *v.tr.* router/acheminer (un envoi).

routeman, *n. NAm:* livreur *m*.

routine, *n.* routine *f*; **office routine,** travail courant de bureau; **routine work,** (*i*) (travail de) routine/affaires courantes (*ii*) travail routinier.

routing, *n.* routage *m*/acheminement *m* (d'un colis, etc.).

royalty, *n.* **royalties,** droits *mpl* d'auteur/ royalties *fpl*/redevances *fpl* (du(e)s à un inventeur, au détenteur de la propriété littéraire ou artistique d'une œuvre); **oil royalties,** redevances pétrolières; **royalty of 10% on the published price,** droit de 10% sur le prix fort.

rule[1], *n.* règle *f*; règlement *m*; **company rules,** règlements internes/de la maison; **operating rules,** règles d'exploitation; **rules and regulations,** statuts *m(pl)* et règlements *m(pl)*.

rule[2], *v.i.* **prices are ruling high,** les prix restent élevés; les prix se maintiennent; **the prices ruling at the moment,** les prix qui se pratiquent en ce moment.

rule off, *v.tr.* **to rule off an account,** clore/ arrêter/régler un compte.

ruling, 1. *a.* **ruling classes,** classes dirigeantes; **ruling price,** cours actuel; cours/prix *m* du jour 2. *n.* décision *f*/jugement *m.*

run¹, *n.* **trial run,** essai *m*; **the run of the market,** les tendances *f* du marché; **run on the market,** ruée *f* (sur les valeurs en bourse); **a run on oils,** une ruée sur les valeurs pétrolières; **a run on the banks,** un retrait massif de dépôts bancaires; **there was a great run on that line,** ces marchandises *fpl* ont été écoulées rapidement.

run², 1. *v.i.* (*a*) **the bill has fifteen days to run,** l'effet a quinze jours à courir; **the lease has only a year to run,** le bail n'a plus qu'un an à courir (*b*) (*of amount, number*) **to run to . . .,** monter/s'élever à . . .; **prices run from . . . to . . .,** les prix varient entre . . . et . . .; **the increase in business may run to tens of thousands (of pounds),** l'augmentation *f* du chiffre d'affaires pourra bien être de l'ordre de dizaines de milliers de livres (*c*) **prices are running high,** les prix sont élevés/en général les prix sont plutôt élevés 2. *v.tr.* (*a*) **to run a cheap line,** vendre un article (à) bon marché/en réclame (*b*) **to run (a business, a shop, a hotel),** diriger (une affaire); tenir (un magasin, un hôtel).

run back, *v.i.* (*of shares*) diminuer de valeur/baisser.

run down, *v.tr.* **the company is being run down,** la société réduit/diminue son niveau d'activité.

rundown, 1. *n.* réduction *f* (du personnel) 2. *a.* **a rundown investment,** une mauvaise affaire/un mauvais investissement.

run into, 1. *v.i.* **to run into debt,** faire des dettes/s'endetter; **the debts run into hundreds of pounds,** la dette s'élève à des centaines de livres 2. *v.tr.* **that will run me into considerable expenses,** cela me coûtera cher/m'entraînera des frais considérables.

runner, *n.* messager *m*/coursier, -ière.

running¹, *a.* 1. **running account,** compte courant 2. **running cost,** frais *mpl* d'exploitation 3. **running days,** jours consécutifs; **for 5 days running,** pendant 5 jours consécutifs/5 jours de suite.

running², *n.* (*a*) marche *f*/fonctionnement *m* (d'une machine, etc.); (*of car, etc.*) **running costs,** frais *mpl* d'entretien (*b*) direction *f* (d'un hôtel, etc.); exploitation *f* (d'une compagnie); **running expenses,** frais d'exploitation.

run up, *v.tr.* (*a*) laisser grossir (un compte); laisser accumuler (des dettes); **I ran up a bill for £100,** à la fin je devais £100 (*b*) (*at auction*) **to run up the bidding,** pousser les enchères.

rush, *n.* 1. **the rush hour,** les heures *f* d'affluence/de pointe; **a rush period,** une poussée (d'affaires, etc.); (*at shop*) heure(s) *f* d'affluence (de la clientèle) 2. hâte *f*/empressement *m*; **rush order,** commande urgente; **rush work/rush job,** travail *m* de première urgence.

rushed, *a.* 1. débordé de travail 2. (travail) fait à la va-vite/bâclé.

S

sabbatical, *n. & a.* **sabbatical (year)**, année *f* sabbatique.

sack[1], *n. F:* **to get the sack**, être renvoyé/mis à la porte/sa(c)qué; **to give s.o. the sack**, renvoyer qn/mettre qn à la porte.

sack[2], *v.tr. F:* renvoyer (qn)/mettre (qn) à la porte/congédier (qn).

sacrifice[1], *n.* vente *f* à perte; **to sell sth. at a sacrifice**, sacrifier (des marchandises); vendre qch. à perte/à toute offre acceptable.

sacrifice[2], *v.tr.* sacrifier un article/vendre à perte/vendre à très bas prix.

s.a.e., (= **stamped addressed envelope**), enveloppe *f* affranchie; enveloppe timbrée avec vos nom et adresse.

safe, **1.** *n.* coffre-fort *m*; *Bank:* **night (deposit) safe**, coffret *m* de nuit **2.** *a.* (*a*) **to place deposit/securities in safe custody**, mettre des valeurs en dépôt (*b*) **safe investment**, placement sûr/de tout repos/de père de famille.

safe-deposit, *n.* coffre-fort *m*; coffre *m*; (*deposit*) dépôt *m* en coffre-fort.

safeguard, *v.tr.* sauvegarder/protéger; **to safeguard the interests of shareholders**, sauvegarder les intérêts des actionnaires.

safe-keeping, *n.* sécurité *f*/sûreté *f*; **to place securities in the bank for safekeeping**, mettre les valeurs *fpl* en dépôt à la banque.

safety, *n.* sûreté *f*/sécurité *f*; **safety regulations**, règles *fpl* de sécurité; **safety stock**, stock *m* de sécurité/stock tampon; *Ind:* **safety factor**, facteur *m*/coefficient *m* de sécurité; **safety margin**, marge *f* de sécurité; **safety standards**, normes *f(pl)* de sécurité; **safety vault**, chambre forte/blindée (d'une banque, etc.).

sag[1], *n.* baisse *f*/diminution *f*/fléchissement *m* (des valeurs, etc.).

sag[2], *v.i.* (*of prices*) baisser/fléchir; **prices are sagging**, les prix *m* fléchissent/baissent.

sagging, **1.** *n.* baisse *f*/fléchissement *m*/affaissement *m*/diminution *f* (des prix, du marché, des valeurs, etc.) **2.** *a.* (*prices, etc.*) en baisse.

salaried, *a.* **1. salaried worker**, employé salarié; **salaried staff**, personnel *m* qui touche un traitement/des appointements; **lower salaried staff**, cadres *m* moyens; **higher salaried staff**, cadres supérieurs **2.** (travail) rétribué/rémunéré/salarié.

salary, *n.* salaire *m*; traitement *m*/appointements *mpl*; rémunération *f*; **to draw one's salary**, toucher son salaire/ses appointements; **fixed salary**, salaire fixe/*F:* fixe *m*; **starting salary**, rémunération *f* de départ; **salary increase**, augmentation *f* de salaire; **salary structure**, structure *f* des salaires/des traitements.

sale, *n.* **1.** (*a*) vente *f*; **bill of sale**, contrat *m*/acte *m* de vente; **cash sale**, vente au comptant; **credit sale**, vente à crédit; **domestic sales**, ventes domestiques; **ready sale**, vente facile; écoulement *m* rapide; **sale contract**, contrat *m* de vente; *StExch:* bordereau *m* de vente; **sale value**, valeur marchande; valeur vénale; **goods for which there is a sure sale**, marchandises de vente/d'un bon débit; **goods for which there is no sale**, articles *m* hors de vente/articles qui n'ont pas de marché; **for sale**, à vendre; **business for sale**, fonds *m* à céder; **house for sale**, maison *f* à vendre; t put sth. **up for sale,** mettre qch. en vente; **not for sale,** (cet article n'est) pas à vendre; **not for general sale/not for sale to the general public,** hors commerce; **for quick sale,** pour vente/liquidation rapide; **on sale,** en vente; **on sale in all leading stores,** en vente/vendu dans tous les grands magasins; **sale by private treaty/ contract/agreement,** vente à l'amiable/de gré à gré; **sale by sealed tender,** vente par soumission cachetée; **sale with option of repurchase,** vente à réméré/avec faculté de rachat; **sale and lease-back,** cession-bail *f*/location *f* après-vente (*b*) *StExch:* **sale for the account,** vente à terme; **closing sale,** vente de couverture (*sur le marché des options*); **closing the sale,** conclure un marché/une affaire; emporter un marché; **opening sale,** vente à découvert (*sur le marché des options*) (*c*) **sales analysis,** analyse *f* des ventes; *Ind:* **sales area,** secteur *m*/territoire *m* (de vente); **sales book,** journal *m* des ventes; facturier *m*; **sales campaign/drive,** campagne *f* de vente; **sales department,** services *mpl* commerciaux/service des ventes; **sales force,** équipe *f* de vente; **sales forecast,** prévision *f* des ventes; **sales manager,** directeur *m*/chef *m* du service des ventes; directeur *m* commercial; **sales policy,** politique *f* de vente; **sales promotion,** promotion *f* de(s) vente(s); **sales room,** salle *f* des ventes (aux enchères); *NAm:* **sales slip,** ticket *m* de caisse; **sales talk,** arguments *mpl* de vente/boniment *m*; **sales tax,** taxe à l'achat; **sales turnover/sales figures/ sales,** chiffre *m* d'affaires (*d*) **sale by auction/auction sale/sale to the highest bidder,** vente à l'enchère/aux enchères; criée *f*/ vente à la criée; vente publique; (*at auction*) **day's sale,** vacation *f*; **sale ring,** cercle *m* d'acheteurs; *Jur:* **compulsory sale,** adjudication forcée **2.** solde *m*; **(clearance) sale,** solde (de marchandises); **(bargain) sale,** vente au rabais; **closing- down sale,** solde de fermeture; liquidation *f*; *NAm:* **on sale,** en solde; **the sales are on,** c'est l'époque des soldes; **to put stock in the sale,** mettre du stock en solde/ solder du stock; **sale goods,** soldes *mpl*; **sale price,** prix *m* de solde.

saleability, *n.* qualité marchande (d'un article); facilité *f* d'écoulement.

saleable, *a.* (*goods, etc.*) vendable/de vente facile; de vente courante; **readily saleable,** qui se vend bien; **saleable value,** valeur marchande.

saleroom, *n.* salle *f* de(s) vente(s).

salesclerk, *n. NAm:* vendeur, -euse.

salesgirl, *n.* vendeuse *f.*

saleslady, *n.f.* vendeuse *f.*

salesman, *n.* vendeur *m*; **door-to-door salesman,** démarcheur *m*; **travelling salesman,** voyageur *m* de commerce/ délégué commercial.

salesmanship, *n.* l'art *m* de vendre.

salesperson, *n.* vendeur, -euse.

saleswoman, *n.* vendeuse *f.*

sample[1], *n.* (*a*) échantillon *m* (de tissu, de vin, etc.); **free sample,** échantillon gratuit; **reference sample,** contre-échantillon *m*; **representative sample,** échantillon type; **to send sth. as a sample,** envoyer qch. à titre d'échantillon; **to buy sth. from sample,** acheter qch. d'après échantillon/ sur montre; **sample book,** collection *f* d'échantillons; **sample card,** carte *f* d'échantillons; **sample packet (of sth.),** paquet *m* échantillon (de qch.); **up to sample,** conforme à l'échantillon (*b*) **random sample,** échantillon aléatoire; **sample survey,** (enquête *f* par) sondage *m.*

sample[2], *v.tr.* prendre/prélever un échantillon/échantillonner; déguster (des vins).

sampling, *n.* (*a*) dégustation *f* (de vins); échantillonnage *m* de marchandises (*b*) **probability sampling,** sondage *m* probabiliste; **random sampling,** échantillonnage aléatoire (*c*) **cluster sampling,** sondage *m* en grappes; **sampling error,** erreur *f* d'échantillonnage/de sondage; **sampling method,** méthode *f* de sondage.

sanction, *n.* **economic/financial sanctions,** sanctions *f* économiques; **sanction**

busting, non-respect *m*/non-observation *f* des sanctions.

satisfaction, *n.* (*a*) acquittement *m*/paiement *m*/liquidation *f* (d'une dette); désintéressement *m* (d'un créancier) (*b*) satisfaction *f*; **consumer satisfaction,** satisfaction du consommateur; **job satisfaction,** satisfaction dans le travail.

satisfy, *v.tr.* payer/liquider (une dette); s'acquitter (d'une dette, d'une obligation); remplir (une condition); satisfaire à (une demande); répondre (aux besoins).

saturate, *v.tr.* saturer (le marché); **the market is saturated,** le marché est saturé.

saturation, *n.* **market saturation,** saturation *f* du marché; **saturation point,** point *m* de saturation; **the market has reached saturation point,** le marché est saturé.

save, 1. *v.tr.* **to save money,** économiser/épargner/mettre de côté (de l'argent); **to save time,** faire une économie de temps/gagner du temps 2. *v.i.* **to save on sth.,** économiser sur qch.; **to save (up),** économiser pour l'avenir/faire des économies/épargner (son argent); **save as you earn (SAYE)** = économie *f* à la source.

saver, *n.* épargnant, -ante.

saving, 1. *n.* (*a*) économie *f*/épargne *f*; **labour saving,** économie de travail; *Ind:* économie de main-d'œuvre (*b*) *pl.* **savings,** économies; **savings account,** compte *m* (de caisse) d'épargne; *NAm:* compte d'épargne (avec intérêt); **Savings plan,** plan d'épargne à long terme; **(National) Savings Bank** = Caisse (Nationale) d'Épargne; **(National) savings certificate** = bon *m* d'épargne; *NAm:* **savings and loan association** (= **Building Society**) = crédit foncier 2. *a.* **saving clause,** clause *f* de sauvegarde/clause restrictive/restriction *f*.

scab, *n.* briseur *m* de grève.

scale¹, *n.* (*a*) échelle *f*; **scale of prices/of charges,** échelle/gamme *f* des prix; **scale of salaries/salary scale,** échelle/barème *m* des salaires/des traitements; **sliding scale,** échelle mobile (des salaires, des prix); (*of*

machine parts sizes, etc.) **standard scale,** échelle des calibres (*b*) échelle (d'une carte etc.); **scale model,** maquette *f*/modèle réduit; **small-scale firm,** petite entreprise; **to do sth. on a small/large scale,** faire qch. sur une petite/une grande échelle.

scale², *v.tr.* **to scale up prices by 5%,** augmenter les prix de 5%; **to scale down production,** ralentir/diminuer la production.

scaling, *n.* graduation *f* (des prix, des salaires, etc.); **scaling down,** réduction *f* à l'échelle; **scaling up,** augmentation *f* à l'échelle.

scalper, *n esp NAm: StExch:* spéculateur, -trice à la journée.

scanning, *n. Mkt:* veille *f* technologique.

scarce, *a.* (*commodities*) rare.

scarceness, scarcity, *n.* rareté *f*; manque *m*/pénurie *f* (de qch.); **scarcity of labour,** manque/pénurie de main-d'œuvre.

schedule¹, *n.* 1. (*a*) *Jur:* annexe *f* (aux statuts d'une société, etc.) (*b*) bordereau *m*/note explicative 2. (*a*) nomenclature *f* (de pièces, etc.); inventaire *m* (de machines, etc.); barème *m* (de prix); **schedule of charges,** liste officielle des taux; tarif *m* (*b*) *Adm:* cédule *f* (d'impôts) (*c*) *Jur:* (*in bankruptcy*) bilan *m* (de l'actif et du passif) 3. (*a*) plan *m* (d'exécution d'un travail, etc.); programme *m*; **to be on schedule,** se poursuivre suivant le planning; **to be behind schedule,** avoir du retard/être en retard sur les prévisions; **to be ahead of schedule,** être en avance sur l'horaire prévu/sur les délais prévus/sur le programme établi; **schedule work,** travail de régime; **tight/detailed schedule,** horaire (strictement) minuté; **work schedule,** horaires *mpl* de travail; **production schedule,** planning *m*/planification *f*/programme *m* de fabrication/barème de production.

schedule², *v.tr.* 1. (*a*) *Jur:* ajouter (un article) comme annexe (aux statuts d'une société, etc.) (*b*) ajouter (une note) en bordereau **2.** inscrire (un article, etc.) sur une liste/sur un inventaire; **progressive scheduled tax,** barème d'imposition progressive; **scheduled prices,** prix *m* tarif; **scheduled taxes,** impôts *m* cédulaires **3.** dresser un plan/un programme de (qch.); arrêter (un programme).

scheduling, *n. Ind:* établissement *m* d'un programme/planification *f*; programmation *f*; ordonnancement *m*.

scheme, *n.* **1.** (*a*) *Jur:* **scheme of composition (between debtor and creditors),** concordat préventif (à la faillite) (*b*) système *m*; **bonus scheme,** système de primes d'encouragement; **incentive scheme,** système de stimulants salariaux; **pension scheme,** régime *m* de retraite; **profit-sharing scheme,** système de participation aux bénéfices; **social benefit schemes for employees,** système de prestations en faveur des employés **2.** plan *m*/projet *m*/ programme *m*; **preliminary scheme,** avant-projet *m*.

schlock, *n. NAm: F:* camelote *f*; **schlock 'house,** magasin *m* qui vend de la camelote.

science, *n.* science *f*; **management science,** science de la gestion.

scientific, *a.* scientifique; **scientific management,** gestion *f* scientifique; organisation *f* scientifique du travail; **scientific research,** recherche(s) *f(pl)* scientifique(s).

scientist, *n.* scientifique *mf*; homme *m*/femme *f* de science; **social scientist,** sociologue *mf*.

scorched earth, *n.* (*against hostile take-over situation*) tactique *f* de la terre brûlée.

scrap[1], *n.* déchets *mpl*; **scrap dealer,** marchand *m* de ferraille; casseur *m*; **scrap value,** valeur *f* à la casse/au rancart; **to sell sth. for scrap,** vendre qch. à la casse.

scrap[2], *v.tr.* mettre (qch.) au rebut; **to scrap a project,** abandonner/rejeter/renoncer à un projet.

screen, *v.tr.* trier/sélectionner (du personnel).

screening, *n.* sélection *f* (du personnel).

scrip, *n. Fin:* (*a*) **scrip (certificate),** certificat *m* d'actions provisoire (*b*) *coll.* valeurs *fpl*/titres *mpl*/actions *fpl*; **registered scrip,** titres nominatifs (*c*) **scrip issue,** attribution *f* d'actions *f* gratuites;/action attribuée gratuitement/action gratuite; *NAm:* **scrip dividend/dividend in scrip,** certificat de dividende provisoire.

scripholder, *n. Fin:* détenteur, -trice de titres.

sea-going, *a.* **sea-going trade,** commerce *m* maritime.

seal[1], *n.* (*a*) (*on deed, etc.*) sceau *m*; (*on letter*) cachet *m*; **contract under seal,** convention scellée (*b*) cachet (de bouteille de vin, etc.); **customs seal,** plomb *m* de la douane; **lead seal,** capsule *f* (de bouteille de vin); plomb (pour sceller une caisse, etc.).

seal[2], *v.tr.* (*a*) sceller (un acte, etc.); cacheter (une lettre, une enveloppe); **sealed tender,** soumission cachetée (*b*) *Cust:* (faire) plomber (des marchandises, etc.).

seaport, *n.* port *m* maritime.

search, *n.* perquisition *f*; enquête *f*; **right of search,** droit *m* de visite; **search warrant,** mandat de perquisition.

season, *n.* **1.** (*a*) saison *f*; **in season,** pendant la saison; **out of season,** hors saison; **low season price,** prix hors saison; **the busy season,** la haute saison; **the slack season/ the off season,** la morte-saison/la saison creuse; **the tourist season/the holiday season,** la saison touristique/des vacances; la haute saison (*b*) **end of season sale,** vente *f* de fin de saison **2. season (ticket),** carte *f* d'abonnement.

seasonal, *a.* (commerce) saisonnier; **seasonal adjustment,** ajustement saisonnier/rectification saisonnière; **seasonal demand,** demande saisonnière; **seasonal fluctuations/variations,** fluctuations/ variations saisonnières; **seasonal unemployment,** chômage saisonnier.

seasonality, *n.* caractère saisonnier.

seasonally, *adv.* **seasonally adjusted/ corrected (rate),** (taux) rectifié/corrigé des variations saisonnières.

seaworthy, *a. MIns:* en état de navigabilité.

second, *a.* second/deuxième; **second mortgage,** deuxième hypothèque *f;* **second debentures,** obligations *f* de deuxième rang; **second endorser,** tiers porteur; **second half-year,** deuxième semestre *m;* **second via,** second routage.

secondary, *a.* secondaire; **secondary industry,** le secteur secondaire/le secondaire; **secondary market,** second marché/marché secondaire.

second-class, *a.* **second-class hotel,** hôtel *m* de deuxième classe; **second-class mail** = tarif *m* réduit; **to travel second-class,** voyager en seconde.

second-grade, *a.* **second-grade article,** article *m* de second choix/de qualité inférieure.

second-hand, *a.* (marchandises) d'occasion/de revente; **second-hand bookshop,** librairie *f* d'occasion; **second-hand car,** voiture *f* d'occasion; **second-hand dealer,** brocanteur *m;* revendeur, -euse; **the second-hand market,** le marché *m* de revente; **second-hand shop/market,** brocante *f.*

second-rate, *a.* (*a*) médiocre/inférieur; de qualité inférieure/de qualité médiocre (*b*) **second-rate stock,** titre *m* de second ordre.

seconds, *n.pl.* articles *m* de qualité inférieure.

secret[1], *n.* secret *m* (professionnel).

secret[2], *a.* **secret ballot,** scrutin secret.

secretarial, *a.* **to do a secretarial course,** suivre un cours/faire des études de secrétariat; **secretarial work,** travail *m* de secrétaire.

secretary, *n.* (*a*) secrétaire *mf;* **private secretary,** secrétaire particulier, -ière/ secrétaire de direction (*b*) **company secretary,** secrétaire général (d'une société);

honorary secretary, secrétaire général bénévole.

section, *n.* (*a*) section *f* (d'un département etc.); division *f*/article *m* (d'un document, etc.) (*b*) *StExch:* rubrique *f.*

sector, *n.* secteur *m;* **building sector,** secteur bâtiment; **economic/industrial sector,** secteur économique/industriel; **growth sector,** secteur/marché *m* en croissance; **services sector,** secteur des services; **the private sector,** le secteur privé; **the public sector,** le secteur public.

secure[1], *a.* **secure investment,** placement sûr/de tout repos.

secure[2], *v.tr.* nantir (un prêteur); garantir; **to secure a debt by mortgage,** hypothéquer une créance; garantir une créance par une hypothèque; **to secure a loan,** obtenir un prêt.

secured, *a.* garanti; nanti; **secured creditor,** créancier privilégié; **secured loan,** emprunt garanti.

security, *n.* **1.** (*a*) sécurité *f*/sûreté *f;* **security of employment/job security,** sécurité de l'emploi (*b*) (*in firm, etc.*) **security police,** services *mpl* de sécurité (*c*) **security margin,** marge *f* de sécurité (*d*) *Adm:* **social security,** sécurité sociale **2.** (*a*) caution *f;* cautionnement *m;* gage *m;* garantie *f*/nantissement *m;* **account opened without security,** compte ouvert sans garantie/sans provision; **security for a debt,** garantie d'une créance; **to give a security,** verser une caution/cautionner; **to pay in a sum as a security,** verser une provision/un cautionnement; **to lodge stock as additional security,** déposer des titres en nantissement; **as security for the sum,** en couverture de la somme; **to lend money on security,** prêter de l'argent sur nantissement/sur garantie; **to lend money without security,** prêter de l'argent à découvert (*b*) (*pers.*) caution *f*/garant, -ante; accréditeur *m; Jur:* répondant, -ante; **to stand/ become security for s.o.,** se porter caution/se porter garant pour qn; répondre de/cautionner qn; **to stand security for a signature/for a debt,** avaliser une signature; assurer une créance 3. *Fin:* **securities,** titres *m*/valeurs *f*/fonds *mpl*; portefeuille *m* titres/*F:* portefeuille; **bearer securities,** titres au porteur; **gilt-edged/government securities,** fonds d'État; **non-marketable securities,** titres non négociables; **outstanding securities;** titres en circulation/ non amortis; **registered securities,** titres nominatifs; **transferable securities,** valeurs négociables/cessibles; **underlying security,** titre sous-jacent; **securities department,** service *m* des titres (d'une banque); **Securities and Investment Board (SIB)**/*NAm:* **Securities and Exchange Commission (SEC),** Commission *f* des Opérations de Bourse.

segment, *v.tr.* **too many models of the same product have completely segmented the market,** les trop nombreux modèles d'un même produit ont totalement morcelé/ fragmenté/dispersé le marché.

seize, *v.tr. Jur:* confisquer/saisir (qch.)/ opérer la saisie de (qch.); **the goods were seized,** les marchandises ont été confisquées; **to seize assets,** mettre des actifs sous séquestre.

select, *v.tr.* sélectionner/choisir (un candidat).

selection, *n.* sélection *f*/choix *m*; **promotion by selection,** promotion *f* au choix; **selection board/committee,** comité *m* de sélection.

selective, *a.* sélectif; **selective selling,** distribution sélective.

self-employed, *a.* indépendant/qui travaille à son (propre) compte; **self-employed person,** travailleur indépendant; *n.* **the self-employed,** les travailleurs indépendants.

self-employment, *n.* travail *m* à son (propre) compte.

self-finance, *v.tr. & i.* autofinancer.

self-financed, *a.* auto-financé.

self-financing[1], *n.* autofinancement *m*; **self-financing ratio,** coefficient *m* d'auto-financement.

self-financing[2], *a.* **the firm is self-financing,** l'entreprise *f* pratique un système d'autofinancement.

self-liquidating, *a.* auto-amortissable.

self-mailer, *n. Mkt:* carte *f*/matériel *m* de publicité directe (*qui est mis à la poste sans enveloppe*); carte-réponse *f.*

self-management, *n.* autogestion *f.*

self-service, *n.* (magasin) libre-service *m*; (restaurant) self-service *m*/*F:* self *m.*

self-sufficiency, *n.* **economic self-sufficiency,** indépendance *f* économique; **national self-sufficiency,** autarcie *f.*

self-sufficient, *a.* indépendant/autosuffisant; **Britain is self-sufficient in oil,** la Grande Bretagne est économiquement indépendante du point de vue pétrole.

sell[1], *n. F:* vente *f*; **hard sell,** vente agressive/ battage *m* publicitaire; **to give (s.o., sth.) the hard sell,** faire du battage (autour de qn, de qch.); **soft sell,** vente facile/vente à publicité discrète.

sell[2], *v.tr.* (*a*) vendre (qch.); **to sell sth. back to s.o.,** revendre qch. à qn; **to sell goods easily,** écouler facilement des marchandises; **difficult to sell,** de vente/d'écoulement difficile; **to sell sth. by auction,** vendre qch. à la criée/aux enchères; **to sell sth. for cash,** vendre qch. (au) comptant; **to sell sth. on credit,** vendre qch. à terme/à crédit; **to sell sth. at a loss,** vendre qch. à perte; **to sell sth. dear,** vendre qch. cher; **to sell sth. cheap,** vendre qch. (à) bon marché; **he sold it to me for a pound,** il me l'a vendu (pour) une livre; *StExch:* **to sell short/to sell a bear,** vendre à découvert; **to sell at best,** vendre au mieux; **to sell forward,** vendre à terme (*b*) **goods that sell well,** marchandises *f* qui se vendent bien; **these pencils are selling at/sell for 8p each,** on vend ces crayons 8p chacun/8p pièce; **certain to sell,** d'un débit assuré; **what are plums selling at?** combien valent les prunes?/quel est le prix des prunes?

sell-by-date, *n.* date *f* limite de vente/date de péremption (d'un produit).

seller, *n.* **1.** (*pers.*) (*a*) vendeur, -euse; *StExch:* **bear seller,** vendeur à découvert; **seller's option,** prime *f* vendeur/pour livrer; **seller's market,** marché *m* à la hausse; **sellers over,** excès *m* de vendeurs (*b*) marchand, -ande/débitant, -ante (de tabac, etc.) **2.** (*article*) **(good) seller,** article *m* de vente/qui se vend bien; **bad seller,** article hors de vente/qui ne se vend pas.

selling, *n.* vente *f*/écoulement *m* (de marchandises, etc.); **direct selling,** vente directe; **hard selling,** vente agressive; **selling cost,** frais *mpl* commerciaux; **selling point,** avantage spécial (d'un produit) susceptible d'intéresser un client; **selling price,** prix *m* de vente; prix marchand/fort; **(conventional) selling weight,** poids vénal; **unique selling proposition (USP),** proposition exclusive de vente (*b*) **selling short/short selling,** vente à découvert/à terme; **selling off,** liquidation *f* (des stocks); *Fin:* (re)vente *f*/réalisation *f* (de titres, etc.); **selling out,** revente *f* de titres impayés (par l'acheteur).

sell-off[1], *n.* solde *m*/liquidation *f* (de stock); dégagement *m*; **a sell-off in the dollar,** vente massive de dollars.

sell off[2], *v.tr.* solder/écouler/vendre à bas prix (des marchandises); se défaire de (marchandises); liquider (son stock, etc.).

sell out, *v.tr.* (*a*) *Fin:* réaliser (un portefeuille); *StExch:* liquider (une position) (*b*) vendre tout son stock de (qch.); **the shop sold out all their furniture,** tous les meubles (du magasin) ont été vendus; **we're sold out of eggs,** nous n'avons plus d'œufs, tout est vendu; **the book is sold out,** l'édition est épuisée (*c*) **to sell out one's business,** vendre/se défaire de son commerce.

sell-out, *n. F:* **this line has been a sell-out,** cet article s'est vendu à merveille (et il ne nous en reste plus); **it was a sell-out,** nous avons absolument tout vendu.

sell-side, *n. NAm:* vendeurs *mpl.*

sell up, *v.tr.* (faire) vendre les biens (d'un failli); **he went bankrupt and was sold up,** il a fait faillite et tout ce qu'il possédait a été vendu.

semi-annual, *a.* semestriel.

semi-automated, *a.* semi-automatisé.

semi-black, *a.* **semi-black market,** marché gris.

semi-finished, *a.* **semi-finished products/ goods,** produits semi-finis/semi-ouvrés; demi-produits *mpl.*

semi-manufactured, *a.* semi-ouvré/semi-fini; **semi-manufactured goods,** demi-produits *mpl.*

semi-manufactures, *n.pl.* semi-produits *mpl*; demi-produits *mpl.*

semi-skilled, *a.* **semi-skilled worker =** ouvrier, -ière spécialisé(e); manœuvre spécialisé.

semi-variable, *a.* (*costs*) semi-variable.

send, 1. *v.tr.* (*a*) envoyer (qn) (*b*) envoyer/ faire parvenir (qch.); expédier (une lettre, un paquet, etc.); remettre (de l'argent, un chèque, etc.); **to send a parcel by post,** expédier un colis par la poste **2.** *v.i.* **to send for s.o./sth.,** envoyer chercher qn/qch.; **to send away for sth.,** écrire pour faire venir qch.; **to send sth. back,** retourner qch.

sender, *n.* expéditeur, -trice (d'une lettre, de marchandises); **return to sender,** retour *m* à l'envoyeur.

send in, *v.tr.* **he has sent in his bill,** il nous a envoyé/fait parvenir son compte; **applications should be sent in before the end of the year,** les demandes devront être reçues avant la fin de l'année; **to send in one's resignation,** envoyer/donner sa démission.

send off, *v.tr.* expédier (une lettre, etc.).

send on, *v.tr.* faire suivre (une lettre).

send out, *v.tr.* expédier; mettre à la poste.

senior, 1. *a.* (*i*) plus âgé (*ii*) qui a plus d'ancienneté (*iii*) plus élevé (en grade); supérieur; **senior clerk,** premier commis/ commis principal; chef *m* de bureau;

senior executive, cadre supérieur; **senior partner,** associé principal; associé majoritaire; **senior in rank,** de grade supérieur; *Fin:* **senior securities,** titres *mpl* prioritaires **2.** *n.* (*i*) le/la plus âgé(e) (*ii*) qui a le plus d'ancienneté (*iii*) le/la plus élevé(e) (en grade).

seniority, *n.* **1.** priorité *f* d'âge; **he is chairman by seniority,** il est président d'âge **2.** ancienneté *f* de service; **to be promoted by seniority,** avancer (en grade)/être promu à l'ancienneté.

sensitive, *a.* **sensitive market,** marché *m* sensible/instable/prompt à réagir.

separate, *a. Jur:* **separate estate,** biens *m* propres (dans un couple marié).

sequester, sequestrate, *v.tr. Jur:* séquestrer (les biens d'un débiteur, etc.); mettre (un bien, des actifs) sous séquestre.

sequestration, *n. Jur:* séquestration *f*; mise *f* sous séquestre; **sequestration order,** ordonnance *f* de mise sous séquestre; **writ of sequestration,** séquestre *m* (judiciaire).

serial, *a.* **serial number,** numéro *m* de série; numéro d'ordre; *Ind: etc:* numéro matricule (d'un moteur, etc.).

series, *n.inv.* série *f*; collection *f*; **pilot series/test series,** présérie *f*.

servant, *n.* **public servants,** employé(e)s d'un service public; **civil servant,** fonctionnaire *m* (de l'État).

serve, *v.tr. & i.* **1. to serve one's apprenticeship,** faire son apprentissage **2.** (*a*) (*in shop*) **to serve a customer,** servir un(e) client(e); **are you being served?** est-ce qu'on s'occupe de vous? (*b*) *v.i.* **to serve in a shop,** être vendeur, -euse.

service¹, *n.* **1.** (*a*) service *m*; **ten years' service,** dix années de service; **promotion according to length of service,** avancement *m* à l'ancienneté *f* (*b*) (*in restaurant, etc.*) service *m*; **service included,** service compris (*c*) *Mkt:* **after sales service/back up service,** service après-vente; **customer service,** service à la clientèle; **service agreement,** contrat *m* de service; **service charge,**

frais *mpl* administratifs/frais d'administration; (*paid by tenants*) prestations *f* locatives; **service flat,** appartement avec service (*compris dans le loyer*); **rent plus service charge,** loyer *m* plus charges; **24-hour service,** service permanent/de 24 heures; permanence *f* (*d*) **to bring/put (a machine, a vehicle) into service,** mettre (un appareil, un véhicule) en service; **service life,** durée *f* de vie/longévité *f* (d'un matériel); durée/potentiel *m* d'utilisation (*e*) *Veh:* **service speed,** vitesse commerciale **2.** *PolEc:* **goods and services,** biens *m* et services; **debt service bill,** charge/service d'une dette; **direct services,** services marchands; **service bureau,** société *f* de services; **service fee,** prestation *f* de service; **service industry,** secteur *m* tertiaire; (*particular company*) société *f* de service; **services sector,** secteur *m* des services **3. the civil service,** l'administration *f*/la fonction publique **4.** (*a*) **public services,** services publics; **postal service,** service postal (*b*) **goods/freight service,** service de marchandises (*c*) **motorway services,** relais *m* d'autoroute (*d*) *NAm:* **service center,** ville commerciale (*qui dessert toute une région*) **5.** (*of car*) révision *f*; **service department,** service de réparation/d'entretien; **service engineer,** technicien *m* d'entretien; **service manual/handbook,** manuel *m* d'entretien; **service station,** station-service *f*.

service², *v.tr.* **1.** réviser/vérifier; **to service a car,** réviser une voiture **2. to service a loan/a debt,** assurer le service d'un emprunt/d'une dette.

servicetill, *n. F:* guichet *m* automatique de banque.

servicing, *n.* (*a*) **debt servicing,** charge *f*/service *m* d'une dette (*b*) entretien *m*/réparation *f* (d'une machine).

session, *n.* (*a*) session *f*; séance *f*; **to have/to hold a session,** se réunir (pour discuter, etc.); **full session,** réunion plénière (*b*) *StExch:* séance/session; **closing session,** session de clôture; **morning session,** matinée *f* de bourse.

set¹, *n.* ensemble *m*; jeu *m* (d'outils, de

boîtes, etc.); série *f* (de poids, de conférences); batterie *f* (d'ustensiles de cuisine); service *m* (à thé, etc.); *Fin:* **set of bills,** effet *m* en plusieurs exemplaires.

set[2], *a.* **set price,** prix *m* fixe.

set[3], *v.tr.* **to set a value on sth.,** évaluer qch.

set aside, *v.tr.* mettre de côté/en réserve.

set against, *v.tr.* **set against your invoice,** à valoir sur votre facture; **to set (off) losses against tax,** déduire les pertes des impôts.

setback, *n.* recul *m* (de prix); revers *m*; **to suffer a setback,** essuyer un revers (de fortune).

set off, *v.tr.* **to set off a debt,** compenser une dette.

set-off, *n.* compensation *f* (d'une dette); *Book-k:* écriture *f* inverse; **as a set-off against ...,** en compensation de ...; en dédommagement de ....

set out, *v.tr.* étaler/disposer (ses marchandises, etc.).

set-out, *n.* étalage *m* (de marchandises, etc.).

setting up, *n.* (*a*) implantation *f* (d'une nouvelle industrie, etc.) (*b*) établissement *m*/création *f*/fondation *f* (d'un comité, d'une maison de commerce).

settle, 1. *v.tr.* (*a*) fixer/déterminer (un jour, un endroit, etc.); **the terms were settled,** on a convenu des conditions; **your appointment is as good as settled,** votre nomination *f* est presque une affaire faite (*b*) résoudre (une question); arranger/liquider (une affaire) (*c*) conclure/terminer (une affaire); régler/solder (un compte); acquitter/régler (une facture); payer (une dette, une amende, un compte, etc.); **to settle (one's bills)/to settle up,** payer/régler ses comptes (*d*) **to settle an annuity on s.o.,** constituer/assigner une annuité à qn; asseoir une annuité sur qn **2.** *v.i.* **to settle for sth.,** accepter qch.; **I settled for £100,** j'ai accepté £100.

settled, *a.* (*a*) (*question, etc.*) arrangé/décidé (*b*) (*bill, etc.*) réglé/soldé/acquitté.

settlement, *n.* (*a*) règlement *m* (d'une affaire, d'un litige); solution *f* (à un problème); détermination *f* (d'une date, etc.) (*b*) règlement/paiement (d'un compte); **settlement of account,** arrêté *m* de compte; **in (full) settlement,** pour solde/ règlement de tout compte; **cash settlement,** règlement des transactions au comptant; **cheque in settlement of an account,** chèque *m* en paiement d'un compte (*c*) *StExch:* liquidation *f*; **the settlement,** le terme; **dealings for settlement,** négociations *f* à terme; **settlement date/day,** jour *m* de (la) liquidation/du règlement; **settlement price,** cours *m* de résiliation; **yearly settlement,** liquidation de fin d'année (*d*) **legal settlement (between merchant and creditors),** concordat *m*/règlement *m* judiciaire (après faillite) (*e*) **settlement of an annuity,** constitution *f* de rente (**on,** en faveur de) (*f*) **wage settlement,** accord *m* sur les salaires.

settling, *n.* (*a*) conclusion *f*/terminaison *f* (d'une affaire); **settling (up),** règlement *m* (d'un compte) (*b*) *StExch:* liquidation *f*; **settling day,** jour *m* de (la) liquidation/du règlement.

set up, 1. *v.tr.* (*a*) créer/organiser/instituer/ constituer (un comité/etc.); fonder (une maison de commerce); monter (un magasin) (*b*) **to set s.o. up in business,** établir qn/lancer qn dans un commerce **2.** *v.i.* **to set up as a chemist,** s'établir pharmacien.

set-up, *n.* organisation *f*/établissement *m*; structure *f*.

seven, *num. a.* **seven-day money/deposits,** dépôts à sept jours; **seven sisters,** cartel des sept pays producteurs de pétrole.

sever, *vtr.* résilier (un contrat de travail).

several, *a.* plusieurs; **several liability,** responsabilité individuelle; **joint and several liability,** responsabilité conjointe et solidaire.

severally, *adv. Jur:* **severally liable,** responsable isolément/individuellement; **jointly and severally,** conjointement et solidairement; par divis et indivis.

severance, *n.* **severance pay,** compensation *f*/indemnité *f* pour perte d'emploi.

shade, *v.tr. NAm:* **to shade prices,** établir des prix dégressifs; **prices shaded for quantities,** tarif dégressif pour le gros.

shady, *a.* **shady deal,** affaire véreuse.

shakeout, *n.* réorganisation *f*/remaniement *m* du personnel (avec licenciements); **shakeout in the market,** assainissement *m* du marché.

shake-up, *n. F:* remaniement *m* (du personnel).

shaky, *a.* **shaky business/shaky undertaking,** entreprise qui périclite.

sham, *a. Fin:* **sham dividend,** dividende fictif.

share[1], *n.* **1.** part *f*/portion *f*; **to have a share in/of the profits,** participer aux bénéfices; **to have a share in a business,** avoir des intérêts dans une affaire **2.** (*a*) contribution *f*/cotisation *f*/quote-part *f*; **to pay one's share,** payer sa (quote-)part (*b*) **to go shares with s.o.,** partager avec qn **3.** *Fin:* (*in a company, etc.*) action *f*/titre *m*/valeur *f*; **A-shares/B-shares, etc,** actions préférentielles de classe A/B etc; **bonus share,** action gratuite; **deferred share,** action différée; **dividend share,** action de jouissance; action de bénéficiaire; **founder's share/deferred ordinary share,** part *f* de fondateur; **fully paid(-up) share,** action entièrement libérée; **gold share/golden share,** action à droit de veto/golden share *m*; **heavy shares,** actions chères/à cours élevé; **non-voting shares,** actions sans droit de vote; **ordinary/common share,** action ordinaire; **participating share,** action de participation; **partly-paid(-up) share,** action non entièrement libérée; **partnership share,** part d'association; **personal/registered share,** action nominative; **preferred/preference/senior share,** action préférentielle; action à dividende prioritaire/préférentiel; action privilégiée/de priorité; **recovery shares,** valeurs de retournement; **redeemable preference shares,** actions à dividende prioritaire remboursables (ADPR)/ actions préférentielles remboursables; **zero dividend share,** action sans dividende; **to allot shares,** attribuer/répartir des actions; **to issue shares,** émettre des actions; **to transfer shares,** céder/transférer des actions; **to hold shares,** posséder/ détenir des actions; être actionnaire; **share capital,** capital-actions *m*/capital *m* actions; **share certificate,** titre d'action(s); certificat *m* d'action(s)/de titre(s); certificat provisoire; **share dealing,** (*between subscribers*) négociation *f* d'actions sur le marché gris; **share prices,** cours *m* des actions; **the share index reached an all-time low,** l'indice *m* des actions est descendu à son plus bas niveau; **share pusher,** courtier marron; placeur *m*/placier *m* de valeurs douteuses; **share pushing,** placement *m* de valeurs douteuses.

share[2], **1.** *v.tr.* partager; **to share an office with s.o.,** partager un bureau avec qn **2.** *v.tr. & ind.tr.* **to share (in) sth.,** prendre part à/avoir part à/participer à/s'associer à qch.; **to share in the profits,** participer/ avoir part aux bénéfices; **to share out the work,** répartir/distribuer le travail.

shareholder, *n. Fin:* actionnaire *mf*/sociétaire *mf* (d'une société anonyme); **nominee shareholder,** actionnaire-paravent/actionnaire faisant du portage; **preference shareholder,** détenteur, -trice d'une action à dividende prioritaire; **registered shareholder,** porteur *m* d'actions nominatives; **shareholders' equity,** fonds *m* propres/ avoir *m* des actionnaires; **shareholders' meeting,** réunion *f* d'actionnaires; **core/ controlling shareholders,** noyau dur.

shareholding, *n.* **1.** possession *f* d'actions/ de titres; actionnariat *m*; **employee shareholding,** actionnariat ouvrier; **he has a major shareholding in the company,** il est un des principaux actionnaires de la société **2. shareholding,** action *f.*

share-out, *n.* partage *m*/distribution *f*/ répartition *f.*

sharing, *n.* **1.** partage *m* (de ses biens, etc.) **2.** participation *f*/partage; **profit sharing,** participation aux bénéfices; association *f* capital-travail; *Cmptr:* **time sharing,** partage de temps/temps partagé.

shark, *n.* *F:* raider *m*/requin *m* (de la finance).

sharp, *a.* **sharp rally,** reprise vigoureuse; **sharp rise/drop in prices,** forte hausse/baisse des prix.

sheet, *n.* feuille *f* (de papier); **order sheet,** bulletin *m*/bon *m* de commande; bordereau *m* d'achat; **sale sheet,** bordereau de vente; *Ind:* **time/work/job sheet,** feuille de présence; **(workman's) time sheet,** semainier *m.*

shelf, *n.* rayon *m*/étagère *f*; **shelf space,** linéaire *m*; (*in supermarket, etc.*) **shelf filler,** réassortisseur, -euse; **shelf life (of a product),** espérance *f*/durée *f* de vie (d'un produit); **shelf talker,** affichette *f* de rayonnage; (*of goods*) **to stay on the shelves,** être difficile à vendre.

shift, *n.* (*a*) **shift in demand,** déplacement *m* de la demande (*b*) équipe *f*/poste *m*/ brigade *f*/relais *m* (d'ouvriers); (*esp. of dockers*) shift *m*; **day shift,** équipe de jour; **night shift,** équipe de nuit; **to work in shifts,** travailler par équipes/se relayer (*b*) journée *f* de travail; **an eight-hour shift,** une période de relève de huit heures; **to work eight-hour shifts,** se relayer toutes les huit heures; faire les trois huits; **I'm on first shift,** je suis du premier huit.

shift-work, *n.* *Ind:* travail *m* par équipes/ par relais; travail posté; **worker who does shift-work/who is on shift-work,** travailleur, -euse posté(e).

shift-working, *n.* travail posté; travail par équipes/par relais.

ship[1], *n.* navire *m*; **container ship,** (navire) porte-conteneurs *m*; **passenger ship,** paquebot *m*; **refrigerator ship,** navire frigorifique.

ship[2], *v.tr.* **1.** embarquer (une cargaison, etc.); mettre (des marchandises) à bord **2.** envoyer/expédier (des marchandises, etc., par voie de mer; *esp. NAm:* par chemin de fer, par la poste, etc.); **to ship coal to France,** expédier du charbon en France.

shipbroker, *n.* courtier *m* maritime.

shipbrokerage, *n.* courtage *m* maritime.

shipment, *n.* **1.** (*a*) embarquement *m*/ mise *f* à bord (de marchandises, etc.) (*b*) expédition *f*/envoi *m* (de marchandises) par mer; **overseas shipment,** envoi outre-mer **2.** (*goods shipped*) chargement *m.*

shipping, *n.* transport *m* maritime; *esp. NAm:* transport routier/par chemin de fer; **shipping agent,** agent *m* maritime; (*for goods*) expéditeur *m*; commissionnaire chargeur *m*; **shipping bill,** connaissement *m*; **shipping charges,** frais *mpl* de transport; *NAm:* **shipping company,** entreprise *f*/ entrepreneurs *mpl* de transport routier; **shipping office,** agence *f* maritime.

shoestring, *n.* **shoestring operation,** opération dotée de moyens financiers très modestes/de très peu de capital.

shoot, *v.tr.* *NAm:* **to shoot crap,** faire un coup de dé/prendre un risque.

shoot up, *v.i.* (*of prices, costs*) augmenter rapidement/brusquement; monter en flèche.

shooting up, *n.* **the shooting up of prices,** la flambée des prix.

shop[1], *n.* **1.** magasin *m*; (*small*) boutique *f*; **baker's shop,** boulangerie *f*; **grocer's shop,** épicerie *f*/(magasin d')alimentation *f*; **mobile shop,** camionnette-boutique *f*; **shoe shop,** magasin de chaussures; **to open a shop/to set up shop,** ouvrir un magasin/s'établir comme commerçant; **to keep a shop,** tenir un magasin/un commerce; **to close a shop,** fermer boutique; **shop front,** devanture *f* de magasin; **shop window,** vitrine *f*; devanture (de magasin); étalage *m*; **in the shop window,** en vitrine/à l'étalage; **shop assistant,** vendeur, -euse (de magasin); employé, -ée de magasin **2.** *Ind: etc:* atelier *m*; **the shop floor,** les ateliers; les ouvriers *m*;

assembly shop, atelier de montage/d'assemblage; **repair shop,** atelier de réparations; **shop foreman,** chef *m* d'atelier; **shop steward,** délégué(e) syndical(e); délégué(e) d'atelier/d'usine/du personnel; **closed shop,** atelier fermé aux (ouvriers) non-syndiqués; = monopole syndical de l'embauche; **open shop,** entreprise *f* qui admet du personnel non syndiqué **3.** *StExch:* introducteurs *mpl*; **shop shares,** actions *f* à introduction.

shop², *v.i.* **to shop/to go shopping,** (aller) faire ses courses/des achats; *(for food)* faire son marché/aller aux provisions; **to shop around,** comparer les prix; chercher des occasions; chercher les prix les plus avantageux.

shopgirl, *n.* vendeuse *f* /employée *f* de magasin.

shopkeeper, *n.* (*a*) commerçant, -ante (*b*) propriétaire *mf* (de magasin).

shoplifter, *n.* voleur, -euse à l'étalage.

shoplifting, *n.* vol *m* à l'étalage.

shopper, *n.* acheteur, -euse; client, -ente.

shopping, *n.* achats *mpl*; courses *fpl*; **to do one's shopping,** faire ses courses; *(for food)* faire son marché/aller aux provisions; *PolEc:* **shopping basket,** panier *m* de la ménagère/panier *m* à provisions; **shopping centre,** centre commercial/*FrC:* centre d'achats; **shopping mall,** galerie marchande; **shopping precinct,** (*i*) centre commercial (*ii*) aire piétonnière; **shopping street,** rue commerçante; **window shopping,** lèche-vitrine *m*/chalandage *m*.

shop-soiled, *a.* (article) défraîchi/abîmé (en magasin)/qui a fait l'étalage.

shopwalker, *n.* (*a*) chef *m* de rayon (*b*) inspecteur, -trice/surveillant, -ante (de magasin).

short, 1. *a.* & *n.* (*a*) *Fin:* **short bills/bills at short date,** billets *m*/traites *f* à courte échéance; billets à vue; **shorts,** *n.* titres courts/obligations courtes; **deposit/loan at short notice,** dépôt *m*/prêt *m* à court terme; **short rate,** taux à court terme (*b*)

(weight, measure, etc.) insuffisant; **to give short weight,** ne pas donner le poids/tricher sur le poids; **the weight is 50 gram(me)s short,** il manque 50 grammes au poids/il y a 50 grammes en moins; **short delivery,** livraison partielle; **to prevent short delivery,** éviter des manquants *m* dans la marchandise (*c*) **to be short of staff,** manquer de/être à court de main-d'œuvre; **I'm short of money,** je suis à court d'argent/je manque d'argent (*d*) *StExch:* **short covering,** couverture *f* d'une position ouverte; **short end,** court terme; **short interest,** découvert/position vendeur; **short seller,** vendeur, -euse à découvert; **short selling,** vente *f* à découvert/à terme **2.** *n. StExch:* vendeur à découvert/à terme **3.** *adv. StExch:* **to go short/to sell short,** vendre à découvert.

shortage, *n.* insuffisance *f*; manque *m*; **shortage of staff/of labour shortage,** manque de personnel/pénurie *f* de main-d'œuvre; **credit shortage,** assèchement *m* du crédit; **dollar shortage,** pénurie de dollars; **housing shortage,** crise *f* du logement; **to make up/make good the shortage,** combler le déficit.

short-dated, *a. Fin:* (billet) à courte échéance; **short-dated securities,** titres courts/obligations courtes.

shortening, *n. Fin:* **shortening of credit,** réduction *f*/amoindrissement *m* de crédit.

shortfall, *n.* déficit *m*; manque *m*.

shorthand, *n.* sténographie *f*; **take this letter down in shorthand,** prenez cette lettre en sténo; **shorthand typist,** sténodactylo *mf*.

shorthanded, *a.* à court de personnel/de main-d'œuvre/d'ouvriers; **to be shorthanded,** manquer de personnel.

shorting, *n.* vente *f* à découvert.

shortlist¹, *n.* **he's on the shortlist,** il a été retenu/sélectionné (comme candidat).

shortlist², *v.tr.* **to shortlist a candidate/an applicant,** sélectionner un candidat/retenir une candidature.

shortlisted, *a.* être parmi les candidats sélectionnés/dont on a retenu la candidature.

shorts, *n.pl.* *Fin* titres courts/obligations courtes.

short-staffed, *a.* **to be short-staffed,** manquer de personnel/de main-d'œuvre.

short-term, *a.* *Fin:* **short-term loan,** prêt *m* à court terme/à courte échéance.

short-time, *a.* **1.** (contrat, etc.) à court terme **2. short-time working,** chômage partiel; **to be on short-time,** être en chômage partiel.

shot, *n.* **mailing shot,** envoi *m*/prospectus *m*/dépliant *m* (de publicité directe).

show[1], *n.* (*a*) exposition *f* (de marchandises, etc.); concours *m*/comice *m* (agricole, etc.); **fashion show,** présentation *f* de collections; **the Motor Show,** le Salon de l'Automobile (*b*) **show house/flat,** maison *f* témoin/appartement *m* témoin (*c*) *F:* **show stopper,** contre-attaque *f* judiciaire contre une OPA hostile.

show[2], *v.tr.* **to show a profit/a loss,** se solder par un profit/un déficit; **the accounts show a net profit of ...,** les comptes *m* se soldent par un bénéfice net de ....

showcard, *n.* (*i*) pancarte *f* (*ii*) étiquette *f* (de vitrine, etc.); affiche *f* à chevalet (*iii*) carte *f* d'échantillons.

showcase, *n.* vitrine *f*.

showroom, *n.* salle *f*/salon *m*/magasin *m* d'exposition (d'une maison de commerce); salle de démonstration (de voitures, etc.).

shredder, *n.* **(document) shredder,** destructeur *m* de documents.

shrink, *a.* **shrink film,** film *m* rétractable; **shrink packaging,** emballage *m* sous film rétractable; **shrink packed/wrapped,** emballé sous film rétractable.

shunting, *n.* *StExch:* arbitrage *m* de place à place.

shut, *v.tr.* **1.** fermer (un magasin, etc.) **2.** (*on*

transfer books of banks, etc.) **shut for dividend,** clôture *f* pour dividende.

shut down, 1. *v.tr.* fermer (une usine, etc.) **2.** *v.i.* (*of factory, etc.*) (*i*) chômer (*ii*) fermer ses portes.

shutdown, *n.* *Ind:* (*i*) fermeture *f*; immobilisation *f* (*ii*) chômage *m* (d'une usine).

shut-out, *n.* *Ind:* lock-out *m* inv.

shuttered, *a.* *NAm:* **shuttered cotton mills,** filature *f* en chômage/qui a fermé ses portes.

shutting, *n.* **shutting down of a factory,** (*i*) fermeture *f* (*ii*) chômage *m* d'une usine.

sick, *a.* malade; **sick leave,** congé *m* de maladie; **sick pay,** indemnité *f*/allocation *f* de maladie.

sickness, *n.* maladie *f*; **sickness benefit,** prestation *f* en cas de maladie; **assurance maladie; to draw sickness benefit,** bénéficier de l'assurance maladie; avoir droit à l'assurance maladie.

side, *n.* **1.** *Book-k:* **credit side,** crédit *m*/avoir *m*; **debit side,** débit *m*/doit *m* **2.** (*on packing cases, etc.*) **this side up,** haut *m* **3. reverse side (of a letter of credit),** dos *m* (d'une lettre de crédit).

sideline, *n.* (*a*) occupation *f*/travail *m* secondaire (*b*) (*of product*) seconde spécialité (*c*) **buyers are on the sidelines,** les acheteurs attendent le bon moment pour rentrer dans le marché.

sight, *n.* (*a*) **bill payable at sight,** effet *m* payable à vue; **bill/draft at sight/sight draft,** effet/papier *m*/traite *f* à vue; **three months after sight,** à trois mois de vue; *StExch:* **sight quotation,** cotation *f* à vue (*b*) **on sale sight unseen,** à vendre tel quel/sur description/sans inspection; *Cust:* **sight entry,** déclaration *f* provisoire.

sighting, *n.* **sighting of a bill,** présentation *f* d'un effet.

sign *v.tr.* signer (son nom, un document, un chèque, etc.); **the letter was signed by the president,** la lettre portait la signature du président; **to sign a bill,** accepter une traite; **to sign a contract,** signer/passer un contrat; **to sign for (reception of) goods,** signer à la réception (de marchandises).

signatory, *a. & n.* signataire *(mf).*

signature, *n.* signature *f;* **stamped signature,** griffe *f;* **to put one's signature to a letter,** apposer sa signature à une lettre/signer une lettre; **for signature,** pour signature; **joint signature,** signature collective; signature des parties intéressées; **the signature of the firm,** la signature sociale.

signing, *n.* signature *f* (d'un document); acceptation *f* (d'une traite); **signing fee,** jeton *m* de signature (d'un directeur de société); **signing officer,** fondé *m* de signature/signataire officiel.

sign off, *v.i.* (*of workers in factories, etc.*) signer le registre (en quittant le travail); pointer au départ.

sign on, 1. *v.tr.* embaucher (un ouvrier) **2.** *v.i.* (*a*) (*of workers*) s'embaucher (*b*) (*of workers in factories, etc.*) signer le registre (en arrivant au travail); pointer à l'arrivée (*c*) *F:* s'inscrire au chômage.

silent, *a.* **silent partner,** associé *m* passif/commanditaire; commanditaire *m;* bailleur *m* de fonds.

silver, *n.* argent *m;* **silver (money),** argent monnayé; **silver coin,** (*i*) pièce *f* d'argent (*ii*) *coll.* (pièces d')argent; **to give a pound in silver,** faire de la monnaie pour une livre (*b*) **silver export point,** silver-point *m* de sortie; **silver import point,** silver-point d'entrée (*c*) **silver wheelchair,** (*term written into employment contract*) = retraite dorée/ = parachute *m* en or.

simple, *a.* (*a*) **simple interest,** intérêts *m* simples (*b*) *Jur:* **simple contract,** convention verbale/tacite; obligation *f* chirographaire; acte *m* sous seing privé; **simple contract creditor,** créditeur *m* chirographaire.

simulation, *n.* simulation *f.*

sincerely, *adv. Corr:* **yours sincerely =** veuillez agréer, Monsieur, Madame, etc.,

l'expression de mes sentiments respectueux/de mes sentiments distingués/de mes sentiments les meilleurs; je vous prie/nous vous prions de croire, Monsieur, Madame, etc., à l'expression de mes/nos sentiments distingués.

single¹, *n. Trans:* billet *m* simple/aller *m* (simple); **a single to Waterloo,** un aller pour Waterloo.

single², *a.* **1. single payment,** règlement *m* en une seule fois; *Ins: etc:* **single premium,** prime *f* unique; *Book-k:* **single-entry book-keeping,** comptabilité *f* en partie simple **2. single ticket,** billet *m* simple/aller *m* (simple).

singly, *adv.* séparément; un(e) à un(e); **articles sold singly,** articles *m* qui se vendent séparément/à la pièce.

sink, 1. *v.i.* baisser/diminuer/s'affaiblir/décliner; **prices are sinking,** les cours *m* baissent/s'affaissent/sont en baisse **2.** *v.tr.* (*a*) **to sink a loan,** amortir un emprunt (*b*) **to sink money into a new business,** investir de l'argent dans une nouvelle entreprise.

sinking, *n.* amortissement *m*/extinction *f* (d'une dette); **sinking fund,** fonds *m*/caisse *f* d'amortissement.

sir, *n. Corr:* **(Dear) Sir,** Monsieur; **Dear Sirs,** Messieurs.

sister, *n.* **sister company,** compagnie *f* sœur/société *f* sœur.

sit-down, *n.* **sit-down strike,** grève *f* sur le tas.

site, *n.* terrain *m;* emplacement *m;* **building site,** terrain à bâtir/chantier de construction.

sit-in, *n.* (grève *f* avec) occupation *f* des lieux.

sitting, *n.* séance *f;* **sitting tenant,** locataire *mf* en possession des lieux.

situation, *n.* **1.** situation *f;* **financial situation,** situation financière; **overall economic situation,** conjoncture *f* économique **2.** emploi *m*/place *f*/position *f;* **to get/obtain a situation,** obtenir un emploi; (*in* *advertisements*) **situations vacant** = offres *f* d'emplois; **situations wanted** = demandes *f* d'emplois.

size, *n.* **1.** (*a*) grandeur *f*/dimension *f*/ mesure *f*; étendue *f*; grosseur *f*/volume *m* (*b*) *Ind:* cote *f*/dimensions **2.** numéro *m* (d'un article); taille *f* (d'un vêtement); pointure *f* (de chaussures, de gants); **collar size,** encolure *f* (de chemise).

skeleton, *n.* **skeleton organization,** organisation *f* squelettique; **skeleton staff,** personnel réduit.

skill, *n.* aptitude *f*/compétence *f*.

skilled, *a.* habile; **skilled worker,** ouvrier, -ière qualifié(e); (ouvrier) professionnel (*m*); **skilled labour,** main-d'œuvre qualifiée/professionnelle.

slack, *a.* **trade/business is slack,** les affaires sont calmes/stagnantes; le commerce est stagnant; **slack period/slack time,** période *f* creuse; période de stagnation; **the slack season,** la morte-saison/la saison creuse.

slacken, *v.tr.* ralentir.

slackness, *n.* stagnation *f*/manque *m* d'activité/marasme *m* (des affaires).

slash, *v.tr.* **to slash prices,** casser les prix; **to slash the budget deficit,** réduire considérablement le déficit budgétaire.

sleeper, *n.* associé *m* passif/commanditaire; commanditaire *m*; bailleur *m* de fonds.

sleeping, *a.* **sleeping partner,** associé *m* passif/commanditaire; commanditaire *m*; bailleur *m* de fonds.

slice, *n.* *F:* **slice of the action,** part *f* des profits.

sliding, *a.* **sliding scale,** échelle *f* mobile (des prix, des salaires, etc.); **sliding-scale tariff,** tarif dégressif.

slip¹, *n.* bordereau *m*/bulletin *m*/bon *m*; **pay (advice) slip,** bulletin *m*/feuille *f* de paie.

slip², *v.i.* glisser; **shares slipped (back) to**

125, le prix des actions *f* a baissé jusqu'à 125.

slippage, *n.* (*a*) fluctuation *f*/variation *f* du cours (*b*) (*under performance of start-up company*) accident *m* de parcours.

slogan, *n.* slogan *m* (publicitaire).

slow, 1. *a.* **slow increase,** augmentation lente; **business is slow,** les affaires *f* ne vont pas/les affaires languissent; **go-slow,** grève perlée **2.** *adv.* **to go slow,** faire une grève perlée.

slow down, *v.tr.* **to slow down production,** ralentir la production.

slowdown, *n.* (*a*) ralentissement *m* (des affaires, etc.) (*b*) *NAm:* **slowdown (strike)** grève perlée.

slowing down, *n.* ralentissement *m* (de la production, etc.).

sluggish, *a.* languissant; **the market is sluggish,** le marché stagne/est lourd.

slump¹, *n.* baisse soudaine/forte baisse/ chute *f*/effondrement *m*/dégringolade *f* (des cours, du marché, etc.); **slump in sales,** mévente *f*; **the slump in the book trade,** la crise du livre; **slump in the pound,** dégringolade de la livre; **the slump,** la crise/la dépression économique.

slump², *v.i.* (*of prices, etc.*) baisser tout à coup/s'effondrer/dégringoler.

slush, *n.* **slush fund,** caisse *f* servant à payer les pots-de-vin/caisse noire.

small, *a.* (*a*) (*in contract, etc.*) **the small print,** ce qui est écrit en petits caractères (*b*) **small income,** revenu *m* modique (*c*) *Journ: F:* **small ads,** petites annonces; **small change,** (petite) monnaie; **banknotes of small denominations,** (billets *m* de banque de) petites coupures; **small firms/ businesses/enterprises,** petites entreprises; **small holder,** petit propriétaire; **the smaller industries,** la petite industrie; **small investors,** petits épargnants; **small shopkeeper,** petit commerçant.

small-scale, *a.* **small-scale business,** entreprise peu importante/de peu d'envergure

smart, *a.* **smart money**, placement astucieux/favorable.

smartcard, *n.* carte *f* à mémoire/à puce.

smash, **1.** *n.* débâcle *f*; effondrement *m*; faillite *f* (commerciale); krach *m* (à la Bourse) **2.** *adv.* **to go smash**, (*of firm*) faire faillite; tomber en faillite; (*of bank*) sauter.

smokestack, *n.* cheminée *f* d'usine; **smokestack industry**, les industries lourdes (*caractérisées par les cheminées*).

smuggle, **1.** *v.tr.* (faire) passer (des marchandises, etc.) en contrebande/en fraude **2.** *v.i.* faire de la contrebande.

smuggler, *n.* contrebandier, -ière; fraudeur, -euse (à la douane).

smuggling, *n.* contrebande *f*; fraude *f* (à la douane).

snake, *n. PolEc:* **the (monetary) snake**, le serpent (monétaire).

snap up, *v.tr.* **to snap up a bargain**, saisir une occasion; sauter sur une occasion; **goods that are quickly snapped up**, marchandises *f* qui s'enlèvent vite.

soar, *v.i.* (*of prices*) monter en flèche.

soaring, *a.* (*of prices, etc.*) qui montent en flèche; **because of soaring prices**, en raison de la (forte) hausse des prix.

social, *a.* **social cost**, coût social.

society, *n.* (*a*) société *f*; **consumer society**, société de consommation; **industrial society**, société industrielle (*b*) **benefit society/friendly society**, société de secours mutuels/société mutuelle; **building society**, caisse *f* d'épargne-logement; = société (commune) de crédit immobilier (hypothécaire); **cooperative society**, société coopérative (de consommation); **loan society**, société de crédit.

soft, **1.** *a.* (*a*) **soft sell**, publicité discrète; **soft selling**, vente *f* par des moyens discrets (*b*) **soft currency**, devise *f* faible **2.** *npl* **softs**, biens *mpl* non durables.

softbound, *a.* (*book*) broché.

software, *n. Cmptr:* logiciel *m*/software *m*; **software bug**, erreur *f* de logiciel; **software package**, progiciel *m*.

sola, *n.* **sola of exchange**, seule *f* de change.

sole, *a.* seul/unique; **sole agent**, agent (commercial) exclusif; seul dépositaire (d'une marque, d'un produit); **sole owner**, seul propriétaire; **sole right**, droit exclusif.

solicitor, *n.* = avoué *m*; avocat *m*; (*for wills, etc.*) notaire *m*; (*in firm*) chef *m* du contentieux; **the solicitor's department**, le bureau du contentieux.

solvability, *n.* solvabilité *f* (d'un commerçant).

solvency, *n.* solvabilité *f*.

solvent, *a.* solvable.

sound, *a.* **1.** (*machine*) en bon état; non endommagé; solide **2.** sain/solide; **sound currency**, monnaie saine; **sound financial position**, situation financière solide.

soundness, *n.* **1.** bon état/bonne condition (des marchandises, etc.) **2.** solvabilité *f*.

source, *n.* source *f* (de revenu, etc.); provenance *f* (de marchandise); **income taxed at source**, salaire imposé à la source; **taxation at source**, retenue *f* à la source.

space, *n.* espace *m*; **floor space**, surface *f* de plancher; **advertising space**, espace publicitaire.

space out, *v.tr.* **to space out payments over ten years**, échelonner des versements/des paiements sur dix ans.

spare, **1.** *a.* (*a*) disponible; **spare capital**, capital *m* disponible; fonds *m* disponibles (*b*) **spare parts**, pièces *f* de rechange/pièces détachées **2.** *n.* pièce de rechange/pièce détachée.

spec, *n.* **to buy sth. on spec**, faire des spéculations; risquer de l'argent (en achetant qch.).

special, *a.* (*a*) spécial; particulier; **special line of business/special class of goods**, spécialité *f*; **special price**, prix *m* de faveur (*b*) (article) hors série; **special order work,** travail *m* à façon.

speciality, *NAm:* **specialty** *n.* spécialité *f* (d'un magasin, etc.); **speciality goods,** produits de spécialité; articles/produits spécialisés; *NAm:* **specialty restaurant,** restaurant spécialisé.

specialization, *n.* spécialisation *f*; **area of specialization,** secteur *m* d'activité.

specialize, *v.i.* se spécialiser (**in,** dans).

specie, *n.* (*no pl*) espèces (monnayées)/ numéraire *m*; **to pay in specie,** payer en espèces.

specification, *n.* **1.** spécification *f*; **job specification,** spécification de la fonction; **standard specification,** norme *f* **2.** (*a*) description précise; devis descriptif; **specifications of a contract,** stipulations *f* d'un contrat (*b*) *Const: Ind: etc:* **specifications,** cahier *m* des charges.

specify, *v.tr.* spécifier/préciser; **specified load,** charge prévue/prescrite; **unless otherwise specified,** sauf indication contraire.

specimen, *n.* spécimen *m*/échantillon *m*/ exemple *m*; **specimen invoice,** modèle *m* de facture; (*of magazine, etc.*) **specimen copy/number,** numéro *m* spécimen; **specimen signature,** spécimen de signature.

speculate, *v.i. Fin:* spéculer; *Pej:* boursicoter; **to speculate on the Stock Exchange,** spéculer en Bourse/jouer à la Bourse; **to speculate in oils,** spéculer sur les valeurs pétrolières; **to speculate for a fall,** spéculer à la baisse; **to speculate for a rise,** spéculer à la hausse.

speculation, *n. Fin:* spéculation *f*; **risky speculation,** spéculation hasardeuse; **to buy sth. as a speculation,** spéculer sur (le prix de) qch.; *StExch:* coup *m* de Bourse.

speculative, *a. Fin:* spéculatif; **speculative buying,** achat(s) spéculatif(s); **speculative selling,** vente(s) spéculative(s); **speculative**

stocks/shares, valeurs spéculatives/de spéculation.

speculator, *n.* (*a*) spéculateur, -trice; **land bought (up) by speculators,** terrains achetés par des spéculateurs (*b*) *StExch:* personne qui joue à la Bourse; agioteur *m*; **small speculator,** boursicotier *m*.

spend, *v.tr.* dépenser (de l'argent).

spending, *n.* dépense(s) *f(pl)*; **spending money,** argent *m* de poche; argent pour dépenses courantes; *PolEc:* **spending power/spending capacity,** pouvoir *m* d'achat.

sphere, *n.* **spheres of activity,** secteurs *mpl* d'activité.

spin-off, *n.* (*a*) produit *m* secondaire/ dérivé *m* (*b*) avantage *m*/bénéfice *m* supplémentaire; retombée *f* (*c*) nouveau marché/nouveau débouché.

spinster, *n.* (femme) célibataire *f*.

spiral[1], *n.* montée *f* (continuelle et rapide) (des prix, etc.)/spirale *f* inflationniste; **wage-price spiral,** spirale des prix et des salaires/montée en flèche des prix et des salaires.

spiral[2], *v.i.* (*of prices, etc.*) monter en spirale/en flèche; monter de façon vertigineuse.

spiv, *n. F:* spéculateur *m* à très court terme.

split[1], *n. StExch:* **share split,** émission *f* d'actions gratuites; **three for two stock split,** distribution gratuite d'une action nouvelle pour deux anciennes.

split[2], *v.tr. Fin:* **to split shares,** partager/ fractionner des actions; **the stock was split 50%, one new share for each two shares held,** les actions ont été fractionnées à raison d'une action nouvelle pour deux anciennes; **split stocks,** stocks scindés.

spoil, 1. *v.tr.* avarier (des marchandises) **2.** *v.i.* (*of fruit, fish, etc.*) s'avarier/se gâter/se détériorer.

sponsor[1], *n.* commanditaire *m*/publifinanceur/sponsor *m*/parraineur *m*.

sponsor[2], *v.tr.* parrainer/commanditer/ publifinancer (un produit, etc.).

sponsoring, *n.* parrainage *m*/publifinançage *m*.

sponsorship, *n.* *Mkt:* patrtnage *m*/parrainage *m*/publifinançage *m*.

spot, *n.* (*a*) **spot cash,** argent comptant; **to pay spot cash,** payer comptant; **spot credit,** crédit ponctuel/crédit spot/à court terme; **spot deal,** opération *f* au comptant; **spot deliveries,** livraisons au comptant/immédiates; **spot market,** marché *m* au comptant; marché spot; **spot goods,** marchandises livrables au comptant; **spot price,** prix du comptant/du disponible; **spot rate,** cours *m* du disponible; **current market spot rate,** cours du marché au comptant; **spot sugar,** sucre payé comptant; **to purchase for spot,** acheter au comptant (*b*) message *m* publicitaire/spot *m* (*c*) **spot check,** (*i*) vérification *f* sur place (*ii*) contrôle-surprise *m*.

spread[1], *n.* écart *m*/différence *f* (entre le prix de fabrique et le prix de vente, entre deux tarifs, etc.); **bid-offer spread,** écart/ marge *f* entre le taux offert et le taux demandé/entre le taux vendeur et le taux acheteur; *StExch:* **jobber's spread,** marge (entre le prix d'achat et le prix de vente) d'un contrepartiste; **bear spread,** écart vertical baissier; **bull spread,** écart vertical haussier.

spread[2], **1.** *v.tr.* **to spread payments over ten months,** échelonner/étaler/répartir des paiements sur dix mois. **2.** vi. *StExch:* spéculer sur les différentiels de cours.

spree, *n.* **spending spree,** grosses/folles dépenses.

square, *v.tr.* **to square the accounts,** apurer les comptes.

squeeze[1], *n.* **credit squeeze,** restriction *f*/ resserrement *m*/encadrement *m* du crédit; **end of credit squeeze,** désencadrement *m* des crédits.

squeeze[2], *v.tr.* *StExch:* **to squeeze credits,** restreindre le crédit; **to squeeze the market,** étrangler le marché/faire pression (*surtout sur les vendeurs à découvert*).

stability, *n.* stabilité *f* (des prix, etc.); **economic stability,** la stabilité économique.

stabilization, *n.* stabilisation *f* (de la monnaie, des prix, etc.).

stabilize, **1.** *v.tr.* stabiliser (les prix, le marché, etc.) **2.** *v.i.* **prices have stabilized,** les prix se sont stabilisés.

stabilizer, *n.* stabilisateur *m*.

stabilizing[1], *a.* stabilisateur; **to have a stabilizing influence on prices,** exercer une influence stabilisatrice sur les prix; **stabilizing policy,** politique *f* de stabilité.

stabilizing[2], *n.* = **stabilization.**

stable, *a.* stable; **stable currency,** monnaie *f* stable; **stable prices,** prix *m* stables.

staff[1], *n.* personnel *m*; employés *mpl*; **to be on the staff,** faire partie du personnel; **clerical staff/office staff,** personnel de bureau; **line and staff organization,** organisation *f* mixte; **senior/managerial staff,** cadres *mpl* supérieurs; **shop/workroom staff,** (personnel de) l'atelier *m*; **staff manager,** chef *m* du personnel; **staff management,** direction *f* du personnel; **staff dining room,** restaurant *m* d'entreprise; (*on notice*) **staff only,** réservé au personnel/entrée interdite (au public).

staff[2], *v.tr.* recruter du personnel (pour un bureau).

staffing, *n.* **staffing policy,** politique *f* de recrutement du personnel.

stag, *n.* *StExch:* loup *m*.

stage[1], *n.* phase *f*/période *f*/étape *f*/degré *m*/palier *m*; **processing stages,** phases de fabrication; **taxation by stages,** taxes imposées par paliers.

stage[2], *v.tr.* organiser (une exposition, etc.); **the market staged a rally,** le marché a repris.

stagflation, *n.* stagflation *f*.

stagger, *v.tr.* échelonner/répartir (des versements); étaler (les vacances, etc.).

stagnant, *a.* (*economy, prices, etc.*) stagnant.

stagnate, *v.i.* (*of trade*) stagner; être/devenir stagnant; être dans un état de stagnation.

stagnation, *n.* stagnation *f*/marasme *m* (des affaires).

stake[1], *n.* **stake (money),** mise *f*/enjeu *m*; **to double the stakes,** doubler la mise; **to have a stake in sth.,** avoir des intérêts/des parts dans une affaire; **minority stake,** participation *f* minoritaire.

stake[2], *v.tr.* mettre (une somme) en jeu; parier/jouer/risquer/hasarder (une somme).

stakeholder, *n.* (*a*) dépositaire *m* de l'enjeu d'un pari (*b*) détenteur, -trice d'une part des actions.

stale, *a.* (*a*) *Fin:* **stale market,** marché lourd/plat (*b*) **stale cheque,** chèque périmé (*c*) **stale goods,** produits *mpl* qui ne sont pas frais.

stalking, *a.* **stalking horse,** prétexte *m*.

stamp[1], *n.* (*a*) timbre *m*; **date stamp,** timbre dateur; **rubber stamp,** tampon *m*/timbre humide; cachet *m*; **stamp pad,** tampon encreur (*b*) timbre/tampon/cachet/marque (apposée); **official stamp,** estampille officielle (*c*) **postage stamp,** timbre(-poste) *m*; **stamp book(let),** carnet *m* de timbres; **revenue stamp,** timbre fiscal; **ad valorem stamp,** timbre proportionnel (*d*) **stamp duty,** impôt *m*/droit *m* de timbre.

stamp[2], *v.tr.* timbrer (un document, un effet, un reçu); apposer un visa sur/viser (un passeport); apposer un tampon sur/*F:* tamponner (un passeport); timbrer/ affranchir (une lettre); estampiller (des marchandises); **stamped addressed envelope (s.a.e.),** enveloppe *f* timbrée à votre adresse; **to stamp "paid" on a bill,** apposer le tampon "pour acquit" sur une facture.

stamping, *n.* timbrage *m* (de documents,

etc.); estampillage *m* (de marchandises, etc.).

stand[1], *n.* **(exhibition) stand,** stand *m* (d'exposition).

stand[2], *v.i.* (*a*) **the agreement stands,** le contrat tient toujours (*b*) **to stand as security for a debt,** assurer une créance; se porter garant/caution d'une créance (*c*) **securities standing in the company's books,** titres portés dans les livres de la société (*d*) **the balance stands at £70,** le reliquat de compte se monte/s'élève à £70.

standard[1], *n.* (*a*) *Fin:* **the gold standard,** l'étalon-or *m*; **gold bullion standard,** étalon-or *m* lingot; **gold exchange standard,** étalon *m* de change-or (*b*) **standard** *m*/niveau *m*/norme *f*; **standard of living,** niveau/standard de vie; **budget standards,** standards budgétaires; **price standards,** standards de prix; **production standards,** normes de production; **safety standards,** normes de sécurité (*c*) **up to standard,** (*i*) conforme à l'échantillon (*ii*) conforme à la norme; **the goods are up to standard in every way,** la marchandise répond à toutes les exigences.

standard[2], *a.* standard/normal; **standard charge** (*i*) redevance *f* forfaitaire (*ii*) tarif habituel; **standard costs,** coûts *m* standards; **standard costing/standard cost accounting,** méthode *f* des coûts standards; **standard deviation,** écart-type *m*; **standard make,** marque courante; (*of car, etc.*) **standard model,** modèle *m* standard; *Ins:* **standard policy,** police *f* (d'assurance) type; **standard price,** prix *m* standard; **standard production,** production *f* en série; **standard rate of pay,** barème normalisé des salaires; **standard specification,** norme *f*; **standard weights,** poids unifiés.

standardization, *n.* standardisation *f*/ production *f* en série (d'après un modèle standard); étalonnage *m*/étalonnement *m* (des poids, etc.); unification *f*/uniformisation *f* (des objets de commerce, etc.); normalisation *f* (dans la fabrication); péréquation *f* (des tarifs, etc.).

standardize, *v.tr.* standardiser/

normaliser/uniformiser (la production, etc.); **standardized production,** fabrication *f* en (grande) série/fabrication standardisée; **standardized products,** produits normalisés.

standby, *n.* ligne *f* de crédit; **standby credit,** crédit *m* de réserve/de soutien; **standby letter of credit,** caution *f* bancaire.

standing[1], *a.* **standing agreement,** accord *m* durable; **standing expenses,** frais généraux; dépenses *f* de maison; **standing order,** *Bank:* ordre de transfert permanent; (*with bookshop, etc.*) commande *f* permanente; **standing price,** prix *m* fixe.

standing[2], *n.* **1. debt of long standing,** dette *f* d'ancienne date **2.** réputation *f*/importance *f* (d'une société, d'une maison); **financial standing of a firm,** surface financière/situation financière d'une maison; **firm of recognized standing,** maison réputée/reconnue.

stand off, *v.tr.* faire chômer (des ouvriers).

stand over, *v.i.* **to let an account stand over,** laisser traîner un compte.

standstill, *n.* arrêt *m*/immobilisation *f*; **standstill agreement,** moratoire *m*.

staple, *a.* principal; **staple commodities,** denrées principales; **staple industry,** industrie principale; **staple trade,** commerce régulier.

starting, *n.* **starting date,** date d'entrée en vigueur; **starting price,** prix initial; **starting salary,** rémunération *f* de départ.

start-up, *n.* nouvelle entreprise/entreprise qui démarre; **business start-up,** lancement *m*/démarrage *m* d'une nouvelle entreprise; **start-up costs,** frais *mpl* de lancement/d'établissement/de démarrage (d'une entreprise).

State[1], *n.* l'État *m*; **State bank,** banque d'État; **state-owned,** étatisé/nationalisé; qui appartient à l'État; **state-aided,** subventionné par l'État.

state[2], *v.tr.* **to state an account,** spécifier un compte.

stated, *a.* **stated account,** compte arrêté; **stated capital,** capital déclaré.

statement, *n.* **1.** exposition *f*/exposé *m*/énoncé *m* (des faits, de la situation, etc.); rapport *m*/compte rendu; **false statement,** fausse déclaration **2. bank statement,** relevé *m* de compte (bancaire); **financial statement,** situation *f* de trésorerie; état financier; bilan *m*; **statement of account,** état *m* de compte; relevé de compte; **monthly statement,** relevé mensuel; **statement of affairs,** bilan *m*; **statement of affairs in bankruptcy,** bilan *m* de liquidation; **statement of expenses,** état/relevé *m* de(s) dépenses; *Ins:* **statement of loss,** certificat *m* d'avarie.

state-of-the-art, *a.* avancé; **state-of-the-art technology,** technologie *f* de pointe.

statistical, *a.* statistique; **statistical control,** contrôle *m* statistique; **statistical expert,** expert *mf* en statistique(s); **statistical tables,** statistiques *f*.

statistician, *n.* statisticien, -ienne.

statistics, *n.pl.* statistique *f*; **employment statistics,** statistiques de l'emploi; **statistics expert,** expert *mf* en statistique(s).

status, *n.* **civil status,** état civil; **financial status,** situation financière; **legal status,** statut *m* légal; **status inquiry,** enquête *f* de solvabilité.

statute, *n.* loi *f*; ordonnance *f*; statuts *mpl*/règlements (d'une société).

statutory, *a.* **1.** établi/fixé/imposé par la loi; réglementaire **2.** statutaire/conforme aux statuts; **statutory dividend,** dividende *m* statutaire.

stay, *n.* *Jur:* **stay of execution,** sursis *m* (d'exécution de peine).

steadily, *adv.* régulièrement; **steadily increasing output,** augmentation régulière et continue de la production.

steadiness, *n.* stabilité *f*/fermeté *f* (des prix, des cours).

steady[1], *a.* **steady demand,** demande suivie; **steady market,** marché soutenu/marché ferme; (*of market, etc.*) **to grow steady,** se stabiliser; **steady prices,** prix *m* stables.

steady², *v.i.* **prices are steadying,** les prix *m* se stabilisent/se raffermissent; **the market has steadied (down),** le marché a repris son aplomb.

steadying, *n.* (*of prices, etc.*) (r)affermissement *m*.

steel, *n.* acier *m*; **steel industry,** sidérurgie *f*.

steelworks, *n.pl.* aciérie *f*.

steep, *a.* (*price*) élevé.

steering, *a.* **steering committee,** comité *m* de restructuration.

sterling, *n.* sterling *m*; **pound sterling,** livre *f* sterling; **five pounds sterling,** cinq livres sterling; **sterling area/sterling zone,** zone *f* sterling; **in sterling,** en livres sterling.

stevedore, *n.* docker *m*/débardeur *m*.

steward, *n.* *Ind:* **shop steward,** délégué(e) d'atelier/d'usine/du personnel; délégué(e) syndical(e).

sticker, *n.* vignette *f* autocollante/autoadhésive; autocollant *m*; *NAm:* **sticker price,** prix de détail/prix marqué.

stiff, *a.* (*a*) (*market, commodity*) (valeur) ferme (*b*) **stiff price,** prix exagéré/prix exorbitant/prix excessif.

stiffening, *n.* (*of prices*) raffermissement *m*.

stimulate, *v.tr.* encourager/activer (la production); **to stimulate trade,** stimuler le commerce/donner de l'impulsion au commerce.

stimulus, *n.* stimulant *m*; **competitive stimulus,** stimulant compétitif.

stipend, *n.* traitement *m*/appointements *mpl*.

stipulate, *v.tr.* **to stipulate that ...,** stipuler que ...; **it is stipulated that construction shall start next month,** il est stipulé que la construction doit commencer le mois prochain; **the stipulated quantity,** la quantité prescrite.

stipulation, *n.* stipulation *f*/condition *f*/clause *f*.

stock¹, *n.* **1.** (*a*) stock *m*/marchandises *f* en magasin; **closing stock,** stock de clôture/stock final; **opening stock,** stock d'ouverture/stock initial; **safety stock,** stock de sécurité; **stock book,** livre *m* de stock; **stock clearance,** liquidation *f* de stock; **stock control,** gestion *f*/contrôle *m* des stocks; **stock turnround/stock turn,** rotation *f* des stocks; **stock valuation,** évaluation *f* des stocks; **stock in hand/stock in trade,** stock existant/fonds de commerce/marchandise *f* en magasin; **to buy the whole stock (of a business),** acheter un fonds (de commerce) en bloc (*b*) **in stock,** en magasin/en stock/en dépôt; **spare parts always in stock,** pièces détachées toujours en stock/toujours disponibles; **to put goods into stock,** stocker des marchandises (*c*) (*of goods*) **out of stock,** (stock) épuisé; **we are out of stock,** nous n'avons plus de .../notre stock est épuisé; **we are running out of stock,** nos stocks s'épuisent/diminuent; notre stock s'épuise/diminue (*d*) **to take stock,** faire/dresser l'inventaire (des marchandises en stock) **2.** *Fin:* valeurs *fpl*/actions *fpl*/titres *mpl*; *NAm:* actions ordinaires; **stocks and shares,** valeurs boursières/mobilières; titres; **active stock,** valeurs traitées activement/valeurs-vedettes *fpl*; **ambulance stock,** valeur de repli; **bank stock,** valeurs de banque; **bearer stocks,** titres au porteur; **capital stock,** capital *m* actions; **common stock,** actions ordinaires; **dated stock,** titres à échéance; **fully paid stock,** titres entièrement libérés; **Government stock,** fonds *m* d'État/rente *f* sur l'État; **high-tech stock,** valeur technologique; **oil stock,** valeurs pétrolières; **preferred stock,** actions à dividende prioritaire/préférentiel; actions privilégiées/de priorité; **takeover stock,** ramassage *m*/titres ramassés; **undated stock,** titres sans date d'échéance; **watered stock,** titres dilués; **stock certificate,** certificat *m* d'action; **stock dividend,** dividende *m* (en) actions;

the (London) Stock Exchange, la Bourse (de Londres); Stock Exchange committee, comité *m* de la Bourse (à Londres); chambre syndicale des agents de change (à Paris); stock index, indice *m* de la Bourse; stock market, marché *m* des titres/des valeurs mobilières/la Bourse; stock market price, cours *m* de la Bourse; stock option, option *f* de titres; stock option plan/stock purchase plan, plan *m* d'option sur titres; stock transactions, opérations *f* de Bourse.

stock², *v.tr.* 1. approvisionner/stocker (un magasin) (with, de); shop well stocked, magasin bien approvisionné 2. avoir/tenir/garder (des marchandises) en magasin/en dépôt; stocker (des marchandises); I don't stock children's bicycles, je ne tiens pas de bicyclettes d'enfants.

stockbroker, *n. Fin:* agent *m* de change; courtier *m* (en valeurs mobilières); outside stockbroker, coulissier *m*; the outside stockbrokers, la coulisse.

stockbroking, *n.* profession *f* d'agent de change.

stockholder, *n.* actionnaire *mf*; sociétaire *mf*.

stockist, *n.* stockiste *m*.

stock-keeper, *n.* magasinier, -ière.

stockjobber, *n. StExch:* courtier *m* intermédiaire de bourse/marchand *m* de titres.

stocklist, *n.* 1. inventaire *m* 2. *StExch:* bulletin *m* de la cote.

stockpile¹, *n.* stocks *mpl* de réserve.

stockpile², *v.tr. & i.* stocker; constituer des stocks de réserve.

stockpiling, *n.* stockage *m*; constitution *f* de réserves.

stockroom, *n.* magasin *m* (de réserve)/entrepôt *m*.

stocktaking, *n.* inventaire *m* (des stocks);

to do the stocktaking, faire l'inventaire; stocktaking sale, solde *m* d'inventaire.

stop¹, *n. StExch:* stop (loss) order, ordre *m* stop.

stop², *v.tr.* (*a*) goods stopped at/by the customs, marchandises *f* en consigne à la douane; marchandises consignées par la douane (*b*) to stop an account, bloquer un compte; to stop bankruptcy proceedings, suspendre une procédure de faillite (*c*) to stop payment, suspendre/arrêter des paiements; to stop (payment of) a cheque, faire opposition à un chèque/au paiement d'un chèque (*d*) to stop s.o.'s wages, retenir le salaire de qn; to stop £20 out of s.o.'s wages, retenir £20/faire une retenue de £20 sur le salaire de qn.

stop loss, *n. StExch:* surpertes *fpl*; stop loss order, ordre stop; stop loss selling, ordre de vente stop/stop-vente *f*.

stoppage, *n.* arrêt *m*/suspension *f* (des affaires commerciales, etc.); stoppage of pay, retenue *f* sur les appointements/sur le salaire; stoppage of payments, suspension/cessation *f* de paiements; stoppage of work, cessation des activités.

storage, *n.* 1. entreposage *m*/emmagasinage *m*/magasinage *m*; storage capacity, capacité *f* d'emmagasinage; storage charges, frais *mpl* de magasinage 2. entrepôts *mpl*/magasins *mpl* (d'une maison de commerce); cold storage, entrepôt frigorifique; he left his furniture in storage, il a mis son mobilier au garde-meuble/il a entreposé ses meubles.

store¹, *n.* 1. entrepôt *m*/magasin *m*; bond store, entrepôt (sous douane); cold store, entrepôt frigorifique 2. magasin; cash store, magasin qui ne fait pas de crédit (à ses clients); chain store, magasin à succursales multiples; co-operative store(s), (société) coopérative *f* de consommation; department store, grand magasin; village store, alimentation *f*/épicerie *f* du village; convenience store, bazarette *f*; store card, carte privative.

store², *v.tr.* mettre (des marchandises) en

magasin/entreposer (des marchandises, des meubles).

storehouse, *n.* magasin *m*/entrepôt *m*/ dépôt *m.*

storekeeper, *n.* **1.** magasinier, -ière **2.** *NAm:* marchand, -ande; boutiquier, -ière.

storing, *n.* entreposage *m.*

straddle, *n. StExch:* ordre lié/opération à cheval; **to take a straddle position,** jumeler simultanément un achat sur une époque avec une vente sur une autre.

straight-line, *a. Fin:* **straight-line method (of depreciation),** méthode *f* (de l'amortissement) linéaire/méthode de l'amortissement constant.

strangle, *n.* strangle *m.*

strategy, *n.* stratégie *f*; **business strategy,** stratégie des affaires; **company/corporate strategy,** stratégie de l'entreprise; **financial strategy,** stratégie financière; **marketing strategy,** stratégie commerciale/de marché/mercatique.

streamline, *v.tr.* moderniser/rationaliser (des méthodes, etc.); **to streamline production,** rationaliser la production.

streamlined, *a.* (*a*) (*car, etc.*) aux lignes aérodynamiques/au profil aérodynamique (*b*) **streamlined production,** production rationalisée.

streamlining, *n.* modernisation *f*/rationalisation *f* (des méthodes, de la production, etc.).

street, *n.* **street market,** marché *m* hors bourse; **street name certificate,** certificat *m* de courtier/titre *m* au porteur; **securities carried in a street name,** titres détenus par une maison de courtage pour le compte de l'acheteur; **the Street,** quartier *m* de la Bourse de New York.

strengthen, *v.tr.* consolider (sa situation financière).

strict, *a.* **strict cost price,** prix de revient calculé au plus juste.

strike¹, *n. Ind:* grève *f*; **go-slow**/*NAm:* **slow-**

down strike, grève perlée; **lightning strike,** grève surprise; **official strike,** grève officielle; **sit-down strike,** grève sur le tas; **strike breaker,** briseur *m* de grève; *Ins:* **strike clause,** clause *f* pour cas de grève; **strike pay/benefit,** allocation *f* de grève/ allocation-gréviste *f*; **sympathy strike,** grève de solidarité; **token strike,** grève d'avertissement/grève symbolique; **unofficial strike/wildcat strike,** grève sauvage; **to be on strike,** faire (la) grève/être en grève; **to go/to come out on strike,** se mettre en grève.

strike², **1.** *v.i. Ind:* se mettre en grève; déclencher une grève; **to strike in sympathy,** se mettre en grève par solidarité; **to strike for better conditions,** se mettre en grève en vue d'obtenir des conditions de travail plus avantageuses **2.** *v.tr.* **to strike an agreement/a deal,** conclure un accord/une affaire/un arrangement.

striker, *n. Ind:* gréviste *mf.*

strip, *US:* démembrement *m.*

structure¹, *n.* structure *f*; **corporate company structure,** structure de l'entreprise; **cost structure,** structure des coûts; **market structure,** structure du marché; **price structure,** structure des prix; **pricing structure,** marge *f* et commissions *fpl*; **salary/wage structure,** structure des salaires.

structure², *v.tr.* structurer.

structuring, *n.* structuration *f* (du travail, etc.).

stub, *n.* souche *f*/talon *m* (de chèque).

study, *n.* étude *f* (du marché, de faisabilité); **case study,** étude de cas.

stunt¹, *n.* **publicity stunt,** coup *m* publicitaire.

stunt², *v.tr.* freiner (la croissance).

style, *n.* (*a*) **style of a firm,** raison sociale/ nom social/commercial (*b*) **made in three styles,** fabriqué en trois genres/en trois modèles.

sub[1], *n.* **1.** avance *f* (de salaire) **2.** = **subscription 3.** = **subeditor**.

sub[2], *v.tr.* **1.** (*a*) obtenir une avance (sur son salaire) (*b*) accorder une avance (d'argent) à un employé **2.** = **subedit**.

sub-agency, *n.* sous-agence *f.*

sub-agent, *n.* sous-agent *m.*

subcommittee, *n.* sous-comité *m*; sous-commission *f.*

subcontract[1], *n.* contrat *m* de sous-traitance.

subcontract[2], *v.tr.* sous-traiter (une affaire)/donner en sous-traitance.

subcontracting, *n.* sous-traitance *f.*

subcontractor, *n.* sous-entrepreneur *m*/ sous-contractant *m.*

subedit, *v.tr.* corriger/mettre au point (un article, un manuscrit).

subeditor, *n.* correcteur, -trice.

subject, *a.* **subject to contract**, sous réserve de la signature du contrat; **prices subject to 5% discount**, prix sous réserve d'une remise de 5%; prix bénéficiant d'une remise de 5%; **transaction subject to a commission of 5%**, opération *f* passible d'un courtage de 5%; **subject to stamp duty**, passible du droit de timbre; soumis au timbre.

sub-lease[1], *n.* sous-bail *m*; sous-location *f.*

sub-lease[2], *v.tr.* sous-louer (un appartement); (*i*) donner en sous-location (*ii*) prendre en sous-location.

sub-leasing, *n.* sous-location *f.*

sub-lessee, *n.* (*a*) sous-locataire *mf* (à bail) (*b*) sous-traitant *m* (d'un travail à l'entreprise).

sub-lessor, *n.* = locataire *m* principal.

sub-let, *v.tr.* (*a*) sous-louer (un appartement); (*i*) donner (un appartement) en sous-location (*ii*) prendre (un appartement) en sous-location (*b*) sous-traiter (un travail, un contrat)/donner en sous-traitance.

sub-letting, *n.* (*a*) sous-location *f* (*b*) sous-traitance *f.*

sub-office, *n.* succursale *f* (d'une banque, etc.); filiale *f*; bureau *m* auxiliaire.

subordinate, **1.** *a.* (rang) inférieur subalterne/secondaire **2.** *n.* subordonné, -ée/ subalterne *mf.*

subordinated, *a.* **subordinated debt**, dette de second rang/subordonnée.

sub-rent, *v.tr.* sous-louer/prendre (un appartment) en sous-location.

subrogation, *n.* subrogation *f*; substitution *f.*

subscribe, *v.i.* (*a*) Fin: **to subscribe for a hundred shares in a company**, souscrire à cent actions d'une société; **to subscribe to a loan/to an issue**, souscrire à un emprunt/ à une émission; **subscribed capital**, capital souscrit (*b*) **to subscribe to a newspaper**, être abonné à un journal.

subscriber, *n.* (*a*) Fin: **subscriber (for shares)**, souscripteur *m* (à des actions) (*b*) signataire *mf* des statuts (d'une nouvelle société) (*c*) **(magazine) subscriber**, abonné, -ée (à une revue) (*d*) **telephone subscriber**, abonné, -ée du téléphone; Tel: **subscriber trunk dialling (STD)**, l'automatique *m.*

subscription, *n.* (*a*) Fin: **subscription to a loan**, souscription *f* à un emprunt; **subscription by conversion of securities**, souscription en titres; **subscription list**, liste *f* de souscriptions; liste des souscripteurs; **subscription right**, droit *m* de souscription (d'actions) (*b*) **to take out a subscription to a newspaper**, s'abonner/prendre un abonnement à un journal; **subscription form**, bulletin *m* d'abonnement; **subscription rate**, prix *m* de l'abonnement.

subsequent, *a.* ultérieur; postérieur.

subsidiary, *a.* & *n.* **subsidiary (company)**, (*i*) filiale *f*/compagnie affiliée (*ii*) compagnie captive.

subsidize, *v.tr.* subventionner.

subsidy, *n.* subvention *f*; subside *m*; prime *f*; **development subsidy**, prime de développement; **food subsidies**, subventions à l'alimentation.

subsistence, *n.* **means/level of subsistence**, moyens *mpl* /niveau *m* de subsistance.

sub-standard, *a.* inférieur à la norme/de qualité inférieure.

substitute[1], *n.* succédané *m*; **substitute products**, produits *mpl* de remplacement.

substitute[2], *v.tr.* substituer (**for**, à).

substitution, *n.* substitution *f*.

subtenancy, *n.* sous-location *f*.

subtenant, *n.* sous-locataire *mf*.

subvention, *n.* *NAm:* subvention *f*; subside *m*; prime *f*.

subventionary, *a.* (paiement, etc.) subventionnel.

sue, *v.tr. Jur:* poursuivre (qn) (en justice).

suicide pill, *n.* (*defensive tactics in takeover*) clause *f* de suicide (*interdit en France*).

suit, *n. Jur:* procès *m*.

sum, *n.* (*a*) total *m*/montant *m* (*b*) **sum (of money)**, somme *f* (d'argent); **large sum**, grosse somme/forte somme; **sum total**, somme totale/somme globale/montant global.

summit, *n.* **summit meeting**, rencontre *f* au sommet.

summons, *n. Jur:* assignation *f*/sommation *f*.

sundry, **1.** *a.* divers; **sundry expenses**, frais *mpl* divers **2.** *n.pl.* **sundries**, (frais) divers *mpl*.

sunbelt, *n.* **sunbelt states**, régions ensoleillées des USA (Californie, Arizona, Floride, etc.).

sunrise, *n.* **sunrise industry**, industrie naissante.

sunset, *n.* **sunset industry**, industrie traditionnelle/déclinante.

superannuation, *n.* retraite *f*; **superannuation fund**, caisse *f* de retraite.

supermajority, *n.* majorité qualifiée.

supermarket, *n.* supermarché *m*; grande surface; (*small*) supérette *f*; **financial supermarket**, supermarché de produits financiers.

superstock, *n. US:* actions *fpl* à droit de vote double.

supertax, *n.* surtaxe *f*.

supervisor, *n.* surveillant, -ante; agent *m* de maîtrise.

supervisory, *a.* (comité, etc.) de surveillance; **supervisory management**, maîtrise *f*; **supervisory staff**, agent(s) de maîtrise.

supplementary, *a.* supplémentaire (**to**, de); additionnel (**to**, à); *Adm:* **supplementary benefit**, allocation *f*/prestation *f* supplémentaire; *Book-k:* **supplementary entry**, écriture *f* complémentaire; **supplementary taxation**, surimposition *f*; **supplementary wage**, sursalaire *m*.

supplier, *n.* fournisseur/approvisionneur (**of**, en, de); **suppliers' credit**, crédit fournisseur.

supply[1], *n.* (*a*) *PolEc:* **supply curve**, courbe de l'offre; **supply and demand**, l'offre *f* et la demande; **supply side (economics)**, économie *f* de l'offre; **supply sider**, économiste *mf* de l'offre; **money supply**, masse monétaire; **supply price**, prix *m* de l'offre (*b*) **we are expecting a new supply of paint**, nous espérons recevoir bientôt un nouveau stock de peinture; **this paper is in short supply**, ce papier est rare; **nous sommes à court de ce (genre de) papier** (*c*) *pl.* **supplies**, fournitures *f*; **supplies of money**, fonds *m*/ressources *f*; **food supplies**, vivres *mpl*.

supply[2], *v.tr.* **to supply s.o. with sth**, fournir/approvisionner qn de qch.

support[1], *n.* appui *m*/soutien *m*; **price support**, subvention *f*/soutien des prix; **support price**, prix *m* de soutien.

support[2], *v.tr.* soutenir; **to support prices by buying,** soutenir des cours par des achats.

surcharge, *n.* supplément *m*/excédent *m*/ surtaxe *f.*

surety, *n.* (*pers.*) caution *f*/garant, -ante; répondant, -ante; donneur *m* d'aval; **surety bond,** cautionnement *m*; **to stand/to go surety for s.o.,** se rendre caution de qn/se porter caution pour qn/se porter garant de qn; **surety for a debt,** garant d'une dette.

surfeit, *n.* surabondance *f.*

surplus, *n.* surplus *m*/excédent *m*; *Fin:* boni *m*; **budget surplus,** excédent budgétaire; **trade surplus,** excédent du commerce extérieur; **surplus products,** surplus/excédent de produits; **surplus to our requirements,** quantité *f* excédentaire.

surrender[1], *n. Ins:* rachat *m* (d'une police); **surrender value,** valeur *f* de rachat.

surrender[2], *v.tr.* abandonner (une option); céder (un droit); *Ins:* racheter (une police d'assurance).

surtax[1], *n.* surtaxe *f.*

surtax[2], *v.tr.* surtaxer.

survey, *n.* expertise *f*; enquête *f*; **business survey,** enquête de conjoncture; **field survey,** enquête sur les lieux.

surveyor, *n.* (*of house*) expert *m*; **(land) surveyor,** géomètre expert; arpenteur *m* (géomètre); **quantity surveyor,** métreur *m* (vérificateur).

suspend, *v.tr.* (*a*) suspendre; **to suspend payment,** suspendre ses paiements/les paiements; **to suspend work for two days,** interrompre le travail pendant deux jours (*b*) **to suspend (s.o.),** suspendre (qn).

suspense, *n.* (*a*) **bills in suspense,** effets *m* en suspens *m*/en souffrance *f* (*b*) **suspense account,** compte *m* d'ordre.

suspension, *n.* (*a*) suspension *f*; **suspension of payment,** suspension de paiements (*b*) suspension (d'un employé).

swap, *n.* (*a*) *Bank:* échange financier/EFI

m; crédit croisé/taux croisé; swap *m*/ opération *f* de swap; **asset swaps,** swaps d'actifs; **debts swap,** échange *m* de dette; **swap agreements,** accords *mpl* d'échanges; **swap facilities,** facilités *f*(*pl*) de crédits réciproques (*b*) *US: StExch:* aller et retour *m.*

swaption, *n.* option *f* de swap; échange *m* de taux croisés.

swing, *n.* **swings and roundabouts,** fluctuations *fpl* des cours.

switch[1], *n.* **switch trading/transaction,** arbitrage *m.*

switch[2], *v.tr. StExch:* **to switch a position,** reporter une position d'une échéance à une autre plus éloignée.

switching, *n.* **equity switching,** rotation *f* de portefeuille-action; **gilt-switching,** rotation de portefeuille-obligation.

sympathy, *n.* **sympathy strike,** grève *f* de solidarité; **to come out in sympathy,** se mettre en grève par solidarité.

syndicate[1], *n.* syndicat *m*; consortium *m*; **banking syndicate,** consortium bancaire/ de banques; **financial syndicate,** syndicat financier; **member of a syndicate,** syndicataire *mf*; **underwriting syndicate,** syndicat financier/de garantie; **to form a syndicate,** se syndiquer.

syndicate[2], **1.** *v.tr.* (*a*) syndiquer (une industrie) (*b*) **syndicated shares,** actions syndiquées **2. syndicated credit,** crédit consortial **3.** *v.i.* se syndiquer.

syndication, *n.* syndication *f*/placement *m*; **primary syndication,** syndication sur le marché primaire.

synergy, *n.* synergie *f.*

synthetic, *a.* synthétique/artificiel.

system, *n.* (*a*) système *m*; **accounting system,** système comptable; **computerized information system,** système d'information par ordinateur; **metric system,** système métrique; **integrated management system,** système intégré de gestion; **systems analysis,** analyse *f* des systèmes; **systems analyst,** analyste-programmeur *mf*;

systems engineering, planification f des systèmes; **systems management,** direction systématisée; **European Monetary System (EMS),** Système Monétaire Européen (SME) (*b*) **quota system,** contingentement *m*.

systematic, *a.* systématique.

systematization, *n.* systématisation *f.*

systematize, *v.tr.* systématiser.

T

table[1], *n.* table *f*/tableau *m*/répertoire *m*/ barème *m* (des prix); **table of contents,** table des matières; **table of weights and measures,** table des poids et mesures; **interest table,** table d'intérêts; *Ins:* **mortality tables/actuaries' tables,** tables de mortalité; **parity table/table of par values,** table de parités; *Fin:* **redemption table,** tableau d'amortissement; **round table,** table ronde.

table[2], *v.tr.* **to table a bill/a motion,** présenter un projet de loi une motion; *NAm:* ajourner un projet de loi/une motion.

tabular, *a.* tabulaire; **in tabular form,** disposé en tableau(x).

tabulate, *v.tr.* (*a*) disposer (des chiffres, etc.) en table(s)/en tableau(x) (*b*) classifier (des résultats); cataloguer (des marchandises).

tabulating, *n.* (*a*) = **tabulation** (*b*) **tabulating machine,** tabulatrice *f*.

tabulation, *n.* (*a*) mise *f*/arrangement *m*/ disposition en tableaux (*b*) classification *f* (de résultats); tabulation *f*.

tabulator, *n.* (*a*) (*in punched-card system, etc.*) tabulatrice *f*; **digital tabulator,** tabulatrice numérique (*b*) (*on typewriter*) tabulateur *m*.

tachograph, *n.* tachygraphe *m*.

tacit, *a.* tacite; **tacit agreement,** accord *m*/ convention *f* tacite.

tactic, *n.* tactique *f*; **crown jewel tactic,** (*against a threatened takeover*) tactique de la vente des joyaux de la Couronne.

tactical, *a.* tactique; **tactical plan,** plan *m* tactique.

tag, *n.* (**price) tag,** étiquette *f* (indiquant le prix); **anti-theft/security tag,** agrafe *f* antivol.

tailspin, *n.* *US:* chute *f* des cours en spirale.

take[1], *n.* (*a*) montant reçu/perçu (*b*) part *f* (de bénéfice).

take[2], *v.tr.* (*a*) **to take an amount out of one's income,** prélever une somme sur son revenu (*b*) **to take so much a week,** se faire tant/faire une recette de tant par semaine; **she takes home only £65 a week,** son salaire net n'est que de £65 par semaine (*c*) **he won't take less,** il refuse d'accepter un prix moins élevé (*d*) **to take stock,** dresser/faire l'inventaire (*e*) (*to secretary*) **will you take (down) a letter?** voulez-vous prendre une lettre? (*f*) **to take a partner,** prendre un associé (*g*) **to take legal advice,** consulter un avocat (*h*) **this bottle will take a litre,** cette bouteille contient un litre (*j*) **we take 'The Financial Times',** nous recevons/nous achetons 'The Financial Times' (tous les jours) (*k*) **it will take £8 to buy it,** cela coûtera £8 (*l*) **does the machine take 10p coins?** est-ce que la machine accepte les pièces de 10p?

tak(e)away, *a. & n.* **tak(e)away (shop)** = restaurant qui vend des plats cuisinés (à emporter); **tak(e)away (meal),** plat(s) cuisiné(s) (à emporter).

take back, *v.tr.* reprendre (un employé, des invendus).

take-home, *a.* **take-home pay,** salaire *m* net (après déductions).

take in, *v.tr.* (*a*) *StExch:* **to take in stock,** reporter des titres; **stock taken in,** titres *mpl* pris en report (*b*) **to take in extra**

work, prendre/accepter du travail supplémentaire.

take off, *v.tr.* (*a*) **to take £2 off (the price of sth.),** déduire/rabattre £2 (sur le prix de qch.); **to take 10% off the price,** réduire le prix de 10%/déduire 10% du prix (*b*) **to take a day off,** prendre un jour de congé.

take on, *v.tr.* (*a*) engager/embaucher (un ouvrier); **these workmen have just been taken on,** on vient d'embaucher ces ouvriers (*b*) entreprendre/se charger de/assumer (une besogne, une responsabilité) (*c*) accepter qn (comme client).

take out, *v.tr.* **to take out a patent,** prendre/obtenir un brevet; **to take out an insurance policy,** contracter une assurance/souscrire à une police d'assurance.

take over, *v.tr.* **to take over from s.o.,** relever qn dans ses fonctions; **to take over a business,** prendre la succession d'une maison de commerce/prendre la suite des affaires; **the firm was taken over,** la société a été achetée; **to take over the liabilities,** prendre les dettes à sa charge/prendre le passif; **to take over the receipts and expenditures,** prendre le contrôle des recettes et des dépenses; *Fin:* **to take over an issue,** absorber une émission.

takeover, *n.* prise *f* de contrôle; reprise *f*/rachat *m*; **takeover bid,** offre publique d'achat/OPA *f*; **(the) Takeover Panel,** organisme chargé de veiller à la régularité des OPA/arbitre *m* des OPA.

taker, *n.* (*a*) (*buyer, lessee*) preneur, -euse (*b*) *StExch:* (*of contangoes*) reporteur *m* (*c*) acheteur, -euse.

taker-in, *n. StExch:* reporteur *m*/contrepartie *f* de report.

take up, *v.tr.* (*a*) **to take up a bill,** honorer un effet; retirer une traite; *StExch:* **to take up an option,** lever une prime; consolider un marché à prime; **to take up a share,** lever un titre; **to take up stock,** prendre livraison de titres (*b*) **to take up a new line**

of goods, se charger d'une nouvelle gamme de produits.

takings, *n.pl.* recette *f*/rentrée *f*; **today's takings,** la recette de la journée; **the takings are good,** la recette est bonne.

talk, *n.* **sales talk,** arguments *mpl* de vente; boniment *m*.

tally[1], *n.* (*a*) **the tally trade,** le commerce à tempérament (*b*) pointage *m*; **to keep (a) tally of goods,** pointer des marchandises (sur une liste); **tally clerk/tally keeper,** pointeur *m*/contrôleur *m*/marqueur *m* (de marchandises, etc.); **tally sheet,** feuille *f* de pointage (à la réception des marchandises, etc.); bordereau *m*.

tally[2], **1.** *v.tr.* pointer/contrôler (des marchandises) **2.** *v.i.* correspondre (**with,** à); s'accorder/concorder (**with,** avec); cadrer (**with,** avec); **these accounts do not tally,** ces comptes ne s'accordent pas.

tallying, *n.* pointage *m*/contrôle *m* (de marchandises, etc.).

tallyman, *n.* (*a*) pointeur *m*/contrôleur *m*/marqueur *m* (de marchandises, etc.) (*b*) marchand *m* qui vend à tempérament (*c*) comptable *m*.

talon, *n.* talon *m* (d'une feuille, de coupons); talon de souche.

tangible, 1. *a.* tangible/matériel; **tangible assets,** actifs corporels **2.** *n.pl.* tangibles = tangible assets.

tank, *n.* **think tank,** laboratoire *m* d'idées.

tap, *n.* **bills on tap,** billets *mpl* placés de gré à gré; **tap buying,** remboursement anticipé par rachat sur le marché; **tap issue,** émission souscrite par les SUT (Spécialistes en Valeurs du Trésor); **tap stock,** valeur *f* du Trésor mise aux enchères.

tape, *n.* (*a*) bande *f*/ruban *m*; *Cmptr:* **magnetic tape,** bande magnétique; **perforated tape/punched tape,** bande perforée (*b*) *F:* **red tape,** paperasserie *f*/bureaucratie *f*.

tare[1], *n.* tare *f*; **actual tare,** tare réelle; **average tare,** tare moyenne/tare par épreuve; **extra tare,** surtare *f*; **to ascertain/to**

allow for the tare, faire la tare; **allowance for tare,** (i) tarage m (ii) la tare.

tare[2], v.tr. tarer (un emballage, etc.); faire la tare.

target, n. but m/objectif m; **production target,** objectif de production; **target company,** société f cible; **target consumers,** consommateurs-cible(s) mpl; **target setting,** fixation f des objectifs.

target at, vi. cibler (un marché, un produit).

tariff[1], n. (a) liste f/tableau m (des prix); **tariff (catalogue),** tarif m (b) **customs tariff,** tarif douanier/tarif d'importation; **full tariff,** plein tarif; **preferential tariff,** tarif préférentiel; **reduced tariff,** tarif réduit; **tariff agreement,** accord m tarifaire; **tariff barriers/tariff walls,** barrières tarifaires/douanières; **tariff laws,** lois f tarifaires; **tariff-level indices,** taux m indices des tarifs; **multi-part tariff/two-part tariff,** tarification séparée des coûts fixes et des coûts mobiles.

tariff[2], v.tr. tarifier (des marchandises, etc.).

tariffing, n. tarification f.

taring n. tarage m.

task, n. tâche f; **task force,** groupe m d'intervention; **task group,** groupe de travail; **task management,** supervision f des travaux; **task work,** travail m à la tâche; travail aux pièces.

tax[1], n. impôt m/contribution f/taxe f; **(profit) after tax,** (profit) après impôt/(profit) net; **airport tax,** taxe d'aéroport; **back tax,** arriéré m d'impôt; **betting tax,** taxe sur les paris; **capital gains tax,** impôt sur les plus-values; **capital transfer tax,** droits mpl de mutation; **cascade tax,** imposition f en cascade; **corporation tax,** impôt sur les sociétés; **inheritance**/NAm: **death/estate tax,** droits de succession; **direct/indirect tax,** impôt direct/indirect; **dividend tax,** impôt sur les dividendes; **entertainment tax,** taxe sur les spectacles; **exceptional/special taxes,** (i) taxes parafiscales (ii) parafiscalité f; **exclusive of**

tax/net of tax, hors taxe (HT); **graduated income tax,** impôt progressif sur le revenu; **hidden tax,** impôt déguisé; **income tax,** impôt sur le revenu; **(income) tax return,** déclaration f de revenu/feuille f d'impôt; **inflation tax,** effect m de seuil fiscal; **input tax,** impôt à la production; **land tax,** impôt foncier; **luxury tax,** taxe sur les produits de luxe; **negative income tax,** déficit fiscal remboursable; **output tax,** impôt à la consommation; **payroll tax,** impôt sur la masse salariale/impôt sur le travail; **profits tax**/NAm: **corporate profits tax,** impôt sur les bénéfices (des sociétés); **excess profits tax,** impôt sur les bénéfices excessifs; **turnover tax,** impôt sur le chiffre d'affaires; **value-added tax (VAT),** taxe à la valeur ajoutée (TVA); **wealth tax,** impôt de solidarité sur la fortune (ISF); **tax adjustment,** redressement m d'impôt; **tax allowance,** déduction f avant impôt; **tax avoidance,** évasion fiscale; **tax base,** assiette f fiscale/de l'impôt; **tax bite,** proportion f du revenu pris par l'impôt; **tax bracket,** tranche f d'imposition; **tax code,** cédule f d'impôt; **tax collection,** perception f/recouvrement m de l'impôt; **tax collector,** percepteur m d'impôt; StExch: **tax credit,** avoir fiscal/crédit d'impôt; **tax cuts,** réduction f/dégrèvement m d'impôt; **tax deducted at source,** impôt retenu à la base/à la source; retenue f à la source; **tax deductible,** déductible de l'impôt; **tax evasion,** fraude fiscale; **tax exemption,** exemption f d'impôt; **tax exile,** personne f qui réside à l'étranger pour minimiser la responsabilité fiscale; **tax-free**/NAm: **tax exempt,** net d'impôt; exonéré d'impôt; **tax form,** déclaration f d'impôt; **tax haven,** asile/paradis fiscal; **tax holiday,** période de grâce accordée pour le paiement des impôts; **tax loss,** déficit fiscal reportable; **tax office,** (bureau m de) perception f; **tax paid,** net d'impôt; **tax rate,** taux m d'imposition; **tax reduction/tax relief,** dégrèvement d'impôt; **tax rules,** lois fiscales; **tax schedule,** barème m d'imposition; **tax shelter,** avantage fiscal; **tax system,** système fiscal; **tax year,** année fiscale; **withholding tax,** retenue à la source/impôt (retenu) à la source/précompte fiscal; **to pay taxes,** payer des taxes/des contributions; **I paid £500 in tax,** j'ai payé £500 d'impôt; **it gives me £25 interest less tax,** je reçois un intérêt de £25 avant impôt; **this benefit is liable to tax,** ce bénéfice est assujetti à l'impôt; **to levy a tax on sth.,** frapper qch. d'un droit.

tax², *v.tr.* (*a*) taxer/imposer (les objets de luxe, etc.); frapper (qch.) d'un impôt; **to tax income,** imposer (des droits sur) le revenu; **fully taxed** = toutes taxes comprises (TTC); **highly taxed/low-taxed goods,** marchandises fortement/faiblement taxées (*b*) imposer (qn); **to be heavily taxed,** être lourdement imposé.

taxable, *a.* (revenu, terrain, etc.) imposable/taxable; **taxable article,** bien *m* taxable; **taxable class of goods,** catégorie *f* de biens taxable; **taxable income,** revenu *m* imposable; **taxable year,** exercice fiscal.

taxation, *n.* (*a*) imposition *f* (de la propriété, etc.); taxation *f*; **the taxation authorities,** l'administration fiscale; **ability-to-pay taxation,** imposition progressive; **benefit taxation,** imposition de l'usager (*b*) charges fiscales; prélèvement fiscal; **commensurate taxation,** équivalence *f* des charges fiscales; **deferred taxation,** impôt différé; **direct taxation,** contributions directes/impôts directs; **excessive taxation,** fiscalité excessive; **highest scale of taxation,** maximum *m* de perception; **indirect taxation,** fiscalité indirecte/impôts indirects; **supplementary taxation,** surimposition *f*/surtaxe *f*; **double taxation relief,** suppression *f* de la double imposition; **profit after taxation,** profit après impôt/profit net; **taxation schedule,** cédule *f* d'impôt (*c*) revenu réalisé par les impôts; impôts *mpl.*

taxman, *n. F:* inspecteur *m* des impôts/des contributions directes.

taxpayer, *n.* contribuable *mf.*

team¹, *n.* équipe *f* (d'ouvriers, etc.); **sales team,** équipe commerciale/de vente.

team², *v.tr. NAm:* camionner (des marchandises).

teamster, *n. NAm:* camionneur *m*/routier *m.*

teamwork, *n.* travail *m* d'équipe.

teaser, *n. Mkt:* **teaser (ad),** aguiche *f.*

teasing, *n. Mkt:* aguichage *m.*

tech, *n.* = **technology; high tech** = **high technology,** technologie *f* de pointe/haute technologie.

technician, *n.* technicien, -ienne.

technique, *n.* technique *f*; **management techniques,** techniques de gestion; **marketing techniques,** techniques commerciales; **merchandising techniques,** techniques marchandes.

technology, *n.* technologie *f*; **advanced/high technology,** technologie de pointe/haute technologie; **new office technology,** bureautique *f.*

Telecom, *n. Rtm:* **British Telecom,** service *m* des télécommunications (en G.-B.).

telebanking, *n.* banque *f* à domicile.

telecommunication, *n.* télécommunication *f.*

telecommuting, *n.* travail *m* à domicile.

teleconference, teleconferencing, *n.* téléconférence *f.*

telecopier, *n.* télécopieur *m.*

telegram, *n.* télégramme *m*/dépêche *f* (télégraphique); **to send s.o. a telegram,** envoyer un télégramme à qn.

telegraph¹, *n.* télégraphe *m*; **telegraph service,** service *m* télégraphique.

telegraph², *v.tr. & i.* télégraphier; câbler; envoyer un télégramme; **to telegraph an order,** câbler/télégraphier une commande.

telegraphic, *a.* télégraphique; **telegraphic address,** adresse *f* télégraphique.

telemarketing, *n.* télémercatique *f.*

telematics, *n.* télématique *f.*

teleorder¹, *n.* commande *f* par ordinateur.

teleorder[2], *v.tr.* commander par ordinateur.

teleordering, *n.* (placement *m* de) commandes *fpl* par ordinateur.

telephone[1], *n.* téléphone *m*; **automatic telephone**, (téléphone) automatique *m*; **house telephone**, téléphone intérieur; **public telephone**, publiphone *m*; **push-button telephone**, téléphone à touches/à clavier; **telephone call**, appel *m* téléphonique; coup *m* de téléphone/de fil; **to speak to s.o. on the telephone**, parler à qn au téléphone; **to be on the telephone**, (*i*) être abonné au téléphone (*ii*) parler au téléphone (*iii*) téléphoner; **telephone directory/book**, annuaire *m* des téléphones/annuaire téléphonique/*F:* bottin *m*; **telephone exchange**, centrale *f* téléphonique; **telephone number**, numéro *m* de téléphone/d'appel; **telephone operator**, téléphoniste *mf*/standardiste *mf*; **telephone subscriber**, abonné, -ée du téléphone; **to have a telephone**, être abonné au téléphone; **telephone banking**, opérations *fpl* bancaires par téléphone; **telephone marketing**, marketing téléphonique; **telephone order**, commande téléphonique/par téléphone; **to order sth. by telephone**, commander qch. par téléphone.

telephone[2], *v.tr. & i.* téléphoner (à qn); **to telephone New York**, appeler New York; **we telephoned him the news**, nous lui avons transmis la nouvelle par téléphone.

telephonist, *n.* téléphoniste *mf*.

teleprinter, *n.* téléscripteur *m*/télétype *m*; **teleprinter operator**, télétypiste *mf*.

teleprinting, *n.* liaison *f* par téléimprimeur.

teleprocessing, *n.* télétraitement *m*; téléinformatique *f*; télégestion *f*.

telesale, *n.* télévente *f*/vente *f* par téléphone; **telesales person**, télévendeur, -euse.

teleshopping, *n.* téléachat *m*.

teletex, *n. Cmptr:* télétex *m*.

teletypewriter, *n. NAm:* = **teleprinter**.

teletypist, *n.* télétypiste *mf*.

telewriter, *n.* = **teleprinter**.

Telex, *n. Rtm:* (*a*) (poste) Télex *m*; **Telex subscriber**, abonné, -ée au service Télex; **Telex user**, usager *m* du Télex; **Telex rate**, tarif *m* Télex; **Telex operator**, télexiste *mf*; **Telex network**, réseau *m* Télex; **to send by Telex**, envoyer par Télex; **we received this order by Telex**, nous avons reçu cette commande par Télex (*b*) (communication) télex *m*; **I received a Telex**, j'ai reçu un télex.

telex, *v.tr.* envoyer par Télex (*Rtm*); **to telex Canada**, envoyer un télex au Canada; **to telex information**, envoyer un renseignement par Télex.

teller, *n.* 1. caissier, -ière; préposé, -ée à la caisse/au guichet; guichetier, -ière 2. caisse *f*; *NAm:* **automatic teller**, guichet *m* automatique de banque/distributeur *m* automatique de billets/billetterie *f*.

temp, *n.* secrétaire *mf* qui fait de l'intérim; intérimaire *f*.

temping, *n.* intérim *m*.

temporary, *a.* temporaire/provisoire; *Cust:* **passed for temporary importation**, admis en franchise temporaire; **temporary measures**, mesures *fpl* provisoires/temporaires; **temporary post**, (*i*) fonction *f* intérimaire/provisoire (*ii*) travail *m* temporaire; intérim *m*; **temporary secretary**, secrétaire *mf* qui fait de l'intérim; **temporary staff**, personnel *m* temporaire.

tenancy, *n.* location *f*; (*period*) occupation *f*; **terms of tenancy**, conditions *fpl* de location; **during my tenancy**, pendant la durée de mon bail/pendant que j'étais locataire.

tenant, *n.* locataire *mf*; **sitting tenant**, locataire en possession des lieux; **tenant's repairs**, réparations locatives; **tenant's**

risks, risques locatifs; **tenants' association,** syndicat *m* des locataires.

tendency, *n.* tendance *f*/inclination *f*/ disposition *f* (**to,** à); **deflationary tendency,** tendance déflationniste; **tendencies of the market,** tendances du marché; **strong upward tendency/bullish tendency,** forte poussée vers la hausse; **strong downward tendency/bearish tendency,** forte poussée vers la baisse.

tender[1], *n.* **1.** offre *f*/soumission *f*; **to put a new hospital out to tender/to invite tenders for a new hospital,** faire un appel d'offres pour la construction d'un nouvel hôpital/mettre en adjudication la construction d'un nouvel hôpital; **allocation to lowest tender,** adjudication *f* au rabais; **by tender,** par voie d'adjudication; **issue by tender,** vente *f* aux enchères; **to send in a tender/to put in a tender,** soumissionner/ faire une soumission; **tender bills,** bons *mpl* du Trésor Public; **tender offer/offer by tender,** *Br:* vente aux enchères; *US:* (*if paid in cash*) offre publique d'achat; (*if paid in kind*) offre publique d'échange; *NAm:* **to make a tender offer,** faire une offre/une soumission; **sealed tender,** soumission cachetée; **tenders for loans,** soumissions d'emprunt; **tender rate,** taux *m* d'appel d'offres **2. legal tender,** monnaie légale; (*of money*) **to be legal tender,** avoir cours légal; avoir pouvoir/force libératoire.

tender[2], **1.** *v.i.* **invitation to tender,** appel *m* d'offres; **to tender for a contract,** faire une soumission (pour une adjudication)/soumissionner (à une adjudication); **to tender for a supply of goods,** soumissionner une fourniture de marchandises; **party tendering for work on contract,** soumissionnaire *m* **2.** *v.tr.* offrir (ses services, une somme, etc.); **to tender one's resignation,** donner sa démission.

tenderer, *n.* soumissionnaire *mf*; **allocation to lowest tenderer,** adjudication *f* au rabais; **successful tenderer for a contract,** adjudicataire *mf*.

tendering, *n.* soumission *f*.

tenor, *n.* durée *f* de vie/teneur *f*/terme *m* (d'une lettre de change).

tentative, *a.* provisoire; **tentative booking,** réservation *f* provisoire; **tentative offer,** première offre/offre provisoire.

tenure, *n.* (période de) jouissance *f*; (période d')occupation *f* (d'une propriété, d'un poste, etc.); **security of tenure,** (*i*) bail assuré (*ii*) stabilité *f*/sécurité *f* d'un emploi; **land tenure,** régime foncier.

term, *n.* **1.** (*a*) (terme d')échéance *f* (d'une lettre de change); **term deposit,** dépôt *m* à terme; **term loan,** prêt *m* à terme (*b*) terme *m*/période *f*/durée *f*; **term day,** (jour du) terme *m* (du loyer); **term of a lease,** terme/ durée d'un bail; **the loan shall be for a term of ten years,** l'emprunt *m* sera conclu pour dix ans; **during his term of office,** pendant la durée de ses fonctions; (*to employee or employer*) **term of notice,** délai *m* de congé **2.** *pl.* (*a*) **terms,** conditions *f*/clauses *f*/termes/teneur *f* (d'un contrat); *Fin:* **terms of an issue,** conditions d'une émission; **terms and conditions of an issue,** modalités *fpl* d'une émission; **terms of trade,** termes de l'échange (*b*) **cash terms,** paiement *m* (au) comptant; **terms of payment,** modalités de paiement; **terms inclusive,** tout compris; **trade terms,** (taux de) remise *f*; **to buy sth. on easy terms,** acheter qch. avec facilités *fpl* de paiement.

terminable, *a.* (*contract, etc.*) résiliable, résoluble; (*annuity*) terminable.

terminal[1], *a.* (*a*) **terminal charges,** charges terminales (*b*) *StExch:* **terminal market,** marché *m* à terme/du terme; **terminal price,** cours *m* du livrable.

terminal[2], *n.* (*of buses, containers, etc.*) terminus *m*; tête *f* de ligne; **air terminal,** aérogare *f*; **computer terminal,** terminal *m* d'ordinateur.

terminate, *v.tr.* (*a*) terminer (*b*) **to terminate a contract,** résilier/résoudre/annuler/ révoquer (un contrat).

termination, *n.* **termination of a contract,** résiliation *f*/annulation *f* d'un contrat.

territory, *n.* (representative's) territory, région (assignée à un représentant); **sales territory**, territoire *m* de vente; **scheduled territory**, zone *f* sterling.

tertiary, *a.* tertiaire; **tertiary industries**, secteur *m* tertiaire; **tertiary market**, marché tertiaire.

test[1], *n.* (*a*) essai *m*/épreuve *f*; test *m*; **aptitude test**, test d'aptitude; **feasibility test**, essai *m* probatoire; **market test**, test de vente; **test drive (for cars)**, essai *m* (de voitures); **test certificate**, certificat *m* d'essai.

test[2], *v.tr.* (*a*) éprouver (qn, qch.); mettre (qn, qch.) à l'épreuve/à l'essai (*b*) essayer (une machine, etc.); contrôler/vérifier (des poids et mesures, etc.); **to test out a scheme**, essayer un projet.

testimonial, *n.* certificat *m*; (lettre *f* de) recommandation *f*; attestation *f*.

testimony, *n.* *Jur:* témoignage *m*/attestation *f*.

testing, *n.* (*a*) essai *m*/épreuve *f* (d'une machine, etc.); contrôle *m* (des poids et mesures, etc.) (*b*) **field testing**, test *m* sur place; **product testing**, test de produit.

text, *n.* texte *m* (d'une police d'assurance, d'un télégramme, etc.).

theme, *n.* thème *m*; **advertising theme**, thème publicitaire.

theory, *n.* théorie *f*; **information theory**, théorie de l'information; **management theory**, théorie de la gestion de l'entreprise.

thin, *a.* *StExch:* **thin market**, marché peu actif; **trading is thin**, il y a peu de transactions.

third[1], *n.* (*a*) tiers *m*; **to lose a third/two thirds of one's money**, perdre le tiers/les deux tiers de son argent; **discount of a third/a third off**, remise *f* d'un tiers (du prix) (*b*) **third of exchange**, troisième *f* de change.

third[2], *a.* (*a*) troisième; **third copy**, triplicata *m* (*b*) **a third party**, une tierce personne/un tiers; *Jur:* **in the hands of a third**

party, en main tierce; **third-party liability**, responsabilité civile/au tiers; **third-party insurance**, assurance *f* au tiers.

threshold, *n.* *EEC:* **threshold price**, prix *m* du seuil.

thrift, *n.* économie *f*/épargne *f*; *NAm:* **thrift institutions/thrifts and loans/thrift**, caisses d'épargne.

thriving, *a.* (*pers.*, *industry*) prospère/florissant.

through, *prep.* *NAm:* **Monday through Friday**, de lundi à vendredi; du lundi au vendredi.

throughput, *n.* (*i*) débit *m*/rendement *m* (*ii*) capacité *f* de traitement.

throw-outs, *n.pl.* rebuts *mpl*/articles défectueux/pièces *fpl* de rebut.

tick[1], *n.* (*a*) *F:* crédit *m*; **to buy sth. on tick**, acheter qch. à crédit (*b*) *StExch:* écart *m* minimum des cours du marché; décalage *m* des cours; **up tick/plus tick**, cours supérieur au cours précédent; **zero-plus tick**, cours inchangé; **down tick**, cours inférieur au cours précédent.

tick[2], *v.tr.* (*on a form*) **tick the appropriate box**, cocher la case correspondante.

ticket, *n.* (*a*) billet *m* (de chemin de fer, de théâtre); ticket *m* (de métro, d'autobus); titre *m* de transport; **book of tickets**, carnet *m* de tickets; **entrance ticket**, billet *m* d'admission; **season ticket**, carte *f* d'abonnement *m*; = carte *f* (orange, etc.); **single ticket**, (billet d')aller *m* ; **return ticket**, (billet d')aller et retour *m* (*b*) **baggage ticket**, bulletin *m*/ticket de bagages; **(price) ticket**, étiquette *f* (portant le prix) (*c*) *StExch:* fiche *f*; **ticket day**, jour *m* de la déclaration des noms.

tie up, *v.tr.* **to tie up money**, immobiliser des capitaux; **to tie up a block of shares**, bloquer une tranche d'actions.

tie-up, *n.* (*a*) **tie-up of capital**, blocage *m*/

immobilisation *f* de capitaux (*b*) association *f* (de maisons de commerce, etc.).

tight, *a.* (*a*) **tight money,** argent *m* rare (*b*) **tight bargain,** transaction *f* qui laisse très peu de marge; **tight discount,** escompte serré.

tighten, *v.tr.* resserrer (le crédit).

tightening, *n.* resserrement *m* (du crédit).

till, *n.* caisse *f*/tiroir-caisse *m*; **till money,** encaisse *f* (d'un magasin); **to do the till,** faire la/sa caisse.

time, *n.* (*a*) temps *m*; **idle time,** temps mort; **time and motion consultant,** organisateur-conseil *m*; **time and methods study,** étude *f* des temps et (des) méthodes; **time and motion study,** étude des temps et (des) mouvements (*b*) heure *f*; **closing time,** heure de fermeture; **opening time,** heure d'ouverture; **time card/time sheet,** feuille *f* de présence; semainier *m*; **time recorder,** horodateur *m*; **time of arrival,** heure d'arrivée; **time of departure,** heure de départ; **time work,** travail *m* à l'heure; **overtime counts (as) time and a half,** les heures supplémentaires sont payées une fois et demie le tarif normal; **to be on short time,** être en chômage partiel; **to get double time on Sundays,** les heures du dimanche sont comptées double (*c*) terme *m*; *NAm:* **time deposit,** dépôt *m* à terme; **time draft,** traite *f* à échéance; *Ins:* **time policy,** police *f* à terme; police à forfait (*d*) délai *m*; **to ask for time (to pay),** demander un délai/un terme de grâce; **in good time,** en temps utile; **latest time,** délai de rigueur; **prescribed time,** délai réglementaire; **time limit,** délai *m*; **strict time limit,** délai péremptoire; **within a reasonable time,** dans un délai raisonnable.

time-share, *n* (*a*) résidence *f* en temps partagé/multi-propriété *f* (*b*) (*job-share*) travail *m* à temps partagé.

timetable, *n.* horaire *m*; indicateur *m* (de chemin de fer).

tinned, *a.* (*food*) en conserve/en boîte.

tip, *n.* (*a*) (*cash*) pourboire *m*/gratification *f*

(*b*) (*information*) renseignement *m*/tuyau *m* (de Bourse, etc.).

title, *n.* **title deed/deed of title,** titre *m* (constitutif) de propriété.

tobacconist, *n.* débitant, -ante de tabac; **tobacconist's (shop),** débit *m* de tabac.

today, *adv.* aujourd'hui; **today's price,** le prix du jour; **today's menu/today's special,** menu *m*/plat *m* du jour.

token, *n.* (*a*) **token payment,** paiement *m* symbolique (*b*) **token money,** monnaie *f* fiduciaire (*c*) **token strike,** grève *f* d'avertissement (*d*) **book token,** chèque-livre *m*; **gift token,** bon-cadeau *m*/chèque-cadeau *m*.

tolerance, *n.* *Cust:* tolérance (permise).

toll, *n.* (*a*) péage *m*; **toll bridge/road,** pont *m*/route *f* à péage (*b*) *NAm: Tel:* frais *mpl* d'interurbain.

tollfree, *a.* *NAm:* **tollfree number,** numéro vert.

ton *n.* **1.** tonne *f*; **long ton/gross ton (of 2240 lb** = 1016.06 kg), tonne forte; **short ton/net ton (of 2000 lb** = 907.185 kg), tonne courte; **metric ton (of 1000 kg** = 2204.6 lb), tonne métrique **2.** *Nau:* (*a*) tonneau *m* (de jauge) (*b*) **measurement ton,** tonne d'arrimage/d'encombrement (*c*) **freight ton,** tonne d'affrètement; **ton mile** = tonne-kilomètre *f*.

tonnage, *n.* *Nau:* tonnage *m*/jauge *f*; capacité *f* de chargement (d'un navire); **gross tonnage,** tonnage brut; jauge brute; **net tonnage,** jauge nette; **deadweight tonnage,** tonnage réel; **register(ed) tonnage,** tonnage net; tonnage de jauge.

tonne, *n.* tonne *f* métrique.

tool, *n.* outil *m*; **to down tools,** (*i*) cesser de travailler (*ii*) se mettre en grève; *pl* **tools,** outillage *m*.

tooling, *n.* usinage *m*.

top¹, *vtr.* **to top an offer,** remporter les enchères/surenchérir.

top², *n.* *StExch:* **to buy at the top and sell at**

the bottom, acheter au plus haut et vendre au plus bas.

top[3], *a.* supérieur; **top management,** haute direction/cadres supérieurs/dirigeants; **top priority,** urgence *f*; **top quality,** (de) première qualité/de qualité supérieure; **to pay the top price,** payer le prix fort.

tot, 1. *v.tr.* additionner/faire le total; **to tot up expenses,** faire le compte des dépenses **2.** *v.i.* (*of expenses, etc.*) **to tot up,** s'élever **(to, à).**

total[1], **1.** *a.* total; entier; complet; global; **total amount,** somme totale/globale; montant total/global; **total assets,** total *m* de l'actif; **total contract value (TCV),** valeur totale du contrat; **total cost,** prix de revient total; **total expenses,** montant total des dépenses; **total liabilities,** total du passif; **total loss,** perte totale; **total output,** production totale; **total quality control (TQC),** qualité globale (QG); **total revenue,** recette totale **2.** *n.* total *m*; montant *m*; **sum total/grand total,** total global; **to calculate the total of the amounts,** faire le total des sommes; **the total comes to £105,** cela fait au total £105.

total[2], *v.tr. & i.* (*a*) additionner/totaliser (les dépenses, etc.) (*b*) **to total (up to)** ..., s'élever à/se monter à ....

totalization, *n.* totalisation *f*.

totalize, *v.tr.* totaliser/additionner (les dépenses, etc.).

touch, *n.* **to be in touch with s.o.,** être en contact avec qn; **to get in touch with s.o.,** se mettre en contact avec qn/prendre contact avec qn/contacter qn/joindre qn.

tour, *n.* visite *f*/voyage *m*/séjour *m* organisé; **conducted tour,** visite guidée; **package tour,** voyage/séjour organisé; **tour operator,** agence *f* de voyages organisés/voyagiste *m*/tour-opérateur *m*; organisateur, -trice de voyages (en groupes).

tourism, *n.* tourisme *m*.

tourist, *n.* touriste *mf*; **tourist bureau/office,** bureau *m* de tourisme; Syndicat *m*

d'Initiative; *Nau: Av:* **tourist information,** renseignements *mpl* touristiques; **the tourist trade,** le tourisme.

town, *n.* ville *f*; cité *f*; **town hall,** hôtel *m* de ville; mairie *f*; **town planning,** urbanisme *m*; **petrol consumption in town,** consommation *f* d'essence en parcours urbain.

trade[1], *n.* (*a*) métier *m*; **to carry on a trade,** exercer un métier (*b*) commerce *m*/négoce *m*/affaires *fpl*; **Board of Trade,** Ministère *m* du Commerce et de l'Industrie; **export trade,** commerce d'exportation; **external trade/foreign trade/overseas trade,** commerce extérieur/avec l'étranger; **home trade/domestic trade,** commerce intérieur; **import trade,** commerce d'importation; **invisible trade,** vente *f*/commerce de services; **visible trade,** vente/commerce de biens; *Nau:* **coastal/coasting trade,** cabotage *m*; **to be in the tea trade,** faire le commerce du thé; **to do a good trade,** faire de bonnes affaires; **to do a roaring trade,** faire des affaires d'or; **to be in trade,** être dans le commerce; être dans le métier; **by way of trade,** commercialement; **trade is at a standstill,** les affaires ne vont pas/le commerce est nul (*c*) échanges commerciaux (entre pays); commerce; **trade agreement,** convention *f*/traité *m* de commerce; **trade allowance,** remise *f*/escompte *m*; **trade balance/balance of trade,** balance commerciale; **trade bank,** banque *f* de commerce/banque commerciale; **trade bills,** effets *mpl* de commerce; **trade card,** carte *f* d'affaires; **trade catalogue,** tarif *m*; catalogue général (complet); **trade credit,** crédit *m* fournisseur; (*in bartering*) = à-valoir *m*; **trade debt,** dettes *fpl* d'exploitation; **trade deficit/gap,** déficit commercial/découvert *m* de la balance commerciale; **trade discount/trade terms,** remise *f* d'usage; **trade fair,** foire commerciale; **trade figures,** chiffre *m* d'affaires; **trade mart,** expomarché *m*; **trade name,** nom commercial/raison commerciale; **trade price,** prix *m* de demi-gros; **trade register,** registre *m* du commerce; **trade route,** route commerciale; **trade secret,** secret professionnel; **trade show,** exposition interprofessionnelle; **trade union,** syndicat *m*; **trade union member,** syndicaliste *mf*; **trade unionist,** syndiqué, -ée; **trade unionism,** syndicalisme *m*; **trade union tariff,** tarif syndical (*d*) *NAm:* (*deal*) marché *m*/affaire *f*; vente *f* ou achat *m*; **they made several trades,** ils ont fait plusieurs ventes ou achats.

trade[2], *v.i.* faire le commerce (**in,** de); faire des affaires/entretenir des relations commerciales (**with s.o.,** avec qn); **he trades in wines,** il est négociant en vins.

trade in, *v.tr.* donner (qch.) en reprise; **I am buying a new car and trading in my old one,** j'achète une nouvelle voiture et donne ma vieille en reprise.

trade-in, *n.* reprise *f*; **trade-in allowance/price,** contre-valeur *f*; prix à la reprise/valeur *f* de reprise.

trademark, *n.* marque *f* de fabrique; **maker's trademark,** cachet *m* du fabricant; **registered trademark,** marque déposée.

tradeoff, *n.* échange *m*; compromis *m*/concession *f*.

trader, *n.* (*a*) négociant, -ante/commerçant, -ante/marchand, -ande; **private trader,** marchand, -ande établi(e) à son propre compte; **sole trader,** chef *m* d'une entreprise individuelle (*b*) *StExch:* cambiste *mf*; courtier *m*; spéculateur, -trice; trader *m*; **day-to-day trader,** spéculateur à la journée; **floor trader,** commis *m*; **position trader,** spéculateur sur plusieurs positions.

tradesman, *n.* marchand *m*/fournisseur *m*; **tradesmen's entrance,** entrée *f* des fournisseurs.

tradespeople, *n.pl.* commerçants, -antes/marchands, -antes/fournisseurs *m*.

trading, *n.* commerce *m*; négoce *m*; marché *m*; échanges commerciaux (entre pays); **paperless trading,** marché *m*/cotation *f* électronique; **trading account,** compte *m* d'exploitation; **trading area,** territoire *m* de vente; **trading assets,** actif engagé; **trading bank,** banque *f* de commerce/banque commerciale; **trading**

capital, capital engagé/capital de roulement; **trading company,** entreprise *f*/société *f* commerciale; **trading estate,** zone industrielle; *StExch:* **trading day,** jour *m* de Bourse; **last trading day,** dernier jour de négociation; **trading floor,** corbeille *f* (à la Bourse); **trading halt,** suspension *f* de séance; **trading port,** port *m* de commerce; *NAm:* **trading post,** corbeille du New York Stock Exchange; **trading profit,** bénéfice *m* d'exploitation/bénéfice brut; *StExch:* **trading range,** écart *m* de prix; **prices are stuck in a trading range,** les prix ne varient pas beaucoup; **trading stamp,** timbre-prime *m*; **trading vessel,** navire marchand/de commerce; **trading year,** exercice *m* comptable; **horse trading,** marchandages *mpl* de maquignons; *StExch:* **late trading,** opérations *fpl* de clôture; **light trading,** marché *m* calme; **basis trading,** spéculation sur la base; **ring trading,** cotation à la corbeille.

traffic, *n.* (*trade*) trafic *m*; **freight traffic/goods traffic,** trafic/mouvement *m* de marchandises; **passenger traffic,** trafic de voyageurs/de passagers; **illegal traffic,** trafic illicite.

train[1], *n.* train *m*; **goods train,** train de marchandises; **passenger and goods train,** train mixte.

train[2], *v.tr.* former/instruire (qn); **to train/to be training as a bricklayer,** être apprenti maçon; **trained personnel,** personnel qualifié/ayant reçu la formation requise.

trainee, *n.* stagiaire *mf*; apprenti, -ie.

training, *n.* éducation *f*/instruction *f*; apprentissage *m*/formation *f*; cours *m* de perfectionnement *m*; **to have had a business training,** avoir reçu une formation commerciale; **on-the-job training,** formation sur le tas; **in-house/in-plant training,** formation dans l'entreprise; **staff training,** formation du personnel; **training levy,** taxe *f* d'apprentissage; **training officer,** directeur, -trice de formation; **training time,** temps *m* de formation; **vocational training,** formation professionnelle.

tranche, *n.* tranche *f.*

tranchette, *n* tranchette *f.*

transact, *v.tr.* **to transact business with s.o.,** faire des affaires avec qn; traiter une affaire.

transaction, *n.* transaction *f*/opération (commerciale); affaire (faite); **the transaction of business,** la conduite des affaires; **cash transaction,** opération/ transaction au comptant; **commercial transaction,** transaction/opération commerciale; **loan transactions,** transactions à crédit; *StExch:* **Stock Exchange/ market transactions,** opérations de Bourse; **transaction for the account,** négociation *f*/opération à terme; **forward exchange transactions,** opérations/négociations de change à terme; **transaction charge,** frais *mpl* de bourse/courtage *m* de place; **transaction costs,** commissions *fpl*/ frais de bourse.

transactor, *n.* négociateur, -trice (d'une affaire); agent *m* économique.

transfer[1], *n.* (*a*) transport *m*/renvoi *m* (de qch. à un autre endroit); déplacement *m*/mutation *f* (d'un fonctionnaire); **staff transfer,** transfert *m* de personnel; *Rail: Av:* transbordement *m* (de marchandises, de voyageurs) (*b*) transfert/transmission *f* (d'un droit, etc.); **transfer of a debt,** cession *f*/revirement *m* d'une créance; **transfer book/transfer register,** journal *m*/registre *m* des transferts; *Jur:* **transfer of property,** mutation *f* de biens; **transfer duty,** droits *mpl* de mutation; *StExch:* **transfer of shares,** transfert d'actions; **transfer fee,** frais *mpl* de transfert; **transfer form,** formule *f* de transfert; **blank transfer,** titre *m* de transfert en blanc; **certificate of transfer,** certificat *m* de transfert (*c*) *Book-k:* contre-passation *f* (d'une écriture); transport/ristourne *f* (d'une somme d'un compte à un autre); **transfer entry,** article *m* de contre-passation; *Bank: etc:* **bank giro transfer,** virement *m* bancaire; **cable/telegraphic transfer,** virement télégraphique; **credit transfer,** virement de crédits; **transfer agent,** agent *m* comptable des transferts;

transfer pricing, prix *m* de transfert/de cession interne; **transfer of account (from one bank to another),** transfert-paiement *m*; **transfer of funds,** virement de fonds (*d*) *Jur:* **transfer deed,** acte *m* de cession; acte translatif (de propriété); *StExch:* (feuille *f* de) transfert (*e*) **transfer payment,** transfert social (*convert par les fonds d'État*).

transfer[2], *v.tr.* (*a*) transférer (des actions, etc.); **to transfer a bill by endorsement,** transférer un billet par voie d'endossement (*b*) *Book-k:* **to transfer a debt,** transporter une créance (*c*) déplacer/ transférer/muter (le personnel); transférer (un bureau, un magasin); *Rail: Av:* transborder (des marchandises) (*d*) virer (une somme) (*e*) *Jur:* céder/transmettre (une propriété, des actions).

transferable, *a.* transférable/transmissible; *Jur:* (droit, bien) cessible; (droit) communicable/transférable; *Fin:* **transferable securities,** valeurs mobilières négociables/cessibles; **transferable share,** action *f* au porteur; (*ticket, etc.*) **not transferable,** non cessible/personnel.

transferee, *n. Jur: Fin:* bénéficiaire *mf*; cessionnaire *mf* (d'un bien, d'un effet de commerce, etc.).

transference, *n.* transfert *m*.

transferor, *n. Jur:* cédant, -ante; endosseur *m* (d'un effet de commerce).

transient, *n. NAm:* voyageur, -euse de passage/*F:* un passage.

transire, *n. Cust:* passavant *m*/laissezpasser *m inv*/acquit-à-caution *m* (délivré au capitaine d'un caboteur).

transit, *n.* (*a*) transit *m*; **(passengers, goods) in transit,** (passagers, marchandises) en transit; **(warehoused) goods for transit,** marchandises de transit; **to convey goods in transit,** transiter des marchandises; **transit bill,** passavant *m*; **transit entry,** déclaration *f* de transit; (*of goods*) **transit trade,** commerce *m* transitaire; *Cust:* **transit visa/permit,** document *m*/visa *m* de transit (*b*) transport *m* (de marchandises);

damage in transit, avarie(s) *f(pl)* en cours de route; **loss in transit,** freinte *f* de route.

transmission, *n.* (*a*) transmission *f* (d'un colis, d'un message, de données) (*b*) **transmission of shares,** cession *f*/transfert *m* d'actions.

transport[1], *n.* **1.** = **transportation 2.** transport *m*; **air transport,** transport aérien/par avion; **public transport,** transports *mpl* en commun; **rail transport,** transport par chemin de fer; **river transport,** transport fluvial; **road transport,** transport routier; **transport by sea,** transport maritime; **means of transport,** moyen *m*/mode *m* de transport; **transport by lorry/by truck,** transport par camion/camionnage *m*; **transport agent,** transitaire *m*; **transport aircraft,** avion *m* de transport; **transport company,** compagnie *f*/société *f*/entreprise *f* de transport.

transport[2], *v.tr.* transporter (des marchandises, des voyageurs); **to transport goods by lorry/by truck,** camionner des marchandises/transporter des marchandises par camion; **to transport goods by rail**/*NAm:* **by railroad,** transporter des marchandises par chemin de fer.

transportable, *a.* (*goods, etc.*) transportable.

transportation, *n.* transport *m*; **transportation method,** méthode *f* des transports.

transporter, *n.* (*pers.*) transporteur *m*/entrepreneur *m* de transports.

travel[1], *n.* voyages *mpl*; **travel agency,** agence *f* de voyages; agence/bureau *m* de tourisme.

travel[2], *v.i.* **to travel for a firm,** représenter une maison de commerce; être représentant d'une société.

travel(l)er, *n.* **1.** **travel(l)er's cheque,** chèque *m* de voyage **2.** (**commercial**) **travel(l)er,** représentant, -ante (de commerce)/délégué, -ée commercial(e).

travelling, *n.* voyages *mpl*; **travelling allowance,** indemnité *f* de déplacement;

travelling expenses, frais *mpl* de représentation; frais de déplacement.

treasurer, *n.* trésorier, -ière; *NAm:* trésorier; **treasurer's report,** rapport financier; **treasurer's office,** trésorerie *f*.

treasury, *n.* (*a*) trésor (public); trésorerie *f*; **treasury bills,** bon *m* du Trésor (à court terme); **treasury bond,** bon *m* du Trésor à long terme (*b*) **purchase of shares for Treasury,** (r)achat *m* par une société de ses propres actions; **Treasury stocks/shares,** actions *fpl* appartenant en propre à une société.

treat, *v.i.* **to treat with one's creditors,** traiter/négocier avec ses créanciers.

treaty, *n.* contrat *m*; accord *m*; **commercial treaty,** traité *m* de commerce; **sale by private treaty,** vente *f* de gré à gré/à l'amiable.

treble[1], **1.** *a.* triple **2.** *n.* triple *m* **3.** *adv.* trois fois plus.

treble[2], *v.tr. & i.* tripler; **prices have trebled in two years,** les prix ont triplé en deux ans; **the value of the house has trebled,** la maison a triplé de valeur.

trend, *n.* (*a*) tendance *f* de fond; **price trend,** tendance des prix; **downward trend,** tendance à la baisse; **economic trend,** tendance/évolution *f* économique; **market trends,** tendances du marché; **the general trend of the market,** les tendances du marché; **upward trend,** tendance à la hausse; **trend reversal,** renversement *m* de tendance (*b*) **the latest trend in footwear,** chaussures dernier cri.

trial, *n.* **1.** essai *m*; **to give sth. a trial,** faire l'essai de qch.; **on trial,** à l'essai; **trial lot,** envoi *m* à titre d'essai; **trial order,** commande *f* à l'essai; **trial period,** période *f* d'essai **2.** *Book-k:* **trial balance,** balance de vérification/d'ordre **3.** *Jur:* procès *m*; **to stand trial,** passer en jugement.

tribunal, *n.* tribunal *m*; **commercial tribunal,** tribunal de commerce.

trigger (off), *v.tr.* déclencher.

trillion, *n.* (*a*) trillion *m* (10^{18}) (*b*) *NAm:* billion *m* (10^{12}).

trip, *n.* **business trip,** voyage *m* d'affaires.

triple[1], **1.** *a.* triple **2.** *adv.* trois fois plus.

triple[2], *v.tr. & i.* tripler.

triplicate[1], *n.* troisième copie; triplicata *m*; **invoice in triplicate,** facture *f* en trois exemplaires.

triplicate[2], *v.tr.* rédiger (un document) en trois exemplaires.

trolley, *n.* (*at supermarket*) caddie *m*.

trouble, *n.* conflit *m*/difficulté *f*; **labour troubles,** conflits ouvriers.

troubleshooter, *n.* médiateur, -trice/ conciliateur, -trice.

trough, *n.* creux *m* (dans la demande).

truck[1], *n.* camion *m*.

truck[2], *v.tr. NAm:* camionner.

trucking, *n. NAm:* camionnage *m*.

trust, *n.* **1.** confiance *f* (**in,** en); **breach of trust,** abus *m* de confiance; **position of trust,** poste *m* de confiance **2.** *Jur:* (*i*) fidéicommis *m* (*ii*) fiducie *f*; **beneficiary of a trust,** fidéicommissaire *mf*; **trust deed,** acte *m* de fidéicommis **3.** *Fin:* (*i*) trust *m*/cartel *m* (*ii*) trust/société *f* holding (*iii*) syndicat *m* (de copropriété); *NAm:* **trust company,** société fiduciaire; **fixed trust,** société d'investissement à capital fixe (SICAF); **flexible trust,** = société d'investissement à capital variable (SICAV); **investment trust,** société de placement(s)/d'investissement(s); **securities in trust,** valeurs mises en trust; **vertical trust,** trust vertical; **to group into a trust,** truster; **organizer/administrator of a trust,** trusteur *m*.

trustee, *n. Jur:* (*a*) (*of testamentary estate*) fiduciaire *mf*/héritier *m* fiduciaire/grevé *m* de fiducie/grevé de restitution (*b*) (*with powers of attorney*) mandataire *mf*; **public trustee,** administrateur *m* judiciaire; curateur *m* aux successions; exécuteur *m* testamentaire (*c*) **board of trustees,** conseil *m* d'administration.

try, *v.tr. Jur:* juger (une cause, un accusé); *NAm:* plaider (une cause).

tumbling, *n.* **tumbling down (of prices, values),** désescalade *f* (des prix, des valeurs).

turn, *n. Fin:* (*a*) **turn (of the market)** marge *f* (entre le prix d'achat et le prix de vente); **jobber's turn,** bénéfice *m* d'un contrepartiste (*b*) **stock turn/***NAm:* **inventory turn,** rotation *f* des stocks.

turn around *v.tr.* = **turn round.**

turnaround, *n. NAm* = **turnround.**

turn down, *v.tr.* **to turn down an applicant,** refuser un candidat; **to turn down a claim,** écarter une réclamation; **to turn down an offer,** rejeter une offre.

turnkey, *a.* **turnkey contract/operation/ project,** (projet *m* de) bâtiment livré clef en main; **turnkey operator,** ensemblier *m*.

turn out, *v.tr.* produire/fabriquer (des marchandises).

turnout, *n.* rendement *m* (d'une machine, d'une usine, etc.).

turn over, *v.tr.* **he turns over £1 000 a week,** son chiffre d'affaires est de £1 000 par semaine; **to turn over capital,** faire rouler les capitaux.

turnover, *n.* (*a*) **(sales) turnover,** chiffre *m* d'affaires; **his turnover is £50 000 per annum,** il fait £50 000 d'affaires par an; **turnover tax,** impôt *m* sur le chiffre d'affaires (*b*) *NAm:* **inventory turnover,** rotation *f* (des stocks); **staff turnover,** rotation roulement *m*/renouvellement *m* du personnel; **turnover rate,** vitesse *f* de rotation des stocks.

turn round, *v.tr.* **the stocks are turned round every four months,** le délai de rotation (des stocks) est de quatre mois.

turnround, *n.* **1.** renversement *m* (de tendances); revirement *m*/retournement *m* (de situation) **2.** (*a*) **turnround of stocks,** rotation *f* des stocks (*b*) **delivery turnround,** délai *m* de livraison.

tycoon, *n.* magnat *m.*

type, *v.tr. & i.* écrire/taper (à la machine)/ dactylographier (une lettre, etc.).

typewriter, *n.* machine *f* à écrire; **golfball typewriter,** machine à écrire à boule/à sphère; **portable typewriter,** machine à écrire portative.

typewritten, *a.* (document, etc.) dac-tylographié/écrit à la machine/tapé (à la machine).

typing, *n.* dactylographie *f*/*F:* dactylo *f*; **typing error,** faute *f* de frappe; **typing paper,** papier *m* (pour) machine (à écrire); **typing pool,** équipe *f* de dactylos; **shorthand typing,** sténodactylographie *f*.

typist, *n.* dactylographe *mf*/dactylo *mf*; **shorthand typist,** sténodactylo *mf*.

U

---

uberrima fides, *Lt. phr. Ins.* la franchise la plus parfaite.

ultimo, *abbr:* **ult,** *adv. Corr:* **your letter of 22 ult(imo),** votre lettre du 22 écoulé.

umbrella, *n.* **umbrella committee,** comité *m* de coordination.

umpirage, *n.* arbitrage *m.*

unabridged, *a.* **unabridged edition,** édition *f* complète/intégrale.

unaccepted, *a.* **unaccepted bill,** effet non accepté.

unaccounted, *a.* **these sixty pounds are unaccounted for in the balance sheet,** ces soixante livres ne figurent pas au bilan; **three articles are still unaccounted for,** il manque toujours trois articles.

unallotted, *a. Fin:* **unallotted shares,** actions non réparties.

unanimous, *a.* unanime; **unanimous consent,** consentement *m* unanime; **unanimous vote,** vote *m* à l'unanimité.

unanimously, *adv.* **he was elected unanimously,** il a été élu à l'unanimité.

unappropriated, *a.* (argent, etc.) inutilisé/disponible; fonds *mpl* sans application déterminée.

unassigned, *a.* **unassigned revenue,** recettes non affectées (en garantie).

unassured, *a. Ins:* non assuré.

unaudited, *a.* **unaudited figures,** chiffres non certifiés.

unauthorized, *a.* non autorisé; sans autorisation; (commerce, etc.) illicite; *P.N:* **no entry to unauthorized person/no unauthor-** ized **access,** accès interdit à toute personne étrangère au service.

unavailability, *n.* indisponibilité *f.*

unavailable, *a.* (*i*) indisponible/non disponible (*ii*) qu'on ne peut se procurer/épuisé.

unavoidable, *a.* inévitable; **unavoidable costs,** frais essentiels/nécessaires.

unbalanced, *a. Book-k:* (*account*) non soldé.

unbankable, *a.* (effet) non bancable/hors de banque/déclassé.

unblock, *v.tr.* désencadrer (les crédits).

unblocking, *n.* **unblocking of credits,** désencadrement *m* des crédits.

unbuilt, *a.* **unbuilt plot,** terrain *m* vague/non construit.

unbundle, *v.tr. NAm:* tarifer séparément; établir des prix séparés.

unbundling, *n. NAm:* séparation *f* des tarifs; facturation/tarification séparée; dégroupage *m* des tarifs.

uncallable, *a. NAm:* **uncallable bonds,** obligations *fpl* non remboursables/obligations sans possibilité d'amortissement anticipé.

uncalled, *a. Fin:* **uncalled capital,** capital non appelé.

uncashed, *a.* **uncashed cheque,** chèque *m* à encaisser/chèque non compensé.

uncertain, *a. StExch:* **to quote uncertain,** donner l'incertain.

unchecked, *a.* (*account, etc.*) non vérifié/non contrôlé.

unclaimed, *a.* (*dividend, etc.*) non réclamé.

uncleared, *a.* (*a*) *Cust:* **uncleared goods,** marchandises non passées en douane/non dédouanées (*b*) (*debt*) non acquitté/non liquidé (*c*) (*cheque*) non compensé.

uncollected, *a.* non réclamé; **uncollected taxes,** impôts non perçus.

unconditional, *a.* (*a*) *Fin:* **unconditional order,** ordre (de payer) pur et simple (*b*) **unconditional · acceptance,** acceptation *f* sans conditions/sans réserve.

unconfirmed, *a.* **unconfirmed credit,** crédit non confirmé.

unconsolidated, *a.* *Fin:* (*debt*) non consolidé.

uncorrected, *a.* (*balance, etc.*) non redressé.

uncovered, *a.* (achat, vente) à découvert; (chèque) sans provision; **uncovered balance,** découvert *m*; **uncovered advance,** avance *f* à découvert; *StExch:* **uncovered bear,** vendeur, -euse à découvert.

uncrossed, *a.* **uncrossed cheque,** chèque non barré; chèque ouvert.

undated, *a.* non daté; sans date; **undated bonds,** obligations *fpl* sans date d'échéance; **undated debenture,** obligation perpétuelle.

undelivered, *a.* **undelivered goods,** marchandises non livrées; **if undelivered please return to sender,** en cas de non-livraison prière de retourner à l'expéditeur.

underbid, *v.tr.* faire des soumissions/offrir des conditions plus avantageuses que (qn); demander moins cher que (qn).

undercapitalization, *n.* sous-capitalisation *f.*

undercapitalized, *a.* sous-capitalisé.

undercut, *v.tr.* (*a*) faire des soumissions plus avantageuses que (qn) (*b*) vendre moins cher/à meilleur prix que (qn).

underdeveloped, *a.* *PolEc:* **under-** **developed countries,** pays *mpl* en voie de développement.

underemployed, *a.* sous-employé.

underemployment, *n.* *PolEc:* sous-emploi *m*/chômage *m.*

underequipped, *a.* sous-équipé.

under-estimate[1], *n.* sous-estimation *f*/ sous-évaluation *f.*

under-estimate[2], *v.tr.* sous-estimer/sous-évaluer.

underfunded, *a.* sous-capitalisé.

underinsure, *v.tr.* **he is underinsured,** ses assurances ne sont pas suffisantes/ne le couvrent pas suffisamment.

undermanned, *a.* à court de personnel/de main-d'œuvre.

undermentioned, *a.* **could you send us the undermentioned items,** pourriez-vous nous faire parvenir les articles suivants/ les articles mentionnés ci-dessous.

underpaid, *a.* mal rétribué/insuffisamment rétribué; **underpaid workers,** ouvriers sous-payés.

underpay, *v.tr.* sous-payer.

underpayment, *n.* insuffisance *f* de paiement.

underpin, *v.tr.* soutenir (un marché, etc).

underprice, *a.* au-dessous de la valeur.

underproduction, *n.* *Ind:* production *f* au-dessous du rendement normal/ production déficitaire/sous-production *f.*

underquote, *v.tr.* faire une soumission plus avantageuse que celle de (qn).

undersell, *v.tr.* (*a*) vendre au-dessous du cours/moins cher que (qn); **we are not knowingly undersold,** à notre connaissance personne ne vend moins cher (que nous); **he undersold his competitors,** il a obtenu le contrat en demandant moins cher que ses concurrents (*b*) vendre (qch.) au-dessous de sa valeur.

undersign, *v.tr.* signer (un document).

undersigned, *a. & n.* soussigné, -ée; **I the undersigned declare that ...,** je soussigné(e) déclare que ....

understaffed, *a.* qui manque de personnel; **to be understaffed,** manquer de/être à court de personnel.

understanding, *n.* (*a*) accord *m*/entente *f* (*b*) condition *f*; **on the understanding that ...,** à condition que.

undertake, *v.tr.* se charger de/entreprendre/s'imposer (une tâche); assumer (une responsabilité); **to undertake a guarantee,** s'engager à donner une garantie.

undertaking, *n.* **(commercial) undertaking,** entreprise commerciale; **joint undertaking,** entreprise en participation.

undervaluation, *n.* estimation *f* (de qch.) au-dessous de sa valeur/sous-estimation *f*/sous-évaluation *f*.

undervalue, *v.tr.* sous-estimer/sous-évaluer (qch.)/estimer (qch.) au-dessous de sa valeur.

underwater, *a. US:* (*share prices*) décoté; **underwater option,** option *f* à prix glissant à la baisse.

underwrite, *v.tr.* (*a*) *Fin:* garantir la souscription d'une émission (*b*) *MIns:* couvrir (un risque, etc.)/garantir (contre un risque) par un contrat d'assurance; **to underwrite a contract,** garantir un contrat; **to underwrite a policy,** souscrire une police.

underwriter, *n.* (*a*) *Fin:* membre *m* d'un syndicat de garantie/syndicataire *mf*; **underwriter agent,** agent souscripteur; **leading underwriter,** apériteur *m*; **the underwriters,** le syndicat de garantie (*b*) *MIns:* assureur *m*/compagnie *f* d'assurance (maritime).

underwriting, *n.* (*a*) *Fin:* garantie *f* d'émission; **underwriting agreement/contract,** contrat *m* de garantie; **under-writing commission,** commission syndicale; **underwriting agent,** agent souscripteur; **underwriting fee,** (*to credit company*) commission de garantie; (*to broker*) commission de placement; **underwriting group,** syndicat *m* de prise ferme; **underwriting share,** part *f* syndicataire; **underwriting syndicate,** syndicat financier/syndicat de garantie/de souscripteurs; **he has been suspended from underwriting,** il a été démis de ses fonctions de souscripteur (*b*) assurance *f* maritime; **insurance underwriting,** souscription d'une police/d'un risque.

undischarged, *a.* (*a*) *Jur:* **undischarged bankrupt,** failli non réhabilité (*b*) **undischarged debt,** dette non acquittée/non liquidée/non soldée.

undisclosed, *a.* (montant) secret/non révélé.

undiscountable, *a.* **undiscountable bill,** billet *m*/effet *m* inescomptable.

undisposed of, *a.* **stock undisposed of,** marchandises non écoulées/non vendues.

undistributed, *a.* non distribué; non réparti; **undistributed earnings,** bénéfices non distribués; **undistributed profit,** bénéfice non distribué.

undivided, *a.* non partagé; **undivided profits,** bénéfices non répartis; **undivided property,** biens indivis.

unearned, *a.* **unearned income,** revenu *m* du capital/revenu non professionnel rente *f*; **unearned increment of land,** plus-value foncière.

uneconomic, *a.* peu économique; **uneconomic proposition,** projet *m* non rentable/peu rentable.

unemployed, *a.* **1.** (*a*) sans travail/sans emploi; en chômage (*b*) *n.pl.* **the unemployed,** les chômeurs *m*; **les sans-travaii** *mf inv*/les sans-emploi *mf inv*; **long-term unemployed,** chômeurs de longue durée **2.** (*capital*) inemployé; **unemployed funds,** fonds inactifs/dormants/inemployés/improductifs.

unemployment, *n.* chômage *m*; **concealed/ disguised unemployment**, chômage déguisé; **cyclical unemployment**, chômage conjoncturel; **frictional unemployment**, chômage résiduel/de mobilité; **long-term unemployment**, chômage de longue durée; **structural unemployment**, chômage structurel/classique; **unemployment benefit/ relief**, allocation *f*/prestation *f*/indemnité *f* de chômage; **unemployment fund**, caisse *f* de chômage; **unemployment insurance**, assurance *f* chômage.

unendorsed, *a.* (*cheque*) non endossé.

unenforceable, *a.* (contrat, etc.) non exécutoire.

unexchangeable, *a. Fin:* **unexchangeable securities**, valeurs *f* impermutables/ inéchangeables.

unexecuted, *a.* (*order*) non exécuté.

unexpended, *a. Fin:* **unexpended balance**, solde non dépensé.

unfair, *a.* injuste; déloyal; **unfair competition**, concurrence déloyale.

unfavourable, *a.* défavorable/peu favorable; (*terms, etc.*) peu avantageux/ défavorable (**to**, à); **unfavourable balance of trade**, balance commerciale défavorable; *Fin:* **unfavourable exchange**, change *m* défavorable.

unfilled, *a. StExch:* (ordre) non exécuté.

unfunded, *a.* sans capitaux suffisants; *Fin:* **unfunded debt**, dette flottante/non consolidée.

ungeared, *a.* (*firm*) sans endettement.

unilateral, *a.* unilatéral; **unilateral contract**, contrat unilatéral.

uninsurable, *a.* non assurable.

uninsured, *a.* non assuré (**against**, contre); *Post:* (colis) sans valeur déclarée.

uninvested, *a.* (argent) non placé/non investi.

union, *n.* (*a*) union *f*; **customs union**, union douanière (*b*) **trade union**/*NAm:* **labor**

union, syndicat *m*; **union agreement**, convention collective; **union card**, carte syndicale; **union meeting**, réunion syndicale; **union member**, syndiqué, -ée; **union representative**, délégué, -ée syndical(e).

unionism, *n.* syndicalisme *m*.

unionist, *n.* syndicaliste *mf*.

unionized, *a.* **non unionized labour/ workers**, ouvriers non syndiqués.

unisex, *a.* **unisex shops/fashion**, boutique *f*/ mode *f* unisexe.

unissued, *a.* **unissued shares**, actions non encore émises.

unit, *n.* 1. (*a*) unité *f*; **each lot contains a hundred units**, chaque lot contient cent unités; **cost unit**, unité de coût; **unit cost**, prix *m* de revient unitaire; **unit price**, prix de l'unité/prix unitaire; **unit sales**, unités vendues; **unit value index**, indice *m* de la valeur unitaire; **accumulation units**, fonds *mpl* de capitalisation (*b*) **visual display unit (VDU)**, console *f* de visualisation/ visuel *m* (*c*) unité (de longueur, de poids, etc.); *Pharm:* unité (*d*) *PolEc:* **monetary unit**, unité monétaire; **unit of consumption/ of production**, unité de consommation/de production; **unit of labour/man work unit**, unité de travail; *EEC:* **unit of account**, unité de compte; **European currency unit (ECU)**, unité de compte européenne (ECU) 2. **unit trust** = Organisme *m* de placement collectif en valeurs mobilières/OPCVM *m*; fonds *m* de placement ouvert.

unitary, *a.* unitaire.

unlawful, *a.* contraire à la loi; illégal.

unlimited, *a.* illimité/non limité.

unlisted, *a. StExch:* non inscrit (à la cote officielle)/hors cote; **unlisted securities**, valeurs non cotées (en Bourse)/valeurs hors cote; **unlisted securities market (USM)**, second marché.

unload, *vi. US:* inonder le marché.

unloading, *n. US:* dumping *m*/ventes massives/vente à perte.

unlock, *v.tr.* **to unlock assets,** débloquer des fonds/mobiliser de l'argent.

unmanufactured, *a.* (à l'état) brut; non manufacturé; **unmanufactured materials,** matières premières/matières brutes.

unmarketable, *a.* (*goods*) invendable; d'un débit difficile; **unmarketable assets,** fonds *m* non réalisables/actif *m* non réalisable.

unmarried, *a.* célibataire.

unmortgaged, *a.* libre d'hypothèques; franc/franche d'hypothèques.

unnegotiable, *a.* (*cheque*) non négociable; **unnegotiable bill,** effet *m* non négociable.

unobtainable, *a.* (*article*) qu'on ne peut obtenir/se procurer.

unofficial, *a.* non officiel/non confirmé; (renseignement) officieux; **unofficial strike,** grève *f* sauvage.

unpaid, *a.* **1.** (*pers.*) non salarié; (*post*) non rétribué; **unpaid agent,** mandataire *m* bénévole; **unpaid services,** services à titre gracieux/non rétribués/bénévoles **2.** (*a*) (*bill*) impayé; (*debt*) non acquitté; **to leave an account unpaid,** laisser traîner un compte/laisser un compte impayé (*b*) (*money*) impayé; non versé.

unpriced, *a.* (article) sans (indication de) prix.

unproductive, *a.* (capital, travail) improductif.

unproductiveness, *n.* improductivité *f.*

unprofitable, *a.* peu profitable/peu lucratif/peu rentable; (travail, etc.) inutile.

unqualified, *a.* **it is our unqualified opinion that,** nous certifions sans réserve que.

unquoted, *a.* *StExch:* **unquoted company,** société privée/non cotée; **unquoted securities,** valeurs non cotées; **unquoted stock,** titre non coté.

unrealizable, *a.* **unrealizable capital,** fonds non réalisables.

unrealized, *a.* (*assets, etc.*) non réalisé.

unreceipted, *a.* non acquitté/sans la mention "pour acquit".

unredeemable, *a.* non remboursable.

unregistered, *a.* non enregistré/non inscrit; (*trademark*) non déposé.

unremunerative, *a.* peu rémunérateur; peu lucratif; peu profitable.

unrepaid, *a.* (emprunt, argent, etc.) non remboursé/non rendu.

unrest, *n.* **social unrest,** mécontentement social/agitation ouvrière.

unsafe, *a.* *Fin:* **unsafe paper,** papier *m* de valeur douteuse.

unsaleable, *a.* (*goods*) invendable.

unsecured, *a.* (*loan, overdraft, etc.*) non garanti/à découvert; (*debt, creditor*) sans garantie; chirographaire.

unsettled, *a.* (*a*) **the unsettled state of the market,** l'incertitude *f* du marché; les fluctuations *f* du marché (*b*) **the debt remained unsettled,** la dette est restée impayée.

unskilled, *a.* non qualifié/non spécialisé; **unskilled labour,** main-d'œuvre non spécialisée; **unskilled job,** travail *m* de manœuvre; **unskilled worker,** manœuvre *m.*

unsocial, *a.* **tariff for unsocial hours,** tarif (plus élevé) payé à qn qui travaille durant les heures de congé ou les jours normalement non ouvrés.

unsold, *a.* invendu; **unsold goods,** marchandises invendues; invendus *mpl.*

unsound, *a.* **it is unsound finance,** c'est de la mauvaise finance; *Ins:* **unsound risk,** mauvais risque.

unspent, *a.* (*sum, balance, etc.*) non dépensé.

unstable, *a.* (marché) instable.

unsteady, *a.* (*prices*) variable; (*market*) agité/irrégulier.

unsubscribed, *a.* (capital) non souscrit.

unsubsidized, *a.* non subventionné/sans subvention.

untax, *v.tr.* détaxer.

untaxed, *a.* exempt/exonéré d'impôt; (produit) non imposé/non taxé.

up, *adv.* **1.** (*on packing case*) **this side up,** haut *m*/dessus *m* **2.** (*shares, etc.*) **to be up,** être en hausse (**at,** à); **shares are up at £5,** les actions ont monté jusqu'à £5; **profits are up (by) 25%,** les profits ont enregistré une hausse de 25%/ont augmenté de 25%; **up to and including page 10,** juqu'à la page 10 inclusivement.

upcoming, *a. NAm:* **upcoming product,** produit *m* qui sera bientôt sur le marché; **upcoming decision,** décision imminente.

update, *v.tr.* mettre à jour.

updating, *n.* mise *f* à jour.

upkeep, *n.* (frais *mpl* d')entretien *m* (d'un établissement, etc.).

upscale, *n. NAm:* **upscale market,** marché *m* de haut de gamme.

upset, *a.* (*at auctions, etc.*) **upset price,** mise *f* à prix.

upside, **1.** *a.* **upside breakout,** mouvement brutal vers la hausse. **2.** *n US:* potentiel *m* de hausse.

upstream, *adv. & a.* (*company*) en amont.

upswing, *n.* essor *m*; mouvement *m* vers la hausse.

uptick, *n. NAm:* **up tick** *n.* transaction *f* à un cours supérieur.

uptrend, *n.* tendance *f* à la hausse.

upturn, *n.* relance *f* (économique); reprise *f*; **upturn in business activity,** reprise des affaires.

upward, *a.* **an upward trend/tendency,** une tendance à la hausse; **an upward movement,** un mouvement de hausse.

urban, *a.* urbain.

urgent, *a.* urgent; **urgent order,** commande urgente.

usance, *n.* (*a*) taux *m* d'intérêt sur un prêt (*b*) revenu *m* du capital (*c*) (*time delay*) usance *f*; **bill at double usance,** effet *m* à double usance; **at thirty days' usance,** à usance de trente jours; **usance bill,** effet *m* à usance.

use [1], *n.* emploi *m*/usage *m*; **direction for use,** mode *m* d'emploi; **in use,** en usage; **joint use,** utilisation *f* en commun; *Cust:* **articles for personal use,** effets usagers/ effets personnels; **to make use of sth.,** se servir de qch./faire usage de qch./ employer qch./utiliser qch.; *Cust:* **home use entry,** sortie *f* de l'entrepôt pour consommation; **goods for home use,** marchandises mises en consommation.

use [2], *v.tr.* employer/utiliser/user de/se servir de/faire usage de (qch.); **used car,** voiture *f* d'occasion.

user, *n.* usager, -ère/utilisateur, -trice.

user-friendly, *a.* (*machine*) convivial.

usual, *a.* usuel/habituel/ordinaire; **usual terms,** conditions *f* d'usage; **it is usual to pay in advance,** il est d'usage de payer d'avance/on paie habituellement d'avance; **the usual practice,** la pratique courante/l'usage courant; **usual hours (of business),** heures *f* réglementaires (d'ouverture).

usufruct, *n. Jur:* usufruit *m*.

usurious, *a.* usuraire.

usury, *n.* usure *f*.

utility, *n.* **public utility services/utilities,** services publics; *NAm:* **utility stocks,** valeurs *fpl* de services publics.

utilization, *n.* utilisation *f* (de qch.); **utilization of a patent,** exploitation *f* d'un brevet (d'invention); *Ind:* **utilization per cent,** taux *m* du rendement; **capacity utilization,** capacité *f* d'emploi.

utilize, *v.tr.* utiliser/se servir de (qch., qn); tirer profit de qch./mettre (qch.) en valeur.

V

vacancy, *n.* **1.** vacance *f*/poste *m* (à pourvoir)/poste vacant; **job vacancy,** poste à pourvoir; **to fill a vacancy,** pourvoir à un emploi/suppléer à une vacance; nommer qn à une vacance **2.** *pl.* (*a*) **vacancies** = chambres *f* à louer; **no vacancies** = complet (*b*) offres d'emploi(s).

vacant, *a.* vacant; (*job*) à pourvoir; (*room, apartment, etc.*) **to be vacant,** être libre; **vacant possession,** libre possession *f* (d'un immeuble); **house to be let with vacant possession,** maison *f* à louer avec jouissance immédiate; (*in advertisements*) **situations vacant,** offres *f* d'emploi(s).

vacate, *v.tr.* quitter (une maison, etc.); *Jur:* **to vacate the premises,** vider les lieux.

vacation, *n. NAm:* vacances *fpl*; **on vacation,** en vacances; **vacation with pay,** congé(s) payé(s).

valid, *a.* (contrat, etc.) valide/valable; (passeport) valide/en règle; **valid receipt,** quittance *f* valable; **to make valid,** valider/rendre valable (un contrat, etc.); **ticket valid for one month,** billet bon/valable pour un mois; **no longer valid,** périmé.

validate, *v.tr.* valider/rendre valable.

validation, *n.* validation *f* (d'un document, d'une signature, etc.)

validity, *n.* validité *f* (d'un contrat, d'un passeport, etc.); **to extend the validity of a credit,** proroger/prolonger la durée d'un crédit.

valium picnic, *n. US:* (*quiet day on New York Stock Exchange*) séance *f* morne/marché creux.

valorization, *n.* valorisation *f.*

valorize, *v.tr.* valoriser.

valuable, *a.* précieux; de valeur; **valuable article,** objet *m* de valeur; *Jur:* **for a valuable consideration,** à titre onéreux.

valuables, *n.pl.* objets *mpl* de (grande) valeur.

valuation, *n.* (*a*) évaluation *f*/estimation *f*/appréciation *f*/expertise *f*; *Jur:* prisée *f* et estimation; **market valuation,** évaluation boursière; **stock valuation,** évaluation des stocks; **to make a valuation (of goods, etc.),** faire l'expertise/expertiser (des marchandises, etc.); **to ask for a valuation,** faire estimer/faire expertiser/soumettre à une expertise (*b*) valeur *f* (estimée); **assessed valuation,** valeur fiscale; **customs valuation,** valeur en douane; (*accounting*) **directors' valuation,** valeur calculée par l'entreprise/évaluation interne à l'entreprise; **at a valuation of,** d'une valeur de; **it is worth £500 at (a) valuation,** l'expertise a établi la valeur à £500; **to set too high/too low a valuation on goods,** surestimer/sous-estimer la valeur de marchandises (*c*) valorisation *f* (d'un produit).

valuator, *n.* expert *m*; commissaire-priseur *m.*

value¹, *n.* (*a*) valeur *f*/prix *m*; **true value,** vraie valeur; **replacement value,** valeur de remplacement; **to be of value,** avoir de la valeur; **this watch is of little/of great value,** c'est une montre de peu de valeur/de grande valeur; **of no value,** sans valeur; **goods to the value of £50,** marchandise *f* d'une valeur de £50; **to lose value/to fall in value,** perdre de sa valeur/diminuer de valeur; se déprécier/se dévaluer/s'avilir; *Fin:* se dévaloriser; **loss of value/loss in value/fall in value,** perte *f*/diminution *f* de valeur; (*of currency*) **value below rate,** décote *f*; **to rise in value,** augmenter de valeur/s'apprécier; *Fin:* dévalorisation *f*; **to set a value (up)on sth.,** évaluer qch.; **to set a low value on the stock,** estimer à un bas prix la valeur des stocks/évaluer les stocks à un bas prix; **to set too high a value on sth.,** surévaluer qch./surestimer qch; **annual value,** rendement annuel (*b*) **book value/written-down value,** valeur comptable/*FrC:* valeur aux livres; **break-up value,** valeur à la casse/de liquidation; **commercial value/market value,** valeur vénale/valeur marchande/valeur négociable; *Fin:* cours *m*/valeur en Bourse; **of no commercial value,** sans valeur commerciale; **customs value,** valeur en douane; **decrease in value,** moins-value *f*; **exchange value/value in exchange,** valeur d'échange/contre-valeur *f*; **extrinsic value,** valeur-temps *f*/valeur extrinsèque; **face value/nominal value,** valeur nominale; **increase in value,** plus-value *f*; **insured value,** valeur assurée; **rateable value,** valeur locative imposable; **resale value,** valeur à la revente; (*of bond, etc.*) **redemption value,** valeur de remboursement; **surrender value of a policy,** valeur de rachat d'une police; **value at maturity,** valeur à l'échéance; **value date,** date *f*/jour *m* de valeur; date d'entrée en vigueur; **for value received,** valeur reçue; **value in use,** valeur d'usage (*c*) *Bank:* **capital value,** valeur en capital; **value in account,** valeur en compte; **value in gold currency,** valeur-or *f* (*d*) **to get good value for one's money,** en avoir pour son argent; **it is very good value,** c'est à un prix très avantageux/ce n'est pas cher.

value², *v.tr.* **to value (goods, damages),** évaluer/estimer/expertiser (des marchandises, des dégâts); faire l'expertise/l'évaluation (de marchandises, de dégâts); **to value furniture,** faire l'expertise/dresser l'état appréciatif d'un mobilier; **to have sth. valued,** soumettre qch. à une expertise/faire évaluer qch.

value-added, *a.* à la valeur ajoutée; **value-added tax (VAT),** taxe *f* à la valeur ajoutée (TVA).

valueless, *a.* sans valeur; **valueless stock** non-valeurs *fpl.*

valuer, *n.* expert *m*; **official valuer (o property, etc.)** commissaire-priseur *m.*

valuing, *n.* évaluation *f*/estimation *f.*

variability, *n.* variabilité *f* (des taux d'in térêt, etc.)

variable, 1. *a.* variable; **variable costs expenses,** frais *m* variables/proportion nels; **variable yield securities,** valeurs *f* à revenu variable; **income from variabl yield investments,** revenu *m* variable; **t quote variable exchange,** coter l'incertai **2.** *n.* variable *f*; *pl.* **variables,** éléments *mp* variables.

variance, *n.* variance *f*/écart *m*; **budge variance,** écart budgétaire; **cost variance** variance/écart des coûts; **variance analysis,** analyse *f* des écarts.

variation, *n.* (*a*) variation *f*; **annual/seas onal variations,** variations annuelles saisonnières (*b*) *Ins:* **variation of risk** modification *f* de risque.

variety, *n.* variété *f*; diversité *f*; *NAm:* **vari ety store,** bazar *m.*

vary, *v.tr.* **to vary the terms of a contract** modifier les clauses d'un contrat.

VAT, *n.* (= **value added tax),** TVA *f* (= taxe à la valeur ajoutée); **exclusive of excluding VAT,** hors TVA; **subject t VAT,** soumis à la TVA; **VATman,** = ins pecteur *m* de la TVA.

VDU, *n. Cmptr:* (= **visual display unit)** console *f* de visualisation/visuel *m.*

vehicle, *n.* (*a*) véhicule *m*; **commercial ve hicles,** véhicules commerciaux/utilitaires **freight vehicle/goods vehicle,** véhicule d transport de marchandises; **heavy good vehicle (HGV),** poids lourd *m*; **motor ve hicle,** voiture *f* (automobile) (*b*) **invest ment vehicle,** société *f* d'investissement; **h controls a property vehicle,** il dirige un société immobilière.

vend, *v.tr. esp. Jur:* vendre.

vending, *a.* **vending machine,** distributeur *m* automatique.

vendor, *n.* (*a*) vendeur, -euse (**of,** de); **street vendor,** marchand, -ande des quatre saisons; vendeur, -euse ambulant(e) (*b*) *Fin:* **vendor's shares,** actions *f* d'apport/de fondation (*c*) *Jur:* vendeur, -eresse.

venture, *n.* entreprise *f*/affaire *f*; projet *m*; **it is a new venture,** c'est une entreprise nouvelle/une affaire nouvelle/un projet nouveau; **joint venture,** coentreprise *f*/ affaire en participation; *FrC:* entreprise *f* en coparticipation; **joint venture assistance,** subvention *f* de groupe; **venture capital,** capital risque *m*.

venturer, *n.* **joint venturer,** coentrepreneur *m*.

verbal, *a.* verbal; **verbal agreement,** convention/entente verbale; **verbal offer,** offre verbale.

verification, *n.* vérification *f*/contrôle *m*.

verify, *v.tr.* vérifier/contrôler (des renseignements, des comptes).

vertical, *a.* vertical; **vertical concentration/ merger,** concentration verticale; **vertical integration,** intégration verticale; **vertical trustification,** cartellisation verticale.

vested, *a.* **vested interests,** droits acquis; **to have a vested interest in a concern,** avoir des capitaux investis dans une entreprise/ être intéressé dans une entreprise.

veto[1], *n.* veto *m*; **right of veto,** droit *m* de veto; **to use one's veto,** exercer son droit de veto.

veto[2], *v.tr.* mettre/opposer son veto (à qch).

viability, *n.* viabilité *f* (d'une entreprise, etc.).

viable, *a.* (*plan, etc.*) viable; durable; **commercially viable,** rentable.

vice-chairman, *n.* vice-président, -ente.

vice-chairmanship, *n.* vice-présidence *f*.

vice-presidency, *n.* vice-présidence *f*.

vice-president, *n.* *NAm:* vice-président, -ente.

video, *n.* vidéo *f*; **video clip,** bande *f* vidéo

promotionnelle/(bande) promo *f*; **video screen,** écran *m* video.

videoconferencing, *n.* vidéoconférence *f*.

videophone, *n.* visiophone *m*; **videophone conference,** visioconférence *f*.

visa[1], *n.* visa *m*; **transit visa,** visa de transit.

visa[2], *v.tr.* viser (un passeport)/apposer un visa à (un passeport).

visible, 1. *a.* visible; **visible exports,** exportations *f* visibles; **visible imports,** importations visibles **2.** *n.pl.* **visibles,** biens *mpl* visibles.

visual, *a.* **visual display unit (VDU),** console *f* de visualisation/visuel *m*.

vitiate, *v.tr.* vicier (un contrat, etc.); **to vitiate a transaction,** rendre une opération nulle.

vocational, *a.* professionnel; **vocational guidance,** orientation professionnelle; **vocational training,** formation professionnelle.

void[1], *a.* (*deed, contract, etc.*) nul; **to render null and void,** rendre nul et non avenu; **to make void,** annuler/rendre nul.

void[2], *v.tr.* résoudre/résilier/annuler (un contrat, etc.); annuler (une facture).

voidable, *a.* (contrat, etc.) résiliable/ annulable.

voidance, *n.* annulation *f* (d'un contrat, etc.).

volatility, *n.* volatilité *f* (d'une option).

volume, *n.* volume *m*; **sales volume,** volume de ventes; chiffre *m* d'affaires; *StExch:* **trading volume,** volume de transactions effectuées; **volume of business,** volume des affaires; **volume of output,** volume de la production; **profit volume ratio,** rapport *m* profit-ventes.

voluntary, *a.* (*a*) volontaire; bénévole; **voluntary export restraint (VER),** restriction *f* volontaire des exportations/auto-limitation *f* des exportations/quotas *mpl* volontaires à l'export; **voluntary liquida-**

tion, liquidation *f* volontaire (*b*) facultatif; **voluntary insurance,** assurance facultative.

vote[1], *n.* (*a*) vote *m*/scrutin *m*; **postal vote,** vote par correspondance; **to take the vote,** procéder au scrutin; **to cast one's vote,** voter; **secret vote,** scrutin secret; **to pass a vote of thanks to s.o.,** voter des remerciements à qn (*b*) (*individual vote*) voix *f*/suffrage *m*; **to give one's vote to s.o.,** donner son vote/sa voix à qn; voter pour qn; **to put a question to the vote/to take a vote on a question,** mettre une question aux voix; **number of votes (cast),** nombre *m* de voix; **(chairman's) casting vote,** voix prépondérante (du président); *coll.* **to lose the trade-union vote,** perdre les suffrages/le vote des syndicalistes (*c*) **to have the vote,** avoir le droit de vote (*d*) motion *f*/résolution *f*; **to carry a vote,** adopter une résolution.

vote[2], **1.** *v.i.* voter (**for, against,** pour, contre); donner sa voix/son vote (**for sth.,** pour qch.); prendre part/participer au vote; **to vote by (a) show of hands,** voter à main levée; **to vote by proxy,** voter par procuration **2.** *v.tr.* (*a*) **to vote a sum,** voter une somme (*b*) **to vote s.o. in,** élire qn; **to vote s.o. out,** rejeter qn.

voter, *n.* votant, -ante.

voting[1], *a.* (*assembly, member*) votant.

voting[2], *n.* (participation *f* au) vote; scrutin *m*; **voting paper,** bulletin *m* de vote; **voting rights,** droit *m* de vote (des actionnaires).

vouch for, *v.tr.* répondre de/se porter garant (de).

voucher, *n.* (*a*) pièce justificative; *Book-k:* pièce comptable (*b*) **voucher for receipt/sales voucher,** récépissé *m*/quittance *f*; **credit card sales voucher,** facturette *f* (*c*) fiche *f*/reçu *m*/reconnaissance *f*/bon *m* d'échange; **cash voucher,** bon de caisse; **gift voucher,** bon d'achat; chèque-cadeau *m*; **luncheon voucher (LV),** chèque-repas *m*/chèque-restaurant *m*.

W

wage, *n.* salaire *m*/paie *f*/paye *f*; **current
rate of wages/current wage rate,** taux
actuel des salaires; **fixed wage,** salaire
fixe/ fixe *m*; **general level of wages/general
wage level,** niveau général des salaires;
minimum wage, salaire minimum; **index-
linked minimum wage** = salaire minimum
interprofessionnel de croissance(SMIC);
hourly wage, salaire horaire; **real wage,**
salaire réel; **supplementary wage,** supplément *m* au salaire normal; sursalaire *m*;
wage(s) agreement, convention *f* des
salaires/accord salarial; **wage(s) bill,**
masse salariale/charges salariales; **wage
claims,** revendications *f* de salaire; **wage
cuts,** réductions *f(pl)* de salaires; **wage
differential,** écart *m* des salaires; hiérarchie *f* salariale; **wage earner,** soutien *m*
de famille; **wage freeze,** blocage *m* des
salaires; **wage fund,** fonds *m* disponible
pour la rétribution du travail; **wage increase,** augmentation *f* de salaire; **wage
negotiations,** négociations salariales;
wage(s) policy, politique salariale/poli-
tique des salaires; **wage-price spiral,** spirale *f* d'inflation par les salaires; **wage
rate,** taux *m* des salaires; **wage scale,**
échelle *f* des salaires; **wage sheet,** feuille
f de salaire/de paie; **wage structure,** structure *f* des salaires; **weekly wage(s),** salaire
hebdomadaire.

wage-earner, *n.* salarié, -ée.

wage-earning, *a.* **wage-earning population,** les salariés *m*.

wager, *n.* pari *m*/gageure *f*.

waiter, *n.* (*in restaurant*) serveur *m*;
StExch: coursier *m*.

waiting, *n.* **waiting time,** temps mort.

waitress, *n.* (*in restaurant*) serveuse *f*.

waitressing, *n.* travail *m* (de serveurs et
serveuses) de restaurant.

waiver, *n.* **waiver of a claim,** désistement *m*
de revendication; **waiver clause,** clause *f*
d'abandon/de désistement; *Jur:* **waiver of
a right,** abandon *m* d'un droit; renonciation *f* à un droit.

walk, *v.i. NAm:* = **walk out.**

walk out *v.i.* (*a*) se mettre en grève (*b*)
partir.

walk-out, *n.* grève *f* (surprise).

wall, *n.* **tariff walls,** barrières douanières.

Wall Street, *n.* (quartier *m* de la) Bourse
de New York; Wall Street.

wanted, *a.* (*in advertisements*) **secretary
wanted,** on demande une secrétaire; **situations wanted,** demandes *fpl* d'emploi;
Fin: **stocks wanted,** valeurs demandées.

war, *n.* guerre *f*; **price war,** guerre des prix;
tariff war, guerre des tarifs.

warehouse[1], *n.* (*a*) entrepôt *m*; magasin *m*;
bonded warehouse, entrepôt de douane; **at
warehouse,** à l'entrepôt/en entrepôt/à
prendre à l'entrepôt; **(price) at /ex warehouse,** prix *m* départ entrepôt; **warehouse
keeper,** magasinier *m;* **warehouse charges,**
frais *mpl* de magasinage/ d'entreposage
(*b*) **furniture warehouse,** garde-meuble *m*.

warehouse[2], *v.tr.* entreposer/mettre en
entrepôt.

warehousing, *n.* (*a*) entreposage *m*; magasinage *m*; **warehousing charges,** droits *mpl*/
frais *mpl* de magasinage/d'entreposage;

269

warehousing system, système *m* d'entrepôt (*b*) parcage *m* d'actions.

warning, *n.* avertissement *m.*

warrant[1], *n.* (*a*) **warrant for goods/warehouse warrant,** certificat *m* d'entrepôt/ warrant *m*; **to issue a warehouse warrant for goods,** warranter des marchandises; **issuing of a warehouse warrant,** warrantage *m*; **goods covered by a warehouse warrant,** marchandises warrantées (*b*) **dividend warrant,** chèque *m* dividende; **interest warrant,** mandat *m* d'intérêts; **warrant indenture,** contrat *m* de droits d'achat d'actions; **share warrant,** warrant/droit *m* d'achat d'actions; **warrant for payment,** ordonnance *f* de paiement (*c*) **search warrant,** mandat *m* de perquisition; **warrant for arrest,** mandat d'arrêt.

warrant[2], *v.tr.* garantir; warranter.

warranted, *a.* garanti; warranté.

warrantee, *n.* porteur, -euse d'une garantie.

warrantor, *n.* répondant *m*/garant *m.*

warranty, *n.* (bulletin *m* de) garantie *f*; (*in contract*) clause pénale; **under warranty,** sous garantie.

wastage, *n.* **1.** (*a*) perte *f*; coulage *m*; **natural wastage,** diminution naturelle de la main-d'œuvre (*par décès, retraite, démission, etc*) (*b*) gaspillage *m* **2.** *coll.* déchets *mpl*/rebuts *mpl.*

waste[1], *a.* (matière, marchandises, etc.) de rebut; (produit) résiduel/non utilisé/ perdu; **waste material,** déchet *m.*

waste[2], *n.* **1.** gaspillage *m* (d'argent, etc.); coulage *m* **2.** déchets *mpl*/rebut(s) *m*(*pl*); **industrial waste,** déchets industriels; **waste disposal,** élimination *f* des déchets.

waste[3], *v.tr.* gaspiller (son argent, son temps, etc.).

wasteful, *a.* **wasteful expenditure,** dépenses *fpl* en pure perte; gaspillage *m.*

way, *n.* **to pay one's own way,** couvrir ses frais; *Jur:* **right of way,** droit *m* de passage; servitude *f.*

waybill, *n.* lettre *f* de voiture/de mouvement; feuille *f* de route; bulletin *m*/ bordereau *m* d'expédition.

weaken, *v.i.* **the market has weakened,** le marché a fléchi.

wealth, *n.* richesse(s) *f*(*pl*); opulence *f*; luxe *m*; **wealth tax,** impôt *m* de solidarité sur la fortune.

wear, *n.* usure *f*/détérioration *f* par l'usure; **wear and tear,** usure; dépréciation *f*/détérioration; dégradation *f* (d'un immeuble); **fair wear and tear,** usure normale.

week, *n.* semaine *f*; **earnings per week,** salaire *m* hebdomadaire.

weekday, *n.* jour *m* ouvrable.

weekly, **1.** *a.* hebdomadaire **2.** *adv.* par semaine; tous les huit jours; hebdomadairement **3.** *n.* journal *m*/revue *f* hebdomadaire/hebdomadaire *m.*

weigh, **1.** *v.tr.* peser (un colis, etc.) **2.** *v.i.* peser; avoir du poids; **parcel weighing two kilos,** paquet *m* qui pèse deux kilos.

weighing, *n.* pesée *f* (de denrées, etc.); **weighing machine,** appareil *m* de pesage *m*; balance *f.*

weight, *n.* **1.** poids *m*; **excess weight,** excédent *m* de poids; **weight when empty,** poids à vide; **to sell by weight,** vendre au poids; **net weight,** poids net; **two kilos in weight,** pesant deux kilos/d'un poids de deux kilos **2.** **weights and measures,** poids et mesures *f.*

weighted, *a.* *PolEc:* **weighted average,** moyenne pondérée; **weighted index,** indice pondéré.

weighting, *n.* **London weighting allowance,** indemnité *f* pour Londres.

wharf, *n.* débarcadère *m*/quai *m*/entrepôt *m* maritime; **ex wharf,** à prendre sur quai; **wharf dues,** droits *m* de quai.

wharfage, *n.* droits *mpl* de quai.

wharfinger, *n.* gardien, -ienne de quai.

wheeler-dealer, *n.* *NAm:* brasseur *m* d'affaires (*plus ou moins en marge de la loi*).

White, *a.* blanc; **white knight,** chevalier blanc; **white squire defence,** technique *f* de sauvetage "page blanc".

wholesale, **1.** *n.* (vente en) gros *m*; **wholesale and retail,** le gros et le détail **2.** *a.* (*a*) en gros/de gros; **wholesale dealer,** marchand, -ande commerçant, -ante en gros; grossiste *mf*; **wholesale goods,** marchandises *f* de gros; **wholesale price,** prix *m* de gros; **wholesale price index,** indice *m* des prix de gros; **wholesale trade,** commerce *m* de gros/le gros; **wholesale shop,** maison *f* de gros (*b*) **wholesale manufacture,** fabrication *f* en série **3.** *adv.* en gros; **to buy/to sell wholesale,** acheter/ vendre en gros; faire le gros.

wholesaler, *n.* (*a*) commerçant, -ante/ marchand, -ante en gros; grossiste *mf* (*b*) **wholesaler's,** maison *f* de gros.

widening, *n.* **widening of capital,** élargisse-ment *m* du capital.

wildcat, *a.* **wildcat strike,** grève *f* sauvage.

will, *n.* testament *m*.

windbill, *n.* billet *m*/effet *m*/traite *f*/papier *m* de complaisance.

windfall, *n.* **windfall profits,** profits inattendus/imprévus.

winding-up, *n.* liquidation *f* (d'une socié-té); **voluntary winding up,** liquidation vo-lontaire; **winding up order,** ordre *m* de mise en règlement judiciaire.

windmill, *n.* = **windbill**.

window, *n.* (shop) window, vitrine *f*; **window display,** étalage *m*; *Book-k* **window dressing,** habillage *m* de bilan.

wind up, *v.tr.* liquider (une société); régler/ clôturer (un compte); **to wind up a meet-ing,** clore une séance.

wipe off, *v.tr.* **to wipe off a debt,** annuler/ liquider une dette.

wipe out, *n.* *NAm:* perte sèche; perte totale.

withdraw, *v.tr.* (*a*) **to withdraw a sum of money,** retirer une somme d'argent (de la caisse d'épargne, etc.)/faire un retrait; **sum withdrawn from the bank,** somme re-tirée/retrait *m* (d'une somme d'argent) d'un compte bancaire (*b*) **to withdraw an order,** annuler une commande.

withdrawal, *n.* retrait *m*; **withdrawal of a sum of money,** retrait d'une somme d'argent; **withdrawal of capital,** retrait de fonds; **withdrawal of labour,** retrait de la main-d'œuvre/grève officielle; *Bank: etc:* **withdrawal notice,** avis *m* de retrait de fonds.

withholding, *n.* *NAm:* **withholding tax,** impôt retenu à la source/retenue fiscale.

within, *adv.* **within 10 days,** dans un délai de 10 jours/d'ici 10 jours.

woman, *n.* femme *f*; **a married woman,** une femme mariée; **a single woman,** une (femme) célibataire; **women's rights,** droits *mpl* de la femme.

work[1], *n.* **1.** travail *m*/ouvrage *m*; **clerical work,** travaux administratifs; **day's work,** (travail d'une) journée; **workday,** jour ouvrable; **factory at work,** usine *f* en ac-tivité; **work assignment,** distribution *f* des tâches; **work in progress,** (*i*) travail en cours (*ii*) produit *m* semi-fini; **work study,** étude *f* du travail **2.** (*employment*) travail/ emploi *m*; **to be out of work,** être sans travail/sans emploi; au chômage **3.** **work to rule,** grève *f* du zèle **4.** *pl.* **works,** usine *f*/atelier *m*; **chemical works,** usine de pro-duits chimiques; **engineering works,** ate-lier de construction de machines; **public works,** travaux *mpl* publics; **steel works,** aciérie *f*; **works committee/council,** comité *m* d'entreprise.

work[2], *v.i.* **1.** travailler; **to work to rule,** faire la grève du zèle **2.** (*of machine, etc.*) fonctionner.

workable, *a.* (projet, plan) réalisable/ exécutable/pratique.

worker, *n.* ouvrier, -ière; travailleur,

-euse; **worker participation,** participation ouvrière; **worker representation,** représentation *f* du personnel.

workforce, *n.* main-d'œuvre *f*; personnel *m.*

working[1], *a.* **1.** (*machine, etc.*) qui fonctionne **2.** **working agreement (between two firms),** accord *m*/entente *f*/convention *f* (entre deux sociétés).

working[2], *n.* **1.** travail *m*; **working conditions,** conditions *fpl* de travail; **working day,** jour *m* ouvrable; **usual working hours,** heures (habituelles) de travail; **the working class,** la classe ouvrière; **working population,** population active **2.** **working account,** compte *m* d'exploitation; **working capital,** capital *m* d'exploitation; fonds *mpl* de roulement; **working capital fund,** compte *m* d'avances; **working expenses,** frais généraux; frais d'exploitation; **working interest,** participation *f* d'exploitation; **working party,** groupe *m* de travail **3.** marche *f*/fonctionnement *m* (d'un appareil); **to be in (good) working order,** (bien) fonctionner.

workload, *n.* travail (assigné).

workman, *n.* ouvrier *m*/artisan *m*; **workmen's compensation insurance,** assurance *f* contre les accidents du travail.

workmanship, *n.* exécution *f*/qualité *f* (d'un travail); fini *m*; façon *f*; maîtrise *f*; **expert workmanship,** travail *m* de spécialiste; **sound/fine workmanship,** travail soigné.

work off, *v.tr.* **to work off a stock of goods,** écouler un stock de marchandises.

work out, **1.** *v.tr.* (*a*) élaborer (un projet); **the plan is being worked out,** le projet est à l'étude (*b*) examiner (un compte); établir/calculer (un prix) **2.** *v.i.* **the total works out at £9,** le montant s'élève à £9.

workshop, *n.* atelier *m.*

workstation, *n.* *Cmptr:* station *f* de travail.

world, *n.* (*a*) **the commercial world,** le commerce; **the financial world,** le monde de la finance; **the third world,** le tiers monde; **the world of high finance,** la haute finance (*b*) **world economy,** conjoncture économique mondiale; **world exports,** exportations mondiales; **world markets,** marchés mondiaux/internationaux; **trends in world trade,** tendances *fpl* du commerce international.

worldwide, *a.* universel/mondial.

worth, **1.** *a.* **to be worth so much,** valoir tant; **to be worth nothing,** ne rien valoir; **what is the franc worth?** combien vaut le franc? **two diamonds worth £50 000 each,** deux diamants *m* valant £50 000 chacun **2.** *n.* valeur *f*; **net worth,** situation *f* nette; valeur nette; **of great worth,** de grande valeur; **of little worth,** de peu de valeur; **of no worth,** d'aucune valeur; **give me ten pound's worth of petrol,** donnez-moi pour dix livres d'essence; **£50 worth of goods,** des marchandises *f* pour une valeur de £50.

worthless, *a.* sans valeur; **worthless bill,** titre *m* sans valeur; non-valeur *f.*

writ, *n.* *Jur:* ordonnance *f*/assignation *f.*

write, *v.tr.* écrire (une lettre, etc.).

write-down[1], *n.* moins-value *f*; dépréciation *f*; décote *f.*

write down[2], *v.tr.* **1.** noter (qch.) par écrit; marquer/noter (ses dépenses, etc.) **2.** *Fin:* réduire (la valeur du capital, des stocks); **written down value,** valeur *f* comptable/*FrC:* valeur aux livres.

write off, *v.tr.* (*a*) *Fin:* **to write off capital,** réduire le capital; amortir le capital (*b*) **to write off a bad debt,** défalquer une mauvaise créance; passer une créance par profits et pertes; **to write so much off for wear and tear,** déduire tant pour l'usure; **my car had to be written off,** ma voiture est une perte totale.

write-off, *n.* perte sèche; **my car is a complete write-off,** ma voiture est une perte totale.

write out, *v.tr.* **to write out a cheque (to**

s.o.), établir/faire/libeller un chèque (à l'ordre de qn).

write up, *v.tr.* mettre (son agenda, sa comptabilité, etc.) à jour.

writing down, *n.* **1.** inscription *f* **2.** *Fin:* réduction *f* (de capital, de stocks).

writing off, *n.* **1.** amortissement *m* (du capital) **2.** défalcation *f* (d'une créance).

X

xerography, *n.* xérographie *f.*

Xerox, *n. R.t.m.* **Xerox copy,** copie *f*
xérographique; photocopie *f*; **Xerox
machine,** machine *f* Xerox; machine à
photocopier/photocopieur *m*/photoco-
pieuse *f.*

Y

year, *n.* an *m*/année *f*; **peak year,** année record; **the year of a wine,** le millésime d'un vin; **base year,** année de référence; **calendar year,** année civile; **company's financial year,** exercice *m* comptable; **financial year/tax year,** année budgétaire; **fiscal year,** année d'exercice; exercice (financier); **current (fiscal) year,** l'exercice en cours; **year end,** fin *f* d'exercice; **year end audit,** vérification *f* comptable de fin d'exercice; **year's purchase,** taux *m* de capitalisation des bénéfices; *Book-k:* **year ended 31 Dec. 1980,** exercice clos le 31 déc. 1980; **year of assessment,** année d'imposition; **the year under review,** l'exercice écoulé; **valid for one year,** valable pour un an.

yearbook, *n. StExch: etc:* annuaire *m*.

year-earlier, *a. US: F:* de l'année précédente.

year-later, *a. US: F:* de l'année prochaine.

yearly, 1. *a.* annuel; **yearly accounts,** comptes annuels; **yearly payment,** annuité *f*; **debt redeemable by yearly payments,** dette *f* annuitaire; **yearly premium,** prime annuelle **2.** *adv.* annuellement.

yellow, *a. Tel:* **yellow pages,** les pages *f* jaunes (de l'annuaire téléphonique).

yield[1], *n.* rendement *m* (d'un capital, etc.); revenu *m* (d'une mise de fonds, etc.); **bond yield,** rendement d'une obligation; **current yield/flat yield,** rendement/taux *m* de rendement; **earnings yield,** rendement; **gross yield,** rendement brut; **annual interest yield gross,** taux *m* de rendement actuariel brut; **fixed yield,** rendement constant; **fixed yield investment,** placement *m* à revenu fixe; *(industry, etc.)* **in full yield,** en plein rapport/en plein rendement; **tax yields,** montant *m* des recettes fiscales; **variable yield investment,** placement *m* à revenu variable; **yield capacity,** productivité *f*; **yield curve,** courbe *f* des taux; **yield gap,** prime *f* de risque; **yield method,** méthode *f* du rendement effectif; **yield to maturity,** rendement à (l')échéance.

yield[2], *v.tr.* **1.** rapporter/produire/donner; **money that yields interest,** argent *m* qui produit des intérêts/argent qui rapporte; **shares that yield high interest,** actions *fpl* à rendement élevé; **to yield an income,** créer un revenu; **to yield (a) 5% (dividend),** produire/rapporter un dividende de 5% **2.** renoncer (à un droit).

yuppie, *n.* (= **young urban professional**), jeune cadre ambitieux/jeune loup *m*/NAP *mf*.

Z

Z, *n*. **Z chart,** diagramme en Z/graphique *m* en dents de scie.

zero, *n*. zéro *m*; (*of shares, etc.*) **to fall to zero,** tomber à zéro; **zero coupon (bonds),** (obligations émises à) coupon zéro; **zero base budgeting (ZBB),** système/technique du budget à base zéro (BBZ).

zero-rated, *a*. **books are zero-rated (for VAT),** il y a un taux zéro (de TVA) sur les livres/les livres sont taxés à un taux zéro.

zero-rating, *n*. taux *m* zéro.

zip code, *n*. *NAm:* **zip code,** code postal.

zone, *n*. zone *f*; **free zone,** zone franche; **sterling/franc zone,** la zone sterling/la zone franc; **time zone,** fuseau *m* horaire; **wage zone,** zone de salaires.

COMMON ABBREVIATIONS—ABRÉVIATIONS USUELLES

a.a.r./AAR	**against all risks,** contre tous risques
a/c, A/C	**account,** compte, c(pte)
acc.	**accepted,** accepté
acce.	**acceptance,** acceptation, acc.
acct.	**account,** compte, c(pte)
accy	**accountancy,** comptabilité
a.c.v.	**actual cash value,** valeur effective au comptant
ad.	**advertisement,** annonce
admin.	**administration,** administration
ad val.	**ad valorem,** ad valorem, ad val.
agcy	**agency,** agence, agce
agt	**agent,** commissionnaire, caire
am	**ante meridiem,** avant midi
amt	**amount,** montant
a/o.	**account of,** pour le compte de
Apr.	**April,** avril
appro.	**approval; on appro.,** à l'essai
approx.	**approximately,** approximativement; environ, env.
a/r.	**all risks,** tous risques
asap	**as soon as possible,** aussitôt/dès que possible; dans les meilleurs délais
ass.	**assurance,** assurance, asse
asst	**assistant,** adjoint; assistant
a/s.	**at sight,** (payable) à vue
Aug.	**August,** août
av.	**average,** (*i*) moyenne (*ii*) avaries
avdp.	**avoirdupois,** avoirdupois
back.	**backwardation,** déport, D.
bal.	**balance,** balance, bce; solde
b&b	**bed and breakfast**
b/d.	**(balance) brought down,** solde à nouveau
b/e., B/E	**bill of exchange,** lettre de change, l/c; traite, T/.
b/f, B/F	**(balance) brought forward,** (solde) reporté/report
bkge	**brokerage,** courtage, cage
B/L	**bill of lading,** connaissement, connt
BO	**1. branch office,** agence/succursale **2. buyer's option**
b/o., B/O	**(balance) brought over,** (solde) reporté
b.p., B/P	**bill payable,** billet à payer, b. à p.; effet à payer, e. à p.
b.r., B/R	**bill receivable,** billet à recevoir, b. à r.; effet à recevoir, e. à r.
Bros	**Brothers,** Frères, Frs
b.s., B/S	**1. balance-sheet,** bilan **2. bill of sale,** acte/contrat de vente
c.	**1. coupon,** coupon, c. **2. centime,** centime, c., cent.
c.a., CA	**1. current account,** compte courant, c/c **2. current assets,** actif
C/A, c/a.	**1. capital account,** compte de capital **2. current account,** compte courant, c/c.
cc	**cubic centimetre,** centimètre cube
c.&f., C&F	**cost and freight,** coût et fret, CF
CB	**cash book,** livre de caisse
CBD	**cash before delivery,** paiement avant la livraison
c.d.	**cum dividend,** coupon attaché, c. at(t).
c/d., C/D	**carried down,** à reporter
cent.	**centime,** centime, c., cent.
cert.	**certificate,** certificat, certif.

CF	**carriage forward,** port dû, p.d.
c/f., C/F	**(to be) carried forward,** à reporter
c.i.f., CIF	**cost, insurance and freight,** coût, assurance, fret, CAF, c.a.f.
cl	**centilitre,** *NAm:* **centiliter,** centilitre, cl
cm	**centimetre,** *NAm:* **centimeter,** centimètre, cm
cmdty	**commodity,** matière première
C/N	1. **credit note,** note de crédit 2. **cover note,** lettre de couverture
Co.	**Company,** compagnie, Cie; société, St^é, Sté
c/o	**care of …,** aux (bons) soins de …
c.o.d.	**cash on delivery,** *NAm:* **collect on delivery,** livraison contre remboursement
com(m).	**commission,** commission, com.
cons.	**consols,** consolidés
cont'd	**continued,** à suivre
convd	**converted,** converti, conv.
corr.	**correspondence,** correspondance, corresp.
corp.	**corporation,** corporation
cp.	**coupon,** coupon, coup.
CP	**carriage paid,** franco, fco; port payé, p.p.
cr.	**credit,** avoir, Av.; crédit, cr.
cu	**cubic,** cube
cum.	**cumulative,** cumulatif, cum.
cum div.	**cum dividend,** coupon attaché, c. at(t).; exercice attaché, ex. att.
c.w.o.	**cash with order,** payable à la commande
cwt	**hundredweight** = 50kg
d.	**day,** jour, jr
DA	**documents against acceptance,** documents contre acceptation, DA
D/A	**deposit account,** compte de dépôt
DAP	**documents against payment,** documents contre paiement, DP
db.	**debenture,** obligation, obl.
d.b.	**day book,** journal, jl
d.d.	1. **days after date,** jours de date, j/d 2. **due date,** échéance
DD	**direct debit,** prélèvement automatique
Dec.	**December,** décembre, déc.
def.	**deferred,** différé, dif.
del.	**delegation,** délégation, dél.
dely	**delivery,** livraison, liv(r).
denom.	**denomination,** coupure, coup.
dept	1. **department,** service, serv. 2. **depot,** dépôt
Dept	*Adm:* **Department,** département, dép.
dft	**draft,** traite, T/., tr.
dir., Dir.	**director,** directeur
disc.	**discount,** escompte, esc.
div.	**dividend,** dividende, div.
do.	**ditto,** idem, id.
dol.	**dollar,** dollar, dol.
doz.	**dozen,** douzaine, douz., dz.
dr., Dr	**debtor,** débiteur, débit, dr.
d.s.	**days after sight,** jours de vue, j/v.
E&OE, e.&o.e.	**errors and omissions excepted,** erreur ou omission exceptée, e.o.o.e., e.&o.e.; sauf erreur ou omission, s.e.&o.
ed.	**edition,** édition, éd(it).
e.g.	**exempli gratia/for example,** par exemple, p.ex.
enc., encl.	**enclosure(s)/enclosed,** pièce(s) jointe(s), PJ; inclus, incl.
esp.	**especially,** spécialement
est.	**established,** fondé

ex.	1. **example**, exemple, ex. 2. **exchange**, échange 3. **extra**, extra; supplément
Exch.	1. **exchange**, échange; Bourse 2. **Exchequer**, Échiquier
excl.	1. **excluding** 2. **exclusive**
ex cp.	**ex coupon**, ex-coupon, ex-c(oup).
ex div.	**ex dividend**, ex-dividende, ex-d.
exec.	1. **executive** 2. **executor**
exp.	1. **expense(s)**, dépense(s) 2. **export**, exportation, exp.
F.	**franc**, franc, F., f.
f.a.a.	**free of all average**, franc de toutes avaries
f.a.s./FAS	**free alongside ship**, franco quai/franco long du bord, FLB
f/c	**for cash**, comptant
Feb.	**February**, février, fév.
fed.	1. **federation**, fédération 2. **Federal**, fédéral
Fed.	**federal reserve (system)**, (système de) Réserve fédérale
f.g.a.	**free of general average**, franc d'avaries communes, FAC
F/H	**freehold**, en toute propriété, en tte ppté
fl.oz.	**fluid ounce**
f.o.b./FOB	**free on board**, franco de bord, FOB, f.o.b./franco à bord, f. à b.
f.o.c./FOC	**free of charge**, franco, fco/gratis; sans frais, SF
f.o.r., FOR	**free on rail**, franco sur rail/franco gare/franco wagon, FOR
f.o.t./FOT	**free on truck**, franco camion
f.p.	**fully paid**, libéré, lib.
f.p.a.	**free of particular average**, franc d'avaries particulières, FAP
Fri.	**Friday**, vendredi
F/S	**financial statement**, situation de trésorerie/état financier
ft	**foot, feet**, pied(s)
g	**gram**, gramme, g
g/a.	**general average**, avaries communes, a.c.
gal	**gallon**, gallon
gds	**goods**, marchandise, mise
Govt	**Government**, gouvernement
GRT	**gross register ton**, tonneau de jauge brute
gr.wt	**gross weight**, poids brut
GT	**gross tonnage**, tonnage brut
GTC	**good-till-cancelled**, ordre à révocation
HO	**head office**, siège social
HP	**hire purchase**, vente à crédit/à tempérament
HQ	**headquarters**, quartier général
hr(s)	**hour(s)**, heure(s), h.
id.	**idem**, idem, id.
i.e.	**id est/that is to say**, c'est-à-dire, c.-à-d.
imp.	**import**, importation, imp.
ind.	**industry**, industrie, ind.
in(s)	**inch(es)**, pouce(s)
Inc.	**Incorporated**
incl.	1. **included**, inclus, incl. 2. **including**, y compris 3. **inclusive**, inclusivement
inf(o).	**information**, information/renseignements, rens.
ins.	**insurance**, assurance, asse
inst.	1. **instant**, courant, ct 2. **institute**, institut
int.	**interest**, intérêt, int.
intl	**international**, international
inv.	**invoice**, facture, fre
IOU	**I owe you**, reconnaissance de dette

J/A	**joint account,** compte (con)joint
Jan.	**January,** janvier, janv.
jnr, jr	**junior,** jeune, Je; fils
Jul.	**July,** juillet
Jun.	**June,** juin
kg	**kilo(gram),** kilo(gramme), kg
kl	**kilolitre,** *NAm:* **kiloliter,** kilolitre, kl
km	**kilometre,** *NAm:* **kilometer,** kilomètre, km
km/h	**kilometres per hour,** kilomètre heure, km/h
kt	**kiloton,** kilotonne, kt
kW	**kilowatt,** kilowatt, KW
kWh	**kilowatt-hour,** kilowatt-heure, KWh
l	**litre,** *NAm:* **liter,** litre, l
lat.	**latitude,** latitude
lb	**pound (weight),** livre
l/c	**letter of credit,** lettre de crédit, l/cr.
led.	**ledger,** grand(-)livre, g.l.
Ltd	**Limited (company),** (*i*) (société) anonyme, SA (*ii*) (société) à responsabilité limitée, SARL; *FrC:* (compagnie) limitée, Ltée
m	**1. metre,** *NAm:* **meter,** mètre, m **2. month,** mois, m
m/a	**my account,** mon compte, m/c.
Mar.	**March,** mars
max.	**maximum,** maximum, max.
memo.	**memorandum,** memorandum
Messrs	**Messieurs,** MM.
mfd	**manufactured,** manufacturé, fabriqué
mfrs	**manufacturers,** fabricants
mg	**milligram,** milligramme
min.	**minimum,** minimum, min.
misc.	**miscellaneous,** divers
mm	**millimetre,** *NAm:* **millimeter,** millimètre, mm
MO	**1. mail order (business),** vente par correspondance, VPC **2. money order,** mandat-poste, MP
m/o	**my order,** mon ordre, m/o.
Mon.	**Monday,** lundi
mortg.	**mortgage,** hypothèque, hyp.
mpg	**miles per gallon** = litres au cent (kilomètres)
mph	**miles per hour** = kilomètre-heure
Mr	**Mister,** Monsieur, M.
Mrs	Madame, Mme
Ms	Madame, Mme; Mademoiselle, Mlle
MS	**manuscript,** manuscrit, MS
m/u, M/U	**making-up-price,** cours de compensation, cc.
n.	**1. name,** nom, N. **2. nominal,** nominal, N.
nat.	**national,** national
NB	**nota bene**
n.c.v.	**no commercial value,** sans valeur commerciale
NF, N/F	**no funds,** défaut de provision
no.	**number,** numéro, n°
nos	**numbers,** numéros, nos
Nov.	**November,** novembre, nov.
NRT	**net register ton,** tonneau de jauge nette
n.s.f.	**not sufficient funds,** insuffisance de provision

o/a	**on account of,** à valoir
o/c	**overcharge,** surcharge
Oct.	**October,** octobre, oct.
o/d., O/D	**1. on demand,** sur demande, à vue **2. overdrawn,** à découvert; **overdraft,** découvert
offs	**offices,** bureaux, burx
o/h	**overheads,** frais généraux, FG
ono	**or near(est) offer**
o.p.	**out of print,** épuisé
ord.	**order,** commande
o.s.	**out of stock,** manque en magasin; épuisé
OT	**overtime,** heures supplémentaires
Our ref.	**our reference,** notre référence, N/Réf.
oz	**ounce,** once
p	**1. penny, pence 2. page,** page, p. **3. premium,** prime
p.a.	**1. per annum,** par an, p.a. **2. particular average,** avaries particulières, a.p.
P&L	**profit and loss,** pertes et profits
p&p	**postage and packing,** port et emballage
pat.	**patent,** brevet
pat.pend.	**patent pending,** demande de brevet déposée
pc.	**1. per cent.** pour cent **2. petty cash,** petite caisse **3. price current,** prix courant
pd	**paid,** acquitté
per pro.	**per procurationem,** par procuration, p. pon
PG	**paying guest,** pensionnaire
pkg.	**1. package,** paquet **2. packing,** emballage
pkt	**packet,** paquet
PN, P/N	**promissory note,** billet à ordre, B/.
PO	**postal order,** mandat-poste, MP
p.p.	**1. per procurationem,** par procuration, p.pon **2. prepaid,** prépayé **3. postpaid,** affranchi
pp.	**pages,** pages, pp.
pr.	**price,** prix, px
pref.	**preference,** (actions de) préférence, préf.
Pres.	**President,** président
prox.	**proximo,** (mois) prochain, pr.
PS	**postscript,** post-scriptum, PS
pt	**1. payment,** paiement **2. pint,** pinte, *FrC:* chopine
PTO	**please turn over,** tournez s'il vous plaît, TSVP
p.v.	**par value,** valeur au pair/parité
qnty, qty.	**quantity,** quantité, q.
qt	**quart**
qtr	**1. quarter,** quart **2. quarterly,** trimestriel
RD	**refer(red) to drawer,** retour au tireur
rd, Rd	**road,** rue, r.
rcvd	**received,** reçu; pour acquit
re.	**regarding,** en ce qui concerne
recpt, rept	**receipt,** reçu/quittance
red.	**redeemable,** amortissable; remboursable, remb.
ref.	**reference,** référence, Réf.
regd	**registered,** recommandé, r.
rep.	**representative,** représentant
rly	**railway,** chemin de fer, ch. de f.
RP	**reply paid,** réponse payée, r.p.
RR	*NAm:* **railroad,** chemin de fer, ch. de f.
RSVP	**please reply,** répondez s'il vous plaît, RSVP

s.a.e.	**stamped addressed envelope,** enveloppe timbrée à votre adresse
s.a.s.e.	*NAm:* **self addressed stamped envelope,** enveloppe timbrée à votre adresse
Sat.	**Saturday,** samedi
sec.	**1. secretary,** secrétaire **2. second,** seconde
Sept.	**September,** septembre, sept.
sgd	**signed,** signé, s.
sh., shr.	**share,** action, act.; titre, t.
sit.	**situation,** emploi; **sits.vac.,** offres d'emploi
Snr	**senior,** aîné; père
s.o.	**1. seller's option,** prime vendeur **2. standing order,** ordre de transfert permanent **3. someone,** quelqu'un, qn
s.o.p.	**standard operating procedure,** procédure normale à suivre
sq	**square,** carré, c
St	**street,** rue, r.
ster.	**sterling,** livre sterling
stk	**stock, 1.** titre, t.; valeur, val., V/. **2.** stock (en magasin)
Sun.	**Sunday,** dimanche
t.	**1. tare,** tare, t. **2. ton,** tonne, t.
TA	**telegraphic address,** adresse télégraphique, ad(r). tél.
tel.	**telephone,** téléphone, tél.; **tel.no., telephone number,** numéro de téléphone, n° tél.
temp.	**temporary secretary,** dactylo intérimaire
Thurs.	**Thursday,** jeudi
tr.	**transfer,** transfert, virement, virt.
TT	**telegraphic transfer,** transfert télégraphique, tt.
Tues.	**Tuesday,** mardi
Tx	**Telex,** Télex
ult.	**ultimo,** (mois) écoulé
u.s.c.	**under separate cover,** sous pli séparé
UV	**ultraviolet,** ultraviolet, UV
U/W	**underwriter,** membre d'un syndicat de garantie
vo.	**verso,** verso, vo., v°
vol.	**volume,** volume
WB	**waybill,** feuille de route/lettre de voiture
w.c.	**without charge,** sans frais/gratis
Wed.	**Wednesday,** mercredi
wk	**week,** semaine
wt	**weight,** poids, p.
xa.	*NAm:* **ex all,** à l'exclusion de tous les avantages supplémentaires comportés par une action.
xc.	**1. ex coupon,** ex-coupon, ex-c(oup) **2. ex capitalization**
xd.	**ex dividend,** ex-dividende, xd., ex-d.
xr.	**ex rights,** ex-droits, ex-dr.
yd	**yard**
yr	**1. year,** an/année **2. your,** votre, v.
Your ref.	**your reference,** votre référence, V/Réf.
&	**ampersand,** et commercial
£	**pound sterling,** livre sterling, L
©	**at,** à
©	**copyright,** droit d'auteur

®	**registered trademark,** marque déposée
%	**per cent,** pour cent
°C	**degrees Celsius/Centigrade,** degrés Celsius/Centigrade
°F	**degrees Fahrenheit,** degrés Fahrenheit

ENGLISH ACRONYMS—SIGLES ANGLAIS

AAAA	**American Association of Advertising Agencies**
AACCA	**Associate of the Association of Certified and Corporate Accountants**
AAIA	**Associate of the Association of International Accountants**
ABAA	**Associate of the British Association of Accountants and Auditors**
ABTA	**Association of British Travel Agents**
ACAS	**Advisory, Conciliation and Arbitration Service**
ACGI	**Associate of the City and Guilds of London Institute**
ACIS	**Associate of the Chartered Institute of Secretaries**
ACMA	**Associate of the Institute of Cost and Management Accountants**
ACPA	**Associate of the Institute of Certified Public Accountants**
ACRA	**Associate of the Corporation of Registered Accountants**
ACT	**Advance Corporation Tax,** impôt anticipé sur les sociétés
ACTU	**Australian Council of Trade Unions**
ADG	**Assistant Director General**
ADP	**Automatic Data Processing,** traitement automatique de l'information
ADR	**American Depositary Receipts**
AEA	**American Economic Association**
AFE	**Authorization for expenditure**
AFL-CIO	**American Federation of Labor and Congress of Industrial Organizations**
AG	**1. Accountant General,** Chef de la Comptabilité **2. Attorney General 3. Agent General**
AGM	**Annual General Meeting,** assemblée générale annuelle
AIA	**1. American Institute of Accountants 2. Associate of the Institute of Actuaries**
AIAA	**Associate of the Institute of Accountants and Actuaries**
AIB	**American Institute of Bankers**
AID	*US:* **Agency for International Development**
AIWM	**American Institute of Weights and Measures**
ALGOL	*Cmptr:* **algorithmic language**
AMEX	**1. American Express Company 2. American Stock Exchange**
AMH	**Automatic/Automated materials handling**
ANPA	**American Newspaper Publishers' Association**
ANSI	**American National Standards Institute** = Association française de normalisation, AFNOR
AO	**1. Accounting officer 2. Administration officer**
AOB	**Any other business**
AP	**Associated Press**
APR	**annualized percentage rate,** taux annualisé
APT	**Advanced Passenger Train** = train grande vitesse, TGV
AR	**Annual return,** revenu annuel
ARAMCO	**Arabian-American Oil Company**
ARICS	**Associate of the Royal Institute of Chartered Surveyors**
ARM	**Adjustable rate mortgage,** hypothèque à taux variable
ASA	**1. Advertising Standards Authority,** Bureau de la vérification de la publicité, BVP **2. American Standards Association**
ASE	**American Stock Exchange**
ASTMS	**Association of Scientific, Technical and Managerial Staff**
ATA	*US:* **1. Air Transport Association 2. American Trucking Association**
ATM	**Automatic telling/***US:* **teller machine,** guichet automatique de banque
AVC	**Additional voluntary contribution,** supplément de cotisation
BA	**British Airways**
BB	*US:* **Bureau of the Budget**
BCom	**Bachelor of Commerce**
BEcon	**Bachelor of Economics**

BHRA	**British Hotels and Restaurants Association**
BID	**Bachelor of Industrial Design**
BIF	**British Industries Fair**
BIM	**British Institute of Management**
BIS	**Bank for International Settlements**
BLL	**Bachelor of Laws**
B of E	**Bank of England**
BNOC	**British National Oil Corporation**
BP	**British Petroleum**
BR	**British Rail**
BRS	**British Road Services**
BSBA	**Bachelor of Science in Business Administration**
BSc	**Bachelor of Science**
BSC	**British Steel Corporation**
BSCP	**British Standard Code of Practice**
BSI	**British Standards Institution** = Association française de normalisation, AFNOR
BSIR	**Bachelor of Science in Industrial Relations**
BSS	**British Standard Specification**
BST	**1. British Summer Time,** heure d'été britannique **2. British Standard Time,** heure légale britannique
BTA	**British Travel Association**
BUPA	**British United Provident Association**
CA	**1. Chartered Accountant**/ *US:* **Certified Accountant,** expert comptable **2. Consumers Association**
CAC	*US:* **Consumers' Advisory Council**
CAP	**1. Common Agricultural Policy,** Politique agricole commune, PAC **2. Code of advertising practice**
CAR	**compound annual return,** taux de rentabilité annualisé/composé annuellement
CARIFTA	**Caribbean Free Trade Area**
CBI	**Confederation of British Industry** = Conseil national du patronat français, CNPF
CC	**Chamber of Commerce**
CCA	**Current cost accounting**
CCC	**Canadian Chamber of Commerce**
CED	**Committee for Economic Development**
CEEC	**Council for European Economic Co-operation**
CEO	*NAm:* **Chief Executive Officer,** directeur général
CET	**Common external tariff,** Tarif douanier commun
CFO	*NAm:* **Chief Financial Officer,** chef comptable
CGI	**City and Guilds Institute**
CGT	**capital gains tax,** impôt sur les plus-values
CH	**corporate hospitality**
CIA	*US:* **Certified Industrial Accountant**
CICA	**Canadian Institute of Chartered Accountants**
CIO	*US:* **Congress of Industrial Organizations**
CIS	**Chartered Institute of Secretaries**
CITB	**Construction Industry Training Board**
CM	**Common Market,** marché commun
CMEA	**Council for Mutual Economic Assistance**
CNAR	**compound net annual rate**
COBOL	*Cmptr:* **common business oriented language**
COD	**Cash on delivery**/ *NAm:* **collect on delivery,** livraison contre remboursement
COI	**Central Office of Information**
COMECON	**Council for Mutual Economic Aid,** Conseil de l'aide économique mutuelle, COMECON
COMEX	Commodity Exchange of New York
COSIRA	**Council for Small Industries in Rural Areas**
CPA	*NAm:* **Certified Public Accountant** = expert comptable

CPI	**Consumer Price Index**
CPM	**Critical Path Method,** méthode du chemin critique
CPR	**Canadian Pacific Railway**
CS	**Civil Service,** Administration civile
CSC	**Civil Service Commission**
CT	**corporation tax,** impôt sur les sociétés
CTT	**capital transfer tax,** droits de mutation
CWS	**Co-operative Wholesale Society,** société coopérative de consommation
DA	*US:* **District Attorney**
DAP	**Documents against payment,** documents contre paiement, DP
DCE	**domestic credit expansion,** croissance de la masse monétaire
DCF	**Discounted cash flow,** cash flow actualisé
DCom	**Doctor of Commerce**
DComL	**Doctor of Commercial Law**
DDD	*NAm:* **Direct distance dialing** = le téléphone automatique/l'automatique
DEcon	**Doctor of Economics**
DERV	**Diesel engined road vehicle**
DHSS	**Department of Health and Social Security**
DIM	**Diploma in Industrial Management**
Dip COM	**Diploma of Commerce**
DipEcon	**Diploma of Economics**
DipPA	**Diploma in Public Administration**
DipTech	**Diploma in Technology**
DPP	**Director of Public Prosecutions**
DPR	**Director of Public Relations** = chef du service des relations publiques
EAAA	**European Association of Advertising Agencies**
EAGGF	**European Agricultural Guidance and Guarantee Fund,** Fonds européen d'orientation et de garantie agricole, FEOGA
EAS	**Enterprise Allowance Scheme,** fonds d'aide à la création d'entreprise
E&OE	**Errors and omissions excepted,** sauf erreur ou omission, s.e.&o.
ECE	**Economic Commission for Europe,** Commission économique pour l'Europe, CEE
ECI	**equity capital for industry,** capital-actions pour l'industrie
ECSC	**European Coal and Steel Community,** Communauté du charbon et de l'acier, CECA
ECU	**European currency unit,** unité de compte européenne, UCE
EDI	**Electronic data interchange,** échange de données électronique
EDP	**Electronic data processing,** informatique
EEA	**Exchange Equalization Account**
EEC	**European Economic Community,** Communauté économique européenne, CEE
EEOC	**Equal Employment Opportunities Commission**
EFT	**Electronic funds transfer,** transfert électronique de fonds
EFTA	**European Free Trade Association,** Association européenne de libre-échange, AELE
EFTPOS	**Electronic funds transfer at point of sale,** transfert électronique de fonds au point de vente
EGM	**Extraordinary general meeting,** assemblée générale extraordinaire
EIB	**European Investment Bank,** Banque européenne d'investissement, BEI
EMA	**European Monetary Agreement,** Accord monétaire européen, AME
EMS	**European Monetary System,** Système monétaire européen, SME
EPOS	**Electronic point of sale,** point de vente électronique
EPP	**executive pension plan,** plan de retraite des cadres
EPS	**earnings per share,** bénéfice/gain par action
EPU	**European Payments Union,** Union européenne des paiements, UEP
ERA	**exchange rate agreement,** accord de taux de change
ERM	**exchange rate mechanism,** mécanisme de taux de change
ERNIE	**Electronic Random Number Indicator Equipment**
ESC	**Economic and Social Committee,** Comité économique et social, CES
ESF	**European Social Fund,** Fonds européen social, FES

ETA	**Estimated time of arrival**
ETO	**European Transport Organization**
FACCA	**Fellow of the Association of Certified and Corporate Accountants**
FAO	**Food and Agriculture Organization,** Organisation pour l'alimentation et l'agriculture
FBAA	**Fellow of the British Association of Accountants and Auditors**
FBIM	**Fellow of the British Institute of Management**
FCA	**Fellow of the Institute of Chartered Accountants**
FCGI	**Fellow of the City and Guilds of London Institute**
FCI	**Fellow of the Institute of Commerce**
FCIA	**Fellow of the Institute of Insurance Agents**
FCMA	**Fellow of the Institute of Cost and Management Accountants**
FDA	*US:* **Food and Drug Administration**
FIA	**Fellow of the Institute of Actuaries**
FIB	**Fellow of the Institute of Bankers**
FICA	**Fellow of the Institute of Company Accountants**
FIFO	**First in first out,** premier entré premier sorti, PEPS
FIMBRA	**Financial Intermediaries and Brokers Regulatory Authority**
FIPM	**Fellow of the Institute of Personnel Management**
FOREX	**Foreign exchange,** devises étrangères
FORTRAN	*Cmptr:* **formular translation**
FRA	**future rate agreement,** accord de garantie de taux
FRICS	**Fellow of the Royal Institute of Chartered Surveyors**
FSA	**Financial Services Act**
FSVA	**Fellow of the Incorporated Society of Valuers and Auctioneers**
FT	**Financial Times**
FTC	*US:* **Federal Trade Commission**
G&A	**General and administrative expenses,** frais généraux et grais de gestion
GAO	**General Accounting Officer**
GATT	**General Agreement on Tariffs and Trade,** Accord général sur les tarifs douaniers et le commerce, AGTDC
GCSE	**General Certificate of Secondary Education**
GDP	**Gross Domestic Product,** produit intérieur brut
GM	**Gross Margin,** marge brute/profit brut
GMP	**Guaranteed Minimum Pension**
GMT	**Greenwich Mean Time,** heure de Greenwich
GMWU	**General and Municipal Workers Union**
GNI	**Gross National Income**
GNP	**Gross National Product,** produit national brut, PNB
HEW	*US:* **Department of Health, Education and Welfare**
HGV	**Heavy goods vehicle,** poids lourd
HMSO	**His/Her Majesty's Stationery Office**
HNC	**Higher National Certificate**
HND	**Higher National Diploma**
HST	**High speed train,** train grande vitesse, TGV
IAF	**International Automobile Federation,** Fédération internationale de l'automobile, FIA
IAM	**Institute of Administrative Management**
IAS	**Internal audit system,** système d'audit interne
IATA	**International Air Transport Association,** Association internationale des transports aériens, AITA
IBM	**International Business Machines**
IBOR	**Interbank offered rate,** taux interbancaire offert
IBRD	**International Bank for Reconstruction and Development,** Banque internationale pour la reconstruction et le développement, BIRD

ICA	**Institute of Chartered Accountants**
ICAO	**International Civil Aviation Organization,** Organisation internationale de l'aviation civile, OIAC
ICC	**International Chamber of Commerce,** Chambre de Commerce internationale
ICMA	**Institute of Cost and Management Accountants**
ICI	**Imperial Chemical Industries**
ICTB	**International Customs Tariffs Bureau,** Bureau international des tarifs douaniers, BITD
IDD	**International Direct Dialling** = l'automatique international
IFC	**International Finance Corporation**
IFTU	**International Federation of Trade Unions,** Fédération syndicale internationale, FSI
ILO	**International Labour Organization,** Organisation internationale du travail, OIT
IMF	**International Monetary Fund,** Fonds monétaire international, FMI
IOB	**1. Institute of Bankers 2. Institute of Book-keepers**
IOM	**Institute of Office Management**
IOU	**I owe you,** reconnaissance de dette
IPM	**Institute of Personnel Management**
IPO	**initial public offering,** introduction en bourse
IPR	**Institute of Public Relations**
IR	**Inland Revenue** = le Fisc
IRR	**Internal rate of return,** taux de rentabilité interne
IRS	*NAm:* **Internal Revenue Service** = le Fisc
ISBN	**International Standard Book Number**
ISFA	**Institute of Shipping and Forwarding Agents**
ISO	**International Standards Organization**
ITO	**International Trade Organisation**
JAL	**Japan Airlines**
JP	**Justice of the Peace**
KAL	**Korean Airlines**
KLM	**Royal Dutch Airlines,** Société royale d'aviation des pays bas, KLM
LBO	**Leveraged Buyout,** rachat d'une société par effet de levier
LC	**Library of Congress**
LCE	**London Commodities Exchange**
LIBOR	**London interbank offered rate,** taux interbancaire offert à Londres
LIFFE	**London International Financial Futures Exchange**
LIFO	**Last in first out,** dernier entré premier sorti, DEPS
LLB	**Bachelor of Laws**
LLD	**Doctor of Laws**
LR	**Lloyds Register**
LSE	**1. London Stock Exchange 2. London School of Economics**
LV	**Luncheon Voucher** = ticket-repas/ticket-restaurant
M&A	**Mergers and Acquisitions**
MBIM	**Member of the British Institute of Management**
MBO	**Management by objectives,** direction par objectifs, DPO
MBWA	**Management by walking/wandering around,** management par écoute et rencontre, MER
MCom	**Master of Commerce**
MD	**Managing Director** = Président-Directeur Général, P-DG
MEcon	**Master of Economics**
MICA	**Member of the Institute of Chartered Accountants**
MIP	**Maximum investment plan,** plan d'investissement maximum
MIRAS	**Mortgage interest relief at source**
MIS	**Management Information System**
MLR	**Minimum Lending Rate,** taux officiel d'escompte

MMB	**Milk Marketing Board**
MRP	**Manufacturer's recommended price**
MSc	**Master of Science**
NALGO	**National and Local Government Officers Association**
NATO	**North Atlantic Treaty Organization,** Organisation du traité de l'Atlantique du nord, OTAN
NASDAQ	*US:* **National Association of Securities Dealers Automated Quotations**
NAV	**Net asset value,** valeur nette des actifs
NC	**National Carriers**
NCI	**New Community Instrument,** Nouvel instrument communautaire, NIC
NEB	**National Enterprise Board**
NEC	**National executive committee**
NEDC	(*also* **Neddy**) **National Economic Development Council**
NHS	**National Health Service**
NI	**National Insurance**
NIC	**Newly industrializing country,** pays nouvellement industrialisé
NIT	**negative income tax,** impôt négatif sur le revenu
NPA	**Newspaper Publishers' Association**
NPO	**Non-profit(-making) organisation,** organisation sans but lucratif
NSB	**National Savings Bank** = Caisse Nationale d'Épargne, CNE
NUPE	**National Union of Public Employees**
NYMEX	**New York Metals Exchange**
NYSE	**New York Stock Exchange**
O&M	**Organization and Methods,** organisation et méthodes, OM
OAP	**Old age pensioner**
OECD	**Organization for Economic Co-operation and Development,** Organisation de coopération et de développement économique, OCDE
OHMS	**On His/Her Majesty's Service**
OIT	**Office of International Trade**
OPEC	**Organization of Petroleum Exporting Countries,** Organisation des pays exportateurs de pétrole, OPEP
OR	**Operational Research,** recherche opérationnelle, RO
OTC	**over-the-counter (market),** (marché des) transactions hors séance/marché THS
PA	**1. Press Association 2. Publishers Association 3. Personal Assistant,** assistant(e) particulier(-ière), AP **4. Public Address System,** sonorisation extérieure
PABX	**Private automatic branch (telephone) exchange**
PAYE	**Pay as you earn** = impôt retenu à la source/à la base
PBDS	**Publishers and Booksellers Delivery Service**
PER/P/E ratio	**Price earnings ratio,** rapport cours-bénéfice/taux de capitalisation des bénéfices
PERT	**Programme, evaluation and review technique** = méthode de programmation optimale, PERT
PET	**Property Enterprise Trust**
PIBOR	**Paris interbank offered rate,** taux interbancaire offert à Paris
PIN	**Personal Identification Number,** code personnel
PLA	**Port of London Authority**
PLC, plc	**Public Limited Company**
PLR	**Public lending right**
PMG	**1. Postmaster General,** directeur général des postes **2. Paymaster General**
PO	**Post Office** = Postes et Télécommunications, P et T
POB	**Post Office Box,** Boîte postale, BP
POP	**Post Office Preferred (envelopes)** = formats postaux normalisés
PPBS	**Planning, programming and budgeting system** = rationalisation des choix budgétaires, RCB
PPP	**Private Patients Plan**
PR	**Public Relations,** relations publiques, RP
PRO	**Public Relations Officer**
PSBR	**Public sector borrowing requirement**

PSV	**Public Service Vehicle**
QANTAS	**Queensland and Northern Territory Aerial Services (Australian International Airline)**
QC	**Queens Counsel** = *FrC:* Conseiller de la Reine, CR
QUANGO	**Quasi autonomous non-governmental organization**
RE	**Royal Exchange,** Bourse du Commerce
REPO	*US:* **repurchase agreement/repossession,** accord de rachat de titres
RFD	*US:* **Rural free delivery service**
RIE	**Recognized investment exchange**
RO	**Receiving Office** = bureau des messageries
ROE	**Return on equity,** rendement des capitaux propres
ROI	**Return on Investment,** rendement du capital investi
RPM	**Resale/retail price maintenance**
RRP	**Recommended retail price**
RSVP	**please reply/answer,** répondez s'il vous plaît, RSVP
SAS	**Scandinavian Airlines System**
SAYE	**Save as you earn**
SCOUT	**Share currency option under tender**
SDR	**Special drawing rights,** droits de tirage spéciaux, DTS
SEAF	**Stock Exchange Automatic Exchange Facility,** Système de Cotation en Continu
SEAQ	**Stock Exchange Automated Quotations**
SEC	*US:* **Securities and Exchange Commission**
SEDOL	**Stock Exchange Daily Official List,** Bulletin de la Cote Officielle
SEPON	**Stock Exchange Pool Nominees**
SERPS	**State earnings related pension scheme**
SIB	**Securities and Investment Board**
SICA	**Society of Industrial and Cost Accountants of Canada**
SRO	**Self-regulating organisation,** conseil/syndicat professionnel.
STD	**Subscriber Trunk Dialling,** l'automatique
SUPSI	**Specific unpublished price sensitive information**
TALISMAN	**Transfer Accounting, Lodgement for Investors, Stock Management for Jobbers,** = Règlement-Livraison de Titres, RELIT
TASS .	**Telegraphic News Agency of the Soviet Union,** agence TASS
TCV	**Total contract value,** valeur totale du contrat
TGWU	**Transport and General Workers Union**
TO	**Telegraphic Office**
TPI	**tax and price index,** indice des impôts et des prix
TQC	**total quality control,** qualité globale, QG
TT	**Telegraphic transfer,** transfer télégraphique, TT
TU	**Trade Union,** syndicat
TUC	**Trade Union Congress**
TWA	**Transworld Airlines**
UAW	*US:* **United Automobile Workers**
UN	**United Nations,** Nations Unies, NU
UNCTAD	**United Nations Conference on Trade and Development,** Conférence des Nations Unies pour le commerce et le développement, UNCTAD
UNIDO	**United Nations Industrial Development Organization**
UNO	**United Nations Organization,** Organisation des Nations Unies, ONU
UPI	**United Press International**
UPU	**Universal Postal Union,** Union postale universelle, UPU
USDAW	**Union of Shop, Distributive & Allied Workers**
USIA	**United States Information Agency**
USM	**1. United States Mint 2. Unlisted Securities Market,** second marché

USP	**Unique selling point,** point de vente unique
USPO	**United States Post Office**
VAT	**Value-added tax,** taxe à la valeur ajoutée, TVA
VDT	**Visual Display Terminal,** écran de visualisation/visuel
VDU	**Visual Display Unit,** écran de visualisation/visuel
VER	**voluntary export restraint**
VIP	**Very important person**
WEU	**Western European Union,** Union de l'Europe occidentale, UEO
WFTU	**World Federation of Trade Unions,** Fédération syndicale mondiale, FSM
ZIP	*US:* **Zone improvement plan**

COUNTRY	PAYS	CURRENCY	MONNAIE
Afghanistan	Afganistan *m*	Afghani	Afghani *m*
Albania	Albanie *f*	Lek	Lek *m*
Algeria	Algérie *f*	(Algerian) **Dinar**	Dinar *m* (algérien)
Andorra	Andorre *f*	(French) **Franc**	Franc (français)
		(Spanish) **Peseta**	Peseta (espagnol)
Angola	Angola *f*	Kwanza	Kwanza *m*
Antigua and Barbuda	Antigua *f* et Barbuda *f*	(E. Caribbean) **Dollar**	Dollar des Caraïbes orientales
Argentina	Argentine *f*	Austral	Austral *m*
Australia	Australie *f*	(Australian) **Dollar**	Dollar *m* (australien)
Austria	Autriche *f*	Schilling	Schilling *m*
Bahamas	Bahamas *mpl*	(Bahamian) **Dollar**	Dollar *m* (des Bahamas)
Bahrain	Bahreïn *m*, Bahrayn *m*	Dinar	Dinar *m* (de Bahreïn)
Bangladesh	Bangladesh *m*	Taka	Taka *m*
Barbados	Barbade *f*	(Barbados) **Dollar**	Dollar (de la Barbade)
Belgium	Belgique *f*	(Belgian) **Franc**	France *m* (belge)
Belize	Belize *f*	(Belize) **Dollar**	Dollar (de Belize)
Benin	Bénin *m*	CFA Franc	Franc CFA
Bermuda	Bermudes *fpl*	Dollar	Dollar *m*
Bolivia	Bolivie *f*	(Bolivian) **Peso, Boliviano**	Peso *m* (bolivien), Boliviano *m*
Brazil	Brésil *m*	Cruzeiro	Cruzeiro *m*
Brunei	Brunei *m*	(Brunei) **Dollar**	Dollar (de Brunei)
Bulgaria	Bulgarie *f*	Lev	Lev *m*
Burkina-Faso	Burkina *m*	CFA Franc	Franc CFA
Burma	Birmanie *f*	Kyat	Kyat *m*
Burundi	Burundi *m*	(Burundi) **Franc**	Franc *m* (du Burundi)
Cambodia	Cambodge *m*	Riel	Riel *m*
Cameroon	Cameroun *m*	CFA Franc	Franc CFA
Canada	Canada *m*	(Canadian) **Dollar**	Dollar *m* (canadien)
Cape Verde	Cap Vert *m*	Escudo	Escudo
Central African Republic	République centrafricaine	CFA Franc	Franc CFA
Chad	Tchad *m*	CFA Franc	Franc CFA
Chile	Chili *m*	(Chilean) **Peso**	Peso *m* (du Chili)
China	Chine *f*	Yuan	Yuan *m*
Colombia	Colombie *f*	(Colombian) **Peso**	Peso *m* (colombien)
Comoro Islands	Iles Comores	CFA Franc	Franc CFA
Congo	Congo *m*	CFA Franc	Franc CFA
Costa Rica	Costa Rica *m*	Colon	Colon *m*
Cuba	Cuba	(Cuban) **Peso**	Peso *m* (cubain)
Cyprus	Chypre	(Cyprus) **Pound**	Livre *f* (cypriote)
Czechoslovakia	Tchécoslovaquie *f*	Crown	Couronne *f* (tchécoslovaque)
Denmark	Danemark *m*	Krone	Couronne *f* (danoise)
Djibouti	Djibouti	Djibouti Franc	Franc (de Djibouti)
Dominican Republic	République Dominicaine	Peso	Peso *m* (dominicain)
Ecuador	Équateur *m*	Sucre	Sucre *m*
Egypt	Égypte *f*	(Egyptian) **Pound**	Livre *f* (égyptienne)
El Salvador	Salvador *m*	Colon	Colon *m*
Equatorial Guinea	Guinée Equatoriale	CFA Franc	Franc CFA
Ethiopia	Éthiopie *f*	Birr	Birr *m*
Fiji	Iles Fidji	(Fiji) **Dollar**	Dollar (fidjien)
Finland	Finlande *f*	Markka	Markka *m*, Mark *m* (finlandais)
France	France *f*	(French) **Franc**	Franc *m* (français)
Gabon	Gabon *m*	CFA Franc	Franc CFA
The Gambia	Gambie *f*	Dalasi	Dalasi *m*
Germany (Federal Republic-GFR)	République Fédérale Allemande-RFA	Mark/Deutschmark	(deutsche) Mark *m*

COUNTRY	PAYS	CURRENCY	MONNAIE
Germany (Democratic Republic-GDR)	République Démocratique Allemande-RDA	Mark/Deutschmark	(deutsche) Mark *m*
Ghana	Ghana *m*	Cedi	Cedi *m*
Gibraltar	Gibraltar *m*	(Gibraltar) Pound	Livre *f* (de Gibraltar)
Greece	Grèce *f*	Drachma	Drachme *m*
Guatemala	Guatemala *m*	Quetzal	Quetzal *m*
Guinea	Guinée *f*	Franc	Franc *m* (guinéen)
Guinea-Bissau	Guinée-Bissau *f*	Peso	Peso *m*
Guyana	Guyana *f*	(Guyana) Dollar	Dollar *m* (de Guyana)
Haiti	Haïti *m*	Goude	Gourde *f*
Honduras	Honduras *m*	Lempira	Lempira *m*
Hong Kong	Hong Kong *m*	(Hong Kong) Dollar	Dollar *m* (de Hong Kong)
Hungary	Hongrie *f*	Forint	Forint *m*
Iceland	Islande *f*	Krona	Couronne *f* (islandaise)
India	Inde *f*	Rupee	Roupie *f*
Indonesia	Indonésie *f*	Rupiah	Rupiah *m*
Iran	Iran *m*	Rial	Rial *m*
Iraq	Iraq *m*, Irak *m*	(Iraqi) Dinar	Dinar *m* (irakien)
Irish Republic	Irlande *f*	(Irish) Pound/Punt	Livre *f* (irlandaise)
Israel	Israël	Shekel	Shekel *m*
Italy	Italie *f*	Lira	Lire *f*
Ivory Coast	Côte-d'Ivoire *f*	CFA Franc	Franc CFA
Jamaica	Jamaïque *f*	(Jamaican) Dollar	Dollar *m* (de la Jamaïque)
Japan	Japon *m*	Yen	Yen *m*
Jordan	Jordanie *f*	(Jordanian) Dinar	Dinar *m* (jordanien)
Kenya	Kenya *m*	Shilling	Shilling *m*
Korea (North)	Corée *f* (du nord)	Won	Won *m*
Korea (South)	Corée *f* (du sud)	Won	Won *m*
Kuwait, Koweit	Koweït *m*	(Kuwait) Dinar	Dinar *m* (koweïtien)
Laos	Laos *m*	Kip	Kip *m*
Lebanon	Liban *m*	(Lebanese) Pound	Livre *f* (libanaise)
Lesotho	Lesotho *m*	Rand	Rand *m*
Liberia	Libéria *m*	(Liberian) Dollar	Dollar *m* (libérien)
Libya	Libye *m*	(Libyan) Dinar	Dinar *m* (libyen)
Luxemburg	Luxembourg *m*	(Luxemburg) Franc	Franc *m* (luxembourgeois)
Madagascar	Madagascar *m*	(Malagasy) Franc	Franc *m* (malgache)
Malawi	Malawi *m*	Kwacha	Kwacha *m*
Malaysia	Malaysia	Rinngit	Rinngit *m*, Dollar *m* (de la Malaysia)
Mali	Mali *m*	CFA Franc	Franc CFA
Malta	Malte	(Maltese) Pound	Livre *f* (maltaise)
Mauritania	Mauritanie *f*	Ouguiya	Ouguiya *m*
Mauritius	Île Maurice	Rupee	Roupie *f* (mauricienne)
Mexico	Mexique *m*	Peso	Peso *m* (mexicain)
Monaco	Monaco *m*	(French) Franc	Franc (français)
Morocco	Maroc *m*	Dirham	Dirham *m*
Mozambique	Mozambique *m*	Metical	Metical *m*
Namibia	Namibie *f*	S.A. Rand	Rand (sud-africain)
Nepal	Népal *m*	Rupee	Roupie *f* (népalaise)
The Netherlands	Pays-Bas	Guilder	Florin *m*
New Zealand	Nouvelle-Zélande	(New Zealand) Dollar	Dollar *m* (néo-zélandais)
Nicaragua	Nicaragua *m*	Cordoba	Cordoba *m*
Niger Republic	République du Niger *m*	CFA Franc	Franc CFA
Nigeria	Nigeria *m*	Naira	Naira *m*
Norway	Norvège *f*	Krone	Couronne *f*

COUNTRY	PAYS	CURRENCY	MONNAIE
Oman	Oman *m*	(Omani) **Rial**	**Rial** *m* (d'Oman)
Pakistan	Pakistan *m*	**Rupee**	**Roupie** *f* (pakistanaise)
Panama	Panama *m*	**Balboa**	**Balboa** *m*
Paraguay	Paraguay *m*	**Guarani**	**Guarani** *m*
Peru	Pérou *m*	**Sol**	**Inti** *m*
Philippines	Philippines *fpl*	**Peso**	**Peso** *m* (philippin)
Poland	Pologne *f*	**Zloty**	**Zloty** *m*
Portugal	Portugal *m*	**Escudo**	**Escudo** *m*
Qatar	Qatar *m*	**Riyal**	**Riyal** *m*
Réunion	Réunion *f*	(French) **Franc**	**Franc** (français)
Romania Rumania	Roumanie *f*	**Leu**	**Leu** *m*
Rwanda	Ruanda *m*, **Rwanda**	(Rwanda) **Franc**	**Franc** *m* (ruandais)
Saudi Arabia	Arabie Saoudite	**Riyal**	**Riyal** *m*
Senegal	Sénégal *m*	**CFA Franc**	**Franc CFA**
Seychelles	Seychelles *fpl*	**Rupee**	**Roupie** (des Seychelles)
Sierra Leone	Sierra Leone *f*	**Leone**	**Leone** *m*
Singapore	Singapour *m*	(Singapore) **Dollar**	**Dollar** *m* (de Singapour)
Somali Republic	Somalie *f*	**Shilling**	**Shilling** *m*
South Africa	Afrique du Sud	**Rand**	**Rand** *m*
Spain	Espagne *f*	**Peseta**	**Peseta** *f*
Sri Lanka	Sri Lanka *m*	(Sri Lanka) **Rupee**	**Roupie** *f* (de Sri Lanka)
Sudan	Soudan *m*	(Sudanese) **Pound**	**Livre** *f* (soudanaise)
Surinam	Surinam(e) *m*	**Guilder**	**Guinée** *f* (de Surinam)
Swaziland	Swaziland *m*	**Lilangeni**	**Lilangeni** *m*
Sweden	Suède *f*	**Krona**	**Couronne** *f* (suédoise)
Switzerland	Suisse *f*	(Swiss) **Franc**	**Franc** *m* (suisse)
Syria	Syrie *f*	(Syrian) **Pound**	**Livre** *f* (syrienne)
Taiwan	Taiwan	(Taiwan) **Dollar**	**Dollar** *m* (de Taiwan)
Tanzania	Tanzanie *f*	**Shilling**	**Shilling** *m*
Thailand	Thaïlande *f*	**Baht**	**Baht** *m*
Togo	Togo *m*	**CFA Franc**	**Franc CFA**
Trinidad & Tobago	Trinité-et-Tobago	(Trinidad & Tobago) **Dollar**	**Dollar** *m* (de la Trinité)
Tunisia	Tunisie *f*	**Dinar**	**Dinar** *m* (tunisien)
Turkey	Turquie *f*	(Turkish) **Lira**	**Livre** *f* (turque)
Uganda	Ouganda *m*	(Uganda) **Shilling**	**Shilling** *m* (ougandais)
United Arab Emirates	Émirats Arabes Unis	**Dirham**	**Dirham** *m*
United Kingdom/UK	Royaume Uni *m*	**Pound** (sterling)	**Livre** *f* (sterling)
United States of America/USA	États-unis *mpl* d'Amérique	(US) **Dollar**	**Dollar** *m* (US)
Uruguay	Uruguay *m*	**Peso**	**Peso** *m* (uruguayen)
U.S.S.R.	U.R.S.S.	**Rouble**	**Rouble** *m*
Venezuela	Venezuela *m*	**Bolivar**	**Bolivar** *m*
Vietnam	Viêt-nam *m*	**Dong**	**Dong** *m*
Yemen (North)	Yémen *m* (du Nord)	(Yemeni) **Riyal**	**Rial** *m* (du Yémen)
Yemen (South)	Yémen *m* (du Sud)	**Dinar**	**Dinar** *m*
Yugoslavia	Yougoslavie *f*	**Dinar**	**Dinar** *m*
Zaïre	Zaïre *m*	**Zaïre**	**Zaïre** *m*
Zambia	Zambie *f*	**Kwacha**	**Kwacha** *m*
Zimbabwe	Zimbabwe *m*	(Zimbabwe) **Dollar**	**Dollar** *m* (du Zimbabwe)

CFA Franc/Franc CFA = Franc de la communauté financière d'Afrique

UNITED STATES: POST OFFICE ABBREVIATIONS—
ABRÉVIATIONS POSTALES: US

AL	ALABAMA		NC	NORTH CAROLINA
AK	ALASKA		ND	NORTH DAKOTA
AR	ARKANSAS		NE	NEBRASKA
AZ	ARIZONA		NH	NEW HAMPSHIRE
CA	CALIFORNIA		NJ	NEW JERSEY
CO	COLORADO		NM	NEW MEXICO
CT	CONNECTICUT		NV	NEVADA
DE	DELAWARE		NY	NEW YORK
FL	FLORIDA		OH	OHIO
GA	GEORGIA		OK	OKLAHOMA
HI	HAWAII		OR	OREGON
IA	IOWA		PA	PENNSYLVANIA
ID	IDAHO		RI	RHODE ISLAND
IL	ILLINOIS		SC	SOUTH CAROLINA
IN	INDIANA		SD	SOUTH DAKOTA
KS	KANSAS		TN	TENNESSEE
KY	KENTUCKY		TX	TEXAS
LA	LOUISIANA		UT	UTAH
MA	MASSACHUSETTS		VA	VIRGINIA
MD	MARYLAND		VT	VERMONT
ME	MAINE		WA	WASHINGTON
MI	MICHIGAN		WDC	WASHINGTON DISTRICT
MN	MINNESOTA			OF COLUMBIA
MO	MISSOURI		WI	WISCONSIN
MS	MISSISSIPPI		WV	WEST VIRGINIA
MT	MONTANA		WY	WYOMING

US ZIP CODES: TOWNS WITH A POPULATION GREATER THAN 300 000—
NUMÉROS DE CODE DES VILLES LES PLUS IMPORTANTES (AU-DELÀ DE 300 000 h.)

ATLANTA	GA	30301		MINNEAPOLIS	MN	55401
BALTIMORE	MD	21233		NASHVILLE	TN	37202
BIRMINGHAM	AL	35203		NEWARK	NJ	07101
BOSTON	MA	02109		NEW ORLEANS	LA	70140
BUFFALO	NY	14240		NEW YORK CITY	NY	10001
CHICAGO	IL	60607		NORFOLK	VA	23501
CINCINNATI	OH	45202		OAKLAND	CA	94617
COLUMBUS	OH	43216		OKLAHOMA CITY	OK	73125
DALLAS	TX	75221		OMAHA	NE	68108
DETROIT	MI	48226		PHILADELPHIA	PA	19104
EL PASO	TX	79940		PHOENIX	AZ	85026
FORT WORTH	TX	76101		PITTSBURG	PA	15230
HONOLULU	HI	96819		PORTLAND	OR	97208
HOUSTON	TX	77052		SAN ANTONIO	TX	78205
INDIANAPOLIS	IN	46204		SAN DIEGO	CA	92101
JACKSONVILLE	FL	32201		SAN FRANCISCO	CA	94101
KANSAS CITY	MO	64108		SAN JOSE	CA	95113
LONG BEACH	CA	90801		SEATTLE	WA	98101
LOS ANGELES	CA	90053		ST LOUIS	MO	63166
LOUISVILLE	KY	40202		ST PAUL	MN	55101
MEMPHIS	TN	38101		TOLEDO	OH	43601
MIAMI	FL	33101		TULSA	OK	74101
MILWAUKEE	WI	53201		WASHINGTON	WDC	20013

NUMÉROS DE CODE DES DÉPARTEMENTS FRANÇAIS
CODE NUMBERS OF FRENCH DEPARTMENTS

01	Ain	25	Doubs	48	Lozère	72	Sarthe
02	Aisne	26	Drôme	49	Maine-et-Loire	73	Savoie
03	Allier	27	Eure	50	Manche	74	Savoie (Haute-)
04	Alpes (Basses-)	28	Eure-et-Loir	51	Marne	75	Paris (Ville de)
05	Alpes (Hautes-)	29N	Nord-Finistère	52	Marne (Haute-)	76	Seine-Maritime
06	Alpes-Maritimes	29S	Sud-Finistère	53	Mayenne	77	Seine-et-Marne
07	Ardèche	30	Gard	54	Meurthe-et-Moselle	78	Yvelines
08	Ardennes	31	Garonne (Haute-)	55	Meuse	79	Sèvres (Deux-)
09	Ariège	32	Gers	56	Morbihan	80	Somme
10	Aube	33	Gironde	57	Moselle	81	Tarn
11	Aude	34	Hérault	58	Nièvre	82	Tarn-et-Garonne
12	Aveyron	35	Ille-et-Vilaine	59	Nord	83	Var
13	Bouches-du-Rhône	36	Indre	60	Oise	84	Vaucluse
14	Calvados	37	Indre-et-Loire	61	Orne	85	Vendée
15	Cantal	38	Isère	62	Pas-de-Calais	86	Vienne
16	Charente	39	Jura	63	Puy-de-Dôme	87	Vienne (Haute-)
17	Charente-Maritime	40	Landes	64	Pyrénées (Basses-)	88	Vosges
18	Cher	41	Loir-et-Cher	65	Pyrénées (Hautes-)	89	Yonne
19	Corrèze	42	Loire	66	Pyrénées-Orientales	90	Belfort (Territ.)
20	Corse	43	Loire (Haute-)	67	Rhin (Bas-)	91	Essonne
21	Côte-d'Or	44	Loire-Atlantique	68	Rhin (Haut-)	92	Hauts-de-Seine
22	Côtes-du-Nord	45	Loiret	69	Rhône	93	Seine-St-Denis
23	Creuse	46	Lot	70	Saône (Haute-)	94	Val-de-Marne
24	Dordogne	47	Lot-et-Garonne	71	Saône-et-Loire	95	Val-d'Oise

NUMÉROS POSTAUX DES VILLES DE FRANCE
FRENCH POSTAL CODES

80100	Abbeville	62100	Calais	53000	Laval	64000	Pau
47000	Agen	59400	Cambrai	93350	Le Bourget	24000	Périgueux
13100	Aix-en-Provence	06400	Cannes	76600	Le Havre	66000	Perpignan
20000	Ajaccio	11000	Carcassonne	72000	Le Mans	86000	Poitiers
61000	Alençon	51000	Châlons/Marne	43000	Le Puy	07000	Privas
80000	Amiens	73000	Chambéry	59000	Lille	29000	Quimper
49000	Angers	74400	Chamonix	87000	Limoges	51100	Reims
16000	Angoulême	08000	Charleville-	14100	Lisieux	35000	Rennes
74000	Annecy		Mézières	65100	Lourdes	17300	Rochefort
06600	Antibes	28000	Chartres	69001	Lyon	59100	Roubaix
33120	Arcachon	36000	Châteauroux	71000	Mâcon	76000	Rouen
13200	Arles	50100	Cherbourg	13001	Marseille	17200	Royan
62000	Arras	63100	Clermont-Ferrand	77000	Melun	22000	Saint-Brieuc
15000	Aurillac	68000	Colmar	57000	Metz	42000	Saint-Étienne
89000	Auxerre	60200	Compiègne	40000	Mont-de-Marsan	50000	Saint-Lô
84000	Avignon	14800	Deauville	34000	Montpellier	35400	Saint-Malo
60000	Beauvais	76200	Dieppe	03000	Moulins	44600	Saint-Nazaire
90000	Belfort	21000	Dijon	68100	Mulhouse	08200	Sedan
25000	Besançon	59500	Douai	54000	Nancy	67000	Strasbourg
64200	Biarritz	59140	Dunkerque	44000	Nantes	83100	Toulon
41000	Blois	88000	Épinal	11100	Narbonne	31000	Toulouse
33000	Bordeaux	74500	Évian	58000	Nevers	59200	Tourcoing
62200	Boulogne/mer	27000	Évreux	06000	Nice	37000	Tours
01000	Bourg-en-Bresse	38000	Grenoble	30000	Nîmes	10000	Troyes
18000	Bourges	06160	Juan-les-Pins	79000	Niort	59300	Valenciennes
29200	Brest	44500	La Baule	45000	Orléans	56000	Vannes
14000	Caen	02000	Laon	94310	Orly	78000	Versailles
46000	Cahors	17000	La Rochelle	75001	Paris	03200	Vichy

NUMÉROS POSTAUX DES VILLES DE BELGIQUE ET DE SUISSE
BELGIAN AND SWISS POSTAL CODES

BELGIQUE

9300 Aaist (Alost)
5220 Andenne
2000 Antwerpen
   (Anvers)
6700 Arlon
7800 Ath
6650 Bastogne
7130 Binche
2650 Boom
1420 Braine-l'Alleud
7490 Braine-le-Comte
8000 Brugge (Bruges)
1000 Bruxelles
6000 Charleroi
6071 Châtelet
6460 Chimay
1010 Cité administra-
   tive de l'État
   Bruxelles
9330 Dendermonde
   (Termonde)

3290 Diest
5500 Dinant
4700 Eupen
5800 Gembloux
9000 Gent (Gand)
1500 Halle (Hal)
3500 Hasselt
5200 Huy
8900 Ieper (Ypres)
5100 Jambes
8500 Kortrijk (Courtrai)
3000 Leuven (Louvain)
4000 Liège
2500 Lier (Lierre)
4890 Malmédy
5400 Marche-en-Famenne
2800 Mechelen (Malines)
8600 Menen (Menin)
7000 Mons
7700 Mouscron
5000 Namur

6620 Neufchâteau
1400 Nivelles
1100 Office des
   Chèques Postaux
   Bruxelles
8400 Oostende (Ostende)
9600 Renaix
8800 Roeselare (Roulers)
6900 Saint-Hubert
2700 St-Niklaas
   (St-Nicolas)
7400 Soignies
4880 Spa
4970 Stavelot
3300 Tienen (Tirlemont)
3700 Tongeren (Tongres)
7500 Tournai
2300 Turnhout
4800 Verviers
1800 Vilvoorde (Vilvorde)
1300 Wavre (Waver)

SUISSE

5400 Baden
4000 Bâle
6500 Bellinzona
3000 Berne
2500 Biel/Bienne
2300 Chaux-de-Fonds
8500 Frauenfeld
1700 Fribourg
1200 Genève
2540 Grenchen
3800 Interlaken
8700 Küsnacht ZH

1000 Lausanne
6600 Locarno
6000 Lucerne
6900 Lugano
1820 Montreux
2000 Neuchâtel
4125 Riehen
9000 Saint-Gall
7500 Saint-Moritz
8200 Schaffhouse
1950 Sion

8800 Thalwil
3600 Thun
8610 Uster
1800 Vevey
8820 Wädenswil
5430 Wettingen
8400 Winterthur
1400 Yverdon
4800 Zofingen
6300 Zug
8000 Zürich

WORLD TIME ZONES—FUSEAUX HORAIRES

GMT = 1200 hours/heures

	Hours/Heures		Hours/Heures
ADELAIDE	2130	LONDON/LONDRES	1200
ALGIERS/ALGER	1300	LUXEMBOURG	1300
AMSTERDAM	1300	MADEIRA/MADÈRE	1100
ANKARA	1400	MADRID	1300
ATHENS/ATHÈNES	1400	MALTA	1300
BEIRUT	1400	MEXICO CITY	0600
BELGRADE	1400	MONTEVIDEO	0830
BERLIN	1300	MONTREAL	7000
BERNE	1300	MOSCOW/MOSCOU	1500
BONN	1300	NAIROBI	1500
BOMBAY	1730	NEW ORLEANS	0600
BRASILIA	0900	NEW YORK	0700
BRISBANE	2200	OSLO	1300
BRUSSELS/BRUXELLES	1300	OTTAWA	0700
BUCHAREST	1400	PANAMA	0700
BUDAPEST	1300	PARIS	1300
BUENOS AIRES	0800	PEKING/PÉKIN	2000
CAIRO/LE CAIRE	1400	PERTH (Austr.)	2000
CALCUTTA	1730	PRAGUE	1300
CAPE TOWN/LE CAP	1400	PRETORIA	1400
CARACAS	0800	QUÉBEC	0700
CHICAGO	0600	RANGOON	1830
COLOMBO	1730	RIO DE JANEIRO	0900
COPENHAGEN	1100	RIYADH/RIYAD	1500
DELHI	1730	ST LOUIS (USA)	0600
DUBAI	1600	SAN FRANCISCO	0400
DUBLIN	1200	SANTIAGO	0800
GIBRALTAR	1300	SINGAPORE	1930
HELSINKI	1400	STOCKHOLM	1300
HOBART	2200	SUEZ	1400
HONG KONG	2000	SYDNEY	2200
ISTANBUL	1400	TEHRAN/TÉHÉRAN	1500
JERUSALEM	1400	TOKYO	2100
KUWAIT CITY	1500	TORONTO	0700
LAGOS	1300	TUNIS	1300
LENINGRAD	1500	VANCOUVER	0400
LIMA	0700	VIENNA/VIENNE	1300
LISBON	1300	WARSAW/VARSOVIE	1300
		WELLINGTON (NZ)	2400

WEIGHTS AND MEASURES—POIDS ET MESURES

Metric Measures—
Mesures métriques

Length—Longueur

1 millimètre (mm)		= 0.0394 in
1 centimètre (cm)	= 10 mm	= 0.3937 in
1 mètre (m)	= 100 cm	= 1.0936 yds
1 kilomètre (km)	= 1000 m	= 0.6214 mile

Weight—Poids

1 milligramme (mg)		= 0.0154 grain
1 gramme (g)	= 1000 mg	= 0.0353 oz
1 kilogramme (kg)	= 1000 g	= 2.2046 lb
1 tonne (t)	= 1000 kg	= 0.9842 ton

Area—Surface

1 cm^2	= 100 mm^2	= 0.1550 sq. in
1 m^2	= 10 000 cm^2	= 1.1960 sq. yds
1 are (a)	= 100 m^2	= 119.60 sq. yds
1 hectare (ha)	= 100 ares	= 2.4711 acres
1 km^2	= 100 hectares	= 0.3861 sq. mile

Capacity—Capacité

1 cm^3		= 0.0610 cu. in
1 dm^3	= 1000 cm^3	= 0.0351 cu. ft
1 m^3	= 1000 dm^3	= 1.3080 cu. yds
1 litre	= 1 dm^3	= 0.2200 gallon
1 hectolitre	= 100 litres	= 2.7497 bushels

Imperial Measures—
Mesures britanniques

Length—Longueur

1 inch		= 2.54 cm
1 foot	= 12 inches	= 0.3048 m
1 yard	= 3 feet	= 0.9144 m
1 rod	= 5.5 yards	= 5.0292 m
1 chain	= 22 yards	= 20.117 m
1 furlong	= 220 yards	= 201.17 m
1 mile	= 1760 yards	= 1.6093 km
1 nautical mile	= 6080 feet	= 1,8532 km

Weight—Poids

1 ounce	= 437.5 grains	= 28.350 g
1 pound	= 16 ounces	= 0.4536 kg
1 stone	= 14 pounds	= 6.3503 kg
1 hundredweight	= 112 pounds	= 50.802 kg
1 ton	= 20 cwt	= 1.0161 tonnes

Area—Surface

1 sq. inch		= 6.4516 cm^2
1 sq. foot	= 144 sq. ins	= 0.0929 m^2
1 sq. yd	= 9 sq. ft	= 0.8361 m^2
1 acre	= 4840 sq. yds	= 4046.9 m^2
1 sq. mile	= 640 acres	= 259.0 hectares

Capacity—Capacité

1 cu. inch		= 16.387 cm^3
1 cu. foot	= 1728 cu. ins	= 0.0283 m^3
1 cu. yard	= 27 cu. ft	= 0.7646 m^3
1 pint	= 4 gills	= 0.5683 litre
1 quart	= 2 pints	= 1.1365 litres
1 gallon	= 8 pints	= 4.5461 litres
1 bushel	= 8 gallons	= 36.369 litres
1 fluid ounce	= 8 fl. drachms	= 28.413 cm^3
1 pint	= 20 fl. oz	= 568.26 cm^3

US: Dry Measures—
Mesures US: matières sèches

1 pint	= 0.9689 UK pt	= 0.5506 litre
1 bushel	= 0.9689 UK bu	= 35.238 litres

US: Liquid Measures—
Mesures US: liquides

1 fluid ounce	= 1.0408 UK fl oz	= 0.0296 litre
1 pint (16 oz)	= 0.8327 UK pt	= 0.4732 litre
1 gallon	= 0.8327 UK gal	= 3.7853 litres

CONVERSION TABLES
TABLEAUX DE CONVERSION

LENGTH/LONGUEUR centimètres	cm or inches	inches	WEIGHT/POIDS kilogrammes	kg or pounds	pounds
2.54	1	0.39	0.45	1	2.20
5.08	2	0.79	0.91	2	4.41
7.62	3	1.18	1.36	3	6.61
10.16	4	1.58	1.81	4	8.82
12.70	5	1.97	2.27	5	11.02
15.24	6	2.36	2.72	6	13.23
17.78	7	2.76	3.18	7	15.43
20.32	8	3.15	3.63	8	17.64
22.86	9	3.54	4.08	9	19.84
25.40	10	3.94	4.54	10	22.05
50.80	20	7.87	9.07	20	44.09
76.20	30	11.81	13.61	30	66.14
101.60	40	15.75	18.14	40	88.19
127.00	50	19.69	22.68	50	110.23
152.40	60	23.62	27.22	60	132.28
177.80	70	27.56	31.75	70	154.32
203.20	80	31.50	36.29	80	176.37
228.60	90	35.43	40.82	90	198.41
254.00	100	39.37	45.36	100	220.46

kilomètres	km or miles	miles	tonnes	tonnes or tons	tons
1.61	1	0.62	1.02	1	0.98
3.22	2	1.24	2.03	2	1.97
4.83	3	1.86	3.05	3	2.95
6.44	4	2.49	4.06	4	3.94
8.05	5	3.11	5.08	5	4.92
9.66	6	3.73	6.10	6	5.91
11.27	7	4.35	7.11	7	6.89
12.88	8	4.97	8.13	8	7.87
14.48	9	5.59	9.14	9	8.86
16.09	10	6.21	10.16	10	9.84
32.19	20	12.43	20.32	20	19.68
48.28	30	18.64	30.48	30	29.5
64.37	40	24.86	40.64	40	39.3
80.47	50	31.07	50.80	50	49.2
96.56	60	37.28	60.96	60	59.0
112.65	70	43.50	71.12	70	68.89
128.75	80	49.71	81.28	80	78.7
144.84	90	55.92	91.44	90	88.5
160.93	100	62.14	101.60	100	98.4

Conversion tables | # Tableaux de conversion

AREA/SURFACE

hectares	hectares or acres	acres
0.41	1	2.47
0.81	2	4.94
1.21	3	7.41
1.62	4	9.88
2.02	5	12.36
2.43	6	14.83
2.83	7	17.30
3.24	8	19.77
3.64	9	22.24
4.05	10	24.71
8.09	20	49.42
12.14	30	74.13
16.19	40	98.84
20.23	50	123.56
24.28	60	148.27
28.33	70	172.98
32.38	80	197.69
36.42	90	222.40
40.47	100	247.11

CAPACITY/VOLUME

litres	litres or gallons	gallons
4.55	1	0.22
9.09	2	0.44
13.64	3	0.66
18.18	4	0.88
22.73	5	1.10
27.28	6	1.32
31.82	7	1.54
36.37	8	1.76
40.91	9	1.98
45.46	10	2.20
90.92	20	4.40
136.38	30	6.60
181.84	40	8.80
227.31	50	11.00
272.77	60	13.20
318.23	70	15.40
363.69	80	17.60
409.15	90	19.80
454.61	100	22.00

SPEED–VITESSE

MPH	20	30	40	50	60	70	80	90	100	$(\times \frac{8}{5})$
KMPH	32	48	64	80	96	112	128	144	160	$(\times \frac{5}{8})$

TEMPERATURE–TEMPÉRATURE

Centigrade
$-18°$ -10 0   10   20   30   40°

0° 10 20 32 40 50 60 70 80 90 100 110°
Fahrenheit

$$C = \frac{5}{9}(F - 32) \quad F = \frac{9}{5}C + 32$$

Balance sheet and statement of a large multinational company

Bilan et résultats d'une grande multinationale

Consolidated Balance Sheet Assets

	DECEMBER 31,	
	1984	1983
	(stated in thousands)	
CURRENT ASSETS		
Cash	$ 41,349	$ 21,564
Short-term investments	3,964,119	3,167,077
Receivables less allowance for doubtful accounts (1984—$25,526; 1983—$27,083)	1,215,143	1,089,599
Inventories	689,748	602,330
Other current assets	87,802	73,181
	5,998,161	4,953,751
INVESTMENTS IN AFFILIATED COMPANIES	731,964	267,693
LONG-TERM INVESTMENTS AND RECEIVABLES	219,982	111,859
FIXED ASSETS less accumulated depreciation	3,145,158	2,621,027
EXCESS OF INVESTMENT OVER NET ASSETS OF COMPANIES PURCHASED less amortization	760,756	366,676
OTHER ASSETS	57,173	32,233
	$ 10,913,194	$ 8,353,239

SEE NOTES TO CONSOLIDATED FINANCIAL STATEMENTS

Bilan consolidé
Actif

	AU 31 DECEMBRE	
	1984	1983
	(en milliers de dollars)	
VALEURS REALISABLES OU DISPONIBLES		
Caisses et banques	$ 41 349	$ 21 564
Dépôts à terme et titres de placement	3 964 119	3 167 077
Clients et autres débiteurs, moins provisions pour créances douteuses		
(1984—$25 526; 1983—$27 083)	1 215 143	1 089 599
Stocks	689 748	602 330
Autres valeurs réalisables ou disponibles	87 802	73 181
	5 998 161	4 953 751
PARTICIPATIONS DANS LES SOCIETES AFFILIEES	731 964	267 693
TITRES DE PARTICIPATION ET CREANCES A LONG TERME	219 982	111 859
IMMOBILISATIONS, moins amortissements cumulés	3 145 158	2 621 027
PRIMES D'ACQUISITION DES TITRES DE PARTICIPATION, moins amortissements cumulés	760 756	366 676
AUTRES ACTIFS A LONG TERME	57 173	32 233
	$ 10 913 194	$ 8 353 239

VOIR NOTES SUR LES ETATS FINANCIERS CONSOLIDES

Consolidated Balance Sheet Liabilities and Stockholders' Equity

	DECEMBER 31,	
	1984	1983
	(stated in thousands)	
CURRENT LIABILITIES		
Accounts payable and accrued liabilities	$ 942,196	$ 796,320
Estimated liability for taxes on income	890,894	597,584
Bank loans	829,555	441,272
Dividend payable	86,597	75,432
Long-term debt due within one year	27,884	12,955
	2,777,126	1,923,563
LONG-TERM DEBT	965,580	455,259
OTHER LIABILITIES	159,806	140,915
MINORITY INTEREST IN SUBSIDIARIES	18,480	14,652
	3,920,992	2,534,389
STOCKHOLDERS' EQUITY		
Common stock	421,583	359,537
Income retained for use in the business	6,908,246	6,049,223
Treasury stock at cost	(127,472)	(449,967)
Translation adjustment	(210,155)	(139,943)
	6,992,202	5,818,850
	$ 10,913,194	$ 8,353,239

SEE NOTES TO CONSOLIDATED FINANCIAL STATEMENTS

Bilan consolidé
Passif et fonds propres

SCHLUMBERGER
LIMITED
(SCHLUMBERGER
N.V., ANTILLES
NEERLANDAISES) ET
SOCIETES FILIALES

	AU 31 DECEMBRE	
	1984	1983
	(en milliers de dollars)	
DETTES A COURT TERME		
Fournisseurs, autres créanciers et frais à payer	$ 942 196	$ 796 320
Provisions pour impôts sur les bénéfices	890 894	597 584
Emprunts bancaires	829 555	441 272
Dividendes à payer	86 597	75 432
Fraction des dettes à long terme payable à moins d'un an	27 884	12 955
	2 777 126	1 923 563
DETTES A LONG TERME	965 580	455 259
AUTRES ELEMENTS DE PASSIF	159 806	140 915
INTERETS MINORITAIRES DANS LES FILIALES	18 480	14 652
	3 920 992	2 534 389
FONDS PROPRES		
Capital—actions ordinaires	421 583	359 537
Bénéfices réinvestis	6 908 246	6 049 223
Actions rachetées par la Société (évaluées au prix d'achat)	(127 472)	(449 967)
Correction pour tenir compte des différences de conversion	(210 155)	(139 943)
	6 992 202	5 818 850
	$ 10 913 194	$ 8 353 239

VOIR NOTES SUR LES ETATS FINANCIERS CONSOLIDES

Consolidated Statement of Income

SCHLUMBERGER LIMITED (SCHLUMBERGER N.V., INCORPORATED IN THE NETHERLANDS ANTILLES) AND SUBSIDIARY COMPANIES

	1984	YEAR ENDED DECEMBER 31, 1983 (stated in thousands)	1982
REVENUE			
Operating	$ 5,978,552	$ 5,513,246	$ 6,025,380
Interest and other income	391,890	284,213	258,430
	6,370,442	5,797,459	6,238,810
EXPENSES			
Cost of goods sold and services	3,652,790	3,388,364	3,478,525
Research & Engineering	393,441	349,377	326,458
Marketing	287,480	270,756	258,875
General	311,402	284,347	303,965
Interest	153,436	115,578	116,634
Taxes on income	389,820	304,738	451,188
	5,188,369	4,713,160	4,935,645
NET INCOME	$ 1,182,073	$ 1,084,299	$ 1,348,165
Net income per share	$ 4.10	$ 3.73	$ 4.60
Average shares outstanding (thousands)	288,580	290,933	293,119

SEE NOTES TO CONSOLIDATED FINANCIAL STATEMENTS

Résultats consolidés

	1984	EXERCICE CLOS LE 31 DECEMBRE 1983 *(en milliers de dollars)*	1982
CHIFFRE D'AFFAIRES			
Exploitation	$ 5 978 552	$ 5 513 246	$ 6 025 380
Intérêts et autres revenus	391 890	284 213	258 430
	6 370 442	5 797 459	6 238 810
DEPENSES			
Coût des ventes et des services	3 652 790	3 388 364	3 478 525
Frais d'études et de recherche	393 441	349 377	326 458
Frais de vente	287 480	270 756	258 875
Frais généraux	311 402	284 347	303 965
Frais financiers	153 436	115 578	116 634
Impôts sur les bénéfices	389 820	304 738	451 188
	5 188 369	4 713 160	4 935 645
BENEFICE NET	$ 1 182 073	$ 1 084 299	$ 1 348 165
Bénéfice net par action	$ 4.10	$ 3.73	$ 4.60
Nombre moyen d'actions en circulation (en milliers)	288 580	290 933	293 119

VOIR NOTES SUR LES ETATS FINANCIERS CONSOLIDES

Consolidated Statement of Stockholders' Equity

SCHLUMBERGER LIMITED (SCHLUMBERGER N.V., INCORPORATED IN THE NETHERLANDS ANTILLES) AND SUBSIDIARY COMPANIES

| | COMMON STOCK | | | | | INCOME RETAINED FOR |
| | ISSUED | | IN TREASURY | | TRANSLATION | USE IN |
	SHARES	AMOUNT	SHARES	AMOUNT	ADJUSTMENT	THE BUSINESS
	(Dollar amounts in thousands)					
Balance, January 1, 1982	302,247,565	$ 307,210	12,978,316	$ 239,889		$ 4,167,312
Translation adjustment, opening					$ (25,561)	
Translation adjustment, 1982					(56,439)	
Purchases for Treasury			1,569,500	63,279		
Issued for Applicon		37,867	(4,005,634)	(1,603)		9,842
Sales to optionees	337,046	7,804	(137,766)	(1,435)		
Net income						1,348,165
Dividends declared ($0.92 per share)						(269,626)
Balance, December 31, 1982	302,584,611	352,881	10,404,416	300,130	(82,000)	5,255,693
Translation adjustment, 1983					(57,943)	
Purchases for Treasury			3,011,000	150,483		
Sales to optionees less shares exchanged	395,170	6,656	(60,425)	(646)		
Net income						1,084,299
Dividends declared ($1.00 per share)						(290,769)
Balance, December 31, 1983	302,979,781	359,537	13,354,991	449,967	(139,943)	6,049,223
Translation adjustment, 1984					(70,212)	
Purchases for Treasury			2,328,000	110,867		
Issued for SEDCO		52,564	(12,996,526)	(433,181)		
Sales to optionees less shares exchanged	391,000	9,482	(17,449)	(181)		
Net income						1,182,073
Dividends declared ($1.12 per share)						(323,050)
Balance, December 31, 1984	303,370,781	$ 421,583	2,669,016	$ 127,472	$ (210,155)	$ 6,908,246

SEE NOTES TO CONSOLIDATED FINANCIAL STATEMENTS

Etat consolidé des fonds propres

| | ACTIONS ORDINAIRES | | | | CORRECTION POUR TENIR COMPTE DES DIFFERENCES DE CONVERSION | BENEFICES REINVESTIS |
| | EMISES | | RACHETEES PAR LA SOCIETE | | | |
	NOMBRE D'ACTIONS	VALEUR	NOMBRE D'ACTIONS	VALEUR		
	(valeurs exprimées en milliers de dollars)					
Solde au 1er janvier 1982	302 247 565	$ 307 210	12 978 316	$ 239 889		$4 167 312
Correction pour tenir compte des différences de conversion au début d'exercice					$ (25 561)	
Correction pour tenir compte des différences de conversion au 31 décembre 1982					(56 439)	
Rachat par la Société de ses propres actions			1 569 500	63 279		
Emission réalisée pour l'acquisition d'Applicon		37 867	(4 005 634)	(1 603)		9 842
Exercice des options d'achat d'actions	337 046	7 804	(137 766)	(1 435)		
Bénéfice net						1 348 165
Dividendes déclarés ($0.92 par action)						(269 626)
Solde au 31 décembre 1982	302 584 611	352 881	10 404 416	300 130	(82 000)	5 255 693
Correction pour tenir compte des différences de conversion au 31 décembre 1983					(57 943)	
Rachat par la Société de ses propres actions			3 011 000	150 483		
Exercice des options d'achat d'actions, déduction faite des actions échangées	395 170	6 656	(60 425)	(646)		
Bénéfice net						1 084 299
Dividendes déclarés ($1,00 par action)						(290 769)
Solde au 31 décembre 1983	302 979 781	359 537	13 354 991	449 967	(139 943)	6 049 223
Correction pour tenir compte des différences de conversion au 31 décembre 1984					(70 212)	
Rachat par la Société de ses propres actions			2 328 000	110 867		
Emission réalisée pour l'acquisition de SEDCO		52 564	(12 996 526)	(433 181)		
Exercice des options d'achat d'actions, déduction faite des actions échangées	391 000	9 482	(17 449)	(181)		
Bénéfice net						1 182 073
Dividendes déclarés ($1,12 par action)						(323 050)
Solde au 31 décembre 1984	303 370 781	$ 421 583	2 669 016	$ 127 472	$ (210 155)	$ 6 908 246

VOIR NOTES SUR LES ETATS FINANCIERS CONSOLIDES

Consolidated Statement of Changes in Financial Position

	1984	YEAR ENDED DECEMBER 31, 1983 *(stated in thousands)*	1982
SOURCE OF WORKING CAPITAL			
Net income	$1,182,073	$1,084,299	$1,348,165
Add (deduct) amounts not affecting working capital			
Depreciation and amortization	735,276	692,194	596,044
Earnings of companies carried at equity less dividends received (1984—$99,000; 1983—$61,164; 1982—$15,272)	77,764	12,328	(62,390)
Other—net	(51,460)	30,910	(20,894)
Working capital provided from operations	1,943,653	1,819,731	1,860,925
Value of shares exchanged for SEDCO	485,745	—	—
Net worth of Applicon acquired for shares	—	—	49,312
Increase in long-term debt	620,572	121,380	192,047
Retirement and sales of fixed assets	59,337	84,179	51,510
Proceeds from sale of shares to optionees	9,663	7,302	9,239
Total working capital provided	3,118,970	2,032,592	2,163,033
APPLICATION OF WORKING CAPITAL			
Net noncurrent assets of SEDCO acquired	1,129,459	—	—
Purchase of Dowell business and assets in North America	438,661	—	—
Increase in excess of investment over net assets of companies purchased	35,417	—	104,029
Increase in other long-term investments and receivables	14,029	57,233	40,971
Additions to fixed assets	726,578	517,030	1,094,334
Dividends declared	323,050	290,769	269,626
Reduction of long-term debt	120,509	126,033	13,336
Effect of exchange rate changes on working capital	24,758	28,114	31,306
Purchases of shares for Treasury	110,867	150,483	63,279
Other—net	4,795	4,084	12,202
Total working capital applied	2,928,123	1,173,746	1,629,083
NET INCREASE IN WORKING CAPITAL	$ 190,847	$ 858,846	$ 533,950
INCREASE IN WORKING CAPITAL CONSISTS OF			
Increase (decrease) in current assets			
Cash and short-term investments	$ 816,827	$ 866,058	$ 640,395
Receivables	125,544	(36,382)	(56,795)
Inventories	87,418	(73,765)	63,711
Other current assets	14,621	(16,368)	26,532
(Increase) decrease in current liabilities			
Accounts and dividend payable	(157,041)	42,611	(76,397)
Estimated liability for taxes on income	(293,310)	20,919	4,545
Bank loans and debt due within one year	(403,212)	55,773	(68,041)
NET INCREASE IN WORKING CAPITAL	$ 190,847	$ 858,846	$ 533,950

SEE NOTES TO CONSOLIDATED FINANCIAL STATEMENTS

Etat consolidé de l'origine et de l'emploi des fonds

SCHLUMBERGER LIMITED (SCHLUMBERGER N.V., ANTILLES NEERLANDAISES) ET SOCIETES FILIALES

| | EXERCICE CLOS LE 31 DECEMBRE | | |
	1984	1983 *(en milliers de dollars)*	1982
ORIGINE DU FONDS DE ROULEMENT			
Bénéfice net	$1 182 073	$1 084 299	$1 348 165
Ajouter (déduire)—montants n'affectant pas le fonds de roulement			
Amortissements des immobilisations corporelles et incorporelles	735 276	692 194	596 044
Participation dans le bénéfice net des sociétés mises en équivalence, moins dividendes reçus (1984—$99 000; 1983—$61 164; 1982—$15 272)	77 764	12 328	(62 390)
Autres—nets	(51 460)	30 910	(20 894)
Fonds de roulement provenant de l'exploitation	1 943 653	1 819 731	1 860 925
Valeurs des actions échangées pour l'acquisition de SEDCO	485 745	—	—
Actif net d'Applicon rémunéré par émission d'actions	—	—	49 312
Accroissement des dettes à long terme	620 572	121 380	192 047
Retraits et cessions d'immobilisations corporelles	59 337	84 179	51 510
Produits de la vente d'actions aux bénéficiaires d'options	9 663	7 302	9 239
Total de l'origine du fonds de roulement	3 118 970	2 032 592	2 163 033
EMPLOI DU FONDS DE ROULEMENT			
Actif net à long term de SEDCO	1 129 459	—	—
Achat de Dowell Schlumberger-Amérique du Nord	438 661	—	—
Augmentation des primes d'acquisition des titres de participation	35 417	—	104 029
Accroissement des titres de participation dans les sociétés non consolidées et des créances à long terme	14 029	57 233	40 971
Achats d'immobilisations corporelles	726 578	517 030	1 094 334
Dividendes déclarés	323 050	290 769	269 626
Remboursement de dettes à long terme	120 509	126 033	13 336
Effet des variations monétaires sur le fonds de roulement	24 758	28 114	31 306
Rachat par la Société de ses propres actions	110 867	150 483	63 279
Autres—net	4 795	4 084	12 202
Total des emplois du fonds de roulement	2 928 123	1 173 746	1 629 083
AUGMENTATION NETTE DU FONDS DE ROULEMENT	$ 190 847	$ 858 846	$ 533 950
AUGMENTATION DU FONDS DE ROULEMENT SE DECOMPOSE COMME SUIT:			
Augmentation (diminution) des valeurs réalisables ou disponibles			
Caisses, banques, dépôts à terme et titres de placement	$ 816 827	$ 866 058	$ 640 395
Clients et autres débiteurs	125 544	(36 382)	(56 795)
Stocks	87 418	(73 765)	63 711
Autres valeurs réalisables ou disponibles	14 621	(16 368)	26 532
(Augmentation) diminution des dettes à court terme			
Fournisseurs, charges et dividendes à payer	(157 041)	42 611	(76 397)
Provisions pour impôts sur les bénéfices	(293 310)	20 919	4 545
Emprunts bancaires et dettes à moins d'un an	(403 212)	55 773	(68 041)
AUGMENTATION NETTE DU FONDS DE ROULEMENT	$ 190 847	$ 858 846	$ 533 950

VOIR NOTES SUR LES ETATS FINANCIERS CONSOLIDES

Notes to Consolidated Balance Sheet

SUMMARY OF ACCOUNTING POLICIES

The Consolidated Financial Statements of Schlumberger Limited have been prepared in accordance with accounting principles generally accepted in the United States. Within those principles, the Company's more important accounting policies are set forth below.

PRINCIPLES OF CONSOLIDATION

The Consolidated Financial Statements include the accounts of majority-owned subsidiaries. Significant 20%–50% owned companies are carried in investments in affiliated companies on the equity method. The pro rata share of revenue and expenses of 50% owned companies is included in the individual captions in the Consolidated Statement of Income. Schlumberger's pro rata share of after tax earnings of other equity companies is included in interest and other income.

TRANSLATION OF NON-U.S. CURRENCIES

Effective January 1, 1982, the Company adopted Financial Accounting Standard No. 52 – Foreign Currency Translation. Under this method, all assets and liabilities recorded in functional currencies other than U.S. dollars are translated at current exchange rates. The resulting adjustments are charged or credited directly to the Stockholders' Equity section of the balance sheet. Stockholders' Equity has been reduced by $70.2 million, $57.9 million and $56.4 million in 1984, 1983 and 1982, respectively. Revenue and expenses are translated at the weighted average exchange rates for the period.

All transaction gains and losses are included in income in the period in which they occur. Transaction gains included in 1984 net income amounted to $9 million compared to $14 million in 1983 and $11 million in 1982.

SHORT-TERM INVESTMENTS

Short-term investments are stated at cost plus accrued interest, which approximates the market, and comprised mainly U.S. dollar time deposits and U.S. Government obligations.

INVENTORIES

Inventories are stated principally at average or standard cost, which approximates average cost, or at market, if lower.

Notes sur les états financiers consolidés

METHODES COMPTABLES ADOPTEES

Les états financiers consolidés de Schlumberger Limited ont été préparés conformément aux principes comptables généralement admis aux Etats-Unis. Dans ce cadre, les principales méthodes comptables en vigueur dans le groupe sont exposées ci-dessous.

PRINCIPES DE CONSOLIDATION

Les états financiers consolidés intègrent les comptes des filiales dans lesquelles Schlumberger détient une participation majoritaire. Les principales sociétés dans lesquelles Schlumberger détient une participation comprise entre 20% et 50% sont incluses dans le bilan sous la rubrique Participations dans les sociétés affiliées, pour une valeur égale à la quote-part de Schlumberger dans leurs actifs nets (mise en équivalence). Les recettes et dépenses des des sociétés détenues à 50% ont été incluses dans les rubriques appropriées des Résultats consolidés, au prorata de la participation de Schlumberger. La quote-part des bénéfices après impôts des autres sociétés mises en équivalence est incluse dans la rubrique Intérêts et autres revenus.

CONVERSION DES DEVISES AUTRES QUE LE DOLLAR DES ETATS-UNIS

Au 1er janvier 1982, la Société a appliqué es principes retenus par la norme comptable américaine n° 52 édictée par le *Financial Accounting Standards Board* et qui concerne la conversion des monnaies étrangères. Selon cette methode, les postes du bilan enregistrés dans des monnaies fonctionnelles autres que le dollar sont convertis au taux de change en vigueur à la fin de l'exercice (taux de change courants). Les pertes ou profits de conversion sont imputés directement aux Fonds propres qui ont été réduits de 70,2 millions, de 57,9 et 56,4 millions de dollars en 1984, 1983 et 1982, respectivement. Les comptes de résultats sont convertis au taux moyen de change de l'exercice.

Tous les profits ou pertes de conversion sont portés aux comptes de résultats de l'année correspondante. Ces conversions se traduisent en 1984 par un gain de 9 millions de dollars par rapport à 14 millions en 1983 et 11 millions en 1982.

PLACEMENTS A COURT TERME

Les placements à court terme sont comptabilisés au prix d'achat majoré des produits financiers à recevoir, proches du taux du marché monétaire, et concernent essentiellement des dépôts à terme en dollars et des bons du trésor des Etats-Unis.

STOCKS

Les stocks sont généralement évalués au prix de revient moyen ou standard (ce dernier étant alors équivalent au prix de revient moyen), ou au prix du marché si celui-ci est inférieur au prix de revient.

FIXED ASSETS AND DEPRECIATION

Fixed assets are stated at cost less accumulated depreciation, which is provided for by charges to income over the estimated useful lives of the assets by the straight-line method. Fixed assets include the cost of Company manufactured oilfield technical equipment. Expenditures for renewals, replacements and betterments are capitalized. Maintenance and repairs are charged to operating expenses as incurred. Upon sale or other disposition, the applicable amounts of asset cost and accumulated depreciation are removed from the accounts and the net amount, less proceeds from disposal, is charged or credited to income.

EXCESS OF INVESTMENT OVER NET ASSETS OF COMPANIES PURCHASED

Costs in excess of net assets of purchased companies having an indeterminate life are amortized on a straight-line basis over 40 years. Accumulated amortization was $59 million and $48 million at December 31, 1984 and 1983, respectively.

DEFERRED BENEFIT PLANS

The Company and its subsidiaries have several voluntary pension and other deferred benefit plans covering substantially all officers and employees, including those in countries other than the United States. These plans are substantially fully funded with trustees in respect to past and current services. Charges to expense are based upon costs computed by independent actuaries.

In France, the principal pensions are provided for by union agreements negotiated by all employers within an industry on a nationwide basis. Benefits when paid are not identified with particular employers, but are made from funds obtained through concurrent compulsory contributions from all employers within each industry based on employee salaries. These plans are accounted for on the defined contribution basis and each year's contributions are charged currently to expense.

TAXES ON INCOME

Schlumberger and its subsidiaries compute taxes on income in accordance with the tax rules and regulations of the many taxing authorities where the income is earned. The income tax rates imposed by these taxing authorities vary substantially. Taxable income may differ from pretax income for financial accounting purposes. To the extent that differences are due to revenue or expense items reported in one period for tax purposes and in another period for financial accounting purposes, an appropriate provision for deferred income taxes is made. The provisions were not significant in 1984, 1983 or 1982.

Approximately $6.5 billion of consolidated income retained for use in the business at December 31, 1984 represented undistributed earnings or consolidated subsidiaries and Schlumberger's pro rata share of 20% – 50% owned companies. It is the policy of the Company to reinvest substantially all such undistributed earnings and, accordingly, no provision is made for deferred income taxes on those earnings considered to be indefinitely reinvested.

Investment credits and other allowances provided by income tax laws of the United States and other countries are credited to current income tax expense on the flow-through method of accounting.

NET INCOME PER SHARE

Net income per share is computed by dividing net income by the average number of common shares outstanding during the year

RESEARCH & ENGINEERING

All research & engineering expenditures are expensed as incurred, including costs relating to patents or rights which may result from such expenditures.

IMMOBILISATIONS ET AMORTISSEMENTS

Les immobilisations sont évaluées à leur prix d'acquisition diminué des amortissements; les amortissements sont calculés et imputés aux résultats selon le mode linéaire basé sur la durée probable d'utilisation des immobilisations. L'équipement technique pétrolier fabriqué par la Société est inclus, au prix de revient, dans les immobilisations. Les dépenses encourues pour les remises en état, remplacements et modernisations des immobilisations sont capitalisées. Les dépenses d'entretien et de réparation sont imputées immédiatement aux frais d'exploitation. Lors de la vente ou de la cession d'une immobilisation, son prix d'acquisition et les amortissements cumulés correspondants sont déduits des comptes du bilan et le montant net, diminué du prix de vente, est passé en perte ou en profit dans les comptes de résultats.

PRIMES D'ACQUISITION DES TITRES DE PARTICIPATION

L'excédent du prix d'acquisition sur la valeur raisonnablement estimée de l'actif net des sociétés acquises représente une prime d'acquisition; ces primes sont en général amorties linéairement sur 40 ans. Les amortissements cumulés constatés à ce titre étaient, respectivement, de 59 millions et de 48 millions de dollars aux 31 décembre 1984 et 1983.

PLANS DE RETRAITE ET D'INTERESSEMENT DIFFERE

La Société et ses filiales ont adopté plusieurs plans facultatifs de retraite et d'intéressement différé en faveur de la presque totalité de leurs cadres et de leur personnel, aux Etats-Unis comme dans les autres pays. Ces plans sont presque intégralement couverts par des versements effectués auprès de trustees, tant pour les services passés que présents. Les charges comptabilisées dans l'exercice sont déterminées par des actuaires indépendants.

En France, les principaux régimes de retraite sont établis par des conventions collectives négociées pour l'ensemble du pays par tous les employeurs et les syndicats d'un même secteur d'activité. Les pensions, lorsqu'elles sont payées, ne le sont pas par l'employeur lui-même; elles sont prélevées sur des fonds alimentés par les cotisations payées obligatoirement par les employeurs dans chaque secteur d'activité et déterminées en fonction du salaire des employés. Les cotisations de l'année sont comptabilisées dans les charges de l'exercice.

IMPOTS SUR LES BENEFICES

Schlumberger et ses filiales calculent l'impôt sur les bénéfices en fonction des divers codes et règlements fiscaux en vigueur dans les nombreux pays dans lesquels les bénéfices sont réalisés. Les taux d'imposition fixés par les autorités fiscales de ces pays varient considérablement. Le bénéfice imposable peut être différent du bénéfice avant impôts tel qu'il ressort des états financiers. Dans la mesure où la différence est due au fait que certains revenus ou frais peuvent être imputables à un exercice donné pour le calcul de l'impôt et à un autre exercice pour la détermination du résultat comptable, des provisions appropriées pour impôts différés sur les bénéfices sont constituées. Ces provisions n'ont pas été significatives en 1984, 1983 et 1982.

Au 31 décembre 1984, environ 6,5 milliards de dollars de bénéfices consolidés réinvestis représentaient les bénéfices non distribués des filiales consolidées ainsi que la quote-part revenant à Schlumberger dans les sociétés détenues de 20% à 50%. La politique de la Société étant de réinvestir la quasi-totalité de ces bénéfices non distribués, il n'a donc pas été constitué de provision pour les impôts qui seraient dûs sur la répartition de ceux-ci, ces bénéfices étant considérés comme réinvestis indéfiniment.

Les crédits d'impôts pour investissements et autres déductions fiscales prévus par les législations fiscales des Etats-Unis et des autres pays sont déduits de l'impôt sur les bénéfices de l'année au cours de laquelle ils ont pris naissance.

BENEFICE NET PAR ACTION

Le bénéfice net par action est calculé en divisant le bénéfice net par le nombre moyen d'actions ordinaires en circulation au cours de l'exercice.

FRAIS D'ETUDES ET DE RECHERCHE

Tous les frais d'études et de recherche, ainsi que les dépenses relatives aux brevets et aux droits qui pourraient en résulter, sont pris en charge immédiatement.

ACQUISITIONS

In April 1984, a subsidiary of the Company acquired 50% of the Dowell business and assets in the United States from The Dow Chemical Company and in July 1984, a subsidiary of the Company acquired 50% of the Canadian operation of Dowell at a combined cost of $439 million. Dowell Schlumberger provides cementing, stimulation and other oilfield services. The acquisitions have been accounted for as purchases and are carried on in investments in affiliated companies, including cost in excess of the fair values of the net assets acquired amounting to $196 million which is being amortized on a straight-line basis over 40 years. The pro rata share of revenue and expenses, from the dates of acquisition, is included in the individual captions in the Consolidated Statement of Income.

On December 24, 1984, a subsidiary of the Company acquired SEDCO, Inc., an offshore drilling contractor operating mainly outside the United States, at a total cost of $968 million ($482 million in cash and approximately 13 million shares of Schlumberger Common Stock valued at $486 million). The acquisition has been accounted for as a purchase and the accounts of SEDCO have been consolidated with those of Schlumberger effective December 31, 1984 after assigning estimated fair values to the individual assets acquired and liabilities assumed. Cost in excess of net assets acquired is currently estimated at $372 million which will be amortized on a straight-line basis over 40 years.

If these acquisitions had taken place on January 1, 1983, the consolidated pro forma unaudited results of Schlumberger would have been:

YEAR ENDED DECEMBER 31,	1984	1983
	(Stated in millions)	
Revenue	$7,035	$6,727
Net income	$1,236	$1,117
Net income per share (dollars)	$ 4.10	$ 3.68
Average shares outstanding (thousands)	301,577	303,930

FIXED ASSETS

A summary of fixed assets follows:

DECEMBER 31,	1984	1983
	(Stated in millions)	
Land	$ 81	$ 66
Buildings & improvements	722	644
Machinery and equipment	4,990	4,068
Total cost	5,793	4,778
Less accumulated depreciation	2,648	2,157
	$3,145	$2,621

Estimated useful lives of buildings & improvements range from 8 to 50 years and of machinery and equipment from 2 to 15 years.

INVESTMENTS IN AFFILIATED COMPANIES

Investments in affiliated companies at December 31, 1984 comprised mainly the Company's 50% investment in the worldwide Dowell Schlumberger business which aggregated $610 million and investments in 50% owned companies acquired through the acquisition of SEDCO. The excess of the Company's investment in all 50% owned affiliated companies over its underlying equity is $261 million, representing primarily the goodwill arising from the acquisition of 50% of the Dowell business and assets in North America.

Combined financial data for all 50% owned affiliated companies are as follows:

DECEMBER 31,	1984
	(Stated in millions)
Current assets	$ 683
Fixed assets	1,039
Other assets	29
	$1,751
Liabilities	$ 857
Equity	894
	$1,751

Equity in undistributed earnings of all 50% owned companies, since acquisition, at December 31, 1984 and 1983, amounted to $172 million and $238 million, respectively.

ACQUISITIONS

En avril 1984, une filiale de la Société a acheté à Dow Chemical 50% des activités et actifs de Dowell aux Etats-Unis et en juillet 1984, une filiale de la Société a acheté 50% des activités et actifs de Dowell au Canada pour un prix d'achat global de 439 millions de dollars. Dowell Schlumberger fournit des services de cimentation et de stimulation et autres services pétroliers. Ces acquisitions ont été comptabilisées comme des achats et figurent à l'actif du bilan consolidé sous la rubrique Participations dans les sociétés affiliées, incluant l'excédent du prix d'acquisition sur la valeur raisonnablement estimée de l'actif net acquis évalué à 196 millions de dollars. Cette prime d'acquisition est amortie linéairement sur 40 ans. Les recettes et dépenses, depuis les dates d'acquisition, ont été incluses dans les rubriques appropriées des Résultats consolidés, au prorata de la participation de Schlumberger.

Le 24 décembre 1984, une filiale de la Société a acheté SEDCO, une société de forage en mer opérant surtout en dehors des Etats-Unis, pour un prix total de 968 millions de dollars (482 millions de dollars en espèces et environ 13 millions d'actions Schlumberger évaluées à 486 millions de dollars). Cette acquisition a été comptabilisée comme un achat et les comptes de SEDCO ont été consolidés avec ceux de Schlumberger au 31 décembre 1984 après avoir attribué des valeurs considérées comme raisonnables à chaque actif acquis et à chaque dette présumée. L'excédent du prix d'acquisition sur la valeur estimée de l'actif net acquis est évalué à 372 millions de dollars qui seront amortis linéairement sur 40 ans.

Si ces acquisitions avaient eu lieu au 1er anvier 1983, les résultats consolidés de Schlumberger, non certifiés par les réviseurs comptables, auraient été:

EXERCICE CLOS LE 31 DECEMBRE	1984	1983
	(en millions de dollars)	
Chiffre d'affaires	$7 035	$6 727
Bénéfice net	$1 236	$1 117
Bénéfice par action (en dollars)	$ 4,10	$ 3,68
Nombre moyen d'actions en circulation (en milliers)	301 577	303 930

IMMOBILISATIONS

Les immobilisations corporelles se répartissent comme suit:

AU 31 DECEMBRE	1984	1983
	(en millions de dollars)	
Terrains	$ 81	$ 66
Immeubles et agencements	722	644
Matériel et équipement	4 990	4 068
Prix de revient total	5 793	4 778
A déduire:		
amortissements cumulés	2 648	2 157
	$3 145	$2 621

Les durées de vie estimées des immeubles et agencements se situent entre 8 et 50 ans, et celles du matériel et de l'équipement entre 2 et 15 ans.

PARTICIPATION DANS LE SOCIETES AFFILIEES

Au 31 décembre 1984, les participations dans les sociétés affiliées comprenaient principalement la participation à 50% de la Société dans les activés mondiales de Dowell Schlumberger qui s'élevaient à 610 millions de dollars et aux participations dans les sociétés détenues à 50% acquises par le biais de l'achat de SEDCO.

Le surplus de l'investissement de la Société dans toutes les filiales détenues à 50% par rapport à leur actif net s'élève à 261 millions de dollars, représentant surtout le fonds de commerce résultant de l'acquisition de 50% des activités et actifs de Dowell en Amérique du Nord.

Les données financières regroupées pour toutes les filiales détenues à 50% s'analysent comme suit:

AU 31 DECEMBRE	1984
	(en milliers de dollars)
Valeurs réalisables ou disponibles	$ 683
Immobilisations	1 039
Autres actifs	29
	$1 751
Dettes	$ 857
Fonds propres	894
	$1 751

L'actif net dans les profits non distribués de toutes les sociétés détenues à 50%, depuis la date d'acquisition, était de 172 millions et 238 millions de dollars aux 31 décembre 1984 et 1983, respectivement.

LONG-TERM DEBT
Long-term debt consisted of the following:

DECEMBER 31,	1984	1983
	(Stated in millions)	
Bank loan due 1990, interest at money market based rates	$800	$350
Other bank loans	166	105
	$966	$455

Long-term debt at December 31, 1984 is payable principally in U.S. dollars and is due $46 million in 1986, $26 million in 1987, $35 million in 1988, $16 million in 1989 and $843 million thereafter.

LINES OF CREDIT
The Company's principal U.S. subsidiary has a Revolving Credit Agreement with a group of banks. The agreement provides that the subsidiary may borrow up to $1.2 billion until December 31, 1990 at money market based rates, of which $800 million was outstanding as of December 31, 1984. In addition, at December 31, 1984, the Company had available unused short-term lines of credit of $258 million.

CAPITAL STOCK
The Company is authorized to issue 500,000,000 shares of Common Stock, par value $.01 per share, of which 300,701,765 and 289,624,790 shares were outstanding on December 31, 1984 and 1983, respectively. The Company is also authorized to issue 200,000,000 shares of cumulative Preferred Stock, par value $.01 per share, which may be issued in series with terms and conditions determined by the Board of Directors. No shares of Preferred Stock have been issued. Holders of Common Stock and Preferred Stock are entitled to one vote for each share of stock held.

Options to officers and key employees to purchase shares of the Company's Common Stock were granted at prices equal to 100% of fair market value at date of grant.

Transactions under stock option plans were as follows:

	NUMBER OF SHARES	OPTION PRICE PER SHARE
Outstanding		
Jan. 1, 1983	3,060,635	$ 1.57 – 74.82
Granted	1,023,550	$43.75 – 56.88
Exercised	(631,044)	$ 1.57 – 54.67
Lapsed or terminated	(226,038)	$ 1.57 – 74.64
Outstanding		
Dec. 31, 1983	3,227,103	$ 1.57 – 74.82
Granted	1,744,800	$37.38 – 51.38
Exercised	(555,005)	$ 1.57 – 43.75
Lapsed or terminated	(400,304)	$ 2.09 – 74.82
Exercisable at		
Dec. 31, 1984	1,120,165	$ 2.09 – 74.72
Available for grant		
Dec. 31, 1983	10,913,635	
Dec. 31, 1984	9,509,329	

INCOME TAX EXPENSE
The Company is incorporated in the Netherlands Antilles where it is subject to an income tax rate of 3%. The Company and its subsidiaries operate in over 100 taxing jurisdictions with statutory rates ranging up to about 50%. Consolidated operating revenue of $6.0 billion in 1984 shown elsewhere in this report includes $2.5 billion derived from operations within the United States. On a worldwide basis, the Company's effective income tax rate was 25% in 1984, 22% in 1983 and 25% in 1982.

DETTES A LONG TERME
Les dettes à long terme s'analysent comme suit:

AU 31 DECEMBRE	1984	1983
	(en milliers de dollars)	
Emprunt bancaire remboursable en 1990, intérêts au taux du marché monétaire	$800	$350
Autres emprunts bancaires	166	105
	$966	$455

Ces dettes sont remboursables principalement en dollars selon l'échéancier suivant exprimé en millions de dollars: 46 (1986), 26 (1987), 35 (1988), 16 (1989) et 843 à une date ultérieure.

LIGNES DE CREDIT
La principale filiale de Schlumberger aux Etats-Unis a passé avec plusieurs banques un accord de crédit renouvelable lui donnant la faculté d'emprunter, jusqu'au 31 décembre 1990, 1,2 milliard de dollars supplémentaires, au taux du marché monétaire, dont 800 millions avaient été utilisés au 31 décembre 1984. De plus, sur les lignes de crédit à court terme dont pouvait disposer la Société, 258 millions de dollars restaient non utilisés au 31 décembre 1984.

CAPITAL
La Société est autorisée à émettre 500 000 000 d'actions ordinaires, d'une valeur nominale de 0,01 dollar, dont, aux 31 décembre 1984 et 1983 respectivement, 300 701 765 et 289 624 790 étaient en circulation. La Société est également autorisée à émettre 200 000 00 d'actions cumulatives préférentielles ayant une valeur nominale de 0,01 dollar, qui pourront à l'avenir être émises par séries aux conditions définies par le Conseil d'administration. Aucune de ces actions préférentielles n'a encore été émise. Les porteurs d'actions ordinaires et préférentielles ont droit à une voix par action détenue.

Les options d'achat d'actions ordinaires de la Société accordées aux directeurs et cadres supérieurs le sont à un prix égal à 100% du cours de l'action à la date où le droit à option a été octroyé.

Les transactions intervenues au titre des plans d'options d'achat d'actions ont été les suivantes:

	NOMBRES D'ACTION	PRIX D'OPTION PAR ACTION
Solde au 1er janvier 1983	3 060 635	$ 1,57−74,82
Options accordées	1 023 550	$43,75−56,88
Options exercées	(631 044)	$ 1,57−54,67
Options caduques ou annulées	(226 038)	$ 1,57−74,64
Solde au 31 décembre 1983	3 227 103	$ 1,57−74,82
Options accordées	1 744 800	$37,38−51,38
Options exercées	(555 005)	$ 1,57−43,75
Options caduques ou annulées	(400 304)	$ 2,09−74,82
Solde au 31 décembre 1984	4 016 594	$ 2,09−74,72
Options pouvant être exercées au 31 décembre 1984	1 120 165	$ 2,09−74,72
Disponibles pour les plans d'options d'achat d'actions au 31 décembre 1983	10 913 635	
au 31 décembre 1984	9 509 329	

IMPOTS SUR LES BENEFICES
La Société est constituée selon les lois des Antilles néerlandaises, où elle est passible d'un impôt sur les bénéfices au taux de 3%. La Société et ses filiales exercent leurs activités dans plus de 100 juridictions fiscales différentes, avec des taux d'imposition pouvant atteindre 50%. Sur le chiffre d'affaires d'exploitation consolidé de 6 milliards de dollars réalisé en 1984 dont il est fait état par ailleurs, 2,5 milliards ont été réalisés aux Etats-Unis. Le taux effectif d'impôts sur les bénéfices mondialement réalisés ressort à 25% en 1984, 22% en 1983 et 25% en 1982.

LEASES AND LEASE COMMITMENTS

Total rental expense was $159 million in 1984, $144 million in 1983 and $149 million in 1982. Future minimum rental commitments under noncancellable leases for years ending December 31 are: 1985 – $74 million; 1986 – $63 million; 1987 – $50 million; 1988 – $40 million; and 1989 – $29 million. For the ensuing three five-year periods, these commitments decrease from $60 million to $13 million. The minimum rentals over the remaining terms of the leases aggregate $11 million.

TAX ASSESSMENTS

The U.S. Internal Revenue Service has completed its examinations for the years 1970 through 1978 and, as previously reported, has proposed assessments based upon income from continuing Wireline operations on the outer continental shelf. Similar assessments are expected for years subsequent to 1978. The Company is contesting these assessments. A trial has been scheduled in the U.S. District Court in Houston for the years 1970 through 1975.

Management of of the opinion that the reserve for estimated liability for taxes on income is adequate and that any adjustments which may ultimately be determined will not materially affect the financial position or results of operations.

CONTINGENCIES

During 1980, a floating hotel, the Alexander Kielland, functioning as a dormitory for offshore work crews in the North Sea, capsized in a storm. The substructure of the floating hotel had been originally built as a drilling rig by an independent shipyard from a design licensed by a subsidiary of the Company. The Company's subsidiary was not involved in the ownership or operation of the drilling rig or in its conversion or use as a floating hotel. The accident has been investigated by a Commission appointed by the Norwegian Government, which has published its report. In October of 1981 and in February of 1982, the Company's subsidiary, the independent shipyard and one of its subcontractors were sued in France by Phillips Petroleum Company Norway and eight others operating in the North Sea and by the Norwegian insurers of the Alexander Kielland seeking recovery for losses resulting from the accident of approximately $75 million (at December 31, 1984 currency exchange rates).

While the Company does not believe it has liability in this matter, the litigation will involve complex international issues which could take several years to resolve and involve substantial legal and other costs. In the opinion of the Company, any liability that might ensue would not be material in relation to its financial position or results of operations.

In 1981, a solvent tank failure was discovered at a Fairchild Semiconductor manufacturing plant in South San Jose, California. The failure allegedly contaminated soil and ground water. Legal actions claiming actual and punitive damages in an unspecified amount resulting from the failure are pending. The Company does not believe it has any material liability in this matter.

PENSION AND DEFERRED BENEFIT PLANS

Expense for pension and deferred benefit plans was $104 million, $90 million and $90 million, and for compulsory contributions for French retirement benefits was $17 million, $20 million and $24 million in 1984, 1983 and 1982, respectively.

Actuarial present value of accumulated benefits at January 1, 1984 and 1983 for U.S. and Canadian defined benefit plans was $235 million and $201 million, respectively, substantially all of which were vested. Net assets available for benefits at January 1, 1984 and 1983 for such plans were $326 million and $276 million, respectively. The assumed rate of return used in determining the actuarial present value of accumulated plan benefits for 1984 and 1983 was 7%.

BAUX ET ENGAGEMENTS DE LOCATION

Le montant total des dépenses de location s'est élevé à 159, 144 et 149 millions de dollars en 1984, 1983 et 1982 respectivement. Les engagements minima de location non résiliables pour les prochains exercices sont les suivants (en millions de dollars): 1985-74; 1986-63; 1987-50; 1988-40 et 1989-29. Ces engagements passeront de 60 à 13 millions de dollars pour les trois périodes quinquennales suivantes. Pour la durée des baux restant à courir ensuite, le montant total des engagements s'élève à 11 millions de dollars.

RAPPEL D'IMPOTS

Comme indiqué précédemment, l'U.S. Internal Revenue Service a terminé son examen des déclarations fiscales de Schlumberger aux Etats-Unis pour les exercices 1970 à 1978 inclus, et a proposé des redressements au titre des bénéfices résultant des activités des services de mesures dans les sondages (logging) sur le plateau continental des Etats-Unis. Des redressements similaires sont prévus pour les années postérieures à 1978. La Société conteste ces redressements. Une instance judiciaire (District Court) de Houston, Texas a été saisie de l'affaire en ce qui concerne les années 1970 à 1975.

La direction estime que les provisions pour impôts sur les bénéfices sont appropriées et que tout ajustement qui pourra se révéler nécessaire n'affectera pas de manière significative la situation financière ou les résultats de la Société.

PASSIFS EVENTUELS

En 1980, l'Alexander Kielland, un hôtel flottant utilisé pour l'hébergement des équipes travaillant en mer du Nord, a chaviré lors d'une tempête. L'infrastructure de cet hôtel flottant était à l'origine celle d'une plate-forme de forage, construite par un chantier naval indépendant, d'après des plans fournis sous licence par une filiale de la Société. Cette filiale n'a pas été propriétaire de la plate-forme et n'a pas participé à son exploitation lors de son utilisation pour les forages ni à sa transformation et exploitation en hôtel flottant. Une commission, nommée par le gouvernement norvégien, a mené une enquête sur cet accident et déposé son rapport. En octobre 1981 et en février 1982, Phillips Petroleum Company, en Norvège, ainsi que huit autres sociétés membres du même groupe d'exploitation du gisement d'Ekofisk, et les assureurs norvégiens ont intenté un procès à la filiale de la Société, au chantier naval et à un sous-traitant, pour obtenir une indemnisation pour les pertes résultant de l'accident d'environ 75 millions de dollars (au taux de change du 31 décembre 1984).

Bien que la Société estime ne pas avoir de responsabilité dans cette affaire, toute procédure portera sur des points complexes de droit international et pourrait s'étendre sur plusieurs années, entraînant ainsi des frais importants. La Société considère que tout passif éventuellement mis à sa charge à l'issue de cette affaire ne devrait pas avoir d'effet significatif sur sa situation financière ou ses résultats.

En 1981, on a constaté une fuite dans un réservoir de solvant à l'usine de San Jose, en Californie. Ce produit a prétendument contaminé, par endroit, le sous-sol et les réserves d'eau voisines. Les actions en justice, ouvertes pour évaluer les dommages actuels et déterminer le montant d'éventuelles indemnités relatives à cette fuite, sont en cours. La Société ne pense pas encourir, en la matière, de responsabilité susceptible de peser notablement sur ses résultats.

PLANS DE RETRAITE ET D'INTERESSEMENT DIFFERE

Les charges comptabilisées au titre des plans de retraite et d'intéressement différé se sont élevées en 1984, 1983 et 1982 à 104 millions, 90 millions et 90 millions de dollars, respectivement; en France les cotisations versées au titre des régimes obligatoires de retraite se sont élevées pour les mêmes exercices à 17 millions, 20 millions et 24 millions de dollars.

La valeur actuelle des avantages acquis par les bénéficiaires des plans constitués aux Etats-Unis et au Canada (calculée à partir de bases actuarielles) s'élevait à 235 millions de dollars au 1er janvier 1983; ces montants représentent dans leur quasi-totalité des avantages acquis sans condition ultérieure d'attribution. La valeur totale des actifs nets représentant les investissements faits au titre de ces plans s'élevait à 326 millions et 276 millions de dollars aux 1er janvier 1984 et 1983.

La valeur actuelle des avantages acquis a été calculée sur la base du taux d'actualisation de 7% pour 1984 et 1983.

SUPPLEMENTARY INFORMATION

Operating revenue and related cost of goods sold and services comprised the following:

YEAR ENDED DECEMBER 31,	1984	1983	1982
	(Stated in millions)		
Operating revenue			
Sales	$2,499	$2,140	$2,045
Services	3,480	3,373	3,980
	$5,979	$5,513	$6,025
Direct operating costs			
Goods sold	$1,561	$1,443	$1,383
Services	2,092	1,945	2,096
	$3,653	$3,388	$3,479

The caption "Interest and other income" includes interest income, principally from short-term investments, of $390 million, $298 million and $254 million for 1984, 1983 and 1982, respectively.

Accounts payable and accrued liabilities are summarized as follows:

DECEMBER 31,	1984	1983
	(Stated in millions)	
Payroll, vacation and employee benefits	$268	$237
Trade	320	251
Other	354	308
	$942	$796

INFORMATIONS SUPPLEMENTAIRES

Le chiffre d'affaires d'exploitation et le coût correspondant des produits vendus et de services fournis s'analysent comme suit:

EXERCICE CLOS LE 31 DECEMBRE	1984	1983	1982
	(en millions de dollars)		
Chiffre d'affaires d'exploitation			
Ventes	$2 499	$2 140	$2 045
Services	3 480	3 373	3 980
	$5 979	$5 513	$6 025
Coûts direct d'exploitation			
Produits vendus	$1 561	$1 443	$1 383
Services	2 092	1 945	2 096
	$3 653	$3 388	$3 479

Dans les Intérêts et autres revenus sont inclus les produits financiers, perçus principalement sur les placements à court terme, qui se sont élevés à 390 millions, 298 millions et 254 millions de dollars en 1984, 1983 et 1982.

Le poste Fournisseurs, autres créanciers et frais à payer se ventile comme suit:

AU 31 DECEMBRE	1984	1983
	(en millions de dollars)	
Rémunérations, congés payés et autres frais de personnel	$268	$237
Fournisseurs	320	251
Autres	354	308
	$942	$796

Typical American
business expressions

Américanismes
Langue des affaires

TYPICAL AMERICAN BUSINESS EXPRESSIONS

A

about-face, faire-demi tour sur une question. *'In the face of such strong opposition, the Government was forced to about-face on their tax policy.'*

acid test ratio, ratio des disponibilités; ratio de trésorerie. *'After applying the acid test ratio to current cash reserves, we have decided to bill our clients upon delivery.'*

act (to clean up one's), améliorer son comportement. *'He was warned that if he didn't clean up his act, he would probably be fired.'*

act (to get in on the), participer à une opération. *'His constant efforts to get in on the act ended up by irritating all concerned.'*

adjustment trigger, critère prédéterminé qui, une fois atteint, déclenche un ajustement (de politique, de taux de change, etc). *'Once interest rates reached the adjustment trigger of 8%, a meeting was called to review the situation.'*

ADR's = American Depositary Receipts, billets émis par les banques américaines pour faciliter les transactions en valeurs étrangères. *'Purchases of South African gold shares are often made in ADR's.'*

advisory funds, fonds gérés par une banque ou tout autre établissement financier, pour le compte de leurs clients. *'In the absence of the client, certain stocks were purchased with the use of advisory funds.'*

after hours dealing/trading, opérations effectuées après la clôture officielle de la Bourse. *'Send those copper orders to be executed in after hours dealing.'*

after-tax real return, rendement net (après déduction du taux de l'inflation). *'With the inflation rate at 2%, the after-tax real rate return will be 4.5%.'*

against actuals, (AA) *StExch:* échange de papier contre la marchandise physique (effectué entre le producteur et l'acheteur final pour dénouer leurs opérations respectives sur le marché à terme). *'The exporter's long position in wheat futures was offset by a trade against actuals.'*

agency bank, organisme qui représente la banque-mère étrangère aux États-Unis (mais qui n'est ni autorisé à accepter de dépôts, ni à accorder de prêts sous son propre nom). *'Funds can be transferred via agency bank in New York.'*

agent bank, banque désignée par un syndicat international de prêt pour protéger les intérêts de ce dernier, tout au long de la durée du prêt. *'The members of the loan syndicate appointed an agent bank to represent them for the duration of the loan.'*

all or none, *StExch:* ordre d'achat (ou de vente) à exécuter au prix du marché (ou à un prix limite) si la totalité spécifiée peut être obtenue. *'The order is to buy 15,000 shares of ITT at 12½, all or none.'*

all-time high/low, niveau/prix le plus haut, le plus bas (qui ait jamais existé). *'Volume recorded on the Paris exchange reached an all-time high.'*

AMEX, deuxième Bourse américaine (située à New York) *'Shares traded on the AMEX (American Stock Exchange) today were slightly higher than on the NYSE.'*

AMEX, American Express. *'Most restaurants in the States accept AMEX (American Express cards).'*

annuals, rapports généraux de gestion. *'Some shareholders never even bother to read the annuals.'*

applied proceeds swap, acquisition d'une tranche d'obligations avec le produit de la vente d'une autre tranche. *'After selling 50,000 long-term bonds, we were able to purchase 50,000 short-term papers in an applied proceeds swap.'*

approved delivery facility, dépôt officiellement approuvé (pour le stockage d'une marchandise livrée contrepartie d'une position sur le marché à terme). *'The bonds were delivered to an approved facility to cover new margin requirements.'*

arbitrager, arbitragiste. *'Arbitragers can cover their positions by trading on different markets or in different delivery months.'*

arms' length, 'à bout de bras', indépendant. *'He finally took an arms' length decision which completely ignored my suggestions.'*

Article Eight currency, monnaie forte, convertible et non assujettie aux contrôles des changes. *'Shipping arrangements are usually made in Article Eight currency.'*

asset play, opération d'ordre spéculatif, destinée à réaliser une plus-value en capital. *'Making an asset play with that particular stock would involve getting in and out of the market very quickly.'*

audit trail, procédé établi par le commissaire aux comptes pour dépister une transaction quelconque. *'They set up an audit trail to reconstitute all pertinent details of the transaction.'*

average down, acheter à intervalles réguliers, au fur et à mesure que le marché baisse (en réduisant le prix moyen). *'Try to establish a long-term position by averaging down whenever the stock loses a point.'*

average up, acheter à intervalles réguliers, au fur et à mesure que le marché monte (en augmentant le prix moyen). *'Some speculators prefer to average up to be sure the market is headed in the right direction.'*

away, *StExch:* loin du prix actuel/loin du marché. *'Your selling price on that stock is well away from the market.'*

B

baby-boomers, ceux qui sont nés dans les années suivant la fin de la 2ème Guerre Mondiale. *'It's hard to realize that the generation of baby-boomers are now in their late forties.'*

to back down/backtrack, faire marche arrière/ rebrousser chemin. *'Management had to back down after taking a premature decision/A certain amount of backtracking was necessary, to check all the salient points of the deal.'*

to backfire, ne pas produire le résultat recherché. *'Their plans backfired badly when the actual costs were revealed.'*

backing and filling, *StExch:* marché qui se consolide. *'The market needs to do a little backing and filling before making any further advances.'*

bag trading, transaction(s) préarangée(s).

to bail out, vendre sa position/sortir hâtivement d'une situation embarrassante. *'When things started to go wrong, he was the first to bail out.'*

bailout, plan de sauvetage; aide financière pour sauver une entreprise en difficulté. *'The bank consortium guaranteed a bailout if the company failed to meet the deadline.'*

balloon loan, emprunt dont le dernier versement est plus important que les versements précédents, ou qui est remboursable dans sa totalité à l'échéance. *'Credit was granted in the form of a balloon-loan, with the final payment representing twice as much as the first six instalments combined.'*

balloon payment, versement forfaitaire et final (d'un emprunt). *'That final balloon-payment represented the same amount as all of the previous year's instalments.'*

ballpark figure, chiffre, montant, approximatif. *'At the preliminary stage, a ballpark figure of 5 million dollars was discussed.'*

bank line, ligne de crédit fournie par une banque; caution bancaire. *'That client is not to exceed his bank line of 30,000 pounds.'*

bar, un million de livres sterling. *'Those particular bonds are now worth at least a bar.'*

basis, *StExch:* différence entre le prix d'une marchandise au comptant et son prix à terme. *'The basis between spot gold and July forwards was then running at 4 dollars and fifty cents.'*

basis grade, *StExch:* spécification d'une marchandise traitée à terme, utilisée comme étalon de base. *'Deliverable commodities have to meet the basis grade designated by each exchange.'*

basis point, unité de mesure, utilisée pour exprimer les fluctuations des taux de change, d'intérêt, etc. *'Interest rates moved up by 1 whole basis point in the course of the week.'*

basket clause, clause couvrant tous les cas non autrement précisés. *'Any other considerations not covered here will be dealt with in a basket clause.'*

beancounter, employé(e) de banque. *'We wouldn't have to stand in line if they employed beancounters who weren't so desperately slow.'*

bear campaign/bear raid/bear tack, effort collectif destiné à faire baisser les cours; ventes massives à découvert. *'The silver market is being dragged down by an aggressive bear campaign/A big group of speculators ran a bear raid on the market/This type of bear tack always makes the market nervous.'*

bear squeeze, étranglement; effort collectif destiné à obliger ceux qui ont vendu à découvert de racheter leurs positions. *'The bear squeeze sent the longs running for cover as soon as the market opened the next morning.'*

beauty contest, concours entre institutions financières pour désigner celle qui s'occupera d'une caisse de retraite ou d'une opération bancaire. *'Morgan Guaranty Trust just entered the beauty contest for that big oil deal.'*

to beef up, renforcer, consolider; augmenter (la production, etc). *'The government decided to beef up their campaign against inflation.'*

belt-tightening measures, mesures d'austérité économiques. *'We can expect fresh belt-tightening measures in the next Budget.'*

Big Blue, *F:* IBM (International Business Machines).

Big Board, la (principale) Bourse de New York. *'Prices on the Big Board were stuck in a narrow range.'*

big business, les grandes entreprises américaines. *'There's no point competing with big business without the funds to back you up.'*

Big Five, les cinq grandes puissances mondiales. *'The Big Five attended a summit meeting this weekend in Paris.'*

big haul/big killing, grand succès; opération qui rapporte de gros bénéfices. *'He made a really big haul when he finally sold out.'*

Big Three, General Motors, Ford, Chrysler; les trois grands de l'industrie automobile (aux USA). *'The Big Three are all having to adapt their production lines to satisfy new pollution controls.'*

to bilk s.o., escroquer qqn; payer qqn en monnaie de singe. *'He realized that he had been bilked out of several thousand dollars.'*

billed, annoncé/programmé (pour la semaine prochaine). *'The next shareholders' meeting is billed for June 8th.'*

to bite, mordre. *'If they intend to take up our offer, they'll have to bite soon';* **no-one will bite,** il n'y a pas de preneurs. *'Although the offer was exceptionally attractive, no-one was ready to bite.'*

blind pool, de l'argent accumulé sans aucun but précis. *'If we have no immediate use for these funds, we can always place them in a blind pool.'*

bloated, gonflé. *'The fund was suddenly bloated by a fat contribution from the mayor.'*

block positioner, maison de courtage spécialisée dans le placement de (gros) block d'actions. *'Place that buy-order for 100,000 shares with a block positioner.'*

blue-sky laws, législation destinée à protéger les investisseurs contre les vendeurs de 'blue-sky securities'. *'Blue-sky laws are supposed to ensure that the public is protected from this type of deal.'*

blue-sky securities, actions sans valeur. *'Little old ladies often fall victims to unscrupulous salesmen offering blue-sky securities.'*

boiler-room, organisation qui vend au public des produits financiers très spéculatifs ou sans valeur. *'These Canadian gold-shares must have been dreamt up in a boiler-room.'*

boiler-room operations, opérations proposées au public au moyen d'une forte pression téléphonique. *'Someone should complain about all those boiler-room operations.'*

bond-washing, vente d'obligations du Trésor américain, avec coupon attaché, et leur rachat ex-coupon; opération qui permet à certains contribuables d'éviter de lourds impôts sur le revenu. *'Bond-washing not only offers a tax advantage to the investor, but also brings in commissions for the reps.'*

boomers, des optimistes. *'He belonged to a group of boomers who always looked on the sunny side.'*

boondoggle, poste sans grande utilité, créé dans la fonction publique pour caser des gens pistonnés. *'They managed to find a comfortable boondoggle for the commissioner.'*

boondoggling, création des postes 'boondoggle'. *'Boondoggling was common under Roosevelt's 'New Deal' as a ploy to reduce unemployment.'*

bottleneck, toute entrave à la production ou à la distribution de produits; goulot d'étranglement. *'The dockers' strike created a bottleneck of goods waiting to be shipped abroad.'*

break-out, mouvement brusque (du marché) à la hausse ou à la baisse; rupture de tendance. *'There was a sudden break-out on the upside, when the copper strike in Peru was announced.'*

bricks and mortar (to invest in), (investir dans le marché de) l'immobilier. *'The French has always thought it a good idea to invest in bricks and mortar.'*

broadside, attaque virulente (souvent d'ordre politique) publiée par la presse. *'The Financial Daily published a particularly virulent broadside against the instigators of the scheme.'*

broke (to be dead/flat/stony), être fauché /ne pas avoir un radis. *'If he sold his car to reimburse his debts, he realized that he would still be dead broke.'*

broke (to go), faire faillite; être ruiné. *'He finally went broke after dreaming up hundreds of impossible schemes.'*

'B' school = Business School, Ecole supérieure de commerce. *'He obtained a Degree in Economics at 'B' School.'*

bubble, activité euphorique en Bourse (consistant à faire monter le prix d'une action à un niveau injustifié). *'Many speculators lost a lot of money when the bubble finally burst.'*

bubble-scheme, entreprise véreuse; duperie. *'Even reputable houses sometimes get unwittingly involved with bubble-scheme operators.'*

to buck the trend, aller contre la tendance. *'Some speculators are forever bucking the trend.'*

bulge, hausse (de prix) rapide et imprévue. *'The sudden bulge in the market was largely due to short-covering.'*

bullet bond, obligation remboursable uniquement à l'échéance. *'There is no chance of early redemption with bullet bonds.'*

bulletin-board, tableau d'affichage. *'The results were posted on the bulletin-board.'*

bum check, chèque sans provision. *'His bank informed him that someone had deposited a bum check in his account.'*

to bunch, rassembler/(re)grouper. *'The subsidiary companies were bunched together to create a new corporation.'*

bundle (to make a), (gagner) une grosse somme d'argent. *'He made a bundle selling options short.'*

burn-out rate, le taux de démission de la part de cadres ne tolérant plus un haut niveau de stress. *'The brokerage industry has one of the highest burn-out rates of all the professions.'*

bust, une descente de la police (surtout contre les trafiquants de drogue). *'A substantial amount of cocaine was discovered in last night's bust in Harlem.'*

busted convertible, obligation convertible qui ne vaut plus rien (par suite de l'effondrement de l'action ordinaire sous-jacente). *'When he saw the price of the stock, he realized he was left with several thousand busted convertibles.'*

to button up a deal, conclure un marché. *'The deal has to be buttoned up very quickly if the deadline is to be met.'*

to buy an idea, accepter/épouser une idée. *'Some guys will buy just about any idea you lay on the table.'*

buy-back, rachat (de titres, etc). *'That buy-back order was to close out my short position in November soybeans.'*

buying-binge/buying-spree (to go on a), (faire) beaucoup d'achats d'une façon irréfléchie. *'It seems as if all the speculators are going on a buying-binge/buying-spree.'*

C

call, *StExch:* courte période (à l'ouverture, à la clôture ou à la mi-séance) pendant laquelle est établi le cours de chaque échéance. *'Wait until they've finished the call before placing that market-order.'*

to can s.o., renvoyer qqn./mettre qqn. à la porte. *'If you're caught with your hand in the till, you can expect to be canned.'*

to cap the risk, limiter son risque en cas de hausse. *'You should place an upside limit to cap the risk on that short position.'*

capped floater, obligation à taux flottant dont une partie du taux d'intérêt est en prime. *'Those capped floaters are attracting a lot of potential buyers.'*

cap rate, taux d'intérêt en prime. *'What's the cap rate on those Danish bonds?'*

car/carload, chargement d'un wagon; lot, contrat de marchandise. *'How many cars of corn do five contracts represent?'*

carryback, avoir fiscal. *'Next year should bring a substantial carryback on those dividends.'*

carryover stocks, (céréales, etc) produites pendant la saison précédente et faisant partie de la réserve actuelle. *'The report on carryover stocks affected the market only slightly.'*

cash cow/cash dog, vache à lait; (filiale qui sert comme dépôt pour des excédents de capital; entreprise qui fait constamment des bénéfices, mais qui n'a aucun potentiel de croissance). *'That Maryland Company is nothing but a cash cow.'*

catered dinner, un dîner assuré par les soins de restaurateurs. *'I won't be able to prepare anything in time, so expect it to be a catered dinner.'*

caucus, sous-division d'un parti politique. *'It didn't suprise anyone that the Women's Caucus of the Democratic Party voted unanimously for equal pay.'*

cemetery accounting, méthode comptable qui interprète la situation financière d'une société de la facon la plus pessimiste possible. *'Our current tax situation calls for someone to do a little cemetery accounting.'*

certified/certificated stocks, marchandises officiellement approuvées et prêtes à livrer. *'Those certified stocks of beans are only deliverable on the Chicago market.'*

chalk up, afficher (de bons résultats, etc). *'This month's results were much better than those we chalked up in February'.* **chalk it up to my account,** mettez-le sur mon compte. *'You'd better chalk it up to my account as I don't have enough cash.'*

chicken feed, chose sans valeur; petite somme d'argent. *'The money he spends on cars is chicken-feed compared to what he loses at the races.'*

Chief Executive Officer (CEO), directeur général. *'His ultimate ambition was to be promoted to CEO.'*

Chief Financial Officer, directeur financier. *'Tell the CFO that those bills are well overdue.'*

Chinese auction, vente aux enchères à rebours (en baissant progressivement le prix, on trouve finalement un acheteur). *'At a Chinese auction, you just hope everyone else is meaner than yourself!'*

chips, argent/fric. *'He couldn't wait to get his hands on the chips!'*

choppy market, marché volatile. *'It was a choppy market showing no real trend.'*

to churn, brasser beaucoup d'affaires pour le compte de ses clients (dans le seul but d'obtenir davantage de commissions). *'The broker was severely reprimanded for churning his client's account.'*

citify, urbaniser. *'The western outskirts will soon be as citified as the town-centre.'*

claim-jumper, individu qui usurpe les droits d'autrui. *'As soon as the new property options were declared, he turned into an aggressive claim-jumper.'*

clawback, retour en arrière. *'They agreed to honour the clawback provision, in the event that circumstances reverted to what they had been six months previously.'*

clean buck, argent gagné honnêtement. *'That rascal never made a clean buck in his life.'*

clean oil, pétrole raffiné. *'How much of a premium is there on that grade one clean oil?'*

to clean s.o. out, ruiner qn. *'His last venture in real-estate really cleaned him out.'*

to clean up, gagner gros. *'He certainly cleaned up on that silver deal.'*

clock-watcher, travailleur peu motivé (qui guette l'heure pour quitter son poste). *'How can we increase productivity with so many clock-watchers on the factory-floor?'*

closed company, société contrôlée par un maximum de cinq personnes. *'They set up a closed company to buy the marine.'*

closed corporation, société dont les actions appartiennent à un nombre limité d'actionnaires et qui n'est pas cotée en Bourse. *'It's quite difficult to get information on those closed corporations.'*

to close out a position, *StExch:* liquider/solder une position. *'Don't wait until the last trading day to close out your position.'*

closing meeting, séance de signature d'un contrat. *'All the interested parties attended the closing meeting.'*

clout, puissance, influence. *'Some companies have more market clout than others when it comes to placing a new issue.'*

C note, billet de banque de cent dollars. *'He pulled out a C note and threw it on the table.'*

coach class, classe touriste. *'Do you want a seat in first class or coach class?'*

coast-to-coast, couvrant toute l'Amérique; de l'Atlantique au Pacifique. *'The news travelled coast-to-coast within a few hours.'*

cold cash, argent comptant. *'She insisted on being paid in cold cash.'*

cold storage, (argent) temporairement planqué/ mis de côté. *'The money we made on that deal is going into cold storage for a while.'*

collectibles, objets/pièces pour collectionneurs, pour amateurs d'art. *'Impressionist paintings are still one of America's favourite collectibles.'*

collegial approach, procédure par laquelle une décision est prise de façon collective. *'A really democratic way to solve the issue would be to use the collegial approach.'*

combat pay, prime *f* de risque(s).

come-on, prime/cadeau pulicitaire. *'The advertising agency had to think up a new come-on for the product.'*

commission house, maison de courtage/de commission. *'Merrill Lynch is the biggest commission house in the States.'*

company raider, chasseur de tête. *'He got his new job after being contacted by a company raider.'*

compensation trade, méthode de paiement par laquelle l'exportateur accepte qu'une partie du prix d'achat se règle en marchandises provenant du pays importateur. *'They worked out a compensation trade which involved exchanging corn for steel.'*

competitive devaluation, dévaluation d'une monnaie (pour avantager le commerce d'exportation). *'The U.S. policy of competitive devaluation has not succeeded in reducing the trade deficit.'*

competitive trader, membre de la Bourse de New York qui fait le commerce d'actions pour un compte dans lequel il détient un intérêt. *'If competitive traders work harder at making money for their clients, they also do it in their own interest.'*

composite index, indice composé de plusieurs indicateurs économiques. *'The composite index is due out next Thursday.'*

computer trading, spéculation basée sur les indications fournies par ordinateur. *'The volume of computer trading became an important factor in the commodity markets.'*

con-artist = confidence man, escroc (qui sait gagner la confiance de ses futures victimes). *'She realized that she had almost entrusted her entire life-savings to a con-artist.'*

congested market, marché peu liquide. *'In this type of congested market, you just have to wait for the break.'*

consolidation merger, fusion de deux ou de plusieurs sociétés pour en créer une toute nouvelle. *'The terms of the consolidation merger between ABC and XYZ Corporation are still being discussed.'*

contract broker, courtier auxiliaire qui aide un commissionnaire agréé à exécuter ses ordres à la corbeille. *'He frequently used the services of contract brokers on very hectic days.'*

contrarian, investisseur ou spéculateur qui joue la tendance contraire à celle favorisée par la majorité. *'The typical contrarian waits for everyone to buy – then sells short.'*

convention, congrès d'ordre politique, professionnel ou commercial. *'Convention facilities in the South of France now attract a new breed of business tourists from all over the world.'*

conversion premium, prime de conversion (payée en cas de remboursement anticipé d'obligations). *'They had to fix a conversion premium in case of early redemption.'*

cooler, money in the cooler, argent temporairement planqué/mis de côté. *'He couldn't wait to get the money out of the cooler.'*

to cop out, se retirer; se dégonfler. *'Don't think you can cop out as easily as that!'*

to cough up, payer/casquer. *'It's about time you coughed up for a change.'*

country risk, risque encouru en investissant dans un certain pays, ou en y prêtant des fonds. *'The country risk lay in the fact that the investment would be made in a Third World country.'*

crafted, mis au point/travaillé. *'The plan had been carefully crafted to ensure a complete success'.* **well-crafted pitch,** argument (de vente) astucieusement préparé. *'His clients knew he would use a well-crafted pitch to convince them.'*

credentials, papiers d'identité; copies certifiées de diplômes; crédibilité (d'une société, etc) basée sur sa compétence antérieure. *'Don't forget to bring your credentials when you come for the interview.'*

cross-over possibilities, possibilité d'échanger sa position dans une affaire pour une autre. *'I'm not sure that giving him cross-over possibilities in that deal is really to our best advantage.'*

crunch, récession. *'England has been going through the crunch for a long time now;* **to feel the crunch,** ressentir les effets de la récession. *'They are feeling the crunch all the more badly after living so well in the past.'*

cum all, y compris tous les avantages supplémentaires (comportés par une action). *'He put in his order to buy 2000 shares cum all.'*

cum new/cum capitalisation, (prix d'une action) y compris celles qui ont été attribuées gratuitement aux actionnaires. *'ABC was trading at 19¼ cum new.'*

curb/curb market, marché non-officiel; marché hors cote (ancien nom de l'American Stock Exchange). *'The stop-order was executed on the curb (market).'*

curb trading, transactions d'après fermeture.

customers' broker, commissionnaire faisant du démarchage auprès d'une clientèle particulière. *'Customers' brokers are not supposed to handle institutional orders.'*

cut-price operator, commerçant vendant sa marchandise au rabais. *'His competitors accused him of being a cut-price operator.'*

czar, magnat. *'The Hunts will always be remembered as the czars of the silver market.'*

D

daylight exposure limit, *Bank:* limite journalière (appliquée aux opérations en devises étrangères). *'We have a daylight exposure limit of just 5 million Swiss francs.'*

day-trade, *StExch:* opération initiée et dénouée au cours d'une seule journée de Bourse. *'Reduced commissions are applied to day-trades.'*

day-trader, opérateur en Bourse qui initie et liquide une même position dans l'espace d'une seule journée; spéculateur du jour. *'He was known to be a day-trader who got in and out of the market several times a day.'*

dead-end, cul-de-sac; impasse. *'Negotiations dragged on for a week and finally came to a dead-end.'*

deadhead, train ou camion roulant à vide. *'Six deadhead wagons are due back in Minneapolis tonight.'*

dead-in-the-water, mort-né.

dealmaker, celui qui organise des affaires. *'He had a good record as a dealmaker, and investors were always ready to participate in his schemes.'*

dealster, celui qui organise des affaires. *'That dealster is always on the look-out for a fresh opportunity.'*

deep pockets, "poches profondes", qui contiennent beaucoup d'argent. *'We could always try to tap the deep pockets for the initial funds.'*

defense dollar, fonds alloués (par le gouvernement) à la défense nationale. *'The U.S. Government announced it was going to increase its expenditure of defense dollars to areospatial research.'*

defensive stock/investment, valeurs sûres/de tout repos. *'His retirement plan would largely be based on defensive stocks.'*

deferred deliveries, échéances reportées. *'Deferred deliveries of oats and rapeseed are hardly ever traded.'*

deficit spending (to indulge in), dépenser plus que prévu dans son budget; vivre au-dessus de ses moyens. *'The Government was accused of indulging in deficit spending, which raised fears of higher inflation.'*

deflator: GNP deflator, différence entre le PNB réel et le PNB nominal (qui reflète le taux d'inflation global de l'économie). *'The GNP deflator was reported to have fallen by half a point this month.'*

delivery months, époques/échéances cotées. *'Which delivery months are the most actively traded in sugar?'*

dime, pièce de dix cents. *'His opinion isn't worth a dime.'*

dirty float, taux de change flottant (contrôlé en partie par le gouvernement). *'If the dollar drops much lower, the Government will probably resort to a dirty float.'*

discount window, facilité de prêt (fournie à certaines institutions par la Réserve Fédérale). *'The Federal Reserve was quoting 4⅛% at the discount window this morning.'*

discovery, découverte de preuves faite avant le procès. *'If we would get a discovery before the trial is held, we could ask for the maximum sentence.'*

disincentive, *PolEc:* frein; obstacle. *'Those new tax laws are going to act as a disincentive to several sectors of industry.'*

distressed merchandise, marchandise soldée. *'He said he would take that distressed merchandise off our hands for half-price.'*

to ditch, rejeter/abandonner (un projet). *'After searching hard for a solution, they finally had to ditch the whole idea.'*

divestiture, dessaisissement/abandon/vente d'une succursale. *'The only answer seemed to lie in the divestiture of the New Jersey company.'*

dividend cover, quotient de dividende/bénéfice (par action). *'What's the dividend cover on XYZ?'*

dividend off, ex-dividende. *'The quotes on those shares are now dividend off.'*

dope, 1. renseignement/tuyau. *'Today's newspaper gave all the dope on that shady deal.'* **2.** drogue. *'All the junkies are waiting for a new dope shipment to arrive in town.'*

dough, *F:* fric. *'Hand over the dough if you don't want to end up in the morgue!'*

down, en panne. *'The electricity strike resulted in the whole communications circuit being down.'*

downswing/downtrend/downturn, repli/régression. *'The market went into a prolonged downswing as soon as Kaufmann made his speech.'*

downtick, fluctuation en baisse (par rapport à celle qui la précédait). *'You can't go short on a stock if the last trade was a downtick.'*

drag, piston; influence. *'She's always had a lot of drag with the boss.'*

droplock loan, obligation à taux flottant, qui devient une obligation à taux fixe en fonction d'une baisse prédéterminée des taux d'intérêt en général. *'If interest rates fall to 6%, they'll peg those droplock loans at a new fixed rate.'*

dry hole, puits de pétrole stérile; opération à rendement (financier) insuffisant. *'If they come up with another dry hole, they'll probably have to close down the entire operation.'*

dual listing, (action) inscrite à la cote de plusieurs Bourses. *'Many U.S. stocks have dual listing on both American and European exchanges.'*

due diligence, diligence (comptable et extra-comptable)/diligence professionnelle. *'The court ruled that the broker had acted with all due diligence in respect of his client's account.'*

dummy directors, hommes de paille (faisant partie du conseil d'administration). *'They had to bring in a few dummy directors to sit on the board.'*

E

eagle, pièce d'or (d'une valeur nominale) de dix dollars. *'He has been collecting eagles ever since he was a child.'*

earnings play, opération d'ordre spéculatif (destinée à exploiter un taux de rendement particulièrement élevé). *'A shrewd move would be an earnings play on XYZ.'*

eligible paper, papier/traite escomptable (dans le commerce ou auprès de la Federal Reserve Bank). *'The bank refused to accept the bills of exchange as eligible paper.'*

end-to-end servicing, service couvrant toutes les phases de la mise au point d'une produit, depuis sa fabrication jusqu'au service après-vente. *'With all the new computers on the market, the manufacturers are having problems with their end-to-end servicing.'*

equity, *StExch:* solde net/situation nette (après liquidation aux cours actuels de toutes les positions ouvertes). *'After liquidating all his open positions at the close of the market, the equity in his account amounted to $155,453.'*

escrow account, compte bloqué. *'The funds were temporarily blocked in an escrow account.'*

to even up a position, solder/liquider une position (en vendant ou en rachetant). *'Many speculators even up their positions before important reports are released.'*

evergreen credit, crédit par acceptation renouvelable. *'He has such a sound reputation that almost any band will grant him evergreen credit.'*

ex all, à l'exclusion de tous les avantages supplémentaires comportés par une action. *'If you really want to purchase the stock immediately, you'll have to take it ex all.'*

executive session, séance (parlementaire ou autre) à huis clos. *'The President called an executive session at 5 a.m. in the morning.'*

exotic currencies, devises rarement traitées sur les marchés des changes internationaux. *'Trading volume in Mexican pesos and other exotic currencies is usually very low.'*

to expense, mettre sur le compte, *'Can you expense all those items to my account?'*

ex pit transactions, opérations négociées en dehors de la corbeille (surtout en matières premières). *'Call the floor-trader in Chicago and tell him we have an ex pit transaction to arrange.'*

F

facility fee, frais de prolongation (de facilités de paiement). *'You'll have to pay a facility fee if you want the credit-line extended until December.'*

fact-finder, enquêteur. *'in order to conduct the survey, several hundred fact-finders had to be hired.'*

fallen angel, ange déchu.

Fannie Mae = Federal National Mortgage Association (FNMA), 1. organisme émetteur de prêts à la construction. *'Fannie Mae just announced a drop in their interest rates.* **2.** Obligations hypothécaires de cet organisme. *'Institutions often hedge their Fannie Mae's on the futures markets.'*

fast as can (FAC), chargement ou déchargement d'une navire accompli aussi rapidement que possible. *'Tell the dockers they have to unload that cargo fast as can.'*

fast lane, voie rapide: chemin à suivre pour se faire un nom. *'After running in the fast lane for the last three years, he's now become a household name.'*

Fed = Federal Reserve, Réserve fédérale (aux USA). *'Paul Volcker has been at the Fed for a long time now.'*

Fed funds = Federal funds, réserves de trésorerie que les banques membres du système de Réserve fédérale se prêtent entre elles du jour au lendemain. *'Fed funds were trading at 6% yesterday.'*

to file (for), soumettre, déposer une demande (pour). *'He filed for admission to the Senators' Club.'*

financial engineering, manipulation financière. *'Even the most respected establishments sometimes indulge in financial engineering.'*

financials, statistiques financières. *'Our economics professor told us to follow the financials every day.'*

to finger/put the finger on s.o., incriminer qqn. *'If he doesn't pay up, we can finger him with the proof.'*

to fire up the salesman, stimuler le vendeur. *'An extra bonus is the only way to fire up those two salesmen.'*

fiscal drag, effet inhibant/lourdeur du poids fiscal. *'Small commerce is beginning to feel the effect of all this fiscal drag.'*

fix, stimulant. *'We need some kind of a quick fix to improve the year-end results.'*

flat (account), (compte) soldé. *'As the account's been flat for more than two years, we can consider it closed.'*

to fleece, voler/plumer qn. *'He's always fleecing his customers, even for petty amounts.'*

fleet policy, assurance couvrant tous les navires appartenant à une seule compagnie maritime. *'Can you set up a fleet policy to cover those four tankers?'*

floater = floating rate bond, obligation à taux variable/flottant. *'Get me the list of quotations for European floaters.'*

floor-broker, commissionnaire qui travaille à la corbeille pour le compte de tierces personnes.

'You have to have a good memory, nerves of steel and strong vocal chords to be a successful floor-broker!'

floor-trader, boursier professionnel qui travaille à la corbeille le plus souvent pour son propre compte. *'Then there was the floor-trader in Chicago who went back to driving a taxi after he went broke...'*

flower bonds, bons du trésor acceptés au pair, en règlement des droits de succession fédéraux. *'Death duties are sometimes settled in the States by handing over flower bonds.'*

to flunk, échouer. *'All of his teachers were amazed that he had flunked his exams.'*

foregone income, manque à gagner. *'Some speculators worry more about foregone income than the money they actually lose!'*

foreign bill, traite payable à l'étranger ou dans un autre état américain. *'He instructed his bank to settle the Japanese payment in foreign bills.'*

Forex = Foreign exchange, devises étrangères. *'The Forex market in London has increased its trading volume dramatically over the last few years.'*

forgivable loan, prêt "excusable" qui n'est pas censé être remboursé. *'Between good friends, I think I can afford to make this a forgivable loan.'*

fortified foods, aliments enrichis. *'The Americans are going through a fad for vitamins and fortified foods.'*

to front, agir en intermédiaire. *'He volunteered to front the company at the coming investigation.'*

to fuel speculation, encourager la spéculation. *'The upcoming summit meeting fuelled a lot of speculation that interest rates would soon be lowered.'*

fundamentalist, investisseur ou analyste qui étudie plutôt les informations fondamentales sur une action que les graphiques; analyste fondamental(e). *'A fundamentalist's analysis can often be directly opposed to that of a chartist.'*

funny money, fausse monnaie. *'The local banks were alerted that a lot of funny money had recently appeared in circulation.'*

to be furloughed, être congédié/licencié/mis temporairement au chômage. *'He couldn't believe that he had actually been furloughed.'*

G

to garage, 1. transférer l'actif ou le passif d'une société pour alléger le montant des impôts à payer. *'The accountant advised the company to garage certain funds a few weeks before year-end.'* **2.** mettre de l'argent en réserve. *'Why not garage 50% of these profits, and wait until another opportunity comes along?'*

Ginnie Mae = Government National Mortgage Association (GNMA), organisme émetteur d'obligations hypothécaires, garanties par l'État. *'Ginnie Mae's are traded just like any other government bonds.'*

G note, billet de banque de mille dollars. *'The car salesman was surprised to see him pull out a bunch of G notes.'*

to glad hand, serrer la main. *'She must get tired of all those people she has to glad hand every day.'*

go-getter, fonceur; arriviste; personne fort dynamique et ambitieuse. *'You have to be a real go-getter if you want to make a living in New York.'*

gogo fund, fonds de placement très spéculatif. *'He convinced three of his betting pals to buy shares in a gogo fund.'*

gogo stocks, actions à la mode. *'He'd never have a blue chip in his portfolio; he's just interested in the latest gogo stocks.'*

gold brick, attrape-nigaud/tromperie. *'He was so naïve that it was inevitable that someone would eventually drop him a gold brick.'*

gold bug, fanatique de l'or. *'Try getting that gold-bug into a more active market.'*

gold fix, détermination du prix de l'or (qui a lieu deux fois par jour parmi les cinq grandes maisons d'or londoniennes). *'Give London a call to see if they've got the gold fix yet.'*

golden handcuffs, (menottes dorées), contrat très avantageux offert par une société à un employé/à un cadre qu'elle veut garder.

golden shares, actions d'une société qui comporte des droits spéciaux tels que des droits de vote. *'They'll have to pay through the nose to recover those golden shares.'*

graft, boulot. *'The new contract meant a lot of real graft, but he was determined to see it through.'*

grain elevator, silo. *'Hundreds of grain elevators are dotted around the countryside in the American corn-belt.'*

grant work, travaux qui bénéficient de subventions. *'Architects and general contractors are always on the look-out for grant work.'*

greenback, billet (de banque) américain; dollar américain; le billet vert. *'You would never have considered it if you'd known how many greenbacks it cost!*

greenfield site, nouvel emplacement pour des bureaux ou des usines le plus souvent dans un environnement de verdure. *'XYZ Corp. has relocated its research department to the new greenfield site near Boston.'*

grifter, escros/trafiquant. *'That's the part of town where the local grifters hang out.'*

ground-floor opportunity, occasion de participer à une entreprise naissante qui est censée rapporter de gros bénéfices. *'This is a* *ground-floor opportunity to get into the company, but you will have to have 3 months' special training.'*

gusher, puits jaillissant. *'For an oilman, there's nothing more exciting than seeing a gusher when it first starts to produce!'*

gutter, marché hors cote. *'Get me a gutter quote on three months' tin!'*

to gyp, escroquer/rouler. *'I sensed he was trying to gyp me, so I pretended I was broke.'*

H

haircut finance, prêt dont le montant représente moins que la valeur totale du nantissement fourni. *'Some lending establishments insist on haircut financing for first-time clients.'*

half-life, période précédant le remboursement de la moitié du principal (d'une obligation). *'What's the half-life on that XYZ paper?'*

hand-to-mouth buying, système d'approvisionnement lié étroitement à l'écoulement des stocks. *'Since there was so little foreign demand, exporters stuck to their policy of hand-to-mouth buying.'*

hardball negotiating, négociations sérieuses/ pouparlers sérieux. *'In the first round of talks, Wendover made himself conspicuous for his hardball negotiating.'*

hard goods, biens durables. *'The figures released this month on hard goods showed a spectacular upturn.'*

head-to-head negotiation, négociation face à face. *'Since there were so many rumours about the takeover, the Company President demanded a head-to-head negotiation.'*

heavy hitters, hommes d'affaires importants. *'His aggressive tactics soon put him into the league of heavy hitters.'*

hedge fund, société d'investissement dont le but est de faire de l'arbitrage sur des positions déjà acquises. *'Since they each held a substantial amount of bonds, they decided to set up a hedge fund to eliminate some of the risk.'*

to hedge one's bets, se couvrir de tous les côtés. *'He decided to play it cautiously and made sure that all his bets were hedged.'*

high flier, personne qui réussit en affaires. *'Even as a young man, his talent and ambition tagged him a high flier.'*

high-price marker, valeur vedette. *'The 10 dollar rise in ABC made it the high-price marker of the week.'*

high roller, spéculateur ou joueur qui risque de grosses sommes d'argent. *'He was known at the race-course for being a high roller.'*

to hike, augmenter. *'We can expect another hike in the price of oil this month.'* **pay hike,** augmentation de salaire. *'They put in a claim for an October pay hike without really expecting to get it.'*

to hit the bid, accepter le cours offert. *'If you wait much longer to sell those shares, somebody else is going to hit the bid.'*

(in) hock, 1. déposé en gage/nantissement/ garantie. *'His long term-assets were placed in hock until he came up with the cash.'* **2. (to be) in hock,** être endetté. *'She was in hock to the grocer for at least $400.'*

hock-shop, Mont-de-Piété. *'He was always in and out of the hock-shop depending on his luck at roulette.'*

hot year, une bonne année (sur le plan financier). *'Just one more hot year and we can retire to the Bahamas!'*

huckster, agent de publicité agressif. *'If that huckster ever comes here again with his lousy deals, I'm going to throw him out.'*

to hustle, se démener/vendre. *'He had been hustling all his life and it finally paid off.'*

hustler, type dynamique/débrouillard. *'You have to be a hustler to succeed in the advertising business.'*

to hype, exagérer le potentiel de qch.; pousser le prix d'une valeur en Bourse, d'une facon injustifiable. *'When they stop hyping that stock, it's going to fall through the floor!'*

hype-up stock, valeurs dont le gain potentiel a été exagéré par les courtiers, la presse etc. *'It still takes a lot of courage to go short on a hyped-up stock.'*

I

ice, diamants. *'You need the advice of a specialist before investing in ice.'*

to impact, avoir des répercussions (sur). *'The advertising campaign impacted much more strongly than anyone had dared hope.'*

import cover, période pour laquelle le coût des importations brutes d'une pays serait couvert par ses réserves monétaires. *'It would be interesting to know exactly how much import cover some of the Third World countries actually have.'*

infant industry, industrie naissante. *'Silicon Valley has been home to a good number of infant industries over the last decade.'*

info rate, cours fourni seulement à titre de renseignement. *'There's so little trading that they'll only give us an info rate.'*

in-plant (training), (formation) qui a lieu dans l'usine même/sur place. *'The personnel were taught how to use the new computers in a series of in-plant training sessions.'*

insightful, plein de perspicacité. *'The boss appreciated his insightful analysis.'*

institutional pot, part d'une émission mise en réserve pour les grandes institutions. *'At least 40% of that new issue will be set aside for the institutional pot.'*

interest cover, solvabilité d'une emprunteur vis à vis des intérêts à payer; couverture de l'intérêt. *'Even if he can't pay back the capital, find out if he's good for the interest cover.'*

intra-day limit, limites imposées sur la position quotidienne d'une cambiste. *'If you buy back 300,000 Swiss francs, you'll be back inside your intra-day limit.'*

inverted market, marché de matières premières à terme dans lequel le prix de la marchandise est plus élevé pour les échéances rapprochées que celui des échéances éloignées (reflétant une pénurie à court terme). *'Strong export demand has created an inverted market in soybeans, with the nearby May contract trading at 50 cents over November.'*

investibles, objets/pièces pour collectionneurs, pour amateurs d'art. *'Old enamel street-signs are now sought after as investibles.'*

J

to jack up, augmenter (la production, etc). *'Even if we jack up production by 15%, we'll never meet the delivery date..'*

jawbone, rhétorique. *'Just how much political jawbone do we have to take?'*

to job (the market), opérer sur la Bourse ou sur les marchés à terme de marchandises, en cherchant à profiter de petits écarts de prix, souvent pendant une seule séance de bourse. *'There was money to be made by jobbing the silver market today.'*

to job out, sous-traiter/donner à un sous-traitant. *'Parts of that contract will have to be jobbed out to sub-contractors.'*

jobber, opérateur professionnel qui cherche à profiter de petits écarts de prix, souvent pendant une seule séance de bourse; cambiste-commis opérateur. *'The jobbers were looking for opportunities to scalp the market.'*

junior bonds, obligations de deuxième rang. *'It might not be a bad idea to add a few junior bonds to your portfolio.'*

junk bonds, obligations à haut rendement mais à haut risque. *'We ought to dump those junk bonds at the earliest opportunity.'*

junk mail, imprimés publicitaires, souvent non personnalisés, distribués par la poste. *'Most of the junk mail we receive goes straight into the waste-paper basket.'*

K

kicker, commission; pourcentage. *'There's a nice kicker in the deal if you want to give it a try.'*

kite, chèque sans provision; traite de complaisance sans valeur. *'He managed to survive the week by flying several kites.'*

to kite a check, émettre un chèque sans provision; faire un tirage en l'air/à découvert. *'If he tries to kite any more checks, the bank will refuse to honour them.'*

kite flying/kiting, escroquerie par tirage à découvert/par tirage en l'air. *'Nearly everyone in town had fallen victim to his kite flying/kiting operations.'*

knock-off, imitation. *'They're producing a whole series of items that are just knock-offs from what we did last year.'*

L

lag time, écart de temps entre une prise de décision et sa mise en œuvre. *'It looks as if the lag time could well be another 6 months.'*

laggard catch-up, *StExch:* rattrapage des actions (qui avaient du retard sur les autres). *'The most notable feature of yesterday's session was the laggard catch-up in the electronics sector.'*

landmark decision, décision d'une importance capitale. *'They were not expecting any landmark decisions to be made at the conference.'*

laundry business, blanchissage; manipulation des prix (en Bourse). *'It looked as if the exchange dealers had been indulging in a little laundry business.'*

lead balloon, projet irréalisable; échec/fiasco. *'As soon as the scheme was launched, it became evident that it was another lead balloon.'*

lead manager, le membre le plus important d'un syndicat de garantie. *'Find out who the lead manager is for that new issue of XYZ.'*

leg (to lift a), liquider la moitié d'une position à cheval. *'Once the news is released, you lift a leg on either the long or the short position.'*

legwork, travail de préparation; rassemblement des informations. *'it always falls to the junior reporters to go and do the legwork.'*

lemon, mauvais coup ou investissement/fumisterie. *'That deal you told me about turned out to be a real lemon.'*

lending margin, différence à payer au prêteur au-dessus du taux de base. *'The lending margin on a three-year loan would be half a point above the base rate.'*

leverage factor, effet de levier; rapport entre le capital d'emprunt d'une société et son capital-actions. *'The leverage factor is always taken into account in assessing a company's overall strength.'* **high leverage factor,** le capital d'emprunt est plus élevé que le capital-actions. *'The fact that they already have a high leverage factor makes them hesitate to borrow more funds.'* **low leverage factor,** le capital-actions est plus élevé que le capital d'emprunt. *'The recent rise in the market has given us a relatively low leverage factor.'*

lifeboat operation, plan de sauvetage; aide financière accordée à une entreprise en difficulté. *'The company president convinced his banker that a short-term lifeboat operation was all that was needed.'*

linkage, rapport/relation. *'What's the linkage between your first theory and what you just said?'*

to load, hausser (le prix de qqch). *'The contract was loaded with unnecessary costs that they hoped would pass unnoticed.'*

to load up (with stock), faire de gros achats de titres. *'Investors who had loaded up with that stock got an unpleasant surprise when the earnings report came out.'*

local, siège régional d'un syndicat. *'There's a strike-meeting next Friday down at the local.'*

to lock in a profit, opérer de façon à s'assurer des bénéfices (au moins théoriquement). *'Certain operators try to lock in a profit by selling options on their stock.'*

locked at the limit, (marché) où il n'y a plus de transactions faute de vendeurs (en limite supérieure) ou d'acheteurs (en limite inférieure). *'The market was locked at the limit throughout the entire session.'*

locked in(to), (spéculateur) qui a fait des bénéfices sur papier qui, une fois réalisés, risquent d'être assujettis aux impôts sur les plus-values. *'He was locked into a tax-situation and decided not to sell until after year-end.'*

locked into a limit-move, (spéculateur) qui ne peut pas liquider sa position, faute de contrepartie. *'Speculators who find themselves locked into a limit-move often try to hedge their position on other months.'*

long dozen, treize. *'Send me a long dozen of your latest samples.'*

long-haul trucking, transport (par camion) à/sur longue distance. *'That long-haul trucking outfit has branches all over the country.'*

long shot, pari très risqué. *'This is a very long shot with a 10% chance of success.'*

to be long the basis, s'arbitrer en vendant à terme après avoir acheté la marchandise au comptant. *'Farmers who are long the basis often wait for a rise in the market before hedging their wheat.'*

low-down, renseignement/tuyau. *'What's the low-down on that new computer outfit?'*

M

machine, organisation d'un parti politique. *'The Republican machine made it clear that they would pass the new legislation in a hurry.'*

Madison Avenue, centre new-yorkais des agences de publicité. *'At least three agencies on Madison Avenue were competing for the company's advertising campaign.'*

marker, reconnaissance de dette. *'Have you received a marker from our old friend Joe?'*

marker-price, prix de base du pétrole (déterminé par l'OPEP). *'The OPEC meeting found it very difficult to come up with a new marker-price.'*

melon, bénéfice à distribuer. *'Under the new agreement, the employees would get 50% of the melon at the end of the year.'*

mezzanine financing, méthode de financement d'une partie du capital nécessaire pour acheter une entreprise (souvent employée par les employés eux-mêmes). *'Rather than see the firm go under, the employees asked the bank to help them set up a mezzanine financing scheme.'*

mole, taupe, informateur. *'As soon as the manager confronted the staff with petty pilfering, they realized that Fred was acting as a mole.'*

mom and pop operation, petite affaire. *'What was once a mom and pop operation has steadily expanded into a flourishing concern.'*

money squeeze, argent rare (en raison de forts taux d'intérêt). *'Smaller businesses are beginning to feel the effects of this latest money squeeze.'*

monkey wrench (to throw a), mettre des bâtons dans les roues. *'All we needed was some idiot to throw a monkey wrench in the works.'*

to mothball, metter (un projet, etc) au rancard; mettre de côté. *'The project was mothballed for lack of ready funds.'*

Movers and shakers, gros bonnets. *'Those movers and shakers have direct contacts in all the international capitals.'*

N

naked position, *StExch:* opération non arbitrée; position non garantie. *'It might be wise to cover those naked positions while the market is going through this choppy phase.'*

nearbys, échéances rapprochées (d'une marchandise traitée à terme). *'The nearbys were trading at a substantial premium over the deferreds.'*

negative pledge, promesse de ne pas solliciter de nouveaux prêts qui privilégieraient les nouveaux créanciers. *'The syndicate undertook a negative pledge for the duration of the loan.'*

nickel, pièce de cinq cents. *'He had had enough of nickel and dime operations and decided to invest in something more solid.'*

notice-day, date de déclaration. *'You must liquidate that April gold position before first notice-day.'*

number cruncher, un adepte de la comptabilité. *'Give those audits to the number cruncher – they'll keep him happy all week!'*

O

odd lot, unité (ou son multiple) de moins de cent actions. *'Those odd-lot orders should be sold at market.'*

online (equipment), (matériel) connecté, en direct. *'The new online processing equipment will be delivered next month.'*

on-site, sur place (dans une usine ou sur un chantier). *'The new training-unit was to be located on-site.'*

open shop, usine employant des ouvriers syndiqués et non syndiqués. *'There are very few open shops in the automobile industry.'*

O.P.M. = other people's money, l'argent d'autrui. *'His talent lies in using O.P.M. to fuel his schemes.'*

outage, coupure/interruption/panne. *'Outage time on that new computer has cost us a lot of money.'*

outplacement advisor, conseiller pour cadres (désirant trouver un emploi après licenciement). *'He made an appointment with an outplacement advisor as soon as they told him he was to be made redundant.'*

over age, *MarIns:* vaisseau qui a plus de 15 ans. *'We have special insurance schemes for ships that are over age.'*

overhang, 1. crédit voté qui dépasse les fonds disponibles. *'There was no alternative but to get approval for an overhang credit.'* **2.** avoirs en devises étrangères, difficilement convertibles en monnaie forte. *'We should never have taken that overhang currency on our books.'*

P

palm (to grease/oil s.o.'s) graisser la patte à qqn. *'We'll have to grease the doorman's palm to get into the club.'*

to palm off, refiler. *'You can palm off those seconds at a third of the price.'*

paperhanger/paperlayer, faux-monnayeur/ émetteur de faux chèques, de chèques sans provision. *'It's about time that paperhanger was indicted for fraud.'*

paralegal, parajuridique. *'If you just want advice, it'll be cheaper to use a paralegal service rather than hire a lawyer.'*

pass (to make a), (faire une) offre. *'There's no point making a pass until we have a fairly accurate idea of the price they're looking for.'*

to pass the buck, passer la responsabilité à qqn d'autre. *'When the manager tried to identify the source of the leak, everyone immediately passed the buck.'*

pathbreaking, innovateur. *'The president's pathbreaking decision encouraged his senior staff to recommend certain other changes.'*

paydown, se dit d'une nouvelle émission d'obligations, lancée par le Trésor américain pour remplacer une émission qui est arrivée à échéance et dont la valeur nominale était supérieure à celle de la nouvelle émission. *'There's a paydown issue of Treasury Bills to replace the ones that expire next week.'*

pay-up, différence entre le prix de vente d'un bloc de valeurs et le prix d'achat d'un autre bloc de valeurs plus chères. *'The net pay-up on that transaction will be $8,500.'*

to peddle, essayer de vendre (sa marchandise, son idée, etc). *'He was forever peddling some new scheme to his associates.'*

peer review, inspection professionnelle. *'He was especially pleased to have done so well in his first peer review.'*

penny-pinching measures, mesures d'austérité (économiques). *'The public had had enough of all these penny-pinching measures.'*

penny stocks, actions (spéculatives) valant moins d'un dollar. *'He was always investing in Canadian penny stocks.'*

peppercorn rent, loyer nominal. *'In return for her doing odd jobs around the house, they only charged her a peppercorn rent.'*

phantom, personne, entreprise, fictive (servant à des fins lucratives et illicites). *'Investigations revealed that the phantom company had embezzled at least $700,000.'*

phon(e)y, bidon/faux/contrefait. *'He immediately suspected that there was something phon(e)y going on.'*

physicals, matières premières disponibles, achetées et vendues au comptant. *'The discount between physicals and the nearby delivery was running at 35 cents a bushel.'*

pickup, avantage obtenu par la vente d'un bloc de valeurs et l'achat d'un autre bloc de valeurs à rendement supérieur. *'The pickup between ABC bonds and XYZ Corp. represents a full two points.'*

piece of the action, participation aux activités. *'Getting a piece of the action will mean putting up 20% of the capital.'*

piece of the pie, une part du gâteau. *'Your timely cooperation on that deal will mean you get an even bigger piece of the pie.'*

piggyback deal, une affaire qui entraîne une deuxième. *'If you give us good results on this first project, it might turn into a piggyback deal.'*

piggyback product, un produit à succès qui sera le premier de toute une série. *'There's no end to the piggyback products we can put on the market now that the first model is such a hit.'*

piggybank shipping, transport de camions chargés, à bord de wagons ouverts. *'The quickest solution is by piggybank shipping from New Orleans.'*

to pike, boursicoter. *'In America, even people in the low-income bracket are tempted to pike.'*

piker, boursicoteur. *'The pikers are always on the lookout for a hot tip.'*

pink sheets, liste quotidienne des cours des valeurs hors cote. *'Get me yesterday's closing prices from the pink sheets.'*

pitch, 1. territoire (d'un vendeur). *'He made sure there was no trespassing on his pitch by new salesmen in the area.'* **2. to make a pitch,** essayer de vendre qch. *'She prepared her arguments well in advance before making any pitch.'*

placing power, capacité d'une maison de courtage de placer les nouvelles émissions auprès des investisseurs. *'Their brokers are well-known for their placing power with new issues.'*

plant, 1. escroquerie/coup monté. *'It was only a few days later that they realised they had been the victim of a plant.'* **2.** planque/cachette pour objets volés. *'He always used the same plant for his stolen merchandise.'*

plateau, terme technique employé pour décrire une phase stable du marché. *'If you look at the charts, you'll see that the market stayed on that plateau for almost two weeks.'*

platform, programme électoral d'un parti politique. *'Once in power, very few politicians can carry out the platform they pushed during their election campaign.'*

to play the field, essayer plusieurs possibilités. *'I'm going to play the field for a while before deciding what I really want to do.'*

(to put in) play, (mettre en) vue. *'They put those shares right in play even before they went public.'*

to play ball, jouer honnêtement; accepter les termes d'un marché. *'If they've finally decided to play ball, we'll sign the contract right away.'*

poison-bill provisions, conditions (d'un marché ou d'un contrat) qui sont difficiles à digérer. *'You'd better take a closer look at those poison-bill provisions before you accept their terms.'*

policy stance, position prise. *'His policy stance on inflation finally produced some positive results.'*

polly, homme politique/fonctionnaire corruptible. *'Just grease the palm of a few pollies to get the building permit.'*

pool, la quantité d'ordres non exécutés dans une situation de limite supérieure ou de limite inférieure. *'The market stayed limit-up for the rest of the session, with 2,400 buy-orders in the pool.'*

position limit, *StExch:* quantité maximum de positions ouvertes autorisée à une seule personne. *'He has a position limit on coffee totalling 50 contracts.'*

position pages, documents préparés à l'avance pour exposer se position dans une discussion. *'Ask the secretary to get the position papers ready by Monday.'*

power retailer, vendeur au détail d'appareils électriques. *'The down-town power retailer stocks a good range of household goods.'*

price-tick, fluctuation de prix. *'The last price-tick was down an eighth.'*

primary reserves, réserves ayant une couverture-or. *'The island's primary reserves amounted to several million dollars.'*

prior charges, frais prioritaires. *'Interest on the loan and insurance premiums were major items among the prior charges.'*

prospect, client éventuel. *'Now brokers first look for prospects among their immediate acquaintances.'*

prospecting, démarchage. *'Prospecting techniques range from reading the Yellow Pages to propping up the bar at the Waldorf Hotel.'*

pull, rendement/influence (de la publicité, etc). *'Those new adds should be a real pull for the product.'* **political pull,** piston/influence. *'We could take advantage of his political pull to get the project approved.'*

puller, annonce/cadeau publicitaire, etc (qui fait vendre). *'Discount coupons used to be a big puller for washing-powders.'*

pump priming, injection de fonds par le gouvernement (pour ranimer l'économie et réduire le chômage). *'The Government will have to do a little pump priming if it really wants to revive the economy.'*

pups, valeurs de qualité douteuse. *'That broker has a knack of always pushing pups to his clients.'*

to put out to pasture, mettre à la retraite. *'Even at 65, he still couldn't face the prospect of being put out to pasture.'*

to put the heat on, exercer une pression sur. *'Management intends to put the heat on to raise productivity levels.'*

to put the lid on, limiter/mettre fin à (des dépenses, etc). *'A sure way to cut our costs is to put the lid on exorbitant travel expenses.'*

Q

quote-sheet, tableau des cours/cotes. *'Every broker should have a copy of the quote-sheet right on his desk.'*

R

to ramp (a stock), faire hausser le prix (d'une action) de façon artificielle. *'They must have ramped that stock for it to have gained $6 in the last two days.'*

rap, condamnation; **tax-rap,** condamnation pour délit fiscal. *'With the changes of administration, tax-raps are likely to be even stiffer.'*

record (to go on), déclarer publiquement. *'He went on record as the first politician to acknowledge the need for extensive tax reforms.'*

red herring, prospectus préliminaire. *'Any clients interested in this new issue must receive a red herring in due time.'*

referral, 1. nouveau client introduit par un habitué de la maison. *'You can open the account for that referral since he was brought in by one of your clients.'* **2.** recommandation (pour un courtier, fournisseur, etc) venant de la part d'un client satisfait. *'Some brokers work hard to get referrals rather than make endless cold calls.'*

referral fee, prime payée pour toute introduction de nouveaux clients. *'He was determined to get a referral fee for bringing a new client to the company.'*

referral scheme/selling, vente (surtout d'articles ménagers) avec possibilité pour l'acheteur de gagner une commission en convaincant ses amis d'acheter le même article. *'Department stores often use referral schemes to encourage housewives to recommend their merchandise to their friends.'*

remake, nouvelle version. *'The model they just brought is nothing more than a remake of an old 'fifties car.'*

repeater, *Jur:* récidiviste. *'When passing sentence, the court took into account the fact that the defendant was a repeater.'*

repo = repurchase agreement, prêt (souvent employé par la Réserve fédérale pour augmenter la masse monétaire) où l'emprunteur vend des fonds d'État avec l'obligation de les racheter ultérieurement. *'The Fed did several repos during the week to increase the money supply.'*

resistance level, palier de résistance. *'The 5-year chart shows a strong resistance level at $14.'*

resting order, *StExch:* **1.** ordre d'achat spécifiant un prix-limite qui est plus bas que le cours actuel. **2.** ordre de vente spécifiant un prix-limite qui est plus haut que le cours actuel. *'Those resting orders ought to be cancelled or changed to a price that is nearer the market.'*

reverse premium, prime offerte à un locataire éventuel (pour l'encourager à prendre un loyer à bail). *'Is there any chance of getting a reverse premium out of the landlord, if I refuse to sign the lease?'*

reverse repo = reverse repurchase agreement, prêt (souvent employé par la Réserve fédérale pour éponger la masse monétaire) où le prêteur vend des fonds d'État avec l'obligation de les racheter ultérieurement. *'The news that the Fed was going to do a reverse repo indicated that the money supply was higher than expected.'*

revolver = revolving credit, crédit (sur acceptation) renouvelable. *'The bank was willing to grant a revolver on certain specific conditions.'*

to rig the books, falsifier les comptes. *'He got away with several thousand dollars before they found out that he'd been rigging the books.'*

road show, exposition qui met en valeur une société, organisée par sa maison de courtage pour intéresser les investisseurs institutionnels. *'XYZ is putting on another road show to convince us that it's a going concern.'*

roll: sales went into a roll, les ventes ont chuté. *'As soon as the rumor hit the market, sales went into a roll.'*

to roll back, baisser un prix (à son niveau précédent). *'After the Budget, the price of petrol was rolled back to what it had been in December.'*

rollback, baisse des prix. *'The government was relieved to see a general rollback in consumer prices.'*

rollercoaster market, marché volatile. *'I don't think I've ever seen such a rollercoaster market as the one we saw today.'*

roll-forward, augmentation des prix (approuvée par le gouvernement). *'The Administration finally approved the roll-forward, even though it meant losing the struggle against inflation.'*

to roll over (a position), se faire reporter à une échéance plus éloignée. *'If you can't contact the client, just roll over the position to a more distant month.'*

roll-over relief, dégrèvement fiscal (à cause d'un réinvestissement immédiat de l'argent provenant d'une vente ou d'un bénéfice exceptionnel). *'You should reinvest those funds immediately if you want to apply for roll-over relief.'*

round-lot, unité (ou son multiple) de cent actions. *'It is easier to fill a round lot order than an order for odd lots.'*

rubber check, chèque sans provision. *'He tried to bounce a rubber check for the goods, but the cashier refused to accept it.'*

runaway plant, usine qui déménage d'un état à un autre pour profiter de conditions plus avantageuses. *'We just learnt of another runaway plant that's moving its headquarters to Idaho.'*

run-till-forbid, valable jusqu'à révocation. *'Those run-till-forbid orders might be executed today if the market continues to slide.'*

S

Samurai bond, obligation libellée en yen, émise au Japon par un emprunteur étranger; obligation par samurai. *'Appreciation in the yen has sparked off a wider interest in Samurai bonds.'*

savvy formula, formule de réconciliation entre partenaires. *'If we can't agree, we'll have to resort to a savvy formula.'*

savvy (investor), (investisseur) perspicace. *'Speculators often ask for a tip from a savvy investor like Munroe.'*

to scale down, acheter à intervalles réguliers au fur et à mesure que le marché baisse. *'My broker suggested that I scale down my buy-orders to take advantage of a dip in the market.'*

to scale up, vendre à intervales réguliers au fur et à mesure que le marché monte. *'He decided to scale up his liquidation orders.'*

to scalp the market, faire de petites opérations en Bourse, en rentrant et sortant très rapidement du marché. *'Floor-traders are well-placed to scalp the market in choppy conditions.'*

scalper, *StExch:* spéculateur à la journée.

schlock, pacotille/camelote. *'He was always trying to hawk his schlock to anyone who would listen.'*

schlock house, magasin qui vend de la pacotille/de la camelote. *'As the quality of their merchandise continued to fall, they became known as the neighbourhood's schlock house.'*

to screw up, gâcher, faire faux pas. *'The presidential candidate really screwed up in his last speech.'*

seam, fraude. *'They promised themselves that if the seam actually worked, they would retire to Florida.'*

seasoned issue, émission d'actions, lancée par une société renommée dont les émissions précédentes ont été généralement bien reçues. *'Serious investors are always keen to subscribe to this type of seasoned issue.'*

seat on an exchange (to have a), (avoir) la qualité de membre d'une Bourse. *'Ever since he left Business School, his intention had been to have a seat on the Exchange.'*

seed money, capital de départ. *'Once we get the seed money together, the bank might take us more seriously.'*

self-trade, mariage. *'Self-trades are illegal on most exchanges.'*

sell-down, part d'une nouvelle émission offerte à des acheteurs potentiels en dehors du syndicat de garantie. *'It is not always a good sign if some of the issue is offered on a sell-down basis.'*

serial bonds, obligations dont les dates d'échéance sont échelonnées. *'Those serial bonds expire at intervals from 1990 through the year 2000.'*

shakedown, 1. extorsion de fonds/chantage. *'Shakedown operators have an uncanny instinct for gullible victims.'* **2.** rançon. *'The kidnappers demanded a shakedown of $500,000.'* **3.** pot-de-vin. *'He made it quite clear that if he cooperated it would cost them a shakedown of 10% of the profits.'*

to shoot the breeze, bavarder. *'Could we please get down to business – we're not here to shoot the breeze.'*

short anchor, effet à très court terme, faisant partie d'un programme de reconsolidation entreprise par le Trésor américain. *'Those short anchor T. Bills are paying 9½%.'*

shots (to call the), imposer ses idées. *'The new boss certainly left no-one in ignorance as to who would be calling the shots.'*

shrinkage, diminution/rétrécissement/réduction (des profits, etc.). *'We've seen a lot of shrinkage in this year's results.'*

shunting, arbitrage de place à place. *'Shunting operations can now be done all around the globe on a 24-hour basis.'*

skids (to be on the), (être sur) la pente qui mène à la ruine. *'He'll soon be on the skids if he doesn't stop gambling.'*

small-time, de petite envergure. *'I have no use for those small-time operations.'*

soak-the-rich policy, réforme fiscale qui pénalise les riches. *'The Socialists applied their soak-the-rich policy as soon as they came to power.'*

soft commodities, matières premières de consommation. *'Sugar, coffee and cotton are examples of soft commodities.'*

soft loan, prêt à long terme à un taux favorable. *'Speculators looking to make a quick buck are hardly likely to be interested in soft loans.'*

soft spots, StExch: valeurs appartenant à un secteur industriel faible. *'Current soft spots include stocks in the cosmetics and paper industries.'*

sourcing, provenance (de matières premières, etc); source d'approvisionnement. *'The sourcing of that wheat may well be in Canada rather than the U.S.'*

spanner in the works, bâtons dans les roues. *'That guy is always looking for an opportunity to put a spanner in the works.'*

spin off, 1. système par lequel une filiale distribue ses actions au prorata aux actionnaires de la société mère. *'The spin off distribution came as an extra bonus to holders of MNO stock.'* **2.** des filiales qui sont partiellement vendues par la société mère qui retient ses actions dans ses anciennes filiales. *'We can always buy back those spin offs at a later date.'*

spoiler, moyen de saccager les projets de ses concurrents. *'They'll soon have a monopoly on that sector if we don't come up with an effective spoiler.'*

spoiling bid, offre publique d'achat qui a pour but de rendre l'opération plus difficile pour ses concurrents. *'That spoiling bid is simply intended to make us pay more.'*

spurt, coup de collier. *'The spurt in the gold market was due to the sudden collapse of the dollar.'* **to put on a spurt,** démarrer subitement. *'The market put on an unexpected spurt after the prime rate was lowered by half a point.'*

square, 1. *(of an account)* soldé. *'Currency dealers prefer their accounts to be square at the end of the day.'* **2. to be square,** être quitte. *If you send me a cheque for $2,000, we'll finally be square.'*

to square a debt, régler une dette. *'He squared all his debts before leaving the country.'*

squeeze play, tactique qui permet de coincer qn. *'It was just another squeeze play to get the bears to cover their shorts.'*

stampede, retraits massifs de dépôts bancaires. *'The rumors created a stampede on the banks.'*

to stash away, cacher/mettre de côté. *'He stashed away his winnings in the garden shed.'*

steer, conseil/renseignement. *'Can't you give me a steer on the way that stock's likely to move?'*

bum steer, faux renseignement/tuyau bidon. *'He dealt me a really bum steer on interest rate futures.'* **hot steer,** tuyau. *'I personally avoid that type of hot steer like the plague.'* **straight steer,** tuyau sûr/fiable. *'He's already given me five or six straight steers.'*

sticker price, prix de détail. *'What's the sticker price on that new delivery?'*

sting, arnaque. *'The whole operation was a sting from start to finish'.* **to get stung,** se faire avoir/se faire arnaquer. *'If you keep listening to that kind of argument, sooner or later you'll get badly stung.'*

stock-in-trade, spécialité (de la maison); activité principale. *'Their stock-in-trade was individually designed villas.'*

straddle, opération à cheval. *'The straddle involved buying March soybeans and selling the November.'* StExch: **to take a straddle position,** jumeler simultanément un achat sur une époque avec une vente sur une autre (sur le même marché et pour une quantité identique de lots). *'His broker advised him to take a straddle position until the announcement was made.'*

straights = straight bonds, obligations non convertibles en actions. *'Conservative investors are quite content to build up a portfolio of straights.'*

the Street = Wall Street, quartier de la Bourse de New York. *'The latest talk on the Street concerns an unwelcome takeover bid for XYZ Corporation.'*

street-price, cours fixé hors cote. *'Find out the current street-price on those over-the-counter shares.'*

sucker, 'poire', investisseur naïf. *'There are not enough suckers around to fall for the bait.'*

sunbelt states, régions ensoleillées des États-Unis (Californie, Arizona, Floride, etc). *'The sunbelt states provide the rest of the country with its daily dose of orange-juice.'*

sunlighting, fait d'avoir deux situations à plein temps.

sunrise industry, industrie naissante. *'The computer companies of Silicon Valley are the best example of a recent sunrise industry.'*

sunset industry, industrie traditionnelle/déclinante. *'Sunset industries such as heavy engineering might not be very glamorous, but they still attract conservative investors.'*

swap, cours de change indiquant la différence entre le taux d'intérêt applicable à deux devises sur une même période. *'What's the swap rate on 3 months deutschmark versus the yen?'*

to sweeten a bid, rendre plus attrayante son offre en proposant des avantages supplémentaires. *'If you agree to sell within the next month, we are prepared to sweeten the bid by paying 50% in ready cash.'*

sweetener, avantage (accordé lors d'une transaction). *'You always have to slip in a sweetener if you want to deal with that guy.'*

sweetheart contract, contrat de travail négocié avec un syndicat, qui est plutôt avantageux pour l'employeur. *'The Union Chiefs virtually delivered a sweetheart contract right to the bosses' door.'*

sweetheart deal, contrat ou transaction qui offre des avantages supplémentaires par rapport à la proposition initiale. *'If you're not prepared to accept our terms, find someone else to offer you a sweetheart deal.'*

r

(to pick up the) tab, (payer) l'addition. *'It was a question of honour to pick up the tab.'*

tail, différence entre le prix moyen et le plus bas accepté (dans une vente aux enchères du Trésor américain). *'I'd like to know what the tail was at the last T'Bill auction.'*

to take a bath, subir une grosse perte. *'He really took a bath in his last currency operation.'*

to take a flier, entreprendre une affaire très risquée. *'It's the last time I take a flier as risky as that one.'*

to take a shot at, essayer de faire qqch. *He's never done this type of work before, but he's willing to take a shot at it.'*

to take down, accepter une attribution d'actions. *'Let us know before next Tuesday if you intend to take down that ABC stock.'*

to be taken to the cleaners, être lessivé/ruiné. *'He used to dabble in commodities, but he was taken to the cleaners on his last three trades.'*

to take s.o. for a ride, duper qn. *'It never occurred to him that he'd been taken for a ride.'*

to tank, chuter. *'The pharmaceutical sector tanked when the public heard that another new drug had been banned.'*

to tap/to touch s.o., emprunter de l'argent à qn. *'Can I tap you for 50 dollars until next Monday?'*
to tap the market, emprunter de l'argent sur le marché des prêt pour financer une opération. *'If you really want to go ahead, you could always tap the market to get the necessary funds.'*

tape-watcher, investisseur qui observe les fluctuations des prix à partir de la bande des cours. *'Since he started to follow the market, he's become a dedicated tape-watcher.'*

tapped out, être 'raide', sans un sou. *'He was completely tapped out and asked his sister to lend him the train fare.'*

tax bite, la proportion de ses revenus payée aux impôts. *'Since you've made more money this year, your tax bite will increase as well.'*

tax-break, 1. avantage fiscal. *'The Government will have to give small industries some form of tax-break if it doesn't want a new wave of bankruptcies.'* **2.** vacances.

taxmanship, l'art de réduire le montant de ses impôts (sans avoir recours à la fraude). *'You'll need an accountant with a flair for taxmanship to get you out of your current difficulties.'*

tax-rap, condamnation pour fraude fiscale. *'The Court gave him a much stiffer tax-rap than he had expected.'*

T'Bill, (Treasury bill) bon du Trésor à court terme.

T'Bond, (Treasury bond) bon du Trésor à long terme.

Ten K/10-K, rapport annuel (exigé des corporations par les US Securities and Exchange Committee). *'Tell Johnson to prepare the Ten K by next Friday at the latest.'*

ten-percenter, intermédiaire qui reçoit 10% sur une affaire conclue par ses soins. *'He made a good living as a ten-percenter on import-export deals.'*

termer, contractant à terme. *Find out if the termer we dealt with last month would be interested in a September delivery of coffee.'*

to be terminated, être mis à la porte. *'He was told he was to be terminated at the end of the month.'*

terms of trade, rapport entre les indices de prix à l'exportation et à l'importation. *'According to the last terms of trade report, the current difference is 65 dollars a ton.'*

third market, marché hors cote. *'Can you send me a third market quote by telex on XYZ?'*

third window, source de crédit à bas taux d'intérêt (fournie aux pays en voie de développement par la Banque Mondiale). *'With any rise in oil-prices, Third World countries would be lining up at the third window.'*

threshold rate, salaire initial. *'in advertising, the threshold rate was once 120 dollars a week.'*

thrift institutions, banques d'épargne. *'Putting your money into a thrift institution is a time-honoured way of saving in the States.'*

thrift shop, magasin qui vend à bas prix. *'I picked up a real bargain at the thrift shop this morning.'*

throwaway, imprimé publicitaire. *'My mail-box is always full of these throwaways.'*

throwback, retour en arrière/recul. *'It's a throwback to the way we did business in the 'fifties.'*

tick, fluctuation de prix. *'Find out if the last tick was up, down or unchanged.'*

ticker, téléscripteur. *'The news came over the ticker just ten minutes ago.'*

ticker-tape, bande de téléscripteur. *'Some people spend their whole day just reading the ticker-tape.'*

ticket, liste des candidats d'un parti politique. *'The Republican ticket will carry several newcomers this year.'*

tied loan, prêt accordé par une nation à une autre, stipulant que celle-ci achète des biens ou des services au pays prêteur. *'The tied loan carries an obligation for the borrower to buy a considerable amount of corn from the U.S. on a yearly basis.'*

tied sale/tie-in deal, vente à condition. *'We're obliged to accept that tied sale, even though the conditions are hard to swallow.'*

top dollar, prix le plus élevé. *'Since they're not in a hurry, they'll wait till they can sell for the top dollar.'*

top-heavy, StExch: se dit d'un marché qui a atteint un palier de résistance et qui risque fort de dégringoler. *'The market feels top-heavy, so it might be wise to do a little unloading.'*

to top and tail, taper ses coordonnées en haut et en bas de la page. *'Would you please top and tail this document before putting it in the mail?'*

topping-up clause, clause stipulant qu'un emprunteur doit augmenter sa garantie sur la simple demande du prêteur. *'If you don't think his credit is all that good, you can always write a topping-up clause into the loan.'*

toppy market, marché nerveux/qui a atteint un palier de résistance. *'With the market looking so toppy, we might see a wave of panic selling.'*

to touch base, maintenir le contact. *'His sales manager told him to touch base at least three times a week when he was out in the field.'*

trade, transaction. *'They made several trades just before the close of the market.'*

trading posts, les corbeilles du New York Stock Exchange. *'If you ever visit the Exchange, you'll be knocked out by the noise and apparent panic at the trading posts.'*

trafficking, négoce (souvent illégal). *'He was known to the police for trafficking in drugs.'*

trigger price, prix d'intervention. *'If the sugar market loses a few more points, the trigger price will go into effect.'*

tripcharter, contrat d'affrétement spécifiant les points de livraison. *'It's a tripcharter that will stop off to deliver the goods in eight different ports.'*

triple A rating = AAA, classement accordé aux obligations de premier rang. *'I won't invest in anything that doesn't have a triple A rating.'*

triple nine, le plus haut titre de l'or/or pur à 99.9 pour cent. *'You usually have to pay a premium for triple nine bars.'*

trustee stocks, valeurs de père de famille. *'You can't go wrong with trustee stocks.'*

tryout, essai. *I don't mind giving it a tryout if you're convinced it's worthwhile.'* **tryout period,** période d'essai. *'They're taking me on for a tryout period of two months.'*

two-timing, duplicité. *'His colleagues soon found out about his two-timing activities.'*

U

Uncle Sam, l'oncle Sam (les initiales US = United States; personnage qui symbolise les États-Unis ou son corps administratif). *'You can always join the Marines if you're keen to serve Uncle Sam.'*

under the counter, en sous-main, illicite. *'He pulled off at least two under-the-counter deals every week.'*

·underhand, clandestin, sournois. *'His underhand dealings soon attracted the attention of the police.'*

unfrocked, rayé, banni d'un corps professionnel. *'He risked being permanently unfrocked if the deal ever came to light.'*

to unload stock, vendre des actions. *'I would try to unload some of those speculative stocks, as the market looks ready for a correction.'*

to unwind a hedge position, défaire/dénouer un arbitrage. *'We have to unwind that hedge position by selling the July's and buying back the November's.'*

upcoming, qui est dû très prochainement. *'The upcoming report on exports was rumoured to be fairly disappointing.'*

to upgrade (a stock), attribuer une classification supérieure (à une valeur). *'Standard and Poor's just upgraded XYZ Corp on the strength of its earnings,'* **to upgrade (an employee),** promouvoir (un employé). *'If we upgrade Jenkins to sales manager old McGee will have something to say!'*

upscale market, marché de haut de gamme. *'Those computer stocks are now moving into the upscale market.'*

USP = unique selling point, point de vente unique/seul point de vente. *'It's a question of prestige to sell through USP's.'*

V

velvet, de velours; gain facile. *'Taking those suckers for a ride was pure velvet.'*

V note/V spot, billet de banque de cinq dollars. *'It'll only cost you a few V notes to join the association.'*

W

to walk, se mettre en grève. *'The vote showed that almost everyone wanted to walk.'*

to want into = **to want to get into.** *'He warned me that he wants into this deal and won't accept a refusal.'*

to warehouse shares, accepter des titres en dépôt. *'The bank accepted to warehouse his shares until he got back from Japan.'*

wash sale, *StExch:* vente fictive (achat et vente effectués simultanément, donc opération fictive et illégale). *'Wash sales are strictly forbidden on the American markets.'*

WASP = **White Anglo-Saxon Protestant,** qui appartient à la race blanche, d'origine anglo-saxonne, et ayant des tendances politiques conservatrices. *'There are a lot of WASPs working on Wall Street.'*

watered stock, actions diluées (actions dont les cours ont baissé, parce que la société concernée a émis trop de titres (parfois gratuitement) par rapport à ses valeurs tangibles). *'That watered stock has lost another 3 dollars over the last week.'*

to wheel and deal, brasser beaucoup d'affaires (terme souvent appliqué à des activités illicites). *'He had a bad reputation for wheeling and dealing in secondhand cars.'*

wheeler-dealer, brasseur d'affaires (plus ou moins en marge de la loi). *'We're just waiting for that wheeler-dealer to make his first mistake.'*

when issued (WI) = **when, as and if issued,** phrase conditionnelle qualifiant le prix d'une action qui n'a pas encore éte émise; à l'émission. *'They announced a price of $9 a share when issued.'*

whipsawed (to get), *StExch:* subir des pertes occasionnées par un marché très volatile. *'It's better to stay out of a nervous market, rather than get whipsawed.'*

whistleblower, 'siffleur', celui qui attire l'attention des autres aux abus pour y mettre fin. *'Every society needs a few whistleblowers to keep an eye on what's going on.'*

to whitewash money, blanchir de l'argent venant d'une source illégale. *'An easy way to whitewash money is to change it at the casino.'*

wirehouse, maison de courtage ayant des lignes téléphoniques et de télex liées directement aux salles de transactions des Bourses. *'The wirehouse of B.J. Jennings has a sound reputation for rapid client service.'*

wirepuller, personne qui cherche à se faire pistonner; intriguant. *'Wirepullers sometimes resort to blackmail if they don't get what they want.'*

wirepulling, piston/patronage/influence; art de tirer les ficelles. *'He got to his present position by wirepulling.'*

write-up, écriture comptable falsifiée. *'They hoped to get out of the mess by using a cleverly disguised write-up.'*

Y

yankee bond, obligation libellée en dollars, émise aux Etats-Unis par un emprunteur étranger. *'The yankee bond market in Europe was especially active today.'*

yard, un milliard (terme employé dans les marchés des changes). *'Can you quote me a yard of sterling to Japanese yen?'*

yes-man, personne qui approuve tout ce qu'on dit, qui dit toujours 'amen'. *'You should find someone who's not afraid of giving his own opinion instead of listening to all these yes-men.'*

Z

zero-sum game/negociation, jeu/négociation à somme nulle. *'Nobody wins and nobody loses in a zero-sum game.'*

Legal and contractual language

Vocabulaire juridique et termes de contrats

LEGAL AND CONTRACTUAL LANGUAGE
COMMON LEGAL AND CONTRACTUAL TERMS AND EXPRESSIONS

acknowledged and agreed to	lu et approuvé
act	acte *m*, décret *m*
act of god	catastrophe naturelle
agreed upon	convenu
agreement	accord *m*
allocation	répartition *f*
amendment	rectification *f*, modification *f*
answerable	responsable, garant
any	n'importe quel, tout, quelconque
any departure from the terms	tout écart aux termes
any one of the following reasons	pour l'une quelconque des raisons suivantes
applicable tariff	tarif *m* en vigueur
as defined in	comme défini dans
as may be allowed	qui pourrait être autorisé
as may be appropriate	selon les besoins
as may be necessary	qui pourrait être nécessaire
as may be required	qui pourrait être exigé
as provided in	comme prévu dans
as regards	concernant
assurance	assurance-vie *f*
as the case may be	selon le cas
attached hereto and made a part thereof	joint au présent accord et qui en fait partie intégrante
at the latest	au plus tard
attributable	imputable
basic requirements	conditions de base
beforehand	au préalable, préalablement
beyond the control	indépendant de la volonté
breach	contravention *f*, infraction *ff*, rupture *f*, violation *f*
breach of contract	rupture *f*, violation *f*, de contrat
bye-law	arrêté *m* émanant d'une autorité locale
by reasons of any breach	en raison de toute rupture
by the term	en vertu de, aux termes de
called	dénommé
clause	clause *f*

clause to assign jurisdiction	clause attributive de juridiction
closure	clôture *f*
commitment	engagement *m* (souvent financier)
compensation	dédommagement *m*
compliance with provisions requirements	conformité aux dispositions *f*, aux conditions *f*
concerned	concerné
concurrence	consentement *m*
consistent with	conforme, compatible, cohérent, en accord avec
consisting of	comprenant
constituted or determined	interprété, considéré ou résolu
contract	contrat *m*
convention	descriptif *m*
cost incurred items	postes *m* à frais courants
damage	dégât *m*
damages	dommages-intérêts *mpl*
deadline	dernier délai, date *f* limite
decree	décret *m*
default	faute *f*, manquement *m*
dispute	litige *m*, différend *m*, controverse *f*
done under this agreement	fait au titre de
due	échu, exigible
due to any of these causes	dû à l'une quelconque des causes ci-dessus
duly	en temps voulu, dûment, en temps utile
enactment	promulgation *f*, acte législatif
encroachment	empiètement *m*
encumbrance	hypothèque *f*
enforceable	exécutoire
ensuing	subséquent, suivant
except as provided in	à l'exception des dispositions prévues
except where otherwise stated	sauf indications contraires
excluding	à l'exception de
expiry of all warrantee periods	expiration de toutes les périodes de garantie
express or implied	exprimé ou implicite

extinctive prescription	prescription *f*	*in good faith*	de bonne foi
fails to fully comply with requirements	ne satisfait pas pleinement aux exigences de la spécification	*in order that*	de façon à, dans le but de
		in respect of	en relation avec
		in respect thereof	à cet égard
		in so far as	pour autant que
failure	manquement *m*, inobservation *f*, non conformité *f*	*installed cost*	coût installé
		in such a way as to	d'une telle manière
failure to comply	non respect de	*insurance*	assurance *f*
failure to meet	défaillance *f* à satisfaire	*in the case of failure*	dans le cas de non respect
failure to pay	non paiement *m*	*in the event of a dispute*	en cas de désaccord
failure to perform	non exécution *f*	*in the event that*	dans le cas où
fixed cost items	postes à frais fixes	*in the first place*	en premier lieu
following reason	raison suivante	*in this respect*	à cet égard
force majeure	force *f* majeure		
for the purpose of	aux fins de	*joint*	solidaire
for the purposes	pour les besoins	*joint cost*	coût installé
forthwith	séance tenante, sur le champ	*law*	loi *f*
further, furthermore	d'autre part	*legal*	légal, juridique
		legal department	service *m* du contentieux
guarantee	garant *m*, garantie *f*, caution *f*, aval *m*	*liable*	responsable, passible de
		likewise	de même
grounds for	cause *f*, motif *m*, raison *f*, matière *f*	*liquidated damages*	pénalités *f*
		litigation	litige *m*
		lump sum	paiement *m* unique
however expressed	quelle que soit la manière dont ils (elles) sont exprimé(e)s	*mandatory*	qui enjoint
		may reasonably require	peut raisonnablement le demander
if	si		
if and when required	si nécessaire et au moment voulu	*non conformance*	non respect de
		not fully compliant	non entièrement conforme
if any	éventuel		
if so required	si nécessaire	*not solely attributable*	non exclusivement imputable
if subsequent to	si postérieurement		
implied	implicite	*notwithstanding*	nonobstant
in accordance with	en tenant compte de, en accord avec	*null and void*	nul et non avenu
in accordance with the law	selon la loi	*on behalf of*	au nom de, pour le compte de
		on or before	au plus tard
in addition to	en plus de	*onus*	charge *f*
in an advisory capacity	à titre consultatif	*optional*	facultatif
in any event	en tout cas	*outstanding*	en suspens, non réglé
in bad faith	de mauvaise foi	*overdue*	en retard, arriéré
in case of	en cas de	*ownership*	propriété *f* (non abstraite)
including but not limited to	y compris sans que la liste soit limitative		
		paid up	à jour, acquitté
in compliance with	en conformité avec	*part hereof*	partie intégrante
in conformity with	en conformité avec	*parties hereto agree to*	(les) parties au présent accord acceptent
in default	en défaut		
indefeasible (right)	(droit) irrévocable	*petition*	requête *f*
in due course	en temps voulu, dûment, en temps utile	*policy*	police *f* (d'assurance)
		prior to commencement	avant de commencer
infringement (of patent)	infraction *f* (aux brevets)	*property*	propriété *f* (biens)

provided for	comme prévu	undertaking	engagement *m*
provided that	à condition que, sous réserve que; attendu que, pourvu que	under the provisions	en vertu de, aux termes de
		undivided shares	parts indivisées
proviso	condition *f*, réserve *f*	unless otherwise stated	en l'absence d'autres précisions indiquées
pursuant to	en vertu de, aux termes de, conformément à		
		upon the following terms and conditions	aux termes et conditions dénommés
quotation	cours *m*, cote *f* cotation *f*	upon delivery	lors de la livraison
		upon issuance	suite à la délivrance
receipt	reçu *m*	upon surrender of the documents	sur remise des documents
referred to below	visé ci-après		
regulation	règlement *m*	usual terms	conditions *f* d'usage
relating to	relatif à		
relevant	s'y rapportant, se rapportant à	vesting of a title	transfert *m* de droit de propriété
		voucher	pièce justificative
remedial	correctif		
rescinding	résiliation *f*	waiver	renonciation *f*, dispense *f*, dérogation *f*
rider	avenant *m*		
rule	règle *f*	warrant	garantie *f*
		whatsoever shall be the case	quelle que soit la cause
shall be binding on the parties	engagera les parties		
		where	si, lorsque
shall be decisive	fera foi	whereas	attendu que, pourvu que
shall be deemed to have been given	sera censé avoir été donné	whether or not	qu'il en soit ainsi ou non
		whole	entier
shall be liable	sera responsable, passible	with a view to	en vue de
shall in no way relieve	ne dégagera en aucune façon	with due regard	compte tenu de
		with respect to	en ce qui concerne
shall not be greater	ne devra pas dépasser	written consent	accord par écrit
shall not be inconsistent	ne devront pas être en désaccord		

COMMON LATIN EXPRESSIONS

shall not in any circumstance	ne devra pas en aucune circonstance	ad hoc	pour ceci
		ad valorem	selon la valeur
shall save the parties harmless	mettra les parties hors de cause	bona fide	de bonne foi
		cum	avec, inclus, y compris
shall under no circumstance be	en aucune circonstance ne sera	de facto	de fait
		de jure	de droit
should it prove necessary	si cela s'avère nécessaire, le cas échéant	e.g. (exempli gratia)	par exemple
		et cetera	etc ...
should the need arise	si le besoin se fait sentir	ex officio	ès qualité
sole	unique, seul, exclusif	ibidem	au même endroit
so that	pour que	i.e. (idem est)	c'est à dire
specified requirements	conditions spécifiées	in camera	à huis clos
subsequent	postérieur, ultérieur	per annum	par an
such	tel, telle, ces	per capita	par tête
suit	procès *m*	per cent	pour cent
		per pro. (p.p.)	par procuration
terms of reference	attributions *f*	prima facie	de prime abord
therefore	ainsi, donc, par conséquent	pro rata	prorata, au marc le franc
to the extent that	dans la mesure où		
to this effect	dans ce sens		
under penalty of	sous peine de		

sic	sic, ainsi
sine die	indéfiniment
sine qua non	condition indispensable
status quo	statu quo
ultra vires	au-delà de la compétence
versus	contre
vice versa	vice versa

FREQUENT ARCHAIC ADVERBS

aforementioned/	sus-mentionné, sus-dit,
aforesaid	précité
as aforesaid	ainsi qu'il a été spécifié plus haut
forthwith	séance tenante, sur le champ
henceforth	désormais
hereafter	dorénavant, désormais, ultérieur, ci-après
hereat	là-dessus
hereby	par le présent, par la présente
herein	en ceci, sur ce point, dans le présent
herein above	ci-dessus
hereinafter/hereinbelow	ci-dessous, ci-après
hereinbefore	ci-devant
hereof	de ceci
hereto	ci-joint
heretofore	auparavant, jusqu'ici
hereunder	ci-dessous, au titre du présent
hereupon	là-dessus
herewith	avec ceci
thereafter	après cela
thereby	de ce fait
therefor	pour cela
therefore	ainsi, donc, par conséquent
therefrom	de là
therein	en cela, à cet égard
thereinafter	plus loin, ci-dessous
thereinbefore	plus haut, ci-dessus
thereinunder	ci-dessous
hereof	de cela
hereto	à cela
heretofore	avant cela
whereas	attendu que
whereby	par lequel, grâce auquel
wherein	en quoi
whereof	duquel, dont
whereon	sur quoi
whereupon	sur lequel

ADVERBS

accordingly	en conséquence
expressly	expressément, formellement
fully	entièrement
irrevocably	irrévocablement
jointly and severally	conjointement et solidairement
mutually	d'un commun accord, réciproquement
reasonably	raisonnablement
severally liable	responsable individuellement
solely	exclusivement
unconditionally	sans réserve
wholly	dans sa totalité

PERSONS

advisor	conseiller *m*
contracting party	partie contractante
contractor	entrepreneur *m*
legal department	(service du) contentieux *m*
party	partie *f*
requesting party	partie demanderesse
said member	ledit membre
sub contractor	sous-traitant *m*
third party	tiers *m*
trustee	adminstrateur *m*, syndic *m*

VERBS
ACTIVE

to abide by the terms	respecter les termes
to act as	agir en qualité de, comme, en tant que
to agree to	consentir, accepter, convenir
to agree with	être d'accord
to allow	permettre (autorisation)
to appear in court	comparaître devant un tribunal
to apply to	s'appliquer à
to approve	agréer, approuver
to arise	découler, se poser, résulter de
to ascertain	s'assurer
to assess	estimer, établir
to assign	attribuer
to avail oneself of	se prévaloir de
to award damages	accorder à titre de dommages et intérêts

to bear on	porter sur	to settle out of court	régler à l'amiable
to bring an action	intenter des poursuites	to sue	poursuivre en justice
to carry a risk	supporter un risque	to sustain a loss	subir une perte
to come into effect	entrer en vigueur	to take legal proceedings	intenter des poursuites
to comply with	se conformer, se soumettre, s'incliner	to take such actions/ measures	prendre toute disposition/ telles mesures
to comprise	inclure, comprendre	to tender	soumettre, soumissionner
to conflict with	être en désaccord, en conflit, en contradiction avec	to undertake	s'engager à
		to waive	déroger, dispenser, renoncer à
to contract to	s'engager à		

PASSIVE

to convene	convoquer
to elapse	s'écouler
to enable	permettre (rendre possible)
to enter into an agreement	conclure un accord
to evidence	attester
to file	déposer, formuler
to file a petition/ complaint	enregistrer une enquête, porter plainte
to fulfil the conditions/ requirements	remplir les conditions
to give rise to	donner naissance à
to go to court/law	aller en justice
to incur loss/debt/risk	subir une perte, contracter une dette, encourir un risque
to indemnify	indemniser, dédommager
to institute proceedings	intenter des poursuites
to invite tenders	faire, lancer, un appel d'offres
to keep and maintain	tenir à jour et conserver
to lead to	conduire à, mener à
to mean	entendre, signifier, vouloir dire
to meet the conditions/ requirements	satisfaire aux conditions
to override	passer outre
to permit	permettre (autorisation)
to pertain to	concerner, appartenir à
to prejudice	porter atteinte à
to prevail	prévaloir, l'emporter sur, dominer
to provoke	occasionner
to reach an agreement	aboutir à un accord
to reach a deadlock	aboutir à une impasse
to recover	recouvrer
to rescind a contract	résilier un contrat
to reserve the right	se réserver le droit
to resort to	avoir recours à
to satisfy the conditions set forth	satisfaire aux conditions énoncées

to be allowed to	être autorisé à
to be awarded	être adjugé, décerné attribué, alloué; se voir décerné, adjugé, attribué, alloué
to be bound by	être lié par
to be charged	être inculpé
to be deemed	être réputé, considéré
to be drawn up	être rédigé
to be entitled to	être en droit de, avoir droit à
to be entrusted to	être confié à
to be entrusted with	se voir confier
to be exempt	être exonéré
to be laid down	être spécifié, prescrit, arrêté, fixé; être couché
to be provided for	être prévu, destiné à
to be relieved	être dégagé
to be required	être exigé, requis, demandé
to be required to	être obligé de, forcé de
to be set forth	être énoncé, décrit, exposé
to be set out	être exposé
to be specified	être spécifié
to be stated	être énoncé
to be stipulated	être stipulé
to be subject to	être sujet à, sous réserve de
to be tried	être jugé

ARCHAIC VERBS

to afford	donner, fournir, accorder (aide)
to afford (sens moderne)	se permettre financièrement
to cease (to stop)	cesser
to commence (to begin)	commencer
to furnish (to provide)	fournir (renseignements)
to furnish (sens moderne)	meubler

FRENCH-ENGLISH

A

abaissement, *n.m.* lowering; **abaissement (des prix, des barrières douanières),** lowering (of prices, of tariff barriers); **abaissement de la valeur du franc,** fall/drop in the value of the franc.

abaisser, *v.tr.* to lower/to reduce (prices, cost, etc.); **abaisser le taux d'escompte,** to lower the minimum lending rate.

abandon, *n.m.* renunciation (of goods, rights, etc.).

abandonner, *v.tr.* to abandon/to surrender/to renounce/to give up; **abandonner la prime,** to relinquish the forfeit/the option money; **abandonner ses biens à ses créanciers,** to surrender one's goods to one's creditors.

abattement, *n.m.* abatement (on declared income); **abattement fiscal,** allowance (against tax); **abattement à la base,** basic personal allowance.

abîmé, *a.* **marchandises abîmées,** damaged/shop-soiled goods.

abonné, -ée, *n.* (*a*) subscriber (to newspaper, etc.); **un abonné du téléphone,** a telephone subscriber; **je suis abonné à cette revue,** I have a subscription to this magazine (*b*) *Rail: etc:* season-ticket holder (*c*) consumer; **les abonnés du gaz,** gas users/consumers.

abonnement, *n.m.* (*a*) subscription (to newspaper, etc.); **bulletin d'abonnement,** subscription form; **prendre un abonnement d'un an à une revue,** to take out a year's subscription to a magazine; **prix de l'abonnement/tarif d'abonnement,** subscription rate; *Ins:* **police d'abonnement,** floating policy (*b*) *Rail: etc:* **(carte d')abonnement,** season ticket/*NAm:* commutation ticket (*c*) *Adm:* (water) rate; (telephone) rental.

abonner, *v.tr.* **abonner qn à un journal,** to take out a subscription to a newspaper for s.o.; **être abonné à (une revue, un journal),** to subscribe to (a magazine, a newspaper).

s'abonner, *v.pr.* (*a*) **s'abonner à un journal,** to subscribe/to take out a subscription to a newspaper; **je me suis abonné à cette revue,** I have taken out a subscription to this magazine (*b*) *Rail: etc:* to buy a season ticket.

abrogation, *n.f.* abrogation/repeal.

abrogatoire, *a.* annulling/rescinding (clause, etc.).

abroger, *v.tr.* to abrogate/to annul/to repeal/to rescind.

absentéisme, *n.m.* absenteeism.

absorber, *v.tr.* to take over (a company).

absorption, *n.f.* takeover (of one company by another).

abus, *n.m.* **abus de confiance,** breach of trust.

accalmie, *n.f.* slack time/lull (in business).

accaparement, *n.m.* **accaparement du marché,** cornering of the market.

accaparer, *v.tr.* to corner (the market).

accéder, *v.tr.* *Cmptr:* **accéder à,** to access.

accélération, *n.f.* **principe d'accélération,** accelerator principle.

acceptabilité, *n.f.* **acceptabilité de la marque,** brand acceptance.

1

acceptant, -ante, *n.* acceptor.

acceptation, *n.f.* acceptance; **acceptation bancaire/de banque,** bank acceptance; **banque d'acceptation,** accepting/acceptance house; (*sur une traite*) **bon pour acceptation,** accepted; **présenter un effet/ une traite à l'acceptation,** to present a bill for acceptance; **refus d'acceptation,** non-acceptance (of goods, bill).

accepté, *a.* (*sur une traite*) accepted; **effet accepté,** accepted bill.

accepter, *v.tr.* to accept; **accepter un effet,** (*i*) to accept/to sign a bill (*ii*) to honour a bill; **ne pas accepter un effet,** to dishonour a bill.

accepteur, -euse, *n.* acceptor/drawee (of bill).

accès, *n.m.* access; **accès libre,** free admission; **droit d'accès,** right of entry; *Cmptr:* **temps d'accès,** access time.

accession, *n.f.* **accession à la propriété,** home ownership; **prêt (aidé) à l'accession à la propriété,** mortgage/loan for the purchase of a home; **prêt pour la première accession,** loans for first time buyers/for first timers.

accessoire, 1. *a.* accessory; **avantages accessoires,** fringe benefits; **clause accessoire,** ancillary clause; **frais accessoires,** incidental expenses; **garantie accessoire,** collateral security **2.** *n.m.pl.* accessories; (*dans un magasin*) **accessoires de/pour la toilette,** toilet requisites.

accident, *n.m.* accident; **accidents du travail,** industrial accident/injuries; **la loi sur les accidents du travail** = the Health and Safety at Work Act/the Factory Acts; *Fin:* **accident de parcours,** hiccup/slippage.

accise, *n.f.* *FrC: & Belgium* excise (duty).

accompagnateur, -trice, *n.* (tourist) guide/courrier.

accord, *n.m.* agreement/contract; treaty; **accord à l'amiable,** private agreement; **accord commercial,** trade agreement; **Accord général sur les tarifs douaniers et le**
commerce, General Agreement on Tariffs and Trade (GATT); **accords internationaux sur les produits de base,** international commodity agreements; **accords réciproques,** reciprocal agreements; **accord tarifaire,** tariff agreement.

accord-cadre, *n.m.* blanket agreement.

accorder, *v.tr.* to grant/to award; **accorder un prêt,** to grant/to extend a loan; **accorder un rabais,** to allow a reduction/ to give a discount.

accrédité, *n.m.* (*a*) holder of a letter of credit; person having credit facilities with/at a bank (*b*) authorized agent.

accréditer, *v.tr.* (*a*) **notre représentant dûment accrédité,** our duly authorized representative (*b*) *Fin:* **accréditer un client,** to open credit facilities for a customer; **il est accrédité auprès de la BNP,** he has credit facilities with/at the BNP.

accréditeur, *n.m.* *Fin:* surety/guarantor.

accréditif, 1. *a.* **carte accréditive,** credit card; **lettre accréditive,** letter of credit **2.** *n.m.* (*a*) letter of credit (*b*) **accréditif permanent,** permanent credit; **loger un accréditif sur une banque,** to open credit facilities with a bank.

accroissement, *n.m.* growth/increase/ increment; **accroissement de la demande,** increase in demand; **accroissement global net,** aggregate net(t) increment; **accroissement de la productivité,** growth of productivity; **accroissement des ventes,** sales growth; **accroissement spontané du capital,** self-induced increase of capital; **coût d'accroissement,** incremental cost; **taux d'accroissement,** rate of increase.

accroître, *v.tr.* to increase/to add/to augment; **accroître le capital,** to increase capital; **accroître la productivité,** to increase/to raise productivity.

accumulation, *n.f.* build-up/buildup (of stocks).

accumulé, *a.* accumulated/accrued; **intérêts accumulés,** accrued interest.

s'accumuler, *v.pr.* (*des intérêts, etc.*) to accrue.

accusé, 1. *n.m.* **accusé de réception,** (*d'une lettre*) acknowledg(e)ment (of receipt) (of a letter); (*d'un colis, etc.*) receipt (of a parcel, etc.); **envoyer un accusé de réception,** to send an acknowledg(e)ment; to acknowledge (sth) **2.** *a.* **baisse (très) accusée,** sharp fall.

accuser, *v.tr.* **1.** to show/to reveal/to indicate; **compte qui accuse une perte,** account which shows a loss **2.** **accuser réception de qch.,** to acknowledge (receipt of) sth.; **j'accuse réception de votre lettre,** I acknowledge receipt of your letter.

achalandage, *n.m.* (*a*) customers; patrons; clientele (*b*) stock; goodwill; **l'achalandage se vend avec l'établissement,** the goodwill is to be sold with the business.

achalandé, *a.* **magasin bien achalandé,** (*i*) shop with a large clientele (*ii*) well-stocked shop.

achat, *n.m.* purchase; **achat au comptant,** cash purchase; **achat d'impulsion/achat spontané,** impulse buying; **achat à crédit/à terme,** (*i*) purchase on credit/for the account (*ii*) buying on hire purchase/ *NAm:* on the instalment plan (iii) forward purchase; **chef des achats,** purchasing manager; head/chief buyer; **service des achats,** buying departments; **droits d'achat,** purchasing rights; **facture d'achat,** invoice; *Book-k:* **journal/livre des achats,** bought ledger; **offre publique d'achat,** takeover bid; **ordre d'achat,** buy(ing) order; indent; **pouvoir d'achat,** purchasing/spending power; **prix d'achat,** cost price/purchase price/actual cost/ prime cost; **aller faire ses achats,** to go shopping; **faire un achat/faire l'achat de qch.,** to make a purchase/to purchase sth./to buy sth.

acheminement, *n.m.* (*a*) **acheminement d'un colis/du courrier,** routing of a consignment of goods/of mail (*b*) flow/ routing (of goods, etc.) (*c*) forwarding/sending/dispatch(ing) (of

goods, etc.); **durée d'acheminement,** forwarding time.

acheminer, *v.tr.* **acheminer qch. sur/vers un endroit,** to send/to forward/to dispatch/to route sth. to a place; **marchandises acheminées sur Nantes,** goods dispatched to Nantes.

achetable, *a.* purchasable.

acheter, *v.tr.* **acheter qch.,** to buy/to purchase sth.; **j'ai acheté ce livre cinq francs,** I bought this book for five francs; **acheter qch. à qn,** (*i*) to buy sth. from s.o. (*ii*) to buy sth. for s.o.; **acheter qch. (à) bon marché,** to buy sth. cheap; **acheter (au) comptant,** to pay cash (for sth.)/to buy for cash; **acheter à crédit/à tempérament,** to buy on credit; to buy on hire purchase/ *NAm:* on the instalment plan; **acheter au détail,** to buy retail; **acheter en gros,** to buy wholesale; **acheter qch. chez l'épicier/ chez Martin,** to buy sth. at the grocer's/at Martin's.

acheteur, -euse, *n.* **1.** buyer/purchaser; customer; *Jur:* vendee; **acheteur éventuel,** intending purchaser; **acheteur potentiel,** potential buyer; **on n'a pas pu trouver d'acheteurs pour …,** there are no buyers for/there is no market for …; **je suis acheteur,** I'll take it **2.** buyer (for department store, etc.); **acheteur principal,** head buyer **3.** **cours acheteur,** buying/bid price; **position acheteur,** bull position; **acheteur non-identifié/anonyme,** undisclosed principal.

achèvement, *n.m.* completion/finishing/ conclusion (of work); **date d'achèvement,** completion date; **date prévue d'achèvement,** target date.

acier, *n.m.* steel.

aciérie, *n.f.* steelworks.

acompte, *n.m.* instalment/down payment/ payment on account; advance; **acompte provisionnel,** advance payment; **payer tant en acompte,** to pay so much on account; **recevoir un acompte sur son salaire,** to receive an advance on one's salary; **verser un acompte de cent francs,** to pay a hundred francs on account (**sur, on**)/to make a down payment/to give an advance of a hundred francs; **acompte sur dividende,** interim dividend; **acompte de préférence,** option money.

acquéreur, -euse, *n.* purchaser/buyer; *Jur:* vendee.

acquis, *a.* **droits acquis,** vested interests.

acquisition, *n.f.* **1.** acquisition; acquiring; **acquisition de données,** data acquisition; **faire l'acquisition de qch.,** to acquire/to purchase sth. **2.** thing bought/acquired; purchase.

acquit, *n.m.* (*a*) receipt; (*sur une facture, etc.*) **pour acquit,** received (with thanks)/ paid (*b*) *Cust:* clearance (certificate) (of ship).

acquit-à-caution, *n.m. Cust:* permit/ transire/excise-bond/bond-note.

acquittement, *n.m.* payment/discharge (of bill, debt, etc.).

acquitter, *v.tr.* (*a*) **acquitter une dette,** to pay/to settle/to discharge a debt; **acquitter les droits sur qch.,** to pay the duty on sth. (*b*) **acquitter une facture,** to receipt a bill; **acquitter un chèque,** to endorse a cheque.

s'acquitter, *v.pr.* **s'acquitter d'une dette,** to pay off/to settle/to discharge a debt.

acte, *n.m. Jur:* (*a*) act/instrument/deed/ agreement; **acte de vente,** bill of sale; sale contract; **acte hypothécaire,** mortgage deed; **acte notarié/acte sur papier timbré,** deed executed and authenticated by a notary; **rédiger/dresser un acte,** to draw up a document (*b*) **acte judiciaire,** writ (*c*) *pl.* **actes,** records (of transactions, proceedings, etc.).

actif[1], *a.* (*a*) **population active,** working population (*b*) **dettes actives,** accounts receivable/debtors.

actif[2], *n.m.* assets; credit (account); **actif circulant,** current/working assets; **actif immobilisé/stable,** fixed assets; **actif brut,** gross assets; **actif net,** net(t) assets; **actif**

incorporel, intangible assets; goodwill; **actif liquide/disponible/négociable/réalisable,** available assets/liquid assets/ quick assets; **actif réel,** real assets; **prêt fondé sur des actifs réels,** asset-based loan; **actif hors exploitation,** non-performing assets; **excédent de l'actif sur le passif,** excess of assets over liabilities; **mettre qch. à l'actif de qn,** to credit s.o. with sth.; **total de l'actif,** total assets; **valeur des actifs,** asset value.

action, *n.f.* **1.** *Fin:* share/stock; equity; security; **actions de capital/de priorité,** senior shares; **actions chères/à cours élevé,** heavy shares; **actions de dividende,** junior shares; **actions à dividende prioritaire remboursables,** redeemable preference shares; **actions de jouissance,** dividend shares; **actions de numéraire,** cash shares; **action différée,** deferred share; **actions à droit de veto,** gold shares; **actions à droit de vote double,** superstock; **actions sans droit de vote,** non-voting shares; **actions gagées,** lien on shares; **action gratuite,** scrip issue/bonus share; **actions indivises,** joint shares; **action libérée,** fully paid-up share; **action non entièrement libérée,** partly paid-up share; **action nominative/ au porteur,** registered share/bearer stock; **action ordinaire,** ordinary share/*NAm:* common stock; **action privilégiée/de priorité/prioritaire,** preference share/preferred share/preferred stock; **actions préférentielles convertibles,** preferred convertible stock; **actions préférentielles de classe A, B, etc,** A-shares, B-shares, etc; **actions préférentielles remboursables,** redeemable preference shares; **société par actions,** joint-stock company; **marché des actions,** stock market; equity market **2.** *Jur:* **action civile,** civil proceedings; **action judiciaire,** action/proceedings; lawsuit; **intenter une action à qn,** to bring an action against s.o./to institute proceedings against s.o./to sue s.o.; **action en paiement,** action for payment; **action en dommages et intérêts,** action/claim for damages; **mandat d'action,** receiving order (in bankruptcy) **3.** *SwFr:* **vente action,** bargain offer **4.** **journée d'action,** day of action.

actionnaire, *n.m.f. Fin:* shareholder/ *NAm:* stockholder.

actionnariat, *n.m.* shareholding; **actionnariat ouvrier**, worker participation/employee shareholding; industrial co-partnership.

activité, *n.f.* **1.** (*a*) briskness; **marché sans activité**, dull market; **le peu d'activité du marché**, the dullness/the slackness of the market (*b*) **graphique des activités**, activity chart; **rapport d'activité**, progress report; **cessation d'activités**, closing-down of business **2.** (*a*) **en activité**, in action/in operation/in progress; **l'usine est en activité**, the factory is in production; **en pleine activité**, in full operation (*b*) **les activités d'une entreprise**, a firm's operations; **activité bancaire**, banking.

actuaire, *n.m.f. Ins: Fin:* actuary.

actualisation, *n.f.* discounting.

actualisé, *a.* discounted; **cash flow actualisé**, discounted cash flow; **valeur actualisée**, discounted present value.

actuariat, *n.m. Ins: Fin:* (*a*) functions of an actuary (*b*) profession of actuary.

actuariel, *a.* (*a*) *Ins:* actuarial (calculation, etc.) (*b*) **taux de rendement actuariel brut**, annual interest yield gross/gross annual interest return.

actuel, *a.* present-day/prevailing/current; **prix actuels**, current/ruling prices; **valeur actuelle (nette)**, (net(t)) present value.

addition, *n.f.* (*a*) adding up; **faire l'addition des chiffres**, to add up the figures (*b*) **en addition au paragraphe 2 ...**, further to paragraph 2 ... (*c*) (*au restaurant, etc.*) bill/*NAm:* check.

additionnel, *a.* additional/extra.

additionner, *v.tr. & i.* to add up.

adjoint, -ointe, *a. & n.* assistant/deputy/ associate; **directeur adjoint/adjoint(e) au directeur**, deputy manager; assistant manager; **directeur général adjoint**, deputy managing director/general manager's assistant/assistant general manager.

adjudicataire, *n.m.f.* (*a*) successful tenderer for a public contract; company which has been awarded a public contract; contractor; **être déclaré adjudicataire de qch.**, to secure the contract for sth. (*b*) highest bidder/purchaser (at auction).

adjudication, *n.f.* (*a*) adjudicating/ adjudging/awarding (public contracts) (*b*) adjudication/allocation/award (of public contract); **obtenir l'adjudication de qch.**, to be awarded a public contract (*c*) knocking down (of sth. to s.o.); **mettre qch. en adjudication**, (*i*) to invite tenders for sth./to put sth. out to tender (*ii*) to put sth. up for sale by auction; **adjudication au rabais**, allocation to lowest tender(er); **adjudication à la surenchère**, allocation to the highest bidder; **par voie d'adjudication**, (*i*) by tender (*ii*) by auction; **prix d'adjudication**, auction price.

adjuger, *v.tr.* **adjuger qch. à qn**, to award/to allocate sth. to s.o.; (*aux enchères*) to knock sth. down to s.o.; **adjuger les fournitures de bureau**, to give the contract for office furniture (after tender).

admettre, *v.tr.* to allow; **admettre un recours**, to allow a claim.

administrateur, -trice, *n.* (*a*) (non-executive) director (of company, bank, etc.); business manager (of newspaper, etc.) (*b*) **administrateur judiciaire**, trustee/ (official) receiver (of estate, business, etc.); receiver in bankruptcy.

administratif, *a.* administrative; **bâtiment administratif**, office building/office block; **détails d'ordre administratif**, administrative details; **frais administratifs**, administration expenses; **méthodes administratives**, systems and procedures.

administration, *n.f.* **1.** (*a*) administration/direction/management (of business, etc.); **l'Administration**, the board of directors; the management; **administration du personnel**, personnel management; **administration des ventes**, sales management; **l'administration du théâtre**, the management of the theatre; **conseil**

d'administration, governing body/board of directors/executive board; **frais d'administration,** administration expenses; **mauvaise administration,** mismanagement; **président du conseil d'administration,** chairman of the board; **réunion du conseil d'administration,** board meeting (b) *Jur:* trusteeship **2. l'Administration,** the Civil Service.

administrer, *v.tr.* to manage/to direct (business, undertaking, estate).

admission, *n.f.* **1.** *Cust:* **admission (en douane),** entry (of goods); **admission en franchise,** duty-free entry; **admission temporaire,** duty-free entry (of products destined for re-export after processing) **2.** *StExch:* **admission à la cote,** admission to quotation.

adopter, *v.tr.* **adopter une résolution,** to adopt/to pass a resolution; **adopter un rapport,** to accept a report; **adopté à l'unanimité,** carried unanimously.

adoption, *n.f.* adoption (of a resolution); acceptance (of a report).

adresse, *n.f.* address; (*d'une société*) **adresse du siège social**/(*d'une personne*) **adresse de bureau,** business address; **adresse du domicile,** home address; **mettre/écrire l'adresse sur une enveloppe,** to address an envelope; (*sur une lettre de change*) **adresse au besoin,** referee in case of need.

adresser, *v.tr.* to address (letter, parcel, etc.).

ad valorem, *Lt.a.phr.* **payer un droit ad valorem,** to pay an ad valorem duty.

aérien, *a. Av:* **compagnie aérienne,** airline; **par voie aérienne,** by air; **poste aérienne,** airmail; **trafic aérien,** air traffic; **transports aériens,** air transport.

aérogramme, *n.m.* air letter (form).

affacturage, *n.m.* (a) factoring; **agent/société d'affacturage,** mercantile agent; **commission d'affacturage,** factoring charges (b) invoice discounting.

affactureur, *n.m.* mercantile agent.

affaire, *n.f.* **1.** (a) business/deal/transaction/bargain; **affaire d'or,** first-class speculation; splendid bargain; **faire une affaire d'or,** to make a killing; **bonne affaire,** sound transaction; good speculation/good bargain/good buy; **grosse affaire,** big deal; **mauvaise affaire,** bad deal/bad bargain; **petite affaire,** small deal; **faire affaire avec qn/être en affaire(s) avec qn,** to do business with s.o./to deal with s.o.; **faire/conclure une affaire,** to make/to conclude a deal; **faire une (bonne) affaire,** to get a bargain; to do a good piece of business; **traiter une affaire avec qn,** to transact business with s.o. (b) business (concern); **une grosse affaire,** a large firm; **son usine est une grande affaire,** his factory is a large concern; **administrer/conduire/gérer/diriger une affaire,** to run a business; **lancer une affaire,** to start a business **2.** *pl.* **affaires,** business/trade; **affaires courantes,** routine business; **agent d'affaires,** (business) agent; **bureau/agence/cabinet d'affaires,** (general) agency; **carte d'affaires,** business card; **centre d'affaires,** business centre; **chiffre d'affaires,** turnover; volume of business/sales volume; **déjeuner d'affaires,** business lunch; **homme/femme d'affaires,** businessman/businesswoman; **le monde des affaires,** the business world; **lettre d'affaires,** business letter; **relations d'affaires,** business connections; **visite d'affaires,** business call; **voyage d'affaires,** business trip; **entrer dans les affaires,** to go into business; **être dans les affaires,** to be in business; **faire des affaires avec qn,** to do business with s.o./to deal with s.o.; **faire de bonnes affaires,** to be successful (in business)/to do good business; **faire de mauvaises affaires,** to be doing badly; to be in difficulties; to work at a loss; **faire des affaires importantes,** to do business on a large scale; to have a big turnover; **parler affaires,** to talk business/*F:* to talk shop; **comment vont les affaires?** how's business? **les affaires vont mal,** business is bad; **je vais à Londres pour affaires,** I am going to London on business; **quel est son genre d'affaires?** what's his line of business?/

what line of business is he in? **s'absenter pour affaires,** to go away on business **3.** *Jur:* case/lawsuit.

affectation, *n.f.* (*a*) **affectation d'une somme à un projet,** assignment/attribution/allocation of money to a purpose; appropriation/earmarking for a purpose; **affectation aux dividendes,** sum available for dividend; **affectations budgétaires,** budget appropriations; **affectation de fonds,** appropriation of funds; **affectation hypothécaire,** mortgage charge (*b*) **affectation des tâches,** job assignment.

affecter, *v.tr.* **affecter des crédits à un certain usage,** to assign funds to; to appropriate/to set aside/to earmark/to allocate funds for a certain use.

affermage, *n.m.* **1.** (*a*) renting (of farm, land, etc.) (*b*) leasing (*c*) contracting (for advertisements, etc.) **2.** rent (of land, farm).

affermer, *v.tr.* **1.** (*a*) to lease (farm, etc.) (*b*) to let out (sth. on contract) **2.** (*a*) to rent; to take (farm, land, etc.) on lease (*b*) to contract for (sth.).

affichage, *n.m.* (*a*) bill-sticking/bill-posting; **panneau d'affichage,** hoarding/*NAm:* billboard (*b*) **publicité par affichage,** poster advertising (*c*) display; **unité d'affichage,** display unit.

affiche, *n.f.* **affiche publicitaire,** poster/bill.

afficher, *v.tr.* to stick (up)/to display (bill, etc.); **afficher une vente,** to put up a poster advertising a sale/to advertise a sale/*NAm:* to post a sale; **prix affiché,** posted price; *PN:* **défense d'afficher,** no bill-sticking/stick no bills/*NAm:* post no bills.

affidavit, *n.m. Jur:* affidavit.

affiliation, *n.f.* affiliation.

affilié, 1. *a.* affiliated; **société affiliée,** associate/affiliate(d) company **2.** *n.* (affiliated) member/associate.

s'affilier, *v.pr.* **s'affilier à,** to become a member of (a syndicate, etc.).

afflux, *n.m.* inflow/influx (of goods, gold, etc.); **afflux de fonds,** capital inflow.

affranchir, *v.tr.* to pay the postage on/of (sth.); to frank/to stamp (letter); **colis affranchi,** parcel with postage paid; **lettre insuffisamment affranchie,** letter with insufficient postage; **machine à affranchir (les lettres),** franking machine/*NAm:* postal meter.

affranchissement, *n.m.* (*a*) stamping/franking (*b*) postage (of letter, parcel, etc.).

affrètement, *n.m.* charter(ing) (of ship, aircraft, etc.); **agent d'affrètement,** chartering agent; **contrat d'affrètement,** charter-party; **affrètement coque nue,** bareboat charter; **affrètement à temps,** time-charter; **affrètement au voyage,** trip-charter.

affréter, *v.tr.* to charter a ship/an aircraft, etc.

affréteur, *n.m.* charterer.

agence, *n.f.* (*a*) agency (office); bureau; **agence d'affaires,** (general) business agency/office; **agence de location,** letting agency; hire/rental company; **agence de placement,** employment agency/employment bureau; **agence de publicité,** advertising agency; **agence de rating,** credit agency/*NAm:* bureau; **agence de renseignement(s),** information bureau; **agence de voyages,** travel agency; **agence de voyages à prix réduits,** bucket shop; **agence en douane,** customs agency; **agence immobilière,** estate agency/*NAm:* real estate agency; **agence maritime,** shipping/forwarding agency; **Agence nationale pour l'Emploi (ANPE)** = Job Centre; **compte d'agence,** agency account; **contrat/mandat d'agence,** agency agreement/contract (*b*) branch office; **la maison a plusieurs agences à l'étranger,** the company has several agencies overseas.

agenda, *n.m.* diary; **agenda de bureau,** desk diary.

agent, *n.m.* (*a*) agent; **agent à demeure,** agent on the spot; **agent comptable,**

accountant; **agent d'affaires,** general agent/(business) agent; **agent d'assurance(s),** insurance broker/agent; **agent attitré,** appointed agent; **agent de location,** letting agent/estate agent; **agent de publicité,** advertising agent/publicity agent; **agent économique,** transactor; **agent en douanes,** customs agent; *Ind* **agent de fabrication,** production worker/worker on a production line; **agent immobilier,** (*i*) land agent (*ii*) estate agent/*NAm:* realtor/real estate agent; **agent maritime,** shipping agent; **seul agent/agent commercial exclusif d'une maison,** sole agent/sole representative of a firm; **il est l'agent exclusif de Toyota,** he has the Toyota agency (*b*) *Fin:* **agent de change,** (*i*) stockbroker/bill broker/exchange broker (*ii*) mercantile broker (*c*) **agent de liaison,** contact man; **agent de maîtrise,** supervisor; **agent de recouvrement,** debt collector.

agétac, *nm.* (*abbr. of Accord général sur les tarifs douaniers et le commerce*) General agreement on tarifs and trade/GATT.

agio, *n.m. Fin:* **1.** agio (of exchange); *Bank:* premium (on gold)/premium offer **2.** (*a*) money-changing (*b*) jobbery/speculation. **3.** *pl. Bank:* **agios,** interest charges on overdrafts.

agiotage, *n.m. Fin: Pej:* stock-jobbing/agiotage/speculation/gambling (on the Stock Exchange).

agioter, *v.i.* to speculate/to gamble (on the Stock Exchange).

agioteur, -euse, *n.* speculator/gambler (on the Stock Exchange).

agitation, *n.f.* **agitation ouvrière,** labour/industrial unrest.

agrafe, *n.f.* **agrafe antivol,** anti-theft/security tag.

agrandir, *v.tr. & i.* (*of industry*) **(s')agrandir,** to expand.

agréé, 1. *a.* **agent agréé,** authorized agent/dealer; *FrC:* **comptable agréé (CA),** chartered accountant (CA) **2.** *n.m. Jur:*

solicitor/counsel/attorney (before a *tribunal de commerce*).

agréer, *v.tr.* to accept/to recognize/to approve (of)/to agree to (sth.); **agréer un contrat,** to approve an agreement; *Corr:* **veuillez agréer/je vous prie d'agréer l'expression de mes sentiments distingués,** yours truly/yours faithfully; yours sincerely.

agricole, *a.* agricultural (country, produce, etc.); **comice(s) agricole(s)/exposition agricole,** agricultural show; **grande exploitation agricole,** (*i*) large scale farming (*ii*) large farm; **petite exploitation agricole,** (*i*) small-scale farming (*ii*) small farm/smallholding; **office commercial des produits agricoles,** agricultural marketing board; **ouvrier agricole,** farm worker; **produits agricoles,** agricultural produce.

agriculteur, *n.m.* agricultur(al)ist; farmer.

agriculture, *n.f.* agriculture; farming.

agrinégoce, *nm.* agribusiness.

agroalimentaire, *a. & n.* food industry based on agriculture; **secteur agroalimentaire,** agri-foodstuffs.

agro-financier, *a.* agri-financial.

agro-industrie, *n.f.* agricultural processing industry.

agro-monétaire, *a.* **mesures agro-monétaires,** agri-monetary measures.

agronome, *n.m.* agronomist/agricultural economist; **ingénieur agronome,** agricultural engineer.

agronomie, *n.f.* agronomy; agronomics.

aguichage, *n.m. Mkt:* teasing.

aguiche, *n.f. Mkt:* teaser (ad).

aide, *n.f.* assistance; grant; **aide économique,** economic aid; **aide personnelle au logement (APL)** = housing loan.

aide-comptable, *n.m.* book(-)keeper; accounts assistant.

ajourner, *v.tr.* **ajourner une réunion,** to

adjourn/to postpone a meeting; **ajourner une motion,** to defer/*NAm:* to table a motion.

ajouté, *n.m.* rider/addition (to MS, contract).

ajustement, *n.m.* adjusting/adjustment (of wages, prices, etc.); **ajustement saisonnier,** seasonal adjustment.

ajuster, *v.tr.* to adjust (an account, etc.).

aléatoire, *a.* aleatory (contract, etc.); risky/uncertain; **sondage/échantillonnage aléatoire,** random sampling.

aliénation, *n.f. Jur:* transfer (of rights, property, etc.).

aliéner, *v.tr.* to transfer (rights, property, etc.).

alignement, *n.m.* making up/balancing (of accounts, etc.); **alignement (des traitements),** bringing (salaries) into line; pay comparability; *Fin:* **alignement monétaire,** (re)alignment of currencies.

aligner, *v.tr. Fin:* to align **(sur,** with)/to bring into line; **aligner les salaires des mineurs sur ceux de l'industrie,** to bring the salaries of miners into line with those of industry; to give miners pay comparability with industry.

aliment, *n.m.* **1.** *Ins:* interest/risk value **2.** food; **aliments et boissons,** food and drink.

alimentaire, *a.* **l'industrie alimentaire,** food industry; **produits/denrées alimentaires,** foodstuff/food products; *Jur:* **pension alimentaire,** alimony/maintenance.

alimentation, *n.f.* **produits d'alimentation,** foodstuff/food products; **(magasin d')alimentation,** grocer's (shop); **(rayon d')alimentation,** food counter/department.

allégement, *n.m.* **allégement fiscal,** tax relief.

aller, *n.m.* outward journey; **cargaison d'aller,** outward cargo; **un aller (simple),** a single (ticket)/*NAm:* a one-way ticket; **un aller (et) retour,** a return (ticket)/*NAm:* a round-trip ticket; **voyage (d')aller et retour,** return journey/*NAm:* round trip; *MIns:* **police à l'aller et au retour,** round policy; *StExch:* **aller-retour,** bed and breakfast deal/round turn/round transaction.

allocataire, *n.m.f.* recipient of an allowance.

allocation, *n.f.* **1.** *(a)* allocation/assignment/granting (of sum of money, etc.); **allocation de fonds,** appropriation of funds *(b) Fin:* allotment (of shares, etc.) **2.** allowance/grant; **allocation d'invalidité,** disability benefit; **allocations familiales** = child benefit; **allocation (de) chômage,** unemployment benefit; **allocation de logement,** rent/housing allowance; **allocation de vieillesse,** old-age/retirement pension; **allocation par tête,** capitation grant.

allonge, *n.f.* **allonge d'une lettre de change,** allonge to a bill of exchange; **allonge d'un document,** rider to a document.

allouer, *v.tr.* to allocate a sum (for a purpose); to grant (a pension); to allocate (shares, etc.); **allouer à qn une somme à titre de dommages-intérêts,** to award s.o. a sum as damages.

alphanumérique, *a. Cmptr:* **caractères alphanumériques,** alphanumerics.

aménagement, *n.m.* planning/development; **aménagement urbain,** town planning; **aménagement du territoire,** town and country planning.

amende, *n.f.* fine; *(pour retard de livraison, etc)* penalty.

amendement, *n.m.* amendment.

amender, *v.tr.* **amender une proposition,** to amend a resolution.

amiable, *a. Jur: (a)* conciliatory; **amiable compositeur,** arbitrator *(b) a. phr.* **à l'amiable,** by mutual agreement; *Jur:* **règlement à l'amiable,** out-of-court settlement; **vente à l'amiable,** sale by private treaty.

amont, *n.m. Mkt:* upside (potential); **en amont,** (*société*) upstream.

amortir, *v.tr.* (*a*) *Fin:* to redeem/to pay off/to extinguish/to amortize (debt); **amortir un emprunt,** to repay a loan; **amortir une obligation,** to redeem a bond (*b*) to allow for depreciation; **amortir (progressivement),** to write down; **amortir (totalement),** to write off.

amortissable, *a. Fin:* redeemable (stock, etc.); **non amortissable,** irredeemable (bonds, etc.).

amortissement, *n.m. Fin:* (*a*) redemption/amortization/repayment (of a debt); **amortissement anticipé,** redemption before due date; **fonds/caisse d'amortissement,** sinking fund (*b*) (amount written off for) depreciation; amortization; **assiette de l'amortissement,** depreciation/*NAm:* depreciable base; **amortissement accéléré,** accelerated depreciation; **méthode de l'amortissement constant/ (méthode de l')amortissement linéaire/ (méthode de l')amortissement en ligne droite,** straight-line method of depreciation; **provision pour amortissement,** depreciation allowance.

amovible, *a.* **personnel amovible,** transferable/mobile staff.

an, *n.m.* year; **par an,** yearly; **obligations à vingt ans,** bonds with a twenty year maturity.

analyse, *n.f.* analysis; **analyse des coûts/ analyse du prix de revient,** cost analysis; **analyse des coûts et rendements/ analyse coût-profit,** cost-benefit analysis; **analyse coût-volume-profit,** cost-volume-profit analysis; **analyse de coût et d'efficacité,** cost-effectiveness analysis; **analyse des écarts,** variance analysis; **analyse des marchés,** market research; **analyse de portefeuille,** portfolio analysis; **analyse des tâches,** job analysis; **analyse des ventes,** sales analysis; **analyse de système/analyse systémique,** systems analysis; **analyse de la valeur,** value analysis; **analyse fondamentale,** fundamental analysis; **analyse sur graphiques,** technical analysis.

analyste, *n.m.f.* analyst; **analyste-programmeur, -euse,** computer analyst; **analyste financier,** financial analyst; **analyste fondamental(e),** fundamental market analyst; **analyste sur graphiques,** chart analyst/*NAm:* technical market analyst.

analytique, *a.* analytic(al); **comptabilité analytique,** analytic(al) accounting/cost accounting.

ancienneté, *n.f.* seniority; **prime d'ancienneté,** seniority pay; **être promu à l'ancienneté,** to be promoted by seniority.

animateur, *n.m.* **animateur des ventes,** marketing executive.

animation, *n.f.* **animation des ventes,** sales drive.

animé, *a.* **marché animé,** brisk/buoyant market.

année, *n.f.* year; **année civile,** calendar year; **année budgétaire/année d'exercise,** financial/fiscal year; **année en cours,** current year; **fin d'année,** year-end; **année record,** peak year; **année de référence,** base year.

annexe, **1.** *a.* **document annexe,** attached document; **industries annexes,** subsidiary industries; **lettre annexe,** covering letter; **revenus annexes,** supplementary income **2.** *n.f.* annexe (to a contract); attached document.

annexer, *v.tr.* to append/to attach (document, etc.).

annonce, *n.f.* **annonce (publicitaire),** advertisement/ad/advert; **annonces classées/ petites annonces,** small ads/classified ads/classified advertisements; **demander qch. par voie d'annonces,** to advertise for sth; **faire paraître une annonce pour recruter les services d'un traducteur,** to advertise for a translator; **insérer une annonce dans les journaux,** to put an advertisement in the papers.

annonceur, *n.m.* advertiser.

annuaire, *n.m.* yearbook; **annuaire du**

commerce, commercial directory; **annuaire des téléphones/du téléphone/ téléphonique,** telephone directory.

annualiser, *vtr.* to annualize; **rythme annualisé,** annually compounded rate; **taux annualisé,** annualized percentage rate/APR.

annualité, *n.f.* yearly recurrence (of tax, etc.).

annuel, *a.* annual/yearly; **rente annuelle,** annuity; **congé annuel/fermeture annuelle,** annual holidays; **loyer annuel,** yearly rent(al).

annuellement, *adv.* annually/yearly.

annuitaire, *a.* (debt) redeemable by yearly payments.

annuité, *n.f.* (*a*) *Fin:* annual instalment (in repayment of debt) (*b*) year of service (*c*) annuity.

annulable, *a. Jur:* voidable/rescindable (contract, etc.); (contract, etc.) that can be annulled/cancelled.

annulation, *n.f. Jur:* annulment; cancelling/cancellation (of contract).

annuler, *v.tr.* to annul/to cancel (contract, etc.); to call off (a deal); to void (a bill, etc.).

anonyme, *a.* anonymous; **société anonyme (par actions),** joint-stock company/ limited(-liability) company.

anticipation, *n.f.* anticipation; **payer par anticipation,** to pay in advance; **paiement par anticipation,** advance (payment)/ prepayment.

anticiper, *v.tr.* (*a*) *Fin:* **anticiper un paiement de dix jours,** to anticipate a payment by ten days; **dividende anticipé,** advanced dividend; **remboursement anticipé,** redemption before due date (*b*) **ventes anticipées,** expected sales.

antidater, *v.tr.* to antedate (contract, cheque, etc.).

anti-inflationniste, *a.* anti-inflationary;

mesures anti-inflationnistes, anti-inflation(ary) measures.

antiprotectionniste, 1. *a.* free-trade (policy, etc.) 2. *n.m.f.* anti-protectionist; free-trader.

antitrust, *a.inv.* anti(-)trust.

apériteur, *n.m. Ins:* leading underwriter.

appareil, *n.m.* apparatus/appliance; **appareil administratif,** administrative machinery.

appel, *n.m.* 1. *Fin:* **appel de marge,** margin call/call for additional cover; **appel d'offres,** invitation to tender; **faire un appel d'offres,** to invite bids/tenders; **taux d'appel d'offres,** tender rate; **avis d'appel de fonds,** call letter; **faire un appel de fonds,** to call up capital 2. telephone/*F:* phone call; **appel avec préavis,** person to person call; **appel en PCV,** transfer charge call/*NAm:* collect call; **prendre un appel,** to take a (phone) call; **recevoir un appel,** to receive a phone call 3. *Jur:* **cour d'appel,** Court of Appeal 4. **article/ produit d'appel,** loss leader.

appelé, *a. Fin:* **capital appelé,** called-up capital.

appellation, *n.f.* **appellation contrôlée,** (*i*) (*d'un vin*) guaranteed vintage (*ii*) guaranteed trade mark; **appellation d'origine =** place of origin guaranteed; **vin d'appellation,** vintage wine; Appellation wine.

appoint, *n.m.* (*a*) **faire l'appoint,** (*i*) to make up (a sum) (*ii*) to pay the right amount/the exact fare; **monnaie d'appoint,** divisional/ fractional money (*b*) **salaire d'appoint,** extra salary.

appointements, *n.m.pl.* salary; **toucher ses appointements,** to draw one's salary.

appointer, *v.tr.* to pay/to give a salary to; **commis appointés,** salaried clerks.

apport, *n.m.* **actions d'apport,** founder's/ promoter's shares; **apport d'argent frais,** injection of new money; **apport de capitaux,** contribution of capital; **capital d'apport,** initial capital.

appréciateur, *n.m.* valuer.

appréciatif, *a.* devis **appréciatif,** estimate; **dresser l'état appréciatif d'un mobilier,** to draw up the valuation of/to value furniture.

appréciation, *n.f.* **1.** valuation/assessment / estimation / estimate / appraisal; **appréciation du personnel,** staff assessment/appraisal; **appréciation des risques,** risk assessment; **faire l'appréciation des marchandises,** to value/to appraise/to make an appraisal of goods **2.** appreciation/rise in value; **appréciation du dollar vis-à-vis de la livre,** improvement of the dollar against the pound.

apprécier, *v.tr.* to appraise/to estimate the value of (sth.); to value (sth.)/to set a value on (sth.).

s'apprécier, *v.pr.* to rise in value; **le dollar s'est apprécié vis-à-vis de la livre,** the dollar has risen/improved against the pound.

apprenti, -ie, *n.* apprentice.

apprentissage, *n.m.* apprenticeship; **mettre qn en apprentissage chez qn,** to apprentice s.o. to s.o.; **faire son apprentissage chez qn,** to serve one's apprenticeship with s.o.; **contrat d'apprentissage,** contract of apprenticeship; indentures; **taxe d'apprentissage,** training levy/ (employers') tax levied as a contribution to training schemes.

approbation, *n.f.* (*a*) approval/approbation; **pour approbation,** for approval/ subject to approval; **soumettre à l'approbation (de qn),** to submit for approval (by s.o.) (*b*) certifying (of accounts, of document); passing (of accounts).

approche, *n.f.* *Mkt:* **approche directe,** cold calls.

appropriation, *n.f.* appropriation; **appropriation de fonds,** embezzlement.

approuver, *v.tr.* to approve; to sanction (expenditure, etc.); **approuver les comptes,** to approve the accounts; **approuver un contrat,** to ratify a contract; **approuver une facture,** to pass an invoice; **approuver une nomination,** to confirm an appointment; **lu et approuvé,** read and approved.

approvisionnement, *n.m.* **1.** provisioning/supplying; procurement; stocking (of shop) **2.** (*a*) supply/stock/ store; **approvisionnements de réserve,** reserve stocks; **faire un approvisionnement de qch.,** to stock up with sth./to lay in a supply of sth. (*b*) *Ind:* raw materials and component parts (*used in processing industry*).

approvisionner, *v.tr.* to supply (**de,** with); to furnish with supplies; to provide with stores; to provision; to procure; to victual (a ship).

s'approvisionner, *v.pr.* to take in/to lay in (stock, a supply of); to stock up with sth.; to lay in stores; **s'approvisionner (chez qn),** to get one's supplies from (s.o.)/to stock up/to shop (somewhere, at s.o.'s).

approvisionneur, -euse, *n.* supplier.

approximatif, *a.* approximate/rough (calculation, estimate); **moyenne approximative,** rough average; **ces chiffres sont très approximatifs,** these figures are only a rough estimate.

après-vente, *a.inv.* **service après-vente,** after-sales service/back up service/sales back-up.

apurement, *n.m.* (*a*) auditing/agreeing (of accounts) (*b*) **apurement du passif,** discharge of all (or part) of one's debts.

apurer, *v.tr.* (*a*) to audit/to pass/to agree (accounts) (*b*) to discharge (debt(s)).

arbitrage, *n.m.* **1.** arbitration; **conseil d'arbitrage,** conciliation/arbitration board (in industrial dispute); **règlement par arbitrage,** settlement by arbitration; **soumettre une question à un arbitrage,** to refer a question to arbitration **2.** *Bank. etc:* arbitrage; **arbitrage de/du change,** arbitrage/arbitration of exchange *StExch:* **arbitrage en reports,** jobbing in contango(e)s; **arbitrage de place en place,** shunting; **faire l'arbitrage de place en place,** to shunt; **arbitrage (à terme),** hedging; **faire une opération d'arbitrage,** to hedge; **arbitrage à la marge/marginal,** margin dealing; **arbitrage sur valeurs du Trésor,** gilt switches.

arbitragiste, *n.m.f.* arbitrager.

arbitral, *a. Jur:* arbitral; **commission arbitrale,** board of referees; **procédure arbitrale,** procedure by arbitration; **solution arbitrale/règlement arbitral,** settlement by arbitration; **tribunal arbitral,** arbitration court/tribunal of arbitration/court of arbitration.

arbitre, *n.m. Jur:* arbitrator/referee/ adjudicator; **arbitre rapporteur,** referee (in commercial suit).

arbitrer, *v.tr. Jur:* to arbitrate.

archivage, *n.m.* filing (of documents).

archives, *n.f.pl.* archives/records.

argent, *n.m.* **1.** silver; **lingot(s) d'argent,** silver bullion; **encaisse or et argent d'un pays,** gold and silver holding of a country **2.** money; cash; **argent mal acquis,** dirty money; **argent liquide,** cash (in hand)/ready money; **argent à bon marché,** cheap money; **argent au jour le jour,** call money/day-to-day money; **argent de poche,** pocket money; **taux de l'argent,** money rate; **payer en argent,** to pay (in) cash; **placer son argent,** to invest one's money; **somme d'argent,** sum/ amount of money; **trouver de l'argent,** to raise money.

arrangement, *n.m.* agreement; settlement; arrangement; **arrangement avec ses créanciers,** composition with one's creditors; **sauf arrangement contraire,** unless otherwise agreed.

s'arranger, *v.pr.* **s'arranger avec qn,** to come to an agreement/to terms with s.o.; **s'arranger avec ses créanciers,** to compound with one's creditors.

arrérager, 1. *v.i. (du loyer, etc.)* to remain unpaid; to be in arrears **2.** *v.pr.* **laisser**

s'arrérager (les termes de) son loyer, to let one's rent fall into arrears.

arrérages, *n.m.pl.* arrears/back interest/ back payment; **arrérages de loyer,** rent arrears/back rent.

arrêt, *n.m.* stoppage; **arrêt de travail,** work stoppage; **arrêt de paiement d'un chèque,** stopping of a cheque.

arrêté, *n.m.* **1. arrêté de compte,** settlement of (an) account **2.** *Jur:* decree; ordinance.

arrêter, *v.tr.* to close/to settle (an account); **arrêter les comptes de l'exercice,** to close the yearly accounts.

arrhes, *n.f.pl. (a)* deposit/down payment; advance payment; **verser des arrhes,** to pay a deposit; to give an advance.

arriéré, 1. *a.* late/in arrears; **paiement arriéré,** overdue/outstanding payment; **intérêts arriérés,** outstanding interest **2.** *n.m.* arrears (of account, correspondence, etc.); backlog (of orders); **arriéré de loyer,** rent arrears/back rent; **arriéré d'impôts,** tax arrears/back taxes.

arrière-boutique, *n.f.* back of the shop/ *NAm:* back-store.

arriérer, *v.tr.* to postpone/to delay/to defer (payment, etc.).

s'arriérer, *v.pr.* to fall into arrears.

arrivage, *n.m.* arrival; consignment (of goods).

arrivée, *n.f.* arrival (of goods).

arrondir, *v.tr.* to round up (a sum of money).

article, *n.m.* **1.** item (of bill, etc.); **articles de dépense,** items of expenditure; **articles divers,** sundries **2.** article/commodity/ item; *pl.* goods/wares; **article (en) réclame,** special offer; **articles d'exportation,** export goods/exports; **articles de ménage,** household requisites; **articles de toilette,** toilet requisites/toiletries; **articles de voyage,** travel goods; **je ne fais pas cet article,** I don't deal in that line; **faire**

l'article, *F:* to plug one's products 3. article (of law, contract).

artisan, -ane, *n.* craftsman/craftswoman.

artisanat, *n.m.* arts and crafts; handicrafts.

assainir, *v.tr.* to stabilize (a budget, etc.); **assainir les finances,** to reorganize the finances; **assainir la monnaie,** to stabilize the currency.

assemblée, *n.f.* assembly/meeting; **assemblée générale annuelle,** Annual General Meeting (AGM); **assemblée (générale) extraordinaire,** extraordinary general meeting (EGM); **assemblée générale d'actionnaires,** general meeting of shareholders.

asseoir, *v.tr.* **asseoir un impôt,** to calculate the basis for a tax.

assiette, *n.f.* **assiette fiscale/de l'impôt,** tax base; taxable income; **détermination de l'assiette de l'impôt,** tax assessment; **assiette d'une hypothèque,** property/funds on which a mortgage is secured.

assignation, *n.f. StExch:* exercise notice.

assigner, *v.tr.* **assigner une somme à un paiement,** to earmark a sum for a payment/to allocate a sum to a payment.

association, *n.f.* (*a*) association; **Association Française des Banques (AFB),** French Bankers' Association (*b*) partnership; **entrer en association avec qn,** to enter into partnership with s.o.; **association de fait,** partnership at will.

associé, -ée, *n.* partner; **associé principal,** senior partner; **associé (en second),** junior partner; **associé commanditaire,** limited partner; **associé commanditaire,** limited partner; **associé commandité,** active partner; **associé passif,** sleeping partner; **associés à part égale,** equal partners; **prendre qn comme associé,** to take s.o. into partnership.

s'associer, *v.pr.* **s'associer à/avec qn,** to enter/to go into partnership with s.o.

assortiment, *n.m.* assortment/variety/mixture (of goods).

assujetti, 1. *n.m.* **les assujettis à l'impôt,** the taxpayers **2.** *a.* **être assujetti à l'impôt,** to be liable to tax.

assurance, *n.f.* (*a*) insurance/assurance; **agent d'assurances,** insurance agent; **compagnie/société d'assurances,** insurance company; **courtier d'assurances,** insurance broker; **frais d'assurance,** insurance charges; **police d'assurance,** insurance policy; **prime d'assurance,** insurance premium; **payer les primes d'assurance/payer l'assurance d'une voiture,** to pay the insurance on a car; **il est dans les assurances,** he's in insurance (*b*) **assurance (contre les) accidents,** accident insurance; **assurance (des patrons) contre les accidents du travail,** employers' liability insurance; = workmen's compensation insurance; **assurance annulation,** cancellation insurance; **assurance auto(mobile),** car/motor insurance; **assurance par capitalisation,** with-profits insurance; **assurance collective,** group insurance; **assurance à cotisations,** contributory insurance; **assurance crédit,** credit insurance; loan repayment insurance; **assurance en cas de décès/assurance décès,** whole life assurance/insurance; whole-of-life policy; term insurance; **assurance forfaitaire,** valued policy; **assurance habitation,** buildings (and contents) insurance; **assurance incendie/assurance contre l'incendie,** fire insurance; **assurance contre l'invalidité,** insurance against injury; personal accident insurance; **assurance longue maladie,** permanent health insurance (PHI); **assurance maladie,** medical insurance; **assurance maritime,** marine insurance; **assurance multirisques,** comprehensive insurance; all-risks insurance; **assurance mutuelle,** mutual insurance; **assurance de perte d'exploitation,** business interruption policy; **assurance responsabilité civile,** public (liability) insurance; **assurance temporaire,** term insurance; **assurance aux tiers/assurances vis-à-vis des tiers,** third-party insurance; **assurance tous risques/** *SwFr:* **assurance casco,** comprehensive insurance; all-risks insurance; **assurance sur la vie/assurance-vie,** life assurance/life insurance; **assurance(-)vie investie/libellée en actions,** equity-linked policy; **assurance(-)vie non défiscalisée,** non-qualifying policy; **assurance en cas de vie,** endowment insurance; **assurance contre le vol/assurance vol,** insurance against theft; **contracter une assurance,** to take out an insurance (policy); **il y a assurance,** the property is insured (c) *Adm:* **assurance-invalidité,** disability pension; **assurance-maladie** = sickness benefit; **assurances sociales** = National Insurance/Social Security; **assurance-vieillesse** = old age pension.

assuré, -ée, *n.* **1.** (a) *Ins:* policy-holder; insured person (b) *Adm:* **assuré social,** member of the National Insurance scheme **2.** *a. Ins:* **la maison est assurée,** the house is insured/covered by an insurance.

assurer, 1. *v.tr.* (a) to ensure; **assurer un service,** to provide a service; **assurer une rente à qn,** to settle an annuity on s.o. (b) *Ins:* **assurer qn,** to insure s.o.; **la Compagnie n'assure pas contre les dégâts causés par la pluie,** the Company will not insure against damage caused by rain; **assurer un immeuble contre l'incendie,** to insure a building against fire **2.** *v.pr.* **s'assurer,** to take out an insurance (policy) (**contre,** against); **s'assurer sur la vie,** to take out a life insurance (policy).

assureur, *n.m. Ins:* (a) insurer (b) underwriter.

atelier, *n.m.* **1.** (work)shop/workroom; **atelier de montage,** assembly (work)shop; **atelier de constructions navales,** shipyard; **il est devenu contremaître après cinq ans d'atelier,** he became a foreman after five years on the shop floor; **chef d'atelier,** (shop) foreman **2.** (a) (shop, workroom) staff (b) industrial unit; work group.

attaché, *n.m.* **attaché commercial,** (i) commercial attaché (ii) sales representative/(sales) rep; **attaché de presse,** press attaché.

attente, *n.f. Corr:* **dans l'attente de votre réponse,** awaiting your reply.

attitré, *a.* appointed/recognized.

attractif, -ive, *a.* **prix attractifs,** attractive prices.

attribuer, *v.tr.* to assign; to allot; **attribuer des actions,** to allot shares.

attributaire, *n.m.f. Jur:* assignee; *Fin:* allottee.

attribution, *n.f.* assigning/allotment/ allocation; **attribution d'actions,** allotment of shares.

audience, *n.f. Jur:* hearing.

audiotypiste, *n.m.f.* audiotypist.

audit, *n.m.* (a) audit; **audit interne,** internal audit (b) auditor; **audit interne,** internal auditor.

augmentation, *n.f.* increase; *Adm:* increment; **un salaire de 80 000 F avec augmentation annuelle de …,** salary of 80 000 F with annual increments of …; **augmentation de salaire,** increase in salary/rise/ *NAm:* raise; **augmentation des prix,** increase in prices; **être en augmentation,** to be on the increase; **chiffre d'affaires en augmentation sur l'année dernière,** turnover showing an increase on last year('s).

augmenter, 1. *v.tr.* to increase; to enlarge; **augmenter le prix de qch.,** to raise/to put up the price of sth.; **cela augmente nos dépenses,** this adds to our expenses; **augmenter qn,** to raise/to increase s.o.'s salary; to give s.o. a rise/*NAm:* a raise; **j'ai été augmenté,** I've had a rise; **édition revue et augmentée,** edition revised and enlarged **2.** *v.i.* to increase; **augmenter de valeur,** to increase in value; **empêcher les frais d'augmenter,** to keep expenses down; **tout a augmenté de prix,** everything has gone up in price; **le chiffre d'affaires a augmenté de 10% par rapport à l'année dernière,** the turnover is 10% up on last year('s).

autarcie, *n.f.* autarky; **autarcie économique,** direct production.

auteur, *n.m.* (a) author; **auteur à succès,** best-selling author/best seller; **droit**

d'auteur, copyright (*b*) **droits d'auteur,** royalties; **recevoir des droits d'auteur de 10%,** to receive royalties/a royalty of 10%.

authentifier, *v.tr.* (*a*) to authenticate/to certify (a signature) (*b*) to legalize (a document, etc.).

authentique, *a.* (*a*) authentic/genuine (*b*) **copie authentique,** certified copy; *Fin:* **cours authentique,** official quotation.

authentiquer, *v.tr.* = **authentifier.**

auto-amortissable, *a.* self-liquidating.

autocontrôle, *n.m.* **(chaîne d')autocontrôle,** loop.

autofinancement, *n.m. Fin:* self-financing; ploughing back of profits; **marge brute d'autofinancement (MBA),** cash flow.

autofinancer, *v.tr.* to self-finance; to plough back; **8 milliards de francs autofinancés à un tiers seulement,** 8 billion francs only a third of which was self-financed.

autogestion, *n.f.* self-management.

autolimiter, *v.tr.* **les Japonais autolimitent leurs exportations de voitures,** the Japanese set voluntary limits to their car exports.

automation, automatisation *n.f.* automation.

automatique, 1. *a.* automatic; **distributeur automatique,** (*i*) vending machine (*ii*) cash dispenser; **guichet automatique de banque,** automatic telling machine/*NAm:* automatic teller **2.** *n.m. Tel:* **l'automatique,** subscriber trunk dialling (STD)/direct dialling; **l'automatique international,** international direct dialling.

automatisation, *n.f.* automation.

automatiser, *v.tr.* to automate.

automobile, *n.f.* car/*NAm:* automobile; **Salon de l'Automobile,** Motor Show; **l'industrie automobile,** the motor/the car in-

dustry; **le marché de l'automobile,** the motor/*NAm:* the automobile market.

autorisation, *n.f.* authorization/permission; permit/licence; **autorisation spéciale,** special permit; **autorisation d'exporter,** export permit; **avoir l'autorisation de vendre qch.,** to be licensed to sell sth.

autoriser, *v.tr.* to authorize.

autorité, *n.f.* (*a*) authority; **agir de pleine autorité,** to act with full powers (*b*) **l'autorité fiscale,** the (income) tax authorities; **autorités financières,** financial authorities.

aval, *n.m.* (*a*) *Fin:* endorsement (on bill); **donner son aval à un billet,** to endorse/to back a bill; **donneur d'aval,** guarantor/backer (of bill) (*b*) *Mkt:* downward (risk); **en aval,** (*société*) downstream.

avaliser, *v.tr.* to endorse/to guarantee/to back (a bill).

avaliseur, -euse, *n.* **avaliste,** *n.m.f.* surety/guarantor/backer.

à-valoir, *n.m.inv.* advance (payment).

avance, *n.f.* **accorder à qn une avance sur son salaire,** to give s.o. an advance on his salary; **avance (de fonds),** advance/loan; **avance bancaire,** bank advance; **avances en devises,** foreign currency loan; **à titre d'avance,** by way of an advance/as an advance; **faire une avance de mille francs à qn,** to advance s.o. a thousand francs; **payé d'avance,** paid in advance/prepaid; **payable à l'avance,** payable in advance.

avancement, *n.m.* **avancement des travaux,** work progress; **compte rendu de l'avancement des travaux,** progress report; **payments proportionnels à l'avancement des travaux,** progress payments.

avancer, *v.tr.* (*a*) to advance/to bring forward; **la réunion a été avancée du 14 au 7,** the meeting has been brought forward from the 14th to the 7th (*b*) **avancer de l'argent à qn,** to advance money to s.o./to lend s.o. money; **avancer un mois d'appointements à qn,** to advance s.o. a month's salary/to pay s.o. a month's salary in advance.

avantage, *n.m.* advantage; **avantage absolu,** absolute advantage; **avantage comparatif,** comparative advantage; **avantages en nature/avantages sociaux,** fringe benefits; perks.

avantageux, *a.* advantageous/favourable; **prix avantageux,** low price; good price.

avant-contrat, *n.m.* preliminary contract.

avant-projet, *n.m.* preliminary scheme/plan.

avarie, *n.f. MIns:* (*a*) **déclaration d'avaries,** (ship's) protest (*b*) **avarie(s)/avaries-frais,** average; **avaries communes/grosses avaries,** general average; **avaries simples/particulières,** particular average; **compromis d'avarie,** average bond; **franc d'avaries,** free from average; **répartition d'avarie,** average adjustment; **répartiteur d'avaries,** average adjuster.

avarié, *a.* damaged/spoiled (goods).

avarier, *v.tr.* to damage/to spoil (goods, etc.).

avenant, *n.m.* endorsement/additional clause (to insurance policy); addendum.

avenu, *a.* **nul et non avenu,** null and void.

avertissement, *n.m.* demand note; tax bill demand.

avilir, *v.tr.* to depreciate/to lower/to bring down (currency, prices, etc.).

'avilir, *v.pr.* to lose value; to fall/to come down (in value, in price); to depreciate.

avilissement, *n.m.* depreciation; fall (in price).

avion, *n.m.* aircraft/aeroplane/*F:* plane/*NAm:* airplane; **en avion,** by air/by plane; **par avion,** (by) airmail; **avion commercial,** commercial aircraft; **avion de transport de marchandises,** freighter.

avion-cargo, *n.m.* freighter/*NAm:* freight plane.

avis, *n.m.* notice/notification; warning; announcement; **avis par écrit,** notice in writing; **donner avis de qch.,** to give notice of sth./to notify s.o. of sth.; **donner avis que ...,** to give notice that ...; **note/lettre d'avis,** advice note/notification of dispatch; **avis de livraison,** delivery note; **jusqu'à nouvel avis,** until further notice; **suivant avis,** as per advice; *StExch:* **avis d'exécution (d'un ordre),** sold (contract) note.

aviser, *v.tr.* **aviser qn de qch.,** to notify s.o. of sth.

avocat, -ate, *n. Jur:* barrister(-at-law)/counsel; *NAm:* lawyer; *Scot:* advocate; **consulter un avocat,** to take legal advice.

avoir, *n.m.* (*a*) property (*b*) **avoir fiscal,** tax credit (on dividends); **système de l'avoir fiscal,** imputation system; **doit et avoir,** debit and credit (*c*) *pl.* **avoirs,** assets; **avoirs disponibles,** liquid assets.

avoué, *n.m.* = sollicitor; *NAm:* attorney-at-law.

ayant droit, *n.m. Jur:* **les ayants droit,** the beneficiaries; persons entitled to (a benefit, etc.).

B

bagages, *n.m.pl.* luggage/*NAm:* baggage; **bagages à main**, hand/cabin luggage; **excédent de bagages**, excess luggage; **franchise de bagages**, luggage/baggage allowance.

bail, *n.m.* lease; **bail à loyer**, rental agreement; **bail à long terme**, long lease; **bail emphytéotique**, long lease (18–99 years)/= leasehold; **prendre une maison à bail**, to take out a lease on a house; to rent a house (for a stated period); **céder/donner une maison à bail**, to lease (out) a house/ to let a house; **signer/passer un bail**, to sign a lease/an agreement; **renouveler un bail**, to renew a lease; **expiration de bail**, expiration of (a) lease; **mon bail expire en mai**, my lease expires/runs out in May.

bailleur, -eresse, *n.* (*a*) *Jur:* lessor (*b*) **bailleur de fonds**, (*i*) sleeping partner (*ii*) (financial) backer/sponsor.

baisse, *n.f.* **baisse (de prix)**, fall/drop/ decline (in prices); **baisse accusée**, sharp fall; **baisse des blés**, drop in wheat; **baisse du franc**, fall in the value of the franc; **baisse du taux officiel d'escompte de 14% à 13%**, lowering of the minimum lending rate from 14% to 13%; *StExch:* **jouer/ spéculer à la baisse**, to operate/to speculate for a fall; to go a bear; **joueur à la baisse**, bear; **marché à la baisse**, falling/ bearish market; buyer's market; **position à la baisse**, bear position; **spéculations à la baisse**, bear speculations; **mouvement de baisse des valeurs**, downward movement of stocks; **acheter en baisse**, to buy on a falling market; **les actions sont en baisse**, shares are falling.

baisser, 1. *v.tr.* **baisser le prix de qch.**, to lower/to reduce/to cut/to bring down the price of sth.; **baisser les loyers**, to lower/to bring down the rents; **baisser le taux officiel de l'escompte**, to lower the minimum lending rate; **faire baisser le coût de la vie**, to reduce/to cut the cost of living; **la concurrence fait baisser les prix**, competition brings prices down 2. *v.i.* (*a*) **nos stocks baissent**, our stocks are running low/ down (*b*) (*des prix*) to fall/to come down/to go down/to drop; **la valeur de ces maisons a baissé**, the value of these houses has gone down/these houses have gone down in value; **le dollar a baissé**, the dollar has weakened; **ses actions baissent**, his shares are going down.

baissier, -ière, *StExch:* 1. *a* (*market, etc*) bearish 2. *n* bear.

balance, *n.f.* 1. scale/scales; weighing machine; **balance à bascule**, pair of scales; **balance automatique**, shop scales/weighing machine 2. (*a*) **balance d'un compte**, balance of an account; **balance de caisse**, cash balance; **balance (reportée) de l'exercice précédent**, balance (brought forward) from the previous account; **balance générale/de vérification**, trial balance; **balance d'inventaire**, balance-sheet; **faire la balance**, to make up the balance(-sheet); **balance de l'actif et du passif**, credit and debit balance; balance of assets and liabilities (*b*) *PolEc:* **balance du commerce/balance commerciale**, trade balance/balance of trade; **balance générale des comptes/balance des paiements**, balance of payments; **balances sterling**, sterling balances.

balancer, *v.tr.* **balancer un compte**, to balance an account; **balancer les comptes**, to close/to make up/to balance the books.

balle, *n.f.* bale (of cotton, etc.); **mise en**

balle, baling; **marchandises en balles,** goods in bales.

bancable, *a. Fin:* bankable/negotiable.

bancaire, *a.* **chèque bancaire,** bank cheque; **commission bancaire,** bank commission; **compte bancaire,** bank/*NAm:* banking account; **crédit bancaire,** bank credit; **dépôt bancaire,** bank deposit; **frais bancaires,** bank charges; **opérations bancaires,** banking operations/transactions; **prêt bancaire,** bank loan; **traite bancaire,** banker's draft; **virement bancaire,** bank giro transfer.

bancarisation, *n.f.* influence of banking institutions on given population; **taux de bancarisation,** percentage of couples with at least one bank account.

banquable, *a. Fin:* bankable/negotiable.

banque, *n.f.* (*a*) bank; **banque d'escompte,** discount house; **la Banque de France,** the Bank of France; **la Banque Mondiale,** the World Bank; **banque d'affaires,** merchant bank; **banque centrale,** central bank/ issuing bank; **banque de placement/banque d'émission,** bank of issue/issuing house; **banque hypothécaire,** mortgage bank; **les grandes banques centrales,** the High Street banks; **billet de banque,** banknote/*NAm:* bill; **carnet/livret de banque,** bank book/ pass-book; **avoir un compte en banque,** to have a bank account/*NAm:* banking account; **avoir un compte en banque au Crédit Lyonnais,** to have an account with/to bank with the Crédit Lyonnais; **crédit en banque,** bank credit; **directeur de banque,** bank manager; **employé(e) de banque,** bank clerk; **prêt de banque à banque,** interbank loan (*b*) banking; **banque à domicile,** telebanking; **opérations de banque,** banking business/transactions; **la haute banque,** high finance (*c*) *Cmptr:* **banque de données,** data bank.

banqueroute, *n.f. Jur:* **banqueroute simple,** bankruptcy (*with irregularities amounting to a breach of the law*); **banqueroute frauduleuse,** fraudulent bankruptcy (*amounting to crime*); **faire banqueroute,** to go bankrupt.

banqueroutier, -ière, *a. & n.* bankrupt (*usu.* fraudulent).

banquier, *n.m.* banker.

baraterie, *n.f. Jur: Nau:* barratry.

barème, *n.m.* (*a*) ready reckoner (*b*) scale (of salaries, etc.) (*c*) (printed) table/ schedule (of prices, charges, etc.); (price) list.

baril, *m.* barrel (of petrol, etc.).

barre, *n.f.* **en dessous de la barre des 3%,** below the 3% mark/below the important chart point of 3%; **or en barre,** ingot; bar gold; bullion; **graphique en barre,** bar chart.

barré, *a.* **chèque barré,** crossed cheque; **chèque non barré,** uncrossed cheque/open cheque.

barrer, *v.tr.* **barrer un chèque,** to cross a cheque.

barrière, *n.f.* barrier; **barrière commerciale,** trade barrier; **barrières douanières,** customs barriers; **barrières à l'entrée,** barrier to entry.

bas¹, *a.* **les prix les plus bas,** rock-bottom prices; **les prix sont au plus bas,** prices have touched rock bottom; **maintenir les prix bas,** to keep prices down/low; **le (taux du) change est bas,** the rate of exchange is low; **marché à bas taux d'intérêt,** cheap money market; **prix basse saison,** low season fare/price; **vendre qch. à bas prix,** to sell sth. cheap.

bas², *adv. StExch:* **les cours sont tombés très bas,** prices have fallen very low.

bas³, *n.m. StExch:* **les hauts et les bas,** highs and lows/highest and lowest prices traded.

base, *n.f.* (*a*) basis; **sur une base nette,** on a net(t) basis (*b*) **contrat de base,** principal contract; **prix de base,** base price/basic price; **produit de base,** basic commodity; **tarifs de base,** basic rates; *Bank:* **taux de**

base (bancaire), base rate; **traitement/ salaire de base,** basic salary.

bâtiment, *n.m.* (*a*) building; premises *pl.*; **nous avons une cantine dans le bâtiment,** we have a canteen on the premises (*b*) **l'industrie du bâtiment/le secteur bâtiment,** (*i*) the building trade (*ii*) the building industry; **entrepreneur de/en bâtiment,** building contractor/builder.

battage, *n.m.* **battage publicitaire,** hard sell; **faire du battage (autour de qn, de qch),** to give (s.o., sth.) the hard sell.

bazarette, *n.f.* convenience store.

bénéfice, *n.m.* profit/gain; **bénéfices fiscaux/imposables,** taxable profits; **bénéfice brut,** gross profit/pre-tax profit/profit before tax; **bénéfices financiers,** interest received; earnings; **bénéfices d'exploitation,** operating profits; **bénéfice net,** clear profit/net profit/profit after tax; **bénéfices non distribués,** undistributed profits/ unappropriated profits/retained earnings; **bénéfice par action,** earnings/income per share; **participation aux bénéfices,** profit-sharing scheme; **part de bénéfice,** bonus; **petits bénéfices,** perks; **rapport cours-bénéfice,** price-earnings ratio; **prise de bénéfices,** profit-taking; **rapporter des bénéfices,** to yield; **donner un bénéfice,** to show a benefit/(a) profit; **réaliser un bénéfice,** to make a profit; **vendre qch. à bénéfice,** to sell sth. at a profit/at a premium.

bénéficiaire, 1. *a.* **bilan bénéficiaire,** balance-sheet showing a profit; **capacité bénéficiaire,** earning power; **compte bénéficiaire,** account showing a credit balance/account (which is) in credit; **marge bénéficiaire,** profit margin; **société bénéficiaire,** firm showing a profit; **solde bénéficiaire,** profit balance **2.** *n.* (*a*) *Ins: etc:* beneficiary (*b*) recipient/payee/ beneficiary (of cheque, money order); **bénéficiaire d'options,** optionee.

Bénélux, *Pr.n.m.* Benelux; **les pays du Bénélux,** the Benelux countries.

bénévole, *a.* unpaid/honorary; **il est employé à titre bénévole,** he is unpaid.

besoin, *n.m.* need; requirement; **analyse des besoins,** needs analysis; **besoins de trésorerie,** cash requirements.

best-seller, *n.m.* bestseller/best-selling author.

bien, *n.m.* (*a*) possessions/property/assets/ wealth/goods; *Jur:* **communauté de biens,** joint estate (*b*) *Jur:* **biens meubles/mobiliers,** personal property/chattels/ movables; **biens immeubles/immobiliers,** real estate; **biens corporels,** tangible assets; *PolEc:* **biens de consommation,** consumer goods; **biens manufacturés,** manufactured goods; **biens permanents/ durables,** durable goods; **biens de production/d'équipement,** capital goods.

bien-fonds, *n.m.* real estate/landed property.

bilan, *n.m.* (*a*) *Fin:* balance sheet; **bilan consolidé/de groupe,** consolidated balance-sheet; **contrôle du bilan,** balance-sheet auditing; **dresser/établir/faire un bilan,** to draw up a balance sheet (*b*) **le bilan hebdomadaire,** the weekly trading report; **dresser le bilan de ses pertes,** to reckon up one's losses (*c*) *Fin:* schedule (of assets and liabilities); **déposer son bilan,** to file one's petition (in bankruptcy) (*d*) *Fin:* balance (of an account); balance; total amount (*e*) statement.

bilatéral, *a.* bilateral; **accord/contrat bilatéral,** bilateral agreement/contract.

bilatéralisme, *n.m. PolEc:* bilateralism.

billet, *n.m.* (*a*) *Trans:* ticket; **billet d'aller (et) retour,** return ticket/*NAm:* roundtrip ticket; **billet simple,** single/one-way ticket; **billet de 1ère classe,** 1st class ticket; **billet d'abonnement,** season ticket (*b*) note/bill; **billet à ordre,** note of hand/promissory note; IOU; **billet au porteur,** bill payable to bearer/bearer bill; **billet à présentation,** bill payable on demand; **billet à vue,** bill payable at sight/sight draft; **billet du Trésor,** Treasury bill; **billet de trésorerie,** commercial paper (*c*) **billet de banque,** banknote/*NAm:* bill; **billet de 50F,** 50F note; *NAm:* **billet de $10,** 10 dollar bill; *F:* **billet vert,** (*american dollar*) greenback

billetterie, *n.f.* cash dispenser; automatic telling machine/ *NAm:* automatic teller.

billion, *n.m.* billion (10^{12})/*NAm:* trillion.

bimensuel, *a.* fortnightly/bi-monthly; **revue bimensuelle,** magazine which comes out every fortnight/every two weeks.

bimestriel, *a.* bi-monthly/two-monthly; **une revue bimestrielle,** a magazine which comes out every other month/every two months.

biodégradable, *a.* biodegradable.

blanc, 1. *a.* **affaire blanche,** profitless/ break-even deal **2.** *n.m.* blank (space); **chèque en blanc,** blank cheque; **endossement en blanc,** endorsement in blank/ blank endorsement.

blanc-seing, *n.m.* paper/document signed in blank.

bloc, *n.m.* (*a*) **bloc monétaire,** currency bloc; **bloc sterling,** sterling bloc (*b*) **bloc de contrôle,** controlling shareholding (*c*) *Ind:* **bloc technique,** design department (in a factory) (*d*) **bloc de marchandises,** job lot of goods; **acheter qch. en bloc,** to buy the whole stock of sth./to buy sth. in one lot/to buy sth. in bulk (*e*) *StExch:* **bloc de titres,** parcel.

blocage, *n.m.* *PolEc:* pegging; *Fin:* freezing; **blocage des prix et des salaires,** price and wage freeze.

bloc-notes, *n.m.* note-pad/memo-pad.

blocus, *n.m.* (economic) blockade.

bloquer, *v.tr.* to stop (a cheque, an account); to block/to stop (an account); **bloquer les salaires,** to freeze wages; **crédits bloqués,** frozen credits.

blue chip, *n.m.* blue chip.

boîte, *n.f.* (*a*) **boîte (de carton),** cardboard box (*b*) **boîte de conserve,** tin/*NAm:* can; **fruits en boîte,** tinned/*NAm:* canned fruit (*c*) **boîte aux lettres,** letter box/post box/*NAm:* mail box (*d*) **boîte postale,** post office box; **BP 57 Lyon,** PO Box 57 Lyons.

bon, 1. *a.* (*a*) good/right/sound; **en bon état de marche,** in good working order; **de bonne foi,** in good faith; bona fide (*b*) good/profitable/advantageous (investment, etc.); **bonne affaire,** good deal/good speculation/bargain; **acheter qch. à bon marché,** to buy sth. cheap/at bargain price (*c*) good/sound/safe (security, credit, etc.); **billet bon pour trois mois,** ticket valid for three months **2.** *n.m.* (*a*) order/voucher/ ticket; **bon d'achat,** gift voucher/gift token; **bon de caisse,** cash voucher; **bon de commande,** purchase order/order form; **bon de commission,** commission note; **bon de livraison,** delivery order (*b*) *Fin:* bond/ bill/draft/note; **bon au porteur,** bearer bond; **bon nominatif,** registered bond; **bon d'épargne,** savings bond/certificate; **bon du Trésor,** Treasury bond/Exchequer bill; tender bill; **bon à vue,** sight draft.

boni, *n.m.* (*a*) (unexpected) profit (*b*) bonus; **recevoir 100F de boni,** to get a 100F bonus.

bonification, *n.f.* (*a*) allowance/rebate/ reduction (*b*) bonus.

bonifier, *v.tr.* to give a bonus (to s.o.); **prêt bonifié/à taux bonifié,** soft loan.

bon-prime, *n.m.* free-gift coupon.

bonus, *n.m.* *Ins:* **un bonus de 35% sur mon assurance,** a 35% no claims bonus.

bonus-malus, *n.m.* *Ins:* **système du bonus-malus** = no claims bonus system.

boom, *n.m.* *Fin:* boom.

bordereau, *n.m.* memorandum/(detailed) statement; invoice/account/docket (of goods, cash, etc.); consignment note; tally sheet; schedule; **bordereau de paie,** pay slip; **suivant bordereau ci-inclus,** as per enclosed statement; *Trans:* **bordereau de chargement,** cargo list; **bordereau d'expédition,** dispatch note/consignment note; cartage/cart note; **bordereau de livraison,** delivery note; *Bank:* **bordereau d'encaissement,** list of bills for collection; **bordereau d'escompte,** list of bills for discount; **bordereau de versement,** paying-in slip; *StExch:* **bordereau d'achat,** bought note/

list of purchases; **bordereau de vente,** sold note/list of sales; **bordereau de crédit,** credit note; **bordereau de débit,** debit note.

bouquinerie, *n.f.* second-hand bookselling/second-hand book trade.

bourse, *n.f.* (*a*) **des prix à portée de votre bourse,** prices to suit your pocket (*b*) **Bourse (des valeurs),** Stock Exchange/ Bourse; **Bourse de commerce/Bourse de(s) marchandises,** commodities exchange; **la Bourse de Londres,** the London Stock Exchange; **à la Bourse/en Bourse,** on the Stock Exchange; **jouer à la Bourse,** to speculate on the Stock Exchange; **coup de Bourse,** deal on the Stock Exchange/ speculation; **opération de Bourse,** Stock Exchange transaction; **le cours de la Bourse,** the market rate; **valeurs de Bourse,** stock/shares; **valeurs cotées en Bourse,** quoted shares; *F:* **pratiquer la bourse buissonnière,** to be a small investor (*c*) **bourse de l'emploi,** job centre (*d*) grant (for studies, etc.).

boursicotage, *n.m.* speculation; speculating; dabbling on the Stock Exchange.

boursicoter, *v.i.* to speculate in a small way/to dabble on the Stock Exchange.

boursicoteur, -euse, *n.,* **boursicotier, -ière,** *n.* speculator; punter.

boursier, -ière, 1. *a.* **opérations boursières,** Stock Exchange transactions **2.** *n.* (*i*) *F:* stockbroker (*ii*) speculator (on the Stock Exchange).

boutique, *n.f.* (*a*) shop/*NAm:* store; **tenir boutique,** to keep/to run a shop; **fermer boutique,** to close down/to fold up; **boutique franche,** duty-free shop (*b*) boutique (*small shop selling fashionable clothes*) (*c*) **boutique (en plein vent),** stall in a market.

boutiquier, -ière, *n.* shopkeeper/ tradesman/tradeswoman.

boycott(age), *n.m.* boycott; boycotting.

boycotter, *v.tr.* to boycott.

brader, *v.tr.* to sell off/to sell cheaply; to get rid of sth. at any price.

braderie, *n.f.* (*a*) clearance sale (*b*) open-air market/street market.

branche, *n.f.* branch/sector (of industry, etc.).

brevet, *n.m.* (*a*) patent; **agent en brevets,** patent agent; **brevet d'inventeur/brevet d'invention,** (letters) patent; **bureau des brevets,** patent office; **demande de brevet déposée,** patent pending/patent applied for; **prendre un brevet,** to take out a patent; **titulaire d'un brevet,** patentee (*b*) *Jur:* **acte en brevet,** contract delivered by notary in original.

breveté, *a.* (*a*) patented (invention); **breveté sans garantie du Gouvernement (SGDG),** patented without Government warranty (of quality) (*b*) **inventeur breveté,** inventor holding letters patent.

breveter, *v.tr.* to patent (an invention); **faire breveter une invention),** to take out a patent for an invention.

briefing, *n.m.* briefing.

brique, *n.f.* **brique de lait/lait en brique,** carton of milk/milk carton.

briseur, *n.m.* **briseur de grève,** scab/blackleg.

brocante, *n.f.* antique shop; junk shop.

brocanter, 1. *v.i.* to deal in second-hand goods **2.** *v.tr. F:* **brocanter ses meubles,** to sell one's furniture (to a second-hand or antique dealer).

brocanteur, -euse, *n.* antique dealer; second-hand dealer; **magasin de brocanteur,** antique shop; junk shop.

brochure, *n.f.* brochure; **brochure publicitaire,** publicity brochure/leaflet; booklet.

brut, 1. *a.* (*a*) raw (material); crude (oil etc.); **produit brut,** primary product (*b*) gross (profit, value, weight, etc.); **marge brute,** gross margin; **montant brut,** gross amount; **produit national brut (PNB)** gross national product (GNP); **recette brute,** gross receipts/gross returns (*c*) *PolEc:* **chiffres bruts,** unweighted figures

données brutes, raw data **2.** *n.m.* **le (pétrole) brut,** crude (oil).

budget, *n.m.* budget; **budget commercial,** sales budget; **budget équilibré,** (well) balanced budget; **budget familial,** household budget; **budget global,** master budget; **budget de publicité,** advertising/publicity budget; **budget de trésorerie,** cash budget; **boucler son budget,** to make both ends meet; **établissement/préparation d'un budget,** budgeting; **inscrire qch. au budget,** to budget for sth.

budgétaire, *a.* **année budgétaire,** fiscal/financial year; **comptabilité budgétaire,** budgeting; **contrainte budgétaire,** budget(ary) constraint; **crédit budgétaire,** budget credit allowance; **déficit budgétaire,** budget deficit; **excédent budgétaire,** budget surplus; **gestion/contrôle budgétaire,** budgetary control; **prévision budgétaire,** budget forecast(ing); **situation budgétaire de l'année,** budget statement for the year.

budgétisation, *n.f. Fin:* inclusion (of an item) in the budget; budgeting.

budgétiser, *v.tr.* to include (sth.) in the budget/to budget for (sth.).

bulletin, *n.m.* (*a*) periodical publication (of a firm, etc.); **Bulletin de la Cote Officielle,** Stock Exchange Daily Official List (SEDOL)/Official List; *Fin:* **bulletin des cours,** official (Stock Exchange) price-list (*b*) ticket/receipt/form/certificate; **bulletin de bagages,** luggage ticket/*NAm:* baggage check; **bulletin de consignation,** consignment note; **bulletin d'expédition,** dispatch note; **bulletin de salaire/de paie,** pay (advice) slip; **bulletin de souscription,** application form; **bulletin de vente,** advice note/slip; sales note; *Rail:* waybill.

bureau, *n.m.* (*a*) desk (*b*) office; **bureau central/principal,** head office; **garçon de**

bureau, office boy; **fournitures de bureau,** stationery; office equipment; **personnel de bureau,** office staff; **travail de bureau,** office work; clerical work; **après les heures de bureau,** after office hours; **organisation des bureaux,** office management (*c*) **bureau de change,** bureau de change; (foreign) exchange office; **bureau de cotation/d'évaluation,** credit agency/*NAm:* bureau; **bureau de douane,** custom(s) house; **bureau d'enregistrement,** (*i*) registry office (*ii*) check-in; **bureau d'expédition,** forwarding office; *Th:* **bureau de location,** box office; **bureau de placement,** employment agency; **bureau de poste,** post office; **bureau de publicité,** advertising agency; **bureau de renseignements,** information/inquiry office; inquiries/information; **bureau de tourisme,** tourist office (*d*) (office) staff (*e*) board/committee/governing body/executive; **constituer le bureau (d'une société, etc.),** to set up a committee (*f*) department; **bureau d'études,** design/planning department; design office; research department; **bureau d'étude technique,** engineering and design department; **bureau administratif,** government department/bureau; **bureau international,** international bureau.

bureaucratie, *n.f.* bureaucracy/officialdom/*F:* red tape.

bureaucratique, *a.* bureaucratic; **style bureaucratique,** formal/official style; officialese.

bureaucratiser, *v.tr.* to bureaucratize.

bureautique, *n.f.* new office technology/office automation (OA)/computerization.

bureautiser, *v.tr.* to automate/computerize (office).

but, *n.m.* goal/target/object(ive); **organisation à but lucratif,** profit-making/profitable organization; **organisation à but non lucratif,** non-profit-making organization.

C

cabinet, *n.m.* office; chambers (of judge, barrister); (doctor's) surgery; **cabinet de conseil en gestion,** management consultancy practice.

câble, *n.m.* cable/cablegram.

câbler, *v.tr.* to cable (a message); **câbler à qn,** to send a cable to s.o./to cable s.o.

cabotage, *n.m. Nau:* coastal trade.

caboteur, *n.m. Nau:* coaster.

cachet, *n.m.* (*a*) seal/stamp (on letter, document); **cachet de douane,** customs seal (*b*) mark/stamp; **cachet d'un fabricant,** maker's trade mark; **cachet de poste,** postmark.

cacheter, *v.tr.* to seal (up) (letter, etc.); **soumission cachetée,** sealed tender.

cadastrage, *n.m.* land registration.

cadastral, *a.* cadastral (register, survey); **extrait cadastral,** land registry certificate.

cadastre, *n.m. Adm:* land register; cadastral survey; cadastre; **bureau du cadastre,** Land Registry Office.

cadastrer, *v.tr.* to enter (property) in the land register.

caddie, *n.m.* (*dans un supermarché*) trolley.

cadre, *n.m.* **1.** (*a*) (*sur un formulaire etc.*) space/box; **cadre réservé à l'administration** = for office use only (*b*) framework; **dans le cadre de ce programme d'expansion,** as part of this expansion programme **2. cadre (d'entreprise),** executive; manager; **cadre commercial,** sales executive; **cadres dirigeants/supérieurs,** managerial staff/senior executives/top

management; **cadres de maîtrise,** supervisory staff; **cadres moyens,** middle management; **jeune cadre,** junior executive; **figurer sur les cadres,** to be on the (company's) books.

caduc, *a. Jur:* (*legs*) null and void; **contrat déclaré caduc,** agreement declared to have lapsed; **dette caduque,** debt barred by the Statute of Limitations.

caducité, *n.f. Jur:* lapsing/nullity.

cahier, *n.m.* **cahier des charges,** conditions; specifications (of a contract).

caisse, *n.f.* **1.** (*a*) (packing-)case; tea chest; box; **caisse à claire-voie,** crate; **caisse en carton,** cardboard box; **mettre des marchandises en caisse,** to case/to crate goods **2.** (*a*) float; cash-box (*b*) **caisse enregistreuse/caisse comptable,** cash register; till; **caisse rapide,** quick service till; **caisse électronique,** electronic service till; **ticket de caisse/**FrC: **reçu de caisse,** (till) receipt (*c*) cash desk/checkout (in super market); cash(ier's) office; **payez à la caisse,** please pay at the desk; **c'est elle qui tient la caisse/qui est préposée à la caisse,** she's the cashier (*d*) (*i*) cash (in hand) (*ii*) takings; **livre de caisse,** cash book; **mouvements de caisse,** cash transactions; **petite caisse,** petty cash; **recettes de caisse,** cash receipts; **solde de caisse,** cash balance; **faire la/sa caisse,** to do the till/to cash up; **avoir tant d'argent en caisse,** to have so much money in hand (*e*) *Bank:* **facilités de caisse,** overdraft facilities (*f*) fund; **caisse d'amortissement,** sinking fund; **caisse de retraite,** pension fund; superannuation fund; **caisse noire,** slush fund (*g*) **caisse régionale,** = local (bank) branch; **Caisse (nationale) d'Ép**

24

argne = (National) Savings Bank; **Caisse des Dépôts,** State bank which manages National Savings Bank funds and local community funds; **caisse de prévoyance,** provident fund (*h*) *Adm:* **caisse de la Sécurité sociale,** social security office.

caissier, -ière, *n.* (*a*) cashier (in shop, cinema, etc.) (*b*) *Bank:* cashier/*NAm:* teller; **caissier principal,** chief cashier/head cashier.

calcul, *n.m.* calculation/reckoning; **faire/effectuer un calcul,** to calculate/to work out (a calculation)/to reckon; **faux calcul/erreur de calcul,** miscalculation.

calculateur, -trice, 1. *n.m.* **calculateur (électronique),** (electronic) calculator 2. *n.f.* **calculatrice,** calculator; **calculatrice de bureau,** desk calculator; **calculatrice de poche,** pocket calculator; **calculatrice imprimante,** print-out calculator/calculator with a listing.

calculer, *v.tr.* to calculate/to work out/to reckon; **calculer un prix,** to arrive at a price/to work out a price; **risque calculé,** calculated risk; **machine à calculer,** calculator; adding machine; **l'impôt se calcule sur ...,** tax is calculated on ....

alculette, *n.f.* pocket calculator.

alendrier, *n.m.* (*a*) calendar; **bloc calendrier,** tear-off calendar (*b*) timetable; *NAm:* schedule; **mon calendrier ne le permet pas,** my timetable does not allow it.

alibrage, *n.m.* grading (of eggs, fruit, etc.).

alibrer, *v.tr.* (*a*) to gauge/to measure (*b*) to grade (eggs, fruit, etc.).

ambial, *a. Fin:* relating to exchange; **droit cambial,** exchange law.

ambiste, *Fin:* 1. *n.m.* trader; foreign exchange dealer/broker 2. *a.* **marché cambiste,** exchange market.

amelote, *n.f. F:* cheap goods/shoddy goods.

cameloter, *v.i. F:* (*i*) to deal in cheap goods (*ii*) to manufacture cheap goods.

camembert, *n.m. F:* pie-chart.

camion, *n.m.* lorry/truck; **camion-citerne,** tanker; **camion de déménagement,** removal van; **camion semi-remorque,** articulated lorry.

camionnage, *n.m.* (*a*) (*prix*) haulage/carriage/*NAm:* truckage (*b*) (*service*) carrying/*NAm:* trucking (trade); **une entreprise de camionnage,** (a firm of) hauliers/haulage contractors/*NAm:* a trucking business.

camionner, *v.tr.* to carry/to haul/*NAm:* to truck (goods).

camionnette, *n.f.* (delivery) van/*NAm:* pick-up (truck).

camionnette-boutique, *n.f.* travelling/mobile shop.

camionneur, *n.m.* (*a*) carrier/(road) haulier; haulage contractor (*b*) van driver/lorry driver/truck driver/*NAm:* trucker/teamster.

campagne, *n.f.* campaign; **campagne de dénigrement,** countermarketing; **campagne de productivité,** productivity campaign/drive; **campagne publicitaire/de publicité,** advertising campaign/publicity drive; **campagne de vente,** sales drive.

canal, *n.m.* channel; **canaux de communication,** communication channels; **canaux de distribution,** distribution channels.

candidat, -ate, *n.* candidate/applicant (**à un emploi,** for a job).

candidature, *n.f.* **formulaire de candidature,** application form; **poser sa candidature à (un poste)/faire acte de candidature,** to apply for (a post); **retirer sa candidature,** to withdraw one's application; **date limite de dépôt de candidatures,** closing date for applications.

capacité, *n.f.* (*a*) **capacité d'achat,** purchasing power; **capacité bénéficiaire,** earning power; earning potential;

capacité d'emprunter, borrowing power; **capacité de production,** manufacturing capacity (b) (d'un tonneau, etc.) content/ capacity; **capacité de storage,** storage capacity.

capital, n.m. Fin: capital/assets; **accumulation de capital,** capital accumulation; **capital(-)actions/capital social,** share capital; equity; **capital appelé,** called-up capital; **capital d'apport,** initial capital; **capital circulant/roulant,** circulating capital; working capital; **capital effectif/libéré/réel,** paid-up capital; **capital émis,** issued capital; **capital d'emprunt,** loan capital; **capital engagé,** tied-up capital; **capitaux exigibles,** current liabilities; **capital d'exploitation/de roulement,** working/NAm: operating capital; **capitaux fébriles/flottants,** hot money; **capital et intérêt,** capital and interest; **capital initial/de départ,** front money/seed money; **capital nominal,** authorized capital; **capital non-appelé/non-libéré,** uncalled capital; nil paid; **capital en numéraire,** cash capital; **capital obligations,** debenture capital; **capitaux permanents/fixes,** fixed capital; **capitaux propres,** shareholders'/stockholders' equity; **capital de réserve,** reserve capital; **capital social,** nominal/registered capital; **capital souscrit,** subscribed capital; **capital technique,** (technical) equipment; **capital versé,** paid-up capital; **compte de capital,** capital account; **dépenses en capital,** capital expenditure; **marché des capitaux,** capital market/money market; **mouvements des capitaux,** capital movements; **société au capital de ...,** company with a capital of .../company capitalized at ...; **avoir des capitaux dans une affaire,** to have vested interests in a business; **faire un appel de capital,** to call for funds; **fournir les capitaux pour un project,** to fund/to finance/to bankroll a project; to put up the funding for a project; **investir/mettre des capitaux dans une affaire,** to invest/to put capital into a business; **association capital-travail,** profit-sharing scheme.

capitalisable, a. capitalizable (interest, etc.).

capitalisation, n.f. capitalization (of interest, etc.); **capitalisation boursière (du pays),** market capitalization; share economy; **fonds de capitalisation,** accumulation units.

capitaliser, v.tr. to capitalize (interest, etc.); **valeur capitalisée,** capitalized value.

capitaliste, n.m. capitalist; investor.

capital-risque, n.m. venture capital/risk capital; **société de capital-risque,** venture-capital company.

captif, a. **compagnie captive,** daughter company/subsidiary company/dependant company.

carat, n.m. carat; **or à 18 carats,** 18-carat gold.

cargaison, n.f. Nau: cargo; freight; **cargaison mixte,** mixed cargo; **cargaison d'aller,** outward cargo; **cargaison de retour,** homeward cargo.

cargo, n.m. (a) Nau: freighter; cargo ship **cargo mixte,** passenger and cargo ship (b) **avion cargo,** (air) freighter.

carnet, n.m. (a) notebook; **carnet de commandes,** order book; **carnet de dépenses,** account book/housekeeping book; **carnet de dépôt,** deposit book Bank: **carnet de banque,** pass book/bank book; **carnet de versements,** paying-in book (b) **carnet de chèques (à souche(s)),** cheque book (with counterfoil/with stub(s)); **carnet de tickets (d'autobus, de métro),** book of (bus, underground tickets; **carnet de timbres,** book of stamp (c) Aut: etc: **carnet de route/de bord,** lo book.

carré, 1. n.m. square 2. a. **mètre carré** (i) square metre (ii) = square yar (approx.).

carrière, n.f. career; **perspectives de carrière,** job expectations.

carte, n.f. (a) **carte d'abonnement,** season ticket; **carte d'affaires,** business card **carte accréditive/de crédit,** credit card **carte bancaire,** cheque (garantee) card cash card; **carte de débit,** payment card/ debit card; **carte à mémoire/à puce,** smartcard; **caste revolving,** revolving credit card; **carte de commerce,** trading licence (*b*) **carte perforée,** punch(ed) card (*c*) **carte d'échantillons,** sample card (*d*) **carte postale,** postcard (*e*) *Ins:* **carte verte,** green card (*f*) (*pour le métro et l'autobus*) **carte orange** = monthly season ticket (*g*) **carte grise** = car registration document.

cartel, *n.m.* cartel/trust; combine; ring; **cartel horizontal,** horizontal combine.

cartellisation, *n.f.* cartel(l)ization.

carton, *n.m.* (*a*) cardboard; **carton ondulé,** corrugated cardboard (*b*) cardboard box; carton.

case, *n.f.* (*a*) **case postale,** post office box/PO box (*b*) (*sur un formulaire*) **cocher la case correspondante,** tick the appropriate box.

cash flow, *n.m.* cash flow; **cash flow net,** net cash flow; **cash flow actualisé,** discounted cash flow (DCF); **cash flow marginal,** incremental cash slow.

casse, *n.f.* (*a*) breakage; damage; **payer la casse,** to pay for breakages; **assurance contre la casse,** insurance against breakage (*b*) **vendre à la casse,** to sell for scrap.

casser, *v.tr.* **casser une tendance/une moyenne à la hausse,** to overshoot.

casuel, *n.m.* perks.

catalogage, *n.m.* cataloguing/*NAm* cataloging.

catalogue, *n.m.* catalogue/*NAm:* catalog; list; **catalogue illustré,** illustrated catalogue; **catalogue de vente par correspondance,** mail order catalogue; **achat/vente sur catalogue,** mail order.

catégorie, *n.f.* category; quality; **viande de première catégorie,** best quality meat/ choice cut; **viande de deuxième catégorie,** poor quality meat/cheap(er) cut.

caution, *n.f.* (*a*) (*pers.*) surety/guarantor;

être **caution de qn/se porter caution pour qn,** to stand surety for s.o. (*b*) surety/ guarantee/security; **caution bancaire,** bank guarantee; **demander une caution,** to ask for security; **fournir caution,** to give security (*c*) deposit; **verser une caution,** to pay a deposit.

cautionnement, *n.m.* (*a*) surety/bond/ guarantee (*b*) security/caution money/ guarantee/guaranty.

cautionner, *v.tr.* to stand surety for (s.o.).

cavalerie, *n.f.* **effet/papier/traite de cavalerie,** accomodation bill/note.

cédant, 1. *a.* **partie cédante,** granting/assigning/transferring (party) **2. cédant, -ante,** *n.* (*a*) grantor/assignor/transferor/ transfer(r)er (of shares, etc.) (*b*) preceding party (to bill).

céder, *v.tr.* (*a*) to give up/to surrender (right); **les droits à eux cédés,** the rights granted to them (*b*) to transfer/to make over/to assign (**à,** to); to dispose of/to sell (lease); **céder à bail,** to lease; **commerce à céder,** business for sale.

cédétiste, *n.m.f.* member of the CFTD (*trade union*).

Cedex, *n.m.* **courrier d'entreprise à distribution exceptionnelle,** commercial PO box service.

cédulaire, *a.* **impôts cédulaires,** scheduled taxes.

cédule, *n.f. Adm:* schedule; **cédule d'impôts,** tax code.

cégétiste, *n.m.f.* member of the CGT (*trade union*).

célibataire, *a. & n.m.f.* unmarried (man, woman, person); **une célibataire,** an unmarried woman/girl; a spinster.

cellulaire, *a.* **gestion cellulaire,** divisional management.

cent[1], *num.a.* (*a*) hundred; **elle a perdu cent francs,** she lost a/one hundred francs (*b*) **pour cent,** percent; **intérêt de sept pour**

cent, seven percent interest; **cent pour cent,** a/one hundred percent (100%).

cent[2], *n.m.* (*pièce de monnaie*) cent.

centaine, *n.f.* (about) a hundred; **une centaine de francs,** about a hundred francs/a hundred francs or so; **quelques centaines de francs,** a few hundred francs.

centième, 1. *num.a.* & *n.* hundredth **2.** *n.m.* hundredth (part); **trois centièmes de la somme globale,** three hundredths of the total amount.

centile, *n.m. Stat:* centile.

centime, *n.m.* centime.

central, 1. *a.* **banque centrale,** central bank; **bureau central,** head office/main office **2.** *n.m.* **central téléphonique,** telephone exchange; **central automatique,** automatic exchange **3.** *n.f.* **centrale d'achats,** central purchasing office; **centrale électrique,** power station; **centrale (syndicale),** group of affiliated trade unions.

centralisation, *n.f.* centralization/centralizing.

centraliser, *v.tr.* to centralize.

centre, *n.m.* (*a*) centre/*NAm:* center; **centre commercial,** shopping centre/shopping precinct; *FrC:* **centre d'achats,** shopping centre; **centre des affaires,** business centre; **centre de traitement de l'information,** data processing centre; **centre de tourisme,** tourist centre; **centre de tri,** sorting office; **centre industriel,** industrial centre (*b*) **centre budgétaire,** budget centre; **centre de coût,** cost centre.

céréale, *n.f.* cereal; grain.

céréalier, -ière, *a.* **coopérative céréalière,** grain/cereal co-operative.

certain, 1. *a.* definite/fixed (price, date) **2.** *n.m. Fin:* **le certain de la livre est de 8,68 F,** the rate of exchange for the pound is 8.68 F.

certificat, *n.m.* (*a*) *Nau:* **certificat de chargement,** certificate of receipt; **certifi-cat de jauge,** tonnage certificate (*b*) *Fin:* **certificat d'action(s),** share/stock certificate; *Ins:* **certificat d'avarie,** certificate of damage/statement of loss; **certificat de conformité,** certificate of compliance; *Cust:* **certificat d'entrepôt,** warrant; **certificat d'homologation,** certificate of approval; **certificat d'investissement privilégié,** non-voting preference share; **certificat de transfert,** transfer certificate; *Fin:* **certificat de trésorerie,** treasury bond; **certificat d'origine,** certificate of origin; **certificat nominatif d'action(s),** registered share certificate; **certificat provisoire,** share certificate/(provisional) scrip; *Ins:* **certificat provisoire d'assurance,** cover note (*c*) (employer's) testimonial; **certificat d'aptitude professionnelle (CAP),** technical/professional diploma.

certification, *n.f.* certification/authentication; **certification d'une signature,** witnessing of a signature.

certifier, *v.tr.* (*a*) *Jur:* to certify/to attest; **certifier une signature,** to witness/to authenticate a signature; **chèque certifié,** certified cheque; **copie certifiée (conforme),** attested copy/certified (true) copy (*b*) **certifier une caution,** to guarantee a surety (*c*) **chiffres (non) certifiés,** (un)audited figures.

cessation, *n.f.* stoppage; termination; **cessation d'un contrat,** termination of a contract; **cessation de paiements,** insolvency; *Jur:* **clause de cessation,** cesser clause; **être en état de cessation de paiements,** to be insolvent/to be in a state of insolvency; **cessation de travail/des activités,** stoppage (of work).

cessibilité, *n.f. Jur:* transferability/assignability (of estate, etc.); negotiability (of pension).

cessible, *a. Jur:* transferable/assignable (*traite, etc.*) negotiable; (*billet*) **non cessible,** not transferable.

cession, *n.f. Jur:* cession/transfer/assignment; **(acte de) cession,** deed of transfer/of assignment; conveyance; **prix de cession**

transfer price; **rédaction d'actes de cession,** conveyancing; **cession de bail,** leaseback/ transference of lease; **cession de biens,** assignment of property (to creditors); **cession d'une créance,** transfer of a debt; **cession en pleine propriété/en usufruit,** renunciation; *Fin:* **cession de parts,** stock transfer; **cession de parts en blanc,** blank transfer.

cession-bail, *n.f.* lease-back/transference of lease.

cessionnaire, 1. *n.m.* transferee/assignee; holder (of bill); *Jur:* cessionary **2.** *a. Jur:* cessionary.

chaîne, *n.f.* **1. chaîne de fabrication,** production line; **chaîne de montage,** assembly line; **chaîne de vente à domicile,** = pyramid selling; **travail à la chaîne,** assembly line work/production line work; **travailler à la chaîne,** to work on an assembly line/on a production line **2. chaîne de magasins/de restaurants/etc.,** chain of stores/restaurants/etc.

chalandage, *n.m.* shopping.

chambre, *n.f.* (*a*) **chambre froide/frigorifique,** cold (storage) room/cold store (*b*) **travailler en chambre,** to work at home (*c*) **Chambre de commerce,** Chamber of Commerce; **Chambre des métiers,** Chamber of Trade; *Fin:* **chambre de compensation/de clearing,** clearing house; **chambre syndicale,** employers' federation; **chambre syndicale des agents de change,** stock exchange committee.

change, *n.m. Fin:* **agent de change,** (*i*) stockbroker (*ii*) exchange broker/dealer; **bureau de change,** bureau de change; **contrôle des changes,** exchange control/ currency control; **cote des changes,** exchange list; **change du dollar,** dollar exchange; **cours/taux du change,** rate of exchange/(foreign) exchange rate; **lettre de change,** bill of exchange; **marché des changes,** foreign exchange market; **opération de change,** foreign exchange transaction; **négociations de change à terme/au comptant,** forward/spot exchange deal-

ings; **prix du change,** exchange premium; agio.

changement, *n.m.* change/alteration; **chagement d'hypothèque,** transfer of mortgage.

changer, *v.tr.* to change; to exchange; **changer un billet de banque,** to change a (bank)note; **changer des dollars contre des francs/en francs,** to change dollars into francs.

changeur, *n.m.* (*a*) (*pers.*) money changer (*b*) **changeur de monnaies,** change machine.

chantier, *n.m.* yard/depot/site; **chantier (de construction),** building site; *Nau:* **chantier de construction navale/chantier naval,** shipyard.

charge, *n.f.* **1.** (*d'un véhicule, etc.*) load/ cargo; capacity; **charge admise/limite,** load limit/*Av:* commercial load; **charge d'un camion/charge complète,** lorry load/ *NAm:* truck load; **charge maximale,** maximum load; **charge normale,** normal load/capacity; **charge par essieu,** axle load; **charge utile,** (*i*) (load-)carrying capacity (*ii*) pay-load/commercial load; *Av:* **charge en vol,** flight load; *Nau:* **charge d'un navire,** shipload; **ligne de charge,** load-line/plimsoll line; **navire de charge,** freighter; **navire en charge,** ship being loaded/ship loading; **prendre charge,** to load (up)/to take in cargo; **rompre charge,** (*i*) to unload cargo (*ii*) to transfer cargo/to transship **2.** (*a*) charge/ responsibility; **prendre en charge,** to take over/to be in charge (*b*) office; **charge d'avoué,** solicitor's practice **3.** charge/ expense; (*impôt*) tax; **cahier des charges,** (*i*) (contract) specifications (*ii*) articles and conditions (of sale, etc.); *Ind:* **charges d'exploitation,** working expenses/running costs; **charge d'une dette,** debt servicing/ *NAm:* debt service; **charges de fonctionnement,** bank charges; **charges financières,** financial expenses; **charges fiscales,** tax (burden); **charges sociales,** National Insurance contributions/social charges (*paid by employer*); **livre des charges,** cost book; **le loyer plus les charges,** rent plus service charge; **les frais de transport sont à notre charge,** the cost of transport is borne by us/payable by us/chargeable to us; **les réparations sont à la charge du locataire,** the repairs are to be paid for by the tenant; **personne à charge,** dependent.

chargé, 1. *a.* (*a*) loaded/laden (*b*) *Post:* **lettre chargée/paquet chargé** = registered letter/parcel (*c*) responsible (for) **2.** *n.* **chargé de budget/chargé de comptes/ chargé d'affaires,** account executive.

chargement, *n.m.* **1.** (*a*) loading(-up) (of lorry, etc.); shipping/loading (of cargo); **navire en chargement,** ship being loaded (*b*) *Post:* registration (of letter, parcel) **2.** (*a*) load/consignment/cargo/freight; **chargement complet,** full load; **chargement réglementaire,** regulation load; *Nau:* **prendre chargement,** to take on cargo (*b*) *Post:* registered letter/ parcel.

charger, *v.tr.* (*a*) to load (up)/to fill (a lorry, a truck, a ship); **charger des marchandises sur un train,** to load goods onto a train; **navire qui charge pour Londres,** ship taking in freight for London (*b*) **charger un compte,** to overcharge (on) an account.

chariot, *n.m.* (*au supermarché*) trolley.

charte, *n.f.* charter; **compagnie à charte,** chartered company.

charte-partie, *n.f. Nau:* charter party.

charter, *n.m.* charter plane; **(vol) charter,** charter flight.

chartiste, *n.m.f. Econ:* chartist.

chasser, *v.tr.* **chasser le découvert,** to raid the bears.

chasseur, *n.m.* **chasseur de têtes,** head hunter.

chef, *n.m.* (*a*) **chef d'atelier,** shop foreman; **chef de bureau,** head clerk/chief clerk; office manager; **chef comptable,** chief accountant; **chef d'entreprise,** busi-

nessman; company manager; **chef d'équipe/de groupe,** team leader; **chef d'établissement,** works/plant manager; *Publ:* **chef de fabrication,** production manager; **chef(-)de(-)file,** leader; lead manager; **chef du personnel,** personnel/ staff manager; **chef de produit,** product manager; **chef de rayon (d'un magasin),** department manager; *Ind:* **chef de service,** department(al) manager; **chef des ventes,** sales manager; **ingénieur en chef,** chief engineer (*b*) **les chefs d'industrie,** the captains of industry (*c*) *Jur:* **chef d'accusation,** count of indictment; charge.

chemin, *n.m.* **1. chemin de fer,** railway/ *NAm:* railroad; **envoi par chemin de fer,** dispatch by rail **2.** *Cmptr:* **méthode du chemin critique,** critical path method (CPM).

chemise, *n.f.* **chemise (cartonnée),** folder/ cardboard file.

chèque, *n.m.* cheque/*NAm:* check; **chèque à ordre,** cheque to order; **carnet de chèques,** cheque book/*NAm:* check book; **chèque de £60,** cheque for £60; **chèque bancaire,** bank cheque; **chèque de banque,** banker's cheque/banker's draft; **chèque barré,** crossed cheque; **chèque en blanc,** blank cheque; **chèque de caisse,** credit voucher; **chèque visé/***FrC:* **certifié,** marked cheque/certified cheque; **chèque ouvert/non barré,** open/uncrossed cheque; **chèque périmé,** out of date cheque; **chèque au porteur,** cheque made payable to bearer/bearer cheque; **chèque postal,** post office cheque; **chèque postdaté,** post-dated cheque; **chèque prescrit,** stale cheque; **chèque sans provision/***F:* **chèque en bois,** unpaid cheque/dud cheque; **il a payé avec un chèque sans provision,** he paid with a cheque that bounced; **chèque de voyage,** traveller's cheque; **service de chèques postaux** = National Girobank; **émettre/faire un chèque,** to write a cheque; **encaisser/ toucher un chèque,** to cash a cheque; **établir/libeller un chèque à l'ordre de ...** to make a cheque out to ...; **faire opposition au paiement d'un chèque,** to stop a cheque; **payer/régler par chèque,** to pay b cheque; **refuser d'honorer un chèque,** to refer a cheque to drawer; **remettre/déposer un chèque à la banque,** to pay a cheque into the bank.

chèque-cadeau, *n.m.* gift cheque/gift token.

chèque-dividende, *n.m.* *Fin:* dividend warrant.

chèque-repas, *n.m.,* **chèque-restaurant,** *n.m.* luncheon voucher.

chéquier, *n.m.* cheque book/*NAm:* check book.

cher, 1. *a.* (*a*) dear/expensive/high-priced/costly; **une voiture chère,** an expensive car; **indemnité de vie chère,** cost-of-living allowance; **ce magasin est trop cher,** this shop is too expensive/this shop charges too much; **c'est trop cher pour moi,** I can't afford it; **un hôtel pas cher,** a reasonably priced/an inexpensive/a cheap hotel (*b*) *Corr:* **Cher Monsieur,** Dear Mr X **2.** *adv.* ça s'est vendu cher, it reached/fetched a very high price; **ça ne vaut pas cher,** it's not worth much; **vendre moins cher (que les autres),** to undercut (others); *F:* **je l'ai acheté pas cher,** I got it cheap.

cherté, *n.f.* **la cherté de la vie,** the high cost of living; **indemnité de cherté de vie,** cost-of-living allowance.

chevalier, *n.m.* (*dans une OPA*) **chevalier blanc/noir,** white/black knight.

chiffre *n.m.* (*a*) figure/number/numeral/digit; **en chiffres ronds,** in round figures; **calculatrice avec (un) affichage de huit chiffres,** calculator with an eight-digit display (*b*) amount/total; **les dépenses de la société atteignent un chiffre de 4 millions (de francs),** the company's spending reaches a figure of/amounts to 4 million (francs); **chiffre d'affaires,** turnover/*NAm:* sales figures/revenue; **la société a un chiffre d'affaires d'un million de francs,** the company has a turnover of a million francs.

chiffrier, *n.m.* counter cash-book.

chirographaire, *a.* *Jur:* depending on a simple contract; **créance chirographaire,** unsecured debt; **créancier chirographaire,** unsecured creditor/simple-contract creditor; **obligation chirographaire,** simple debenture.

choix, *n.m.* (*a*) choice/selection; **ce magasin a un très grand choix de chaussures,** this shop has a good selection/a wide range of shoes; **au choix de l'acheteur,** at the buyer's option (*b*) **article de choix,** choice article; **de tout premier choix,** (of the) best quality/first-class/high-grade (*c*) **au choix** = all at the same price.

chômage, *n.m.* unemployment; **au chômage,** out of work; **être/s'inscrire au chômage,** to be/to go on the dole; **allocation/indemnité de chômage,** unemployment benefit/*F:* dole; **caisse de chômage,** unemployment fund; **chômage conjoncturel,** cyclical unemployment; **chômage de longue durée,** long-term unemployment; **chômage déguisé,** concealed/disguised unemployment; **chômage résiduel/de mobilité,** frictional unemployment; **chômage saisonnier,** seasonal unemployment; **chômage structurel/classique,** structural unemployment; **chômage technique,** lay off; **être en chômage technique,** to have been laid off; **être en chômage partiel,** to work short time/to be on short time/to be on short-time working.

chômer, *v.i.* to be unemployed; **les usines chôment,** the works are at a standstill; **laisser chômer son argent,** to let one's money lie idle.

chômeur, -euse, *n.* unemployed; **les chômeurs,** the unemployed; **chômeurs de longue durée,** long-term unemployed; **chômeur partiel,** short-time worker.

chute, *n.f.* **chute des prix,** (heavy) fall/drop in prices; **chute des cours en spirale,** tailspin; **chute des ventes,** fall-off in sales.

chuter, *v.i.* **faire chuter les cours,** to cause a heavy fall in prices.

cible, *n.f.* target; objective; **détermination de la cible,** target setting; **société-cible,** target company.

cibler, *v.tr.* to target at (a market, etc).

ci-contre, *adv. Book-k:* **porté ci-contre,** as per contra.

ci-inclus, *a. Corr:* **la copie ci-incluse,** the enclosed copy; **(vous trouverez) ci-inclus copie de sa lettre,** (please find) herewith/enclosed a copy of his letter.

ci-joint, *a.* attached/herewith/hereto (annexed); **les pièces ci-jointes,** the enclosed/attached documents; **veuillez trouver ci-joint mon chèque,** please find cheque enclosed.

circonscription, *n.f.* district; constituency; **circonscription électorale,** electoral district; ward; constituency.

circuit, *n.m.* circuit; **les circuits commerciaux,** commercial/trading/marketing channels; **circuit de distribution,** distribution/marketing network; chain of distribution.

circulaire, 1. *a.* circular (letter, etc.); **billet circulaire,** (*i*) circular note (*ii*) *Trans:* return/*NAm:* round-trip ticket **2.** *n.f.* circular (letter); memorandum.

circulant, *a. Fin:* **billets circulants,** (bank)notes in circulation; **capitaux circulants,** working capital/circulating capital.

circulation, *n.f.* (*a*) circulation; **mettre un livre en circulation,** to put a book into circulation; **libre circulation des marchandises,** free movement of goods (*b*) *Fin:* **circulation monétaire,** money in circulation (*c*) **actions ordinaires en circulation,** common shares outstanding.

circuler, *v.i.* (*argent*) to be in circulation; **faire circuler des effets,** to keep bills afloat.

citoyen, *n.m.*, **citoyenne,** *n.f.* citizen.

civil, *a.* civil; **année civile,** calendar year; **droit civil,** civil law; **état civil,** civil status; **assurance responsabilité civile,** public liability insurance; **génie civil,** civil engineering.

civique, *a.* civic; **droits civiques,** civic rights.

clair, *a.* **profit tout clair,** clear profit.

classe, *n.f.* (*a*) class/division/category/order; *Adm: etc:* rank; grade; **produits de première classe,** top quality goods; **hôtel de première classe,** first class hotel (*b*) **classe de revenu,** income bracket (*c*) *Rail:* **compartiment de première classe,** first class compartment; *Av:* **classe affaires,** club class; **classe économique,** economy class; **classe touriste,** tourist class.

classement, *n.m.* (*a*) classification (*b*) filing (of documents).

classer, *v.tr.* (*a*) to class/to classify/to rate; *Fin:* **valeurs classées,** investment stock (*b*) to file (documents).

classeur, *n.m.* loose-leaf file; jacket-file; filing cabinet; **classeur à fiches,** card-index file; **tiroir classeur,** filing drawer; *Adm:* **classeur des entrées et sorties,** tally file.

classification, *n.f.* classification/classifying; **classification de fonctions,** job classification; **classification des impôts locaux,** rating.

clause, *n.f. Jur:* clause; **clause additionnelle,** additional clause; rider; **clause compromissoire,** arbitration clause; **clauses d'un contract,** terms of a contract; **clause échappatoire,** escape clause; **clauses de maintien de cours/clauses de vérité des prix,** fair price provisions; **clause pénale,** penalty clause; **clause résolutoire,** avoidance clause; **clause restrictive,** restrictive clause; **clause de sauvegarde,** saving clause; *Ins:* **clause de régularisation,** clause stating that insurance starts after payment of the first premium.

clavier, *n.m.* keyboard; *Cmptr:* **introduire (des données) par clavier,** to keyboard/to key in (data).

clé, *n.f.* = **clef.**

clearing, *n.m. Fin:* (*a*) clearing house (*b*)

clearing; **accord de clearing,** clearing agreement; **banque de clearing,** clearing bank.

clef, *n.f.* (*a*) key; **industrie clef,** key industry; **poste clef,** key post (*b*) **prix clefs en mains,** all-inclusive price; **(projet de bâtiment) livré clef(s) en main(s),** turnkey operation/project/contract.

client, -ente, *n.* customer/client; **client mystère,** mystery shopper; **client régulier,** regular customer/patron; **comptes clients,** receivables.

clientèle, *n.f.* (*i*) custom (*ii*) customers; **attirer la clientèle,** to attract custom; **clientèle de passage,** irregular customers; passing trade; **service à la clientèle,** customer service; **avoir une grosse clientèle,** to have a large clientele/a lot of customers; **accorder sa clientèle à ...,** to patronize ....

clos, *a.* **exercice clos le 31 déc. 1980,** year ended 31 Dec. 1980.

clôture, *n.f.* (*a*) *StExch:* close; **cours/prix de clôture,** closing price/price at the finish; (*prix*) **être ferme en clôture,** to close firm; **opérations de clôture,** late trading/ trading at the finish (*b*) closing (of account); making up/balancing (of books).

clôturer, 1. *v.tr.* to close (accounts, etc.); *Jur:* **clôturer une faillite,** to close a bankruptcy **2.** *v.i.* **le dollar a clôturé à 11,35F,** the dollar closed at 11.35F.

coacquéreur, *n.m.* joint purchaser.

coacquisition, *n.f.* joint purchase.

coadministrateur, -trice *n.* co-director; *Jur:* co-trustee.

coassocié, -ée, *n.* copartner/joint partner.

coassurance, *n.f.* mutual assurance; joint insurance/coinsurance.

cocher, *v.tr.* to tick/*NAm:* to check; (*sur un formulaire*) **cocher la case correspondante,** tick/check the appropriate box.

cocontractant, -ante, *a. & n. Jur:* contracting (partner).

code, *n.m.* code; **code (à) barres,** bar code; **code de commerce,** commercial law; **code personnel,** (*pour carte barcaire*) personal identification number/PIN; **code postal,** postcode/*NAm:* zip code.

code-barre, *n.m.* bar code.

codébiteur, -trice, *n. Jur:* joint debtor.

codétenteur, -trice, *n. Jur:* joint holder.

codirecteur, -trice, *n.* co-director; joint manager.

codirection, *n.f.* joint directorship; joint management.

coefficient, *n.m.* coefficient/factor; **coefficient d'activité,** activity ratio; **coefficient beta,** relative strength; **coefficient de capital,** output ratio; **coefficient de capitalisation des résultats,** price-earnings ratio; **coefficient d'exploitation,** working coefficient/operating ratio; **coefficient de liquidité,** liquidity ratio/ratio of liquid assets to current liabilities; **coefficient saisonnier,** seasonal index; **coefficient de solvabilité,** solvency coefficient; **coefficient de trésorerie,** cash ratio.

coentrepreneur, *n.m.* joint venturer.

coentreprise, *n.f.* joint venture.

coffre, *n.m. Bank:* safe-deposit box.

coffre-fort, *n.m.* safe; **dépôt en coffre-fort,** safe deposit.

cofinancement, *n.m.* joint venture.

cofinancer, *v.tr.* to finance jointly.

cogérance, *n.f.* joint management; coadministration.

cogérant, -ante, *n.* joint manager/ manageress; co-administrator.

cogérer, *v.tr.* to manage jointly.

cogestion, *n.f.* joint management.

cogniticien, -ienne, *n.* knowledge engineer.

colicitant, -ante, *n.m. Jur:* co-vendor.

col, *n.m.* **col blanc,** white collar worker; **col bleu,** blue collar worker; **col doré,** gold collar worker.

colis, *n.m.* parcel/package; **(envoyer qch.) par colis postal,** (to send sth.) by parcel post.

collecte, *n.f.* **collecte de fonds,** fund raising.

collecter, *v.i.* to raise funds.

collectif, *a.* collective/joint (action, report, etc.); **billet collectif,** group ticket; **contrat collectif,** collective contract; **décision collective,** joint/group decision; **convention collective,** collective bargaining agreement; **propriété collective,** collective ownership; **signature collective,** joint signature.

collectivisme, *n.m.* collectivism.

collectivité, *n.f.* group; organization; **collectivités locales,** local communities.

colocataire, *n.m.f.* joint tenant/cotenant.

colonne, *n.f.* column (of figures, etc.); **colonne créditrice,** credit column; **colonne débitrice,** debit column.

combler, *v.tr.* to make up/to make good (a loss); to bridge a gap.

comestible, **1.** **aliments/denrées comestibles,** consumable goods **2.** *n.m.* **les comestibles,** consumables.

comité, *n.m.* committee/board; **comité consultatif,** advisory board/commission; **comité de direction,** board of directors/executive board; **comité d'entreprise,** works council; **comité de restructuration,** steering committee.

commande, *n.f.* order; **bon/bulletin de commande,** order form; **commandes en attente,** backlog of orders; **commande téléphonique/par téléphone,** (tele)phone order; **commande(s) par ordinateur** (*i*) teleorder(s) (*ii*) teleordering; **commandes par quantités,** bulk orders; **commande renouvelée,** repeat order; **conformément à**

votre commande, as per (your) order; **commande pour l'exportation,** export order; **commande passée par un acheteur étranger (à un exportateur),** indent; **carnet de commandes,** order book; **exécuter une commande,** to fill an order; **faire/passer une commande (de qch.) au fabricant,** to place an order (for sth.) with the manufacturer/to order (sth.) from the manufacturer; **passer une commande de qch. à qn,** to indent on s.o. for sth.; **fait sur commande,** made to order; customized; **payable à la commande,** cash with order; **livrer une commande,** to deliver an order.

commander, *v.tr.* to order (goods, etc.); **commander qch. chez un fournisseur,** to order sth. from a supplier/a stockist; **commander qch. par téléphone,** to order sth. by telephone/to (tele)phone an order; **commander par ordinateur,** to teleorder; (*au café, etc.*) **il a commandé une bière,** he ordered a beer.

commanditaire, **1.** *a. & n.m.* **(associé) commanditaire,** limited partner **2.** *n.m. Mkt:* sponsor.

commandite, *n.f.* (*a*) **(société en) commandite simple,** limited partnership; **commandite par actions,** partnership limited by shares (*b*) interest of capital invested by sleeping partner(s).

commandité, -ée *a. & n.* **(associé) commandité,** active partner.

commanditer, *v.tr.* (*a*) to subscribe capital to/to finance (a firm, etc.) (as a limited partner) (*b*) *Mkt:* to sponsor.

commerçant, **1.** *a.* commercial/business (district, etc.); **rue commerçante,** shopping street; **ville commerçante,** trading town **2.** *n.* tradesman; shopkeeper; merchant dealer; **commerçant en détail,** retailer **commerçant en gros,** wholesaler; **petit commerçant,** small trader/shopkeeper; **être commerçant,** to be a shopkeeper/to be in trade; **les commerçants,** tradespeople.

commerce, *n.m.* (*a*) commerce/trade; **le commerce,** (*i*) trade (*ii*) the commercial world; **le petit commerce,** (*i*) smal traders (*ii*) shopkeeping; **être dans le commerce,** to be in trade; **Chambre de commerce,** Chamber of Commerce; **Ministère du Commerce et de l'Industrie,** Board of Trade; *NAm:* Department of Commerce; **commerce de biens,** visible trade; **commerce de services,** invisible trade; **commerce de détail/en gros,** retail/wholesale trade; **commerce extérieur,** foreign trade; **commerce intérieur,** home market; **effet de commerce,** bill of exchange; commercial paper; **hors commerce,** not for retail sale/not for general sale/not on sale to the general public; **livres de commerce,** account books; **registre de commerce,** trade/commercial register; **représentant/voyageur de commerce,** (sales) representative/*F:* rep (*b*) business; **commerce à céder,** shop/business for sale; **fonds de commerce,** business/goodwill; **maison de commerce,** firm; **tenir un commerce,** to run a business; **vendre un fonds de commerce,** to sell a business (as a going concern).

commercer, *v.i.* to trade/to deal (**avec,** with).

commercial, *a.* commercial; **attaché commercial,** commercial attaché; **balance commerciale,** trade balance; **animateur/cadre commercial,** sales/marketing executive; **centre commercial,** shopping centre; **délégué commercial,** sales representative/*F:* rep; **directeur commercial,** sales manager/marketing manager; **direction commerciale,** sales management; **droit commercial,** commercial law; **effet commercial,** commercial paper; **nom commercial,** trade name; name of a shop; **service commercial,** sales department; **stratégie commerciale,** marketing strategy; **tendances commerciales,** trade trends; **usages commerciaux,** trade practices.

commercialement, *adv.* commercially.

commercialisation, *n.f.* (*a*) commercialization (*b*) marketing; **accord de commercialisation,** marketing agreement;

délai de commercialisation, launching period (of a product).

commercialiser, *v.tr.* (*a*) *Fin:* to negotiate (a bill) (*b*) to commercialize; **produit non encore commercialisé,** product not yet on sale to the public/not yet marketed/not yet on the market.

commettant, *n.m. Jur:* principal (to a deal)/actual purchaser/actual vendor (*when represented by agent*); **commettant et mandataire,** principal and agent.

commis, *n.m.* (*a*) clerk; *StExch:* floor trader; **commis aux écritures,** accounting clerk/accounts clerk; **commis d'agent de change,** stockbroker's clerk; **commis principal/premier commis,** head/chief clerk (*b*) **2.** (*dans un magasin*) sales assistant/shop assistant; salesman/*NAm:* sales clerk.

commissaire, *n.m.* **commissaire aux comptes,** auditor.

commissaire-priseur, *n.m.* (*a*) appraiser/valuer (*b*) auctioneer.

commissariat, *n.m.* **commissariat des comptes,** auditorship.

commission, *n.m.* **1.** (*a*) commission; factorage; brokerage; **commission d'arrangement,** over-riding commission; **commission de bourse,** transaction costs; **commission de change,** agio; **commission de gestion,** agency fee; **commission de chef de file,** management fee (*b*) **il reçoit une commission de 5% sur chaque vente,** he gets (a) commission of 5% on each sale **2.** commission/order; **maison de commission,** (firm of) commission agents/commission agency; **courtier à la commission,** commission agent; **vente à la commission,** sale on commission **3. Commission d'enquête,** Board of Inquiry; **Commission des opérations de Bourse (COB),** = *US:* Securities and Exchange Commission (SEC).

commissionnaire, *n.m.* commission agent; **commissionnaire d'achat,** buyer; **commissionnaire en gros,** factor; *Fin:* **commissionnaire en banque,** outside broker; **commissionnaire en douane,** customs broker; **commissionnaire en gros,** factor;

commissionnaire expéditeur/de transport/ de roulage, forwarding agent/shipping agent/carrier; **commissionnaire exportateur,** export agent; **commissionnaire d'importation,** import agent.

commissionner, *v.tr.* (*a*) to commission; to appoint (s.o.) as buyer (on commission) (*b*) to order (goods).

commun, *a.* (*a*) common (to two or more); **fonds commun de placement,** investment fund; **le Marché Commun,** the Common Market; **faire bourse commune,** to share expenses; to pool resources (*b*) **tare commune,** average tare/mean tare (*c*) **créer une société en commun avec qn,** to start a company in partnership/jointly with s.o.; **mise en commun de fonds,** pooling of funds; **transports en commun,** public transport.

communauté, *n.f.* *Jur:* **communauté de biens,** joint estate; **la Communauté Économique Européenne (CEE),** the European Economic Community (EEC).

communication, *n.f.* (*a*) communication; **avoir communication d'un dossier,** to have access to a document; **demander communication des livres d'une société,** to demand access to the books of a company; **se mettre en communication avec qn,** to get in touch with s.o. (*b*) **réseau de communications,** communications network (*c*) **communication téléphonique,** (telephone) call; **communication interurbaine,** trunk call/*NAm:* long distance (call); **communication urbaine,** local call; **obtenir une communication par l'automatique,** to dial direct.

commutatif, *a.* *Jur:* commutative (contract, etc.).

compagnie, *n.f.* (*a*) company; **compagnie de navigation,** shipping company; **compagnie aérienne,** airline (*b*) **(la maison) Thomas et Compagnie** (*usu.* **et Cie**), (the firm of) Thomas and Company (*usu* & Co.).

compensable, *a.* payable; **chèque compensable à Paris,** cheque domiciled in Paris.

compensateur, *a.* compensatory; countervailing.

compensation *n.f.* compensation (for damages); clearing; offset; *Fin:* clearance (of cheques); **accord de compensation,** clearing agreement; **chambre de compensation,** clearing house; **compte de compensation,** clearing account; *StExch:* **cours de compensation,** making-up price.

compensatoire, *a.* compensatory; countervailing; **demande compensatoire,** counterclaim; *EEC:* **montant compensatoire monétaire,** monetary compensation amount.

compenser, *v.tr.* to compensate/to make up for (sth.)/to offset; **compenser une perte,** to make good a loss; *Fin:* **compenser un chèque,** to clear a cheque (*through a clearing house*).

compétence, *n.f.* competence/proficiency/ skill/ability; *Jur:* area of jurisdiction; **degré de compétence,** standard of efficiency; **compétence technique,** technical skill.

compétent, *a.* *Jur: etc:* competent (tribunal, authority, etc.); **commis compétent,** (*i*) competent clerk (*ii*) qualified clerk; **transmettre au service compétent,** to pass on to the department concerned.

compétitif, *a.* competitive; **prix compétitifs,** competitive prices.

compétition, *n.f.* competition.

compétitivité, *n.f.* competitiveness.

complaisance, *n.f.* **billet/effet/traite/ papier de complaisance,** accommodation bill.

complémentaire, *a.* (*a*) **pour renseignements complémentaires s'adresser à ...,** for further information apply to ... (*b*) *Book-k:* **écriture complémentaire,** supplementary entry.

complet, *a.* complete/whole/full; (*à l'hôtel*) **complet,** no vacancies; **rapport complet détaillé,** comprehensive report.

compléter, *v.tr.* **compléter un billet à ordre,** perfecting the sight.

complexe, *n.m.* **complexe industriel,** industrial complex/industrial estate.

comportement, *n.m.* behaviour; **comportement du consommateur,** consumer behaviour.

composé, *a.* *Fin:* **intérêts composés,** compound interest.

composer, **1.** *v.i.* to compound (**avec,** with); to make a composition (with creditors, etc.) **2.** *v.tr.* **composer un numéro (de téléphone),** to dial a (phone) number.

comprendre, *v.tr.* to comprise/to cover/to include; **service compris,** service (charge) included; **service non compris,** service not included/service extra; **six mille francs par mois tout compris,** six thousand francs a month (all) inclusive/all in; **y compris,** including.

compression, *n.f.* *Fin:* **compression des dépenses budgétaires/compressions budgétaires,** retrenchment; cuts in budgetary expenditure; **compression de personnel,** reduction of staff/staff cutbacks.

compromis, *n.m.* compromise/arrangement; **mettre une affaire en compromis,** to submit a matter to arbitration; **obtenir un compromis,** to compound (with creditors); *MIns:* **compromis d'avarie,** average bond.

compromissoire, *a.* *Jur:* **clause compromissoire,** arbitration clause (*in agreement*).

comptabiliser, *v.tr.* to account for (sth.)/to enter (sth.) in the accounts.

comptabilité, *n.f.* (*a*) book-keeping; accountancy; **comptabilité à/en partie double,** double-entry book-keeping; **comptabilité à/en partie simple,** single-entry book-keeping; **comptabilité analytique des coûts variables,** direct cost accounting; **comptabilité de coût de revient,** cost accounting; **comptabilité en coûts de remplacement/en coûts déflatés/en coûts réels,** current cost accounting;

comptabilité de gestion, management accounting; **comptabilité publique,** public accountancy; **commission de comptabilité,** audit committee; **livre de comptabilité,** account book; **tenir la comptabilité d'une maison,** to keep the books/the accounts of a firm; *Ind:* **comptabilité matières,** stock record/stores accounts; **(service de) la comptabilité,** accounts department; **chef de la comptabilité,** chief accountant.

comptable, **1.** *a.* accounting (work, etc.); **caisse comptable,** cash register; **machine comptable,** accounting machine; **méthode comptable,** accounting policies/method; **pièce comptable,** accountable receipt; voucher; **plan comptable,** accounting system; **quittance comptable,** formal receipt; **service(s) comptable(s),** accounts department; **valeur comptable,** book value **2.** *n.m.* accountant; **chef comptable,** chief accountant; **expert comptable/**FrC: **comptable agréé (CA),** (*i*) = chartered accountant (CA)/NAm: certified public accountant (*ii*) auditor; **comptable agréé** = certified accountant; **vérificateur comptable,** auditor.

comptant, **1.** *a.* **argent comptant,** ready money/cash; **payer cent francs comptant(s),** to pay a hundred francs cash (down)/in cash **2.** *adv.* **payer comptant,** to pay (in) cash/in ready money **3.** *n.m.* **acheter qch. (au) comptant,** to buy sth. for cash/to pay cash for sth.; **marché/opération au comptant,** cash transaction; **payable (au) comptant,** (*i*) cash terms (*ii*) payable on presentation; **paiement (au) comptant,** cash payment; **prix (au) comptant,** cash price; **valeurs au comptant,** securities dealt in for cash; **le marché du comptant,** spot market; **livraison au comptant,** spot delivery; **prix du comptant,** cash/spot price; **vente au comptant contre rachat à terme,** put and take.

compte, *n.m.* (*a*) reckoning/calculation; **faire le compte des dépenses,** to add up/to reckon (up)/to work out expenses; **le compte y est,** the total/the amount is correct; **compte rond,** round sum/even money; **acheter qch. à bon compte,** to buy sth. cheap (*b*) account; **compte d'achats,**

purchase account; **compte (de) caisse,** cash account; **compte de capital,** capital account; **comptes de clôture,** annual accounts; **compte de contrepartie,** contra account; **compte créditeur,** credit account; **compte débiteur,** debit account; **compte d'actif/comptes clients,** accounts receivable/*NAm:* receivables; **compte bloqué,** frozen account/*NAm:* escrow account; **compte de passif/comptes fournisseurs,** accounts payable/*NAm:* payables; **compte des dépenses et recettes,** income and expenditure account; **compte détaillé,** detailed/itemized account; **compte d'exploitation,** trading account/ *NAm:* operating account; **compte de pertes et profits,** appropriation account; **compte de résultat,** profit and loss account; **comptes semestriels/trimestriels,** interim accounts; **livres de comptes,** account books; **arrêter un compte,** to close an account; **vérifier les comptes d'une société,** to audit the books of a company; **faire ses comptes,** to do one's accounts; (*dans un magasin*) to do the till/to cash up (*c*) **compte crédit/ compte d'abonnement,** budget account; **compte permanent** = credit account/ *NAm:* charge account; **compte client,** customer account; **être en compte avec qn,** to have an account with s.o.; **(se faire) ouvrir un compte chez qn,** to open an account with s.o.; **payer/régler un compte,** to pay a bill; to settle an account; **passer une somme en compte/mettre qch. sur le compte de qn,** to enter sth./to put sth. down to s.o.'s account; **mettez-le/ inscrivez-le à mon compte,** charge it to my account; **publié à compte d'auteur,** published at the author's (own) expense; **la Cour des comptes** = Audit Office (*d*) **être/travailler à son compte,** to work for oneself/to have one's own business; **s'installer/prendre/se mettre à son compte,** to set up in business on one's own account (*e*) *Bank:* **compte à découvert,** overdrawn account; **compte de dépôt à vue,** demand deposit; drawing account; **compte bancaire/compte en banque,** bank account/ *NAm:* banking account; **compte courant,** current account; **compte courant postal/ compte chèque postal (CCP)** =

(National) Girobank account; **compte (de caisse) d'épargne/compte sur livret,** savings account; **compte de dépôt/compte rémunéré/compte à terme,** deposit account; **compte (de) chèques (CC),** (personal) cheque account/*NAm:* checking account; **compte de prêt/d'avances,** loan account; **compte (con)joint,** joint account; **compte étranger,** foreign account; **compte numéroté,** numbered account; **compte personnel/compte propre,** personal account; **compte professionnel/commercial,** office/ business account; **numéro de compte,** account number; **relevé de compte,** bank statement; statement (of account); **se faire ouvrir un compte en banque,** to open a bank account; **titulaire d'un compte,** account holder; **verser de l'argent à son compte/alimenter son compte/faire créditer son compte d'une somme,** to pay money into one's account (*f*) fund; **compte du Trésor Public,** consolidated fund; **compte sous mandat de gestion,** discretionary fund.

compter, 1. *v.tr.* (*a*) to count (up)/to reckon (up) (numbers, etc.); to add up; **mal compter,** to miscount 2. *prep.phr.* **à compter de ...,** (reckoning) from ...; **à compter du 1ᵉʳ janvier,** as from January 1st/starting from January 1st (*b*) to charge; **je vous compterai cent francs pour cet article,** I'll charge you a hundred francs for this article.

comptoir, *n.m.* 1. counter 2. (*en Extrême-Orient*) go-down 3. *Fin:* (*a*) bank; **comptoir d'escompte,** discount house (*b*) branch (of bank).

comptoir-caisse, *n.m.* pay desk/cash desk.

concentration, *n.f.* concentration; integration (of enterprises); merger.

concepteur, *n.m.* (project) designer; **concepteur rédacteur,** copywriter.

conception, *n.f.* design; **conception de(s) produit(s),** product design; **conception assistée par ordinateur,** computer aided design; **étude de conception,** design engineering.

concerner, *v.tr.* **en/pour ce qui concerne ...** as regards .../with regard to .../in respect of .../in relation to ....

concessible, *a.* concessible.

concession, *n.f.* concession; **concession exclusive et réciproque**, tied outlet.

concessionnaire, **1.** *a.* concessionary (company, etc.) **2.** *n.m.* (*a*) concessionaire/concessionary/licence-holder (*b*) dealer/agent; **consultez votre concessionnaire le plus proche**, see your nearest dealer.

conclure, *v.tr.* to conclude (an agreement); **conclure un marché/une affaire**, to make a deal; to settle a deal; to close the sale; **conclure un accord/un arrangement**, to strike a deal/to strike an agreement/to cut a deal (with s.o.).

concordat, *n.m.* (bankrupt's) certificate; **concordat préventif (à la faillite)**, (*i*) scheme of composition (*ii*) composition/legal settlement (*between businessmen and creditors*).

concordataire, *a.* **failli concordataire**, certificated (bankrupt); **procédure concordataire**, composition proceedings.

concurrence, *n.f.* competition; **capacité de concurrence**, competitive power/rivalry; **concurrence acharnée**, cut-throat competition; **concurrence déloyale**, unfair competition; industrial sabotage; **concurrence pure et parfaite**, perfect/pure competition; **être/entrer en concurrence avec qn**, to compete with s.o.; **nos prix défient toute concurrence**, our prices are unbeatable/our prices are the lowest; **articles sans concurrence**, unrivalled goods.

concurrencer, *v.tr.* to compete with (s.o., sth.) (in trade, in the open market); **leur nouvelle gamme ne peut concurrencer la nôtre**, their new line can't compete with ours.

concurrent, *n.m.* competitor; rival (company); **analyse des concurrents**, competitor analysis.

concurrentiel, *a.* **prix concurrentiels**, competitive prices.

condition, *n.f.* (*a*) condition; stipulation; *pl.* terms; **condition à remplir/nécessaire/requise**, requirement; **conditions d'admission**, admission requirements; **conditions d'emploi**, conditions of employment; **conditions de faveur**, preferential terms; **conditions de paiement**, terms (of payment); **condition préalable**, pre-requisite; **condition(s) provisionnelle(s)**, proviso(s); **conditions d'un contrat**, terms/articles of a contract; **conditions d'une vente**, conditions of a sale; **faire de meilleures conditions**, to give s.o. better terms; **marchandises envoyées à condition**, goods sent on approval/*F:* on appro; **prêt à condition**, tied loan; **marchandises sous condition**, goods on sale or return; **offre sans condition**, unconditional offer; **signer qch. sans condition**, to sign sth. unconditionally/*F:* with no strings attached; **signer un engagement sous condition**, to sign an agreement conditionally/provisionally (*b*) **conditions de travail (dans une usine, etc.)**, working conditions (in a factory, etc.); **conditions de vie**, living conditions; **les conditions économiques (du marché)**, the economic situation.

conditionné, *a.* **viande conditionnée**, pre-pack(ag)ed meat.

conditionnel, *a.* conditional (sale); qualified (acceptance); **clause conditionnelle**, provisory clause; **offre conditionnelle**, conditional offer; **endos conditionnel**, qualified endorsement.

conditionnement, *n.m.* (*a*) package (*b*) packaging; **industries de conditionnement**, packaging industries.

conditionner, *v.tr.* to package; to pre-pack.

conditionneur, **-euse**, *n.* (*pers.*) packer.

confection, *n.f.* (ready-to-wear) clothing industry; **magasin de confection**, shop/store selling ready-to-wear clothes; **vêtements de confection**, off-the-peg clothes.

confectionner, *v.tr.* to manufacture (clothing, etc.); **confectionnés sur demande,** made up to order.

conférence, *n.f.* conference; meeting; **conférence de presse,** press conference; **il est en conférence,** he's in a meeting.

confidentiel, *a.* confidential; (*sur document, lettre, etc.*) private and confidential.

confirmation, *n.f.* confirmation (of a credit, a booking, a telephone message, etc.).

confisquer, *v.tr.* to confiscate, to seize (goods).

conflit, *n.m.* dispute; **conflits du travail,** industrial/labour disputes; **opinions en conflit,** conflicting opinions.

conforme, *a.* copie conforme (à l'original), true copy; **pour copie conforme,** certified true copy; **conforme à la demande,** as per order; **conforme à l'échantillon,** up to/true to sample; *Book-k:* **écriture conforme,** corresponding entry.

conformément, *adv.* in accordance/in compliance (**à,** with); as per; **conformément à votre demande du 13 courant,** in accordance with/as per your request of 13th inst.

conformité, *n.* certificat de conformité, clear report of findings.

confrère, *n.m.* colleague; fellow member (of association, profession, society, etc.).

congé, *n.m.* **1.** (*a*) leave (of absence); **congé de maladie,** sick leave; **congé de maternité,** maternity leave; **congé de paternité/de naissance,** paternity leave (*b*) holiday/*esp. NAm:* vacation; **congé annuel,** annual leave/annual holiday(s); **congé payé,** holiday with pay/paid leave; **congé sans solde,** unpaid leave/holiday; **être en congé,** to be on holiday; **prendre un congé d'une semaine,** to take a week off/a week's holiday; **un après-midi de congé,** an afternoon off **2.** (*a*) (notice of) dismissal; **donner (son) congé à qn,** to give s.o. notice/ to dismiss s.o.; **demander son congé,** to hand in one's resignation; to give in one's notice (*b*) **donner congé à un locataire,** to give a tenant notice to quit; **donner congé à son propriétaire,** to give one's landlord notice of leaving **3.** (*pour un apprenti*) recevoir son congé d'acquit, to take up one's indentures **4.** authorization/permit; **congé pour le transport des vins,** release of wine from bond.

congédiement, *n.m.* dismissal/sacking (of employee).

congédier, *v.tr.* to dismiss (employee); **congédier tout le personnel,** to dismiss/to sack the whole staff.

congelé, *a.* frozen; **produits congelés,** frozen foods.

conglomérat, *n.m.* conglomerate.

congrès, *n.m.* congress.

conjoint, *a.* joint; **compte conjoint,** joint account; **dette conjointe,** joint debt; **responsabilité conjointe,** joint liability.

conjointement, *adv.* jointly; **conjointement et solidairement,** jointly and severally.

conjoncture, *n.f. PolEc:* **conjoncture économique,** economic situation; **fluctuations de la conjoncture,** fluctuations in the market; **(période de) basse conjoncture,** slump; **haute conjoncture,** boom; **ralentissement de la conjoncture,** slowing down of economic activity.

conjoncturel, *a. PolEc:* cyclical (unemployment, fluctuations, etc.); **prévisions conjoncturelles,** economic prospects; **stratégie conjoncturelle,** economic strategy; **tendances conjoncturelles,** economic trends.

conjoncturiste, *n.m.f.* economic planner.

connaissement, *n.m. Nau:* bill of lading/shipping bill; **connaissement direct (avec rupture de charge),** through bill of lading (with transhipment).

connexe, *a.* related; allied.

conseil, *n.m.* **1.** (*a*) *Jur:* **avocat-conseil,** counsel (*b*) **ingénieur conseil,** consulting/consultant engineer; **cabinet d'ingénieur(s) conseil(s),** consultancy/firm of consultants; **conseil financier,** finance consultant/adviser; **conseil fiscal,** tax consultant; **conseil en gestion,** management consultant; **conseil en recrutement,** recruitment consultant **2.** council/committee/board; **conseil d'administration,** board of directors; **président du conseil d'administration,** chairman of the Board; **réunion du conseil d'administration,** board meeting; **salle de réunion du conseil d'administration,** boardroom; **la banque fait partie du conseil,** the bank is represented on the board; **conseil de surveillance,** board of trustees; **Conseil de l'aide économique mutuelle,** Council for mutual economic aid (COMECON); **Conseil national du crédit,** National credit council **3.** advice; **conseil en placement,** investment advice.

conseiller, -ère, *n.* counsellor/adviser/advisor; **conseiller de direction/de gestion,** management consultant; **conseiller économique,** economic adviser; **conseiller fiscal** = tax consultant; **conseiller juridique,** legal adviser; **conseiller en placements,** investment adviser; **conseiller technique,** technical adviser.

consentement, *n.m.* consent; **consentement exprès,** formal consent; **par consentement mutuel,** by mutual consent.

consentir, 1. *v.i.* to consent/to agree (**à**, to); **assurances sur la vie consenties par l'industrie automobile,** life assurances agreed (to) by the motor industry **2.** *v.tr.* **consentir un prêt,** to grant a loan; **consentir une remise à qn,** to allow a discount to s.o./to give s.o. a discount.

conservateur, *n.m.* **conservateur des hypothèques,** registrar of mortgages.

conserve, *n.f.* tinned/canned food.

conserverie, *n.f.* canning industry.

considération, *n.f. Corr:* **veuillez agréer** l'assurance de ma haute considération, yours faithfully.

consignataire, *n.m.f.* (*a*) *Jur:* depository; trustee (*b*) consignee.

consignateur, -trice, *n.* consignor/shipper.

consignation, *n.f.* **1.** lodging/deposit (of money) **2.** consignment (of goods); **envoyer qch. à qn en consignation,** to consign sth. to s.o./to send sth. to s.o. on consignment; **marchandises en consignation,** goods on consignment; **facture de consignation,** consignment invoice.

consigne, *n.f.* (*a*) **marchandises en consigne à la douane,** goods stopped/held up at the customs (*b*) left luggage (office); *NAm:* checkroom (*c*) deposit (on a bottle).

consigner, *v.tr.* (*a*) to deposit (money, etc.); **bouteille non consignée,** non-returnable bottle (*b*) **consigner sa valise,** to leave one's suitcase at the left luggage (office) (*c*) to consign (goods, etc.) (*d*) **marchandises consignées par la douane,** goods stopped/held up at the customs.

consolidation, *n.f.* (*a*) consolidation (of accounts, position, power, etc.) (*b*) *Fin:* financing/funding (of floating debt).

consolidé, *a. Fin:* **bénéfices nets consolidés,** net consolidated income/profit; **bilan consolidé,** consolidated account; consolidated balance-sheet; **chiffre d'affaires consolidé,** group turnover; **dette consolidée,** funded debt; **dette non consolidée,** floating debt; **les fonds consolidés/** *n.m.pl.* **les consolidés,** consolidated stock/annuities; consols.

consolider, *v.tr.* **1.** to consolidate (position, etc.) **2.** *Fin:* to fund/to finance (debt); to consolidate (accounts, rates).

consommable, *a.* consumable (goods).

consommaction, *n.f.* consumerism.

consommateur, -trice, *n.* (*a*) consumer; **consommateur cible,** target consumer; **producteurs et consommateurs,** producers and consumers; **(mouvement de) défense**

des consommateurs, consumerism (b) customer (in restaurant, etc.).

consommation, n.f. 1. consumption (of wheat, petrol); biens de (grande) consommation, (mass) consumer goods/products; Aut: consommation d'essence aux 100 kilomètres = petrol consumption (in miles per gallon); consommation mondiale, world consumption; concours de consommation, economy run; crédit à la consommation, consumer credit; dépenses de consommation, consumer spending; industrie de consommation, consumer industry; société de consommation, consumer society; Institut national de la consommation = Consumers' Association; indice des prix à la consommation, consumer price index 2. drink/snack (in café, bar).

consommatique, n.f. consumer research.

consommatisme, n.m. consumerism.

consommer, v.tr. to consume; cette voiture consomme environ 10 litres aux 100 km en parcour urbain = this car does about thirty miles to the gallon in town.

consommérisme, n.m. consumerism.

consomptible, a. consumable (goods).

consortial, a. relating to a consortium; crédit consortial, syndicated credit.

consortium, n.m. consortium; syndicate.

constant, a. francs/dollars constants, constant francs/dollars.

constat, n.m. Jur: constat à l'amiable, agreed statement of facts (on motor vehicle accident)/accident statement.

constaté, a. Fin: valeur constatée, registered value.

constitué, a. corps constitué, corporate body.

constituer, v.tr. to set up (committee, etc.); to form/to incorporate (a company).

constitutif, a. constitutive/conferring a

right; titres constitutifs (d'une propriété), title deeds.

constitution, n.f. constitution/establishing; constitution d'une société, incorporation of a company; acte de constitution (d'une société), instrument/articles of incorporation; memorandum of association; constitution du capital social, capital clause; frais de constitution (d'une société), preliminary expenses (in promoting a company); constitution d'un comité, setting up of a committee.

constructeur-promoteur, n.m. property developer.

consultant, -ante, n. consultant.

consultatif, a. consultative/advisory/consulting (committee, board, document, etc.); avoir une voix consultative, to be present in an advisory (but non-voting) capacity; à titre consultatif, in an advisory capacity.

container, n.m. = conteneur.

conteneur, n.m. Trans: container; transports maritimes par conteneurs, container shipping.

conteneurisation, n.f. Trans: containerization.

conteneuriser, v.tr. Trans: to containerize; to put into containers.

contenir, v.tr. (a) to contain; to hold (b) to control; contenir l'inflation, to check inflation.

contentieux, n.m. bureau/service du contentieux, legal department (of bank, company, etc.); disputed claims office; chef du contentieux, (company's) solicitor; les contentieux en cours, the claim being disputed.

contenu, n.m. content(s) (of parcel, bottle, etc.); le contenu de sa lettre, the subject matter/the content of his letter.

contingent, n.m. quota; contingent

(d'exportation, d'importation), (export, import) quotas.

contingentement, *n.m. Adm:* (*i*) quota system of distribution (*ii*) apportioning/fixing of quotas.

contingenter, *v.tr. Adm:* to establish/to fix quotas for (imports, etc.).

contractant, *Jur:* **1.** *a.* contracting (party) **2.** *n.m.* contracting party.

contracter, *v.tr.* (*a*) to incur/to contract (debt) (*b*) **contracter une assurance,** to take out an insurance policy; **contracter un emprunt,** to contract a loan.

contractuel, *a. Jur:* contractual (obligation, etc.); **action contractuelle,** action for breach of contract; **date contractuelle,** contract date/date of agreement; **main-d'œuvre contractuelle,** contractual labour; **droits contractuels,** rights granted by contract.

contrat, *n.m.* (*a*) contract/agreement; deed; **contrat d'assurance,** (*i*) contract of insurance (*ii*) insurance policy; **contrat collectif,** collective agreement/group contract; **contrat de location,** hiring/leasing agreement; **contrat de productivité,** productivity deal; **contrat de société,** deed/articles of partnership; **contrat de travail,** contract of employment/*NAm:* labor contract; **contrat de vente,** bill of sale/(sales) agreement; **contrat translatif de propriété,** conveyance; **rupture de contrat,** breach of contract; **lié par contrat,** bound by contract/under contract; **passer un contrat (avec qn)/s'engager par contrat,** to enter into/to conclude an agreement (with s.o.); **rédiger/dresser un contrat,** to draw up a contract; **résilier un contrat,** to annul/to terminate/to cancel a contract; **signer un contrat,** to sign a contract (*b*) *Fin: StExch:* **contrats à terme,** futures; **contrats à terme d'instruments financiers (CATIF),** financial futures; **contrat à terme de gré à gré,** forward contract.

contre, *prép.* **le franc est faible contre les autres devises,** the franc is weak against the other currencies.

contre-analyse, *n.f.* check analysis.

contre-assurance, *n.f.* reinsurance.

contre-attaque, *n.f.* countermove.

contrebalancer, *v.tr.* to counter-balance/to offset.

contrebande, *n.f.* **marchandises de contrebande,** smuggled goods.

contre-écriture, *n.f. Book-k:* contra-entry.

contre-épreuve, *n.f.* cross-check.

contre-expertise, *n.f.* re-survey/counter-valuation.

contrefaçon, *n.f.* **1.** counterfeiting; fraudulently copying or imitating (trademark, etc.); infringement (of patent, copyright)/*F:* piracy; **procès en contrefaçon,** action for infringement (of copyright, etc.) **2.** forgery/fraudulent imitation; pirated edition of book.

contrefaire, *v.tr.* to forge/to falsify.

contremaître, -tresse, *n.* foreman/forewoman.

contremarché, *n.m.* countermove.

contre-offensive, *n.f.* countermove.

contre-offre, *n.f.* counter-offer.

contre-OPA, *n.f.* tactic/strategy against a hostile takeover bid.

contrepartie, *n.f.* **1.** *StExch:* **contrepartie dissimulée/occulte,** market making/rigging; **faire de la contrepartie,** to operate against one's client; **centrepartie de report,** taker-in **2.** (*a*) *Book-k:* contra; **en contrepartie,** per contra (*b*) counterpart/duplicate (of document) **3.** *NAm:* hedging (position).

contre-passation, *n.f.* **1.** *Fin:* return (of bill to drawer) **2.** *Book-k:* (*a*) reversing/transferring (of item, entry) (*b*) contra entry.

contre-passer, *v.tr.* **1.** *Fin:* to return/to endorse/to back (bill to drawer) **2.**

Book-k: to reverse/to contra/to transfer (item, entry).

contre-poser, *v.tr. Book-k:* to enter (item) on the wrong side of the ledger.

contre-position, *n.f. Book-k:* mis-entry (in ledger).

contreseing, *n.m.* counter-signature.

contresigner, *v.tr.* to countersign.

contre-valeur, *n.f. Fin:* exchange value.

contribuable, *n.m.f.* taxpayer; **contribuable à l'impôt foncier** = ratepayer.

contribution, *n.f.* tax; rate; **contributions (directes, indirectes),** (direct, indirect) taxation; **contribution foncière,** land tax; **(bureau des) contributions,** tax office/ = Inland Revenue/*NAm:* Internal Revenue; **lever/percevoir une contribution,** to collect/to levy a tax; **payer ses contributions,** to pay one's taxes.

contrôle, *n.m.* **1.** (*a*) control; **contrôle de (la) qualité,** quality control; **contrôle de la comptabilité,** accounting control; auditing; *Fin:* **contrôle des changes,** (foreign) exchange control/restrictions; **contrôle des prix,** price control; **contrôle des stocks,** stock control/*NAm:* inventory control; **contrôle budgétaire,** budget control; *Mkt:* **contrôle continu,** monitoring; **contrôle financier,** financial control (*b*) **prise de contrôle,** takeover **2.** (*a*) auditing/checking (of accounts, etc.) (*b*) **contrôle (de gestion),** management control (*c*) **contrôle de présence,** timekeeping **3. poinçon de contrôle,** hallmark (on gold and silver).

contrôler, *v.tr.* **1.** to check/to audit (accounts) **2.** to hallmark (gold, silver).

contrôleur, -euse, *n.* (*a*) **contrôleur des contributions,** inspector of taxes; **contrôleur des comptes d'une société,** auditor of a company's accounts; **contrôleur de gestion,** controller/comptroller (*b*) inspector/examiner/supervisor (of work, etc.)

convenir, *v.i.* to agree; to come to an agreement; **convenir d'un prix avec qn,** to agree on a price/to settle on a price with s.o.; **prix convenu,** agreed price.

convention, *n.f.* (*a*) agreement; covenant; **convention par écrit,** agreement in writing; **projet de convention,** draft agreement; **convention collective** = collective bargaining agreement/union agreement (*b*) *Jur:* article/clause (of deed, etc.).

conventionné, *a.* (*price, etc*) agreed/set.

conversion, *n.f.* (*a*) *StExch:* conversion; **conversion de titre(s),** conversion of stock; **taux de conversion (de l'argent),** rate of exchange/exchange rate (of currency) (*b*) **conversion de devise,** foreign currency translation (*c*) **conversion de la rente de 5% en 3½%,** conversion of Government 5% stock into 3½%.

convertibilité, *n.f.* convertibility (of currencies, etc.).

convertible, *a.* convertible (**en,** into); **obligation convertible (en actions),** convertible bond; **monnaies convertibles,** convertible currencies.

convertir, *v.tr.* to convert (**en,** into); to translate (foreign currency); **convertir des rentes,** to convert stock.

convertissement, *n.m. StExch: Fin:* conversion (of securities into money).

convivial, *a.* (*computer, machine*) userfriendly.

convoquer, *v.tr.* to convene (meeting); to call (creditors); to summon (shareholders).

coopératif, *a.* **société coopérative,** cooperative society.

cooperative, *n.f.* co-operative stores/*F:* co-op; **coopérative agricole,** agricultural co-operative; **coopérative de consommation,** (*i*) consumers' cooperative (*ii*) cooperative stores; **coopérative ouvrière,** workers' co-operative; **coopérative de production,** producers' co-operative; **coopérative vinicole,** wine co-operative.

coparticipant, -ante, *n.m. Jur:* copartner.

coparticipation, *n.f. Jur:* copartnership; *Ind:* **coparticipation des employés dans les bénéfices,** profit-sharing by the employees.

copie, *n.f. (a)* copy/transcript; **copie sur (support) papier/copie en clair,** hard copy; *Jur:* **pour copie conforme,** certified true copy *(b)* carbon copy (of letter).

copieur, *n.m.* (photo)copier.

coporteur, *n.m. Fin:* joint holder (of stock).

coposséder, *v.tr.* to own jointly/to have joint ownership of (sth.).

copossesseur, *n.m. Jur: (a)* joint owner *(b)* co-tenant.

copossession, *n.f. Jur: (a)* joint ownership *(b)* co-tenancy.

copreneur, -euse, *n. Jur:* co-lessee/co-tenant.

coproduction, *n.f.* coproduction.

copropriétaire, *n.m.f. Jur:* coproprietor; joint owner/part owner/co-owner.

copropriété, *n.f. Jur:* co-property; joint ownership/co-ownership.

copyright, *n.m.* copyright.

corbeille, *n.f. StExch:* trading post/pit/floor; **corbeille des obligations,** bond trading ring; **cotation à la corbeille,** on-floor trading.

corporation, *n.f.* corporation/corporate body/public body.

corporel, *a.* **biens corporels,** tangible assets.

correspondance, *n.f.* correspondence; **entrer en correspondance avec qn,** to enter into correspondence with s.o.; **maison de vente par correspondance,** mail-order firm; **vente par correspondance (VPC),** *(i)* mail order (selling) *(ii)* mail order (sales).

correspondancier, -ière, *n.* correspondence clerk; **secrétaire correspondancière,** (correspondence) secretary.

cosignataire, *n.m.* co-signatory.

cotation, *n.f. Fin:* quotation/quote; quoting; *NAm:* listing; **cotation en continu,** continuous trading; **cotation de l'or,** golden fixing; **cotation par téléphone,** telephone dealing; **cotation (traditionnelle) à la corbeille,** (traditional) floor trading; ring trading; **cotation au cours du marché,** market quotation/quote; **cotation par appel de marge,** margin dealing.

cote, *n.f. (a)* quota/share/proportion (of expense, taxes, etc.); **cote mal taillée,** compounding in gross (of account)/rough and ready settlement *(b) Adm:* assessment; **cote foncière,** assessment on land; **cote mobilière,** assessment on property *(c) StExch:* quotation; **cote officielle,** official list; listed market; **cote des prix,** *(i)* official (share) list *(ii) (dans le commerce)* list of prices; **actions inscrites à la cote/ valeurs admises à la cote (de la Bourse),** listed shares/shares quoted on the Stock Exchange/quoted shares; **(actions) hors cote,** unlisted (shares)/(shares that are) not (officially) quoted on the Stock Exchange; **marché hors cote,** over the counter market/unlisted securities market; **admission à la cote,** admission to quotation/to the official list; **faire une demande d'admission à la cote,** to seek admission to quotation/a share quotation; **valeur à la cote,** quoted market value.

coter, *v.tr.* to quote (price, etc.); **coter l'ouverture,** to open; **valeurs cotées en Bourse,** quoted shares/shares quoted on the Stock Exchange/listed shares; **valeurs non cotées en Bourse,** unlisted/unquoted securities.

cotisant, -ante, *n.* paying member; subscriber (**de,** to).

cotisation, *n.f. (a)* quota/share; contribution (to common fund); **assurance à cotisations,** contributory insurance; **cotisations maladie** = health insurance contributions; **cotisation patronale,** employer's contribution; **cotisation ouvrière,** employee's contribution; **cotisation syndicale,** political levy; **cotisations sociales,** (National Insurance and National Health) contributions; **cotisations à la Sécurité sociale =** National Insurance contributions; **régime de retraite financé par les cotisations patronales et ouvrières,** contributory pension plan (*b*) subscription (to club, etc.).

cotiser, *v.tr.* to pay one's share; **cotiser à la Sécurité sociale =** to pay one's National Insurance (contributions).

coulage, *n.m.* **tenir compte du coulage,** to allow for (*i*) wastage (*ii*) petty theft (*iii*) leakage.

coulisse, *n.f. StExch:* **la coulisse,** the outside market/the kerb.

coulissier, *n.m. StExch:* outside/kerb broker.

coupe, *n.f.* cut/cutback; **coupe (sombre),** (drastic) cut (in personnel, in estimates).

coupon, *n.m.* coupon; *Fin:* **coupon d'actions,** coupon; **avec coupon,** cum right; **coupon d'intérêt,** interest coupon; **coupon de dividende,** dividend coupon; **coupon attaché,** cum dividend; with/cum coupon; **coupon détaché,** ex dividend/ex coupon; **coupon arriéré,** coupon in arrears; **coupon couru,** accrued interest.

coupon-prime, *n.m.* gift voucher.

coupon-réponse, *n.m. Post:* **coupon-réponse international,** international reply coupon.

coupure, *n.f. Fin:* (bank)note/*NAm:* bill; **coupure de dix francs,** ten-franc note; **petite coupure,** note of small denomination.

cour, *n.f.* court/tribunal; **Cour d'Appel,** Court of Appeal; **la Cour des comptes,** the Audit Office.

courant, 1. *a.* (*a*) *Bank:* **compte courant,** current account (*b*) **l'année courante,** the present/current year; **le cinq du mois cou-** rant/le cinq courant/le 5 ct., the 5th inst.; **fin courant,** at the end of this month (*c*) **affaires courantes,** (*i*) routine/everyday business (*ii*) business in/on hand; **dépenses courantes,** running expenses; **dette courante,** floating debt; **marchandises de vente courante,** goods that have a ready sale; **monnaie courante,** legal currency; **prix courant,** current price; **prix courants,** (current) price list; **prix courants du marché,** current market prices (*d*) **marque courante,** standard make; **taille courante,** standard size **2.** *n.m.* **le courant économique actuel,** the present economic situation.

courbe, *n.f.* curve; graph; **courbe des taux,** yield curve; **courbe des ventes,** sales chart/graph.

courir, *v.i.* **les intérêts courent à partir de ...,** interest accrues (as) from ...; **les intérêts qui courent,** the accruing interest; **intérêts courus,** accrued interest; **le bail n'a plus qu'un an à courir,** the lease has only one year to run.

courrier, *n.m.* mail/post; letters; **par retour du courrier,** by return (of post); **dépouiller son courrier,** to open/to go through one's mail; *Cmptr:* **courrier électronique,** electronic mail.

cours, *n.m.* **1. année en cours,** current year; **affaires en cours,** outstanding business; **négociations en cours,** negotiations in progress; **travail en cours,** work in progress; work in/on hand; **en cours de production,** in production **2.** circulation (of money); (*devise*) **avoir cours (légal),** to be legal tender; to be in circulation; **cours forcé,** forced currency **3.** *StExch:* quotation/price; **bulletin des cours,** official list of quotation; **cours commerciaux,** commodity prices; **cours de base,** exercise/striking price; **cours de clôture/dernier cours,** closing/close price; **cours d'ouverture/premier cours,** opening price; **le cours de l'or,** the price of gold; **cours du change,** rate of exchange; **cours au/du comptant,** cash price/rate; spot price/rate; **cours du marché/cours de la Bourse,** market price/rate; **cours du marché au**

comptant, current market spot rate; **cours étranger,** foreign exchange; **cours des devises,** foreign exchange rate; **cours à terme,** price for the account; forward rate; **cours d'achat/cours acheteur,** offer price/ buying price/buying rate; **cours vendeur,** selling/bid price; **cours de rachat,** buying-in price; **cours de compensation,** making-up price; **cours pivot,** average/target price; **cours de résiliation,** settlement price; **cours offerts,** prices offered/asked; **cours en Bourse/cours officiel,** official price; (*à Londres*) house price; **cours hors Bourse/ cours hors cote,** unofficial price; **à cours limité,** at limit; **acheter au cours (du jour),** to buy at the price/rate of the day; **cours (des changes) à terme,** forward (exchange) rates; **quel est le cours du sucre?** what is sugar quoted at?

coursier, -ière, *n.* runner.

court, *a.* short; **crédit à court terme,** short-term credit; **effet à courte échéance,** short-dated bill; *Fin:* **papiers courts,** short-dated bills; **titres courts/obligations courtes,** short-dated securities/*n.* shorts; **tonne courte,** short ton.

courtage, *n.m.* (*a*) broking/brokerage; **faire le courtage,** to be a broker; **courtage en immeubles,** real estate agency (*b*) **droit/ frais de courtage,** brokerage/commission; **courtage de place,** transaction charge.

courtier, *n.m.* broker; agent; **courtier d'assurances,** insurance broker; **courtier de Bourse,** stockbroker; **courtier de change,** exchange dealer; bill broker; **courtier de commerce/de marchandises,** general broker/commercial broker; **courtier en valeurs mobilières,** (stock)broker; **courtier libre,** outside broker; **courtier maritime,** ship broker; **courtier membre du parquet,** floor broker; **courtier(-négociant du parquet),** trader; **courtier sur actions,** equities trader; **courtier marron/non autorisé,** outside broker; **bureau de courtier marron,** bucket-shop; *Publ:* **courtier en librairie,** trade sales rep(resentative)/*NAm:* book agent.

couru, *a. Fin:* **intérêts courus,** accrued interest.

coût, *n.m.* (*a*) cost; **coût, assurance, fret (CAF),** cost, insurance, freight (CIF); **coût d'accroissement,** incremental cost; **coût d'opportunité/d'option/ de substitution,** opportunity cost; **coûts constants/ fixes,** fixed costs/expenses; **coût du capital,** capital cost; **coût économique,** economic cost; **(comptabilisation au) coût moyen pondéré,** average cost pricing; **étude/ analyse coût-efficacité,** cost-effectiveness analysis; **évaluation du coût,** costing; **facteur coût,** cost factor; **méthode de coûts variable/proportionnel,** direct costing; **méthode de capitalisation du coût entier,** full costing/full cost accounting; **structure des coûts,** cost structure (*b*) **le coût de la vie,** the cost of living; **indice du coût de la vie,** cost of living index (*c*) *Mkt:* **coût média,** above-the-line; **coût promotion,** below-the-line.

coûtant, *a.m.* **au/à prix coûtant,** at cost price.

coût-efficacité, *n.f.* cost-effectiveness.

coûter, *v.i.* to cost; **cela coûte cinq francs,** it costs five francs; **coûter cher,** to be expensive; **ne pas coûter cher,** to be inexpensive.

coûteux, *a.* costly/expensive; **peu coûteux,** inexpensive.

couvert, *n.m.* 1. **être à couvert,** to be covered (for a credit); *StExch:* **vendre à couvert,** to hedge; to sell for (future) delivery/to sell for futures 2. (*au restaurant*) **(frais de) couvert,** cover charge.

couverture, *n.f.* (*a*) cover; margin; hedge; **commande sans couverture,** order without security/without cover; **couverture (boursière) obligatoire,** margin requirement; **converture sur opération spéculative,** speculative margin; **couverture optionnelle,** closing purchase; **couverture d'une position ouverte,** short covering; **exiger une couverture de 20% en espèces,** to claim a margin of 20% in cash; **opération de couverture,** hedging; **opérer avec couverture,** to operate with cover; to hedge; **couverture sur indice,** index arbitrage (b) *Ins:* cover; covering (of risks); **lettre de couverture,** cover note (c) coverage; **couverture du marché,** sales coverage.

couvrir, 1. *v.tr.* to cover; **le prix de vente couvre à peine les frais,** the selling price barely covers the cost; **cette assurance ne couvre pas les risques de vol,** this insurance doesn't cover us against theft; **couvrir un emprunt,** to cover a loan; **couvrir les frais de port,** to refund the postage/the carriage; **couvrir une enchère,** to make a higher bid **2.** *v.pr. StExch:* to cover (oneself)/to hedge; **se couvrir en achetant à long terme,** to hedge by buying at long date; **se couvrir en rachetant,** to cover oneself by buying back.

covendeur, -euse, *n.* co-vendor/joint seller.

crayonné, *n.m. Mkt:* simple/rough layout.

créance, *n.f.* **1. lettre de créance,** letter of credit **2.** debt; *Jur:* claim; **créance contractuelle,** contractual claim; **créances exigibles,** debts due; **créance garantie,** secured debt; **créances gelées,** frozen credits; **créance privilégiée,** preferential/ preferred debt; **nos créances,** monies owing to us; receivables; **mauvaises créances/créances douteuses,** bad debts; doubtful accounts; **amortir une créance,** to write off a debt.

créancier, -ière, *n.* creditor; holder of debt claim; **créancier d'exploitation,** trade creditor; **créancier hypothécaire,** mortgagee; **créancier entièrement nanti,** fully-secured creditor.

créateur, *n.m.* **créateur d'entreprise(s),** entrepreneur/enterpriser.

créatif, -ive, *n. Mkt:* designer.

création, *n.f.* **création d'emploi,** job creation (scheme); **création d'une entreprise,** founding/establishment (of a company, a firm); **création d'un nouveau produit,** creation of a new product; **création de produits,** product generation;

nos dernières créations, our latest models; our latest creations.

crédibilité, *n.f.* credibility.

crédirentier, -ière, *n. Jur:* recipient of an allowance/of an income/of an annuity.

crédit, *n.m.* **1.** (a) credit; **crédit bancaire,** bank credit; **crédit en blanc/à découvert,** blank/open credit; **crédit de campagne,** seasonal loan; **carte de crédit,** credit card; **crédit commercial,** trade credit; commodity credit; **crédit à la consommation,** consumer credit; **crédit à court terme/à long terme,** short/long term credit; **crédit croisé,** swap; **crédit différé,** deferred credit; **crédit documentaire,** documentary letter of credit; **crédits d'équipement,** equipment financing; **crédits à l'exportation,** export credit; **crédit renouvelable/ permanent/revolving,** revolving/*NAm:* revolver credit; **crédit ponctuel,** spot credit; **crédits de trésorerie,** (short term) credit facilities/cash advances; **crédit d'impôt,** (i) tax rebate (ii) tax credit (on dividends) (iii) allowance; **crédit relais,** briding loan; **lettre de crédit,** letter of credit; **ligne de crédit,** credit line; **marché du crédit,** credit market; **note de crédit,** credit note; **acheter/vendre à crédit,** to buy/to sell sth. (i) on credit/*F:* on tick (ii) on hire purchase/*NAm:* on the installment plan; **faire crédit à qn,** to give s.o. credit; **ouvrir un crédit à qn,** to open a credit account in s.o.'s favour/in s.o.'s name; **ouvrir un crédit chez qn,** to open a credit account/*F:* an account with s.o.; **crédit sur la marché,** credit worthiness (b) **banque de crédit,** credit bank; **société (commune) de crédit immobilier (hypothécaire)** = building society/*NAm:* building and loan association **2.** credit side (of ledger, balance-sheet); **porter une somme au crédit de qn,** to credit s.o. with a sum/to enter a sum to s.o.'s credit.

crédit-bail, *n.m* leasing; **crédit-bail mobilier,** equipment leasing.

créditer, *v.tr.* **créditer qn du montant d'une somme,** to credit s.o./s.o.'s account with a sum; **créditer un compte,** to credit an account; **faire créditer son compte d'une somme,** to pay money into one's account.

créditeur, -trice, 1. *n.* creditor **2.** *a.* **compte créditeur,** account in credit; **solde créditeur,** credit balance.

crédit-relais, *n.m.* bridge financing.

créneau, *n.m.* gap/opening/opportunity in the market; **créneau porteur,** strong gap in the market.

crever, *v.tr.* **crever le plafond des 10%,** to break the 10% ceiling.

creux, *a.* **année creuse,** poor/lean year; **heures creuses,** off-peak hours; **marché creux,** sagging market; **saison creuse,** slack season.

criée, *n.f.* auction; **chambre des criées,** (public) auction room/saleroom/*NAm:* salesroom; **vente à la criée,** sale by auction.

crier, *v.tr.* to put (furniture, etc.) up for auction/to auction (furniture).

crise, *n.f.* crisis; **crise économique,** economic crisis; slump; **crise de l'emploi,** unemployment crisis/job shortage; **la crise du logement,** the housing shortage/crisis.

croisé, *a.* **crédit croisé,** swap; **participation croisée,** cross holding.

croissance, *n.f.* growth; **secteur/marché en croissance,** growth sector; **croissance économique,** economic growth; **croissance par habitant/per capita,** economic development; **courbe de croissance,** growth curve; **industrie en croissance rapide,** growth industry; **ralentissement du taux de croissance,** slowing down of the growth rate; *Fin:* **valeur de croissance,** growth stock.

croissant, *a.* increasing (wealth, etc.); **coût croissant,** increasing cost; **rendements croissants,** increasing returns.

croître, *v.i.* to grow/to increase.

cube, *a.* **mètre cube,** cubic metre.

culbute, *n.f.* F: **faire la culbute,** (*i*) to go bankrupt (*ii*) to make 100% profit.

cumulatif, *a.* cumulative (shares, etc.); **assurance cumulative,** double insurance; **action à dividende cumulatif,** cumulative share; **dividende cumulatif,** cumulative dividend.

cycle, *n.m.* cycle; **cycle économique,** business/trade cycle; **cycle de vie (d'un produit),** life cycle (of a product).

cyclique, *a.* cyclical; **valeurs cycliques,** cyclicals; **variations cycliques,** cyclical variations.

D

dactylo, 1. *n.m.f.* typist; **équipe/pool de dactylos,** typing pool **2.** *n.f.* typing **3.** *n.m. FrC:* typewriter.

dactylographie, *n.f.* typing.

dactylographier, *v.tr.* to type; **lettre dactylographiée,** typed/typewritten letter.

datation, *n.f.* dating; **datation d'un contrat,** dating of a contract.

date, *n.f.* date; **la lettre porte la date du 12 juin,** the letter is dated June 12th/12th (of) June; **en date du 15 courant,** dated the 15th inst.; **en date de Paris,** dated from Paris; **à trente jours de date,** thirty days after date; **date d'échéance,** date of maturity/due date; expiry date; **date d'émission,** date of issue; **date de naissance,** date of birth; **date d'entrée en vigueur,** effective date (of regulation, etc.); **date limite,** deadline; **date limite de vente/date de péremption,** sell-by date; **date de valeur,** value date; **sans date,** *(lettre, etc.)* undated.

dater, 1. *v.tr.* to date (letter, etc.); **votre lettre datée d'hier,** your letter dated yesterday; **lettre datée du 13 mars,** letter dated the 13th (of) March/dated March 13th **2.** *v.i.* to date **(de,** from); **à dater de ce jour,** *(i)* from today *(ii)* from that day; **à dater du 15,** on and after the 15th; (starting) from the 15th/as from the 15th/as of the 15th.

dateur, *a.* **timbre dateur,** date stamp.

débâcle, *n.f. Fin:* **débâcle (financière),** crash.

déballage, *n.m.* unpacking.

déballer, *v.tr.* to unpack (goods, etc.); to display (goods for sale).

débarquer, *v.tr.* to unload (goods); to land/disembark (passengers).

débattre, *v.tr.* to discuss; **débattre un prix,** to discuss a price; **prix à débattre,** price to be agreed/price by arrangement; **salaire à débattre,** salary negotiable.

débauchage, *n.m. Ind:* laying off (of workers).

débaucher, *v.tr. Ind:* to lay off (workers)/ to make (workers) redundant.

débet, *n.m. Fin:* debit balance; **être en débet,** to settle an account partially.

débit¹, *n.m. (a)* (retail) sale; **marchandises de bon débit/d'un débit facile,** goods with a ready market/which sell well; **ces marchandises ont peu de débit,** there is little demand for these goods *(b)* (retail) shop; *esp.* **débit de tabac,** tobacconist's (shop); **débit de boissons** = pub/bar *(c)* output (of machine).

débit², *n.m.* debit; *Book-k:* debit side; **note bordereau de débit,** debit note; **article porté au débit (d'un compte),** debit entry **inscrire/porter au débit,** to debit; **porter une somme au débit de qn/au débit d'un compte,** to debit s.o. with an amount/to debit s.o.'s account with an amount.

débitant, -ante, *n. (a)* retailer *(b)* **débitant (de tabac),** tobacconist.

débiter¹, *v.tr.* **1.** to retail/to sell (goods) retail; **on débite beaucoup dans cette boutique,** this shop has a large turnover **2.** to yield; **machine qui débite beaucoup d'ouvrage,** machine with a large output.

débiter², *v.tr.* to debit; **débiter le compte de qn,** to debit s.o.'s account (with); **débiter qn (d'une somme),** to debit s.o. with a amount; **débiter les frais de poste au client,** to charge (the) postage to the customer.

débiteur,-trice, 1. *n.* debtor **2.** *a.* **colonne débitrice,** debit column/debit side; **compte débiteur,** debit account; **solde débiteur,** debit balance; *Bank:* overdraft.

déblocage, *n.m. Fin:* unblocking/release/ unfreezing (of credits, capital); decontrolling (of wages, prices).

débloquer, *v.tr. Fin:* to unblock/to release/to unfreeze (credits, capital, etc.); **débloquer (les prix, les salaires),** to decontrol (prices, wages); **débloquer des fonds/ des capitaux,** to unlock assets; to release funds.

déboguer, *v.tr. Cmptr:* to debug (system, program).

débonification, *n.f.* withdrawal of bonus.

débordement, *n.m. Mkt:* overlap.

débouché, *n.m.* (*a*) outlet/opening/ market; **créer de nouveaux débouchés pour un produit,** to open up new markets/to create new outlets for a product; **examen des débouchés,** market analysis (*b*) job opportunity; **l'industrie offre des débouchés aux économistes,** industry has (job) prospects/job opportunities for economists.

déboucler, *v.tr. StExch:* **déboucler sa position,** to close one's position.

débours, *n.m. usu. pl.* out-of-pocket expenses/outgoings; **faire des débours,** to lay out/to pay out money; **rentrer dans ses débours,** to recover one's outlay.

déboursement, *n.m.* outlay/disbursement; expenditure.

débourser, *v.tr.* to spend/to lay out/to pay out (money).

débudgétisation, *n.f.* debudgeting.

débudgétiser, *v.tr.* to debudget.

décaissement, *n.m.* (*a*) withdrawal of a

sum of money/of funds (for payment) (*b*) sum withdrawn.

décaisser, *v.tr.* to withdraw a sum of money/funds (for payment); to pay out.

décalage, *n.m.* gap; *StExch:* **décalage des cours,** tick.

décentralisation, *n.f.* (*a*) decentralization; **décentralisation administrative,** devolution (*b*) relocation of offices.

décentraliser, *v.tr.* (*a*) to decentralize (administration) (*b*) to relocate (offices, etc.) (away from large towns).

décès, *n.m.* death; **mutation par décès,** transmission on death.

décharge, *n.f.* **1. décharge d'un impôt,** tax rebate **2. porter une somme en décharge,** to mark a sum as paid **3.** discharge/ release (from debt, etc.).

déchargement, *n.m.* unloading (of ship).

décharger, *v.tr.* **1.** to unload (a ship, cargo, goods) **2. décharger qn d'un impôt,** to exempt s.o. from (paying) a tax; **décharger qn d'une dette,** to remit a debt; **failli (non) déchargé,** (un)discharged bankrupt; **décharger un compte,** to discharge an account.

déchéance, *n.f.* forfeiture (of rights, etc.); **déchéance de titres,** forfeiture of shares; **action en déchéance de brevet,** action for forfeiture of patent.

déchet, *n.m.* **1.** loss/decrease/diminution (of weight, value, quantity); **déchet de route,** loss in value (*during transit, manufacture, etc*) **2.** waste product; *usu. pl. Ind: etc:* **déchets,** waste/refuse.

décideur 1. *a.* **organisme décideur,** decision-making body **2.** *n.m.* decision maker.

décile, *n.m. Stat:* decile.

décision, *n.f.* **prise de décision,** decision-making.

déclaratif, *a.* **jugement déclaratif de faillite,** decree in bankruptcy.

déclaration, *n.f.* (*a*) declaration; statement/report; **déclaration sous serment,** sworn statement/affidavit; **déclaration de revenu/déclaration fiscale,** income-tax return; **envoyer sa déclaration à l'inspecteur des contributions directes** = to make a tax return/*NAm:* to file one's tax return; **fausse déclaration,** (*i*) misrepresentation (*ii*) false return/false declaration; *Adm:* **déclaration de versement/de quittance,** receipt; *Rail:* **déclaration d'expédition,** invoice (*b*) *Cust:* **déclaration de/en douane,** customs declaration/bill of entry; **déclaration d'entrée en entrepôt,** warehousing entry; **déclaration de transit,** transit entry (*c*) *Nau:* **déclaration d'avarie,** (ship's) protest (*d*) *StExch:* **jour de la déclaration des noms,** ticket day.

déclarer, *v.tr.* to declare; **déclarer un dividende,** to declare a dividend; **déclarer ses revenus au fisc** = to make one's tax return/*NAm:* to file one's tax return; *Cust:* **avez-vous quelque chose à déclarer?** (have you) anything to declare? **rien à déclarer,** nothing to declare; **valeur déclarée,** declared value; *Fin:* **transferts déclarés,** certified transfers; *StExch:* **se déclarer vendeur,** to put the shares.

déclassé, *a. Fin:* **valeurs déclassées,** displaced stock.

déclassement, *n.m. StExch:* displacement (of shares).

décommander, *v.tr.* **décommander (une commande, une livraison),** to cancel (an order, a delivery); **décommander une réunion,** to cancel/to call off a meeting.

décomposer, *v.tr.* **décomposer un compte,** to analyse/to break down an account.

décomposition, *n.f.* **décomposition des dépenses,** breakdown of expenses; **décomposition des tâches,** job breakdown.

décompte, *n.m.* **1.** (*a*) **faire le décompte,** to deduct sth. (from the price); to make a deduction (from sum to be paid) (*b*) **payer le décompte,** to pay the balance due (on an account) **2.** detailed account; breakdown (of account).

décompter, *v.tr.* to deduct (sum from price).

déconcentration, *n.f.* **déconcentration industrielle,** relocation of offices/businesses (*away from large towns*).

déconcentrer, *v.tr.* to relocate (offices, businesses) (*away from large towns*).

déconfiture, *n.f.* financial collapse; *Jur:* insolvency; bankruptcy (of non-trader).

déconsigner, *v.tr.* (*a*) to return/to pay back the deposit on (bottles, etc.) (*b*) **déconsigner ses bagages,** to take one's luggage out of (the) left luggage (office).

décote, *n.f.* (*a*) tax relief; tax exemption; tax credit (*b*) *Fin:* value (of currency) below rate (*c*) depreciation/loss in value/write-down.

découvert, 1. *n.m.* (*a*) *Bank: etc:* overdraft; overdrawn balance; **accorder à qn un découvert de £500,** to allow s.o. an overdraft of £500/to allow s.o. to overdraw to the amount of £500; **avoir un découvert de 2 000 francs à la banque,** to have an overdraft of 2 000 francs/to be 2 000 francs overdrawn at the bank; **découvert en blanc,** unsecured overdraft (*b*) *Ins:* parts/things not covered by insurance (*c*) *Adm:* (budgetary) deficit; *PolEc:* **découvert de la balance commerciale,** trade gap; *StExch:* **chasser le découvert,** to raid the bears **2.** *adv. phr. Bank:* **compte à découvert,** overdrawn account; **mettre (son compte) à découvert/tirer à découvert,** to overdraw (one's account); **crédit à découvert,** unsecured credit; **faire couvrir le découvert,** to force the bears to cover their short position; **vente à découvert,** sale for futures/short sale/short selling; **vendre à découvert,** to sell short; to go a bear.

dédit, *n.m.* forfeit/penalty (for breaking contract, etc.).

dédommagement, *n.m.* indemnity/compensation/damages; **réclamer un dédommagement,** to claim compensation; **recevoir une somme en dédommagement (de qch.)/à titre de dédommagement,** to receive a sum in/by way of compensation (for sth.).

dédommager, 1. *v.tr.* to indemnify/to compensate (s.o.) **(de qch.,** for sth.) **2.** *v.pr.* **se dédommager de ses pertes,** to recoup one's losses.

dédouanage, *n.m.* **dédouanement,** *n.m.* Cust: (*i*) customs clearance (*ii*) taking out of bond.

dédouaner, *v.tr.* Cust: (*i*) to clear through customs (*ii*) to take out of bond (*iii*) to remove the customs duty from an article.

déductible, *a.* deductible; **déductible de l'impôt,** tax deductible.

déduction, *n.f.* (*a*) deduction; allowance; **après déduction des impôts,** after deduction of tax; **déduction forfaitaire,** fixed deduction; **déduction faite des frais,** after deducting the expenses; **faire déduction des sommes payées d'avance,** to allow for/to deduct sums paid in advance; **somme qui entre en déduction de ...,** amount deductible from ...; **sous déduction de 10%,** less/minus 10% (*b*) Adm: allowance; tax relief.

déduire, *v.tr.* to deduct; to mask off (against sth.); **déduire 5%,** to take off/to allow/to deduct 5%; **les frais de poste sont à déduire du prix total,** postage to be deducted from the total price.

de facto, *Lat. phr:* de facto.

défaillance, *n.f.* Fin: **défaillance du franc,** weakening of the franc; **défaillance du marché,** sagging of the market.

défaillant,-ante, 1. *a.* **partie défaillante,** defaulting party **2.** *n.* defaulter.

défalcation, *n.f.* (*a*) deduction/deducting; writing off (of bad debt); **défalcation faite des frais,** after deducting the expenses (*b*) sum/weight deducted; allowance; abatement (from income tax).

défalquer, *v.tr.* to deduct/to take off (sum from total); to mark off (against sth.); **dé-**

falquer une mauvaise créance, to write off a bad debt.

défaut, *n.m.* **1.** (*a*) default/absence/deficiency/insufficiency/(total) lack (of sth.); **à défaut de paiement,** failing payment/in default of payment; **défaut de paiement,** failure to pay/non(-)payment; **intérêts pour défaut de paiement,** default interest; Bank: **défaut de provision,** no funds (*b*) Jur: default; StExch: **agent en défaut,** defaulter **2. défaut de fabrication,** fault/defect (in manufacture); flaw (in fabric, etc.).

défavorable, *a.* Fin: **balance de paiements défavorable,** adverse trade balance; **change défavorable,** unfavourable exchange.

défectueux, *a.* **articles défectueux,** imperfect goods; rejects; seconds.

défendeur, -eresse, *n.* Jur: defendant.

déficit, *n.m.* deficit/shortfall (in cash, balance-sheet); deficiency (in revenue); shortage (in cash, weight); **être en déficit/accuser un déficit/présenter un déficit,** to show a deficit; **combler un déficit,** to make up/to make good a deficit; **compte qui présente un déficit,** account showing a deficit/debit balance; **déficit budgétaire,** budget deficit; **déficit commercial,** trade gap; trade deficit; **déficit de la balance commerciale,** trade deficit; **déficit fiscal remboursable,** negative income tax; **déficit fiscal reportable,** tax loss.

déficitaire, *a.* showing a deficit; lossmaking; **balance/solde déficitaire,** adverse balance/debit balance; **être déficitaire,** to show a deficit/F: to be in the red; **rétablir un budget déficitaire,** to balance an adverse budget.

défiscaliser, *v.tr.* to give (total) tax relief to; **défiscalisé,** tax free.

déflation, *n.f.* deflation; **politique de déflation,** deflationary policy.

déflationniste, *a.* PolEc: **mesures déflationnistes,** deflationary measures.

défraîchi, *a.* **articles défraîchis,** shop-soiled goods.

défrayer, *v.tr.* **défrayer qn,** to pay/to meet/to settle s.o.'s expenses.

dégagement, *n.m.* sell-off.

dégager, *v.tr.* to redeem/to pledge.

dégât, *n.m.* damage.

dégeler, *v.tr.* to unfreeze/to unblock (assets, credits, etc.).

degré, *n.m.* degree; **degré de liquidité,** degree of liquidity/liquidity ratio.

dégressif, *a.* decreasing/graded; **impôt dégressif,** sliding scale taxation/graduated tax; **frais dégressifs,** decreasing costs; **tarif dégressif,** decreasing tariff/sliding scale tariff.

dégressivité, *n.f.* grading/decrease; sliding scale.

dégrèvement, *n.m.* (*a*) reduction/abatement (of tax); **dégrèvement pour entretien d'immeubles,** allowance for repairs (*b*) relief from taxation/derating (of industry); **quotité du dégrèvement fiscal,** extent of taxation relief.

dégrever, *v.tr.* to reduce tax/duty (on products); to relieve (s.o.) of a tax; to reduce (s.o.'s) taxes; to derate (industry); to reduce the assessment on (a property).

dégringolade, *n.f.* **dégringolade du franc,** collapse of the franc; **dégringolade des prix,** slump in prices.

dégringoler, *v.i.* (*prix*) to slump.

déguisé, *a.* hidden (tax, unemployment, etc).

délai, *n.m.* (*a*) delay; *Corr:* **veuillez nous répondre sans délai,** please reply immediately/without delay (*b*) time allowed (for completion of a job, etc.); **dans un délai de trois ans,** within three years/within a three year limit; **dans le plus bref délai/le plus court délai/dans les meilleurs délais,** in the shortest possible time/as soon as possible/at your earliest convenience; **dans les délais prescrits,** within the prescribed/

required time; **délai de livraison un mois,** (*i*) delivery within a month/allow one month for delivery (*ii*) delivery turnround/*NAm:* delivery lead time one month; **délai de paiement,** term of payment; **délai de récupération (du capital investi),** payback period (of capital invested); **livrable dans un délai de trois jours,** can be delivered at three days' notice/within three days (*c*) *Jur:* **un délai franc de 5 jours,** 5 clear days' grace; **délai de grâce,** days of grace; **délai de préavis/de congé,** period of notice (to employee, to employer).

délai-congé, *n.m. Jur:* term/period of notice (*to employee or employer*).

délaissé, *a. StExch:* **valeurs délaissées,** neglected stocks.

délaissement, *n.m.* abandonment (of ship to insurer).

délégation, *n.f.* **1.** (*a*) delegation (of authority) (*b*) *Jur:* assignment/transfer (of debit) **2.** delegation; **une délégation commerciale japonaise,** a Japanese trade delegation/mission.

délégué, -ée, *a. & n.* (*a*) **délégué général,** managing director; **administrateur délégué,** acting managing director (*b*) delegate; representative; **délégué commercial,** sales representative/sales rep; *Ind:* **délégué syndical,** (trade) union representative; **délégué d'usine/du personnel/d'atelier,** shop steward.

déléguer, *v.tr.* (*a*) **déléguer ses pouvoirs/son autorité,** to delegate one's powers/one's authority (*b*) **déléguer une créance,** to assign a debt.

délit, *n.m.* offense; *Fin:* **délit d'initié(s),** insider dealing/trading.

délivrance, *n.f.* delivery/issue (of patent, certificate, etc.).

délivrer, *v.tr.* to deliver (goods, etc.); to deliver/to issue (certificate, ticket, receipt); **délivrer un brevet à qn,** to grant a patent to s.o.

déloyal, *a.* unfair (practice, proceedings); **concurrence déloyale,** unfair competition.

demande, *n.f.* (*a*) request/application (**de,** for); (**faire une**) **demande d'argent/de crédits,** (to put in a) request for money/for funds; **faire une demande (d'emploi, etc.),** to apply for (a job, etc.); **faire une demande par écrit,** to write (off) for/to send for; **suite à votre demande,** as requested; **sur demande,** on application/on request; (**envoi d')échantillons sur demande,** samples (are sent) on request/on application; **argent payable/remboursable sur demande,** loan payable at call; call money; **chèque payable sur demande,** cheque payable on demand/at sight; *Journ:* **demandes d'emploi,** situations wanted (*b*) demand; *Ind: etc:* **construit/fabriqué sur demande,** made to customer's specifications/custom-built/custom-made; **demande croissante,** increasing demand; **demande régulière,** steady demand; **évaluation de la demande,** demand assessment; *PolEc:* **l'offre et la demande,** supply and demand; **travailler à la demande,** to work to order (*c*) *Ins:* **demande d'indemnité,** claim.

demander, *v.tr.* **1.** to ask (for); **demander des dommages-intérêts,** to claim damages; **combien demandez-vous de l'heure?** how much do you charge per hour/an hour? **demander un emploi/un poste,** to apply for a job; **demandez notre catalogue,** write for/send for our catalogue **2.** to want/to need/to require; **article très demandé,** article in great demand; **prix demandé,** asked price; *Journ:* **on demande vendeuse,** sales assistant wanted/needed.

demandeur, -eresse, *n. Jur:* claimant.

démantèlement, *n.m.* **démantèlement d'entreprise,** asset stripping.

démarchage, *n.m.* door-to-door selling.

démarcher, *v.tr.* to canvass.

démarcheur, -euse, *n.* (*a*) canvasser; door-to-door salesman/saleswoman (*b*) finder; **prestation de démarcheur,** finder's fee.

démarque, *n.f.* marking down (of goods in sales).

démarquer, *v.tr.* to mark down (goods in sales).

démembrement, *n.m.* strip(ping).

démettre, 1. *v.tr.* **démettre qn de ses fonctions,** to remove s.o. from his post **2.** *v.pr.* **se démettre (de ses fonctions),** to resign/to hand in one's notice.

demeure, *n.f.* (*a*) (place of) residence (*b*) **mise en demeure,** formal notice.

demi-douzaine, *n.f.* half-dozen.

demi-gros, *n.m.inv.* wholesale dealing in small quantities; **libre-service de demi-gros,** cash and carry.

demi-page, *n.f.* (*annonce*) half-page (advertisement).

demi-pension, *n.f.* (*dans un hôtel*) half(-)board.

demi-produit, *n.m. Ind:* semi-manufactured product.

demi-salaire, *n.m.* half-pay/half-salary.

démission, *n.f.* resignation; **donner sa démission,** to tender/to hand in one's resignation.

démissionner, *v.i.* to resign (**de,** from).

demi-tarif, *n.m. & a.* **billet (à) demi-tarif,** half-price ticket; half fare.

démographie, *n.f.* demography.

démographique, *a.* demographic.

démonétisation, *n.f.* demonetization; calling in/withdrawal from circulation (of coinage, etc.).

démonétiser, *v.tr.* to demonetize; to call in/to withdraw (coinage, etc.) from circulation.

démonstrateur, -trice, *n.* demonstrator.

démonstration, *n.f. Mkt:* demonstration (*of an article on show or for sale*); **appareil de démonstration,** demonstration model; **démonstration sans engagement,**

(ask for) free demonstration; **salle de démonstration,** showroom.

dénationalisation, *n.f.* denationalization (of an industry, etc.).

dénationaliser, *v.tr.* to denationalize (an industry, etc.).

dénombrement, *n.m.* census (of population).

dénommer, *v.tr.* to name/to designate; *Ins:* **personne dénommée,** nominee (for life annuity); *(dans un contrat, etc.)* **ci-après dénommé ...,** hereinafter referred to as ....

denrée, *n.f. usu. pl.* commodity; *esp.* foodstuff/produce; **denrées alimentaires,** food products/foodstuffs; **denrées du pays,** home produce; **denrées périssables,** perishable goods; *StExch:* **matières premières et denrées,** commodities.

déontologie, *n.f.* professional etiquette; **code de déontologie boursière,** model code.

dépareillé, *a.* odd/unmatched; **articles dépareillés,** oddments/job lot.

départ, *n.m.* (*a*) **courrier au départ,** outgoing mail (*b*) **départ d'un compte,** opening/starting date of an account; **prix départ usine,** price ex works; *(à une vente aux enchères)* **prix de départ,** upset price; **salaire/rémunération de départ,** starting salary; **valeur de départ,** initial value (*c*) **départ volontaire,** voluntary redundancy.

département, *n.m.* department; **département commercial,** sales department.

dépens, *n.m.pl.* (legal) costs; **être condamné aux dépens,** to be ordered to pay costs.

dépense, *n.f.* expenditure/expense/spending/outlay (of money); **compte des dépenses,** expense account; **dépenses courantes,** current/running expenditure; **dépenses diverses,** general/sundry expenses; **dépenses en capital/dépenses d'établissement/dépenses d'investissement/ dépenses en immobilisations,** capital expenditure; **dépenses d'exploitation/de**

fonctionnement, operating costs/working expenses; **dépenses publiques,** government expenditure; **pièce de dépenses,** cash expenditure note; **recettes et dépenses,** income and expenditure; **contrôler les dépenses,** to check expenditure; **faire des dépenses,** to incur expenses; **faire trop de dépenses,** to overspend; **les dépenses excèdent les recettes,** expenditure exceeds income; **on ne regardait pas à la dépense,** no expense was spared.

dépenser, *v.tr.* to spend (money); **trop dépenser,** to overspend.

déplacement, *n.m.* (*a*) **frais de déplacement,** (*i*) travelling expenses (*ii*) removal expenses; **prime/indemnité de déplacement,** relocation/removal allowance (*b*) **déplacement de l'offre et de la demande,** shift/swing in supply and demand.

déplafonnement, *n.m.* removal of the upper limit (of prices, etc.).

déplafonner, *v.tr.* to remove the upper limit of (prices, etc.).

dépliant, *n.m.* folder/brochure; leaflet.

déport, *n.m. StExch:* (*i*) backwardation (*ii*) premium (of exchange).

déposant, -ante, *n.* (*a*) depositor (of money in bank, etc.) (*b*) *Jur:* **(témoin) déposant,** witness who testifies.

déposer, *v.tr.* (*a*) to deposit (documents etc.) (in a safe place); **déposer de l'argent à la banque,** to deposit money (at the bank)/to pay money into the bank (*b* **déposer une demande de brevet,** to file an application for a patent; **déposer une marque de fabrique,** to register a trade mark; **modèle déposé,** registered design/pattern; **marque déposée,** registered trademark (*c*) *Jur:* **déposer son bilan,** to file one's petition (in bankruptcy).

deposit, *n.m. Fin:* initial margin.

dépositaire, 1. *a.* **établissement dépositaire,** financial institution holding securities on trust 2. *n.m.f.* (*a*) trustee; *NAm:* depository; **dépositaire de valeurs,** holde of securities on trust (*b*) dealer/stockist; **seul dépositaire/dépositaire exclusif des produits de qn,** sole agent for s.o.'s products.

dépôt, *n.m.* **1.** (*a*) registration (of trademark); **effectuer/opérer le dépôt d'une marque (de fabrique),** to register a trademark (*b*) *Publ:* **dépôt légal,** legal deposit **2.** (*a*) depositing; deposit (of money, etc.); **dépôt à échéance fixe,** fixed deposit; **dépôt à sept jours de préavis,** deposit at seven days' notice; **dépôt à terme,** short-term investment; **dépôt à court terme,** call money; **dépôt à vue,** demand deposit; **dépôt de garantie,** deposit of guarantee/security (deposit); **dépôt en coffre-fort,** safe-deposit; **dépôt en banque/dépôt bancaire,** bank deposit; **dépôt initial/de marge,** initial margin; **effectuer un dépôt de fonds à la banque,** to deposit/to lodge funds at a bank/with a bank (*b*) **banque de dépôt,** (deposit) bank; **bordereau de dépôt,** paying-in slip; **compte de dépôt,** deposit account; **livret de dépôt,** deposit book (*c*) **en dépôt,** on/in trust; **mettre (des documents, des valeurs) en dépôt dans une banque,** to deposit (documents, securities) with a bank; **marchandises en dépôt,** (*i*) *Cust:* goods in bond (*ii*) goods on sale or return/on consignment **3.** warehouse/depot; **dépôt de marchandises,** warehouse/goods depot; **en dépôt chez ...,** stocked by ... **4.** stock.

dépouillement, *n.m.* **dépouillement d'un compte,** breaking down of an account; **dépouillement de la correspondance,** opening of the mail; **dépouillement d'un rapport,** examination/analysis of a report.

dépouiller, *v.tr.* **dépouiller un compte,** to break down an account; **dépouiller le courrier,** to open/to go through the mail; **dépouiller un rapport,** to examine/to analyse a report; **dépouiller des renseignements,** to process information.

dépréciation, *n.f.* (*a*) depreciation; fall/drop in value; write-down; **comptabilité de la dépréciation,** depreciation accounting; **dépréciation fonctionnelle,** obsolescence; **provisions pour dépré-**

ciation, allowance(s) made for depreciation (*b*) wear and tear.

déprécier, **1.** *v.tr.* (*a*) to depreciate (currency, gold, etc.) (*b*) to undervalue (goods, etc.) **2.** *v.pr.* **se déprécier,** (*l'argent, etc.*) to depreciate/to fall in value.

déprédation, *n.f.* misappropriation/corrupt administration (of funds, etc.).

dépression, *n.f. StExch:* depression (of stock); **dépression du marché,** market depression; *PolEc:* **dépression économique,** economic depression/slump/recession.

déprimé, *a.* **marché déprimé,** depressed market.

dérégulation, *n.f.* deregulation.

déréguler, *v.tr.* to deregulate.

dérivé, *a. & n.m.* **(produit) dérivé,** by-product.

dernier, *a.* (*a*) last; *StExch:* **derniers cours,** closing prices; **dernier paiement,** final payment; **dernier rappel,** final demand; **le plus offrant et le dernier enchérisseur,** the highest bidder (*b*) latest; **voiture dernier modèle,** car of the latest design.

dérogatoire, *a. Jur:* **clause dérogatoire,** overriding clause.

désaisonnalisé, *a.* seasonally adjusted.

désaisonnaliser, *v.tr.* to seasonally adjust (figures).

désassortir, *v.tr.* **désassortir un marchand de qch.,** to buy all the stock of a shop(keeper).

description, *n.f.* description; **conforme à la description,** as represented; **description de brevet,** patent specification; **description de poste,** job description.

désemballage, *n.m.* unpacking/unwrapping (of goods).

désemballer, *v.tr.* to unpack/to unwrap/to undo (parcel, goods, etc.).

désencadrement, *n.m.* **le désencadrement**

des crédits, unblocking of credits/end of credit squeeze.

désendettement, *n.m.* degearing.

déséquilibre, *n.m.* **déséquilibre de la balance commerciale,** unfavourable/adverse trade balance; **déséquilibre financier,** financial imbalance/instability.

désescalade, *n.f.* tumbling down (of prices, shares); downturn.

déshypothéquer, *v.tr.* to disencumber/to free (a property) from mortgage.

désignation, *n.f.* **désignation de marchandises,** description of goods.

designer, *n.m.* designer.

désindexation, *n.f.* removal from index.

désindexé, *a.* (*salaire*) not index-linked.

désinflation, *n.f.* disinflation.

désinflationniste, *a.* **politique désinflationniste,** deflationary policy.

désintéressement, *n.m.* buying out (of partner, etc.); satisfying/paying off (of creditor, etc.); **commission de désintéressement,** drop dead fee; **taux/cours dedésintéressement,** drop dead rate.

désintéresser, *v.tr.* to buy out (partner); to satisfy/to pay off (creditor); to reimburse (s.o.).

désintermédiation, *n.f.* disintermediation.

désinvestissement, *n.m.* disinvestment; **désinvestissement marginal,** marginal disinvestment.

désœuvré, -ée, *n.m.f.* jobless/unemployed person; *pl.* **les désœuvrés,** the jobless/the unemployed.

dessin, *n.m.* (*a*) **dessin publicitaire,** publicity drawing (*b*) design/pattern; **dessin du produit,** product design; **dessin industriel,** design engineering.

déstabilisateur, *a.* destabilizing.

déstabiliser, *v.tr.* to destabilize (government, etc.).

destinataire, *n m.f.* addressee/recipient (of letter, etc.); consignee (of goods).

destination, *n.f.* destination; **marchandises à destination de la province et de l'étranger,** goods for consignment to the provinces and abroad; **navire à destination de Bordeaux,** ship bound for Bordeaux.

destiner, *v.tr.* **destiner une somme d'argent à un achat,** to allot/to assign a sum of money to a purchase; **marchandises destinées à l'exportation,** goods (intended) for export.

déstocker, *v.tr. & i.* to destock.

déstockage, *n.m.* destocking/reduction of stock.

destructeur, *n.m.* **destructeur de documents,** (document) shredder.

désuet, *a.* **équipement désuet,** obsolete equipment.

désuétude, *n.f.* **désuétude calculée,** planned/built-in obsolescence.

détachement, *n.m.* **détachement du coupon,** detaching/detachment of the coupon.

détacher, *v.tr.* **détacher un coupon d'une action,** to detach a coupon from a bond; **le coupon de ces actions se détache le 1er août,** this stock goes ex-coupon on (the) 1st (of) August; **coupon détaché,** ex-coupon.

détail, *n.m.* 1. (*a*) **pour de plus amples détails s'adresser à ...,** for further particulars apply to ...; **faire le détail d'un compte,** to itemize an account/to break down an invoice; **détails d'un compte,** items of an account; **paiements dont détails ci-dessous,** payments as per details/as specified below (*b*) **détails techniques,** technical features/specifications 2. retail; the retail trade; **le commerce en gros et au détail,** the wholesale and retail business/trade; **magasin de détail,** retail shop; **marchand au détail/marchand qui fait le détail,** retail dealer/retailer; **prix de dé-**

tail/de vente au détail, retail price; **vente au détail,** retail; **vendre au détail,** to retail.

détaillant, -ante, n. (**marchand**) **détaillant,** retailer/shopkeeper.

détaillé, a. **état détaillé de compte,** detailed/itemized statement of account.

détailler, v.tr. (a) to retail/to sell retail (b) to itemize (an account).

détaxe, n.f. (a) remission of tax/of duty; **détaxe postale,** refund on postage paid in error (b) decontrolling (of the price of sth.).

détaxer, v.tr. (a) to take the duty/the tax off (sth.) (b) **détaxer la viande,** to decontrol the price of meat.

détenir, v.tr. **détenir des titres,** to hold stock; **société détenue à 50%,** 50% owned company; **détenu par des intérêts privés,** privately-held.

détenteur, -trice, n. (a) holder (of securities, account, etc.); **détenteur de titres,** shareholder/stockholder/scripholder (b) owner (of copyright, etc.).

déterminer, v.tr. to determine/ascertain; **déterminer le revenu imposable,** to assess taxable income.

détournement, n.m. misappropriation/fraudulent misuse/embezzlement; **détournement de fonds,** misappropriation of funds; **auteur d'un détournement de fonds,** embezzler.

détourner, v.tr. to misappropriate/to embezzle (funds) (à, from).

dette, n.f. debt; **acquitter une dette/s'acquitter d'une dette,** to pay off a debt; **avoir des dettes,** to be in debt; **avoir pour 10 000 francs de dettes,** to be 10 000 francs in debt; **contracter/faire des dettes,** to run into debt; **dettes à court terme,** current liabilities; **dettes actives,** debts owed to us/accounts receivable; **dettes bancaires,** bank debts; **dettes compte,** book debts; **dettes d'exploitation,** trade debt; **dette consolidée,** funded debt/consolidated debt; **dette exigible,** debt due for (re)payment; **dette extérieure,** external debt; **dette publique flottante/non consolidée/courante,** floating debt/unfunded debt; **dette non acquittée,** unpaid/undischarged debt; **dettes passives,** debts owed by us/accounts payable/liabilities; **dette de premier rang/dette senior,** senior debt; **dette privilégiée,** privileged debt; **dette subordonnée/dette mezzanine,** mezzanine debt; **reconnaissance de dette,** IOU; **assurer le service d'une dette,** to service a debt; **la dette de l'État/la dette publique,** the National debt; **consolidation de la dette,** debt financing; **le grand-livre de la dette publique,** the National Debt Register.

deuxième, a. & n. second; **deuxième de change,** second of exchange.

dévalorisation, n.f. (a) fall in value/loss of value (b) Fin: devaluation (of currency).

dévaloriser, 1. v.tr. Fin: to devalue (currency); **dévaloriser une monnaie de 10%,** to devalue a currency by 10% 2. v.pr. **se dévaloriser,** to fall in value/to depreciate.

dévaluation, n.f. Fin: PolEc: devaluation.

dévaluer, v.tr. to devalue/devaluate (currency).

devanture, n.f. (a) shop front/shop window (b) goods in the window.

développement, n.m. development; expansion; **développement d'un commerce/d'une entreprise,** growth/expansion of a business; **développement du produit,** product development; **développement des ventes,** sales expansion; **programme de développement,** development programme; **prime de développement,** development subsidy; **zone de développement,** development area; **pays en (voie de) développement,** developing country.

devis, n.m. estimate (of work to be done, etc.); quotation; **devis descriptif,** specification; **établir un devis estimatif,** to draw up an estimate (of quantities and costs); **le devis des réparations s'élève à trois mille**

francs, the estimate/the quotation for the repairs comes to three thousand francs.

devise, *n.f. Fin:* currency; **le yen est la devise japonaise,** the yen is the Japanese currency; **cours officiel des devises,** official exchange rate; **devise convertible,** convertible currency; **devises étrangères,** foreign currency; **devise faible,** soft currency; **devise forte,** hard/scarce currency; **devise sontenue,** firm currency; **effet en devise(s),** bill in foreign currency; **marché des devises (étrangères),** foreign exchange market.

devoir, *v.tr.* devoir qch. à qn, to owe s.o. sth.; **il me doit mille francs,** he owes me a thousand francs; **la somme qui m'est due,** the amount owing to me/owed to me/due to me.

diagramme, *n.m.* diagram; chart; graph; **diagramme de circulation,** flow (process) chart; **diagramme à bâtons,** bar chart/bar diagram; **diagramme à secteurs,** pie chart.

dialoguer, *v.i.* to communicate.

dictaphone, *n.m. Rtm:* Dictaphone.

dictée, *n.f.* dictation; **écrire qch. sous la dictée de qn,** to take down a dictation.

dicter, *v.tr.* to dictate; **dicter une lettre à sa secrétaire,** to dictate a letter to one's secretary; **machine à dicter,** dictating machine.

différé, *a.* deferred (payment, etc.); **crédit différé,** deferred credit; **assurance à capital différé,** endowment insurance (plan).

différence, *n.f.* difference; spread (between bid and asked price).

différentiel, *a.* differential; **droits différentiels,** differential duties; **tarif différentiel,** differential tariff; **différentiel de taux,** interest rate differential.

différer, *v.tr.* to defer/to postpone/to put off/to hold over (payment, etc.); **différer l'échéance d'un effet,** to let a bill lie over.

diffuser, *v.tr.* to distribute/to circulate (books, newspapers, etc.).

diffusion, *n.f.* distribution/circulation (of books, newspapers, etc.); **liste de diffusion,** mailing list.

digraphie, *n.f.* double-entry bookkeeping.

dilapider, *v.tr.* to waste/to squander (public money, etc.); to misappropriate (trust funds, etc.).

diluer, *v.tr.* **to dilute equity,** diluer le bénéfice par action.

dilution, *n.f. Fin:* dilution; **dilution du bénéfice par action,** dilution of equity/equity dilution; **dilution des actions,** dilution of a shareholding; **effet de dilution,** dilutive effect; **dilution négative,** antidilutive effect.

diminuer, *v.tr.* **montant net diminué du prix de vente,** net amount less purchase price.

diminution, *n.f.* reduction/decrease/lowering (of price, etc.); cutting down (of expenses); **diminution d'impôts,** (*i*) lowering of taxation (*ii*) drop in taxation; **diminution de prix/sur le prix,** reduction in price; **faire une diminution sur un compte,** to allow a rebate on an account.

dinausore, *n.m.* (*corps constitué*) elephant.

direct, *a.* direct; **coûts directs/charges directes,** direct expenses; **impôts directs,** direct taxes; **publicité directe,** direct advertising/direct mail(ing); **vente directe,** direct selling.

directeur, -trice, **1.** *n.* director; *NAm:* executive officer; executive manager/manageress; head (of industrial concern, etc.); **directeur adjoint,** deputy manager; **directeur commercial/directeur des ventes,** sales manager/marketing manager; **directeur général,** general manager/managing director; **président-directeur général (P-DG),** chairman and managing director/*NAm:* chief executive officer (CEO); **directeur d'hôtel,** hotel manager; **directeur de la publicité,** advertising/publicity manager; *Bank:* **directeur de banque,** bank manager; **directeur de succursale,** branch manager; **directeur du personnel,** personnel manager; **directeur**

régional, district manager **2.** *a.* **comité directeur,** steering committee; **prix directeur,** price leader.

direction, *n.f.* (*a*) board (of directors); management (of company, etc.); **conseil en direction,** management consultant; **direction commerciale/des ventes,** sales management; **direction générale,** general management/top management; **direction du personnel,** (*i*) personnel department (*ii*) personnel management; **direction par objectifs (DPO),** management by objectives (MBO); **équipe de direction,** management team; **haute direction,** top management; **membre du comité de direction,** executive member; **secrétaire de direction,** director's secretary/private secretary/executive secretary (*b*) (*i*) board (of directors) (*ii*) administrative staff; **la direction,** the management (*c*) (*i*) offices (of the board); director's/manager's office (*ii*) head office (of firm, etc.); **direction régionale,** district/regional headquarters.

directoire, *n.m.* board of directors; **président du directoire,** chairman of the board (of directors).

directorial, *a.* **bureau directorial,** manager's/director's office.

dirigé, *a.* controlled/planned; **économie dirigée,** planned economy; *Fin:* **monnaie dirigée,** managed/controlled currency.

dirigeant, *n.m.* executive; director; manager; **les dirigeants (d'une société),** (the) management.

diriger, *v.tr.* to manage; to run (business, etc.); **diriger la production,** to control production.

dirigisme, *n.m.* (*a*) *PolEc:* planning; **dirigisme économique,** economic planning (*b*) controlled finance.

dirigiste, *n.m.f.* *PolEc:* advocate/exponent of planned economy.

disant, *n.m.* **le moins disant,** the lowest bidder.

discontinu, *a.* discontinuous; **production discontinue,** production in batches.

discount, *n.m.* discount; **magasin de discount,** discount store.

discounté, *a.* **tarif discounté,** discount price.

dispendieux, *a.* expensive/costly (product, etc.).

disponibilité, *n.f.* (*a*) *pl.* liquid assets; **disponibilités monétaires,** money supply (*b*) **disponibilités du stock,** items available in stock.

disponible, 1. *a.* available; disposable; **actif disponible/valeurs disponibles,** available assets/liquid assets/current assets; **capital disponible,** spare capital; **encaisse disponible,** cash in hand; **fonds disponibles,** available funds; **revenus disponibles,** disposable income **2.** *n.m.* **le disponible,** items available in stock; *Fin:* available assets/liquid assets; *StExch:* **marché du disponible,** spot market; **cours/prix du disponible,** spot rate/price.

disposer, *v.tr.* (*a*) **disposer de capitaux importants,** to have a large capital at one's disposal (*b*) **disposer sur qn,** to draw on s.o.

disposition, *n.f.* **disposition(s) du marché/de la Bourse,** tone of the market.

disque, *n.m.* record; *Cmptr:* **disque dur,** hard disk; **disque souple,** floppy disk/diskette; **unité de disques,** disk drive.

disquette, *n.f.* *Cmptr:* floppy disk/diskette.

dissimulation, *n.f.* *Jur:* **dissimulation d'actif,** (fraudulent) concealment of assets.

dissolution, *n.f.* *Jur:* dissolution/termination (of contract); winding up (of company).

distraire, *v.tr.* to misappropriate (funds, supplies, etc.).

distribuable, *a.* **bénéfices distribuables,** (*i*) distributable profits (*ii*) attributable profits.

distribuer, *v.tr.* to distribute; **bénéfices**

non distribués, undistributed profit(s)/retained earnings.

distributeur, *n.m.* (*a*) distributor; **distributeur agréé,** authorized stockist/distributor (*b*) **distributeur automatique,** vending machine; **distributeur automatique (de billets),** *Bank:* cash dispenser/*NAm:* automatic teller; *Rail: etc:* ticket machine; **distributeur de monnaie,** change machine/money changer.

distribution, *n.f.* distribution; allotment (of shares); *Post:* delivery; **distribution de dividendes (aux actionnaires),** distribution of dividends (to the shareholders); **circuit/réseau de distribution,** distribution network; **canaux de distribution,** distribution channels.

divers, 1. *a.pl.* **articles divers,** sundry articles/sundries; **frais divers,** sundry expenses/sundries 2. *n.m.pl.* sundries.

diversification, *n.f.* diversification; **diversification industrielle,** diversification/lateral integration of industry; **diversification des produits,** product diversification.

diversifier, *v.tr.* **diversifier sa production,** to diversify production.

dividende, *n.m.* dividend; **avec dividende,** cum div(idend)/*NAm:* dividend on; **sans dividende/ex-dividende,** ex div(idend)/*NAm:* dividend off; **acompte de dividende/acompte sur dividende/dividende intérimaire,** interim dividend; **certificat de dividende provisoire,** scrip dividend/dividend in scrip; **chèque-dividende,** dividend warrant; **dividende cumulatif,** cumulative dividend; **dividende d'actions,** dividend on shares; **dividende par action,** dividend per share; **dividende fictif,** sham dividend; **dividende privilégié/prioritaire,** preference dividend; **dividende prioritaire cumulatif,** preference cumulative dividend; **solde de dividende,** final dividend; **politique de dividendes,** dividend policy; **toucher un dividende,** to draw a dividend.

division, *n.f.* division; *Adm:* department/branch; **gestion de division,** divisional management.

divisionnaire, *a.* **monnaie divisionnaire,** fractional/divisionary coins.

dock, *n.m.* 1. *Nau:* (*a*) dock (*b*) dock(s)/dockyard; **droits de dock,** dock dues 2. (dock) warehouse; bonded warehouse.

docker, *n.m.* docker; stevedore; *NAm:* longshoreman.

document, *n.m.* document.

documentaire, *a.* documentary; **crédit documentaire,** documentary credit; **traite documentaire,** draft with documents attached; documentary bill of exchange.

documentation, *n.f.* (*a*) documentation (*b*) documents; information; literature.

documenter, *v.tr.* to document (material); **rapport bien documenté,** well-supported report/statement.

doit, *n.m.* debit/liability; **doit d'un compte,** debit (side) of an account; **doit et avoir,** debit and credit/debtor and creditor.

dollar, *n.m.* dollar; **dollar des États-Unis/dollar américain,** US dollar; *F:* greenback; **billet de 5 dollars,** 5 dollar note/*NAm:* 5 dollar bill; **cours du dollar,** exchange rate of the dollar; **prime sur le dollar,** dollar premium; **zone dollar,** dollar area.

domaine, *n.m.* (*a*) estate (*b*) **ouvrage tombé dans le domaine public,** work on which the copyright has lapsed/run out; work out of copyright; **invention tombée dans le domaine public,** invention the patent of which has expired.

domicile, *n.m.* (*a*) domicile; place of residence; permanent residence (*b*) **prise de colis à domicile,** collection of parcels; **notre épicier livre à domicile,** our grocer has a delivery service; **travail à domicile,** work done at home; **faire du travail/travailler à domicile,** to work at home.

domiciliataire, *n.m.* paying agent (of bill of exchange).

domiciliation, *n.f.* domiciliation (of bill of exchange).

domicilier, *v.tr.* (*a*) to domicile (bill of exchange, etc.) (*b*) **salaire domicilié**, pay/wages paid direct into bank account (*c*) **être domicilié à Londres**, to be domiciled in London.

dommage, *n.m. usu. pl.* (*a*) damage (to goods, property, etc.); **dommages corporels**, bodily injuries; **dommages matériels**, damage to property/material damages; **réparer les dommages**, to repair/to make good the damage; to make up the losses (*b*) *Jur:* **dommages et intérêts** = **dommages-intérêts**.

dommages-intérêts, *n.m. pl. Jur:* damages; **actionner/poursuivre qn en dommages-intérêts**, to sue s.o. for damages/to bring an action for damages against s.o.; **se faire accorder/obtenir des dommages-intérêts**, to be awarded damages.

données, *n.f.pl. Cmptr: Stat:* data; **banque de données**, data bank; **base de données**, data base; **collecte de données**, data acquisition; **données brutes**, raw data; **entrée/introduction de données**, data input; **rassemblement de données (statistiques)**, data gathering; **recherche/récupération de données**, information retrieval.

donneur, -euse, *n.* (*a*) *Fin:* **donneur d'aval**, guarantor/backer of bill; **donneur de caution**, guarantor; **donneur d'ordre**, principal (*b*) *Fin:* seller; *StExch:* **donneur d'ordres**, client (of a broker).

dormant, *a.* (*capital*) unproductive/lying idle.

dos, *n.m.* **signer au dos d'un chèque**, to endorse a cheque/to sign (on the back of) a cheque.

dossier, *n.m.* dossier; file; **dossier de candidature**, application; application form; *Mkt:* **dossier de presse**, press pack/kit.

dotation, *n.f.* (*a*) **fonds de dotation**, endowment fund (*b*) **dotation au compte de provisions**, appropriation to the reserve.

douane, *n.f.* customs; **bureaux de douane**, customs (house); **déclaration de/en douane**, customs declaration; bill of entry; (**droits de) douane**, customs duties/customs dues; **entrepôt de (la) douane**, bonded warehouse; **exempt de douane/ (importé) en franchise de douane**, duty-free; **préposé(e) à la douane**, customs officer/employee; **soumis aux droits de douane**, dutiable; **visite de la douane**, customs examination/formalities; **acquitter la douane**, to pay the (customs) duty (on sth.); **passer des marchandises en douane**, to clear goods; **passer par la douane**, to pass/to get through (the) customs; **procéder aux formalités de la douane**, to effect customs clearance.

douanier, -ière 1. *a.* (pertaining to the) customs; **barrières douanières**, tariff walls; **poste douanier**, (frontier) customs (post); **tarif douanier**, customs tariff; **union douanière**, customs union; **visite douanière**, customs examination/customs formalities **2.** *n.* customs officer.

double, 1. *a.* double (quantity, etc.); *Book-k:* **article qui fait double emploi**, duplicated item; **comptabilité en partie double**, double-entry book-keeping; **double imposition**, double taxation; **double option**, double option; put and call; **quittance double**, receipt in duplicate **2.** *n.m.* (*a*) double; **je l'ai vendu pour le double de ce qu'il m'a coûté**, I sold it for twice as much as it cost me/for double the price/for twice the price (*b*) duplicate; carbon copy; **facture en double**, invoice in duplicate.

drainage, *n.m.* drain (of money, capital).

drainer, *v.tr.* to tap (capital, etc.); to draw/to attract (trade, workers, etc.).

drawback, *n.m. Cust:* drawback.

dresser, *v.tr.* to prepare/to draw up/to draft (plan, report, contract, bill, etc.); to make out (invoice, etc.); to make out/to draw up (list).

droit, *n.m.* **1.** (*a*) fair claim; *Publ:* right; **avoir droit à qch.**, to be entitled to sth., **ce qui revient de droit**, entitlement; **être dans**

son droit, to be within one's rights; **faire droit à une réclamation,** to allow a claim; to satisfy a claim; **faire valoir ses droits,** to establish one's rights; **droit de préférence,** right of first refusal; **renoncer à ses droits,** to waive one's rights; **droits de fabrication,** manufacturing rights; *Publ:* **droit d'auteur,** copyright; **droits étrangers,** foreign rights; **droits d'édition,** publishing rights; **tous droits réservés,** all rights reserved/copyright reserved (*c*) *Jur:* **les ayant droit,** rightful claimants; beneficiaries; **à qui de droit,** to whom it may concern **2.** (*a*) charge/fee/due; **droits d'auteur,** royalties; **exemplaires hors droits,** royalty-free copies (*b*) *Cust:* **droit de douane,** duty; **droit d'entrée,** import duty; **marchandises assujetties aux droits,** dutiable goods; **marchandises exemptes/ en franchise de droits,** duty-free goods; **droits de passage,** ferry dues; **droits de port,** harbour rates/port dues (*c*) *Jur:* **droits de succession,** inheritance tax/death duties; *NAm:* death/inheritance/estate tax; **droits de mutation,** capital tansfer tax (*d*) **droit d'inscription,** registration fee; *Adm:* **droit de timbre,** stamp duty **3.** law; **droit civil,** civil law; **droit commercial,** commercial law; **droit maritime,** maritime law; **droit des obligations** = contract law; **droit des sociétés,** company law/*NAm:* corporation law.

dû, 1. *a.* (*a*) owing; **en port dû,** carriage forward (*b*) proper; **contrat rédigé en bonne et due forme,** contract drawn up in due form/formal contract **2.** *n.m.* due(s); **payer son dû,** to pay the amount owed/to pay one's dues.

ducroire, *n.m.* (*a*) del credere (commission)/guarantee commission (*b*) delcredere/guarantee agent.

dûment, *adv.* duly/in due form; **dûment expédié/reçu,** duly dispatched/received; **représentant dûment accrédité,** duly authorized representative.

dumping, *n.m.* dumping; **faire du dumping,** to dump (goods).

duopole, *n.m.* duopoly.

duopsone, *a.* **marché duopsone,** duopsony market.

duplicata, *n.m.inv.* duplicate (copy); **duplicata de reçu,** duplicate receipt; **reçu en duplicata,** receipt in duplicate.

duplicateur, *n.m.* duplicator (of circulars, etc.)/duplicating machine; copier.

durable, *a.* **biens (de consommation) durables,** (consumer) durables; **accord durable,** standing agreement.

durée, *n.f.* duration; **sur une durée de dix ans,** over a period of ten years/during ten years; **durée d'un bail,** duration/term of a lease; **durée de vie,** tenor; **durée d'un prêt,** life of a loan; **durée (utile) de vie d'un produit,** product life expectancy/shelf-life.

dynamique, *a.* **concurrence dynamique,** brisk competition.

E

écart, *n.m.* (*a*) discrepancy/divergence/ disparity/gap/variance; **analyse des écarts,** variance analysis; **écart de cent francs entre deux comptes,** discrepancy of a hundred francs between two accounts; **écart budgétaire,** budgetary variance; **écart des bénéfices,** profit gap; **écart des coûts,** cost variance; **écart déflationniste,** deflationary gap; **écart inflationniste,** inflationary gap; *StExch:* **écart minimum des cours du marché,** tick; **écart de cours maximal/minimal,** maximum/minimum price fluctuation; **écart vertical baissier,** bear spread; **écart vertical haussier,** bull spread (*b*) **écart de prix,** price differential; **écarts de salaire,** wage differentials; **écart entre le prix d'achat et le prix de vente,** spread between bid and asked prices; **écart entre le taux d'inflation et les tranches d'imposition,** bracket creep; **écart entre taux offert et taux demandé,** bid-offer spread.

échange, *n.m.* (*a*) exchange; swap; **échange d'actions,** exchange of shares; **valeur d'échange,** exchange value; **échange de dette,** debts swap (*b*) barter; trading; **échanges commerciaux,** trade; trading; **libre échange,** free trade; **termes de l'échange,** terms of trade (*c*) **échanges en volume,** tonnage; **échanges en valeurs,** turnover.

échangeable, *a.* exchangeable (**contre,** for).

échanger, *v.tr.* (*a*) to exchange; **on n'échange pas les articles achetés,** no goods exchanged (*b*) to barter; to swap.

échangiste, *n.m.f. Jur:* exchanger.

échantillon, *n.m.* sample (of cloth, etc.); **conforme à l'échantillon,** up to sample; **échantillon aléatoire,** random sample;

échantillon gratuit, free sample; **échantillon témoin,** check sample; **échantillon type,** representative sample; **échantillon représentatif,** true/fair sample; **paquet échantillon,** sample packet; *Post:* **échantillons sans valeur,** samples of no (commercial) value.

échantillonnage, *n.m.* **1.** (*a*) making up of samples (*b*) range of samples **2.** verifying/checking against the samples.

échantillonner, *v.tr.* **1.** to prepare patterns/samples of (sth.) **2.** to verify/to check (articles) by the samples.

échappatoire, *a.* **clause échappatoire,** escape clause.

échéance, *n.f.* (*a*) (**date d')échéance,** due date; **avis d'échéance,** notice to pay; **dépôt à échéance fixe,** fixed deposit; **échéance commune,** equation of payment (of bill of exchange); **échéance moyenne,** average due date; **effet à courte échéance,** short-dated/short-term bill; **effet à longue échéance,** long-dated/long-term bill; **emprunter à longue/à courte échéance,** to borrow long/short; **prêter à longue/à courte échéance,** to lend long/short; **échéance à long/moyen terme,** long-term/ medium-term maturity; **à trois mois d'échéance,** at three months' date/three months after date; **faire face à une échéance,** to meet a bill; **il n'a pas pu faire face à l'échéance,** he couldn't meet his end of (the) month payments; **l'intérêt n'a pas été payé à l'échéance,** the interest is overdue; **payable à l'échéance,** payable at maturity; **venir à échéance,** to fall due/to mature; maturing (bills) (*b*) expiration (of tenancy, etc.).

échéancier, *n.m.* *Fin:* bills-receivable

book/bills-payable book; bill book/bill diary; **échéancier des devises livrables à terme,** forward book.

échéant, *a. Fin:* falling due.

échelle, *n.f.* (*a*) scale; **économies de grande échelle,** large-scale economies; **à l'échelle internationale,** on a world wide scale (*b*) **échelle mobile,** (*i*) sliding scale (of prices, of salaries, etc.) (*ii*) escalator clause; **échelle des prix,** price range; **échelle des salaires,** salary scale.

échelonnement, *n.m.* (*a*) spreading out (of payments) (*b*) staggering (of holidays).

échelonner, *v.tr.* (*a*) to spread out (payments); **versements échelonnés sur dix ans,** instalments spread over ten years (*b*) to stagger; **congés échelonnés,** staggered holidays.

échoir, *v.i.* (*a*) *Fin:* to fall due/to become due/to mature; **billets échus,** bills (over)due; **capitaux dont la date de paiement est échue,** matured capital; **intérêts échus,** outstanding interest; **intérêts à échoir,** interest falling due (*b*) (*d'un bail*) to expire.

économat, *n.m.* (*a*) staff shop (*provided by employer*) (*b*) bursar's office.

économe, *n.m.* bursar.

économétrique, *a.* econometric.

économie, *n.f.* **1.** (*a*) economy; management (*b*) **l'économie de la France,** (*i*) the French economy (*ii*) the French economic system; **économie active,** buoyant economy; **économie capitaliste/libérale,** capitalist economy; **économie dirigée,** controlled economy; **économie d'échelle/ de dimension,** economy of scale; **économie de marché,** (*i*) market economy (*ii*) indirect production; **économie mixte,** mixed economy; **économie planifiée,** planned economy; **économie politique,** political economy; **économie souterraine,** black economy; **économie stagnante,** run-down economy; **économie de troc/non monétaire,** natural economy; **économie à dominante**

de services, service economy; **économie d'actionnariat populaire/de participation,** share economy; **économie à ressources sous-exploitées,** sleeping economy; **économie salariale,** wage economy **2.** economy/saving; **économie de main d'œuvre,** labour-saving; **vous faites une économie de 20%,** you make a saving of 20% **3.** *pl.* savings; **faire des économies,** to save (money); to cut down (on) expenditure; to save (up); **politique d'économies,** policy of retrenchment.

économique, *a.* **1.** (*a*) economic; **aide économique,** economic aid; **climat économique,** economic climate; **conjoncture économique,** economic situation/trend; **crise économique,** economic crisis; **croissance économique,** economic growth; **politique économique,** economic policy; **reprise économique,** economic recovery; **sciences économiques,** economics; **série économique,** economic batch; **série économique de production/quantité économique de fabrication,** economic manufacturing quantity; **vie économique (d'un produit),** economic life (of a product) (*b*) **Communauté économique européenne (CEE),** European Economic Community (EEC) **2.** economical/inexpensive; **une voiture économique,** an economical car to run; *Av:* **voyager en classe économique,** to travel economy class.

économiquement, *adv.* (*a*) economically; **les économiquement faibles,** the lower-income groups/(people in) the lower-income bracket (*b*) inexpensively.

économiser, *v.tr.* to economize/to save (money, time); **il faut économiser sur qch.,** we must economize/cut down on sth.

économiste, *n.m.f.* (political) economist; **économiste d'entreprise,** business economist.

écoulé, *a.* (*a*) of last month/ult(imo); **votre lettre du 25 écoulé,** your letter of 25th ult(imo); **payable fin écoulé,** due at the end of last month (*b*) **l'exercice écoulé,** the last financial year; the year under review.

écoulement, *n.m.* sale; selling; **marchandises d'écoulement facile,** goods which sell well/that have a ready sale.

écouler, 1. *v.tr.* to sell (off)/to dispose of/to get rid of (goods, etc.); **écouler (qch.) à bas prix,** to sell (sth.) off at a low price/ cheaply **2.** *v.pr.* **notre stock s'écoule rapidement,** our stock is (*i*) selling fast (*ii*) running low.

écraser, *v.tr.* **écraser les prix,** to hammer prices.

écrémer, *v.tr.* **écrémer le marché,** to cream the market.

écrire, *v.tr.* (*a*) to write; **écrire à qn,** to write to s.o.; **écrire une lettre à qn,** to write s.o. a letter (*b*) **écrire une lettre à la machine,** to type a letter; **écrit à la machine,** typewritten/typed; **machine à écrire,** typewriter (*c*) to write (sth.) down; **écrire l'adresse de qn,** to write down s.o.'s address (*d*) **écrire la comptabilité,** to write up the books.

écrit, 1. *n.m.* (*a*) writing; **consigner/coucher qch. par écrit,** to put sth. down in writing; **convention par écrit,** agreement in writing/ written agreement (*b*) (written) document; **droit écrit,** statute law; **signer un écrit,** to sign a document **2.** *a.* written; **convention/déclaration écrite,** written agreement/statement.

écriture, *n.f.* **1.** handwriting **2.** (*a*) *pl.* (legal, commercial) papers/documents/ records; **écritures administratives,** paperwork (*b*) **commis/employé aux écritures,** book-keeper/(invoicing) clerk; **tenir les écritures,** to keep the accounts/the books (*c*) entry/item; **arrêter les écritures,** to close the accounts; **écritures en partie double,** double-entry bookkeeping; **passer une écriture,** to make an entry (in the books); **passer les écritures,** to post (up) the books.

écu, *n.m.* ecu (*European currency unit*); **compte en écus,** account in ecu.

éditeur, *n.m.* **1.** (book) publisher **2.** *Cmptr:* **éditeur de textes,** word processor.

édition, *n.f.* (book) publishing; **maison d'édition,** publishing firm/company/ house.

effectif, 1. *a.* effective; *Fin:* **circulation effective,** active circulation; **coût effectif,** effective cost; **monnaie effective,** effective money; **rendement effectif,** actual yield; **revenu effectif,** real income; **taux effectif,** effective rate; **taux d'imposition effectif,** effective/*NAm:* average tax rate; **valeur effective,** real value **2.** *n.m.* (*a*) **effectif budgétaire,** budgetary strength/*NAm:* authorized strength; **effectifs,** manpower; **crise d'effectifs,** shortage of manpower; **gestion des effectifs,** manpower management (*b*) *Ind:* stock (of material, etc.) (*c*) **effectif de série économique,** economic batch quantity.

effectuer, *v.tr.* to effect/to carry out; to make (a calculation); to incur (expenses); to carry on (business dealings); to effect/ to make (payment); **paiements effectués par la caisse,** cash payments.

effet, *n.m.* **1.** effect/result; **les effets de la crise économique,** the effects of the economic crisis; **sans effet,** ineffective **2.** (*a*) **facture avec effet rétroactif,** backdated bill; **nul et sans effet,** null and void; **prendre effet,** to take effect; to become operative (*b*) *Ins:* commencement (of policy) **3. effet bancaire,** bank bill; **effet de commerce,** bill (of exchange)/negotiable instrument; trade bill; **effets à payer,** bills payable; **effets à recevoir,** bills receivable; **effet à vue,** sight draft; **effet de complaisance,** accommodation bill; *Fin:* **effets au porteur,** bearer securities; **effets nominatifs,** registered stock; **effets publics,** government stock/securities **4.** *pl.* **effets mobiliers,** personal effects.

efficace, *a.* effective; efficient; **direction efficace,** effective management.

efficacement, *adv.* effectively/efficiently.

efficacité, *n.f.* effectiveness; efficiency; **efficacité économique,** economic efficiency; **efficacité de la direction,** managerial effectiveness; **efficacité parfaite,** absolute efficiency; **efficacité publicitaire,** advertising effectiveness; **efficacité relative,** relative efficiency.

efficience, *n.f.* efficiency (of business, etc.); **efficience absolue,** absolute efficiency; **efficience relative,** relative efficiency.

efficient, *a.* efficient/effective.

effondrement, *n.m. StExch:* **effondrement des cours,** slump in prices/collapse of prices; **l'effondrement du dollar,** the collapse of the dollar.

effondrer(s'), *v.pr.* (*cours, etc.*) to slump/ to collapse; **le marché s'est effondré,** the bottom has fallen out of the market.

effritement, *n.m. StExch:* **effritement des cours,** crumbling of prices.

effriter(s'), *v.pr. StExch:* (*cours, etc.*) to crumble.

égal, *a.* equal (à, to); **associés à part égale,** equal partners.

égalité, *n.f.* equality; **principe d'égalité des salaires,** principle of equal pay; **à égalité,** on a par (with).

élaborer, *v.tr.* **élaborer un plan,** to elaborate/to work out/to think out/to prepare/to formulate/to draw up a plan.

élasticité, *n.f. PolEc:* **l'élasticité de l'offre et de la demande,** the elasticity of supply and demand.

élastique, *a. PolEc:* **offre/demande élastique,** elastic supply/demand.

électrique, *a.* electric; **centrale électrique,** power station.

électroménager, *a. & n.m.* **appareil électroménager,** electrical (household) appliance; labour-saving device.

électronique, 1. *a.* electronic; **calculateur électronique,** electronic computer; **génie électronique,** electronic engineering; **machine à écrire électronique,** electronic typewriter; **industrie électronique,** electronics industry **2.** *n.f.* electronics.

élément, *n.m.* component/constituent (of

sth.); factor; **élément du prix de revient,** cost factor; **élément d'un compte,** item of an account.

élévation, *n.f.* rise; **élévation des prix,** rise in prices/price rise/escalation (of prices).

élevé, *a.* **devise à change élevé,** hard currency; **les dépenses sont élevées,** expenditure is running high; **(à des) prix élevés,** (at) high prices; **taux d'intérêt élevé,** high interest rate.

élever, 1. *v.tr.* to raise (prices); **élever qn à un rang supérieur,** to promote s.o. **2.** *v.pr.* (*a*) **chaque mois les prix s'élèvent un peu,** prices are going up a little every month (*b*) **le compte s'élève à mille francs,** the bill comes to/amounts to a thousand francs.

éluder, *v.tr.* **éluder le paiement de l'impôt,** to evade payment of tax.

émargement, *n.m.* receipting/initialling/ signing (of account, etc.) in the margin; **feuille/liste d'émargement,** payroll.

émarger, *v.tr.* (*a*) *Adm: etc:* **émarger un compte,** to receipt/to initial an account (in the margin) (*b*) to draw one's salary; **émarger au budget,** to be on the payroll.

emballage, *n.m.* (*a*) packing/packaging/ wrapping (of parcels, goods, etc.) (*b*) packing department (*c*) container/pack/ packing cases/crates; **l'emballage est consigné,** there is a deposit on the container; **emballage géant,** giant pack; **emballage sous film rétractable,** shrinkwrap(ped) pack; **emballage perdu,** no-deposit/non-returnable container; disposable/throw-away container; **emballage transparent,** blister pack; **emballage sous vide,** vacuum pack (*d*) **frais de port et d'emballage,** postage and packing; **poids net à l'emballage,** net weight when packed.

emballage-bulle, *n.m.* bubble pack/blister pack.

emballement, *n.m. StExch:* **emballement du marché,** sudden activity of the market.

emballer, *v.tr.* to pack (goods, etc.); to wrap up (article in paper, etc.); **(produit)**

emballé sous vide, vacuum packed (product).

embarcadère, *n.m. Nau:* landing stage; wharf/quay; loading dock.

embargo, *n.m. Nau:* embargo; **lever l'embargo,** to raise the embargo; **mettre l'embargo (sur un navire),** to lay an embargo (on a ship)/to place (a ship) under (an) embargo; **mettre un embargo sur l'importation de qch.,** to put an embargo on the import(ation) of sth.

embarquement, *n.m.* (*a*) *Nau:* embarkation (of passengers); shipment/shipping (of goods); **port d'embarquement,** port of embarkation (*b*) *Rail: Av:* loading/putting (goods) into (a train, a plane); **quai d'embarquement,** loading platform (for goods) (*c*) boarding; **heure d'embarquement,** boarding time.

embarquer, 1. *v.tr.* (*a*) *Nau:* to embark (passengers); to ship (goods)/to take (goods) aboard (*b*) to load up; to put (goods) into/onto (a lorry, train, plane, etc.); **poids net embarqué,** loaded net weight **2.** *v.pr.* **s'embarquer,** to go aboard/to go on board/to board (a ship, a train, a plane, etc.).

embarras, *n.m.* difficulty/trouble; **des embarras d'argent,** financial difficulties; financial distress.

embauchage, *n.m.* taking on/engaging/ *NAm:* hiring (of workers).

embauche, *n.f.* **1.** = **embauchage 2.** *F:* job; **chercher de l'embauche,** to look for a job.

embaucher, *v.tr.* to take on/to engage/ *NAm:* to hire (staff, workers).

emboîtage, *n.m. Publ:* box/casing.

émergent, *a.* **marché émergent,** emerging market.

émetteur, -trice, 1. *n. Fin: etc:* issuer (of banknotes, shares, etc.) **2.** *a.* issuing; **banque émettrice,** issuing bank.

émettre, *v.tr.* to issue (banknotes, shares, cheques, etc.); **émettre un emprunt,** to issue/to float a loan; **capital émis,** issued capital; **le chèque a été émis le 24 mars,** the cheque is dated 24th March.

émission, *n.f. Fin: etc:* (*i*) issue (*ii*) issuing (of banknotes, shares, etc.); **(lancement d'une) émission (de titres),** (*i*) issue (*ii*) flotation/float (of loan); **émission d'obligations,** bond issue; **émission réservée/en placement privé,** placing; **émission par séries,** block issues; **garantir une émission,** to underwrite an issue; **prix/valeur d'émission,** issue price; **banque d'émission,** issuing bank; **émission de timbres-poste,** issue of postage stamps.

emmagasinage *n.m.,* **emmagasinement** *n.m.* (*a*) (*i*) storage (*ii*) storing/warehousing (of goods) (*b*) storage (charges)/warehouse charges.

emmagasiner, *v.tr.* to store/to warehouse (goods).

émoluments, *n.m.pl.* fee/salary/pay/ emoluments.

empaquetage, *n.m.* **1.** packing (of goods, etc.); doing up (of goods) into parcels; **empaquetage automatique,** automatic packaging; **poids net à l'empaquetage, 250 g,** net weight when packed, 250 g **2.** packing (material).

empaqueter, *v.tr.* to package; to pack (sth.) up/to make (sth.) into a parcel.

emphytéose, *n.f. Jur:* long lease (18 to 99 years).

emphytéote, *n.m.f. Jur:* lessee/holder of a long lease.

emphytéotique, *a. Jur:* **bail emphytéotique,** long lease (18 to 99 years)/= leasehold; building lease; **redevance emphytéotique,** ground rent.

emplette, *n.f.* (*a*) shopping; **faire ses emplettes,** to do one's shopping (*b*) (*objet acheté*) purchase.

emploi, *n.m.* **1.** (*a*) **mode d'emploi,** directions for use (*b*) **emploi du temps,** timetable/schedule (of work) (*c*) *Book-k:* **double emploi,** duplication (of entry);

faire double emploi avec ..., to duplicate with ... **2.** employment/occupation/post/job; **chercher un emploi,** to look for a job; **créer de nouveaux emplois,** to create new jobs; **la crise de l'emploi,** the unemployment crisis; **emploi à temps complet/à plein temps,** full-time employment/job; **emploi à temps partiel,** part-time employment/job; **être sans emploi,** to be unemployed; *PolEc:* **planification de l'emploi,** manpower planning; **plein emploi,** full employment; **sécurité de l'emploi,** job security; *Journ:* **demandes d'emploi,** situations wanted; **offres d'emploi,** situations vacant.

employé, -ée, *n.* employee/member of (the) staff; **employé de magasin,** sales assistant/shop assistant/*NAm:* clerk; **employé de banque,** bank clerk; **employé de bureau,** office worker; **employé au classement,** filing clerk; **employé aux écritures,** book-keeper; **employé de l'expédition,** dispatch clerk; shipping clerk; **employé d'administration,** government employee/civil servant; **employé de la régie,** customs and excise officer.

employer, *v.tr.* **1.** *Book-k:* **employer une somme en recette,** to put/to enter an amount in the receipts **2.** to employ (workers, etc.); **employer qn comme secrétaire,** to employ s.o. as secretary.

employeur, -euse, *n.* employer.

emporter, *v.tr.* (*a*) to take away; **plats (cuisinés) à emporter,** food to take away/take away food (*b*) **emporter un marché,** to close the sale.

empressé, *a. Corr:* **veuillez agréer mes salutations empressées,** (I remain) yours faithfully.

emprunt, *n.m.* **1.** borrowing; **capital d'emprunt,** borrowed capital; **faire un emprunt à qn,** to borrow money from s.o.; **j'ai fait un emprunt de 2000F à la banque,** I borrowed 2000F from the bank **2.** loan; **emprunt à 8%,** loan (bearing interest) at 8%; **emprunt consolidé,** consolidated loan; funded debt; **emprunt à découvert,** unsecured loan; **emprunt d'État,** govern-

ment loan; **emprunt d'État indexé,** granny bond; **emprunt forcé,** forced loan; **emprunt garanti,** secured loan; **emprunt indexé,** indexed loan; **emprunt obligataire,** debenture loan; bond issue; **emprunt or,** gold loan; **emprunt perpétuel,** perpetual loan; **emprunt personnel,** personal loan; **emprunt remboursable sur demande,** call loan/loan repayable on demand; **emprunt de remboursement,** refunding loan; **emprunt à terme,** loan at notice; **emprunt à court terme,** short term loan; **emprunt à long terme,** long term loan; **emprunt sur titres,** loan on securities/on stock; **amortir un emprunt,** to redeem/to repay a loan; **contracter un emprunt,** to raise a loan; **couvrir un emprunt,** to cover a loan/to subscribe to a loan; **émettre un emprunt/lancer un emprunt,** to issue/to float a loan; **placer un emprunt,** to place a loan; **procéder à un nouvel emprunt,** to make a new issue of capital/a new loan issue; **rembourser un emprunt,** to repay/to redeem a loan; **souscrire un emprunt,** to subscribe a loan.

emprunter, *v.tr.* to borrow; **emprunter (de l'argent) à qn,** to borrow (money) from s.o.; **la société a dû emprunter pour s'acquitter de ses dettes,** the company had to borrow to pay off its debts; **emprunter (de l'argent) sur titres,** to borrow (money) on securities/on stock; **emprunter à long/à court terme,** to borrow long/short; **emprunter à intérêt,** to borrow at interest.

emprunteur, -euse, 1. *n.* borrower **2.** *a.* borrowing (corporation, etc.).

encadrement, *n.m.* (*a*) *Ind: Adm:* management; **personnel d'encadrement,** managerial staff; **poste d'encadrement,** managerial position (*b*) **encadrement du crédit,** credit squeeze/credit ceilings/credit control(s); **encadrement des loyers,** rent control.

encaissable, *a. Fin:* (en)cashable/collectable (bill); **ce chèque est encaissable à la banque,** this cheque can be cashed at the bank.

encaissage, *n.m.* boxing/casing/packing (of goods).

encaisse, *n.f.* cash (in hand)/ready cash; cash balance; **encaisse d'un magasin,** money in the till/takings; **encaisse or et argent de la Banque de France,** gold and silver reserves/holdings of the Bank of France; **encaisse métallique,** gold and silver reserves; bullion; *Bank:* **pas d'encaisse,** no funds.

encaissement, *n.m. Fin:* cashing (of cheque); receipt/collection (of money or bills).

encaisser, *v.tr.* to cash; to receive/to collect (money, bill); **encaisser un chèque,** to cash a cheque; **effets à encaisser,** accounts receivable.

encaisseur, **1.** *n.m.* collector/receiver (of bill, cheque, money, etc.); payee (of cheque, etc.); (bank) cashier **2.** *a.* collecting (banker, etc.).

encan, *n.m.* (public) auction; **mettre qch. à l'encan,** to put sth. up for auction; **vendre qch. à l'encan,** to auction sth./to sell sth. by auction.

enchère, *n.f.* bid(ding); **mettre/porter une enchère,** to make a bid; **couvrir une enchère,** to make a higher bid/*F:* to up the bidding; **l'enchère a monté jusqu'à deux cents francs,** the bidding rose to two hundred francs; **faire une enchère de cent francs,** to bid another hundred francs; **mettre qch. aux enchères,** to put sth. up to/for auction; **mettre une enchère,** to make a bid (on sth); **vente aux enchères,** (sale by) auction/auction sale; **enchères au rabais,** Dutch auction; **vente sur folle enchère,** re-auctioning of goods with lower reserve prices (*when taker cannot pay*).

enchérir, *v.i.* to make a higher bid; **enchérir de dix francs,** to bid another ten francs; **enchérir sur qn,** to outbid s.o.

enchérisseur, -euse, *n.* bidder; **vendre au (plus offrant et) dernier enchérisseur,** to sell to the highest bidder.

encombrement, *n.m.* glut (of goods on the market).

encombrer, *v.tr.* **encombrer le marché,** to glut/to overstock the market.

encouragement, *n.m.* encouragements, incentives; **encouragements à la production,** production incentives.

encourir, *v.tr.* **encourir des frais,** to incur expenses.

encours, en-cours, *n.m.* **1.** *Bank:* total of the bills (remitted by the customer to the bank) outstanding at any one time; **encours de crédit,** outstanding credits; **l'encours de la dette,** the outstanding debt **2.** *Ind:* **encours de fabrication,** material undergoing processing; **encours de route,** material/stock awaiting transfer (*to another department*).

endetté, *a.* in debt.

endettement, *n.m.* (*a*) running into debt (*b*) **endettement extérieur,** external debt; *Fin:* **endettement à long terme,** long-term/deferred liabilities; **ratio d'endettement,** gearing/debt ratio; **ratio d'endettement sur fonds propres,** debt-for-equity; **diminution/réduction du ratio d'endettement,** de-gearing; **plafond d'endettement,** debt ceiling/limit.

endetter, **1.** *v.tr.* **l'achat de sa maison l'a endetté,** the purchase of his house got him into debt **2.** *v.pr.* **s'endetter,** to get/to run into debt; to run up bills.

endiguement, *n.m.* hedging.

endos, *n.m.* endorsement (on bill, cheque); **endos en blanc,** blank endorsement.

endossataire, *n.m.f.* endorsee.

endossement, *n.m.* (*a*) endorsing (*b*) endorsement (on bill, cheque); **endossement en blanc,** blank endorsement.

endosser, *v.tr.* to endorse (cheque, bill, etc.); to back (bill).

endosseur, -euse, *n.* endorser (of bill, etc.).

énergétique, *n.f.* energetics; **la facture énergétique,** energy (consumption) bill.

énergie, *n.f.* energy; **énergie nucléaire,** nuclear energy.

engagement, *n.m.* **1.** (*a*) pawning/pledging; mortgaging (of property) (*b*) tying up/locking up (of capital); downside; **engagement bancaire,** (bank) commitment; **engagement hors bilan,** contingent liabilities; *Adm:* **engagement de dépenses,** commitment of funds; **créances et engagements,** claims and liabilities (*c*) receipt (for object pledged) **2.** (*a*) promise/agreement; contract; liability; commitment; **sans engagement,** without obligation; **contracter/prendre un engagement,** to enter into a contract/into an agreement (*b*) engagement/appointment (of employee); indenture.

engager, 1. *v.tr.* (*a*) to pledge/to pawn; to mortgage (property); **tous les frais engagés seront remboursés,** all expenses incurred will be reimbursed; **cette lettre ne vous engage pas,** this letter does not bind you/does not commit you (*b*) **engager du personnel,** to take on/*NAm:* to hire staff; **nous avons dû engager une nouvelle vendeuse,** we had to take on a new sales assistant (*c*) *Fin:* **engager son capital,** to lock up/to tie up one's capital; **engager des frais,** to incur expenses; **actif engagé,** trading assets (*d*) to begin/to start; **engager des négociations,** to enter into negotiations; *Jur:* **engager des poursuites,** to bring an action/to take legal action/to take legal proceedings/to institute proceedings (**contre,** against) **2.** *v.pr.* **s'engager (par contrat),** to bind oneself (by contract)/to contract (**à faire,** to do).

engorgement, *n.m. PolEc:* **l'engorgement (des marchés),** glutting (of markets).

engorger, *v.tr. PolEc:* to glut (the market).

enlever, 1. *v.tr.* (*a*) **enlever des marchandises,** to snap up goods; *Fin:* **enlever une émission d'actions,** to snap up an issue of shares (*b*) **il a enlevé l'affaire,** he got the order/the contract **2.** *v.pr.* **marchandises qui s'enlèvent,** goods that sell quickly/that are snapped up.

enquête, *n.f.* inquiry/investigation; **commission d'enquête,** board/commission of inquiry; **enquête d'opinion,** attitude/opinion survey; **enquête par sondage,** sample survey; opinion poll; **enquête pilote,** pilot survey; **enquête sur les lieux,** field study.

enregistrement, *n.m.* registration/record(ing); **enregistrement d'une commande,** booking/entering (up) of an order; **enregistrement d'une compagnie,** incorporation of a company; **enregistrement des bagages,** registration of luggage; *Av:* **se présenter à l'enregistrement,** to check in; *Adm:* **l'Enregistrement,** (the) Registration department; **droits d'enregistrement,** registration fees.

enregistrer, *v.tr.* to register/to record; **enregistrer une commande,** to book/to enter (up) an order; **enregistrer une perte,** to carry a loss; **société enregistrée,** incorporated company; **(faire) enregistrer ses bagages,** (*i*) to register one's luggage (*ii*) *Av:* to check in one's luggage.

ensemblier, *n.m.* turnkey operator.

entamer, *v.tr.* **entamer son capital,** to break into one's capital; **entamer des négociations,** to open negotiations; *Jur:* **entamer des poursuites,** to take legal proceedings/to institute proceedings (**contre,** against).

entente, *n.f.* (*a*) agreement/understanding (**entre,** between) (*b*) **entente (industrielle),** (*i*) combine; cartel (*ii*) restrictive practice.

en-tête, *n.m.* heading (of letter, document, bill, etc.); **papier à en-tête,** headed notepaper; **feuille de papier à en-tête d'une société,** company letter heading.

entièrement, *adv.* entirely/completely; **capital entièrement versé,** fully paid(-up) capital.

entrée, *n.f.* **1.** (*a*) entry (in account books, etc.) (*b*) *pl.* (*i*) goods received (*ii*) takings/receipts (*c*) **entrée de capitaux,** capital inflow **2.** (*a*) admission/admittance; entrance fee; **billet d'entrée,** entrance ticket; **entrée gratuite,** admission free; **entrée**

libre, (*i*) = no obligation to buy (*ii*) admission free (*b*) import(ation); *Cust:* entry; **droit d'entrée/taxe à l'entrée,** import duty; **entrée en douane,** clearance inward/entry inward (*c*) **entrée en fonctions,** taking up of duties; **entrée en jouissance,** taking possession; **entrée en séance,** opening of a meeting (*d*) **entrée d'un marché,** entry **3.** way in/entrance; **entrée des fournisseurs,** tradesmen's entrance.

entre-fin, *a.* medium-quality (goods).

entreposage, *n.m.* warehousing/storing; *Cust:* bonding.

entreposer, *v.tr.* to warehouse/to store; *Cust:* to bond; to put (goods) in bond; **marchandises entreposées,** bonded goods.

entreposeur, *n.m.* (*a*) warehouse keeper/warehouseman; *Cust:* officer in charge of a bonded store (*b*) wholesaler selling goods under Government monopoly (*e.g. tobacco, matches, salt*).

entrepositaire, *n.m.f.* warehousekeeper.

entrepôt, *n.m.* (*a*) warehouse/store/repository; **entrepôt frigorifique,** cold store; **marchandises en entrepôt,** goods in store; **à prendre à l'entrepôt/en entrepôt,** at warehouse (*b*) *Cust:* **entrepôt réel/entrepôt de (la) douane,** bonded warehouse; **entrepôt fictif,** unbonded warehouse; **entrepôt maritime,** wharf; **marchandises en entrepôt,** bonded goods/goods in bond; **mettre des marchandises en entrepôt,** to bond goods; to put goods in bond (*c*) entrepôt; **Londres est un grand centre d'entrepôt,** London has a large entrepôt trade; **port d'entrepôt,** entrepôt port.

entrepreneur, *n.m.* (*a*) contractor; **entrepreneur (en bâtiments),** building contractor; **entrepreneur de transports/de roulage,** carrier/haulage contractor (*b*) entrepreneur/enterpriser; **(activités) d'entrepreneur,** entrepreneurial (activities).

entreprise, *n.f.* **1.** (*a*) undertaking/venture; **entreprise en participation,** joint venture (*b*) enterprise/business/firm; **chef d'entreprise,** head/manager (of company, firm, etc.); **créateur d'entreprise(s),** entre-

preneur; **entreprise artisanale,** (*i*) small-scale enterprise (*ii*) cottage industry; **entreprise agricole,** farm business/enterprise; **entreprise commerciale,** business undertaking/business concern; **entreprise familiale,** family business/firm; **entreprise industrielle,** manufacturing industry; **entreprise de navigation,** shipping company; **les grosses entreprises,** big/large(-scale) industry; **petites et moyennes entreprises (PME),** small and medium-sized firms; **entreprise phare,** leading/model company; **entreprise privée,** private enterprise; **entreprise publique,** public corporation; **entreprise de service public,** statutory company; **la libre entreprise,** free enterprise (*c*) **comité d'entreprise,** works council; **croissance de l'entreprise,** corporate growth; **formation dans l'entreprise,** in-house/in-plant training; **planification de l'entreprise,** company planning (*d*) **entreprise de transports/de roulage,** road haulage company/haulage contractors **2. (contrat d')entreprise,** contract (for work, supply of goods, etc.); **entreprise de travaux publics,** contract for public works; **travail à l'entreprise,** contract work; **mettre/donner qch. à l'entreprise,** to put sth. out to contract; **prendre qch. à l'entreprise,** to contract for sth.; **avoir l'entreprise de construire une route,** to hold a contract for building a road.

entrer, 1. *v.i.* (*a*) to enter; **entrer en association avec qn,** to enter into partnership with s.o.; **entrer en correspondance avec qn,** to enter into correspondence with s.o. (*b*) to import; **les marchandises qui entrent en France sont soumises à des droits de douane,** goods entering France are subject to customs duty (*c*) **entrer en vigueur,** to come into force/to take effect **2.** *v.tr.* **entrer des marchandises en contrebande/en fraude,** to smuggle in goods.

entretenir, *v.tr.* to keep (sth.) in good repair/in good (working) order; to maintain (sth.).

entretien, *n.m.* **1.** upkeep/maintenance (of property, machines, etc.); **entretien systé-**

matique, planned maintenance; **entretien et réparations,** servicing and repairs; **personnel d'entretien,** maintenance staff **2.** (*a*) interview; **j'ai demandé un entretien avec les directeurs,** I asked to talk to the managers/I asked for a meeting with the managers (*b*) *pl.* **entretiens,** talks/ negotiations.

enveloppe, *n.f.* **1.** envelope (of letter); wrapper/wrapping (of parcel); **mettre une lettre sous enveloppe,** to put a letter in/into an envelope; **enveloppe autocollante,** self-seal envelope; **enveloppe à fenêtre,** window envelope; **enveloppe gommée,** adhesive envelope; **enveloppe kraft,** brown envelope; **enveloppe-réponse,** reply-paid envelope; **joindre une enveloppe timbrée à votre adresse,** enclose a stamped addressed envelope (s.a.e.) for reply **2.** *Fin:* **enveloppe budgétaire,** provision; budget allocation; appropriation.

envoi, *n.m.* **1.** (*a*) sending/dispatch(ing)/ forwarding/consignment; **envoi (par mer, par terre, par fer, par air),** shipment; **envoi à titre d'essai,** sent on approval; **envoi contre remboursement,** cash on delivery (c.o.d.); **j'ai bien reçu votre envoi du 10 octobre,** I acknowledge receipt of your dispatch/consignment of 10th October; **faire un envoi tous les mois,** to send/to dispatch goods every month; **bordereau d'envoi,** dispatch note; **lettre d'envoi,** advice letter/note (*b*) **envoi de fonds,** remittance (of funds); **faire un envoi de fonds à qn,** to remit funds to s.o. **2.** consignment; parcel; shipment; **faire un envoi de fleurs,** to send flowers.

envoyer, *v.tr.* to send; to dispatch; **envoyer une lettre à qn,** to send s.o. a letter; **envoyer qch. par (chemin de) fer,** to send sth. by rail; **envoyer qch. par la poste,** to post/to mail sth.; **je lui ai envoyé un chèque par la poste,** I sent him a cheque by post; **envoyer des fonds,** to remit funds.

envoyeur, -euse, *n. Post:* sender/forwarder (of goods, letter, etc.); **retour à l'envoyeur,** return to sender.

épargnant, *n.m.f.* saver/investor; **petits épargnants,** small savers/small investors.

épargne, *n.f.* saving; economy; **caisse d'épargne,** savings bank; **Caisse nationale d'épargne,** = National Savings Bank; **livret de caisse d'épargne,** savings bank book; **plan d'épargne,** savings account; savings plan; **épargne complément de retraite,** pension fund savings; **l'épargne privée,** private investors; **la petite épargne,** small savers/small investors.

épargne-logement, *n.m.* **caisse d'épargne-logement** = building society/*NAm:* building/savings and loan association; **plan d'épargne-logement** = building society (savings) account; **prêt d'épargne-logement** = (building society) mortgage/loan.

épargner, *v.tr.* to save (up).

épongeage, *n.m. Fin:* absorbing/mopping up/draining off.

éponger, *v.tr. Fin:* to absorb/to mop up/to drain off; **éponger le pouvoir d'achat excédentaire,** to mop up excess purchasing power.

épuisé, *a.* (*a*) **lettre de crédit épuisée,** invalid letter of credit (*b*) (*produit, etc.*) out of stock; sold out; (*livre*) out of print.

épuisement, *n.m.* running out (of stocks, goods, etc.); **jusqu'à épuisement des stocks,** while stocks/supplies last.

épuiser, **1.** *v.tr.* to run out of (goods, stocks, etc.); **épuiser un stock,** to sell out (of) an article **2.** *v.pr.* **s'épuiser,** (*i*) to run out (*ii*) to run low.

équilibration, *n.f.* balancing (of the budget).

équilibre, *n.m.* equilibrium; balance; **parvenir à rétablir l'équilibre budgétaire,** to manage to balance the budget; **prix d'équilibre,** equilibrium price.

équilibrer, *v.tr.* **équilibrer le budget,** to balance the budget.

équipe, *n.f.* (*a*) **équipe de jour,** day shift; **équipe de nuit,** night shift; **travailler par**

équipes, to work in shifts; **travail par équipes,** shift work; **chef d'équipe,** (*i*) foreman (*ii*) team leader (*b*) team; **équipe de direction,** management team; **équipe de vente/équipe commerciale,** sales team/force; **travail d'équipe,** teamwork.

équipement, *n.m.* equipment; **biens d'équipement,** capital goods; **budget d'équipement,** capital budget; **équipement industriel,** plant.

équivalent, *a. & n.m.* equivalent (à, to).

ergonome, *n.m.f.* ergonomist/efficiency expert.

ergonomie, *n.f.* ergonomics/biotechnology/human engineering.

ergonomiste, *n.m.f.* = **ergonome.**

érosion, *n.f.* **érosion monétaire,** depreciation of money.

erreur, *n.f.* error/mistake; **erreur de calcul,** miscalculation; **marge d'erreur,** margin of error; **il y a une erreur dans votre compte,** there is a mistake in your account; **sauf erreur ou omission,** errors and omissions excepted (e. & o.e.).

escalade, *n.f.* escalation (of prices, etc.); **escalade des taux d'intérêt,** escalation of interest rates.

escomptable, *a. Fin:* discountable (securities, etc.).

escompte, *n.m* 1. discount; **accorder/faire un escompte,** to allow a discount; **escompte (sur paiement) au comptant/ escompte de caisse,** discount for cash; **escompte d'usage,** trade discount 2. *Fin:* **banque d'escompte,** discount house; **escompte (de banque),** discount; **taux (officiel) d'escompte,** minimum lending rate (MLR); *NAm:* prime rate; **escompte en dedans,** true discount; **escompte en dehors,** commercial/bank discount; **escompte de traites/de créances,** invoice discounting; **présenter une traite à l'escompte,** to have a bill discounted; **prendre à l'escompte un effet de commerce,** to discount a bill of exchange 3. *StExch:*

call for delivery (of securities) before settlement.

escompter, *v.tr.* (*a*) *Fin:* **escompter un effet,** to discount a bill; **faire escompter une traite,** to have a bill discounted (*b*) *StExch:* to call for delivery of (securities) before settlement.

escompteur, 1. *n.m. Fin:* discounter/ discount broker 2. *a.* **banquier escompteur,** discounting banker.

escroquer, *v.tr.* to swindle; to defraud.

escroquerie, *n.f.* swindle; fraud.

espèces, *n.f.pl. Fin:* **payer en espèces,** to pay in cash; **contre espèces,** for a consideration/for cash.

espérance, *n.f.* **espérance de vie d'un produit,** product life expectancy; shelf life (of a product).

essai, *n.m.* (*a*) trial/test(ing); **à titre d'essai,** subject to approval; **acheter qch. à l'essai,** to buy sth. on approval/on appro; **commande d'essai,** trial order; **essai gratuit,** free trial; **faire l'essai d'un produit,** to test/to try out a product; **faire l'essai d'une voiture,** to test-drive a car (*b*) **période d'essai,** probation/trial period; **prendre/ engager à l'essai (un employé),** to take on (an employee) for a probationary period/ for a trial period/on probation.

essayer, *v.tr.* to try; **essayez notre nouvelle voiture,** test-drive our new car.

essor, *n.m.* **essor économique,** economic expansion; **industrie en plein essor,** booming/expanding industry; **période d'essor,** boom.

estampillage, *n.m.* stamping/marking (of goods, etc.).

estampille, *n.f.* (*sur un document, etc.*) (official) stamp; (*sur un colis, un produit, etc.*) identification mark; brand; trademark; postmark; **l'estampille a oblitéré le timbre,** the postmark has cancelled the stamp.

estampiller, *v.tr.* to stamp (weights,

documents, etc.); to mark (goods); to hallmark (gold, silver).

estimateur, -trice, *n.* appraiser/valuer.

estimatif, *a.* estimated (cost, etc.); **devis estimatif,** estimate.

estimation, *n.f.* (*a*) estimation/estimate (of the value, price, of sth.); valuing/appraising (of goods, etc.); assessment (of damage); **estimation approximative/estimation au jugé,** rough estimate/*F:* guesstimate (*b*) estimate/valuation; **estimation faite par un expert,** expert valuation.

estimer, *v.tr.* to estimate/to value/to appraise (goods); to assess (damage).

établir, 1. *v.tr.* (*a*) to establish/to set up (firm, etc.) (*b*) to draw up; **établir un budget,** to draw up/to work out a budget; **établir un compte,** to draw up/to make up an account; **établir un contrat,** to draw up a contract; **établir un prix,** to price (sth.)/to fix a price (for sth.) **2.** *v.pr.* **s'établir à son compte,** to start up (a business) on one's own/to set up in business on one's own; to become self-employed.

établissement, *n.m.* (*a*) drawing up/making up (of accounts, contract, etc.); **établissement des prix,** pricing; **établissement des prix de revient,** costing (*b*) setting up/start-up (of a business, a firm, etc.); **frais d'établissement/coût de premier établissement,** initial outlay/investment/expenditure; set-up/start-up costs; *Ind:* **capital d'établissement,** invested capital (*c*) institution; **établissement de crédit,** bank/loan society (*d*) **chef d'établissement,** works manager; **établissement commercial,** commercial premises; **établissement industriel,** factory; industrial premises; **établissement principal,** main branch/head office (of a business); **les établissements Renault,** the Renault works; **établissement de service public,** statutory company.

étalage, *n.m.* (*a*) display (of goods, etc.); **étalage de marchandises sur la voie publique,** street trading (*b*) tax paid by street trader (*c*) window-display; window-

dressing; **faire l'étalage,** (*i*) to put (goods) on display (*ii*) to dress the window(s); **mettre qch. à l'étalage,** to display sth. in the window; **article qui a fait l'étalage,** shop-soiled article.

étalager, *v.tr.* to display (goods) for sale; to put (goods) on display (in shop window, on counter, etc.).

étalagiste, *n.m.f.* (*a*) street trader/stallholder (*b*) window-dresser.

étalement, *n.m.* **1.** displaying (of goods, etc.) **2.** staggering/spreading out (of holidays, payments).

étaler, *v.tr.* **1. étaler sa marchandise,** to display one's goods (for sale) **2.** to stagger/to spread out (holidays, payments); **versements étalés sur deux ans,** instalments spread (out) over two years.

étalon, *n.m.* standard (of weights, measures, etc.): *Fin:* **étalon or,** gold standard; **étalon de change-or,** gold exchange standard; **étalon-or lingot,** gold bullion standard.

étalonnage *n.m.,* **étalonnement,** *n.m.* standardization (of weights, etc.).

étalonner, *v.tr.* to standardize (weights, etc.).

état, *n.m.* **1.** state/condition; **machine en bon/mauvais état (de marche),** machine in good/bad working order **2.** (*a*) statement/report/list/return; **état de compte,** statement of account; **état détaillé d'un compte,** breakdown of an account; **état financier,** financial statement; **état de fortune,** financial standing/situation; *Jur:* **état de frais,** bill of costs; **état de paiements,** schedule of payments (*b*) **état 'néant',** 'nil' return (*c*) **état des lieux,** inventory of fixtures (*as between landlord and tenant*) (*d*) *Ind: etc:* **état périodique,** progress report (*e*) *Adm:* **état civil,** (*i*) (civil) status (*ii*) registry office (*f*) **état estimatif/appréciatif,** estimate **3. l'État,** the State; **banque d'État,** State bank; **obligations d'État,** Government bonds.

étatisation, *n.f.* nationalization.

étatisé, *a.* State-controlled/State run/State owned/government run/nationalized; **industrie étatisée,** nationalized industry.

étatiser, *v.tr.* to establish State control over (industry, etc.); to nationalize.

état-major, *n.m.* top management (of factory, etc.).

étiquetage, *n.m.* labelling (of luggage, etc.); ticketing (of goods, etc.); **étiquetage du prix,** price labelling.

étiqueter, *v.tr.* to label (luggage); to ticket (goods).

étiquette, *n.f.* label/docket/ticket; **étiquette à bagages,** luggage label; **étiquette autocollante,** stick-on label; self-adhesive sticker/label; **étiquette à œillets,** tie-on label; tag; **étiquette de prix,** price ticket/price tag; **étiquette de qualité,** quality label.

étoile, *n.f.* **un hôtel deux étoiles,** a two-star hotel.

étranger, *a.* foreign; **monnaie/devise étrangère,** foreign currency.

étude, *n.f.* (a) research (work); investigation; survey; **étude de cas,** case study; **étude de conception,** design engineering; **étude de marché,** market research/survey; **étude de produit,** product analysis; **étude des charges,** cost analysis; **étude des méthodes,** methods analysis; **étude du travail,** work study; **étude économique,** economic research; **étude préliminaire,** preliminary/pilot study; **étude des temps et des mouvements,** time and motion study; **études et recherches,** research and engineering **2.** office (of solicitor); chambers (of barrister).

eurochèque, *n.m.* Eurocheque; **carte eurochèque,** Eurocheque card.

eurocrate, *n.m.* eurocrat.

eurodevise, *n.f.* Eurocurrency; **marché des eurodevises,** Eurocurrency market.

eurodollar, *n.m. Fin:* Eurodollar.

euromarché, *n.m.* Euromarket.

euromonnaie, *n.f.* Eurocurrency.

euro-obligation, *n.f.* Eurobond.

euroyen, *n.m.* Euroyen.

évaluable, *a.* appraisable/assessable (goods, property).

évaluation, *n.f.* evaluation; valuation (of stock); appraisement (of property, etc.); appraisal (of the market); assessment (of demand, project, damages); estimate (of weight, losses, etc.); **évaluation des coûts,** cost analysis/costing; **évaluation d'un emploi,** job evaluation; **évaluation approximative,** rough estimate/*F:* guesstimate; **évaluation interne à l'entreprise,** directors' valuation; **évaluation prudente,** conservative estimate.

évaluer, *v.tr.* to evaluate/to value/to appraise/to estimate; to assess (damages).

évasion, *n.f.* **évasion des capitaux,** flight of capital; **évasion fiscale,** tax avoidance.

éventail, *n.m. PolEc: etc:* range; **éventail des prix,** price range; **éventail de produits,** range of products; **éventail des salaires,** salary range.

éventualité, *n.f.* possibility/contingency/eventuality.

éventuel, *a.* possible/contingent; *Fin:* **passif éventuel,** contingent liabilities; **client éventuel,** potential/prospective customer.

évolutif, *a.* **poste évolutif,** post with possibility of advancement.

évolution, *n.f.* **graphique d'évolution,** flow chart.

examen, *n.m.* examination; **examen des comptes,** inspection/scrutiny of accounts; **examen financier,** financial review; **la question est à l'examen,** the question is under consideration/we are looking into it.

examiner, *v.tr.* to examine; to investigate; to look into/to go into; **examiner les comptes,** to go through/to inspect the accounts; **examiner une question,** to look into/to go into/to consider a matter.

excédent, *n.m.* excess/surplus; **budget en excédent,** budget showing a surplus; **somme en excédent,** sum in excess; **nous avons un excédent de dépenses,** we are overspending; we have a deficit; **excédent de l'encaisse/de caisse,** over in the cash/overs; **excédents et déficits,** overs and shorts; **excédents de 10%,** 10% overs; **payer 50 francs d'excédent,** to pay (a) 50 francs excess (charge)/to pay a surcharge of 50 francs; **excédent de bagages,** excess luggage; **excédent de production d'un pays,** surplus produce of a country; **excédent des exportations sur les importations,** excess of exports over imports; **excédent (de production) de blé,** wheat surplus; **excédent (brut) d'exploitation,** (gross) operating profit.

excédentaire, *a.* (in) excess/(in) surplus; **la balance commerciale est excédentaire,** the trade balance shows a surplus/a credit; **écouler la production excédentaire sur les marchés extérieurs,** to dump surplus/excess production on foreign markets.

excéder, *v.tr.* to exceed/to go beyond (a certain limit); **excéder le montant de son compte (en banque),** to overdraw one's account; **nos pertes excèdent nos profits,** our losses are greater than our profits.

exceptionnel, *a.* **éléments exceptionnels/résultat exceptionnel/compte exceptionnel,** exceptional items; **prix exceptionnels,** special (bargain) prices; **profits exceptionnels/pertes exceptionnelles,** extraordinary items; **taxe exceptionnelle,** special/exceptional tax.

excès, *n.m.* excess; surplus; **excès des dépenses sur les recettes,** excess of expenditure over revenue; **excès de l'offre sur la demande,** excess of supply over demand; *StExch:* **excès de vendeurs,** sellers over.

exclusif, *a.* exclusive/sole (right, etc.); **affaire exclusive,** one-off deal; **agent exclusif,** sole agent; **importateur exclusif pour la France,** sole importer (of a pro-

duct) for France; **produit exclusif,** exclusive article; speciality.

exclusivité, *n.f.* sole/exclusive rights; **nous avons l'exclusivité de la vente de ce produit,** we have the (sole) rights for this product.

ex-coupon, *adv.phr. Fin:* ex coupon.

ex-dividende, *adv.phr. Fin:* ex dividend; **actions citées ex-dividende,** shares quoted ex dividend.

ex-droit, *adv.phr. Fin:* **titre ex-droit,** stock ex rights.

exécuter, *v.tr.* **1.** to carry out (work, etc.); to fulfil/to carry out/to execute (a contract); to put (project, etc.) into action **2.** (*a*) *Jur:* **exécuter un débiteur,** to distrain upon a debtor (*b*) *StExch:* **exécuter un spéculateur,** to hammer a defaulter; **exécuter un client,** (*i*) to buy in (*ii*) to sell out against a client.

exécuteur, -trice *n.* **exécuteur testamentaire/d'un ordre,** executor.

exécutif, 1. *a.* executive; **comité exécutif,** executive committee; **le pouvoir exécutif,** the executive **2.** *n.m.* (*a*) executive committee; **un exécutif de cinq membres,** an executive of five (*b*) **l'exécutif,** the executive.

exécution, *n.f.* **1.** carrying out; implementation (of plan, agreement, etc.); **travaux en voie d'exécution,** work in progress **2.** (*a*) *Jur:* distraint (*b*) *StExch:* hammering (of defaulter).

exécutoire, *Jur:* **1.** *a.* (*contrat, etc.*) enforceable; to be carried into effect; **obligation exécutoire,** operative obligation **2.** *n.m.* writ of execution; **exécutoire des dépens,** order to pay costs.

exemplaire, *n.m.* (*a*) copy (of books, etc.); *Adm:* **exemplaire d'archives,** file copy (*b*) **en double exemplaire,** in duplicate; **en triple exemplaire,** in triplicate.

exempt, *a.* **exempt d'impôts,** exempt from taxes/tax-exempt; *Cust:* **exempt de droits,**

free of duty/duty-free; **exempt de frais,** free of charge.

exempter, *v.tr.* **exempter qn d'un impôt,** to exempt s.o. from a tax.

exemption, *n.f.* exemption (**de,** from); immunity (from tax, etc.); *Cust:* **lettre d'exemption,** bill of sufferance.

exercice, *n.m.* 1. exercise; **dans l'exercice de ses fonctions,** in the exercise of one's duties 2. visit of inspection (of excise officer) 3. (*a*) (*i*) financial year/year's trading/accounting period (*ii*) budgetary year/fiscal period; **clôture d'un exercice,** year end/end of financial year; **exercice comptable/exercice social,** company's financial year; **l'exercice de ce mois,** this month's trading; **l'exercice en cours,** the current (fiscal) year; **fin d'exercice,** year end; **bilan de fin d'exercice,** end of year balance-sheet (*b*) **exercice 1989 attaché,** cum dividend 1989.

exigence, *n.f.* demand(s)/requirement(s); **exigences de poste,** job requirements; **la marchandise répond à toutes les exigences,** the goods are up to standard in every way; **satisfaire aux exigences de ses clients,** to meet one's customers' requirements.

exiger, *v.tr.* to exact/to demand/to require (**de,** from); **exiger un paiement,** to exact a payment.

exigibilités, *n.f.pl.* current liabilities.

exigible, *a.* claimable (**de,** from); (payment) due; **exigible à vue,** payable at sight; **dette exigible,** debt due for payment; **passif exigible,** current liabilities.

existant, 1. *a.* existing; **majorer les tarifs existants,** to increase existing tariffs **2.** *n.m.* **l'existant en caisse,** (the) cash in hand; **l'existant en magasin/les existants,** stock (in hand).

existence, *n.f.* **existence en magasin,** stock (in hand).

exode, *n.m. PolEc:* **exode des capitaux,** flight of capital.

exonération, *n.f.* exemption (**de,** from) (fees, taxes, etc.).

exonérer, *v.tr.* (*a*) to exonerate (**de,** from); **être exonéré de l'impôt sur le revenu,** to be exempted from income tax/tax free/free of tax (*b*) **exonérer des marchandises,** to exempt goods from import duty.

expansion, *n.f.* expansion (of a firm, etc.); **expansion monétaire,** currency expansion; **industrie en pleine expansion,** booming/ expanding industry; **taux d'expansion économique,** economic growth rate.

expansionnisme, *n.m. PolEc:* expansionism.

expansionniste, *a. & n.m.f. PolEc:* expansionist.

expatrier, *v.tr. Fin:* **expatrier des capitaux,** to invest money/capital abroad.

expédier, *v.tr.* (*a*) *Jur:* to draw up (contract, deed) (*b*) to forward/to send (letter, parcel, goods); to dispatch; **expédiez ceci par le premier courrier,** get this off by the first post; **expédier des marchandises par navire,** to ship goods; **expédier (un colis) par la poste,** to post/to mail (a parcel); to send (a parcel) through the post/by post.

expéditeur, -trice, *n.* 1. sender (of telegram, letter, etc.); (*sur une enveloppe, etc.*) (*abbr.* **exp.**) from .../sender ... 2. (*a*) shipper/consignor (of goods) (*b*) forwarding agent (*c*) dispatcher.

expédition, *n.f.* (*a*) *Jur:* copy (of deed, contract, etc.); **première expédition,** first authentic copy; **en double expédition,** in duplicate (*b*) delivery/dispatch(ing)/forwarding/sending/consignment (of parcels, etc.); **bulletin/bordereau d'expédition,** waybill; **expédition par mer,** shipping/ shipment; **frais d'expédition,** delivery/ forwarding/shipping charges; **maison d'expédition,** forwarding house; **expédition franco à partir de 1000 francs,** orders of 1000 francs and over delivered free.

expert, 1. *a.* expert/skilled (**en, dans,** in); **la main d'œuvre la plus experte,** the most highly-skilled labour **2.** *n.m.* (*a*) expert (*b*) valuer/appraiser/surveyor; **expert en assurances,** claims/insurance adjuster.

expert-comptable, *n.m.* = chartered accountant/*NAm:* certified public accountant.

expert-conseil, *n.m.* Ind: etc: consultant.

expertise, *n.f.* **1.** (expert) appraisal/valuation; *Nau:* survey (of ship for damage); **expertise d'avarie,** damage survey; **faire l'expertise des dégâts,** to appraise the damage; **faire une expertise,** to make a valuation/a survey; **faire l'expertise,** to appraise/to value; **cabinet d'expertise comptable,** chartered accountant practice; **frais d'expertise,** consultancy fee **2.** expert's report/expert opinion.

expertiser, *v.tr.* **1.** to appraise/to value/to estimate; *Nau:* to survey (ship for damage); **faire expertiser qch.,** to have sth. surveyed/to obtain an expert opinion on sth. **2.** to give an expert opinion.

expiration, *n.f.* expiry/expiration/termination/end (of lease, contract, term of office, etc.); **venir à expiration,** to expire; **l'expiration des délais,** lapsing of the time limit.

expirer, *v.i.* to expire; **notre bail a expiré hier,** our lease expired/ran out yesterday; **ce passeport expire le 5 mai,** this passport expires on May 5th.

explicatif, *a.* explanatory; **note/notice explicative,** instructions/directions for use.

exploitant, 1. *a.* **société exploitante,** development company; **exploitant (d'une entreprise),** operator **2.** *n.m.* (*a*) **exploitant agricole,** farmer; **les petits exploitants,** small farmers/smallholders (*b*) owner/manager (of a cinema, etc.).

exploitation, *n.f.* **1.** (*a*) running/operation (of company, etc.); **bénéfices d'exploitation,** trading/*NAm:* operating profits; **exploitation agricole,** farming; **exploitation d'entreprise,** operatorship; **frais d'exploitation,** working costs; running/ *NAm:* operating expenses; **société d'exploitation,** development company (*b*)

compte d'exploitation, trading account/ *NAm:* operating report; **budget d'exploitation prévisionnel,** forecast(ed) operating budget; **capital d'exploitation,** working capital (*c*) **exploitation d'une invention,** utilization of a patent **2.** (*a*) **exploitation commerciale,** commerce; commercial enterprise; **exploitation industrielle,** industrial concern/undertaking (*b*) farm; **petite exploitation,** smallholding.

exploiter, *v.tr.* (*a*) to run/to operate/to work; **exploiter un commerce,** to run/to carry on a business (*b*) **ouvriers exploités,** sweated labour.

expomarché, *n.m.* trade mart.

export, *n.m.* **prix à l'export/prix export,** export price; **quotas volontaires à l'export,** voluntary export restraint (VER); **taux de crédit export,** export credit rate.

exportable, *a.* exportable.

exportateur, -trice, 1. *n.* exporter **2.** *a.* exporting (country, etc.); **les pays exportateurs de pétrole,** the oil exporting countries.

exportation, *n.f.* export/*NAm:* exportation; **articles d'exportation,** exports; **faire l'exportation,** to export; **les exportations,** (*i*) the export trade (*ii*) exports; **commerce d'exportation,** export trade; **exportation de capitaux,** export of capital; **exportations visibles/invisibles,** visible/invisible exports; **nos exportations de beurre s'élèvent à deux millions de tonnes,** our butter exports total two million tons; **licence d'exportation,** export licence/*NAm:* license; **prime d'exportation,** export subsidy; **restrictions volontaires des exportations/auto-limitation des exportations,** voluntary export restraint (VER); **taxe à l'exportation,** export tax.

exporter, *v.tr.* to export (goods) (**à, en,** to).

exposant, -ante, *n.* exhibitor (of goods at show, trade fair, etc.).

exposer, *v.tr.* to exhibit/to show/to display (goods, etc.); **exposer des marchandises en vente,** to display goods for sale.

exposition, *n.f.* exhibition/show (of

goods, etc.); **exposition internationale,** international exhibition; **exposition interprofessionnelle,** trade show; **salle d'exposition,** (*i*) (large) exhibition hall/ exhibition room (*ii*) showroom.

exprès, *a.inv. & n.m. Post:* **(lettre, colis) exprès,** express (letter, parcel); **par exprès,** by special delivery.

expropriation, *n.f. Jur:* expropriation; **expropriation (pour cause d'utilité publique),** compulsory purchase (order) (of private property); compulsory surrender (of real estate).

exproprier, *v.tr.* to expropriate (*i*) a proprietor (*ii*) property.

expulser, *v.tr.* to evict (a tenant).

expulsion, *n.f.* eviction (of a tenant).

ex-répartition, *adv.phr. Fin:* ex allotment.

extérieur, 1. *a.* foreign/external (trade, etc.); **déficit extérieur,** external deficit/ balance of payments deficit; **dette extérieure,** foreign/overseas debt **2.** *n.m.* **nos relations commerciales avec l'extérieur,** our (commercial) dealings with foreign countries.

extinction, *n.f.* paying off/wiping out (of debt); termination (of contract).

extourne, *n.f. Fin:* **faire une extourne,** to recredit.

extrabudgétaire, *a. Fin:* extrabudgetary/outside the budget.

extrait, *n.m.* abstract (of deed, account); **extrait de compte,** statement of account.

extraordinaire, *a.* extraordinary; **assemblée (générale) extraordinaire,** extraordinary (general) meeting; **budget extraordinaire,** emergency budget; **frais/ dépenses extraordinaires,** (*i*) extras (*ii*) non-recurring expenditure; **impôt extraordinaire,** emergency tax; exceptional tax.

extrinsèque, *a.* **valeur extrinsèque,** legal/ fictitious value (of currency).

F

fabricant, *n.m.* maker/manufacturer; **fabricant de chaussures,** shoe manufacturer.

fabrication, *n.f.* (*a*) manufacture/making/production (of sth.); workmanship; **article de bonne fabrication,** well-made article/article of good workmanship; **contrôle de fabrication,** manufacturing control; **coût de fabrication,** manufacturing cost; **défaut de fabrication,** defect/fault/flaw (in the manufacture of an article); faulty workmanship; **fabrication à la chaîne,** mass production; **fabrication en série,** mass production; **fabrication par lots,** batch production; **frais de fabrication,** manufacturing/factory overheads; **numéro de fabrication,** serial number; **programme de fabrication,** production plan/schedule sheet; **(produit) de fabrication française,** (product, article) made in France/French-made (product, article); **secret de fabrication,** trade secret; **unité de fabrication,** factory unit (*b*) *Publ:* **chef de fabrication,** production manager (*c*) manufactured goods; **notre fabrication,** our products.

fabrique, *n.f.* **1.** making/manufacture; **prix de fabrique,** cost price/manufacturer's price; **marque de fabrique,** trademark/brand **2.** factory/works; **fabrique de chaussures,** shoe factory; **valeur en fabrique,** cost price.

fabriquer, *v.tr.* to manufacture (cloth, bicycles, etc.); **fabriqué en France,** made in France; **fabriqué en grande série,** mass-produced; **fabriqué sur commande,** made to order; **fabriqué sur mesure(s),** made to measure.

façade, *n.f. Ins:* fronting.

face, *n.f.* **opération de face à face,** back to back loan.

facial, *a.* **valeur faciale (d'une action),** face value/nominal value (of a share).

facilité, *n.f. Bank:* **facilités de caisse,** overdraft facilities; **facilités de crédit,** credit terms; **facilités de paiement,** easy terms/easy payments/deferred payment.

facob, *n.m.* (*abbr. of traité facultatif obligatoire*) *Ins:* open cover.

façon, *n.f.* (*i*) making; fashioning (of jewellery, etc.) (*ii*) workmanship/labour; **matière et façon,** material and labour; **tailleur à façon,** bespoke tailor; **travail à façon,** suits/dresses made to measure.

facsim, *n.m.* hard copy.

fac(-)similaire, *a.* (copy, etc.) in facsimile; **contrat fac(-)similaire,** contract in facsimile.

fac-similé, *n.m.* facsimile/exact copy (of signature, etc.); hard copy.

factage, *n.m.* (*a*) carriage (and delivery); transport (of goods); **entreprise/service de factage,** delivery service; **payer le factage,** to pay the carriage (*b*) delivery (of letters).

facteur, *n.m.* factor; **analyse des facteurs de profit,** profit factor analysis; **facteur coût/prix,** cost factor; **facteur de charge,** load factor; **facteur humain,** human factor; **facteur de production,** production factor; input; **facteur d'utilisation,** duty factor/cycle.

factoring, *n.m.* factoring.

facturation, *n.f. Book-k:* invoicing; **service de facturation,** invoice department.

facture, *n.f.* invoice/bill (of sale);

acquitter une facture, (*i*) to pay a bill (*ii*) to receipt an invoice/a bill; **facture détaillée,** itemized invoice; **faire/dresser/établir une facture,** to make out an invoice; **facture pro forma/provisoire,** pro forma invoice; **payer/régler une facture,** to settle an invoice/to pay a bill; **prix de facture,** invoice/*NAm:* billing price; **selon/suivant facture,** as per invoice; **valeur de facture,** invoice value.

facturer, *v.tr.* to invoice; to charge for (sth.) (on an invoice)/to put (sth.) on a bill/*NAm:* to bill s.o. for (sth.); **le papier nous a été facturé 60 francs,** we were charged 60 francs for the paper; **marchandises facturées,** invoiced goods; **machine à facturer,** invoicing machine.

facturette, *n.f.* credit card sales voucher.

facturier, -ière, 1. *n.m.* sales book **2.** *n.m.f.* invoice clerk **3.** *n.f.* **facturière,** invoicing machine **4.** *a.* **dactylo(graphe) facturière,** invoice typist.

faculté, *n.f.* option/right; **louer un immeuble avec faculté d'achat,** to rent a building with the option of purchase; **facultés contributives,** ability to pay; *StExch:* **faculté du double,** call of more.

faible, 1. *a.* **faible demande,** slack demand; **prix faible,** (*i*) low price (*ii*) discount price; **faible quantité,** small quantity; **faible revenu,** low/small income **2.** *n.m.f. pl.* **les économiquement faibles,** (people in) the lower-income bracket/lower income groups.

failli, 1. *a.* **commerçant failli,** bankrupt businessman **2.** *n.* (adjudicated) bankrupt; **failli (non) réhabilité,** (un)discharged bankrupt.

faillite, *n.f.* bankruptcy/insolvency; **être en faillite/en état de faillite,** to be bankrupt/insolvent; **être près de la faillite,** to be on the verge of bankruptcy; **maison en faillite,** bankrupt firm; **mettre qn en faillite,** to bankrupt s.o.; **prononcer la faillite de qn,** to adjudicate/to adjudge s.o. bankrupt; **tomber en faillite/faire faillite,**

to go bankrupt/to fail; **se mettre en faillite,** to file a petition in bankruptcy.

faire, *v.tr.* **1.** (*a*) to make; **faire un paiement/un versement,** to make a payment (*b*) **faire un chèque,** to write a cheque/to raise a cheque; **faire un chèque de £10,** to make out a cheque for £10 (*c*) **nous ne faisons que le gros,** we only trade wholesale/we only deal (in) wholesale (*d*) **faire sa fortune,** to make one's fortune; **faire une offre,** to make an offer; to (make a) bid; **faire des pertes,** to meet with/to sustain losses; **il se fait 10 000 francs par mois,** he makes 10 000 francs a month **2.** (*a*) to do; **faire des affaires avec qn,** to do business with s.o.; **faire les cuirs,** to deal in leather (*b*) **faire son apprentissage,** to serve one's apprenticeship; **faire les magasins,** to go round the shops (*c*) to amount to; **combien cela fait-il?** how much does that come to?/does it amount to? **3.** **faire monter/baisser les prix,** to force prices up/down; **faire coïncider le prix avec le coût marginal,** to equate price with marginal cost; **faire marcher un commerce/une affaire,** to run a business.

faisabilité, *n.f.* **étude de faisabilité,** feasibility study.

faisable, *a.* practicable/feasible.

falsification, *n.f.* falsification; forgery/faking (of documents, etc.).

falsifier, *v.tr.* to falsify; to forge/to fake (documents, etc.); **falsifier les comptes,** to falsify/to fake/to tamper with the accounts.

famille, *n.f.* household.

familial, *a.* (*a*) *Adm:* **allocation familiale,** family allowance; **revenu familial,** family income (*b*) **entreprise familiale,** family firm/business (*c*) **pot familial,** family-size(d) jar.

fantaisie, *n.f.* **objets de fantaisie,** fancy goods; **magasin de fantaisies,** novelty shop.

faussaire, *n.m.* counterfeiter.

faux, 1. *a.* false; forged; **fausse déclaration,**

false declaration/misrepresentation; **faux chèque,** forged cheque; **faux bilan,** fraudulent balance sheet; **faux frais,** incidental/sundry expenses **2.** *n.m. Jur:* fake/forgery; **s'inscrire en faux contre qch.,** to take action to dispute the validity of sth.

faveur, *n.f.* favour; **billet de faveur,** complimentary ticket; **prix de faveur,** preferential/special price; **taux de faveur,** special rates; **le solde est en votre faveur,** the balance is in your favour.

favorable, *a.* favourable; **à des conditions favorables,** on favourable terms; **balance commerciale favorable,** favourable trade balance.

favoriser, *v.tr.* to help/to encourage (sth.); **favoriser l'essor de la production,** to encourage production; **favoriser la croissance,** to promote growth.

fébrile, *a.* **capitaux fébriles,** hot money.

fédération, *n.f.* federation; **fédération de syndicats,** amalgamated union; **fédération syndicale,** trade(s) union.

férié, *a.m.* **jour férié** = public holiday/ *Adm:* bank holiday.

ferme[1], **1.** *a.* (*a*) firm/steady; **maintenir ses prix fermes,** to keep one's prices steady; **le marché reste très ferme,** the market continues very steady (*b*) **acheteur ferme,** firm buyer; **offre ferme,** firm/definite offer **2.** *adv.* **vendre ferme,** to make a firm sale **3.** *n.m. StExch:* **valeur ferme,** firm stock.

ferme[2], *n.f.* farming lease; **prendre une terre à ferme,** to take lease of/to rent a piece of land; **donner à ferme,** to farm out.

fermer, 1. *v.tr.* to close/to shut; **fermer boutique/fermer ses portes,** to close down; **fermer un compte,** to close an account; **fermer une usine,** to close down a factory **2.** *v.i.* **les magasins ferment à cinq heures,** the shops close/shut at five (o'clock); **hôtel qui ferme pour l'hiver,** hotel that closes down for the winter; *StExch:* **les actions ont fermé à . . . ,** shares closed at . . . .

fermeté, *n.f.* firmness/steadiness (of stocks, etc.).

fermeture, *n.f.* (*a*) **fermeture des ateliers,** period when a workshop is closed; (*causée par la faillite*) closure/closing down of the workshops; (*réponse à une grève*) lock-out (*b*) **fermeture annuelle,** annual closure/annual holiday; **heure de fermeture,** closing time (of shop) (*c*) **fermeture d'un compte,** closing of an account.

ferroviaire, *a.* **réseau ferroviaire,** railway network.

fête, *n.f.* **fête légale** = public holiday/ *Adm:* bank holiday.

feuille, *n.f.* **feuille de paie/des salaires/des appointements,** payroll/pay sheet/pay slip; **feuille d'impôt,** notice of tax assessment; **feuille de présence,** time sheet; attendance list; **feuille de route,** waybill; **feuille de service,** (duty) roster; *Bank:* **feuille de versement,** paying-in slip.

fiche, *n.f.* (*a*) (*i*) docket/slip (of paper) (*ii*) card/form/list/sheet; **fiche de contrôle,** docket; check-list/check sheet/tally sheet; **fiche de pesage,** weight slip; **fiche technique,** data sheet; **remplir une fiche,** to fill in/(*esp. NAm:*) to fill out a form (*b*) (index) card; **boîte à fiches,** card-index box; **fiche de renseignement,** data card/ information card; **fiche perforée,** perforated/punch(ed) card; **jeu de 100 fiches,** pack/packet of 100 cards; **mettre (des informations) sur fiches,** to card-index; **mise sur fiche(s),** card-indexing.

fichier, *n.m.* (*a*) card-index cabinet/file/ box; filing cabinet; **fichier principal,** master file (*b*) card index.

fichiste, *n.m.f.* card indexer.

fictif, *a.* (*a*) false/fictitious; *Fin:* **actif fictif,** fictitious assets; **compte fictif,** impersonal account; **dividende fictif,** sham dividend; **prix fictif,** nominal price (*b*) **profits fictifs,** paper profits; *Fin:* **valeur fictive (de la monnaie fiduciaire),** face value (of notes coinage).

fidéicommis, *n.m. Jur:* trust.

fidéicommissaire, *n.m. Jur:* beneficiary (of a trust).

fidélisation, *n.f.* (development of) customer loyalty.

fidéliser, *v.i.* to develop customer loyalty.

fiduciaire, 1. *a.* (*a*) fiduciary (loan, etc.); **monnaie fiduciaire,** fiduciary currency (= *paper money, coinage of low intrinsic value*); **circulation fiduciaire,** fiduciary currency (= *paper money*); **en dépôt fiduciaire,** in escrow; **avoirs des banques en monnaie fiduciaire,** cash holdings of banks; **une circulation fiduciaire excessive entraîne l'inflation,** too much paper money (in circulation) leads to inflation; **titres fiduciaires,** paper securities (*b*) **société fiduciaire** = *NAm:* Trust company; **certificat fiduciaire,** trustee's certificate **2.** *n.m.* trustee.

fiducie, *n.f. Jur:* trust; **grevé de fiducie,** trustee.

figer, *v.tr. PolEc:* to freeze; **les salaires ont été figés,** (the) salaries have been frozen.

figurer, *v.i.* to appear/to figure; **ces articles figurent dans le catalogue,** these articles appear/are listed in the catalogue; **faire figurer la réserve au passif,** to show the reserve among the liabilities.

filiale, *n.f.* subsidiary (company); affiliated firm/*NAm:* affiliate.

filialiser, *v.tr.* to affiliate (company).

filière, *n.f.* **1. il faut que cette demande passe par la filière administrative,** this request must go through the usual official channels **2.** (*a*) transfer note (*b*) *StExch:* **établir la filière,** to draw up/to trace the succession of previous holders (of shares).

fin, *n.f.* (*a*) **fin courant,** the end of the (current) month; **fin du mois,** end of the month; **fin prochain,** the end of next month; **facture payable fin juin,** bill payable at the end of June; *Bank:* **sauf bonne fin,** under reserve (*b*) **fins de série,** discontinued line; oddments.

final, *a.* (*a*) **règlement final,** final settlement; **solde final,** final balance (*b*) **compte final,** account for the financial year (*c*) **produit final,** end-product.

finance, *n.f.* (*a*) finance; **le monde de la finance,** the financial world; **la haute finance,** (*i*) (the world of) high finance (*ii*) the financiers/the bankers; **finance d'entreprise,** corporate finance (*b*) *pl.* finances/financial resources; **les finances de la compagnie vont mal,** the company's finances are in a bad state; **les finances publiques,** public resources/funds; **ministère des Finances** = the Treasury; **Inspecteur des Finances** = (high) Treasury official.

financement, *n.m.* financing/funding; **financement (à court, à long terme),** (short-term, long-term) financing; **financement par emprunt,** debt financing; **le financement du projet sera assuré par la compagnie,** the financing/funding of the project will be undertaken by the company/the company will finance the project.

financer, *v.tr.* to finance/to fund (undertaking, etc.); to put up the money/the funding for (sth.); to back (s.o.); *NAm:* to bankroll (s.o., a project); **opération entièrement financée par emprunt,** operation 100% debt financed; **BP financera le projet à 50%,** BP will put up half of the funding (for the project).

financier, 1. *a.* (*a*) financial (system, etc.); **analyste financier,** financial analyst; **conseil financier,** financial consultant/adviser; **contrôle financier,** financial control; **crise financière,** financial crisis; **embarras financiers/difficultés financières,** financial difficulties/trouble; **examen financier,** financial review; **directeur financier,** financial director; **direction/gestion financière,** financial management; **frais/coûts financiers,** interest charges; **produits financiers,** interest received/interest income; **société financière,** finance company; **stratégie financière,** financial strategy; **solide au point de**

vue financier, financially sound (*b*) **groupe financier,** group (of interrelated companies) (*c*) **le marché financier,** (*i*) the financial market/capital market (*ii*) the securities market; **rapport financier,** financial/treasurer's report **2.** *n.m.* financier; **financier d'entreprise,** corporate finance manager.

financièrement, *adv.* financially.

firme, *n.f.* business/firm/concern.

fisc, *n.m.* the Inland Revenue/*NAm:* the Internal Revenue; **les employés du fisc/le fisc,** Inland Revenue officials/tax officials/*F:* the tax people/the taxman; **frauder le fisc,** to evade tax(es).

fiscal, *a.* fiscal; **administration fiscale,** the taxation authorities/the tax authorities/ *NAm:* the taxing authorities; **abri/asile/ paradis fiscal,** tax haven; **avantage fiscal,** tax shelter; **avoir fiscal,** tax credit (on dividend); **charges fiscales/prélèvement fiscal,** taxation; **dans un but fiscal,** for tax purposes; **dégrèvement fiscal,** tax reduction; tax relief; **droit fiscal,** tax legislation/law; **droits fiscaux,** State dues; taxes; customs and excise dues; **évasion fiscale,** tax avoidance; **exercice fiscal,** financial year; **fraude fiscale,** tax evasion/ *F:* tax dodging; **politique fiscale,** fiscal policy; **recettes fiscales,** revenue derived from taxes; **montant des recettes fiscales,** tax yields; **ressources fiscales de l'État,** financial resources of the State; **système fiscal,** tax system.

fiscaliser, *v.tr.* to tax.

fiscaliste, *n.m.f.* tax consultant.

fiscalité, *n.f.* financial and taxation system (of a country); **fiscalité excessive,** excessive taxation; **fiscalité indirecte,** indirect taxation; **poids de la fiscalité,** tax burden.

fixation, *n.f.* fixing (of date, indemnity, etc.); setting (of date); **fixation des impôts,** assessment of taxes; **fixation des dommages-intérêts,** assessment of damages; **fixation des indemnités,** determination of compensation; **fixation des objectifs,**

target setting; **fixation des prix,** price fixing/pricing.

fixe, *a.* fixed/regular/settled; **actif fixe,** fixed assets; **agent fixe,** local agent; **capital fixe,** fixed capital; *StExch:* **cours fixe,** firm quotation; **coûts fixes,** fixed costs; **dépôt à terme fixe,** fixed deposit; **frais fixes,** fixed expenses/costs; **placement à revenu fixe,** fixed-yield investment; **prix fixe,** fixed price; **repas à prix fixe,** set menu/meal; **traitement/salaire fixe/***n.m.* **le fixe,** fixed salary; **valeurs à intérêt fixe,** fixed-interest securities.

fixer, *v.tr.* to fix/to determine; to set/to arrange (time); **fixer le prix de qch.,** to determine/to fix the price of sth.; **fixer un jour pour la réunion,** to fix a day/a date for the meeting; **fixer des conditions,** to lay down conditions/to stipulate terms; *StExch:* **fixer un cours,** to make a price.

flambée, *n.f.* **flambée des prix,** jump in prices/price escalation.

flèche, *n.f.* **les prix sont montés en flèche,** prices have shot up/rocketed/soared; **montée en flèche des prix et des salaires,** wage-price spiral.

fléchir, *v.i.* (*marché*) to sag/to weaken; **les prix des actions fléchissent,** share prices are easier/are down today.

fléchissement, *n.m.* (*a*) **fléchissement des dépôts en banque,** falling off of bank deposits (*b*) falling (of prices); *StExch:* **fléchissement des cours,** sagging/easing of prices.

flexibilité, *n.f. Fin:* **flexibilité (d'une entreprise),** flexibility (of a company).

flexible, *a.* flexible (budget, prices, etc.); **horaire flexible,** flexible (working) hours/ flexible time-table/flexi-time.

flottaison, *n.f.* = **flottement.**

flottant, *a.* **1.** floating/fluctuating; **capitaux flottants,** floating capital/assets; **dette flottante,** floating debt; *Ins:* **police flottante,** floating policy; **titres flottants,** shares available on the market; **taux de**

change flottant, floating exchange rate 2. *n.m. StExch:* float.

flottement, *n.m.* le flottement de la livre sterling, the floating of the pound sterling.

flotter, *v.i. & tr.* les prix flottent entre ... et ..., prices fluctuate between ... and ...; faire flotter la livre, to float the pound.

fluctuation, *n.f.* fluctuation; fluctuations du change, fluctuations in exchange rates; fluctuations des cours, swings and roundabouts; fluctuations du marché, market fluctuations/ups and downs of the market; fluctuation défavorable des prix, adverse price movements; fluctuations saisonnières, seasonal fluctuations.

fluctuer, *v.i. Fin:* to fluctuate.

fluidité, *n.f. PolEc:* fluidity/free interplay of supply and demand.

flux, *n.m.* flow; *Fin:* flux monétaire/financier, flow of money/monetary flow; flux réel, flow of goods.

FOB, *a.inv. (abbr. de free on board)* (vente) FOB, (sale) free on board (FOB).

foi, *n.f.* acheteur de bonne foi, bona fide purchaser; détenteur de mauvaise foi, mala fide holder; texte qui fait foi, authentic text.

foire, *n.f.* (trade) fair; foire du livre, book fair.

foire-échantillon, *n.f.* trade fair.

foire-exposition, *n.f.* trade fair.

foncier 1. *a.* crédit foncier, mortgage/loan (on property or land); Crédit foncier = building society; *NAm:* Savings and Loan Association; Crédit foncier de France, government-controlled building society; impôt foncier, land tax/property tax; propriété foncière, landed property; real estate; petite propriété foncière, smallholding; propriétaire foncier, landlord; landowner; registre foncier, land register; rente foncière, ground rent 2. *n.m.* le foncier, land tax/property tax; foncier bâti,

landed property; foncier non bâti,, building land/land for development.

fonction, *n.f.* 1. job; classification de la fonction, job classification; dans l'exercice de ses fonctions, in the exercise of one's duties; définition de la fonction, job description; entrer en fonction, to take up one's appointment/to start one's job; se démettre de ses fonctions, to give in one's notice/to resign; spécification de la fonction, job specification; voiture de fonction, company car 2. *(a)* les fonctions de président, the functions/duties of a chairman; fonctions de direction, managerial functions; fonctions complémentaires, support activities *(b)* en fonction de, according to/with respect to; les appointements offerts seront fonction de l'expérience, the salary offered will be commensurate with/according to/in accordance with experience.

fonctionnaire, *n.* official/*esp.* civil servant; hauts fonctionnaires, top/high ranking civil servants; petits fonctionnaires, minor officials/minor civil servants.

fonctionnariser, *v.tr. (a)* to organize on the lines of the civil service *(b)* to transfer to the civil service/to make part of the civil service.

fonctionnarisme, *n.m.* officialdom/*F:* red tape.

fonctionnel, *a.* functional; organisation fonctionnelle, functional staff/organization; responsabilité fonctionnelle, functional responsibility.

fonctionnement, *n.m. (a)* bon fonctionnement d'une entreprise, efficiency/smooth running of a firm *(b)* operation/running/working (of a machine, etc.); en (bon) état de fonctionnement, in (good) working order; frais/coûts de fonctionnement, operating costs/expenses.

fondateur, -trice, *n.* founder (of a business, etc.); *Fin:* promoter/founder (of a company); membre fondateur, founder member; **parts de fondateur,** founder's shares.

fondé, *n.m. Jur:* **fondé de pouvoir,** agent (holding power of attorney); proxy; attorney; **il est le fondé de pouvoir (de),** he holds a power of attorney (for).

fonder, *v.tr.* (*a*) to found/to establish (business, etc.); **fonder un commerce/une maison de commerce,** to start/to set up a business; **fonder une société,** to float/to launch/to form a company; **fondé en 1928,** established in 1928 (*b*) *Fin:* to fund (debt).

fondre (se), *v.pr.* to amalgamate; to merge; **une société qui se fond avec une autre,** a company which amalgamates with another.

fonds, *n.m.* **1. fonds (de commerce),** business/goodwill; **fonds (de commerce) à vendre,** business for sale (*as a going concern*); **fonds d'épicier,** grocery business/shop; **fonds social,** company funds **2.** *pl.* (*a*) funds; **fonds de roulement,** working/operating capital; **fonds disponibles,** liquid assets; **fonds propres,** shareholders'/stockholders' equity; equity (capital); **quasi fonds propres,** quasi-equity; **faire les fonds,** to provide for a bill of exchange; **faire/fournir les fonds d'une entreprise,** to supply the capital/to put up the funds for an undertaking; **faire un appel de fonds,** to call up capital; **mettre des fonds dans une entreprise,** to invest money in a business; **mise de fonds,** (*i*) putting up of capital (*ii*) paid-in capital; **ma première mise de fonds a été de £1 000,** my initial outlay was £1 000; **rentrer dans ses fonds,** to recover one's outlay/to get one's outlay back/to get one's money back (*b*) fund; **fonds communs,** pool; **fonds commun de placement,** investment fund; mutual fund; **fonds dédié/fonds de capital-risque maison,** captive fund; **fonds à faible frais d'entrée,** low-load fund; **fonds géré,** managed fund; **fonds à gestion indicielle/fonds indiciel,** index fund; **fonds d'amortissement,** sinking fund; **fonds fédéraux,** federal fund; **Fonds Monétaire International (FMI),** International Monetary

Fund (IMF); **fonds de placement sur le marché monétaire/fonds monétaire,** money market fund; **fonds de prévoyance,** contingency reserve; **fonds de retraite maison/d'entreprise/de groupe,** occupational pension scheme; **fonds de stabilisation des changes,** exchange equalization account (*c*) means/resources; cash; **placer son argent/investir à fonds perdus,** to purchase a life annuity; **prêter à fonds perdus,** to lend money without security; **dépôt de fonds,** depositing (of money in a bank); **retrait de fonds,** withdrawal; taking money out of a bank account; *Adm:* **subvention à fonds perdu,** capital grant; **être en fonds,** to be in funds; **fonds de caisse,** cash in hand (*d*) *Fin:* stocks/securities/funds; **fonds consolidés,** funded/consolidated debt; consols; **fonds publics/fonds d'État,** Government stock.

fongibilité, *n.f. Bank: Jur:* fungibility.

fongible, *a.* fungible/interchangeable.

force, *n.f.* (*a*) **forces économiques,** economic forces; **forces du marché,** market forces (*b*) *Ins:* **(cas de) force majeure,** force majeure/act of God (*c*) *Mkt:* **force de vente,** sales force.

forcé, *a.* forced/compulsory; **cours forcé,** forced currency; **emprunt forcé,** forced/compulsory loan; **liquidation forcée,** compulsory liquidation; **vente forcée,** forced/compulsory sale.

forclore, *v.tr.* to foreclose.

forclusion, *n.f.* foreclosure.

forfait, *n.m.* (*a*) (contract for a) fixed price; flat rate; lump sum; **travailler à forfait,** to work by contract; **voyage à forfait** (all-)inclusive/package tour; **verser un forfait,** to pay a fixed sum (*b*) **vente à forfait,** outright sale.

forfaitaire, *a.* (*a*) **prix forfaitaire,** fixed price; flat rate; inclusive price; contract price; **voyage à prix forfaitaire,** package tour (*b*) **vente forfaitaire,** outright sale.

formalité, *n.f.* formality; **formalités de douanes,** customs formalities.

format, *n.m.* format/size; **grand format,** large-size(d); **petit format,** small size(d); **format de poche,** pocket-size(d); **format A4,** A4 (size) paper; **formats postaux normalisés,** Post Office preferred (format).

formation, *n.f.* (*a*) forming; development; **formation des prix sur le marché,** market pricing; **formation de réserves,** building up of reserves; **société en voie de formation,** developing company (*b*) education/training; **formation professionnelle,** professional/vocational training; **formation dans l'entreprise,** in-house/in-plant training; **formation des cadres,** management training/executive training; **formation du personnel,** staff training; **formation sur le tas,** on-the-job training.

forme, *n.f.* **la quittance est en (bonne) forme,** the receipt is in order; **un reçu en bonne et due forme,** a regular receipt.

former, *v.tr.* to form; **former une société,** to form a company.

formulaire, *n.m.* (printed) form; questionnaire; **formulaire de candidature,** application form; **remplir un formulaire,** to fill in a form/*esp. NAm:* to fill out a form.

formule, *n.f.* **1.** *Jur:* **formule d'un contrat,** wording of a contract **2.** method; **il existe trois formules de paiement,** there are three methods of payment/you can pay in three different ways; **nous offrons deux formules différentes de voyage organisé,** we can offer two different types of package tour **3.** (printed) form (*to be filled in*); **formule d'effet de commerce,** form for bill of exchange; **formule de chèque,** cheque form/*NAm:* blank check; **remplir une formule,** to fill in/*esp. NAm:* to fill out a form.

formuler, *v.tr.* to formulate; **formuler un acte,** to draw up a document in due form/to formulate a document.

fort, *a.* (*a*) strong; *Fin:* **devise forte,** strong currency (*b*) **forte baisse des prix,** sharp/big drop in prices; **forte hausse des prix,** sharp/big rise in prices; **prix en forte hausse,** soaring prices; **forte perte,** heavy loss; **forte somme,** large sum of money; **il a un fort salaire,** he has a high salary/he is highly paid (*c*) **prix fort,** full price/catalogue price/list price.

fortement, *adv.* strongly/heavily/highly; **fortement rémunéré,** highly paid; **fortement taxé,** heavily taxed.

fortune, *n.f.* **1.** fortune/chance; *MIns:* **fortune de mer,** (*i*) perils of the sea; accidents at sea (*ii*) goods on which a maritime lien applies **2.** fortune/wealth; **faire fortune,** to make a fortune; **avoir une fortune personnelle,** to have independent means; **impôt de solidarité sur la fortune,** wealth tax.

fourchette, *n.f.* *Stat:* bracket; range; **fourchette salariale/de salaire,** wage bracket; **fourchette de taux,** rate band; **une fourchette de 10 à 20%,** a 10 to 20% band; *StExch:* **fourchette de cotation,** trading range; **fourchette de cours d'ouverture/de clôture,** opening/closing range.

fournir, 1. *v.tr.* to supply/to provide; to find (a security); **fournir qch. à qn/fournir qn de qch.,** to supply s.o. with sth.; **fournir un restaurant en pain,** to supply a restaurant with bread; **ce magasin nous fournit tout le matériel de bureau,** this shop supplies us with all our office equipment (*b*) **fournir une lettre de crédit sur qn,** to issue a letter of credit on s.o.; **fournir en nantissement,** to lodge as collateral; **fournir une traite sur qn,** to draw a bill on s.o.; **fournir sur la BNP,** to draw (a cheque) on the BNP (*c*) **magasin bien fourni,** well-stocked shop **2.** *v.i.* **fournir aux dépenses,** to contribute to the expenses **3.** *v.pr.* **il se fournit chez nous,** he is a customer of ours/he's one of our customers; we supply him.

fournissement, *n.m.* *Fin:* **1.** contribution in shares (to a company); holding in shares **2. compte de fournissement,** repartition account.

fournisseur, -euse, *n.* (*a*) supplier/purveyor; dealer/stockist; caterer; **fournisseur exclusif,** sole supplier (*b*) **les**

fournisseurs de cette ville, the tradesmen of this town; **entrée des fournisseurs,** tradesmen's entrance (c) *Fin:* **comptes fournisseurs,** accounts payable/*NAm:* payables; **crédit fournisseur,** supplier's credit/trade credit.

fourniture, *n.f.* (a) supplying/providing (b) *pl.* supply of goods/supplies/requisites; **fournitures de bureau,** office equipment/(office) stationery; **contrat de fourniture,** supply contract; **main-d'œuvre et fournitures/façon et fournitures,** labour and material.

fraction, *n.f.* fraction; **par 10 francs ou fraction de 10 francs,** for each 10 francs or fraction/or fractional part thereof.

fractionnaire, *a.* fractional; **couvertures fractionnaires,** fractional reserves; **livre fractionnaire,** day book/book of prime entry.

fractionner, *v.tr.* to divide into parts; to split (up) (shares, etc.).

frais, *n.m.pl.* expenses/cost; **frais d'administration/de gestion,** administration costs/management expenses; *Nau:* **frais d'agence,** agency fees/attendance fees; **frais d'amortissement,** (i) amortization charges (ii) (amount written off for) depreciation (of building, plant, etc.); **frais bancaires/de banque,** bank charges; **frais de Bourse,** transaction charge; transaction costs; **frais de bureau,** office allowance/office expenses; **frais de déplacement,** travel allowance/travel expenses; **frais d'expédition,** delivery charges; shipping cost/charges; **frais directs,** direct costs; **frais divers,** sundry charges/sundries; *Fin:* **frais d'entrée/de sortie,** charges/commission on purchase/on sale of shares; **frais d'entreposage/de magasinage,** storage charges/warehouse charges; **frais d'entretien (du matériel, etc.),** upkeep/maintenance expenses; cost of upkeep/of maintenance; **frais d'établissement,** capital expenditure; **frais d'expertise,** consultancy fees; **frais d'exploitation,** operating costs; current expenditure; **exempt de frais/sans frais,** free of charge; no expen-

ses; **frais de fabrication,** production costs; **faux frais,** incidental/additional expenses; contingencies; extras; **frais fixes/permanents,** fixed charges; standing costs/expenses/charges; **frais généraux,** general (running) expenses; overheads/oncost; **à grands frais,** at great cost; expensively; **à peu de frais,** at little cost; inexpensively; **frais d'installation,** initial/preliminary expenses; **frais de justice,** legal costs *Ind:* **frais de lancement d'une fabrication,** set-up costs; **frais de main-d'œuvre,** labour costs; **aux frais de la maison,** at the firm's expense; **frais de manutention,** handling costs/expenses; **menus frais,** petty expenses; **frais à payer,** outstanding expenses; **frais de port,** carriage; **frais de représentation,** (i) business expenses (ii) entertainment allowance; **frais de transport,** transport charges; carriage; freightage; **frais de trésorerie,** finance costs; **total des frais effectués/encourus,** total expenses incurred; **tous frais payés,** (i) all expenses paid (ii) all-inclusive; **le voyage (organisé) coûte 2 400 francs tous frais payés,** the (package) holiday costs 2 400 francs all-inclusive; **faire les frais de qch.,** to bear the cost of/the expense of sth.; **faire/couvrir ses frais,** (i) to cover one's expenses/to get back one's money (ii) to get out of a transaction without loss (iii) to pay its way; **se mettre en frais,** to go to (great) expense; **rentrer dans ses frais,** to get one's money back.

franc[1], *n.m.* franc; **franc (belge, français, suisse),** (Belgian, French, Swiss) franc; **franc lourd,** new franc; **franc or,** gold franc; **franc vert,** green franc; **compte (tenu) en francs,** franc account; **pièce de 5 francs,** 5 franc coin.

franc[2], *a.* 1. free; **franc de tout droit,** duty-free/free of duty; **franc d'impôts,** exempt from taxation; **franc de port,** carriage paid; *Cust:* **zone franche,** free zone; *Nau:* **franc d'avaries,** free of average; **port franc,** free port 2. complete/whole; **huit jours francs/délai franc de huit jours,** eight clear days.

franchisage, *n.m.* franchising; **contrat de franchisage,** franchise.

franchise, *n.f.* **1.** exemption; **importer/ faire entrer qch. en franchise,** to import sth. free of duty/duty-free: **franchise de bagages,** (free) luggage/baggage allowance; *Post:* (en) **franchise postale (f.p.)** = official paid; **en franchise d'impôt,** exempt from tax/tax free **2. franchise d'assurance,** (*i*) excess clause (*ii*) franchise; **assurance en franchise,** franchise policy **3.** franchise.

franchisé, 1. *n.m.* franchisee **2.** *a.* **boutique franchisée,** franchise outlet.

franchiseur, *n.m.* franchisor.

franco, 1. *adv.* **franco (de port),** free/ carriage free; carriage paid/postage paid; **livré franco/franco (à) domicile,** delivery free; carriage paid; **franco de bord (FOB),** free on board (f.o.b.); **franco long du bord (FLB)/franco quai,** free alongside ship (f.a.s.); free on quay/at wharf; *NAm:* ex quay/ex wharf; **franco gare,** free on rail; **livraison franco frontière française,** delivered free as far as the French frontier; **prix franco,** franco price **2.** *n.m. StExch:* single commission (*on double operation*).

frappe, *n.f.* (*a*) minting (of coins) (*b*) typing; **faute de frappe,** typing error.

frapper, *v.tr.* (*a*) **frapper des marchandises d'un droit,** to impose/to levy a duty on goods (*b*) to mint (coins) (*c*) to type (letter, etc.).

fraude, *n.f.* **1.** fraud/deception; *Jur:* **fraude civile,** fraud/wilful misrepresentation; **fraude fiscale,** tax evasion; tax dodging; **fraude douanière,** illegal entry/illegal importation (of goods)/smuggling; **en fraude,** (*i*) fraudulently/unlawfully (*ii*) secretly; **faire entrer/introduire qch. en fraude,** to smuggle sth. in/to smuggle sth. through (the) customs **2.** fraudulence/ deceit; **par fraude,** under false pretences.

frauder, *v.tr.* to defraud/to swindle/to cheat (s.o.); **frauder la douane,** to defraud the customs/to smuggle; **frauder le fisc,** to evade/to dodge tax.

fraudeur, -euse, *n.* (*a*) defrauder/cheat/ swindler (*b*) smuggler (*c*) tax dodger.

frauduleusement, *adv.* fraudulently/by fraud.

frauduleux, *a.* fraudulent; *Jur:* **banqueroute frauduleuse,** fraudulent bankruptcy.

freiner, *v.tr.* to curb (inflation); **freiner la production,** to check/to restrain production.

freinte, *n.f.* loss in value (*during transit, manufacture, etc*).

fret, *n.m.* (*a*) freight (for sea, air, road, transport); **fret aérien,** air freight; **payer le fret,** to pay the freight/freight charges; *Rail: etc:* **fret au poids,** freight by weight; **taux du fret,** freight rates (*b*) chartering; **donner un navire à fret,** to freight (out) a ship; **prendre un navire à fret,** to charter a ship (*c*) load/cargo (of ship, aircraft, lorry); **prendre du fret,** to take in freight/ to embark cargo; **fret d'aller,** outward freight; **fret de retour,** home freight; **faux fret,** dead freight.

fréter, *v.tr.* to freight (out) a ship; to hire a car/a lorry; to charter (a plane, etc.).

fréteur, *n.m.* person who freights (out) a ship/shipowner; **fréteur et affréteur,** owner and charterer.

fuite, *n.f.* **fuite des capitaux (à l'étranger),** flight of capital (abroad).

fumeur, *n.m. Trans:* **compartiment fumeurs,** smoking compartment/smoker; **compartiment non fumeurs,** non-smoking compartment/non-smoker.

fusion, *n.f. Fin:* merger; **fusion de deux compagnies,** merger of two companies; **opérer une fusion,** to amalgamate.

fusionner, *v.i.* to amalgamate/to merge.

futur, *a.* **futur acheteur,** intending purchaser/prospective customer; **ventes futures,** future sales; **valeur future,** prospective value.

G

gâchage, *n.m.* **gâchage des prix,** price cutting.

gage, *n.m.* (*a*) security; **emprunt sur gage,** loan against security; *Jur:* **contrat de gage,** bailment (*b*) wages (*c*) pawned article; pledge; **laisser qch. en gage,** to leave sth. as security/on deposit; to pledge sth. as security; **mettre qch. en gage,** to pawn/to pledge sth.; **mise en gage,** pawning/pledging; **prêteur sur gages,** pawnbroker; **ma montre est en gage,** my watch is in pawn.

gagé, *a. Jur:* **créance gagée,** secured loan; **recettes non gagées,** unassigned/un-pledged revenue.

gager, *v.tr.* to guarantee/to secure (loan, etc.).

gagiste, *n.m.* (**créancier**) **gagiste,** secured creditor; pledgee.

gagner, *v.tr.* to earn; **gagner de l'argent,** to earn money; **gagner cinq mille francs par mois,** to earn five thousand francs a month; **gagner gros,** (*i*) to earn a lot of money (*ii*) to make large profits; **il gagne bien sa vie,** he earns a good salary/he makes good money.

gain, *n.m.* (*a*) gain/profit; **gains d'une entreprise,** profits of a company (*b*) earnings; **gains d'un ouvrier,** a worker's earnings; **gain de la femme mariée,** wife's earned income/wife's personal income; **gain d'opportunité,** notional income.

gamme, *n.f.* (*a*) range/series/scale; **gamme de produits,** range/line of products; **gamme des prix,** price range/scale of prices (*b*) **haut de gamme,** up market; **bas de gamme,** down market; **quartier de haut de gamme,** up market area/fashionable area.

gammiste, *n.m.f.* (**ingénieur-/technicien-) gammiste,** process development engineer/technician.

garant, -ante, *n.* guarantor/*esp. NAm:* warrantor; surety/bail; **garant d'une dette,** surety for a debt; **se porter garant pour qn,** to stand/to go surety/to go bail for s.o.

garantie[1], *n.f. Jur:* guarantee/*esp. NAm:* warantee.

garantie[2], *n.f.* (*a*) guarantee/pledge (of execution of contract); guaranty (of payment); **garantie accessoire,** collateral (security); **garantie bancaire,** bank guarantee; **garantie d'exécution,** contract bond; **fonds déposés en garantie,** funds lodged as security; **titres détenus en garantie,** stocks held as security; *Fin:* **garantie de la circulation,** backing of the currency (*b*) guarantee/warranty (of quality, etc.); **bulletin de garantie,** (certificate of) guarantee; **avec garantie,** guaranteed; **sans garantie,** having no guarantee/no warranty; **sous garantie,** under guarantee (*c*) *Fin:* underwriting; **syndicat de garantie,** under-writers; **contrat de garantie,** underwriting contract (*d*) **caisse/fonds de garantie (d'un emprunt),** guarantee fund.

garantir, *v.tr.* (*a*) to warrant/to guarantee; **créance garantie,** secured debt; **garantir le paiement d'une dette,** to guarantee a debt (*b*) **montre garantie (pour) deux ans,** watch under a two-year guarantee/guaranteed for two years (*c*) *Fin:* to underwrite (issue of shares, etc.); **garantir un contrat,** to underwrite a contract (*d*) **garantir un emprunt,** to back a loan (*e*) **son assurance le garantit contre le vol,** his insurance cover him against theft/he is covered against theft (by his insurance).

garçon, *n.m.* **garçon de bureau,** office boy; (office) messenger.

garde, *n.f.* **garde (en dépôt),** (safe) keeping/ (safe) custody; **déposer des titres en garde,** to place securities in safe custody.

gare, *n.f.* (*a*) railway/*NAm:* railroad station; **gare d'arrivée,** (*pour passagers*) arrival station; (*pour marchandises*) receiving station; **gare de départ,** (*pour passagers*) departure station; **gare d'expédition/gare expéditrice,** forwarding station/dispatch station; **gare de marchandises,** goods depot/goods station/*NAm:* freight depot (*b*) **gare routière,** (*i*) (bus, coach) station/terminal (*ii*) road haulage depot (*c*) **gare maritime,** harbour station.

gâter, *v.tr.* to spoil/to damage; **gâter le marché,** to spoil the market.

gel, *n.m.* **gel des crédits,** credit freeze/ squeeze.

gelé, *a.* frozen; *Fin:* **capitaux gelés,** frozen capital; **dettes gelées,** frozen debts.

général, *a.* general; **assemblée générale,** general meeting; **directeur général,** (*i*) managing director (*ii*) general manager; **frais généraux,** overheads/general (running) expenses; **hausse générale des prix,** general increase in prices; *PolEc:* **commerce général,** total/global trade (*including entrepôt trade*).

générique, *a. & n.m. Pharm:* generic; **(produit) générique de fantaisie,** branded generic; **(produit) générique vrai,** commodity generic.

génie, *n.m.* engineering; **génie électronique/ civil,** electronic/civil engineering.

gérance, *n.f.* (*a*) management (of business); **contrat de gérance,** management agreement (*b*) managership/administratorship; **pendant sa gérance,** during his period as manager/under his administration.

gérant, -ante, *n.* manager/manageress; **gérant d'une succursale,** branch manager.

gérer, *v.tr.* **gérer un commerce,** to manage/ to run a business; **mal gérer ses finances,** to mismanage one's finances.

gestion, *n.f.* management; administration; control; **comptabilité de gestion,** management accounting; **conseil en gestion,** management consultant; **contrôle de la gestion,** management audit; **frais de gestion,** management fees; **gestion administrative,** administration; **gestion autonome,** independent administration; **gestion cellulaire/par département,** divisional management; **gestion financière (d'une affaire),** financial administration (of a business); **gestion indicielle,** indexed portfolio; **gestion participative/paritaire,** participative management; **gestion passive/gestion indicielle répliquée,** passive management; **gestion prévisionnelle/budgétaire,** budgetary control; **gestion des affaires,** business management; **gestion des effectifs,** manpower management; **gestion du personnel,** personnel management; **gestion de portefeuille,** portfolio management; **gestion de la production,** production control; **gestion de qualité totale/gestion zéro-défaut,** total quality management (TQM); **gestion des stocks,** stock control/*NAm:* inventory control; **gestion de trésorerie,** cash management; **rapport de gestion,** management report; **science de la gestion,** management science; **techniques de gestion,** management techniques.

gestionnaire, 1. *a.* **compte gestionnaire,** management account 2. *n.* manager/ manageress; administrator; **gestionnaire de(s) stock(s),** stock controller/*NAm:* inventory controller; **gestionnaire de fonds/ de portefeuille,** fund/portfolio manager.

global, *a.* total/overall; aggregate; gross; lump (sum); **budget global de publicité,** overall publicity budget; **contrat global,** package deal; **montant global/somme globale,** total amount; **production globale,** aggregate output; **revenu global,** gross income.

gold-point, *n.m. Fin:* gold point; **gold-point d'entrée/d'importation,** import gold point; **gold-point de sortie/d'exportation,** export gold point; **maintenir le change au-dessus du gold-point,** to maintain the exchange above the gold point.

gondole, *n.f. Mkt:* (*présentoir*) gondola; island shelves.

gouverneur, *n.m.* governor; **conseil des gouverneurs,** board of governors.

gracieux, *a.* free (of charge); **à titre gracieux,** gratis/free of charge; **billet donné à titre gracieux,** complimentary ticket.

gramme, *n.m. Meas:* gram (*abbr:* g) (= 0.0353 oz.).

grand-livre, *n.m.* (general) ledger; **grand-livre d'achats,** bought/purchases ledger; **grand-livre de ventes,** sales ledger; **porter qch. au grand-livre,** to post an entry/to enter an item in the ledger.

graphe, *n.m.* graph/chart; **graphe en ligne,** line chart.

graphique, *n.m.* diagram; graph; chart; **graphique d'acheminement,** flow (process) chart; **graphique des activités,** activity chart; **graphique à secteurs/graphique circulaire,** pie chart; **tracer un graphique,** to plot a graph.

gratification, *n.f.* gratuity/tip; bonus.

gratis, 1. *adv.* gratis/free (of charge) **2.** *a.* free (ticket, etc.); **entrée gratis,** admission free.

gratuit, *a.* free (of charge); **échantillon gratuit,** free sample; **entrée gratuite,** admission free; **essai gratuit,** free trial; **crédit gratuit,** interest-free credit.

gratuitement, *adv.* free of charge.

gré, *n.m.* **au gré de l'acheteur,** at buyer's option; **au gré du vendeur,** at seller's option; **bail renouvable au gré du locataire,** lease renewable at the option of the tenant; **de gré à gré,** by (mutual) agree-

ment; **vendre de gré à gré,** to sell by private treaty/contract; to sell privately.

greffe, *n.m.* **1.** *Jur:* office of the clerk of the court **2.** *Fin:* registry (of joint stock company); **droits de greffe,** registry dues.

greffier, *n.m. Jur:* clerk of the court.

grève, *n.f.* strike/walkout; **allocation de grève,** strike pay; **briseur de grève,** strike breaker/*F:* blackleg/scab; **grève d'avertissement/symbolique,** token strike; **grève générale,** general strike; **grève perlée,** go-slow; **grève sauvage,** unofficial strike, wildcat strike; **grève surprise,** lightning strike; walkout; **grève sur le tas,** sit-down strike; sit-in; **grève tournante,** staggered strike; **grève du zèle,** work to rule; **faire la grève du zèle,** to work to rule; **piquet de grève,** (strike) picket; **faire grève,** to (be on) strike; **lancer un ordre de grève/ordonner une grève,** to call a strike; **se mettre en grève,** to go/to come out on strike; to take strike action; **ils se sont mis en grève par solidarité avec les mineurs,** they came out (on strike) in sympathy with the miners.

grever, *v.tr.* to burden/to encumber; **contribuable grevé d'impôts,** taxpayer saddled with taxes; **propriété grevée d'hypothèques,** encumbered estate.

gréviste, *n.m.f.* striker.

grille, *n.f.* grid; **grille de gestion,** managerial grid; **grille des salaires,** salary scale.

gris, *a.* **carte grise** = car licence/*NAm:* automobile license; **marché gris,** grey market; **zone grise,** grey zone.

gros, 1. *a.* (*a*) big/large; **gros bénéfices,** large profits; **grosse somme d'argent,** large sum of money; **la plus grosse partie de nos affaires,** the bulk of our business (*b*) **gros propriétaire,** big landowner **2.** *adv.* **gagner gros,** to make a lot (of money) **3.** *n.m.* (*a*) bulk/mass; **le gros de la cargaison,** the bulk of the cargo (*b*) **en gros,** roughly/broadly/approximately; **évaluation en gros,** rough estimate (*c*) wholesale (trade); **faire le gros et le détail,** to dea wholesale and retail; **maison/commerce de gros,** wholesale business; **commerçant en gros,** wholesale dealer/wholesaler; **prix de gros,** wholesale price; **indice des prix de gros,** wholesale price index.

grosse, *n.f.* (*a*) gross/twelve dozen; **six grosses de crayons,** six gross (of) pencils (*b*) *Jur:* engrossed document/engrossment/written instrument; **grosse (exécutoire),** first authentic copy of agreement or title.

grossiste, *n.m.f.* wholesaler/wholesale dealer.

grossoyer, *v.tr. Jur:* to engross (document).

groupage, *n.m.* bulking (of parcels); consolidation (of orders, etc.); **service de groupage,** joint cargo service/consolidation service.

groupe, *n.m.* (*a*) group (of companies); **le Groupe Shell,** the Shell Group; **comptes de groupe,** group accounts; *PolEc:* **Groupe des 7,** Group of Seven; *Ind: etc:* **groupe de pression,** pressure group; **groupe de travail,** working party; *Ins:* **contrat de groupe,** group insurance (*b*) *StExch:* crowd.

groupement, *n.m.* **1.** (*a*) *Stat:* **groupement de données,** classification/grouping of data (*b*) pooling (of interests, etc.) **2.** (*a*) group (of companies); **groupement de consommateurs,** consumer group; **groupement financier,** financial pool; **groupement syndical,** trade union bloc (*b*) *Ind:* pool.

grouper, *v.tr.* to group; to consolidate (orders, etc.); **grouper des colis,** to collect parcels (for forwarding in bulk).

guelte, *n.f.* commission/percentage (on sales).

guerre, *n.f.* war; **guerre des prix,** price war; **guerre des tarifs,** tariff war.

guichet, *n.m.* (*a*) *Bank: Post:* position; **guichet fermé,** position closed; **payer au guichet,** to pay at the counter (*b*) booking office (window); *Th:* box office (window) (*c*) *Bank:* **guichet automatique bancaire/de banque/guichet libre-service,** cash dispenser/*NAm:* automatic teller.

guichetier, -ière, *n. Bank:* counter clerk/ *NAm:* teller; *Post:* counter assistant/ clerk; *Th: Cin:* booking clerk; box office assistant.

H

habiliter, *v.tr.* **il est habilité (à faire qch.),** he is empowered/entitled (to do something).

habillage, *n.m.* (*a*) packaging (of goods); **habillage transparent,** blister pack (*b*) **habillage du bilan,** window-dressing of the balance-sheet.

habiller, *v.tr.* (*a*) **habiller un article pour la vente,** to label/to box/to package an article for sale (*b*) **habiller le bilan,** to window-dress the balance-sheet.

habitant, *n.m.* inhabitant; **par habitant,** per person/per capita.

habitation, *n.f.* **habitation à loyer modéré (HLM)** = council house/flat; **immeuble à usage d'habitation,** residential building.

***hallage,** *n.m.* **(droits de) hallage,** market dues; stallage.

***halle,** *n.f.* (covered) market; **halle aux blés,** corn exchange; **halle aux poissons,** fish market; **halle aux vins,** wine market.

***hausse,** *n.f.* (*a*) rise; **les affaires sont à la hausse,** business is looking up (*b*) **hausse du coût de la vie,** rise in the cost of living; **hausse des prix,** price increase/rise in prices; **hausse de prix déguisée,** hidden price increase; **les prix sont à la hausse,** prices are hardening; prices are going up; **les prix ont subi une forte hausse,** prices have gone up considerably/prices have shot up; **hausse du prix du pain,** rise/increase in the price of bread; **(la) hausse du prix du pétrole,** (the) increase in oil prices; **hausse graduelle/pas à pas,** incremental increase (*c*) **hausse du taux officiel d'escompte,** the raising of the minimum lending rate; **accuser une hausse,** to show a rise; to go up (*d*) *StExch:* **actions en hausse,** shares that are rising/that are going up; **marché à la hausse,** rising market; **spéculateur à la hausse,** bull; **tendance à la hausse,** bullish tendency; **jouer/spéculer à la hausse,** to speculate on a rising market/to go a bull; **position à la hausse,** bull/long position; **pousser les actions à la hausse,** to bull the market; **provoquer une hausse factice,** to rig the market.

***hausser, 1.** *v.tr.* to raise; **hausser les prix,** to raise/to put up prices; **hausser le taux (officiel) de l'escompte,** to raise/to put up the minimum lending rate **2.** *v.i.* to rise; to go up/to increase; **faire hausser les prix,** to send up/to force up prices.

***haussier** *StExch:* **1.** *a.* bullish **2.** *n.m.* bull.

***haut, 1.** *a.* (*a*) high; **la haute direction,** top management; **la haute finance/la haute banque,** (*i*) high finance (*ii*) the financiers/bankers; **haut fonctionnaire,** top civil servant; high ranking official (*b*) **haut salaire,** high salary; **les prix sont hauts,** prices are high **2.** *n.m.* top/upper part; (*sur une boîte, etc.*) **haut,** this side up; *StExch:* **les hauts et les bas (des cours),** highs and lows.

hebdomadaire, 1. *a.* weekly; **bilan hebdomadaire,** weekly return/weekly (trading) report; **salaire hebdomadaire,** weekly salary/wage **2.** *n.* **un hebdomadaire,** a weekly (paper, magazine).

héritage, *n.m.* inheritance; heirloom.

hériter, *v.tr.* to inherit; **j'ai hérité de mon père,** I inherited from my father **2.** *v.i.* **la**

maison dont il vient d'hériter, the house he just inherited.

héritier, -ière, *n.* heir, heiress.

heure, *n.f.* hour; time; **heure d'arrivée,** arrival time/time of arrival; **heure de départ,** departure time/time of departure; **aux heures de bureau/d'affaires,** during office/business hours; **en dehors des heures d'affaires/de bureau,** out of office hours; **heures d'ouverture/heures d'affaires,** (*i*) times of opening/opening hours (*ii*) business/office hours; **heures d'affluence/de pointe,** rush hour/peak period(s); *StExch:* **heurs de cotation,** trading time; **heures creuses,** off-peak hours; **engager qn à l'heure,** to employ s.o. by the hour; **être payé à l'heure,** to be paid by the hour; **il est payé 15 francs (de) l'heure,** he is paid 15 francs an hour; **ouvrier à l'heure,** hourly-paid worker; casual worker; **heure de travail/heure d'ouvrier,** man-hour; **la semaine de quarante heures,** the forty-hour week; **il travaille 8 heures par jour,** he works an 8-hour day; **heures supplémentaires,** overtime.

hexagonal, *a.* French.

Hexagone, *n.m.* **l'Hexagone,** France.

*****hiérarchie,** *n.f. Adm:* classification of grades/ranking; managerial structure.

*****hiérarchique,** *a.* **cadre hiérarchique,** line officer; **directeur hiérarchique,** line director; line manager; **structure hiérarchique,** line organization.

*****hiérarchiser,** *v.tr.* **hiérarchiser le personnel,** to grade the staff.

histogramme, *n.m.* histogram.

*****holding,** *n.m. Fin:* holding; **société holding,** holding company.

homme, *n.m.* man, *pl.* men; **l'homme moyen,** the man in the street; **homme d'affaires,** businessman.

homme-sandwich, *n.m.* sandwich man.

homologation, *n.f. Ind:* homologation

d'un prototype, type approval/type certification.

homologuer, *v.tr.* (*a*) to ratify; to approve; to obtain legal ratification (of document); to probate (a will) (*b*) *Adm:* **prix homologués,** authorized charges/prices.

honneur, *n.m.* (*a*) honour; *Fin:* **faire honneur à une traite,** to honour/to meet a bill; **ne pas faire honneur à une traite,** to dishonour a bill; **acceptation par honneur,** acceptance (of a bill) for honour (*b*) **prêt d'honneur,** loan on trust.

honorabilité, *n.f.* **maison d'une honorabilité reconnue,** firm of recognized standing.

honorable, *a.* **maison honorable,** firm of high standing.

honoraire, 1. *a.* honorary (member, etc.) 2. *n.m.pl.* fee(s) (of doctor, lawyer, etc.); honorarium.

honorer, *v.tr. Fin:* to honour/to meet/to retire (bill); **ne pas honorer une traite,** to dishonour a bill; *Jur:* **refuser d'honorer un contrat,** to repudiate a contract.

horaire, 1. *a.* hourly; *Ind:* **débit horaire,** hourly output/output per hour; **puissance horaire,** output per hour; **salaire horaire ouvrier,** worker's hourly rate/pay; **salarié horaire,** hourly-paid worker 2. *n.m.* timetable; schedule; times of opening (of a shop); **horaire souple/variable/flexible,** flexitime/flex-time/flexible working time/flexible working hours.

horizontal, *a.* (*a*) **organisation horizontale,** functional organization/staff organization (*b*) **concentration horizontale,** horizontal merger; **intégration horizontale,** horizontal integration.

horodaté, *a.* stamped with time and date.

horodateur, -trice 1. *a.* **horloge horodatrice,** time clock 2. *n.m.* time recorder; time (and date) stamp.

*****hors,** *prep.* 1. **hors bourse,** after hours; **hors pointe,** off-peak (hours); **prix hors**

saison, off-peak prices/fares; **modèle hors série,** made-to-order model/custom-built model; **hors taxe (HT),** exclusive of tax **2.** *prep. phr.* **mettre un associé hors d'intérêt,** to buy out a partner; **c'est hors de prix,** it is too expensive; the price is prohibitive.

*hors-cote, *a.* **actions hors-cote,** unlisted shares/shares not quoted on the Stock Exchange; **marché hors-cote,** unofficial market/over-the-counter market/*NAm:* off-board market.

hôtel, *n.m.* **1. l'Hôtel de la Monnaie,** the Mint; **hôtel de ville,** town hall **2.** *(a)* hotel; **hôtel de luxe,** luxury hotel/first-class hotel; **hôtel de tourisme,** tourist (class) hotel *(b)* **hôtel meublé/garni,** lodging house/residential hotel/*NAm:* rooming house.

hôtelier, -ière, 1. *n.* hotelier/hotel manager/hotel proprietor **2.** *a.* **l'industrie hôtelière,** the hotel trade.

hôtellerie, *n.f.* **l'hôtellerie,** the hotel trade.

huissier, *n.m.* bailiff; process server.

humidité, *n.f.* humidity; *(sur un colis)* **craint l'humidité,** keep in a dry place/to be kept dry.

hyperinflation, *n.f.* hyperinflation.

hypermarché, *n.m.* hypermarket.

hypothécable, *a.* mortgageable; **biens hypothécables,** mortgageable property.

hypothécaire, *a.* **contrat hypothécaire,** mortgage deed; **créance hypothécaire,** mortgage claim; **créancier hypothécaire,** mortgagee; **débiteur hypothécaire,** mortgagor; **garantie hypothécaire,** mortgage security; **obligation hypothécaire,** mortgage bond/debenture; **prêt hypothécaire,** mortgage loan/loan on mortgage; **prêt hypothécaire à montant fixe,** closed-end mortgage.

hypothécairement, *adv.* by/on mortgage; **créance garantie hypothécairement,** debt secured by mortgage; **emprunter hypothécairement,** to borrow on mortgage.

hypothèque, *n.f.* mortgage; **première hypothèque/hypothèque de premier rang,** first mortgage; **deuxième hypothèque,** second mortgage; **propriété grevée d'hypothèques,** encumbered/burdened estate; **hypothèque générale,** blanket mortgage; **prêt sur hypothèque,** mortgage loan; **acheter une maison sur hypothèque/contracter une hypothèque pour acheter une maison,** to buy a house on a mortgage; **avoir une hypothèque sur une maison,** to have a mortgage on a house/to have one's house mortgaged; **emprunter sur hypothèque,** to borrow on mortgage; **prendre une hypothèque,** to raise a mortgage; **purger une hypothèque,** to pay off/to redeem a mortgage.

hypothéquer, *v.tr.* **1.** to mortgage (estate, etc.); **hypothéquer des titres,** to mortgage securities; to lodge stock as security **2.** to secure (debt) by mortgage.

I

identité, *n.f.* identity; **carte d'identité**, identity card; **papiers d'identité**, identification papers.

illégal, *a.* illegal/unlawful; **exercise illégal d'une profession**, unlawful practice of a profession.

illégalement, *adv.* illegally/unlawfully.

illégalité, *n.f.* (*a*) illegality/unlawfulness (*b*) unlawful act.

illicite, *a.* illicit; **profits illicites**, illicit profits.

illimité, *a.* unlimited; **crédit illimité**, unlimited credit; *Fin:* **responsabilité illimitée**, unlimited liability.

îlôt, *n.m. Mkt:* **îlôt de vente**, (display) stand/island.

image, *n.f.* image; **image de marque**, (*i*) brand image (*ii*) corporate image/corporate identity; **image de produit**, product image.

imbattable, *a.* unbeatable; **prix imbattables**, (highly) competitive prices/unbeatable prices/lowest prices.

imitation, *n.f.* imitation; copy; forgery; **imitation de signature**, forging of signature.

immatériel, *a.* **valeurs immatérielles**, intangible assets/intangibles.

immatriculation, *n.f.* registering/registration (of deed, company, etc.); **droit d'immatriculation**, registry/registration fee; **plaque d'immatriculation (d'une voiture)**, registration plate (of a car).

immatricule, *n.f.* registration (of deed, etc.).

immatriculer, *v.tr.* to register (document, company, etc.).

immeuble, **1.** *a. Jur:* **biens immeubles**, real estate/property; immovable property/immovables **2.** *n.m.* (*a*) real estate/landed property/*esp. NAm:* realty; **gérant d'immeubles**, property manager; **immeuble(s) de rapport**, rented property; **placer son argent en immeubles**, to invest in property (*b*) building; **immeuble (de bureaux)**, office block; **immeuble (d'appartements)** block of flats; **immeuble à usage d'habitation**, residential building (*c*) premises *pl*; **immeuble (à usage) commercial**, business premises.

immobilier, **1.** *a. Jur:* **biens immobiliers**, real estate/*esp. NAm:* realty; immovable property/immovables; **agence immobilière**, estate agency/*NAm:* real estate agency; **agent immobilier**, estate agent/*NAm:* real estate agent/realtor; **crédit immobilier**, property loan; **investissement immobilier**, property investment; **marché (de l')immobilier**, property market; **propriété immobilière**, real estate; **société (commune) de crédit immobilier (hypothécaire)**, = building society; **société immobilière**, = real estate company; property company; **vente immobilière**, sale of property **2.** *n.m.* (*a*) real estate/realty; immovable property/immovables (*b*) (the) property/real estate business; **il a fait (sa) fortune dans l'immobilier**, he made his money in property.

immobilisation, *n.f.* **1.** (*a*) *Jur:* conversion (of personalty) into real estate (*b*) *Fin:* capitalization (of expenditure) **2.** (*a*) immobilization/locking up/tying up/tie-up (of capital) (*b*) *pl.* **immobilisations (corporelles)**, tangible assets/fixed assets/ capital assets; **immobilisations incorpo-**

relles, intangible assets; **faire de grosses immobilisations,** to carry heavy stocks.

immobilisé, *a.* **actif immobilisé/valeurs immobilisées,** fixed assets; **capital immobilisé,** tied-up/locked-up capital.

immobiliser, *v.tr.* **1.** *Jur:* to convert (personalty) into real estate **2.** to immobilize/ to lock up/to tie up (capital).

immunité, *n.f.* immunity; **immunité fiscale,** tax immunity/exemption from taxation.

impasse, *n.f.* (*a*) deadlock (*b*) *Fin:* **impasse (budgétaire),** budget deficit.

impayé, (*a*) *a.* unpaid (debt, bill, etc.); **comptes impayés,** unsettled accounts (*b*) *a. & n.m.* dishonoured (bill); **les impayés,** outstanding payments; dishonoured bills.

impenses, *n.f.pl. Jur:* expenses incurred for the maintenance or improvement of property; **impenses nécessaires,** maintenance expenses; **impenses utiles,** expenditure on improvements (*which give increased value to the property*); **impenses voluptuaires,** expenditure on luxury items (*which do not really increase the value of the property*).

implantation, *n.f.* (*a*) **l'implantation d'une industrie dans une région,** the setting up/ establishment of an industry in a region (*b*) layout (of factory, equipment, etc.); **implantation fonctionnelle,** functional layout.

implanter, *v.tr.* **implanter une industrie nouvelle,** to set up/to establish a new industry.

importable, *a.* **produits importables,** importable products/products that may be imported.

importance, *n.f.* (*a*) size; extent; **usine de moyenne importance,** medium-sized factory; **importance des dégâts,** extent of the damage (*b*) position/standing; **importance d'une société,** standing of a company.

important, *a.* large/considerable; **une**

somme importante, a considerable/large sum of money; **nous ne pouvons pas vous accorder un crédit plus important,** we cannot allow you credit beyond this limit.

importateur, -trice, 1. *n.* importer; **importateur exclusif pour la France,** sole importer for France **2.** *a.* importing (firm, etc.); **les pays importateurs de pétrole,** the oil-importing countries.

importation, *n.f.* **1.** importing (of goods); **commerce d'importation,** import trade; **contingents d'importation,** import quotas; **droit d'importation,** import duty; **excédent/surplus d'importation,** import surplus; **importation en franchise,** duty-free import; **licence d'importation,** import licence; **maison d'importation,** importer; **prix à l'importation,** import price; **règlements à l'importation,** importers' entry of goods; **restrictions d'importation,** import restrictions; **tarifs d'importation,** import tariffs **2. (article d')importation,** import; *pl.* **importations,** imports/imported goods; **importations visibles,** visible imports; **importations invisibles,** invisible imports; **contingentement des importations,** import quota system.

importer, *v.tr.* to import (goods); **importer des marchandises des États-Unis en France,** to import goods from the United States into France; **la France importe du café,** France is an importer of coffee.

import-export, *n.m.* **une entreprise d'import-export,** an import-export business.

imposable, *a.* (*a*) taxable/liable to tax; **matière imposable/revenu imposable,** taxable income (*b*) rateable/assessable (property); **valeur locative imposable,** rateable value.

imposé, 1. *a.* **imposé par la loi,** statutory; **prix imposés** = resale price maintenance (RPM)/*NAm:* administered price **2. marchandises imposées,** taxed goods **3.** *n.* (*a*) taxpayer (*b*) ratepayer.

imposer, *v.tr.* (*a*) *Adm:* **imposer des droits sur qch.,** to impose/to put a tax on sth.; to tax sth.; **objets lourdement imposés,** goods heavily taxed (*b*) **imposer qn,** (*i*) to tax s.o. (*ii*) to rate s.o.; **imposer qch.,** to make sth. liable to tax; to tax sth./to put a tax on sth.; **imposer les automobiles,** to tax cars; **imposer un immeuble,** to levy a rate on a building.

imposition, *n.f.* taxation; **année d'imposition,** year of assessment; tax year; **barème d'imposition,** tax schedule; **capacité d'imposition,** ability to pay tax; **double imposition,** double taxation; **taux d'imposition,** rate of taxation; **taux d'imposition effectif,** effective/*NAm:* average tax rate; **imposition en cascade,** cascade tax; **imposition progressive,** ability-to-pay tax.

impôt, *n.m.* tax/duty; **avant impôt,** before tax; **après impôt,** after tax; **(être) assujetti à l'impôt,** (to be) liable to tax; **cédule d'impôt,** tax code; **crédit d'impôt,** tax credit; **exempt d'impôt,** tax-free/exempt from tax; **déclaration/feuille d'impôts,** income tax return; tax form; **dégrèvement d'impôt,** tax cuts; tax relief/reduction; **impôt à la consommation,** output tax; **impôt déguisé,** hidden tax; **impôt différé,** deferred taxation; **impôt direct,** direct tax; **impôt foncier,** land tax; **impôt indirect,** indirect tax; **impôts locaux,** rates; **impôt à la production,** input tax; **impôt progressif,** graduated income tax; **impôt retenu à la base/à la source,** (*i*) pay as you earn (tax)/ PAYE/witholding tax/*NAm:* pay as you go (*ii*) tax deducted at source; **impôt sur les bénéfices (des sociétés),** profit tax; **impôt sur le capital,** capital levy; **impôt sur le chiffre d'affaires,** turnover tax; **impôt de solidarité sur la fortune,** wealth tax; **impôt sur le revenu,** income tax; **impôt sur les dividendes,** dividend tax/tax on dividend; **impôt sur la masse salariale/sur le travail,** payroll tax; **impôt sur les plus-values,** capital gains tax; **impôt sur les sociétés,** corporation tax; *NAm:* corporate/corporation income tax; **impôt du timbre,** stamp duty; **frapper qch. d'un impôt,** to tax sth./to levy a tax on sth.; **net d'impôts,** tax paid/net of tax; **perception/ recouvrement de l'impôt,** tax collection; **payer 5000F d'impôts,** to pay 5000 francs

in tax(es); **les impôts sont très élevés,** taxation is very high.

imprévu, *a.* unforeseen/unexpected; **dépenses imprévues,** unforeseen expenses; incidental expenses/extras.

imprimante, 1. *n.f. Cmptr:* printer; **calculatrice à imprimante,** calculator with a listing; **imprimante à marguerite,** daisy wheel printer; **imprimante par points,** dot matrix printer; **sortie d'imprimante,** printout; listing **2.** *a.* **calculatrice imprimante,** printout calculator.

imprimé, 1. *a.* printed **2.** *n.m.* (*a*) printed paper; **remplir un imprimé,** to fill in a form; **imprimé publicitaire,** advertising leaflet/publicity handout (*b*) *Post:* **imprimés,** printed matter; **tarif imprimés,** printed paper rate.

improductif, *a.* unproductive/nonproductive (assets); **argent improductif,** money earning no interest/yielding no returns.

improductivité, *n.f.* unproductiveness (of capital, etc.).

impulsion, *n.f.* **achat d'impulsion,** impulse buying.

imputable, *a.* chargeable; **frais imputables sur un compte,** expenses chargeable to an account.

imputation, *n.f.* **imputation des charges,** cost allocation; **imputation d'un paiement,** appropriation of money (*to the payment of a debt*).

imputer, *v.tr.* **imputer qch. sur qch.,** (*i*) to deduct sth. from sth. (*ii*) to charge sth. to sth.; **imputer des frais à un compte,** to charge expenses to an account.

inabordable, *a.* prohibitive (price); **l'essence est inabordable cette année,** the price of petrol is astronomical/prohibitive this year.

inacceptation, *n.f.* non-acceptance (of a bill, etc.).

inacquitté, *a.* unreceipted (bill, etc.).

inactif, *a.* inactive; dormant; **fonds**

inactifs, unemployed capital; **marché inactif,** dull market; **population inactive,** non-working population.

inamical, *a.* **OPA inamicale,** hostile takeover bid.

inamovible, *a.* (*a*) **fonctionnaire inamovible,** civil servant holding an appointment for life (*b*) (post) held for life.

inanimé, *a.* **marché inanimé,** dull market.

incapacité, *n.f.* (*a*) **incapacité (professionnelle),** inefficiency/incompetence (of person in his work) (*b*) **incapacité de travail,** (industrial) disablement.

incendie, *n.m.* fire; *Ins:* **assurance contre l'incendie,** fire insurance.

incertain, *n.m. Fin:* variable exchange; **coter/donner l'incertain,** to quote uncertain.

incertifié, *a.* uncertified.

incessible, *a.* not negotiable; non transferable.

inchangé, *a.* unchanged (price, etc.).

incidence, *n.f.* (*a*) **incidence d'un impôt sur le consommateur,** the incidence of a tax on the consumer (*b*) **l'incidence des salaires sur les prix de revient,** the impact/the repercussion of wage levels on production costs.

incitation, *n.f.* **incitations à la vente,** sales incentives; **incitations fiscales,** tax incentives.

inclure, *v.tr.* (*a*) to enclose; **inclure un chèque dans une lettre,** to enclose a cheque with/in a letter (*b*) to include; **le service est inclus (dans le prix),** (the) service is included (in the price) (*c*) *Jur:* to insert (clause in contract, etc.).

inclus, *a.* enclosed; **chèque inclus dans la lettre,** cheque enclosed with the letter.

inclusivement, *adv.* inclusively; **du vendredi au mardi inclusivement,** from Friday to Tuesday inclusive/*NAm:* Friday through Tuesday; **jusqu'au 30 avril inclu-** sivement, up to and including April 30th/*NAm:* through April 30th.

incompensé, *a.* uncompensated (loss, etc.).

incompétent, *a.* (*a*) *Jur:* not competent (to deal with sth.) (*b*) incompetent/inefficient.

inconvertible, *a.* inconvertible (paper money, etc.).

incorporation, *n.f. Fin:* **incorporation de réserves au capital,** capitalization of reserves.

incorporel, *a.* **actif incorporel/valeurs incorporelles,** intangible assets; **biens incorporels,** intangible property.

incoterms, (*abbr de international commercial terms,* termes de commerce international) incoterms.

indemnisable, *a.* entitled to compensation.

indemnisation, *n.f.* indemnification; compensation.

indemniser, *v.tr.* to indemnify/to compensate; **indemniser totalement qn,** to pay full indemnity/compensation to s.o.; **indemniser qn de ses frais,** to reimburse s.o. his expenses/to pay s.o.'s expenses.

indemnitaire, 1. *n.m.f.* receiver of an indemnity/of compensation **2.** *a.* **prestation indemnitaire,** allowance/benefit; **obligation indemnitaire,** indemnity bond.

indemnité, *n.f.* (*a*) **indemnité compensatrice,** indemnity/indemnification/compensation (for loss); **indemnité en argent,** cash compensation; **indemnité de licenciement,** redundancy pay/severance pay; **indemnité de départ,** golden handshake; **indemnité contractuelle de départ/de licenciement,** golden parachute; **demander une indemnité (en dommages-intérêts),** to put in a claim (for damages) (*b*) compensation to the other party; penalty (for delay, nondelivery, etc.) (*c*) allowance; **indemnité pour accidents de travail,** industrial injury benefit; **in-**

demnité de cherté de vie/de vie chère, cost-of-living allowance; **indemnité de chômage,** unemployment benefit/*F:* dole; **indemnité de déplacement/de route,** travelling expenses/allowance; **indemnité de fonction,** entertainment allowance; **indemnité kilométrique** = mileage allowance; **indemnité de maladie,** sickness benefit; **indemnité de résidence/de logement,** housing/accommodation allowance.

indépensé, *a.* unspent.

indexation, *n.f. PolEc:* index-linking (of prices, salaries, pensions, etc.); **clause d'indexation,** escalator clause.

indexer, *v.tr. PolEc:* to index-link (prices, salaries, pensions, etc.); **assurance indexée,** index-linked insurance; **emprunt indexé,** index-linked loan; **salaires indexés sur l'indice du coût de la vie,** salaries linked to the cost of living/index-linked salaries.

indicateur, 1. *a.* **chiffre indicateur,** index number **2.** *n.m.* (*a*) (railway, bus) timetable (*b*) indicator; **indicateur statistique,** statistical indicator; *PolEc:* **indicateurs d'activité économique/indicateurs d'alerte,** economic indicators/ business indicators; **indicateur de marché,** market indicator.

indicatif, *n.m. Tel:* (dialling) code; **indicatif interurbain/départemental/***FrC:* régional, area code/STD code; **indicatif du pays,** country code.

indication, *n.f.* **indication de provenance/ d'origine,** place of origin; *Adm:* **sauf indication contraire,** unless otherwise stated.

indice, *n.m.* (*i*) index (number) (*ii*) factor/ coefficient (*iii*) rating; *PolEc:* **indice de croissance,** growth index; **indice du coût de la vie,** cost-of-living index; **indice (des prix) de gros,** wholesale price index; **indice (des prix) de détail,** retail price index; **indice pondéré,** weighted index; **indice des prix à la consommation,** consumer price index; *StExch:* **indice des**

actions, share index; **indice du Financial Times,** Financial Times/FT index; **indice général des cours,** all-items indicator.

indirect, *a.* indirect; **coûts indirects/dépenses indirectes,** indirect expenses; **impôts indirects/contributions indirectes,** indirect taxation; **vente indirecte,** indirect selling.

indisponibilité, *n.f.* unavailability/nonavailability (of funds, etc.).

indisponible, *a.* unavailable (capital, etc.).

individuel, *a.* (*a*) individual; private (fortune, etc.); **consommateur individuel,** individual consumer (*b*) *Jur:* **responsabilité individuelle,** several liability.

individuellement, *adv.* (*a*) individually (*b*) *Jur:* severally; **responsables individuellement,** severally liable.

indivis, *a.* (*a*) *Jur:* undivided/joint (estate) (*b*) **actions indivises,** joint shares/shares held jointly; **propriétaires indivis,** joint owners.

indivisaire, *n.m.f. Jur:* joint owner.

indivisément, *adv. Jur:* jointly.

indivisible, *a. Jur:* joint (obligation, etc.).

indivision, *n.f. Jur:* joint possession.

indu, *n.m.* **paiement de l'indu,** payment of money not owed.

induit, *a.* induced; **demande induite,** induced demand; **investissement induit,** induced investment.

industrialisation, *n.f.* industrialization.

industrialiser, 1. *v.tr.* (*a*) to industrialize; **pays (nouvellement) industrialisé,** (newly) industrialized country (*b*) **fromage industrialisé,** processed cheese **2.** *v.pr.* **s'industrialiser,** to become industrialized; **le (commerce du) lait s'industrialise,** the milk trade is becoming industrialized.

industrialisme, *n.m.* industrialism.

industrie, *n.f.* (*a*) industry; **industrie artisanale,** cottage industry; **industrie de base,** basic industry; **industrie de consom-**

mation, consumer goods industry; **industrie connexe,** allied/related industry; **industrie en croissance rapide,** growth industry; **industrie de pointe,** advanced technology industry; **industrie de précision,** precision industry; **industrie légère,** light industry; **industrie lourde,** heavy industry; **industrie de luxe,** luxury goods industry; **industrie manufacturière,** manufacturing industry; **industrie naissante,** sunrise industry; **industrie nationalisée,** nationalized industry/state-owned industry; **industrie primaire,** primary industry; **industrie traditionelle/déclinante,** sunset industry; **industrie de transformation,** processing industry (*b*) **industrie aéronautique,** aircraft industry; **industrie alimentaire,** food industry; **industrie agroalimentaire,** agri-foodstuffs industry; **industrie automobile,** car/motor industry; **industrie du bâtiment,** building trade/building industry; **industrie chimique,** chemical industry; **industrie électronique,** electronics industry; **industrie hôtelière,** hotel trade/industry; **industrie des constructions navales,** shipbuilding industry; **industrie de l'informatique,** computer industry; **industrie du livre,** book trade; **industrie mécanique,** engineering; **industrie minière,** mining industry; **industrie pétrochimique,** petrochemical/plastics industry; **industrie pétrolière/du pétrole,** oil industry; **industrie textile,** textile industry (*c*) firm/business; **diriger une industrie prospère,** to run a successful business.

industrie-clef, *n.f.* key industry.

industriel, 1. *a.* (*a*) **centre industriel,** industrial centre; **complexe industriel,** industrial complex/industrial estate; **établissement industriel/société industrielle,** manufacturing firm; **faubourg industriel,** industrial suburb; **génie industriel,** industrial engineering; **produit industriel,** industrial product; **secteur industriel,** branch/sector of industry; **véhicule industriel,** industrial vehicle/goods vehicle; **ville industrielle,** industrial town; **zone industrielle,** (*i*) industrial estate (*ii*) industrial area (*b*) *Fin:* **banque industrielle,** industrial bank; **valeurs industriel-**

les, industrial shares/industrials **2.** *n.m.* manufacturer/industrialist.

industriellement, *adv.* industrially; (produced) in industry.

inéchangeable, *a.* unexchangeable; **valeurs inéchangeables,** unexchangeable securities; **les articles vendus en solde sont inéchangeables,** sales goods cannot be exchanged.

inemployé, *a.* unemployed/unused (capital, etc.).

inescomptable, *a. Fin:* undiscountable.

inexact, *a.* inaccurate/incorrect; wrong.

inexécuté, *a.* unfulfilled (contract, etc.); **travaux inexécutés,** work not carried out.

inexécution, *n.f.* non-fulfilment (of contract, etc.).

inexécutoire, *a.* unenforceable/nonenforceable (contract, etc.).

inexigible, *a.* (*dette*) (*i*) not due (*ii*) not claimable.

inférieur, 1. *a.* (*a*) inferior; **d'un rang inférieur,** of a lower rank/inferior in rank (*b*) poor; **des marchandises inférieures/de qualité inférieure,** poor quality/second rate goods (*c*) **votre paiement est inférieur de 1 000 francs à la somme prévue,** your payment falls short of the agreed amount by 1 000 francs **2.** *n.* subordinate.

inflation, *n.f. PolEc:* inflation; **inflation par les coûts,** cost-push inflation; **inflation par la demande,** demand-pull inflation; **inflation fiduciaire,** inflation of the currency; **inflation contenue,** repressed/suppressed inflation; **inflation galopante,** galloping/rampant inflation; **inflation monétaire,** monetary inflation; **politique d'inflation,** inflationary policy; **inflation des prix,** price inflation; **inflation rampante,** creeping inflation; **inflation des salaires,** wage inflation; **taux d'inflation,** rate of inflation; **tendances à l'inflation,** inflationary tendencies; **contenir l'inflation,** to contain inflation; **le gouvernement**

a eu recours à l'inflation, the government resorted to inflation.

inflationnisme, *n.m. PolEc:* inflationism.

inflationniste, 1. *n.m.f.* inflationist **2.** *a.* inflationary; **politique inflationniste,** inflationary policy; **tendance inflationniste,** inflationary tendency.

informaticien, -ienne, *n.* computer scientist; **ingénieur informaticien,** computer engineer.

information, *n.f.* (*a*) information; **service d'informations/marché de l'information,** information services; **centre d'information(s),** information centre; **(devoirs d')information financière,** disclosure; **je vous l'envoie à titre d'information,** I am sending it to you for your information (*b*) *Cmptr:* **traitement de l'information,** data processing; **théorie de l'information,** information theory.

informatique, 1. *n.f. Cmptr:* data processing/information processing; **(science de l')informatique,** computer science **2.** *a.* **gestion informatique,** computer control; **service informatique,** computer service.

informatisation, *n.f.* computerization.

informatiser, *v.tr.* to computerize; **informatiser les salaires,** to computerize salaries/wages.

infrastructure, *n.f. Adm: PolEc:* infrastructure.

infructueux, *a.* unprofitable (investment, etc.).

ingénierie, *n.f. Ind:* (*i*) engineering (*ii*) engineering department; **ingénierie financière,** financial engeering.

ingénieur, *n.m.* (*a*) (graduate, qualified) engineer; **ingénieur chimiste,** chemical engineer; **ingénieur civil,** civil engineer; **ingénieur constructeur/ingénieur des travaux publics,** civil engineer; **ingénieur électricien,** electrical engineer; **ingénieur électronicien,** electronic engineer; **ingénieur mécanicien,** mechanical engineer

(*b*) specialist engineer; **ingénieur commercial,** sales engineer; **ingénieur conseil,** (*i*) engineering consultant/consulting engineer (*ii*) patent engineer; **ingénieur d'études/ingénieur projecteur,** design engineer; **ingénieur informaticien,** computer engineer; **ingénieur en organisation,** work study engineer.

initial, *a.* (*a*) initial (cost, capital, etc.) (*b*) **prix initial,** starting price.

initié, *n.m. StExch:* **les initiés,** the insiders; **délit d'initié(s),** insider dealing/trading.

initiative, *n.f.* **Syndicat d'Initiative =** tourist (information) office.

injecter, *v.tr.* **injecter du capital dans une entreprise,** to inject capital into a business.

innommé, *a. Jur:* **contrat innommé,** innominate (contract).

inondation, *n.f.* **l'inondation du marché par des produits étrangers,** the flooding of the market with foreign goods.

inonder, *v.tr.* to flood/to glut (the market).

inopérant, *a. Jur:* inoperative/invalid; **clause inopérante,** inoperative clause.

inscription, *n.f.* **1.** (*a*) entering/recording (in account book, etc.) (*b*) registration/enrolment; **inscription d'une entreprise au Registre de Commerce,** registration of a firm in the Register of Companies **2.** entry (in account book, etc.) **3.** (*a*) *Fin:* scrip; **inscription sur le grand-livre,** (French) Treasury scrip (*b*) *StExch:* **inscription à la cote,** quotation in/on the (official) list; **faire une demande d'inscription à la cote,** to apply for admission to the official list/to seek a share quotation/quote.

inscrire, *v.tr.* (*a*) *Fin:* **valeur inscrite à la cote officielle,** listed stock; **valeur non inscrite,** unlisted stock/over-the-counter stock; **la dette inscrite,** the Consolidated Debt.

insérer, *v.tr.* to insert; **insérer une clause dans un contrat,** to insert a clause in an agreement; **insérer une annonce dans un journal,** to put/to insert an advertisement in a newspaper.

insertion, *n.f.* insertion; **tarif des insertions,** advertising rates.

insignifiant, *a.* unimportant; nominal (rent); trifling (sum, loss).

insolvabilité, *n.f.* insolvency.

insolvable, *a.* insolvent.

inspecter, *v.tr.* to inspect/to examine (factory, machine, company books, etc.).

inspecteur, -trice, *n.* inspector; supervisor (in shop); foreman (in factory, etc.); **inspecteur du travail,** factory inspector; **inspecteur des contributions directes,** tax inspector; **inspecteur des contributions indirectes,** customs and excise official; **Inspecteur des Finances** = (high) Treasury official; **inspecteur des impôts,** tax inspector/*F:* taxman; **inspecteur de la TVA,** VATman.

inspection, *n.f.* **1.** (*a*) inspection; inspecting; examination; examining; **faire l'inspection de ...,** to inspect/to examine ...; **inspection du travail,** factory inspection; **effectuer/passer une inspection,** to make an inspection/to inspect (*b*) tour of inspection **2.** (*a*) inspectorship; **obtenir une inspection,** to be appointed inspector (*b*) inspectorate; body of inspectors.

inspectorat, *n.m. Adm:* (*a*) inspectorship (*b*) inspectorate; body of inspectors.

instabilité, *n.f.* **l'instabilité du marché,** the unsettled state of the market; **l'instabilité du change,** fluctuation in the rates of exchange.

instable, *a.* unsteady (prices, etc.); **marché instable,** jumpy market.

installation, *n.f.* **1.** installing/setting-up (of machine, etc.); fitting out/equipping (of workshop, etc.) **2.** (*a*) fittings (in workshop, etc.); **installations électriques,** electrical fittings/equipment (*b*) plant; equipment; facilities; **installation frigorifique,** refrigerating plant.

installer, *v.tr.* to install; to set up (machine, etc.); to fit out/to equip (factory, etc.).

institut, *n.m.* (*a*) institute/institution; **l'Institut d'Assurances Maritimes de Londres** = the Institute of London Underwriters (*b*) establishment; **institut de beauté,** beauty parlour (*c*) **institut monétaire,** lender (of the last resort).

institution, *n.f.* (*a*) instituting/establishing (*b*) institution.

institutionnel, *a.* **investisseurs institutionnels,** *n.pl.* **les institutionnels,** institutional investors.

instructions, *n.f. pl.* **instructions permanentes,** standing instructions/*NAm:* standard operating procedure; **conformément aux instructions,** as directed; **aux termes des instructions qui lui avaient été données, la commission était chargée de ...,** under its terms of reference the commission was instructed to ...; *Corr:* **nous attendons vos instructions,** we await your instructions.

instruire, *v.tr.* **instruire qn de qch.,** to inform s.o. of sth.

instrument, *n.m.* (*a*) instrument; **instrument de commerce/de crédit,** instrument of commerce/of credit; **instrument de couverture/de négociation/de placement,** hedging/trading/investment instrument (*b*) *Jur:* (legal) instrument (*deed, contract, writ, etc.*) (*c*) **instruments de précision,** precision instruments.

insuffisance, *n.f.* insufficiency; shortage; **insuffisance de personnel,** shortage of staff.

insuffisant, *a.* insufficient; inadequate; **poids insuffisant,** short weight; **salaire insuffisant,** inadequate salary.

intégral, *a.* entire/complete; **paiement intégral,** payment in full; **libération intégrale d'une action,** payment in full of a share.

intégralement, *adv.* completely/fully/in full; **rembourser intégralement une**

somme, to repay a sum in full; **capital intégralement versé,** fully paid(-up) capital.

intégration, *n.f.* integration; **intégration économique,** economic integration; **intégration horizontale,** horizontal integration; **intégration verticale,** vertical integration.

intégré, *a.* integrated; **système intégré de gestion,** integrated management system.

intenter, *v.tr.* **intenter un procès, une action à/contre qn.,** to bring an action/institute proceedings against s.o.

interbancaire, *a.* interbank; **dépôt interbancaire,** interbank deposit; **taux interbancaire offert,** interbank offered rate/IBOR; **taux de référence interbancaire,** interbank reference rate.

interdépartemental, *a.* interdepartmental.

interdiction, *n.f.* **interdiction d'exportation,** export ban; **interdiction d'importation,** import ban.

interdire, *v.tr.* to forbid/to prohibit; **l'exportation de l'or est formellement interdite,** the export of gold is strictly prohibited; *PN:* **entrée interdite (au public)** = no admittance.

interdit, *n.m.* **interdit bancaire,** account holder forbidden by bank to write cheques (*usu. for one year*).

interentreprises, *a.* inter-firm.

intéressant, *a.* attractive (offer, etc.).

intéressé, 1. *a.* interested; **être intéressé dans une entreprise,** to have a financial interest in a venture; **les parties intéressées,** the interested parties **2.** *n.m.pl.* **les intéressés,** the interested parties.

intéressement, *n.m.* profit-sharing (scheme); benefit (plan); **intéressement du personnel aux fruits de l'expansion/aux bénéfices,** profit-sharing by the employees.

intéresser, *v.tr.* **intéresser les employés**

(aux bénéfices), to initiate a profit-sharing scheme; **je ne suis pas intéressé dans cette entreprise,** I have no financial interests in this firm.

intérêt, *n.m.* **1.** share/stake (in business, etc.); **avoir des intérêts dans une compagnie,** to have a financial interest/vested interests/a stake in a company; **mettre qn hors d'intérêt,** to buy s.o. out **2.** advantage; **agir dans l'intérêt de la société,** to act in the interest(s) of the company **3.** *Fin:* **intérêt du capital,** interest on capital; **intérêts composés,** compound interest; **intérêt couru,** accrued interest; **intérêts échus,** outstanding interest; interest due/payable; **intérêt élevé,** high interest; **intérêt fixe,** fixed interest; *Bank:* **intérêts à payer,** interest charges; **intérêt simple,** simple interest; **intérêt sur mille francs,** interest on a thousand francs; **intérêt sur prêt,** interest on a loan; **coupon d'intérêt,** interest coupon; **prêt à intérêt,** interest-bearing loan; **revenu d'intérêt,** earned interest/interest income; **sans intérêt,** interest-free; **taux d'intérêt/de l'intérêt,** interest rate/rate of interest; **taux d'intérêt de 4%,** interest rate of 4%; **taux d'intérêt à long terme,** long-term interest rate; **emprunter à intérêt,** to borrow at interest; **laisser courir des intérêts,** to allow interest to accumulate; **payer des intérêts,** to pay interest; **placer son argent à 7% d'intérêt,** to invest one's money at 7% interest; **porter intérêt,** to bear interest/to yield; **actions qui portent intérêt au taux de 5%,** shares that yield (a) 5% interest.

interface, *n.f. Cmptr:* interface.

intérieur, 1. *a.* **commerce intérieur,** home/internal trade; **consommation intérieure,** home consumption; **marché intérieur,** home market; **produit intérieur brut,** gross domestic product; *Post:* **(tarif d')affranchissement en régime intérieur,** inland postage rate **2.** *n.m.* home (country); **Ministère de l'Intérieur,** Home Office/*NAm:* Department of the Interior; *Post:* **colis à destination de l'intérieur,** inland parcels.

intérim, *n.m.* interim; **assurer l'intérim,** to

take over s.o.'s duties temporarily; **faire l'intérim (de qn),** to deputize (for s.o.); **secrétaire par intérim,** acting secretary/interim secretary; **secrétaire qui fait de l'intérim,** temp.

intérimaire, 1. *a.* temporary/provisional; **directeur intérimaire,** acting manager; **dividende intérimaire,** interim dividend; **dactylo intérimaire,** temp; **personnel intérimaire,** personnel from a temp agency; temporary staff; **rapport intérimaire,** interim report **2.** *n.m.f.* official holding a temporary appointment; deputy.

intermédiaire, 1. *a.* intermediate; **biens intermédiaires,** intermediate products; **commerce intermédiaire,** middleman's business **2.** *n.m.f.* (*a*) middleman (*b*) *StExch:* jobber; **marge d'un intermédiaire,** jobber's turn (*c*) intermediary/agency; **négocier par l'intermédiaire de ...,** to negotiate through the intermediary/the agency of ....; **intermédiaire agréé,** accredited agent; authorized dealer; **intermédiaire financier,** financial intermediary.

international, *a.* international; **commerce international,** international trade; **droit international,** international law; **réserves monétaires internationales,** international monetary reserves.

interne, *a.* internal; **contrôle/vérification interne,** internal auditing; **vérificateur, -trice interne,** internal auditor.

interprofessionnel, *a.* interprofessional; **salaire minimum interprofessionnel de croissance/SMIC** = index-linked minimum wage.

interrogation, *n.f.* interrogation; *Cmptr:* **interrogation de banque de données,** information retrieval.

intersyndical, *a. Ind: etc:* inter-union.

interurbain, *a.* **appel téléphonique interurbain,** STD call/trunk call/long-distance call.

intervenant, -ante, *n.* (*a*) intervening party; acceptor (of bill) for honour (*b*)

intervenant sur le marché, market participant.

intervenir, *v.i.* to happen/to occur; **un accord est intervenu entre la direction et les syndicats,** (an) agreement has been reached between management and unions.

intervention, *n.f.* (*a*) *EEC:* **cours/prix d'intervention,** intervention price; **taux d'intervention,** intervention rate (*b*) *Jur:* intervention/becoming a third party (in a contract, etc.); **paiement par intervention,** payment on behalf of a third party (*c*) **acceptation par intervention,** acceptance (of protested bill) for honour.

intestat 1. *a.* **décéder/mourir intestat,** to die intestate **2.** *n.m.* intestacy.

intitulé, *n.m.* (*a*) **intitulé d'un compte,** name of an account (*b*) *Jur:* **intitulé d'un acte,** premises of a deed.

intransférable, *a.* not transferable; *Jur:* unassignable (right, etc.).

introducteurs, *n.m.pl. StExch: F:* the shop.

introduction, *n.f.* (*a*) bringing in; importing (of goods from abroad, etc.) (*b*) **l'introduction de la semaine de cinq jours,** the introduction of the five-day week; **lettre d'introduction,** letter of introduction (**de la part de,** from; **auprès de,** to) (*c*) *StExch:* bringing out (of shares); **introduction en bourse,** initial public offering (IPO); **délai d'introduction en bourse,** IPO window; **actions à l'introduction,** *F:* shop shares; **(cours d')introduction,** debut.

introduire, *v.tr.* to introduce; to bring in/to import (goods from abroad, etc.); *StExch:* to introduce/to bring out (shares).

invalidation, *n.f. Jur:* invalidation (of document, contract, etc.).

invalide, *a. Jur:* invalid/null and void.

invalidité, *n.f. Jur:* invalidity (of contract, etc.).

invendable, *a.* unsaleable/unmarketable;

article/marchandise **invendable,** drug on the market.

invendu, 1. *a.* unsold **2.** *n.m.pl.* **invendus,** unsold goods; unsold copies (of newspapers, etc.); remainders/*NAm:* overstocks (of books).

inventaire, *n.m.* (*a*) inventory; **faire/dresser un inventaire,** to draw up an inventory; **inventaire d'entrée,** ingoing inventory; **inventaire de sortie,** outgoing inventory; **meubles dont l'inventaire se monte à 100 000 francs,** the inventory for the furniture comes to 100 000 francs (*b*) stock list; stocktaking/*NAm:* inventory; **inventaire permanent,** perpetual/continuous/rolling inventory; **nous faisons/nous dressons l'inventaire,** we're stocktaking/*NAm:* we're taking the inventory; **soldes après inventaire,** stocktaking sale (*c*) *Book-k:* **inventaire (comptable),** book inventory; **inventaire de fin d'année,** accounts for/to the end of the financial year; **livre d'inventaire,** balance book (*d*) *Fin:* valuation (of investments, securities, etc.) (*e*) list/schedule.

inventer, *v.tr.* to invent.

inventeur, -trice, *n.* inventor.

invention, *n.f.* invention; **brevet d'invention,** patent (for an invention).

inventorier, *v.tr.* **1.** (*a*) to inventory/to do the stocktaking/*NAm:* to take the inventory (*b*) to value (goods, bills, etc.) **2.** to enter (article) on an inventory/on a stock list.

investi, *a.* **capitaux investis,** invested/funded capital.

investir, *v.tr.* to invest (money); **investir des capitaux à l'étranger,** to invest capital abroad.

investissement, *n.m.* investment; investing (of capital); **biens d'investissement,** capital goods; **crédit d'investissement,** investment credit; **dépenses d'investissement,** capital expenditure; **gestion des investissements,** investment management; **investissements à l'étranger,** foreign investment/capital movements; **investissements immobiliers,** investments in real estate; **investissement industriel,** investment in industry; **investissement en valeurs de redressement/de retournement,** failure investment; **plan d'investissement,** investment plan; **programme d'investissement,** investment programme; **rendement des investissements,** return on investment; **société d'investissements,** investment company; **société d'investissements à capital fixe,** closed-end investment company; **société d'investissements à capital variable/SICAV,** open-end investment company; unit trust/*NAm:* mutual fund; **faire des investissements,** to invest (money)/to place money.

investisseur, *n.m. Fin:* investor; **investisseur institutionnel,** institutional investor; **investisseur-or/investisseur patrimonial en or,** gold bug; **investisseur privé,** private investor.

invisible, *PolEc:* **1.** *a.* invisible; **exportations invisibles,** invisible exports; **importations invisibles,** invisible imports **2.** *n.m.pl.* **invisibles,** invisibles.

invitation, *n.f.* invitation; **invitations de complaisance,** = corporate hospitality.

irréalisable, *a. Fin:* **valeurs irréalisables,** unrealizable securities.

irrégularité, *n.f.* **irrégularité comptable,** accounting irregularity/irregularity in the accounts.

J

jargon, *n.m.* jargon; **jargon publicitaire,** advertising jargon.

jauge, *n.f.* (*a*) gauge; capacity (*b*) *Nau:* tonnage/burden; **jauge brute,** gross register(ed) tonnage; **jauge nette,** net register(ed) tonnage; **jauge de douane/ jauge de registre,** register(ed) tonnage.

jaugeage, *n.m. Nau:* measurement (of tonnage).

jauger, *v.tr.* **1.** to gauge/to measure capacity; **jauger un navire,** to measure the tonnage of a ship **2.** *Nau:* **pétrolier qui jauge quarante mille tonneaux,** forty thousand ton tanker.

jaune, *a.* **les pages jaunes (de l'annuaire téléphonique),** the yellow pages (of the telephone directory).

jetable, *a.* disposable (nappies, bottle, etc.).

jeter, *v.tr.* to throw; to throw away; **jeter des marchandises sur le marché,** to throw goods on(to) the market.

jeton, *n.m.* **jeton de présence,** director's fees.

jeu, *n.m.* (*a*) *StExch:* speculating; **jeu de bourse,** gambling on the Stock Exchange/ Stock Exchange speculations; **jeu sur les reports,** speculating in contangoes (*b*) **jeu d'outils,** set of tools (*c*) *Book-k:* **jeu d'écritures,** paper transaction.

joindre, *v.tr.* (*a*) to add (à, to); **joindre l'intérêt au capital,** to add the interest to the capital; **l'échantillon joint à votre lettre,** the sample attached to your letter (*b*) to get in touch with s.o.; **essayer de joindre un client,** to try to get in touch with a client; **j'ai téléphoné, mais je n'ai pas réussi à le** joindre, I phoned but couldn't get in touch with him/get hold of him.

joint, *a.* joined; *Corr:* **pièces jointes (PJ),** enclosures (*abbr.* encl.).

jouer, *v.i.* **1.** *Fin:* to speculate; to play the market; **jouer à la Bourse,** to speculate/to gamble on the Stock Exchange; **jouer à la hausse,** to speculate on a rising market/to bull the market; **jouer à la baisse,** to speculate on a fall/to bear the market; **jouer sur les mines,** to speculate in mining securities **2.** to be operative/to become operative/to operate; **l'augmentation des salaires joue depuis le 1ᵉʳ janvier,** the rise in salaries has been operative since January 1st.

joueur, -euse, *n. StExch:* speculator/ operator; **joueur à la hausse,** bull; **joueur à la baisse,** bear.

jouissance, *n.f.* (*a*) *Jur:* **jouissance en commun (d'un bien),** communal tenure; **avoir la jouissance de certains droits,** to enjoy certain rights; **maison à vendre avec jouissance immédiate,** house for sale with vacant possession (*b*) *Fin:* right to interest/dividends; **date de jouissance (de bons du Trésor, etc.),** date from which interest begins to run; **action de jouissance,** redeemed share that continues to participate in dividends.

jour, *n.m.* (*a*) day; **jour franc,** clear day; **préavis de dix jours francs,** ten clear days' notice; **quinze jours,** a fortnight (*b*) **intérêts à ce jour,** interest to date; *Fin:* **prêts au jour le jour,** money at call/call money (*c*) **mettre (une liste, etc.) à jour,** to bring (a list, etc.) up to date/to update (a list, etc.); **tenir les livres à jour,** to keep the books/ the accounts up to date (*d*) *Adm:* **jour**

férié = bank/public holiday; **jour ouvrable**, working day; *StExch:* **jour de Bourse**, trading day; **jour non-ouvrable**, non-trading day; **fixer un jour pour qch.**, to fix a date/to appoint a day/to make an appointment for sth. (*e*) **le prix du jour**, today's price.

journal, *n.m.* **1.** *Book-k:* **(livre) journal**, account book; journal; **journal des achats**, bought ledger; **journal des ventes**, sales ledger **2.** (news)paper; journal; **journal d'entreprise**, company/house magazine.

journalier, *a.* daily (consumption, etc.).

journaliser, *v.tr. Book-k:* to enter/to write up (an entry) in the books.

journalisme, *n.m.* journalism.

journaliste, *n.m.f.* journalist.

journée, *n.f.* **journée de travail**, (*i*) day's work (*ii*) working day; **faire la journée continue**, (*magasin*) to remain open at lunchtime; (*personne*) to work through lunch; **travailler à la journée**, to work by the day.

judiciaire, *a.* (*a*) judicial/legal; **administrateur judiciaire**, official receiver; **assistance judiciaire**, legal aid; **frais judiciaires**, legal charges/costs (in an action); **poursuites judiciaires**, (*i*) proceedings (*ii*) prosecution; **règlement judiciaire**, bankruptcy; **vente judiciaire**, sale by order of the court (*b*) **le pouvoir judiciaire**, (*i*) judicial power (*ii*) the Bench.

judiciairement, *adv.* judicially.

juge, *n.m.* judge; **juge d'instruction**, examining magistrate; **juge d'instance**, conciliation magistrate (*in commercial cases*); police-court magistrate; **juge consulaire/ juge au tribunal de commerce**, judge in commercial court.

jugement, *n.m.* (*a*) *Jur:* judgement; decision; award; (*dans une cause criminelle*) sentence; **jugement déclaratif de faillite**,

adjudication in bankruptcy (*b*) trial (of case).

juger, *v.tr.* (*a*) to judge; *Jur:* **juger un procès**, to try/to judge a case; **juger une réclamation**, to adjudicate a claim (*b*) to adjudicate (**entre**, between).

juguler, *v.tr.* **juguler l'inflation**, to check inflation.

juridiction, *n.f.* jurisdiction; **question tombant sous la juridiction du tribunal**, matter within the jurisdiction of the court.

juridique, *a.* juridical/judicial; legal; **conseiller juridique**, legal advisor; **frais juridiques**, lawyer's fees/legal charges (in a transaction).

juriste, *n.m.* lawyer.

jury, *n.m.* jury.

juste, **1.** *a.* right/fair; **juste salaire**, fair wage **2.** (*a*) right/exact/accurate; **balance juste**, accurate scales; **chiffres justes**, correct figures; **mesure juste**, full measure (*b*) **au plus juste prix**, at rockbottom price **3.** *adv.* exactly; precisely; **prix calculé au plus juste**, strict price.

justice, *n.f.* (*a*) justice (*b*) law/legal proceedings; **action en justice**, action at law; **recourir à la justice**, to go to law; **poursuivre qn en justice**, to institute legal proceedings against s.o./to take legal action against s.o.

justificatif, **1.** *a.* supporting/justificatory; *Jur:* **pièces justificatives**, (*i*) written proof (*ii*) relevant documents **2.** *n.m.* (*a*) voucher (copy) (*b*) (*d'un journal, etc.*) tear sheet/advertiser's copy.

justification, *n.f.* proof; *Typ:* justification.

justifier, *v.tr.* **1.** to justify; to warrant (expenditure, etc.); to prove **2.** *Typ:* to justify.

K

kilo, kilogramme, *n.m. Meas:* kilo, kilogram (*abbr.* kg) (= 2.2 lbs); **5 kilos/5 kg de beurre,** 5 kilos/5 kg of butter.

kilométrage, *n.m.* (*a*) length in kilometres (*b*) = mileage.

kilomètre, *n.m. Meas:* kilometre (*abbr.* km) (= 0.624 mile); *Av:* **kilomètre-passager** = passenger-mile; *Rail:* **kilomètre-voyageur** = passenger-mile; **tonnes-kilomètres marchandises,** ton kilometres.

kilométrique, *a.* kilometric; *Aut:* **coût kilométrique,** cost per kilometre; **indemnité kilométrique** = mileage allowance.

kiosque, *n.m.* **kiosque à journaux,** newspaper kiosk/stand.

krach, *n.m.* (financial) crash; **krach boursier,** crash on the Stock Exchange.

krugerrand, *n.m.* Krugerrand.

L

label, *n.m.* label; seal of approval; trade-union mark; **label d'exportation,** export label; **label de garantie,** guarantee label; **label d'origine,** certificate of origin; **label de qualité,** quality label.

laboratoire, *n.m.* **laboratoire d'idées,** think tank.

laissé-pour-compte, *a. & n.m.* returned/rejected/unsold (article).

laissez-faire, *n.m.* **politique du laissez-faire,** laissez-faire policy.

laissez-passer, *n.m.inv.* pass/permit; *Cust:* transire.

lancement, *n.m.* floating/launching (of company); launching (of new product, publicity campaign); **prix de lancement,** introductory offer/price.

lancer, *v.tr.* to float/to promote (a new company); to float (a loan); **lancer un nouveau produit (sur le marché),** to put a new product on the market/to launch a new product/to market a new product; **lancer une souscription,** to start a fund.

lanceur, -euse, *n.* promoter (of company); **lanceur d'affaires,** business promoter.

languissant, *a.* dull/sluggish (market); slow (business).

leasing, *n.m.* lease financing.

légal, *a.* legal; **fête légale,** statutory holiday; bank holiday; **monnaie légale,** legal tender; *Fin:* **taux d'intérêt légal,** official rate of interest.

légalement, *adv.* legally/lawfully.

légalisation, *n.f.* legalization; (*d'une signature, etc.*) authentication/certification.

légaliser, *v.tr.* to legalize; to authenticate/to certify (signature, etc).

légalité, *n.f.* legality.

légataire, *n.m.f.* legatee/heir.

léger, *a.* **industrie légère,** light industry.

législation, *n.f.* legislation; **législation anti-dumping,** anti-dumping laws; **législation anti-trust,** anti-trust legislation; **législation fiscale,** tax laws; **législation bancaire/douanière,** banking/customs legislation; **législation du travail/législation ouvrière,** industrial/labour legislation.

légitime, *a.* legitimate; **propriétaire légitime,** legal owner.

legs, *n.m.* legacy/bequest; **legs particulier,** personal/private legacy; **legs universel,** residuary legacy.

léguer, *v.tr.* to leave/to bequeath (money, etc.).

léonin, *a. Jur:* **contrat léonin,** unconscionable/one-sided bargain.

lessivage, *n.m.* laundering; **on fait le lessivage de l'argent,** money is laundered.

lessiver, *v.tr.* **lessiver l'argent,** to launder money.

lettre, *n.f.* **1. lettres majuscules,** capital letters/capitals; **écrire une somme en (toutes) lettres,** to write an amount in words (not figures) **2.** (*a*) lettre; **lettre d'affaires/lettre commerciale,** business letter; **lettre d'envoi/lettre d'introduction,** covering letter; *Post:* **lettre exprès,** express letter; **lettre d'intention,** letter of intent; **lettre de rappel,** (letter of) reminder; **lettre de réclamation,** (letter of) complaint; **lettre recommandée,** (*i*) registered letter (*ii*) (letter sent by) recorded delivery; **lettre de recommandation,** reference; **lettre de relance (à un client),** follow-up letter (to a customer); **envoyer une lettre à tarif normal,** to send a letter first class; **envoyer une lettre à tarif réduit,** to send a letter second class (*b*) **lettre d'avis,** advice note; **lettre de change,** bill of exchange; **lettre de change à l'extérieur,** foreign bill; **lettre de crédit,** letter of credit; **lettre de crédit circulaire,** circular letter of credit; **lettre de crédit documentaire,** documentary letter of credit; *Av:* **lettre de transport aérien,** air waybill; **lettre de voiture,** waybill/consignment note (*c*) *StExch:* **lettre d'allocation,** letter of allotment.

levée, *n.f.* (*a*) lifting (of embargo); closing/ adjourning (of meeting) (*b*) collecting (of taxes); *Post:* collection (of letters); *Fin:* **levée des actions,** taking (up) (of stock); **levée d'une option,** taking up (of) an option; *Bank:* **levées de compte,** personal withdrawals.

lever, *v.tr.* **1.** (*i*) to close (a meeting) (*ii*) to adjourn (a meeting); to lift/to raise (embargo, etc.); **la séance a été levée à trois heures,** the meeting (*i*) was adjourned (*ii*) was closed at three o'clock **2.** to collect (taxes); *Post:* **lever les lettres,** to collect the mail; *Fin:* **lever des actions,** to take up (delivery of) stock; **lever une option/une prime,** to take up/exercise an option.

levier, *n.m. Fin:* **effet de levier,** gearing/ leverage; **achat d'entreprise par effet de levier,** leveraged buyout.

liaison, *n.f.* (*a*) **liaison aérienne,** air link; **liaison ferroviaire,** rail link; **liaison postale,** postal link; **liaison rail-aéroport,** rail-air link; **liaison routière,** road link; **la liaison téléphonique Paris-Londres,** (telephone) communications between Paris and London; **travailler en liaison avec qn,** to liaise with s.o./to work in conjunction with s.o. (*b*) **liaisons hiérarchiques,** manager-staff relations/line relations.

libellé, *n.m.* wording/terms used (in a document); **libellé d'une écriture,** particulars of an item.

libeller, *v.tr.* to draw up/to word (a document, etc.); **libeller un chèque au nom de qn,** to make out/to write (out) a cheque to s.o.; **chèque libellé à l'ordre de Mme X,** cheque made out to Mrs X; **être libellé au porteur,** to be made out to/to be made payable to bearer; **chèque libellé en devises étrangères,** cheque denominated in foreign currency.

libéralisation, *n.f.* **la libéralisation du commerce,** the easing of trade restrictions; **libéralisation du cours du dollar,** freeing of the dollar.

libéraliser, *v.tr.* to free/to ease (currency, trade restrictions, etc.).

libération, *n.f.* (*a*) payment (in full); discharge; **libération d'une dette,** discharging/ redeeming of a debt; *Fin:* **libération d'une action,** paying up of a share; **libération de capital,** paying up of capital (by shareholders) (*b*) **libération des échanges commerciaux,** relaxing/freeing of exchange controls.

libératoire, *a.* (*a*) **paiement libératoire,** payment in full discharge from debt/of debt; **prélèvement libératoire,** deduction (of tax) at source (*b*) (*argent*) **avoir force/ pouvoir libératoire,** to be legal tender.

libéré, *a. Fin:* (fully) paid-up (share); **non (entièrement) libéré/partiellement libéré,** partly paid-up.

libérer, 1. *v.tr.* to free (s.o., an institution, etc.) from/of debt; **libérer un garant,** to discharge a surety; **libérer qn de la responsabilité légale,** to relieve s.o. of legal liability; **titre de 1000 francs libéré de 750 francs/libéré à 75%,** 1000 franc share of which 750 francs are paid (up) **2.** *v.pr.* **se libérer (d'une dette),** to redeem a debt/to clear oneself of a debt; **se libérer d'un engagement,** to free oneself from a commitment/an obligation.

liberté, *n.f.* (*a*) **liberté du commerce,** freedom of trade (*b*) **liberté syndicale,**

right of a worker to belong to a union of his own choosing.

libraire, *n.m.f.* bookseller; **libraire-éditeur,** bookseller and publisher.

librairie, *n.f.* bookshop.

libre, *a.* (*a*) free; **cours libre,** free market rate; **libre concurrence,** free competition; **libre entreprise,** free enterprise; **marché libre,** free market; **marché libre des capitaux,** open money market; **produit en vente libre,** product on general sale (*b*) **entrée libre,** (*i*) admission free (*ii*) no obligation to buy (*c*) **libre possession,** vacant possession (*d*) free (from mortgage).

libre-échange, *n.m. PolEc:* free trade; **politique de libre-échange,** free-trade policy; **zone de libre-échange,** free-trade area.

libre-échangiste, **1.** *n.m.* free trader **2.** *a.* **politique libre-échangiste,** free-trade policy.

libre-réponse, *n.f. Post:* Freepost.

libre-service, *n.m.* self-service; **(magasin) libre-service,** self-service store; **(restaurant) libre-service,** self-service restaurant.

licence, *n.f.* licence/*NAm:* license; **détenteur d'une licence,** licensee; **licence de débit de boissons,** licence to sell beer, wines and spirits/*NAm:* liquor license; **licence d'exploitation d'un brevet,** licence to use a patent; **licence d'exportation,** export licence; **licence de fabrication,** manufacturing licence; **licence exclusive,** exclusive licence; **fabriqué sous licence,** made/manufactured under licence; **licence d'importation,** import licence.

licenciement, *n.m.* dismissal; laying-off/lay-off (of workers); **licenciement abusif,** unfair dismissal; **licenciement économique,** redundancy; **indemnité de licenciement,** redundancy pay/compensation; **lettre/préavis de licenciement,** notice of dismissal; **licenciement sans préavis,** dismissal without notice.

licencier, *v.tr.* to make s.o. redundant/to dismiss s.o.; to lay s.o. off.

licite, *a.* licit/lawful/permissible.

licitement, *adv.* licitly/lawfully.

lier, *v.tr.* (*a*) to bind; **contrat qui lie qn,** agreement binding (up)on s.o.; **ce contrat vous lie,** you are bound by this agreement (*b*) **marchés liés,** related markets; **opération liée,** combined deal; **emprunts liés,** tied loans.

lieu, *n.m.* **1.** (*a*) locality; place; **lieu de livraison,** place of delivery; *Adm:* **lieu de naissance,** place of birth; *Mkt:* **lieu de vente,** point of sale (*b*) *pl.* **lieux,** house/premises; **état des lieux,** inventory of fixtures (*as between landlord and tenant*); **vider les lieux,** to vacate the premises **2.** **avoir lieu,** to take place; **la réunion aura lieu vendredi,** the meeting will take place/will be held on Friday.

ligne, *n.f.* (*a*) line; *Fin:* **ligne de crédit/de découvert/d'escompte,** line of credit (*b*) **amortissement en ligne droite,** straight line depreciation (*c*) **ligne aérienne,** airline; **ligne maritime,** shipping line; **ligne d'autobus,** bus route; **ligne de métro,** underground route/line (*d*) *Tel:* telephone line; **ligne partagée,** party line; **vous avez Paris sur la ligne,** you have Paris on the line (*e*) *Book-k:* **(dépenses) au-dessus de la ligne,** above-the-line (expenditures) (*f*) *Cmptr:* **en ligne,** on-line.

limitatif, *a.* limiting; restrictive; *Jur:* **clause limitative,** limiting clause.

limitation, *n.f.* limitation/restriction; **limitation des prix,** price control; **limitation de responsabilité,** limitation of liability; **limitation des salaires,** wage restraint; **ils appliquent une limitation volontaire de leurs exportations,** they set voluntary limits to their exports.

limite, *n.f.* (*a*) limit; **limite d'âge,** age limit; **limites de prix,** price limits; **limite de poids,** weight limit; **prix limite,** upper price limit (*b*) **cas limite,** borderline case; **date limite,** latest date/deadline; (*sur un produit*) **date limite de vente,** sell-by date (*c*) *StExch:* **ordre limite,** limit (order);

limite de la hausse/de la baisse/supérieure/inférieure, limit up/limit down.

limité, *a.* limited; *StExch:* **cours limités,** limited prices; *Publ:* **édition à tirage limité,** limited edition; **société à responsabilité limitée (SARL),** limited liability company; *FrC:* **Desrochers et Cie Ltée,** Desrochers and Co. Ltd.

linéaire 1. *a.* (*a*) **programmation linéaire,** linear programming (*b*) **mode/méthode (d'amortissement) linéaire,** straight line (depreciation) method **2.** *n.m.* shelf space.

lingot, *n.m.* **lingot d'or,** gold ingot/bar; **or en lingots,** gold bullion.

liquidateur,-trice, *n.* **1.** *Jur:* liquidator; **liquidateur d'une société,** liquidator of a company **2.** *Fin:* **liquidateur officiel (à la Bourse),** official assignee (on the Stock Exchange).

liquidatif, *a. Jur:* pertaining to liquidation; **acte liquidatif de société,** winding-up resolution/order; **valeur liquidative,** value at liquidation.

liquidation, *n.f.* **1.** (*a*) liquidation; **frais de liquidation,** closing-down costs; **liquidation forcée,** compulsory liquidation; **liquidation volontaire,** voluntary liquidation; **entrer en liquidation,** to go into liquidation; to wind up a business (*b*) clearing (of accounts); *StExch:* settlement; **chambre de liquidation,** (bankers') clearing house; *StExch:* **jour de la liquidation,** account day/settlement day; **liquidation de quinzaine,** fortnightly account **2.** selling off (of stocks); clearance sale.

liquide, 1. *a.* liquid; **actif liquide,** liquid assets; **argent liquide,** ready money/cash; **capital liquide,** liquid capital; **dette liquide,** liquid debt; **fonds liquides,** available funds **2.** *n.m.* (*a*) liquid/fluid; **measures (de capacité) pour les liquides,** fluid measures (*b*) ready money/cash; **je n'ai pas de liquide,** I haven't any cash.

liquider, *v.tr.* **1.** (*a*) to wind up (a business); to wipe out (a debt) (*b*) to clear/to settle (account); to close (transaction); to settle (a deal) **2. liquider le stock,** to sell off stock/to have a clearance sale.

liquidité, *n.f.* **1.** liquidity; **coefficient/taux de liquidité,** liquidity ratio; **liquidité du portefeuille,** portfolio liquidity **2.** *pl.* **liquidités,** liquid assets; **liquidités excédentaires,** excess liquidities.

listage, *n.m. Cmptr:* listing.

liste, *n.f.* list; register; **liste d'attente,** waiting list; **liste de candidats,** list of applicants; **liste de contrôle/de vérification,** checklist; **liste d'envoi/liste des abonnés/liste d'adresses/liste de diffusion,** mailing list; **liste des importations,** import list; *Cust:* **liste des marchandises importées en franchise,** free list; **liste officielle de taux,** schedule of charges; *FrC:* **liste de paie,** payroll; *Fin:* **liste des souscripteurs (à un emprunt),** list of applications; **dresser/établir une liste,** to draw up/to make out a list.

lister, *v.tr. Cmptr:* to list.

listing, *n.m.* = **listage.**

litige, *n.m.* litigation; lawsuit; dispute; **litige commercial,** commercial dispute.

litre, *n.m. Meas:* litre/*NAm:* liter (*abbr.* l) (1000 cubic cm = *approx.* 1¾ pints); **ma voiture consomme onze litres aux 100 kilomètres (11 L/100 km)** = my car does 25 miles per gallon (25 mpg)/25 miles to the gallon.

livrable, 1. *a.* (*a*) *Fin:* deliverable (*b*) ready for delivery; **commandes livrables à domicile,** orders delivered (to your door) **2.** *n.m.* **prix du livrable,** forward/terminal market.

livraison, *n.f.* (*a*) delivery; **bordereau de livraison,** delivery note; **conditions de livraison,** delivery terms; **défaut de livraison,** non-delivery; **délai de livraison,** delivery period/lead time; **délai de livraison un mois,** delivery within a month; **frais à percevoir à la livraison,** charges forward; **livraison à domicile,** door-to-door delivery/we deliver to your door; **livraison franco,** delivered free/free delivery;

livraison immédiate, immediate delivery; **livraison lendemain,** next day delivery; **livraison contre remboursement/paiement à la livraison,** cash on delivery (COD)/*also NAm:* collect on delivery (COD); **payable à la livraison,** payable on delivery; **voiture de livraison,** delivery van; **faire livraison de qch.,** to deliver sth.; **prendre livraison de qch.,** to take delivery of sth. (*b*) issue (of magazine, revue); **nous avons lu dans votre livraison de septembre,** we read in the September issue (of your magazine) (*c*) *Fin:* delivery; **livraisons à terme,** future deliveries (*d*) *Const:* **livraison (d'un bâtiment) clé en main,** turnkey operation.

livre[1], *n.f.* **1.** (*poids*) pound (*abbr.* lb) (= 500 grams); **une livre de sucre,** a pound/half a kilo of sugar; **vendre qch. à la livre,** to sell sth. by the pound **2.** (*argent*) **livre (sterling),** pound (sterling); **billet de cinq livres,** five pound note; **livre verte,** green pound.

livre[2], *n.m.* (*a*) book; **l'industrie du livre,** the book trade (*b*) *Book-k:* **livre des achats,** bought ledger; **livre de caisse,** cash book; **livres de commerce/de comptabilité/des comptes,** account books/the books; **livre d'échéance,** bill book; **livre des inventaires,** stock book; **livre journal,** journal/day book; **livre de magasin,** warehouse book; **livre de paie,** payroll; **livre de petite caisse,** petty cash book; **livre des réclamations,** claims book; **livre des ventes,** sales ledger; **teneur de livres,** book-keeper; **tenue de livres,** book-keeping; **tenir les livres,** to keep the accounts/the books.

livrer, *v.tr.* (*a*) to deliver (goods, etc.); **livrer une commande,** to deliver an order; **livrer à domicile,** to deliver to the customer's address (*b*) *StExch:* **prime pour livrer,** seller's option; **vente à livrer,** sale for delivery.

livret, *n.m.* booklet; catalogue (of exhibition); **livret de dépôts,** deposit book; **livret de Caisse d'Épargne,** savings-bank book; passbook; **compte sur livret,** savings account; **se faire ouvrir un livret,** to open a savings account (*at the Caisse d'Épargne*).

livret-portefeuille, *n.m.* savings-bank book.

livreur, *n.m.* delivery man/boy.

local, 1. *a.* local (authority, industry, etc.); **impôts locaux,** rates; **classification des impôts locaux,** rating **2.** *n.m.* premises; building; **locaux commerciaux,** business premises/commercial property; **locaux à louer,** premises to let; **local professionnel,** premises (used) for professional purposes.

locataire, *n.m.f.* (*a*) (*i*) tenant (*ii*) lodger; *Jur:* **locataire (à bail),** lessee/lease-holder (*b*) hirer/renter (of equipment, etc.).

locateur, -trice, *n.* lessor.

locatif, *a.* **impôts locatifs** = rates; **logement locatif,** rented accommodation; **marché locatif,** rental market; **réparations locatives,** repairs incumbent on the tenant; **revenu locatif,** rental income; rent; **risques locatifs,** tenant's risk; **valeur locative,** rental (value); **valeur locative imposable,** rateable value; **jouissance locative,** tenure.

location, *n.f.* (*a*) (*d'une voiture, etc.*) (*i*) hiring/renting (*ii*) hire/rental; **location d'équipement,** plant hire; **location de voitures (sans chauffeur),** (self-drive) car hire/car rental; **location à long terme,** leasing; **donner qch. en location,** to hire sth. out; **contrat de location,** rental agreement; **prendre qch. en location,** to hire sth.; **verser £200 pour la location d'une salle,** to pay £200 for the hire of a hall; **voiture de location,** hire car/rented car (*b*) (*d'une maison, d'un appartement*) (*i*) renting; tenancy (*ii*) letting; **location à vie,** life tenancy; **location avec option d'achat,** lease financing; **agent de location,** estate agent/letting agent; **prix de location,** rent (*c*) *Th: etc:* booking/reservation (of seats); **(bureau de) location,** box office/booking office.

location-gérance, *n.f.* agreement with liquidator to manage a company in liquidation.

location-vente, *n.f.* hire purchase (of

property, equipment); rent back; **contrat de location-vente,** hire purchase agreement; **acheter qch. en location-vente,** to buy sth. on hire purchase.

lock-out, *n.m.inv. Ind:* lock(-)out.

lock-outer, *v.tr. Ind:* to lock out (the personnel).

loco, *adv.* loco; **prix loco,** loco price.

logement, *n.m.* accommodation; lodgings.

logiciel, *n.m. Cmptr:* software; **erreur de logiciel,** software bug.

logotype, *n.m.* logotype/logo.

loi, *n.f.* law; **loi de Finances,** Finance Act; **loi de l'offre et de la demande,** law of supply and demand; **loi des rendements décroissants,** law of diminishing returns; **loi sur les sociétés,** Companies' Act; *NAm:* corporation/corporate law.

lombard, *a.* **taux lombard,** lombard rate.

long, *a.* long; **bail à long terme/à longue échéance,** long lease; **contrat à long terme,** long-term contract; **crédit à long terme,** long-term credit; **emprunt à long terme,** long-term loan; **effets à longue échéance/** *F:* **papiers longs,** long-dated bills; **titres longs/obligations longues,** long-dated securities/longs; **placements à long terme,** long-term investments; **politique à long terme,** long-term policy; **emprunter à long terme,** to borrow long.

longévité, *n.f.* life (of product, etc.); **matériel à longévité élevée,** long-life equipment; **longévité des capitaux durables,** (length of) life of durable assets.

lot, *n.m.* **1.** (*a*) (*dans une loterie*) prize; **gros lot,** first prize/jackpot (*b*) *Fin:* **emprunt à lots,** lottery loan; **obligation à lots,** prize bond **2.** (*a*) (*aux enchères*) lot (*b*) parcel (of goods); batch (of goods, etc.); **contrôle par lots,** batch control; **fabrication par lots,** batch production; **lot d'envoi,** consignment (*c*) plot (of land); lot.

loterie, *n.f.* **billet de loterie,** lottery ticket;

loterie (publicitaire), lottery; **loterie nationale,** national lottery.

lotir, *v.tr.* (*a*) to divide (sth.) into lots/into batches (*b*) to divide (land) into building plots; **terrains à lotir,** land to be sold in lots.

lotissement, *n.m.* **1.** (*a*) dividing (of goods, etc.) into lots; parcelling out (*b*) division into plots (of building land) **2.** (*a*) building plot (*b*) housing estate/development.

lotisseur, -euse *n.* (*a*) person in charge of dividing goods into lots (*b*) property developer.

louage, *n.m.* **contrat de louage,** rental agreement/contract; **louage de services,** contract of employment; **voiture de louage,** rented car/hired car/hire car.

louer, *v.tr.* (*a*) to hire out/to let (out) (**à,** to); **louer à bail,** to lease; **maison à louer,** house to let; **voitures à louer,** cars for hire (*b*) to rent (house, car, etc.) (**de,** from); to take on (seasonal workers) (*c*) **louer une place d'avance,** to reserve/to book a seat (in advance).

loueur, -euse, *n.* hirer (out); renter.

lourd, *a.* heavy; **l'industrie lourde,** heavy industry; **les industries lourdes,** smokestack industries; **poids lourd,** heavy goods vehicle; **investissement lourd,** heavy investment; *Fin:* **marché lourd,** dull/sluggish market.

loyal, *a.* honest/fair; **qualité loyale et marchande,** fair market/fair average quality; **bon et loyal inventaire,** true and accurate inventory.

loyalement, *adv.* honestly/fairly.

loyauté, *n.f.* honesty/fairness; good faith; **loyauté en affaires,** fair (and square) dealing.

loyer, *n.m.* **1.** rent/rental; **arriéré de loyer,** rent arrears/back rent; **loyer de bureau,** office rent; **loyer élevé/gros loyer,** high rent; **loyer modéré,** fair rent; **loyer trimestriel,** quarterly rent; **devoir trois mois de**

loyer, to owe three months' rent; **donner à loyer,** to let; **prendre une maison à loyer,** to rent a house; **quittance de loyer,** rent receipt **2.** *Bank: Fin:* **le loyer de l'argent,** the rates of interest (for money on loan)/the price of money.

lucratif, *a.* lucrative/profitable/paying; **(association) à but lucratif,** profit-making (association); **(association) sans but lucratif,** non-profit-making (association); **entreprise lucrative,** profitable/lucrative business; **travail lucratif,** well-paid job; **travail peu lucratif,** badly-paid job.

luxe, *n.m.* luxury; **articles/produits de luxe,** luxury goods; **boutique de luxe,** shop selling luxury goods; **industrie de luxe,** luxury goods industry; **impôt/taxe de luxe,** luxury tax; **voiture de luxe,** de luxe car.

lyophilisé, *a.* freeze-dried.

M

machine, *n.f.* (*a*) machine; **machine à additionner,** adding machine; **machine à calculer,** calculator/calculating machine; **machine comptable,** accounting machine; **machine à dicter,** dictating machine/*Rtm:* Dictaphone; **machine à écrire,** typewriter; **machine à écrire à boule/à sphère,** golfball typewriter; **machine à (poly)copier,** copying machine/duplicator; **écrire/taper une lettre à la machine,** to type a letter; **machine de traitement de texte(s),** word processor (*b*) *Ind: etc:* machine; **les machines,** (the) machinery; **atelier des machines,** machine shop; **fait à la machine,** machine-made; **machine-outil,** machine-tool; **machines agricoles,** agricultural machinery; **production à la machine,** machine production; **travail à la machine,** machine work (*c*) **la machine administrative,** administrative/bureaucratic machinery.

machinerie, *n.f. Ind:* machinery; plant.

macro-économie, *n.f.* macro-economics.

macro-économique, *a.* macro-economic.

Madame, *n.f.* **Madame**/*abbr:* **Mme,** Mrs/Ms; *Corr:* **Madame,** Dear Madam; **Chère Madame,** Dear Mrs X; **Madame la Présidente,** Madam Chairman; *pl.* **Mesdames X et Y/Mmes X et Y,** Mrs X and Mrs Y.

Mademoiselle, *n.f.* **Mademoiselle**/*abbr:* **Mlle,** Miss/Ms; *Corr:* **Mademoiselle,** Dear Madam; **Chère Mademoiselle,** Dear Miss X; *pl.* **Mesdemoiselles**/*abbr:* **Mlles X et Y,** Miss X and Miss Y.

magasin, *n.m.* (*a*) shop/*esp. NAm:* store; **chaîne de magasins,** chain of shops; **devanture de magasin,** shop front/shop window; **employé de magasin,** shop assistant/employee; **grand magasin,** department store; **magasin d'alimentation,** grocery shop/store; **magasin de (vente au) détail,** retail shop/store; **magasin à grande surface,** hypermarket; **magasin libre-service,** self-service store; **magasin populaire/magasin à prix unique,** oneprice store/popular store; **magasin spécialisé,** specialized store; **magasin sous franchise exclusive,** tied outlet; **magasin à succursales multiples,** chain store/multiple store/multiple; **rayon de magasin,** department; counter; **vitrine de magasin,** shop window; **tenir un magasin,** to keep a shop (*b*) store/warehouse; **magasins généraux,** bonded warehouse(s); **marchandises en magasin,** stock in hand; **avoir qch. en magasin,** to have sth. in stock.

magasinage, *n.m.* **1.** warehousing/storing of goods **2. (droits de) magasinage,** warehouse dues; storage charges **3.** *FrC:* shopping.

magasiner, *v.i. FrC:* **aller magasiner,** to go shopping.

magasinier, -ière *n.m.* warehouseman/ stock keeper.

magazine, *n.m.* (illustrated) magazine.

magistrat, *n.m.* judge; justice; magistrate.

magnat, *n.m.* magnate (of industry, etc.)/tycoon.

magnétique, *a.* **bande magnétique,** magnetic tape.

magouille(s), *n.f.* (*pl.*) *Pol: F.* fiddling/ scheming/graft.

main, *n.f.* **1.** (*a*) hand; **bagages à main,** hand luggage (*b*) **camion d'occasion de pre-**

mière main, second hand truck (*with only one previous owner*); **changer de mains,** to change hands; **la propriété a changé de mains en janvier,** the property changed hands in January (*c*) **payer de la main à la main,** to hand over (the) money directly (*without receipt or other formality*); **remettre (qch.) en main(s) propre(s),** to hand over (sth.) personally (*d*) **faire/fabriquer qch. à la main,** to do/to make sth. by hand; **fait (à la) main,** hand-made (*e*) **travailler de ses mains,** to have a manual job **2.** (*a*) hand(writing) (*b*) **main courante,** rough book; *Bank:* **main courante de caisse,** counter cash book; **main courante de dépenses/de recettes,** paid/received cash book.

main-d'œuvre, *n.f.* (*a*) labour; manpower; workforce; **main-d'œuvre occasionnelle,** casual labour; **main-d'œuvre directe,** direct/productive labour; **main-d'œuvre féminine,** female labour; **main-d'œuvre indirecte,** indirect labour; **main-d'œuvre qualifiée,** skilled labour; **main-d'œuvre spécialisée,** semi-skilled labour; **embaucher de la main-d'œuvre,** to take on workers (*b*) **frais de main-d'œuvre,** cost of labour; **matériel et main-d'œuvre,** material and labour (*c*) workmanship.

mainlevée, *n.f. Jur:* **mainlevée de saisie,** restoration of goods (taken in distraint); replevin; **mainlevée d'une hypothèque,** release of mortgage.

mainmise, *n.f.* seizure of/distraint upon (property); **mainmise économique,** economic stranglehold.

maintenance, *n.f. Ind: etc:* maintenance (service); **maintenance périodique,** routine maintenance; **programme de maintenance,** maintenance programme.

maintenir, 1. *v.tr.* to maintain; to keep; **dividende maintenu à 5%,** dividend maintained at 5%; **maintenir le change au-dessus du gold-point,** to maintain the exchange above the gold-point; **maintenir les prix fermes,** to keep prices firm/steady **2.** *v.pr.* **la hausse des prix se maintient à 4%,** the rise in prices remains at/is

sustained at 4%; *StExch:* **ces actions se maintiennent à ...,** these shares remain firm at ....

maintien, *n.m.* maintenance/keeping; **maintien de la prospérité économique,** maintenance of economic prosperity; **maintien continu de plein emploi,** continuous full employment.

maison, *n.f.* **1.** (*a*) house; **maison de rapport,** block of (rented) flats (*b*) home; **dépenses de la maison,** household expenses; **(fait) maison,** home-made **2. maison (de commerce),** firm/company; **maison affiliée,** affiliated company/affiliate; **maison de courtage,** brokerage house; **maison de détail,** retail company/firm; retailer; **maison d'édition,** publishing firm/house; **maison d'escompte,** discount house; **maison d'exportation,** export(ing) firm; **maison de gros,** wholesale firm; **maison d'importation,** import(ing) firm; **maison(-)mère,** parent company/head office.

maître, *n.m.* (*a*) **être maître du marché,** to lead the market (*b*) skilled tradesman (*self-employed*); **maître charpentier,** master carpenter (*c*) works owner (*d*) employee in charge; **maître d'œuvre,** (*i*) foreman (*ii*) prime contractor.

maîtrise, *n.f. Ind:* supervisory staff; **agent de maîtrise,** foreman/supervisor.

majeur, *a.* (*a*) major/greater; **la majeure partie de nos exportations,** the major part of our exports (*b*) **affaire majeure,** well-established business (*c*) **(cas de) force majeure,** force majeure; act of God.

majoration, *n.f.* **1.** (*a*) overestimation/overvaluation (of assets, etc.) (*b*) (*sur une facture*) additional charge/surcharge; **frapper un immeuble d'une majoration de cinq pour cent,** to put five per cent on to the valuation of a building; **majoration d'impôt,** surcharge **2.** increase (in price); mark-up.

majorer, *v.tr.* **1.** to overestimate/to overvalue (assets, etc.) **2.** (*sur une facture*) to make an additional charge; **majoré de**

notre commission de 10%, to which we have added our commission of 10%; **majorer une facture de 10%,** (*i*) to put 10% on an invoice (*ii*) to overcharge by 10% on an invoice **3.** to raise/to put up/to increase/to mark up the price of (sth.); **majorer un prix,** to increase a price.

majoritaire, (*a*) *a.* **vote majoritaire,** majority vote (*b*) *Fin:* **actionnaire majoritaire,** majority shareholder; **participation majoritaire,** majority holding/interest/stake; **se rendre (largement) majoritaire,** to acquire majority interest/to acquire a majority shareholding.

majorité, *n.f.* majority; **majorité absolue,** absolute majority; **majorité qualifiée,** supermajority; **une majorité de(s) deux tiers,** a two-thirds majority; **décision prise à la majorité (des voix),** majority decision.

mal, *adv.* badly; **mal calculer un compte,** to miscalculate an account; **mal gérer une affaire,** to mismanage a business; **mal renseigner (qn),** to misinform (s.o.); **mal représenter les faits,** to misrepresent the facts; **il est très mal payé,** he is very badly paid.

maladie, *n.f.* **assurance-maladie/indemnité de maladie,** sickness benefit; **certificat de maladie,** medical certificate; **congé de maladie,** sick leave; **maladie professionnelle,** occupational disease.

malfaçon, *n.f.* (*a*) bad work(manship) (*b*) defect.

malversation, *n.f.* embezzlement/corrupt administration (of funds).

management, *n.m.* management; **système d'information de management,** management information system.

manageur, -euse *n. Ind:* manager.

mandant, *n.m. Jur:* principal (in transaction); **mandant et mandataire,** principal and agent.

mandat, *n.m.* **1.** (*a*) mandate; commission; terms of reference (of committee) (*b*) *Jur:* power of attorney; proxy **2.** warrant; *Jur:* **lancer un mandat,** to issue a warrant; **mandat d'arrêt,** warrant of arrest; *Fin:*

mandat du Trésor, Treasury warrant **3.** *Bank: Post:* order to pay; money order; draft; **mandat sur la Banque de France,** order on the Bank of France; **mandat international,** international money order; **mandat de paiement,** (*i*) order to pay (*ii*) (French) treasury money order; **mandat postal/mandat(-)poste,** postal order; **mandat de virement,** transfer order; **toucher un mandat,** to draw on/to cash a money order.

mandataire, *n.m. & f.* **1.** (*à une réunion*) proxy; representative **2.** *Jur:* authorized agent; attorney; assignee; **mandataire général,** general agent; **mandataire(-)liquidateur,** official receiver.

mandat-carte, *n.m. Post:* postal order/money order (*in postcard form*).

mandat-contributions, *n.m. Post:* (special) money order (*for paying income tax*).

mandatement, *n.m.* (action of) paying by means of a money order.

mandater, *v.tr.* **1.** to elect/to appoint/to commission (representative, etc.) **2.** (*a*) to write out a money order (*b*) to pay by money order.

mandat-lettre, *n.m. Post:* postal order/money order (*which may be sent as a letter in an envelope*).

mandat-poste, *n.m. Post:* postal order/money order.

maniement, *n.m.* handling/management (of business, etc.); **maniement de fonds publics,** handling of public money.

manier, *v.tr.* to handle/to manage/to control (business, etc.).

manieur, -euse *n.* **manieur d'argent,** financier.

manifeste, *n.m. Av: Nau:* **manifeste (de douane),** customs manifest; **manifeste de chargement,** (ship's, aircraft's) manifest; **manifeste d'entrée,** inward manifest

manifeste de fret, freight manifest; **manifeste de sortie,** outward manifest.

anifold, *n.m.* multi-part form.

anipulation, *n.f.* **manipulation de cours sur l'indice,** market tending.

anœuvre, *n.f.* (*a*) **manœuvre de Bourse,** manipulation on the stock market (*b*) *pl. Jur:* **manœuvres frauduleuses,** swindling **2.** *n.m.* unskilled labourer/worker; **manœuvre qualifié,** skilled worker; **manœuvre spécialisé,** semi-skilled worker; **travail de manœuvre,** unskilled labour/work.

anquant,-ante, 1. *a.* (*a*) missing/absent (*b*) lacking (*c*) out of stock **2.** *n.* absentee **3.** *n.m.* deficiency; **manquant en caisse,** short(age) in the cash; **éviter des manquants dans la marchandise,** to prevent short delivery.

anque, *n.m.* deficiency/shortage; **manque d'affaires,** slackness/slack market; **manque de fonds,** lack of funds; **manque à gagner,** (*i*) lost opportunity of doing business (*ii*) loss of profit/earnings; **manque à l'embarquement,** short-shipped goods; **manque à la livraison,** short delivery; **manque de poids,** deficiency in weight; **dix kilos de manque,** ten kilos short.

anquer, 1. *v.i.* (*a*) **manquer de qch.,** to lack/to be short of sth.; **manquer d'argent,** to be short of money; **manquer de personnel,** to be short of staff/to be under-staffed; **manquer de sucre,** to be out of sugar/to have run short of sugar; **il nous manque les capitaux nécessaires,** we lack/are short of the necessary capital (*b*) to be lacking/deficient; **manquer en magasin,** to be out of stock; **il me manque dix francs,** I'm ten francs short; **il manque 50 grammes au poids,** the weight is 50 grams short (*c*) (*personne*) to be absent; **manquer à un rendez-vous,** to fail to keep an appointment **2.** *v.tr.* to miss/to lose; **manquer une affaire,** to miss one's chance of doing business; **manquer un contrat,** to lose a contract.

anuel, 1. *a.* manual (labour, etc.) **2.** *n.m.* (*a*) manual worker/blue collar worker

(*b*) *n.m.* manual/handbook/instruction book.

manufacturé, *a.* manufactured; factory-made; **biens/produits manufacturés,** manufactured goods.

manufacturer, *v.tr.* to manufacture (industrial products).

manufacturier, *a.* manufacturing (town, industry, etc.).

manutention, *n.f.* handling (of stores, materials, etc.); **appareils de manutention,** handling equipment/machines; **frais de manutention,** handling charges/costs; **manutention industrielle,** industrial handling.

manutentionnaire, *n.m. Ind: etc:* warehouseman; handler.

manutentionner, *v.tr.* to handle (stores, materials).

maquette, *n.f.* (*a*) *Publ:* dummy (of book); lay-out (of page, etc.) (*b*) *Ind:* mock-up (*c*) (scale) model.

maquignon, *n.m. Pej:* shark/swindler/trickster.

maquignonnage, *n.m.* sharp practice.

maquignonner, *v.tr.* to fiddle/rig (business); **affaire maquignonnée,** put-up job.

maquillage, *n.m.* forging/faking (of documents, etc.); disguising (of stolen property).

maquiller, *v.tr.* **maquiller un chèque,** to forge a cheque.

maraîchage, *n.m.* market gardening/*NAm:* truck farming.

maraîcher, *a.* **industrie maraîchère,** market-gardening (industry)/*NAm:* truck farming; **produits maraîchers,** market-garden produce/*NAm:* truck.

marasme, *n.m.* **le marasme des affaires,** the stagnation/slackness of business; the slump in business; **économie dans le marasme,** stagnating/sagging economy.

marc, *n.m. Jur:* **au marc le franc,** pro rata/

proportionally; **au marc le franc de la valeur,** in proportion to the value.

marchand, -ande, 1. *n.* dealer; shop-keeper; tradesman/tradeswoman; **marchand ambulant/des quatre saisons,** coster/hawker; **marchand de biens** = estate agent; property dealer; **marchand au détail,** retailer; **marchand en gros,** wholesaler/wholesale dealer; **marchand de journaux,** newsagent; **marchand de poisson(s),** fishmonger; **marchand de tabac,** tobacconist; **marchand de vin,** wine merchant **2.** *a.* (*a*) **denrées marchandes,** saleable/marketable goods; **prix marchand,** trade price; **qualité marchande,** standard/average quality; **techniques marchandes,** merchandising; **valeur marchande,** commercial value/market-(able) value (*b*) **galerie marchande (d'un aéroport),** shopping arcade; **quartier marchand,** shopping centre; commercial centre; **ville marchande,** commercial town (*c*) **marine marchande,** merchant navy; **navire marchand,** merchant ship/trading vessel.

marchandage, *n.m.* (*a*) bargaining/haggling (*b*) *Ind: Jur:* (illegal) subcontracting of labour (*whereby the worker receives less than a fair wage*).

marchander, *v.tr.* **1. marchander qch. avec qn,** to haggle/to bargain with s.o. over sth. **2.** *Ind:* to sub-contract (job) (illegally).

marchandeur, -euse, *n.* **1.** haggler/bargainer **2.** *Ind:* (illegal) sub-contractor of labour.

marchandisage, *n.m.* marketing/merchandising.

marchandise, *n.f.* merchandise/commodity/*pl.* goods; **gare de marchandises,** goods depot/goods station/*NAm:* freight depot; **marchandises au détail,** retail goods; **marchandises en gros,** wholesale goods; **marchandises en magasin,** stock in hand; **marchandises livrables au comptant,** spot goods; **marchandises périssables,** perishable goods/perishables; (*à la Bourse de commerce*) **marchandises et**

biens physiques/marchandises livrées au comptant, actuals; **train de marchandises,** goods train/*NAm:* freight train; **livrer des marchandises,** to deliver goods.

marche, *n.f.* (*a*) running/working (of machine, etc.); **en état de marche,** in working order (*b*) **bonne marche d'une entreprise,** smooth running of a firm (*c*) course (of events, etc.); **marche à suivre,** course to be followed/to adopt; procedure.

marché, *n.m.* **1.** (*a*) **faire son marché,** to do one's shopping (*b*) deal/bargain/contract; **marché au comptant,** cash transaction; **marché de fournitures,** supply contract; **marché de gré à gré,** mutual agreement/private contract; **être en marché avec qn,** to negotiate a deal with s.o.; **faire/conclure un marché,** to strike a bargain/to clinch a deal; **faire un marché avec qn pour un travail,** to make/to sign a contract with s.o. for a piece of work (*c*) **(à) bon marché,** cheap(ly); **articles bon marché,** low-priced/cheap goods/bargains; **à meilleur marché,** more cheaply/cheaper; **acheter qch. à bon marché,** to buy sth. cheaply/cheap; **avoir qch. à très bon marché,** to get a very good bargain; **vendre qch. à très bon marché,** to sell sth. cheap(ly) **2.** (*a*) market; **marché en plein air,** open-air market; **marché couvert,** covered market; **marché aux bestiaux,** cattle market; **marché aux poissons,** fish market; **jour du marché,** market day; **la place du marché,** the market place; **aller au marché,** to go to the market (*b*) **Marché commun,** the Common Market; **marché extérieur/d'outre-mer,** foreign overseas market; **marché gris,** grey/semi black market; **marché intérieur,** home market; **marché libre,** open/free market; **marché marginal,** fringe market; **marché mondial,** world market; **marché noir,** black market; **faire du marché noir,** to buy and sell on the black market; **marché parallèle,** = underground economy; **marché réglementé,** regulated market (*c*) *StExch: Fin:* **marché boursier,** stock exchange; **marché calme,** quiet/dull market; **marché des changes/des devises,** foreign exchange market; **marché des changes à terme,** fo ward exchange market; **marché de contrats à terme,** futures market; **marché au/du comptant/marché du disponible,** spot market; cash market; **marché en coulisse,** outside market; **marché des (denrées et) matières premières,** commodity market/exchange; **marché d'équipement,** capital goods market; **marché étroit,** limited market; **marché ferme/soutenu,** steady market; **marché gouverné par les prix,** quote driven market; **marché gouverné par les ordres,** order driven market; **marché financier/marché des capitaux,** financial market/capital market; **marché baissier/marché à la baisse/marché acheteur,** bear/buyer's market; **marché haussier/marché à la hausse/marché vendeur,** bull/seller's market; **marché hors cote,** unofficial market/third market; **marché instable,** jumpy market; **marché de l'immobilier,** property market; **marché monétaire,** money market; **marché des obligations,** bond market; **marché officiel,** official market; **marché à options/à primes,** options market; **marché de l'or,** gold market; **marché primaire,** primary market; **marché secondaire,** secondary market; **second marché,** unlisted securities market (USM); **marché à terme/**(à la Bourse de Paris) **marché du règlement mensuel (RM),** forward market; **marché à/du terme,** futures exchange; **marché à terme d'instruments financiers (MATIF),** financial futures market; **marché des transactions hors séance/marché THS/marché (des valeurs) hors bourse,** over-the-counter market/OTC market; **marché des valeurs mobilières,** stock exchange (d) **accaparement du marché,** cornering of the market; **analyse du marché,** market analysis; **cours du marché,** market price/rate; **étude du marché,** market research; **évaluation du marché,** market appraisal; **forces du marché,** market forces; **prix du marché,** market price; **prévision du marché,** market forecast; **tendances du marché,** market trends (e) **accaparer/monopoliser un marché,** to corner a market; **inonder le marché,** to flood/to glut the market; **mettre/lancer un nouveau produit sur le marché,** to put/to launch a new product on the market; **percer/entrer sur les marchés de l'Ouest,** to break into Western markets; **travailler le marché/agir sur le marché,** to manipulate the market.

marchéage, *n.m.* marketing mix.

marcher, *v.i.* (a) (d'un projet) to proceed/to progress; **les affaires marchent,** business is brisk; **les affaires ne marchent plus,** business is at a standstill/is slack (b) (affaire, appareil) to work/to run/to operate.

marge, *n.f.* (a) **marge d'erreur,** margin of error; **marge de sécurité,** safety margin; *Ind:* **marge de tolérance,** tolerance margin; **laisser une bonne marge pour les déchets,** to make a generous allowance for waste (b) *Fin:* margin; spread; **marge entre taux vendeur et taux acheteur,** bid-offer spread; **appel de marge,** margin call/call for margin/call for/additional cover; **marge bénéficiaire,** profit margin; **marge brute,** gross margin (of profit); **marge brute d'autofinancement (MBA),** cashflow; **marge commerciale,** trading profit; **marge étroite,** fine price; **marge (nette) d'exploitation,** operating margin; **marge de fluctation (d'une monnaie),** margin of fluctuation (of a currency); **marge initiale,** initial margin; **marge d'intérêt,** margin of interest; **marge nette,** net margin (of profit).

marginal, *a.* marginal; **analyse marginale,** marginal analysis; **bénéfice marginal,** marginal profit; **coût marginal,** marginal cost; **comptabilité marginale/méthode des coûts marginaux,** marginal costing/cost pricing; **entreprise marginale,** firm with only a marginal profit; **marché marginal,** fringe market; **prix marginal,** marginal price; **productivité marginale,** marginal productivity; **rendement marginal du capital,** marginal return on capital; **utilité marginale,** marginal utility.

marginalisme, *n.m. PolEc:* marginalism.

margoulin, *n.m. F:* (a) *St Exch:* petty speculator (b) shark/swindler.

marguerite, *n.f. Typ:* daisy wheel.

mariage, *n.m.* marriage; **contrat de mariage,** marriage contract; **extrait d'acte de mariage,** marriage certificate.

marine, *n.f.* marine marchande/de commerce, merchant navy/fleet.

maritime, *a.* maritime; **agent maritime,** shipping agent; **assurance maritime,** marine insurance; **commerce maritime,** maritime trade; **courtier maritime,** shipbroker; **droit/législation maritime,** maritime law; *Rail:* **gare maritime,** harbour station; *Ins:* **risque maritime,** maritime risk; **transport maritime,** shipping.

mark, *n.m.* (German) mark/Deutschmark.

marketing, *n.m.* marketing; **chef/directeur du marketing,** marketing manager/director; **marketing mix,** marketing mix; **service de marketing,** marketing department; **marketing direct/téléphonique,** cold call sales.

marquage, *n.m.* marking (of price, weight, date, etc.).

marque, *n.f.* (*a*) brand/make; **acceptabilité de la marque,** brand acceptance; **bonne marque de cigares,** good brand of cigars; **fidélité à la marque,** brand loyalty; **grande marque,** famous make/well-known brand; **image de marque,** brand image; **marque d'appel,** brand on offer; **marque collective,** label; **marque courante,** standard make; **marque déposée,** registered trademark; **marque de distributeur,** distributor's brand name; **marque de fabricant,** manufacturer's brand name; **marque de fabrique/de commerce,** trademark/brand (name); **marque de garantie,** certification mark; **marque de service,** mark of quality/quality guarantee (*on range of services offered by company or manufacturer*); **produits de marque,** (*i*) well known brand of goods (*ii*) branded goods; **publicité de marque,** brand advertising; **vin de marque,** wine of a well-known brand; vintage wine (*b*) **taux de marque,** mark-up rate/cost-plus (*c*) **marque de la douane,** customs stamp.

marquer, *v.tr.* **prix marqué,** catalogue price/list price; marked price; **acheter un article au prix marqué,** to buy an article at the marked price/at the price marked on the label.

marqueur, -euse, *n.* 1. (*personne*) marker 2. *n.f. Ind:* stamping machine (*for bars o, chocolate, soap, etc.*).

marron, *a.* unlicensed (trader, etc.); **courtier marron,** unlicensed broker.

masse, *n.f.* (*a*) *Jur:* **masse des créanciers,** (general) body of creditors; *Fin:* **masse des obligataires,** body of debenture holders/bondholders (*b*) *Fin:* **fund masse active,** assets; **masse passive,** liabilities; **masse monétaire,** money supply; **masse salariale,** total wages bill.

mass(-)media, *n.m.pl.* mass media.

matelas, *n.m.* buffer stock (of shares).

matériau, *n.m.* 1. *Const: Ind:* (building material 2. **matériaux,** *n.m.pl. Cons* materials; **matériaux de construction,** building materials.

matériel, 1. *a.* material; **valeurs matérielles,** tangible assets 2. *n.m.* (*a*) equipment material; stock in trade; plant (c factory); **matériel de bureau,** office equipment; **matériel lourd,** heavy equipment plant; **main-d'œuvre et matériel,** labour and material (*b*) *Mkt:* **matériel de PLV (publicité sur le lieu de vente),** point-of-sale material; **matériel de présentation,** display material; **matériel publicitaire,** advertising material 3. *n.m. Cmptr:* hardware.

matière, *n.f.* 1. material; **matières premières/de base,** raw materials; basic commodities; **marché des matières premières,** commodity market; **comptabilité matières,** (raw) materials accounting; **matière brute/non travaillée,** unprocessed/unrefined material; **matière plastiques,** plastics; **matière synthétique,** synthetic material 2. matter; **matière imposable,** taxable income; **matière juridique,** legal matters; (*dans un catalogue etc.*) **table des matières,** (table of) contents.

matinée, *n.f.* **matinée de bourse,** morning session.

matraquage, *n.m. Mkt:* **matraquage publicitaire,** plugging.

matricule, 1. *n.f.* (*a*) register/list (*b*) registration **2.** *n.m.* number.

maturité, *n.f.* maturity; **économie en pleine maturité,** mature economy.

mauvais, *a.* (*a*) bad; poor; inadequate; **mauvaise administration/mauvaise gestion,** mismanagement; **mauvais marché,** losing market; **mauvaise période/saison,** slack/poor season; **de mauvaise qualité,** of poor quality; inferior; **faire de mauvaises affaires,** to be doing badly (in business); **nous faisons de mauvaises affaires en ce moment,** business is bad/poor at the moment (*b*) wrong; **mauvaise mesure,** short measure (*c*) **mauvaise créance,** bad debt.

maximal, *a.* (*a*) maximum (efficiency, etc.) (*b*) maximal.

maximalisation, *n.f.* maximization/ maximalization; maximizing; **maximalisation du profit/des profits,** profit maximization; **la maximalisation de l'utilité totale,** the maximization of total utility.

maxim(al)iser, *v.tr.* to maximize.

maximum, 1. *n.m.* maximum; **maximum de rendement,** highest performance/ maximum efficiency; **au maximum,** to the maximum; to the highest degree; **chiffre d'affaires de 3 millions au maximum,** turnover of 3 millions at the most/at the outside; **porter la production au maximum,** to raise production to a maximum/to maximize production **2.** *a.* **prix maximums/maxima,** maximum prices/ highest prices; **rendement maximum,** maximum/peak output; **tarif maximum,** maximum tarif; **taux maximum,** top rate.

mécanisation, *n.f.* mechanization.

mécanisé, *a.* mechanized.

mécaniser, *v.tr.* to mechanize (an industry, etc.).

mécanisme, *n.m.* mechanism/machinery; **mécanisme administratif,** administrative machinery; **mécanisme bancaire,** banking machinery/mechanism; **mécanisme**

budgétaire, budgetary mechanism; **mécanismes économiques,** economic machinery; **mécanisme des prix,** price mechanism.

mécénat, *n.m.* patronage.

mécompte, *n.m.* miscalculation; error in reckoning/in account.

mécontentement, *n.m.* **mécontentement social,** social unrest.

média, media, *n.m.pl.* **les média,** the media; **mixte média,** media mix; **plan média,** media planning.

médialisation, *n.f.* media planning.

médialiste, *n.m.f.* media planner.

médialogie, *n.f.* media research.

médiaplaneur, *n.m.* media planner.

médiateur, -trice, 1. *n.* mediator; *Ind:* conciliator; *Adm:* ombudsman; **agir en médiateur/servir de médiateur entre la direction et les employés,** to act as mediator between management and employees **2.** *a.* mediatory/mediating.

médiation, *n.f.* mediation.

médiatique, *a.* of/concerning the media; **couverture médiatique,** media coverage.

médiatisation, *n.f.* diffusion via/by the media.

médiatiser, *v.tr.* to diffuse/publisize.

médical, *a.* medical; **certificat médical,** medical certificate; **visite médicale,** medical examination.

méga-, *pref.* mega-; **méga-fusion,** mega-merger.

meilleur, *a.* **1.** better; **meilleur marché,** cheaper/less expensive; **acheter qch. (à) meilleur marché,** to buy sth. cheaper; **payer (qch.) meilleur marché,** to pay less (for sth.); **obtenir du crédit à meilleur compte,** to obtain cheaper credit; **produit de meilleure qualité,** better quality product/product of a better quality **2. le meilleur/la meilleure,** (*i*) the best (of several) (*ii*) the better (of two); *Corr:*

veuillez agréer, Monsieur, l'expression de mes sentiments les meilleurs/de mes meilleurs sentiments = yours faithfully.

membre, *n.m.* member; **carte de membre,** membership card; **club de mille membres,** club with a thousand members/with a membership of a thousand; **membre du conseil d'administration,** member of the board/board member; **membre fondateur,** founding member; **les pays membres de la CEE,** the member countries of the EEC.

mémoire, *n.m.* 1. (contractor's) account/bill; **présenter un mémoire,** to send a detailed account (of costs) 2. **pour mémoire,** as a record/as a memorandum 3. *n.f. Cmptr: etc:* storage/memory; **calculatrice à mémoire,** calculator with storage/memory (function).

mémomarque, *n.f. Mkt:* brand name recall.

mémorandum, *n.m.* 1. memorandum/memo/note 2. written order (to a supplier).

ménage, *n.m.* household/family.

ménager[1], *a.* **appareils ménagers,** household equipment/appliances; *NAm:* housewares; **Salon des Arts Ménagers** = Ideal Home Exhibition.

ménager[2], *v.tr.* to use (sth.) economically.

meneur, *n.m.* **meneur de grève,** strike leader.

mensualisation, *n.f.* (*a*) paying (of employees) by the month; monthly salary system (*b*) transfer (of employees) to a monthly salary system.

mensualiser, *v.tr.* (*a*) to pay (employees) by the month (*b*) to put (employees) on a monthly salary system (*c*) **mensualiser l'impôt,** to collect/pay taxes by monthly payments.

mensualité, *n.f.* (*a*) monthly payment; **payer par mensualités,** to pay by monthly instalments (*b*) monthly salary.

mensuel, -uelle, 1. *a.* monthly; **rapport mensuel,** monthly report; **publication**

mensuelle, monthly publication 2. (*a*) *n.m.* monthly magazine (*b*) *n.m.f.* monthly paid employee.

mensuellement, *adv.* monthly/each month/every month; once a month.

mention, *n.f.* (*a*) mention; **faire mention (de qn, de qch.),** to mention (s.o., sth.)/to refer to (s.o., sth.) (*b*) note/comment; *Adm: etc:* **rayer les mentions inutiles,** delete where inapplicable.

mentionner, *v.tr.* to mention; **mentionné ci-dessus,** above-mentioned/aforesaid.

menu, 1. *a.* small/minor; **menus dépôts,** small deposits; **menus frais,** petty/incidental expenses; **menue monnaie,** small/loose change 2. *n.m.* menu; **menu à prix fixe,** set menu; **menu touristique,** tourist/economy menu.

mercantile, *a.* mercantile; commercial.

mercantilisme, *n.m.* mercantilism.

mercaticien, -ienne, *n.* marketing specialist/consultant.

mercatique, *n.f.* marketing.

merchandising, *n.m.* merchandising.

mercuriale, *n.f.* market price-list/market prices (of commodities).

mère, *n.f.* **maison mère/société mère,** parent company; head office.

mérite, *n.m.* merit; **appréciation du mérite,** merit rating.

message, *n.m.* message; *TV: WTel:* **message publicitaire,** spot/commercial; **message téléphonique,** telephone message; **laisser un message pour qn,** to leave a message for s.o.; **je lui transmettrai le message,** I'll give him the message.

messagerie, *n.f.* 1. **messagerie (électronique),** electronic mail 2. *pl.* **bureau de messageries,** (*i*) shipping office (*ii*) *Rail:* parcels office; **entreprise de messageries,** parcel delivery firm/company; **service de messageries,** parcel post/delivery service; **messageries aériennes,** air-freight company; **messageries maritimes** (*i*) transport of goods by sea (*ii*) shipping line; **messageries de presse,** press distribution service.

mesure, *n.f.* 1. (*a*) measure; **mesure de longueur,** linear measure; **mesure de capacité pour les liquides,** fluid measure; **mesure (de capacité) pour les matières sèches,** dry measure; **mesure de superficie,** square measure; **mesure de volume,** cubic measure; **poids et mesures,** weights and measures; **prendre la mesure de qch.,** to measure sth. (*b*) *Tail:* **fait sur mesure,** made to measure; **se faire faire un costume sur mesure,** to have a suit made to measure 2. measure/step; **mesures déflationnistes,** deflationary measures; **mesures provisoires,** temporary measures; **mesures de sécurité,** safety measures/ safety precautions; **par mesure de sécurité,** as a safety precaution; **mesures d'urgence,** emergency measures.

mesurer, *v.tr.* 1. (*a*) to measure (dimensions, quantity); to measure out (corn, etc.); to measure up (wood, etc.); to measure off (cloth, etc.); **mesurer deux kilos de sucre,** to weigh two kilos of sugar (*b*) *Tail:* **mesurer un client,** to take a customer's measurements 2. **mesurer ses dépenses sur ses profits,** to proportion one's expenditure to one's profits.

métal, *n.m.* metal; **métal fin,** pure gold/ silver; **industrie des métaux,** the metal/ metallurgical industry.

méthode, *n.f.* (*a*) method/system/way; **méthodes administratives,** systems and procedures; **méthode de classement,** filing system; **méthode expérimentale,** experimental method; **méthode d'exploitation,** method of working/method of operation; **méthodes et organisation,** organization and methods (O&M) (*b*) **méthode du chemin critique,** critical path method; *Fin:* **méthode de capitalisation du coût entier,** full cost accounting (method); **méthode des coûts variables,** direct costing (*c*) *Ind:* **bureau/service des méthodes,** methods office; **étude des méthodes,** methods engineering/methods study; **étude des temps et des méthodes,** time and methods

study; **ingénieur de méthodes,** methods engineer.

métier, *n.m.* (*a*) trade/craft/profession/ occupation; **argot de métier,** trade/technical jargon; **Chambre des métiers,** Chamber of Trade; **corps de métier,** guild/ trade association; **homme du métier,** expert/professional; **métier manuel,** manual trade/craft; **risques de métier,** occupational hazards; **terme de métier,** technical term; **exercer/faire un métier,** to carry on a trade/a profession; **il est du métier,** he's in the trade/the business (*b*) craftsmanship.

métrage, *n.m.* 1. (*a*) measuring/ measure(ment) (*b*) *Const: etc:* quantity surveying 2. (metric) length (of fabric).

mètre, *n.m.* (*a*) *Meas:* metre (*abbr.* m)/*NAm:* meter (= 3.281 ft.); **mètre carré,** square metre; **mètre courant,** linear metre; **mètre cube,** cubic metre (*b*) (metre) rule; **mètre à ruban,** tape measure.

métrer, *v.tr.* 1. to measure (by the metre) 2. *Const: etc:* to survey.

métrique, *a.* metric; **le système métrique,** the metric system; **adopter le système métrique,** to go metric; **adoption/introduction du système métrique,** metrication; **tonne métrique,** metric ton; tonne; **unité métrique,** metric unit.

mettre, *v.tr.* 1. to put/to place; **mettre une annonce dans les journaux,** to put an advertisement/an ad in the newspapers; **mettre sa signature à un contrat,** to put one's signature to a contract/to sign a contract 2. **mettre son argent en immeubles,** to put/to invest one's money in property; **mettre en vente une maison,** to put a house up for sale; **je ne peux pas y mettre tant que ça,** I can't afford as much as that.

meuble, 1. *a.* movable; *Jur:* **biens meubles,** movables; personal property/personalty 2. *n.m.* piece of furniture; **meubles de bureau,** office furniture 3. *n.m.pl. Jur:* movables; personal property/personalty; **meubles corporels,** tangible assets/

movables; **meubles incorporels,** intangible movables/assets.

meublé, 1. *a.* furnished (room, etc.); **appartement meublé,** furnished flat/apartment **2.** *n.m.* furnished flat/apartment.

mévente, *n.f.* slump (in sales)/slack period.

micro-économie, *n.f.* micro-economics.

micro-économique, *a.* micro-economic.

microfiche, *n.f.* microfiche.

microfilm, *n.m.* microfilm.

micro-informatique, *n.f. Cmptr:* micro-computing/microprocessing.

micro-ordinateur, *n.m.* microcomputer.

microplaquette, *n.f.* micro/silicon chip.

microprocesseur, *n.m.* microprocessor.

mieux, *adv.* **acheter au mieux,** to buy at best.

milieu, *n.m.* **milieux commerciaux,** business circles; **milieux financiers,** financial circles.

mille, *num.a. inv. & n.m. inv.* thousand; **mille francs,** a/one thousand francs; **deux mille francs,** two thousand francs; **billet de mille,** thousand-franc note.

millésime, *n.m.* (*a*) date (on coin, etc.) (*b*) year of manufacture; (*d'un vin*) year/vintage.

millésimé, *a.* **vin millésimé,** vintage wine.

milliard, *n.m.* a thousand million(s); *NAm:* a billion; **10 milliards de dollars,** 10 billion dollars.

milliardaire, *a. & n.m.f.* multi-millionaire; *NAm:* billionaire.

millier, *n.m.* (about a) thousand; a thousand (or so); **des milliers de francs,** thousands of francs.

milligramme, *n.m. Meas:* milligram(me) (*abbr.* mg).

millilitre, *n.m. Meas:* millilitre/*NAm:* milliliter (*abbr.* ml).

millimètre, *n.m. Meas:* millimetre/*NAm:* millimeter (*abbr.* mm).

millimétrique, *a.* **échelle millimétrique,** millimetre scale.

million, *n.m.* million; **un million de francs,** a million francs; **chiffre d'affaires de deux millions,** turnover of two million; **une machine coûtant deux millions de livres,** a two-million-pound machine.

millionnaire, *a. & n.m.f.* millionaire.

mine, *n.f.* mine; **mine d'or,** gold mine; **mine de charbon,** coal mine.

minerai, *n.m.* **minerai de fer,** iron ore.

mineur, *n.m.* miner.

minier, *a.* **industrie minière,** mining industry; **droits miniers,** mineral rights.

minimal, *a.* minimal; **valeur minimale,** minimal value.

minimarge, *n.m.* **(magasin) minimarge,** discount store.

minimisation, *n.f.* minimization; **minimisation du coût de production,** minimization/minimizing of production costs.

minimiser, *v.tr.* to minimize.

minimum, 1. *n.m.* **réduire les frais au minimum,** to reduce expenses to a minimum; *PolEc:* **minimum vital,** minimum living wage **2.** *a.* **pertes minimums/minima,** minimum/minimal losses; **poids minimum,** minimum weight; **prix minimum,** minimum price; **quantité minimum,** minimum/minimal amount; **salaire minimum interprofessionnel de croissance (SMIC)** = index linked minimum wage **3.** *adv.phr.* **au minimum** as a minimum; at least; **il y en aura 5 au minimum,** there will be a minimum of 5.

mini-ordinateur, *n.m.* minicomputer.

ministère, *n.m.* ministry; department.

ministre, *n.m.* minister; **Premier Ministre** Prime Minister/Premier.

minoritaire, *a.* **actionnaire minoritaire;** minority shareholder; **participation minoritaire,** minority holding/interest/ stake.

minorité, *n.f.* minority; **être en minorité,** to be in the/in a minority.

minutage, *n.m.* drafting (of document).

minutaire, *a.* **document minutaire,** document in draft (form); **acte minutaire,** original document.

minute, *n.f.* **1.** (*a*) minute (*b*) **clef minute,** key-cutting (while you wait); **talon minute,** heel bar **2.** (*a*) minute/draft (of contract, etc.); **faire la minute d'un contract,** to minute/to draft a contract (*b*) record (of deed, etc.).

minuté, *a.* timed; **horaire minuté,** (*i*) tight schedule (*ii*) detailed schedule.

minuter, *v.tr.* **1.** (*a*) to minute/to draw up/to draft (agreement, etc.) (*b*) to record (deed, etc.) **2.** to time; **sa journée est soigneusement minutée,** his day is carefully planned; his day is run on a tight schedule.

mise, *n.f.* **1.** (*a*) **mise en place de qch.,** placing/positioning (of sth.); **mise en bouteille,** bottling; **mise en dépôt,** warehousing; *Typ:* **mise en page,** page make-up (*b*) *Mkt:* **mise en avant,** special display; **mise en circulation (de l'argent),** putting into circulation (of money); **mise au courant (du personnel),** induction (of staff); *Jur:* **mise en demeure,** formal notice (of summons, etc.); **mise en demeure de payer,** final demand; **mise en distribution,** distribution; distributing; **mise à jour,** bringing up to date/updating; **mise en œuvre,** implementation; **mise au point,** (*d'un travail*) clarification/explanation; (*d'une construction, etc.*) finishing touch; **mise en service,** putting into service; **mise en vente,** putting up for sale; bringing (of product) onto the market; launching (of new product); publication (of book) **2.** (*a*) (*à une vente aux enchères*) bid; **mise à prix,** reserve price/upset price; **doubler la mise,** to double the stakes (*b*) *Fin:* **mise de**

fonds, (*i*) putting up of money (*ii*) capital outlay; **faire/fournir une mise de fonds,** to put up capital; **mise en commun de fonds,** pooling of capital; **mise hors,** (*i*) disbursement (of money) (*ii*) sum advanced; **mise en jeu,** downside; **mise en paiement (du dividende),** payment (of dividend); **mise sociale,** capital brought into a business by a partner; **mise en valeur,** (*d'un investissement*) turning to account; (*d'une propriété*) improving; **mise en valeur d'un terrain,** land development.

miser, *v.tr. & i.* (*a*) to speculate (on a rise, etc.) (*b*) (*à une vente aux enchères*) to bid.

mi-temps, *adv. phr.* **emploi à mi-temps,** part-time job.

mitoyen, *a.* **mur mitoyen,** party wall; (*between two rooms*); **cloison mitoyenne,** dividing wall; **maison mitoyenne,** semi-detached house.

mitoyenneté, *n.f.* *Jur:* (*d'un mur, etc.*) joint ownership/use.

mixte, *a.* (*a*) mixed; *Nau:* **cargaison mixte,** mixed cargo; **économie mixte,** mixed economy; **organisation mixte,** line and staff organization; *Ins:* **risques mixtes,** mixed risks (*b*) serving a double purpose; **billet mixte,** combined road and rail ticket.

mobile, 1. *n.m.* (*a*) **motif/mobile d'achat,** buying inducement/motive; purchasing motivator (*b*) *Mkt:* **mobile (publicitaire),** (advertising) mobile **2.** *a.* mobile; **échelle mobile,** sliding scale (of prices, salaries, etc.); **moyenne mobile,** moving average.

mobilier, 1. *a.* *Jur:* movable; **biens mobiliers,** movables/personal estate/ personalty; *Adm:* **contribution mobilière,** movable property tax; **cote mobilière,** assessment on property; *Fin:* **valeurs mobilières,** stocks and shares; transferable securities **2.** *n.m.* **mobilier de bureau,** office furniture.

mobilisable, *a.* (*capital*) that can be made available; **fonds mobilisables,** realizable funds.

mobilisation, *n.f.* mobilization (of real estate); realization (of capital).

mobiliser, *v.tr.* to mobilize; to realize; to unfreeze/to free (capital, money); to unlock (assets).

mobilité, *n.f.* mobility (of capital, labour, etc.).

modalités, *n.f.pl.* ways and means; *Jur:* **modalités d'application de la loi,** means/method of enforcing the law; *Fin:* **modalités d'une émission,** terms and conditions of an issue; **modalités de financement,** financing terms/conditions; **modalités de paiement,** methods of payment; **modalités de souscription,** conditions of application.

mode¹, *n.f.* fashion; **journal de mode(s),** fashion magazine.

mode², *n.m.* method; **mode d'emploi,** directions for use; **mode de paiement,** method/means of payment.

modèle, *n.m.* (*a*) model/pattern; **maison/appartement modèle,** show house/flat; **modèle de démonstration,** demonstration model; **modèle déposé,** registered design/pattern; **modèle d'une lettre de change,** form of wording for a bill of exchange; specimen of a bill of exchange; **modèle périmé,** obsolete model/type; **modèle réduit,** (scale) model; **nouveau modèle (d'une voiture),** new model (of a car); **modèle de signature,** specimen signature (*b*) *PolEc:* **modèle décisionnel,** decision model; **modèle d'entreprise,** corporate model; **modèle prévisionnel,** econometric model (*c*) **(article) grand modèle,** large-size(d) (article); **échantillon modèle,** standard sample.

modem, *n.m. Cmptr:* (= **modulateur-démodulateur**), modem (= modulator-demodulator).

modération, *n.f.* **modération de droit,** tax reduction/rebate.

modéré, *a.* moderate; reasonable (price); **habitation à loyer modéré (HLM)** = council house/flat.

modernisation, *n.f.* modernization/modernizing.

moderniser, *v.tr.* to modernize.

modicité, *n.f.* **la modicité de son revenu ne lui permet pas d'acheter une voiture,** he can't afford a car with his low income.

modification, *n.f.* modification/amendment/change/rectification.

modifier, *v.tr.* to modify/to amend/to rectify/to change; *Book-k:* to rectify (an entry).

modique, *a.* modest/low (price, income, rent).

moindre, *a.* 1. less(er); **vendre une quantité moindre,** to sell a smaller quantity 2. **les moindres détails,** the smallest details.

moins, *adv.* (*a*) less; **dix francs de moins,** (*i*) ten francs less (*ii*) ten francs short; **moins de dix francs,** less than ten francs; **paquet qui pèse moins de 10 kilos,** parcel weighing less than 10 kilos; **vendre qch. à moins du prix de revient,** to sell sth. at less than cost price; **je ne peux pas vous le laisser à moins,** I can't let you have it for less; **à moins d'avis contraire,** unless I hear to the contrary (*b*) **le moins,** the least; **le moins disant,** the lowest bidder (*c*) **vous compterez cela en moins,** you may deduct that.

moins-perçu, *n.m.* amount due and not received; short payment.

moins-value, *n.f.* (*a*) capital loss; **moins-value sur titres,** paper loss (*b*) depreciation/drop in value.

mois, *n.m.* (*a*) month; **mois civil,** calendar month; **mois légal,** thirty days; **au mois d'août,** in (the month of) August; **le 12 de ce mois,** the 12th of this month/the 12th inst.; **le mois dernier,** last month (*b*) **un mois de crédit,** a month's credit; *Fin:* **papiers à trois mois (d'échéance),** bills at three months; *Bank:* **relevé de fin de mois,** monthly statement (of account); **salaire de cinq mille francs par mois,** salary of five thousand francs a month; **devoir trois mois de loyer,** to owe three months'/a quarter's rent; **être payé au mois,** to be paid by the month; **louer qch. au mois,** to rent/to hire sth. by the month (*c*) monthly salary; **mois double/treizième mois** = (Christmas) bonus; **toucher son mois,** to receive one's (month's) pay/salary.

moitié, *n.f.* half; **à moitié prix,** at half price; **la première moitié de l'année,** the first half of the year; **bénéfices réduits de moitié,** profit(s) reduced by half; **être de moitié dans une entreprise,** to have a half share/a partnership in a business; **perdre la moitié de son capital,** to lose half (of) one's capital; **partager les frais moitié-moitié,** to share the cost fifty-fifty.

monde, *n.m.* (*a*) world (*b*) **le monde des affaires,** the business community; **le monde de la haute finance,** the world of high finance/the financial world/financial circles.

mondial, *a.* world(-wide); **commerce mondial,** world trade; **prix mondiaux,** world (market) prices; **production mondiale,** world output.

mondialisation, *n.f.* application worldwide.

mondialiser, *v.tr.* to apply (budget) worldwide.

monétaire, *a.* monetary; **circulation monétaire,** monetary circulation; **marché monétaire,** money market; **masse monétaire,** money supply; **politique monétaire,** monetary policy; **système monétaire d'un pays,** monetary system of a country; **unité monétaire,** monetary/currency unit; **zone monétaire,** monetary area; **Fonds monétaire international (FMI),** International Monetary Fund (IMF); **système monétaire européen (SME),** European Monetary system (EMS).

monétarisme, *n.m.* monetarism.

monétique, *n.f. Rtm:* computerized and electronic banking system; *F:* electronic money.

moniteur, *n.m.* (publicity) monitor.

monnaie, *n.f.* **1.** (*a*) monetary unit; **cours d'une monnaie,** rate of a currency; dé-

valuation d'une monnaie, devaluation of a currency; **monnaie étrangère,** foreign currency (*b*) coinage; currency; money; **fausse monnaie,** counterfeit coinage; **monnaie d'argent,** silver money; **monnaie de compte,** money of account; **monnaie divisionnaire/monnaie d'appoint,** divisional/fractional money; **monnaie électronique** = plastic money; **monnaie faible,** soft currency; **monnaie fiduciaire,** (*i*) token money (*ii*) = fiduciary currency; **monnaie flottante,** floating currency; **monnaie forte,** hard currency; **monnaie légale,** legal tender; **monnaie de marchandise,** commodity money; **monnaie d'or,** gold money; **monnaie de papier/papier-monnaie,** paper money/banknotes; **monnaie de réserve,** reserve currency; **monnaie scripturale/monnaie de banque,** bank deposits; **pièce de monnaie,** coin; **Hôtel de la Monnaie/la Monnaie** = the Mint; **frapper de la monnaie,** to coin/to mint money **2.** change; **petite monnaie/menue monnaie,** small change; **donner la monnaie de 50 francs,** to give change for 50 francs/for a 50 franc note; **faire de la monnaie,** to give change (for a note).

monnayage, *n.m.* minting/coining.

monnayer, *v.tr.* to mint/to coin.

monométallisme, *n.m. Fin:* monometallism.

monopole, *n.m.* monopoly; **monopole d'État,** state monopoly; **monopole des prix,** price ring; **monopole syndical de l'embauche,** closed shop; **avoir le monopole de qch.,** to have the monopoly of sth./*NAm:* on sth.

monopoleur, -euse, *a. & n.* monopolist; **service monopoleur,** monopoly service.

monopolisateur, -trice, 1. *a.* monopolistic **2.** *n.* monopolist/monopolizer.

monopolisation, *n.f.* monopolization; monopolizing.

monopoliser, *v.tr.* to monopolize; to have the monopoly of (sth.)/*NAm:* on (sth.).

monopoliste, 1. *a.* monopolist(ic);

compagnie pétrolière monopoliste, oil company with a monopoly **2.** *n.m.f.* monopolist.

monopolistique, *a.* monopolistic; **contrôle monopolistique,** monopoly control.

monopsone, *n.m.* monopsony.

Monsieur, *n.m.* **Monsieur/***abbr:* **M.,** Mr; *Corr:* **Monsieur,** Dear Sir; **Cher Monsieur,** Dear Mr X; **Monsieur le Président,** Mr President/Mr Chairman; *pl.* **Messieurs/** *abbr.* **MM,** Messrs.

montage, *n.m.* **1.** installation; fixture; assembling (of apparatus); fitting out (of workshop); **notice de montage,** instructions for assembly **2.** *Ind: etc:* assembling/assembly; **chaîne de montage,** assembly line.

montant, *n.m.* amount/(sum) total/total amount (of account, bill); proceeds (of sale, etc.); **montant brut,** gross amount/ total; **montant net,** net amount/total; **j'ignore le montant de mes dettes,** I do not know what my debts amount to/come to.

monté, *a.* **boutique bien montée,** well-stocked shop.

monte-charge, *n.m.inv.* hoist; service lift/ goods lift/*NAm:* elevator.

monter, 1. *v.i.* (*a*) to rise; (*prix*) to rise/to go up/to increase; **empêcher les prix de monter,** to keep prices down; **faire monter les prix,** to raise prices; to send prices up; **les enchères ont monté à cent mille francs,** the bidding went up to a hundred thousand francs; **les prix montent en flèche,** prices are soaring (*b*) **la somme monte à cent francs,** the total comes to a hundred francs **2.** *v.tr.* to fit out/to equip (workshop, etc.); to set up/to install (apparatus, etc.); to assemble (a machine); **monter une affaire,** to set up a business **3.** *v.pr.* **se monter,** to amount; **frais qui se montent à des milliers de francs,** expenses that mount up to thousands of francs; **la note se monte à mille francs,** the bill amounts to/adds up to/comes to a thousand francs.

monteur, *n.m.* **monteur d'affaires,** business promoter.

moral, *a.* **personne morale,** legal entity/ corporate body.

morale, *n.f.* **morale professionnelle,** business ethics.

moratoire, *Jur:* **1.** *a.* (payment) delayed by agreement; **intérêts moratoires,** interest on overdue payments **2.** *n.m.* moratorium; standstill agreement; **décréter un moratoire,** to announce a moratorium; **le moratoire des loyers,** the moratorium on rents.

moratorié, *a.* (bill, etc.) for which a moratorium has been granted.

moratorium, *n.m. Jur:* moratorium.

mort, *a.* (*a*) **marché mort,** dead market (*b*) **argent mort,** money bringing in no interest/lying idle (*c*) *Stat:* **point mort** break-even point.

morte-saison, *n.f.* slack season/of season.

motel, *n.m.* motel.

motif, *n.m. Mkt:* **motif d'achat,** buying inducement/motive.

motion, *n.f.* motion/proposal; **faire une motion,** to propose/to bring forward a motion; **adopter une motion,** to carry a motion; **la motion fut adoptée,** the motion was carried; **présenter une motion,** to put/to move/*Br:* to table a motion; **ajourner une motion,** to defer/*NAm:* to table a motion.

motionner, *v.i.* to propose a motion.

motivation, *n.f.* motivation; **motivation par le profit,** profit motive; *PolEc: Mkt:* **études de motivation,** motivational research; **motivation du consommateur,** consumer motivation.

mouvement, *n.m.* **1.** (*a*) movement/ motion; **étude des temps et des mouvements,** time and motion study; **mouvement de caisse/mouvement d'espèces,** cash transaction; **mouvement de capitaux**

de fonds, movement of capital; **mouvement du personnel,** staff turnover; **mouvement des stocks,** stock turnover/turnround (b) traffic; **mouvement d'un aéroport,** air(port) traffic; **mouvement d'un port,** harbour/port traffic; **mouvement des marchandises,** goods/freight traffic **2.** *Fin:* **mouvement de baisse,** downward movement; **mouvement de hausse,** upward movement; **mouvement du marché,** market fluctuations; **mouvement des prix,** change/fluctuation/trend in prices.

moyen[1], *a.* (a) middle; **les cadres moyens,** middle management (b) average/mean (price, etc.); **l'homme moyen,** the man in the street; *StExch:* **cours moyen,** middle price (c) medium (quality, etc.); **de taille/de grandeur moyenne,** medium-sized; **moyenne entreprise,** medium-sized firm; **rendement moyen,** average yield; **prix moyen,** moderate/reasonable price.

moyen[2], *n.m.* (a) means; **moyens de communication,** means of communication; **moyens de paiement,** means of payment; **moyens de transport,** means of transport (b) *Fin:* **voies et moyens,** ways and means; **répartition des moyens,** distribution of resources/resource allocation; **vivre au-dessus de ses moyens,** to live beyond one's means.

moyennant, *prep.* for; in consideration of; **moyennant paiement de dix francs,** subject to/on payment of ten francs.

moyenne, *n.f.* average; mean; **au-dessus de la moyenne,** above average; **au-dessous de la moyenne,** below average; **en moyenne,** on average; **il gagne en moyenne 40 francs (de) l'heure,** on average he earns 40 francs an hour; **moyenne mobile,** moving average; **moyenne horaire,** average speed, wage, etc.; **moyenne pondérée,** weighted average; **les recettes donnent une moyenne de mille francs par jour,** takings average a thousand francs a day; **établir la moyenne (des pertes, etc.),** to average (the losses, etc.).

multilatéral, *a.* multilateral; **accord multilatéral,** multilateral agreement; **commerce multilatéral,** multilateral trade.

multilatéralisme, *n.m. PolEc:* multilateralism.

multimillionnaire, *a. & n.m.f.* multimillionaire.

multinational *a. & n.f.* **une (société) multinationale,** a multinational (company).

multiple, *a.* multiple; **direction multiple,** multiple management; **maison à succursales multiples,** multiple store/multiple shop/chain store.

multiplication, *n.f.* multiplication.

multiplier, *v.tr. & v.i.* to multiply (**par,** by); **multiplier deux nombres l'un par l'autre,** to multiply two numbers together.

multipropriété, *n.f.* multiple ownership (of building, etc.); time-share.

multirisque, *a.* **assurance multirisque,** all-in/all risks insurance (policy); (*for car and house*) comprehensive insurance policy.

municipal, *a.* municipal; **taxes municipales** = rates.

mutation, *n.f.* (a) *Jur:* change of ownership; transfer (of property) (b) **mutation de personnel,** transfer of staff (c) **mutation d'entrepôt,** transfer of bonded goods (*to another bonded warehouse*).

mutualiste, *n.m.f.* member of a mutual insurance company/of a friendly society.

mutualité, *n.f.* mutual insurance; **société de mutualité,** friendly society.

mutuel, 1. *a.* mutual (service, insurance, etc.); **compagnie d'assurances mutuelles,** mutual insurance company **2.** *n.f.* **mutuelle,** mutual insurance company; friendly society.

N

nantir, *v.tr. Jur:* to give security to/to secure (creditor); to pledge (securities); **créancier entièrement nanti,** fully secured creditor; **valeurs nanties,** pledged securities.

nantissement, *n.m. Jur:* (*a*) hypothecation/pledging/bailment; **nantissement d'un fonds de commerce,** pledging of a business (as security) (*b*) pledge/collateral (security)/cover; **avances sur nantissement,** advances against collateral; **droit de nantissement,** lien on goods; **nantissement d'actions,** lien on shares; **lettre de nantissement,** letter of hypothecation; **prêt sur nantissement,** loan on collateral; **déposer des titres en nantissement,** to hypothecate securities/to lodge stock as security; **emprunter sur nantissement,** to borrow on security.

natalité, *n.f.* birth rate.

nation, *n.f.* nation; **Nations Unies,** United Nations.

national, *a.* national; **banque nationale,** national bank; **dette nationale,** national debt; **fortune nationale,** national wealth; **produit national brut (PNB),** gross national product (GNP); **revenu national brut,** gross national income; **revenu national net,** net national income.

nationalisation, *n.f.* nationalization; social ownership.

nationalisée, *n.f.* **les nationalisées,** nationalised industries.

nationaliser, *v.tr.* to nationalize; **entreprises nationalisées,** nationalized/state owned industries.

nationalité, *n.f. Adm:* nationality; *Nau:* acte de nationalité, (ship's) certificate of registry; **prendre la nationalité française,** to take French nationality.

nature, *n.f.* nature/kind; **nature du contenu,** nature of (the) contents; **payer en nature,** to pay in kind.

naturel, *a.* natural; **droit naturel,** unwritten law; **cause naturelle,** Act of God.

naval, *a.* **chantier naval,** shipyard; **construction navale,** shipbuilding.

navette, *n.f.* **faire la navette (entre sa résidence et son travail),** to commute.

navigabilité, *n.f. Nau: Av:* **certificat de navigabilité,** certificate of seaworthiness/certificate of airworthiness.

navigation, *n.f.* navigation; shipping; **compagnie de navigation aérienne,** airline; **compagnie de navigation (maritime),** shipping company; **ligne de navigation,** shipping line; **navigation côtière,** coastal trade; **droits de navigation,** shipping dues.

navire, *n.m.* ship; **navire de charge,** freighter; cargo boat; **navire de commerce/navire marchand,** merchant ship; **navire mixte,** mixed passenger and cargo ship; **navire de passagers,** passenger ship; **navire porte-conteneurs,** container ship; lift-on lift-off ship.

navire-citerne, *n.m. Nau:* tanker.

néant, *n.m. Adm:* none; nothing to report; nil; **état néant,** nil return.

nécessité, *n.f.* necessity; **denrées de première nécessité,** essential foodstuffs; staple commodities.

négatif, *a.* negative; **épargne négative,** negative saving.

négligé, *a. StExch:* **fonds négligés,** neglected stocks.

négligence, *n.f.* (*a*) negligence/carelessness; neglect; **par négligence,** through negligence (*b*) *Jur:* **négligence grave,** gross negligence; **négligence coupable/criminelle,** criminal negligence (*c*) *Ins:* **clause (de) négligence/**_MIns:_ **négligence-clause,** negligence clause.

négoce, *n.m.* trade/trading/business; **faire le négoce du vin,** to trade in wines/to be a wine trader.

négociabilité, *n.f.* negotiability (of a bill).

négociable, *a.* negotiable; transferable (bond, bill, cheque); marketable; **actif négociable,** liquid assets; **négociable en banque,** bankable; **non négociable,** not negotiable/non negotiable; **titres négociables en Bourse,** stocks negotiable on the Stock Exchange; **valeur négociable,** market value.

négociant, -ante *n.m.* (*a*) wholesale merchant/dealer; wholesaler; **négociant en vins,** wine merchant (*b*) *StExch:* trader; **négociant courtier,** broker dealer.

négociateur, -trice, *n.* **1.** (*a*) negotiator (*b*) middleman/intermediary **2.** transactor (of deal).

négociation, *n.f.* **1.** negotiation; negotiating (of loan, bill); trading; **en négociation,** under negotiation; *PolEc:* **négociations (de conventions) collectives,** collective bargaining; **négociation syndicale d'un contrat de productivité,** productivity bargain; **pouvoir de négociation,** bargaining power; *StExch:* **négociations à prime/ à option,** option dealings/tradings; **négociations à terme,** dealings for the settlement; **négociations de bloc,** block trading; **engager/entamer des négociations,** to enter into negotiations; **rompre des négociations,** to break off negotiations; **des négociations sont en cours,** negotiations are in progress **2.** transaction; **négociations de Bourse,** Stock Ex-

change transactions; **négociations de change,** exchange transactions.

négocier, 1. *v.tr. & i.* to negotiate (sale, loan, bill, etc.); **négocier une affaire,** to negotiate a deal; **négocier les salaires,** to negotiate/discuss salaries (*b*) to place (loan) **2.** *v.pr.* (*effet, etc.*) **se négocier,** to be negotiated.

net, 1. *a.* (*a*) **(actif, poids, prix, montant, revenu) net,** net(t) (assets, weight, price, amount, income); **(base, perte, marge, valeur) nette,** net(t) (basis, loss, margin, value); **bénéfice net,** net/clear profit; after-tax profit; **bénéfice net par action,** net income per share; **bénéfice clair et net,** clear profit; (*à l'hôtel, etc.*) **prix net,** all inclusive/inclusive price; **ventes nettes,** net sales; **il reçoit un salaire net de £80 par semaine,** he gets £80 clear a week (*b*) **net de ...,** free from ...; **net d'impôt,** tax free/free of tax **2.** *n.m.* (*sur le bulletin de paie*) **net à payer** = net pay **3.** *adv.* **cela m'a rapporté 100 francs net,** I cleared/I netted 100 francs; I made a net profit of 100 francs.

neuf, *a.* new (garment, product, etc.); **remis à neuf,** reconditioned/restored; **à l'état (de) neuf,** as new/in new condition; (*timbre, etc.*) in mint condition/mint.

niche, *n.f. Mkt:* niche.

niveau, *n.m.* level (of prices, salaries, etc.); **niveau de vie (élevé),** (high) standard of living; **niveau sans précédent,** record level; **niveau de cours des actions,** stock price level; **l'indice des actions est descendu à son plus bas niveau/est monté à son plus haut niveau,** the share index reached an all-time low/an all-time high; **maintenir les prix à un niveau élevé,** to maintain prices at a high level; **produit de haut niveau,** high standard product.

niveler, *v.tr.* to level/to even up (prices, rates, etc.); **niveler au plus bas,** to level down.

nivellement, *n.m* levelling (of income, etc.).

nocturne, *n.m.* **nocturne le vendredi,** late opening Friday.

noir, *a.* black; **caisse noire,** slush fund; **liste noire,** black list; **marché noir,** black market; **acheter au noir,** to buy on the black market; **travail (au) noir,** moonlighting; **travailler au noir,** to moonlight; **travailleur, -euse au noir/personne qui travaille au noir,** moonlighter.

nolisement, *n.m.* chartering (of ship, etc.).

noliser, *v.tr.* to charter (ship, plane, etc.); **avion nolisé,** charter (plane).

nom, *n.m.* **1.** (*a*) name; **nom (de famille),** surname; **nom et prénoms,** full name; **nom de jeune fille,** maiden name (*b*) **nom du bénéficiaire,** name of the payee; **nom commercial,** name of a company; firm/corporate name; **nom déposé,** registered (trade) name; **nom d'un produit,** name of a product (*c*) **agir au nom de qn,** to act in s.o.'s name; **les actions sont à mon nom,** the shares are in my name **2.** name/reputation; **un nom bien connu dans le monde des affaires,** a big name in the business world.

nombre, *n.m.* (*a*) number; **nombre élevé,** high number; **nombre de trois chiffres,** three-digit number; **nombre d'heures de travail,** number of hours worked; *PolEc:* **nombre index,** index number (*b*) **le nombre suffisant/voulu/minimum (de membres),** the (full) quorum (*at meeting*); **ne pas être en nombre,** not to have a quorum.

nomenclature, *n.f.* list; catalogue; schedule; **nomenclature douanière,** customs classification; **numéro de nomenclature,** catalogue number/inventory number.

nominal, 1. *n.m.* nominal value **2.** *a.* nominal (price, etc.); *Fin:* **capital nominal,** nominal capital/authorized capital; **taux nominal,** nominal rate/yield; **valeur nominale (d'un effet, etc.),** nominal value/par value/face value/*NAm:* face amount (of bill, etc.).

nominatif, 1. *a. Fin:* nominal; **action nominative,** registered share; **certificat nominatif d'actions,** registered share

certificate; **liste nominative (des actionnaires),** nominal list (of shareholders); **porteur d'actions nominatives,** registered shareholder; **titres nominatifs,** registered securities/scrip **2.** *n.m. Fin:* **dividende de tant au nominatif,** dividend of so much on registered securities.

nomination, *n.f.* (*a*) nomination (for an appointment) (*b*) appointment; **recevoir sa nomination,** to be appointed (**à un poste,** to a post).

nommer, *v.tr.* (*a*) to name; to give a name to (sth.); **nommé ci-après ...,** hereinafter called/named ... (*b*) **nommer un jour,** to appoint a day (*c*) to appoint/to nominate (s.o. to an office or post); **nommer des experts,** to appoint experts; **nommer qn à un poste,** to nominate s.o. to/for a post; **nommer qn président,** to appoint s.o. chairman/president.

non-acceptation, *n.f.* non-acceptance (of bill); refusal (of goods).

non-accomplissement, *n.m.* non-fulfilment.

non-disponibilité, *n.f.* non-availability (of supplies, etc.).

non-exécution, *n.f.* non-fulfilment (of agreement, etc.); non-performance.

non-lieu, *n.m. Jur:* withdrawal/dismissal (of case, suit, etc.); non-suit.

non-livraison, *n.f.* non-delivery (of goods).

nonobstant, *prep. Jur:* notwithstanding; in spite of; **nonobstant toute clause contraire,** notwithstanding any provision to the contrary.

non-paiement, *n.m.* non-payment; **en cas de non-paiement,** in case of non-payment.

non-réception, *n.f.* non-delivery (of goods).

non-reconduction, *n.f. Adm:* failure to renew (a contract, etc.).

non-résident, *a.* non-resident/non-domiciled.

non-responsabilité, *n.f. Jur:* non-liability; **clause de non-responsabilité,** non-liability clause.

non-salarié, -ée, *n.* non-wage-earning person.

non(-)syndiqué, -ée, 1. *a.* non-union; **employé non(-)syndiqué,** non-union employee **2.** *n.* non-member of a union/ non-union worker.

non-valeur, *n.f.* **1.** (*i*) bad debt (*ii*) worthless security; *Adm:* **fonds de non-valeur,** provision for possible deficit (in budget estimates) **2.** unproductiveness; **terres en non-valeur,** unproductive land.

non-vente, *n.f.* no sale.

normal, *a.* (*a*) normal; **prix normaux,** normal prices; **valeur normale,** normal value (*b*) standard; **échantillon normal,** average sample; **poids normal,** standard weight.

normale, *n.f.* standard; **au-dessus/au-dessous de la normale,** above/below standard.

normalisation, *n.f.* normalization; standardization (of manufacture, etc.); **commission de normalisation,** standardization committee.

normaliser, *v.tr.* to normalize; to standardize; **production normalisée,** standardized production.

norme, *n.f.* norm/standard/(standard) specification; **conforme à la norme,** up to standard/up to specification; **normes financières,** financial standards; **norme de prix de revient,** cost standard; **normes de production,** production standards; **normes publicitaires,** advertising standards; **normes de sécurité,** safety standards.

notaire, *n.m. Jur:* (*i*) notary (public) (*ii*) = solicitor; **dressé par-devant notaire,** drawn up before a notary.

notarial, *a. Jur:* notarial (function, etc.).

notarié, *a. Jur:* **acte notarié,** deed executed and authenticated by a notary.

notation, *n.f.* (*a*) notation (*b*) markings/ scoring/rating; **notation du personnel,** personnel rating/*NAm:* merit rating/ performance evaluation.

note, *n.f.* (*a*) note/memo(randum); **note d'avis,** advice note; *Ins:* **note de couverture,** cover note; **note de crédit/note d'avoir,** credit note; **note de débit,** debit note; *Cust:* **note de détail,** details/description (of parcel, etc.); **note de frais,** (note of) expenses; **note de poids,** weight note; **note de service,** memorandum; **prendre note d'une commande,** to book/to make note of an order (*b*) annotation; **note explicative/marginale,** explanatory/ marginal note (*c*) notice (*d*) account/bill/invoice; **note d'hôtel,** hotel bill; **suivant la note ci-jointe,** as per account enclosed; **régler/payer une note,** to pay a bill/to settle an account; **faut-il le porter sur la note?** shall I put it on the bill?/shall I charge (for) it on the bill?

noter, *v.tr.* (*a*) to note; **il est à noter que ...,** it should be noted that ... (*b*) to jot down (sth.)/to write down (sth.)/to make a note of (sth.).

notice, *n.f.* information; directions; **notice explicative,** (*i*) directions for use (*ii*) instructions book; **notice publicitaire,** advertising brochure; (*dans un journal*) advertisement; **notice technique,** technical instructions/technical handbook; data sheet; *Fin:* **notice (d'information),** (information) prospectus.

notificatif, *a.* **lettre notificative,** letter of notification.

notification, *n.f.* notification/notice; **recevoir notification de qch.,** to be notified of sth.

notifier, *v.tr.* **notifier qch. à qn,** to notify s.o. of sth.; **veuillez notifier par écrit,** please advise in writing.

notoriété, *n.f.* (*a*) *Fin:* **avances sur notoriété,** unsecured advances; **crédit sur notoriété,** unsecured credit (*b*) *Mkt:* **notoriété de la marque,** brand awareness; **notoriété publicitaire,** advertising awareness.

nourrir, *v.tr.* **cinq cents francs par mois logé et nourri,** five hundred francs a month with board and lodging.

nouveau, *a.* (*a*) new; **deux actions nouvelles pour cinq anciennes,** two new shares for each five shares held; a seven-for-five stock split; **nouveau modèle,** up-to-date model; **nouvelle émission d'actions,** new issue of shares; **créer de nouveaux débouchés au commerce,** to open up new channels for trade (*b*) new/recent/fresh; **vin nouveau,** new wine (*c*) another/further/additional; **jusqu'à nouvel ordre,** until further notice; *StExch:* until cancelled; **un nouvel acompte de cent francs,** a further hundred francs on account; **pour une nouvelle période de trois mois,** for a further period of three months (*d*) *Book-k:* **solde à nouveau,** balance brought forward; **report à nouveau (de l'exercice précédent),** balance brought forward (from previous account).

nouveauté, *n.f.* **1.** new invention; new publication **2.** *pl.* **nouveautés,** fancy articles/fancy goods; latest fashions.

nouvelle, *n.f.* (piece of) news; **nouvelles économiques,** economic intelligence.

novation, *n.f. Jur:* novation/substitution (*of new obligation, contract, for an old one*); **novation de créance,** substitution of debt.

nover, *v.tr. Jur:* to substitute (debt).

noyau, *n.m.* **noyau dur,** core/controlling shareholders.

nue-propriété, *n.f. Jur:* bare ownership/ownership without usufruct.

nuit, *n.f.* night; **être de nuit,** to be on night shift; to work nights; **travail de nuit,** night work.

nul, *a.* (*a*) **solde nul,** nil balance; *Jur:* **nul et de nul effet/nul et non avenu,** null and void; **considérer une lettre comme nulle et non avenue,** to consider a letter as cancelled; **rendre nul,** to invalidate/to nullify/to render void (*b*) non-existent; **capitaux presque nuls,** almost non-existent capital.

nullité, *n.f.* **1.** invalidity/nullity (of deed, etc.); *Jur:* **action en nullité,** action for annulment/avoidance of contract; **nullité de l'assurance,** invalidity of the insurance; **frapper une clause de nullité,** to render a clause null and void **2.** (*a*) non-existence (of means); **nullité des affaires,** slackness/standstill in trade (*b*) incompetence (of employee, etc.).

numéraire, **1.** *a.* (*d'une pièce de monnaie*) **valeur numéraire,** legal-tender value **2.** *n.m.* metallic currency/specie; cash; **actions en numéraire,** cash shares; **avance en numéraire,** cash advance; **numéraire fictif,** paper currency; **versement en numéraire,** payment in cash; **payer en numéraire,** to pay in cash.

numérique, *a.* (*a*) numerical (value, ratio, list, etc.) (*b*) **analyse numérique,** numerical analysis; **calculateur numérique,** digital computer; **données numériques,** numerical data.

numériquement, *adv.* numerically.

numéro, *n.m.* (*a*) number; **numéro de chèque,** cheque number; **numéro de commande,** order number; **numéro de compte,** account number; **numéro d'immatriculation,** registration number; **numéro de lot,** lot number; **numéro de référence,** reference number; **numéro de série/numéro de fabrication,** serial number (*b*) *Tel:* **numéro de téléphone,** telephone/phone number; **faux numéro,** wrong number; **composer/faire un numéro,** to dial a number; **numéro vert,** Freephone number; **numéro sur la liste rouge,** ex-directory number (*c*) issue/number (of magazine, etc.); **le dernier numéro,** the latest issue (*d*) **le numéro un français du verre,** the leader of the French glass industry.

numérotage, *n.m.,* **numérotation,** *n.f.* numbering (of pages, etc.); allocation of a (classification) number (to document, etc.).

numéroter, *v.tr.* to number (consecutively).

numéroteur, *n.m.* numbering machine/numbering stamp.

nu-propriétaire, *n.m.f. Jur:* bare owner.

O

objectif, *n.m.* aim/target/objective; **direction par objectifs (DPO)**, management by objectives (MBO); **établissement des objectifs**, target setting; **objectif à court terme**, short-term objective; **objectifs globaux de l'entreprise**, overall company objectives; **objectif lointain**, long-term objective; **objectif de production**, production target; **objectif de profit**, profit target; **objectif de vente**, sales target.

objet, *n.m.* (*a*) object/aim; **la société a pour objet …**, the aim of the company is … ; **objet d'un contrat**, purpose of a contract (*b*) article; **objet de luxe**, luxury article; **objet de valeur**, valuable/article of value.

obligataire, 1. *n.m.* *Fin:* (*a*) bondholder/ debenture holder; **registre des obligataires**, debenture register (*b*) *Jur:* obligee (*whose bill has been backed, etc.*) 2. *a.* **créancier obligataire**, bond creditor; **dette obligataire**, debenture debt; **émission obligataire**, bond issue; **emprunt obligataire**, debenture loan; **intérêts obligataires**, bond interest; **marché obligataire**, bond market.

obligation, *n.f.* 1. *Fin:* bond; debenture; **certificat d'obligation**, debenture bond; **indice des obligations**, bond index; **marché des obligations**, bond market; **obligations amortissables/remboursables**, redeemable bonds; **obligations à bons de souscription d'actions (Obsa)**, equity warrant bonds; **obligation cautionnée**, guaranteed bond; **obligations classiques**, straight bonds; **obligations convertibles en actions**, convertible bonds/convertibles *n.*; **obligation hypothécaire**, mortgage debenture; **obligation indexée**, indexed bond; **obligation nominative**, registered bond; **obligation au porteur**, bearer bond; **obligations remboursables en actions (ORA)**, redeemable bonds; **obligation à revenu variable**, variable income bond; **obligation d'État**, government bond/Treasury bond; **obligation de société**, corporate bond; **porteur d'obligations**, bondholder 2. *Jur:* (*a*) obligation; bond· **contracter une obligation (envers qn)**, to enter into a binding agreement (with s.o.) (*b*) **obligation contractuelle**, privity of contract (*c*) **obligation d'information**, disclosure.

obligatoire, *a.* compulsory; **assurance obligatoire**, compulsory insurance; *StExch:* **couvertures boursières obligatoires**, margin requirements.

obligé, *n.* (*a*) person under obligation; *Jur:* obligee (*b*) *Fin:* obliger (*guaranteeing a bill*).

oblitérer, *v.tr.* to cancel (a stamp).

observateur, -trice *n.* observer.

obsolescence, *n.f.* obsolescence; **obsolescence calculée/obsolescence prévue (systématiquement)**, built-in obsolescence.

obsolescent, *a.* obsolescent.

obtenir, *v.tr.* to obtain/to get; to secure; to achieve (result); **obtenir du crédit à meilleur compte**, to get cheaper credit; **obtenir un délai**, to obtain an extension (of time); **où peut-on l'obtenir?** where can you get it?

occasion, *n.f.* (*a*) bargain; **occasions exceptionnelles**, outstanding sales bargains (*b*) **voiture d'occasion**, secondhand/used car; **acheter qch. d'occasion**, to buy sth. secondhand.

occasionnel, *a.* **travailleur/employé occasionnel**, casual worker.

occupant, -ante 1. *a.* occupying/in possession (of property, etc.) **2.** *n.* occupier; occupant; *Jur:* **premier occupant,** occupant.

occupation, *n.f.* (*a*) occupancy/occupation/possession (of a house, etc.); **grève avec occupation d'usine,** sit-in (strike) (*b*) business/work/employment; **occupation pendant les heures de loisir,** spare-time job; **être sans occupation,** to be unemployed/to be out of work.

occupé, *a.* busy; *Tel:* **la ligne est occupée,** the line's engaged/busy.

occuper, 1. *v.tr.* **occuper un poste important,** to occupy/to hold an important post (*b*) to give employment to; **occuper vingt ouvriers,** to employ twenty workmen **2.** *v.pr.* **est-ce qu'on s'occupe de vous?** are you being attended to?/are you being served?

octroi, *n.m.* concession/grant(ing) (of a privilege, etc.); **octroi de crédits,** credit grant.

octroyer, *v.tr.* to grant/to allow (**à,** to).

offert, *a.* offered; **prix offert,** offered/selling price.

office, *n.m.* (*a*) office/post; **faire office de secrétaire,** to act as secretary (*b*) bureau/office; **office de publicité,** advertising agency; **office de régularisation de vente,** marketing board; **office du tourisme,** tourist board (*c*) *adv.phr.* **d'office,** ex officio; **être nommé d'office,** to be automatically appointed/to be appointed as a matter of course; **être mis à la retraite d'office,** to be automatically retired.

officiel, 1. *a.* official (statement, journal, source); **congé officiel,** official holiday; *Fin:* **cote officielle,** official quotation/official list (of securities); **marché officiel,** official market; **réserves en or officielles,** official gold reserves; **le taux officiel de l'escompte,** the minimum lending rate; **à titre officiel,** officially/formally **2.** *n.* official.

officiellement, *adv.* officially.

officieusement, *adv.* unofficially/off the record.

officieux, *a.* unofficial.

offrant, *n.m.* (*à une vente aux enchères*) **le plus offrant (et dernier enchérisseur),** the highest bidder.

offre, *n.f.* (*a*) offer; proposal; **offre par écrit,** offer in writing; *Journ:* **offres d'emploi,** situations vacant; **offre d'essai,** trial offer; **offre ferme,** firm offer; **offre publique,** general offer; *Fin:* **offre publique d'achat (OPA),** takeover bid; **offre publique d'échange (OPE),** exchange offer; **offre publique de vente (OPV),** offer by prospectus; *Mkt:* **offre spéciale,** special offer (*b*) (*à une vente aux enchères*) bid (*c*) *PolEc:* **l'offre et la demande,** supply and demand (*d*) tender; **appel d'offre,** invitation to tender (*e*) **économie de l'offre,** supply side economics; **économiste de l'offre,** supply sider.

offrir, *v.tr.* (*a*) **offrir ses services,** to offer one's services; **on lui a offert un emploi,** he has been offered a job (*b*) **offrir cent francs,** (*i*) to offer 100 francs (*ii*) to bid 100 francs; **combien m'en offrez-vous?** how much will you offer me/how much will you give me for it? **offrir des marchandises en vente,** to offer goods for sale; **enchérir sur les prix offerts,** to improve on the prices offered; **être offert à ...,** to be on offer at ...; *StExch: etc:* **cours offerts,** prices offered.

off-shore, *a.* **pétrole/gisement off-shore,** offshore oil/field.

oisif, *a.* **capital oisif,** uninvested/idle capital.

oligopole, *n.m. PolEc:* oligopoly.

oligopoliste, *a. PolEc:* oligopolistic (market, etc.).

oligopsone, *n.m.* duopsony.

olographe, *a.* **testament olographe,** holograph/hand-written will.

omission, *n.f.* **sauf erreur ou omission,** errors and omissions excepted (E & OE).

omnium, *n.m.* *StExch:* (*a*) the aggregate value of the different stocks in which a loan is funded (*b*) **omnium (de valeurs)**, omnium investment company.

once, *n.f. Meas:* ounce (*abbr.* oz) (= 28.35 grammes).

onéreux, *a.* heavy (expenditure, tax, etc.); **charge onéreuse pour le budget**, heavy charge on the budget; *Jur:* **à titre onéreux**, subject to certain liabilities; subject to payment; for a valuable consideration.

on-shore, *a.* **pétrole/gisement on-shore**, on-shore oil/field.

OPA, *n.f.* (*abbr. de offre publique d'achat*) takeover bid; **OPA amicale**, friendly (takeover) bid; **OPA inamicale/hostile/sauvage**, hostile takeover bid.

opéable, *a.* (*société*) vulnerable to takeover bids.

open-market, *n.m.* open-market; **politique d'open-market**, open-market policy.

opérateur, -trice, *n.* (*a*) (machine) operator (*b*) *StExch:* operator; **opérateur à la hausse**, operator for a rise/bull; **opérateur à la baisse**, operator for a fall/bear.

opération, *n.f.* **1.** (*a*) *Bank: Fin:* transaction; deal; operation; **opération blanche**, break-even transaction; **opération de clearing**, clearing transaction; **opération comptable**, accounting operation; **opération au comptant**, cash transaction; **opération d'escompte**, discount operation; **opération de prêt**, loan transaction (*b*) *StExch:* transaction; deal; speculation; **opérations de Bourse**, Stock Exchange business/transactions; **opération à la baisse**, bear transaction; **opération de change**, exchange transaction; swap; **opération de change à terme**, forward exchange transaction; **opération au comptant**, spot deal/spot transaction; **opération à la hausse**, bull transaction; **opérations à prime**, option dealing(s); **opération à terme**, *StExch:* transaction for the settlement; futures transaction; **opération à découvert**, (to take a) short

position; **opération à terme sur marchandises**, commodity futures (trading) **2.** gestion des opérations, operations management; **planification des opérations**, operational planning **3.** **le procédé comporte trois opérations**, the process involves three operations.

opérationnel, *a.* (*a*) **audit opérationnel**, *NAm:* operational audit; **coûts opérationnels**, operational costs; **efficacité opérationnelle**, operational efficiency; **recherche opérationnelle (RO)**, operational research; *NAm:* operations research (OR) (*b*) **ce système sera opérationnel en 1984**, this system will be operational/will be in operation in 1984.

opérer, **1.** *v.i.* **opérer à découvert**, to operate without cover; to take a short position/to go short **2.** *v.tr.* (*a*) *PolEc: etc:* **opérer un sondage**, to take a sample test; to conduct an opinion poll (*b*) to make/to effect (payment, etc.).

opinion, *n.f.* opinion (**de**, of; **sur**, about); view/judgment; **sondage d'opinion (publique)**, opinion poll/survey.

opportunité, *n.f.* opportunity; **coût d'opportunité**, opportunity cost.

opposition, *n.f.* (*a*) **faire opposition à un chèque/au paiement d'un chèque**, to stop (payment of) a cheque; *StExch:* **opposition à la cote**, objection to mark.

optimal, *a.* **conditions optimales**, optimum conditions; **répartition optimale des ressources**, optimal resource allocation.

optim(al)isation, *n.f.* **optim(al)isation du profit**, profit optimization.

optim(al)iser, *v.tr.* to optimize.

optimum, **1.** *n.m.* optimum **2.** *a.* **emploi optimum des ressources**, optimum employment of resources.

option, *n.f.* **1.** **option d'achat**, option of purchase; **prendre une option sur l'achat d'un immeuble**, to have the option of purchase on a building **2.** *StExch:* option; **double option**, double option; **marché à/des options**, options market; **opérations**

à option, option dealing/trading; **option d'achat,** call option; **option d'achat vendue à découvert,** naked aption; **option cotée,** traded option; **option en dedans/en dehors,** in-the-money/out-of-the-money option; **option à l'argent/à la monnaie/au cours,** at-the-money option; **option du double,** call of more; **option à prix glissants à la baisse,** underwater option; **option de titres,** stock option; **option de vente,** put option; **lever une option,** to take up an option; **plan d'option sur titre,** stock option plan.

optionnel, a. **plan optionnel d'achat d'actions,** stock option plan.

optique, n.f. outlook; **optique de la direction,** top management approach; **optique publicitaire,** advertising approach.

or, n.m. 1. Fin: StExch: gold; **cours de l'or,** price/rate of gold; **encaisse or et argent,** gold and silver holdings; **étalon(-)or,** gold standard; **étalon change-or,** gold exchange standard; **franc or,** gold franc; **marché de l'or,** gold market; **obligation or,** gold bond; **or en barres/en lingots,** gold bars; ingots; gold bullion; **réserves d'or,** gold reserves; **(acheter, vendre) à prix d'or,** (to buy, to sell) at an exorbitant price; **marché/affaire d'or,** excellent deal/business; excellent bargain 2. **or monnayé/monnaie d'or/pièces d'or,** gold specie/gold coins.

ordinaire, a. Fin: **actions ordinaires,** ordinary shares/NAm: common stock.

ordinateur, n.m. Cmptr: computer; **comptabilité par ordinateur,** computer accounting; **gestion par ordinateur,** computer control; **ordinateur analogique,** analog computer; **ordinateur électronique,** electronic computer; **ordinateur de gestion,** business computer; **ordinateur individuel,** small (business) computer; **unités d'ordinateur,** computer equipment; **mettre (des données) sur ordinateur,** to computerize/to put (data) on computer; **mise (de données) sur ordinateur,** computerization.

ordonnance, n.f. Adm: **ordonnance de paiement,** order/warrant for payment.

ordonnancement, n.m. (a) scheduling/sequencing (of production, orders, etc.); **ordonnancement de la production des pièces de rechange,** scheduling/sequencing of spares (b) Adm: order to pay.

ordonnancer, v.tr. Adm: to pass (account) for payment; to sanction (expenditure); to initial (account).

ordonnateur, -trice, n. person authorized to pass accounts.

ordre, n.m. 1. (a) **ordre alphabétique,** alphabetical order; **certificats délivrés par ordre de date,** certificates issued in order of date; **numéro d'ordre,** serial number (b) Jur: **ordre utile,** ranking (of creditor) 2. **ordre du jour,** agenda (of a meeting); **questions à l'ordre du jour,** items/business on the agenda 3. class/category; **de premier ordre,** first-class/first-rate (firm, employee, etc.); Fin: **obligation de premier ordre,** prime bond; **la hausse de l'inflation sera de l'ordre de 5%,** the rise in inflation will be in the region of 5% 4. (a) Bank: Fin: **billet à ordre,** promissory note; bill of exchange payable to order; **chèque à ordre,** cheque to order; **compte d'ordre,** suspense account; **ordre de Bourse,** (Stock Exchange) order/instruction; **ordre d'achat/ de vente,** buy/sell order; **ordre à cours limite,** limit order; **ordre à révocation,** good-till-cancelled (GTC)/open order/resting order; **ordre lié,** straddle; **ordre tout ou rien,** all or none order; **ordre de vente stop,** stop-loss selling; **exécuter un ordre,** to fill an order; **ordre de transfert permanent/ordre de virement automatique,** banker's order; standing order; **ordre de virement,** order/instructions for transfer (of money, funds, etc.); StExch: **ordre stop,** stop order/stop loss order; (sur un chèque) **non à ordre,** not negotiable; **libeller un chèque à l'ordre de qn,** to make a cheque payable to s.o./to make out a cheque to s.o.; **payez à l'ordre de ...,** pay to the order of ....

organe, n.m. (a) **organe de publicité,** advertising medium (b) Adm: **organe distributeur,** distributing agency.

organigramme, n.m. (a) administrative

chart (of organization etc.); organization chart/organogram (*b*) *Cmptr:* flowchart/flow diagram.

organigraphe, *n.m.* charting template.

organisateur,-trice, 1. *a.* organizing; **efficacité organisatrice,** organizational effectiveness **2.** *n.* organizer; **organisateur de voyages,** tour operator.

organisateur-conseil, *n.m.* time and motion consultant.

organisation, *n.f.* **1.** (*a*) organizing; organization; planning; **comité d'organisation,** organizing/planning committee (*b*) organization/management; **organisation fonctionnelle/horizontale,** functional organization/staff organization; **organisation hiérarchique/verticale,** line organization; **organisation mixte,** line and staff organization; **organisation scientifique du travail (OST),** scientific management; **organisation du travail,** organization of work **2.** (*a*) organization; **organisation (internationale, politique, etc.),** (international, political, etc.) organization/body (*b*) (business, etc.) organization/*F:* set-up.

organisé, *a.* organized; **voyage organisé,** package trip/tour.

organiser, *v.tr.* to organize; to arrange (a meeting, etc.).

organisme, *n.m.* organization/body; **organisme professionnel,** professional body; **organisme de placement,** mutual fund; **organisme de placement collectif (OPCVM),** unit trust.

orientation, *n.f.* **orientation du client,** customer orientation; **orientation du marché,** market trend; **orientation professionnelle,** vocational/careers guidance.

orienté, *a.* oriented; **économie orientée vers les exportations,** export-oriented economy; **marché orienté à la baisse,** falling market; **marché orienté à la hausse,** rising market.

originaire, *a.* **membre originaire,** original member; founder member; **vice originaire,** original defect.

original, -aux, 1. *a.* original (text, etc.); **facture originale,** original invoice **2.** *n.* original; top copy; **original d'une facture,** original of an invoice; **copier qch. sur l'original,** to copy sth. from the original.

origine, *n.f.* (*a*) **pays d'origine,** country of origin; **produits d'origine nationale,** home(-grown) produce (*b*) *Fin:* **capital d'origine,** original capital; *Cust:* **certificat d'origine,** certificate of origin; **emballage d'origine,** original packing; **marchandises d'origine** = origin of goods guaranteed; *Ind:* **pièce d'origine,** original/factory-installed component; **valeur à l'origine,** original value.

oscillant, *a.* *Fin:* fluctuating (market).

oscillation, *n.f.* *Fin:* **les oscillations du marché,** the fluctuations of the market/the ups and downs of the market; **oscillations saisonnières,** seasonal fluctuations.

osciller, *v.i.* to fluctuate/to swing; *Fin:* (*marché, valeurs*) to fluctuate.

outillage, *n.m.* plant/equipment/machinery (of factory).

outre-mer, *adv.* overseas; **commerce d'outre-mer,** overseas trade.

ouvert, *a.* (*a*) open; **les bureaux sont ouverts de dix heures à cinq heures,** the offices are open from ten to five (*b*) *Fin:* **compte ouvert,** open account; **crédit ouvert,** open credit; *Trans:* **billet ouvert,** open ticket (*c*) *PolEc:* **politique de la porte ouverte,** open-door policy.

ouverture, *n.f.* (*a*) opening (up) (of a shop, business, etc.); opening (of an account, of a credit); **ouverture de négociations,** opening of negotiations; **l'ouverture de nouveaux débouchés,** the opening (up) of new markets/of new channels (of trade) (*b*) **heures d'ouverture,** business hours (of shop) (*c*) *StExch:* **cours d'ouverture,**

opening price; *Book-k:* **écriture d'ouverture,** opening entry.

ouvrable, *a.* **jour ouvrable,** working day.

ouvrage, *n.m.* (*a*) workmanship (*b*) piece of work/product (*c*) **il n'a pas d'ouvrage,** he is out of work/out of a job.

ouvragé, *a.* worked; finished (product).

ouvré, *a.* worked (jewellery, timber); finished/manufactured (article, product).

ouvrier, -ière, 1. *n.m.f.* worker/workman; operative; **ouvrier agricole,** agricultural worker; **ouvrier hautement qualifié (HQ),** highly skilled worker; **ouvrier à la journée,** day labourer; **ouvrier aux pièces,** piece worker; **ouvrier professionnel (OP)/ouvrier qualifié,** skilled worker; **ouvrier spécialisé (OS),** semi-skilled worker; **ouvrier syndiqué,** worker belonging to a union **2.** *a.* **agitation ouvrière,** industrial unrest; labour unrest; **association ouvrière,** workers' association; **heures d'ouvrier,** man-hours; **législation ouvrière,** industrial legislation; **participation ouvrière,** worker participation; **syndicat ouvrier,** trade union.

ouvrir, 1. *v.tr.* (*a*) **ouvrir une région au commerce,** to open up a region to trade (*b*) **ouvrir boutique,** to set up shop; **ouvrir des négociations,** to open/to begin negotiations; **ouvrir un nouveau magasin,** to open a new shop (*c*) *Fin:* **(se faire) ouvrir un compte bancaire,** to open a bank account; **ouvrir un crédit,** to open a (line of) credit; **ouvrir un emprunt,** to open a loan **2.** *v.i.* (*a*) **nous ouvrons tous les jours à huit heures,** we open every day at eight (o'clock); **les banques n'ouvrent pas les jours de fête,** the banks do not open on public holidays (*b*) *StExch:* **les valeurs pétrolières ont ouvert ferme,** oils opened firm.

P

pacte, *n.m.* **le pacte pour l'emploi** = job creation scheme (for young people); *Jur:* **pacte de paiement**, pay(ments) agreement; **pacte de préférence**, preference clause.

page, *n.f.* page; **annonce en première page**, front page advertisement; *Tel:* **pages jaunes**, yellow pages.

paie, *n.f.* pay/wages; **feuille/bulletin de paie**, pay (advice) slip; **jour de paie**, pay day; **livre de paie**, payroll; **toucher sa paie**, to draw one's pay/to be paid.

paiement, *n.m.* (*a*) payment; **défaut de paiement**, non(-)payment; **délai de paiement**, deferment of payment; **facilités de paiement**, credit facilities/easy terms; **modalités de paiement**, terms of payment; **suspension de paiement**, stoppage of payment; **paiement à la livraison**, cash on delivery/COD; **paiement anticipé**, advance payment; **paiement comptant**, cash payment; **paiement différé**, deferred payment; **paiement d'un compte**, settlement of an account; **autoriser le paiement d'un compte**, to authorize the payment of an account; **paiement d'un impôt**, payment of a tax; **paiement intégral**, payment in full; **paiement libératoire**, payment in full discharge; **paiement par chèque**, payment by cheque; **faire opposition au paiement d'un chèque**, to stop (payment of) a cheque; **paiement partiel**, payment on account; **paiement par versements (échelonnés)**, payment by/in instalments; **plan/programme de paiement**, payment plan/schedule; *Jur:* **être en état de cessation de paiements**, to be insolvent (*b*) **paiement en espèces/en numéraire**, payment in cash; **paiement en nature**, payment in kind; **paiement électronique**, electronic payment/money; **contre paie-**ment **de 100 francs**, on payment of 100 francs; **effectuer/faire un paiement**, to pay for sth.; to make a payment; **recevoir un paiement**, to receive (a) payment; **suspendre/cesser les paiements**, to stop payments.

pair, 1. *a.* even (number) 2. *n.m. Fin:* par; **au-dessous du pair**, below par; **au-dessus du pair**, above par; **pair du change**, par of exchange; **remboursable au pair**, repayable at par; **valeur au pair**, par value; **émettre des actions au pair/au-dessus du pair/au-dessous du pair**, to issue shares at par/at a premium/at a discount.

palette, *n.f.* pallet; **marchandises sur palette(s)**, palletized goods.

palettisation, *n.f.* palletization (of goods).

palettiser, *v.tr.* to palletize (goods).

palier, *n.m.* stage/level; **l'inflation a atteint un nouveau palier**, inflation has reached/found a new level; **taxes imposées par paliers**, graduated taxation.

panel, *n.m. Mkt:* panel; **panel de consommateurs**, consumer panel.

panier, *n.m.* 1. (*a*) *PolEc:* **le panier de la ménagère**, the shopping basket (*b*) *Mkt:* **panier (présentoir)/panier vrac**, dumpbin; **panier à la sortie**, checkout display (stand) (*c*) *PolEc:* **panier de monnaies**, basket of currencies 2. package deal.

panneau, *n.m.* board/panel; **panneau d'affichage/panneau à affiches/panneau publicitaire**, hoarding/*NAm:* billboard.

panneau-réclame, *n.m.* hoarding.

paperasserie, *n.f.* paperwork; **paperasserie (administrative)**, red tape.

papeterie, *n.f.* 1. (*a*) paper manufacturing (*b*) paper mill/factory (*c*) paper trade 2. (*a*) stationery trade (*b*) stationer's (shop) (*c*) stationery.

papier, *n.m.* 1. paper; **feuille/morceau de papier**, sheet/piece of paper; **papier buvard**, blotting paper; **papier carbone**, carbon paper; **papier d'emballage/papier kraft**, wrapping paper/brown paper; **papier à en-tête**, headed notepaper; **papier journal**, newsprint; **papier à lettres**, writing paper/notepaper; **papier pour machine à écrire/F: papier machine**, typing paper; **papier pelure**, air mail paper; flimsy 2. (*a*) *Adm: etc:* document/paper; **papier de bord**, ship's papers; **papiers d'expédition**, clearance papers; **papiers d'identité**, identity papers; **papier libre**, official paper on which stamp duty has not been paid/unstamped paper; **papier timbré**, official paper on which stamp duty has been paid/stamped paper (*b*) *Fin:* bill(s); **papier bancable/papier non bancable**, bankable paper/unbankable paper; **papier commercial/de commerce**, commercial/mercantile/trade paper; **papier de complaisance**, accommodation bill; **papier à court terme/papier court**, short (-dated) bill; **papier sur l'étranger**, foreign bill; **papier fait**, guaranteed paper/backed bill(s); **papier à long terme/papier long**, long(-dated) bill; **papier négociable**, negotiable paper; **papiers valeurs**, paper securities.

papier-monnaie, *n.m.* paper money/paper currency.

papillon, *n.m.* **papillon (d'un document)**, rider.

paquebot, *n.m.* **paquebot mixte**, mixed passenger and cargo boat; **paquebot transatlantique**, liner.

paquet, *n.m.* (*a*) parcel/package; **expédier un paquet par la poste**, to post a parcel/to send a parcel by post (*b*) **paquet (de lessive, de cigarettes, etc.)**, packet/*NAm:* pack (of washing powder, of cigarettes, etc.); **paquet géant**, giant packet/*NAm:* pack (*c*) *Fin:* **paquet d'actions**, block of shares.

parafe, *n.m.* = **paraphe**.

parafer, *v.tr.* = **parapher**.

parafiscal, *a. Adm:* **taxe parafiscale**, exceptional tax; special levy.

parafiscalité, *n.f. Adm:* special levies.

paragraphe, *n.m.* (*a*) paragraph (of letter, etc.) (*b*) sub-clause/paragraph (of contract, etc.).

parallèle, *a.* parallel (à, to/with); **économie parallèle**, black economy; **marché parallèle**, parallel/black market.

paralyser, *v.tr.* to paralyse; **grèves qui paralysent l'industrie**, strikes that cripple industry.

paraphe, *n.m. Adm: Jur:* signature; initials.

parapher, *v.tr. Adm: Jur:* to initial (a document).

parapluie, *n.m.* **parapluie doré**, golden parachute.

parc, *n.m.* **parc automobile**, (*d'un pays*) number of cars on the road; (*d'une entreprise*) fleet (of cars); **parc locatif de 1 million de logements**, 1 m rented dwellings; 1 m dwellings available for rent; **parc d'ordinateurs**, computer population/(the total) number of computers in service.

parcage, *n.m.* **parcage d'actions**, warehousing.

parcours, *n.m.* **consommation d'essence en parcours urbain**, petrol consumption in town.

parère, *n.m. Jur:* certificate attesting particular usage.

pari passu, *Lt. phr.* pari passu (**avec**, with).

paritaire, *a.* **commission paritaire**, equal representation committee; **gestion paritaire**, participative management; **négociations paritaires**, joint negotiations; **réunion paritaire**, round-table conference.

parité, *n.f.* parity; equality (of value, etc.); *Fin:* **change à (la) parité**, exchange at par/at parity; **parité à crémaillère/ rampante,** sliding/crawling peg; **parité de change,** exchange parity/equivalence of exchange; **parité fixe,** fixed parity; **rapport de parité,** parity ratio.

Parquet, *n.m. StExch:* le **Parquet** = (*i*) the Ring (*ii*) the stockbrokers.

parrainage, *n.m.* sponsoring.

parrainer, *v.tr.* to sponsor.

part, *n.f.* **1.** (*a*) *Fin:* share/part; **associé à part entière,** full partner; **part d'association,** partnership share; **parts de fondateur/parts bénéficiaires,** founder's share(s); **part du marché,** share of the market/market share (*b*) **avoir part aux bénéfices,** to have a share in the profits/to share in the profits; **mettre qn de part (dans une affaire),** to give s.o. a share in the profits **2. faire part de qch. à qn,** to inform s.o. of sth. **3. de la part de,** on behalf of; (*au téléphone*) **c'est de la part de qui?** who's calling, please?

partage, *n.m.* division (into shares); allotment/distribution (of goods, etc.); *Jur:* partition (of real property).

partager, *v.tr.* **1.** (*a*) to divide (into shares); to parcel out; to apportion (property, etc.) **2.** to share; **partager les bénéfices avec son associé,** to share the profits with one's partner; *Fin: etc:* **partager proportionnellement,** to divide pro rata.

partenaire, *n.m.* partner; **partenaires sociaux,** the two sides of industry.

partenariat, *n.m.* (trading) partnership; **convention/accord de partenariat,** partnership agreement.

participant,-ante, 1. *n.* participant; contributor (to a fund, etc.) **2.** *a.* **action participante,** participating share.

participation, *n.f.* (*a*) participation (**à qch.,** in sth.); **participation aux frais,** cost sharing; **participation ouvrière,** worker participation (*b*) share/interest (**à,** in); (part of) ownership (in a company); **entreprise en participation,** joint venture; **participation aux bénéfices,** profit sharing;

participation croisée, cross holding; **participation des travailleurs aux bénéfices,** profit-sharing scheme; **participation des salariés aux fruits de l'expansion,** earnout; **participation majoritaire,** majority holding/controlling interest; **participation minoritaire,** minority holding/ minority interest.

participer, *v.i.* (*a*) **participer (aux bénéfices, etc.),** to have an interest/a share, (in the profits, etc.) (*b*) **participer (aux frais, etc.),** to pay one's share (of the costs, etc.)/to contribute to (the costs, etc.) (*c*) **participer (à la gestion d'une entreprise, à une réunion),** to take part in (the running of a firm, a meeting).

particulier, -ière, 1. *n.* **(simple) particulier,** (private) individual **2.** *a.* private; personal (account); **assistant, -ante particulier/particulière,** personal assistant (PA); **secrétaire particulier/particulière,** private secretary/personal assistant.

partie, *n.f.* (*a*) part; **faire partie du personnel,** to be on the staff/to be a member of staff (*b*) **comptabilité en partie double,** double-entry book-keeping; **comptabilité en partie simple,** single-entry book-keeping (*c*) *Jur:* party (to a dispute, a suit, etc.); **les parties contractantes,** the contracting parties; **les parties concernées,** the interested parties.

partiel, *a.* (*a*) partial/incomplete; **acceptation partielle d'une traite,** partial acceptance of a bill; *Nau:* **expédition partielle/chargement partiel,** part shipment; **paiement partiel,** part payment; **perte partielle/sinistre partiel,** partial loss (*b*) **employé(e) qui travaille à temps partiel,** part-time worker/part-timer; **être en chômage partiel,** to be on short time; **travailler à temps partiel,** to work part time/to have a part-time job.

partiellement, *adv.* partially/in part; **créancier partiellement nanti,** partially secured creditor; **payer partiellement,** to pay in part.

partir, *v.i.* (*a*) to start; **à partir d'aujourd'hui,** starting from today/from today (onwards); **à partir du 15,** on and after the 15th; **le directeur sera libre à partir de 10 heures,** the manager will be free from ten (o'clock) onwards/any time after ten; **robes à partir de 100 francs,** dresses from 100 francs.

parution, *n.f. Publ:* publication; **date de parution,** publication date.

parvenir, *v.i.* to arrive; **faire parvenir qch. à qn,** to send/to forward sth. to s.o.; **votre lettre m'est parvenue,** your letter has reached me; I (have) received your letter; **votre demande doit nous parvenir avant la fin du mois,** your application must reach us by the end of the month.

pas-de-porte, *n.m.* (*i*) goodwill (of shop) (*ii*) key money.

passage, *n.m.* (*a*) **passage d'un représentant,** call of a representative (*b*) **nous n'avons que la clientèle de passage/***F:* **que les passages,** we only get the passing trade.

passager, -ère, *n.* passenger; traveller.

passation, *n.f.* (*a*) drawing up/signing (of an agreement); making (of a contract); placing (of orders); entering into (a contract, a lease, etc.) (*b*) *Book-k:* making/posting (of entries); entering (of items).

passavant, *n.m. Adm:* permit; *Cust:* transire.

passe, *n.f.* **passe de caisse,** allowance to cashier for errors.

passeport, *n.m.* passport.

passer, 1. *v.i.* (*a*) **notre chiffre d'affaires est passé de deux millions à trois millions en cinq ans,** our turnover has increased from two million to three million in five years (*b*) (*représentant*) **passer chez un client,** to call on a client/a customer **2.** *v.tr.* (*a*) **passer des marchandises en fraude,** to smuggle in goods (*b*) **passer une commande,** to place an order (**de qch. à qn,** for sth. with s.o.)/to order sth. (*c*) *Tel:* **passez-moi M. Lecuyer,** put me through to/get me Monsieur Lecuyer (*d*) *Jur:* **acte passé par-devant notaire,** document drawn

up before a solicitor; **passer un accord,** to sign a contract; to enter into a contract (*e*) *Book-k:* **passer un article au grand-livre,** to post an entry in the ledger; **passer écriture d'un article,** to post an entry; **passer une somme au débit,** to debit (an account) with a sum; **passer (une somme) en perte,** to charge (an amount to) an account; **passer (une somme) en profit,** to credit (an amount to) an account.

passible, *a.* liable; **passible d'une amende,** liable to a fine; **passible d'une taxe,** subject to tax.

passif, 1. *a. Fin: Book-k:* **dettes passives,** liabilities; creditors; **solde passif,** debit balance **2.** *n.m. Fin: Book-k:* liabilities/debt(s); **l'actif et le passif,** assets and liabilities; **passif éventuel,** contingent liabilities; **passif exigible,** current liabilities; **passif à long terme,** long-term liabilities; **passif reporté,** deferred liabilities.

patentable, *a.* (trade, etc.) subject to a licence/*NAm:* license; requiring a licence.

patente, *n.f.* (*a*) licence (to exercise a trade or profession) (*b*) tax (paid by merchants and professional men); **payer patente,** to be duly licensed.

patenté, *a.* licensed (trader, etc.).

patenter, *v.tr.* to license.

patrimoine, *n.m.* heritage; *Fin:* property; *Jur:* patrimony; **patrimoine culturel,** cultural heritage.

patron, -onne, *n.* employer; head; owner; *F:* boss (of firm, of business); proprietor/proprietress (of hotel).

patronage, *n.m. Mkt:* sponsorship/sponsoring.

patronal, *a. Ind:* of/pertaining to employers; **cotisation patronale,** employer's contribution; **organisation patronale,** organization of employers; **syndicat patronal,** employers' federation.

patronat, *n.m. Ind:* (the) employers.

patronner, *v.tr. Mkt:* to sponsor/to back

payable, *a.* payable; **effet payable au 1er juillet**, bill due on July 1st; **payable sur demande**, payable on demand; **payable à 30 jours**, payable at 30 days' date; **payable à la commande**, cash with order; **payable à la livraison**, payable on delivery; **payable à l'échéance**, payable at maturity; **payable au porteur**, payable to bearer; **payable à présentation**, payable on presentation; **payable à vue**, payable on sight.

payant, *a.* (*a*) (agency, etc.) charging a fee; **téléphone payant**, pay phone (*b*) **affaire payante**, business that pays/that is profitable; **travail payant**, paid work.

paye, *n.f.* = **paie**.

payement, *n.m.* = **paiement**.

payer, 1. *v.tr.* (*a*) to pay sth.; **payer (une facture, des impôts, des intérêts, son loyer)**, to pay (a bill, tax(es), interest, one's rent); **payer une amende**, to pay a fine; **payer une dette**, to pay (off)/to settle/to discharge a debt; **payer un effet**, to honour a bill; **refuser de payer une traite**, to dishonour a bill (*b*) **payer qch.**, to pay for sth.; **payer 100 francs à qn**, to pay s.o. 100 francs; **il le lui a payé 50 francs**, he paid him 50 francs for it; **combien payez-vous le thé?** how much do you pay for tea? **vous l'avez payé trop cher**, you've paid too much for it; **payer d'avance**, to pay in advance; **payer (argent) comptant/au comptant**, to pay cash (down); **payer par chèque**, to pay by cheque; **payer à l'échéance**, to pay at maturity/at due date; **payer en espèces**, to pay in cash; **payer intégralement/en totalité**, to pay in full; **payer des marchandises**, to pay for goods; (*sur un chèque*) **payer à l'ordre de . . .**, pay to the order of . . .; **payer à l'ordre de moi-même**, pay cash/pay self; **payer à vue/à présentation**, to pay on demand/at sight/on presentation; *Post:* **port payé**, carriage paid/post paid; **réponse payée**, reply paid (*c*) to pay s.o.; **payer un créancier**, to pay a creditor; **payer l'épicier**, to pay the grocer (*d*) **payer un employé**, to pay an employee; **être payé (à l'heure, à la semaine, au mois)**, to be paid (by the hour, by the week, by the month); **être payé à la pièce**, to be on

piece work; **congé payé**, paid holiday/holiday with pay; **maison qui paie mal**, firm which pays badly/which doesn't give very good wages; **travail bien payé**, well-paid work/job **2.** *v.i. F:* **un métier qui paie**, a job that pays well/a well-paid job.

payer-prendre, *n.m.* cash and carry (store).

payeur, -euse, **1.** *n.* payer; **c'est un bon payeur**, he is a good payer/a prompt payer **2.** *n.m. Adm: etc:* paying cashier.

pays, *n.m.* (*a*) country; **pays de provenance**, country of origin; **nouveau pays industriel (NPI)**, rim country (*b*) region/district/locality; **denrées du pays**, home(-grown) produce; **vin de pays/du pays**, local wine.

péage, *n.m.* **pont à péage**, toll bridge; **route à péage**, toll road/*NAm:* turnpike; **télévision à péage**, pay TV.

PCV, *abbr: Tel:* **appel en PCV**, transfer(red) charge call; **faire un appel en PCV**, to reverse the charges (on a call)/to make a transfer(red) charge call.

pécuniaire, *a.* pecuniary; **aide pécuniaire**, financial help; **embarras pécuniaires**, financial difficulties; **peine pécuniaire**, fine; **perte pécuniaire**, pecuniary loss; **améliorer sa situation pécuniaire**, to improve one's financial position/situation.

peine, *n.f.* penalty; **peine contractuelle**, penalty for non-performance (of contract).

pénal, *a.* **clause pénale**, penalty clause (in contract).

pendant, *a.* **la question est toujours pendante**, the matter in still in abeyance.

pénétration, *n.f.* **pénétration d'un marché**, entry.

pénétrer, *v.tr.* **pénétrer des marchés étrangers**, to penetrate foreign markets.

pension, *n.f.* **1.** pension/allowance; **pension sur l'État**, government pension; **pension de retraite**, retirement/old-age pension; **pension viagère**, life annuity **2.** (payment for) board and lodging; **cham-**

bre et pension, room and board; **chambre avec demi-pension,** room with half board; **chambre avec pension complète,** room with full board.

pensionnaire, *n.m.f.* boarder; guest/ resident (in hotel); **prendre des pensionnaires,** to take paying guests.

pensionné, -ée 1. *a.* pensioned (employee) **2.** *n.* pensioner.

pensionner, *v.tr.* to pension; to grant a pension to (s.o.).

pénurie, *n.f.* scarcity/shortage/(severe) lack (of money, goods, staff, etc.); *PolEc:* **pénurie de dollars,** dollar gap; **il y a pénurie de matières premières,** there is a scarcity of raw materials.

pépinière, *n.f.* **(zone de) pépinière d'entreprises,** enterprise zone.

percée, *n.f.* **percée commerciale,** market thrust; **percée technologique,** technological breakthrough.

percepteur, *n.m.* collector of taxes/tax collector.

perception, *n.f.* collection/receipt (of taxes, duties, rents); levying (of tax); **(bureau de) perception,** tax collector's office/revenue office.

percer, *v.i.* **percer sur les marchés de l'Ouest,** to break into Western markets.

percevoir, *v.tr.* to collect (taxes, rents, etc.); to levy (taxes); **cotisations à percevoir,** contributions still due; **percevoir des intérêts,** to receive interest.

perdre, *v.tr.* (*a*) to lose (one's money, a court case, etc.); **perdre un client,** to lose a customer (*b*) **perdre de sa valeur,** to lose value.

perdu, *a.* **argent placé à fonds perdu,** money invested in an annuity; **emballage perdu,** no-deposit / non-returnable / throw-away (container, pack(ing), bottle).

père, *n.m. Fin:* **valeurs de père de famille,** gilt-edged securities; blue chips.

péremption, *n.f.* **date de péremption,** sell-by date/best before date.

péréquation, *n.f.* equalization (of taxes, salaries); *Rail: etc:* **péréquation des prix,** standardizing of freight charges/of tariffs; **faire la péréquation des salaires,** to equalize wages.

perfectionnement, *n.m.* (*a*) perfecting (of machine, method, process); improving; **brevet de perfectionnement,** patent relating to improvements (*b*) (further) training; **perfectionnement des cadres,** management/executive training; **perfectionnement en cours d'emploi,** in-service training.

perfectionner, *v.tr.* to improve/to perfect (machine, method, process).

performance, *n.f.* performance; achievement; **appréciation des performances,** performance appraisal.

performant, *a.* efficient; with a high degree of (efficiency, productivity, etc.); **entreprise performante,** highly competitive firm; **résultats performants,** good profit performance.

péril, *n.m. Ins:* **péril de mer,** risk and peril of the seas; sea risk.

périmé, *a.* out-of-date (coupon, etc.); expired (bill, passport); (ticket) no longer valid; lapsed (money order, ticket, etc.); **matériel périmé,** out-of-date/ old-fashioned equipment.

périmer, *v.i. Jur:* to lapse/to become out-of-date; **laisser périmer un droit,** to allow a right to lapse; to forfeit a right.

périmètre, *n.m.* **périmètre de consolidation,** consolidation perimeter.

période, *n.f.* period; **pendant une période de trois mois,** for a period of three months; for a three month period; **période de grâce/de remise d'impôt sur les sociétés,** tax holiday; **période de récupération/de remboursement,** payback period; **période comptable,** financial period/accounting period; **période boursière,** trading account.

périodique, 1. *a.* periodic(al); **publication périodique,** periodical (publication) 2. *n.m.* periodical (publication)/ magazine.

périphérique, *n.m. Cmptr:* peripheral.

périssable, *a.* perishable; **denrées périssables,** perishable goods/perishables.

perlé, *a.* **grève perlée,** go-slow; **faire la grève perlée,** to go slow.

permanence, *n.f.* (*a*) (duty) office (*b*) **il y a une permanence le dimanche,** there is a 24 hr service on Sundays; the office is manned on Sundays/a skeleton staff is (always) on duty on Sundays; **être de permanence,** to be on duty/on call.

permanent, -ente 1. *a.* permanent (job, etc.); standing (committee); **capitaux permanents,** fixed assets; **éducation permanente,** continuous education; **instructions permanentes,** standing instructions/*NAm:* standard operating procedure; **inventaire permanent,** perpetual inventory/continuous stocktaking; *Bank:* **ordre de transfert permanent,** standing order/banker's order 2. *n.* paid staff (of organization).

permis, *n.m.* permit; licence/*NAm:* license; **permis de construire,** building permit; planning permission; *Cust:* **permis de chargement,** loading permit; *Aut:* **permis de conduire,** driving licence/ *NAm:* driver's license; **permis poids lourds,** heavy goods vehicle licence/ HGV licence; **permis de travail,** work permit.

perquisition, *n.f.* search; **mandat de perquisition,** search warrant.

personnaliser, *v.tr.* to personalize; **chèque personnalisé,** personalized cheque; **publicité personnalisée,** personalized sales technique.

personne, *n.f.* person; **par personne,** per capita; **le prix est de 20 francs par personne,** it costs 20 francs per head/per person; *Jur:* **personne morale,** legal entity; artificial person; corporate body;

personnes physiques, individual entities; **personne à charge,** dependent.

personnel, 1. *a.* personal (business, letter, etc.); *Jur:* **biens personnels,** personal estate/property; **fortune personnelle,** private means/personal wealth; **prêt personnel,** personal loan 2. *n.m.* (*a*) personnel/staff/employees/workforce (of factory, firm, shop, etc.); staff/employees (of hotel, etc.); **personnel administratif,** administrative staff/personnel; **personnel amovible/volant,** mobile/transferable staff; **personnel de bureau,** office staff/ clerical staff/secretariat staff; **personnel dirigeant/d'encadrement,** managerial staff/supervisory personnel; *Av:* **personnel rampant,** ground staff; **personnel volant,** flight staff; **personnel réduit,** reduced/skeleton staff; **personnel de service,** staff on duty (*b*) **appréciation du personnel,** staff appraisal/personnel rating; **bureau/service/direction du personnel,** personnel department/office; **chef/ directeur du personnel,** personnel manager/officer; **mouvement/mutation du personnel,** (*i*) staff transfers (*ii*) staff turnover; **réduction du personnel,** staff reduction/cutbacks; **faire partie du personnel,** to be on the staff/to be a member of staff/to be on the payroll; **manquer de personnel,** to be understaffed/shorthanded.

personnellement, *adv.* personally; in person.

perspective, *n.f.* prospect/outlook; **perspectives de carrière,** job expectations; **perspectives commerciales,** market prospects; **perspectives économiques,** economic prospects; **perspectives de profit,** profit outlook.

perte, *n.f.* 1. loss; **perte de clientèle,** loss of custom; **perte de marché,** loss of market; **perte maximale,** downside (*b*) *Ins:* loss/ damage; **perte présumée,** presumptive loss; **perte sèche,** dead loss; **perte totale,** total loss; (*d'un véhicule*) write-off 2. deficit; loss (of money); **perte d'arbitrage/de trading/de gestion,** trading loss; **compte de pertes et de profits,** appropriation account/*NAm:* profit and loss statement; **dépense en pure perte,** wasteful expenditure; **pertes et profits exceptionnels,** extraordinary items; **vente à perte,** sale at a loss; **passer une perte par profits et pertes,** to write off a loss; **subir de grandes pertes,** to suffer heavy losses; **vendre qch. à perte,** to sell sth. at a loss.

petit, *a.* small; minor; **petites annonces,** classified advertisements/small ads; **petite caisse,** petty cash; **petit commerçant,** small trader; shopkeeper; **petite entreprise,** small firm; **petits épargnants,** small savers; **la petite industrie,** small-scale industry.

pétrodollar, *n.m.* petrodollar.

pétrole, *n.m.* petroleum/oil; **pétrole brut,** crude oil; **raffinerie de pétrole,** oil refinery; *StExch:* **les pétroles,** oils/oil shares.

pétrolier, 1. *a.* **l'industrie pétrolière,** the petroleum/the oil industry; *StExch:* **marché pétrolier,** oil market; **pays pétroliers,** oil producing countries; **prix pétroliers,** oil prices; **produits pétroliers,** oil products; **grandes sociétés pétrolières,** large/big oil companies; *NAm:* Big oil; **valeurs pétrolières/n. les pétrolières,** oil shares/oils **2.** *n.m.* **pétrolier,** tanker.

pétromonnaie, *n.f.* petrocurrency.

phase, *n.f.* phase/stage; *Ind:* **phases de fabrication,** processing stages.

photocopie, *n.f.* photocopy.

photocopier, *v.tr.* to photocopy.

photocopieur, *n.m.,* **photocopieuse,** *n.f.* photocopier/photocopying machine.

photostat, *n.m.* photostat.

photostyle, *n.m. Cmptr:* light pen.

pièce, *n.f.* **1.** (*a*) **pièce de monnaie,** coin; **pièce d'or,** gold coin; **pièce de deux francs,** two-franc coin; **pièce de bon aloi,** genuine coin (*b*) **ils coûtent dix francs la pièce,** they cost ten francs each; **ils se vendent à la pièce,** they are sold separately/singly (*c*) **travail à la pièce,** piece work; **être payé à la pièce,** to be paid piece work (rates); **tra**vailler à la pièce/aux pièces,** to be on piece work/to do piece work (*d*) *Jur: Adm: etc:* document; **pièce annexe/pièce jointe (PJ),** enclosure (enc.); **pièces justificatives,** (*i*) written proof (*ii*) relevant documents **2. pièces de rechange/pièces détachées,** spare parts/spares.

pignoratif, *a. Jur:* **contrat pignoratif,** contract of sale with option of redemption.

pilote, *n.m.* experimental/pilot (factory, farm, store, study); **échantillon pilote,** pilot sample; **prix pilotes,** experimental/trial prices.

pilule, *n.f.* (*contre-OPA*) **pilule empoisonnée,** poison pill.

piquet, *n.m. Ind: etc:* picket; **piquets de grève,** strike pickets; **piquets de grève volants,** flying pickets.

piquetage, *n.m.* picketing (by strikers, etc.).

piqueter, *v.tr.* to picket (approaches to factory, place of work, etc.).

placard, *n.m.* poster/bill; *Typ:* **épreuves en placards,** galley proofs; **placard (de réclame),** advertisement (in newspaper).

place, *n.f.* **1.** job/position; **perdre sa place,** to lose one's job; **trouver une place de sténodactylo,** to find a job as a shorthand typist **2.** (*a*) **sur place,** on-the-spot; **achats sur place,** local purchases; **personne engagé sur place,** staff engaged locally; **prix sur place,** loco price; *Mkt:* **test sur place,** field test(ing) (*b*) *Bank: Fin:* **affaires sur la place de Paris,** business on the Paris market; **chèque encaissable sur la place,** cheque cashable locally; (*commerçant, etc.*) **avoir du crédit sur la place,** to have credit (facilities) locally/with local banks (*c*) **place du marché,** market place **3.** *Th: Trans:* seat; **réserver une place,** to reserve/to book a seat.

placement, *n.m.* **1.** *Fin:* investment; **titre de placement,** investments; *F:* **placement de père de famille,** gilt-edged investment/ blue chip; **placement privé,** placement; **placements financiers,** stock market invest ment; **placements obligataires,** bond investment; **revenus d'un placement,** income/returns on an investment; **faire des placements,** to invest (money)/to make investments; **faire un bon placement/un placement avantageux,** to make a good investment; **conseil en placements,** investment advice **2. agence/bureau de placements,** employment agency/bureau.

placer, 1. *v.tr.* (*a*) to place (s.o.); to find a job/a post for (s.o.) (*b*) to invest (capital, money); to place (shares); **placer (de l'argent) dans les pétroles,** to invest in oils (*c*) to sell (goods); **marchandises qui se placent facilement,** goods that sell readily; **valeurs difficiles à placer,** bills difficult to negotiate **2.** *v.pr.* **se placer,** to obtain/to find a post; **chercher à se placer chez qn,** to try to find a job/employment with s.o.

placier, -ère, *n.* (*a*) sales representative/travelling salesman/*NAm:* drummer (*b*) door-to-door salesman; **placier en librairie,** (publisher's) trade representative.

plafond, *n.m.* ceiling; **plafond de crédit,** credit ceiling/limit; **prix plafond,** ceiling (price); **crever le plafond,** to exceed the limit; to break the ceiling; **fixer un plafond à un budget,** to fix a ceiling to a budget.

plafonné, *a.* **salaire plafonné,** wage ceiling (*above which no percentage reduction is made for national insurance contributions*).

plafonnement, *n.m.* **protester contre le plafonnement des salaires,** to protest against the ceiling imposed on salaries.

plafonner, *v.i.* **les prix plafonnent à ...,** prices have reached the ceiling of ...; **la production plafonne,** output has reached its ceiling.

plage, *n.f.* band; **plage de taux,** rate band.

plaignant, -ante, *n. Jur:* plaintiff.

plan, *n.m.* **1.** plan; blueprint; **plans et devis,** drafts and estimates **2.** (*a*) plan/scheme/project; **plan de campagne,** plan of campaign; **plan d'échantillonnage,** sampling

project; *Mkt:* **plan de marketing,** marketing plan; **plan média,** media planning; **plan de travail,** planning (*b*) *Fin: PolEc:* **plan d'austérité,** austerity policy; **plan comptable,** accounting plan; **plan économique,** economic plan; **plan d'épargne,** savings account/plan; *StExch:* **plan d'options sur titres,** stock option plan; **plan quinquennal,** five-year plan; **plan de trésorerie,** cash plan.

plancher, *n.m.* **prix plancher,** bottom price.

planificateur, -trice 1. *a.* planning; **autorité planificatrice,** planning authority **2.** *n. PolEc: etc:* planner.

planification, *n.f. PolEc: etc:* **planification (à court terme/à long terme),** (short-term/long-term) planning; **planification économique,** economic planning; **planification de l'entreprise,** company/corporate planning; **planification de l'emploi,** manpower planning; **planification du produit,** product planning; **service de planification,** planning department.

planifié, *a. PolEc:* **économie planifiée,** planned economy.

planifier, *v.tr. PolEc: etc:* to plan (production, etc.).

planisme, *n.m. PolEc:* planning.

planiste, *n.m. PolEc:* planner.

planning, *n.m. Ind: PolEc:* planning; scheduling; **bureau/service de planning,** planning department; **planning de distribution,** distribution planning; **planning de la production,** production planning; *Ind:* **(tableau de) planning,** work schedule.

plein, 1. *a.* (*a*) *Nau:* **plein chargement,** full cargo; **valeur pleine,** full value (*b*) **agir de plein droit,** to act by right; **avoir plein(s) pouvoir(s),** to have full power/*Jur:* to have power of attorney; (*usine*) **être en plein travail,** to be in full production; **payer plein tarif,** to be charged full fare/rate; **voyager en pleine saison,** to travel at the height of the season/in the high season; **travailler à plein temps,** to work full-time/to have a full time job **2.** *n.m.* **faire le plein (d'essence),** to fill up (with petrol).

plein-emploi, *n.m. PolEc:* full employment.

pli, *n.m.* cover/envelope (of letter); **sous pli cacheté,** in a sealed envelope; **sous pli séparé,** under separate cover; **nous vous envoyons sous ce pli ...,** please find enclosed/herewith ....

plomber, *v.tr. Cust:* to seal (package, goods wagon).

plus, 1. *adv.* (*a*) more; **gagner plus de mille francs,** to earn more than/over a thousand francs (*b*) **(le) plus,** most; **le taux le plus élevé,** the highest rate of interest (*c*) plus/in addition; **deux cents francs d'amende plus les frais,** two hundred francs fine plus costs; **le prix du repas plus la TVA,** the price of the meal plus VAT (*d*) **en plus,** in addition/extra; **le vin est en plus,** the wine is extra.

plus-value, *n.f.* (*a*) increase in value/ appreciation (of property, shares); **actions qui ont enregistré une plus-value,** shares that show an appreciation; **impôt sur les plus-values,** capital gains tax; **plus-value sur titres,** paper profit (*b*) surplus; excess (of receipts over expenses); profit.

poids, *n.m.* **1.** weight; **poids de 5 kilo(gram-me)s,** 5 kilo(gram) weight; *Adm:* **poids et mesures,** weights and measures; **vendre au poids,** to sell by weight; **vendre à faux poids,** to give short weight **2.** load; **poids brut,** gross weight; **poids en charge,** laden weight; *Aut:* **poids lourd,** heavy goods vehicle (HGV); **poids mort,** dead weight; **poids net,** net weight; **poids utile,** payload/ load-carrying capacity.

poinçon, *n.m.* (*sur l'or et l'argent*) hallmark.

point, *n.m.* **1.** (*a*) point/place (of arrival, departure); **point de chargement,** loading point/place; **point de déchargement,** unloading point/place; **point d'entrée de l'or,** import/incoming gold-point; **point de sortie de l'or,** export/outgoing gold-

point (*b*) *Fin:* **point mort,** break-even point (*c*) **point de vente,** point of sale (POS); sales outlet; stockist; **point de vente électronique,** electronic point of sale; **terminaux-points de vente,** point of sale terminals; **plus de 400 points de vente en France,** over 400 stockists/outlets in France; *Bank:* **point retrait,** cashpoint **2.** *Fin:* **point de base,** basis point; **(hausse, baisse, d')un point,** one point (up, down); **amélioration de trois points,** improvement of three points/three-point improvement.

pointage, *n.m.* (*a*) checking/ticking off (of items, account, names on list, etc.) (*b*) *Ind:* clocking (in, out); **carte de pointage,** time card.

pointe, *n.f.* (*a*) **heures de pointe,** (*de consommation de gaz, etc.*) peak period/peak hours; (*de la circulation*) peak hours/rush hour(s) (*b*) **industrie de pointe,** advanced technology industry.

pointer, *v.tr.* (*a*) to check/to tick off (items, names on a list, etc.); to tally (goods) (*b*) *Ind:* **pointer à l'arrivée,** to clock in/on; **pointer à la sortie,** to clock out/off (*c*) **pointer à l'ANPE,** = to register at the job centre.

pointeur, -euse *n.* checker; tallyman; timekeeper.

police, *n.f.* (*a*) *Ins:* policy; **police d'assurance (sur la) vie,** life (insurance) policy; **police conjointe,** joint policy; **police à forfait,** policy for a specific amount; **police générale,** master/general policy; **police au porteur,** policy to bearer; **police tous risques,** all risks/fully comprehensive policy; **police type,** standard policy; **titulaire/détenteur d'une police,** policy holder; **établir une police,** to draw up/to make out a policy; **souscrire à/prendre une police d'assurance,** to take out an insurance policy (*b*) *MIns:* **police d'assurance maritime,** marine insurance policy; **police d'abonnement/police flottante/police ouverte,** floating policy/open policy; **police sur corps,** hull/ship policy; **police à temps,** time policy; **police à terme,** time policy; **police à voyage,** voyage policy.

politique, 1. *a.* **économie politique,** political economy; economics **2.** *n.f.* (*a*) **politique d'achats centralisés,** central purchasing; **politique d'arrêt et d'accélération de l'économie,** stop-go policy; **politique déflationniste/de déflation,** policy of deflation/deflationary policy; **politique de distribution,** dividend policy; **politique inflationniste/d'inflation,** policy of inflation/inflationary policy; **politique de libre échange,** free-trade policy; **politique de la porte ouverte,** open-door policy; **politique des prix et des salaires,** prices and incomes policy (*b*) **politique économique,** economic policy; **politique en matière de change,** exchange policy; **politique de l'entreprise,** company policy; **politique financière,** financial policy; **politique d'investissement,** investment policy; **politique de lancement d'un produit,** product policy; **politique monétaire,** monetary policy; **politique de promotion,** promotional policy; **politique de vente,** sales policy; **nous avons pour politique de satisfaire nos clients,** our policy is to satisfy our customers/we try to keep our customers satisfied (*c*) **la politique,** politics.

pollution, *n.f.* pollution; **pollution atmosphérique,** air pollution.

polycopie, *n.f.* duplicating (process).

polycopié, *n.m.* (duplicated) copy.

polycopier, *v.tr.* to duplicate; **machine à polycopier,** duplicating machine.

polyvalent, *a.* multi-purpose (tool, etc); **être polyvalent,** to have several skills/qualifications; **homme/femme d'affaires polyvalent(e),** businessman/businesswoman with several (business) interests.

ponction, *n.f.* **ponction sociale,** = National Insurance/Social Security contributions.

ponctionner, *v.tr.* to tax.

ponctuel, *a.* unique/one-off/*NAm:* one-of-a-kind; **crédit ponctuel,** spot credit.

ponctuellement, *adv.* from time to time.

pondérateur, *a.* balancing/stabilizing; **éléments pondérateurs du marché,** stabilizing factors of the market.

pondération, *n.f.* balance; *PolEc etc.* weighting.

pondéré, *a. PolEc:* **indice pondéré,** weighted index; **moyenne pondérée,** weighted average; **moyenne non pondérée,** unweighted average.

pondérer, *v.tr. PolEc:* **pondérer un indice,** to weight an index.

pont, *n.m.* **faire un pont d'or à qn,** to offer a golden hello to s.o.

pool, *n.m.* (*a*) *PolEc:* pool; common stock/fund; combine; syndicate; **pool bancaire,** banking pool; **pool de l'or,** gold pool (*b*) **pool de dactylos/pool dactylographique,** typing pool.

population, *n.f.* population; **la population active,** the working population.

port¹, *n.m.* harbour/port; **droits de port,** harbour dues/port charges; **port autonome,** independent/autonomous port; **port d'attache,** home port; **port de commerce/port marchand,** commercial port; **port d'escale/port de relâche,** port of call; **port franc,** free port; **port fluvial,** river port; **le port de Paris,** the port of Paris; **port ouvert,** open port; **port de pêche,** fishing port; **port pétrolier,** oil port.

port², *n.m.* **1.** cost of transport; carriage/shipping (charges); delivery charges; postal charges/postage (of parcel, letter); **port compris,** postage included; **(en) port dû,** carriage forward; **port et emballage,** postage and packing; **(en) port payé/franco de port/franc de port,** carriage paid/free; post paid **2.** *Nau:* (*a*) burden, tonnage (of ship) (*b*) **port en lourd,** dead weight.

portable, *a.* **dette portable,** debt payable at the address of payee.

portage, *n.m. StExch:* **société de portage,** nominee company.

portatif, *a.* portable; **machine à écrire portative,** portable typewriter.

porte(-)à(-)porte, *n.m.* door-to-door (transport, selling); **faire du porte à porte,** to be a door-to-door salesman/saleswoman/salesperson.

porte-conteneurs, *n.m.inv. Trans:* (avion) **porte-conteneurs,** container aircraft; **(navire) porte-conteneurs,** container ship; **poste à quai pour navire porte-conteneurs,** container berth; **(train) porte-conteneurs,** container train.

porte-documents, *n.m.inv.* document case/brief case/executive case.

portée, *n.f.* **1.** *Nau:* burden/tonnage (of ship); **portée en lourd,** deadweight (capacity); **portée utile,** load-carrying capacity **2.** range/reach; scope; **des prix à la portée de tout le monde,** prices to suit every pocket.

portefeuille, *n.m.* (a) portfolio (for papers, etc.) (b) wallet/notecase/*NAm:* billfold (c) *Fin:* **effets en portefeuille/ portefeuille effets,** bills in hand/holdings; **gestion de portefeuille,** portfolio management; **portefeuille (titres),** investments; securities; **portefeuille indexé,** indexed portfolio; **portefeuille avec mandat,** discretionary portfolio; **société de portefeuille,** holding company; **société de gestion de portefeuille,** unit trust; **valeurs/ titres en portefeuille,** securities (in portfolio) (d) **portefeuille d'assurances,** portfolio (of insurance broker)/insurance book.

porter, 1. *v.tr.* (a) **la lettre porte la date du 28 novembre,** the letter is dated 28th November (b) **placement qui porte intérêt,** interest-bearing investment (c) **je porterai votre proposition à la connaissance du conseil d'administration,** I shall bring your suggestion to the notice of the board (d) to enter/to inscribe; **porter qch. en compte à qn,** to charge sth. to s.o.'s account;

portez cela sur/à mon compte, put that down on my account/charge it to my account/*NAm:* bill it to me/bill it to my account; **portez-le sur la note,** put it/ charge it on the bill; **porter une somme au crédit de qn,** to credit s.o.'s account with a sum (f) to raise/to carry; **porter la production au maximum,** to raise production to a maximum; **si vous pouviez porter la somme à deux mille francs,** if you could raise/increase the amount to two thousand francs (g) to declare/to state; **avec une clause conditionnelle portant que ...,** with a proviso to the effect that ....

porteur, -euse, 1. *a.* (*marché*) buoyant/ bullish. **2.** *n.* (a) bearer/carrier (of message, etc.); **prière de donner la réponse au porteur,** please hand the reply to bearer (b) (railway, etc.) porter (c) *Fin: etc.* holder/bearer; (*sur un chèque*) **payer au porteur,** pay bearer; **effets au porteur** bearer stocks; **payable au porteur,** payable to bearer; **porteur d'actions,** shareholder/ stockholder; **petit porteur,** small shareholder; **porteur d'un chèque,** bearer/payee of a cheque; **porteur d'un effet,** bearer/ holder/payee of a bill of exchange; **porteur d'obligations,** debenture holder/ bondholder; **titre au porteur,** bearer bond; negotiable instrument (d) *n.m. Av:* **(avion) gros porteur,** airliner/large transport aircraft.

portuaire, *a.* **autorité portuaire,** port authority; **capacité portuaire,** port capacity; **équipement/installation portuaire** harbour/port equipment; **Montréal es une ville portuaire,** Montreal is a port.

position, *n.f.* (a) position; **position concurrentielle,** competitive position; **position clef,** key position (b) *StExch:* **position acheteur,** bull position; **position ouverte nue,** open position; **position de place** market position; **position vendeur/baissière,** bear/short position; **liquider un position,** to close (out) a position; **prendr une position inverse sur le marché,** to offse (c) *Fin: Bank:* position/situation; **feuill de position,** statement; **position de trésorerie,** cash(flow) situation; **demander**

position de son compte (en banque), to ask for the balance of one's account.

positionnement, *n.m.* **1.** *Bank:* calculation of the balance of an account **2.** *Mkt:* **positionnement du produit,** product positioning.

positionner, *v.tr.* **1.** *Bank:* to calculate the balance of (an account) **2.** *Mkt:* to position (a product)/to define the market (of a product).

possesseur, *n.m.* possessor/owner; occupier; holder (of shares).

possession, *n.f.* possession (of property, shares, etc.); *Ind:* **coût de possession d'un article (en stock),** storage (cost); **libre possession d'un immeuble,** vacant possession (of a property); *Jur:* **possession de fait,** actual possession; **être en possession de qch.,** to be in possession of sth.; **prendre possession d'une maison,** to take possession of a house.

possibilité, *n.f.* possibility; opportunity (of employment); **possibilités d'exportation,** export possibilities.

possible, *a.* possible; **aussitôt que possible/ le plus tôt (qu'il vous sera) possible,** at your earliest convenience; as early/as soon as possible.

postal, *a.* **boîte postale 270,** post office box 270/PO Box 270; **carte postale,** postcard; **code postal,** postcode/*NAm:* zip code; **mandat postal,** postal order; **service postal aérien,** airmail service; **tarifs postaux,** postage/postal rates/postal charges.

postdater, *v.tr.* to postdate (cheque, etc.).

poste[1], *n.f.* (*a*) post; **les Postes et Télécommunications (P et T)** = the Post Office; **par poste aérienne,** by airmail; **poste restante,** poste restante; **envoyer (une lettre, un paquet) par la poste,** to send (a letter, a parcel) by post/*NAm:* by mail; **mettre une lettre à la poste,** to post/*NAm:* to mail a letter (*b*) **(bureau de) poste,** post office; **employé(e) des postes,** post office clerk/ post office employee.

poste[2], *n.m.* **1.** (*a*) post, station (of worker); **poste de travail,** operation station (in factory) (*b*) **poste de nuit,** night shift; **poste de 12 heures,** 12-hour shift **2.** *Tel:* **poste (intérieur, supplémentaire),** extension; **poste 106,** extension 106 **3.** post/position/ job; **description de poste,** job description; **exigences de poste,** job requirements; **poste vacant/poste à pourvoir,** (job) vacancy; **M. X s'est vu confié le poste de directeur général,** Mr X was appointed general manager **4.** *Book-k:* (*a*) entry (in books) (*b*) heading.

posté, *a.* **travail posté,** shift-work(ing); **travailleur posté,** worker on shift-work.

poster, *v.tr.* to post/to mail (letter, etc.).

pot-de-vin, *n.m.* F: bribe; hush money.

potentiel, 1. *a.* **acheteur potentiel,** potential buyer; **marché potentiel,** potential market; **ressources potentielles,** potential resources **2.** *n.m.* potential; **potentiel de croissance,** growth potential; **potentiel industriel,** industrial potential; **potentiel du marché,** market potential; **potentiel publicitaire,** advertising potential; **potentiel de vente,** sales potential.

pourboire, *n.m.* tip/gratuity.

pourcentage, *n.m.* percentage (of commission); rate (of interest); **pourcentage de bénéfices,** percentage of profit.

pourchasser, *v.tr. StExch:* **pourchasser le découvert,** to raid the shorts/the bears.

pourcompte, pour-compte, *n.m.* undertaking to sell goods on behalf of a third party.

poursuite, *n.f. usu.pl. Jur:* lawsuit/action/ prosecution; suing (of a debtor); **engager/ intenter des poursuites (judiciaires) contre qn,** to take/to institute proceedings against s.o.; to take (legal) action against s.o.

poursuivre, *v.tr. Jur:* **poursuivre qn (en justice),** to prosecute s.o./to take legal action against s.o.; to sue (debtor).

pourvoir, *v.i.* *(a)* **pourvoir aux frais d'un voyage,** to pay the cost of a journey *(b)* **pourvoir à un emploi,** to fill a vacancy/ a post; **poste à pourvoir à Paris,** (job) vacancy in Paris.

poussée, *n.f.* **poussée inflationniste,** inflationary surge.

pousser, *v.tr.* **pousser la vente de qch.,** to push the sale of sth.; **pousser un article aux enchères,** to up the bidding for sth; **pousser les enchères,** to run up the bidding.

pouvoir, *n.m.* **1. pouvoir d'achat,** purchasing power **2.** authority; **les pouvoirs publics,** the authorities; **pouvoir exécutif,** executive power; **le pouvoir judiciaire,** the judiciary; **pouvoir législatif,** legislative power **3.** *Jur:* **être fondé de pouvoir,** to have power of attorney.

pratique, *n.f.* **pratiques déloyales,** unfair (business) dealings.

pratiquer, *v.tr.* **pratiquer des prix trop élevés,** to be too expensive; **prix pratiqués sur le marché,** current market prices.

préalable, 1. *a.* *(a)* **accord préalable,** prior agreement; **sans avis préalable,** without prior notice *(b)* preliminary (agreement, arrangement, etc.) **2.** *n.m.* prerequisite/ precondition; preliminary.

préavis, *n.m.* *(a)* prior notice/advance notice; *(au travail)* **préavis (de congé),** notice; **donner un préavis d'un mois,** to give a month's notice; **exiger un préavis de trois mois,** to require three months' notice *(b)* *Bank:* **dépôt à sept jours de préavis,** deposit at seven days' notice.

précaution, *n.f.* **ils font des achats de précaution,** they're panic buying.

précis, *n.m.* **précis d'un article,** abstract of an article.

précompte, *n.m.* *Fin:* *(a)* advance deduction (from an account) *(b)* deduction at

source (of income tax, national insurance, etc., from wages).

précompter, *v.tr.* *(a)* to deduct in advance *(b)* to deduct (income tax, etc.) at source; **précompter la Sécurité Sociale sur le salaire de qn,** to deduct National Insurance from s.o.'s pay.

préconditionné, *a.* pre-packed/prepackaged (goods).

préconditionner, *v.tr.* to pre-pack/to pre-package (goods).

prédécesseur, *n.m.* predecessor.

préemballé, *a.* pre-packaged.

préemballer, *v.tr.* to pre-package (goods).

préemption, *n.f.* pre-emption; **droit de préemption,** right of first refusal/pre-emptive right.

préférence, *n.f.* *(a)* *Jur:* **droits de préférence,** priority rights/preferential claims; **pacte de préférence,** preference clause; **préférence d'un créancier,** priority of a creditor *(b)* *Fin:* **actions de préférence,** preference/preferred shares; *PolEc:* **préférence pour la liquidité,** liquidity preference *(c)* *Cust:* **préférences douanières,** (customs) preference/ preferential duty.

préférentiel, *a.* *(a)* preferential (treatment); *Cust:* **tarif/taux préférentiel,** preferential tariff/rate; *Adm:* concessionary fare/tariff *(b)* *Fin:* **droit préférentiel de souscription,** rights issue; **action à dividende préférentiel/action préférentielle,** preference share/preferred stock.

préfinancement, *n.m.* prefinancing; **(crédits de) préfinancement d'exportations,** prefinancing of export transactions.

préjudice, *n.m.* prejudice/detriment; **au préjudice de ...,** to the prejudice of ...; **sans préjudice de mes droits,** without prejudice (to my rights).

préjudiciable, *a.* detrimental.

prélèvement, *n.m.* *(a)* deduction in advance; setting aside (of a certain portion); *EEC:* **prélèvements agricoles,** agricultural levies; **prélèvement fiscal,** taxation; **prélèvement social =** National Insurance Contribution; **prélèvement sur le capital,** capital levy; **prélèvement à l'exportation,** export levy; **(méthode de) prélèvement des frais (d'achat) sur les premiers versements,** front-end loading (*b*) amount deducted; *Bank:* **prélèvement bancaire (automatique),** direct debit.

prélever, *v.tr.* to deduct/to set aside (portion or share from whole) (in advance); to draw on (an account); **prélever dix pour cent sur une somme,** to make an advance deduction of 10% from a sum of money/ to deduct 10% in advance; **prélever une commission de deux pour cent sur une opération,** to charge a 2% commission on a transaction; **dividende prélevé sur le capital,** dividend paid out of capital.

premier, -ière, 1. *a.* (*a*) first; **le premier juin,** the first of June; **coût premier,** prime cost; **frais de premier établissement,** initial outlay/initial expenses; **premier cours,** opening price; *Publ: Journ:* **première édition,** first edition; **première page,** front cover (*b*) *Ind:* **matières premières,** raw materials; *StExch:* **marché des matières premières,** commodity market; **premier cours,** opening price (*c*) best; **(produit de) premier choix/première qualité,** best/first quality (product); *Fin:* **obligation de premier ordre,** prime bond; *Trans:* **billet de première classe,** first class ticket; **voyager en première,** to travel first class **2.** *n.* (*a*) *n.m.* **premier entré, premier sorti (PEPS),** first in first out (FIFO) (*b*) *n.f.* **première de change,** first of exchange.

renant, *a. Fin:* **partie prenante,** (*i*) payee (*ii*) receiver/recipient.

rendre, *v.tr.* **1.** (*a*) **prendre la direction d'une affaire,** to take over the management of a business (*b*) **prendre mille francs sur son salaire du mois prochain,** to get an advance of a thousand francs on next month's salary (*c*) **prendre 40 francs (de) l'heure,** to charge 40 francs an hour (*d*) **prendre (de l'essence, etc.),** to get/to buy

(petrol, etc.); **prendre une chambre,** to take/to reserve/to book a room; **prendre (une place, un billet),** to book/to buy (a place, a ticket) **2.** (*a*) **prendre un jour de congé,** to take a day's holiday/to take a day off; **prendre rendez-vous/prendre date,** to fix a date (for a meeting, etc.); **voulez-vous prendre une lettre?** will you take (down) a letter?/take a letter, please! (*b*) **prendre un associé,** to take a partner; **prendre un ouvrier,** to take on/to engage/ *NAm:* to hire a worker; **prendre qn comme secrétaire,** to engage s.o. as one's secretary (*c*) **prendre des marchandises,** to take in cargo **3. prendre (l'avion, le bateau, le train),** to take/to catch (the plane, the boat, the train); to go (by air, by boat, by train).

preneur, -euse, *n.* (*a*) buyer/purchaser; taker; **avoir (trouvé) preneur pour qch.,** to have (found) a purchaser for sth.; **je suis preneur,** I'll take it (*b*) **preneur d'une lettre de change,** payee of a bill (*c*) *Jur:* **preneur (à bail),** lessee/leaseholder.

préparation, *n.f.* preparation; **préparation des commandes,** order preparation; *Ind:* **préparation d'un travail,** organization of a job; **temps de préparation,** tooling-up time.

prépayer, *v.tr.* to prepay; **réponse prépayée,** prepaid answer.

préposé, -ée, *n.* (*a*) employee; clerk; **préposé(e) à la caisse,** cashier; *Rail:* **préposé(e) à la distribution des billets,** booking clerk; **préposé(e) des douanes,** customs officer (*b*) **préposé(e) des PTT,** postman/postwoman (*c*) *Jur:* **commettant et préposé,** principal and agent.

préposer, *v.tr.* **préposer qn à une fonction,** to appoint s.o. to a position; to put s.o. in charge of a job; **préposer qn à la direction d'un service,** to appoint s.o. (as) head of department.

préretraite, *n.f.* early retirement.

prescrit, *a.* stipulated; **dans délai prescrit,** in the required time.

présence, *n.f.* **feuille de présence,** attendance sheet/work sheet.

présentateur,-trice, 1. *n.* presenter (of a bill, etc.) **2.** *a.* **banque présentatrice,** presenting bank.

présentation, *n.f.* (*a*) presentation (of bill, etc. for payment); **payable à présentation,** payable on demand/on presentation/at sight (*b*) *Mkt:* display; exhibit (at trade fair, etc.); **présentation du produit,** product display; **présentation en masse,** mass display; **présentation au sol,** floor display; **présentation à la sortie,** checkout display; **présentation en vrac,** dump display.

présenter, *v.tr.* (*a*) **présenter une traite à l'acceptation,** to present a bill for acceptance; **présenter un chèque à l'encaissement,** to cash a cheque (*b*) **présenter une motion à l'assemblée,** to put a motion to the meeting; **compte qui présente un solde créditeur de 50 000 francs,** account that shows a credit balance of 50 000 francs (*c*) *Mkt:* to display (goods).

présentoir, *n.m.* *Mkt:* display (stand, unit); merchandiser; **(panier) présentoir,** dumpbin; dump display; **présentoir au sol,** floor display/floor stand; **présentoir à la sortie,** checkout display.

présérie, *n.f.* *Ind:* (*a*) pre-production/pilot run (*b*) test series; pilot series.

présidence, *n.f.* chairmanship/presidency; **être nommé à la présidence de ...,** to be appointed chairman of ....

président, -ente, *n.* (*a*) chairman/chairperson/chairwoman/president (of a meeting, committee, etc.); **être élu président,** to be voted into the chair/to be elected president (*b*) **président (du conseil d'administration),** chairman (of the board)/*NAm:* president; **président-directeur général (P-DG),** Chairman and Managing Director/*NAm:* Chief Executive Officer (CEO).

présider, *v.tr. & i.* to preside/to be in the chair/to chair; **présider (à) une réunion,** to preside at/over a meeting; to chair a meeting.

presse, *n.f.* **la presse,** the press; the (news)-papers; **presse (nationale, régionale),** (national, provincial) press/papers; **(agence, attaché, campagne, conférence) de presse,** press (agency, attaché, campaign, conference); **service de presse,** (*i*) press office; publicity (department) (*ii*) press copies (*b*) *Typ:* **(livre, journal) sous presse,** (book, newspaper) in the press; **prêt à mettre sous presse,** ready for press; **nous mettons sous presse,** we're going to press.

pression, *n.f.* pressure; **groupe de pression,** pressure group/*NAm:* lobby group; **pression inflationniste,** inflationary pressure.

prestataire, *n.m. & f. Adm:* person receiving benefits/allowances.

prestation, *n.f.* (*a*) *Ins:* benefit; *Adm:* allowance/benefit; **prestations familiales** = family allowances/maternity benefits; **prestations maladie,** sickness benefit; **prestations sociales** = national insurance benefits; **verser les prestations,** to pay out benefits (*b*) **prestation de démarcheur,** finder's fee; **prestation de service,** (*i*) service fee/charge; (*ii*) service fee/charge; **prestations locatives,** service charges (*paid by tenants*).

prestige, *n.m.* **publicité de prestige,** prestige advertising.

préstockage, *n.m.* prestocking.

prêt[1], *a.* ready; prepared; **vêtements prêts à porter,** ready-made/ready-to-wear clothes.

prêt[2], *n.m.* **1.** loan; **prêts aux particuliers,** personal loans; **prêt bonifié/à taux bonifié,** soft loan; **prêts bonifiés d'aide à l'investissement/au développement des entreprises,** loan guarantee scheme (LGS); **prêt conditionnel,** tied loan; **prêt à découvert,** unsecured loan/loan on overdraft; **prêt sur gage/sur nantissement,** loan on collateral/against security; **prêt garanti,** secured loan; **prêt à la grosse,** bottomry loan; **prêt d'honneur,** loan on trust;

prêt hypothécaire, loan on mortgage; **prêts immobiliers conventionnés (PIC),** property loan discounted by the Crédit Foncier; **prêt à intérêt,** loan at interest; **prêt à la petite semaine,** loan by the week; **prêt au jour le jour,** money at call/call money; **prêt remboursable sur demande,** loan at call/loan repayable on demand; **prêt à terme,** loan at notice; **prêt à terme fixe,** term loan; **prêt à court terme,** short(-term) loan; **prêt à long terme,** long(-term) loan; **prêt sur titres,** advance on securities; **demande de prêt,** application for a loan; **intérêt sur prêt,** interest on a loan; **caisse de prêt,** loan bank; **maison de prêt,** loan office/company; **octroi d'un prêt,** granting of a loan; **titre de prêt,** loan certificate; **accorder/consentir un prêt,** to allow/to grant a loan; **demander/solliciter un prêt,** to apply for a loan **2.** advance (on salary, wages).

prêt-à-porter, *n.m.* ready-to-wear clothes; **magasin de prêt-à-porter,** shop selling ready-to-wear/off-the-peg/ready-made clothes.

prétention, *n.f.* (*a*) claim (à, to); **exposé détaillé des prétentions du demandeur,** detailed statement of claim (*b*) (*dans une annonce d'offre d'emploi*) **envoyer curriculum vitae et prétentions (de salaire),** send curriculum vitae/CV and state salary requirements/expected salary.

prêter, *v.tr.* to lend/*esp. NAm:* to loan; **prêter de l'argent à intérêt,** to lend money at interest; **prêter sur garantie/sur gage(s),** to lend against security; **prêter à la petite semaine,** to make a short-term loan at a high rate of interest.

prêteur,-euse, *n.* lender (*esp.* of money); *Jur:* bailor; **prêteur sur gages,** (*i*) *Jur:* pledgee (*ii*) pawnbroker.

preuve, *n.f.* proof/evidence.

préventif, *a.* preventive; **entretien préventif,** preventive maintenance; **mesures préventives,** preventive measures.

prévision, *n.f.* forecast(ing); expectations; outlook; **prévisions budgétaires,** budget estimates/budget forecasts; **prévision du marché,** market forecast(ing); **prévision des ventes,** sales forecast(ing)/sales projections; **prévision économique par graphique,** chartism.

prévisionnel, *a.* (*a*) estimated/provisional (costs, etc.) (*b*) **budget d'exploitation prévisionnel,** forecast operating budget; **gestion prévisionnelle,** budgetary control; **plan prévisionnel,** forecast plan; **résultats prévisionnels,** earnings forecast.

prévisionniste, *n.m.f. Econ:* chartist.

prévoir, *v.tr.* (*a*) to foresee/to forecast; **ventes prévues,** projected sales; **il prévoit une baisse de 4% au mois de mai,** he's projecting a 4% slide in May; **l'installation de cet ordinateur est prévue pour l'année prochaine,** this computer is scheduled/is due for installation next year; **la réunion est prévue pour demain,** the meeting is arranged for/will be held tomorrow (*b*) to provide in advance for (sth.); **dépenses prévues au budget,** expenses provided for/allowed for in the budget.

prévoyance, *n.f.* **caisse de prévoyance,** (*i*) contingency fund (*ii*) *Adm:* (staff) provident fund/scheme; **société de prévoyance,** provident society.

prier, *v.tr. Corr:* **je vous prie de bien vouloir accepter l'assurance de mes sentiments les meilleurs** = yours sincerely; *Ind: etc:* **le personnel est prié d'arriver à neuf heures précises,** staff are requested to arrive punctually at nine o'clock.

prière, *n.f.* request; **prière de nous couvrir par chèque,** kindly remit by cheque; *Post:* **prière de faire suivre,** please forward.

primaire, *a.* primary; *PolEc:* **secteur primaire,** primary industries (*agriculture and extractive industries*).

prime, *n.f.* **1.** (*a*) *Ins:* premium; **assurance à prime réduite,** low-premium insurance; **prime annuelle,** annual premium; **prime nette,** pure premium (*b*) *Fin: StExch:* premium; option; **acheteur/vendeur de prime,** giver/taker of an option; **marché à primes,** option market; **opérations à prime,**

options dealing/trading; **prime de conversion,** conversion premium; **prime du change,** agio; **prime d'émission,** issue premium; **prime de l'or,** premium on gold; **prime de remboursement,** premium on redemption; **(jour de la) réponse des primes,** declaration of options/option day; **abandonner la prime,** to forfeit/to surrender the option (money); **acheter à prime,** to give for the call; **donner la réponse/répondre à une prime,** to declare an option; **faire prime,** to stand at a premium; **lever la prime,** to exercise/to take up an option **2.** subsidy/grant; *Ind:* **prime de développement,** (government) development subsidy/grant **3.** (*a*) bonus; **prime (payée) aux employés,** bonus paid to employees; **prime d'ancienneté** = bonus for long service; **prime de déménagement,** removal allowance; **prime de rendement,** productivity/output bonus; **prime de risque,** yield gap; **prime de transport,** travel/transport allowance; **prime de vie chère,** cost-of-living bonus (*b*) *PolEc:* **prime à l'exportation,** export bonus **4.** *Mkt:* free gift; **prime échantillon,** free sample; **recette donnée en prime avec ce produit,** free (gift) recipe given with this product/when you buy this product.

principal, 1. *a.* principal/chief; **agent principal,** main agent; **associé principal,** senior partner; **produit principal d'un pays,** main/staple commodity of a country; **un des principaux actionnaires,** a major shareholder **2.** *n.m.* **principal d'une dette,** debt principal.

principe, *n.m.* (*a*) principle; **principes économiques,** economic principles (*b*) **aboutir à un accord de principe,** to reach an agreement in principle.

prioritaire, *a.* priority; **action (à dividende) prioritaire,** preference share/preferred stock; **droits prioritaires,** priority rights; **être prioritaire,** to have priority.

priorité, *n.f.* priority; *Jur:* priority of claim; *StExch:* **actions de priorité,** preference shares/preferred stock; **créancier de priorité,** preferred creditor; **droits de prio-**

rité, priority rights; **dividende de priorité,** preferential dividend; **avoir la priorité,** to have priority.

prise, *n.f.* (*a*) **prise de contrôle (majoritaire),** takeover; acquisition; direct action; **prise de décision(s),** decision making; *Fin:* **prise de participation,** acquisition of shareholding; takeover (*b*) *StExch:* **prise de bénéfices,** profit taking.

prisée, *n.f. Jur:* **prisée (et estimation),** valuation (of goods); appraisal (before auction).

privatif, *a.* exclusive; private; **droit privatif,** exclusive right.

privatisation, *n.f.* privatization.

privatiser, *v.tr.* to privatize.

privé, *a.* private (bank, enterprise, property, etc.); **société privée,** privately-held company; **le secteur privé,** the private sector (of industry).

privilège, *n.m.* **1.** licence/charter; **le privilège de la Banque de France,** exclusive right of the Bank of France to issue banknotes **2.** preferential right; **privilège du créancier,** creditor's preferential claim; **privilège général,** general lien; **avoir un privilège sur qch.,** to have a lien/a charge on sth.

privilégié, *a.* (*a*) licensed; **banque privilégiée,** chartered bank (*b*) **action privilégiée,** preference share/preferred stock; **créance privilégiée,** preferential debt/preferred debt/privileged debt; **créancier privilégié,** preferred creditor.

privilégier, *v.tr.* to license; to grant a charter to (bank, etc.); to give preference (to a claim, a creditor).

prix, *n.m.* (*a*) price; consideration; quotation; **bas prix,** low price; **à moitié prix,** half price; **prix élevé,** high price; **affichage des prix,** displaying of prices; *PolEc:* **blocage des prix,** price pegging/price freezing; **contrôle des prix,** price control; **détermination des prix,** pricing/price fixing; **différences des prix,** price differentials; **échelle/éventail des prix,** price range;

fixation des prix, price-fixing; **forte réduction des prix,** price cutting/slashing; **guerre des prix,** price war; *PolEc:* **indice des prix,** price index; **magasin à prix unique,** one-price store/popular store; **monopole des prix,** price ring; **niveau des prix,** price level; **prix affiché/à la vente,** sticker price/displayed price; **prix d'achat/ prix coûtant,** purchase price/cost; **prix d'appel,** cut/reduced price; **prix catalogue/ prix public/prix fort (de vente),** catalogue price/list price/full price; **prix chocs,** drastic reductions/(incredible) bargain prices; **prix cassés,** knock-down prices; **prix (au) comptant,** cash price; **prix (du) comptant,** sell price; **prix compétitif,** competitive price; **prix concurrenciel,** fine price; **prix conseillé/recommandé,** manufacturer's recommended price (MRP)/recommended retail price (RRP); **prix convenu,** agreed price; **prix courant/ actuel/pratiqué,** current price; **prix demandé,** asking price; **prix de détail,** retail price; **prix démarqués/soldés,** double pricing; **prix de demi-gros,** trade price; cash-and-carry price; **prix directeur,** price leader; **prix d'équilibre/de marché,** choice price/average price/target price; **prix exceptionnel/de solde,** bargain price; **prix à l'exportation,** export price; **prix de fabrique,** cost price/manufacturer's price; **prix ferme,** firm/steady price; **prix fixe/prix forfaitaire,** fixed price; **prix franco,** delivered pricing; **prix de gros,** wholesale price/direct price; **prix à l'importation,** import price; **prix imposé,** retail price maintenance (RPM)/*NAm:* administered price; **prix initial,** basic price; prime cost; **prix intéressant,** attractive price; *EEC:* **prix d'intervention,** intervention price; **prix de lancement,** introductory price; **prix du marché,** market value; **prix marqué,** marked price; **prix minimum,** minimum price; **prix modéré/modique,** moderate price; **prix moyen,** average price; **prix net,** net price; *(sur un menu)* price inclusive of service; **prix officiel/prix taxé,** standard price; *PolEc:* **prix plafond,** ceiling price; *PolEc:* **prix plancher/prix seuil,** floor price; minimum price; **prix préférentiel,** preferential price; **prix à la**

production/prix départ usine, price ex warehouse/factory price; **prix de rabais/ prix réduit,** cut/reduced/discount price; **prix réel,** actual price; **prix de revient/prix coûtant,** cost price; **comptabilité de prix de revient,** cost accounting; *EEC:* **prix du seuil,** threshold price; **prix tout compris/ prix tous frais compris/prix toutes taxes comprises (TTC),** all-inclusive price; **prix à terme,** forward price; **prix unitaire,** unit price; **prix de vente,** selling price; **régime des prix/mécanisme des prix,** price mechanism/system; **réglementation des prix,** price regulation; **soutien des prix,** price support; **acheter qch. à bas prix,** to buy sth. at a low price/to buy sth. cheap; **augmenter de prix,** to increase in price; **augmenter/baisser les prix,** to mark up/to mark down prices; **coûter un prix fou,** to cost the earth; **déterminer/fixer le prix de qch.,** to price sth.; **établir le prix (de revient) d'un travail,** to cost a job; **faire un prix,** to quote/to name a price; **faire un prix à qn,** to quote s.o. a price; **je vous ferai un prix (d'ami),** I'll let you have it cheap/I'll give you special terms; **faire monter les prix,** to push up prices; **mettre un prix à qch.,** to price sth./to put a price to sth.; **quel est le prix de ce livre?** what is the price of this book? how much is this book? *(b) StExch: Fin:* **actions cotées au prix de ...,** shares quoted at the rate of ...; **effondrement des prix,** price slump; **hausse/baisse des prix,** rise/fall in prices; **prix du change,** (exchange) premium; agio; **prix de l'argent,** price of money; **prix d'émission (d'actions, etc.),** issue price (of shares, etc.); **prix d'exercice,** exercise price; **prix du marché,** market price; **acheter/vendre au prix du marché,** to buy/to sell at market price/at (the) market; **prix de l'option,** option price; **prix du report,** contango rate *(c)* charge; **prix d'un trajet/du voyage,** fare; **le prix des places est de 25 francs,** the seats are 25 francs each.

prix-courant, *n.m.* price list; catalogue.

prix(-)étalon, *n.m.* standard cost/price.

problème, *n.m.* problem; **évaluation de problème(s),** problem appraisal.

procédé, *n.m. Ind: etc:* process/way; method (of working); **procédé de fabrication,** manufacturing process; **procédé de travail,** operating process.

procédure, *n.f.* **1.** procedure; **(mode de) procédure,** procedure (at a meeting, etc.) **2.** *Jur:* proceedings; **procédure de faillite,** bankruptcy proceedings.

procès, *n.m.* proceedings at law; action (at law); case; law-suit; **intenter un procès à qn,** (*i*) to file a suit against s.o.; to institute proceedings against s.o.; to sue s.o. (*ii*) to prosecute s.o.

processif, *a. PolEc:* progressive; **processif ou récessif,** progressive or recessive.

processus, *n.m.* method/process; **commande/régulation de processus,** process control; **processus décisionnel/de décision,** decision making.

procès-verbal, *n.m.* (official) report; proceedings/minutes (of meeting); **dresser un procès-verbal,** to draw up a report; **tenir le procès-verbal des réunions,** to keep the minutes of the meetings; **le procès-verbal de la dernière séance a été approuvé,** the minutes of the last meeting were approved; *Nau:* **procès-verbal des avaries,** protest.

procuration, *n.f.* procuration/proxy; power of attorney; **procuration générale,** full power of attorney; **signé par procuration,** signed by proxy/on behalf of/per pro/pp; **agir par procuration,** to act by proxy.

procurer, *v.tr.* **où puis-je me procurer ce livre,** where can I get/buy that book? **il est impossible de se procurer ce livre,** this book is unobtainable.

procureur, *n.m. Jur:* attorney.

producteur, -trice, 1. *a.* productive (**de,** of); producing; **capital producteur d'intérêt,** interest-bearing capital; **les pays producteurs de pétrole,** oil producing countries; **régions productrices d'un pays,** productive regions of a country **2.** *n.* producer.

productif, *a.* productive; *PolEc:* **personnel productif/main-d'œuvre productive,** productive labour.

productique, *n.f.* production engineering.

production, *n.f. PolEc: Ind: etc:* (*a*) production/output; **chaîne de production,** production line; **chute/baisse de production,** fall/drop in production; **excédent de production,** surplus production; **production agricole,** agricultural production; **production à la chaîne,** production line system/mass production; **production sur commande,** production to order; **production continue,** continuous flow production; **production dirigée/planifiée,** planned production; **production globale,** aggregate output/production; **production par lots,** batch production; **production en masse/en série,** mass production; **production manufacturée,** secondary production; **production de matières premières,** primary production; **taux de production,** rate of production; **augmenter la production,** to increase production/output; **ralentir la production,** to slow down production/to reduce output (*b*) **biens de production,** (*i*) capital goods (*ii*) producer goods; **capacité de production,** production capacity; **chef/directeur de la production,** production manager; **coûts/frais de production,** production costs; **délai de production,** lead time; **gestion de production,** production control; **moyens de production,** means/method of production; **organisation de la production,** production engineering; **production intérieure brute (PIB),** gross domestic product; **service de la production,** production department.

productivité, *n.f.* productivity; productive capacity/yield capacity; **campagne de productivité,** productivity drive/productivity campaign; **contrat de productivité,** productivity deal; **prime de productivité,** incentive/productivity bonus; **productivité financière d'une entreprise,** productiveness of a firm.

produire, *v.tr.* **1.** to produce (documents etc.) **2.** to produce/to yield; **argent qui produit de l'intérêt,** money that yields interest; **produire mille voitures par jour,** t produce/to turn out a thousand cars a day.

produit, *n.m.* (*a*) product; produce; **produits agricoles,** agricultural produce; **produits alimentaires,** food products; *Mkt:* **produit d'appel,** loss leader; impulse item; **produit de base,** (*i*) basic (*ii*) staple commodity/product; **produits de consommation,** consumer goods; **produit chimique,** chemical; **produits dérivés,** by-products/derivatives; **produits étrangers,** foreign produce/goods; **produit fini/ouvré,** finished/end product; **produit industriel,** industrial product; **produits manufacturés,** manufactured goods/products; **produit de première nécessité,** essential/staple product; **produits du pays,** home produce; **produits de rejet,** waste products; **produit semi-fini/semi-ouvré,** semi-finished/semi-manufactured product; **analyse de produit,** product analysis; **conception de produit,** product design; **mise au point d'un produit,** product development (*b*) proceeds/yield; revenue; **produit moyen,** average revenue; **produit net,** net earnings/proceeds; **produit brut,** gross earnings/proceeds; *PolEc:* **Produit Intérieur Net,** net domestic product; **produit national brut (PNB),** gross national product (GNP); *Fin:* **produits accessoires,** sundry income; **produits financiers,** interest income.

profession, *n.f.* profession/occupation/trade; **les membres des professions libérales,** professional people.

professionnel, *a.* **accident professionnel,** occupational accident; **association professionnelle,** trade association; professional association; **frais professionnels,** professional fees; **maladie professionnelle,** occupational disease; **secret professionnel,** professional secrecy; trade secret.

profil, *n.m.* profile; **profil de la clientèle,** customer profile; **profil d'entreprise,** company profile; **profil du marché,** market profile.

profit, *n.m.* profit; **profit brut,** gross profit; **profit net,** clear profit; **profits et pertes,** profit and loss; **profits de l'exercice,** year's profits/earnings; **profits théoriques/fictifs/non matérialisés,** paper profits; **profits mis en réserve,** capital reserves; **objectif de profits,** profit target; **optimisation des profits,** profit optimization; **vendre à profit,** to sell at a profit.

profitabilité, *n.f.* (*i*) profitability (*ii*) earning power.

profitable, *a.* profitable; advantageous; **affaire profitable,** paying concern; profitable business.

profiteur, -euse, *n. Pej:* profiteer.

pro forma, *a.phr.inv.* **facture pro forma,** pro forma invoice.

progiciel, *n.m. Cmptr:* software package; **progiciel de comptabilité,** accounting package.

programmation, *n.f.* (*a*) programming; scheduling; planning; **programmation à long terme,** long-range planning; **programmation linéaire,** linear programming; **programmation de la production,** production scheduling; **personnel chargé de la programmation,** scheduling staff; **service (de la) programmation,** programming department (*b*) *Cmptr:* programming; **langage de programmation,** computer language.

programme, *n.m.* (*a*) programme/*NAm:* program; schedule; **programme de développement,** development programme; **programme de fabrication/de production,** production programme/schedule; *Fin:* **programme d'investissement,** investment programme; **programme à long terme,** long-range plan; **programme de recherche(s),** research programme; *Mkt:* **programme des ventes,** sales programme/schedule; **arrêter un programme,** to draw up/to arrange a programme (*b*) *Cmptr:* program.

programmé, *a. Cmptr:* programmed; **gestion programmée,** programmed management.

programmer, *v.tr. Cmptr:* to program.

programmeur, -euse, *n. Cmptr:* programmer.

progrès, *n.m.* progress.

progressif, *a.* (*a*) progressive; **impôt progressif,** progressive/graduated tax (*b*) gradual (growth, development); **l'amélioration progressive du rendement,** the gradual improvement in productivity.

progression, *n.f. Fin:* **progression des bénéfices,** increase in profits.

progressivité, *n.f. Fin:* **progressivité de l'impôt,** progressive increase in taxation.

prohibé, *a.* prohibited; **marchandises prohibées,** prohibited goods.

prohibitif, *a.* prohibitive (price, duty).

prohibition, *n.f.* **prohibition d'entrée,** import prohibition/ban; **prohibition de sortie,** export prohibition/ban.

projection, *n.f.* projection; **projection des ventes,** sales projection.

projet, *n.m.* (*a*) plan/project; scheme; **étude de projet,** project analysis; **étude de projet d'investissement,** capital project evaluation; **projet de budget,** budget estimates; **projet de contrat,** draft contract; **projet de loi,** bill.

projeter, *v.tr.* to plan.

prolongation, *n.f.* extension; renewal.

promesse, *n.f.* promise; **promesse d'achat,** agreement/undertaking to purchase; **promesse de payer,** undertaking/promise to pay; **promesse de vente,** undertaking/promise to sell.

promo, *n.f. F:* promotion; **(bande) promo,** promotional video.

promoteur, -trice, *n.* promoter; **promoteur-constructeur/promoteur immobilier,** property developer; **promoteur des ventes,** sales promoter.

promotion, *n.f.* **1.** promotion; **promotion à l'ancienneté,** promotion by seniority; **promotion des cadres,** executive promotion **2. promotion immobilière,** (promoting of)

property development projects; *Mkt:* **promotion des ventes,** sales promotion; **promotion sur le lieu de vente (PLV),** point-of-sale (POS) promotion; **en promotion,** on promotion/on offer.

promotionnel, *a. Mkt:* **équipe promotionnelle,** promotion team; **vente promotionnelle** = special offer/bargain offer.

promouvoir, *v.tr.* (*a*) to promote (s.o.); **être promu,** to be promoted (*b*) to promote (sales, products); **promouvoir la recherche scientifique,** to encourage scientific research.

pronostic, *n.m.* forecast; **pronostic du marché,** market forecast.

propension, *n.f. PolEc:* **propension à consommer,** propensity to consume; **propension moyenne à épargner,** average propensity to save.

proportion, *n.f.* proportion; ratio; percentage.

proportionnalité, *n.f. Fin:* **proportionnalité de l'impôt,** fixed rate system of taxation.

proportionnel, *a.* proportional (à, to); proportionate; **compensation proportionnelle au dommage subi,** compensation proportional to the damage; **distribution proportionnelle,** proportionment; *Cust:* **droit proportionnel,** ad valorem duty; *Fin:* **impôt proportionnel,** proportional tax.

proportionnellement, *adv.* proportionally/in proportion (à, to); pro rata; *Fin: etc:* **partager proportionnellement,** to prorate.

proposer, *v.tr.* to propose/to recommend; **proposer un candidat,** to nominate a candidate; **être proposé pour un emploi,** to be recommended for a job.

proposition, *n.f.* proposal/proposition; **proposition d'assurance,** proposal of insurance; **faire/formuler une proposition,** (*i*) to make a proposal (*ii*) to put/to propose a motion (at a meeting).

propriétaire, *n.m. f.* (*a*) proprietor/

proprietress (of business, hotel, etc.); owner (of car, house, etc.); holder (of shares, etc.); **nu propriétaire,** bare owner; **propriétaire foncier,** (*i*) ground landlord (*ii*) landowner; *Jur:* **propriétaire indivis,** joint owner; **propriétaire légitime,** rightful owner; **propriétaire unique,** sole owner (*b*) landlord/landlady.

propriétaire-occupant, -ante *n.* owner-occupier.

propriété, *n.f.* (*a*) proprietorship/ownership; **propriété collective,** collective ownership; social ownership; **propriété commerciale,** commercial tenant's (right to) security of tenure or compensation; **propriété commune,** joint ownership; **propriété individuelle,** individual ownership; **propriété indivise,** joint ownership; **propriété industrielle,** patent rights; **propriété littéraire/artistique,** literary property/copyright; **titres de propriété,** title deeds (*b*) property/estate/holding; **propriété foncière,** landed property/landed estate; **propriété immobilière,** real estate/realty; **propriété mobilière,** personal estate; **propriété privée,** private property; **propriété à vendre,** property for sale.

prorata, *n.m.inv.* proportional part/proportion; **au prorata de qch.,** in proportion to sth./proportionately to sth.; **distribution au prorata,** proportionment; **paiement au prorata,** payment pro rata; **rémunération au prorata du travail accompli,** payment in proportion to work done.

prorogation, *n.f.* extension of time/of time limit (for payment to be made, etc.); **prorogation de bail,** renewal of lease.

proroger, *v.tr.* to extend (time limit); **proroger l'échéance d'un billet,** to prolong/to extend maturity of a bill.

prospecté, -ée, *n. Mkt:* prospect/prospective customer/potential buyer; potential supplier.

prospecter, *v.tr. Mkt:* to investigate/to examine (potential market, etc.); **pros-**

pecter la clientèle, to canvass for customers.

prospecteur, -trice, *n.* canvasser.

prospectif, *a.* prospective; **étude prospective du marché,** market study/survey.

prospection, *n.f. Mkt:* canvassing; **prospection des marchés,** market exploration; **prospection sur le terrain,** field research.

prospectus, *n.m.* (*a*) *Fin:* **prospectus d'émission,** prospectus (*b*) *Mkt:* **prospectus publicitaire,** brochure; (publicity) handout/leaflet.

prospère, *a.* prosperous/thriving (business, etc.).

prospérer, *v.i.* to thrive/to prosper.

prospérité, *n.f.* prosperity; **vague de prospérité,** boom/wave of prosperity.

protecteur, *a. PolEc:* protective (duty, tariff, etc.); **système protecteur,** protection(ism).

protection, *n.f.* (*a*) protection/safeguarding; *Mkt:* **protection du consommateur,** consumer protection (*b*) *PolEc:* protection(ism).

protectionnisme, *n.m. PolEc:* protectionism.

protéger, *v.tr.* (*a*) to protect; **protéger qch. par un brevet,** to patent sth. (*b*) *PolEc:* to protect/to safeguard (industry, etc.).

protester, *v.tr.* **protester (un effet, une lettre de change),** to protest (a bill).

protêt, *n.m.* protest; **protêt authentique,** certified protest; **protêt faute d'acceptation,** protest for non-acceptance; **protêt faute de paiement,** protest for non-payment; **dresser/lever/faire protêt (d'un effet, d'une lettre de change),** to protest (a bill); **signifier un protêt,** to give notice of a protest.

protocole, *n.m.* **il a signé le protocole d'accord,** he signed heads of agreement.

prototype, *n.m.* prototype; **voiture prototype,** prototype car.

provenance, *n.f.* (*a*) origin; **de provenance**

française, of French origin; **pays de provenance,** country of origin *(b) pl. Cust:* **les provenances,** imports.

provenir, *v.i.* to come **(de,** from); to originate **(de,** in); **revenu provenant d'un investissement,** income coming from/accruing from an investment.

provision, *n.f.* **1.** *(a) Fin: Bank:* funds/cover/reserve; **insuffisance de provision,** insufficient funds (to meet cheque, etc.); **manque de provision,** no funds; **chèque sans provision,** cheque without cover/*F:* dud cheque; **il m'a payé avec un chèque sans provision,** his cheque bounced; **provision d'une lettre de change,** consideration for a bill of exchange; **faire provision pour une lettre de change,** to provide for/to protect a bill of exchange; **verser une provision,** to pay a deposit/to deposit funds *(b) Book-k:* provision/reserve; **provision pour créances douteuses,** reserve for bad debts; loan–loss provision; **provision pour dépréciation/pour amortissement,** provision for depreciation/depreciation allowance *(c)* retainer (given to lawyer, etc.) **2.** *(a)* store/stock/supply; **provision de papier,** paper supply *(b)* **faire ses provisions,** to do one's shopping.

provisionnel, *a. Fin:* **acompte provisionnel,** payment (of income tax) made on provisional assessment.

provisionner, *v.tr.* to give consideration for (a bill); *Bank:* **provisionner un compte,** to pay money into an account.

provisoire, *a.* provisional; temporary; **dividende provisoire,** interim dividend; **gérant provisoire,** acting manager; **nommé à titre provisoire,** appointed provisionally.

prud'hommes, *n.m.pl.* **conseil de(s) prud'hommes,** conciliation board/industrial tribunal *(of employers and workers, in industrial disputes).*

psychologie, *n.f.* psychology; **psychologie commerciale,** psychology of marketing; **psychologie industrielle,** industrial psychology; **psychologie de la publicité,** advertising psychology.

psychotechnique, *n.f.* industrial psychology.

pub, *abbr.* = **publicité.**

public, 1. *a.* public; **dépense publique,** public expenditure; **la dette publique,** the National Debt; *Jur:* **marché public,** market overt; *Fin:* **offre publique d'achat (OPA),** takeover bid; **les pouvoirs publics,** the (public) authorities; **relations publiques,** public relations (PR); **secteur public,** public sector; **services de santé publique,** National Health services; **société d'utilité publique,** public utility company; **le Trésor public,** the (French) Treasury **2.** *n.m.* **le public,** the public (sector); *(société)* **placer des actions dans le public,** to go public; **le grand public,** the general public.

publication, *n.f.* *(a)* publication/publishing; **publication des comptes,** disclosure (of accounts) *(b)* publication/published work; **publication périodique,** periodical/magazine.

publicitaire, 1. *a. Mkt:* **agence publicitaire,** advertising agency; *Journ:* **annonce publicitaire,** advertisement/*F:* ad; **baratin publicitaire,** blurb; **budget publicitaire,** publicity/advertising budget; **dépenses publicitaires,** publicity/advertising expenses; **espace publicitaire,** advertising space; *TV:* **message publicitaire,** (advertising) spot/commercial; **normes publicitaires,** advertising standards; **supports publicitaires,** advertising media; **vente publicitaire,** promotional sale **2.** *n.m. f.* advertising executive; publicity man/woman; publicist; *F:* adman.

publicité, *n.f. Mkt:* advertising/publicity; build-up; advertisement; **agence/bureau de publicité,** advertising agency/ad agency/publicity bureau; **agent de publicité,** advertising agent; **budget de publicité,** *(i)* publicity/advertising budget *(ii)* (advertising) account; **campagne de publicité,** advertising/publicity campaign; publicity drive; **chef de (la) publicité,**

advertising manager; **envoi/prospectus/ dépliant de publicité (directe),** mailing piece/shot; **exemplaire de publicité,** press copy; **frais de publicité,** advertising/ publicity costs; **(service de) la publicité,** publicity department; **publicité par affichage/par affiches,** poster advertising; **publicité d'amorçage,** advance publicity; **publicité aggressive,** hard sell; **publicité collective,** group advertising; **publicité concurrentielle,** competitive advertising; **publicité directe,** direct mailing; **publicité-médias,** media advertising; **publicité mensongère/trompeuse,** misleading advertising; **publicité au point de vente,** in-store promotion; **publicité subliminale,** subliminal advertising; **publicité tapageuse,** display advertising; **publicité télévisée,** television advertising/televized advertising; **faire de la publicité (pour un produit),** to advertise/to publicize (a product).

publifinançage, *n.m.* sponsoring.

publifinancer, *v.tr.* to sponsor.

publifinanceur, *n.m.* sponsor.

publiphone, *n.m.* public telephone; **publiphone à carte,** cardphone; **carte de publiphone,** phonecard.

publipostage, *n.m. Mkt:* mailing.

puce, *n.f. Cmptr:* microchip; **carte à puce,** smartcard.

purger, *v.tr.* **purger une hypothèque,** to redeem/to pay off a mortgage.

pyramide, *n.f.* **pyramide des salaires,** wage pyramid.

Q

quadrimestre, *n.m.* *Book-k:* four monthly (accounting) period.

quadrimestriel, *a.* four-monthly.

quadruple, *a. & n.m.* quadruple; **payer le quadruple du prix,** to pay four times the price.

quadrupler, *v.tr. & i.* to quadruple; to increase (one's assets, etc.) fourfold.

quai, *n.m.* (*a*) *Nau:* quay; wharf; pier; **droit(s) de quai,** quayage; wharfage; **marchandises à prendre/livrables à quai,** goods ex quay/ex wharf; **rendu/livré franco à quai,** free on quay (*b*) *Rail:* platform; **billet de quai,** platform ticket; **quai d'arrivée,** arrival platform; **quai de départ,** departure platform; **quai de chargement,** loading platform; *Trans:* loading bay; **quai de déchargement,** offloading platform.

qualification, *n.f.* **1.** *Fin:* qualifying (*by acquisition of shares*) **2.** qualification; **qualifications professionnelles,** professional qualifications; **posséder les qualifications nécessaires pour un poste,** to have the necessary qualifications for a job.

qualifié, *a.* qualified; **ouvrier qualifié,** skilled worker; **ouvrier non qualifié,** unskilled worker; **être qualifié pour faire qch.,** to be qualified to do sth.

qualité, *n.f.* **1.** (*a*) quality; **de bonne qualité/de qualité supérieure,** (of) good/high quality; **marchandises de mauvaise qualité/de qualité inférieure,** poor quality goods; **de première qualité,** high-grade/(of the) best quality; **qualité marchande,** (fair) average quality; **qualité prescrite,** stipulated quality (*b*) **contrôle de la qualité,** quality control (QC); **qualité globale**

(QG), total quality control; **garantie de qualité,** guarantee/warranty of quality; quality guarantee; **marchandises de qualité,** quality goods (*c*) **qualité du travail,** workmanship **2.** qualification/capacity; **avoir qualité pour agir,** to be qualified/ authorized to act; **posséder les qualités requises pour un poste,** to have the necessary qualifications for a post; to be qualified for a post; **en sa qualité de ...,** in his capacity as ....

quantième, *n.m.* *Adm:* day (of the month).

quantitatif, *a.* quantitative; *PolEc:* **théorie quantitative,** quantity theory.

quantité, *n.f.* quantity; **une petite quantité,** a small quantity (**de,** of); **une (grande) quantité de ...,** a (large) quantity of ...; **acheter qch. en quantité considérable/en grande quantité,** to buy sth. in bulk/in large quantities; **remise sur la quantité,** quantity discount; *Cust:* **la quantité permise (de tabac, etc.),** the quantity (of tobacco, etc.) permitted; *Ind:* **quantité économique de production,** economic manufacturing quantity; **quantité économique à commander/quantité économique de réapprovisionnement,** economic order quantity/economic lot size (ELS); **déterminer la quantité de qch.,** to quantify sth.

quantum, *n.m.* amount/proportion/ratio; **fixer le quantum des dommages-intérêts,** to fix the amount of damages/to assess the damages.

quarante, *num.a.inv. & n.m.inv.* forty; **semaine de quarante heures,** forty-hour week.

quart, *n.m.* (*a*) quarter/fourth (part); **trois quarts,** three quarters; **remise du quart,** discount of 25%; **je peux l'avoir au quart**

du prix, I can buy it for a quarter (of) the price (b) **un quart (de beurre, de café),** a quarter of a kilo/250 grammes (of butter, of coffee).

quartier, *n.m.* district; **quartier des affaires,** business district/area/*NAm:* downtown; **quartier commercant,** shopping district/area; **quartier résidentiel,** residential district/area.

quasi-contrat, *n.m. Jur:* quasi contract/ implied contract.

quasi-monnaie, *n.f.* quasi-money/near money.

questionnaire, *n.m.* questionnaire.

quinquennal, *a.* **plan quinquennal,** five-year plan.

quintal, *n.m. Meas:* **quintal** = 100 kilogrammes; *FrC:* a hundredweight.

quinzaine, *n.f.* **1.** (about) fifteen; **une quinzaine de francs,** fifteen francs or so **2.** (a) fortnight (b) fortnight's pay/wages.

quinze, *num.a.inv.* (a) fifteen; **le 15 décembre,** on 15th December (b) **quinze jours,** a fortnight.

quittance, *n.f.* receipt; *Jur:* discharge; **carnet de quittances,** receipt book; **quittance comptable,** accountable receipt; **quittance double,** duplicate receipt; **quittance en double,** receipt in duplicate;

quittance libératoire/finale, receipt in full (discharge); **quittance de loyer,** rent receipt; **quittance pour solde,** receipt in full.

quittancer, *v.tr.* to receipt (bill).

quitus, *n.m.* receipt in full; *Jur:* final discharge (from debt, liability, etc.); **donner à qn quitus de sa gestion,** to give s.o. final discharge from his financial administration.

quorum, *n.m.* quorum; **constituer un quorum,** to have/to form a quorum; **le quorum n'est pas atteint,** we don't have/we don't form a quorum.

quota, *n.m.* quota; **quota d'exportation,** export quota; **quota d'importation,** import quota; **quota de ventes,** sales quota; **sondage par quotas,** quota sampling; **système des quotas,** quota system.

quote-part, *n.f.* share/quota/portion; contribution pro rata; **quote-part des bénéfices,** share in the profits; **apporter/payer sa quote-part,** to contribute one's share.

quotidien, *n.m.* daily (newspaper).

quotient, *n.m.* quotient/ratio.

quotité, *n.f.* quota/share/amount/proportion/percentage; **impôt de quotité,** coefficient tax; **quotité imposable,** taxable quota; **la quotité du dégrèvement fiscal,** the extent of tax relief.

R

rabais, *n.m.* reduction (in price); allow-ance/rebate/discount; **rabais de 10 francs,** 10 francs off/reduction of 10 francs/10 franc reduction; **maison de rabais,** dis-count store; **acheté à rabais,** bought at a reduced price/bought (on the) cheap; **faire/accorder un rabais sur qch.,** to make a reduction on sth./to reduce sth.; to give a discount on sth.; **vendre qch. au rabais,** to sell sth. at a discount/at a reduced price/*NAm:* at cut-rate prices.

rabaissement, *n.m.* lowering (of prices).

rabaisser, *v.tr.* to reduce/to lower (price).

rabattre, *v.tr.* to reduce; **rabattre 5% du prix,** to take/*F:* to knock 5% off the price; to reduce sth. by 5%.

rachat, *n.m.* (*a*) buying back/repurchase; buying in (of goods); *StExch:* **rachat d'actions,** covering purchases; *StExch:* **rachat des vendeurs à découvert,** bear/short covering; bear closing; **rachat d'entreprise par les salariés (RES)/rachat par une société de ses propres actions,** management buyout; *Jur:* **pacte de rachat,** covenant of redemption; **(vente) avec faculté de rachat,** (sale) with option of re-purchase/of redemption; repurchase agreement; **remboursement anticipé par rachat sur le marché,** tap-bying (*b*) *Ins:* surrender (of policy); redemption (of annuity, etc.); **valeur de rachat,** surrender value.

rachetable, *a.* repurchasable; redeemable (stock).

racheter, *v.tr.* **1.** (*a*) to repurchase; to buy (sth.) back; to buy (sth.) in; *StExch:* **se couvrir en rachetant,** to buy back a short position; to cover (a short position) by buying back; **racheter des titres,** to cover short sales/shorts (*b*) to redeem (debt, pledge, etc.) (*c*) *Ins:* to surrender (policy); to redeem (annuity) **2.** to buy again; to make a further purchase of (sth.); **racheter du fromage,** (*i*) to buy some more cheese (*ii*) to buy some more of the same cheese.

radiation, *n.f.* erasure/crossing out (of an item in an account, etc.); cancellation (of debt, etc.); **radiation d'une société de la Bourse,** going private.

radier, *v.tr.* to erase; to cross (sth., s.o.) off (a list, etc.).

radiorecherche, *n.f.* **radiorecherche de personne,** radiopaging.

radiotéléphone, *n.m.* radiotelephone.

raffermir, **1.** *v.tr.* to steady (prices, etc.); **raffermir le crédit d'une maison,** to rees-tablish a firm's credit **2.** *v.pr.* **les prix se raffermissent,** prices are steadying/are hardening.

raffermissement, *n.m.* hardening/steadying (of prices).

raffinage, *n.m.* (oil, etc.) refining.

raffinerie, *n.f.* (oil, etc.) refinery.

raid, *n.m.* raid; direct action; **raid financier,** asset stripping.

raider, *n.m.* raider/shark.

raison, *n.f.* **1. raison sociale,** name/style (of a firm, company); trade name/corporate name **2. travail payé à raison de 35 francs l'heure,** work paid at the rate of 35 francs an hour.

raisonnable, *a.* (*a*) reasonable; **prix raisonnable,** reasonable/fair/moderate price (b) **revenu raisonnable,** reasonable/adequate income.

rajustement, *n.m.* readjustment; **les syndicats réclament un rajustement des salaires,** the unions are demanding a readjustment of the wage structure/a wage increase in line with the cost of living.

rajuster, *v.tr.* **rajuster les salaires,** to re-adjust the wage structure; to bring wages into line with the cost of living.

ralenti, *n.m.* *Ind:* **travail au ralenti,** go-slow; **travailler au ralenti,** to go slow.

ralentir, *v.tr.* to slow down; **ralentir la production,** to slow down production.

ralentissement, *n.m.* slackening/slowing down; **ralentissement des affaires,** falling off of business; **ralentissement de la demande,** fall-off/slow-down in demand; **ralentissement de la production,** slowing down of production.

ramassage, *n.m.* takeover stock.

ramasse-monnaie, *n.m.* (*au guichet*) tray for change.

ramener, *v.tr.* **ramener le prix d'un article à ...,** to bring the price of an article down to ...; **ramener la semaine de 40 à 35 heures,** to reduce the working week from 40 to 35 hours.

rang, *n.m.* (a) **se mettre sur les rangs,** to come forward as a candidate; to apply for a job (b) **avoir/prendre (le) même rang que ...,** (*une personne, une dette, une hypothèque*) to rank equally with ...; (*une action, etc.*) to rank pari passu with ...; **actions de premier rang,** preference shares; **obligations de deuxième rang,** junior bonds (c) standing/rank/status; **d'un rang élevé,** high ranking.

rappel, *n.m.* **1.** payment of arrears **2.** (a) reminder (of account, etc.); **dernier rappel,** final reminder (b) **rappel de traitement,** back pay **3.** *Mkt:* (*à la radio*) mention (of advertiser's name)/*F:* plug.

rappeler, *v.tr.* **1.** *Corr:* **dans votre réponse rappeler a référence FK/FJ,** when re-plying quote ref(erence) FK/FJ; **prière de rappeler ce numéro,** (in reply) please quote this number **2.** *Tel:* to call back/to ring back.

rapport, *n.m.* **1.** yield/return/profit; **d'un bon rapport,** profitable/that brings in a good return/that pays well; **actions d'un bon rapport,** shares that yield a good return; **capital en rapport,** interest-bearing/productive capital; **immeuble/maison de rapport,** rented property which brings in income/revenue; **rapport d'un investissement,** return on an investment; **terre de bon rapport,** land yielding a good return **2.** *Adm:* *Jur:* account/report/statement; return (of expenses, etc.); survey; *Nau:* **rapport d'avaries,** damage report; **rapport collectif,** joint report; **rapport du commissaire aux comptes,** auditor's report; **rapport financier,** treasurer's report; **rapport de gestion (d'une société),** annual report (of a company); **rapport périodique/rapport d'avancement des travaux,** progress report; **rapport du président,** chairman's/president's report; **envoyer un rapport,** to send in a report; **faire/rédiger un rapport sur qch.,** to make/to draw up a report on sth.; **présenter/soumettre un rapport à qn (sur qch.),** to present/to submit a report to s.o. (on sth.) **3.** **avoir rapport à qch.,** to relate/to refer to sth. **4.** ratio/proportion; **rapport cours-bénéfice,** price-earnings ratio; **rapport profit sur ventes,** profit-volume ratio; **rapport qualité-prix,** quality-price ratio; value for money **5.** relations (between people); **avoir des rapports avec,** (i) to have dealings with s.o. (ii) to be in touch with s.o.; **avoir de bons rapports avec la filiale française,** to be on good terms with the French subsidiary; **mettre qn en rapport avec qn,** to bring s.o. into contact with s.o./to put s.o. in touch with s.o.; **rapports patrons--syndicats,** relations between the employers and the unions/union--employer relations.

rapporter, *v.tr.* to bring in/to yield/to bear/to produce; **placement qui rapporte 5%,** investment that yields/brings in/

bears 5%; **cela ne rapporte rien,** it doesn't pay; **affaire qui rapporte,** profitable/paying business; **la publicité rapporte,** it pays to advertise.

ratio, *n.m. Fin:* ratio; **ratio de capitalisation,** assets-to-equity ratio; **ratio de capital-travail,** capital-labour ratio; **ratio comptable,** accounting ratio; **ratio cours-bénéfices,** price-earnings ratio (P/E ratio); **ratio de distribution,** distribution ratio; **ratio d'endettement,** debt ratio; gearing; **ratio de fonds de roulement net,** acid-test ratio; **ratio d'intensité de capital,** capital-output ratio; **ratio de levier,** leverage; **ratio de liquidité,** liquid assets ratio; **ratio de rentabilité (nette),** (net) profit ratio.

rationalisation, *n.f. PolEc:* rationalizing/streamlining (of industry).

rationaliser, *v.tr. PolEc:* to rationalize/to streamline (industry).

rationnel, *a.* rational; **l'organisation rationnelle de l'industrie,** the rationalization/streamlining of industry.

rattrapage, *n.m. PolEc:* adjustment (of wages in relation to the cost of living, etc.).

rayer, *v.tr.* to strike out/to delete; (*sur un formulaire*) **rayer les mentions inutiles,** delete where inapplicable.

rayon, *n.m.* **1. rayon d'action d'une campagne publicitaire,** range of an advertising campaign; **rayon de livraison,** delivery area; **cette entreprise a étendu son rayon d'action,** this firm has extended its range of activities **2.** (*dans un magasin*) department; counter; **chef de rayon,** department manager; **magasin à rayons,** department store; **rayon de l'alimentation,** food hall/food department/food counter; **rayon des bagages,** luggage department; **rayon des soldes,** bargain counter/bargain basement; (*au supermarché*) **le cinquième rayon,** the non-food section.

rayonnage, *n.m.* shelving/shelves.

réaction, *n.f.* reaction; *StExch:* **vive ré-**

action du sterling sur le marché des changes, sharp reaction of sterling on the (foreign) exchange market.

réactique, *n.f.* business intelligence system.

réajustement, *n.m.* = **rajustement.**

réajuster, *v.tr.* = **rajuster.**

réalignement, *n.m.* **réalignement des taux de change,** realignment of exchange rates; **réalignement monétaire,** realignment of currencies.

réalisable, *a.* **1. projet réalisable,** workable plan **2.** *Fin:* realizable; available; **actif réalisable/valeurs réalisables,** current/liquid assets.

réalisation, *n.f.* **1.** realization (of plan, project, etc.); **réalisation des buts,** target achievement **2.** (*a*) *Fin: Bank:* realization; concluding (of bargain, transaction, etc.); **réalisation d'actions,** selling out of shares (*b*) **réalisation d'un bénéfice,** making a profit (*c*) **réalisation du stock,** clearance sale.

réaliser, *v.tr.* (*a*) to make/to realize (a profit) (*b*) *Fin: etc:* **réaliser des valeurs,** to realize/to sell out shares (*c*) **réaliser des économies,** to economize.

réapprovisionnement, *n.m.* restocking/reordering; **quantité économique de réapprovisionnement,** economic order quantity/economic lot size (ELS).

réapprovisionner, 1. *v.tr.* to reorder; to restock (shop) (**en,** with) **2.** *v.pr.* **se réapprovisionner,** to stock up again.

réassortiment, *n.m.* (*a*) restocking (*b*) new stock.

réassortir, *v.tr.* to restock (shop).

réassurance, *n.f.* reinsurance/reassurance; **courtier de réassurance,** reinsurance broker; **police de réassurance,** reinsurance policy.

réassurer, *v.tr.* to reinsure/to reassure.

réassureur, *n.m.* reinsurer.

rebaisser, *v.i.* **les prix ont remonté puis re-**

baissé, prices have gone up and then fallen again.

rebut, *n.m.* (*a*) waste/scrap; *Ind:* **pièces de rebut/les rebuts,** rejects (*b*) *Post:* **service des rebuts,** dead letter office.

recel, *n.m.* receiving of stolen goods.

recensement, *n.m. Adm:* (*i*) census (*ii*) inventory.

recentrage, *n.m.* **recentrage du marché,** recentring of the market.

récépissé, *n.m.* (acknowledgement of) receipt; *Bank: Fin:* **récépissé de dépôt,** deposit receipt; **récépissé de douane,** customs receipt; **récépissé d'entrepôt,** warehouse receipt; **récépissé postal,** postal receipt; *Fin:* **récépissé de souscription à des actions,** application receipt for shares.

récepteur, *n.m.* receiver; **récepteur de poche/récepteur de volume réduit,** radio-pager.

réception, *n.f.* **1.** (*a*) receipt (of letter, order, etc.); **accusé de réception,** acknowledgement (of receipt); **accuser réception de qch.,** to acknowledge receipt of sth.; **avis de réception,** advice of delivery (*b*) receipt/reception/taking delivery (of goods); **à la/dès réception de (votre envoi),** on receipt of (the goods forwarded); **payer à la réception,** to pay on receipt (*c*) *Ind:* acceptance/taking over (of equipment, machines, etc., from manufacturer) **2.** (*à l'hôtel, etc.*) reception (desk); **chef de la réception,** chief receptionist.

réceptionnaire, 1. *a.* receiving (agent, clerk) **2.** *n.m.f.* (*a*) receiver/consignee (of goods, shipment) (*b*) chief receptionist (in hotel).

réceptionner, *v.tr.* to check and sign for (goods on delivery); to take delivery of (parcel, etc.).

réceptionniste, *n.m.f.* receptionist.

réceptivité, *n.f.* **réceptivité des consommateurs,** consumer acceptance.

récession, *n.f. PolEc:* recession.

recette, *n.f.* **1.** receipts/returns/takings; **dépenses et recettes,** expenses and receipts; outgoings and incomings; *Fin:* expenditure and income; **recettes brutes,** gross takings/earnings; **recette nette,** net takings/earnings; **la recette d'une semaine,** a week's takings/the weekly takings; **recettes fiscales,** tax revenue **2.** (*a*) collection (of bills, by bank messenger, etc.); **faire la recette (des traites, etc.),** to collect money due/owing **3.** tax (collector's) office/(inland) revenue office.

receveur, -euse, *n.* **1.** receiver (of sth.); addressee (of telegram, etc.) **2.** *Adm:* **receveur des contributions,** tax collector/inland revenue officer; **receveur des douanes,** collector of customs; **receveur des Finances,** district collector (of taxes); **receveur des postes,** postmaster.

recevoir, *v.tr.* (*a*) to receive (letter, etc.); **bien reçu,** duly received; *Corr:* **nous avons bien reçu votre lettre,** thank you for your letter/we acknowledge receipt of your letter/we are in receipt of your letter; **recevez, Monsieur, l'assurance de mes sentiments distingués,** yours faithfully (*b*) *Book-k:* **effets à recevoir,** bills receivable; **intérêts à recevoir,** interest receivable/to come; accrued interest.

rechange[1], *n.m.* replacement; **matériel de rechange,** duplicate/standby equipment; **pièce de rechange,** spare part; *pl.* **rechanges,** spares/spare parts.

rechange[2], *n.m. Fin: Bank:* re-exchange (of a bill); redraft.

recherche, *n.f.* research; **recherche appliquée,** applied/industrial research; **recherche des besoins des consommateurs,** consumer research; **recherche opérationnelle,** operational research; **recherche de personne,** paging (service); **recherche de produits,** product research; **recherche scientifique,** scientific research; **service/centre de recherche,** research department/centre.

recherché, *a.* **article (très) recherché,** article in great demand; **article peu recherché,** article in limited demand.

recherche-développement, *n.f. Econ:* research and development.

réciprocité, *n.f.* **réciprocité (de concessions)**, reciprocity.

réciproque, *a.* **facilités de crédits réciproques**, swap (credit) facilities.

réclamation, *n.f.* **1.** complaint; **bureau/service des réclamations**, complaints office/department; **toutes réclamations devront être adressées à ...**, all complaints to be addressed to ...; **faire/déposer une réclamation**, to make a complaint/to lodge a complaint/to complain **2.** claim; **chef du service des réclamations**, claims manager; **formulaire de réclamation**, claim form; *Jur:* **réclamation en dommages-intérêts**, claim for damages; **réclamation d'indemnité**, claim for compensation; **déposer/faire une réclamation**, to make/to put in a claim.

réclame, *n.f.* (*a*) advertising; **en réclame**, on offer; **article (en) réclame**, special offer; *Mkt:* loss leader; **vente réclame**, bargain sale; **faire de la réclame**, to advertise (*b*) advertisement; **réclame lumineuse**, illuminated/neon sign.

réclamer, **1.** *v.i.* to complain/to lodge a complaint (**auprès de qn**, with s.o.) **2.** *v.tr.* (*a*) to claim (sth.); **réclamer des dommages-intérêts**, to claim damages; **dividende non réclamé**, unclaimed dividend (*b*) to claim (sth.) back; **réclamer son argent**, to ask for one's money back.

recommandataire, *n.m. & f.* (*pour une lettre de change*) referee in case of need.

recommandation, *n.f.* **1.** recommendation/recommending (of s.o., of hotel, etc.); **(lettre de) recommandation**, (*i*) letter of introduction (*ii*) (letter of) reference/testimonial **2.** *Post:* registration (of letter, parcel).

recommandé, *a.* (*a*) approved/recommended (hotel, product, etc.) (*b*) *Post:* registered (letter, parcel); **envoi en recommandé/***F: n.m.* **un recommandé**, registered letter/parcel.

recommander, *v.tr.* **1.** to recommend;

recommander un hôtel, to recommend a hotel **2.** *Post:* to register (letter, parcel).

reconduction, *n.f. Jur:* renewal (of hiring agreement, of lease, etc.)

reconduire, *v.tr.* to renew (hiring agreement, lease, etc.).

reconnaissance, *n.f.* (*a*) acknowledgement (of debt, etc.) (*b*) **reconnaissance de dettes**, note of hand/IOU (*c*) *Mkt:* **test de reconnaissance**, recognition test.

reconstitution, *n.f.* reconstitution/reconstruction (of a company, etc.).

reconversion, *n.f.* (*a*) **reconversion technique (de l'économie)**, adaptation to new (economic) techniques (*b*) redeployment (of workers).

record, *n.m.* record (production); maximum/peak (output, etc.); **année record**, peak year; **chiffre record**, record figure.

recoupement, *n.m.* cross-checking; **moyen de recoupement**, cross-reference.

recouponnement, *n.m. Fin:* renewal of coupons (of share certificate).

recouponner, *v.tr. Fin:* to renew the coupons (of share certificate).

recours, *n.m.* (*a*) recourse/resort; **recours à l'arbitrage**, appeal to arbitration; *Jur:* **droit de recours**, right of recourse/appeal; **se réserver le recours**, to reserve the right of recourse (*b*) **recours contre des tiers**, recourse against third parties; *Ins:* **s'assurer contre le recours des tiers**, to insure against a third-party claim.

recouvrable, *a.* recoverable (money, etc.); collectable (debt).

recouvrement, *n.m.* **1.** recovery/collection (of bill, debts, tax, etc.); **recouvrement de créances**, debt collection; **faire un recouvrement**, to recover/to collect a debt **2.** *pl.* outstanding debts; **recouvrements restant à faire en fin d'exercice**, (book) debts outstanding at the end of the financial year.

recouvrer, *v.tr.* to recover/to collect (debts, taxes, etc.); **créances à recouvrer,** outstanding debts (due to us).

recrutement, *n.m.* recruitment/recruiting (of personnel); **conseil en recrutement,** recruitment consultant.

recruter, *v.tr.* to recruit (staff).

rectificatif, 1. *a.* rectifying; *Book-k:* **écriture rectificative,** correcting entry; **facture rectificative,** amended invoice **2.** *n.m. Adm:* corrigendum (to circular, to payroll, etc.).

rectification, *n.f.* rectification; amendment/correction (of document, etc.); adjustment/correction (of account, prices, etc.).

rectifier, *v.tr.* to rectify; to amend/to correct (document, etc.); to adjust/to correct (account, prices).

reçu, *n.m.* (*a*) receipt; voucher; **reçu certifié,** accountable receipt (*b*) **au reçu de votre lettre,** on receipt of your letter.

recul, *n.m.* setback/downturn (in business); **les ventes ont subi un recul,** sales have suffered a setback.

récupérabilité, *n.f. Ind:* salvage value.

récupérable, *a. Ind:* **heures récupérables,** time to be made up.

récupération, *n.f.* (*a*) *Jur:* recuperation/recovery (of debt); **récupération du capital investi,** payback; **délai de récupération,** payback period (*b*) *Ind:* recovery (of waste products, etc.); salvage (*c*) recoupment (of losses).

récupérer, *v.tr.* **1.** to recover (debt, etc.) **2.** (*a*) *Ind: etc:* to recover (waste products); to salvage (*b*) to give a new job to/to find alternative employment for s.o. **3.** (*a*) to recoup (a loss) (*b*) to make up (lost time, etc.); **la journée chômée sera récupérée,** the lost day will be made up.

recyclage, *n.m. Ind: etc:* (*a*) retraining (of staff); **suivre un stage de recyclage,** to take a refresher course/to retrain (*b*) recycling/re-processing.

recycler, *v.tr.* **1.** (*a*) to retrain (staff) (*b*) to re-process/to recycle (paper, etc.) **2.** *v.pr.* **se recycler,** to retrain/to take a refresher course.

rédacteur, -trice, *n. Journ: Publ:* (*i*) editor (*ii*) sub-editor; **rédacteur en chef,** chief editor; **rédacteur publicitaire,** copywriter.

rédaction, *n.f.* **1.** *Journ: Publ:* (*a*) editorial staff (*b*) editorial offices **2.** drafting (of contract, deeds).

reddition, *n.f.* rendering (of account); *Jur:* **action en reddition de compte,** action for an account.

redéploiement, *n.m. Econ:* redeployment.

redéployer, *v.tr. Econ:* to redeploy.

redevable, *a.* **être redevable de qch. à qn,** to be accountable to s.o. for sth.; **redevable de l'impôt,** liable for tax.

redevance, *n.f.* (*a*) dues; tax; charges (*b*) rent; **redevance emphytéotique,** ground rent (*c*) royalty; **redevances d'auteur,** (author's) royalties; **redevance pétrolière,** oil royalty (*d*) fee; (*d'une télévision, etc.*) licence fee; **redevance téléphonique,** rental charge.

redevoir, *v.tr.* to owe a balance of (a sum on an account, etc.); **il me redoit cent francs,** he still owes me a hundred francs; **somme redue,** balance due/amount owed.

rédiger, *v.tr.* to draw up/to draft/to write (out) (agreement, invoice, letter, etc.); **rédiger la correspondance d'une maison,** to conduct the correspondence of a firm.

redressement, *n.m.* (*a*) **redressement économique,** economic recovery (*b*) adjustment (of account); *Book-k:* **écriture de redressement,** correcting entry; **redressement fiscal/redressement d'impôt,** back tax/tax adjustment.

redresser, 1. *v.tr.* to rectify (mistake); to

adjust (account) **2.** *v.pr.* (*une action, l'éco-nomie*) **se redresser,** to recover/to rally.

redresseur, *n.m.* **redresseur d'entreprise,** company doctor.

redû, *n.m.* balance due/amount owed.

réductible, *a.* reducible (amount, etc.).

réduction, *n.f.* (*a*) reduction/abatement (of amount, taxation, etc.); curtailment/restriction/cutting back (of expenditure); *Fin:* **réduction du capital social,** reduction of share capital; **réduction des coûts,** cost minimization; *Ind:* **réduction d'heures de travail,** cut in working hours; **réduction de personnel,** staff cutback; **réduction de salaires,** wage/salary cuts; **reductions d'impôts,** tax cuts (*b*) **réduction (de prix),** (price) reduction; **réductions sur la quantité,** concessions for quantity; bulk discount/discount on bulk (purchases, orders); **faire une réduction,** to make a reduction/to give a discount/to give a rebate.

réduire, *v.tr.* to reduce; *Fin:* **réduire le capital,** to write down the capital; **réduire ses dépenses,** to reduce/to curtail/to cut back on one's expenses; **réduire le prix d'un article,** to reduce/to lower/to bring down/to cut the price of an article; **réduire les stocks,** to run down stocks.

réduit, *a.* reduced (price, etc.); *Ins:* **assurance à prime réduite,** low-premium insurance; **billet à prix réduit/à tarif réduit,** cheap ticket/cheap rate/cheap fare; concessionary fare; **débouchés réduits,** restricted market.

réel, *a.* real; **coût réel,** real/actual cost; **revenu réel,** real income; **salaire nominal et salaire réel,** nominal wage rate and net earnings; **valeur réelle,** real value/actual value; *Cmptr:* **temps réel,** real time.

réembaucher, *v.tr.* to re-employ (s.o.).

réemploi, *n.m.* re-employment.

réemployer, *v.tr.* = **remployer.**

rééquilibrer, *v.tr.* **rééquilibrer le budget,** to rebalance the budget.

rééquipement, *n.m.* re-equipment.

rééquiper, *v.tr.* to re-equip.

réescompte, *n.m. Fin:* rediscount/new discount.

réescompter, *v.tr. Fin:* to rediscount; to discount (bill) again.

réévaluation, *n.f.* revaluation (of currency); new assessment/appraisal (of property, etc.); *Fin:* **réévaluation de l'actif (d'une entreprise),** revaluation of the assets (of a company).

réévaluer, *v.tr.* to revalue/to appraise again; to estimate again.

réexpédier, *v.tr.* (*a*) to forward/to send on/to redirect (a letter, a parcel, etc.) (*b*) to return (to sender).

réexpédition, *n.f.* (*a*) forwarding/sending on/redirecting (of a letter, a parcel, etc.) (*b*) returning (of letter, etc.).

réexportation, *n.f.* (*a*) re-exportation/re-exporting (*b*) re-export.

réexporté, *a.* **produits réexportés,** re-exports.

réexporter, *v.tr.* to re-export.

réfaction, *n.f.* allowance/reduction/rebate/drawback (*on goods not up to sample, for loss or damage in transport, etc.*).

référence, *n.f.* (*a*) reference; **indemnité fixée par référence au traitement,** compensation fixed according to salary (*b*) *Corr: etc:* reference (on letter, document, etc.); **N/Réf(érence),** our ref(erence); **V/Réf(érence),** your ref(erence); **adresser sous référence RL3U/référence à rappeler RL3U,** when replying please quote ref(erence) RL3U (*c*) sample; pattern (*d*) *pl.* **références,** (employee's) reference/testimonial; **avoir de bonnes références,** to have good references.

référencer, *v.tr.* to classify (sample, pattern) in a sample book.

refinancement, *n.m.* refinancing.

reflation, *n.f.* reflation (of the economy).

réforme, *n.f.* reform; **réforme monétaire,** monetary reform.

refuge, *n.m.* shelter; **valeur refuge,** safe investment.

refus, *n.m.* refusal; **refus d'acceptation,** refusal to accept/non-acceptance; **refus de paiement,** refusal to pay/non payment; **il a été condamné à une amende pour refus de paiement,** he was fined for non-payment.

refuser, *v.tr.* to refuse/to decline (sth.); to turn down (offer); **refuser de payer une traite,** to dishonour a bill.

régie, *n.f.* 1. (*a*) administration (of property, undertaking, etc.); **en régie,** (*i*) in the hands of trustees (*ii*) under State control; **mise sous régie d'une industrie,** bringing of an industry under State control; **régie du dépôt légal,** copyright department (*b*) **régie (directe),** State-owned company; public corporation; **la régie Renault,** the Renault Company; **la régie des tabacs** = State Tobacco Corporation 2. **régie des impôts indirects/des contributions indirectes,** excise (administration); **la Régie,** Customs and Excise.

régime, *n.m.* system/regime/regulations; **régime douanier,** customs regulations; **régime préférentiel,** customs preference/preferential rates of duty/preferential customs duties; **régime de retraite,** pension plan/scheme; **régime d'assurance vieillesse,** old age pension fund/plan.

égir, *v.tr.* to govern/to rule; **les prix sont régis par ...,** prices are governed by ...; **les conditions régissant votre compte,** the terms for the conduct of your account.

egistre, *n.m.* 1. register/record; **Registre de commerce** = trade register; Register of Companies; **registre de comptabilité,** account book; ledger; **registre d'un hôtel,** hotel register; **registre des salaires,** payroll; **inscrire/rapporter un article sur un registre,** to enter/to post an item in a register 2. *Cmptr:* register/counter.

ègle, *n.f.* (*a*) rule; **règles d'exploitation,** operating rules; **règles de sécurité,** safety regulations (*b*) **passeport en règle,** valid passport/passport in order; **reçu en règle,** formal receipt/receipt in due form; **tenir sa comptabilité en règle,** to keep one's accounts in order.

règlement, *n.m.* 1. (*a*) settlement (of account, etc.); payment (of bill, debt, etc.); **en règlement de ...,** in settlement of ...; **mode/lieu de règlement,** method/place of payment; **pour règlement de tout compte,** in full settlement; **règlement en espèces,** cash payment/cash settlement; **faire un règlement par chèque,** to pay by cheque; **règlement en nature,** settlement in kind (*b*) *StExch:* **jour du règlement,** settlement day/account day; (*à la Bourse de Paris*) **(marché du) règlement mensuel (RM),** forward market (*c*) *Jur:* **règlement à l'amiable,** out-of-court settlement; **règlement par arbitrage,** settlement by arbitration; **règlement judiciaire,** legal settlement; **être en règlement judiciaire,** to be in the hands of the receiver; **se mettre en règlement judiciaire,** to go into receivership; to call in the receiver 2. *pl.* regulations; **les règlements de la douane,** (the) customs regulations; **règlements intérieurs,** internal regulations (of a company, etc.); by(e)-laws.

réglementaire, *a.* statutory; prescribed.

réglementation, *n.f.* 1. regulating/regulation; **réglementation des changes,** exchange control; **réglementation des prix,** price control 2. regulations; rules; **la réglementation du travail,** labour regulations/regulations concerning the employment of labour.

réglementer, *v.tr.* to regulate; to make rules for (sth.); **industries réglementées,** regulated industries; **réglementer les prix,** to control prices.

régler, 1. *v.tr.* to settle (account, deal, debt, etc.); to pay (bill, invoice, supplier, shopkeeper, etc.); **régler sa dépense,** to restrict one's expenses; **régler un sinistre,** to settle a claim 2. *v.i.* **régler par chèque,** to pay by cheque.

régression, *n.f.* decline/downturn (in business, etc.); drop (in sales, etc.); **analyse de régression,** regression analysis.

regrèvement, *n.m.* tax increase.

régularisation, *n.f.* regularizing; *Fin:* equalization (of dividends); *Book-k:* adjustment; **écriture de régularisation,** adjusting entry; *EEC:* **fonds de régularisation,** equalization fund.

régulariser, *v.tr.* to regularize; to put (document, etc.) into proper order; to equalize (dividends, etc.).

régulateur, *a.* regulating (force, mechanism); *PolEc:* **stocks régulateurs,** buffer stocks.

régulation, *n.f.* regulation/control; *Ind:* **régulation d'un procédé,** process control.

réhabilitation, *n.f.* (*d'un failli*) discharge in bankruptcy.

réhabiliter, *v.tr.* to discharge (a bankrupt).

réimportation, *n.f.* (*a*) reimportation/reimporting (*b*) reimport.

réimporter, *v.tr.* to reimport.

réinscription, *n.f.* re-entry/re-entering; re-registering/re-registration.

réinscrire, *v.tr.* to re-enter; to re-register.

réintégration, *n.f.* reinstatement (of civil servant, etc.).

réintégrer, *v.tr.* to reintegrate; to reinstate; **réintégrer qn (dans ses fonctions),** to reinstate s.o.; **réintégrer des employés,** to take employees on again; to re-engage/to reinstate employees.

réinvestir, *v.tr.* to reinvest; **réinvestir les bénéfices,** to plough back the profits; **bénéfices réinvestis,** ploughback.

rejet, *n.m.* rejection (of proposal, etc.); *Jur:* setting aside (of claim, etc.); disallowance (of expenses).

rejeter, *v.tr.* to reject/to refuse (sth.); **rejeter une dépense,** to disallow an expense;

rejeter une offre, to reject/to turn down an offer.

relais, *n.m.* (*a*) *Ind:* relay/shift; **travail par relais,** shift work (*b*) *Fin:* **crédit-relais,** bridge financing (*c*) **relais d'autoroute,** motorway services.

relance, *n.f.* (*a*) boost; upturn (in business); **relance économique,** economic revival (*b*) *Ind: etc:* follow-up (of work in hand); following up (of customer) (*c*) *Mkt:* follow-up (system); **lettre de relance,** reminder (letter)/follow-up letter.

relancer, *v.tr.* to revive/to boost; **relancer l'économie,** to revive/to boost/to reflate the economy.

relation, *n.f.* (*a*) relation; connection; **relations d'affaires,** business relations; **être en relations d'affaires avec qn,** to have business relations with s.o./to deal with s.o. (*b*) **relations industrielles/syndicales,** industrial relations; **relations ouvrières/du travail,** labour relations (*c*) **relations publiques,** public relations; **chef du service des relations avec le public,** public relations officer.

relevé, *n.m.* abstract/summary/statement; **relevé de caisse,** cash statement; **relevé de compte(s),** statement (of account); **relevé de compte bancaire,** bank statement; **relevé des dépenses,** statement of expenditure; **relevé des dettes actives et passives,** statement of assets and liabilities; **relevé de fin de mois,** end-of-the-month statement; **relevé remis,** account tendered.

relèvement, *n.m.* (*a*) recovery/revival (of business) (*b*) increase (in wages); raising (of tariff, tax, etc.); **relèvement du taux officiel de l'escompte,** raising of/rise in the minimum lending rate.

relever, 1. *v.tr.* (*a*) **relever (les salaires, les prix),** to raise/to increase (wages, prices); **relever le cours du franc,** to raise the value of the franc (*b*) **relever un compte,** to make out a statement of account (*c*) to revive (an industry) (*d*) **relever le compteur (du gaz),** to read the (gas) meter **2.** *v.pr.* **se relever,** to pick up; **les affaires se**

relèvent, business is looking up; **les cours se relèvent,** prices are recovering.

reliquat, *n.m.* remainder; unexpended balance; **reliquat d'un compte,** balance of an account.

remballage, *n.m.* (*a*) repacking (of goods) (*b*) new packaging.

remballer, *v.tr.* to repack; to pack (goods) (up) again.

remboursable, *a.* (re)payable/reimbursable/refundable; redeemable (annuity, etc.); **remboursable sur une période de 25 ans,** repayable over (a period of) 25 years.

remboursement, *n.m.* reimbursement/repayment/refund; payout; redeeming/redemption (of annuity, etc.); reduction (of debt); **délai de remboursement,** payback period; **livraison contre remboursement,** cash on delivery/*also NAm:* collect on delivery/COD; *Cust:* **remboursement des droits de douane,** drawback; **remboursement d'un effet,** retirement of a bill; **remboursement d'un emprunt,** repayment of a loan.

rembourser, *v.tr.* (*a*) to repay/to refund (expenses, etc.); to redeem/to pay off (annuity, bond); **rembourser un effet,** to retire a bill; **rembourser un emprunt,** to pay off/to repay a loan (*b*) **rembourser qn,** to reimburse/to repay s.o.; **on m'a remboursé,** I got my money back; **frais remboursés (par un employeur),** expenses paid (by an employer).

réméré, *n.m. Jur:* **faculté de réméré,** option of repurchase; **vente à réméré,** sale subject to right (of vendor) to repurchase/sale with option of repurchase.

remettant, *n.m. Bank:* person who pays money/cheque into a current account.

remettre, 1. *v.tr.* **remettre un chèque à l'encaissement,** to cash a cheque; **remettre sa démission,** to hand in one's notice **2.** to remit (debt) **3.** to postpone/to adjourn (meeting); to postpone/to put off (decision); to put off/to put back (appointment, delivery date, etc.).

remise, *n.f.* **1.** delivery (of letter, parcel, etc.); remitting (of money); **payable contre remise du coupon,** payable on presentation of the coupon **2.** (*a*) remission (of debt, tax, etc.); **faire remise d'une dette,** to remit/to cancel a debt (*b*) adjournment/postponement (of meeting, etc.) **3.** (*a*) remittance; **faire une remise (de fonds) à qn,** to send s.o. a remittance/to remit a sum to s.o. (*b*) commission (*paid to agent*) (*c*) discount/rebate; **remise d'usage,** trade discount; **remise sur la quantité,** discount on bulk purchases/orders; **taux de remise,** trade terms; trade discount (rate); **remise de 10%,** discount of 10%/10% off; **faire/consentir/accorder une remise sur un article,** to allow a discount/to make a reduction on an article.

remisier, *n.m. StExch:* intermediate broker/half-commission man.

remonter, 1. *v.i.* **les valeurs pétrolières ont remonté,** oil shares have gone up again **2.** *v.tr.* **remonter un magasin,** to restock a shop.

remplacement, *n.m.* (*a*) replacement; **dactylo qui fait des remplacements,** temporary (typist)/temp (*b*) **coût de remplacement,** replacement cost; **débouchés/marchés de remplacement,** replacement/alternative markets; **produit de remplacement,** substitute product; *Ins:* **valeur de remplacement,** replacement value (*of lost or damaged property*).

remplacer, *v.tr.* to replace; to take the place of (s.o., sth.); to deputize for (s.o.).

remplir, *v.tr.* (*a*) to fill in/*NAm:* to fill out/to complete (a form, a questionnaire, etc.) (*b*) to comply with/to fulfil (a condition, an obligation).

remploi, *n.m. Jur:* reinvestment (of the proceeds of a sale of property, etc.).

remployer, *v.tr.* (*a*) to re-employ (s.o.) (*b*) to re-use (sth)/to make use of (sth.) again (*c*) *Jur:* to reinvest/to re-use (money, funds).

remue-méninges, *n.m. Mkt:* brainstorming.

rémunérateur, _a._ remunerative (work, price, investment, etc.); lucrative/profitable; **peu rémunérateur,** not very profitable/unprofitable; **ce travail n'est pas rémunérateur,** this work doesn't pay.

rémunération, _n.f._ (_a_) remuneration/ payment (**de,** of); **en rémunération de vos services,** as payment for your services; in consideration of your services; **rémunération au temps passé,** time rate; **rémunération du capital,** return on capital (_b_) salary; **rémunération de départ,** starting salary.

rémunérer, _v.tr._ (_a_) to pay for (services) (_b_) to pay (wages); **employés rémunérés,** paid/salaried employees.

rencaissement, _n.m._ receiving back (of money).

rencaisser, _v.tr._ to receive back (money); to have (money) refunded.

renchérir, 1. _v.tr._ to make (sth.) dearer/to raise the price of (sth.) **2.** _v.i._ (_a_) (_produits, main-d'œuvre_) to get dearer; to increase/to rise in price; **tout renchérit,** everything is going up (in price) (_b_) **renchérir sur qn,** to outbid s.o.

renchérissement, _n.m._ rise/advance/ increase in price.

rendement, _n.m._ (_a_) _Fin: etc:_ yield/return/ profit (on transaction); earnings (of shares); _NAm:_ payoff; **actions à gros rendement,** shares that bear/yield high interest; **(taux de) rendement,** current yield/ flat yield; **rendement annuel,** annual value; **rendement brut,** gross yield/return; **rendement constant,** fixed yield; **rendement des investissements,** return on investment; **rendement d'une obligation,** bond yield; **taux de rendement,** rate of return; _PolEc:_ **loi du rendement non-proportionnel,** law of diminishing returns (_b_) output (of worker); output/production (of factory, works, etc.); yield; throughput/ _NAm:_ thruput (of computer); **augmentation de rendement,** rise in production; **diminution de rendement,** fall in output; **rendement d'ensemble/global/total,**

aggregate output; **rendement à l'heure/ rendement horaire,** output per hour; **rendement individuel,** output per person; **rendement journalier moyen,** average daily output; **rendement optimal/ maximum,** maximum output; **rendement minimum,** minimum output; **travailler à plein rendement,** to work to full capacity (_c_) (_d'une machine_) efficiency; **rendement économique,** commercial efficiency; **rendement effectif,** performance rating; **rendement global,** overall efficiency.

rendez-vous, _n.m.inv._ appointment; **rendez-vous d'affaires,** business appointment; **fixer un rendez-vous/donner rendez-vous (à qn),** to make/to fix an appointment (with s.o.).

rendre, _v.tr._ **1.** (_a_) to give back/to return; **rendre de l'argent,** to repay/to pay back money; **rendre un dépôt,** to return a deposit; **rendre la monnaie d'un billet de cent francs,** to give change for a hundred franc note; **rendre un article,** to return an article (to a shop) (_b_) (_terre_) to yield; (_impôts, etc._) to produce/to yield (so much); **placement qui rend 10%,** investment that brings in 10% **2.** to convey/to deliver; **rendre des marchandises à destination,** to deliver goods (to their destination); **rendu à domicile,** delivered to your door; **rendu franco à bord,** (delivered) free on board/f.o.b.; **prix rendu,** delivery price.

rendu, _n.m._ returned article; return; **faire un rendu,** to return an article; to exchange an article.

renflouer, _v.tr._ **renflouer une entreprise,** to set a business on its feet again/to refloat a business; _F:_ **renflouer qn,** to keep s.o. afloat (financially).

renouvelable, _a._ renewable.

renouveler, _v.tr._ (_a_) **renouveler son personnel,** to renew one's staff (_b_) **renouveler une commande,** to repeat an order; **commandes renouvelées,** repeat orders; **renouveler son passeport,** to renew one's passport (_c_) _Fin: Jur:_ to renew/to extend (bill, lease, contract); **renouveler un crédit,** to extend a credit.

renouvellement, *n.m.* (*a*) restocking/reordering (of goods); *Ind:* replacement (of equipment); **renouvellement du personnel,** staff turnover; **taux de renouvellement,** entry and exit (of companies) (*b*) (*d'un bail, d'un contrat*) renewing/renewal; *Ins:* **prime de renouvellement,** renewal premium; **renouvellement d'un crédit,** extension of a credit.

renseignement, *n.m.* (*a*) (piece of) information; *Tel: etc:* **renseignements,** enquiries/inquiries; **bureau de renseignements,** enquiry office/information (bureau); **demande de renseignements,** enquiry/request for information; **tous les renseignements utiles,** all the necessary information; **pour de plus amples renseignements, s'adresser à/écrire à ...,** for further information/further particulars/further details, apply to ...; **donner des renseignements (sur qch.),** to give information/particulars (on, about sth.); **prendre des renseignements sur qch.,** to make enquiries about sth.; **je vous envoie à titre de renseignement ...,** I am sending you for your information/by way of information ... (*b*) **renseignements (techniques),** data; **renseignements statistiques,** statistical data.

enseigner, 1. *v.tr.* to inform/to give (some) information **2.** *v.pr.* **se renseigner sur qch.,** to get information about sth./to make enquiries about sth.; to enquire/to ask/to find out about sth.

entabilisation, *n.f.* making sth. pay/making sth. show a profit.

entabiliser, *v.tr.* to make (sth.) pay/to make (sth.) show a profit; **l'industrie exige de gros investissements longs à rentabiliser,** industry requires heavy investment which takes a long time to show a profit.

entabilité, *n.f.* profitability/profit-earning capacity; pay-off (of project); **limite de rentabilité,** limit of profitability; **rentabilité des capitaux investis/rentabilité d'un investissement,** return on capital invested/return on an investment; **rentabilité des ventes,** return on sales; **seuil de rentabilité,** break-even point; *PolEc:* **taux de rentabilité,** rate of return/rate of profitability.

rentable, *a.* profitable; profit-earning; paying (proposition); **ce n'est pas rentable,** it isn't profitable/it doesn't pay; **affaire/marché rentable,** profitable deal; economic proposition; **loyer rentable/peu rentable,** economic/uneconomic rent; **société qui devient rentable,** company that moves into profit.

rente, *n.f.* **1. rente foncière,** ground rent **2.** *usu. pl.* (unearned) income; **avoir cent mille francs de rente(s),** to have a private income of a hundred thousand francs; **vivre de ses rentes,** to live on one's private income **3.** annuity/pension/allowance; **rente à paiement différé,** deferred annuity; **rente à terme,** terminable annuity; **rente viagère,** life annuity/life interest **4. rente(s) sur l'État,** Government stock(s)/funds/bonds; **rentes, actions et obligations** = stock and shares; **rentes amortissables,** redeemable stock/loans; **rentes perpétuelles,** perpetual stock/loans.

rentier, -ière, *n.* (*a*) *Fin:* stockholder/shareholder (*esp.* holder of Government stocks) (*b*) **rentier viager,** annuitant (*c*) person of independent means/who lives on unearned income; *PolEc:* rentier.

renting, *n.m.* rental/hire/renting (of machines, material, etc.); plant hire.

rentrée, *n.f.* (*a*) taking in/receipt/encashment (of money); income; revenue (of taxes); **faire des rentrées d'argent,** to get money in; **opérer une rentrée,** to collect a sum of money (*b*) *pl. Bank:* bills and cheques paid in.

rentrer, *v.i.* **rentrer dans ses frais,** (*i*) to get one's money back (*ii*) to get one's expenses (paid).

renvoi, *n.m.* **1.** sending back/return(ing) (of goods, letter, etc.) **2.** dismissal; **menace de renvoi,** threat of dismissal; **renvoi d'un**

employé, sacking/dismissal of an employee **3.** putting off/postponement; adjournment **4.** (*a*) referring/reference (of a project, etc. to higher, competent authority) (*b*) **numéro de renvoi,** reference number.

renvoyer, *v.tr.* **1.** to return/to send back (goods, letter, etc.) **2.** to dismiss/to sack (employee) **3.** to put off/to postpone/to adjourn (a matter, decision, meeting) **4.** **renvoyer qch. à qn,** to refer sth. to s.o.

réorganisation, *n.f.* reorganization/reorganizing; redeployment (of staff, resources, etc.).

réorganiser, *v.tr.* to reorganize; to redeploy (staff, resources, etc.).

réouverture, *n.f.* reopening (of a market, a store, etc.); resumption (of negotiations, trading).

réparation, *n.f.* **1.** repair/repairing (of equipment, etc.); **réparation d'entretien,** maintenance; **être en réparation,** to be under repair **2.** *Jur:* **réparation civile,** compensation; **réparation de dommages,** damages; **réparation légale,** legal redress.

réparer, *v.tr.* **réparer ses pertes,** to make good one's losses.

répartir, *v.tr.* (*a*) to distribute/to divide/to share out (**entre,** among); **répartir un dividende,** to distribute a dividend; **versements répartis sur plusieurs années,** payments spread over several years (*b*) to apportion/to assess; *Fin:* **répartir des actions,** to allot/to allocate shares; **répartir des impôts,** to assess taxes.

répartiteur, *n.m. Adm:* **(commissaire) répartiteur,** tax assessor; *Ins:* **répartiteur d'avaries,** average/loss adjuster.

répartition, *n.f.* (*a*) distribution (of wealth, etc.) (*b*) dividing up/sharing out/allocation (of expenses, responsibilities, work, etc.); distribution/appropriation (of profit); distribution/allotment (of functions); *Jur:* **répartition entre créanciers,** distribution among creditors (*c*) (*distribution pro rata*) apportionment/

allocation (of expenses, losses, rights, liabilities, etc.); assessment (of taxes); *Book-k:* appointment (of costs, expenses, to different accounts); **répartition proportionnelle des pertes entre les commanditaires,** (pro rata) apportionment of losses among the sleeping partners (*d*) *Fin:* allotment (of shares); **(lettre d')avis de répartition,** letter of allotment; **libération/versement intégral à la répartition,** payment in full on allotment (*e*) dividend/distribution; **première répartition,** first dividend/distribution; **nouvelle répartition,** second dividend/distribution; **dernière répartition,** final dividend/distribution.

répercuter, *v.tr.* **la taxe sera répercutée/se répercutera sur les consommateurs,** the tax will be passed on to the consumers.

répertoire, *n.m.* index/table/list/catalogue; **répertoire d'adresses,** (*i*) directory (*ii*) address book; **répertoire maritime,** shipping directory.

répertorier, *v.tr.* (*a*) to index (file, etc.) (*b*) to index (item); to enter (item) in an index.

répéter, *v.tr.* to repeat (an order, etc.).

répétition, *n.f. Jur:* claiming back; **répétition d'indu,** recovery of payment made in error.

repli, *n.m. StExch:* fall/drop (in the value of shares).

replier (se), *v.pr. Fin: StExch:* to fall back.

répondant, -ante *n.* (*a*) *Jur:* surety security/guarantor/warrantor (*b*) referee reference.

répondre, *v.i.* **1.** to reply/to answer; **répondre à une lettre,** to reply to a letter/to answer a letter **2.** *Fin:* **répondre à une prime,** to declare an option.

réponse, *n.f.* **1.** answer/reply; **en réponse à votre lettre du 20 ct,** in reply to your letter/further to your letter of the 20th inst.; *Post:* **réponse payée,** reply paid 2

Fin: **réponse des primes,** declaration of options.

report, *n.m.* **1.** *Book-k:* (*au bas d'une page*) (balance) carried forward; (*au haut d'une page*) (balance) brought forward; **report des exercices antérieurs,** amount brought in; **report à nouveau,** amount carried forward/balance to next account; **report déficitaire sur les exercises précédents/sur les exercises ultérieurs,** loss carry back/loss carry forward (*c*) posting (*of journal entries to the ledger accounts*) **2.** *StExch:* (*a*) contango(ing)/continuation; **titres en report,** stock taken in/stock carried over; **prendre des actions en report,** to take in stock (*b*) **(taux de) report,** contango (rate)/continuation rate.

eporté, *n.m.* *StExch:* giver (of stock); payer (of contango).

eporter, *v.tr.* **1.** *Book-k:* (*a*) to carry forward; to bring forward; to carry over (balance, total) (*b*) to enter up/to transfer (sum to ledger accounts); **solde à reporter,** balance (to be) carried forward **2.** *StExch:* to continue/to contango; to carry over; **(faire) reporter des titres,** to take in/to carry stock; **(faire) reporter un emprunteur,** to take in stock for a borrower; **se faire reporter,** to be carried over/to lend stock.

eporteur, *n.m.* *StExch:* taker (of stock); receiver (of contango).

epos, *n.m.* *Fin:* **valeurs de tout repos,** safe investments; gilt-edged securities; blue chips.

eprendre, 1. *v.tr.* (*a*) to take back; **reprendre un employé,** to take back/to re-engage an employee; **reprendre des invendus,** to take back unsold goods; **nous reprendrons les invendus,** the goods are on sale or return (*b*) **reprendre le travail,** to resume work **2.** *v.i.* **les affaires reprennent,** business is improving/is looking up.

epreneur, *n.m.* buyer of company in financial difficulties.

eprésentant, -ante, *n.* **représentant (de commerce),** (*i*) agent (*ii*) (sales) represent-

ative/(sales) rep/(commercial) traveller; **représentant dûment accrédité,** duly authorized representative; **représentant exclusif,** sole agent; **représentant à cartes multiples/représentant multicarte,** representative/rep for several firms; general agent.

représentation, *n.f.* **1.** agency; **représentation exclusive d'une maison,** sole agency for a firm; **avoir la représentation exclusive de ...,** to be sole agents for ... **2. frais de représentation,** entertainment allowance/expenses.

représenter, *v.tr.* (*a*) to represent/to act for (s.o.); **nous représentons la maison X et Cie,** we represent/we are agents for Messrs X & Co. (*b*) to correspond to/to account for; **ceci représente 10% du budget,** this accounts for 10% of the budget.

repris, *a.* **emballage non repris,** non-returnable packing.

reprise, *n.f.* **1.** (*a*) **marchandises en dépôt avec reprise des invendus,** goods on sale or return; **reprise (locative)** = fixtures and fittings (f & f); **reprise d'une voiture,** trade-in (allowance) on a car (*b*) (car, etc., taken in) part exchange (*c*) **reprise d'entreprise par les/ses salarés (RES),** leveraged management buyout (LMBO) **2.** (*a*) resumption (of negotiations, etc.); **reprise de travail,** return to work (after absence); **reprise des travaux,** resumption of work (*b*) **reprise économique/reprise des affaires,** recovery/revival of business; upturn/upswing; **reprise des cours,** recovery of prices; **mouvement de reprise,** upward movement.

reproduction, *n.f.* reproduction/reproducing; duplicating (of documents, etc.).

reproduire, *v.tr.* (*a*) to reproduce/to duplicate/to copy (document, etc.) (*b*) **modèle reproduit en grande série,** mass-produced model.

requérant, -ante *a. & n. Jur:* plaintiff; **partie requérante,** claimant.

requin, *n.m.* **requin (de la finance),** shark/raider.

rescindable, *a.* that may be annulled/cancelled.

rescinder, *v.tr. Jur:* to rescind/to annul/to cancel/to void (contract).

rescision, *n.f. Jur:* rescission/annulment/voiding (of contract).

réseau, *n.m.* network; **réseau de distribution,** distribution network; **réseau téléphonique,** telephone system/network; **réseau de vente/réseau commercial,** sales network.

réservation, *n.f.* (hotel, plane, etc.) reservation; **bureau de réservation,** booking office.

réserve, *n.f.* 1. reservation; *Jur:* **sous toutes réserves,** without prejudice; **sous réserve de ...,** subject to ...; **sous réserve de la signature du contrat,** subject to contract; **acceptation sous/sans réserve,** qualified/unconditional acceptance 2. (*a*) reserve (of provisions, etc.); stock/reserve; **avoir qch. en réserve,** to have sth. in stock/in reserve (*b*) storeroom/warehouse (*c*) *Fin:* reserve (of money, etc.); **réserve d'achat,** = credit limit; **réserves bancaires,** bank reserves; **réserve pour créances douteuses,** bad debts reserve; **réserve latente/occulte,** hidden/secret reserve; **réserve légale,** legal reserve; **réserve liquide,** liquid assets; **réserves non distribuées,** capital reserves; **réserves obligataires,** federal fund; **réserve de prévoyance,** contingency reserve; **réserve statutaire,** statutory reserve/reserve provided for by the articles; **réserve visible,** visible reserve; **fonds de réserve,** reserve fund; **incorporation de réserves,** capitalization of reserves; **mettre de l'argent en réserve,** to put/to set money aside; **puiser dans les réserves,** to draw on the reserves.

réserver, *v.tr.* (*a*) to reserve/to book (hotel room, table in restaurant, etc.); to set aside (goods for a customer, etc.); *Trans:* **réserver une place,** to reserve a seat; *Publ:* **tous droits (de reproduction) réservés,** all rights reserved (*b*) to set aside/to earmark (money for a purpose).

résiliable, *a.* that may be annulled/cancelled.

résiliation, *n.f.* cancelling/cancellation/annulling/annulment/termination (of contract, lease, etc.).

résilier, *v.tr.* to annul/to cancel/to terminate/to void (contract, etc.).

résistance, *n.f. Mkt:* **résistance des consommateurs,** consumer resistance.

résoluble, *a.* annullable/cancellable/terminable/voidable (contract).

résolution, *n.f.* 1. termination/cancellation/annulment (of contract, owing to breach, etc.); cancelling (of sale); **action en résolution,** action for rescission of contract 2. **prendre/adopter une résolution,** to pass/to carry/to adopt a resolution; **résolution extraordinaire,** special resolution.

résolutoire, *a. Jur:* **clause résolutoire,** avoidance clause; **condition résolutoire,** condition of avoidance (in contract).

résorber, *v.tr.* to absorb (deficit, surplus), to reduce/to bring down (inflation, unemployment).

résoudre, *v.tr.* to annul/to cancel/to void/to terminate/to rescind (contract, etc.).

respecter, *v.tr.* to respect; **respecter une clause dans un contrat,** to respect/to comply with a clause in a contract.

responsabilité, *n.f.* responsibility/liability (**de,** for); *Jur:* **responsabilité civile,** third party liability/civil liability; **responsabilité de l'employeur,** employer liability; **responsabilité hiérarchique,** linear responsibility; **société à responsabilité limitée (SARL),** limited (liability) company; *NAm:* incorporated (Inc) company.

responsable, 1. *a.* responsible/accountable/answerable; **être responsable de qch.,** to be responsible for sth.; **être responsable du dommage,** to be liable for the damage 2. *n.m.f.* (*a*) person responsible (**de,** for (*b*) person in charge/person authorized to take decisions; **responsable de budget,** account manager/executive; **responsable des relations publiques,** public relations officer (PRO); **responsable commercial,** (*i*) business manager (*ii*) marketing manager (*iii*) sales manager; **responsable syndical,** union official.

esserrement, *n.m.* (*a*) *PolEc:* **resserrement du crédit,** credit squeeze (*b*) tightness/scarcity (of money).

essort, *n.m.* (*i*) jurisdiction (*ii*) competence (of a court, etc.).

essources, *n.f.pl.* (*a*) resources/means; **affectation/allocation des ressources,** resource allocation; **ressources du budget,** budgetary resources; **ressources de l'État,** government resources; **ressources financières,** financial resources; **ressources personnelles,** private means (*b*) **ressources naturelles (d'un pays),** natural resources (of a country).

estaurant, *n.m.* restaurant; **restaurant d'entreprise,** staff dining room/canteen; **restaurant libre-service,** self-service restaurant.

staurateur, -trice, *n.* restaurant owner/restaurateur; caterer.

stauration, *n.f.* catering; **restauration rapide,** fast-food; **travailler dans la restauration,** to work in catering/in the restaurant business.

ste, *n.m.* rest/remainder; **payer le reste par versements,** to pay the balance in instalments/*NAm:* installments.

stituable, *a.* returnable/repayable.

stitution, *n.f.* restitution/refund; *Cust:* **restitution des droits d'entrée,** drawback; *EEC:* **restitution à l'exportation,** export restitution/refund; **restitution d'impôts,** return of taxes; *Jur:* **restitution d'indu,** return of payment made in error.

streignant, *a.* restricting (clause, etc.).

streindre, *v.tr.* to restrict/to curb; **restreindre les dépenses,** to restrict/to cut down expenses; **restreindre la production,** to restrict/to cut back production.

restreint, *a.* restricted/limited; **crédit restreint,** restricted credit; **moyens restreints,** limited means.

restrictif, *a.* restrictive (practice); limitative (clause in contract); **endossement restrictif,** restrictive endorsement.

restriction, *n.f.* restriction; limitation (of authority); **restriction de concurrence,** trade restraint; **restriction du crédit,** credit squeeze/restrictions; **restrictions sur les importations,** import restrictions; **restrictions salariales,** wage restraint; *Fin:* **restrictions de transfert,** transfer restrictions.

restructuration, *n.f.* restructuring; reorganizing the structure (of an industry, etc.).

restructurer, *v.tr.* to restructure; to reorganize the structure (of an industry, etc.).

résultat, *n.m.* result/outcome; **résultat de l'exercice,** statement of income/income statement; **résultat économique,** economic profit; **résultats financiers/résultat d'exploitation,** trading/company results/ *NAm:* operating result; **résultat brut,** gross result/income; **résultat net,** net result/income; **résultat net consolidé,** consolidated statement of net income.

résumé, *n.m.* summary; synopsis.

rétablir, *v.tr.* to re-establish/to restore; **rétablir un budget déficitaire,** to balance an adverse budget.

retard, *n.m.* delay; **commandes en retard,** back orders; **compte en retard,** account outstanding/overdue; **paiement en retard,** late payment/payment overdue; **être en retard pour payer son loyer,** to let one's rent fall into arrears; **retard de livraison,** delay in delivery.

retarder, *v.tr.* to delay; **retarder un paiement,** to defer payment.

retenir, *v.tr.* (*a*) **retenir une somme sur le**

salaire de qn, to keep back/to deduct a sum from s.o.'s salary (*b*) to make a reservation; to reserve/to book (a seat, a place); **retenir (une chambre d'hôtel, une table au restaurant),** to reserve/to book (a hotel room, a table in a restaurant) (*c*) **retenir une offre,** to accept an offer.

rétention, *n.f. Jur:* reservation; retaining (of pledge); **droit de rétention de marchandises,** (possessory) lien on goods.

retenue, *n.f.* (*sur un salaire*) deduction/stoppage; **faire une retenue de 5% sur les salaires,** to stop/to deduct/to withold 5% from the wages; *Adm:* **retenue à la source** = pay as you earn/P.A.Y.E./ *NAm:* pay as you go; (*sur les investissements*); withholding tax; **traitement soumis à retenue,** salary from which a sum is withheld (for pension, etc.).

retirer, 1. *v.tr.* (*a*) **retirer de l'argent de la banque,** to withdraw/to take out (some) money from the bank; **retirer des marchandises de la douane,** to take goods out of bond; to clear goods (*b*) **retirer un profit de qch.,** to derive/to get a profit from sth. (*c*) **retirer un effet,** to retire/to withdraw/to take up a bill 2. *v.pr.* **se retirer,** to retire; **se retirer des affaires,** to retire from business.

retombées, *n.f.pl.* spin-off effects; **la grève aura des retombées sur les prix,** the strike will have repercussions on prices.

retour, *n.m.* 1. (*a*) *Trans:* **(billet de) retour/ (billet d')aller (et) retour,** return (ticket)/ *NAm:* round-trip (ticket); **prix/tarif d'aller (et) retour,** return fare; **voyage (d')aller et retour,** return journey; **prendre un aller (et) retour,** to buy a return ticket (*b*) *Post:* **par retour (du courrier),** by return (of post)/*NAm:* by return mail; **retour à l'expéditeur,** return to sender (*c*) **cargaison/chargement/fret de retour,** return cargo/freight; homeward cargo/ freight; **retour en charge,** loaded return; **retour à vide,** empty return (*d*) **effet de retour,** feed-back effect 2. (*a*) return (of goods, of dishonoured bill, etc.); **marchandises de retour/***F:* retours, re-

turned goods/returns; **vendu avec faculté de retour,** on sale or return (*b*) dishonoured bill/bill returned dishonoured 3. **en retour d'une somme de 50 francs,** in consideration of a sum of 50 francs.

retourner, *v.tr. Fin:* **retourner un effet impayé,** to return a bill dishonoured *Post:* **retourner (une lettre, un paquet),** to return/to send back (a letter, a parcel) **marchandises retournées,** returned goods/ returns; **prière de nous retourner l'accusé de réception ci-joint, revêtu de votre signature,** please sign and return the enclosed acknowledgment.

retrait, *n.m.* (*a*) withdrawal (of order bill, licence, etc.); **retrait d'une somme d'argent de la banque,** withdrawal of a sum of money from the bank; **retrait d'espèces,** cash withdrawal; **retrait de fonds,** withdrawal of capital; *Fin:* **lettre de retrait,** letter of withdrawal (*b*) **retrait d'un ordre de grève,** calling off a strike; **retrait de monnaies,** withdrawal of currency from circulation/calling in of currency (*c*) **retrait d'une société de la Bourse,** going private.

retraite[1], *n.f.* (*a*) retirement (from work) **âge de la retraite,** age of retirement/ retiring age; **retraite anticipée,** early retirement; **retraite sur demande,** optional retirement; **retraite d'office/forcée,** compulsory/mandatory retirement; **être à la retraite,** to be retired; **mettre qn à la retraite,** to pension s.o. off/to retire s.o.; **prendre sa retraite,** to retire (on a pension) (*b*) **caisse de retraite,** pension fund/ superannuation fund; **pension de retraite/ retraite de vieillesse,** retirement pension; **régime de retraite,** pension plan/scheme **régime de retraites complémentaires/ retraite des cadres** = graduated pension scheme; **régime de retraite financé par les cotisations patronales et ouvrières,** contributory pension plan; **(régime de) retraite proportionnelle/(régime de) retraite indexée sur le revenu,** earnings-related pension (plan); **régime de retraite des artisans, commerçants et professions libérales,** self-employed pension; **retrai-**

par capitalisation, loanback pension; **retraite complémentaire,** private pension; **retraite minimum,** guaranteed minimum pension (GMP).

retraite[2], *n.f.* re-draft/re-exchange; renewed bill; **faire retraite sur qn,** to re-draw on s.o.

retraité,-ée, 1. *a.* retired; pensioned **2.** *n.* (*i*) (old age) pensioner (*ii*) retired person/ *NAm:* retiree.

retraiter, *v.tr.* to pension off/to retire/to superannuate (s.o.).

rétribuer, *v.tr.* to pay/to remunerate (employee, service); **fonctionnaires bien rétribués,** highly-paid officials; **travail mal rétribué,** badly-paid work.

rétribution, *n.f.* remuneration/reward/ payment (for services rendered); salary.

rétroactif, *a.* retrospective/retroactive; **augmentation avec effet rétroactif au 1er septembre,** increase backdated to September 1st.

rétrocéder, *v.tr.* (*i*) *Jur:* to reassign/to retrocede (*ii*) to sell sth. one has just bought (*usu.* for profit); **rétrocéder une commission,** to return a commission.

rétroprojecteur, *n.m.* overhead projector (OHP).

rétroprojection, *n.f.* overhead projection.

réunion, *n.f.* meeting; **réunion du conseil d'administration,** board meeting; **réunion préparatoire,** briefing.

Réunion-Téléphone, *n.f.* conference call.

réunir, 1. *v.tr.* **réunir une somme,** to collect/to get together a sum of money; **réunir un comité,** to convene a committee/ to call a committee meeting **2.** *v.pr.* **se réunir,** (*a*) (*pers.*) to meet/to convene (*b*) (*sociétés*) to amalgamate.

revalorisation, *n.f. Fin:* revalorization/ revaluation (of the franc, etc.).

revaloriser, *v.tr.* **1.** *Fin:* to revalorize/to revalue (currency) **2.** to stabilize (prices) at a higher level.

revenant-bon, *n.m.* surplus; bonus; unexpected/casual profit.

revendable, *a.* resaleable.

revendeur, -euse, *n.* (*a*) retailer; middleman; **escompte/rabais pour revendeurs,** trade discount (*b*) secondhand dealer.

revendicatif, *a. Ind:* **action revendicative/ mouvement revendicatif,** industrial action; **lutte revendicative,** (wage) claims dispute.

revendication, *n.f.* (*a*) *Ind:* claim/demand (**sur,** on); **revendications de salaires,** wage claims; **les revendications syndicales,** union demands/claims (*b*) **revendication de brevet,** patent claim; **mener une action en revendication,** to lodge a claim against s.o.

revendiquer, *v.tr.* to claim/to demand (higher wages, etc.).

revendre, *v.tr.* to resell; *Fin:* **revendre des titres,** to sell out stock.

revenir, *v.i.* to cost; **sa maison lui revient à 75 000 francs,** his house cost him 75 000 francs; **cet article vous reviendra à 100 francs,** this article will cost you 100 francs.

revente, *n.f.* **1.** resale; reselling; **droit de revente,** right of resale; **valeur à la revente,** resale value **2.** selling out; *esp. Fin:* **revente de titres,** selling out of stock.

revenu, *n.m.* (*a*) income (of person, of company); revenue (of the State); incomings; **déclaration de revenus,** income-tax return; **impôt sur le revenu,** income tax; **revenu annuel,** annual income; **revenu disponible,** disposable income; **revenu fixe,** fixed income; **revenu imposable,** taxable income; *PolEc:* **revenu national brut,** gross national income; **revenu brut/net global,** total gross/net income; **revenu(s) obligataire(s)/des obligations,** interest on bonds/income from bonds; **revenu résiduel,** residual income; **revenu du travail,** earned income; **valeur à revenu fixe,**

fixed-interest security; **valeurs à revenu variable,** variable-interest securities; equities; **créer un revenu,** to yield/to generate an income; **dépenser plus que son revenu,** to live beyond one's income (*b*) yield (of investment, etc.).

reversement, *n.m.* Fin: transfer (*of funds from one account to another*).

reverser, *v.tr.* to transfer/to carry (*an item from one account to another*).

réversion, *n.f.* Jur: reversion (à, to); **droit de réversion,** right of reversion; **rente viagère avec réversion,** reversionary annuity.

revêtir, *v.tr.* **revêtir un document,** to sign/to validate a document.

revient, *n.m.* **(prix de) revient,** cost price/manufacturing cost/prime cost; **prix de revient comptable,** book cost; **établissement des prix de revient,** costing; **établir le prix de revient d'un article,** to cost an article.

révisable, *a.* **prix révisable,** (*i*) price subject to alteration/to modification (*ii*) price open to offer; **prix non révisable,** firm/fixed price.

réviser, *v.tr.* to revise/to check; **réviser un compte,** to (re)check an account.

révision, *n.f.* (*a*) revision/check (of list, account, etc.) (*b*) **clause de révision,** revision clause; **révision des prix,** price review.

révoquer, *v.tr.* **1.** to revoke/to countermand (an order, etc.); **révoquer un ordre de grève,** to call off a strike **2.** to dismiss; to remove (an official) from office.

revue, *n.f.* journal; review; magazine.

riche, 1. *a.* rich/wealthy **2.** *n.m.f.* wealthy person.

richesse, *n.f.* wealth; **la richesse publique,** public wealth; **richesse en matières premières,** resources in raw materials; *Mkt:* **la richesse vive,** household/consumer purchasing power.

risque, *n.m.* risk; **risque accru/double**

risque, overexposure; **capital risque,** risk capital/venture capital; **risques de change,** exchange risks; currency exposure; **risque de marché,** market risk; **risques du métier,** occupational hazards; **aux risques et périls du propriétaire,** at owner's risk (*b*) *Ins:* **assurance tous risques,** comprehensive/all-risks insurance; **risque assuré,** risk subscribed/taken up; **risque collectif,** collective risk; **risque d'incendie,** fire risk; **risque locatif,** tenant's third-party risk; **risque de mer/maritime,** sea risks; **risque de perte,** loss risk; **risque du recours du tiers,** third-party risk; **risque de vol,** theft risk; **couvrir un risque,** to cover a risk; **souscrire un risque,** to underwrite a risk.

risque-pays, *n.m.* country risk.

ristourne, *n.f.* (*a*) *Adm: Fin:* refund; return (of amount overpaid) (*b*) rebate/discount (*c*) *MIns:* cancelling/cancellation/annulment (of policy) (*d*) *Ins:* repayment (to party insured) (*e*) commission (*f*) dividend (from co-operative society).

ristourner, *v.tr.* (*a*) to refund/to return (amount overpaid) (*b*) *MIns:* to cancel/to annul (policy) (*c*) to give (s.o.) a discount (on sth.) (*d*) to pay a dividend (to a member of a co-operative society).

robotique, *n.f.* robotics.

rôle, *n.m.* roll; **rôle d'impôt,** tax roll.

rompu, *n.m.* fraction (of share, stock).

rond, *a.* round; **en chiffres ronds,** in round figures; **compte rond,** round sum/even figure.

rotation, *n.f.* turnover (of stocks); **rotation des capitaux,** turnover of capital; **rotation du personnel,** staff turnover/turnover of staff; **rotation de portefeuille,** churning; **rotation de portefeuille-action,** equity switching; **rotation de portefeuille-obligation,** gilt switching; **rotation des stocks,** stock turnround/*NAm:* inventory turn; **le délai de rotation (des stocks) est de quatre mois,** stocks are turned round every four months; **taux de rotation,** rate of turnover.

rouge, *a. & n.m.* red; **la société est retombée**

dans le rouge, the company is in the red again.

roulage, *n.m.* carriage/haulage (of goods); **entreprise de roulage,** (firm of) hauliers/haulage contractors/*NAm:* trucking business; **frais de roulage,** (cost of) carriage/haulage.

roulant, *a.* **fonds roulants,** circulating/floating capital.

roulement, *n.m.* **roulement de fonds,** circulation of capital; **fonds de roulement,** working/operating capital; **roulement du personnel,** staff turnover.

rouler, *v.i.* **l'argent roule,** money circulates freely.

routage, *n.m.* (*i*) bundling up (*ii*) dispatching/routing (of newspapers, circulars, letters, etc.).

route, *n.f.* (*a*) road; **transport par route,** road transport (*b*) route; **feuille de route,** waybill; **frais de route,** travelling expenses; **marchandises avariées en cours de route,** goods damaged in transit; **route**

commerciale, commercial route/trade route.

routier, 1. *a.* **transports routiers,** road transport/road haulage; **gare routière,** road haulage depot 2. *n.m.* long-distance lorry driver/*NAm:* truck driver/teamster; **(restaurant de) routier(s)** = transport café.

routine, *n.f.* **travail de routine,** routine work.

rouvrir, *v.tr.* to reopen (an account, etc.).

rubrique, *n.f.* heading; column (in newspaper, etc.); **mentionné sous cette rubrique,** mentioned under this heading.

rupture, *n.f.* (*a*) breaking (off); **rupture de contrat,** breach of contract; **rupture des négociations,** breaking off of negotiations; **en rupture de stock,** out of stock (*b*) **rupture de charge,** transhipment of cargo.

rural, *a.* **économie rurale,** rural economy.

rythme, *n.m.* **rythme de livraisons,** delivery rate.

S

sabbatique, *a.* **année sabbatique,** sabbatical (year).

sac, *n.m.* bag; **sac publicitaire,** carrier bag/plastic bag (displaying name of shop, etc.).

sacquer, *v.tr. F:* to sack/to fire (s.o.)/to give (s.o.) the sack; **être sacqué,** to get the sack/to be fired.

saisie, *n.f. Jur:* seizure (of goods, etc.); distraint; embargo; **saisie d'une hypothèque,** foreclosure/foreclosing of a mortgage; **ordonnance de saisie,** garnishee order; **vente sur saisie/marchandises vendues sur saisie,** distress merchandise.

saisie-arrêt, *n.f.* **ordonnance de saisie-arrêt,** garnishee order.

saisir, *v.tr.* **1.** *Jur:* to distrain upon/to seize/to impound (goods); to lay an embargo on sth.; **saisir une hypothèque,** to foreclose a mortgage **2. saisir un tribunal d'une affaire,** to refer a matter to a court/to lay a matter before a court.

saison, *n.f.* (*a*) season; **la saison creuse/la morte-saison,** the off season/the slack season; **la haute saison,** the busy season/the high season/the peak season; the tourist season/the holiday season; **la saison touristique,** the tourist season (*b*) **hors saison,** off season; low season; **pendant la saison,** in season; **prix hors saison,** low-season price; **vente de fin de saison,** end-of-season sale.

saisonnier, -ière, 1. *a.* seasonal (employment, etc.); **chômage saisonnier,** seasonal unemployment; **demande saisonnière,** seasonal demand; **fluctuations saisonnières,** seasonal fluctuations; **(taux) corrigé des variations saisonnières,** seasonally adjusted/corrected rate **2.** *n.* seasonal worker.

salaire, *n.m.* salary/wage(s)/pay; **augmentation/hausse de salaire,** salary increase/pay rise; **blocage des salaires,** wage freeze; **écart des salaires,** wage differentials; **feuille/bulletin de salaire,** pay slip; **politique des salaires,** wage policy; **revendications de salaire,** wage claims; **salaire de base,** basic salary/wage; **salaire brut,** gross pay; **salaire de départ,** starting salary; **salaire élevé,** high salary/wage; **salaire fixe,** fixed salary/wage; **salaire hebdomadaire,** weekly pay/wage; **salaire horaire,** hourly wage/pay; **salaire indexé,** index-linked salary/wage; **salaire indirect,** fringe benefits; **salaire mensuel,** monthly salary; **salaire minimum,** minimum wage; **salaire minimum interprofessionnel de croissance (SMIC),** index-linked guaranteed minimum wage; **salaire net,** net salary/pay; **salaire nominal,** nominal wages; **salaire réel,** real wage; **structure des salaires,** salary/wage structure; **taux des salaires,** wage rate; **toucher son salaire,** to draw one's wages/one's salary.

salarial, *a.* **dépenses salariales,** wage expenditure; **fourchette salariale,** wage bracket; **hiérarchie salariale,** (*i*) wage differentials (*ii*) salary structure; **masse salariale/charges salariales,** (total) wages bill; **négociations salariales,** wage negotiations/pay talks; **politique salariale,** pay policy; **revenus salariaux,** earned income; **signer des accords salariaux,** to sign wages agreements.

salariat, *n.m.* wage-earning population/the wage earners; salaried staff; **le salariat et le patronat,** employees and employers.

salarié, -ée, 1. *a.* (*a*) salaried/wage-earning; **employé salarié,** wage earner;

personnel **salarié,** salaried staff (b) paid (work) **2.** n. wage earner; salaried worker; **les salariés et les patrons,** employees and employers.

salarier, v.tr. to pay a wage/a salary to (s.o.)

salle, n.f. **salle d'accueil/salle de réception (de la clientèle),** reception room; **salle d'attente,** waiting room; **salle de conférence,** conference room; **salle d'exposition,** showroom; **salle des ventes,** auction room/salesroom; StExch: **salle des changes,** dealing room.

salon, n.m. trade exhibition/show; **le Salon des Arts ménagers** = the Ideal Home Exhibition; **le Salon de l'automobile** = the Motor Show.

sanction, n.f. PolEc: **sanctions économiques,** economic/financial sanctions.

sans-emploi, n.m.f.inv. unemployed person; **les sans-emploi,** the unemployed.

sans-travail, n.m.f.inv. unemployed person; **les sans-travail,** the unemployed.

sapiteur, n.m. MIns: valuer (of cargo).

saquer, v.tr. F: = **sacquer.**

satisfaction, n.f. satisfaction; **satisfaction du consommateur,** consumer satisfaction; **satisfaction dans le travail,** job satisfaction.

saturation, n.f. Mkt: **campagne de saturation,** all-out (publicity) campaign; **point de saturation,** saturation point; **saturation du marché,** market saturation.

saturé, a. **le marché est saturé,** the market is saturated/has reached saturation point.

saturer, v.tr. to saturate (the market).

sauf, prep. except; **sauf avis contraire,** unless I/we hear to the contrary; **sauf stipulation contraire,** unless otherwise stated.

saupoudrage, n.m. Adm: Fin: allocation (of small amounts of credit to a large number of recipients).

sauter, v.i. (banque) to crash; (entreprise) to go bankrupt/to fail.

sauvegarde, n.f. **clause de sauvegarde,** saving clause; PolEc: **droits de sauvegarde,** safeguarding duties.

sauvegarder, v.tr. to safeguard/to protect; **sauvegarder les intérêts des actionnaires,** to protect the interests of shareholders.

savoir-faire, n.m. know-how.

sceau, n.m. seal; **apposer son sceau à un document,** to set one's seal to a document.

schéma, n.m. (a) summary; outline (b) diagram; (sketch) plan; schema.

schématique, a. diagrammatic; schematic; **organisation schématique,** skeleton organization; **plan schématique,** outline (plan).

schématiser, v.tr. (a) to schematize; to simplify (b) to make a diagram (of sth.).

science, n.f. science; **homme/femme de science,** scientist; **science de la gestion,** management science.

scientifique, 1. a. scientific; **chercheur, -euse scientifique,** researcher/research worker; **gestion scientifique,** scientific management; **recherche scientifique,** scientific research **2.** n.m.f. scientist.

scinder, v.tr. to divide/to split (up); Fin: **stocks scindés,** split stocks.

scission, n.f. **scission d'actif,** splitting/divestment of assets.

script, n.m. Fin: scrip/subscription receipt.

scriptural, a. Bank: **monnaie scripturale,** bank credit; financial credit; bank deposits.

scrutin, n.m. vote; ballot; **dépouiller le scrutin,** to count the votes.

séance, n.f. (a) sitting/session/meeting; StExch: **séance de clôture,** closing session; **séance supplémentaire,** additional session (b) **séance (de travail, d'entraînement),** (working, training) period/session.

second, a. second; taking second place/

inferior; **article de second choix,** inferior/ second-grade article; *Trans:* **billet de seconde,** second-class ticket; **second associé,** junior partner; *StExch:* **second marché,** secondary market.

secours, *n.m.* help/relief/assistance; **caisse/ fonds de secours,** emergency/relief fund; **société de secours mutuels,** benefit society/ friendly society; **secours d'argent,** financial assistance.

secret, *n.m.* **secret professionnel,** trade secret; professional secrecy.

secrétaire, *n.m. f.* secretary; *Adm:* **secrétaire général(e) (d'une société),** company secretary; **secrétaire de direction,** director's/executive secretary; private secretary; **secrétaire particulier/particulière,** private secretary; personal assistant (PA).

secteur, *n.m.* (*a*) **graphique à secteurs,** pie diagram/chart (*b*) area/district; **secteur de ventes,** sales area/trading area (*c*) *PolEc: etc:* **secteurs d'activité,** field/sphere of activity; area of specialisation; **secteur bâtiment,** building industry/ sector; **secteur en croissance,** growth sector; **secteur diffus,** (*maisons individuelles*) individual housing/houses; **secteur économique,** economic sector; **secteur groupé,** (*maisons en villages*) housing estate(s); **secteur industriel,** industrial sector; **secteur primaire,** primary industry; **le secteur privé,** the private sector; **le secteur public,** the public sector; **secteur secondaire,** secondary industry; **secteur tertiaire/secteur des services,** tertiary/service industries; services sector; service economy.

section, *n.f. Adm:* section/branch (of department, etc.).

sécurité, *n.f.* (*a*) security; reliability (of statistics, machinery, etc.); **sécurité de l'emploi,** security of employment/job security; *Adm:* **Sécurité sociale =** Social Security (*b*) safety; **service de sécurité,** security staff/guards (in firm, etc.); *Ind: etc:* **co-efficient de sécurité,** security factor; **marge de sécurité,** security margin; **règles de sécurité,** safety regulations.

seing, *n.m. Jur:* **acte sous seing privé,** simple contract; private agreement; contract in writing signed but not sealed or witnessed.

séjour, *n.m.* stay; **permis de séjour,** residence permit.

self, *n.m. F:* = **self-service.**

self-service, *n.m.* **(magasin, restaurant) self-service,** self-service (store, restaurant).

semaine, *n.f.* (*a*) week; working week; week's work; **semaine de quarante heures,** forty-hour week; **faire la semaine anglaise,** to work a five-day week; to have Saturday off (*b*) week's pay/weekly wages.

semainier, *n.m.* (*a*) (workman's) time sheet (*b*) desk diary (*with sections for each day of the week*).

semestre, *n.m.* (*a*) half-year; six-month period; **bénéfices du premier semestre,** first-half profits (*b*) six months' pay/ income (*c*) six months' rent.

semestriel, *a.* half-yearly/six-monthly.

semestriellement, *adv.* semi-annually/ half-yearly/every six months; **réviser les salaires semestriellement,** to review salaries every six months.

semi-fini, *a.* semi-finished (product).

semi-ouvré, *a.* semi-finished (product).

semi-produit, *n.m.* semi-manufactured product.

sensible, *a.* marked/noticeable/appreciable/considerable; **amélioration sensible,** marked improvement; **une hausse sensible des prix,** a big price rise/a marked rise in prices; **subir des pertes sensibles,** to incur heavy/extensive/large losses.

sept, *a.* **dépôts à sept jours,** seven-day money/deposits; **cartel des sept pays producteurs de pétrole,** seven sisters.

séquestre, *n.m. Jur:* sequestration; **ordonnance de mise sous séquestre,** receiving order (*in bankruptcy proceedings*); sequestration order; **mettre des actifs sous sé-**

questre, to sequester/sequestrate assets; to seize assets.

séquestrer, *v.tr. Jur:* to sequester/to sequestrate (property).

série, *n.f.* (*a*) set (of documents, tools, etc.); range (of colours, sizes, samples, etc.); **numéro de série,** serial number; *PolEc:* **série économique,** economic batch; **valeurs remboursables par séries,** securities redeemable in series (*b*) range/line (of goods, products, etc.); **article hors série,** custom-made/custom-built article; **chaîne de fabrication en série,** production line; **fabrication/production en (grande) série,** mass production; **fabrication/ production en (petite) série,** small-scale manufacture/batch production; **fins de série,** end of lines; oddments/remnants; *Adm: etc:* **prix de série,** contract prices; **série de produits,** product line; **fabriquer en série,** to mass-produce.

sérieux, *a.* (*a*) genuine; **acheteur sérieux,** genuine purchaser; **offre sérieuse,** bona fide offer (*b*) reliable; **client sérieux,** good customer; **maison sérieuse,** reliable firm.

serment, *n.m.* oath; **prêter serment,** to take an oath; to be sworn (in); **déclaration sous serment,** sworn statement; **faire un faux serment,** to commit perjury.

serpent, *n.m. EEC:* **le serpent (monétaire),** the (monetary) snake.

serveur, *n.m. Cmptr:* on-line data service.

service, *n.m.* **1.** (*a*) **porte/entrée de service,** tradesmen's entrance (*b*) service/tip (in hotel, restaurant, etc.); **service compris,** service included/inclusive of service; **service non compris,** service not included/ exclusive of service (*c*) **libre-service,** self-service (in restaurant, shop, etc.) (*d*) **service à la clientèle,** customer service; **service permanent/de 24 heures,** 24-hour service; **service après-vente,** after-sales service; back-up service (*e*) *Adm:* **nécessités de service,** service requirements; **service contractuel,** contract service **2.** duty; **service de jour,** day duty; **service de nuit,** night duty; **tableau de service,** duty

roster/chart; **être de service,** to be on duty **3.** *PolEc:* **biens et services,** goods and services; **prestation de service,** (*i*) service (*ii*) service fee/charge; **société de services,** service bureau; company providing a service/providing services; **service d'informations sur le marché,** market data service; **services marchands,** direct services; **service de la dette,** debt servicing/ *NAm:* debt service; **assurer le service d'un emprunt,** to service a loan **4.** (*a*) *Adm:* branch/department/service; **services publics,** public utility services/*NAm:* utilities; *StExch:* **valeurs de services publics,** public utility stocks/*NAm:* utilities; **services administratifs,** administrative department; **service central,** headquarters; **service des douanes,** customs service; **service postal/des postes,** postal service(s); **service des transports,** transport (services); **chef de service,** head of department (*b*) department (of firm); **service des achats,** purchasing department; *Ind:* **service commercial,** commercial department; **service de (la) comptabilité,** accounts department; **service des expéditions,** forwarding/dispatch department; **service de groupage,** joint-cargo service; **service de livraison,** delivery service; **service du personnel,** personnel department; **service de presse,** (*i*) press department (*ii*) *Publ:* (distribution of) press copies/review copies; **service de publicité,** advertising/publicity department; **service technique,** technical branch/engineering department; **service des ventes,** sales department **5.** (*machine, etc.*) **en service,** in use/in operation; **hors de service,** out of order/not in use; **mettre en service,** to put/to bring into service (*b*) *Trans:* service (of train, aircraft, ferry, etc.); **service de marchandises,** goods/freight service; **service régulier,** regular service; **service de voyageurs/de passagers,** passenger service.

servir, *v.tr.* (*a*) **servir un client,** to serve/to attend to a customer; **(est-ce qu')on vous sert?** are you being attended to? are you being served? (*b*) to supply (s.o. with goods) (*c*) **servir une rente à qn,** to pay an annuity to s.o.

seuil, *n.m.* threshold; *EEC:* **prix du seuil,** threshold price; **seuil de réapprovisionnement,** reorder point; **seuil de pauvreté,** poverty line; **seuil de rentabilité/point de seuil,** break-even point; **en dessous du seuil psychologique de 3%,** below the psychologically important 3% mark/below the important chart point of 3%.

SICAV, *n.f.* (*Société d'investissement à capital variable*) open-end fund; **SICAV actions,** open-end fund invested in equity; **SICAV obligations,** open-end fund invested in bonds.

siège, *n.m.* **siège social,** head office/registered office (of a company).

signataire, *n.m.f.* signatory (of a contract, etc.).

signature, *n.f.* **1.** signature; **apposer/mettre sa signature au bas d'un document,** to put one's name to a document; **signature d'un contrat,** signing of a contract; **avoir la signature,** to be authorized to sign (on behalf of firm, etc.); **la lettre portait la signature du président,** the letter was signed by the chairman; **fondé de signature,** signing officer; **pour signature,** for signature; **signature collective,** joint signature; **la signature sociale,** the signature of the firm **2.** *Publ:* signature (of a book).

signer, *v.tr.* to sign (a document, a letter, etc.); **signer un chèque,** to sign a cheque; **signer un contrat,** to become party to an agreement/to sign an agreement; **signer à la réception (de marchandises),** to sign (for goods) on reception; **signez au bas de la page,** sign at the bottom of the page.

simple, *a.* **billet simple,** one-way ticket; **intérêts simples,** simple interest.

simulation, *n.f.* simulation.

sinistre, *n.m.* disaster; *Ins:* contingency insured against.

situation, *n.f.* **1.** (*a*) *Fin:* state/condition; **situation financière,** financial status; **quelle est la situation (financière) de la maison?** what is the (financial) position of the firm? **situation de trésorerie,** cash(flow) situation; **situation en banque d'un client,** customer's financial position/ situation; (*d'une société*) **situation nette,** net assets/net worth (*b*) report/return; *Fin:* statement of finances; **situation de caisse,** cash statement; **situation hebdomadaire (de la Banque de France),** weekly report (of the Bank of France) **2.** position/ job; **avoir une belle situation,** to have a good job; **chercher une situation,** to look for a job; **perdre sa situation,** to lose one's job.

slogan, *n.m. Mkt:* slogan.

SMIC = **salaire minimum international de croissance,** minimum salary.

smicard, -arde, *n.* person who is paid a minimum salary/the SMIC.

social, *a.* (*a*) **année sociale,** company's trading year; **capital social,** share capital; **exercice social,** accounting period/tax year; **nom social/raison sociale,** name/ style of a company; **siège social,** head office (*b*) **assurances sociales** = National Insurance; **Sécurité Sociale** = Social Security.

sociétaire, *n.m.f.* (*a*) (full) member (of corporate body); **carte de sociétaire** membership card (*b*) **sociétaire d'une société anonyme,** shareholder/stockholder.

société, *n.f.* company/firm; partnership *NAm:* corporate body; corporation; **société anonyme (SA),** (*i*) public company (*ii*) limited (liability) company; **société anonyme par actions,** joint-stock company/*NAm:* incorporated company; **société de bourse,** stockbroking firm/firm of stockbrokers; **société en commandite (simple),** limited partnership; **société en commandite par actions,** limited partnership (with shares); **société coopérative** cooperative society; **société cotée en Bourse,** listed company; **société cotée à la Cote officielle,** quoted company; **société (commune) de crédit immobilier (hypothécaire),** building society; **société de crédit mutuel,** friendly society; **société d'économie mixte,** semi-public company; **société d'exploitation,** development company; **société d'exploitation en commun,** joint-venture company; **société de famille,** family company; **société de finances,** finance company; **société immobilière,** real-estate company; property developer; **société d'investissement,** investment company; **société d'investissement à capital fixe (SICAF),** closed-end investment company/closed-end fund; **société d'investissement à capital variable (SICAV),** open-end investment company/open-end fund; **société mère,** parent company; **société mutuelle,** friendly society; **société de navigation,** shipping company; **société en nom collectif,** general partnership; **société de personnes,** partnership; **société de placement,** investment trust; **société de portefeuille/société de contrôle/société holding,** holding company; **société de prévoyance,** provident society; **société privée/non cotée,** unquoted company; **société à responsabilité infinie,** unlimited company; **société à responsabilité limitée (SARL)** = limited liability company; **société de services,** company providing a service/providing services; **société de transport,** transport company; **société d'utilité publique,** public utility company; **acte/contrat de société,** deed of partnership/articles of association; **droit des sociétés,** Company Law/*NAm:* corporation law; **impôt sur les sociétés,** corporation tax; **loi sur les sociétés,** company law; **revenus de société,** corporate income/company revenue; **constituer une société,** to form/to incorporate a company; **liquider une société,** to liquidate/to wind up a company.

société-écran, *n.f.* front company.

solde, *n.m.* **1.** balance; **solde bancaire/en banque,** bank balance; **solde en caisse,** balance in hand; **solde de compte,** balance of account; **solde créditeur,** credit balance; **solde débiteur,** debit balance/balance due; *Bank:* overdraft; **solde à découvert,** outstanding balance; **solde déficitaire,** debit balance; **solde de dividende,** final dividend; **solde d'une facture,** balance outstanding on an invoice; **solde de fin de mois,** end-of-month

balance; **solde d'ouverture,** opening balance; **solde à nouveau/solde reporté,** balance brought forward; **solde à reporter,** balance (to be) carried forward; **pour solde,** in settlement; **pour solde de tout compte,** in full settlement; to close the account; **régler le solde,** to pay the balance **2.** (*a*) surplus stock/remnant; *pl.* **soldes,** sale goods/bargains (*b*) sale; reduction; **solde (de marchandises),** (clearance) sale; sell-off; **solde d'édition,** remainders; **solde de fermeture,** closing-down sale; **soldes de fin de saison,** end-of-season sales; **solde après inventaire,** stocktaking sale; **c'est l'époque des soldes,** the sales are on; **prix de solde,** sale price; **en solde,** to clear; reduced; **mettre du stock en solde,** to sell off stock; **je l'ai eu en solde,** I got it in the sales; I got it cheap.

solder, *v.tr.* **1.** (*a*) to balance (an account); **les comptes se soldent par un bénéfice net de ...,** the accounts show a net profit of ... (*b*) to settle/to discharge/to pay (off) (an account) **2.** to sell off (goods at sale price, at bargain price); to clear (surplus, unsold stock); *Publ:* to remainder (books).

solderie, *n.f.* reject shop.

soldeur, -euse, *n.* person who buys and deals in (*i*) end-of-season fashions (*ii*) seconds/imperfect goods (*iii*) clearance lines/*Publ:* remainders.

solidaire, *a. Jur:* joint and several; jointly liable/responsible; **obligation solidaire,** obligation binding on all parties; **responsabilité (conjointe et) solidaire,** joint and several liability.

solidairement, *adv.* jointly; *Jur:* **conjointement et solidairement,** jointly and severally.

solidarité, *n.f.* **1.** *Jur:* joint and several obligation or liability; joint responsibility **2.** solidarity; **faire grève/débrayer par solidarité,** to come out in sympathy.

solide, *a.* sound; **garantie solide,** reliable/trustworthy guarantee; **solide au point de vue financier,** financially sound.

solvabilité, *n.f.* solvency; **réputation/ degré de solvabilité,** credit rating.

solvable, *a.* (financially) solvent.

sommaire, *n.m.* **sommaire d'un article,** abstract of an article.

somme, *n.f.* (*a*) sum; total; amount; **la somme s'élève à 100 francs,** the total amounts to 100 francs; **somme totale,** total sum/total amount/sum total; **somme versée,** amount paid (*b*) **somme (d'argent),** sum of money; **payer une grosse/forte somme,** to pay a large sum/ amount of money; **dépenser une somme de 500 francs,** to spend (a sum of) 500 francs.

sommier, *n.m.* *Adm: etc:* register.

sonal, *n.m.* (advertising) jingle.

sondage, *n.m.* **contrôle par sondage,** random check; **enquête par sondage,** sample survey; **méthode de sondage,** sampling method; **sondage aléatoire,** random sampling; **sondage d'opinion,** opinion poll.

sonder, *v.tr.* **sonder l'opinion,** to make a survey of public opinion; to carry out/to conduct an opinion poll.

sortant, *a.* **administrateurs sortants (d'une société),** retiring directors (of a company); **membres (de comité) sortants,** retiring/ outgoing members (of a committee).

sortie, *n.f.* (*a*) going out; coming out; departure; exit; *Adm:* issue of stores; **bon/ facture de sortie,** issue voucher; *Nau:* **fret de sortie,** outward freight; **inventaire de sortie,** outgoing inventory; *Cust:* **sortie d'entrepôt,** clearing/taking out of bond (*b*) retirement (of official) (*c*) *Mkt:* launching (of new product); publication/ coming out (of book, magazine, etc.) (*d*) export (of goods); **connaissement de sortie,** outward bill of lading; **déclaration de sortie,** entry outwards; **droit de sortie,** export duty; **prohibition des sorties,** export ban/prohibition of exports; **tarif de sortie,** export tariff (*e*) **sorties de fonds,** expenses/ outgoings; **ce mois-ci il y a eu plus de sorties que de rentrées,** this month's out-

goings have exceeded payments received; we are down on this month's trading/ takings (*f*) *Fin:* **gold-point de sortie,** export gold-point; **sortie de devises/de capitaux,** currency/capital outflow; flight of currency/of capital; **les sorties d'or,** gold withdrawals.

souche, *n.f.* counterfoil/stub (of cheque, ticket, etc.); tally (of receipt); **carnet/ livret à souche(s),** counterfoil book.

souffrance, *n.f.* **délai/jours de souffrance,** days of grace; **en souffrance,** pending/in abeyance; *Fin:* **coupons en souffrance,** outstanding/unpaid coupons; **dette en souffrance,** outstanding debt; **effets en souffrance,** bills held over; bills overdue/ outstanding; **marchandises en souffrance,** goods held up in transit/awaiting delivery; **travail en souffrance,** work waiting to be dealt with/work pending.

soulte, *n.f.* *Jur:* balance/cash adjustment (to equalize shares, etc.).

soumettre, *v.tr.* to submit/to refer/to put (question, etc.); **soumettre un document à la signature,** to submit/to present a document for signature.

soumis, *a.* subject (à, to); **dividendes soumis à l'impôt sur le revenu,** dividends liable to income tax; **soumis au (droit de) timbre,** subject to stamp duty; **soumis aux fluctuations du marché,** subject to fluctuations in the market.

soumission, *n.f.* (*a*) tender; bidding (for public works, etc.); **offre de soumission,** call for tenders; **par (voie de) soumission,** by tender; **soumission cachetée,** sealed tender; **faire une soumission pour un travail,** to tender for a piece of work; **la soumission la plus basse,** the cheapest and best bidding (*b*) *Cust:* **soumission (en douane),** bond; **soumission cautionnée,** secured bond.

soumissionnaire, *n.m.* party tendering for work on contract; tenderer; bidder.

soumissionner, *v.tr.* to tender for/to put in a tender for (job, public works, etc.); **soumissionner à une adjudication,** to tender for a contract; to bid for/on a contract; **soumissionner la construction du nouvel hôpital,** to bid for/to bid on/to tender for the new hospital.

source, *n.f.* source; *Fin:* **imposé à la source,** taxed at source; **retenue (de l'impôt sur le revenu) à la source,** pay as you earn (PAYE)/*NAm:* pay as you go.

sous-affrètement, *n.m.* sub-charter (-ing).

sous-affréter, *v.tr.* to sub-charter (ship, etc.).

sous-affréteur, *n.m.* sub-charterer.

sous-agence, *n.f.* sub-agency.

sous-agent, *n.m.* sub-agent.

sous-bail, *n.m.* sublease.

sous-capitalisation, *n.f. PolEc:* under-capitalization.

sous-capitalisé, *a. PolEc:* under-capitalized/underfunded (project).

sous-chef, *n.m.* (*a*) deputy chief clerk (*b*) (*i*) assistant manager (*ii*) under manager.

sous-comité, *n.m.,* **sous-commission,** *n.f.,* sub-committee.

sous-consommation, *n.f. PolEc:* under-consumption.

sous-contractant, **-ante,** *n.* sub-contractor.

souscripteur, *n.m. Fin:* (*a*) subscriber; applicant (for shares, etc.) (*b*) drawer (of bill of exchange) (*c*) subscriber (to a magazine, etc.).

souscription, *n.f.* **1.** *Fin:* subscription; application; **souscription d'actions/à des titres,** application for shares; **bulletin de souscription,** allotment letter; application/ order-form; **droits de souscription,** application/subscription rights; **droit préférentiel de souscription,** rights issue; **souscription en titres,** subscription by conversion of securities; **souscription à une nouvelle émission,** subscription to a new issue; **garantir la souscription d'une**

émission, to underwrite an issue **2.** subscription; contribution (of a sum of money); **verser une souscription,** to pay a subscription.

souscrire,1. *v.tr.* (*a*) to sign/to execute (deed); to subscribe/to sign (bond, contract, etc.); *Ins:* **souscrire une police,** to underwrite a policy; **souscrire une lettre de change,** to subscribe/to sign a bill of exchange; *Fin:* **souscrire des actions,** to subscribe shares/to apply for shares; **capital souscrit,** subscribed/issued capital (*b*) to subscribe; **souscrire à une publication,** to take out a subscription to a publication; *Fin:* **souscrire à des actions,** to take up shares; **souscrire à une émission,** to apply for/to subscribe to an issue; **souscrire à un emprunt,** to subscribe to a loan; **souscrire à titre irréductible,** to apply as of right for new shares; **souscrire à titre réductible,** to apply for excess shares **2.** *vi* **souscrire pour (la somme de) mille francs,** to subscribe a thousand francs.

sous-développé, *a.* (*a*) *PolEc:* **pays sous-développés,** underdeveloped countries/ developing countries (*b*) underequipped/ undermechanized (factory, etc.).

sous-directeur, **-trice,** *n.* assistant manager/manageress; deputy manager/ deputy manageress.

sous-emploi, *n.m. PolEc:* underemployment.

sous-entrepreneur, *n.m.* subcontractor.

sous-estimation, *n.f.,* **sous-évaluation,** *n.f.,* undervaluation.

sous-estimer, **sous-évaluer,** *v.tr.* to underestimate/to undervalue/to underrate.

sous-fréter, *v.tr.* to underfreight/to underlet (a ship).

sous-locataire, *n.m.f.* subtenant/ sublessee.

sous-location, *n.f.* (*a*) subletting/ subrenting (*b*) subtenancy; sublease.

sous-louer, *v.tr.* (*a*) to sublet/to sublease (house) (*b*) to rent (house) from a tenant.

sous-main, *n.m.inv.* blotting pad; blotter.

sous-palan (en), *adv.phr. Nau:* **livraison en sous-palan,** delivery (of goods) ready for shipping.

sous-payer, *v.tr.* to underpay; **ouvriers sous-payés,** underpaid workers.

sous-production, *n.f.* underproduction.

sous-produit, *n.m.* by-product; secondary product; spin-off.

sous-seing, *n.m.* private agreement/private contract.

soussigné, -ée, *a. & n.* undersigned; **je soussigné déclare que ...,** I, the undersigned, declare that ....

sous-traitance, *n.f.* subcontracting; **donner en sous-traitance,** to subcontract/to contract out.

sous-traitant, *n.m.* subcontractor; **on a donné le travail à un sous-traitant,** the work was contracted out/farmed out to s.o.

sous-traité, *n.m.* subcontract.

sous-traiter, *v.tr.* to subcontract/to contract out/to farm out.

sous-vendre, *v.tr.* to resell (portion of goods purchased to a third party).

sous-vente, *n.f.* resale (of goods to a third party).

soutenir, *v.tr.* **1.** to support/to back (undertaking, person, etc.); to back (s.o., sth., financially); to underpin; **soutenir des cours par des achats,** to support prices by buying **2. soutenir une dépense,** to meet an expense.

soutenu, *a.* sustained; **marché soutenu,** steady market; **marché moins soutenu,** easier market.

soutien, *n.m.* support; **prix de soutien,** support(ed)/pegged price; **soutien des prix,** price pegging; **soutien de famille,** wage earner.

spécial, *a.* special.

spécialisation, *n.f.* specialization.

spécialisé, *a.* specialized; **ouvrier spécialisé (OS),** skilled worker; **main-d'œuvre non spécialisée,** unskilled labour.

spécialiser (se), *v.pr.* **se spécialiser dans qch.,** to specialize in sth.

spécialiste, *n.m.f.* specialist; expert; **spécialiste du marketing,** marketing expert.

spécialité, *n.f.* speciality/special feature; special line of business; *Fin:* **spécialité budgétaire,** budgetary speciality; **spécialité pharmaceutique,** patent medicine; **c'est la spécialité de la maison,** it's our speciality.

spécification, *n.f.* specification (of product, etc.); **spécification de la fonction,** job specification.

spécifier, *v.tr.* to specify (conditions, etc.); **compte spécifié,** detailed/itemized account; *StExch:* **spécifier un cours,** to make a price.

spécimen, *n.m.* specimen; sample; *Mkt:* (*d'une revue, etc.*) specimen copy; sample copy; **spécimen de signature,** specimen signature.

spéculateur, -trice, *n. Fin:* speculator; **terrains achetés par des spéculateurs,** land bought up by speculators; *StExch:* **spéculateur à la baisse,** bear; **spéculateur à la hausse,** bull; **spéculateur à la journée,** day to day trader/*esp. NAm:* scalper; **spéculateur sur plusieurs positions,** position trader.

spéculatif, *a. Fin:* speculative (deal, etc.); **achat spéculatif,** speculative buying; **capitaux spéculatifs,** risk capital; **valeurs spéculatives,** speculative stocks; **vente spéculative,** speculative selling.

spéculation, *n.f. Fin:* speculation; **spéculation à la baisse,** bear operations; **spéculation sur la base,** basis trading

spéculation hasardeuse, risky speculation; **spéculation à la hausse,** bull operations; **spéculations immobilières,** property speculation.

spéculer, *v.i. Fin:* to speculate; **spéculer en Bourse,** to speculate on the Stock Exchange; **spéculer à la baisse,** to speculate for a fall/on a falling market; to go a bear; **spéculer à la hausse,** to speculate for a rise/on a rising market; to go a bull; **spéculer sur les différentiels de cours,** to spread; **spéculer sur les valeurs pétrolières,** to speculate in oils.

spirale, *n.f.* spiral; **spirale inflationniste,** inflationary spiral; **spirale prix-salaires,** wage-price spiral; (*prix*) **monter en spirale,** to spiral.

spontané, *a.* **achat spontané,** impulse buying.

spot, *n.m.* (*a*) *Fin:* **crédit spot,** spot credit; **marché spot,** spot market (*b*) *Mkt:* **spot (publicitaire),** (advertising) spot/commercial; **spot télé,** TV commercial.

stabilisateur, 1. *a.* stabilizing; **exercer une action stabilisatrice sur les prix,** to have/to exert a stabilizing action on prices **2.** *n.m.* stabilizer.

stabilisation, *n.f.* stabilization (of currency); pegging (of prices, market, etc.); **fonds de stabilisation des changes,** exchange equalization account.

stabiliser, *v.tr.* to stabilize (currency, prices, market, etc.); **les prix se sont stabilisés,** prices have stabilized.

stabilité, *n.f.* stability/steadiness (of prices, etc.); **politique de stabilité,** stabilizing policy; **stabilité économique,** economic stability.

stable, *a.* stable/firm/steady; balanced; **monnaie stable,** stable currency.

stage, *n.m.* period of training; course of instruction; probationary period; **faire un stage,** to attend/to go on a (training) course.

stagflation, *n.f. PolEc:* stagflation.

stagiaire, 1. *a.* training (period); probationary (period) **2.** *n.m.f.* trainee.

stagnant, *a.* stagnant; **économie stagnante,** stagnant economy.

stagnation, *n.f.* stagnation; (*commerce, marché*) **en stagnation,** at a standstill/stagnant.

stagner, *v.i.* to stagnate.

stand, *n.m.* **stand d'exposition,** exhibition stand.

standard, 1. *a.* standard; **coûts standards,** standard costs; **modèle standard,** standard model; **prix standard,** standard price **2.** *n.m.* (*a*) standard; **standards budgétaires,** budgetary standards (*b*) *Tel:* switchboard.

standardisation, *n.f.* standardization.

standardiser, *v.tr.* to standardize; **production standardisée,** standardized production.

standardiste, *n.m.f. Tel:* switchboard operator.

stand by, *n.m. Fin:* standby agreement.

station, *n.f. Cmptr:* **station de travail,** workstation.

statisticien, -ienne, *n.* statistician.

statistique, 1. *a.* statistical; **données statistiques,** statistical data **2.** *n.f.* (*a*) statistics (*b*) *pl.* statistical tables; **statistiques pour 1980,** statistics/figures for 1980.

statistiquement, *adv.* statistically.

statuer, *v.tr.* to decree.

statut, *n.m.* **1.** (*a*) statute/article (of company, etc.); **statuts d'une société,** (memorandum and) articles (of association) of a company (*b*) **statuts et règlements,** rules and regulations **2. statut civil,** civil status.

statutaire, *a.* statutory; **actions statutaires,** qualifying shares; *Fin:* **dividende statutaire,** statutory dividend; **gérant**

statutaire, manager appointed according to the articles.

statutairement, *adv. Fin:* in accordance with the articles; under the articles.

stellage, *n.m. Fin:* double option/put and call.

sténo, *n.f.* (*abbr. de sténographie*) *F:* stenography/shorthand; **prendre en sténo,** to take down in shorthand.

sténodactylo, *n.m.f.* shorthand typist.

sténodactylo(graphie), *n.f.* shorthand typing.

sténographie, *n.f.* stenography/shorthand.

sténographier, *v.tr.* to take down/to write in shorthand.

sterling, *a.m.inv.* sterling; **balances sterling,** sterling balances; **livre sterling,** pound sterling; **cinq livres sterling,** five pounds sterling; **zone sterling,** sterling area.

stimulant, *n.m.* stimulus/incentive; **stimulants de la production,** production incentives; **stimulants de vente,** sales incentives.

stimuler, *v.tr.* to stimulate/to give a stimulus to (trade, etc.); **l'exportation stimule la production,** exports stimulate production.

stipulation, *n.f.* **stipulations d'un contrat,** stipulations of a contract; conditions laid down in an agreement; **stipulation particulière,** special provision.

stipuler, *v.tr.* to stipulate; to lay down (that ...); **il est stipulé que ...,** it is stipulated that ...; **le contrat stipule que toutes les réparations seront à la charge du locataire,** the contract stipulates that the tenant shall be responsible for all repairs.

stock, *n.m.* (*a*) stock (of goods)/*NAm:* inventory; **évaluation des stocks,** stock valuation; **gestion des stocks,** stock control/*NAm:* inventory control; **liquidation de stock,** stock clearance; **livre de stock,** stock book; **renouvellement des stocks,** restocking; **rotation des stocks,** stock turnround; **stock de clôture/stock final,** closing stock; **stock de dépannage/de sécurité,** safety stock/buffer stock; **stocks de réserve,** stockpile; **stock existant/stock en magasin,** stock in hand; **stock d'ouverture/stock initial,** opening stock; **avoir en stock,** to have in stock; **pièces détachées toujours en stock,** spare parts always in stock; **constituer des stocks,** to build up stocks; **épuisement des stocks,** stock depletion; **épuiser les stocks,** to deplete/to exhaust stocks; **notre stock est épuisé,** we are out of stock; **nos stocks s'épuisent,** our stocks are running out/we are running out of stock (*b*) **stock d'or** (*d'une Banque d'État*) gold reserve.

stockage, *n.m.* **1.** stocking/keeping in stock (of goods); storage; **stockage mécanisé,** mechanized stocking **2.** (*a*) stocking/building up of stocks (*b*) stockpiling.

stocker, *v.tr.* (*a*) to stock (goods) (*b*) to stockpile.

stockiste, *n.m.f.* stockist; agent; dealer.

stop, *n.m. StExch:* **ordre stop,** stop order/stop loss order.

stop-vente, *n.f.* stop-loss selling.

stratégie, *n.f.* strategy; **stratégie des affaires,** business strategy; **stratégie commerciale/de marché,** marketing strategy; marketing mix; **stratégie de l'entreprise,** company/corporate strategy; **stratégie financière,** financial strategy; **stratégie d'actions/d'investissement en valeurs mobilières,** equity play.

structuration, *n.f.* structuring.

structure, *n.f.* structure; **structure des coûts,** cost structure; **structure de l'entreprise,** corporate/company structure; **structure du marché,** market structure; **structure de(s) prix,** price structure; **structure des salaires,** wage structure.

stylicien, -ienne, *n.* designer.

stylique, *n.f.* design(ing).

structurer, *v.tr.* to structure.

subalterne, *a.* subordinate; **employé subal-**

terne, junior employee; employee in a minor position.

subliminal, *a.* subliminal; **publicité subliminale,** subliminal advertising.

subrogation, *n.f. Jur:* subrogation.

subside, *n.m.* subsidy.

substitution, *n.f.* substitution; **produits de substitution,** substitute products.

subvention, *n.f.* subsidy/grant (of money); **subventions à l'alimentation,** food subsidies; **subventions en capital,** capital grants; **subvention d'équipement,** equipment subsidy; **subvention d'exploitation,** operating subsidy.

subventionnel, *a.* subventionary (payment).

subventionner, *v.tr.* to subsidize; to grant financial aid to (undertaking, etc.); **industries subventionnées,** subsidized industries; **subventionné par l'État,** State-aided.

succès, *n.m.* **succès de librairie,** bestseller.

successeur, *n.m.* successor **(de,** to).

succession, *n.f.* inheritance; **droits de succession,** death duties/inheritance tax.

succursale, *n.f.* branch (of store, etc.); branch (of bank); branch office; **magasin à succursales (multiples),** multiple (store)/chain store.

succursalisme, *n.m.* multiple/chain of stores.

suite, *n.f.* follow-up; *Corr:* **comme suite à votre lettre du 15 août,** with reference to/further to/in response to your letter of 15th August; **(comme) suite à notre conversation téléphonique,** further to your telephone call; **à la suite de votre demande,** in reply to/further to/with reference to your request; *(d'un produit)* **sans suite,** cannot be repeated/discontinued; **donner suite à,** *(i)* to deal with/to carry out (an order) *(ii)* to follow up a letter.

suivant, 1. *prep.* in accordance with/following (instructions); **suivant inven-**

taire, as per stock list **2.** *a.* following; **aux conditions suivantes,** on the following terms.

suivi, 1. *a.* close (business relations); steady/persistent (demand); **achats suivis,** consistent buying; **correspondance suivie,** close/regular correspondence **2.** *n.m. Mkt: etc:* follow-up (of product, market, order, etc.).

suivre, *v.tr.* faire suivre une lettre, to forward/to redirect a letter; *(sur une lettre)* **(prière de) faire suivre,** please forward; **suivre une affaire,** to follow up (a piece of) business; **nous n'avons pas suivi cet article,** we have given up/discontinued this line.

sujet, *a.* subject/liable (à, to); **contrat sujet au droit de timbre,** agreement subject to stamp duty; **marchandises sujettes à un droit de ...,** goods subject to/liable to a duty of ....

superbénéfices, *n.m.pl.* excess profits/surplus profits; (very) large profits.

superdividende, *n.m. Fin:* surplus dividend.

supérette, *n.f.* minimarket/small supermarket.

superficie, *n.f.* area.

superflu, *a.* superfluous.

supérieur,-eure, 1. *a. (a)* superior (à, to); **supérieur à la moyenne,** above average/better than average *(b)* **cadre supérieur,** senior executive; *pl.* **cadres supérieurs,** managerial staff/top management *(c)* **offre supérieure,** higher bid *(d)* (goods, products) of superior quality **2.** *n.* superior; **il est mon supérieur,** he is above me in rank.

supermarché, *n.m.* supermarket.

superminimarge, *n.m.* off-price/cut-price store.

superprofits, *n.m.pl.* very high/large profits.

supplément, *n.m. (a)* supplement/addition; **en supplément,** extra/additional; **vin en supplément,** wine not included/wine extra (b) extra/additional payment; **supplément de prix,** extra charge/surcharge; **payer le supplément,** to pay the additional charge/the surcharge/the extra.

supplémentaire, a. supplementary/additional/extra/further; **dépenses supplémentaires,** additional expenses; Ind: **heures supplémentaires,** overtime; Post: **port supplémentaire,** extra postage; **demander un crédit supplémentaire,** to ask for (an) additional credit/for (a) further credit.

support, n.m. **support de publicité/ support publicitaire,** publicity medium/advertising medium.

supporter, v.tr. **supporter les frais de qch.,** to bear the cost of sth.

suppression, n.f. **suppression d'un produit,** abandonment of a product; Adm: **suppression de la double imposition,** double taxation relief; **600 suppressions d'emploi,** 600 jobs lost/600 job reductions; **suppression de solde,** suspension of pay.

supputation, n.f. calculation/reckoning; working out (of interest, etc.).

supputer, v.tr. to calculate/to reckon; to work out (interest, expenses).

sûr, a. safe/secure; **maison sûre,** firm of good/established standing; **placement sûr,** safe investment.

surabondance, n.f. surfeit/glut (of produce, etc.).

suracheté, a. **marché suracheté,** overtrading; **le marché est suracheté,** the market is over-bought/over-traded.

surassurance, n.f. over-insurance.

surcapacité, n.f. PolEc: surplus production capacity.

surcapitalisation, n.f. Fin: over-capitalization.

surcapitalisé, a. over-capitalized (company).

surcharge, n.f. (a) Ind: overloading;

surcharge permise, permissible overload (b) excess weight (of luggage) (c) **surcharge de travail,** excess/extra work (d) extra/excess tax (e) overcharge/surcharge; additional charge (on account rendered).

surcharger, v.tr. (a) Fin: **surcharger le marché,** to glut the market (b) to overtax; to overcharge.

surchauffe, n.f. PolEc: **surchauffe (économique),** overheating (of the economy).

surchoix, n.m. finest quality; **viande surchoix,** prime quality meat; choice meat.

surconsommation, n.f. PolEc: overconsumption.

surcotisation, n.f. extra contribution (paid to National Insurance, etc.).

surcoût, n.m. extra charge/cost/ expense.

surcroît, n.m. addition/increase; **surcroît de dépenses,** additional expenditure; **avoir un grand surcroît de travail,** to have a great deal of extra work.

surdéveloppé, a. PolEc: (a) highly developed (economy) (b) **un secteur surdéveloppé de l'économie,** an over-developed sector of the economy.

surdéveloppement, n.m. PolEc: over-development.

surdon, n.m. (a) compensation (allowable to purchaser) for damage to goods (b) right to non-acceptance (of damaged goods).

sureffectif, n.m. overmanning.

surélévation, n.f. (excessive) increase (of price, etc.).

surélever, v.tr. to raise (prices, tariff, etc.) higher; to force up (prices, etc.).

suremballage, n.m. Mkt: overwrap; outer wrap(per).

surémission, n.f. over-issue (of paper money).

suremploi, n.m. PolEc: overemployment

surenchère, n.f. higher bid/outbidding

counter-bid; **faire une surenchère sur qn,** to outbid s.o.

surenchérir, *v.i.* (*a*) to bid higher; **surenchérir sur qn,** to bid higher than s.o.; to outbid s.o. (*b*) to rise higher in price.

surenchérissement, *n.m.* further rise in prices.

surenchérisseur, -euse, *n.* outbidder.

surendetté, *a.* **pays surendetté,** country with more debts than it can repay.

surendettement, *n.m.* state of having more debts than one can repay.

suréquilibre, *n.m.* overbalance; **budget en suréquilibre,** overbalanced budget.

suréquipement, *n.m. PolEc:* overequipment.

suréquiper, *v.tr. PolEc:* to overequip.

surestarie, *n.f. MIns:* demurrage.

surestimation, *n.f.* overestimate/overvaluation.

surestimer, *v.tr.* to overestimate/to overvalue (price, cost).

sûreté, *n.f.* (*a*) safety/security/safe-keeping (*b*) *Jur:* surety/security/guarantee; **sûreté (en garantie) d'une créance,** security/surety for a debt; **sûreté personnelle,** surety; **sûreté réelle,** (real) security.

surévaluation, *n.f.* overvaluation/overestimate.

surévaluer, *v.tr.* to overestimate/to overvalue.

surexploitation, *n.f.* over-exploitation/excessive exploitation (of natural resources, etc.).

surface, *n.f.* (*a*) surface; **les grandes surfaces,** hypermarkets/(large) supermarkets; **surface de présentation (dans un magasin),** display space (in a store); **surface de vente,** sales/selling area (*b*) **surface financière,** financial standing.

surfaire, *v.tr.* **surfaire la valeur de qch.,** to

overcharge for (sth.)/to ask too much for (sth.)/to oversell (sth.).

surfait, *a.* **prix surfaits,** excessive prices; **restaurant surfait,** overrated restaurant.

surfin, *a.* superfine; of the highest quality.

surgelé, *a.* frozen (food).

surimposer, *v.tr.* (*a*) to increase the tax on (sth.) (*b*) to overtax.

surimposition, *n.f.* (*a*) increase of taxation (*b*) overtaxation.

surindustrialisation, *n.f.* overindustrialization.

surinvestissement, *n.m. Fin:* overinvestment.

surmarquage, *n.m.* overpricing; overcharging.

surmarquer, *v.tr.* to overprice (an article); to overcharge.

suroffre, *n.f.* (*a*) better offer; higher bid; counter-bid (*b*) offer exceeding demand.

suroffreur, *a.* **marché suroffreur,** market exceeding demand.

surpaie, *n.f.* = **surpaye.**

surpasser, *v.tr. Fin:* to oversubscribe (loan, etc.).

surpaye, *n.f.* overpaying/overpayment.

surpayer, *v.tr.* to overpay (s.o.); to pay too much for (sth.).

surpertes, *n.f.pl.* stop loss.

surplus, *n.m.* surplus/excess; **payer le surplus,** to pay the difference; **surplus agricoles,** agricultural surplus; *Fin:* **surplus monétaire,** monetary surplus; **surplus de productivité,** productivity surplus.

surprime, *n.f. Ins:* extra/additional premium; loaded premium.

surprix, *n.m.* excess price.

surproduction, *n.f. PolEc:* overproduction.

surproduire, *v.tr. & i. PolEc:* to over-produce.

surprofit, *n.m. PolEc:* (*i*) abnormally high profit (*ii*) excessive profit.

surremise, *n.f.* special discount; extra/additional discount.

surréservation, *n.f.* double booking/overbooking.

sursalaire, *n.m.* supplementary wage/extra pay; bonus.

sursaturer, *v.tr.* to supersaturate (the market).

sursis, *n.m. Jur:* respite/delay; **sursis d'exécution de peine,** stay of execution; **sursis de paiement,** respite of payment.

sursouscrire, *v.tr. Fin:* to oversubscribe (a loan, an issue).

sursouscrit, *a Fin:* oversubscribed.

surtare, *n.f.* extra tare.

surtaux, *n.m.* over-assessment; **présenter une réclamation en surtaux,** to claim a reduction of assessment.

surtaxe, *n.f.* (*a*) surtax/extra tax; **surtaxe à l'importation,** import surcharge; **surtaxe sur les marchandises,** surcharge on goods; **surtaxe progressive,** progressive surtax (*b*) excessive tax; over-assessment.

surtaxer, *v.tr.* to overtax; to over-assess.

survaleur, *n.f.* overvalue (of currencies).

surveillance, *n.f.* (*a*) supervision; *Ind:* **personnel chargé de la surveillance,** maintenance staff; **surveillance de la production,** production control (*b*) **surveillance des prix,** monitoring of prices.

surveillant,-ante, *n.* supervisor; (*dans un magasin*) shopwalker.

survendre, *v.i.* to oversell/to overcharge; **le marché est survendu,** the market is oversold.

survente, *n.f.* (*a*) (*vieilli*) overselling/(*b*) overcharging.

survie, *n.f. Ins:* **tables de survie,** expectation of life/life expectancy tables.

sus, *adv.phr.* **en sus,** in addition/extra; **frais de poste en sus,** postage extra.

susdit,-ite, *a. & n. Jur:* aforementioned/above-mentioned/aforesaid.

susmentionné, *a. & n. Jur:* aforementioned/above-mentioned.

susnommé, *a. & n. Jur: Adm:* aforenamed/above-named.

suspendre, *v.tr.* (*a*) to suspend; to stop (payment); **suspendre le travail pour deux jours,** to stop/to suspend work for two days; **suspendre le paiement d'un chèque,** to stop a cheque (*b*) **suspendre un fonctionnaire,** to suspend an official.

suspens, *adv.phr.* **en suspens,** pending; in abeyance; **effets en suspens,** bills held over/bills outstanding.

suspension, *n.f.* **suspension de paiements,** suspension of payment; **suspension d'un employé,** suspension of an employee; *StExch:* **suspension de la cotation/de séance,** trading halt.

swap, *n.m. Bank:* **(opération de) swap,** swap; **swap d'actifs,** asset swaps; **option de swap,** swaption.

symbolique, *a.* **loyer symbolique,** nominal rent; **paiement symbolique,** token payment; *Jur:* **obtenir le franc symbolique de dommages-intérêts,** to be awarded token damages.

syndic, *n.m.* (*avant 1985*) **syndic de faillite,** official receiver (in bankruptcy).

syndical, *a.* 1. **chambre syndicale (des agents de change)** = Stock Exchange Committee; **commission syndicale,** underwriting commission; **part syndicale,** underwriting share 2. **carte syndicale,** union card; **délégué syndical,** shop steward/(trade) union representative; **mouvement syndical,** trade-union movement; **relations syndicales,** industrial relations; **réunion syndicale,** union meeting.

syndicalisme, *n.m.* **syndicalisme (ouvrier),** trade unionism.

syndicaliste, *n.m.f.* trade unionist.

syndicat, *n.m.* **1.** syndicate; **syndicat d'enchères,** tender pool; **syndicat financier,** (financial) syndicate; **syndicat de garantie/de prise ferme,** underwriting syndicate; pool; **syndicat industriel,** pool; **Syndicat d'Initiative** = tourist information office; **syndicat patronal,** employers' federation; **syndicat de producteurs,** producers' association; **syndicat professionnel,** trade association **2. syndicat (ouvrier),** trade union/*NAm:* labor union; **les syndicats,** the unions; **syndicat des mineurs,** miners' union.

syndicataire, 1. *a.* of/pertaining to a syndicate **2.** *n.* (*a*) member of a syndicate (*b*) *Fin:* underwriter.

syndication, *n.f.* syndication.

syndiqué, *a.* **1.** belonging to a syndicate **2. ouvriers syndiqués,** trade unionists; **travailleurs non syndiqués,** non-union workers/workers who are not members of a union.

syndiquer, 1. *v.tr.* to form into a trade union; to unionize (an industry, etc.) **2.** *v.pr.* **se syndiquer** (*a*) to form a syndicate/to syndicate (*b*) to form a trade union (*c*) to join a union.

synergie, *n.f.* synergy.

synthétique, *a.* synthetic.

systématique, *a.* systematic; **entretien systématique,** planned maintenance.

systématisation, *n.f.* system(at)ization/system(at)izing.

systématiser, *v.tr.* to systematize.

système, *n.m.* **analyse de systèmes,** systems analysis; **système bancaire,** bank(ing) system; **système comptable,** accounting system; **système de direction,** management system; **système d'information par ordinateur,** computerized information system; **système intégré de gestion,** integrated management system; **système métrique,** metric system; **système monétaire européen (SME),** European monetary system (EMS); **système de traitement de l'information/système informatique,** data processing system/computer system.

T

table, *n.f.* table; *Ins:* **table(s) d'actualisation**, present value tables; **tables de mortalité/d'espérance de vie**, expectation of life tables/life expectancy tables/ actuaries' tables; **table d'intérêts**, interest table; **table des parités**, parity table/table of par values; **table de poids et mesures**, table of weights and measures; **table ronde**, round table.

tableau, *n.m.* **1.** board; **tableau d'affichage**, notice board; *Rail: etc:* indicator board; **tableau des arrivées**, arrivals board; **tableau des départs**, departures board **2.** (*a*) list/table; **tableau d'avancement**, promotion table; **tableau de bord**, management chart; *Rail: etc:* **tableau des horaires**, timetable; **tableau de marche**, progress schedule; **tableau de prix**, price list; **tableau statistique**, statistical table; **tableau de travail**, work schedule/timetable; **sous forme de tableau**, in tabular form/ tabulated; **disposer (des chiffres) en tableau**, to tabulate (figures) (*b*) *Fin:* **tableau d'amortissement**, redemption table; **tableau comptable**, (financial) statement; **tableau emplois-ressources/tableau de financement**, statement of source and application of funds.

tabloïd, tabloïde, *n.m.* tabloid (newspaper).

tabulatrice, *n.f.* tabulator/tabulating machine (*in punched-card system, etc.*); **tabulatrice numérique**, digital tabulator.

tâche, *n.f.* job; **affectation des tâches**, job assignment; **analyse des tâches**, job analysis/operations analysis; **fixation des tâches**, job specification; **ouvrier à la tâche**, (*i*) piece worker (*ii*) jobbing worker; **travail à la tâche**, (*i*) piece work (*ii*) work

(paid) by the job; **travailler à la tâche**, to be on piecework.

tachistoscope, *n.m. Mkt:* tachistoscope.

tachygraphe, *n.m. Trans:* tachograph.

tacite, *a.* tacit; **convention tacite**, tacit agreement; *Jur:* **tacite reconduction**, renewal (of lease) by tacit agreement.

tactique, **1.** *a.* tactical; **plan tactique**, tactical plan(ning) **2.** *n.f.* tactics; **tactique commerciale**, marketing tactics; **tactiques de défense contre-OPA**, defensive tactics; **tactique de la terre brûlée**, scorched earth.

taille, *n.f.* (*d'un vêtement*) size; **les grandes tailles**, the large sizes; outsizes; **petite taille**, small size; **taille courante**, standard size/stock size; **taille de l'entreprise**, size of the firm.

talon, *n.m.* **talon d'un chèque**, counterfoil/ stub of cheque; *Fin:* talon (of sheet, of coupons).

tampon, *n.m.* **1.** (*a*) (inking) pad (*b*) rubber stamp; **apposer le tampon "acquitté" sur une facture**, to stamp "paid" on a bill; to receipt a bill (*c*) **tampon de la poste**, postmark **2. stock tampon**, buffer stock/safety stock.

tant, *n.* **le tant pour cent sur cette opération**, the percentage on this transaction; **gagner tant par mois**, to be paid so much a month; **payé à tant par jour**, paid (at a rate of) so much per day/a day.

tantième, *n.m.* percentage/share/quota (of profits, etc.); **tantièmes des administrateurs**, directors' percentage of profit.

taper, *v.tr.* **taper une lettre (à la machine)**, to type a letter; **dactylo qui tape au toucher**, touch-typist.

tapeur, -euse, *n.f.* **tapeur de fonds,** fund raiser.

tarage, *n.m.* taring; allowance for tare.

tare, *n.f.* 1. depreciation/loss in value (*owing to damage or waste*) 2. tare; **tare moyenne/tare par épreuve,** average tare; **tare réelle,** actual tare; **faire la tare,** to allow for/to ascertain the tare.

tarer, *v.tr.* to tare/to ascertain the weight of (packing case, etc.).

tarif, *n.m.* (*a*) tariff/price list; **tarif de nuit,** night charge/rate/fare; (*dans un café*) **tarif des consommations,** price list/bar prices; *Cust:* **tarif d'entrée,** import list; **tarif de sortie,** export list (*b*) tariff/scale (of charges); rate; **abaissement des tarifs,** lowering of tariffs; **relèvement des tarifs,** raising of tariffs; **tarif dégressif,** sliding-scale tariff/tapering charge; **tarif en vigueur,** rate in force; **tarif forfaitaire,** fixed rate/charge; **tarif d'un impôt,** rate of a tax; *Journ: etc:* **tarif de la publicité,** advertising rates; **tarif réduit,** reduced rate; **tarif des salaires,** scale of wages; **tarif uniforme,** flat rate; **taux indices des tarifs,** tariff-level indices (*c*) *Cust:* **tarif ad valorem,** ad valorem tariff; **tarif différentiel,** discriminating duty; **tarif douanier,** customs tariff; **tarif douanier commun,** common external tariff; **tarif de faveur/tarif préférentiel,** preferential rate/tariff (*d*) *Post:* **tarifs postaux,** postal rates; **tarif (des) imprimés,** printed paper rate; **tarif (des) lettres,** letter rate; **tarif normal,** ordinary rate/first(-)class (rate); **tarif réduit,** reduced rate/second(-)class (rate) (*e*) *Trans:* **plein tarif,** (*i*) full fare; adult fare (for passengers) (*ii*) full tariff (for goods, etc.); **tarif par kilomètre,** fare/tariff per kilometre; **tarif (des) marchandises,** goods/freight rate.

arifaire, *a.* relating to tariffs; **accord tarifaire,** tariff agreement; **barrières tarifaires,** tariff barriers; **barrières non tarifaires,** non-tariff barriers; **lois tarifaires,** tariff laws.

arifer, *v.tr.* to tariff; to fix the rate of (duties, etc.); to fix the price of (goods, etc.).

tarification, *n.f.* tariffing; fixing the rate/rate fixing (of duties); fixing the price (of goods, etc.).

tas, *n.m.* **formation sur le tas,** on-the-job training; **grève sur le tas,** sit-down strike.

tassement, *n.m. Fin: StExch:* setback; **tassement du marché,** weakening of the market; **tassement des prix,** sagging of prices.

se tasser, *v.pr.* (*en parlant d'un marché, des valeurs*) to weaken.

taux, *n.m.* 1. (*a*) rate; **taux de l'impôt,** rate of income tax (*b*) **taux des salaires,** wage rate; **taux horaire,** hourly rate/pay; **être payé au taux de £5 l'heure,** to be paid at the rate of £5 an hour 2. (*a*) percentage/rate; **taux d'intérêt,** interest rate/rate of interest; **taux d'intérêt facial,** nominal rate; **taux légal,** legal rate; **taux de rendement/de rentabilité (d'un placement),** rate of return (on investment); **prêter au taux de 12%,** to lend at (the rate of) 12%; **taux d'inflation,** rate of inflation (*b*) *Bank:* **taux de base (bancaire)/taux de référence,** base rate; **taux d'escompte/*FrC:* taux préférentiel,** minimum lending rate/bank rate/*NAm:* prime rate (*c*) **taux de/du change,** rate of exchange/exchange rate; **taux de change fixe,** fixed exchange rate; **le taux du jour,** today's rate (*d*) *StExch:* **taux de conversion,** conversion rate; **taux de déport,** backwardation rate; **taux de report,** contango rate; **taux plafonné,** cap 3. (*a*) *Fin:* ratio; **taux de capitalisation des bénéfices,** price earnings ratio; **taux de corrélation,** relative strength; **taux de couverture,** cover ratio; **taux de profit net,** net profit ratio; **taux de marge,** mark-up ratio; **taux de rotation des stocks,** rate of turnover (*b*) **taux de mortalité/de natalité,** death/birth rate.

taxation, *n.f.* 1. fixing of prices/wages/etc. 2. *Adm:* (*a*) taxation (*b*) assessment.

taxe, *n.f.* 1. (*a*) fixed price; fixed rate (of pay); **marchandises vendues à la taxe,** goods sold at the controlled price (*b*) charge (for service); rate; *Tel:* call charge; **taxe forfaitaire,** flat rate; **taxe postale,**

postage; **taxe supplémentaire,** surcharge **2.** tax/duty/rate; **taxe d'aéroport,** airport tax; **taxe sur le chiffre d'affaires,** turnover tax; **taxe à l'importation,** import duty; **taxe locale/taxe d'habitation** = rates; **taxe de luxe,** tax on luxury goods/luxury tax; *Adm:* **taxe parafiscale/taxe exceptionnelle,** exceptional tax/special levy; **taxe professionnelle,** business licence; **taxe sur les spectacles,** entertainment tax; **taxe sur le tabac,** tax on tobacco; **taxe à la valeur ajoutée (TVA)/***FrC:* **taxe sur les ventes,** value-added tax (VAT)/*NAm:* = sales tax; **hors taxes (HT),** exclusive of tax; **toutes taxes comprises (TTC),** inclusive of tax; fully taxed.

taxer, *v.tr.* **1.** to regulate/to fix (prices); to regulate the rate of (wages, postage); **taxer une denrée,** to fix a controlled price for a food product **2.** to tax/to impose a tax on (s.o., luxury goods, cars, etc.); **marchandises faiblement taxées,** low-duty goods; **marchandises fortement taxées,** high-duty goods.

technicien, -ienne, *n.* technician.

technico-commercial, *a.* **agent technico-commercial,** sales technician.

technique, 1. *a.* technical; **directeur technique,** technical manager/works manager; **service technique,** engineering department **2.** *n.f.* **techniques commerciales,** marketing techniques; **techniques de défense contre-OPA,** defensive tactics; **techniques de gestion,** management techniques; **techniques marchandes,** merchandising techniques; **techniques de la vente,** sales engineering.

techniquement, *adv.* technically.

technocrate, *n.m.f.* technocrat.

technocratie, *n.f. PolEc:* technocracy.

technocratique, *a.* technocratic.

technologie, *n.f.* technology; **haute technologie,** high technology/high tech.; **technologie de pointe,** advanced technology.

technologique, *a.* technological; **chô-**

mage technologique, unemployment resulting from automation.

téléachat, *n.m.* teleshopping.

Télécarte, *n.f. Rtm:* Phonecard (*Rtm:*).

télécommunication, *n.f.* telecommunication(s).

téléconférence, *n.f.* teleconferencing.

télécopie, *n.f.* facsimile/Fax (*Rtm:*).

télécopier, *v.tr.* to facsimile/to Fax (*Rtm:*).

télécopieur, *n.m.* facsimile/Fax (*Rtm:*) machine.

télégestion, *n.f. Cmptr:* teleprocessing.

télégramme, *n.m.* telegram; **envoyer un télégramme à qn,** to send a telegram to s.o.

télégraphe, *n.m.* telegraph.

télégraphier, *v.tr. & i.* to telegraph/to wire; to cable; **télégraphier à Paris,** to cable/to send a cable to Paris; **j'ai télégraphié la nouvelle,** I cabled the news.

télégraphique, *a.* telegraphic; **adresse télégraphique,** telegraphic address; **dépêche télégraphique,** telegram; **service télégraphique,** telegraph service.

téléimprimeur, *n.m.* teleprinter/*NAm:* teletypewriter; **liaison par téléimprimeur,** teleprinting.

téléinformatique, *n.f. Cmptr:* teleprocessing.

télématique, *n.f.* telematics.

télémercatique, *n.f.* telemarketing.

téléphone, *n.m.* telephone/phone; **abonné du téléphone,** telephone subscriber; **annuaire du téléphone/des téléphones,** telephone directory/phone book; **commande par téléphone,** telephone/phone order; **coup de téléphone,** telephone/phone call; **numéro de téléphone,** telephone/phone number; **téléphone à touches/à clavier,** push-button telephone/*NAm:* touch dialing telephone; **téléphone automatique,**

STD (system)/automatic telephone system/direct dialling; **téléphone intérieur,** house telephone/house phone/internal phone; **ventes par téléphone,** telesales; **appeler qn au téléphone/donner un coup de téléphone à qn,** to phone s.o./to call s.o. (up)/to ring s.o.; **être abonné au téléphone,** to be on the phone; **commander qch. par téléphone,** to order sth. by telephone/phone; **parler à qn au téléphone,** to speak to s.o. on the phone.

téléphoner, *v.tr. & i.* (*a*) to telephone/to phone (a piece of news, etc.) (*b*) **téléphoner à qn,** to ring s.o. (up)/to phone s.o./to call s.o. (up); **je vous téléphonerai demain,** I'll give you a ring/a call tomorrow; I'll ring you (up)/I'll phone you/I'll call you tomorrow.

téléphonique, *a.* **annuaire téléphonique,** telephone directory/phone book; **appel téléphonique,** telephone/phone call; **cabine téléphonique,** call box/phone box; **centrale téléphonique,** telephone exchange; **commande téléphonique,** telephone/phone order; **marketing téléphonique,** telephone marketing; **redevance téléphonique,** rental charge; **taxe téléphonique,** call charge.

téléphoniste, *n.m.f.* telephonist; telephone operator.

téléscripteur, *n.m.* teleprinter/*NAm:* teletypewriter.

télétraitement, *n.m. Cmptr:* teleprocessing.

télétypiste, *n.m.f.* teletypist; teletype(writer) operator/teleprinter operator.

télévendeur, -euse, *n.* telesales person.

télévente, *n.f.* telesales(s).

télex, *n.m. Rtm:* (*a*) Telex (machine); **abonné au service Télex,** Telex subscriber; **réseau Télex,** Telex network; **tarif Télex,** Telex rate; **envoyer par Télex,** to send by Telex/to telex; **nous avons reçu cette commande par Télex,** we received this order by Telex (*b*) telex (message);

envoyer un télex au Canada, to telex Canada/to send a telex to Canada.

télexer, *v.tr.* to send by Telex/to telex.

télexiste, *n.m.f.* Telex operator.

témoignage, *n.m.* testimony; evidence.

témoin[1], *n.m.* witness.

témoin[2], *a.* **appartement/maison témoin,** show flat/show house.

tempérament, *n.m.* **acheter à tempérament,** to buy on credit/to buy by instalments/to buy on easy terms/to buy on hire purchase (HP)/*NAm:* to buy on the installment plan; **achat à tempérament,** credit purchase/purchase on credit; **crédit à tempérament,** instalment credit; **vente à tempérament,** sale on hire purchase/on credit.

temporaire, *a.* **mesures temporaires,** temporary measures; **personnel temporaire,** temporary staff; **travail temporaire,** temporary work; *Cust:* **admis en franchise temporaire,** passed for temporary importation.

temps, *n.m.* (*a*) **emploi à plein temps,** full-time employment; **emploi à temps partiel/à mi-temps,** part-time employment; **emploi/travail à temps partagé,** job-share/time-share; **travailler à temps complet/à plein temps,** to work full time; **résidence en temps partagé,** time-share (*b*) time/period; *Mkt:* **temps d'antenne,** airtime/airspace/broadcasting time; *Ind:* **temps mort/temps d'arrêt/temps improductif,** down time/idle time/waiting time (*c*) **en temps utile,** in good time; **étude des temps et des méthodes,** time and methods study; **étude des temps et des mouvements,** time and motion study (*d*) *Cmptr:* **temps d'accès,** access time; **temps partagé,** shared time (*e*) **industrie du temps libre,** leasure industry.

tenante, *n.f.* holding company.

tendance, *n.f.* tendency/trend; **tendance à la baisse/tendance baissière,** downward trend/tendency; downtrend; *StExch:* bearish tendency; **tendance à la hausse,**

upward trend/tendency; *StExch:* bullish tendency; **tendance de croissance,** growth trend; **tendance déflationniste,** deflationary tendency; **tendance économique,** economic trend; **tendance générale,** general trend/tendency; **les tendances du marché,** market trends/general trend of the market; **renversement de tendance,** trend reversal.

teneur[1], **-euse,** *n.* **teneur de livres,** bookkeeper; **teneur de marché,** market maker.

teneur[2], *n.f.* **1.** tenor/(exact) wording/terms (of document, etc.) **2.** (*a*) *Ind: etc:* amount/content/percentage (*b*) **teneur payante,** payable grade (of ore); **teneur en or,** gold content.

tenir, 1. *v.tr.* (*a*) to keep; **tenir la caisse,** to be in charge of the cash/the till; **elle tient la caisse,** she is the cashier; **tenir la comptabilité/les livres,** to keep the accounts; **tenir un magasin,** to keep/to run a shop (*b*) to keep/to stock (groceries, etc.) **2.** *v.i.* **mon offre tient toujours,** my offer still stands.

tenu, *a. StExch:* firm/hard (prices).

tenue, *n.f.* **1.** keeping/managing/running (shop, etc.); **tenue de livres,** bookkeeping; **tenue de livres à/en partie double/tenue de livres à/en partie simple,** double-entry/single-entry bookkeeping **2.** *Fin:* steadiness/firmness (of prices); tone (of the market); **la bonne tenue du franc,** the firmness of the franc/the strong position of the franc.

terme[1], *n.m.* **1.** (*a*) **prévisions à court terme/à long terme,** short-range/long-range forecasts (*b*) *Fin: Bank:* **à court terme,** short-term/short-dated; **à long terme,** long-term/long-dated; **argent à court terme,** money at short notice/at call; **crédit à court terme/à long terme,** short-term/long-term credit; short/long credit; **dépôt à terme,** fixed deposit; **court terme,** short end; **dettes à court terme,** current liabilities; **effet à court terme/à long terme,** short-dated/long-dated bill; **emprunt à court terme,** short(-term) loan; **placement à long terme,** long-term invest-

ment; **prêt à terme,** time loan; term loan; **acheter à terme,** to buy on credit (*c*) *StExch:* **le terme,** the settlement; **cours à terme/taux pour les opérations à terme,** forward rate(s)/price for the account; **livrable à terme,** for future delivery; **livraisons à terme,** futures; **marché à terme,** (*i*) futures market/forward market (*ii*) terminal market; **opérations/transactions à terme,** forward deals/sales/trading; futures; **opération de change à terme,** forward exchange contract; **valeurs à terme,** securities dealt in for the account; **acheter à terme,** to buy forward/to buy for the account; **vendre livrable à terme,** to sell forward (*d*) delay (for payment); *Jur:* **accorder un terme de grâce,** to allow (a debtor) extra time to pay; **terme de rigueur,** latest (possible) date (*e*) instalment; **acheter à terme,** to buy on credit; **remboursable par paiements à terme,** repayable by instalments **2.** (*a*) quarter (of rent); term (*b*) quarter's rent (*c*) quarter day.

terme[2], *n.m.* (*a*) term; **terme de métier,** technical term (*b*) *pl.* wording (of clause, etc.); terms/conditions; **termes d'un contrat,** terms of a contract; **aux termes de l'article 12,** in accordance with the terms of article 12; by/under article 12.

terminal, *n.m.* (*a*) (air, container, etc.) terminal (*b*) *Cmptr:* terminal (*c*) **terminaux points de vente,** point-of-sale terminals.

terminer, 1. *v.tr.* to terminate; to end/to finish/to bring to a close (meeting, etc.) **2.** *v.i.* **les actions ont terminé à ...,** shares finished/closed at ... **3.** *v.pr.* **se terminer,** to end/to come to an end; **exercice se terminant au 31 décembre,** year ending 31st December.

terrain, *n.m.* **1.** (*a*) ground; piece of ground; plot (of land); **terrains à lotir,** development site/building land; **terrain à bâtir,** a building plot; **mettre en valeur un terrain à construire,** to develop building site (*b*) **la livre a perdu du terrain,** sterling has lost ground **2.** *Mkt:* **sur le terrain,** in the field; **prospection sur**

terrain, field research; **travaux sur le terrain,** fieldwork.

terre, *n.f.* **1.** ground/land; **impôt sur la vente des terres,** tax on the sale of land; **prix courant de la terre,** current price of land **2.** estate/property; **emprunter de l'argent sur une terre,** to borrow money on the security of an estate.

terrestre, *a. Ins:* **assurance terrestre,** land insurance.

territoire, *n.m. Mkt:* **territoire de vente,** sales territory.

tertiaire, *a. PolEc:* **secteur tertiaire,** tertiary industries/service industries.

test, *n.m.* test/trial; **test d'aptitude,** aptitude test; **test auprès des consommateurs,** consumer test(ing); **test sur place,** testing in the field/field testing; **test de produit,** product test(ing); **test de vente,** market test.

testament, *n.m. Jur:* will.

tête, *n.f.* head; **par tête,** per capita/per person.

texte, *n.m.* (*d'un contrat, etc.*) text/wording; *Cmptr:* **machine de traitement de textes,** word processor.

thème, *n.m.* theme; **thème publicitaire,** advertising theme.

théorie, *n.f.* theory; **théorie de l'information,** information theory.

théorique, *a.* **profits théoriques,** paper profits.

ticket, *n.m.* (*a*) ticket; coupon; **ticket d'admission,** entrance ticket; **ticket d'admission dans un parking,** car park ticket; **ticket d'autobus/de métro,** bus/underground ticket; **ticket de caisse,** till receipt (*b*) *Adm:* **ticket modérateur,** patients' contribution towards cost of medical treatment.

ticket-repas *n.m.,* **ticket-restaurant,** *n.m.* = luncheon voucher (*Rtm:*).

tierce, *a.f. see* **tiers.**

tiercisme, *n.m. Mkt:* third-party branding/sub-branding.

tiers, 1. *a.* (*a*) **tierce caution,** contingent liability; **une tierce personne,** a third person; **tiers porteur,** second endorser (of a bill); **taux de change entre devises tierces,** cross rates of exchange; *Jur:* **en main tierce,** in the hands of a third party; **déposé en main tierce,** held in escrow (*b*) **tiers monde,** third world (*c*) *EEC:* **marché tiers,** market outside the (European) community **2.** *n.m.* (*a*) third (part); **remise d'un tiers (du prix),** discount of a third/a third off (the price) (*b*) third party; **assurance au tiers/vis-à-vis des tiers,** third-party insurance; **tiers bénéficiaire,** beneficiary (of a cheque, a bill of exchange, etc.); *Adm:* **tiers payant,** direct payment of medical expenses by social security or insurance company; **tiers provisionnel,** interim tax payment (*equal to one third of tax paid in the previous tax year*); *Fin:* **tiers souscripteur,** third-party subscriber.

tiers-saisi, *n.m.* garnishee.

timbre, *n.m.* **1.** (*a*) stamp (on document, etc.); **timbre à empreinte,** embossed stamp; **timbre du jour,** date (stamped on document) (*b*) (postage) stamp; **carnet de timbres,** book of stamps (*c*) *Adm:* **droit de timbre,** stamp duty; **timbre fiscal,** revenue stamp; **timbre proportionnel,** ad valorem stamp; **timbre de quittance,** receipt stamp (*d*) **timbre dateur,** date stamp; **timbre humide/timbre de caoutchouc,** rubber stamp **2.** crest/mark (of a firm).

timbre-poste, *n.m.* postage stamp.

timbre-prime, *n.m.* trading stamp.

timbre-quittance, *n.m.* receipt stamp.

timbrer, *v.tr.* (*a*) to stamp (passport, document, etc.); to stamp the postmark on (letter, etc.); **lettre timbrée de Paris,** letter with a Paris postmark/letter postmarked Paris; *Adm:* **papier timbré,** official paper on which stamp duty has been paid (*b*) **timbrer une lettre,** to stamp/to put a stamp on a letter; **joindre une enveloppe timbrée**

pour la réponse, to enclose a stamped addressed envelope (s.a.e.) for reply.

tirage, *n.m.* **1.** drawing (of bonds, of lottery, etc.); *Fin:* **tirage au sort,** drawing of lots; **bons sortis au tirage,** drawn bonds; **les obligations sont rachetées par voie de tirage,** debentures are redeemed by lot **2.** (*a*) *Bank: Fin:* drawing/issue (of cheque, bill of exchange); **tirage en l'air/en blanc,** *F:* kite flying/kiting (*b*) *Fin:* **droits de tirage spéciaux (du FMI),** special drawing rights (of the IMF) **3.** *Publ: Journ:* printing/print-run; circulation (of newspaper); edition (of book); **journal à fort tirage,** newspaper with a large circulation; **un tirage de 30 000 exemplaires,** a circulation/a print-run of 30 000 copies; **tirage limité,** limited edition **4.** *Cmptr:* hard copy.

tiré, -ée, *n.* drawee.

tirer, *v.tr.* **1.** to draw/to obtain; **tirer un profit de qch.,** to get/to make a profit from sth. **2.** to draw (bill of exchange, cheque); **tirer un chèque sur une banque,** to draw a cheque on a bank; **tirer à vue sur qn,** to draw on s.o. at sight **3.** *Publ: Journ:* to print; **bon à tirer,** passed for press; **journal qui tire à 30 000 exemplaires,** newspaper with a circulation of 30 000; **tirer un livre à 5 000 exemplaires,** to print 5 000 copies of a book.

tireur, -euse, *n.* drawer (of bill of exchange, of cheque).

tiroir-caisse, *n.m.* till.

tissu, *n.m.* fabric/material.

titre, *n.m.* **1.** title; form of address; *Jur:* **propriétaire en titre,** legal owner/titular owner; **sans titre officiel,** without any official status **2.** (*a*) **titre (de propriété),** title deed (*b*) **titre de créance,** proof/evidence of debt; debt security; **titre de crédit,** proof of credit; **titre de paiement,** (document of) payment/remittance; **le titre de paiement doit être envoyé à ...,** remittance by cheque or money order to be sent to ... (*c*) *Fin: StExch:* warrant/bond/certificate; *pl.* stocks and shares; **titre à lots,** lottery loan bond; **titres dilués,**

watered stock; **titres négociables,** negotiable stock; **titre nominatif,** registered security; **titre de participation,** share; participation certificate; **titres de placement,** investment securities; **titres en portefeuille,** securities (in portfolio); **titre au porteur,** bearer security; **titre de prêt,** loan certificate; **titre provisoire,** scrip certificate; **titres ramassés,** takeover stock; **titre de rente,** government bond; **titre sous-jacent,** underlying security; **titres subordonnés à durée indéterminée (TSDI),** subordinated perpetuals; **certificat de titres/titre d'action(s),** share certificate; **marché des titres,** stock market; **plan d'options sur titres,** stock option plan; **prendre livraison de titres,** to take delivery of stock; **vendre des titres,** to sell stock **3.** claim/right; **titre juridique à qch.,** legal claim to sth. (*b*) **à titre de ...,** by way of ...; as a ...; **à titre gratuit,** free (of charge); *Jur:* **à titre onéreux,** subject to certain liabilities/subject to payment; **à titre provisoire,** provisionally; **marchandises envoyées à titre d'essai,** goods sent on approval.

titulaire, 1. *a.* titular **2.** *n. m.f.* holder (of passport, etc.); **titulaire d'un brevet,** patentee; *Bank:* **titulaire d'un compte,** account holder; **titulaire d'une carte de crédit,** (credit) cardholder; **titulaire d'un poste,** holder of a post.

titularisation, *n.f. Adm:* establishment (of civil servant, etc.) in a job/post; **en stage de titularisation,** on probation.

titulariser, *v.tr. Adm: etc:* to confirm (s.o.) in his post/appointment.

tolérance, *n.f. Cust:* **tolérance (permise),** tolerance/allowance.

tomber, *v.i.* (*prix, valeurs, etc.*) to fall (back)/to drop.

tonnage, *n.m.* **1.** tonnage (of ship) **2.** tonnage (of a port) **3.** **(droit de) tonnage,** (duty based on) tonnage.

tonne, *n.f.* (*a*) ton (= 1 000 kg); **tonne courte,** short ton (= 907.185 kg); **tonne forte,** long ton/gross ton (= 1016.06 kg); **tonne kilomètre** = ton mile; **tonne ki-**

lométrique, kilometric ton; **tonne métrique,** tonne/metric ton (*b*) *Nau:* **affrètement à la tonne,** freighting per ton; **tonne de jauge,** gross ton/register ton.

tonneau, *n.m.* **1.** cask/barrel **2.** *Nau:* **tonneau d'affrètement,** freight ton; **tonneau de capacité,** measurement ton; ton measurement; **tonneau de jauge,** gross ton/register ton; **navire de 5 000 tonneaux,** 5 000-ton ship/ship of 5 000 tons burden.

tontine, *n.f. Ins:* tontine.

total, **1.** *a.* total/complete/entire/whole; **coût total,** total cost; **dépenses totales,** total expenses; **montant total,** total amount; **nombre total d'actions,** total number of shares; **somme totale,** sum total **2.** *n.m.* whole/total; **total global,** sum total/grand total; **le total des recettes et des dépenses,** total revenue and expenditure; **faire le total des bénéfices,** to add up the profits/to calculate the total profit; **total de l'actif/du passif,** total assets/liabilities.

totalisation, *n.f.* totalizing/totalization; adding up (of amounts).

totaliser, *v.tr.* to totalize/to total up/to add up; **l'actif se totalise par deux millions,** the assets add up to two million.

totalité, *n.f.* totality/whole; **versements faits en totalité,** payments made in full.

touchable, *a.* (cheque) that can be cashed; collectable (bill).

toucher, *v.tr.* **toucher son traitement,** to be paid; to draw/to receive one's salary; **toucher un chèque,** to cash a cheque; **toucher des intérêts,** to receive interest; **toucher une traite,** to collect a bill.

tour, *n.m. Bank: Fin:* **tour de table,** pool.

tourisme, *n.m.* tourism; tourist trade; **agence/bureau de tourisme,** travel agency/tourist agency; **office du tourisme,** tourist board.

touriste, *n.m.f.* tourist; *Nau: Av:* **classe touriste,** tourist class.

touristique, *a.* tourist; **menu touristique,**

tourist menu; **renseignements touristiques,** tourist information; **ville/centre touristique,** tourist centre.

tour-opérateur, *n.m.* tour operator.

trader, *n.m.* trader.

trafic, *n.m.* **1.** (*a*) illicit trading; trafficking (*b*) *Jur:* **trafic d'influence,** (corrupt) favour trading **2.** *Trans:* traffic; **trafic ferroviaire/des chemins de fer,** rail(way) traffic; **trafic routier/aérien,** road/air traffic; **trafic (de) marchandises,** goods/freight traffic.

trafiquant,-ante, *n.* trafficker; **trafiquant du marché noir,** black marketeer.

trafiquer, *v.tr.* to traffic in sth.

train, *n.m.* **1.** train; **train de marchandises,** goods/freight train; **train mixte,** passenger and goods train **2.** **train de vie,** standard of living **3.** **train de propositions,** package deal.

traite, *n.f.* (*a*) *Fin:* (banker's) draft; bill (of exchange); **traite avalisée,** guaranteed bill; **traite à courte échéance,** short-dated bill; **traite à longue échéance,** long-dated bill; **traite à terme,** time draft; **traite en l'air,** fictitious bill/*F:* kite; **traite sur l'étranger/sur l'extérieur,** foreign bill; **traite sur l'intérieur,** inland bill; **traite à vue,** sight bill; **encaisser une traite,** to collect a bill; **escompter une traite,** to discount a bill; **présenter une traite à l'acceptation,** to present a bill for acceptance; **tirer une traite,** to draw a bill (*b*) (hire purchase) payment/instalment; **je rembourse les traites,** I pay the instalments.

traité, *n.m. Ins:* **traité facultatif obligatoire,** open cover.

traitement, *n.m.* **1.** (*a*) processing; *Ind:* **capacité de traitement,** handling capacity; **traitement par lots,** batch processing (*b*) *Cmptr:* **traitement de l'information/de données,** data processing; **traitement de textes,** word processing; **machine de traitement de textes,** word processor; **unité centrale de traitement,** main frame (computer) **2.** salary; **structure des traitements,**

salary structure; **toucher un traitement fixe,** to draw/to be paid a fixed salary.

traiter, 1. *v.tr.* (*a*) *Ind:* to process (*b*) to handle (business); **traiter une affaire avec qn,** to transact a piece of business with s.o. **2.** *v.i.* to negotiate/to deal; **traiter avec ses créanciers,** to negotiate with one's creditors.

traiteur, *n.m.* (outside) caterer.

tranche, *n.f.* (*a*) **tranche de revenus,** income bracket; **la tranche des salariés moyens,** the middle-income bracket (*b*) block/ portion (of an issue of shares, etc.); *Adm:* **par tranche de 1 000 francs ou fraction de 1 000 francs,** for every complete sum of 1 000 francs or part thereof; **émettre un emprunt en tranches,** to issue a loan in instalments.

transaction, *n.f.* (*a*) transaction; **transaction commerciale,** commercial transaction; **transaction au comptant,** cash transaction/cash deal; **transactions à crédit,** loan transactions/credit transactions; **transactions à terme,** futures; forward trading (*b*) *StExch: etc:* dealing/deal/trading; **transaction automatisée sur écran,** screen-based automated dealing; **transaction hors bourse,** after hours dealing.

transbordement, *n.m.* transhipment (of cargo, passengers from ship, vehicle).

transborder, *v.tr.* to tranship (cargo, passengers from ship, vehicle).

transcription, *n.f.* **1.** transcript/copy **2.** *Book-k:* posting (of journal).

transcrire, *v.tr.* (*a*) to transcribe/to write out (*b*) *Book-k:* **transcrire le journal au grand(-)livre,** to transfer journal entries into the ledger.

transférable, *a.* transferable/negotiable (securities, etc.).

transférer, *v.tr.* to transfer (shares, bills of exchange, etc.); to transfer (funds) (*from one bank account to another*); to assign; **transférer un billet par voie d'endossement,** to transfer a bill by endorsement; **transférer le titre de propriété,** to transfer the title deed.

transfert, *n.m.* transfer/making over/ assignment (of stock, rights, property, etc.); *Bank:* transfer (of funds); **transfert électronique de fonds,** electronic funds transfer (EFT); **transfert électronique de fonds au point de vente,** electronic funds transfer at point of sale (EFTPOS); **ordre de transfert permanent,** standing order/ banker's order; *Jur:* **acte de transfert,** deed of assignment (in favour of creditors); **formule de transfert,** transfer form; *StExch:* **frais de transfert,** transfer fee; *Fin:* **journal/registre des transferts,** transfer register; **transfert de personnel,** staff transfer.

transfert-paiement, *n.m. Fin:* transfer of account (*from one savings bank to another*).

transfert-recette, *n.m. Fin:* (*caisse d'épargne*) opening of transferred account.

transformation, *n.f. PolEc:* **industrie de transformation,** processing industry; **transformation active,** inward processing; **transformation passive,** outward processing.

transiger, *v.i.* **transiger avec ses créanciers,** to come to terms with one's creditors.

transit, *n.m. Cust:* transit; **visa de transit,** transit permit/visa; **maison de transit,** forwarding agency; **marchandises de transit,** (warehoused) goods for transit; **marchandises en transit,** goods in transit; **passagers en transit,** passengers in transit.

transitaire, 1. *a.* relating to transit of goods; **commerce transitaire,** transit trade; **pays transitaire,** country through which goods are conveyed in transit **2.** *n.m.* forwarding agent/transport agent.

transiter, 1. *v.tr.* to convey (goods) in transit **2.** *v.i.* to be in transit.

translatif, -ive, *a. Jur:* **rédaction d'actes translatifs de propriété,** conveyancing.

translation, *n.f. Jur:* **translation de propriété,** conveyancing; conveyance.

transmettre, *v.tr. Jur:* to transfer/to

convey (property, etc.); to assign (shares, patents, etc.).

transmissible, *a. Jur:* **bien transmissible par (voie de) succession,** hereditament; **effet transmissible par (voie de) succession,** hereditable bond.

transmission, *n.f.* **1.** passing on/transmission (of message, orders, etc.) **2.** *Jur:* transfer(ence)/conveyance (of estate, etc.); assignment (of shares, patent, etc.).

transport, *n.m.* **1.** (*a*) transport; carriage; haulage; **transport aérien/par air,** air transport; **transport par (chemin de) fer,** rail transport; **transport fluvial,** river transport; **transport de marchandises,** goods transport; **transport maritime,** transport by sea; shipping; **transport routier,** road transport/*also NAm:* shipping; **transports en commun,** public transport (*b*) **avion de transport,** transport aircraft; **compagnie/société de transport,** transport company; carrying/forwarding company; **entrepreneur de transports,** haulage contractor/shipping company; haulier/carrier; **frais de transport,** freight (charges); carriage **2.** (*a*) *Jur:* = **transport-cession** (*b*) *Book-k:* transfer (*from one account to another*).

transportation, *n.f.* transport/transportation/conveyance (of goods, etc.).

transport-cession, *n.m. Jur:* transfer/assignment/conveyance (of property, rights, etc.).

transporter, *v.tr.* **1.** to transport/to carry (goods, etc.); **transporter des marchandises (par avion, par chemin de fer, par mer),** to transport goods (by air, by rail, by sea); **transporter des marchandises en camion,** to transport goods by road/by lorry/by truck; *NAm:* to truck goods/to ship goods **2.** (*a*) *Jur:* **transporter (des droits, etc.) à qn,** to transfer/to assign (rights, etc.) to s.o. (*b*) *Book-k:* to transfer.

transporteur, *n.m.* carrier/forwarding agent.

travail, *n.m.* **1.** (*a*) work; **travail de bureau,** office work; **travail à la chaîne,** assembly line work/production line work; **travail en cours,** work in progress; **travail à domicile,** telecommuting; **travail à l'entreprise,** contract work; **travail à façon,** job work; **travail (au) noir,** moonlighting; **travail de nuit,** night work; **travail à la pièce/aux pièces,** piece work (*b*) **accidents du travail,** industrial injuries; **conditions de travail,** working conditions; **étude du travail,** work study; **groupe de travail,** working party; **heure de travail,** man-hour; **jour de travail,** work(ing) day; **organisation scientifique du travail (OST),** scientific management; **planification du travail,** job scheduling; **revenu du travail,** earned income (*c*) occupation/employment/job; **être sans travail,** to be out of work/to be unemployed; **Ministère du Travail** = Department of Employment (*d*) place of work; **il est à son travail,** he's at work (*e*) **travaux publics,** public works **2.** (*a*) piece of work; job (of work); **entreprendre un travail,** to undertake a piece of work; to take on a job (*b*) workmanship.

travailler, *v.i.* (*a*) to work; **travailler pour soi-même/pour son compte/à son compte,** to work for oneself; to be self-employed; to work freelance; **travailler huit heures par jour,** to work an eight-hour day (*b*) **faire travailler son argent,** to put one's money out at interest.

travailleur, -euse, *n.* worker; **travailleur indépendant,** self-employed person; **travailleur manuel,** manual worker.

trésor, *n.m.* treasury; **le Trésor (public),** the (French) Treasury; **le trésor public,** public funds/finances; **bons du Trésor,** Treasury bills/bonds/notes.

trésorerie, *n.f.* **1.** treasury; **la Trésorerie générale/la trésorerie,** the Treasury; the Exchequer **2.** (*a*) treasurership (*b*) treasurer's office **3.** funds; cash; **budget de trésorerie,** cash budget; **gestion de trésorerie,** management of funds/cash management; **avoir des problèmes de trésorerie,** to have cashflow problems.

trésorier, *n.m.* treasurer; **commis trésorier,** treasury clerk; *Adm:* **trésorier-**

payeur général, paymaster general (*for a department*).

tribunal, *n.m.* tribunal; court of law/law court; (the) magistrates; **décision du tribunal,** court ruling; **tribunal de commerce,** commercial tribunal/court; **tribunal d'instance** = magistrates' court.

trillion, *n.m.* (= 10^{18}) trillion.

trimestre, *n.m.* (*a*) quarter; three months; **par trimestre,** quarterly; **abonnements au trimestre,** quarterly subscriptions (*b*) quarter's salary; quarter's rent.

trimestriel, *a.* quarterly (payment, account, review).

trimestriellement, *adv.* quarterly; every three months.

triple, 1. *a.* treble/triple; **facture en triple exemplaire,** invoice in triplicate **2.** *n.m.* **il gagne le triple de mon salaire,** he earns three times as much as I do/he earns treble my salary.

tripler, *v.tr. & i.* to treble/to triple.

triplicata, *n.m.inv.* triplicate; third copy.

tripotage, *n.m.* F: **tripotage financier,** market jobbery/manipulation.

tripoter, 1. *v.i.* to engage in underhand dealings/in shady business; **tripoter dans l'immobilier,** to engage in shady property

deals/speculation **2.** *v.tr.* to deal dishonestly with (money).

tripoteur, -euse, *n.* F: shady speculator.

troc, *n.m.* barter; swap; **accord de troc,** barter agreement.

trop-perçu, *n.m.* Fin: overpayment (of taxes); **rembourser le trop-perçu,** to refund the excess payment.

troquer, *v.tr.* to barter; to swap.

trust, *n.m.* Fin: trust; **trust de placement,** investment trust; **trust de valeurs,** holding company; **trust vertical,** vertical trust; **valeurs mises en trust,** securities in trust.

truster, *v.tr.* **1.** to group into a trust **2.** F: to monopolize.

trusteur, *n.m.* organizer/administrator of a trust.

tuteur, -trice, *n. Jur:* (legal) guardian.

tuyau, *n.m.* tip; **tuyau de bourse,** stock exchange tip.

TVA, *n.f.* (= taxe à la valeur ajoutée), VAT (= value added tax); **soumis à la TVA** subject to VAT.

type, *n.m.* type; standard model; sample piece; pattern; **échantillon type,** representative sample; **police (d'assurance) type,** standard policy.

U

térieur, *a.* later (date, etc.); **commandes ultérieures,** further orders; orders to come.

anime, *a.* unanimous (vote, etc.); **consentement unanime,** unanimous consent/ agreement.

ification, *n.f.* standardization (of weights and measures, tariffs, etc.).

ifié, *a.* unified; standard(ized) (weights, tariffs, etc.).

ifier, *v.tr.* to unify; to standardize (weights and measures, etc.).

iforme, *a.* uniform; regular; **tarif uniforme,** flat rate.

ilatéral, *a.* unilateral/one-sided/ex parte (contract, etc.).

ion, *n.f.* (*a*) union/association; **union douanière,** customs union; **union économique,** economic union; **union monétaire,** monetary union (*b*) *Jur:* **union des créanciers/contrat d'union,** agreement (on the part of creditors) to take concerted action.

ique, *a.* sole; single; *Adm:* **allocation de salaire unique,** allowance to single-income family; *Ins:* **prime unique,** single premium; **prix unique,** flat price; **articles à prix unique,** articles (all) at one price/at the same price; **magasin à prix unique,** one-price store/popular store.

itaire, *a.* **prix unitaire,** unit price/price per unit; **indice de la valeur unitaire,** unit value index.

ité, *n.f.* 1. (*a*) unit; **unité de coût,** cost unit; **prix de l'unité,** price of one article/ unit price/price per unit; *Fin:* **actions émises en unités,** shares issued in ones; **la**

production a dépassé les 3 000 unités, production has passed the 3 000 unit mark (*b*) *Adm: Ind: etc:* department; unit; plant; **unité administrative,** administrative unit (*c*) *Cmptr:* unit/module; **unité d'affichage,** display unit; **unité centrale (de traitement),** central processing unit 2. unit (of measure, value, size, etc.); *Fin: EEC:* **unité de compte,** unit of account; **unité de compte européenne (ECU),** European currency unit (ECU); *PolEc:* **unité de consommation/de production,** unit of consumption/of production; **unité monétaire,** monetary unit/unit of currency; **unité de poids,** unit of weight; **unité de travail,** unit of labour/man-work unit.

urbain, *a.* urban; *Tel:* **communication urbaine,** local call; **consommation d'essence en parcours urbain,** petrol consumption in town; **aménagement urbain,** urban/ town planning.

urbanisme, *n.m.* town planning.

urbaniste, *n.m.f.* town planner.

urgence, *n.f.* (*a*) urgency; emergency (*b*) *adv.phr.* **d'urgence,** immediately; **veuillez répondre d'urgence,** please reply without delay; **mesures d'urgence,** emergency measures.

urgent, *a.* urgent; **commande urgente,** rush order; **travail urgent,** urgent work.

usage, *n.m.* 1. (*a*) use/using; **à usages multiples,** multi-purpose (equipment, etc.); **locaux à usage commercial,** business/ commercial premises; **valeur d'usage,** value as a going concern (*b*) wear/service; **biens/produits d'usage,** durable goods 2. *Jur:* **droit/clause d'usage,** customary right/ clause; **avoir l'usage (d'un bien, etc.),** to have the right to (possession of) (property, etc.) **3.** usage; custom; practice; **je peux vous fournir les références d'usage,** I can supply (you with) the usual references.

usagé, *a.* used (article); secondhand (car, etc.).

usager,-ère, 1. *n.* user (of sth.) **2.** *a. Cust:* **effets usagers,** articles for personal use; personal effects.

usance, *n.f.* usance; **lettre (de change) à deux usances,** bill payable at double usance; **à usance de trente jours,** at thirty days' usance.

usinage, *n.m.* (*a*) manufacturing (of end product) (*b*) machining; tooling.

usine, *n.f.* factory; works; plant; **usine d'automobiles,** car factory; **apprentissage/ formation en usine,** in-plant training; **directeur d'usine,** works manager; **ouvrier d'usine,** factory worker; **prix (sortie) usine,** price ex works; **travailler dans une usine,** to work in a factory.

usiner, *v.tr.* (*a*) to manufacture (end product) (*b*) to machine; to tool.

usinier, *a.* **groupe usinier,** group of factories; **ville usinière,** factory town.

usufruit, *n.m. Jur:* usufruct.

usure[1], *n.f.* usury; charging of illegal rate of interest.

usure[2], *n.f.* wear and tear (of machinery etc.); **usure en magasin,** shelf depreci ation.

utile, *a.* (*a*) **charge utile,** (*i*) (load-)carryin capacity (*ii*) pay-load/commercial loa (*b*) **en temps utile,** in (good) time; withi the prescribed time; duly; *Jur:* **jour utiles,** prescribed time; days relevant t an action; **prendre toutes disposition utiles,** to make all necessary arrange ments.

utilisable, *a.* usable; available; **crédi utilisable à vue,** credit available at sight

utilisateur,-trice, *n.* user/utilizer; **att tude des utilisateurs,** user attitude.

utilisation, *n.f.* utilization/using (of sth. **frais d'utilisation,** running costs; **mod d'utilisation,** method of use; **instructio** for use; **période d'utilisation,** econom life.

utiliser, *v.tr.* to use; to utilize; to make u of (sth.).

utilitaire, *a.* utilitarian; **véhicules uti taires,** commercial vehicles.

utilité, *n.f.* utility/use(fulness); servic **utilité marginale,** marginal utility.

V

vacance, *n.f.* **1.** vacancy; **suppléer à une vacance/nommer qn à une vacance,** to fill a post/a vacancy **2.** *pl.* holiday(s)/*NAm:* vacation; **un mois de vacances,** a month's holiday/a month off; **les grandes vacances,** the summer holidays; **période/saison des vacances,** holiday period; **étaler les vacances,** to stagger holidays.

vacant, *a.* vacant; **poste vacant,** (job) vacancy.

vache, *n.* cow; *F:* **vache à lait,** cash cow.

vague[1], *n.f.* wave; **vague de baisse,** wave of depression; **vague de hausses de salaire,** wave of wage increases; **vague de spéculation,** wave of speculation.

vague[2], *a.* **terrain vague,** wasteland.

valable, *a.* valid/good; **billet valable pour un mois,** ticket valid for one month; **quittance valable,** proper receipt; **lettre de crédit valable dans le monde entier,** worldwide letter of credit; *StExch:* **valable jusqu'à nouvel ordre,** good until cancelled.

valeur, *n.f.* **1.** (*a*) (relative) value/worth; **mettre une terre en valeur,** to develop a piece of land; *PolEc:* **valeur ajoutée,** added value; **taxe à la valeur ajoutée (TVA),** value-added tax (VAT); **valeur d'échange,** exchange value/value in exchange; **valeur marginale,** marginal value (*b*) (monetary) value/worth; **articles/objets de valeur,** articles of value/valuable articles/valuables; **sans valeur commerciale,** of no commercial value; **date de valeur,** value date; **valeur actuelle,** real value; **valeur à la casse/de liquidation,** break-up value; **valeur à la casse/de liquidation,** break-up value; **valeur comptable,** book value/written-down value; *Bank:*

valeur en compte, value in account; **valeur à l'échéance,** value at maturity; **valeur extrinsèque,** extrinsic value; **valeur de facture,** invoice value; **valeur locative imposable,** rateable value; **valeur intrinsèque,** intrinsic value; **valeur négociable/valeur marchande/valeur vénale,** market value/commercial value; **valeur nette,** net value/worth; **valeur au pair,** par value; **valeur de remplacement,** replacement value; **valeur nominale,** face value/nominal value/*NAm:* face amount; **valeur de rendement (d'une entreprise),** profitability value; *Cust:* **valeur en douane,** customs value; *Post:* **colis/paquet avec valeur déclarée,** insured parcel (*c*) *Fin:* **valeur d'achat d'une action,** cost of a share; **valeurs d'actif (net),** (net) asset value; **valeur boursière,** market value; **valeur d'un remboursement,** redemption value (of a bond, etc.); **valeur en hausse/en baisse,** gainer/loser; (*sur les marchés à terme*) **valeur du contrat,** total contract value (TCV) (*d*) *Ins:* **valeur assurable,** insurable value; **valeur assurée,** insured value; **valeur de rachat (d'une police),** surrender value (of policy); **valeur à neuf,** replacement value (as new)/new for old (policy) **2.** *Fin:* (*a*) asset; **valeurs actives,** assets; **valeur en capital,** capital value; **valeur en espèces,** (*i*) cash (*ii*) bullion; **valeurs immobilisées,** fixed assets; **valeurs incorporelles,** intangible assets; intangibles; **valeurs matérielles,** tangible assets; tangibles (*b*) *pl.* shares/securities/stocks; **bourse des valeurs,** stock market; **indice des valeurs industrielles,** industrial share index; **valeurs au comptant,** securities dealt in for cash; **valeurs cotées,** quoted/listed securities; **valeurs non cotées,** unquoted/unlisted securities; **valeurs de croissance,** growth shares/stocks; **valeurs**

immobilières, real property shares; **valeurs à lot,** lottery bonds/prize bonds; **valeurs mobilières,** stocks and shares; transferable securities; **valeurs mobilières de placement,** quoted investment; **valeurs nominatives,** registered securities; **valeurs de placement/de portefeuille,** investment securities/stocks; **valeurs au porteur,** bearer securities; bearer bonds; **valeurs de père de famille/valeurs vedettes/valeurs de tout repos/valeurs de premier choix/valeurs de premier ordre,** gilt-edged securities; blue chips; active stock; **valeurs de repli,** ambulance stock; **valeurs de retournement,** recovery shares; **valeurs à revenu fixe,** fixed-yield securities; **valeurs à revenu variable,** variable-yield securities; equities/equity shares; **valeurs technologiques,** high-tech stock; **valeurs à terme,** forward securities.

valeur-or, *n.f. Fin:* value in gold currency.

valeur-temps, *n.f.* extrinsic value.

validation, *n.f.* validation; authentication (of document, signature, etc.).

valide, *a.* (*a*) valid (contract, etc.) (*b*) **billet valide pour un mois,** ticket valid for one month.

valider, *v.tr.* to make valid; to ratify (contract, etc.); to authenticate (document, etc.).

validité, *n.f.* validity (of contract, passport, etc.).

valoir, *v.tr. & i.* (*a*) to be worth (in money, quality); **valoir son prix,** to be worth its price; **valoir cher,** to be expensive; to be worth a lot (of money); **tissu qui vaut douze francs le mètre,** material (which is) worth twelve francs a metre/which sells at twelve francs a metre (*b*) **à valoir sur (qch., une somme),** on account of (sth., a sum); **à valoir sur votre facture,** set against your invoice; **payer 200 francs à valoir,** to pay 200 francs on account (*c*) **faire valoir son argent,** to invest one's money to good account/to invest one's money at a profit;

faire valoir ses droits à ..., to assert one's claims to ....

valorisation, *n.f.* (*a*) valuation (of product, etc.); stabilization (of price of commodity); **valorisation des stocks,** costing/pricing (of stocks) (*b*) *Bank:* **valorisation (de chèques) sur Paris,** valuing (of cheques) on Paris.

valoriser, *v.tr.* (*a*) to valorize; to stabilize (price of commodity) (*b*) to raise the price of (a commodity) (*c*) *Bank:* to value (cheques, etc.).

variabilité, *n.f.* variability (of interest rates, etc.).

variable, *a.* variable; **frais variables,** variable expenses; **méthode des coûts variables,** direct costing; **prêt à taux variable,** variable interest loan; **revenu variable,** income from variable-yield investments; **valeurs à revenu variable,** variable-yield securities; **société d'investissement à capital variable (SICAV),** open-end investment company.

variance, *n.f. Stat:* variance.

variation, *n.f.* variation; **variations (annuelles, saisonnières),** (annual, seasonal) variations; **variations du cours du franc,** fluctuations of the franc; **variation maximale autorisée,** maximum fluctuation; **variation de cours minimale,** minimum fluctuation.

varier, *v.i.* to vary; to fluctuate.

variété, *n.f.* variety (**de,** of); **grande variété de produits,** wide range of products.

vedette, *n.f.* **valeur vedette,** blue chip stock.

véhicule, *n.m.* **véhicules commerciaux/utilitaires,** commercial vehicles; **véhicule de transport de marchandises,** freight vehicle/goods vehicle.

véhiculer, *v.tr. Mkt:* **véhiculer une image,** to convey an image/to serve as a vehicle for an image.

veille, *n.f. Mkt:* **veille technologique,** scanning.

vénal, *a.* **poids vénal,** conventional selling weight; **valeur vénale,** market value.

vendable, *a.* saleable/marketable; **peu vendable,** hard to sell; unsaleable.

venderesse, *n.f. Jur:* vendor.

vendeur, -euse, *n.* (*a*) seller (*b*) *Jur:* vendor (*c*) salesperson; salesman; saleswoman/saleslady; sales assistant/shop assistant/*NAm:* sales clerk; **vendeur à domicile,** door-to-door salesman; **vendeur, -euse par téléphone,** telesales person (*d*) *StExch:* **vendeur à découvert,** short seller/bear seller/uncovered bear; **position vendeur,** bear/short position; **cours vendeur,** selling/offered price.

vendre, *v.tr.* to sell; **vendre qch. à qn,** to sell sth. to s.o.; **vendre à bon marché,** to sell cheap; **vendre comptant,** to sell for cash; **vendre au détail,** to sell retail/to retail; **vendre en gros,** to sell wholesale; **vendre moins cher que qn,** to undersell s.o.; **vendre à perte,** to sell at a loss; **vendre à terme/à crédit,** to sell on credit; *StExch:* **vendre à terme,** to sell (for) forward (delivery)/for future delivery; **vendre à découvert,** to sell short;/to go a bear; **article qui se vend cher,** article that fetches a high price; **articles qui se vendent bien,** articles that sell well/ready sellers; **marchandises qui ne se vendent pas,** slow sellers; **maison à vendre,** house for sale.

vente, *n.f.* (*a*) sale/selling; **vente agressive,** hard sell(ing); **vente au comptant,** cash sale; **vente par correspondance (VPC)/vente sur catalogue,** mail order selling; **vente à crédit/à tempérament,** credit sale/sale on hire purchase/*NAm:* sale on the installment plan; **vente au détail,** retail sale; **ventes domestiques,** domestic sales; **vente aux enchères/à l'enchère,** sale by auction/auction (sale); *StExch:* issue by tender; *Br:* tender offer; **vente à l'essai,** sale on approval; **vente de couverture** (*sur le marché des options*) closing sale; **vente-débarras,** garage sale; *StExch:* **vente à découvert,** sale for futures/short sale/short selling/shorting; (*sur le marché des options*) opening sale; **vente directe,** direct selling; cold call sales; **vente de gré à gré/vente à l'amiable,** sale by private agreement/contract/treaty; private sale; **vente ferme,** firm sale; **vente forcée,** forced sale; **vente de liquidation,** closing-down sale; **vente à perte,** sale at a loss; **vente à prix réduit,** sale at a reduced price; **vente promotionnelle/publicitaire,** promotional sale; **vente publique,** public sale/public auction; **vente pyramidale,** pyramid selling; **vente rapide,** quick/ready sale; **vente réclame,** bargain sale; **vente à réméré,** sale with option of repurchase; **ventes par téléphone,** telesales/telephone selling; *StExch:* **vente à terme,** forward sale/sale for the account (*b*) **acte de vente,** bill of sale; **bureau de vente,** sales office; **campagne de vente,** sales campaign/sales drive; **contrat de vente,** contract of sale; **directeur/chef des ventes,** sales manager; **équipe des ventes,** sales force; **point/lieu de vente,** point of sale (POS); **publicité lieu de vente (PLV),** point of sale material/POS material; **prévision des ventes,** sales forecast; **prix de vente,** selling price; **promotion des ventes,** sales promotion; **réseau de vente,** sales network; **service des ventes,** sales department; **vente de biens/de services,** visible/invisible trade (*c*) **en vente,** on sale; for sale; **en vente dans tous les grands magasins,** on sale at all leading stores; **hors de vente,** (*i*) withdrawn from sale/no longer on sale (*ii*) unsal(e)able; **mettre en vente,** to put up for sale; **retirer de la vente,** to withdraw from sale; **articles de bonne vente/de vente facile,** articles which sell well/which have a ready market; **marchandises de vente difficile,** goods that are hard to sell.

ventilation, *n.f. Book-k:* allocation/apportionment/breakdown (of prices, expenses, etc.); **ventilation des prix de revient,** cost distribution.

ventiler, *v.tr. Book-k:* to apportion/to allocate/to break down; **ventiler les dépenses,** to break down expenses.

verbal, *a.* **convention verbale,** verbal agreement; *Jur:* simple contract; **offre verbale,** verbal offer.

véreux, *a. F:* **créances/dettes véreuses,** bad debts; **financier véreux,** shady financier; **firme/société véreuse (travaillant au téléphone),** bogus company/ *NAm:* boilerroom (firm).

vérificateur, -trice, *n.* inspector/ examiner; **vérificateur de(s) comptes/ vérificateur comptable,** auditor/*NAm:* comptroller; **vérificateur interne,** internal auditor; **vérificateur des poids et mesures,** inspector of weights and measures.

vérification, *n.f.* inspection/examination/ checking (of work, measures, etc.); **balance de vérification,** trial balance; **vérification des comptes/vérification comptable,** audit(ing) of accounts; **vérification en douane,** customs examination (of goods); **vérification fiscale,** tax audit; **vérification des stocks,** stock control.

vérifier, *v.tr.* to inspect/to examine/to check (work, measures, etc.); to audit (accounts); **vérifié et revérifié,** checked and double-checked; cross-checked; **vérifier des comptes,** to audit accounts; **vérifier des références,** to take up references.

versement, *n.m. Fin: Bank:* payment/ paying in/deposit; **bulletin de versement,** paying-in slip; deposit slip; **carnet de versement,** paying-in book; **dernier versement,** final instalment; **versement annuel,** yearly payment; **versement à la commande,** down payment; **versement comptant,** cash payment; **versement en compte courant,** payment into a current account; **versement partiel,** instalment; **payer en plusieurs versements/par versements échelonnés,** to pay by/in instalments.

verser, *v.tr.* (*a*) *Fin:* to pay (in); to deposit (money); **verser des arrhes,** to make a deposit; **verser au comptant,** to pay (in) cash; **verser des fonds dans une affaire,** to invest capital in/to put money into an undertaking; **verser des intérêts,** to pay interest; **verser un salaire,** to pay a salary; **capitaux versés,** paid-up capital (*b*) **verser un document au dossier,** to add a document to the file/to file a document.

verso, *n.m.* verso/back/reverse (of a sheet of paper); back (of a bill, cheque, etc.).

vert, *a. F:* **la banque verte,** the *Crédit Agricole*; *EEC:* **franc vert,** green franc; **livre verte,** green pound; **monnaies vertes,** green currencies; **taux vert,** green rate.

vertical, *a.* vertical; **concentration verticale,** vertical concentration; **intégration verticale,** vertical integration; **organisation verticale,** line organization.

veto, *n.m.* veto; **droit de veto,** right of veto; **mettre/opposer son veto à une décision,** to veto a decision.

viabilité, *n.f.* viability/workability (of a project, system, etc.).

viable, *a.* viable (plan, project); **l'entreprise est viable,** the firm is paying its way/is viable.

viager, 1. *a.* for life; **rente viagère,** life annuity/life interest; **rentier viager,** annuitant **2.** *n.m.* life interest; **placer son argent en viager,** to invest one's money in a life annuity; to buy an annuity; **acheter une propriété en viager,** to acquire a property by paying pre-determined instalments until the death of the owner(s).

vice, *n.m.* fault/defect/flaw; **vice caché,** hidden/latent defect; **vice de construction,** defect in construction/construction fault.

vice-gérance, *n.f.* deputy managership.

vice-gérant, *n.m.* deputy manager.

vice-présidence, *n.f.* vice-presidency; vice-chairmanship.

vice-président, -ente, *n.* vice-president; vice-chairman.

vidéo, *a. & n.f.* video; **bande vidéo promotionnelle,** promotional video; video clip; **écran vidéo,** video screen.

vidéoconference, *n.f.* videoconferencing.

vie, *n.f.* (*a*) life; **assurance sur la vie,** life assurance; **le coût de la vie,** the cost of living; **indemnité de cherté de vie,** cost-of-living allowance; **niveau de vie,** standard of living; **gagner sa vie,** to earn one's living (b) **espérance/durée de vie d'un produit,** shelf life of a product; **vie économique d'un produit,** economic life of a product.

vieillesse, *n.f.* old age; **(caisse d')assurance vieillesse,** old-age pension (fund).

vignette, *n.f.* (a) manufacturer's label (of quality, guarantee, etc.) (b) *Aut:* tax disc/road fund licence; *Adm:* price label on medicines for reimbursement by the Social Security.

vigueur, *n.f.* (*en parlant d'un règlement, d'une loi, etc.*) **en vigueur,** in force; **entrer en vigueur,** to come into force/into effect; to become operative; **cesser d'être en vigueur,** to lapse; **taux en vigueur,** current/present rate (of exchange).

village, *n.m.* **le village planétaire,** the global village.

violation, *n.f.* breach; infringement.

virement, *n.m.* (a) *Bank:* transfer; **chèque de virement,** giro cheque; **mandat de virement,** order to transfer; **virement bancaire,** bank giro transfer; **virement de crédit,** credit transfer; **virement postal =** Girobank transfer; **payer par virement bancaire,** to pay by bank (giro) transfer; **comptoir général de virement,** (banker's) clearing house (b) *Adm:* **virement de fonds,** transfer (often illegal) of funds from one article of the budget to another.

virer, *v.tr. Bank:* to transfer (a sum) (*from one account to another*).

virgule, *n.f.* **virgule décimale =** decimal point.

visa, *n.m.* (a) visa (on passport); **visa de la douane,** customs visa (b) signature (on document, etc.); initials (of supervisor, etc., on bankslip, etc.); **visa de chèque,** certification (of cheque) (c) **visa (de la COB),** permission to deal.

vis-à-vis, *prep.phr.* **le dollar a gagné 7% vis-à-vis du franc,** the dollar is up 7% against/on the franc.

viser, *v.tr.* (a) to visa (passport) (b) to

countersign/to initial (document); to certify (cheque).

visible, *a.* visible; **biens visibles,** visibles; **exportations visibles,** visible exports; **importations visibles,** visible imports.

visioconférence, *n.f.* videophone conference.

visiophone, *n.m.* videophone.

visite, *n.f.* **1. visites (d'un représentant),** calls (by a representative) **2.** search/inspection/examination; **droit de visite,** right of search; *Cust:* **visite de douane,** customs examination.

visiter, *v.tr.* **1.** to call on (a client) **2.** to inspect/to examine (machinery, etc.); *Cust:* to examine (luggage, etc.).

visualisation, *n.f. Cmptr:* **console/écran de visualisation,** visual display unit (VDU)/visual display terminal (VDT).

visualiseur, *n.m. Mkt:* roughman.

visuel, *n.m. Cmptr:* visual display unit (VDU)/visual display terminal (VDT).

vitesse, *n.f.* (a) (*en parlant de la production, de l'économie*) **perdre de la vitesse,** to slow down/to be losing ground/to flag/to sag (b) **expédier un travail à toute vitesse,** to rush a job through (c) *PolEc:* **vitesse de transformation des capitaux,** income velocity of capital; *Fin:* **vitesse de rotation (des stocks),** turnover rate/turnround rate (of stocks).

vitrine, *n.f.* (a) shop window/*NAm:* store window/shop front; **articles en vitrine,** goods (on show) in the window; **article qui a fait la vitrine,** article that has been in the window; shop-soiled article; **faire la vitrine,** to dress the window; **lécher les vitrines,** to go window-shopping/to window-shop (b) goods displayed in a shop window (c) display case.

vivre, *n.m.* (a) **le vivre et le couvert,** board and lodging (b) *pl.* (food) supplies; provisions.

vœu, *n.m.* wish; **le comité a adopté des vœux**

demandant que ..., the committee has adopted a resolution in favour of ....

voie, *n.f.* **1.** way/road; route; **par voie de mer**, by sea; **par voie de terre**, by land; overland; **par voie ferrée**, by rail; **par la voie hiérarchique**, through the official channels **2.** (*a*) *Adm: Fin:* **voies et moyens**, ways and means; **en voie d'achèvement**, nearing completion; **pays en voie de développement**, developing countries (*b*) *Jur:* **voie de droit**, recourse to legal proceedings; **voie de recours**, grounds for appeal (to a higher court).

voiture, *n.f.* **1.** **lettre de voiture**, waybill/ consignment note **2.** (*a*) car/*NAm:* automobile; **voiture de fonction/voiture de société**, company car; **voiture de livraison**, delivery van; **voiture de location/de louage**, hire car (*b*) *Rail:* carriage/car/ wagon.

voix, *n.f.* (individual) vote; **donner sa voix à qn**, to vote for s.o.; **mettre une question aux voix**, to put a question to the vote; to take a vote on a question; **voix prépondérante**, casting vote.

vol[1], *n.m. Av:* flight.

vol[2], *n.m.* (*a*) theft; **assurance vol**, insurance against theft; **vol à l'étalage**, shoplifting (*b*) rip off.

volant, **1.** *a.* **personnel volant**, (*i*) mobile/ transferable staff (*ii*) *Av:* flight/flying staff **2.** *n.m.* **talon et volant**, counterfoil and leaf (of cheque).

volatilé, *n.f.* volatility (of an option).

voler, *v.tr.* to steal.

volet, *n.m.* (*d'un chèque, etc.*) tear-off/detachable section.

voleur, -euse, *n.* thief; **voleur à l'étalage**, shoplifter.

volontaire, *a.* **liquidation volontaire**, voluntary liquidation.

volonté, *n.f.* **billet payable à volonté**, promissory note payable on demand.

volume, *n.m.* volume; bulk; size; **volume des affaires**, volume of business; **volume d'affaires**, trading volume; **volume d'une entreprise**, size of a firm; **volume de la production courante**, volume of current output; **volume de ventes**, sales volume.

votant, -ante, *n.* voter.

vote, *n.m.* (*a*) vote; **vote de confiance**, vote of confidence; **vote par correspondance**, postal vote (*b*) **bulletin de vote**, ballot paper; **vote au scrutin secret**, secret ballot; **déclarer le résultat d'un vote**, to declare the result of the voting; **donner son vote à qn**, to vote for s.o.; **prendre part au vote**, to vote/to take part in the voting.

voter, **1.** *v.i.* to vote; **voter à main levée**, to vote by a show of hands; **voter par procuration**, to vote by proxy **2.** *v.tr.* to vote (money, credits, etc.); **voter une loi**, to pass a law; **voter des remerciements à qn**, to pass a vote of thanks to s.o.

voyage, *n.m.* journey/trip; **agence/bureau de voyages**, travel agency; **chèque de voyage**, traveller's cheque; **frais de voyage**, travelling expenses; **voyage d'affaires**, business trip; **voyage organisé**, organised tour/trip; package tour.

voyager, *v.i.* **1.** (*a*) to travel; to make a journey/a trip; **voyager pour affaires**, to travel on business (*b*) **voyager pour une maison de commerce**, to travel for a firm/to represent a firm **2.** (*en parlant de marchandises, etc.*) to be transported; **vin qui ne voyage pas**, wine that does not travel well.

voyageur, -euse, *n.* (*a*) traveller/*NAm:* traveler; *Trans:* passenger; **train de voyageurs**, passenger train (*b*) **voyageur (de commerce)/voyageur représentant placier (VRP)**, travelling salesman/ (commercial) traveller/representative/rep.

voyagiste, *n.m.* tour operator.

vrac, *n.m.* **en vrac**, loose; in bulk; **cargaison en vrac**, bulk cargo; **marchandises en vrac**, loose goods (*not packed*); **faire le vrac**, **transporter le vrac**, to transport goods in bulk.

ue, *n.f.* (*a*) **papier (payable) à vue,** bill payable at sight/sight bill/demand bill; **à sept jours de vue,** seven days after sight; **dépôt à vue,** demand/call deposit; **traite à vue,** draft (payable) at sight; sight draft (*b*) **en vue,** on view; **mettre des marchandises bien en vue,** to display goods prominently.

W

wagon, *n.m.* *Rail:* (passenger) carriage/ *NAm:* passenger car; **wagon de première classe,** first-class carriage; **wagon de marchandises,** goods van/goods wagon/ *NAm:* freight car; **wagon complet,** truckload/wagon load; **wagon frigorifique,** refrigerated van; **franco wagon,** free on rail; **prix par wagon (complet),** price per truckload; **prix sur wagon,** price on rail.

wagon-poste, *n.m.* *Rail:* mail van.

wagon-restaurant, *n.m.* *Rail:* restaurant/ dining car.

warrant, *n.m.* (*a*) *Jur:* (warehouse) warrant (*b*) **warrant agricole,** agricultural warrant; **warrant hôtelier,** hotel warrant; **warrant industriel,** industrial warrant.

warrantage, *n.m.* issuing of a warehouse warrant (for goods).

warranter, *v.tr.* to issue a warehouse warrant for (goods); **marchandises warrantées,** goods covered by a warehouse warrant.

X

---

xérographie, *n.f.* xerography.

xérographique, *a.* **copie xérographique,** xerocopy/Xerox (*Rtm*) copy.

Xerox, *n.m. Rtm:* **machine Xerox,** Xerox machine.

Z

zèle, *n.m.* **grève du zèle,** work to rule.

zéro, *n.m.* zero; nought; **valeur qui est tombée à zéro,** share which has fallen to zero; **(obligations émises à) coupon zéro,** zero coupon (bonds); **système/technique du budget à base zéro (BBZ),** zero base budgeting (ZBB); **taux zéro,** zero rating; **taxer à un taux zéro,** to zero rate.

zinzins, *n.m.pl. F:* (*investisseurs institutionnels*) institutional investors.

zone, *n.f.* (*a*) *PolEc:* **zone franche,** free zone; **zone de libre-échange,** free-trade area; **zone monétaire,** monetary area; **zone (dollar, franc, sterling),** (dollar, franc, sterling) area (*b*) **zone de développement d'entreprises/zone franche,** enterprise zone; **zone industrielle,** industrial estate/ trading estate; industrial area; *Adm:* **zone à urbaniser en priorité (ZUP),** priority development area (*c*) *Adm:* **zone de salaire,** wage zone/wage bracket.

232

ABRÉVIATIONS USUELLES—COMMON ABBREVIATIONS

ab.	**abandonné,** relinquished (right, etc.)
ac.	**acompte,** (payment) on account
a.c.	1. **argent comptant,** cash 2. **année courante,** current year 3. **avaries communes,** general average, g/a.
acc.	**acceptation,** acceptance (of bill), acc.
act.	**action,** share, sh(r).
ad(r).	**adresse,** address; **ad(r). tél., adresse télégraphique,** telegraphic address, TA
ad val.	**ad valorem,** ad valorem, ad val.
agce.	**agence,** agency, agcy.
AP	1. **à protester,** to be queried 2. **avis de paiement,** advice/notice of payment
a.p.	**avaries particulières,** particular average, p.a.
appt	**appartement,** apartment, flat
AR	**accusé de réception,** acknowledgement
arrdt	**arrondissement,** district
asse	**assurance,** insurance, ins.; assurrance, ass.
ass.extr.	**assemblée extraordinaire,** extraordinary (general) meeting, EGM
à t.p.	**à tout prix,** at any cost
Av.	**avoir,** credit, cr.
à vdre	**à vendre,** for sale, to be sold
b.	1. **billet,** bill 2. **bénéfice,** profit
B/.	**billet à ordre,** promissory note PN, P/N
b. à p.	**billet à payer,** bill payable, b.p., B/P
b. à r.	**billet à recevoir,** bill receivable, b.r., B/R
bce.	**balance,** balance, bal.
Bd	**Boulevard,** boulevard
beau	**bordereau,** memorandum, memo
B.P.	**Boîte Postale,** Post Office Box, P.O. Box
bt.	1. **billet,** bill 2. **brut,** gross
bté	**breveté,** patented
burx	**bureaux,** offices, offs
c	**carré,** square, sq.
c.	1. **centime,** centime, c., cent. 2. **coupon,** coupon, c(p). 3. **cours,** quotation 4. **compte,** account, a/c., A/C, acct
c/.	**contre,** contra
c.a.f./CAF	**coût, assurance, fret,** cost, insurance, freight, c.i.f., CIF
cage	**courtage,** brokerage, bkge
caire	**commissionnaire,** agent, agt
c.-à-d.	**c'est-à-dire,** that is to say, i.e.
c. at(t).	**coupon attaché,** cum dividend, cum div., c.d.
c	1. **cours de compensation,** making-up price, m/u, M/U 2. **centimètre cube,** cubic centimetre
/c.	**compte courant,** current account, c.a., c/a, CA, C/A
ce	**commerce,** commerce
ent	**centime,** centime, cent., c.
ertif.	**certificat,** certificate, cert.
CF	**coût et fret,** cost and freight, c&f., C&F
h. de f.	**chemin de fer,** railway, rly, *NAm:* railroad, RR
h.f.	**change fixe,** fixed exchange
ie	**Compagnie,** Company, Co.
/j.	**courts jours,** short-dated (bills)
l	**centilitre,** centilitre, cl

cm	**centimètre,** centimetre, cm
c/o.	**compte ouvert,** open account
com.	**commission,** commission, com(m).
connt	**connaissement,** bill of lading, B/L
conv.	**converti,** converted, convd
corresp.	**correspondance,** correspondence, corr.
coup.	**1. coupon,** coupon, cp. **2. coupure,** denomination, denom.
cpt	**comptant,** cash, ready money
cpte	**compte,** account, A/C, a/c
cr.	**crédit,** credit, cr.
ct	*Corr:* **courant,** instant, inst.
cu.	**cours unique,** sole quotation
CU	**charge utile,** payload
cum.	**cumulatif,** cumulative, cum.
D.	**1. doit, débit,** debit, debtor, dr **2. déport,** backwardation **3. départ,** starting date
DA	**documents contre acceptation,** documents against acceptance, DA
déb.	**débit,** debit, debtor, dr., Dr.
déc.	**décembre,** December, Dec.
dél.	**délégation,** delegation, del.
dép.	*Adm:* **département,** department, Dept
dest.	**destinataire,** addressee/to …
dét.	**détaché,** (coupon) detached
dif.	**différé,** deferred (stock), def.
Dir.	**Direction,** management
div.	**dividende,** dividend, div.
dol.	**dollar,** dollar, dol.
douz.	**douzaine,** dozen, doz.
DP	**documents contre paiement,** documents against payment, DAP
dr	**débiteur, débit,** debtor, dr., Dr.
dr.c.	**derniers cours,** last quotation
dt	**débit,** debit, dr., Dr.
dz.	**douzaine,** dozen, doz.
e. à p.	**effet à payer,** bill payable, b.p., B/P
e. à r.	**effet à recevoir,** bill receivable, b.r., B/R
éd(it).	**édition,** edition, ed.
en tte. ppté	**en toute propriété,** freehold, F/H
e.o.o.e./e.&o.e.	**erreur ou omission exceptée,** errors and ommissions excepted, E.&O.E., e.&o.e.
env.	**environ,** approximately, approx.
esc.	**escompte,** discount, disc.
est.	**estampillé,** stamped
Éts	**établissements,** factory
ex.	**1. exemple,** (for) example, e.g. **2. exercice,** financial year
ex.att.	**exercice attaché,** cum dividend, cum div.
ex-bon.	**ex-bonification,** ex bonus
ex-c(oup).	**ex-coupon,** ex coupon; ex cp.; **ex-c.div., ex-coupon de dividende,** ex-dividend coupon; **ex-c.int., ex-coupon d'intérêt,** ex-interest coupon
ex-d.	**ex-dividende,** ex dividend, ex div.
ex-dr.	**ex-droits,** ex rights, xr.
exp.	**1. exportation,** export, exp. **2. expéditeur,** sender/from …
expn	**expédition,** dispatch(ing)
ex-rép.	**ex-répartition,** ex bonus
F., f.	**franc,** franc, F.
f. à b.	**franco à bord,** free on board, FOB, f.o.b.
FAC	**franc d'avaries communes,** free of general average, f.g.a.

FAP	**franc d'avaries particulières,** free of particular average, f.p.a.
fco	**franco,** free of charge, FOC, f.o.c.; carriage paid, CP
f. ct	*Corr:* **fin courant,** at the end of this month
fév.	**février,** February, Feb.
FG	**frais généraux,** overheads, o/h
FLB	**franco long du bord,** free alongside ship, FAS, f.a.s.
FOB, f.o.b	**franco de bord,** free on board, f.o.b., FOB
FOR	**franco sur rail,** free on rail, FOR, f.o.r.
f.p.	**1. (en) franchise postale,** official paid **2.** *Corr:* **fin prochain,** at the end of next month
fre	**facture,** invoice, inv.
Frs	**Frères,** Brothers, Bros
FS	*Post:* **faire suivre,** please forward
g	**gramme,** gram, g
g.l.	**grand(-)livre,** ledger, led.
h.	**1. heure(s),** hour(s), hr(s) **2.** *StExch:* **hier,** yesterday
ha	**hectare**
h.c.	**1. hors cadre,** not on the staff **2. hors commerce,** not for sale
HS	**hors de service,** not in service/not in use
HT	**hors taxe(s),** exclusive of tax
hyp.	**hypothèque,** mortgage, mortg.
id.	**idem,** idem, id./ditto, do.
imp.	**1. impayé,** dishonoured (bill, etc.) **2. importation,** import, imp.
incl.	**inclus,** (*i*) enclosed, enc(l). (*ii*) included, incl.
ind.	**industrie,** industry, ind.
nt.	**intérêt,** interest, int.
J	**Joule,** joule
anv.	**janvier,** January, Jan.
/d	**jours de date,** days after date, d.d.
Je	**jeune,** junior, jnr, jr
J	**journal,** day-book, d.b./journal
r	**jour,** day, d.
/v.	**jours de vue,** days after sight, d.s.
kg	**kilo(gramme),** kilo(gram), kg
kJ	**kilojoule,** kilojoule
l	**kilolitre,** kilolitre, *NAm:* kiloliter, kl
m	**kilomètre,** kilometre, *NAm:* kilometer, km; **km/h, kilomètre heure,** kilometres per hour, km/h
t	**kilotonne,** kiloton, kt
W	**kilowatt,** kilowatt, kW
Wh	**kilowatt-heure,** kilowatt-hour, Kwh
,	**livre sterling,** pound sterling, £
l	**litre,** litre, *NAm:* liter, l
c.	**1. leur compte,** their account **2. lettre de change,** bill of exchange, b/e., B/E
CR	**lettre de change relevé**
cr.	**lettre de crédit,** letter of credit, l/c
b.	**libéré,** fully paid, f.p.
q.	**liquidation,** settlement
v(r).	**livraison,** delivery, dely
o.	**leur ordre,** their order
tée	*FrC:* **(compagnie) limitée,** limited (company), Ltd.

M.	1. **Monsieur**, (Mister), Mr 2. **mille**, thousand
m	1. **mètre**, metre, *NAm:* meter, m 2. **mois**, month, m
max.	**maximum**, maximum, max.
m/c.	**mon compte**, my account, m/a
M^e	**Maître**, (lawyer)
min.	**minimum**, minimum, min.
mise	**marchandise**, goods, gds
Mlle	**Mademoiselle**, Miss, Ms
Mlles	**Mesdemoiselles**, Misses
MM.	**Messieurs**, Messrs
mm	**millimètre**, millimetre, *NAm:* millimeter, mm
m/m	**moi-même**, (my)self
Mme	**Madame**, Mrs, Ms
Mmes	**Mesdames**
mn.	**minute**, minute, min.
m/o.	**mon ordre**, my order, m/o
MP	**mandat-poste**, postal order, PO; money order, MO
MS	**manuscrit**, manuscript, MS
mx	**au mieux**, at best
N.	1. **nom**, name, n. 2. **nominal**, nominal, n.
n.	**notre**, our
NB	**nota bene**
n/c.	**notre compte**, our account
nég.	**négociable**, negotiable
NF	**nouveau(x) franc(s)**, new franc(s)
NFC	**nouvelle feuille de coupon**, new sheet of coupons
n°	**numéro**, number, no.; **n° tél.**, **numéro de téléphone**, telephone number, tel. no.
nom.	**nominatif**, registered (security)
nos	**numéros**, numbers, nos
nov.	**novembre**, November, Nov.
N/Réf.	**notre référence**, our reference, Our ref.
o/...	**à l'ordre de ...**, to the order of ...
OB	1. **opération bancaire**, bank transaction 2. **ordre de bourse**
obl.	**obligation**, debenture, db.; bond
oct.	**octobre**, October, Oct.
off.	**offert**, offered
o/m/m.	**à l'ordre de moi-même**, to my/our own order
p.	1. **page**, page, p. 2. **pair**, par 3. **papier**, paper 4. **poids**, weight, wt
p.a.	**par an**, per annum, p.a.
PA	1. **pour amplification**, true copy 2. **propriété assurée**, insured property
pable	**payable**, payable
p.c.	1. **pas coté**, unlisted 2. **pour cent**, per cent
p/c.	**pour compte**
PCC	**pour copie conforme**, certified true copy
p.d.	**port dû**, carriage forward, CF
p.ex.	**par exemple**, for example/exempli gratia, e.g.
PJ	**pièce(s) jointe(s)**, enclosure(s), encl./enclosed, enc.
pp.	**pages**, pages, pp.
p.p.	**port payé**, carriage paid, CP
p.pon	**par procuration**, per procuration, per pro./p.p.
pptaire	**propriétaire**, proprietor, owner
ppté	**propriété**, property
pr.	**(mois) prochain**, proximo, prox.
préf.	**préférence**, preference, pref.
priv.	**privilégié**, preferential (share)

PS	post-scriptum, postscript, PS
te	perte, loss
x	prix, price, pr.

q.	1. quai, quay 2. quantité, quantity, qnty, qty
QL	quittance de loyer, rent receipt
n	quelqu'un, someone, s.o.
q	quelques, some
qf	quelquefois, sometimes

r	1. rue, street, St/road, Rd 2. reçu, received, rcvd 3. *Post:* recommandé, registered, regd
RA	*Rail:* régime accéléré, fast goods service/Rail Express Parcels/Red Star
réf.	référence, reference, ref.
emb.	1. remboursable, redeemable 2. remboursement, redemption
ens.	renseignements, information, inf(o).
ep.	report, contango
ép.	répartition, allotment
O	*Rail:* régime ordinaire, normal, usual goods service
p.	réponse payée, reply paid, RP
SVP	Répondez s'il vous plaît, please reply, RSVP

s	signé, signed, sgd
b.	son billet, his bill
b.f.	sauf bonne fin/sous réserve de bonne fin, under usual reserve
c.	seul cours, sole quotation
c.	1. son compte, his account 2. *Corr:* sous couvert, under cover
e.&o.	sauf erreur ou omission, errors and omissions excepted, E&OE, e.&o.e.
pt.	septembre, September, Sept.
rv.	service, department, dept.
f	sans frais, free of charge, FOC, f.o.c.
l.	sauf livraison, against delivery
o.	sauf omission, omissions excepted
o.	son ordre, his order
té, Sté	Société, Company, Co.
v.	sans valeur, of no value, worthless
VP	s'il vous plaît, please

t	1. titre, security, stock, stk; share, sh(r). 2. tonne, (metric) tonne 3. tare, tare, t.
.	traite, draft, dft
.	toutes coupures, all denominations (of banknotes)
C	taxe complémentaire, supplementary charge; additional tax
l.	1. téléphone, telephone, tel. 2. télégraphique, telegraphic
.	tout payé, all expenses paid
	traite, draft, dft
R	tarif réduit, reduced rate
S	1. tarif spécial, special rate 2. taxe supplémentaire, supplement
S.V.P.	tournez s'il vous plaît, please turn over, P.T.O.
	transfert télégraphique, telegraphic transfer, TT
c.	toutes taxes comprises, inclusive of tax

u	unité, unit
v	ultraviolet, ultraviolet, UV

v	1. vendeur, seller 2. votre, your, yr
.,val.	valeur, security, stock, stk; share, sh(r)
c.	votre compte, your account

virt	**virement,** transfer. tr.
vo., v°	**verso,** verso, vo.
VPC	**vente par correspondance,** mail order (business). MO
V/Réf.	**votre référence,** your reference. Your ref.
vte	**vente,** sale
XP	*Post:* **exprès payé,** express paid
&	**et commercial,** ampersand
©	**droit d'auteur,** copyright
%	**pour cent,** per cent

SIGLES FRANÇAIS—FRENCH ACRONYMS

AC	1. Appellation contrôlée 2. Agent de change
ACAC	Administration centrale de l'aviation civile
ACSI	Analyse et Conception de Systèmes Informatiques
ACTIM	Agence pour la coopération technique, industrielle et économique
ADR	Accord pour le transport des marchandises dangereuses par route
AELE	Association européenne de libre-échange, European Free Trade Association, EFTA
AETR	Accord européen de transports internationaux par route
AFB	Association française des banques, French Bankers' Association
AFDEP	Association française pour le développement de la productivité
AFNOR	Association française de normalisation = 1. British Standards, BSI 2. American National Standards Institute, ANSI
AFP	1. Agence France-Presse 2. Association française de prévention des accidents du travail
AG	Assemblée générale annuelle, Annual general meeting, AGM
AGEMCO	Agence européenne d'emballage et conditionnement
AGTDC	Accord général sur les tarifs douaniers et le commerce, General Agreement on Tariffs and Trade, GATT
AID	Association internationale de développement
AITA	Association internationale des transports aériens, International Air Transport Association, IATA
ALE	1. Agence locale pour l'emploi 2. Association de libre-échange, Free Trade association
AME	Accord monétaire européen, European Monetary Agreement, EMA
AMM	Autorisation de mise sur le marché
ANAS	Association nationale des avoués et agréés syndics
AP	Assistant(e) particulier(-ière), personal assistant, PA
APL	Aide personnelle au logement
ANPE	Agence nationale pour l'emploi = Job Centre
ASBL	Association sans but lucratif, non profit-making organisation
ASF	Association pour la structure financière
ASSEDIC	Association pour l'emploi dans l'industrie et le commerce
ATC	Assistant technique du commerce
ATI	Assistant technique de l'industrie
ATM	Assistant technique des métiers
ATP	Autorisation de transferts préalable
ATVA	Association de transports et voyages aériens
BAII	Banque arabe et internationale d'investissements
BALO	Bulletin d'annonces légales obligatoires
BB	1. Banque de Bretagne 2. Banque de Belgique
BC	Banque de Commerce
BCI	Banque de crédit international
BEC	Brevet d'enseignement commercial
BEH	Brevet d'enseignement hôtelier
BEI	1. Banque européenne d'investissement 2. Brevet d'enseignement industriel
BF	Banque de France
BFCE	Banque française du commerce extérieur
BFI	Banque de financement industriel
BGL	Banque générale du Luxembourg
BI	1. Brevet d'invention, patent 2. Brevet industriel
BIA	Banque internationale arabe
BIC	Banque internationale du commerce
BIPE	Bureau d'informations et de prévisions économiques

BIRD	**Banque internationale pour la reconstruction et le développement,** International Bank for Reconstruction and Development, IBRD
BITD	**Bureau international des tarifs douaniers,** International Customs Tariffs Bureau; ICTB
BNB	**Banque nationale belge**
BNP	**Banque nationale de Paris**
BODAC	**Bulletin officiel des annonces commerciales**
BP	**1. Boîte postale,** Post Office box, PO box **2. Brevet professionnel**
BPA	**Bénéfices par action**
BPF	**Bon pour francs,** value in francs
BPGF	**Banque privée de gestion financière**
BSGD	**Breveté sans garantie du Gouvernement,** patent without Government warranty of quality
BT	**Brevet de technicien**
BTP	**Bâtiments, travaux publics,** construction industry
BTS	**Brevet de technicien supérieur**
BVP	**Bureau de la vérification de la publicité,** Advertising Standards Authority, ASA
CA	**Chiffre d'affaires,** turnover
CAO	**Conception assistée par ordinateur**
CAP	**Certificat d'aptitude professionnelle**
CAPES	**Certificat d'aptitude pédagogique à l'enseignement secondaire**
CAPET	**Certificat d'aptitude pédagogique à l'enseignement technique**
CATIF	**Contrat à terme d'instruments financiers,** financial futures
CB	**Carte bancaire,** cheque/banker's/payment card
CCHCI	**(Caisse centrale de) crédit hôtelier, commercial et industriel**
CC	**Compte courant,** current account, CA, C/A
CCF	**Crédit commercial de France**
CCI	**Chambre de commerce internationale,** International Chamber of Commerce, ICC
CCP	**Compte courant postal/Compte chèque postal** = (National) Girobank account
CD	**Corps Diplomatique,** Diplomatic Corps
CDE	**Comptoir des Entrepreneurs**
CDF, CdF	**Charbonnage de France**
CE	**1. Comité d'entreprise,** works council **2. caisse d'épargne,** savings bank
CEA	**Caisse d'épargne en actions**
CECA	**Communauté du charbon et de l'acier,** European Coal and Steel Community, ECSC
CEDEX	**Courrier d'entreprise à distribution exceptionnelle**
CEE	**1. Communauté économique européenne,** European Economic Community, EEC **2. Commission économique pour l'Europe,** Economic Commission for Europe, ECE
CERC	**Centre d'études des revenus et des coûts**
CES	**Comité économique et social,** Economic and Social Committee
CESP	**Centre d'études des supports de publicité**
CFDT	**Confédération française démocratique du travail**
CGAF	**Confédération générale de l'artisanat français**
CGC	**Confédération générale des cadres**
CGT	**Confédération générale du travail**
CI	**Certificat d'importation,** import certificate
CIC	**Crédit industriel et commercial**
CIDA	**Centre international du droit des affaires**
CIP	**Certificat d'investissement privilégié**
CISI	**Compagnie internationale de services en informatique**
CITT	**Compagnie internationale du travail temporaire**
CL	**Crédit Lyonnais**
Cler	**Compte libre d'épargne et de retraite**
CM	**Crédit mutuel**
CMB	**Crédit mutuel de Bretagne**
CMCC	**Crédit de mobilisation de créances commerciales**

CNB	Caisse nationale des banques
CNC	Conseil national du crédit
CNE	1. Caisse nationale d'épargne = National Savings Bank, NSB 2. Comptoir national d'escompte
CNI	Caisse nationale de l'industrie
CNME	Conseil national des marchés de l'État
CNPF	Conseil national du patronat français = Confederation of British Industry, CBI
CNRS	Centre national de la recherche scientifique
CNT	Confédération national du travail
COB	Commission des opérations de Bourse
Codefi	Comité départemental d'examen des problèmes de financement des entreprises
COFACE	Compagnie française d'assurance pour le commerce extérieur
COMECON	Conseil pour l'aide économique mutuelle, Council for Mutual Economic Aid, COMECON
CV	Curriculum vitae, curriculum vitae, CV
DAB	Distributeur automatique de billets, cash dispenser
DEUG	Diplôme universitaire d'études générales
DEUS	Diplôme universitaire d'études scientifiques
DPO	Direction par objectifs, management by objectives, MBO
DTS	Droits de tirage spéciaux, Special drawing rights, SDR
ECU	Unité de compte européenne
EDF, EdF	Électricité de France
ENA	1. École nationale d'administration 2. École nationale d'agriculture
ENSET	École normale supérieure de l'enseignement technique
ESC	École supérieure de commerce
ETAM, etam	Employés techniques et agents de maîtrise
É.-U.	États-Unis, United States
EUR	Europe, Europe
EXIM	Exportation–Importation
FAC	Fonds d'aide et de coopération
FB	Franc Belge, Belgian Franc
FCFA	Franc de la communauté financière d'Afrique
FCP	Fonds communs de placement, investment fund
FDES	Fonds de développement économique et social
FEOGA	Fonds européen d'orientation et de garantie agricole, European Agricultural Guidance and Guarantee Fund, EAGGF
FF	Franc Français, French Franc
FG	Frais généraux, overheads
Fidei	Financière de développement industriel
FMI	Fonds monétaire international, International Monetary Fund, IMF
FS	Franc Suisse, Swiss Franc
FSE	Fonds social européen, European Social Fund
FSI	Fédération syndicale internationale, International Federation of Trade Unions, IFTU
FSM	Fédération syndicale mondiale, World Federation of Trade Unions, WFTU
GAN	Groupe d'assurances nationales
GICEX	Groupement interbancaire pour les opérations de crédit à l'exportation
GMF	Générale Mutuelle de France
GPL	Gaz de pétrole liquéfiés
HLM	Habitation à loyer modéré = council flat
HT	Hors taxes, exclusive of tax
IDI	Institut de développement industriel

IMEX	**Importation–exportation**
INSEE	**Institut national des statistiques et des études économiques**
IS	**Impôt sur les sociétés**
ISF	**Impôt de Solidarité sur la Fortune,** wealth tax
JAL	**Japan Airlines**
JO	**Journal Officiel**
KAL	**Korean Airlines**
KLM	**Société royale d'aviation des pays bas,** Royal Dutch Airlines, KLM
L.ès L.	**Licencié ès lettres** = Bachelor of Arts, BA
L.ès Sc.	**Licencié ès sciences** = Bachelor of Science, BSc
MATIF	**Marché à terme d'instruments financiers,** futures market
MBA	**Marge brute d'autofinancement,** cash flow
MER	**Management par écoute et rencontre,** Management by walking around
MM	**1. Marine marchande,** Merchant Navy **2. Messageries maritimes**
MUTI	**Mutuelle des travailleurs indépendants**
NF	**Normes françaises** = British Standards
NIC	**Nouvel instrument communautaire,** New Community Instrument, NCI
NU	**Nations unies,** United Nations, UN
OAT	**Obligation assimilable du Trésor**
OCDE	**Organisation de coopération et de développement économique,** Organisation for Economic Co-operation and Development, OECD
OECE	**Organisation européenne de coopération économique,** Organization for European Economic Co-operation, OEEC
OHQ	**Ouvrier hautement qualifié,** highly skilled worker
OIAC	**Organisation internationale de l'aviation civile,** International Civil Aviation Authority, ICAO
OIC	**Organisation internationale du commerce**
OIT	**Organisation internationale du travail,** International Labour Organization, ILO
OM	**Organisation et méthodes,** Organization and Methods, OM
ONS	**Ouvriers non syndiqués,** non-union workers
ONU	**Organisation des nations unies,** United Nations Organization, UNO
OP	**Ouvrier professionel,** skilled worker
OPA	**Offre publique d'achat,** takeover bid
OPCVM	**Organisme de Placements Collectifs en Valeurs Mobilières,** unit trust
OPE	**Offre publique d'échange,** exchange offer
OPEP	**Organisation des pays exportateurs de pétrole,** Organization of Petroleum Exporting Countries, OPEC
OPV	**Offre publique de vente,** offer by prospectus
ORA	**Obligations remboursables en actions**
ORT	**Obligations renouvelables du Trésor,** renewable treasury bills
OS	**Ouvrier spécialisé,** semi-skilled worker
OST	**Organisation scientifique du travail,** scientific management
OTAN	**Organisation du traité de l'Atlantique du nord,** North Atlantic Treaty Organization, NATO
PAC	**Politique agricole commune,** Common Agricultural Policy, CAP
PAO	**Publication assistée par ordinateur,** desktop publishing
PAP	**1. Port autonome de Paris 2. Prêt (aidé) à l'accession à la propriété**
PCC	**Pour copie conforme,** true copy
PCV	*Tel:* **Paiement contre vérification; appel en PCV,** transfer(red) charge call

P-DG	**President-directeur général,** Chairman and Managing Director/*NAm:* Chief Executive Officer, CEO
PEPS	**Premier entré premier sorti,** first in first out, FIFO
PER	**Price-earnings ratio, rapport-cours bénéfice**
PERT	**Méthode de programmation optimale,** Programme evaluation and review technique, PERT
P et T	**Postes et Télécommunications** = the Post Office, PO
PIB	**Produit intérieur brut/Production intérieure brute,** gross domestic product, GDP
PIC	**Prêts immobiliers conventionnés**
PIM	**Programmes intégrés méditerranéens**
PJ	**Pièce(s) jointe(s),** enclosure(s)/enclosed, enc., encl.
PLV	**Publicité sur le lieu de vente,** point-of-sale advertising, POS
PME	**(Confédération des) petites et moyennes entreprises**
PMI	**Petite et moyenne industrie**
PN	**1. poids net,** net weight **2. prix normal**
PNB	**Produit national brut,** gross national product, GNP
PNN	**Produit national net,** net national product
PP	**1. port payé,** carriage paid, cp **2. payable au porteur,** payable to bearer **3. Pertes et Profits,** Profit and loss, P&L
PR	**1. Poste restante 2. Procureur de la République 3. Prix de revient,** cost price
PROMODES	**Procédé moderne de distribution et de standardisation**
PV	**Procès-verbal**
RC	**Registre du commerce**
RCB	**Rationalisation des choix budgétaires** = planning, programming and budgeting system, PPBS
RCI	**Rentabilité des capitaux investis,** return on capital employed, ROCE
RELIT	**Règlement-Livraison des Titres,** = Transfer Accounting, Lodgement for Investors, Stock Management for Jobbers, TALISMAN
RES	**Rachat/Reprise d'entreprise par les salariés,** management buyout
RM	**Règlement mensuel** = forward market
RP	**Relations publiques,** public relations, PR
RSVP	**Répondez s'il vous plaît,** please reply, RSVP
SA	**Société anonyme,** (*i*) public company (*ii*) limited (liability) company
SARL	**Société à responsabilité limitée** = limited (liability) company
SBF	**Société des Bourses françaises**
SCM	**Société de caution mutuelle**
SDR	**Société de développement régional**
SERNAM	*Rail:* **Service national des messageries**
SFDD	**Société française de développement et de distribution**
SGDG	**Sans garantie du Gouvernement,** (patent) without Government warranty of quality
SI	**1. Syndicat d'Initiative** = tourist (information) office **2. Système international**
SICAF	**Société d'investissement à capital fixe,** closed-end investment fund
SICAV	**Société d'investissement à capital variable**
SICOMI	**Société immobilière pour le commerce et l'industrie**
SICOVAM	**Société interprofessionnelle pour la compensation des valeurs mobilières**
SIMCA	**Société industrielle de mécanique et de construction automobile**
SL	**Société Lyonnaise**
SM	**Système métrique,** metric system
SME	**System monétaire européen,** European Monetary System, EMS
SMIC	**Salaire minimum interprofessionnel de croissance**
SNC	**Société en nom collectif**
SNCF	**Société nationale des chemins de fer français**
SOCAR	**Société de cartons**
SOFINNOVA	**Société pour le financement de l'innovation**
SOFRES	**Société française d'enquêtes et de sondages**
SOGEBAIL	**Société générale pour le développement des opérations de crédit-bail immobilier**

SS	Sécurité sociale = (*i*) National Health Service, NHS (*ii*) Social Security
SVF	Société des vins de France
SVP	S'il vous plaît, please
SVT	Spécialiste en Valeurs du Trésor, gilt-edge market-maker
TAF	Taxe sur les activités financières
TBB	Taux de base bancaire
TCA	Taxe sur le chiffre d'affaires, turnover tax
TEG	Taux effectif global
TGV	Train grande vitesse = advanced passenger train, APT
TIR	Transports internationaux routiers, International road transport
T4M	Taux moyen mensuel du marché monétaire
TP	1. Trésor public 2. Tiers provisionnel 3. Taxe à la production 4. Taxe proportionnelle
TPG	Trésorier payeur général
TPS	Taxe sur les prestations de service
TR	Tarif réduit, reduced rate
TS	1. Tarif spécial, special rate 2. taxe de séjour
TSDI	Titres subordonnés à durée indéterminée, subordinated perpetuals
TT	Transfert télégraphique, telegraphic transfer, TT
TTC	Toutes taxes comprises, inclusive of (all) tax
TU	Temps universel, Universal time, UT; Greenwich mean time, GMT
TVA	Taxe à la valeur ajoutée, value-added tax, VAT
UBAF	Union des banques arabes et françaises
UCA	Unité de compte agricole
UCE	Unité de compte européenne, European currency unit, ECU
UEO	Union de l'Europe occidentale, Western European Union, WEO
UEP	Union européenne des paiements, European Payments Union, EPU
UFB	Union française des banques
UFC	Union fédérale des consommateurs
Ugap	Union des groupements d'achats publics
UIS	Union pour le financement d'immeubles de sociétés
UNEDIC	Union nationale pour l'emploi dans l'industrie et le commerce
UPU	Union postale universelle, Universal Postal Union, UPU
UTA	Union des transporteurs aériens
VDQS	Vin délimité de qualité supérieure
VN	1. *Ins:* valeur à neuf = new for old (policy) 2. valeur nominale
VPC	Vente(s) par correspondence, mail-order selling/sales
VRP	Voyageur, représentant, placier, representative/(travelling) salesman
XP	*Post:* Exprès payé, express paid
ZAD	Zone à aménagement différé
ZUP	Zone à urbaniser en priorité, priority development area